COMPREHENSIVE ROAD ATLAS BRITAIN AND IRELAND

RAC Bartholomew Comprehensive Road Atlas Britain and Ireland

Published jointly by
Bartholomew,
An Imprint of HarperCollins*Publishers*,
77-85 Fulham Palace Road, London W6 8JB
and
RAC Publishing
RAC House
Bartlett Street
South Croydon CR2 6XW

New 1996 Edition

Printed in Great Britain by The Edinburgh Press Ltd

ISBN 0 7028 2906 4

HB 7874

CONTENTS

iv-v	Route Planning and Weather Hazards
vi-vii	Airport Plans
viii-ix	Port Plans
x	Channel Tunnel Terminals
xi	Channel Ferries
xii	Distance Chart
1	Key to Road Map Symbols
2-107	Road Maps
108	Town Plan Contents
109-117	London Maps
118-124	Index to London Maps
125-144	Town Plans
145	Key to Ireland Maps
146-155	Ireland Road Maps
156-160	Index to Ireland Maps
161-212	Index to Place Names

Route Planning & Weather Hazards

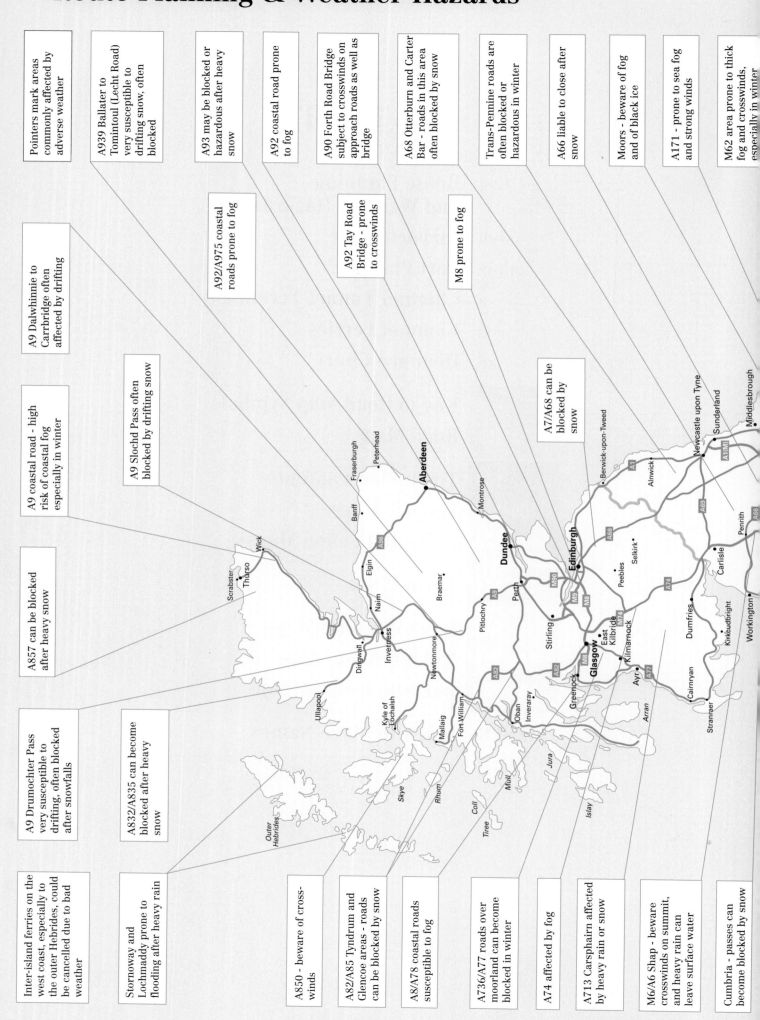

Pointers mark areas commonly affected by adverse weather

A939 Ballater to Tomintoul (Lecht Road) very susceptible to drifting snow, often blocked

A93 may be blocked or hazardous after heavy snow

A92 coastal road prone to fog

A90 Forth Road Bridge subject to crosswinds on approach roads as well as bridge

A68 Otterburn and Carter Bar - roads in this area often blocked by snow

Trans-Pennine roads are often blocked or hazardous in winter

A66 liable to close after snow

Moors - beware of fog and of black ice

A171 - prone to sea fog and strong winds

M62 area prone to thick fog and crosswinds, especially in winter

A9 Dalwhinnie to Carrbridge often affected by drifting

A92/A975 coastal roads prone to fog

A92 Tay Road Bridge - prone to crosswinds

M8 prone to fog

A9 coastal road - high risk of coastal fog especially in winter

A9 Slochd Pass often blocked by drifting snow

A7/A68 can be blocked by snow

A857 can be blocked after heavy snow

A9 Drumochter Pass very susceptible to drifting, often blocked after snowfalls

A832/A835 can become blocked after heavy snow

Inter-island ferries on the west coast, especially to the outer Hebrides, could be cancelled due to bad weather

Stornoway and Lochmaddy prone to flooding after heavy rain

A850 - beware of cross-winds

A82/A85 Tyndrum and Glencoe areas - roads can be blocked by snow

A8/A78 coastal roads susceptible to fog

A736/A77 roads over moorland can become blocked in winter

A74 affected by fog

A713 Carsphairn affected by heavy rain or snow

M6/A6 Shap - beware crosswinds on summit, and heavy rain can leave surface water

Cumbria - passes can become blocked by snow

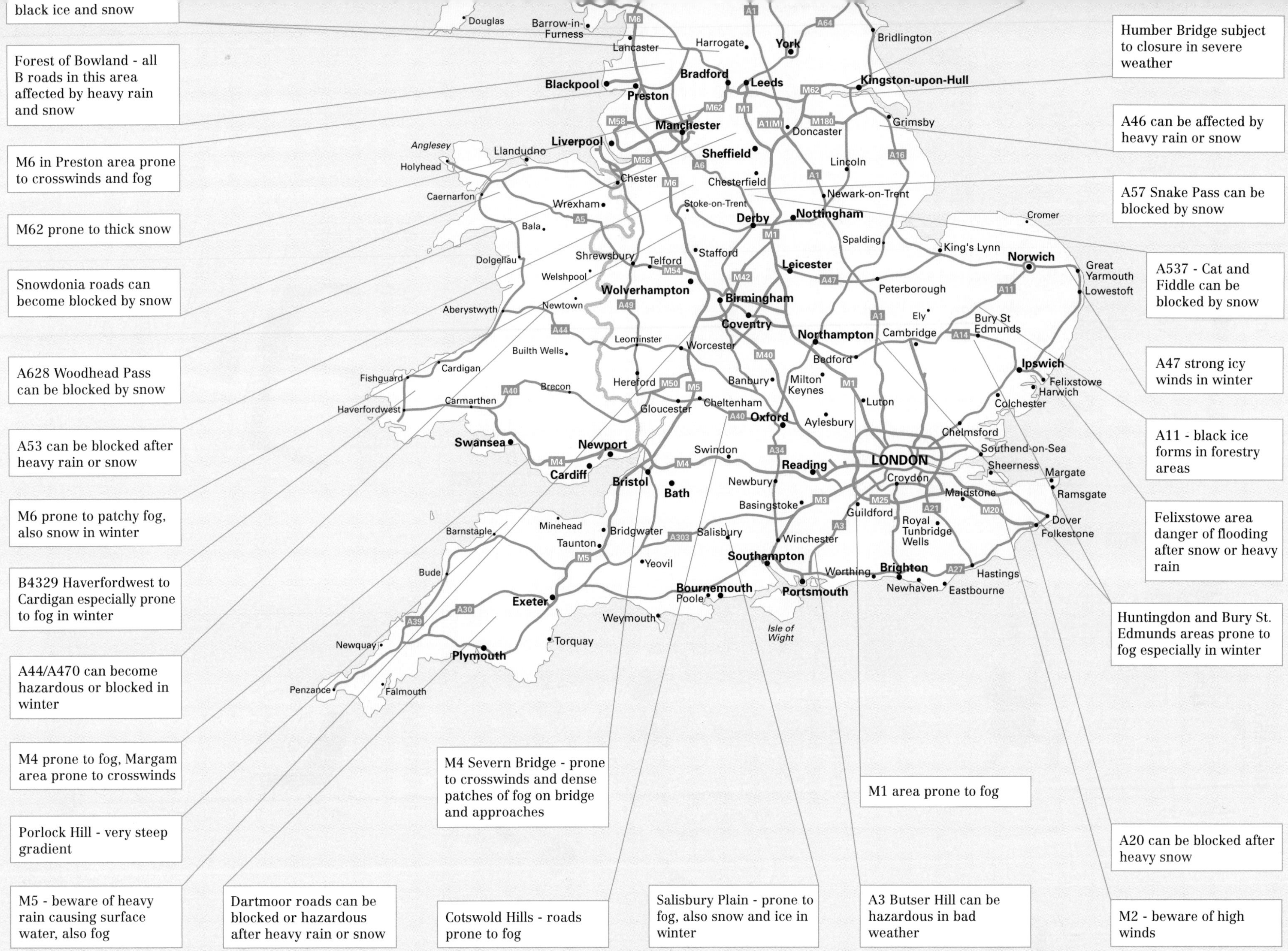
black ice and snow
Forest of Bowland - all B roads in this area affected by heavy rain and snow
M6 in Preston area prone to crosswinds and fog
M62 prone to thick snow
Snowdonia roads can become blocked by snow
A628 Woodhead Pass can be blocked by snow
A53 can be blocked after heavy rain or snow
M6 prone to patchy fog, also snow in winter
B4329 Haverfordwest to Cardigan especially prone to fog in winter
A44/A470 can become hazardous or blocked in winter
M4 prone to fog, Margam area prone to crosswinds
Porlock Hill - very steep gradient
M5 - beware of heavy rain causing surface water, also fog
Dartmoor roads can be blocked or hazardous after heavy rain or snow
M4 Severn Bridge - prone to crosswinds and dense patches of fog on bridge and approaches
Cotswold Hills - roads prone to fog
Salisbury Plain - prone to fog, also snow and ice in winter
M1 area prone to fog
A3 Butser Hill can be hazardous in bad weather
M2 - beware of high winds
A20 can be blocked after heavy snow
Huntingdon and Bury St. Edmunds areas prone to fog especially in winter
Felixstowe area danger of flooding after snow or heavy rain
A11 - black ice forms in forestry areas
A47 strong icy winds in winter
A537 - Cat and Fiddle can be blocked by snow
A57 Snake Pass can be blocked by snow
A46 can be affected by heavy rain or snow
Humber Bridge subject to closure in severe weather
Douglas
Barrow-in-Furness
Lancaster
Harrogate
York
Bridlington
Blackpool
Preston
Bradford
Leeds
Kingston-upon-Hull
Manchester
Grimsby
Doncaster
Liverpool
Sheffield
Anglesey
Llandudno
Holyhead
Caernarfon
Chester
Chesterfield
Lincoln
Newark-on-Trent
Wrexham
Stoke-on-Trent
Derby
Nottingham
Bala
Cromer
Spalding
King's Lynn
Norwich
Great Yarmouth
Lowestoft
Dolgellau
Shrewsbury
Telford
Stafford
Leicester
Welshpool
Wolverhampton
Birmingham
Peterborough
Newtown
Coventry
Ely
Aberystwyth
Bury St Edmunds
Northampton
Cambridge
Leominster
Worcester
Builth Wells
Ipswich
Cardigan
Bedford
Felixstowe
Harwich
Fishguard
Hereford
Banbury
Milton Keynes
Luton
Brecon
Colchester
Carmarthen
Cheltenham
Haverfordwest
Gloucester
Oxford
Aylesbury
Chelmsford
Swansea
Newport
Swindon
Southend-on-Sea
LONDON
Cardiff
Reading
Sheerness
Margate
Bristol
Bath
Newbury
Croydon
Ramsgate
Maidstone
Basingstoke
Guildford
Dover
Folkestone
Minehead
Royal Tunbridge Wells
Barnstaple
Bridgwater
Salisbury
Winchester
Taunton
Southampton
Yeovil
Worthing
Brighton
Hastings
Bude
Bournemouth
Poole
Newhaven
Eastbourne
Portsmouth
Exeter
Weymouth
Isle of Wight
Newquay
Torquay
Plymouth
Penzance
Falmouth
M6
A1
A64
M62
M1
M58
A1(M)
M180
M56
A6
A16
M6
A5
M54
M42
A47
A11
A49
A1
A44
A14
M40
M50
M5
M1
A40
A40
A34
M4
M4
M3
M25
A21
M20
A3
A303
M5
A27
A30
A39

Airport Plans

BELFAST

01232 22888

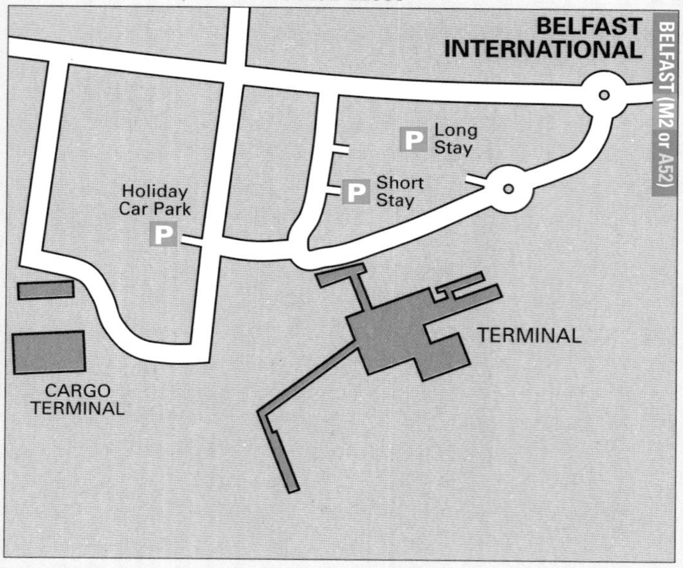

BIRMINGHAM

0121 767 5511

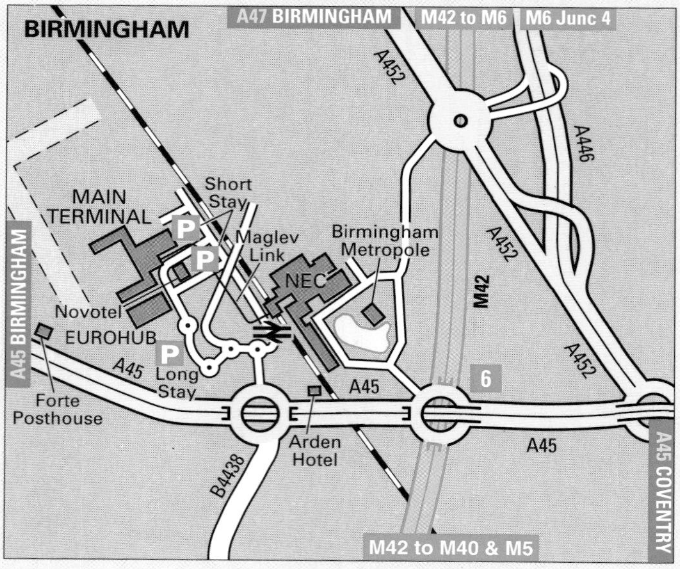

DUBLIN

00 353 1 8444900

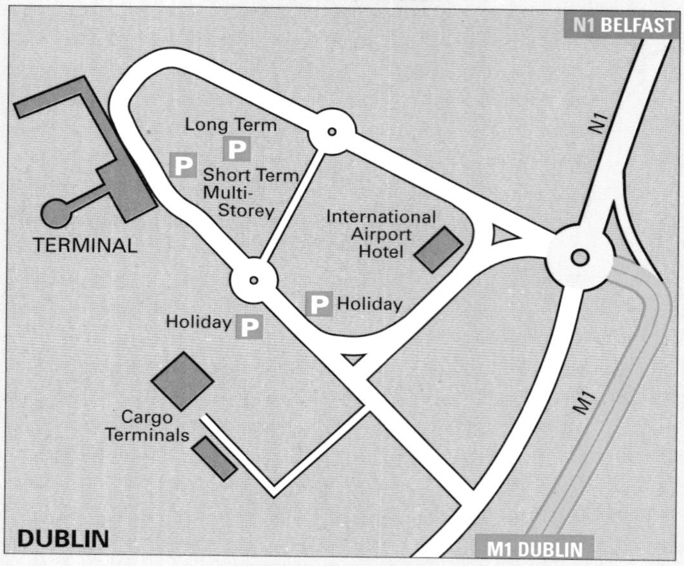

EAST MIDLANDS

01332 810621

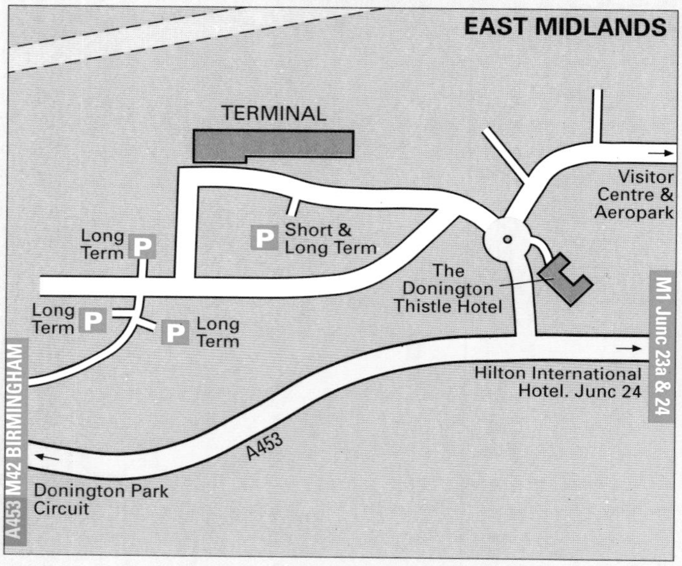

EDINBURGH

0131 333 1000

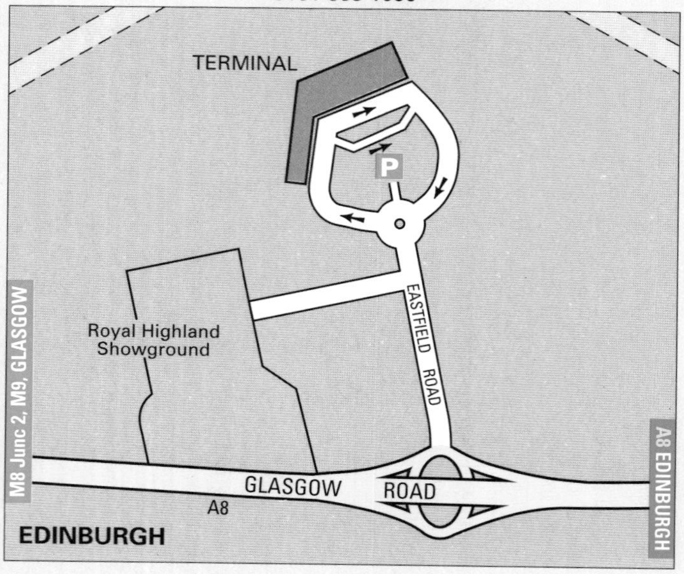

GLASGOW

0141 887 1111

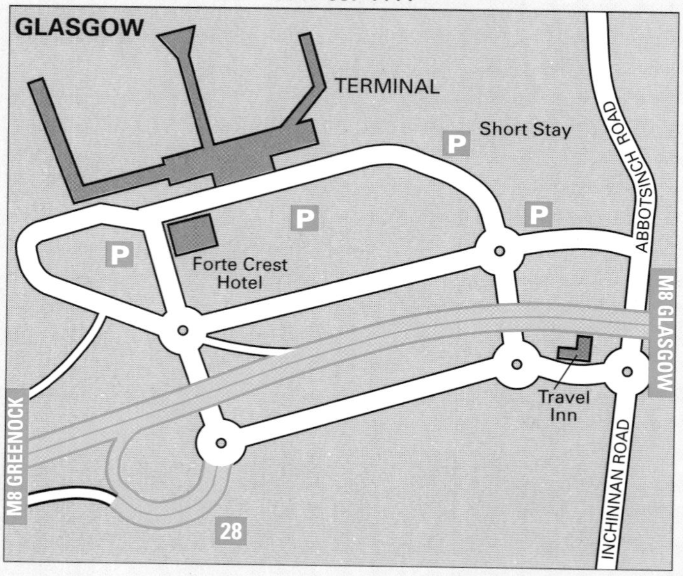

Airport Plans

GATWICK

01293 535353

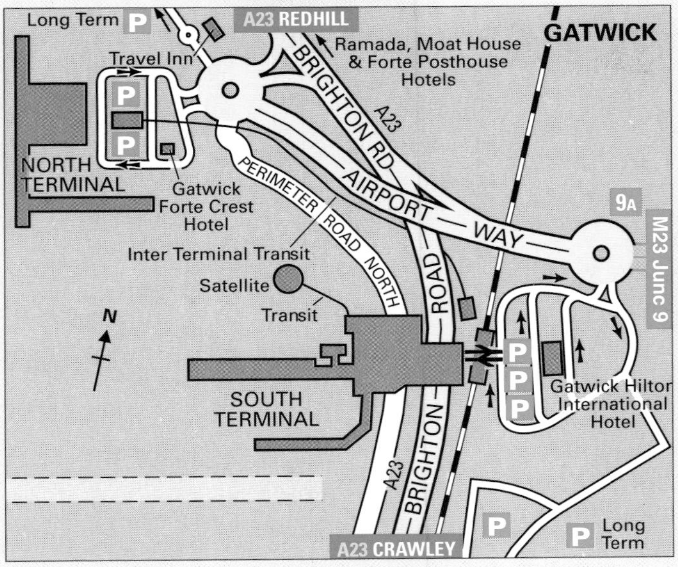

HEATHROW

0181 759 4321

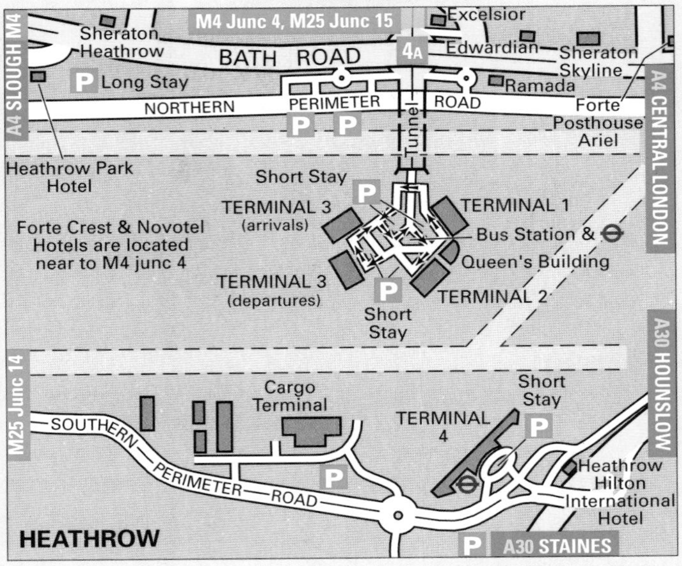

LONDON CITY

0171 474 5555

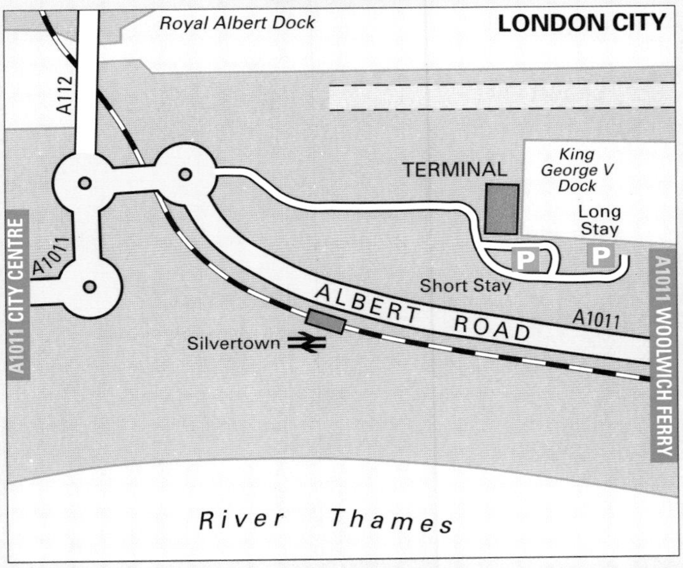

LUTON

01582 405100

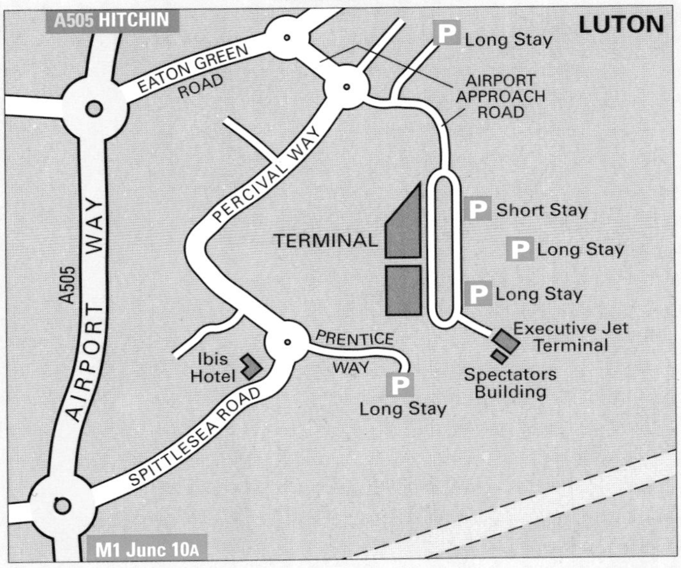

MANCHESTER

0161 489 3000

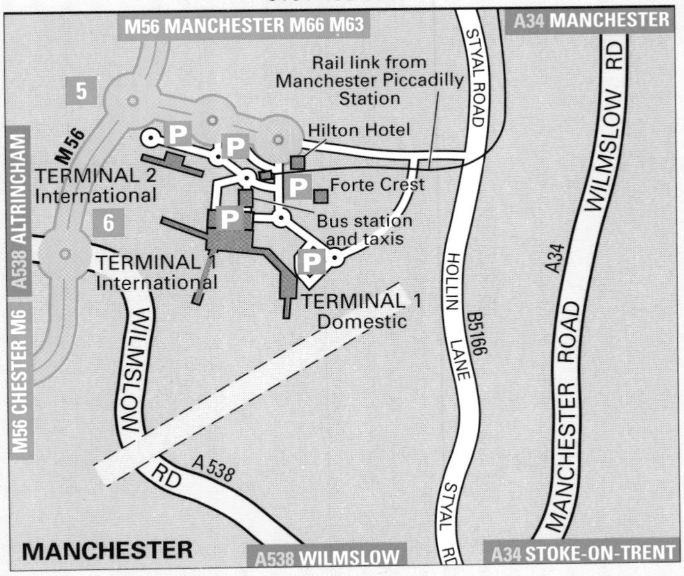

STANSTED

01279 680500

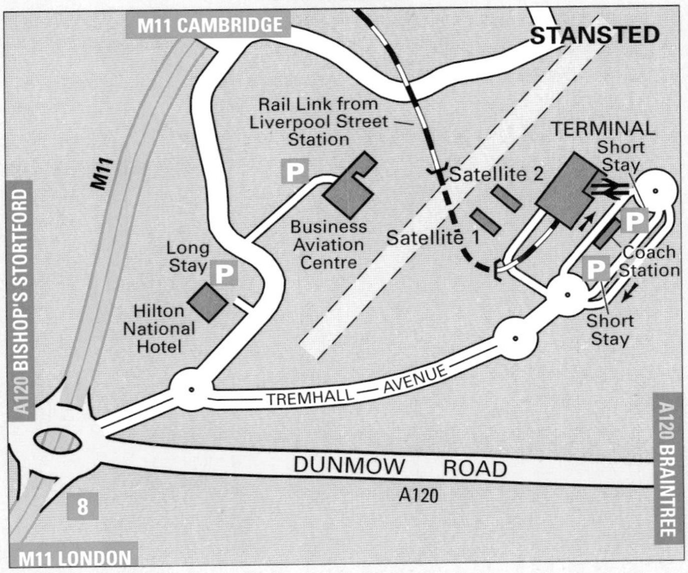

Port Plans

CAIRNRYAN

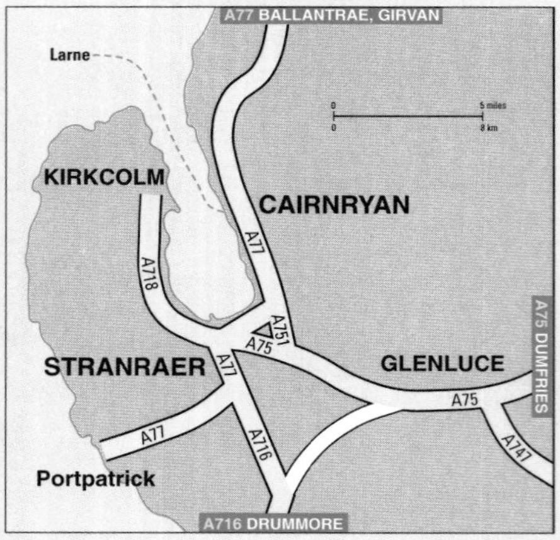

CORK

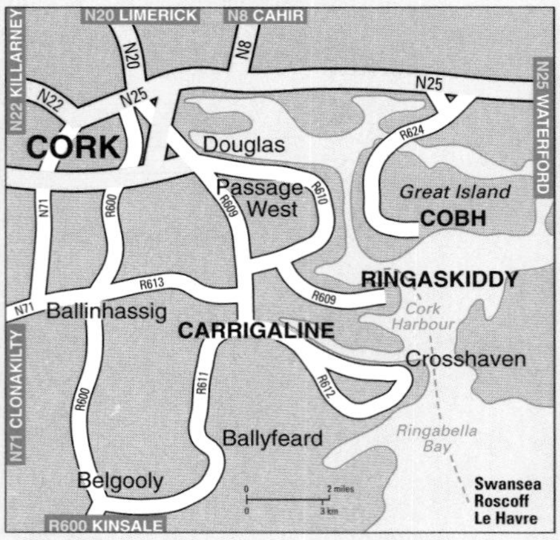

DOVER

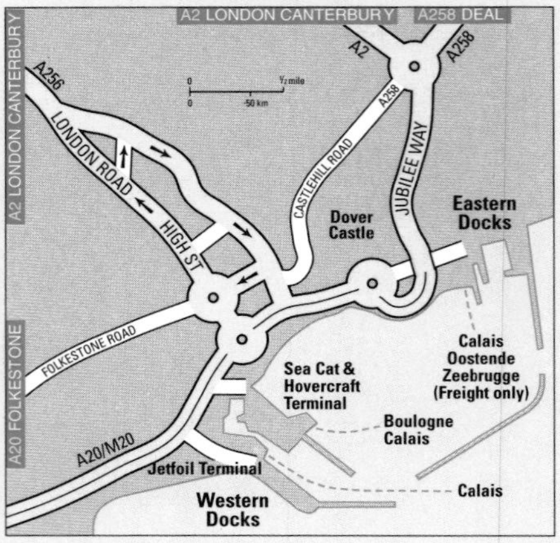

DUBLIN

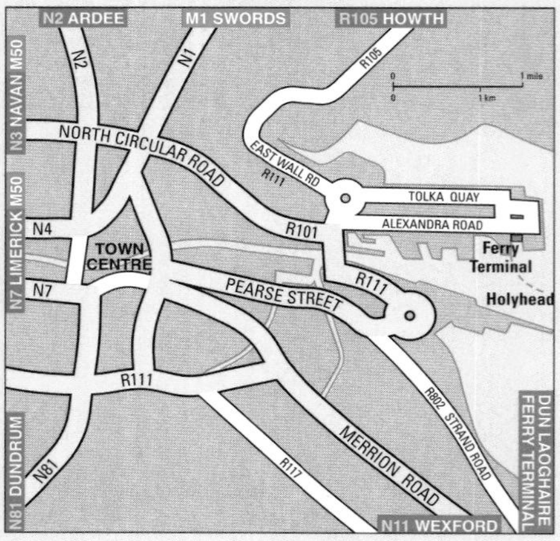

DUN LAOGHAIRE

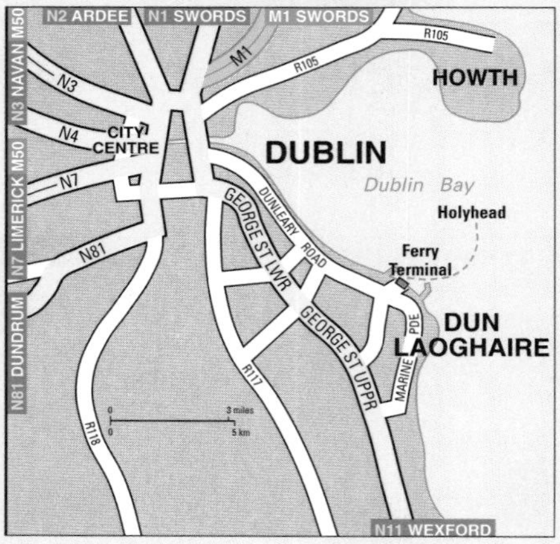

FELIXSTOWE

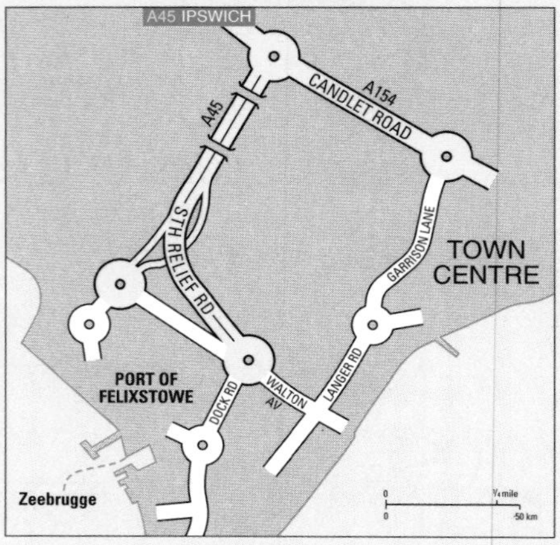

FISHGUARD

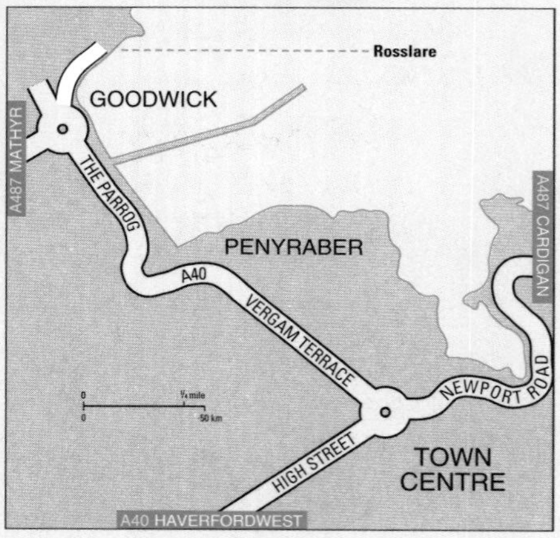

FOLKESTONE

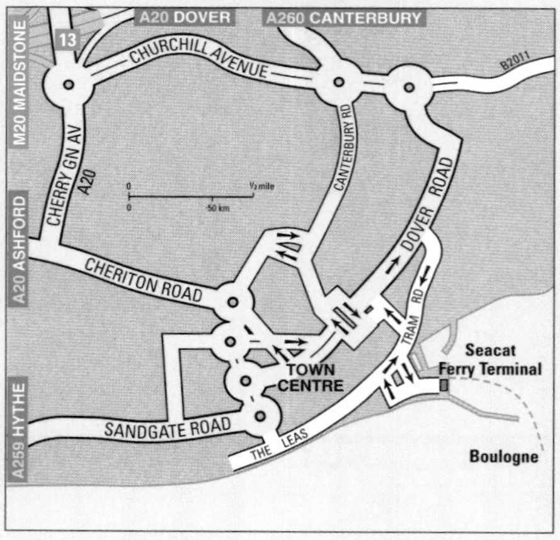

HARWICH

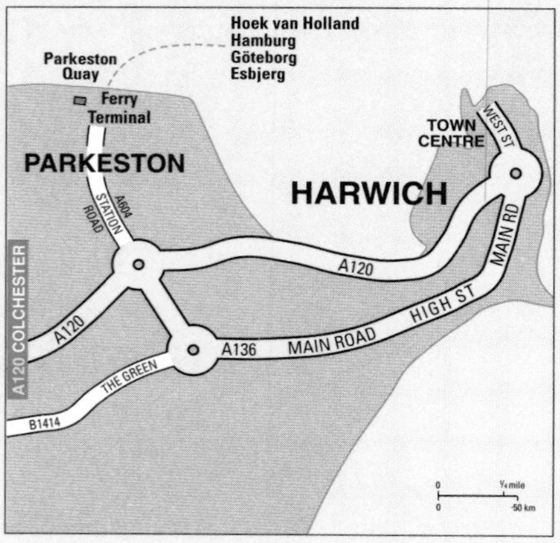

HOLYHEAD

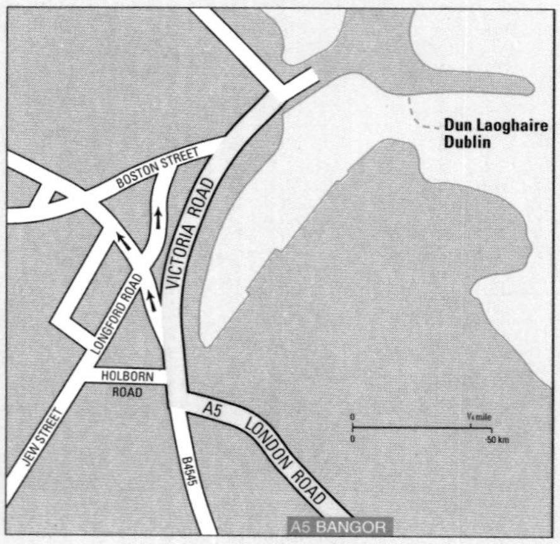

HULL

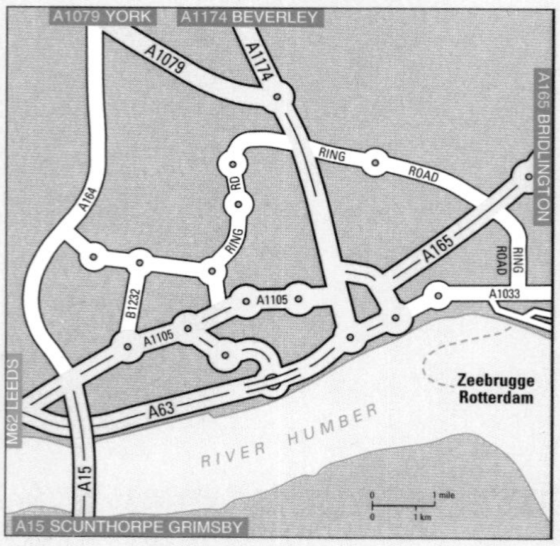

LARNE

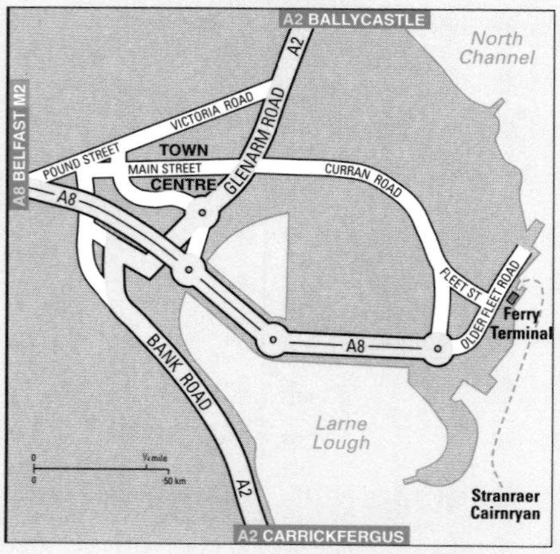

Port Plans

NEWCASTLE UPON TYNE

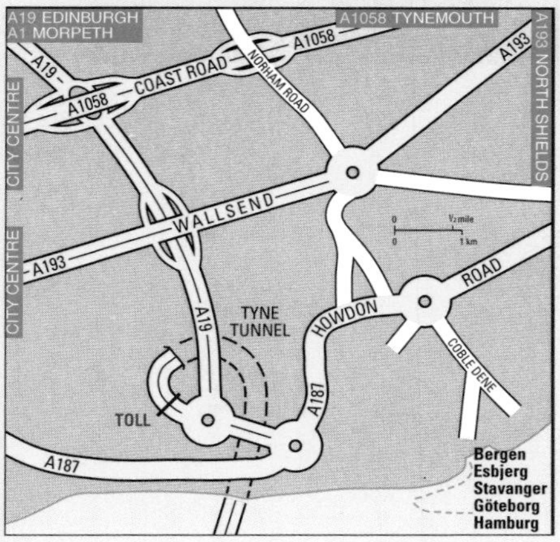

NEWHAVEN

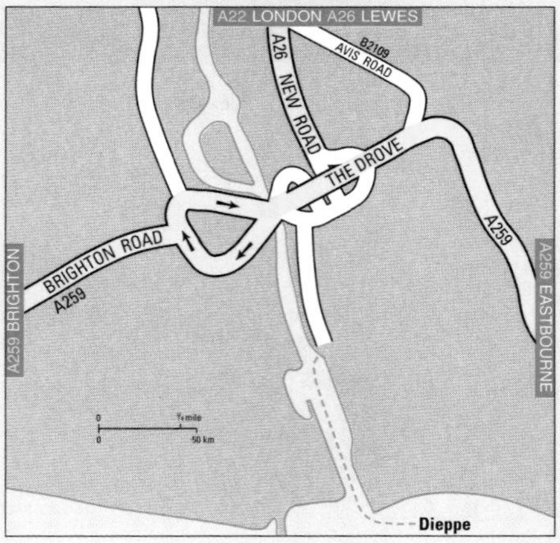

PEMBROKE DOCK

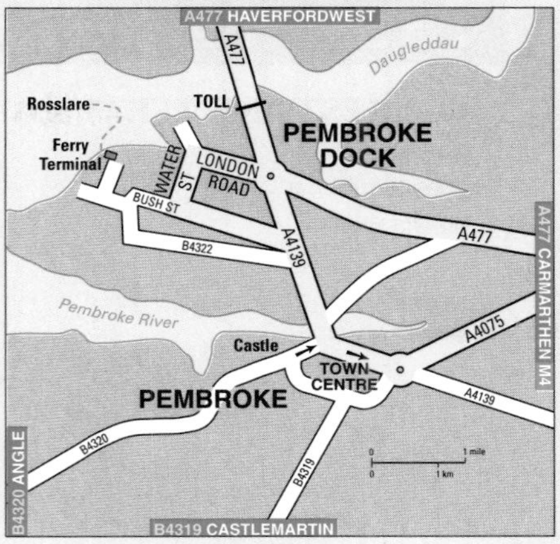

PLYMOUTH

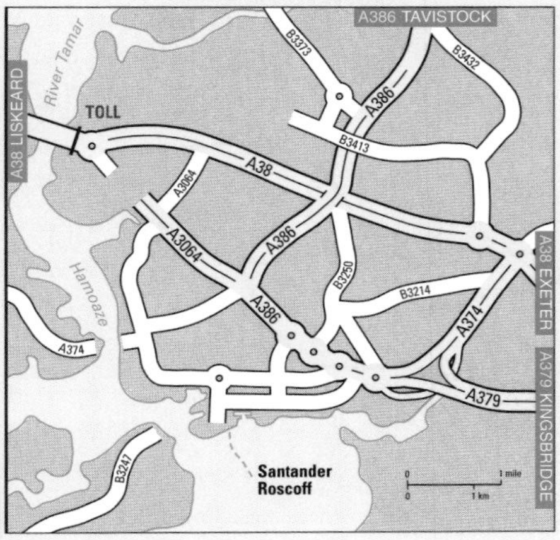

POOLE

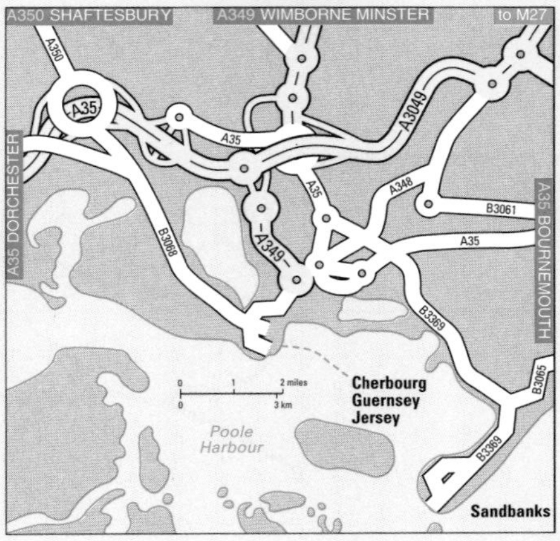

PORTSMOUTH

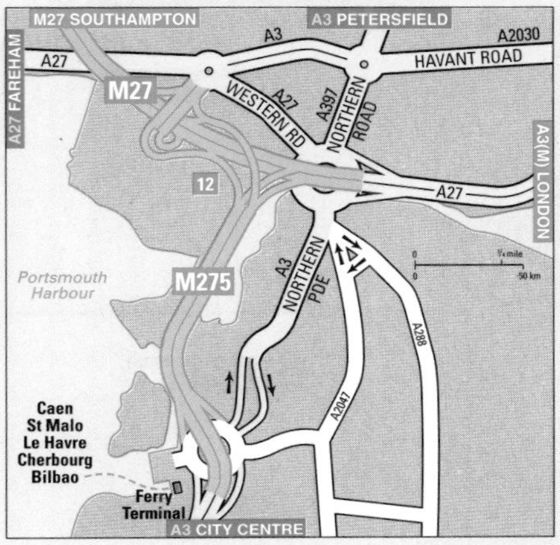

RAMSGATE

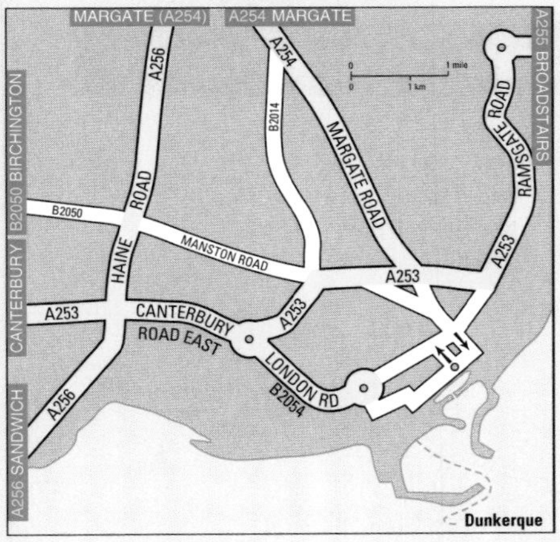

ROSSLARE

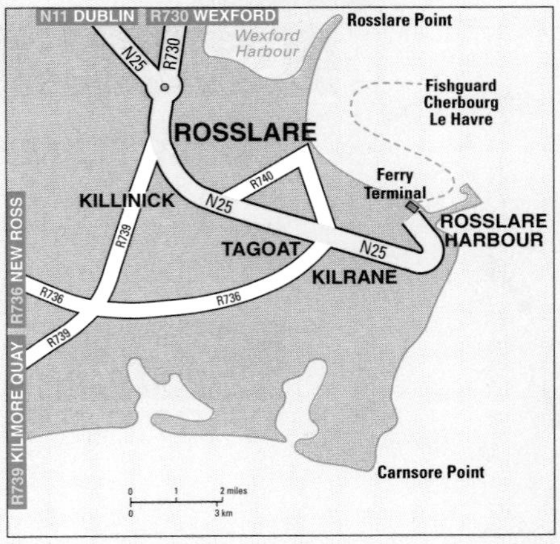

SHEERNESS

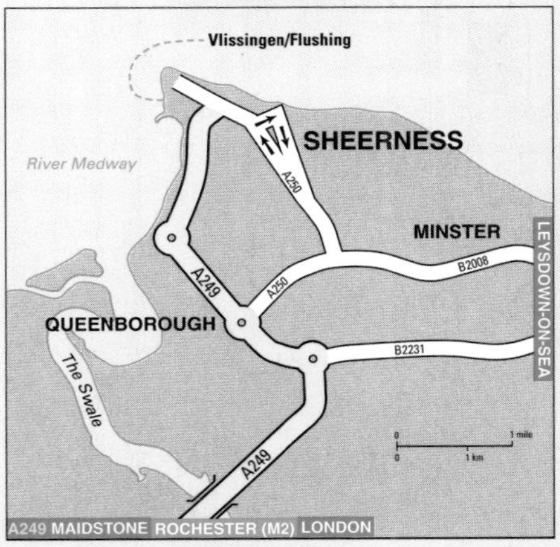

SOUTHAMPTON

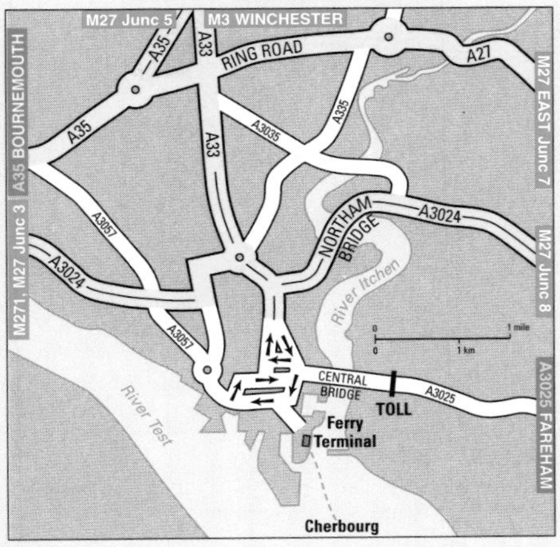

STRANRAER

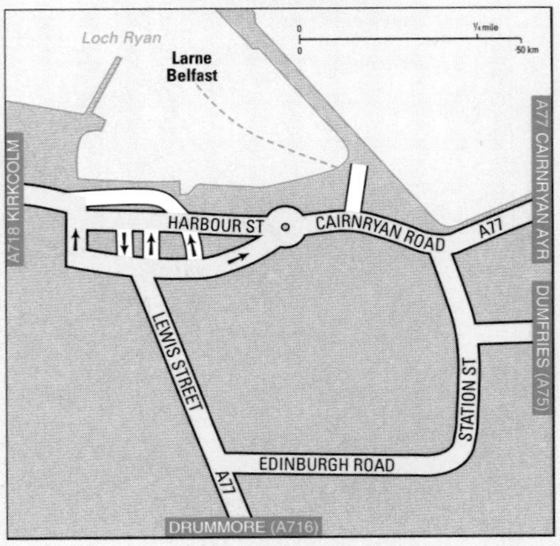

SWANSEA

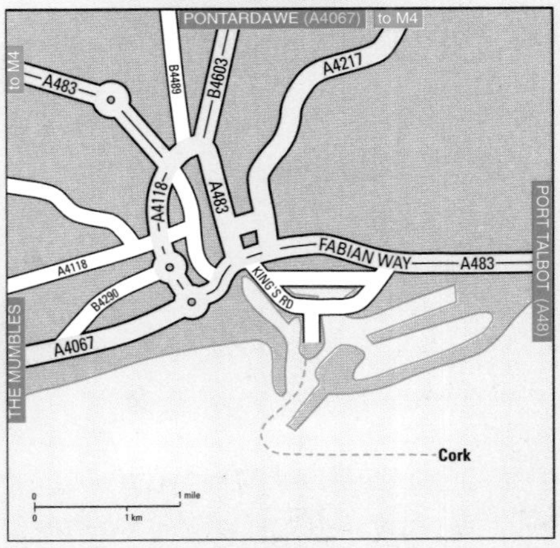

Channel Tunnel Maps

Le Shuttle: Access from the UK

FOLKESTONE TERMINAL

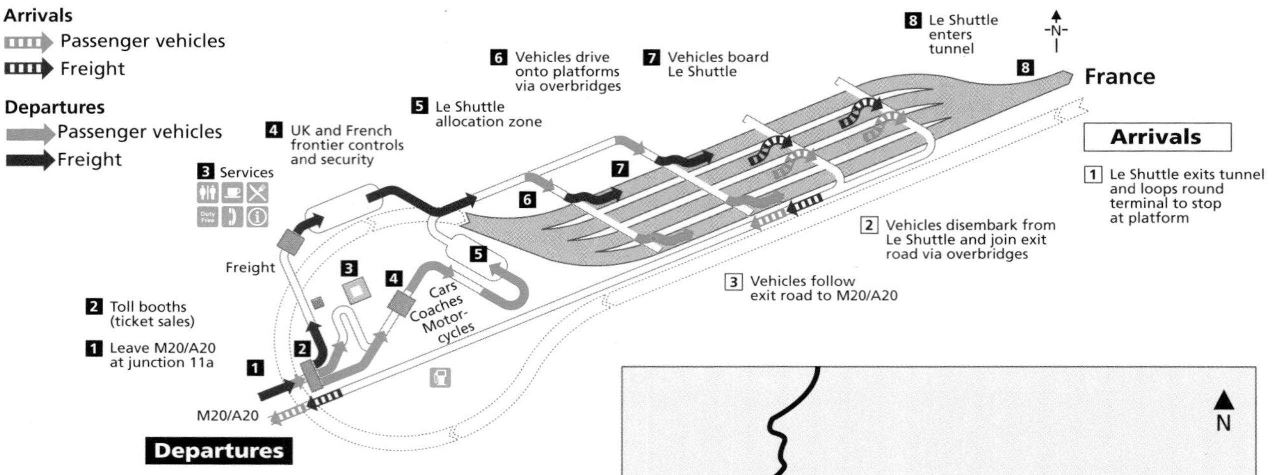

Arrivals
Passenger vehicles
Freight
Departures
Passenger vehicles
Freight
1 Leave M20/A20 at junction 11a
2 Toll booths (ticket sales)
3 Services
4 UK and French frontier controls and security
5 Le Shuttle allocation zone
6 Vehicles drive onto platforms via overbridges
7 Vehicles board Le Shuttle
8 Le Shuttle enters tunnel
N
France
Freight
Cars Coaches Motor-cycles
M20/A20
Departures
Arrivals
1 Le Shuttle exits tunnel and loops round terminal to stop at platform
2 Vehicles disembark from Le Shuttle and join exit road via overbridges
3 Vehicles follow exit road to M20/A20

FOLKESTONE ACCESS MAP

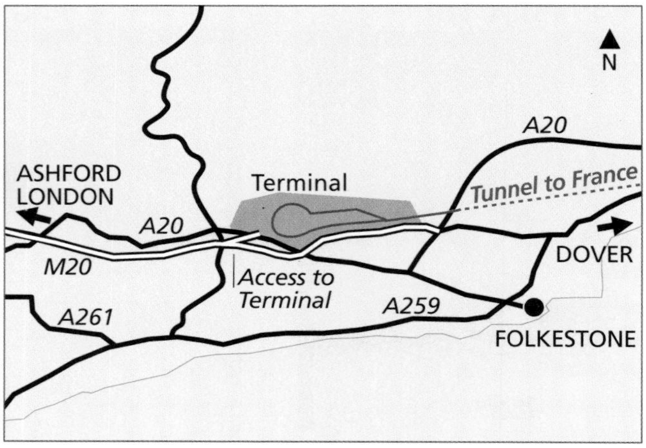

N
A20
ASHFORD
LONDON
Terminal
Tunnel to France
A20
M20
Access to Terminal
DOVER
A261
A259
FOLKESTONE

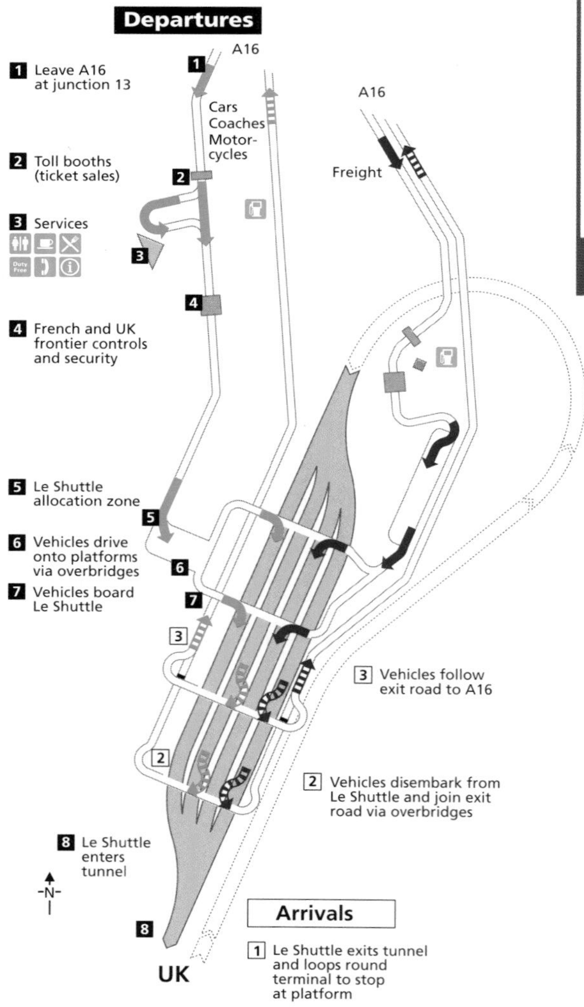

Departures
1 Leave A16 at junction 13
2 Toll booths (ticket sales)
3 Services
4 French and UK frontier controls and security
5 Le Shuttle allocation zone
6 Vehicles drive onto platforms via overbridges
7 Vehicles board Le Shuttle
8 Le Shuttle enters tunnel
A16
A16
Cars
Coaches
Motor-cycles
Freight
N
UK
Arrivals
1 Le Shuttle exits tunnel and loops round terminal to stop at platform
2 Vehicles disembark from Le Shuttle and join exit road via overbridges
3 Vehicles follow exit road to A16

Le Shuttle: Access from France

CALAIS TERMINAL

Arrivals

Passenger vehicles

Freight

Departures

Passenger vehicles

Freight

CALAIS ACCESS MAP

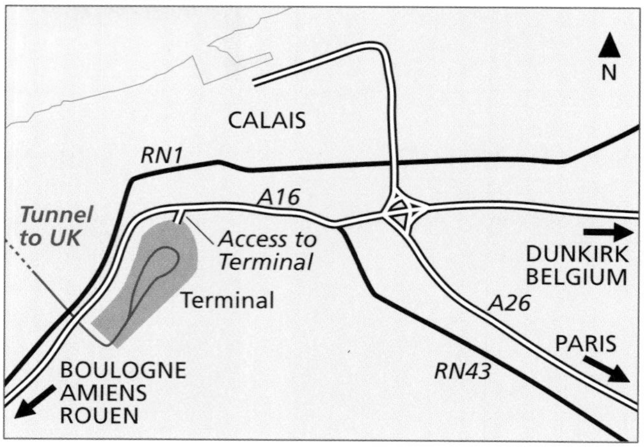

N
CALAIS
RN1
A16
Tunnel to UK
Access to Terminal
Terminal
DUNKIRK
BELGIUM
A26
PARIS
RN43
BOULOGNE
AMIENS
ROUEN

Channel Ferries

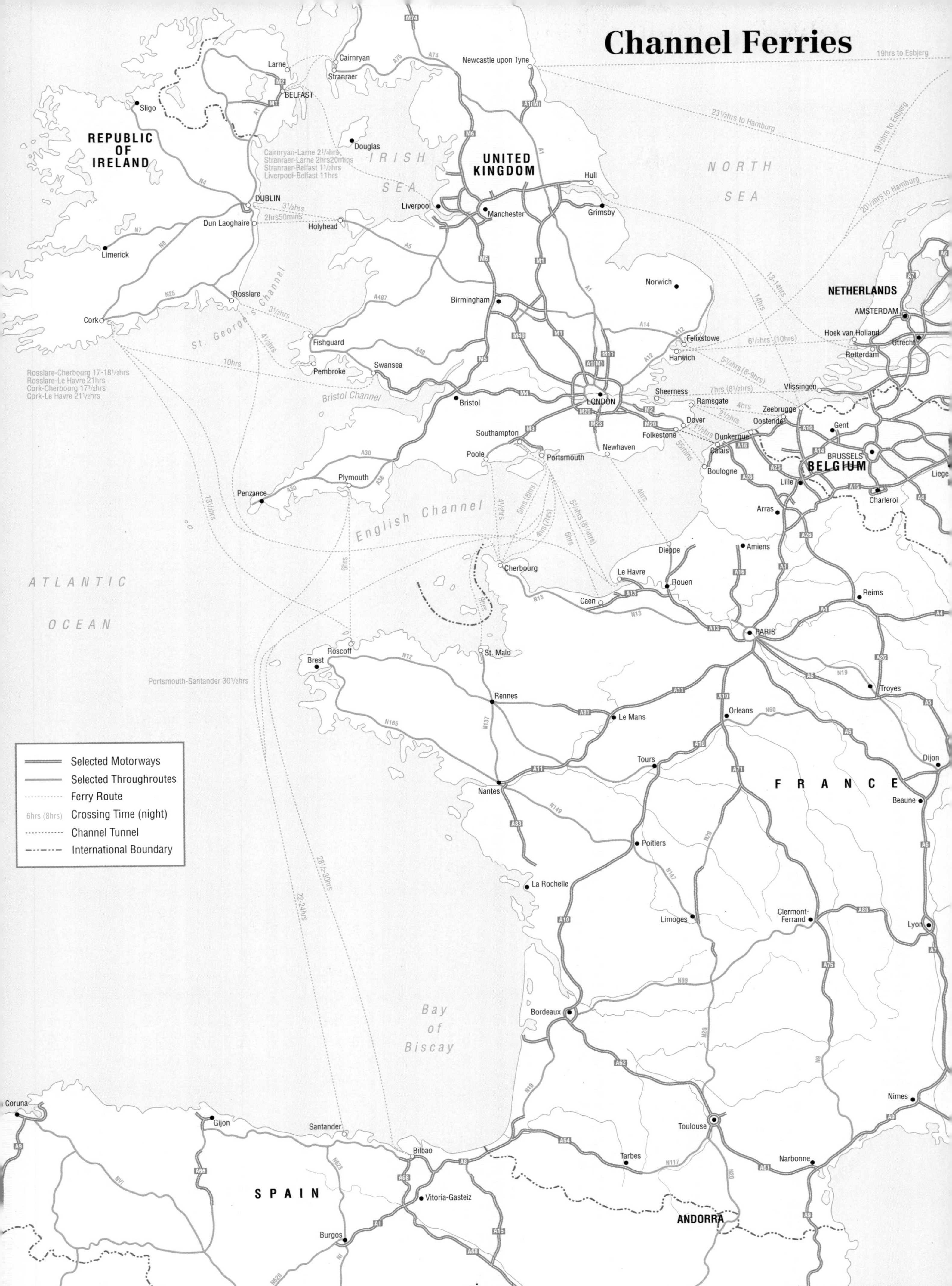

Distance Chart

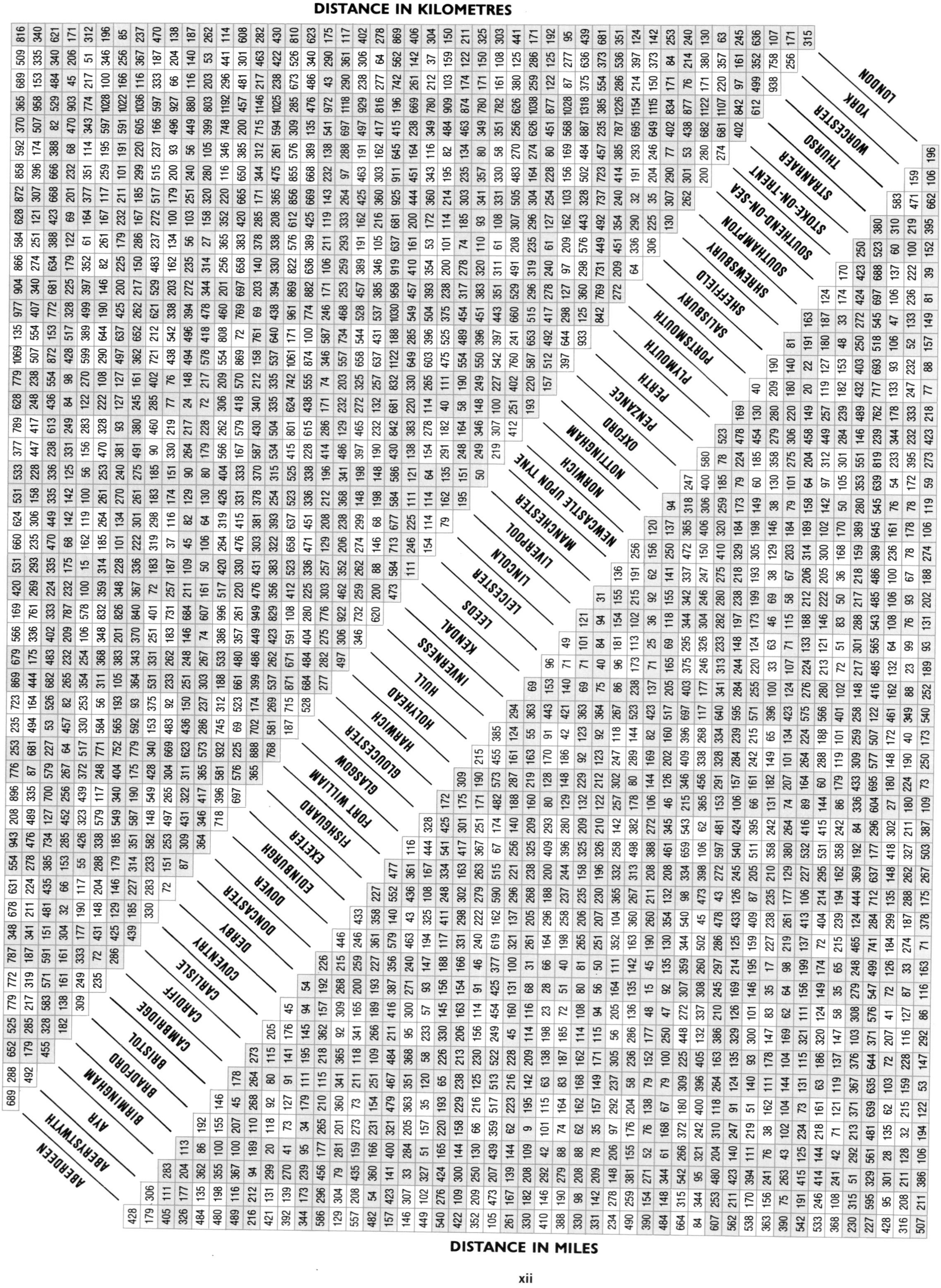
DISTANCE IN KILOMETRES
ABERDEEN
ABERYSTWYTH
AYR
BIRMINGHAM
BRADFORD
BRISTOL
CAMBRIDGE
CARDIFF
CARLISLE
COVENTRY
DERBY
DONCASTER
DOVER
EDINBURGH
EXETER
FISHGUARD
FORT WILLIAM
GLASGOW
GLOUCESTER
HARWICH
HOLYHEAD
HULL
INVERNESS
KENDAL
LEEDS
LEICESTER
LINCOLN
LIVERPOOL
MANCHESTER
NEWCASTLE UPON TYNE
NORWICH
NOTTINGHAM
OXFORD
PENZANCE
PERTH
PLYMOUTH
PORTSMOUTH
SALISBURY
SHEFFIELD
SHREWSBURY
SOUTHAMPTON
SOUTHEND-ON-SEA
STOKE-ON-TRENT
STRANRAER
THURSO
WORCESTER
YORK
LONDON
DISTANCE IN MILES

Key to Main Map Symbols

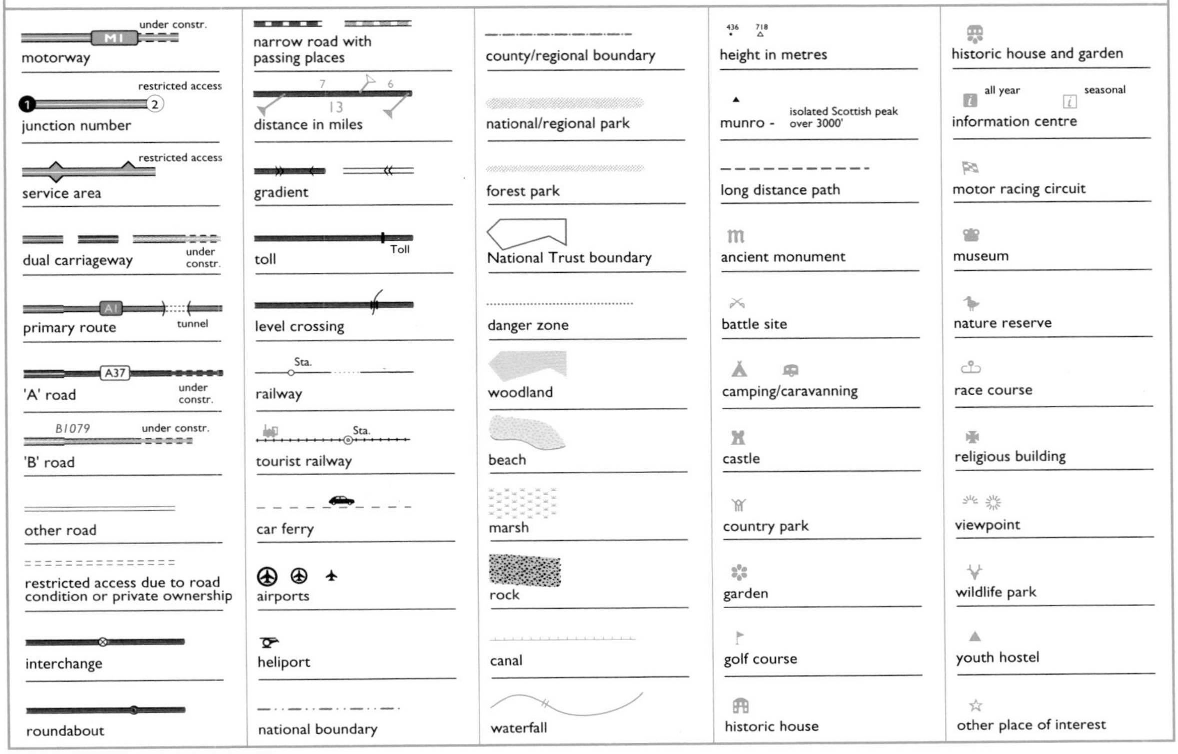

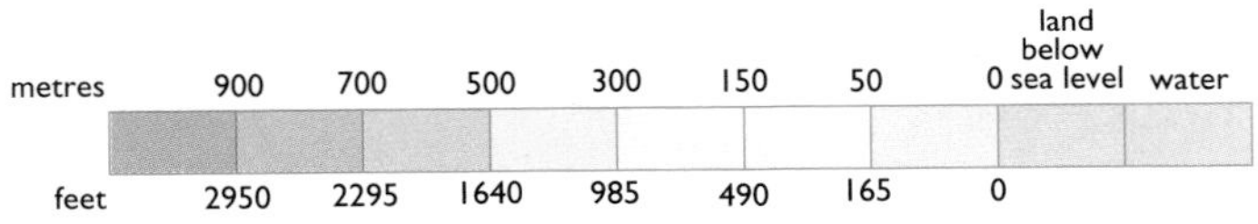

Scale

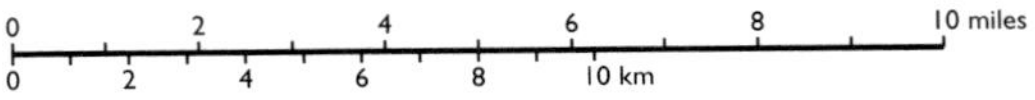

St Helen's
White Island
Lower Town
St Martin's
Old Grimsby
Tean
Middle Town
Higher Town
New Grimsby
Bryher
Tresco
Eastern Isles
Samson
Crow Sound
North West Channel
The Road
CHAMBERED CAIRNS
Maypole
Hugh Town
A3110
St Mary's
PORTH HELLICK DOWN BURIAL CHAMBER
The Garrison
Scilly Isles
Old Town
GARRISON WALLS
Crim Rocks
Broad Sound
Annet
St Mary's Sound
Gugh
St Agnes
ISLES OF SCILLY
Western Rocks
Smith Sound
Bishop Rock
same scale as main map
Kelsey Head
West Pentire
Holywell Bay
Penhale Point
Ligger Pt
Ligger or Perran Bay
Perranporth
Bawden Rocks or Man and his Man
Trevellas
St Agnes Head
St Agnes
Mithian
Goonbell
A3075
Porthtowan
Mount Hawke
Three Burrows
A30
Tregavethan
A390
Mawla
Portreath
B3300
Blackwater
Illogan
Bridge
Chacewater
Crane Islands
Navax Point
Godrevy Island
Scorrier
St Day
Coombe
Pool
Redruth
Gwithian
Kehelland
Tuckingmill
Carn Brea
Pennance
Carharrack
Gwennap
Twelveheads
Carn Naun Pt
The Carrack's
BARBARA HEPWORTH MUSEUM
The Island
St Ives Bay
St Ives
Carbis Bay
Halsetown
Connor Downs
Roseworthy
Camborne
Lanner
A393
Gurnard's Head
Zennor
Phillack
Angarrack
Four Lanes
Perranarworthal
Trendrine Hill
Towednack
A3074
Lelant
Barripper
Troon
Penhalvean
Ponsanooth
Porthmeor
B3306
Gwinear
Carnhell Green
Amalebra
Cripplesease
Hayle
Stithians
A393
Pendeen Watch
Nancledra
Trencrom Hill
St Erth Praze
Rosewarne
Lower Boscaswell
Morvah
CHYSAUSTER ANCIENT VILLAGE
Canon's Town
Fraddam
B3280
Praze-an-Beeble
Burras
Stithians Res
Bojewyan
Pendeen
Trewellard
New Mill
St Erth
Leedstown
Crowan Beacon
Long Downs
Penryn
B3318
Ludgvan
A30
Whitecross
Crowan
Porkellis
Rame
Botallack
Carnyorth
Townshend
Mabe Burnthouse
Madron
Crowlas
Relubbus
Edgcumbe
Cape Cornwall
St Just
Newbridge
Heamoor
Gulval
Longrock
St Hilary
B3302
Nancegollan
A394
Treverva
Budock Water
The Brisons
A3071
TRENGWAINTON
GODOLPHIN HOUSE
Godolphin Cross
Wendron
CARN LESKYS
Bosavern
Tremethick Cross
Chyandour
Marazion
Crowntown
Seworgan
Kelynack
Sancreed
Buryas Bridge
Penzance
St Michael's Mount
Goldsithney
Trescowe
Tregonning Hill
Penjerrick
Brane
Lower Drift
THE EGYPTIAN HOUSE
Perranuthnoe
Germoe
Sithney
Brill
Whitesand Bay
Tredavoe
A30
Catchall
Newlyn
Ashton
Breage
Constantine
Mawnan Smith
Crows-an-wra
Kerris
Paul
Cudden Point
Praa Sands
Rinsey
Helston
Porth Navas
Sennen Cove
B3283
Mousehole
Gweek
Longships
Sennen
St Buryan
St Clement's Isle
Trewavas Head
Porthleven
A3083
Mawgan
Helford
Trevescan
Boleigh
MOUNT'S BAY
Garras
Manaccan
LAND'S END
B3315
STONE CIRCLE
St Martin
Lamorna Cove
Porthcurno
Treen
Gunwalloe
Berepper
Newtown in St Martin
Tregidden
St Levan
Cribba Head
Logan Rock
Cury
St Keverne
Gwennap Head
Crosslanes
TUMULI
Traboe
Poldhu Cove
Poldhu Point
Goonhilly Downs
Mullion
B3296
Penhale
Porth Mellin
Mullion Cove
Gwenter
Mullion Island
Ruan Major
Kuggar
Predannack Wollas
Ruan Minor
A3083
Vellan Head
Grade
Cadgwith
Kynance Cove
Toll
Landewednack
Lizard
Hot Point
LIZARD POINT
Wolf Rock
0 2 4 6 8 10 miles
0 2 4 6 8 10 km

14
15
16
17
18
A
B
C
D
E
F
G
Newland
Rumps Point
The Mouls
Pentire Point
Pentireglaze
New Polzeath
Port Isaac
Portquin
Port Gaverne
Trelights
Westdowns
Lanteglos
Trewalder
Helstone
Valley Truddle
Tresinney
Lower Moor
Buttern Hill
Bray Down
Fivelanes
Altarnun
Polyphant
Kennards House
South Petherwin
Lewannick
Gulland Rock
Polzeath
Trebetherick
St Endellion
Pendoggett
Michaelstow
Garrow Tor
Codda
BODMIN MOOR
Congdon's Shop
Trebullett
Lezant
Treburley
Coad's Green
Gunver Head
Trevose Head
Quies
Crugmeer
Pityme
Rock
Stoptide
St Minver
St Kew
Trelill
St Breward
Row
Bolventor
Trebartha
North Hill
Constantine Bay
St Merryn
Trevone
Padstow
Chapel Amble
St Kew Highway
St Tudy
Trewornan
Kelly
Bodieve
Treyarnon
Shop
Little Petherick
Trevanson
Wadebridge
Egloshayle
St Mabyn
Blisland
Temple
Colliford Reservoir
Dozmary Pool
Smallacombe Downs
Kilmar Tor
Henwood
Linkinhorne
Bray Shop
Rilla Mill
South Hill
Porthcothan Beach
Porthcothan
Tregolds
St Breock
St Issey
Hellandbridge
Helland
Cardinham Moor
Browngelly Downs
Siblyback Resr
Minions
Upton Cross
Golberdon
Park Head
Penrose
St Ervan
Rumford
Tredinnick
Burlawn
Washaway
Lane-end
Maidenwell
Warleggan
Caradon Hill
Common Moor
Darite
Pensilva
Hayes
Trevigro
Bedruthan Steps
St Eval
Dunmere
Cardinham
Mount
St Neot
St Cleer
Tremar
Middlehill
Trenance
St Breock Downs
The Fiddler
Rutherbridge
Nanstallon
Bodmin
Mawgan Porth
Berryl's Point
Vale of Mawgan or Lanherne
St Mawgan
Winnards Perch
St Lawrence
Withiel
Ley
Doublebois
Dobwalls
Merrymeet
St Ive
Tregurrian
Watergate Bay
Talskiddy
St Columb Major
St Wenn
Lanivet
Bodmin Parkway Station
East Taphouse
Liskeard
Pengover Green
Quethiock
Porth
St Columb Minor
Tregonetha
Victoria
Trebyan
Trevelmond
St Pinnock
Lamellion
Menheniot
Blunts
Colan
Mountjoy
Black Cross
Trebudannon
Ruthvoes
Belowda
Lockengate
Sweetshouse
Restormel Castle
West Taphouse
Boconnoc
Quintrell Downs
White Cross
Trevarren
Roche
Bodwen
Redmoor
Lostwithiel
Bridgend
St Keyne
Herodsfoot
Trewidland
Horningtops
Tideford
Kestle Mill
St Columb Road
Indian Queens
Bilberry
Lanlivery
Couch's Mill
Duloe
Bylane End
Retyn
Fraddon
St Dennis
Bugle
Luxulyan
Bocaddon
Widegates
Trerule Foot
Newlyn East
St Enoder
Blue Anchor
Hensbarrow Downs
Stenalees
Lanreath
Muchlarnick
Tredinnick
Hessenford
Retew
Penwithick
Penpillick
Lerryn
Sandplace
Morval
Summercourt
Treviscoe
Nanpean
Carthew
Ruddlemoor
Frethurgy
Tywardreath Highway
St Blazey
St Veep
Pelynt
St Martin
Chapel Town
Foxhole
Newlyn Downs
Mitchell
Brighton
Scarcewater
Whealmartyn
St Blazey Gate
Tywardreath
Golant
Penpoll
East Looe
Downderry
Portwrinkle
Carland Cross
St Stephen
ST AUSTELL
Boscoppa
Par
Lescrow
Trenewan
West Looe
Trelassick
New Mills
Coombe
High Street
Trewoon
Holmbush
Carlyon Bay
Polkerris
Lansallos
Porthallow
St George's or Looe Island
Trethan
St Allen
Ladock
St Mewan
Charlestown
Fowey
Bodinnick
Polperro
Trispen
Tregear
Grampound Road
Sticker
Polgooth
St Austell Bay
Menabilly
Polruan
Pencarrow Head
Lantivet Bay
Whitsand
St Erme
CORNWALL
Probus
Grampound
Hewas Water
Porthpean
Trenarren
Gribbin Head
Black Head
Pentewan
Penare Point
Mevagissey Bay
Tresillian
Creed
St Ewe
Trewithen
Kenwyn
Truro
Polmassick
Mevagissey
Merther
St Clement
Tregony
Chapel Point
Malpas
Trewarthenick
Trevarrick
Gorran Churchtown
Ruan Lanihorne
Old Kea
St Michael Penkevil
Lamorran
St Michael Caerhays
Gorran Haven
Maenease Point
Playing Place
Portholland
Boswinger
Trelissick
Philleigh
Veryan
Portloe
Veryan Bay
Penare
Dodman Point
Feock
Carne
Gerrans
Nare Head
Trewithian
St Just in Roseland
Portscatho
Gerrans Bay
St Mawes
Greeb Point
Castle Pt
Pendennis Point
St Anthony
Bohortha
Zone Point
Falmouth Bay
The Manacles
ALDERNEY
The Swinge
Fort Quesnard
St Anne
same scale as main map
GUERNSEY
Grand Havre
Bordeaux
Weymouth
L'Islet
Vale (ruins)
St Sampson
Herm
Saumarez Park
Vazon Bay
St Peter Port
Castle Cornet
Lihou
Dolmen
Jethou
King's Mills
Rocquaine Bay
Fort Grey
St Saviour
Sausmarez Manor
La Seigneurie
SARK
Brecqhou
St Martin
Pleinmont Pt
German Occupation Mus.
St Helier
Jerbourg Pt
Little Sark
Alderney
Guernsey
Herm
Sark
Jersey
CHANNEL ISLANDS location map
JERSEY
Plemont Pt
Greve de Lecq Bay
Grosnez (ruins)
St John
Bouley Bay
Battle of Flowers Museum
St Ouen
Tropical Gardens
Carrefour Selous
German Underground Hosp.
Zoo
St Martin
St Catherine's Bay
St Ouen's Bay
St Peter
Maufant
Mt Orgueil
St Brelade
St Aubin
St Aubin's Bay
Five Oaks
Gorey
Grouville
La Cotte
Elizabeth Castle
St Peter Port & Weymouth
Noirmont Pt
St Helier
St Malo
La Rocque Pt
A30
A38
A39
A389
A390
A391
A392
A3058
A3059
A3076
A3078
A3082
A387
A10
A11
A12
A13
A3
A4
A5
A6
A8
A9
B3314
B3266
B3267
B3276
B3274
B3275
B3287
B3269
B3268
B3359
B3254
B3257
B31
B33
B55
B27
B28
B41

16
17
18
19
20
A
B
C
D
E
F
G
6
3
CORNWALL
BODMIN MOOR
Widemouth Bay
Coppathorne
Dizzard Point
Poundstock
Tregole
Trewint
St Gennys
Crackington Haven
Cambeak
Wainhouse Corner
Crackington
Fire Beacon Point
Tresparrett Posts
Tresparrett
Boscastle
Trevalga
Tintagel Head
TINTAGEL OLD POST OFFICE
Bossiney
Tintagel
Trewarmett
Trebarwith
Start Point
Rockhead
Delabole
Treligga
Westdowns
Port Isaac
Port Isaac Bay
Port Gaverne
Portquin
Portquin Bay
Trelights
The Mouls
St Endellion
St Minver
Chapel Amble
St Kew
St Kew Highway
Pendoggett
Trelill
St Teath
Trewalder
Lanteglos
Camelford
Valley Truckle
Helstone
Michaelstow
St Tudy
St Mabyn
Kelly
Bodieve
Trevanson
Wadebridge
Egloshayle
St Breock
Burlawn
Washaway
Lane-end
Dunmere
Nanstallon
Bodmin
St Lawrence
Ruthernbridge
St Breock Downs
St Wenn
Withiel
Tregonetha
Victoria
Belowda
Roche
Lanivet
Trebyan
Lockengate
Bodwen
Bilberry
Bugle
Redmoor
Lostwithiel
Lanlivery
Luxulyan
St Dennis
Stenalees
Hensbarrow Downs
Carthew
Penwithick
Trethurgy
St Blazey
St Blazey Gate
Par
Tywardreath
Tywardreath Highway
Penpillick
Nanpean
Foxhole
St Stephen
ST AUSTELL
High Street
Trewoon
St Mewan
Holmbush
Boscoppa
Charlestown
Carlyon Bay
Polgooth
Sticker
Hewas Water
Porthpean
Trenarren
St Austell Bay
Black Head
Pentewan
Penare Point
St Ewe
Polmassick
Mevagissey
Mevagissey Bay
Chapel Point
Trevarrick
Gorran Churchtown
St Michael Caerhays
Gorran Haven
Maenease Point
Boswinger
Penare
Dodman Point
Veryan Bay
Polkerris
Fowey
Menabilly
Gribbin Head
Polruan
Pencarrow Head
Lantivet Bay
Bodinnick
Golant
Lerryn
Penpoll
Lanreath
Lansallos
Polperro
Pelynt
Trenewan
Muchlarnick
Sandplace
Porthallow
Talland
Looe
East Looe
West Looe
Looe Bay
St George's or Looe Island
St Martin
Morval
Duloe
Tredinnick
Herodsfoot
Trewidland
Horningtops
St Keyne
Couch's Mill
Bocaddon
Boconnoc
Bridgend
Sweetshouse
West Taphouse
East Taphouse
Trevelmond
St Pinnock
Doublebois
Dobwalls
Liskeard
Lamellion
Menheniot
Merrymeet
Pengover Green
Quethiock
Blunts
Pillaton
St Ive
Tremar
Darite
Common Moor
St Cleer
St Neot
Ley
Mount
Warleggan
Maidenwell
Cardinham
Cardinham Moor
Blisland
Temple
Colliford Reservoir
Browngelly Downs
Dozmary Pool
Bolventor
Codda
St Breward
Row
Garrow Tor
Brown Willy
Rough Tor
Buttern Hill
Bray Down
Lower Moor
Tresinney
New Park
St Clether
Davidstow
Trewassa
Tremail
Hallworthy
Treneglos
Tremaine
Warbstow
Trelash
Otterham
Canworthy Water
Marshgate
Lesnewth
Collamoor Head
Langdon
Jacobstow
Week St Mary
Whitstone
Treskinnick Cross
Titson
Bridgerule
Yeomadon
Pyworthy
Chesty
Hollacombe
Tinney
Herdicott
Clawton
Cofcott Green
North Tamerton
Trebarrow
Tetcott
Lana
Luffincott
Ashwater
Henford
Halwill Forest
Halwill
Halwill Junction
Beaworthy
Upcott
Quoditch
Broadbury
Eworthy
Germansweek
Chapman's Well
Virginstow
East Panson
Northcott
Boyton
Gridley Corner
Bratton Clovelly
Roadford Resr
Broadwoodwidger
Cross Green
Thrushelton
Stowford
Lewdown
Lewtrenchard
Portgate
Allerford
Liftondown
Lifton
Tinhay
Coryton
Marystow
Chillaton
Kelly
Bradstone
Felldownhead
Milton Abbot
South Brentor
Longcross
Dunterton
Rezare
Lamerton
Sydenham Damerel
Horsebridge
Cholwell
Latchley
Gulworthy
Gunnislake
Chilsworthy
Hingston Down
St Ann's Chapel
Albaston
Higher Metherell
Morwellham
Calstock
Buckland Monachorum
Bere Alston
Milton Combe
Bere Ferrers
Tamerton Foliot
Landulph
Cargreen
Carkeel
Botusfleming
Hatt
Landrake
Tideford
Trematon
Saltash
Markwell
St Stephen's
St Budeaux
St Germans
Polbathic
Hessenford
Widegates
Bylane End
Trerule Foot
Seaton
Downderry
Portwrinkle
Crafthole
Sheviock
Antony
Torpoint
Devonport
Stonehouse
Cremyll
Mount Edgcumbe
Millbrook
St John
Kingsand
Cawsand
Cawsand Bay
Rame
Rame Head
Penlee Point
Whitsand Bay
Danger Zone
Freathy
Eddystone Rocks
Santander (summer only)
Roscoff
Launceston
St Stephens
Newport
Kennards House
Tregadillett
Piper's Pool
Red Down
Trewen
Laneast
Downhead
Polyphant
Altarnun
Fivelanes
Lewannick
South Petherwin
Lawhitton
Lezant
Trebullett
Trekenner
Treburley
Congdon's Shop
Coad's Green
Trebartha
North Hill
Kilmar Tor
Smallacombe Downs
Bathpool
Linkinhorne
Rilla Mill
Henwood
Upton
Upton Cross
Minions
Siblyback Resr
Caradon Hill
Pensilva
Middlehill
Golberdon
Kelly Bray
Haye
Trevigro
Callington
Harrowbarrow
Kit Hill
Ashton
St Dominick
Newbridge
St Mellion
South Hill
Downgate
Luckett
Stoke Climsland
Bray Shop
North Petherwin
Egloskerry
Tresmeer
Tregeare
Yeolmbridge
Langore
Werrington
Ladycross
Polapit Tamar
Bridgetown
St Giles on the Heath
Bennacott
Troswell
Brazacott
Caudworthy
Maxworthy
Clubworthy
South Wheatley
West Curry
Yeolmbridge
0 2 4 6 8 10 miles
0 2 4 6 8 10 km

21
22
23
24
25
A
B
C
D
E
F
G
7
DEVON
DARTMOOR
NATIONAL PARK
Jacobstowe
Exbourne
Honeychurch
Sampford Courtenay
North Tawton
Bow
Clannaborough Barton
Copplestone
Sandford
Creedy Park
Thorverton
Up Exe
Silverton
Hele
Shilstone
Broadnymett
Nymet Tracey
Knowle
Crediton
Shobrooke
Bradninch
Clyst St Lawrence
Inwardleigh
Oak Cross
Folly Gate
Belstone Corner
Itton
Yeoford
Uton
Hookway
Newton St Cyres
Brampford Speke
Nether Exe
Rewe
Stoke Canon
Poltimore
Upton Pyne
Westwood
Broad Clyst
Whimple
Taw Green
Spreyton
Court Barton
Oldridge
Dog Village
Cowley
Southcott
Okehampton
Sticklepath
South Tawton
Hittisleigh
Cheriton Bishop
Tedburn St Mary
Pinhoe
Rockbeare
Thornton Cross
Yelland
Belstone
Okehampton Camp
South Zeal
Crockernwell
Cheriton Cross
Whitestone
Exwick
Whipton
EXETER
Pocombe Bridge
Clyst Honiton
Sowton
Exeter
Aylesbeare
Meldon
Danger Zone
Cawsand Hill
550
Whiddon Down
Longdown
Countess Wear
Clyst St Mary
Farringdon
Yes Tor
619
High Willhays
621
Throwleigh
Drewsteignton
Sourton
Wonson
Dunsford
Ide
Alphington
Shillingford St George
Clyst St George
Woodbury Salterton
White Cross
Bridestowe and Sourton Common
Gidleigh
Easton
Murchington
Chagford
Doccombe
Dunchideock
Doddiscombsleigh
Topsham
Exminster
Ebford
Woodbury
Shortacombe
Okement Hill
Hangingstone Hill
604
Amicombe Hill
Great Kneeset
568
Whitehorse Hill
601
Frenchbeer
Moretonhampstead
Bridford
Christow
Higher Ashton
Kennford
Kenn
Exton
Yettington
Black Hill
Downton
Beardon
Fernworthy Resr
Lettaford
North Bovey
Sanduck
Coombe
Lower Ashton
Bickham House
Powderham
Lympstone
Sittaford Tor
537
Cut Hill
604
Easdon Tor
Kenton
Starcross
Withycombe Raleigh
Willsworthy
Danger Zone
White Ridge
Warren House
Manaton
Lustleigh
Hennock
Trusham
Mamhead
Cockwood
EXMOUTH
Littleham
Lynch Tor
517
Cowsic Head
Grimspound
Hameldown Tor
Hamel Down
Bonehill Down
Becka Falls
Chudleigh
Ashcombe
Langdon House
Horndon
Cudliptown
Cocks Hill
Rough Tor
Higher White Tor
Postbridge
Bovey Tracey
Chudleigh Knighton
Ideford
Dawlish Warren Sta.
Dawlish
Peter Tavy
Cox Tor
442
Great Mis Tor
Danger Zone
Bellever
Cator Court
Widecombe in the Moor
Haytor Vale
Ilsington
Brimley
Heathfield
Luton
Little Haldon
Merrivale
436
Rundlestone
Two Bridges
Babeny
Corndon Tor
Dunstone
Rippon Tor
Danger Zone
Liverton
Coldeast
Preston
Sandygate
Bishopsteignton
Holcombe
Merrivale Prehistoric Settlement
Princetown
Royal Hill
407
Hexworthy
Dartmeet
Ponsworthy
Horridge
Sigford
Bickington
Teigngrace
Highweek
Kingsteignton
Shaldon
Teignmouth
Sampford Spiney
Walkhampton Common
445
Buckland in the Moor
Poundsgate
Caton
Rew
Combe Cross
Newton Abbot
Netherton
Combeinteignhead
Whiteworks
Ashburton
West Ogwell
East Ogwell
Wolborough
Abbotskerswell
Milber
Stokeinteignhead
Walkhampton
Ryder's Hill
Holne
Woodland
Denbury
Haccombe
Lower Gabwell
Higher Gabwell
Babbacombe Bay
Dousland
Burrator Resr
Cater's Beam
Scorriton
Coffinswell
Maidencombe
Yelverton
Sheepstor
Buckfast
Forder Green
Torbryan
Kingskerswell
Daccombe
Meavy
Dean Moor
Buckfastleigh
Landscove
Ipplepen
North Whilborough
Barton
Edginswell
St Marychurch
Clearbrook
468
480
Woolston Green
Broadhempston
Shiphay
Babbacombe
Cadover Bridge
Stall Moor
Dean
Riverford Bridge
Staverton
Compton
TORQUAY
Hope's Nose
Shell Top
475
Brent Moor
Dean Prior
Red Post
Marldon
Cockington
Shaugh Prior
Penn Moor
Shipley Bridge
Harbourneford
Dartington
Littlehempston
Bickleigh
Didworthy
Rattery
Shinner's Bridge
Berry Pomeroy
Lee Moor
Ugborough Moor
Harford Moor
South Brent
Tigley
Totnes
Blagdon
PAIGNTON
Plym Forest
Drakeland Corner
Cornwood
376
Belsford
Collaton St Mary
Tor Bay
Plym Bridge
Lutton
Harford
Ugborough Beacon
Harberton
Sharpham House
Goodrington
Buckland
Sparkwell
Avonwick
Lincombe
Bittaford
Diptford
Ashprington
Stoke Gabriel
Berry Head
Lee Mill Bridge
Plympton
Ivybridge
North Huish
Harbertonford
Tuckenhay
Galmpton
Churston Ferrers
Brixham
Cornworthy
East Cornworthy
Dittisham
Higher Brixham
Sharkham Point
Ugborough
Bickham Bridge
Washbourne
Hillhead
MOUTH
Westlake
Gara Bridge
Halwell
Capton
Allaleigh
Downton
Woodhuish
Elburton
Ermington
Brownston
Moreleigh
Hemborough Post
Boohay
Scabbacombe Head
Plymstock
Brixton
Yealmpton
Sequer's Bridge
Modbury
Coleton Fishacre
Goosewell
Kitley
Dunstone
Flete
Topsham Bridge
Blackawton
Dartmouth
Kingswear
Torr
Ford
Holbeton
Millcombe
Mew Stone
Knighton
East Allington
Bowden
Battisborough Cross
Ashford
Loddiswell
Woodleigh
Stoke Fleming
Newton Ferrers
Noss Mayo
Kingston
St Ann's Chapel
Aveton Gifford
Coombe
Worswell
Houghton
Venn
Cole's Cross
Merrifield
Strete
Netton
Stoke Point
Beacon Pt
Ringmore
Bigbury
Goveton
Churchstow
Buckland-tout-Saints
Start Bay
Bigbury-on-Sea
Burgh Island
Kingsbridge
Sherford
Slapton
Slapton Ley
Buckland
West Alvington
South West Coast Path
Bantham
Upton
Thurlestone
South Milton
Frogmore
Stokenham
Chillington
West Charleton
East Charleton
Torcross
Bigbury Bay
South Huish
Galmpton
South Pool
Ford
Beeson
Beesands
Hope
Dunstone
Bolt Tail
Bolberry
Malborough
Kellaton
Chivelstone
South Allington
Hallsands
Salcombe
East Portlemouth
Soar
Start Point
Overbecks Museum & Garden
Bolt Head
East Prawle
Lannacombe Bay
Prawle Point
A30
A386
A3072
A377
A396
A38
A380
A382
A383
A381
A384
A385
A3022
A379
A3121
A3122
A376
A3052
M5
B3215
B3217
B3260
B3219
B3193
B3212
B3357
B3387
B3199
B3192
B3196
B3197
B3205
B3392
B3186
B3147

18
19
20
21
22
North West Point
LUNDY
(NT)
Rat Island
Shutter Rock
same scale as main map
Heddon's Mouth
Trentishoe
Martinhoe
Widmouth Head
Ilfracombe
Hele
Berrynarbor
Combe Martin
Heale
Bull Point
Lee
Slade
Sterridge
Parracombe
Morte Point
Mortehoe
Mullacott Cross
Woolacombe
Morte Bay
Trimstone
Berry Down Cross
Kentisbury
Kentisbury Ford
Blackmoor Gate
West Down
East Down
Patchole
Bittadon
Arlington Beccott
Arlington
Baggy Point
Pickwell
North Buckland
Georgeham
Croyde Bay
Croyde
Halsinger
Milltown
Muddiford
Knightacott
Loxhore
Bratton Fleming
Knowle
Marwood
Shirwell
Shirwell Cross
Pippacott
Kings Heanton
Prixford
Saunton
Saunton Sands
Danger Zone
Braunton
Braunton Burrows
Wrafton
Heanton Punchardon
Ashford
Benton
Goodleigh
Stoke Rivers
Toll
Pilton
Barnstaple
Newport
Northleigh
Gunn
Charles
BARNSTAPLE
OR
BIDEFORD BAY
The Neck
Bickington
Fremington
Yelland
West Buckland
East Buckland
Appledore
Instow
Bickleton
Landkey
Swimbridge Newland
Yarnacott
Tawstock
Bishop's Tawton
Swimbridge
Westward Ho!
Northam
Tapeley
St John's Chapel
Westleigh
Horwood
Newton Tracey
Hartland Point
Windbury Point
Titchberry
Gallantry Bower
Bideford
Eastleigh
Loveacott
Herner
Cobbaton
Filleigh
Hartland Abbey
East-the-Water
Abbotsham
Woodtown
Hiscott
Ensis
Chittlehampton
Clovelly
Clovelly Bay
Fairy Cross
Ford
Alverdiscott
Gammaton Moor
Fishley Barton
Hudscott
Clapworthy
Stoke
Hartland
Dyke
Buck's Mills
Yeo Vale
Littleham
Landcross
Yarnscombe
Umberleigh
Milford
Philham
Edistone
Clovelly Cross
Buck's Cross
Horns Cross
Goldworthy
Langridge
Atherington
Warkleigh
Satterleigh
Elmscott
Tosberry
Cranford
Parkham Ash
Parkham
Weare Giffard
Huntshaw Cross
Langridgeford
High Bickington
Woolfardisworthy
Almiston Cross
Buckland Brewer
Monkleigh
High Bullen
Sherwood Green
Chittlehamholt
South Hole
Knaps Longpeak
Welcombe
Ashmansworthy
Melbury
Frithelstock
Frithelstock Stone
Great Torrington
St Giles in the Wood
Meddon
Powler's Piece
Taddiport
Kingscott
Head Bridge
Kismeldon Bridge
Little Torrington
Northcote Manor
Roborough
Gooseham
Eastcott
Youlstone
Dinworthy
East Putford
West Putford
Burrington
Morwenstow
Langtree
Villavin
Elstone
Shop
Bradworthy
Bulkworthy
Stibb Cross
Beaford
Colleton
Lower Sharpnose Point
Woodford
Brendon
Peters Marland
Riddlecombe
Copy Lake
Taylors Cross
Abbots Bickington
Woollaton
Winswell
Ashreigney
Coombe
Kilkhampton
Alfardisworthy
Sutcombe
Newton St Petrock
Merton
Heanton Satchville
Dolton
Ashley
Upper Tamar Lake
Lower Tamar Lake
Stibb
Soldon Cross
Milton Damerel
Huish
Hollocombe
Eggesford Barton
Youldonmoor Cross
Shebbear
North Town
Dowland
Wembworthy
Youldon
Thornbury
Buckland Filleigh
Petrockstow
Poughill
Hersham
Holsworthy Beacon
Ash
Iddesleigh
Winkleigh
Nymet
Flexbury
Bude Haven
Grimscott
Chilsworthy
Bradford
Meeth
Brushford Barton
Bude
Stratton
Launcells Cross
Pancrasweek
Sheepwash
Hele Bridge
BUDE
Launcells
Cookbury
Black Torrington
Broadwood Kelly
Taw Bridge
Red Post
Holsworthy
Anvil Corner
Brandis Corner
Monkokehampton
BAY
Helebridge
Marhamchurch
Rydon
Dunsland Cross
Highampton
Hatherleigh
Bondleigh
Widemouth Bay
Bridgerule
Pyworthy
Chasty
Hollacombe
Graddon Moor
Lydacott
Bassett's Cross
Honeychurch
Sampford Courtenay
North Tawton
Yeomadon
Halwill Forest
Exbourne
Coppathorne
Titson
Week Orchard
Jacobstowe
Shilstone
Halwill
Halwill Junction
Inwardleigh
Point
Poundstock
Treskinnick Cross
Herdicott
Tinney
Cofcott Green
Clawton
Beaworthy
Northlew
Belstone Corner
Tregole
Trewint
Whitstone
Upcott
Ashbury
Oak Cross
Folly Gate
Itton
Week St Mary
North Tamerton
Quoditch
Broadbury
Taw Green
Wainhouse Corner
Jacobstow
Trebarrow
Tetcott
Lana
Ashwater
Eworthy
Southcott
Okehampton
South Tawton
Luffincott
Henford
Germansweek
Boasley Cross
Thornton Cross
Yelland
Sticklepath
Belstone
Collamoor Head
Marshgate
Langdon
South Wheatley
Maxworthy
West Curry
Chapman's Well
Northcott
Clubworthy
Virginstow
Hewton
Okehampton Camp
Finch Foundry
South Zeal
Canworthy Water
Otterham
Caudworthy
Troswell
Bennacott
Boyton
East Panson
Roadford Resr
Bratton Clovelly
Danger Zone
Cawsand Hill
550
Trelash
Warbstow
Brazacott
St Giles on the Heath
Gridley Corner
Meldon
Yes Tor
619
Throwleigh
Tremaine
North Petherwin
Bridgetown
Polapit Tamar
Broadwoodwidger
Bridestowe
Sourton
High Willhays
621
Wonson
Hallworthy
Treneglos
Tresmeer
Yeolmbridge
Ladycross
Werrington
Cross Green
Thrushelton
Bridestowe and Sourton Common
Okement Hill
DARTMOOR
413
Gidleigh
Tremail
CORNWALL
Langore
Stowford
Lewdown
Shortacombe
Hangingstone Hill
604
Tregeare
Egloskerry
Red Down
St Stephens
Liftondown
Portgate
Lewtrenchard
Amicombe Hill
Great Kneeset
568
Cranmere Pool
Whitehorse Hill
601
Frenchbeer
Downhead
Piper's Pool
Newport
Launceston
Lifton
Finhay
Allerford
Lydford
Downtown
Laneast
Tregadillett
Coryton
Beardon
Fernworthy Resr
New Park
Trewen
Kennards House
Lawhitton
Marystow
Lydford Gorge
NATIONAL
SETTLEMENTS
Cut Hill
604
Sittaford Tor
537
PARK
Buttern Hill
346
Bray Down
346
Polyphant
Altarnun
Kelly
Chillaton
Black Down
North Brentor
Willsworthy
White Ridge
Fivelanes
Lewannick
South Petherwin
Bradstone
Felldownhead
Brent Tor
South Brentor
Lynch Tor
Danger Zone
DARTMOOR
Warren House
Brown Willy
420
369
Congdon's Shop
Lezant
Abbot
Horndon
Blackdown
Cowsic Head
Rough Tor
Codda
Trebullett
Trekenner
Dunterton
Mary Tavy
Cudlipptown
517
Higher White Tor
Postbridge
BODMIN
Trebartha
Coad's Green
Treburley
Rezare
Lamerton
Peter Tavy
Danger Zone
Bellever
A
B
C
D
E
F
G
A39
A361
A399
A3123
A377
A386
A388
A3072
A3079
A30
A395
A3124
B3230
B3343
B3231
B3233
B3237
B3248
B3227
B3220
B3217
B3254
B3226
B3216
B3219
B3215
B3260
B3262
B3358
B3212

BRIDGWATER BAY
EXMOOR
EXMOOR NATIONAL PARK
SOMERSET
DEVON
23
24
25
26
27
A
B
C
D
E
F
G
19
8
5
Lynton
Lynmouth
Countisbury
Foreland Point
Brendon
Leeford
Barbrook
Hillsford Bridge
Malmsmead
Oare
Culbone
Porlock
Porlock Weir
West Porlock
Bossington
Allerford
Selworthy
Selworthy Beacon
Minehead
Alcombe
Dunster
Blue Anchor Bay
Blue Anchor
Watchet
Doniford
St Decumans
Williton
West Quantoxhead
East Quantoxhead
Kilve
Hinkley Pt
Stolford
Nether Stowey
Quantock Hills
Simonsbath
Exford
Withypool
Winsford
Dunkery Hill
Dunkery Beacon
Wootton Courtenay
Luccombe
Timberscombe
Carhampton
Cutcombe
Wheddon Cross
Brendon Hills
Exton
Bridgetown
Brompton Regis
Wimbleball Lake
Clatworthy Reservoir
Raleigh's Cross
Wiveliscombe
Milverton
Dulverton
Bampton
Brushford
Exebridge
Morebath
Molland
North Molton
South Molton
Bishop's Nympton
Knowstone
Rose Ash
Witheridge
Tiverton
Bolham
Sampford Peverell
Halberton
Uffculme
Culmstock
Hemyock
Wellington
Vale of Taunton Deane
Bishop's Lydeard
Norton Fitzwarren
TAUNTON
Blackdown Hills
Cullompton
Bradninch
Silverton
Thorverton
Cadbury
Bickleigh
Crediton
Copplestone
Morchard Bishop
Kentisbeare
Dunkeswell
Upottery
Honiton
Ottery St Mary
Sidmouth
Sidbury
Branscombe
Beer
Seaton
Colyton
Broad Clyst
EXETER
Topsham
Exminster
Kenton
Powderham
Starcross
Dawlish Warren
Lympstone
EXMOUTH
Budleigh Salterton
East Budleigh
Otterton
Woodbury
Dunsford
Moretonhampstead
North Bovey
Chudleigh
Chagford
Drewsteignton
Tedburn St Mary
South West Coast Path
A39
A396
A361
A38
A30
A35
A373
A377
A3072
A3052
A376
A379
A380
A382
M5
B3223
B3224
B3227
B3190
B3191
B3137
B3181
B3174
B3178
B3179
B3183
B3193

27
28
29
19
30
31
A
B
C
D
E
F
G
7
S O M E R S E T
D E V O N
D
O
L Y M E B A Y
BRIDGWATER
TAUNTON
YEOVIL
Glastonbury
Street
Wellington
Ilminster
Chard
Crewkerne
Honiton
Axminster
Lyme Regis
Bridport
Sidmouth
Budleigh Salterton
Ottery St Mary
Somerton
Langport
Williton
West Quantoxhead
St Audries
Stogursey
Holford
Stringston
Dodington
Nether Stowey
Over Stowey
Bicknoller
Monksilver
Stogumber
Crowcombe
Quantock Forest
Quantock Hills
Elworthy
Lower Vexford
Flaxpool
Combwich
Cannington
Fiddington
Coultings
Spaxton
Four Forks
Charlinch
Wembdon
Pawlett
Puriton
Dunball
Down End
Huntspill Level
Chilton Trinity
Bawdrip
Knowle Hall
Woolavington
Cossington
Chilton Polden
Edington
Catcott
Stawell
Chedzoy
Sutton Mallet
Moorlinch
Shapwick
Ashcott
Greinton
Pedwell
Walton
Westhay
Burtle
Godney
Polsham
Coxley
Worminster
Southway
North Wootton
Queen's Sedge Moor
West Pennard
Edgarley
West Bradley
Parbrook
Overleigh
Baltonsborough
Butleigh Wootton
Butleigh
Ham Street
Southwood
Westonzoyland
SEDGEMOOR 1885
Middlezoy
Greylake
Othery
Thorngrove
King's Sedge Moor
Polden Hills
Nythe
Henley Corner
Henley
Dundon
Compton Dundon
Barton St David
Littleton
Kingweston
Keinton Mandeville
Lydford-on-Fosse
Charlton Mackrell
Charlton Adam
Babcary
Kingsdon
Podimore
Huntworth
Durleigh
Enmore
Goathurst
Lower Aisholt
Merridge
Courtway
Woolmersdon
North Petherton
Northmoor Green or Moorland
Broomfield
Cothelstone
Toulton
Cushuish
Kingston St Mary
Thurloxton
North Newton
Hedging
Adsborough
West Monkton
Cheddon Fitzpaine
Monkton Heathfield
Durston
Lyng
West Lyng
Burrow Bridge
Athelney
Stathe
Curload
Stoke St Gregory
Mare Green
North Curry
Knapp
Creech St Michael
Bathpool
Ruishton
Ham
Thorn Falcon
Henlade
Greenway
West Sedge Moor
Curry Rivel
Drayton
Muchelney
Pibsbury
Huish Episcopi
Long Sutton
Long Load
Low Ham
High Ham
Pathe
Aller
Bramwell
Pitney
Wearne
Brompton Ralph
Willett
Lydeard St Lawrence
Tolland
Combe Florey
East Combe
Bishop's Lydeard
Ash Priors
Clatworthy
Pitsford Hill
Tarr
Langley Marsh
Ford
Fitzhead
Halse
Wiveliscombe
VALE OF TAUNTON DEANE
Heathfield
Staplegrove
Norton Fitzwarren
Milverton
Oake
Hillfarrance
Nunnington Park
Bathealton
Stawley
Kittisford
Langford Budville
Chipley Park
Nynehead
Runnington
Appley
Thorne St Margaret
Bradford-on-Tone
Rumwell
Bishop's Hull
Wilton
Trull
Orchard Portman
Stoke St Mary
West Hatch
Hatch Beauchamp
Thurlbear
Curry Mallet
Isle Abbotts
Isle Brewers
Fivehead
Swell
Wrantage
Beercrocombe
Hambridge
Westport
Puckington
Barrington
East Lambrock
West Lambrock
Kingsbury Episcopi
Thorney
Stapleton
Martock
Coat
South Petherton
Shepton Beauchamp
Stocklinch
Whitelackington
Seavington St Michael
Seavington St Mary
Over Stratton
Lopen
Merriott
Dinnington
Hinton St George
Chillington
Cudworth
Chaffcombe
Cricket St Thomas
Hewish
Misterton
Wayford
Clapton
Seaborough
Winsham
Drimpton
Mosterton
North Perrott
South Perrott
Haselbury Plucknett
Chiselborough
West Chinnock
East Chinnock
Norton sub Hamdon
Stoke sub Hamdon
Montacute
Odcombe
Preston Plucknett
Barwick
West Coker
North Coker
East Coker
Stoford
Hardington Mandeville
Pendomer
Closworth
Hardington Marsh
Ryme Intrinseca
Halstock
Melbury Osmond
East Chelborough
West Chelborough
Corscombe
Chedington
Benville Lane
Evershot
Toller Down Gate
Rampisham
Uphall
Toller Whelme
Lower Wraxall
Hooke
Higher Kingcombe
Lower Kingcombe
Toller Porcorum
Toller Fratrum
Wynford Eagle
West Compton
Uploders
Loders
Askerswell
Powerstock
North Poorton
West Milton
Nettlecombe
Eggardon Hill
Mapperton
Melplash
Beaminster
Stoke Abbott
Broadwindsor
Whetley Cross
Netherbury
Waytown
Salwayash
South Bowood
Broadoak
Dottery
Bradpole
Walditch
Bothenhampton
Shipton Gorge
Chilcombe
Litton Cheney
Long Bredy
Kingston Russell
Puncknowle
Swyre
Littlebredy
West Bexington
Abbotsbury
Burton Bradstock
West Bay
Eype
Seatown
Chideock
Symondsbury
Morcombelake
Ryall
Whitchurch Canonicorum
Charmouth
Golden Cap
Marshwood
Marshwood Vale
Bettiscombe
Pilsdon
Pilsdon Pen
Birdsmoor Gate
Marshalsea
Burstock
Blackdown
Thorncombe
Holditch
Hawkchurch
Fishpond Bottom
Wootton Fitzpaine
Raymond's Hill
Uplyme
Pinhay
Rousdon
Combpyne
Dowlands
Axmouth
Seaton
Beer
Seaton Bay
Beer Head
Branscombe
Vicarage
Weston
Salcombe Regis
Sidford
Sidbury
Harcombe
Colyford
Colyton
Southleigh
Musbury
Whitford
Seaton Junction
Shute
Kilmington
Weycroft
Smallridge
Dalwood
Wilmington
Widworthy
Offwell
Northleigh
Farway
Broad Down
Church Green
Cotleigh
Monkton
Combe Raleigh
Stockland
Furley
Membury
Chardstock
Tytherleigh
Alston
Chard Junction
South Chard
Tatworth
Forton
Wambrook
Yarcombe
Newcott
Howley
Marsh
Whitestaunton
Northay
Combe St Nicholas
Wadeford
Buckland St Mary
Crock Street
Donyatt
Kingstone
Dowlish Wake
Cricket Malherbie
Ilton
Horton
Horton Cross
Broadway
Windmill Hill
Ashill
Hatch Green
Bickenhall
Curland
Staple Fitzpaine
Staple Hill
Pitminster
Blagdon Hill
Corfe
Angersleigh
Blackmoor
Ford Street
Wrangway
Sampford Arundel
Holywell Lake
Rockwell Green
West Buckland
Greenham
Holcombe Rogus
Burlescombe
Ayshford
Ashayne
Appledore
Waterloo Cross
Uffculme
Culmstock
Craddock
Hackpen Hill
Hemyock
Culm Valley
Clayhidon
Rosemary Lane
Blackdown Hills
Black Down
Churchstanton
Fyfett
Stapley
Bishopswood
Churchinford
Bolham Water
Madford
Smeatharpe
Smithincott
Ashill
Bradfield
Blackborough
Sheldon
Kentisbeare
Dunkeswell
Upottery
Luppitt
Rawridge
Beacon
Kerswell
Broadhembury
Norman's Green
Colliton
Luton
Upton
Godford Cross
Awliscombe
Higher Tale
Payhembury
Colestocks
Buckerell
Higher Cheriton
Feniton
Talaton
Fenny Bridges
Hamlet
Gittisham
Alfington
Fairmile
Putts Corner
West Hill
Wiggaton
Tipton St John
Venn Ottery
Harpford
Bowd
Newton Poppleford
Colaton Raleigh
Pinn
East Budleigh
Knowle
South West Coast Path
St Catherines Chapel
Chesil
White Hill
Dorchester
A39
A38
A358
A361
A372
A37
A303
A3088
A30
A356
A3066
A378
A3065
A373
A375
A35
A3052
A358
B3153
B3151
B3165
B3168
B3162
B3167
B3164
B3163
B3157
B3174
B3176
B3178
B3224
B3227
B3187
B3188
B3391
B3261
M5
23
24
25
26
384
0 2 4 6 8 10 miles
0 2 4 6 8 10 km

WILTSHIRE
DORSET
Shaftesbury
Blandford Forum
Sherborne
Dorchester
WEYMOUTH
POOLE
BOURNEMOUTH
Wareham
Swanage
Wimborne Minster
Gillingham
Mere
Wilton
Wincanton
Bruton
Castle Cary
Sturminster Newton
Stalbridge
Milborne Port
Fortuneswell
ISLE OF PORTLAND
Bill of Portland
ISLE OF PURBECK
Poole Harbour
Poole Bay
Studland Bay
Brownsea Island
Weymouth Bay
Ringstead Bay
Worbarrow Bay
Lulworth Cove
St Aldhelm's or St Alban's Head
Durlston Head
Peveril Point
The Foreland or Handfast Point
Ballard Point
Cranborne Chase
Blackmoor Vale
Great Ridge
Grovely Wood
Wylye Valley
Verwood
Ferndown
Cranborne
Broadstone
Upton
Puddletown
Charminster
Maiden Newton
Bere Regis
Wool
Corfe Castle
Milborne St Andrew
Tolpuddle
Hindon
Tisbury
Fovant
Chicklade
Ringwood Forest
Guernsey & Jersey
St Malo (summer only)
Cherbourg
Danger Zone
Chesil Beach
South West Coast Path
32
33
34
35
36
20
10
A
B
C
D
E
F
G

WILTSHIRE
DORSET
THE NEW FOREST
SALISBURY
Amesbury
Wilton
Shaftesbury
Fordingbridge
Ringwood
Verwood
Ferndown
Wimborne Minster
Blandford Forum
Wareham
Swanage
POOLE
BOURNEMOUTH
CHRISTCHURCH
LYMINGTON
Lyndhurst
Brockenhurst
Romsey
Totton
New Milton
Highcliffe
Milford on Sea
Totland
Yarmouth
Cranborne
Cranborne Chase
Downton
Whiteparish
Tisbury
Hindon
Mere
Sandbanks
Studland
Corfe Castle
Kimmeridge
Poole Harbour
Poole Bay
Christchurch Bay
Hengistbury Head
The Needles
Durlston Head
St Aldhelm's or St Alban's Head
Isle of Purbeck
Wylye Valley
Danger Zone
St. Malo (summer only)
Cherbourg
0 2 4 6 8 10 miles
0 2 4 6 8 10 km
35 36 37 38 39
A B C D E F G
A36
A30
A338
A31
A35
A350
A354
A303
A337
M27

H A M P S H I R E
WINCHESTER
EASTLEIGH
Southampton
FAREHAM
GOSPORT
PORTSMOUTH
Southsea
HAVANT
Waterlooville
Petersfield
Alton
Haslemere
Midhurst
CHICHESTER
Selsey
Selsey Bill
Bognor
ISLE OF WIGHT
Cowes
East Cowes
RYDE
Newport
Sandown
Shanklin
Ventnor
Bembridge
Yarmouth
St Catherine's Point
Culver Cliff
Dunnose
THE SOLENT
Southampton Water
Portsmouth Harbour
Langstone Harbour
Chichester Harbour
Hayling Island
Thorney Island
Bracklesham Bay
Sandown Bay
Brighstone Bay
S O U T H   D O W N S
Santander (winter only)
Bilbao
St Malo
Cherbourg
Caen and Le Havre
M3
M27
M275
A3(M)
A3
A27
A31
A32
A272
40
41
42
43
44
21
22
12
A
B
C
D
E
F
G

43
44
45
46
47
A
B
C
D
E
F
G
CAMBERLEY
FRIMLEY
FLEET
FARNBOROUGH
ALDERSHOT
FARNHAM
WOKING
GUILDFORD
DORKING
LEATHERHEAD
Godalming
Haslemere
Alton
Petersfield
Midhurst
Petworth
HAVANT
CHICHESTER
BOGNOR REGIS
Littlehampton
Arundel
WORTHING
PORTSMOUTH
Selsey
Selsey Bill
Bembridge Foreland
Hayling Island
Emsworth
Pulborough
Storrington
Billingshurst
Cranleigh
Hindhead
Liphook
Bordon
Hook
Odiham
Sandhurst
Byfleet
Cobham
Steyning
Bramshill Forest
Danger Zone
N O R T H D O W N S
S U R R E Y
W E S T S U S S E X
S O U T H
South Downs Way
M3
M25
A3
A3(M)
A27
A29
A24
A31
A272
A283
A286
A285
A259
10 miles
10 km

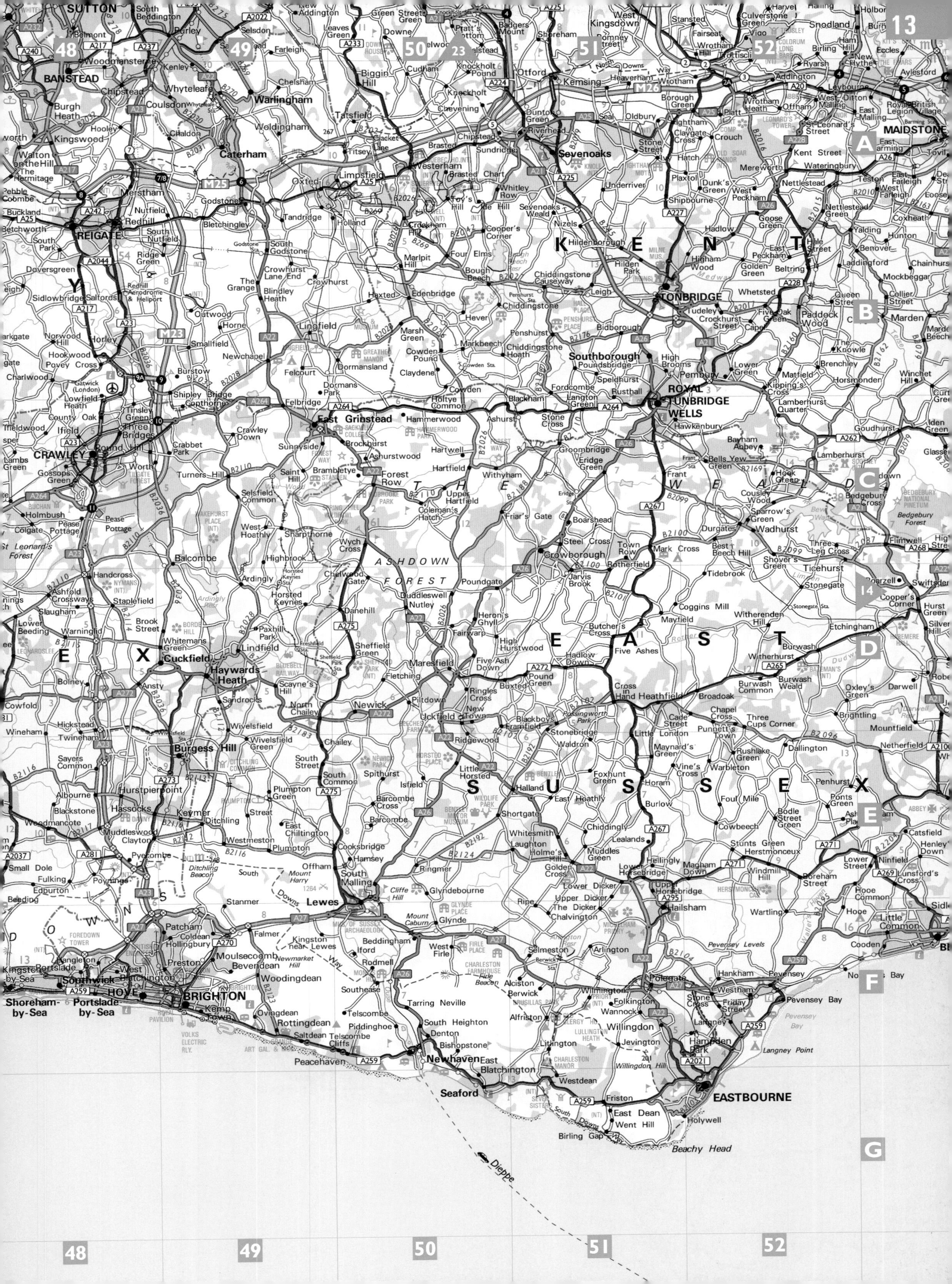
SUTTON
BANSTEAD
REIGATE
Redhill
CRAWLEY
Horley
Caterham
Warlingham
Oxted
Westerham
Sevenoaks
MAIDSTONE
TONBRIDGE
ROYAL TUNBRIDGE WELLS
Southborough
East Grinstead
Lingfield
Crowborough
Wadhurst
Ticehurst
Cuckfield
Haywards Heath
Burgess Hill
Uckfield
Heathfield
Hailsham
Lewes
BRIGHTON
HOVE
Shoreham-by-Sea
Portslade-by-Sea
Newhaven
Seaford
EASTBOURNE
Beachy Head
Pevensey Bay
Langney Point
Dieppe
ASHDOWN FOREST
K E N T
W E A L D
E A S T
S U S S E X
M25
M26
M23
A23
A22
A21
A26
A27
A259
A264
A267
48
49
50
51
52
A
B
C
D
E
F
G
14
23

Queensborough
ROCHESTER
GILLINGHAM
CHATHAM
SITTINGBOURNE
MAIDSTONE
Sevenoaks
TONBRIDGE
Southborough
ROYAL TUNBRIDGE WELLS
Crowborough
Hailsham
EASTBOURNE
BEXHILL
HASTINGS
Rye
Tenterden
Seaford
Newhaven
Cranbrook
Paddock Wood
Wadhurst
Heathfield
Battle
Hawkhurst
Headcorn
Marden
Lenham
Charing
Ashford
K E N T
E A S T S U S S E X
NORTH DOWNS
THE WELD
ISLE OF OXNEY
Rye Bay
Pevensey Bay
Pevensey Levels
M2
M20
M25
M26
A21
A26
A22
A27
A28
A229
A259
A262
A268
51
52
53
54
55
A
B
C
D
E
F
G

56
57
58
59
60
A
B
C
D
E
F
G
25
Warden Point
Leysdown-on-Sea
Shell Ness
WHITSTABLE
HERNE BAY
Swalecliffe
Reculver
Seasalter
Chestfield
West End
Herne
Herne Common
Yorkletts
Graveney
Clapham Hill
Hillborough
Beltinge
Broomfield
Hunters Forstal
Highstead
St Nicholas at Wade
Boyden Gate
Chislet
Maypole
Hoath
Sarre
Gore Street
Birchington
Westgate on Sea
MARGATE
Cliftonville
Foreness Point
Long Nose Spit
White Ness
North Foreland
St Peter's
BROADSTAIRS
ISLE OF THANET
Acol
Manston
Minster
Monkton
Cliffs End
RAMSGATE
Oostende
Dunkerque
Pegwell Bay
Sandwich Flats
Sandwich Bay
Stonar Cut
Great Stonar
Sandwich
Woodnesborough
Worth
Hacklinge
DEAL
Walmer
Kingsdown
Sholden
Northbourne
Finglesham
Great Mongeham
Ripple
Sutton
Ringwould
St Margaret's at Cliffe
St Margaret's Bay
West Cliffe
South Foreland
DOVER
Guston
East Langdon
West Langdon
Whitfield
Temple Ewell
Buckland
River
Maxton
Farthingloe
Capel le Ferne
Hougham
Hawkinge
Alkham
Drellingore
Densole
Swingfield Minnis
Ewell Minnis
Acrise Place
Paddlesworth
Etchinghill
Newbarn
Postling
Lyminge
Elham
Selstead
Wootton
Denton
Wingmore
Lydden
Coldred
Shepherdswell or Sibertswold
Eythorne
Woollage Green
Barfreston
Womenswold
Aylesham
Nonington
Easole Street
Tilmanstone
Elvington
Ashley
Betteshanger
East Studdal
Knowlton
Eastry
Goodnestone
Chillenden
Staple
Marshborough
Wingham
Ash
Cop Street
Westmarsh
Preston
Elmstone
Grove
Ware
Hoaden
Wickhambreaux
Ickham
Littlebourne
Bramling
Stodmarsh
Westbere
Upstreet
West Stourmouth
East Stourmouth
Stour
Hersden
Sturry
Fordwich
Calcott
Broadoak
Tyler Hill
Honey Hill
Pean Hill
Blean
Hales Place
Rough Common
CANTERBURY
Harbledown
Thanington
Dunkirk
Boughton Street
Hernhill
Dargate
Goodnestone
Preston
Oversland
Chartham Hatch
North Street
Sheldwich
Selling
Old Wives Lees
Chartham
Shalmsford Street
Street End
Lower Hardres
Bridge
Nackington
Bekesbourne
Patrixbourne
Adisham
Bishopsbourne
Kingston
Petham
Upper Hardres Court
Barham
Derringstone
Breach
Bladbean
Stelling Minnis
Bossingham
Waltham
Sole Street
Crundale
Shottenden
Chilham
Godmersham
Challock
Bilting
Boughton Lees
Hassell Street
Bodsham Green
Wye
Kennington
Brook
Hastingleigh
Sixmile Cottages
Rhodes Minnis
Ottinge
Lymbridge Green
Stowting
Willesborough Lees
Hinxhill
Willesborough
Sevington
Brabourne
Brabourne Lees
Smeeth
Mersham
Sellindge
Stanford
Beachborough
Newington
Cheriton
FOLKESTONE
Sandgate
Saltwood
Hythe
West Hythe
Lympne
Court-at-Street
Aldington
Bonnington
Stonestreet Green
Cheeseman's Green
Bilsington
Ruckinge
Burmarsh
Newchurch
Dymchurch
St Mary in the Marsh
St Mary's Bay
Ivychurch
Snave
Old Romney
New Romney
Littlestone-on-Sea
Romney Sands
Greatstone-on-Sea
Lydd
Lydd-on-Sea
Denge Marsh
Denge Beach
Dungeness
Danger Zone
Danger Zone
East Wear Bay
East Road
Road
ROMNEY MARSH
NORTH DOWNS
STRAIT OF DOVER
Calais
Channel Tunnel
Boulogne
A2
A20
A28
A252
A256
A257
A258
A259
A260
A261
A290
A291
A299
A253
A254
A255
M20
B2068
B2046
B2205
B2011
B2067
B2075
Stone Street
Roman Road
North Downs Way
Lyminge Forest
0
2
4
6
8
10 miles
0
2
4
6
8
10 km

PEMBROKESHIRE COAST
NATIONAL PARK
ST BRIDE'S BAY
Rosslare
Cork (summer only)
13
14
15
16
17
A
B
C
D
E
F
G
Strumble Head
Pen Caer
Goodwick
Fishguard
Fishguard Bay
Dinas Head
Newport
Newport Bay
Nevern
Eglwyswrw
Crymych
Mynydd Preseli (Prescelly Mts)
Foel Cwmcerwyn
536
Mynachlog-ddu
Maenclochog
Rosebush
Greenway
Puncheston
Letterston
Mathry
Trevine
Abercastle
Porthgain
Abereiddy
Croesgoch
St David's Head
St David's
Whitesands Bay
Ramsey Sound
Ramsey Island
Bishops and Clerks
North Bishop
South Bishop
Carreg Rhoson
Solva
Newgale
Newgale Sands
Roch
Camrose
Nolton
Druidston
Haroldston West
Broad Haven
Stack Rocks
Little Haven
Talbenny
St. Brides
Marloes
Skomer Island
Mew Stone
Gateholm Island
Wooltack Point
Broad Sound
Hoopers Point
The Stack
The Head
Skokholm Island
Dale
Dale Point
Thorn I.
St Ann's Head
Sheep Island
Angle
Angle Bay
MILFORD HAVEN
Milford Haven
Neyland
Pembroke Dock
Pembroke
Lamphey
Manorbier
Tenby
Saundersfoot
Amroth
Kilgetty
Penally
Caldey Island
St Catherine's Island
Giltar Point
Chapel Point
Old Castle Head
Stackpole Head
St Govan's Head
Saddle Head
Bosherston
Castlemartin
Freshwater West
Linney Head
Crow Rock
Toes
Danger Zone
Haverfordwest
Narberth
Wiston
Llawhaden
Clarbeston Road
Spittal
Treffgarne
Wolf's Castle
Fishguard
Newgale
A40
A487
A477
A478
A4075
A4076
A4139
A4115
B4329
B4313
B4330
B4331
B4341
B4327
B4319
B4320
B4322
B4325
B4314
B4316
B4318
B4585
B4584
B4586
0 2 4 6 8 10 miles
0 2 4 6 8 10 km

D Y F E D
W E S T G L A M O R G A N
C A R M A R T H E N
B A Y
S W A N S E A
B A Y
Newcastle Emlyn
Llandysul
Carmarthen
Llandeilo
Ammanford
Kidwelly (Cydweli)
Burry Port
LLANELLI
Gorseinon
SWANSEA
PORT TALBOT
St Clears
Laugharne
Pendine
Glanaman
Brynamman
Pontardawe
The Mumbles
Mumbles Head
Port Eynon
Rhossili
Worms Head
Llangennith
Llanmadoc
Whitford Point
Burry Holms
Oxwich Bay
Oxwich
Pwlldu Head
Port Eynon Point
Cefn Sidan Sands
Pembrey
Pembrey Forest
Danger Zone
Ferryside
Llansteffan
Llanstephan
St Ishmael
Pontardulais
Llangyfelach
Morriston
Skewen
Gowerton
Loughor
Dunvant
Killay
Sketty
Bishopston
Pennard
Parkmill
Ilston
Penmaen
Nicholaston
Reynoldston
Knelston
Llanddewi
Middleton
Horton
Overton
Llanrhidian
Oldwalls
Fairyhill
Cheriton
Landimore
Crofty
Penclawdd
Llanmorlais
Three Crosses
Upper Killay
Tycroes
Pontamman
Garnant
Betws
Gwaun-Cae-Gurwen
Cwmgors
Cross Hands
Tumble
Gorslas
Penygroes
Llandybie
Carmel
Drefach
Porthyrhyd
Llanddarog
Nantycaws
Llangendeirne
Pontyates
Pont-Henri
Pontyberem
Meinciau
Four Roads
Llansaint
Llandyry
Trimsaran
Pwll
Dafen
Bynea
Llangennech
Llwynhendy
Felinfoel
Hendy
Fforest
Llannon
Sylen
Horeb
Five Roads
Carway
Croesyceiliog
Cwmffrwd
Llangain
Llangynog
Llanybri
Llandeilo Abercywyn
Llansadurnen
Llanmiloe
Llanddowror
Llandawke
Whitland Abbey
Meidrim
Bancyfelin
Sarnau
Merthyr
Trelech
Talog
Abernant
Cynwyl Elfed
Llanpumsaint
Pontarsais
Rhydargaeau
Brechfa
Alltwalis
Gwyddgrug
Pencader
New Inn
Abergorlech
Llansawel
Talley
Crugybar
Caeo
Porthyrhyd
Halfway
Llansadwrn
Llanwrda
Llangadog
Bethlehem
Ffairfach
Trap
Carreg Cennen
Derwydd
Golden Grove
Dryslwyn
Llanarthney
Llanegwad
Pontargothi
Nantgaredig
Abergwili
White Mill
Capel Dewi
Llangunnor
Johnstown
Tanerdy
Rhosmaen
Manordeilo
Salem
Capel Isaac
Maerdy
Llanfynydd
Felingwmuchaf
Cenarth
Cwmcoy
Henllan
Llandyfriog
Pentrecagal
Drefach
Felindre
Penrherber
Cwm-Morgan
Cwmpengraig
Capel Iwan
Clydey
Glaspant
Tegryn
Llanfyrnach
Dinas
Blaenwaun
Llanwinio
Cwmbach
Cwmfelin Mynach
Gellywen
Castell Gorfod
Llangynin
Blaen-y-coed
Hermon
Gorllwyn
Cwmduad
Esgair
Rhos
Bwlch-clawdd
Saron
Penboyr
Llangeler
Pentre-cwrt
Pontwelly
Abergiar
Llanllwni
Rhydcymerau
Llidiadnenog
Pen-y-garn
Cwmdu
Edwinsford
Llandovery
Blaenos
Llwyn-y-brain
Cilycwm
Aber Bowlan
Twynllanan
Penllergaer
Tirdeunaw
Cadle
Fforest-fach
Waunarlwydd
Cockett
Landore
Bon-y-maen
Pentre-chwyth
Kilvey Hill
Birchgrove
Llansamlet
Clydach
Ynystawe
Craigcefnparc
Felindre
Bolgoed
Pontlliw
Grovesend
Pont-lasau
Alltwen
Trebanos
Vardre
Godre'r-graig
Rhydyfro
Rhyd-y-fro
Llangiwg
Cwmllynfell
Lower Brynamman
Pantyffynnon
Capel Hendre
Saron
Garnswllt
Pont Abraham
Pentre Gwenlais
Blaengweche
Tir-y-dail
West Cross
Black Pill
Newton

WEST GLAMORGAN
MID GLAMORGAN
SOUTH GLAMORGAN
AFAN FOREST PARK
EXMOOR NATIONAL PARK
SWANSEA BAY
BRIDGWATER BAY
SWANSEA
NEATH
PORT TALBOT
MAESTEG
Pontycymer
Glyncorrwg
Aberdare
MOUNTAIN ASH
MERTHYR TYDFIL
Rhymney
Tredegar
EBBW VALE
BARGOED
GELLIGAER
PONTYPRIDD
CAERPHILLY
Ystrad
Treorchy
Tonypandy
Bridgend
Porthcawl
Cowbridge
BARRY
Barry Island
Llantwit Major
Llantrisant
Pontardawe
Ystalyfera
Ystradgynlais
Brynamman
Hirwaun
Penderyn
Glyn-Neath
Resolven
Seven Sisters
Kenfig
Pyle
Ogmore-by-Sea
Southerndown
Nash Point
Breaksea Pt
Sully Island
Lynton
Lynmouth
Countisbury
Foreland Point
The Valley of Rocks
Martinhoe
Parracombe
Blackmoor Gate
Challacombe
Simonsbath
Exford
Porlock
Minehead
Dunster
Watchet
Williton
Blue Anchor Bay
Dunkery Beacon
Wheddon Cross
Lilstock
A
B
C
D
E
F
G
17
23
24
25
26
27
7

19
28
29
30
31
32
Monmouth (Trefynwy)
Forest of Dean
AND WYE VALLEY
Blaenavon
ABERTILLERY
Abersychan
PONTYPOOL
G W E N T
Usk
Raglan
Chepstow
CWMBRAN
Caerleon
NEWPORT
Risca
Rogerstone
Magor
Caldicot
Lydney
Sharpness
Berkeley
Thornbury
G L O S
Vale of Berkeley
Wotton-under-Edge
Chipping Sodbury
Yate
Severn Road Bridge
Severn Tunnel
Danger Zone
Due open Spring 1996
Caldicot Level
St Mellons
Rumney
Peterstone Wentlooge
CARDIFF
MOUTH OF THE SEVERN
Avonmouth
Portishead
Battery Point
Clevedon
Nailsea
BRISTOL
Mangotsfield
KINGSWOOD
Keynsham
Hanham
A V O N
Bath
Flat Holm
Steep Holm
WESTON-SUPER-MARE
Weston Bay
Brean Down
Sand Bay
Congresbury
Yatton
Wrington
Chew Magna
Bristol (Lulsgate)
Banwell
Axbridge
Cheddar
Mendip Forest
M E N D I P H I L L S
Midsomer Norton
Radstock
Paulton
Burnham-on-Sea
Highbridge
Berrow Flats
Gore Sand
Stert Flats
Wedmore
Wells
Shepton Mallet
Glastonbury
S O M E R S E T
Queen's Sedge Moor
Tadham Moor
M4
M5
M32
M48
M49
A A
B
C
D
E
F
G
20
8
9

G L O U C E S T E R S H I R E
C O T S W O L D H I L L S
A V O N
W I L T S H I R E
S A L I S B U R Y P L A I N
Newnham
Arlingham
Boxbush
Hardwicke
Rodley
Longney
Brookthorpe
Brimpsfield
Elkstone
Chedworth
Stowell
Eastington
Fossebridge
Upper Soudley
Moreton Valence
Harescombe
Painswick
Whiteway
Winstone
Rendcomb
Coln St Dennis
Coln Rogers
Winson
Aldsworth
Awre
Frampton on Severn
Wheatenhurst
Whitminster
Putloe
Edge
Pitchcombe
Slad
The Camp
Miserden
Duntisbourne Abbots
Woodmancote
Calmsden
North Cerney
Ablington
Bibury
Blakeney
Nibley
The Noose
New Grounds
Stroud Green
Randwick
Whiteshill
Stonehouse
Stroud
Sudgrove
Edgeworth
Duntisbourne Leer
Duntisbourne Rouse
Bagendon
Arlington
Barnsley
Coln St Aldwyns
Hatherop
Eastington
Bisley
Daglingworth
Baunton
Quenington
Slimbridge
Cambridge
Leonard Stanley
King's Stanley
Rodborough
Eastcombe
Bournes Green
Oakridge
Bussage
Chalford
Sapperton
Stratton
Sharpness
Halmore
Frocester
Coaley
Woodchester
Thrupp
Frampton Mansell
Ampney Crucis
Ampney St Mary
Sunhill
Wanswell
Amberley
Hyde
Cirencester
Preston
Ampney St Peter
Poulton
Fairford
Breadstone
Lower Cam
Nympsfield
Box
Minchinhampton
Coates
Berkeley
Cam
Stinchcombe
Dursley
Uley
Nailsworth
Tarlton
Siddington
Harnhill
Driffield
Meysey Hampton
Whelford
Ham
Horsley
Barton End
Cherington
Rodmarton
Kemble
Ewen
South Cerney
Dunfield
Kempsford
Bevington
Newport
Kingscote
Tiltups End
Avening
Marston Meysey
Down Ampney
Woodford
Stone
North Nibley
Newington Bagpath
Tetbury Upton
Culkerton
Poole Keynes
Shorncote
Cerney Wick
Latton
Castle Eaton
Michaelwood
Ozleworth
Beverstone
Ashley
Chelworth
Somerford Keynes
Ashton Keynes
Cricklade
Hannington Wick
Falfield
Tortworth
Wotton-under-Edge
Lasborough
Tetbury
Chedglow
Crudwell
Oaksey
Eastcourt
Leigh
Seven Bridges
Hannington
Whitfield
Kingswood
Charfield
Wortley
Tresham
Leighterton
Long Newton
Broad Blunsdon
Morton
Cromhall
Churchend
Alderley
Doughton
Hankerton
Upper Minety
Purton Stoke
Blunsdon St Andrew
Stanton Fitzwarren
Milbury Heath
Cromhall Common
Hillesley
Westonbirt
Shipton Moyne
Brokenborough
Charlton
Minety
Tytherington
Oldbury on the Hill
Willesley
Knockdown
Garsdon
Purton
Haydon Wick
Wickwar
Hawkesbury Upton
Hawkesbury
Didmarton
Easton Grey
Foxley
Malmesbury
Lea
Cleverton
Callow Hill
Lydiard Millicent
Nine Elms
Stratton St Margaret
Itchington
Bagstone
Rangeworthy
Sopworth
Sherston
Shaw
Hook
Latteridge
Engine Common
Horton
Little Badminton
Norton
Little Somerford
Brinkworth
SWINDON
Iron Acton
Yate
Chipping Sodbury
Little Sodbury
Luckington
Corston
Rodbourne
Great Somerford
Startley
Grittenham
Wootton Bassett
Nibley
Old Sodbury
Badminton
Alderton
Hullavington
Dauntsey
North Wroughton
Wroughton
Coalpit Heath
Acton Turville
Littleton Drew
Grittleton
Stanton St Quintin
Lower Stanton St Quintin
Lower Seagry
Upper Seagry
Tockenham Wick
Lyneham
Elcombe
Dodington
Wapley
Codrington
Leigh Delamere
Burton
Nettleton
Sutton Benger
Bradenstoke
Tockenham
Chiseldon
Westerleigh
Dodington Ash
Castle Combe
Christian Malford
Church End
Preston
Bushton
Broad Town
Uffcott
Tormarton
West Kington
Kington St Michael
Kington Langley
Foxham
Goatacre
Clyffe Pypard
Broad Hinton
Pucklechurch
Hinton
Dyrham
Yatton Keynell
North Wraxall
Langley Burrell
Charlcutt
East Tytherton
Spirthill
Hilmarton
Clevancy
Winterbourne Bassett
Marlborough Downs
Ogbourne St George
Mangotsfield
Soundwell
KINGSWOOD
Abson
West Littleton
Upper Wraxall
Ford
Hardenhuish
West Tytherton
Highway
Berwick Bassett
Ogbourne St Andrew
Doynton
The Shoe
Slaughterford
Chippenham
Bremhill
Stanley
Compton Bassett
Winterbourne Monkton
Rockley
Pennsylvania
Marshfield
Cold Ashton
Biddestone
Studley
Yatesbury
Windmill Hill
Bridgeyate
Wick
Thickwood
Cross Keys
Colerne
Calne
Cherhill
Avebury
Oldland
Upton Cheyney
St Catherine
Corsham
Easton
Derry Hill
Quemerford
Beckhampton
Marlborough
Bitton
North Stoke
Langridge
Lansdown
Swainswick
Northend
Ditteridge
Hawthorn
Notton
Gastard
Bowden Hill
Sandy Lane
Mile Elm
Calstone Wellington
West Kennett
Fyfield
Saltford
Woolley
Charlcombe
Batheaston
Box
Neston
Lacock
Bewley Common
Chittoe
Blackland
Stockley
East Kennett
West Overton
Lockeridge
Manton
Chewton Keynsham
Kelston
Weston
Bathford
Bathampton
Shaw
Beanacre
Melksham Forest
Bromham
Heddington
Netherstreet
St Edith's Marsh
Bishops Cannings
Burnett
Twerton
BATH
Monkton Farleigh
Atworth
Norrington Common
Sandridge
Roundway Hill
Wansdyke
Milk Hill
Huish
Oare
St Loe
Englishcombe
Claverton
South Wraxall
Broughton Gifford
Melksham
Rowde
Roundway
Allington
Alton Priors
West Stowell
Stanton Prior
Odd Down
Combe Down
Monkton Combe
Bradford-on-Avon
Holt
Sells Green
Coate
All Cannings
Stanton St Bernard
Alton Barnes
Wilcot
Marksbury
Inglesbatch
Southstoke
Winsley
Limpley Stoke
Staverton
Seend Cleeve
Seend
Devizes
Pewsey
Priston
Combe Hay
Midford
Freshford
Westwood
Semington
Poulshot
Etchilhampton
Woodborough
Manningford Bruce
Dunkerton
Carlingcott
Wellow
Twinhoe
Trowle Common
Hilperton
Great Hinton
Keevil
Potterne
Stert
Beechingstoke
Patney
Manningford Abbots
Peasedown St John
Hinton Charterhouse
Trowbridge
Ashton Common
Bulkington
Worton
Potterne Wick
Urchfont
Wedhampton
Marden
Hilcott
Camerton
Farleigh Hungerford
Wingfield
Steeple Ashton
Marston
Chirton
Wilsford
North Newnton
Manningford Bohune
Pewsey Down
Paulton
Clandown
Shoscombe
Norton St Philip
Southwick
West Ashton
Charlton
Radstock
Tellisford
North Bradley
Yarnbrook
Coulston
Erlestoke
Great Cheverell
Easterton
Eastcott
Rushall
Upavon
Midsomer Norton
Writhlington
Faulkland
Rode
Woolverton
Hemington
Laverton
Hawkeridge
Heywood
Little Cheverell
Market Lavington
Littleton Panell
West Lavington
Wilsford Down
West Chisenbury
East Chisenbury
Kilmersdon
Hardington
Beckington
Bratton
Edington
Black Heath
Charlton Down
Compton Down
Longstreet
Enford
Stratton-on-the-Fosse
Lullington
Buckland Dinham
Oldford
Rudge
Westbury
Littleton Down
Gore Cross
Highbury
Mells
Great Elm
Vobster
Frome
Dilton Marsh
Berkley
Westbury Leigh
Warminster Down
Summer Down
West Lavington Down
Danger Zone
Tilshead
West Down
Orcheston Down
Enford Down
Fittleton
Netheravon
Coleford
Whatley
Leigh upon Mendip
Chapmanslade
Corsley
Upton Scudamore
Figheldean
Stoke St Michael
Chantry
Downhead
Holwell
Nunney
Cley Hill
Warminster
Boreham
Orcheston
Knighton Down
Milston
Durrington
Dean
Cranmore
Cloford
Trudoxhill
Tytherington
Corsley Heath
West Woodlands
Bishopstrow
Norton Bavant
Chitterne
Shrewton
Larkhill
Bulford
Doulting
Leighton
Longleat
Heytesbury
Knook
Rollestone
Countess
Amesbury
Chesterblade
Horningsham
Crockerton
Sutton Veny
Tytherington
Upton Lovell
Winterbourne Stoke
Stonehenge
West Amesbury
Wanstrow
Witham Friary
Gare Hill
Shear Cross
Longbridge Deverill
Corton
Codford St Peter
Codford St Mary
Fisherton de la Mere
Wilsford
Lake
Westcombe
Upton Noble
Batcombe
Maiden Bradley
Tytherington Hill
Boyton
Sherrington
Deptford
Berwick St James
Upper Woodford
Great Durnford
Stoney Stratton
Milton
North Brewham
Monkton Deverill
Stockton
Wylye
Wylye Valley
Steeple Langford
Stapleford
M5
M4
A38
A46
A417
A419
A4135
A433
A429
A435
A4311
A3102
A4361
A420
A4174
A4175
A431
A4
A342
A350
A365
A36
A363
A361
A367
A366
A362
A3098
A360
A345
A303
A3028
A359
B4066
B4058
B4060
B4040
B4014
B4042
B4069
B4122
B4005
B4006
B4534
B4425
B4465
B3109
B3353
B3107
B3101
B3098
B3099
B3086
B3083
B390
B3414
B3092
B3139
B3115
Ridgeway
Hackpen Hill
Ermin Way
Fosse Way
Roman Road
19
20
29
33
34
35
36
37
9

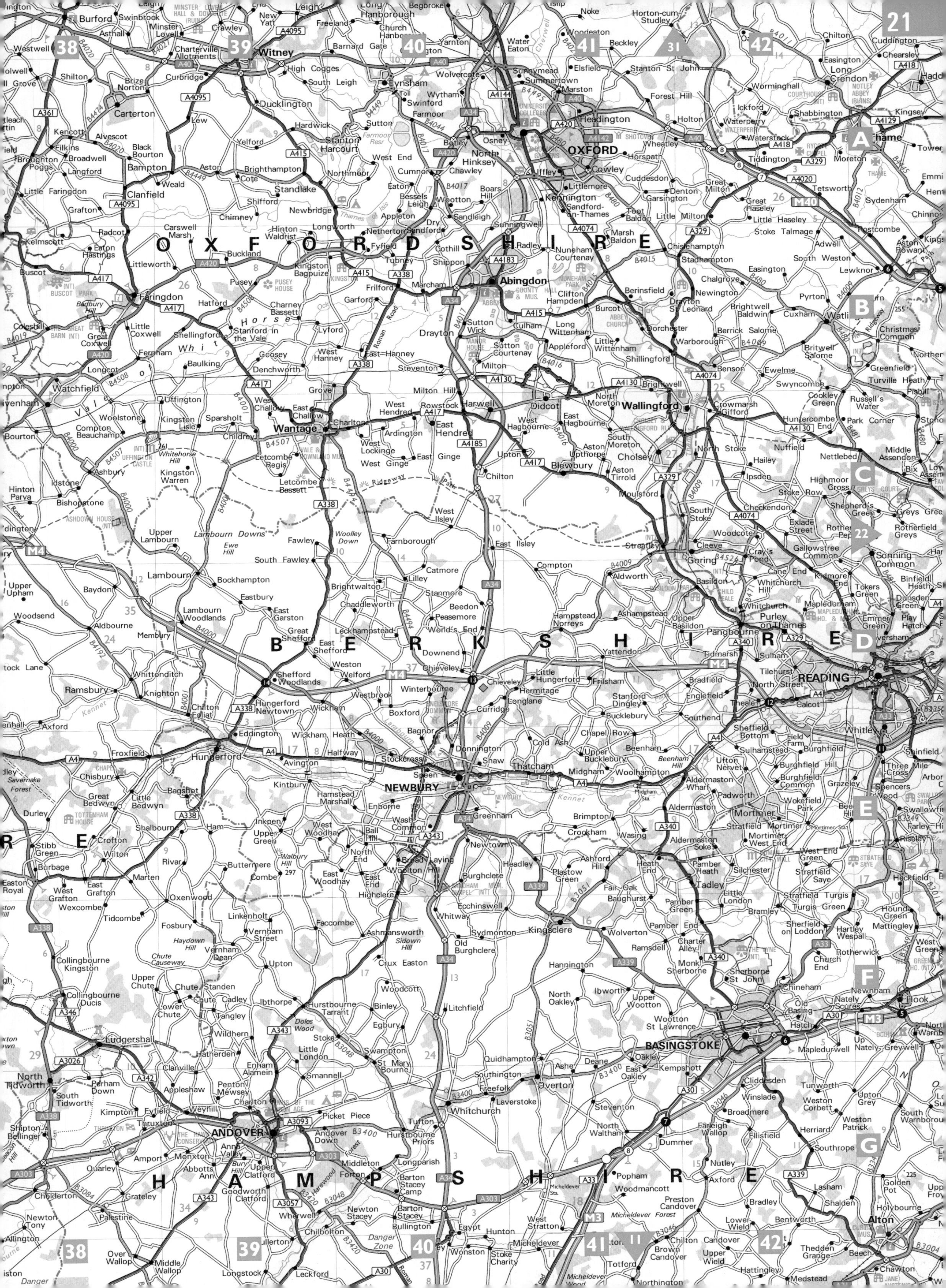

O X F O R D S H I R E
B E R K S H I R E
H A M P S H I R E
OXFORD
Witney
Abingdon
Wantage
Wallingford
Didcot
Faringdon
Carterton
Burford
Bampton
Eynsham
Headington
Cowley
Kennington
Harwell
Lambourn
Hungerford
NEWBURY
Thatcham
READING
Pangbourne
Goring
Theale
Tadley
Kingsclere
Whitchurch
Overton
BASINGSTOKE
ANDOVER
Ludgershall
Alton
Hook
Thame
Chinnor
Watlington
Benson
Dorchester
Cholsey
Streatley
Compton
Chieveley
Lambourn Downs
38
39
40
41
42
31
22
11
A
B
C
D
E
F
G
M4
M40
M3
A34
A4
A338
A339
A303
A420
A415
A417
A4074
A329

BUCKINGHAM
BERKSHIRE
HERT
SUR
G R
HIGH WYCOMBE
HEMEL HEMPSTEAD
WATFORD
RICKMANSWORTH
HARROW
HILLINGDON
EALING
HOUNSLOW
SLOUGH
MAIDENHEAD
WINDSOR
Eton
READING
Henley-on-Thames
Marlow
Beaconsfield
Amersham
CHESHAM
Berkhamsted
Tring
Wendover
Thame
Haddenham
Princes Risborough
Great Missenden
Hazlemere
Chorleywood
Uxbridge
STAINES
Egham
SUNBURY
WALTON-ON-THAMES
ESHER
Weybridge
Chertsey
WOKING
GUILDFORD
DORKING
LEATHE
Godalming
FARNHAM
ALDERSHOT
FARNBOROUGH
FLEET
CAMBERLEY
FRIMLEY
BRACKNELL
Wokingham
Twyford
Sandhurst
Bagshot
Ascot
Windlesham
Chobham
Cobham
Alton
Hook
Odiham
Crondall
Tilford
Milford
Elstead
Cranleigh
Shere
Ripley
Byfleet
Addlestone
Shepperton
Ashford
Feltham
Southall
Hayes
Ruislip
Pinner
Northwood
Bushey
Radlett
ST ALBA
KINGS UP THA
M40
M4
M25
M3
M1
A404(M)
A329(M)
Chiltern Hundreds
Windsor Great Park
Danger Zone
43
44
45
46
47
32
21
12
A
B
C
D
E
F
G

WELWYN GARDEN CITY
Hertford
HODDESDON
HARLOW
Epping
CHESHUNT
Waltham Abbey
POTTERS BAR
BARNET
ENFIELD
CHIGWELL
BRENTWOOD
BILLERICAY
CHELMSFORD
BASILDON
Chipping Ongar
WALTHAM FOREST
REDBRIDGE
Romford
HAVERING
BARKING & DAGENHAM
NEWHAM
ISLINGTON
HACKNEY
CAMDEN
Tower Hamlets
City of Westminster
City of London
KENSINGTON & CHELSEA
GREENWICH
SOUTHWARK
LAMBETH
WANDSWORTH
LEWISHAM
BEXLEY
DARTFORD
GRAYS
Tilbury
GRAVESEND
Northfleet
Swanscombe
ROCHESTER
MAIDSTONE
MERTON
BROMLEY
CROYDON
SUTTON
BANSTEAD
REIGATE
Redhill
Caterham
Sevenoaks
TONBRIDGE
ROYAL TUNBRIDGE WELLS
Southborough
East Grinstead
Oxted
Westerham
ESSEX
GREATER LONDON
KENT
SURREY
M25
M11
M20
M26
M23
M2
48
49
50
51
52
33
24
13

50
51
52
53
54
33
34
23
13
14
A
B
C
D
E
F
G
E S S E X
K E N T
HARLOW
CHELMSFORD
Maldon
CHESHUNT
Waltham Abbey
Epping
Chipping Ongar
CHIGWELL
BRENTWOOD
BILLERICAY
Wickford
RAYLEIGH
BASILDON
WALTHAM FOREST
REDBRIDGE
Romford
HAVERING
BARKING & DAGENHAM
NEWHAM
TOWER HAMLETS
GREENWICH
LEWISHAM
BEXLEY
BROMLEY
DARTFORD
GRAYS
Tilbury
Northfleet
GRAVESEND
SOUTH BENFLEET
CANVEY ISLAND
Leigh-on-Sea
Westcliff-on-Sea
ROCHESTER
CHATHAM
GILLINGHAM
MAIDSTONE
Sevenoaks
TONBRIDGE
ROYAL TUNBRIDGE WELLS
Southborough
East Grinstead
Swanley
Orpington
THAMES

55
56
57
58
59
A
B
C
D
E
F
G
0 2 4 6 8 10 miles
0 2 4 6 8 10 km
Salcott
West Mersea
Mersea Flats
Jaywick
Seawick
Colne Point
Tollesbury
Cobmarsh I
The Nass
Virley Channel
B1023
Blackwater
Bradwell Waterside
Bradwell-on-Sea
Sales Point
St Peter's Flat
Ramsey Island
St Lawrence
Tillingham
Dengie Flat
Steeple
B1021
Dengie
Mayland
Asheldham
Dengie Marshes
Southminster
Ray Sand
Monsale
Deal Hall
Stoneyhills
Ostend
Burnham-on-Crouch
Holliwell Point
Foulness Sands
Foulness Point
Wallasea Island
Courtsend
Danger Zone
Churchend
Foulness Island
Paglesham Churchend
Paglesham Eastend
Potton Island
Barling
Little Wakering
Havengore Island
Maplin Sands
Great Wakering
B1017
A13
Danger Zone
North Shoebury
Shoeburyness
Thorpe Bay
Danger Zone
Shoebury Ness
Vlissingen
Sheerness
A250
West Minster
Halfway Houses
Minster
B2008
Warden Point
Warden
Eastchurch
Leysdown-on-Sea
B2231
ISLE OF SHEPPEY
Eastchurch Marshes
Elmley Island
Shell Ness
Isle of Harty
KINGSHILL
The Swale
Conyer
Uplees
Murston
SITTINGBOURNE
Luddenham Court
Oare
Graveney
Teynham
Faversham
Rodmersham
Lynsted
Ospringe
Preston
Goodnestone
Hernhill
Boughton Street
Dunkirk
M2
A2
Whitehill
Newnham
Doddington
Eastling
North Street
Sheldwich
Oversland
Selling
A251
Frith
Throwley
Badlesmere
Old Wives Lees
Shottenden
Chilham
Otterden Place
Leaveland
Stalisfield Green
Warren Street
Molash
A252
Challock
Godmersham
Bilting
Lenham Heath
Charing
Charing Heath
Westwell Leacon
Boughton Aluph
Eastwell Park
Westwell
Boughton Lees
Wye
Little Chart
Ram Lane
Pluckley
Pluckley Thorne
Hothfield
ASHFORD
Kennington
A20
A28
Great Chart
South Willesborough
Willesborough
Sevington
Hinxhill
Willesborough Lees
Mersham
Kingsnorth
Cheeseman's Green
Bull Green
Shadoxhurst
A2070
M20
Smeeth
Sellindge
Stanford
Postling
Brabourne
Brabourne Lees
Stonestreet Green
Westenhanger Sta.
Brook
Hastingleigh
Lymbridge Green
Sixmile Cottages
Rhodes Minnis
Stowting
Ottinge
Lyminge
Elham
Acrise Place
Swingfield Minnis
Densole
Paddlesworth
Newbarn
Etchinghill
Beachborough
Newington
Hawkinge
Capel le Ferne
Cheriton
East Wear Bay
Whitstable
Swalecliffe
Seasalter
Chestfield
West End
Herne
Herne Common
Yorkletts
Clapham Hill
Pean Hill
Dargate
Honey Hill
Blean
Tyler Hill
Broadoak
Rough Common
Hales Place
Sturry
Fordwich
Calcott
Maypole
Hoath
Hersden
Westbere
Stodmarsh
CANTERBURY
Harbledown
Chartham Hatch
Thanington
Chartham
Shalmsford Street
Nackington
Bridge
Street End
Lower Hardres
Bishopsbourne
Petham
Upper Hardres Court
Kingston
Barham
Derringstone
Sole Street
Crundale
Waltham
Bossingham
Hassell Street
Bodsham Green
Stelling Minnis
Breach
Bladbean
Wingmore
Wootton
Denton
Selstead
A260
HERNE BAY
Reculver
Hillborough
Beltinge
Broomfield
Hunters Forstal
Highstead
Boyden Gate
Chislet
St Nicholas at Wade
Sarre
Gore Street
Monkton
Birchington
Westgate on Sea
MARGATE
Cliftonville
Kingsgate
St Peter's
BROADSTAIRS
RAMSGATE
Manston
Minster
Cliffs End
Acol
ISLE OF THANET
A28
A299
A253
A254
A255
A256
A257
A258
A291
A290
Upstreet
West Stourmouth
East Stourmouth
Westmarsh
Grove
Preston
Ware
Elmstone
Hoaden
Wickhambreaux
Ickham
Littlebourne
Wingham
Bramling
Ash
Cop Street
Marshborough
Staple
Goodnestone
Eastry
Woodnesborough
Sandwich
Sandwich Bay
Sandwich Flats
Pegwell Bay
Stonar Cut
Great Stonar
Toll
Worth
Ham
Hacklinge
Finglesham
DEAL
Northbourne
Sholden
Betteshanger
Great Mongeham
Walmer
Ripple
Kingsdown
Sutton
Ringwould
East Studdal
Ashley
West Langdon
East Langdon
Martin Mill Sta.
St Margaret's at Cliffe
St Margaret's Bay
South Foreland
Guston
West Cliffe
DOVER
Bekesbourne
Patrixbourne
Adisham
Chillenden
Knowlton
Aylesham
Nonington
Easole Street
Tilmanstone
Elvington
Womenswold
Barfreston
Woollage Green
Eythorne
Shepherdswell or Sibertswold
Coldred
Lydden
Whitfield
Temple Ewell
Ewell Minnis
Buckland
Alkham
Drellingore
West Hougham
Maxton
Farthingloe
B2011
B2046
B2068
Long Nose Spit
Foreness Point
White Ness
North Foreland
South Channel
Oostende
Dunkerque
Calais
North Downs Way
Stone Street
Roman Road
NORTH DOWNS

17
18
19
20
21
A
B
C
D
E
F
G
0 2 4 6 8 10 miles
0 2 4 6 8 10 km
C A R D I G A N
B A Y
Aberystwyth
The Bar
Penparcau
Rhydyfelin
Blaenplwyf
Llanddeiniol
Carreg Ti-pw
Llanrhystud
Llansantffraid
Llanon
Nebo
Cross Inn
Aberarth
Aberaeron
Pennant
Monachty
Ffos-y-ffin
Llanaeron
Cilcennin
New Quay Head
New Quay Bay
New Quay
Llwyn-onn
Gilfachrheda
Llwyncelyn
Neuadd
Ciliau-Aeron
Oakford
Bwlch-llan
Brynog
Trefilan
Tal-sarn
Cwmtudu
Llanarth
Nanternis
Cross Inn
Dihewyd
Ystrad Aeron
Mydroilyn
Garth
Abermeurig
Ynys-Lochtyn
Llwyndafydd
Synod Inn
Temple Bar
Caledrhydiau
Llangranog
Wervil Brook
Plwmp
Pencribach
Cardigan Island
Penbryn
Pentregat
Parcllyn
Aberporth
Tresaith
Brynhoffnant
Talgarreg
Cribyn
Capel St Silin
Silian
Cemaes Head
Gwbert
Verwig
Blaenannerch
Tan-y-groes
Sarnau
Wstrws
Gorsgoch
Pen-yr-afr
Pwllygranant
Cippyn
Tre-Rhys
Penparc
Tremain
Blaenporth
Glynarthen
Capel Cynon
Aber
Cwrt-newydd
Lampeter
Ceibwr Bay
St Dogmaels
Cardigan
Pantgwyn
Noyadd Trefawr
Beulah
Bettws Evan
Rhydlewis
Ffostrasol
Moel y Mor
Castell Howell
Llanwnen
Cwmsychbant
Alltyblaca
Llangoedmor
Brongest
Hawen
Penrhiw-pal
Pontshaen
Llanwenog
Dre-fach
Pencarreg
Bwa
Monington
Ponthirwaun
Troedyraur
Maesllyn
Tre-groes
Rhydowen
Llanybydder
Tredrissi
Glanrhyd
Cilgerran
Llechryd
Llandygwydd
Capel Tygwydd
Croes-lan
Pren-gwyn
Highmead
Bridell
Llantood
Manordeifi
Pont Ceri
Teifi Valley
Horeb
Capel Dewi
Pen Tas-eithin
Berry Hill
Trewilym
Cenarth
Cwmcoy
Llandyfriog
Aber-banc
Penrhiw-llan
Llanfair-Orllwyn
Maesycrugiau
Abergiar
Nevern
Rhos Hill
Abercych
Newcastle Emlyn
Aberarad
Henllan
Bangor Teifi
Llandysul
Pontwelly
Llanllwni
Newport
Velindre
Newchapel
Clynfyw
Penrherber
Pentrecagal
Drefach
Llangeler
Pentre-cwrt
Llanfihangel-ar-arth
Rhydcymerau
Eglwyswrw
Cilwendeg
Boncath
Felindre
Glynteg
Saron
Banc-y-ffordd
Llidiadnenog
Carningli Common
Llanfair-Nant-Gwyn
Cwmpengraig
Penboyr
New Inn
Cilgwyn
Crosswell
Blaenffos
Bwlch-y-groes
Glaspant
Capel Iwan
Moelfre
Bwlch-clawdd
Pencader
Gwyddgrug
Brynberian
Whitechurch
Freni-fawr
Star
Clydey
Cilrhedyn
Cwm-Morgan
Rhos
Dol-gran
Gwernogle
Tafarn-y-bwlch
Crymych
Gorllwyn
Abergorlech
Foel Eryr
Mynydd Preseli (Prescelly Mts)
Foel Cwmcerwyn
Tegryn
Hermon
Alltwalis
Mynachlog-ddu
Llanfyrnach
D Y F E D
Greenway
Foel Drych
Pentre-galar
Trelech
Dinas
Hermon
Cwmduad
Brechfa
Rosebush
Glandwr
Llanpumsaint
Llanllawddog
Henry's Moat
Maenclochog
Hebron
Esgair
Pontarsais
Llanfynydd
Llangolman
Blaenwaun
Blaen-y-coed
Cynwyl Elfed
Plas
New Moat
Llanglydwen
Cwmbach
Llanwinio
Trelech a'r Betws
Rhydargaeau
Efailwen
Cefn-y-pant
Talog
Felingwmuchaf
Lys-y-fran
Via Julia
Cwmfelin Mynach
Bwlchnewydd
Llanycefn
Login
Maesgwynne
Gellywen
Abernant
Newchurch
Llanfihangel uwch-gwili
Pentre
Llandre
Llanboidy
Broadoak
Llandissilio
Nant Cynnen
Ffynnon-ddrain
Capel Gwyn
Court Henry
Bletherston
Henllan Amgoed
Castell Gorfod
Tre-vaughan
Tanerdy
Abergwili
Nantgaredig
Pontargothi
Felindre
Rhydywrach
Meidrim
Merthyr
Carmarthen
Johnstown
Llangunnor
White Mill
Capel Dewi
Llanegwad
Dryslwyn
Gelly
Clynderwen
Llanfallteg
Llanfallteg West
Cwmfelin Boeth
Llangynin
Bron-y-Gaer
Sarnau
Llanllwch
Pensarn
Nantycaws
Llanarthney
Golden Grove
Bethesda
Llawhaden
Llanddewi Velfrey
Whitland Abbey
Bancyfelin
Penrhiwgoch
Robeston Wathen
Whitland
Pwll Trap
Cwmffrwd
Maesybont
Canaston Bridge
Redstone Bank
Trevaughan
St Clears
Croes-y-ceiliog
Llanddarog
Cwmisfael
Porthyrhyd
Narberth
Crinow
Lampeter Velfrey
Llwyn-y-brain
Llangynog
Llangain
Heol-ddu
Cefneithin
Gorslas
Cold Blow
Brandy Hill
Llanddowror
Llandeilo Abercywyn
Cwmllyfri
Llangendeirne
Crwbin
Drefach
Cross Hands
Cross Hands
Templeton
Princes Gate
Tavernspite
Red Roses
Llandawke
Llanybri
Pontantwn
Llandefaelog
Bancffosfelen
Pontyberem
Tumble
Ludchurch
Laugharne
Llansteffan
Meinciau
Reynalton
Thomas Chapel
Llanteg
Marros
Llansadurnen
Broadway
Ferryside
Cliff
Broadway
Pont-Henri
Loveston
Stepaside
Amroth
Pendine
Brook
Llanmiloe
Danger Zone
East Marsh
Laugharne Burrows
Pendine Sands
Ginst Point
St Ishmael
Llansaint
Kidwelly
Pontyates
Cynheidre
Llannon
Mynydd Sylen
Begelly
Kilgetty
Jeffreyston
A487
A482
A486
A475
A485
A484
A478
A40
A48
A477
A4066
A4115
A4075
B4577
B4342
B4337
B4459
B4476
B4336
B4338
B4334
B4333
B4332
B4329
B4582
B4546
B4548
B4570
B4571
B4335
B4299
B4298
B4300
B4310
B4306
B4317
B4312
B4328
B4314
B4315
B4313
B4297

POWYS
BRECON BEACONS NATIONAL PARK
FFOREST FAWR
Mynydd Epynt
Tywi Forest
Crychan Forest
Glasfynydd Forest
Brecon
Builth Wells
Llandrindod Wells
Llandovery
Llanwrtyd Wells
Rhayader
Tregaron
Devil's Bridge
Pontrhydfendigaid
Strata Florida
Llanidloes
Llangurig
Aberystwyth
Capel Dewi
Capel Bangor
Goginan
Ponterwyd
Old Goginan
Rhydybeddau
Dyffryn Castell
Pant Mawr
Tyn-y-Cwm
Cwmbelan
Tylwch
Llanbadarn Fynydd
Llanbister
Abbeycwmhir
St Harmon
Bwlch-y-sarnau
Pant-y-dwr
Dolfach
Elan Village
Llansantffraed-Cwmdeuddwr
Gaufron
Nantmel
Gwystre
Crossgates
Penybont
Fron
Dolau
Llanyre
Nant-y-groes
Nant-glas
Llanwrthwl
Argoed Mill
Newbridge-on-Wye
Disserth
Howey
Crossway
Ridgebourne
Llanelwedd
Cwmbach
Builth Road
Cilmery
Llanafan-fawr
Pentre-llwyn-llwyd
Llwyn-Madoc
Beulah
Abergwesyn
Llanlleonfel
Garth
Llangammarch Wells
Tyn-y-graig
Llanafan-fechan
Llanddewi'r Cwm
Alltmawr
Pen-y-garreg
Cwm Owen
Pentre Dolau Honddu
Upper Chapel
Gwenddwr
Erwood
Crickadarn
Llanstephan
Boughrood
Llyswen
Bronllys
Castle Madoc
Lower Chapel
Llandefalle
Garthbrengy
Talachddu
Felinfach
Llanfilo
Tredomen
Llandefaelog Fach
Llanddew
Battle
Aberyscir
Llanspyddid
Penpont
Llanfaes
Ffrwdgrech
Cefn Cantref
Llanhamlach
Llanfrynach
Pencelli
Talybont-on-Usk
Llangasty-Talyllyn
Libanus
Merthyr Cynog
Blaen Dyryn
Llandeilo'r-Fan
Llanfihangel Nant Bran
Pont-faen
Pwllgloyw
Pentre'r-felin
Trallong
Sennybridge
Defynnog
Trecastle
Llywel
Halfway
Myddfai
Cilgwyn
Llangadog
Felindre
Dolgarreg
Llanwrda
Lansadwrn
Llwyn-y-brain
Blaenos
Pentre-ty-gwyn
Babel
Pen-y-bont
Abercrychan
Cynghordy
Glanbran
Cilycwm
Rhandirmwyn
Ystradffin
Porthyrhyd
Caeo
Pumsaint
Crugybar
Aber Bowlan
Llansawel
Talley
Llandeilo
Ffairfach
Maerdy
Trap
Blaengweche
Glanaman
Garnant
Brynamman
Lower Brynamman
Gwaun-Cae-Gurwen
Cwmllynfell
Ystradowen
Cwm-twrch Isaf
Ystradgynlais
Abercraf
Caehopkin
Coelbren
Penrhos
Craig-y-nos
Penwyllt
Pen-y-cae
Cray
Heol Senni
Ystradfellte
Aber-llia
Pontsticill
Vaynor
Trefil
Princetown
Tredegar
Rhymney
Llechryd
Dukestown
Sirhowy
Abercynafon
Nant-ddu
Pontbren Llwyd
Seven Sisters
Pont Nedd Fechan
Tycroes
Pantyffynnon
Betws
Pontamman
Tir-y-dail
Llanfair Clydogau
Llanddewi-Brefi
Llangybi
Llandre
Ffarmers
Llanycrwys
Garthynty
Lledrod
Tynygraig
Ystrad Meurig
Swyddffynnon
Bronnant
Ffair-Rhos
Ysbyty Ystwyth
Pont-rhyd-y-groes
Cwmystwyth
Llanafan
Rhos-y-garth
Cnwch Coch
New Cross
Gors
Llanfihangel-y-Creuddyn
Aberffrwd
Ysbyty Cynfyn
Brynamman
Llangadog
A44
A470
A483
A4120
A485
A482
A40
A4069
A4067
A4215
A4059
A465
A4109
A479
A438
A481
A4081
B4518
B4343
B4340
B4574
B4358
B4520
B4519
B4567
B4594
B4302
B4337
B4342
B4578
B4575
B4577
B4356
B4560
B4558
B4599
22
23
24
25
26
28
37
18

SHROPSHIRE
POWYS
HEREFORD
GWENT
Radnor Forest
Black Mountains
BRECON BEACONS NATIONAL PARK
Llaithddu
Newcastle
Bettws-y-crwyn
Quabbs
Clun
Clunton
Brampton
Aston on Clun
Craven Arms
Stokesay
Culmington
Beguildy
Llanbadarn Fynydd
Dutlas
Llanfair Waterdine
Knucklas
Lloyney
Hobarris
New Invention
Chapel Lawn
Bedstone
Bucknell
Stowe
Hopton Castle
Hoptonheath
Clungunford
Onibury
Stanton Lacy
Bromfield
Ludlow
Ludford
Llanbister
Crug
Llangunllo
Knighton
Milebrook
Brampton Bryan
Leintwardine
Kinton
Walford
Adforton
Burrington
Downton on the Rock
Abbeycwmhir
Llanddewi Ystradenni
Bleddfa
Rhos-y-Meirch
Pilleth
Whitton
Norton
Wigmore
Leinthall Starkes
Leinthall Earls
Richard's Castle
Orleton
Brimfield
Little Hereford
Dolau
Llanfihangel Rhydithon
Cascob
Pentre
Maes-Treylow
Discoed
Presteigne
Stapleton
Kinsham
Byton
Combe
Lingen
Aymestrey
Yatton
Mortimer's Cross
Lucton
Yarpole
Bircher
Luston
Moreton
Eye
Ashton
Gwystre
Crossgates
Penybont
Llandegley
Kinnerton
Evenjobb
Nash
Rodd
Llandrindod Wells
New Radnor
Old Radnor
Walton
Knill
Titley
Staunton on Arrow
Stansbatch
Shobdon
Ledicot
Kingsland
Cobnash
Eyton
Leominster
Stockton
Kimbolton
Ridgebourne
Howey
Crossway
Llanfihangel-nant-Melan
Wolfpits
Yardro
Burlingjobb
Eywood
Pembridge
Eardisland
Shirl Heath
Lawton
Cholstrey
Monkland
Betws Disserth
Gwaithla
Gladestry
Dolyhir
Kington
Lyonshall
Marston
Lower Barewood
Barewood
Moorcot
Luntley
Sollers Dilwyn
Dilwyn
Stretford Court
Ivington
Ivington Green
Wharton
Brierley
Stoke Prior
Hundred House
Glascwm
Colva
Upper Hergest
Lower Hergest
Huntington
Kingswood Common
Holme Marsh
Broxwood
Haven
Knapton Green
Birley
Hope under Dinmore
Bowley
Cregrina
Veaullt
Newchurch
Hengoed
Brilley Mountain
Michaelchurch-on-Arrow
Upper Welson
Lower Welson
Woonton
Almeley
Upcott
Weobley
Weobley Marsh
Bush Bank
King's Pyon
Westhope
Bodenham
Bodenham Moor
Maund Bryan
Llanfaredd
Aberduhonw
Llanbadarn-y-garreg
Rhulen
Bryngwyn
Rhosgoch
Dolleycanney
Brilley
Hurstway Common
Eardisley
Kinnersley
Sarnesfield
Ledgemoor
Canon Pyon
Urdimarsh
Felton
Whitney
Rhydspence
Clifford
Winforton
Willersley
Norton Wood
Norton Canon
Yarsop
Wormsley
Wellington
Wellington Marsh
Marden
Preston Wynne
Llanbedr
Painscastle
Bronydd
Priory Wood
Pen-y-Park
Merbach
Letton
Staunton on Wye
Moorhampton
Yazor
Foxley
Mansell Gamage
Mansell Lacy
Tillington
Tillington Common
Brinsop
Moreton on Lugg
Sutton St Nicholas
Erwood
Crickadarn
Llanstephan
Llowes
Clyro
Hay-on-Wye
Cusop
Hardwicke
The Bage
Bredwardine
Brobury
Moccas
Portway
Monnington on Wye
Preston on Wye
Byford
Bishopstone
Kenchester
Credenhill
Burghill
Stretton Sugwas
Swainshill
Holmer
Shelwick
Pipe and Lyde
Withington
Boughrood
Cwmbach
Glasbury
Llanigon
Dorstone
Snodhill
Blakemere
Ploughfield
Bridge Sollers
Lulham
Canon Bridge
Upper Breinton
Breinton
White Cross
HEREFORD
Tupsley
Lugwardine
Hampton Bishop
Llyswen
Pipton
Three Cocks
Tregoyd
Velindre
Hinton
Peterchurch
Tyberton
Madley
Eaton Bishop
Shenmore
Lower Bullingham
Mordiford
Bronllys
Talgarth
Llanelieu
Craswall
Turnastone
Vowchurch
Upper Maes-coed
Webton
Kingstone
Clehonger
Grafton
Allensmore
Dinedor
Holme Lacy
Twyford Common
Talachddu
Felinfach
Llanfilo
Tredomen
Trefecca
Llandefaelog-tre'r-graig
Michaelchurch Escley
Middle Maes-coed
St Margarets
Bacton
Thruxton
Whitfield
Didley
Kerry's Gate
Callow
Dewsall Court
Aconbury
Fownhope
Pengenffordd
Capel-y-ffin
Llanveynoe
Lower Maes-coed
Abbey Dore
Wormbridge
Kilpeck
Much Dewchurch
Wormelow Tump
Much Birch
Little Birch
Kingsthorne
Little Dewchurch
Bolstone
Ballingham
Carey
Brecon
Llechfaen
Llanywern
Heol Lly Goden
Llanfihangel-Tal-y-llyn
Llangorse
Llanthony
Clodock
Longtown
Ewyas Harold
Howton
Kenderchurch
Orcop Hill
Llanwarne
Llandinabo
Hoarwithy
Kings Caple
Penallt
Talyllyn
Llanhamlach
Llangasty-Talyllyn
Cathedine
Pencelli
Scethrog
Llansantffraed
Rowlstone
Pontrilas
Bagwyllydiart
Harewood End
Pencoyd
Sellack
Kentchurch
Garway Hill
Orcop
Michaelchurch
Sandyway
St Owen's Cross
Peterstow
Bridstow
Walterstone
Oldcastle
Grosmont
Little Garway
St Weonards
Tretire
Talybont-on-Usk
Bwlch
Cwmdu
Tretower
Cwmyoy
Pandy
Hoaldalbert
Garway
Glewstone
Patrishow
Llanfihangel Crucorney
Llangattock Lingoed
Cross Ash
Skenfrith
Broad Oak
Llangarron
Pencraig
Coed-yr-ynys
Gaer
Llanbedr
Crickhowell
Llangynidr
Ffawyddog
Llangattock
Llangenny
Cwrt-y-gollen
Blaenawey
Llantilio Pertholey
Llanvetherine
Upper Green
Bont
Crossway
Llanrothal
Llangrove
Marstow
Goodrich
Welsh Bicknor
Whitchurch
Ganarew
Newcastle
Welsh Newton
Abercynafon
Glangrwyney
Gilwern
Llanelly
Mardy
Abergavenny
Llantilio Crossenny
Llangattock Vibon-Avel
Rockfield
Symonds Yat
Trefil
Clydach
Govilon
Croes Hywel
Llanvapley
Llanddewi Rhydderch
Llanvihangel-Ystern-Llewern
Wernyrheolydd
Dixton
Rassau
Beaufort
Blackrock
Llanfoist
Coed Morgan
Monmouth (Trefynwy)
Christchurch
Staunton
Tafarnaubach
Princetown
Dukestown
Brynmawr
Nantyglo
Newtown
Llanellen
Llanarth
Penrhos
Pen-yr-heol
Great Oak
Bryngwyn
Tregare
Dingestow
Wonastow
Penallt
Berry Hill
Crossways
Coleford
Newland
Llechryd
Tredegar
Rhymney
EBBW VALE
Coalbrookvale
Blaina
Blaenavon
Coedcae
Llanover
Mardy
Rhyd-y-meirch
The Bryn
Raglan
Pen-y-clawdd
Mitchel Troy
Mitcheltroy Common
Clearwell
MERTHYR

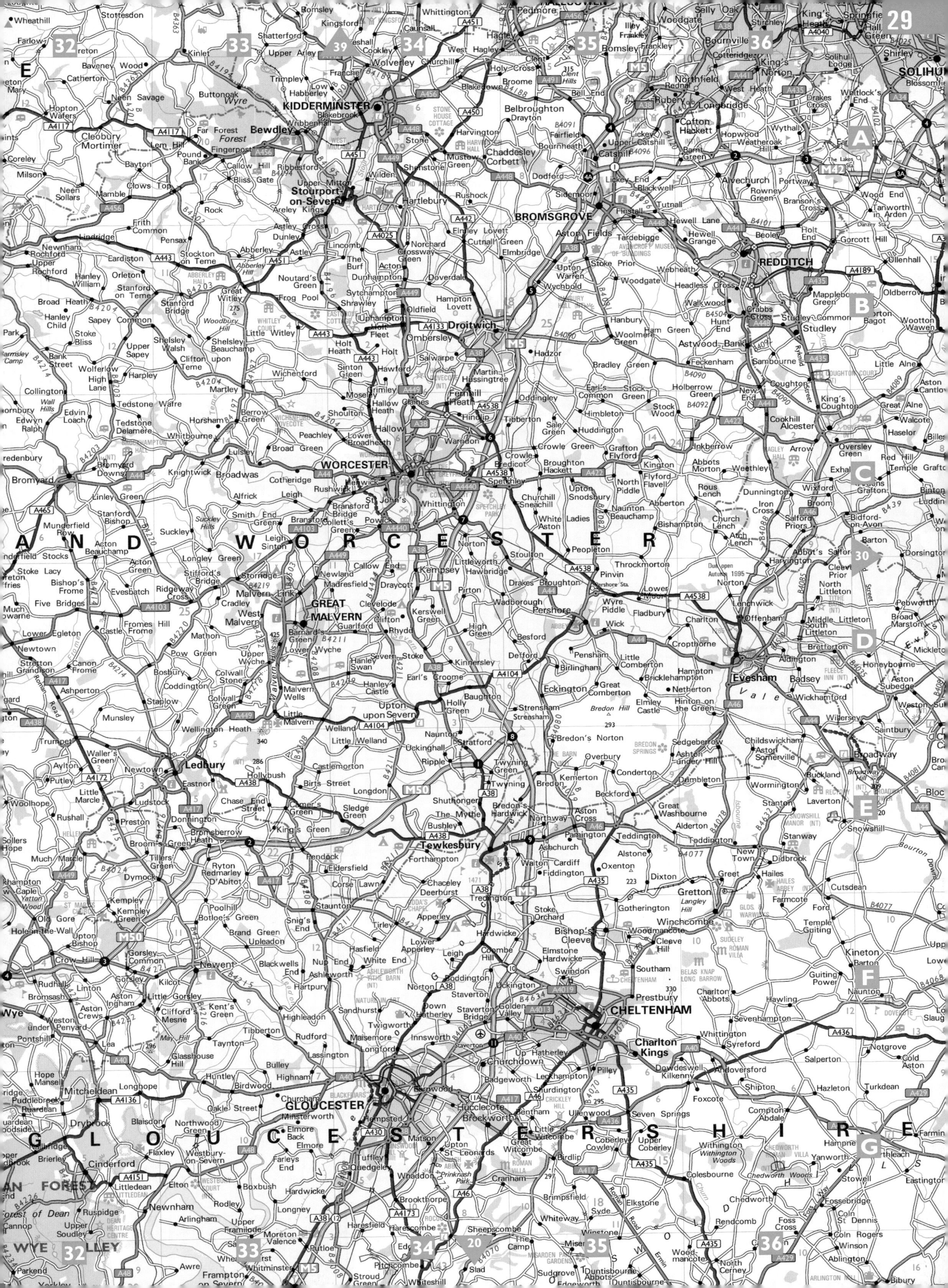
KIDDERMINSTER
Bewdley
Stourport-on-Severn
BROMSGROVE
REDDITCH
SOLIHULL
Droitwich
WORCESTER
GREAT MALVERN
Ledbury
Tewkesbury
Evesham
Pershore
CHELTENHAM
GLOUCESTER
Newent
Alcester
Studley
Broadway
Winchcombe
Charlton Kings
Cinderford
AND WORCESTER
GLOUCESTERSHIRE
Vale of Evesham
Forest of Dean
WYE VALLEY
Wyre Forest
Malvern Hills
Bredon Hill
A
B
C
D
E
F
G
32
33
34
35
36
39
30
20
M5
M50
M42

35
36
37
38
39
40
A
B
C
D
E
F
G
29
150
SOLIHULL
COVENTRY
Kenilworth
BROMSGROVE
REDDITCH
ROYAL
LEAMINGTON SPA
Warwick
Droitwich
W A R W I C K S
H E R E F O R D
&
W O R C E S T E R
Alcester
Studley
Stratford-upon-Avon
Evesham
VALE OF EVESHAM
Pershore
Broadway
Chipping
Campden
Shipston on
Stour
Moreton-
in-Marsh
Stow-on-
the-Wold
Chipping
Norton
Tewkesbury
CHELTENHAM
Winchcombe
Charlton
Kings
Bourton-
on-the-Water
Burford
Witney
Charlbury
Shipton-
under-
Wychwood
G L O U C E S T E R S H I R E
O X F O
Henley-
in-Arden
Hagley
Bournville
Meriden
Northfield
Knowle
Balsall
Common
M5
M42
M40
A44
A46
A38
A435
A429
A3400
A422
A424
A436
A40
A361
A4189
A439
A435
Due open
Autumn 1995

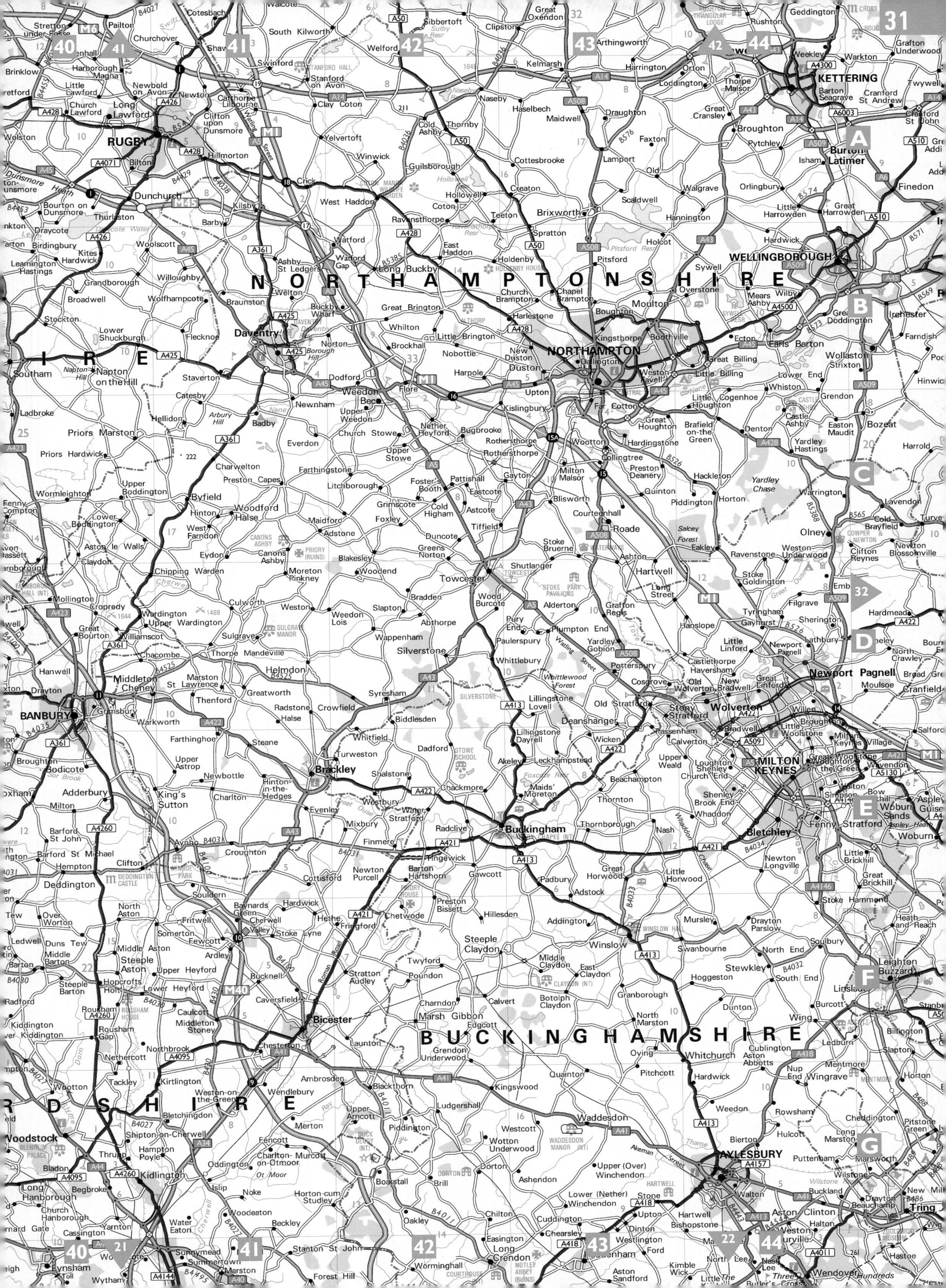
NORTHAMPTONSHIRE
BUCKINGHAMSHIRE
KETTERING
WELLINGBOROUGH
NORTHAMPTON
RUGBY
Daventry
BANBURY
Towcester
Brackley
Buckingham
Bicester
MILTON KEYNES
Wolverton
Newport Pagnell
Bletchley
Stony Stratford
Winslow
AYLESBURY
Leighton Buzzard
Olney
Kidlington
Woodstock
Thame
Wendover
Tring
Dunchurch
Long Buckby
Brixworth
Rushden
Burton Latimer
Finedon
Earls Barton
Deddington
Adderbury
Silverstone
Roade
Hanslope
Woburn
Long Crendon
Waddesdon
Whitchurch
Wing
Steeple Claydon
Middleton Cheney
Byfield
Weedon Bec
Moulton
Welford
Naseby
Crick
Kilsby
Braunston
Southam
Napton on the Hill
Woburn Sands
Fenny Stratford

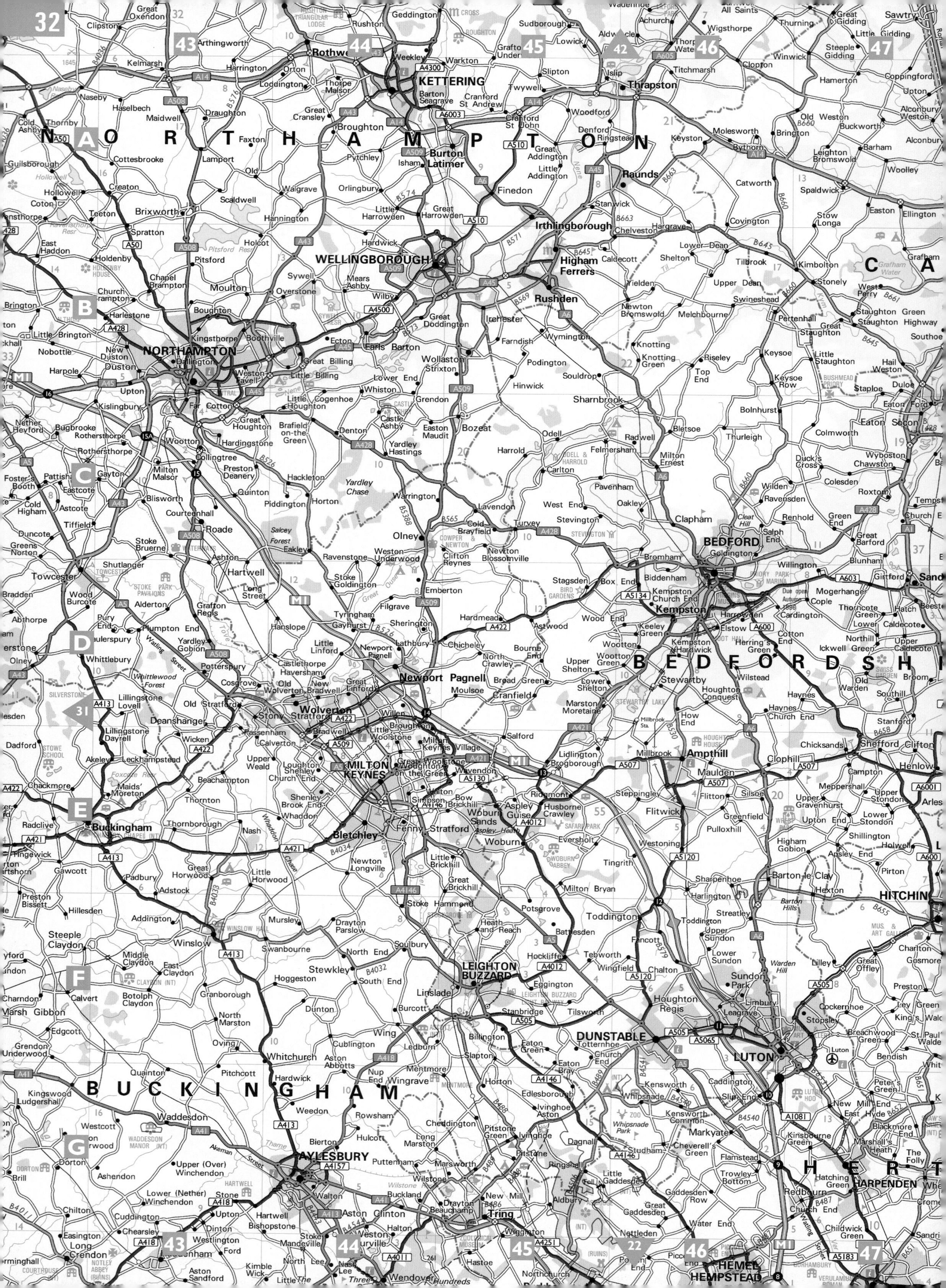
NORTHAMPTON
BEDFORDSH
BUCKINGHAM
HERT
KETTERING
Rothwell
Burton Latimer
Thrapston
Raunds
Irthlingborough
WELLINGBOROUGH
Higham Ferrers
Rushden
NORTHAMPTON
Earls Barton
Wollaston
Olney
Newport Pagnell
Wolverton
Stony Stratford
MILTON KEYNES
Bletchley
Fenny Stratford
Towcester
Buckingham
Winslow
LEIGHTON BUZZARD
Linslade
DUNSTABLE
LUTON
Houghton Regis
AYLESBURY
Tring
Wendover
HEMEL HEMPSTEAD
HARPENDEN
HITCHIN
BEDFORD
Kempston
Ampthill
Flitwick
Shefford
Woburn
Woburn Sands
Aspley Guise
Bozeat
Sharnbrook
Yardley Hastings
Stewartby
Brixworth
Moulton
Guilsborough
Long Crendon
Haddenham
Wing
Whitchurch
Waddesdon
Stewkley
Toddington
Barton-le-Clay
Sundon Park
Leagrave
Stopsley
Whipsnade
Ivinghoe
Edlesborough
Great Billing
Little Billing
Finedon
Kimbolton
Colmworth
Clapham
Cranfield
Salford
M1
A5
A6
A14
A43
A45
A421
A422
A413
A418
A41
A428
A509
A508
A505
A507
A600
A603
32
33
37
31
22
42
43
44
45
46
47

CAMBRIDGESHIRE
ESSEX
HERTFORDSHIRE
CAMBRIDGE
Ely
Huntingdon
St Ives
Newmarket
Haverhill
Royston
Saffron Walden
BISHOP'S STORTFORD
STEVENAGE
HARLOW
WELWYN GARDEN CITY
Hertford
Ware
HODDESDON
Sawbridgeworth
Baldock
Buntingford
Great Dunmow
Thaxted
Linton
Sawston
Soham
Burwell
Fordham
Mildenhall
Lakenheath
Chatteris Fen
Somersham
Warboys
Sutton
Haddenham
Cottenham
Histon
Girton
Waterbeach
Milton
Fulbourn
Trumpington
Grantchester
Great Shelford
Melbourn
Duxford
Great Chesterford
Audley End
Stansted Mountfitchet
Takeley
Hatfield Heath
Sheering
Papworth Everard
Caxton
Gamlingay
Potton
Ashwell
Newport
Clavering
Braughing
Puckeridge
Much Hadham
Knebworth
Hatfield
Broxbourne
Bedford Level (South Level)
Middle Fen
Gog Magog Hills
Danger Zone
Great Ouse
Granta
Cam
M11
A1
A10
A14
A11
A120
A1198
A505
A603
A1307
A1303
A1304
A1101
A1123
A142
A602
A414
A1060
48
49
43
50
51
52
34
23
A
B
C
D
E
F
G

Queen Adelaide
Prickwillow
Level
Lakenheath
Wangford Warren
FOREST
Thetford Warren
Thetford
Brettenham
Shadwell
West Harling Heath
Lopham
South Lopham
Fersfield
Rushford
Garboldisham
Gasthorpe
Knettishall
Smallworth
Blo Norton
Lakenheath Warren
The Delph
Kennyhill
Middle Fen
Mildenhall Fen
Eriswell
Elveden
Euston
Fen Street
Hopton
Thelnetham
Redgrave
Stuntney
Great Fen
Holywell Row
Berner's Heath
Barnham
Coney Weston
Market Weston
Wortham
Broad Hill
Isleham Fen
Thistley Green
Beck Row
Mildenhall
Little Fakenham
Barningham
Hinderclay
Botesdale
West Row
Sapiston
Rickinghall
Burgate
Soham Mere
Soham
Isleham
Worlington
Barton Mills
PARK
Honington
Bardwell
Hepworth
Wattisfield
Icklingham
Ixworth Thorpe
Stanton
Walsham le Willows
Little Green
Down Field
Freckenham
Tuddenham
Wordwell
Troston
Cranmer Green
Wicken
Fordham
Chippenham
Red Lodge
Lackford
West Stow
Ampton
Great Livermere
Four Ashes
Crowland
Fordham Abbey
Herringswell
Cavenham
Flempton
Ingham
Culford
Ixworth
Langham
Finningham
Westhorpe
Little Fen
Landwade
Snailwell
Kennett
Hengrave
Timworth Green
Stowlangtoft
Badwell Ash
Hunston
Long Thurlow
Wyverstone
Wyverstone Street
Burwell
Kentford
Fornham All Saints
Fornham St Martin
Stanton Street
Great Ashfield
Earl's Green
Cotton
Bacton
Reach
Great Barton
Pakenham
Norton
Ward Green
Higham
Risby
BURY ST EDMUNDS
Thurston
Beyton Green
Haughley Green
Prior
Moulton
Westley
Elmswell
Swaffham Bulbeck
Newmarket
National Horseracing Museum
Gazeley
Barrow
Little Saxham
Great Saxham
Beyton
Tostock
Woolpit
Wetherden
Old Newton
Blackthorpe
Rougham
Haughley
Haughley New Street
Dunstall Green
Dalham
Denham
Horringer
Rushbrooke
Hessett
Drinkstone
Middlewood Green
Cheveley
Ashley
Rougham Green
Stowupland
Hargrave
Nowton
Little Welnetham
Bradfield St George
Harleston
Stowmarket
Ousden
Chevington
Sicklesmere
Drinkstone Green
Stetchworth
Saxon Street
Upend
Lady's Green
Hawstead
Great Welnetham
Rattlesden
Great Finborough
Woodditton
Lidgate
Chedburgh
Whepstead
Bradfield Combust
Bradfield St Clare
Gedding
Buxhall
Dullingham
Ditton Green
Kirtling
Depden
Poystreet Green
Combs Ford
Six Mile Bottom
Westley Waterless
Rede
Cross Green
Great Green
Stanningfield
Felsham
Combs
Badley
Kirtling Green
High Street Green
Burrough End
Burrough Green
Thorns
Clopton Green
Brockley Green
Lawshall
Thorpe Green
Cockfield
Little Finborough
Needham Market
Brinkley
Cowlinge
Wickhambrook
Brettenham
Battisford
Weston Colville
Wickham Street
Somerton
Thorpe Morieux
Battisford Tye
Great Bradley
Stradishall
Denston
Hartest
Shimpling Street
Ringshall
Carlton
Little Bradley
Hawkedon
Cross Green
Charles Tye
Wattisham
Ringshall Stocks
Barking
Weston Green
Stansfield
Shimpling
West Wratting
Little Thurlow
Alpheton
Preston
Hitcham
Great Bricett
Willisham
Balsham
Boxted
Kettlebaston
Great Thurlow
Barnardiston
Stanstead
Bridge Street
The Priory Guildhall
Lavenham
Little Hall
Bildeston
Nedging Tye
Offton
West Wickham
Great Wratting
Hundon
Poslingford
Brook Street
Monks Eleigh
Naughton
Nettlestead
Withersfield
Glemsford
Kentwell Hall
Brent Eleigh
Chelsworth
Somersham
Linton
Horseheath
Little Wratting
Kedington
Chilton Street
Blacklands Hall
Cavendish
Washmere Green
Semer
Elmsett
Flowton
Haverhill
Nether Hall
Pentlow
Long Melford
Melford Hall
Milden
Whatfield
Bartlow
Clare
Little Waldingfield
Aldham
Camps
Foxearth
Liston
Acton
Lindsey
Wolves Wood
Castle Camps
Sturmer
Wixoe
Stoke by Clare
Clare Castle
Belchamp St Paul
Rodbridge Corner
Great Waldingfield
Kersey
Ashdon
Camps End
Helions Bumpstead
Baythorn End
Ovington
Borley
St James Chapel
Hadleigh
Chattis
Church End
Ashen
Belchamp Otten
Sudbury
Ballingdon
Edwardstone
Little Walden
Olmstead Green
Steeple Bumpstead
Birdbrook
Ridgewell
Knowl Green
Puttock End
Newton
Groton
Red Oaks Hill
Little Yeldham
Belchamp Walter
Bulmer
Great Cornard
Boxford
Layham
Sewards End
Middleton
Sackers Green
Walden
Wimbish
Hempstead
Stambourne
Great Yeldham
Gestingthorpe
Bulmer Tye
Henny Street
Assington
Polstead
Raydon
Radwinter
Cornish Hall End
Toppesfield
Pool Street
Great Henny
Twinstead
Leavenheath
Shelley
Great Wenham
Great Sampford
Barr Hall
Wickham St Paul
Lamarsh
Stoke-by-Nayland
Holton St Mary
Wimbish Green
Highstreet Green
Castle Hedingham
Alphamstone
Honey Tye
Thorington Street
Higham
Debden
Little Sampford
Sible Hedingham
Great Maplestead
Bures Green
Stratford St Mary
East Bergholt
Howe Street
Little Maplestead
Bures
Nayland
Wissington
Debden Green
Finchingfield
Pebmarsh
Mount Bures
Wormingford
Boxted
Langham
Dedham
Saffron Walden... Thaxted
Bardfield End Green
Little Bardfield
Wethersfield
Blackmore End
Halstead
Whiteash Green
Colne Engaine
Little Horkesley
Boxted Cross
Blacksmith's Corner
Lamb Corner
Great Horkesley
Langham Moor
Manningtree
Great Bardfield
Gosfield Hall
Gosfield
White Colne
Colne Valley
Wakes Colne
Rose Green
Horkesley Heath
Ardleigh
Chickney
Monk Street
Oxen End
Shalford
Beazley End
Earls Colne
Chappel
Swan Street
West Bergholt
Mile End
Fox Street
Broxted
Lindsell
Church End
Shalford Green
Jasper's Green
Greenstead Green
Fordstreet
Crockleford Heath
Duton Hill
Duck End
Bardfield Saling
Mill End Green
High Garrett
Great Tey
Eight Ash Green
Great
Bran End
Great Saling
Bocking Churchstreet
Stisted
Little Tey
Aldham
Marks Tey
Stanway
Beacon End
Shrub End
Little Easton
Butcher's Pasture
Stebbing
Stebbing Green
Panfield
Blake End
Bocking
BRAINTREE
Pattiswick
Broad Green
Copford Green
COLCHESTER
Elmstead Market
Wivenhoe
Bamber's Green
Churchend
Great Dunmow
Throws
Rayne
Bradwell
Coggeshall
Blackheath
Takeley
Little Dunmow
Bannister Green
Black Notley
Tye Green
Cressing
Coggeshall Hamlet
Feering
Easthorpe
Heckfordbridge
Rowhedge
Danger Zone
Hope End Green
Felsted
Willows Green
Hawbush Green
Silver End
Hardy's Green
Birch
Fingringhoe
Broadgroves
Barnston
Causeway End
Cobler's Green
Young's End
White Notley
Kelvedon
Messing
Layer de la Haye
Bacon End
Bishop's Green
North End
Abberton
Great Canfield
Hounslow Green
Hartford End
Little Leighs
Great Leighs
Rank's Green
Faulkbourne
Rivenhall
Smythe's Green
Layer Breton
Langenhoe
High Roding
Ford End
Littley Green
Fairstead
Rivenhall End
Inworth
Layer Marney
Layer Marney Tower
Peldon
Aythorpe Roding
High Easter
Stagden Cross
Fuller Street
Terling
Chipping Hill
Tiptree
Tiptree Heath
Tolleshunt Knights
Great Wigborough
Mersea Island
East Mersea
Cudmore Grove
White Roding
Keeres Green
Howe Street
Gamble's Green
Witham
Little Braxted
Great Braxted
Oxley Green
Virley
Salcott
Leaden Roding
Pleshey
Great Waltham
Little Waltham
Wickham Bishops
Great Totham
West Mersea
Abbess Roding
Margaret Roding
Good Easter
Mashbury
Chignall Smealy
Chignall St James
Little Totham
Tolleshunt D'Arcy
Great Cob
Cobmarsh I
The Nass
Beauchamp Roding
Broomfield
Hatfield Peverel
Tolleshunt Major
Berners Roding
Shellow Bowells
Crix
Nounsley
Boreham
Broad Street Green
Pickerells
Roxwell
Langford
Heybridge
Goldhanger
Sales Point
St Peter's
Fyfield
Willingale
Ulting
Little Baddow
Bradwell Waterside
52
53
54
55
56
44
33
24
25
A
B
C
D
E
F
G
S
U
F
E
S
S
E
X

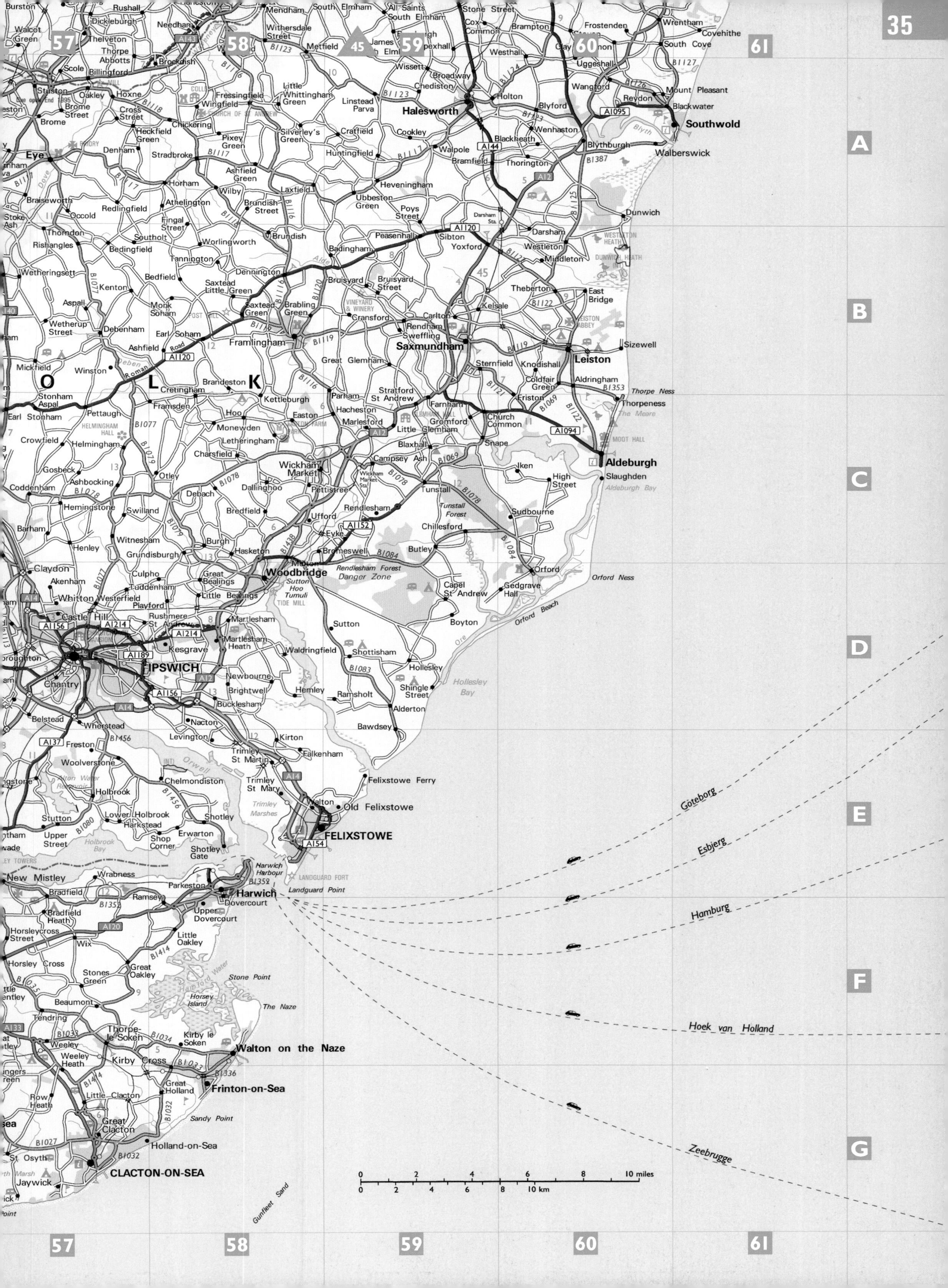
57
58
59
60
61
A
B
C
D
E
F
G
Burston
Rushall
Mendham
South Elmham
All Saints South Elmham
Stone Street
Brampton
Frostenden
Wrentham
Covehithe
Walcot Green
Thelveton
Dickleburgh
Needham
Withersdale Street
Metfield
Cox Common
South Cove
Thorpe Abbotts
Brockdish
Westhall
Uggeshall
Scole
Billingford
Wissett
Broadway
Stuston
Oakley
Hoxne
Little Whittingham Green
Chediston
Holton
Wangford
Mount Pleasant
Reydon
Brome
Brome Street
Cross Street
Fressingfield
Wingfield
Linstead Parva
Halesworth
Blyford
Blackwater
Southwold
Chickering
Heckfield Green
Pixey Green
Silverley's Green
Craffield
Cookley
Wenhaston
Blackheath
Blythburgh
Walberswick
Eye
Denham
Stradbroke
Huntingfield
Walpole
Bramfield
Thorington
Ashfield Green
Horham
Wilby
Laxfield
Heveningham
Braiseworth
Occold
Redlingfield
Athelington
Brundish Street
Ubbeston Green
Poys Street
Dunwich
Thorndon
Fingal Street
Brundish
Peasenhall
Sibton
Yoxford
Darsham
Westleton
Rishangles
Bedingfield
Southolt
Worlingworth
Badingham
Middleton
Wetheringsett
Tannington
Dennington
Bruisyard
Bruisyard Street
Theberton
East Bridge
Kenton
Bedfield
Saxtead Little Green
Aspall
Monk Soham
Saxtead Green
Brabling Green
Cransford
Carlton
Kelsale
Wetherup Street
Debenham
Earl Soham
Framlingham
Rendham
Sweffling
Saxmundham
Sizewell
Ashfield
Leiston
Mickfield
Winston
Great Glemham
Sternfield
Knodishall
Coldfair Green
Aldringham
Thorpe Ness
Thorpeness
The Meare
Brandeston
Stonham Aspal
Cretingham
Kettleburgh
Parham
Stratford St Andrew
Earl Stonham
Pettaugh
Framsden
Hoo
Easton
Hacheston
Farnham
Friston
Church Common
Monewden
Marlesford
Little Glemham
Gromford
Snape
Crowfield
Helmingham
Letheringham
Blaxhall
Aldeburgh
Charsfield
Campsey Ash
Iken
Slaughden
Aldeburgh Bay
Gosbeck
Ashbocking
Wickham Market
Otley
High Street
Coddenham
Debach
Dallinghoo
Pettistree
Tunstall
Tunstall Forest
Hemingstone
Swilland
Bredfield
Rendlesham
Sudbourne
Barham
Ufford
Chillesford
Witnesham
Henley
Grundisburgh
Burgh
Eyke
Bromeswell
Butley
Hasketon
Melton
Claydon
Culpho
Great Bealings
Woodbridge
Rendlesham Forest Danger Zone
Orford
Orford Ness
Akenham
Tuddenham
Sutton Hoo Tumuli
Capel St Andrew
Gedgrave Hall
Whitton
Westerfield
Playford
Little Bealings
Tide Mill
Castle Hill
Rushmere St Andrew
Martlesham
Boyton
Orford Beach
Martlesham Heath
Sutton
Kesgrave
Waldringfield
Shottisham
Ipswich
Chantry
Newbourne
Brightwell
Hemley
Hollesley
Hollesley Bay
Ramsholt
Shingle Street
Bucklesham
Alderton
Belstead
Wherstead
Nacton
Bawdsey
Levington
Freston
Kirton
Falkenham
Trimley St Martin
Woolverstone
Chelmondiston
Felixstowe Ferry
Trimley St Mary
Holbrook
Trimley Marshes
Walton
Old Felixstowe
Stutton
Lower Holbrook
Shotley
Harkstead
Erwarton
Felixstowe
Upper Street
Holbrook Bay
Shop Corner
Shotley Gate
Harwich Harbour
Landguard Fort
Landguard Point
New Mistley
Wrabness
Parkeston
Harwich
Bradfield
Ramsey
Dovercourt
Bradfield Heath
Upper Dovercourt
Horsleycross Street
Wix
Little Oakley
Horsley Cross
Great Oakley
Stones Green
Stone Point
Horsey Island
The Naze
Beaumont
Tendring
Thorpe-le-Soken
Kirby le Soken
Weeley
Weeley Heath
Walton on the Naze
Kirby Cross
Great Holland
Frinton-on-Sea
Row Heath
Little Clacton
Great Clacton
Sandy Point
Holland-on-Sea
St Osyth
Jaywick
Clacton-on-Sea
Gunfleet Sand
Göteborg
Esbjerg
Hamburg
Hoek van Holland
Zeebrugge
0 2 4 6 8 10 miles
0 2 4 6 8 10 km
A12
A14
A120
A140
A143
A144
A1094
A1095
A1120
A1152
A1156
A1189
A1214
A137
A133
A154
B1078
B1079
B1083
B1084
B1069
B1119
B1121
B1122
B1353
B1116
B1117
B1118
B1123
B1125
B1387
B1456
B1080
B1352
B1414
B1033
B1034
B1032
B1027
B1336

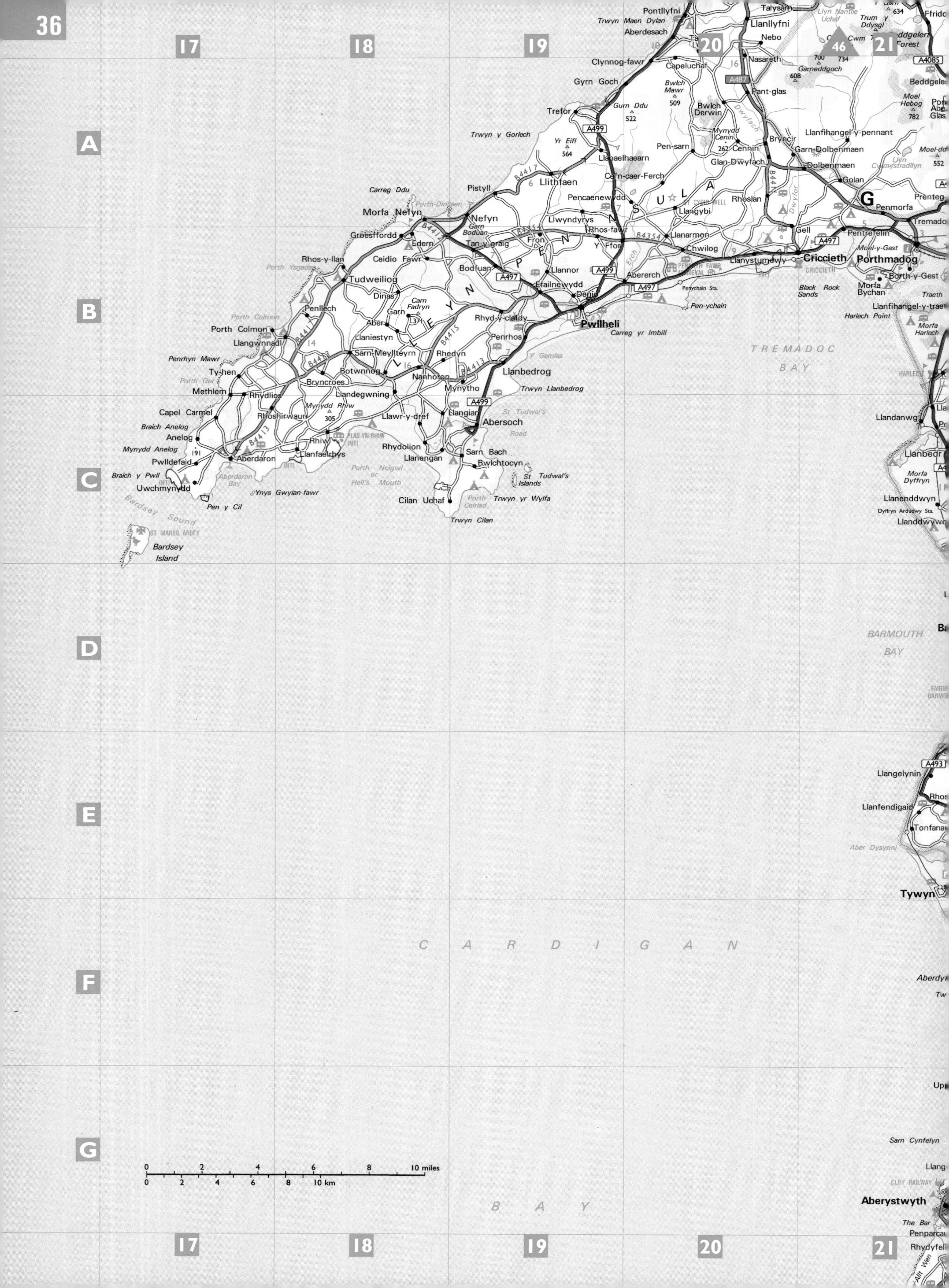
17
18
19
20
21
46
A
B
C
D
E
F
G
Pontllyfni
Trwyn Maen Dylan
Aberdesach
Talysarn
Llanllyfni
Nebo
Llyn Nantlle Uchaf
Trum y Ddysgl
Cwm
Beddgelert Forest
634
700
734
A4085
Clynnog-fawr
Capeluchaf
Nasareth
Garneddgoch
608
A487
Pant-glas
Beddgelert
Gyrn Goch
Bwlch Mawr
509
Gurn Ddu
522
Bwlch Derwin
Dwyfach
Moel Hebog
782
Trefor
A499
Trwyn y Gorlech
Yr Eifl
564
Llanaelhaearn
Mynydd Cennin
262
Cennin
Pen-sarn
Bryncir
Llanfihangel-y-pennant
Garn-Dolbenmaen
Glan-Dwyfach
Dolbenmaen
Llyn Cwmystradllyn
552
B4417
Llithfaen
Cefn-caer-Ferch
Golan
Carreg Ddu
Pistyll
Porth-Dinllaen
Pencaenewydd
ST CYBI'S WELL
Rhoslan
Dwyfor
Penmorfa
Prenteg
Tremadog
Morfa Nefyn
Nefyn
Garn Boduan
Llwyndyrys
Llangybi
Groesffordd
B4412
Edern
B4354
Fron
Rhos-fawr
Llanarmon
Gell
Pentrefelin
A497
Tan-y-graig
Y Ffor
Chwilog
Moel-y-Gest
Rhos-y-llan
Porth Ysgadan
Ceidio Fawr
Bodfuan
Llannor
A499
Abererch
Erch
PENARTH FAWR MEDIEVAL HOUSE
Llanystumdwy
Criccieth
CRICCIETH
Porthmadog
Tudweiliog
A497
Efailnewydd
Penychain Sta.
Borth-y-Gest
Morfa Bychan
Black Rock Sands
Traeth
Dinas
Carn Fadryn
371
Deneio
Pen-ychain
Llanfihangel-y-traethau
Harlech Point
Morfa Harlech
Porth Colmon
Penllech
Garn
Rhyd-y-clafdy
Pwllheli
Carreg yr Imbill
Porth Colmon
Aber
B4415
Llaniestyn
Penrhos
TREMADOC BAY
Llangwnnadl
B4417
Penrhyn Mawr
14
Sarn Meyllteyrn
Rhedyn
Y Gamlas
Ty-hen
B4413
Botwnnog
16
B4413
Llanbedrog
Porth Oer
Bryncroes
Nanhoron
HARLECH
Methlem
Rhydlios
Llandegwning
Mynytho
Trwyn Llanbedrog
A499
Capel Carmel
Mynydd Rhiw
305
Llawr-y-dref
Llangian
St Tudwal's Road
Llandanwg
Braich Anelog
Rhoshirwaun
Abersoch
Anelog
PLAS-YN-RHIW (NT)
Mynydd Anelog
191
B4413
Rhiw
Rhydolion
Pwlldefaid
Aberdaron
Llanfaelrhys
Llanengan
Sarn Bach
Llanbedr
Braich y Pwll
Aberdaron Bay
Porth Neigwl or Hell's Mouth
Bwlchtocyn
St Tudwal's Islands
Morfa Dyffryn
Uwchmynydd
Ynys Gwylan-fawr
Cilan Uchaf
Porth Ceiriad
Trwyn yr Wylfa
Llanenddwyn
Pen y Cil
Dyffryn Ardudwy Sta.
Bardsey Sound
Trwyn Cilan
Llanddwywe
ST MARYS ABBEY
Bardsey Island
BARMOUTH BAY
Llangelynin
A493
Llanfendigaid
Tonfanau
Aber Dysynni
Tywyn
CARDIGAN
BAY
Sarn Cynfelyn
CLIFF RAILWAY
Aberystwyth
The Bar
Penparcau
Rhydyfelin
Allt Wen
0
2
4
6
8
10 miles
0
2
4
6
8
10 km

GWYNEDD
CLWYD
POWYS
DYFED
SNOWDONIA
NATIONAL
PARK
COED Y BRENIN
FOREST PARK
CAMBRIAN MOUNTAINS
Berwyn
Blaenau Ffestiniog
Ffestiniog
Bethania
Tanygrisiau
Maentwrog
Gellilydan
Penrhyndeudraeth
Trawsfynydd
Bronaber
Ganllwyd
Llanelltyd
Dolgellau
Penmaenpool
Abergwynant
Arthog
Friog
Cader Idris
Minffordd
Corris
Corris Uchaf
Aberllefenni
Tal-y-llyn
Abergynolwyn
Dolgoch
Pantperthog
Machynlleth
Derwenlas
Glaspwll
Aberdyfi
Eglwys Fach
Furnace
Tre'r-ddol
Taliesin
Talybont
Bow Street
Capel Bangor
Ponterwyd
Eisteddfa Gurig
Llangurig
Llanidloes
Staylittle
Dylife
Llanbrynmair
Talerddig
Carno
Clatter
Caersws
Newtown (Y Drenewy)
Tregynon
Llanfair Caereinion
Llanerfyl
Llangadfan
Foel
Pen-y-bont
Llanwddyn
Lake Vyrnwy
Abertridwr
Penybontfawr
Llangynog
Bala
Llyn Tegid (Bala Lake)
Llanuwchllyn
Llangower
Llanfor
Llandderfel
Frongoch
Rhyd-uchaf
Cerrigydrudion
Glasfryn
Pentrefoelas
Ysbyty Ifan
Glan-Conwy
Dolwyddelan
Penmachno
Corwen
Druid
Maerdy
Bettws Gwerfil Goch
Gwyddelwern
Llandrillo
Cynwyd
Dinas-Mawddwy
Mallwyd
Cwm-Cewydd
Aber-cywarch
Llanymawddwy
Cemmaes
Glantwymyn
Commins Coch
Abergwydol
Darowen
Penegoes
Llan
Bont Dolgadfan
Pennant
Plynlimon
Pumlumon-Arwystli
Dyfi Forest
Trefeglwys
Llandinam
Oakley Park
Dolfor
Mochdre
Pant Mawr
Tyn-y-Cwm
Aberffrwd
Ysbyty Ystwyth

WREXHAM
Rhostyllen
Ruabon
Llangollen
Corwen
Chirk
Oswestry
Ellesmere
Overton
Whitchurch
Malpas
Wem
SHREWSBURY
Welshpool
(Y Trallwng)
Llanfyllin
Llanrhaeadr-ym-Mochnant
Montgomery
(Trefaldwyn)
Newtown
(Y Drenewydd)
Bishop's
Castle
Church Stretton
Pontesbury
Clun
C L W Y D
P O W Y S
S H R O P S
A5
A483
A495
A490
A458
A488
A489
A49
A528
A525
A539
A41
A5112
A53

Nantwich
Newcastle-under-Lyme
Stoke-on-Trent
Market Drayton
Stone
Uttoxeter
Cheadle
Stafford
Eccleshall
Newport
Rugeley
Cannock
Telford
Wellington
Penkridge
Hednesford
Lichfield
Brownhills
Bloxwich
Aldridge
Wednesfield
Walsall
Wolverhampton
Bridgnorth
Sedgley
Dudley
West Bromwich
Sutton Coldfield
Stourbridge
Halesowen
Warley
Birmingham
Solihull
S T A F F O R D S
I R E
W E S T
M I D L A N D S
Cannock Chase
M6
M54
M5
A38(M)
32
33
34
35
36
49
40
29
A
B
C
D
E
F
G

STAFFORDSHIRE
WEST MIDLANDS
NEWCASTLE-UNDER-LYME
STOKE-ON-TRENT
Ashbourne
Stone
Uttoxeter
STAFFORD
BURTON UPON TRENT
RUGELEY
CANNOCK
LICHFIELD
BROWNHILLS
TAMWORTH
BLOXWICH
ALDRIDGE
WEDNESFIELD
WALSALL
WOLVERHAMPTON
SUTTON COLDFIELD
WEST BROMWICH
DUDLEY
BIRMINGHAM
STOURBRIDGE
HALESOWEN
WARLEY
KIDDERMINSTER
Newport
Shifnal
Hednesford
Cannock Chase
Needwood Forest
Trent Valley
Tutbury
Cheadle
Leek
Longton
Fenton
Hanley
Burslem
Tunstall
Eccleshall
Penkridge
Codsall
Sedgley
Coleshill
Meriden
Solihull
Erdington
Castle Bromwich
Fazeley
Alrewas
Yoxall
Abbots Bromley
Rocester
Alton
Cheddleton
Froghall
Kingsley
Barlaston
Trentham
Madeley
Keele
Audley
Talke
M6
M42
M5
A38(M)
A5
A50
A38
A34
A51
A52
A449
A518
A519
A515
A513
34
35
36
37
38
39
50
29
A
B
C
D
E
F
G

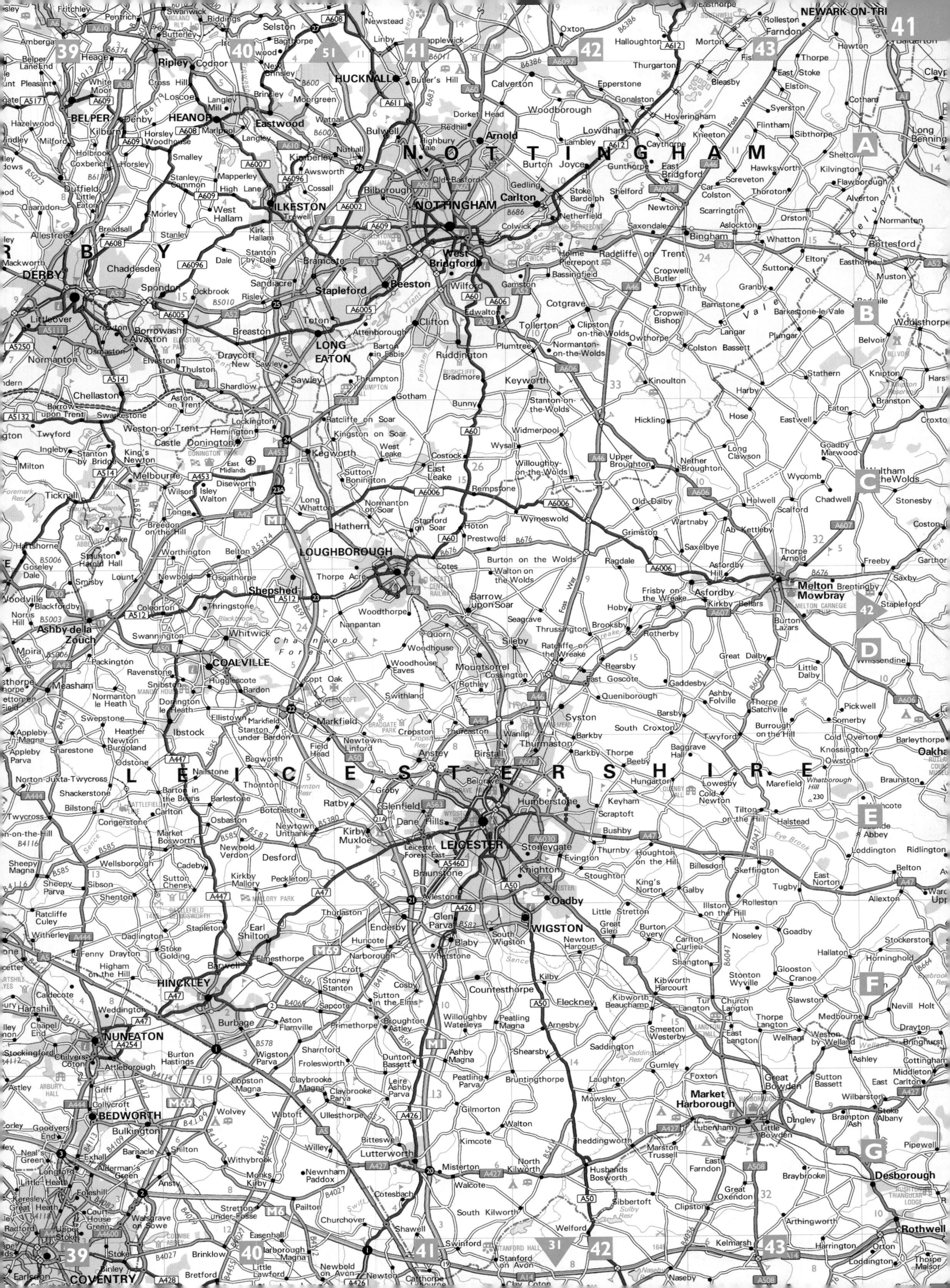
NOTTINGHAM
LEICESTERSHIRE
NOTTINGHAM
DERBY
LEICESTER
LOUGHBOROUGH
HUCKNALL
ILKESTON
HEANOR
BELPER
Ripley
Eastwood
Arnold
Carlton
Beeston
Stapleford
West Bridgford
LONG EATON
Shepshed
COALVILLE
Ashby-de-la-Zouch
Melton Mowbray
HINCKLEY
NUNEATON
BEDWORTH
COVENTRY
WIGSTON
Oadby
Market Harborough
Lutterworth
Desborough
Rothwell
Bingham
Radcliffe on Trent
Castle Donington
Kegworth
Melbourne
Syston
Sileby
Asfordby
Bottesford
NEWARK-ON-TRENT
Vale of Belvoir
Charnwood Forest
East Midlands
M1
M69
M6
A
B
C
D
E
F
G
39
40
41
42
43
51
31

NOTTS
LINCOL
LEICESTER
NORTHAMPTON
NEWARK-ON-TRENT
GRANTHAM
Sleaford
Bourne
Melton Mowbray
Oakham
Stamford
Uppingham
CORBY
Market Harborough
KETTERING
Oundle
Rothwell
Desborough
Bingham
Radcliffe on Trent
Bottesford
Market Deeping
Deeping St James
Thrapston
Leadenham
Cranwell
Leasingham
Ruskington
Dorrington
North Kyme
South Kyme
Anwick
Heckington
Helpringham
Billingborough
Horbling
Folkingham
Ancaster
Wilsford
Caythorpe
Claypole
Long Bennington
Barrowby
Great Gonerby
Sedgebrook
Colsterworth
Corby Glen
Castle Bytham
Ryhall
Empingham
Ketton
Collyweston
Wansford
Barnack
Helpston
Glinton
Whittlesey
Yaxley
Sawtry
Warmington
Nassington
Kings Cliffe
Bulwick
Deene
Weldon
Brigstock
Geddington
Rushton
Broughton
Asfordby
Frisby on the Wreake
Rearsby
Syston
Queniborough
Tilton on the Hill
Billesdon
Hallaton
Medbourne
Rockingham
Cottingham
Caldecott
Lyddington
Ketton
Wittering
Oakham
Rutland Water
Vale of Belvoir
Vale of Catmose
Rockingham Forest
A1
A17
A15
A52
A46
A606
A607
A47
A43
A427
A6003
A6116
A605
A151
A16
B1176
41
43
44
45
46
47
52
32
A
B
C
D
E
F
G

48
53
49
50
51
52
A
B
C
D
E
F
G
44
33
Wildmore Fen
Leake
Common Side
Wrangle
Friskney Flats
Gipsey Bridge
Sibsey
Old Leake
Leake Hurn's End
Langrick
Fishtoft Drove
Langriville
Frith Bank
Hill Dyke
Leverton
Leverton Outgate
Amber Hill
Witham
Brothertoft
Benington
Benington Sea End
Holland Fen
Hubbert's Bridge
BOSTON
Butterwick
Halltoft End
Freiston
Butterwick Low
Roger Sand
Swineshead Bridge
Kirton Holme
Skirbeck
Frampton West End
Fishtoft
Freiston Shore
Fenhouses
Scrane End
Toft Sand
Swineshead
Wyberton
The Haven
Black Buoy Sand
Gat Sand
Drayton
Kirton End
Frampton
The Scalp
THE
WASH
Kirton
Mare Tail
Hoffleet Stow
Sandholme
Skeldyke
Wigtoft
Old South
Donington
Sutterton
Algarkirk
Fosdyke
Church End
Quadring Eaudike
Bicker Haven
Gosberton
Boston Deeps
Long Sand
Lynn Deeps
Lynn Channel
Old Lynn Channel
Seal Sand
Peter Black Sand
Bulldog Sand
Danger Zone
Holbeach St Matthew
Holbeach St Marks
Welland
Whaplode Marsh
Holbeach Marsh
Gedney Marsh
Dawsmere
Gedney Drove End
Surfleet
Surfleet Seas End
Moulton Seas End
Holbeach Bank
Holbeach Hurn
Lutton Marsh
Glen
Spalding Marsh
Saracen's Head
Holbeach Clough
Crossgate
Pinchbeck
Loosegate
Fleet Hargate
Gedney Dyke
Lutton
Guy's Head
Weston
Whaplode
Holbeach
Chapelgate
Little London
Moulton
Gedney
Fleet
Long Sutton
Spalding
Gedney Broadgate
Delph Bank
Sutton Bridge
Sutton Crosses
Weston Hills
Whaplode Fen
Whaplode St Catherine
Tydd St Mary
Moulton Chapel
Holbeach St Johns
Cowbit
Sutton St James
Tydd Gote
Four Gotes
Moulton Fen
Deeping St Nicholas
Tydd St Giles
Aswick Grange
Whaplode Drove
Tydd St Giles Fen
Newton
Great Postland
Sutton St Edmund
Fitton End
Holbeach Drove
Shepeau Stow
Gorefield
Crowland
Gedney Hill
Leverington
Crowland Abbey
Peckover House (NT)
Wisbech
North Fen
Church End
Parson Drove
Borough Fen
Murrow
Wisbech St Mary
Morris Fen
Wryde Croft
Tholomas Drove
Elm
Bedford Level
Eye Green
Thorney
Waldersey
Eye
North Level
Guyhirn
Adventurers' Land
Ring's End
Hobbs Lots Bridge
Coldham
Friday Bridge
Outwell
Upwell
Laddus Fens
Priors Fen
Newark
North Side
Eldernell
PETERBOROUGH
Morton's Leam
Nene
White Moor
Westry
Whittlesey
Twenty Foot River
Fletton
Eastrea
Coates
March
Binnimoor Fen
Stanground
King's Delph
West Fen
Town End
Flag Fen
Farcet Fen
Glass Moor
Ransom Moor
Wimblington
Whittlesey Mere
Pondersbridge
White Fen
Bedford Level
Level
Doddington
The Herne
Benwick
Middle Moor
Mere Side
Middle Level
Wimblington Fen
Manea
Manea Sta.
Ramsey Mereside
Forty Foot or Vermuden's Drain
Sixteen Foot Drain
Ramsey St Mary's
Ramsey Forty Foot
West Moor
Horseway
Purls Bridge
Chatteris
Ramsey Heights
Ramsey Hollow
Ramsey Abbey Gatehouse (NT)
Ramsey
Langwood Fen
Welches Dam
Tick Fen
Bury
CAMBRIDGE
Upwood
Horseley Fen
Somersham High North Fen
Great Raveley
Wistow
Pidley Fen
Little Raveley
Warboys
Fenton
Pidley
Chatteris Fen
Broughton
Somersham
Abbots Ripton
Wennington
Holme next the Sea
Titchwell
Thornham
Hunstanton
Ringstead
Heacham
Sedgeford
Snettisham
Fring
Peddars Way
Southgate
Ingoldisthorpe
Great Bircham
Shernborne
Dersingham
Anmer
Wolferton
Sandringham
West Newton
Flitcham
Babingley
Castle Rising
Hillington
North Wootton
Trinity Hospital
Congham
Roydon
South Wootton
Grimston
Terrington Marsh
Ongar Hill
Great Ouse
Breast Sand
Wingland Marsh
Terrington St Clement
Little London
KING'S LYNN
St Georges Guildhall (NT)
Gaywood
Pott Row
Clenchwarton
Walpole Cross Keys
West Lynn
Gayton
Ashwicken
Walpole St Andrew
Tilney All Saints
Tilney High End
Walpole St Peter
West Winch
East Winch
East Walton
Saddle Bow
Terrington St John
North Runcton
Middleton
St John's Highway
Tilney St Lawrence
Wiggenhall St Germans
Blackborough End
Pentney
Setchey
West Walton
Walpole Highway
Wiggenhall St Mary the Virgin
Wiggenhall St Peter
Nar
Narborough
West Walton Highway
St John's Fen End
Wormegay
Walsoken
Wiggenhall St Mary Magdalen
Tottenhill
Magdalen Road Sta.
St Mary
Watlington
Marham
New Walsoken
Marshland Fen
Runcton Holme
Shouldham
Emneth
Thorpland
South Runcton
Shouldham Thorpe
Emneth Hungate
Stowbridge
Fincham
Roman Road
Holly End
NORFOLK
Stow Bardolph
Stow Bardolph Fen
Barroway Drove
Wimbotsham
Stradsett
Middle Level Main Drain
Crimplesham
Bexwell
Downham Market
Upwell North District
Denver
Boughton
Nordelph
Wereham
Oxborough
Three Holes
West Dereham
Eximoor Fen
Wretton
Stoke Ferry
Upwell Fen
Fordham
South District
Hilgay
Whittington
Wissey
Christchurch
Ten Mile Bank
Lakesend
Upwell Fen
Old Bedford River
Delph
Southery
Hilgay Fen
Methwold Hythe
Welney
Southery Fens
Methwold Fens
Queen's Ground
Gold Hill
THETFORD
Brandon Creek
Feltwell
Apes Hall
Feltwell Fens
Hockwold cum Wilton
Brandon Bank
Mare Fen
Burnt Fen
Hockwold Fens
Fodder Fen
Littleport
Little Ouse
Shippea Hill Sta.
Wangford Fen
Grime Fen
Wangford
Pymore
New Bedford River or Hundred Foot Drain
Little Downham
Chettisham
Lakenheath
Coveney
Bedford Level
Padnal Fen
Prickwillow
Wardy Hill
West Fen
South Level
Queen Adelaide
The Delph
Kennyhill
Mepal
Witcham
Ely
Middle Fen
Sutton
Wentworth
Witchford
Stuntney
Great Fen
Mildenhall Fen
Eriswell
A1121
A52
A16
A17
A151
A16
A152
A1073
A47
A605
A1101
A141
A142
A10
A1122
A134
A149
A148
A1078
A1065
A1101
B1184
B1183
B1192
B1391
B1357
B1168
B1165
B1515
B1359
B1390
B1169
B1187
B1166
B1167
B1443
B1040
B1093
B1095
B1096
B1098
B1099
B1101
B1050
B1381
B1411
B1382
B1094
B1057
B1160
B1106
B1112
B1386
B1145
B1153
B1440
B1439
B1454
B1154

52
53
54
55
56
A
B
C
D
E
F
G
Lynn Deeps
THE WASH
Brancaster Bay
Holkham Bay
Blakeney Point
Peddars Way & Norfolk Coast Path
Hunstanton
Holme next the Sea
Titchwell
Thornham
Brancaster
Burnham Deepdale
Burnham Norton
Burnham Market
Burnham Overy
Overy Staithe
Burnham Thorpe
Holkham
Wells-next-the-Sea
Stiffkey
Morston
Blakeney
Cley next the Sea
Newgate
Wiveton
Glandford
Cockthorpe
Warham
Langham
Binham
Wighton
Saxlingham
Field Dalling
Letheringsett
Westgate
Ringstead
Heacham
Sedgeford
Summerfield
Docking
Stanhoe
North Creake
South Creake
Creake Abbey
Egmere
Little Walsingham
Great Walsingham
Houghton St Giles
Hindringham
Lower Green
Bale
Sharrington
Thornage
Hunworth
Brinton
Stody
Gunthorpe
Briningham
Melton Constable
Briston
Swanton Novers
Barney
Thursford
Great Snoring
Little Snoring
North Barsham
East Barsham
West Barsham
Kettlestone
Fulmodeston
Hindolveston
Thurning
Snettisham
Southgate
Ingoldisthorpe
Fring
Bircham Newton
Barmer
Great Bircham
Bircham Tofts
Bagthorpe
Syderstone
Sculthorpe
Shernborne
Dersingham
Wolferton
Sandringham
West Newton
Anmer
Houghton Hall
New Houghton
Flitcham
East Rudham
West Rudham
Tattersett
Dunton
Shereford
Tatterford
Hempton
Fakenham
Toftrees
Helhoughton
Harpley
Little Ryburgh
Great Ryburgh
Stibbard
Wood Norton
Guestwick
Wood Dalling
Seal Sand
Peter Black Sand
Bulldog Sand
Babingley
Castle Rising
North Wootton
South Wootton
Ongar Hill
Hillington
Little Massingham
Great Massingham
Congham
Roydon
Grimston
Colkirk
Oxwick
West Raynham
South Raynham
East Raynham
Whissonsett
Horningtoft
Guist
Twyford
Foulsham
Themelthorpe
Gateley
North Elmham
Bintree
Foxley
Bawdeswell
Reepham
Little London
KING'S LYNN
Gaywood
Clenchwarton
West Lynn
Pott Row
Weasenham St Peter
Weasenham All Saints
Wellingham
Tittleshall
Rougham
Massingham Heath
Stanfield
Brisley
Billingford
East Bilney
Worthing
Sparham
Tilney All Saints
Tilney High End
Gayton
Ashwicken
Gayton Thorpe
West Lexham
East Lexham
Litcham
Mileham
Beetley
Bittering
Mill Street
Lyng
Elsing
Hoe
Swanton Morley
Woodgate
Primrose Green
Saddle Bow
West Winch
East Winch
Wiggenhall St Germans
North Runcton
Middleton
Blackborough End
West Bilney
East Walton
Castle Acre
Newton
Gressenhall
Longham
Beeston
Great Dunham
Norfolk Rural Life Museum
Northall Green
East Dereham
North Tuddenham
Wiggenhall St Mary the Virgin
Wiggenhall St Peter
Setchey
Pentney
Narborough
West Acre
South Acre
Great Fransham
Little Dunham
Wendling
Scarning
Toftwood
Mattishall
Mattishall Burgh
Clint Green
Yaxham
South Green
East Tuddenham
Wiggenhall St Mary Magdalen
Watlington
Tottenhill
Wormegay
Runcton Holme
Marham
Shouldham
Shouldham Thorpe
Thorpland
Stowbridge
Great Palgrave
Sporle
Little Fransham
Ivy Todd
Daffy Green
Westfield
Whinburgh
Welborne
Swaffham
Oakleigh House
Swaffham Heath
Necton
East Bradenham
West Bradenham
Holme Hale
South Runcton
Fincham
Roman Road
Stow Bardolph
Wimbotsham
Stradsett
Barton Bendish
Beechamwell
North Pickenham
Shipdham
Garvestone
Runhall
Thuxton
Brandon Parva
Coston
Reymerston
Cranworth
Southburgh
Hardingham
Kimberley
Carleton Forehoe
Crimplesham
Downham Market
Bexwell
Denver
Nordelph
Cockley Cley
Iceni Village
South Pickenham
Ashill
Woodrising
Crownthorpe
Wicklewood
Boughton
Wereham
Oxborough
Gooderstone
Saham Toney
Ovington
Carbrooke
Hingham
Hackford
Scoulton Mere
Great Cressingham
Threxton Hill
Watton
Watton Green
Scoulton
Deopham
Morley St Botolph
West Dereham
Wretton
Stoke Ferry
Hilborough
Fordham
Whittington
Foulden
Bodney
Little Cressingham
Griston
Northacre
Little Ellingham
Deopham Green
Hilgay
Wissey
Northwold
Danger Zone
Merton
Caston
Rockland St Peter
Great Ellingham
Ten Mile Bank
Little London
Tottington
Thompson
Stow Bedon
Rockland All Saints
Besthorpe
Attleborough
Southery
Methwold
Cranwich
Ickburgh
Methwold Hythe
Mundford
West Tofts
Breckles
Shropham
North End
Puddledock
Old Buckenham
Hilgay Fen
Southery Fens
Methwold Fens
Queen's Ground
Great Hockham
Eccles Road
Cake Street
Brandon Creek
Feltwell
Feltwell Fens
THETFORD
Lynford
Weeting Castle
BRECKLAND
Wretham
Illington
Snetterton
Wilby
Apes Hall
Brandon Bank
Hockwold cum Wilton
Weeting
Grime's Graves
Larling
Banham
Burnt Fen
Little Ouse
Hockwold Fens
Santon Downham
Croxton
Quidenham
Kenninghall
Brandon
Town Street
Wangford Fen
Wangford
Brandon Park
Wangford Warren
Thetford Warren Lodge
Thetford Warren
Roudham
East Harling
Bridgham
Middle Harling
Winfarthing
Grime Fen
Kilverstone
Thetford
Brettenham
Shadwell
West Harling Heath
North Lopham
South Lopham
Fersfield
Prickwillow
Padnal Fen
Level
Lakenheath
The Delph
FOREST PARK
Ancient House Mus.
Rushford
Garboldisham
Queen Adelaide
Middle Fen
Kennyhill
Lakenheath Warren
Elveden
Gasthorpe
Knettishall
Knettishall Heath
Smallworth
Blo Norton
Bressingham
Bressingham Live Steam Museum & Gardens
Stuntney
Great Fen
Mildenhall Fen
Eriswell
Barnham
Euston
Hopton
Thelnetham
Market
Redgrave
Mere
Scoulton
A149
A148
A1067
A1065
A47
A17
A10
A134
A1122
A1075
A11
A1066
A1101
A1088
A1078
B1155
B1153
B1454
B1355
B1105
B1110
B1145
B1146
B1388
B1156
B1354
B1440
B1439
B1077
B1108
B1106
B1386
B1112
B1160
B1107
B1111
B1114
B1113
B1077
B1135
B1057
B1382
43
34
WALSINGHAM ABBEY
HOLKHAM HALL
SHIREHALL MUSEUM
WELLS & WALSINGHAM LIGHT RLY
SAXON CATHEDRAL & EARTHWORKS
SNETTERTON
TRINITY HOSPITAL
ST GEORGE'S GUILDHALL (NT)
OXBOROUGH HALL (NT)
NORFOLK

57
58
59
60
61
0 2 4 6 8 10 miles
0 2 4 6 8 10 km
A
B
C
D
E
F
G
Sheringham
West Runton
Cromer
Weybourne
Beeston Regis
East Runton
Upper Sheringham
Overstrand
Sidestrand
Trimingham
Aylmerton
Felbrigg
West Beckham
East Beckham
Crossdale Street
Northrepps
Gresham
Metton
Baconsthorpe
Roughton
Gimingham
Southrepps
Mundesley
Bessingham
Sustead
Hanworth
Thurgarton
Matlaske
Aldborough
Alby Hill
Thorpe Market
Trunch
Paston
Little Barningham
Wickmere
Knapton
Bacton
Keswick
Suffield
Bradfield
Antingham
Edingthorpe
Walcott
Erpingham
Swafield
Calthorpe
Colby
Witton Bridge
Ridlington
Happisburgh
Itteringham
Saxthorpe
North Walsham
Spa Common
Crostwight
Corpusty
Ingworth
Banningham
Whimpwell Green
Oulton
Felmingham
Happisburgh Common
Hempstead
Oulton Street
Blickling
Lessingham
Tuttington
Bengate
Honing
Aylsham
Westwick
East Ruston
Sea Palling
Waxham
Burgh next Aylsham
Skeyton
Worstead
Stalham
Ingham
Southgate
Brampton
Swanton Abbot
Dilham
Stalham Green
Hickling
Cawston
Marsham
Oxnead
Smallburgh
Low Street
Hickling Green
Sloley
Sutton
Booton
Eastgate
Buxton Heath
Lamas
Fairstead
Scottow
Market Street
Barton Common
Hickling Heath
Horsey
Buxton
Little Hautbois
Beeston St Lawrence
Barton Turf
Hevingham
Sco Ruston
Catfield
Neatishead
Stratton Strawless
Tunstead
Ashmanhaugh
Irstead
Potter Heigham
East Somerton
Swannington
Coltishall
West Somerton
Winterton-on-Sea
Alderford
Horstead
Waterloo
Hainford
Belaugh
Hoveton
Ludham
Martham
Felthorpe
St Helena
Frettenham
Wroxham
Horning
Bastwick
Hemsby
Newport
Attlebridge
Newton St Faith
Crostwick
Repps
Weston Longville
Horsford
Upper Street
Thurne
Rollesby
Ormesby St Margaret
Scratby
Spixworth
Woodbastwick
Clippesby
California
Taverham
Horsham St Faith
Rackheath
Salhouse
Ranworth
Burgh St Margaret
Ormesby St Michael
Ringland
Drayton
Panxworth
Billockby
Filby
Catton
New Rackheath
South Walsham
Upton
Upton Green
Mautby
Caister-on-Sea
Costessey
Sprowston
Little Plumstead
Thrigby
West Caister
Easton
Thorpe End Garden Village
Hemblington
North Burlingham
Runham
West End
New Costessey
Hellesdon
Great Plumstead
Acle
Stokesby
Marlingford
Thorpe St Andrew
Blofield
Lingwood
Damgate
Bawburgh
Bowthorpe
Brundall
Tunstall
Colney
Earlham
Eaton
NORWICH
Postwick
Strumpshaw
Beighton
Moulton St Mary
THE BROADS
Halvergate
Great Melton
Little Melton
Eakenham
Trowse Newton
Kirby Bedon
Surlingham
Buckenham
South Burlingham
Hassingham
Freethorpe
Berney Arms
Wrampingham
Hethersett
Cringleford
Keswick
Bramerton
Southwood
Freethorpe Common
Wickhampton
Burgh Castle
Southtown
GREAT YARMOUTH
High Green
Arminghall
Rockland St Mary
Claxton
Cantley
Limpenhoe
Intwood
Caistor St Edmund
Framingham Pigot
Hellington
Gorleston on Sea
Bradwell
Ketteringham
Swardeston
Framingham Earl
Yelverton
Ashby St Mary
Belton
Dunston
Alpington
Reedham
Hobland Hall
Wymondham
East Carleton
Mulbarton
Stoke Holy Cross
Poringland
Bergh Apton
Thurton
Langley Street
Hardley Street
Fritton
Hopton
Swainsthorpe
Howe
Chedgrave
Norton Marshes
Lower Thurlton
Silfield
Bracon Ash
Shotesham
Brooke
Sisland
Loddon
Norton Subcourse
Thurlton
Lound
Wreningham
Newton Flotman
Saxlingham Nethergate
Kirstead Green
Seething
Mundham
Heckingham
Hales
Thorpe
Herringfleet
Blundeston
Corton
Ashwellthorpe
Flordon
Saxlingham Thorpe
The Laurels
Ravenningham
Haddiscoe
Somerleyton
Hapton
Fundenhall
Saxlingham Green
Maypole Green
Pleasurewood Hills Theme Park
Tacolneston
Tasburgh
Forncett St Mary
Tharston
Hempnall
Thwaite St Mary
Kirby Cane
Toft Monks
Oulton
Lowestoft End
Lowestoft Ness
Bunwell Street
Stratton St Michael
Woodton
Wheatacre
Camps Heath
Burgh St Peter
Forncett End
Forncett St Peter
Hedenham
Stockton
Bunwell
Long Stratton
Fritton
Topcroft
Hempnall Green
Aldeby
Oulton Broad
LOWESTOFT
Morningthorpe
Topcroft Street
Kirby Row
Geldeston
Gillingham
Kirkley
Hargate
Aslacton
Wacton
Great Moulton
Shelton
Shelton Green
Ditchingham
Ellingham
Broome
Beccles
Shipmeadow
Barsham
Worlingham
Barnby
Pakefield
Hardwick
Great Green
Carlton Colville
Tibenham
North Green
Earsham
Bungay
Mettingham
North Cove
Danger Zone
Gisleham
Denton
Ringsfield
Mutford
Bush Green
Tivetshall St Margaret
Alburgh
Flixton
Ilketshall St Andrew
Ringsfield Corner
Rushmere
Kessingland
Tivetshall St Mary
Piccadilly Corner
Ilketshall St Margaret
Hulver Street
Henstead
Kessingland Beach
Gissing
Pulham Market
Pulham St Mary
Homersfield
Ellough
Wortwell
St Margaret South Elmham
St Michael South Elmham
Ilketshall St Lawrence
Redisham
Sotterly
Shadingfield
West End
Benacre
Starston
Redenhall
St Cross South Elmham
Brampton
Burston
Shimpling
Harleston
Mendham
All Saints South Elmham
Stone Street
Rushall
Dickleburgh
Needham
Withersdale Street
Rumburgh
Cox Common
Brampton
Frostenden
Wrentham
Covehithe
Stoven
Walcot Green
Thelveton
St James South Elmham
Spexhall
Clay Common
South Cove
Thorpe Abbotts
Weybread
Metfield
Westhall
Billingford
Brockdish
35
Broadway
Wangford
Mount Pleasant
Chediston
Stuston
Oakley
Fressingfield
Little Whittingham Green
Linstead
Holton
Reydon
Hoxne
Wingfield
Blyford
Blackwater

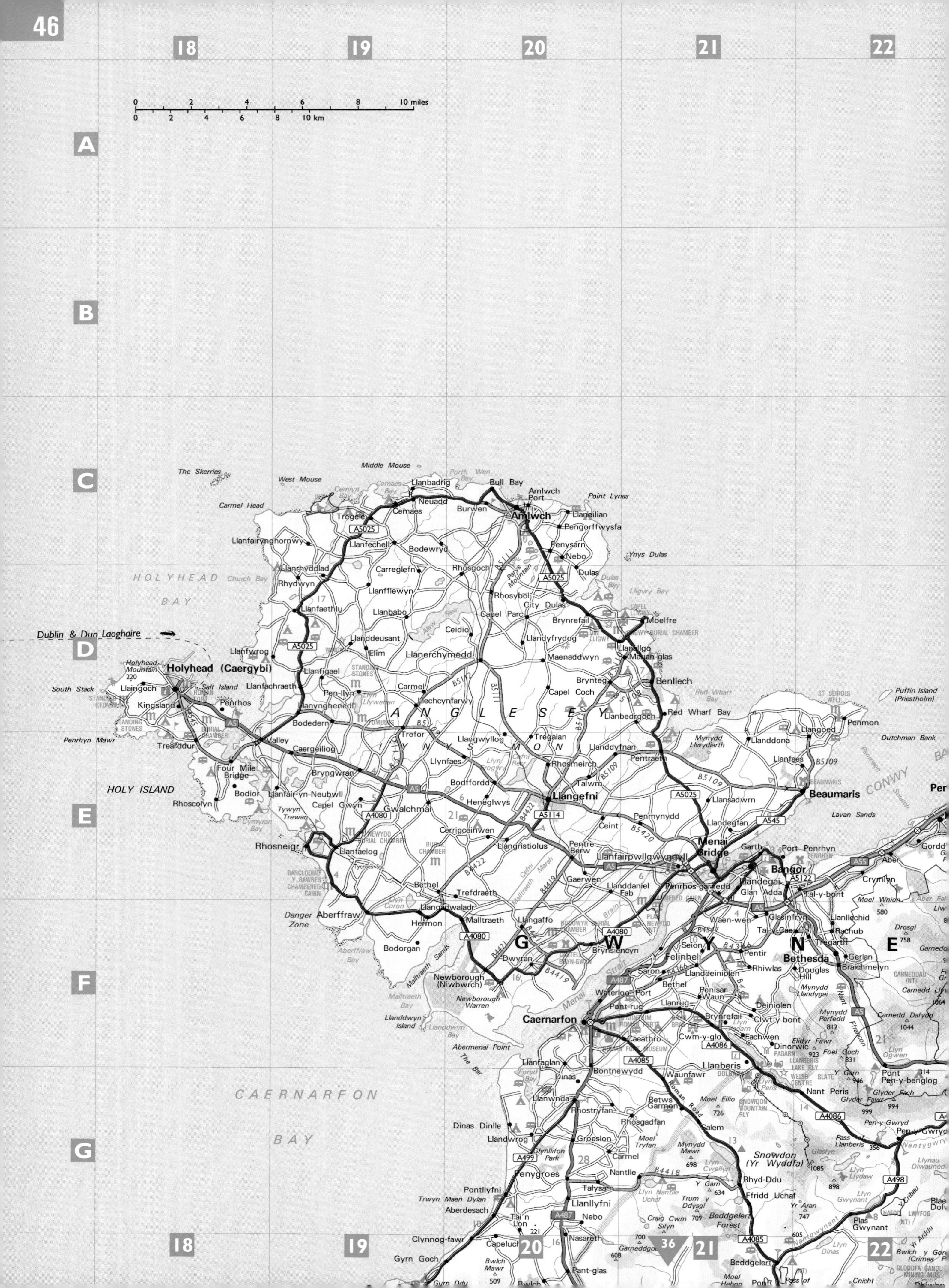

18
19
20
21
22
A
B
C
D
E
F
G
0 2 4 6 8 10 miles
0 2 4 6 8 10 km
The Skerries
Middle Mouse
West Mouse
Carmel Head
Cemlyn Bay
Cemaes Bay
Porth Wen Bay
Llanbadrig
Bull Bay
Amlwch Port
Point Lynas
Neuadd
Burwen
Tregele
Cemaes
Amlwch
Llaneilian
Pengorffwysfa
A5025
Llanfechell
Llanfairynghornwy
Bodewryd
Penysarn
Nebo
Ynys Dulas
Llanrhyddlad
Carreglefn
Rhosgoch
Parys Mountain
Dulas
HOLYHEAD
Church Bay
Rhydwyn
Llanfflewyn
Dulas Bay
Lligwy Bay
BAY
Rhosybol
City Dulas
Llanfaethlu
Llanbabo
Capel Parc
Brynrefail
Moelfre
Alaw Resr
Ceidio
Dublin & Dun Laoghaire
Llanddeusant
Llandyfrydog
LLIGWY BURIAL CHAMBER
Llanfwrog
Elim
Llanerchymedd
Llanallgo
Marian-glas
Holyhead Mountain
220
Holyhead (Caergybi)
Llanfigael
STANDING STONES
Maenaddwyn
South Stack
Llaingoch
Salt Island
Llanfachraeth
Pen-llyn
Llyn Llywenan
Carmel
Brynteg
Benllech
Kingsland
Penrhos
Llechcynfarwy
Capel Coch
Red Wharf Bay
Puffin Island (Priestholm)
ST SEIRIOLS WELL
STANDING STONES
Llanynghenedl
A N G L E S E Y
Llanbedrgoch
Red Wharf Bay
Penmon
Bodedern
Trefor
Llangoed
Dutchman Bank
Penrhyn Mawr
Trearddur
Valley
Caergeiliog
Llangwyllog
Tregaian
Mynydd Llwydiarth
Llanddona
Y N Y S M O N
Llanddyfnan
Pentraeth
Four Mile Bridge
Bryngwran
Llynfaes
Llyn Frogwy
Cefni Resr
Rhosmeirch
Llanfaes
B5109
HOLY ISLAND
Bodffordd
Talwrn
BEAUMARIS
CONWY
Bodior
Llanfair-yn-Neubwll
Heneglwys
Llangefni
A5025
Beaumaris
Rhoscolyn
Tywyn Trewan
Capel Gwyn
Gwalchmai
Llansadwrn
A4080
A5114
Penmynydd
Lavan Sands
Cymyran Bay
Cerrigceinwen
Ceint
Llandegfan
A545
Rhosneigr
Llanfaelog
Llangristiolus
Pentre Berw
Menai Bridge
Garth
Port Penrhyn
Llanfairpwllgwyngyll
Bangor
Aber
Gorddi
BARCLODIAD Y GAWRES CHAMBERED CAIRN
Malltraeth Marsh
Gaerwen
Llanddaniel Fab
Penrhos-garnedd
Llandegai
Glan Adda
A5122
Crymlyn
Bethel
Trefdraeth
Tal-y-bont
Moel Wnion
580
Llyn Coron
Danger Zone
Aberffraw
Llangadwaladr
A5
Glasinfryn
Llanllechid
Hermon
Malltraeth
Llangaffo
BODOWYR BURIAL CHAMBER
A4080
Waen-wen
Tal-y-Cae
Rachub
Drosgl
758
Bodorgan
G W Y N E
Tregarth
Aberffraw Bay
Dwyran
Brynsiencyn
Seion
Pentir
Bethesda
Gerlan
Malltraeth Sands
Felinheli
Rhiwlas
Braichmelyn
Newborough (Niwbwrch)
Saron
Llanddeiniolen
Douglas Hill
CARNEDDAU (NT)
Menai Strait
Bethel
Mynydd Llandygai
Carnedd Llywelyn
Malltraeth Bay
Newborough Warren
Waterloo Port
Penisar Waun
1064
Llanddwyn Island
Llanddwyn Bay
Pont-rug
Llanrug
Deiniolen
Mynydd Perfedd
812
Carnedd Dafydd
1044
Caernarfon
Brynrefail
Clwt-y-bont
Cwm-y-glo
A4086
Fachwen
Abermenai Point
Caeathro
Elidyr Fawr
Dinorwic
923
Foel Goch
831
A4085
Llyn Padarn
Llyn Ogwen
The Bar
Llanfaglan
Llanberis
Glyder Fach
994
Dinas
Bontnewydd
Foryd Bay
Waunfawr
Y Garn
946
Pont Pen-y-benglog
314
Nant Peris
Glyder Fawr
999
C A E R N A R F O N
Llanwnda
Betws Garmon
Moel Eilio
726
Rhostryfan
Rhosgadfan
A4086
Pen-y-Gwryd
Dinas Dinlle
Salem
Llandwrog
Groeslon
Moel Tryfan
Mynydd Mawr
698
Pass of Llanberis
356
B A Y
A499
Glynllifon Park
Carmel
Snowdon (Yr Wyddfa)
Glaslyn
1085
Llyn Llydaw
898
Penygroes
Nantlle
B4418
Llyn Cwellyn
Rhyd-Ddu
A498
Pontllyfni
Talysarn
Y Garn
634
Ffridd Uchaf
Llyn Gwynant
Trwyn Maen Dylan
Llyn Nantlle Uchaf
Trum y Ddysgl
Yr Aran
747
Aberdesach
Llanllyfni
A487
Nebo
Craig Cwm Silyn
709
Beddgelert Forest
Plas Gwynant
Tai'n Lôn
221
Clynnog-fawr
Capeluch
Nasareth
700
Garneddgoch
608
36
A4085
605
Llyn Dinas
Gyrn Goch
Bwlch Mawr
509
Pant-glas
Beddgelert
Gurn Ddu
Bwlch
Moel Hebog
Pont
Pass of
Cnicht

LIVERPOOL BAY
Formby Po
East Hoyle Bank
Hoylake
Moreton
Hilbre Island
West Kirby
Grange
Frankby
Saughall Massie
Caldy
Thurstaston
THE WIRRAL (NT)
Dawpool Bank
DEE
West Hoyle Bank
Welsh Channel
Point of Ayr
Talacre
Mostyn Bank
Ffynnongroyw
Mostyn Quay
Mostyn
Glan-y-don
Llannerch-y-mor
Holywell Bank
Greenfield
Bagillt
Bagillt Bank
Holywell
Bedol
Flint
Prestatyn
Gronant
Gwespyr
Meliden
Gwaenysgor
Llanasa
Trelogan
Downing
Whitford
Mertyn
Lloc
Gorsedd
Carmel
Pantasaph
Brynford
Babell
Pentre Halkyn
Halkyn
Lixwm
Ysceifiog
Caerwys
Afon-wen
Walwen
Rhes-y-cae
Rhosesmor
Northop
Rhydymwyn
Nannerch
Cilcain
Mold
Cadole
Gwernymynydd
Maeshafn
Llanferres
Tafarn-y-Gelyn
Moel Famau
Loggerheads
Eryrys
Treuddyn
Graianrhyd
Llanarmon-yn-Ial
Gelli
Rhydtalog
Llandegla
Pen-y-stryt
Pentre-bwlch
Horseshoe Pass
World's End
Moel y Gamelin
Mynydd Gricor
Nant y Garth Pass
Graig-fechan
Pentre-celyn
Moel Gaeregog
Llanfair Dyffryn Clwyd
Ruthin
Llanbedr-Dyffryn-Clwyd
Rhewl
Hirwaen
Llanynys
Llangynhafal
Llandyrnog
Ffordd-las
Llangwyfan
Waen
Moel y Parc
Ddol
Bodfari
Tremeirchion
Graig
Rhuallt
Pen-y-cefn
Dyserth
Trelawnyd
Marian Cwm
Cwm
Offa's Dyke
Gop Hill
St Asaph (Llanelwy)
Llannerch
Trefnant
Henllan
Denbigh
Gwaynynog
Llanrhaeadr
Pentre Llanrhaeadr
Pant-pastynog
Pentre Saron
Nantglyn
Meifod
Cyffylliog
Bontuchel
Llanfwrog
Efenechtyd
Clocaenog
Clocaenog Forest
Craig Bron-banog
Nilig
Clawdd-newydd
Derwen
Cefn Coch
Llanelidan
Melin-y-Wig
Bryneglwys
Gwyddelwern
Rhyl
Kinmel Bay
Towyn
Pensarn
Morfa Rhuddlan
Rhuddlan
Plas Llwyd
Pengwern
Bodelwyddan
St George
Abergele
Abergele Roads
Llanddulas
Llysfaen
Rhyd-y-foel
Llanelian-yn-Rhos
Dolwen
Betws-yn-Rhos
Dawn
Moelfre Isaf
Moelfre Uchaf
Groesffordd Marli
Llannefydd
Plas-yn-Cefn
Llanfair Talhaiarn
Pentre Isaf
Plasisaf
Llangernyw
Hafodunos
Llansannan
Deunant
Tan-y-fron
Groes
Bylchau
Gell
Mwdwl Eithin
Rhos-y-mawn
Wenlli
Pandy Tudur
Gwytherin
Sportsman's Arms
Bryn Trillyn
Gorsedd Bran
Aled Isaf Resr
Llyn Aled
Moel Llyn
Llyn Alwen
Mynydd Hiraethog
Alwen Resr
Llyn Brenig
Hafod-Dinbych
Pont yr Alwen
Pentrefoelas
Llyn y Cwrt
Rhydlydan
Glasfryn
Cefn-brith
Llanfihangel Glyn Myfyr
Cerrigydrudion
Garn Prys
Ysbyty Ifan
C L W Y D
COLWYN BAY
Old Colwyn
Mochdre
Rhos-on-Sea
Llandrillo-yn-Rhos
Penrhyn Bay
Little Ormes Head
Great Ormes Head
Gogarth
Llandudno
Penrhyn-side
Llanrhos
Conwy Sands
Deganwy
Tywyn
Llandudno Junction
Conwy
Gyffin
Capelulo
Llansantffraid Glan Conwy
Pentrefelin
Bryn-y-maen
Henryd
Roewen
Ty'n-y-groes
Caerhun
Tal-y-cafn
Graig
Eglwysbach
Llanbedr-y-cennin
Tal-y-bont
Vale of Conwy
Dolgarrog
Pont Dolgarrog
Trefriw
Llanddoged
Llanrwst
Pentre-tafarn-y-fedw
Melin-y-coed
Oaklands
Nebo
Capel Garmon
Betws-y-coed
Pont-Cyfyng
Glyn
GWYDYR FOREST
Pont-y-pant
Dolwyddelan
Pentre-bont
Rhydlanfair
Glan-Conwy
Penmachno
Gwydyr Forest
Foel Lus
Talyfan
Moel Penamnen
TELFORD BRIDGE (NT)
ABERCONWY HOUSE
GREAT ORME TRAMWAY
A55
A470
A548
A547
A525
A5151
A541
A543
A544
A5
A542
A5104
A5119
A494
B5115
B5113
B5381
B5382
B5383
B5384
B5435
B5401
B5105
B5429
B5428
B5430
B5106
23
24
25
26
27
A
B
C
D
E
F
G
48
37
38

SOUTHPORT
LIVERPOOL BAY
MERSEYSIDE
LIVERPOOL
BIRKENHEAD
WALLASEY
BOOTLE
CROSBY
LITHERLAND
KIRKBY
ORMSKIRK
SKELMERSDALE
WIGAN
CHORLEY
ST HELENS
WIDNES
RUNCORN
ELLESMERE PORT
CHESTER
WREXHAM
Mold
Flint
Holywell
Denbigh
Ruthin
Formby
Hoylake
West Kirby
Heswall
Neston
Connah's Quay
Buckley
DELAMERE
CLWYD
Douglas, Isle of Man
Belfast
10 miles
10 km

DARWEN
Withnell
Ramsbottom
Edgworth
Tottington
Horwich
BOLTON
BURY
HEYWOOD
ROCHDALE
Littleborough
Ripponden
Elland
Whitworth
Wardle
Milnrow
Slaithwaite
Marsden
Meltham
Shaw
Royton
Radcliffe
FARNWORTH
Whitefield
MIDDLETON
CHADDERTON
OLDHAM
Uppermill
Hindley
ATHERTON
Tyldesley
WORSLEY
PRESTWICH
Swinton
FAILSWORTH
Mossley
LEIGH
SALFORD
ECCLES
MANCHESTER
Droylsden
ASHTON-UNDER-LYNE
STALYBRIDGE
Dukinfield
Audenshaw
Hollingworth
Hadfield
URMSTON
STRETFORD
DENTON
HYDE
Glossop
GREATER MANCHESTER
SALE
Bredbury
Romiley
STOCKPORT
CHEADLE
GATLEY
Marple
ALTRINCHAM
WARRINGTON
Lymm
Bowdon
Hale
HAZEL GROVE
Bramhall
Disley
New Mills
Chapel-en-le-Frith
Poynton
WILMSLOW
Whaley Bridge
Knutsford
Alderley Edge
Bollington
Northwich
Chelford
MACCLESFIELD
Buxton
CHESHIRE
Winsford
Middlewich
Holmes Chapel
CONGLETON
PEAK DISTRICT NATIONAL PARK
Sandbach
Biddulph
Leek
CREWE
Alsager
KIDSGROVE
Nantwich
STAFFS
NEWCASTLE
Hanley
STOKE
M6
M56
M60
M62
M66
M67
M602

34
35
36
37
38
56
49
40
A
B
C
D
E
F
G
W
E
S
T
Y
O
R
K
GREATER
MANCHESTER
CHESHIRE
STAFFS
PEAK
DISTRICT
NATIONAL
PARK
Bacup
Newchurch
Waterfoot
Stacksteads
Britannia
Helmshore
Walsden
Lumbutts
Sowerby
Triangle
Ripponden
Norland Town
Greetland
BRIGHOUSE
Rastrick
Elland
Heckmondwike
Roberttown
Mirfield
Ravensthorpe
Ossett
Holywell Green
Barkisland
Stainland
Edenfield
Ramsbottom
Whitworth
Warland
Summit
Calderbrook
Littleborough
Wardle
Clough
Shuttleworth
Stubbins
Edgworth
Tottington
Harwood
BURY
ROCHDALE
HEYWOOD
Milnrow
Castleton
Smallbridge
Firgrove
Newhey
Denshaw
Rishworth
Rishworth Moor
Booth Wood
Moselden Height
Pole Moor
Golcar
Outlane
Quarmby
Lindley
HUDDERSFIELD
Kirkheaton
Upper Hopton
Whitley Lower
Thornhill
Middlestown
Grange Moor
Flockton
Milnsbridge
Linthwaite
Almondbury
Lepton
Slaithwaite
Marsden
Meltham
Honley
Netherthong
Brockholes
Farnley Tyas
Highburton
Kirkburton
Shelley
Skelmanthorpe
Clayton West
Emley
West Bretton
Thurstonland
New Mill
Shepley
Holmfirth
Upperthong
Denby Dale
Cawthorne
Scholes
Hepworth
Holme
Austonley
Silkstone
Hoyland Swaine
Ingbirchworth
Upper Denby
Thurlstone
Penistone
Oxspring
Langsett
Carlecotes
Dunford Bridge
Thurlstone Moors
Midhopestones
Upper Midhope
Stocksbridge
Bolsterstone
Ewden
Wightwizzle
Broomhead Moor
Bradfield Moors
High Bradfield
Low Bradfield
RADCLIFFE
Whitefield
Prestolee
Kearsley
PRESTWICH
MIDDLETON
CHADDERTON
OLDHAM
Royton
Shaw
Crompton
Heyside
Moorside
Delph
Diggle
Uppermill
Greenfield
Lees
Grasscroft
Saddleworth Moor
Black Hill
Heyden Moor
Swinton
Pendlebury
SALFORD
ECCLES
MANCHESTER
FAILSWORTH
Droylsden
ASHTON-UNDER-LYNE
Mossley
Micklehurst
STALYBRIDGE
Dukinfield
Audenshaw
Tintwistle
Hollingworth
Hadfield
Mottram in Longdendale
Old Glossop
Glossop
Broadbottom
Charlesworth
Chisworth
Chunal
HYDE
DENTON
Haughton Green
Gorton
Rusholme
Levenshulme
Reddish
Trafford
STRETFORD
Chorlton-cum-Hardy
Withington
Burnage
Didsbury
Heaton Moor
SALE
Ashton upon Mersey
Baguley
Timperley
STOCKPORT
Bredbury
Romiley
Compstall
Marple
Mellor
Little Hayfield
Hayfield
Kinder Scout
Edale
Edale Moor
Snake Pass
Featherbed Top
Bleaklow Hill
HIGH PEAK ESTATE
CHEADLE
Cheadle Hulme
GATLEY
Bowdon
Hale
Halebarns
Heaviley
Offerton
HAZEL GROVE
Bramhall
Disley
Newtown
New Mills
Low Leighton
Birch Vale
Thornsett
Chinley Head
Chinley
Furness Vale
Buxworth
Whaley Bridge
Chapel-en-le-Frith
Sparrowpit
Peak Forest
Castleton
Hope
Aston
Thornhill
Bamford
Hathersage
Brough
Bradwell
Abney
Hope Valley
Win Hill
High Neb
Redmires Reservoirs
Ashley
Styal
Handforth
Woodford
Poynton
Middlewood
Morley Green
WILMSLOW
Mobberley
Knolls Green
Knutsford
Ollerton
Marthall
Mottram St Andrew
Alderley Edge
Nether Alderley
Adlington
Kettleshulme
Pott Shrigley
Bollington
Kerridge
Prestbury
Rainow
Taxal
Fernilee
Horwich End
Lower Crossings
Combs
Dove Holes
Peak Dale
Upper End
Wormhill
Tideswell
Litton
Wheston
Great Hucklow
Little Hucklow
Grindlow
Foolow
Eyam
Stoney Middleton
Calver
Froggatt
Grindleford
Nether Padley
Chelford
Over Peover
Peover Heath
Henbury
Monks Heath
Tytherington
Broken Cross
MACCLESFIELD
Hurdsfield
Langley
Sutton Lane Ends
Macclesfield Forest
Cat and Fiddle Inn
Goyt's Moss
Burbage
Buxton
Fairfield
King Sterndale
Harpur Hill
Taddington
Chelmorton
Blackwell
Miller's Dale
Little Longstone
Great Longstone
Ashford in the Water
Rowland
Hassop
Baslow
Pilsley
Bakewell
Edensor
Beeley
Over Haddon
Rowsley
Sheldon
Flagg
Monyash
Youlgreave
Alport
Middleton
Stanton in Peak
Birchover
Elton
Winster
Wensley
Darley
Blackden Heath
Withington Green
Siddington
Warren
Gawsworth
Oakgrove
Wildboarclough
Jodrell Bank
Goostrey
Cranage
Swettenham
Lower Withington
Gleadsmoss
Marton
Highlane
Rodeheath
North Rode
Bosley
Allgreave
Wincle
Danebridge
Gradbach
Flash
Hollinsclough
Longnor
Crowdecote
Earl Sterndale
Holmes Chapel
Brereton Green
Brereton Heath
Hulme Walfield
Eaton
CONGLETON
Astbury
Arclid
Brookhouse Green
Sandbach
Hassall Green
Wheelock
Spen Green
Key Green
Timbersbrook
Hightown
Bridestones
Rushton Spencer
Heaton
Upper Hulme
Meerbrook
Fawfieldhead
Newtown
Pilsbury
Sheen
Hartington
Heathcote
Biggin
Pikehall
Grangemill
Aldwark
Ible
Bonsall
Cromford
Middleton
Wirksworth
Fourlanes End
Brownlow Heath
Biddulph Moor
Biddulph
Gillow Heath
Rode Heath
Church Lawton
Alsager
Scholar Green
Mow Cop
Knypersley
Horton
Rudyard
Leek
Ball Haye Green
Thorncliff
Upper Elkstone
Warslow
Hulme End
Ecton
Butterton
Wetton
Alstonefield
Alsop en le Dale
Longcliffe
Ballidon
Brassington
Parwich
Carsington
Hopton
Bradbourne
KIDSGROVE
Harriseahead
Newchapel
Brindley Ford
Brown Edge
Horse Bridge
Longsdon
Bradnop
Onecote
Grindon
Waterfall
Ilam
Thorpe
Tissington
Fenny Bentley
Kniveton
Hognaston
Kirk Ireton
Idridgehay
Atlow
Biggin
Mapleton
Goldenhill
Tunstall
Burslem
Talke
Butt Lane
Audley
Radway Green
Balterley
Halmer End
Chesterton
Alsagers Bank
Endon
Stanley
Norton in the Moors
Smallthorne
Milton
Baddeley Green
Bagnall
Cheddleton
Basford Green
Wetley
Abbey Hulton
Bucknall
Hanley
Consall
Ipstones
Froghall
Cellarhead
Foxt
Whiston
Winkhill
Waterhouses
Calton
Cauldon
Blore
Swinscoe
M62
M66
M60
M602
M67
M63
M56
M6
A627(M)
A6
A34
A523
A54
A53
A515
A57
A628
A635
A62
A58
A56
A537
A536
A50
A500
A527
A52
A520
A5012
A6024
A625
A623
A621
A619
A6013
A6016
A624

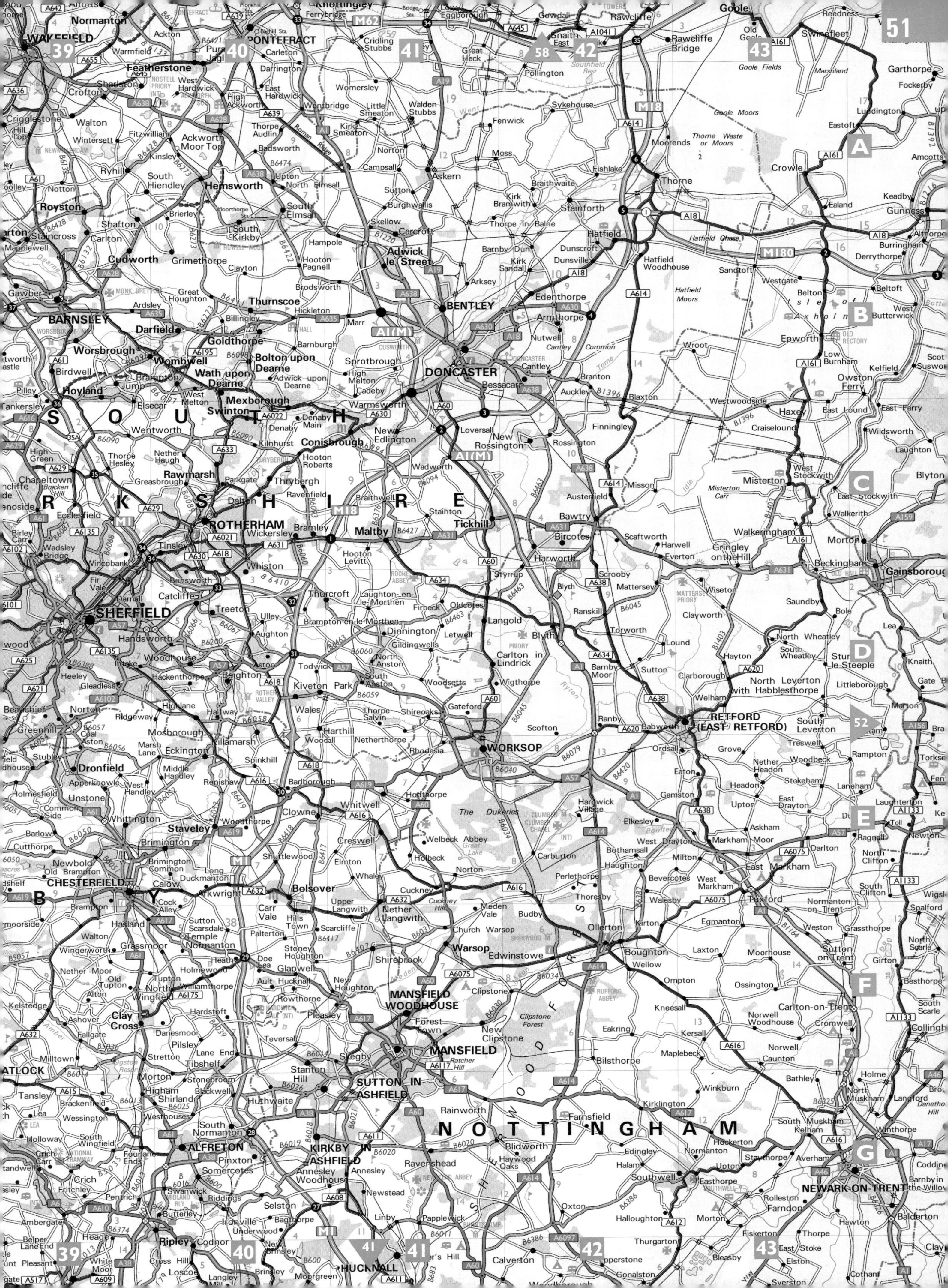
WAKEFIELD
PONTEFRACT
Featherstone
Normanton
Knottingley
Goole
Snaith
Rawcliffe
Rawcliffe Bridge
Swinefleet
Garthorpe
Luddington
Eastoft
Crowle
Thorne
Keadby
Gunness
Hemsworth
Royston
Cudworth
South Elmsall
South Kirkby
Askern
Adwick le Street
Hatfield
Stainforth
BARNSLEY
Darfield
Goldthorpe
Thurnscoe
BENTLEY
DONCASTER
Armthorpe
Epworth
Haxey
Wombwell
Hoyland
Mexborough
Swinton
Wath upon Dearne
Bolton upon Dearne
Conisbrough
Sprotbrough
Bessacarr
Rossington
Finningley
Misterton
ROTHERHAM
Rawmarsh
Maltby
Tickhill
Bawtry
Bircotes
Harworth
Gainsborough
SHEFFIELD
Dinnington
Langold
Blyth
Kiveton Park
WORKSOP
RETFORD (EAST RETFORD)
Dronfield
Eckington
Killamarsh
Staveley
CHESTERFIELD
Bolsover
Clowne
Whitwell
The Dukeries
Tuxford
Ollerton
Edwinstowe
Warsop
MANSFIELD WOODHOUSE
MANSFIELD
SUTTON IN ASHFIELD
KIRKBY IN ASHFIELD
ALFRETON
Clay Cross
Ripley
HUCKNALL
Ravenshead
Blidworth
Southwell
NEWARK-ON-TRENT
Farndon
Balderton
SOUTH YORKSHIRE
NOTTINGHAM
SHERWOOD FOREST
39
40
41
42
43
58
52
A
B
C
D
E
F
G

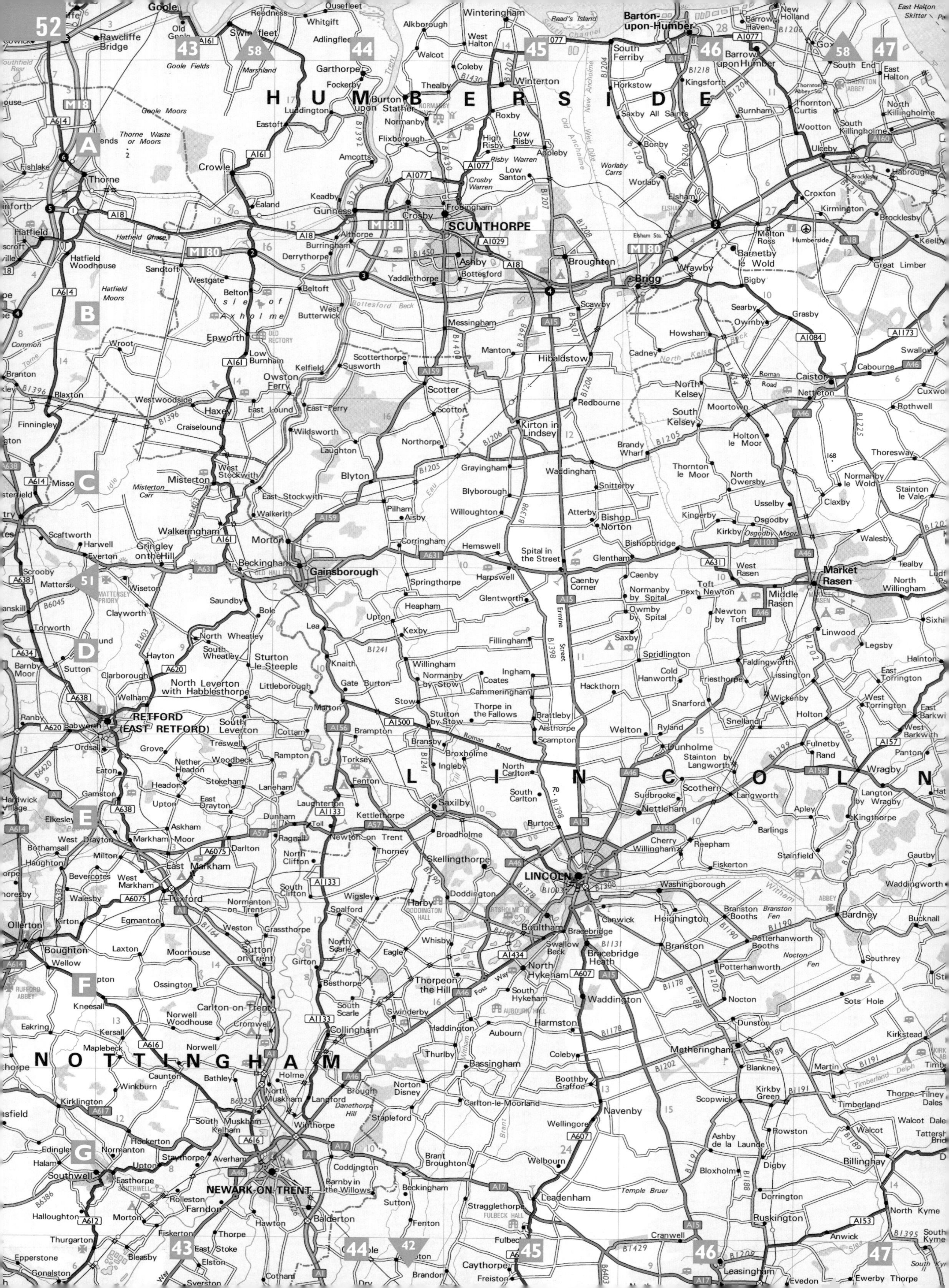
HUMBERSIDE
LINCOLN
NOTTINGHAM
Goole
Old Goole
Reedness
Ousefleet
Whitgift
Adlingfleet
Swinefleet
Rawcliffe Bridge
Goole Fields
Marshland
Goole Moors
Thorne Waste or Moors
Thorne
Fishlake
Crowle
Eastoft
Luddington
Garthorpe
Fockerby
Amcotts
Ealand
Keadby
Gunness
Althorpe
Burringham
Derrythorpe
Hatfield
Hatfield Chase
Hatfield Woodhouse
Hatfield Moors
Sandtoft
Westgate
Belton
Isle of Axholme
Epworth
Low Burnham
Wroot
Owston Ferry
Kelfield
Haxey
Westwoodside
Craiselound
East Lound
Blaxton
Finningley
Branton
Misterton
West Stockwith
East Stockwith
Walkerith
Walkeringham
Gringley on the Hill
Beckingham
Gainsborough
Morton
Scaftworth
Harwell
Everton
Scrooby
Mattersey
Wiseton
Clayworth
Torworth
Saundby
Bole
North Wheatley
South Wheatley
Hayton
Sturton le Steeple
Sutton
Barnby Moor
Clarborough
Welham
North Leverton with Habblesthorpe
Littleborough
RETFORD (EAST RETFORD)
Babworth
Ranby
Ordsall
Grove
Eaton
Gamston
Headon
Upton
Nether Headon
Woodbeck
Stokeham
South Leverton
Treswell
Cottam
Rampton
Laneham
East Drayton
Askham
Markham Moor
Dunham
West Drayton
Elkesley
Bothamsall
Haughton
Milton
East Markham
West Markham
Darlton
Ragnall
Bevercotes
Walesby
Tuxford
Kirton
Ollerton
Boughton
Wellow
Egmanton
Normanton on Trent
Weston
Grassthorpe
Laxton
Moorhouse
Sutton on Trent
Ossington
Kneesall
Eakring
Kersall
Maplebeck
Carlton-on-Trent
Norwell Woodhouse
Cromwell
Norwell
Caunton
Bathley
Winkburn
Kirklington
North Muskham
South Muskham
Holme
Kelham
Hockerton
Edingley
Halam
Normanton
Southwell
Upton
Staythorpe
Averham
Easthorpe
Rolleston
Halloughton
Morton
Farndon
Fiskerton
Thurgarton
Thorpe
Bleasby
East Stoke
Epperstone
Elston
Gonalston
Syerston
NEWARK-ON-TRENT
Hawton
Balderton
Barnby in the Willows
Coddington
Winthorpe
Langford
Beckingham
Sutton
Fenton
Brandon
Cotham
Winteringham
West Halton
Alkborough
Whitton
Walcot
Coleby
Thealby
Burton upon Stather
Normanby
Flixborough
Winterton
Roxby
High Risby
Low Risby
Risby Warren
Appleby
Low Santon
Crosby Warren
Frodingham
Crosby
SCUNTHORPE
Ashby
Bottesford
Yaddlethorpe
Beltoft
West Butterwick
Messingham
Broughton
Scawby
Manton
Hibaldstow
Scotter
Scotton
Scotterthorpe
Susworth
Wildsworth
Laughton
East Ferry
Northorpe
Redbourne
Kirton in Lindsey
Blyton
Grayingham
Pilham
Aisby
Blyborough
Willoughton
Corringham
Hemswell
Springthorpe
Harpswell
Heapham
Glentworth
Upton
Kexby
Fillingham
Lea
Knaith
Willingham
Normanby by Stow
Gate Burton
Stow
Coates
Ingham
Cammeringham
Marton
Sturton by Stow
Thorpe in the Fallows
Brattleby
Aisthorpe
Scampton
Bransby
Brampton
Torksey
Broxholme
Ingleby
North Carlton
South Carlton
Fenton
Saxilby
Laughterton
Kettlethorpe
Newton on Trent
Broadholme
Thorney
Skellingthorpe
North Clifton
South Clifton
Wigsley
Harby
Doddington
Spalford
Whisby
North Scarle
Eagle
Girton
Thorpe on the Hill
Besthorpe
South Scarle
Swinderby
Collingham
Haddington
Aubourn
Thurlby
Bassingham
Brough
Norton Disney
Carlton-le-Moorland
Stapleford
Danethorpe Hill
Brant Broughton
Welbourn
Wellingore
Navenby
Leadenham
Stragglethorpe
Fulbeck
Caythorpe
Frieston
Boothby Graffoe
Coleby
Harmston
Waddington
South Hykeham
North Hykeham
Swallow Beck
Bracebridge
Bracebridge Heath
Boultham
LINCOLN
Canwick
Burton
Nettleham
Sudbrooke
Cherry Willingham
Reepham
Fiskerton
Washingborough
Heighington
Branston
Branston Booths
Potterhanworth
Potterhanworth Booths
Nocton
Dunston
Metheringham
Blankney
Martin
Scopwick
Kirkby Green
Timberland
Rowston
Ashby de la Launde
Digby
Bloxholm
Dorrington
Ruskington
Anwick
Leasingham
Cranwell
Temple Bruer
Evedon
Ewerby
Ewerby Thorpe
Barton-upon-Humber
Barrow Haven
Barrow upon Humber
New Holland
Goxhill
South Ferriby
Horkstow
Kingsforth
Saxby All Saints
Bonby
Worlaby
Elsham
Wrawby
Brigg
Barnetby le Wold
Melton Ross
Kirmington
Croxton
Ulceby
Thornton Curtis
Wootton
Burnham
Thornton Abbey
East Halton
South End
North Killingholme
South Killingholme
Habrough
Brocklesby
Great Limber
Bigby
Searby
Owmby
Grasby
Howsham
Cadney
North Kelsey
South Kelsey
Moortown
Caistor
Nettleton
Cabourne
Swallow
Cuxwold
Rothwell
Holton le Moor
Thoresway
Brandy Wharf
Waddingham
Snitterby
Thornton le Moor
North Owersby
Normanby le Wold
Stainton le Vale
Usselby
Claxby
Kingerby
Osgodby
Kirkby
Walesby
Atterby
Bishop Norton
Bishopbridge
Spital in the Street
Glentham
Caenby
Caenby Corner
Normanby by Spital
Owmby by Spital
Saxby
West Rasen
Toft next Newton
Newton by Toft
Middle Rasen
Market Rasen
Tealby
North Willingham
Linwood
Legsby
Spridlington
Faldingworth
Lissington
Cold Hanworth
Friesthorpe
Hackthorn
Snarford
Wickenby
East Torrington
West Torrington
Holton
Snelland
Welton
Ryland
Dunholme
Stainton by Langworth
Scothern
Langworth
Fulnetby
Rand
Wragby
Langton by Wragby
Apley
Kingthorpe
Barlings
Stainfield
Bardney
Southrey
Sots Hole
Kirkstead
Walcot
Billinghay
North Kyme
South Kyme
Woodhall
Ermine Street
Roman Road
Foss Way

48
49
50
51
52
A
B
C
D
E
F
G
0 2 4 6 8 10 miles
0 2 4 6 8 10 km
Patrington
Holmpton
Out Newton
Welwick
Weeton
Haven Side
Salthaugh Grange
Sunk Island
Old Hall
Easington
Skeffling
Skeffling Clays
Kilnsea
Kilnsea Clays
Sunk Island Sands
Immingham Dock
HUMBER
MOUTH OF THE HUMBER
Spurn Head
Rotterdam & Zeebrugge
GRIMSBY
CLEETHORPES
WELLHOLME GALLERIES
West Marsh
Great Coates
Laceby
Bradley
Scartho
New Waltham
Humberston
Waltham
Holton le Clay
Tetney Lock
Tetney
Barnoldby le Beck
Brigsley
Ashby cum Fenby
Hatcliffe
Grainsby
North Cotes
Marsh Chapel
Danger Zone
Donna Nook
East Ravendale
West End
Eskham
Wragholme
North Thoresby
Churchthorpe
Wold Newton
Fulstow
Grainthorpe
Covenham Resr
Meals
North Somercotes
Ludborough
Covenham St Bartholomew
Ludney
Conisholme
Church End
Saltfleet
North Ormsby
Covenham St Mary
South Somercotes
Skidbrooke
Binbrook
Utterby
Yarburgh
Fotherby
Little Grimsby
Alvingham
North Cockerington
Saltfleetby St Clements
Saltfleetby All Saints
Kelstern
North Elkington
South Elkington
Keddington
South Cockerington
Saltfleetby St Peter
Theddlethorpe St Helen
Theddlethorpe All Saints
Welton le Wold
Louth
Grimoldby
Manby
Stewton
Gayton le Wold
Hallington
Little Carlton
Mablethorpe
Great Carlton
Legbourne
Trusthorpe
Raithby
Gayton le Marsh
South Reston
North Reston
Strubby
Donington on Bain
Tathwell
Little Cawthorpe
Withern
Thorpe
Sutton on Sea
Sutton le Marsh
Sandilands
Benniworth
Stenigot
Haugham
Authorpe
Tothill
Maltby le Marsh
Market Stainton
CADWELL PARK
Muckton
Beesby
Cawkwell
Asterby
Goulceby
Ranby
Maidenwell
Burwell
Claythorpe
Hannah
Scamblesby
Farforth
Ruckland
Belleau
Aby
Markby
Saleby
Oxcombe
White Pit
Bilsby
Huttoft
Ketsby
South Thoresby
Swaby
Alford
Flint Hill
Little London
South Ormsby
Rigsby
Anderby
Mumby
Authorpe Row
Hemingby
Belchford
Tetford
Farlesthorpe
Driby
Well
Ulceby Cross
Cumberworth
West Ashby
Salmonby
Brinkhill
Ulceby
Chapel St Leonards
Hogsthorpe
Fulletby
Ashby Puerorum
Somersby
Harrington
HARRINGTON HALL
Claxby
Low Toynton
Bag Enderby
Willoughby
Edlington
Greetham
Aswardby
Langton
Sloothby
Thimbleby
High Toynton
Hagworthingham
Sausthorpe
Skendleby
Welton le Marsh
Ingoldmells
Ingoldmells Point
Langton
Horncastle
Lusby
Addlethorpe
Thornton
Mareham on the Hill
Hameringham
Raithby
Partney
Scremby
Candlesby
Orby
Asgarby
Mavis Enderby
Ashby by Partney
GUNBY HALL (NT)
Burgh le Marsh
Winthorpe
Claxby Pluckacre
Hareby
Hundleby
Spilsby
Halton Holegate
Bratoft
Orby Marsh
Burgh Marsh
Dalderby
Old Bolingbroke
Roughton
Moorby
Miningsby
Irby in the Marsh
CHURCH FARM MUSEUM
Skegness
Haltham
Toynton All Saints
Great Steeping
Wood Enderby
West Keal
East Keal
Toynton St Peter
Little Steeping
Firsby
Hagnaby
Kirkby on Bain
Mareham le Fen
Revesby
East Kirkby
Keal Cotes
Toynton Fen Side
Thorpe Culvert
Croft
Fendike Corner
Thorpe St Peter
Seacroft
Croft Marsh
Havenhouse Sta
Tumby
Stickford
Coningsby
Moor Side
Wainfleet Bank
Wainfleet All Saints
Gibraltar
Tattershall
New Bolingbroke
New Leake
Key's Toft
Gibraltar Pt.
TATTERSHALL
Tumby Woodside
Midville
Friskney Eaudike
Hawthorn Hill
Stickney
Eastville
Wainfleet Sand
New York
Carrington
East Fen
Friskney
Scrub Hill
West Fen
Lade Bank
Northlands
Wildmore Fen
Leake Commonside
Wrangle Lowgate
Boston Deeps
Gipsey Bridge
Frithville
Sibsey
Wrangle
Friskney Flats
Old Leake
Fishtoft Drove
Leake Hurn's End
Langriville
Frith Bank
Hill Dyke
Leverton
Leverton Outgate
Hobhole Drain
43
Sand
THE WASH
S H I R E
THE WOLDS
A180
A46
A1098
A1031
A16
A18
A631
A157
B1200
A1104
A1111
B1449
A52
A1028
A153
B1225
A158
B1195
B1183
A155
B1191
B1192
B1184
B1201
B1203
A52

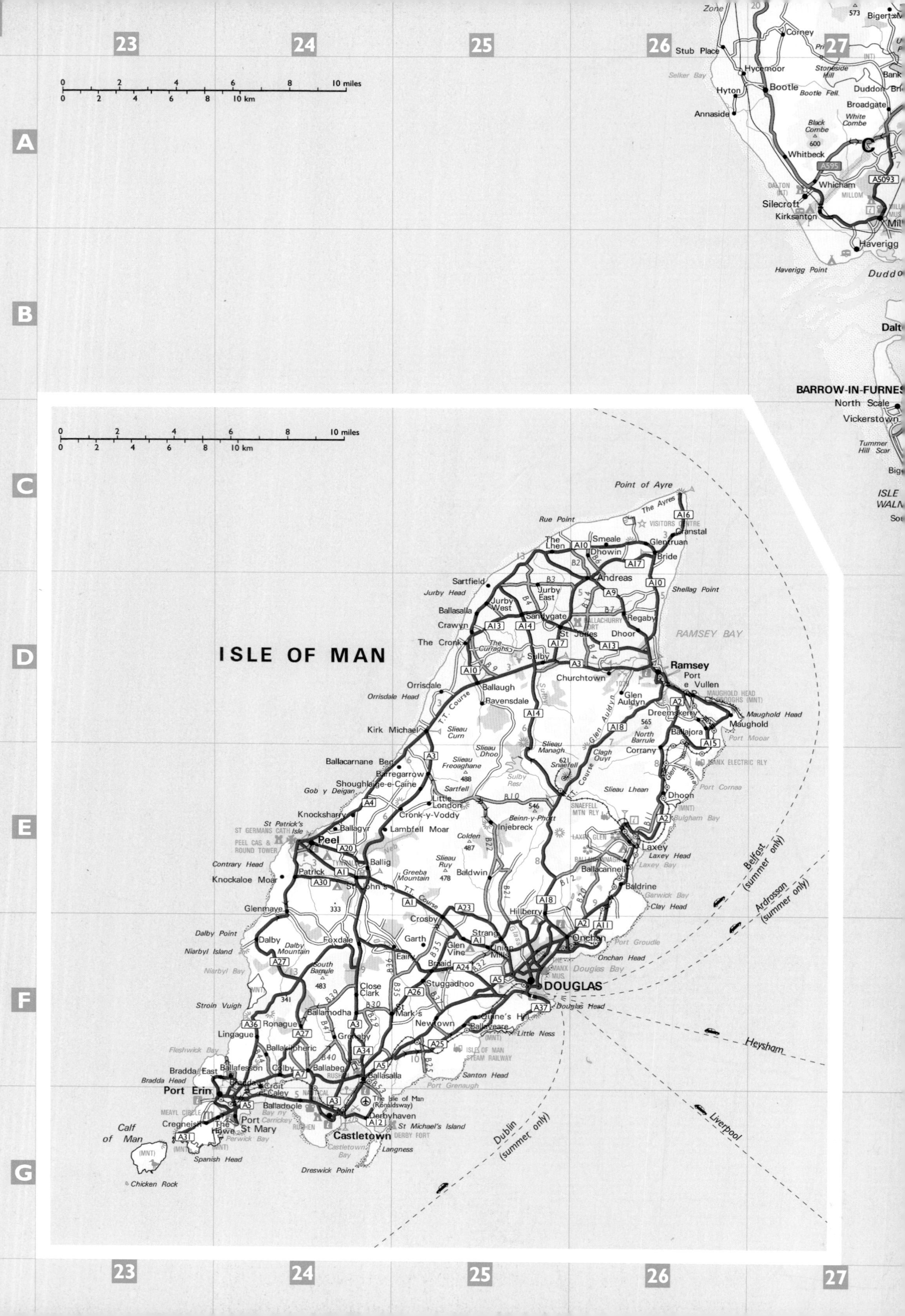
ISLE OF MAN
0 2 4 6 8 10 miles
0 2 4 6 8 10 km
23
24
25
26
27
A
B
C
D
E
F
G
Point of Ayre
The Ayres
Rue Point
Smeale
Glentruan
Cranstal
The Lhen
Dhowin
Bride
Andreas
Sartfield
Jurby Head
Jurby West
Jurby East
Shellag Point
Ballasalla
Sandygate
Regaby
Crawyn
St Judes
Dhoor
The Cronk
The Curraghs
RAMSEY BAY
Sulby
Ramsey
Churchtown
Port e Vullen
Orrisdale
Ballaugh
Glen Auldyn
Orrisdale Head
Ravensdale
Dreemskerry
Maughold Head
Maughold
Kirk Michael
Slieau Curn
Ballajora
North Barrule
Corrany
Port Moar
Slieau Dhoo
Slieau Managh
Clagh Ouyr
Snaefell
Ballacarnane Beg
Barregarrow
Slieau Freoaghane
Shoughlaige-e-Caine
Gob y Deigan
Sartfell
Sulby Resr
Slieau Lhean
Port Cornaa
Little London
Dhoon
Knocksharry
Cronk-y-Voddy
Beinn-y-Phott
Injebreck
Bulgham Bay
St Patrick's Isle
Ballagyr
Lambfell Moar
Colden
Peel
Laxey
Laxey Head
Laxey Bay
Contrary Head
Ballig
Slieau Ruy
Baldwin
Ballacannell
Knockaloe Moar
Patrick
Greeba Mountain
St John's
Baldrine
T.T. Course
Garwick Bay
Clay Head
Glenmaye
Hillberry
Crosby
Belfast (summer only)
Ardrossan (summer only)
Dalby Point
Strang
Onchan
Port Groudle
Niarbyl Island
Dalby
Dalby Mountain
Foxdale
Garth
Glen Vine
Union Mills
Onchan Head
Niarbyl Bay
South Barrule
Eairy
Braaid
Douglas Bay
DOUGLAS
Stuggadhoo
Close Clark
Stroin Vuigh
St Mark's
Douglas Head
Ballamodha
Cronk's Hill
Ronague
Newtown
Ballavere
Lingague
Grenaby
Little Ness
Heysham
Fleshwick Bay
Ballakilpheric
Bradda East
Ballafesson
Colby
Ballabeg
Ballasalla
Santon Head
Bradda Head
Port Erin
Croit Caley
Port Grenaugh
Balladoole
The Isle of Man (Ronaldsway)
Cregneish
Port St Mary
Derbyhaven
St Michael's Island
Liverpool
Calf of Man
The Howe
Perwick Bay
Castletown
Castletown Bay
Langness
Dublin (summer only)
Spanish Head
Chicken Rock
Dreswick Point
Zone
Bigert
Corney
Stub Place
Hycemoor
Selker Bay
Bootle
Bootle Fell
Hyton
Duddon Bri
Broadgate
Annaside
Black Combe
White Combe
Whitbeck
Whicham
Silecroft
Kirksanton
Haverigg
Haverigg Point
BARROW-IN-FURNES
North Scale
Vickerstown
Tummer Hill Scar
ISLE WALN

FOREST PARK
C U M B R I A
L A N C A S H I R E
M O R E C A M B E
B A Y
Forest of Bowland
Kendal
Sedbergh
Satterthwaite
Sunny Bank
Underbarrow
Grigghall
Killington Lake
West Mostard
Broughton in Furness
Lower Hawthwaite
High Nibthwaite
Force Mills
Rusland
Finsthwaite
Lakeside
Newby Bridge
Staveley-in-Cartmel
Bowland Bridge
Cartmel Fell
Pool Bank
Witherslack Hall
Brigsteer
Natland
Sedgwick
Levens
Stainton
Endmoor
Old Hutton
Middleshaw
Millholme
Killington
Harprigg
Gawthrop
Dent
Middleton
Aye Gill Pike
Deepdale
Crag Hill
Whernside
Lowick
Colton
Oxen Park
Bouth
Spark Bridge
Backbarrow
Haverthwaite
Low Wood
Penny Bridge
Greenodd
Broughton Beck
Gawthwaite
Grizebeck
Beck Side
Mansriggs
Arrad Foot
Stribers
Field Broughton
Ayside
High Newton
Witherslack
Town End
Lindale
Meathop
Hincaster
Crooklands
Leasgill
Heversham
Woodhouse
Milnthorpe
Nook
Lupton
Farleton
Mansergh
Barbon
Rigmaden Park
Old Town
Bullpot Farm
Casterton
Kearstwick
Kirkby Lonsdale
Storth
Beetham
Holme
Arnside
Grange-over-Sands
Cartmel
Holker
Allithwaite
Cark
Flookburgh
Kents Bank
Ulverston
Pennington
Ireleth
Marton
Lindal in Furness
Great Urswick
Little Urswick
Bardsea
Stainton with Adgarley
Newton
Dendron
Scales
Gleaston
Aldingham
Baycliff
Leece
Newbiggin
Roosecote
Rampside
Roa Island
Foulney Island
Piel Island
Hilpsford Point
Humphrey Head Point
Cartmel Sands
Silverdale
Yealand Redmayne
Yealand Conyers
Warton
Warton Sands
Burton West
Burton-in-Kendal
Clawthorpe
Hutton Roof
Moor End
Whittington
Newton
Cowan Bridge
Leck
Ireby
Nether Burrow
Westhouse
Skirwith
Weathercote
Ingleborough Common
Ingleton
Slatenber
Newby
Cantsfield
Tunstall
Burton in Lonsdale
Priest Hutton
Borwick
Arkholme
Capernwray
Melling
Carnforth
Over Kellet
Gressingham
Wennington
High Bentham
Low Bentham
Tatham
Hornby
Wray
Mill Houses
Keasden
Nether Kellet
Bolton-le-Sands
Danger Zone
Aughton
Claughton
Hest Bank
Slyne
Halton
Caton
Brookhouse
Caton Moor
Lowgill
Moor Cock
Tatham Fells
Goodber Common
Middle Salter
Crossgill
Higher Thrushgill
Bottom Head
MORECAMBE
West End
Torrisholme
Sandylands
Oxcliffe Hill
HEYSHAM
LANCASTER
Heaton
Scotforth
Middleton
Stodday
Overton
Quernmore
Blanch Fell
Haylot Fell
Salter Fell
Clougha Pike
Ward's Stone
White Hill
Wolfhole Crag
Mallowdale Fell
Douglas, Isle of Man
Sunderland Bank
Sunderland Point
Glasson
Conder Green
Lower Thurnham
Upper Thurnham
Galgate
Cockersand Abbey
Cockerham
Lee Fell
Tarnbrook
Lower Green Bank
Lee
Abbeystead
Wyresdale Tower
Trough of Bowland
Marshaw
Whins Brow
Beatrix Fell
Dolphinholme
Street
Forton
Hawthornthwaite Fell
Sykes
Hareden
Dunsop Bridge
Newton
Slaidburn
Meanley
Easington Fell
Bernard Wharf
Braides
North Wharf
Rossall Point
Knott End-on-Sea
Pilling Lane
Pilling
Fisher's Row
Stake Pool
Winmarleigh
Scorton
Calder Fell
Totridge Fell
Fair Snape Fell
Oakenclough
Calder Vale
Whitewell
Marl Hill Moor
FLEETWOOD
Preesall
Stalmine
Staynall
Eagland Hill
Nateby
Garstang
Bowgreave
Churchtown
Catterall
Parlick
Chipping
Bashall Eaves
West Bradford
Waddington
Burn Naze
Trunnah
Cleveleys
Hambleton
Moss Side
Out Rawcliffe
Ratten Row
Little Bispham
Norbreck
Thornton
Whin Lane End
St Michael's on Wyre
Claughton
White Chapel
Hesketh Lane
Longridge Fell
Bashall Town
Low Moor
Bispham
Carleton
Great Eccleston
Bilsborrow
Inglewhite
Priest Hill
Stonyhurst College
Great Mitton
Poulton-le-Fylde
Singleton
Elswick
Crossmoor
Inskip
Cuddy Hill
Barton
Goosnargh
Knowle Green
New Row
Moor Nook
Barrow
North Shore
BLACKPOOL
Normoss
Thistleton
Roseacre
Esprick
Newsham
Longridge
Hurst Green
Staining
Wharles
Catforth
Greenhalgh
Broughton
Haighton Green
Ribchester
Billington
Great Marton
Weeton
Swillbrook
Woodplumpton
Grimsargh
Langho
Coniston Green
South Shore
Great Plumpton
Wesham
Treales
Cottam
Sharoe Green
Salesbury
Wilpshire
Great Harwood
Squires Gate
Common Edge
Kirkham
Fulwood
Ribbleton
Elston
Balderstone
Mellor Brook
Osbaldeston
Clayton-le-Moors
Westby
Wrea Green
Lea Town
Samlesbury
Mellor
Rishton
Blackpool
Higher Ballam
Moss Side
Clifton
PRESTON
Fishwick
St Anne's
Ansdell
Saltcotes
Freckleton
Penwortham
Walton-le-Dale
Higher Walton
Samlesbury Bottoms
BLACKBURN
Church
Oswaldtwistle
LYTHAM ST ANNE'S
Lytham
Salter's Bank
Warton
Hutton
New Longton
Bamber Bridge
Pleasington
Ewood
Belthorn
Longton
Lostock Hall
Tardy Gate
Hoghton
Feniscowles
Earcroft
Lower Darwen
Banks Sands
Walmer Bridge
Midge Hall
Farington
Brindle
Tockholes
Abbey Village
Haslingden
Hesketh Bank
Becconsall
Much Hoole
Leyland
Clayton-le-Woods
Withnell
Brinscall
DARWEN
Hoddlesden
Hundred End
Tarleton
Bretherton
Whittle-le-Woods
Wheelton
Ryal Fold
Banks
Horse Bank
Heapey
Marshside
Crossens
Euxton
White Coppice
Angry Brow
Churchtown
Mere Brow
Anglezarke Moor
Turton Moor
SOUTHPORT
Eccleston
CHORLEY
Ribble
Wyre
Lune
Piel Bar
Mort Bank
Yeoman Wharf
Cartmel Wharf
Lancaster Sound
Heysham Lake
M6
M55
M61
M65
A6
A65
A590
A591
A683
A684
A588
A585
A586
A587
A583
A584
A59
A5085
A5105
A589
A6070
A601(M)
A592
A5074
A5084
A5092
A595
A5087
A5230
A565
A581
A675
A674
A666
A677
A6119
A679
B6254
B5278
B5277
B5271
B5282
B6385
B6254
B5290
B5272
B5270
B6377
B5266
B5268
B5260
B5269
B5259
B5261
B6245
B6243
B6246
B6478
B6480
B5247
B5248
B5256
B6391
B6232
B6535
28
29
30
31
32
60
61
56
48
A
B
C
D
E
F
G

CUMBRIA
YORKSHIRE DALES NATIONAL PARK
NORT
LANCASHIRE
Forest of Bowland
The Forest of Pendle
The Forest of Trawden
Forest of Rossendale
Langstrothdale Chase
Kendal
Oxenholme
Sedbergh
Dent
Hawes
Kirkby Lonsdale
Milnthorpe
Carnforth
Ingleton
High Bentham
Clapham
Settle
Giggleswick
Malham
Hellifield
Gargrave
Slaidburn
LANCASTER
Garstang
Clitheroe
Whalley
Longridge
Barnoldswick
Earby
Colne
NELSON
Brierfield
BURNLEY
Padiham
PRESTON
Fulwood
BLACKBURN
Great Harwood
Clayton-le-Moors
Rishton
ACCRINGTON
Oswaldtwistle
Haslingden
RAWTENSTALL
Bacup
Todmorden
Whitworth
Ramsbottom
DARWEN
Leyland
CHORLEY
Whernside 736
Ingleborough 724
Pendle Hill 557
A6
M6
A65
A59
A56
A682
M65
M61
A601(M)
A666
A671
A680
A646
A B C D E F G
31 32 33 34 35
55
48
49
61

YORKSHIRE
WEST YORKSHIRE
HARROGATE
LEEDS
BRADFORD
WAKEFIELD
KEIGHLEY
HALIFAX
Ripon
Knaresborough
Thirsk
Bedale
Masham
Middleham
Leyburn
Wetherby
Tadcaster
Otley
Ilkley
BINGLEY
SHIPLEY
Baildon
Guiseley
Yeadon
Horsforth
PUDSEY
MORLEY
ROTHWELL
GARFORTH
CASTLEFORD
PONTEFRACT
DEWSBURY
BATLEY
BRIGHOUSE
Elland
Heckmondwike
Cleckheaton
Mirfield
Ossett
Horbury
Normanton
Featherstone
Knottingley
Boroughbridge
Pateley Bridge
Easingwold
Sowerby
Topcliffe
Dishforth
Kirkby Malzeard
Aldborough
Spofforth
Boston Spa
Bramham
Aberford
Sherburn in Elmet
South Milford
Kippax
Swillington
Oulton
Stanley
Lofthouse
Wyke
Queensbury
Denholme
Cullingworth
Haworth
Addingham
Burley in Wharfedale
Menston
Pool
Bramhope
Pannal
Follifoot
Ripley
Hampsthwaite
Killinghall
Dacre
Summer Bridge
Lofthouse
Ramsgill
Leighton
Healey
Fearby
Ellingstring
Well
Snape
Carthorpe
Burneston
Exelby
Leeming
Crakehall
Finghall
Spennithorne
Harmby
Wensley
Redmire
Preston-under-Scar
Coverham
Carlton
Melmerby
West Witton
Swinithwaite
North Otterington
South Otterington
Newsham
South Kilvington
North Kilvington
Sutton-under-Whitestonecliffe
Thirkleby
Husthwaite
Coxwold
Dalton
Tholthorpe
Linton-on-Ouse
Newton-on-Ouse
Great Ouseburn
Whixley
Green Hammerton
Kirk Hammerton
Long Marston
Bilton
Hessay
Rufforth
Ulleskelf
Church Fenton
Saxton
Barkston
Monk Fryston
Hillam
Birkin
Brotherton
Ferrybridge
Cridling Stubbs
Womersley
Wentbridge
Ackworth
Crofton
Sharlston
Kirkheaton
Upper Hopton
Netherton
Middlestown
Outlane
Lindley
Holywell Green
Greetland
Rastrick
Southowram
Hipperholme
Northowram
Shelf
Ovenden
Luddenden
Midgley
Sowerby Bridge
Triangle
Ripponden
M1
M62
M606
M621
A1
A61
A59
A65
A64
A63
A6108
A684
A168
A170
A19

NORTH YORKSHIRE
Thirsk
Sowerby
Helmsley
Kirkbymoorside
Pickering
Thornton Dale
Malton
Norton
Old Malton
Easingwold
Boroughbridge
Aldborough
Wetherby
Tadcaster
YORK
Selby
Goole
Howden
CASTLEFORD
PONTEFRACT
GARFORTH
Knottingley
Ferrybridge
Featherstone
Normanton
Pocklington
Market Weighton
Stamford Bridge
Strensall
Haxby
Shipton
Sheriff Hutton
Castle Howard
Slingsby
Hovingham
Ampleforth
Coxwold
Kilburn
Dunnington
Wilberfoss
Elvington
Escrick
Riccall
Cawood
Sherburn in Elmet
Snaith
Rawcliffe
Drax
Barlby
Bubwith
Holme-on-Spalding-Moor
Gilberdyke
Swinefleet
Howardian Hills
Hambleton Hills
Wolds Way
Marston Moor
Aberford
Boston Spa
Bramham
Clifford
Thorner
Rufforth
Bishopthorpe
Copmanthorpe
Fulford
Heslington
Osbaldwick
Acomb
Upper Poppleton
Skelton
Huntington
New Earswick
Rawcliffe
Brayton
Hemingbrough
Eastrington
Airmyn
Hook
Old Goole
Carlton
South Milford
Brotherton
Kippax
Allerton Bywater
Methley
Woodlesford
Swillington
Oulton
Darrington
Womersley
Whitley
Eggborough
Hensall
Pollington
Wheldrake
Crockey Hill
Naburn
Stillingfleet
Bolton Percy
Ulleskelf
Church Fenton
Saxton
Barkston
Monk Fryston
Hambleton
Ledsham
Ledston
Great Preston
Kirk Deighton
North Deighton
Cattal
Hunsingore
Kirk Hammerton
Green Hammerton
Whixley
Flaxby
Goldsborough
Knaresborough
Great Ouseburn
Little Ouseburn
Linton-on-Ouse
Newton-on-Ouse
Tollerton
Alne
Huby
Stillington
Crayke
Brandsby
Terrington
Bulmer
Welburn
Whitwell-on-the-Hill
Kirkham
Westow
Buttercrambe
Sand Hutton
Bossall
Flaxton
Claxton
Towthorpe
Wigginton
Skipwith
North Duffield
Wressle
Spaldington
Bursea
Foggathorpe
Harlthorpe
Everingham
Seaton Ross
Melbourne
Allerthorpe
Barmby Moor
Bishop Wilton
Fangfoss
Full Sutton
Youlthorpe
Kirby Underdale
Thixendale
Acklam
Leavening
Burythorpe
Langton
Settrington
Scagglethorpe
Rillington
Wykeham
Scampston
Ryton
Amotherby
Swinton
Broughton
Barton-le-Street
Appleton-le-Street
Great Habton
Little Habton
Kirby Misperton
Great Barugh
Little Barugh
Salton
Normanby
Marton
Middleton
Aislaby
Wrelton
Sinnington
Keldholme
Kirkby Mills
Nawton
Beadlam
Wombleton
Harome
Sproxton
Oswaldkirk
Gilling East
Stonegrave
Nunnington
Cawton
Coulton
Yearsley
Oulston
Husthwaite
Carlton Husthwaite
Thirlby
Felixkirk
Kilvington
Knayton
Boltby
Cowesby
Kepwick
Upsall
Kirby Knowle
Cold Kirby
Old Byland
Rievaulx
Scawton
Sutton-under-Whitestonecliffe
Bagby
Thirkleby
Dalton
Topcliffe
Asenby
Dishforth
Cundall
Norton-le-Clay
Helperby
Brafferton
Raskelf
Tholthorpe
Myton-on-Swale
Fawdington
Crakehill
Sessay
Hutton Sessay
Thormanby
Skipton-on-Swale
Carlton Miniott
Catton
Kirby Hill
Langthorpe
Roecliffe
Minskip
Grafton
Marton
Staveley
Arkendale
Ferrensby
Coneythorpe
Scriven
Sicklinghall
Linton
Collingham
East Rigton
Walton
Wighill
Healaugh
Bilbrough
Askham Bryan
Askham Richard
Hutton Wandesley
Long Marston
Bilton
Bickerton
Tockwith
Cowthorpe
Kirk Deighton

45
46
47
48
49
63
A
B
C
D
E
F
G
0 2 4 6 8 10 miles
0 2 4 6 8 10 km
Silpho
Burniston
Cromer Point
Broxa
Langdale End
Suffield
Ness
Scalby
North Bay
Wykeham Forest
Everley
PARK
SCARBOROUGH
Irton Moor
Falsgrave
South Bay
West Ayton
East Ayton
Black Rocks
Sawdon
Hutton Buscel
Osgodby
Cayton Bay
Ruston
Wykeham
Irton
Eastfield
WYKEHAM ABBEY
Seamer
Cayton
Snainton
Brompton
Lebberston
The Wyke
Gristhorpe
Filey Brigg
The Carrs
Hertford
Flixton
Folkton
Filey
Willerby
Staxton
Muston
East Heslerton
Sherburn
Ganton
Filey Bay
Wolds Way
Hunmanby
West Heslerton
Sherburn Wold
Fordon
Reighton Sands
Reighton
Crab Rocks
Speeton
Foxholes
Wold Newton
Buckton
Burton Fleming
Bempton
Butterwick
Grindale
Flamborough Head
Weaverthorpe
Helperthorpe
Flamborough
West Lutton
East Lutton
Octon
Thwing
SEWERBY HALL
Sewerby
Swaythorpe
Boynton
Langtoft
Rudston
BRIDLINGTON
Gypsey Race
Cowlam Manor
Sledmere
Roman Road
Carnaby
Hilderthorpe
Cottam
Bessingby
SLEDMERE HOUSE
Haisthorpe
BRIDLINGTON
West End
Kilham
BURTON AGNES HALL
Thornholme
Carnaby Moor
Burton Agnes
Ruston Parva
Fraisthorpe
Harpham
Garton-on-the-Wolds
Wetwang
Elmswell
Lowthorpe
Gransmoor
Nafferton
BAY
Great Driffield
Little Driffield
Great Kelk
Lissett
Barmston
Tibthorpe Wold
Gembling
Old Howe
Eastburn
Kelleythorpe
Wansford
Foston on the Wolds
Ulrome
Tibthorpe
Kirkburn
Southburn
SKIPSEA
Skipsea
Skerne
Old Sunderlandwick
Beeford
Dalton
Brigham
Church End
North Frodingham
Bainton
Hutton Cranswick
Dunnington
Rotsea
Middleton-on-the-Wolds
Atwick
Watton
WATTON PRIORY
Hempholme
Bewholme
Lund
Watton Carrs
NUNKEELING
Kilnwick
Burshill
Beswick
Hornsea
Holme on the Wolds
Lockington
Little Burton
Brandesburton
Seaton
Thorpe
Hornsea Mere
Aike
Hull
South Dalton
Leven
Catwick
Sigglesthorne
Rolston
Kiplingcotes
Goxhill
Etton
Scorborough
Arram
Little Catwick
Mappleton
Leconfield
Danger Area
Great Cowden
Great Hatfield
BERSIDE
Gardham
Cherry Burton
Routh
Tickton
Rise
Long Riston
Molescroft
Withernwick
Bishop Burton Wold
Bishop Burton
BEVERLEY
MUSEUM OF ARMY TRANSPORT
New Ellerby
South Skirlaugh
Marton
West Newton
Aldbrough
Woodmansey
Old Ellerby
Newbald Wold
North Newbald
Walkington
Wawne
Holderness Drain
BURTON CONSTABLE HALL
Thearne
South Newbald
High Hunsley
Swine
Flinton
Garton
Dunswell
Coniston
Bentley
Little Weighton
Sproatley
Humbleton
Ganstead
Skidby
Cottingham
Rowley
Stoneferry
Owstwick
Tunstall
South Cave
Riplingham
Sutton-on-Hull
Bilton
Lelley
Elstronwick
Burton Pidsea
Roos
Epleworth
Preston
Brantingham
Willerby
Marfleet
Waxholme
Wadworth Hill
Kirk Ella
West Ella
Hedon
Withernsea
Elloughton
Welton
Anlaby
KINGSTON UPON HULL
WILBERFORCE HOUSE
Burstwick
Rimswell
Brough
Swanland
Halsham
Thorngumbald
North Ferriby
Hessle
To Rotterdam & Zeebrugge
Paull
Whitton Ness
Redcliff Channel
Keyingham
Humber Bridge
Hollym
Whitton
Ottringham
Winestead
Humber
Paull Holme Sands
East Halton Skitter
Holmpton
Winteringham
Read's Island
South Channel
New Holland
Barton-upon-Humber
Barrow Haven
Patrington
Foulholme Sands
Out Newton
West Halton
South Ferriby
Goxhill
Haven Side
Welwick
Salthaugh Grange
Weeton
Barrow upon Humber
South End
Sunk Island
Skeffling
Easington
Horkstow
Winterton
Thornton Abbey Sta.
THORNTON ABBEY
Old Hall
Skeffling Clays
Burnham
Thornton Curtis
North Killingholme
Saxby All Saints
New Ancholme
52
53
A165
A171
A170
A64
A1039
A166
A1035
A1079
A164
A1174
A1033
A1034
A1105
A63
A1077
A15
A165
B1261
B1249
B1253
B1252
B1248
B1229
B1255
B1259
B1242
B1244
B1243
B1230
B1233
B1237
B1238
B1240
B1239
B1362
B1445
B1206
B1218
B1204
B1207

Blackshaw Bank
Bowness-on-Solway
Port Carlisle
Glasson
69
Drumburgh
Burgh by Sands
Rockcliffe
Blackford
Harker
Houghton
Beaumont
Cargo
Monkhill
Kingstown
Kirkandrews-upon-Eden
Grinsdale
Moorhouse
Stanwix
Boustead Hill
Longburgh
Easton
Hadrian's Wall
Criffell
569
Carse Bay
Kirkbean
Carsethorn
Cavens
Borron Point
Caulkerbush
Mainsriddle
Arbigland
Preston Merse
Mersehead Sands
Southerness
Southerness Point
Gillfoot Bay
Barnhourie Sands
25
26
27
28
29
Firth
Solway
Cardurnock
Bowness Common
Anthorn
Whitrigg
Angerton
Fingland
Kirkbride
Studholme
Kirkbampton
Thurstonfield
Oughterby
Little Bampton
Great Orton
Little Orton
Newby West
CARLISLE
Cummersdale
Carleton
Brisco
Durdar
Dalston
Grune Point
Skinburness
Moricambe
Newton Arlosh
Silloth
Calvo
Seaville
Causewayhead
Blitterlees
Wedholme Flow
Bigland
Aikton
Gamelsby
Wiggonby
Baldwinholme
Micklethwaite
Thursby
Oulton
Lessonhall
Waverbridge
Kelsick
Abbeytown
Highlaws
Dundraw
Beckfoot
Pelutho
Buckabank
Curthwaite
Wigton
Blencogo
Waverton
Bromfield
Aikshaw
Langrigg
Mawbray
Dubmill Point
Red Dial
Warblebank
Raughton Head
Gaitsgill
Southwaite
Stockdalewath
Welton
Rosley
Westward
Edderside
Westnewton
Allonby
Allonby Bay
Bolton Low Houses
Fletchertown
Brocklebank
Ivegill
Sebergham
Aspatria
Hayton
Baggrow
Blennerhasset
Mealsgate
Boltongate
Faulds Brow
Sowerby Row
Caldbeck
Whelpo
Parkend
Hesket Newmarket
Allerby
Crosscanonby
Arkleby
Plumbland
Torpenhow
Bothel
Parsonby
Whitrigg
Ireby
Maryport
Crosby
Gilcrux
High Ireby
Uldale
Longlands
Branthwaite
Millhouse
Lamonby
Ellonby
Ellenborough
Dearham
Moota Hill
Sunderland
Ruthwaite
Caldbeck Fells
High Pike
658
Binsey
Tallentire
Blindcrake
Bewaldeth
Flimby
Broughton Moor
Bridekirk
Dovenby
Uldale Fells
Knott
710
Carrock Fell
Hutton Roof
Johnby
Greystoke Forest
Mosedale
Little Broughton
Papcastle
Bassenthwaite
Camerton
Seaton
Great Broughton
Cockermouth
Embleton
Great Calva
690
Greystoke
Berrier Hill
Great Clifton
Brigham
Skiddaw Forest
Skiddaw
931
Mungrisdale
WORKINGTON
Bridgefoot
Greysouthen
Little Clifton
Eaglesfield
WHINLATTER FOREST PARK
Thornthwaite Forest
Bassenthwaite Lake
Mire House
Saddleback or Blencathra
868
Scales
Motherby
Penruddock
Westfield
High Harrington
Deanscales
Lorton Vale
Lord's Seat
Millbeck
Applethwaite
Threlkeld
Hutton
Dean
Pardshaw
High Lorton
Thornthwaite
Latrigg
Great Mell Fell
Branthwaite
Ullock
300
Whinlatter Pass
Portinscale
Keswick
Distington
Gilgarran
Mockerkin
Grisedale Pike
790
Braithwaite
Castlerigg Stone Circle
Matterdale End
Little Mell Fell
Clough Head
726
Matterdale Common
Watermillock
Ulcat Row
Moresby
Pica
Hopegill Head
Brackenthwaite Fell
Grasmoor
851
Loweswater
Lamplugh
Causey Pike
Stair
Derwent Water
St John's Beck
Dowthwaitehead
Great Dodd
856
Dockray
Aira Force
Parton
Asby
Arlecdon
Blake Fell
572
Loweswater Fell
Little Town
Stybarrow Dodd
840
WHITEHAVEN
Rowrah
Murton Fell
Crummock Water
Kirkland
Derwent Fells
C
U
M
Hensingham
Frizington
Croasdale
Scale Force
Buttermere
340
Robinson
737
Grange
High Seat
608
Glenridding
Place Fell
657
Saltom Bay
Cleator Moor
Ennerdale Bridge
Great Borne
616
Watendlath
Thirlmere
Patterdale
Sandwith
Buttermere
Red Pike
High Stile
806
Dale Head
754
Helvellyn
949
Striding Edge
Grisedale
Beda Fell
St Bees Head
Moor Row
Wath Brow
Ennerdale Water
Seatoller
Rosthwaite
Borrowdale
Bridgend
Cleator
Ennerdale Fell
Scarth Gap Pass
Hay Stacks
Honister Pass
358
Stonethwaite
Wythburn
Dollywagon Pike
Hartsop
Rottington
Bigrigg
Pillar
892
Black Sail Pass
Borrowdale Fells
Wythburn Fells
Brothers Water
St Bees
Egremont
Wilton
Lank Rigg
Steeple
Haycock
841
Caw Fell
Kirk Fell
Great Gable
899
Seathwaite
Ullscarf
726
Dunmail Raise
Fairfield
873
Seat Sandal
Hayeswater
How Man
Leconfield Commons
797
Glaramara
LAKE
DISTRICT
Snellings
Middletown
Nethertown
Haile
Wasdale Head
Sty Head
High Raise
762
Rydal Fell
Middle Dodd
Kirkstone Pass
454
Seatallan
692
Lingmell
Great End
Allen Crags
Stake Pass
Dungeon Ghyll Force
Beckermet
Calder Bridge
Copeland Forest
Scafell Pike
977
Esk Hause
Langdale Pikes
Grasmere
Dove Cottage
Rydal Mount
Braystones
Calder Abbey
Scafell
964
Bow Fell
902
Rydal
Ponsonby
Wellington
Nether Wasdale
The Screes
Crinkle Crags
Chapel Stile
Elterwater
Ambleside
Sellafield
Wastwater
Burnmoor Tarn
Whin Rigg
Eskdale Fell
NATIONAL
Pike of Blisco
702
Skelwith Bridge
Waterhead
Clappersgate
Troutbeck
Gosforth
Hardknott Roman Fort
Wrynose Pass
390
Brathay
Seascale
Santon Bridge
Eskdale Green
Boot
Hardknott Pass
393
Cockley Beck
Furness Fells
Holmrook
Drigg
Gubbergill
Beckfoot
Harter Fell
649
Stanley Force
Levers Water
Seathwaite Tarn
Outgate
Wray Castle
High Wray
Troutbeck
Windermere
Danger Zone
Kokoarrah
Ravenglass & Eskdale Railway
Ravenglass
Muncaster
Devoke Water
Dow Crag
803
Coniston
The Old Man of Coniston
Hawkshead
Claife Heights
Bowness-on-Windermere
Woodend
Seathwaite
Dunnerdale
Bowmanstead
Grizedale
Near Sawrey
Broad Oak
Ulpha Fell
Hall Dunnerdale
Caw
529
Torver
Brantwood
Mitchelland
Stainton Fell
Whitfell
573
Lane End
Ulpha
Bigert Mire
Hoses
GRIZEDALE FOREST PARK
Satterthwaite
Winster
Danger Zone
Sunny Bank
Corney
Ulpha Park
Broughton Mills
Blawith Fells
255
Force Forge
Stub Place
Prior Park
Nibthwaite
Hycemoor
Bank End
Water Yeat
Bootle
Hyton
Bootle Fell
Duddon Bridge
Broughton in Furness
Blawith
Oxen Park
Finsthwaite
Lakeside
Broadgate
Selker Bay
Woodland Fell
54
55

NORTHUMBERLAND
DURHAM
CUMBRIA
NORTH YORKSHIRE
Laversdale
Newtown
Irthington
Brampton
Milton
Tindale
Hallbankgate
Midgeholme
Lambley
Castle
Featherstone
Rowfoot
Plenmeller Common
Whitfield
Bearsbridge
Catton
Allendale Town
Dalton
Dotland
Whitley Chapel
Slaley
Slaley Forest
Dipton Wood
Newby East
Hayton
Little Corby
Warwick Bridge
How
Faugh
Heads Nook
Great Corby
Talkin
Farlam
Castle Carrock
Forest Head
Cold Fell
Halton Lea Gate
Stonehouse
Ashholme Common
Glendue Fell
Burnstones
Knarsdale
King's Forest of Geltsdale
Williamston Common
Whitfield Law
Whitfield Moor
Ninebanks
Studdon
Hexhamshire Common
Broadwell House
Blanchland Moor
Cumwhitton
Hall's Tenement
Slaggyford
Geltsdale Middle
Sinderhope
Allendale Common
Hangman Hill
Hope Fell
Blanchland
Cumrew
Hornsby Gate
Cotehill
Hornsby
Newbiggin
Croglin Fell
Kirkhaugh
Ayle
Mohope Moor
Spartylea
Hartley Moor
Hunstanworth
Nookton Fell
Holmwrangle
Croglin
Grey Nag
Carr Shield
Green Hill
Aiketgate
Ainstable
Armathwaite
Watch Hill
Renwick Fell
Raise
Alston
Nenthead
Bayles
Allenheads
Coalcleugh
Bolt's Law
High Hesket
Scale Houses
Ruckcroft
Black Fell
Gilderdale Forest
Hartside Height
Middle Fell
Killhope Moor
Redburn Common
Renwick
Haresceugh
Leadgate
Rookhope
Stanhope Common
Staffield
Kirkoswald
Garrigill
Cornriggs
Middlehope Moor
Cowshill
Wearhead
Fiend's Fell
Alston Moor
Rotherhope Fell
Burnhope Reservoir
Westgate
Eastgate
Lazonby
Gamblesby
Glassonby
Ireshopeburn
St John's Chapel
Daddry Shield
Brotherlee
Melmerby Fell
Ousby Fell
Burnhope Seat
Plumpton
Salkeld Dykes
Great Salkeld
Little Salkeld
Melmerby
Ireshope Moor
Green Fell
Round Hill
Chapel Fell
Chapelfell Top
Hunsonby
Ousby
Row
Plumpton Head
Winskill
Cross Fell
Bellbeaver Rigg
Three Pikes
Westernhope Moor
Snowhope Hill
Langwathby
Milburn Forest
Viewing Hill
Harwood
Langdon Common
Outberry Plain
Middleton Common
Catterlen
Edenhall
Skirwith
Kirkland
Great Dun Fell
Langdon Beck
Newbiggin Common
Carrs Hill
Newton Reigny
Penrith
Blencarn
Widdybank Fell
Forest-in-Teesdale
Knock Fell
Eamont Bridge
Culgaith
Milburn
Cow Green Reservoir
Dufton Fell
High Force
Newbiggin
Monks Moor
Stainton
Brougham
Roman Road
Cauldron Snout
Temple Sowerby
Knock
Backstone Edge
Pennine Way
Cronkley Fell
Holwick
Holwick Fell
Tirril
Clifton
Whinfell Forest
Kirkby Thore
Dufton
High Cup Nick
Middleton-in-Teesdale
Mickleton
Pooley Bridge
Lowther Castle
Melkinthorpe
Cliburn
Long Marton
Keisley
Mickle Fell
Askham
Lowther
Bolton
Brampton
Murton Fell
Danger Zone
Lune Moor
Lune Forest
Bowbank
Thringarth
Helton
Hackthorpe
Great Strickland
Morland
Crackenthorpe
Murton
Little Fell
Fish Lake
Grassholme
Romaldkirk
Whale
Kings Meaburn
Appleby-in-Westmorland
Burton Fell
Warcop Fell
Mickleton Moor
Grassholme Resr
Selset Reservoir
Hunderthwaite
Barton Fell
Newby
Little Strickland
Colby
Hilton
Brackenber
Hunderthwaite Moor
Hury
Hury Resr
Coupland
Iron Band
Blackton Resr
Baldersdale
Bampton
Sleagill
Burrells
Stainmore Common
Balderhead Resr
Clove Lodge
Cotherstone Moor
Rosgill
Reagill
Maulds Meaburn
Hoff
Great Ormside
Sandford
Deep Dale
Bampton Common
Shap
Shap Abbey
Wickerslack
Drybeck
Warcop
Hillbeck
Brough
North Stainmore
Keld
Ralfland Forest
Crosby Ravensworth
Great Asby
Bleatarn
Great Musgrave
Little Musgrave
Verteris Roman Fort
Brough Sowerby
Beldoo Hill
Haweswater Resr
Swindale Beck
Seat Robert
Wet Sleddale Resr
Shap Summit
Kaber
Mardale Common
Soulby
Bowes Moor
Stainmore Forest
Winton
Crosby Ravensworth Fell
Grange Scar
Crosby Garrett
Hartley
Gatescarth Pass
Shap Fells
Great Yarlside
Orton
Raisbeck
Smardale
Waitby
Kirkby Stephen
Winton Fell
Kaber Fell
Taylor Rigg
Tan Hill
Sleightholme Moor
Scargill High Moor
Cleasby Hill
Nettle Hill
Nateby
Bastifell
Nine Standards Rigg
Sadgill
Tebay
Greenholme
Bretherdale Head
Begin Hill
Ash Fell
Newbiggin-on-Lune
Kelleth
Tailbridge Hill
Arkengarthdale Moor
Water Crag
Whaw
Long Sleddale
Borrowdale
Ravenstonedale
Southwaite
Stonesdale Moor
Rogan's Seat
Great Pinseat
Staveley Head Fell
Forest Hall
West Fell
Langdale Fell
Simon's Seat
Ravenstonedale Common
Harter Fell
Outhgill
High Seat
Birkdale
Birkdale Common
Whitsundale Beck
West Stonesdale
Keld
Melbecks Moor
Hard Level Gill
Whinfell Beacon
Uldale Head
Wild Boar Fell
Mallerstang Common
Garnett Bridge
Watchgate
Yarlside
Angram Common
Thwaite
Gunnerside
Kearton
Blades
Feetham
Low Row
Staveley
Grayrigg
Lowgill
The Calf
Low Haygarth
Bluecaster
Uldale House
Swarth Fell
Great Shunner Fell
Muker
Ivelet
Crackpot
Beck Foot
Brant Fell
West Baugh Fell
Holmes Moss
Abbotside Common
Butter Tubs
Butter Tubs Pass
Oxnop Ghyll
Windermere
Meal Bank
Burneside
Crook
Lambrigg Fell
Firbank
Cautley
Askrigg Common
Kendal
Fisher Tarn Resr
Ingmire Hall
Sedbergh
Baugh Fell
Knoutberry Haw
East Baugh Fell
Garsdale Head
Cotterdale
Fossdale
High Shaw
Askrigg
Newbiggin
Killington Lake
New Hutton
Garths
Killington Resr
Millthrop
Clough
Mid Mossdale
Hardraw
Sedbusk
Woodhall
Oxenholme
Millholme
Middleshaw
West Mostard
Garsdale
Mossdale Moor
Hawes
Wensleydale
Bainbridge
Brigsteer
Natland
Killington
Aye Gill Pike
Great Knoutberry Hill
Widdale Fell
Burtersett
Thornton Rust
Countersett
Thoralby
Sizergh Castle
Old Hutton
Cotes
Sedgwick
Harprigg
Gawthrop
Dentdale
Middleton
Dent Sta
Cowgill
Weather Fell
A689
A69
A686
A6
A66
M6
A685
A683
A684
A591
A65
A6
B6305
B6295
B6294
B6306
B6277
B6276
B6278
B6282
B6413
B6412
B6260
B6261
B6259
B6270
B6257
B5284
31
32
33
34
35
56
62
70
A
B
C
D
E
F
G
H

Dilston
Riding Mill
Stocksfield
Mickley Square
Prudhoe
Blaydon
Winlaton
Dunston
Pelaw
Cleadon
East Boldon
West Boldon
BOLDON
WHICKHAM
GATESHEAD
FELLING
A194(M)
Whitburn Bay
Broomhaugh
Dipton Wood
Greenside
Leadgate
Rowlands Gill
Highfield
Winlaton Mill
Marley Hill
Sunniside
Lamesley
Wrekenton
Springwell
Southwick
Roker
Fulwell
Monkwearmouth
SUNDERLAND
Hendon
Slaley
Healey
Hedley on the Hill
Chopwell
Hamsterley
Lintzford
Burnopfield
Kibblesworth
Castletown
Hylton
South Hylton
Washington
Birtley
Whittonstall
Newlands
Kiln Pit Hill
Ebchester
Hobson
Tanfield
Tantobie
Ouston
New Silksworth
Silksworth
Ryhope
Barleyhill
Medomsley
Dipton
Beamish
Pelton
Fatfield
Penshaw
Shiney Row
Herrington
Shotley Bridge
Shotleyfield
STANLEY
South Moor
Newfield
Grange Villa
Chester-le-Street
Bournmoor
Carterway Heads
Blanchland
Ruffside
Edmundbyres
Muggleswick
CONSETT
Leadgate
Annfield Plain
Craghead
Waldridge
Fence Houses
HOUGHTON LE SPRING
SEAHAM
Allensford
Castleside
Delves
Iveston
Maiden Law
Greencroft Hall
Edmondsley
Great Lumley
Colliery Row
Seaton
Cross Rigg
Healeyfield
Rowley
Knitsley
Burnhope
Holmside
Plawsworth
Kimblesworth
West Rainton
East Rainton
Hetton-le-Hole
Dalton-le-Dale
Nose's Point
Muggleswick Common
Smiddy Shaw Resr
Waskerley
Lanchester
Sacriston
Pity Me
Murton
Cold Hesledon
Butsfield
Langley Park
Esh
Witton Gilbert
Framwellgate Moor
Easington Lane
South Hetton
Hawthorn
Skaylock Hill
Waskerley Resr
Cornsay
Satley
Cornsay Colliery
Quebec
Bearpark
Ushaw Moor
DURHAM
Pittington
Littletown
Carrville
Sherburn
Haswell
Easington
Easington Colliery
Little Thorpe
Stanhope Common
Collier Law
Wolsingham Moor
Tunstall Resr
Esh Winning
Waterhouses
East Hedleyhope
Shadforth
Ludworth
Shotton Colliery
Horden
Peterlee
Crawleyside
Stanhope
Eastgate
Langley Moor
Brandon
Shincliffe
Thornley
Shotton
Blackhall Colliery
Blackhall
Wolsingham
Tow Law
Sunniside
DURHAM
Sunderland Bridge
Durham Hett
Bowburn
Cassop
Quarrington Hill
Wheatley Hill
Wingate
Station Town
Castle Eden
Hesleden
Frosterley
Thornley
Billy Row
Brancepeth
Oakenshaw
Croxdale
Coxhoe
Kelloe
Trimdon Colliery
Hutton Henry
Hart
Hill End
Harvey Hill
Crook
Willington
Tudhoe
Byers Green
Trimdon Grange
Sheraton
South Wingate
Knitsley Fell
Fir Tree
Howden-le-Wear
Spennymoor
Cornforth
Trimdon
High Throston
St John's
Pikeston Fell
Newfield
Middlestone Moor
Ferryhill
Hurworth Burn Resr
Pawlaw Pike
Bedburn
Witton-le-Wear
High Grange
Hunwick
Westerton
Dean Bank
Bishop Middleham
Fishburn
Elwick
Dalton Piercy
Low Redford
Hamsterley
Kirk Merrington
Chilton
Crookfoot Resr
Hamsterley Common
Witton Park
Coundon
BISHOP AUCKLAND
Rushyford
Hardwick Hall
Brierton
Monks Moor
Hamsterley Forest
Low Etherley
High Etherley
St Helen Auckland
Coundon Grange
Bradbury
Sedgefield
Morley
Toft Hill
Woodland
Butterknowle
Eggleston Common
Shildon
Middridge
Woodham
Mordon
Thorpe Larches
Newton
Woodland Fell
Copley
Evenwood
West Auckland
Newton Aycliffe
Foxton
Wolviston
Billingham
Langleydale Common
Cockfield
Bildershaw
Redworth
Elstob
Stillington
Mickleton
Eggleston
Burnt Houses
Raby
Wackerfield
Bolam
Houghton Bank
Aycliffe
Whitton
Thorpe Thewles
Romaldkirk
Kinninvie
Hilton
Heighington
Great Stainton
Carlton
Norton
Hunderthwaite
Staindrop
Ingleton
Houghton-le-Side
Brafferton
Bishopton
Redmarshall
MIDDL
Hury
Hury Resr
Cotherstone
Stainton
Cleatlam
Langton
Headlam
Killerby
Denton
Walworth
Coatham Mundeville
Little Stainton
Stockton-on-Tees
Lartington
Summer-house
Archdeacon Newton
Barmpton
Hartburn
Barnard Castle
Little Newsham
Gainford
Great Burdon
Sadberge
Elton
Thornaby-on-Tees
Startforth
The Bowes Mus.
Westwick
Winston
High Coniscliffe
Mowden
Haughton Le Skerne
Longnewton
Whorlton
Piercebridge
DARLINGTON
Urlay Nook
Preston Park Museum
Boldron
Eggleston
Greta Bridge
Ovington
Wycliffe
Caldwell
Low Coniscliffe
Eastbourne
Tees-side Airport Sta.
Tees-side
Eaglescliffe
Ingleby Barwick
Bowes
Gilmonby
Brignall
Hutton Magna
Eppleby
Manfield
Forcett
Cleasby
Blackwell
Middleton St George
Middleton One Row
Aislaby
Egglescliffe
Yarm
Maltby
Lane Head
Aldbrough St John
Stapleton
Hurworth-on-Tees
Low Dinsdale
High Leven
Hilton
Scargill
Barningham
West Layton
Stanwick Camp
Croft-on-Tees
Neasham
Low Worsall
Kirklevington
Middleton-on-Leven
Newsham
East Layton
Newton Morrell
Eryholme
Scargill High Moor
Cleasby Hill
Barningham Moor
Dalton
Melsonby
Barton
Dalton-on-Tees
Girsby
Picton
Ravensworth
Roman Road
Crathorne
Gayles
Kirby Hill
Sockburn
Hope Moor
Holgate Moor
Kexwith Moor
Washton
Gilling West
Middleton Tyas
Low Entercommon
Hutton Rudby
Appleton Wiske
Enterpen
Danger Zone
Scotch Corner
High Entercommon
Hornby
Great Smeaton
Whaw
Hurst Moor
High Moor
North Cowton
West Rounton
East Rounton
Potto
Great Pinseat
Langthwaite
Washfold
Marske Moor
Moulton
Atley Hill
East Cowton
Birkby
Welbury
Hurst
Skeeby
Richmond
Uckerby
Deighton
Ingleby Arncliffe
Calver Hill
Skelton
Marrick Moor
Marske
Hudswell
Brompton on Swale
Hutton Bonville
East Harlsey
Ingleby Cross
Reeth
Fremington
Grinton
Marrick
Scorton
Bolton-on-Swale
Whitwell
Streetlam
Oaktree Hill
Battle of Standard 1138
Cleveland Tontine
Kearton
Blades
Healaugh
Feetham
Low Row
Ellerton Priory
Downholme
Catterick Camp
Catterick
Ellerton
Danby Wiske
Mount Grace Priory
Osmotherley
Crackpot
Harkerside Moor
Hipswell Moor
Kiplin
Great Langton
Ellerbeck
Gibbon Hill
Stainton
Scotton
Tunstall
Brompton
Stainton Moor
East Appleton
Kirby Fleetham
Yafforth
Kirby Sigston
Thimbleby
Redmire Moor
Preston Moor
Bellerby Moor
East Bolton Moor
Barden
East Hauxwell
Hackforth
Great Fencote
Thrintoft
Romanby
Northallerton
Over Silton
Nether Silton
Castle Bolton
Leyburn Moor
Bellerby
Hunton
Hornby
Arrathorne
Little Fencote
Scruton
Ainderby Steeple
Crosby Court
Newbiggin
Redmire
Preston-under-Scar
Burton Hall
Patrick Brompton
Little Holtby
Langthorne
Crakehall
Morton-on-Swale
Warlaby
Woodhall
Carperby
Low Bolton
Leyburn
Harmby
Constable Burton
Kirkbridge
Thornton-le-Beans
Kepwick
Wensley
Newton-le-Willows
Leeming Bar
North Otterington
Borrowby
Cowesby
Thornton Rust
Aysgarth
West Witton
Finghall
Spennithorne
Thornton Resr
Bedale Hall
Leeming
Londonderry
Aiskew
Bedale
Thornton-le-Moor
Boltby Moor
Kirby Knowle
Thoralby
West Burton
Middleham
Agglethorpe
Thornton Steward
Rookwith
Cowling
Burrill
Exelby
Gatenby
Newby Wiske
Maunby
South Otterington
Knayton
Upsall
D U R H A M
N O R T H Y O R
A
B
C
D
E
F
G
36
37
38
39
40
71
61
57
A1(M)
A66(M)
A1
A19
A167
A66
A67
A68
A684
A689
A690
A691
A692
A693
A694
A695
A6108
A6136
A6072
A688
A177
A181
A182
A183
A1018
A1027
A1044
A1045
A1046
A135
A168
A179
A195
A1231
A1290
A184
A194
A1050
B6278
B6279
B6282
B6275
B6274
B6270
B6277
B6271
B6263
B1264
B1283
B1285
B1286
B1284
B6296
B6300
B6302
B6301
B6287
B6288
B6291
B1278
B6168
B6173
B6309
B6306
B6313
B6316
B1275

41
42
43
44
45
A
B
C
D
E
F
G
0 2 4 6 8 10 miles
0 2 4 6 8 10 km
Middleton
HARTLEPOOL
Hartlepool Bay
Tees
Seaton Carew
Bay
Seal Sands
Tees Mouth
Warrenby
Coatham
Redcar
CLEVELAND
Dormanstown
Kirkleatham
Marske-by-the-Sea
Saltburn-by-the-Sea
KIRKLEATHAM HALL MUSEUM
Clarence
Grangetown
New Marske
Warsett Hill
Cargo Fleet
South Bank
Lazenby
Yearby
Upleatham
Brotton
Skelton
Skinningrove
Cleveland Way
Wilton
Dunsdale
Eston
Normanby
Skelton Green
Carlin How
Boulby
Staithes
Kilton
North Skelton
Guisborough
Boosbeck
Loftus
Easington
Dalehouse
Port Mulgrave
Hinderwell
Marton
Margrove Park
Lingdale
Roxby
Runswick Bay
Kettle Ness
Runswick
Nunthorpe
SKI CENTRE
Stanghow
Liverton
Borrowby
Newton Mulgrave
Kettleness
Goldsborough
Pinchinthorpe
Newton under Roseberry
Gisborough Moor
Lockwood Beck Resr
Moorsholm
Roxby Low Moor
Ellerby
Lythe
Sandsend Ness
Sandsend
Scaling
Roseberry Topping
Freebrough Hill
Scaling Resr
Mickleby
East Barnby
West Barnby
Great Ayton
Moorsholm Moor
Roxby High Moor
Whitby
Saltwick Bay
Commondale Moor
Commondale
Danby Low Moor
Ugthorpe
Dunsley
Little Ayton
Easby Moor
Kildale
Danby Beacon
Lealholm Moor
Newholm
Cleveland Way
Easby
Kildale Moor
Danby
Ruswarp
Stainsacre
Battersby
Castleton
Houlsyke
Lealholm
Aislaby
Great Broughton
Baysdale Beck
Ainthorpe
Egton Low Moor
Sneaton
High Hawsker
Ingleby Greenhow
Baysdale
Esk Dale
Egton
Sleights
Ugglebarnby
Low Hawsker
Ness Point or North Cheek
Kirkby
Westerdale
NORTH YORK MOORS RAILWAY
Sneatonthorpe
Great Busby
Baysdale Moor
Street
Grosmont
Raw
Robin Hood's Bay
Glaisdale
Egton Bridge
Littlebeck
Fylingthorpe
Westerdale Moor
Danby High Moor
Beck Hole
Sleights Moor
Low Moor
Old Peak or South Cheek
Urra
Round Hill
Falling Foss
Seave Green
NORTH
YORK
MOORS
Ravenscar
Cockayne Ridge
Glaisdale Moor
Egton High Moor
Goathland
Chop Gate
Bilsdale East Moor
Farndale Moor
Pike Hill Moss
Mallyan Spout
Flask Inn
Fylingdales Moor
Rosedale Moor
Danger Zone
Burn Howe Rigg
Staintondale
Cockayne
Hunt House
Church Houses
Wheeldale Moor
Cleveland Way
Snilesworth Moor
Bilsdale West Moor
WHEELDALE MOOR ROMAN ROAD
Harwood Dale
Grange
Thorgill
Lockton High Moor
Rosedale Abbey
Allerston High Moor
Cloughton Newlands
Fangdale Beck
Low Mill
Cropton Forest
Broxa Forest
Cloughton
NATIONAL
PARK
NORTH
RIDING
Stape
Silpho
Spaunton Moor
Lockton Low Moor
Burniston
Kelldy Castle
Levisham
Langdale End
Broxa
Helmsley Moor
Gillamoor
Lastingham
Newton-on-Rawcliffe
Hackness
Suffield
Hawnby
Wether Cote
Hutton-le-Hole
Spaunton
Lockton
Scalby
Fadmoor
Cropton
Dalby Forest
FOREST
PARK
Irton Moor
Falsgrave
Kirkbymoorside
Keldholme
Carlton
58
59
A1049
A1085
A1042
A1053
A66
A174
A1053
B1380
A171
A173
B1267
B1268
A172
B1365
B1366
B1266
B1447
B1416
A169
B1257
A165
B1269

16
17
18
19
20
A
B
C
D
E
F
G
67
Ailsa Craig
Dipple
Dowhill
Kilkerran
Craig
Maratz Hill
Tairlaw
Low Craighead
Dailly
Chapeldonan
Grangeston
Old Dailly
Penkill
Hadyard Hill
Garleffin Fell
429
Lintern Loch
Loch Bradan Reservoir
Loch Finlas
Girvan
Saugh Hill
Penwhapple Reservoir
Glendoune
Glengennet
North Balloch
South Balloch
Waterhead
Craiglee
LOCH DOON
Black Neuk
Glendrissaig
Pinminnoch
Changue Forest
Nick of the Balloch Pass
Shiel Hill
Ardwell
Kennedy's Pass
Grey Hill
297
Barr
341
Stinchar
Starr
Shalloch
Loch Riecawr
S T R A T H C L Y D E
C A R R I C K
Loch Macaterick
565
Polmaddie Hill
479
Shalloch on Minnoch
Lendalfoot
Water of Lendal
MOTTE
Pinmore
Aldons
Carleton Fishery
Daljarrock
GALLOWAY
Bennane Head
Poundland
Pinwherry
Muck Water
Kirriereoch Hill
786
Kirriereoch Loch
Colmonell
Dalreoch
Glenduisk
FOREST
Merrick
843
Dry Loch
Loch Enoch
Ballantrae Bay
Knockdolian
Craigneil
Black Clauchrie
Garwall Hill
Palgowan
Craignaw
Mains of Tig
Water of Tig
Ballochmorrie
Loch Neldricken
Ballantrae
Auchairne
Balkissock
Shiel Hill
Barrhill
Feoch Burn
Loch Goosey
PARK
Buchan Hill
Loch Valley
Glen Trool Lodge
Downan Point
Glenapp Castle
Smyrton
Lochton
Eldrick
Corwar House
30
22
Kilantringan Loch
Beneraird
439
Mulldonoch
Craigie Fell
Milljoan Hill
Drumlamford Loch
Glentrool
Lamachan Hill
716
Carlock Hill
Altimeg Hill
Chirmorrie
Drumlamford Ho
Bargrennan
Larg Hill
Millfore
Glen App
Loch Dornal
Loch Ochiltree
Pulniskie Burn
Larne & Belfast
Finnarts Point
Milleur Point
Loch Maberry
Clachaneasy
Larg
Markdhu
STANDING STONES
Polbae
D U M F R I
Garlick Hill
Corsewall Point
Miltonise
Knockville
Barnhills
LOCH RYAN
Glenwhilly
Knowe
North Cairn
Dalnigap
Urrall Fell
Southern Upland Way
Penninghame
Garlies Castle
A712
South Cairn
Corsewall
Kirkcolm
Cairn Point
Cairnryan
Glenrazie
Boreland
Dallash
Airies
Ervie
Main Water of Luce
Cross Water of Luce
Black Burn
Carseriggan
Cumloden
Portobello
A718
St Mary's Croft
Braid Fell
Artfield Fell
Challoch
Minnigaff
Bargaly
Soleburn Bridge
Beoch Burn
Balminnoch
Newton Stewart
Blackcraig
Knocknain
Leswalt
Culvennan Fell
Cairnsmore
B7043
Innermessan
New Luce
Tarf Bridge
Loch Ronald
Shennanton
Nether Barr
Palnure
LOCHNAW
Auchmantle
Benfield
Linn of Barhoise
A718
Lochinch Castle
A751
Galdenoch
Craig Fell
15
Baltersan
Spittal
Stranraer
Black Loch
CASTLE KENNEDY
White Loch
Carscreugh
Barlae
Craighlaw
Kirkcowan
Barraer
Portslogan
Loch Magillie
Castle Kennedy
25
Tarf Water
Causeway End
Barholm
Broadsea Bay
Soulseat Loch
Dunragit Moor
Whitecairn
Carsegowan
Creetown
Whiteleys
Dunragit
Demaglar Loch
Spittal
ABBEY
Bishop Burn
Lochans
Whitecrook
Glenluce
STONE CIRCLE
Black Head
Kildrochet
Genoch
Knock Moss
Culquhirk
Wigtown Sands
Dunskey Burn
Cairn Pat
B7077
Genoch Square
B7084
CASTLE OF PARK
A747
Knock Fell
Bladnoch
B7005
MARTYRS' MONUMENT
Dinvin
Colfin
Whitefield Loch
Fell Loch
Portpatrick
DUNSKEY
Awhirk
A716
Sands of Luce
OLD PLACE OF MOCHRUM
Bladnoch
Wigtown
Stoneykirk
Crow's Nest
Castle Loch
Corsemalzie
Baldoon Sands
Port of Spittal Bay
Auchenmalg
Mochrum Loch
Malzie
B7005
B7052
Balgreggan
Sandhead
Auchenmalg Bay
Barnbarroch
Kirkinner
Orchardton
Cairngarroch Bay
Alticry
Culshabbin
Loch Head
Whauphill
Stewarton
Money Head
CHAPEL FINIAN
Elrig Loch
B7052
KIRKMADRINE STONES
A747
Elrig
MOTTE OF DRUCHTAG
Kirkland of Longcastle
Clachanmore
Sorbie
Ardwell
L U C E B A Y
Barr Point
Mochrum
Airyhassen
T H E
Garlieston
Ardwell Bay
Chapel Rossan
ARDWELL HOUSE
STANDING STONES
M A C H A R S
Drumbreddan Bay
Logan
Danger Zone
Port William
White Loch
Barwinnock
A746
Cults
Balgowan
New England Bay
Castlewigg
Mull of Logan
LOGAN BOTANIC GARDENS
Barsalloch Point
FORT
Monreith
B7021
Port Logan
Terally
Monreith Bay
Craigdhu
RISPAIN CAMP
PRIORY
Whithorn
A716
A747
Clanyard Bay
Kilstay
Cairndoon
Glasserton
Fell of Carleton
B7004
Kirkmaiden
Laggantalluch Head
Drummore
Kidsdale
Damnaglaur
Cailiness Point
St Ninian's Cave
Port Castle Bay
B7041
Maryport
Cutcloy
Crammag Head
Dunman
Burrow Head
Scares
Devil's Bridge
Portankill
Nick of Kindram
East Tarbert
West Tarbert
Mull of Galloway
A77
A714
B734
B741
B7044
B7027
B738
B798
A75
B735
B733
B7085
B7084
B7042
B7063
Rinns of Galloway

DUMFRIES & GALLOWAY
SOLWAY FIRTH
WIGTOWN BAY
Dumfries
Castle Douglas
Kirkcudbright
Dalbeattie
New Galloway
Gatehouse of Fleet
Thornhill
Moniaive
St John's Town of Dalry
Carsphairn
Penpont
Closeburn
Dunscore
Holywood
Locharbriggs
Maxwelltown
New Abbey
Kirkbean
Crossmichael
Parton
Mossdale
Laurieston
Twynholm
Tongland
Ringford
Dundrennan
Auchencairn
Palnackie
Rockcliffe
Kippford or Scaur
Colvend
Southerness
Crocketford or Ninemile Bar
Kirkpatrick Durham
Springholm
Haugh of Urr
Clatteringshaws
Forest of Ae
Dalbeattie Forest
Criffell 569
Maryport
Flimby
Workington
Danger Zone
Abbey Head
Little Ross
Balcary Point
Hestan Island
Mersehead Sands
Barnhourie Sands
Borron Point
Southerness Point
0 2 4 6 8 10 miles
0 2 4 6 8 10 km
21 22 23 24 25
A B C D E F G
68
69

12
13
14
15
16
A
B
C
D
E
F
G
72
73
Bellochantuy
Meall Buidhe
374
ABBEY (RUINS)
Saddell
Saddell Bay
Lussa Loch
Corrylach
Killocraw
Sgreadan Hill
397
KINTYRE
Tangy Loch
Tangy
Skeroblingarry
Ballochgair
Ugadale Point
Westport
Low Ballivain
Drumgarve
Glen Lussa
Callyburn
Machrihanish Bay
A83
Kilchenzie
Peninver
Ardnacross Bay
East Darlochan
Kilmichael
B842
Campbeltown (Machrihanish)
Drumore
Machrihanish
Campbeltown
Witchburn
Campbeltown Loch
Davaar Island
Drumlemble
B843
Dalivaddy
Kilkerran
Davaar
Chiscan
Glenramskill
Knocknaha
New Orleans
Oatfield
Kilchrist
Beinn Ghuilean
352
Earadale Point
Chiscan Water
The Slate
385
Arinarach Hill
Killellan
Cnoc Moy
446
Rubha Duin Bhain
Largybaan
Conie Water
Conie Glen
Cnoc Reamhar
277
Cnoc Odhar
Glen Kerran
Feochaig
Ru Stafnish
Glen Breackerie
Brecklate
Sheanachie
Keprigan
Kildavie
Strone Glen
Carrine
Macharioch
Polliwilline Bay
Beinn na Lice
428
Keil
Southend
Mull of Kintyre
Garveld
Feorlan
Carskey Bay
Borgadelmore Point
Sanda Sound
Sheep Island
Sanda Island
Ballycastle (proposed)
KILBRANNAN SOUND
Machrie Bay
MACHRIE MOOR STONE CIRCLES
Ard Bheinn
512
Tormore
KING'S CAVE
Ballymichael
Bhreac
HUT CIRCLES
Cnoc a'Chapuill
417
Torbeg
Shiskine
FORT
ARRAN
Blackwaterfoot
Drumadoon Bay
Kilpatrick
Brown Head
A841
Glen Scorrodale
Tighvein
458
Corriecravie
CAIRN BAN
Sliddery
Kilmory Water
Lagg
Glen Ashdale
CHAMBERED CAIRNS
Shannochie
Bennan Head
Levencorroch
Sound of Pladda
Pladda
Kildonan
Dippin
Dippin Head
Largybeg
Largybeg Point
Largymore
Whiting Bay
Knockenkelly
Kiscadale
Kingscross
Kingscross Point
Glenkiln
Benlister Glen
Lamlash
Lamlash Bay
Margnaheglish
Clauchlands
Holy Isle
Ailsa Craig
Bennane Head
Ballantrae Bay
Ballantrae
Downan Point
Larne
Belfast
Finnarts Point
Milleur Point
Glen App
Corsewall Point
Barnhills
North Cairn
B738
Corsewall
Kirkcolm
LOCH RYAN
South Cairn
Dounan Bay
Airies
Ervie
A718
Cairn Point
Cairnryan
B798
Portobello
St Mary's Croft
Soleburn Bridge
Knocknain
Leswalt
Slouchnawen Bay
B7043
LOCHNAW
A718
B738
Stranraer
Broadsea Bay
Portslogan
A77
Whiteleys
0 2 4 6 8 10 miles
0 2 4 6 8 10 km

17
18
19
20
21
74
A
B
C
D
E
F
G
68
64
65
STRATHCLYDE
CARRICK
GALLOWAY
FOREST
PARK
DUMFRIES & GALLOWAY
Lady Isle
Ayr Bay
Heads of Ayr
Culzean Bay
Maidenhead Bay
Turnberry Bay
Troon
Barassie
Loans
Symington
Bogend
Coodham
Craigie
Boydston
Whitelees
Middleyard
Auchmannoch Muir
Distinkhorn
Wedder Hill
Mid Hill
Dun Rig
Netherwood
Adamhill
Lochlea
Blairkip
Rosemount
Fail
Monkton
Prestwick
Mossgiel
Mauchline
Ballochmyle
Sorn
Nethershield
Wellwood
Tarbolton
Failford
Catrine
Gilmilnscroft
Boghead
Prestwick
New Prestwick
Mossblown
Barskimming
Darnconner
Cronberry
St Quivox
Whitletts
Auchincruive
Stair
Auchinleck
Carbellow
Annbank
Trabboch
Ochiltree
Holmhead
Lugar
Logan
AYR
WALLACE TOWER
Belston
Sundrum
Schaw
Cumnock
Netherthird
Seafield
Holmston
Joppa
Coylton
Drongan
Dalblair
Alloway
Burnton
Skares
Lagg
Fisherton
Dunure
Brown Carrick Hill
Nether Auchendrane
Mount Oliphant
Sinclairston
Lochhill
Dunure Mains
Sauchrie
Culroy
Dalrymple
Hollybush
Littlemill
Carsgailoch Hill
Pathhead
ELECTRIC BRAE
Minishant
Skeldon
Rankinston
New Cumnock
Knoweside
Stannery Knowe
Dalgig
Connel Park
Afton Bridgend
CULZEAN CASTLE & COUNTRY PARK (NTS)
Pennyglen
Grimmet
Dalvennan
Kilmein Hill
Patna
Lethanhill
Laight
Burnside
Maybole
Maidens
Morriston
Kirkmichael
Waterside
Maneight
Loch Spallander Reservoir
Benbeoch
TURNBERRY
Kirkoswald
CROSSRAGUEL ABBEY
SOUTER JOHNNIE'S COTTAGE (NTS)
Keirs Hill
Burnton
Clawfin
Enoch Hill
Blackcraig Hill
Crosshill
Blairquhan
Dalmellington
Craigdarroch
Turnberry
Cloyntie
Gass
Straiton
Bogton Loch
Windy Standard
Craigoch
Kirk Hill
Dalcairnie
Tooden Hill
Afton Resr
Kilkerran
Craigengillan
Wallacetown
Dipple
Dowhill
Craig
Maratz Hill
Deil's Elbow
Ness Glen
Low Craighead
Dailly
Tairlaw
Benbrack
Eriff
Chapeldonan
Bargany
Grangeston
Old Dailly
Penkill
Hadyard Hill
Garleffin Fell
Loch Finlas
Loch Bradan Reservoir
Loch Doon
Cairnsmore of Carsphairn
Dodd Hill
Girvan
Penwhapple Reservoir
Saugh Hill
Linfern Loch
Drumjohn
Glendoune
Glengennet
North Balloch
Lamloch
Black Shoulder
Black Neuk
Glendrissaig
South Balloch
Waterhead
Craiglee
LOCH DOON
Brochloch
Craig of Knockgray
Kennedy's Pass
Ardwell
Pinminnoch
Changue Forest
Shiel Hill
Coran of Portmark
Garryhorn
Carsphairn
Knockgray
Grey Hill
Barr
Nick of the Balloch Pass
Shalloch
Starr
Loch Head
Loch Riecawr
Marscalloch Hill
Meaul
Bardennoch
Polmaddie Hill
Shalloch on Minnoch
Loch Macaterick
Pinmore
Kendoon Loch
Dalshangan
Carleton Fishery
Aldons
Daljarrock
Carlin's Cairn
Kirriereoch Hill
Poundland
Pinwherry
Kirriereoch Loch
Corserine
Forrest Lodge
Colmonell
Dalreoch
Loch Harrow
Burnhead
Carsfad Loch
Craigneil
Glenduisk
Merrick
Loch Enoch
Millfire
Rhinns of Kells
Loch Dungeon
Knocknalling
Mains of Tig
Ballochmorrie
Black Clauchrie
Loch Moan
Garwall Hill
Palgowan
Craignaw
Meikle Millyea
Earlstoun Loch
Loch Neldricken
Balkissock
Shiel Hill
Barrhill
Loch Goosey
Eldrick
Buchan Hill
Loch Valley
St John's Town of Dalry
Garroch
Lochton
Corwar House
Glen Trool Lodge
Darrou
Glenlee
Beneraird
Glentrool
Mulldonoch
Loch Dee
Craigencallie
Bennan
BRUCE'S STONE
New Galloway
Drumlamford Loch
Lamachan Hill
Clatteringshaws Loch
Chirmorrie
Drumlamford Ho
Bargrennan
Larg Hill
Darnaw
Cairnsmore of Dee
KENMURE
Clatteringshaws
Loch Maberry
Loch Dornal
Loch Ochiltree
Pulnskie Burn
Millfore
Forest Drive (summer only)
Markdhu
Clachaneasy
Larg
STANDING STONES
Polbae
Garlick Hill
WILD GOAT PARK
Miltonise
Knowe
Knockville
Round Fell
Shaw Hill
Black Water of Dee
Bennan
Glenwhilly
Fell of Fleet
Dalnigap
Urrall Fell
Penninghame
Garlies Castle
Craignelder
Loch Grannoch
Loch Fleet
Auchencloy Hill
Airie Hill
Stroan Loch
Slogarie
Glenrazie
Boreland
Cumloden
Dallash
Loch Skerrow
Artfield Fell
Carseriggan
Challoch
Cairnsmore of Fleet
Bargaly
Minnigaff
Newton Stewart
Blackcraig
Balminnoch
New Luce
Tarf Bridge
Culvennan Fell
Loch Ronald
Cairnsmore
Door of Cairnsmore
White Top of Culreoch
Darngarroch
Auchmantle
Shennanton
Benfield
Nether Barr
Palnure
Castle Kennedy
Galdenoch
Linn of Barhoise
Baltersan
Loch Whinyeon
Crag Fell
Barraer
Spittal
Castramont
Carscreugh
Barlae
Craighlaw
Kirkcowan
Causeway End
Glenquicken Moor
Glengap
Dunragit Moor
Whitecrook
Glenluce
Dernaglar Loch
ABBEY
Spittal
STONE CIRCLE
Carsegowan
GEM ROCK MUSEUM
Creetown
Cassencarie
Glen
Lauchentyre
Barlay
Gatehouse
Dunragit
A70
A71
A75
A76
A77
A78
A79
A712
A713
A714
A719
A762
B7000
B7023
B7024
B7027
B7034
B7035
B7036
B7045
B7046
B705
B729
B730
B734
B741
B742
B743
B744
B796

STRATHCLYDE
DUMFRIES AND GALLOWAY
NITHSDALE
LOWTHER HILLS
Middleyard
Crosshands
Blairkip
Lochlea
Mossgiel
Mauchline
Ballochmyle
Sorn
Catrine
Failford
Barskimming
Gilmilnscroft
Netherwood
Nethershield
Nether Wellwood
Smallburn
Muirkirk
Kames
Glenbuck
Parish Holm
Hazelside
Glespin
Redshaw
Carmacoup
Glentaggart
Crawfordjohn
Boghead
Darnconner
Auchinleck
Cronberry
Carbellow
Ochiltree
Schaw
Holmhead
Lugar
Logan
Cumnock
Netherthird
Drongan
Burnton
Skares
Sinclairston
Dalblair
Littlemill
Rankinston
Lochhill
Pathhead
New Cumnock
Afton Bridgend
Connel Park
Laight
Dalgig
Burnside
Maneight
Waterside
Benbeoch
Burnton
Clawfin
Dalmellington
Craigdarroch
Fingland
Kirkland
Lagrae
Kirkconnel
Kelloholm
Drambuie
Crawick
Sanquhar
Ulzieside
Corsebank
Carco
Wanlockhead
Leadhills
Lettershaws
Crawford
Abington
Cold Chapel
Wandel
Roberton
Newton
Wiston
Elvanfoot
Glenochar
Watermeeting
Mennock
Eliock
Ardoch
Enterkinfoot
Durisdeer
Gateslack
Breckonside
Polgown
Dalgonar
Glenmanna
Holm of Drumlanrig
Carronbridge
Dabton
Thornhill
Burnhead
Penpont
Gatelawbridge
Auchenbrack
Auchenhessnane
Benbuie
Clonrae
Tynron
Keir Mill
Closeburn
Croalchapel
Carroch
Moniaive
Crawfordton
Kirkland
Craigdarroch
Glencrosh
Crossford
Barndennoch
Blackwood
Glenhead
Allanton
Dunscore
Milton
Stroquhan
Speddoch
Sundaywell
Castlefairn
Holmhead
Lochurr
Waterhead
Craigenputtock
Drumwhirn
Corriedoo
St John's Town of Dalry
Bogue
Blackcraig
Eriff
Drumjohn
Lamloch
Brochloch
Carsphairn
Garryhorn
Knockgray
Bardennoch
Dalshangan
Forrest Lodge
Burnhead
Knocknalling
Garroch
Glenlee
Craigencallie
New Galloway
Balmaclellan
Clatteringshaws
Knocklearn
Gibbshill
Corsock
Slongaber
Margreig
Scaur
Glen
Shawhead
Terregles
DUMFRIES
Maxwelltown
Holywood
Newtonairds
Gribton
Locharbriggs
New Bridge
Cargenbridge
Goldielea
Lochfoot
Henderland
Crofts
Brooklands
Brae
Crocketford or Ninemile Bar
Merkland
Square Point
Glenlair
Drumrash
Walton Park
Kirkpatrick Durham
Springholm
Milton
Beeswing
Dalskairth
Cargen
Mabie
Gillfoot
Kirkconnell
Shambellie
New Abbey
Kinharvie
Bennan
Mossdale
Parton
Slogarie
Craig
Dallash
Crossmichael
Auchendolly
Old Bridge of Urr
Hermitage
Stonehouse
Kirkgunzeon
Haugh of Urr
Mollance
Clarebrand
Laurieston
Glenlochar
Townhead of Greenlaw
Hillowton
Darngarroch
Castle Douglas
Dalbeattie
Buchan
Bridge of Dee
Castramont
Rusko
Barlay
Ringford
Gatehouse
Barcaple
Cairnsmore
Bargaly
Spittal
Barholm
Creetown
Cassencarie
Wigtown
Glen
Lauchentyre
Palnackie
Gelston
Caulkerbush
Kirkbean
A76
A70
A713
A702
A712
A762
A75
A711
A710
A745
A74(M)
M74
21
22
23
24
25
75
67
65
A
B
C
D
E
F
G

BORDERS
ETTRICK FOREST
DUMFRIES AND GALLOWAY
Selkirk
Hawick
Moffat
Lockerbie
Lochmaben
Langholm
Annan
Gretna
Longtown
Brampton
Newcastleton
Canonbie
Ecclefechan
Eskdalemuir
Beattock
Tweedsmuir
Ettrickbridge
Yarrowford
Broadmeadows
Yarrow
Yarrow Feus
Mountbenger
Dryhope
Cappercleuch
Tibbie Shiels Inn
Birkhill
Muchra
Crosslee
Cacrabank
Hopehouse
Ettrick
Ettrickhill
Buccleuch
Roberton
Borthwickbrae
Burnfoot
Branxholm Bridgend
Branxholme
Newmill
Harwood on Teviot
Broadhaugh
Northhouse
Craik
Howpasley
Teviothead
Castleweary
Linhope
Mosspaul Hotel
Hermitage
Newlands
Steele Road
Dinlabyre
Castleton
Kershopefoot
Kershope Forest
Cauldside
Nook
Catlowdy
Rowanburn
Oakshaw Ford
Haggbeck
Roadhead
Lyneholmeford
Stapleton
Kirkcambeck
Boltonfellend
Hethersgill
Kirklinton
Smithfield
Westlinton
Todhills
Scaleby
Scalebyhill
Laversdale
Irthington
Newtown
Blackford
Harker
Houghton
Kingstown
Rockcliffe
Cargo
Monkhill
Kirkandrews-upon-Eden
Grinsdale
Linstock
Little Corby
Hayton
Newby East
Burgh by Sands
Longburgh
Boustead Hill
Glasson
Port Carlisle
Bowness-on-Solway
Bowness Common
Anthorn
Whitrigg
Cardurnock
Grune Point
Drumburgh
Easton
Fingland
Torduff Point
Sarkfoot Point
Rockcliffe Marsh
Blackshaw Bank
Solway Firth
Eastriggs
Dornock
Rigg
Springfield
Gretna Green
Hollee
Kirkpatrick-Fleming
Creca
Kirtlebridge
Brydekirk
Eaglesfield
Chapelknowe
Milltown
Evertown
Solwaybank
Wallacehall
Springkell
Waterbeck
Middlebie
Burnswark
Tundergarth Mains
Bankshill
Dunnabie
Callisterhall
Bigholms
Auchenrivock
Collin Hags
Debate
Paddockhole
Gillenbie
Corrie Common
Heithat
Corsehill
Boreland
Sibbaldbie
Hangingshaw
Dinwoodie Mains
Johnstonebridge
Annandale Water
Newton
St Ann's
Poldean
Laverhay
Dumcrieff
Craigieburn
Capplegill
Bodesbeck
Granton House
Ericstane
Oliver
Hearthstane
Stanhope
Glenbreck
Talla Linnfoots
Meggethead
Kirkstile
Arkleton
Bentpath
Billholm
Allangillfoot
Castle O'er
Castle O'er Forest
Holm
Garwald
Garwaldwaterfoot
Davington
Fingland
Glendearg
Foulbog
Nether Dalgliesh
Glenkerry
Langshawburn
Craigcleuch
Jamestown
Craik Forest
Templand
Cumrue
Millhousebridge
Nethermill
Kirkland
Blackacre
Heck
Hightae
Castlemilk
Kettleholm
Dalton
Carrutherstown
Clarencefield
Ruthwell
Cummertrees
Powfoot
Mouswald
Cleuchbrae
Woodside
Collin
Torthorwald
Racks
Bankend
Shearington
Blackshaw
Philiphaugh
Aikwood Tower
Sundhope
Kirkhope
Gilmanscleuch
Newburgh
Ashkirk
Woll
Lindean
Midlem
Lilliesleaf
Clerklands
Riddell
Hassendean
Clarilaw
Appletreehall
Wilton
Borthwickshiels
Deanburnhaugh
Grey Mare's Tail
Devil's Beef Tub
James Hogg Monument
Telford Memorial
Carlyle's Birthplace
Hart Fell
Broad Law
White Coomb
Culter Fell
Loch Skeen
St Mary's Loch
Megget Reservoir
Talla Resr
Fruid Resr
Black Esk Resr
A7
A74(M)
A701
A708
A709
A75
A6071
A69
B709
B7009
B7068
B723
B722
B725
B7020
B6357
B6318
B6399
26
27
28
29
30
60
61
70
75
76

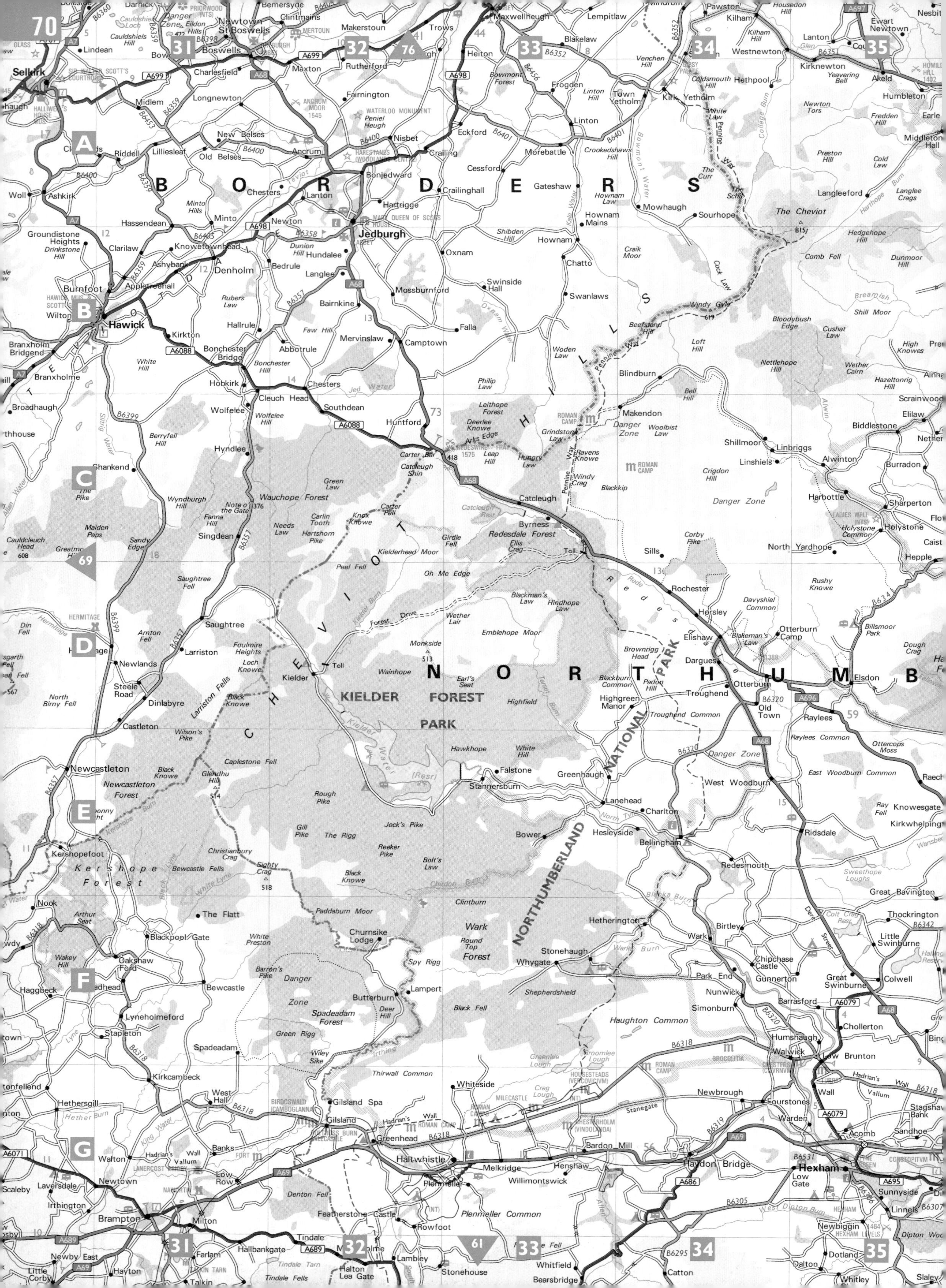

70
31
32
33
34
35
76
69
61
A
B
C
D
E
F
G
BORDERS
NORTHUMB
CHEVIOT HILLS
KIELDER FOREST PARK
NORTHUMBERLAND NATIONAL PARK
Selkirk
Lindean
Newtown St Boswells
Boswells
Bemersyde
Clintmains
Makerstoun
Trows
Maxwellheugh
Lempitlaw
Pawston
Kilham
Lanton
Ewart
Newtown
Nesbit
Westnewton
Kirknewton
Akeld
Humbleton
Charlesfield
Maxton
Rutherford
Heiton
Blakelaw
Frogden
Linton
Town Yetholm
Kirk Yetholm
Hethpool
Midlem
Longnewton
Fairnington
Eckford
Nisbet
Crailing
Morebattle
Riddell
Lilliesleaf
New Belses
Old Belses
Ancrum
Bonjedward
Cessford
Gateshaw
Mowhaugh
Sourhope
Langleeford
The Cheviot
Woll
Ashkirk
Chesters
Lanton
Crailinghall
Hartrigge
Minto
Newton
Jedburgh
Hownam
Hownam Mains
Hassendean
Groundistone Heights
Clarilaw
Knowetownhead
Denholm
Bedrule
Hundalee
Oxnam
Chatto
Ashybank
Appletreehall
Burnfoot
Wilton
Hawick
Langlee
Mossburnford
Swinside Hall
Swanlaws
Bairnkine
Kirkton
Hallrule
Falla
Mervinslaw
Camptown
Branxholm Bridgend
Bonchester Bridge
Abbotrule
Branxholme
Hobkirk
Chesters
Cleuch Head
Southdean
Blindburn
Broadhaugh
Wolfelee
Huntford
Makendon
Hyndlee
Carter Bar
Shillmoor
Linbriggs
Alwinton
Burradon
Biddlestone
Shankend
Catcleugh
Harbottle
Sharperton
Holystone
Byrness
Singdean
Sills
North Yardhope
Hepple
Rochester
Horsley
Saughtree
Otterburn Camp
Elishaw
Larriston
Dargues
Newlands
Kielder
Otterburn
Elsdon
Steele Road
Dinlabyre
Troughend
Highgreen Manor
Old Town
Raylees
Castleton
Newcastleton
Falstone
Stannersburn
Greenhaugh
West Woodburn
Lanehead
Charlton
Bower
Hesleyside
Bellingham
Ridsdale
Kershopefoot
Redesmouth
Nook
The Flatt
Hetherington
Birtley
Blackpool Gate
Churnsike Lodge
Wark
Stonehaugh
Whygate
Chipchase Castle
Gunnerton
Park End
Nunwick
Simonburn
Oakshaw Ford
Haggbeck
Bewcastle
Lampert
Butterburn
Barrasford
Chollerton
Lyneholmeford
Stapleton
Spadeadam
Humshaugh
Walwick
Low Brunton
Kirkcambeck
Whiteside
West Hall
Gilsland Spa
Newbrough
Fourstones
Wall
Hethersgill
Gilsland
Greenhead
Warden
Acomb
Sandhoe
Banks
Walton
Haltwhistle
Melkridge
Henshaw
Bardon Mill
Haydon Bridge
Hexham
Newtown
Laversdale
Scaleby
Low Row
Willimontswick
Irthington
Brampton
Milton
Featherstone Castle
Rowfoot
Low Gate
Sunnyside
Linnels
Newbiggin
Tindale
Hallbankgate
Farlam
Lambley
Whitfield
Catton
Dotland
Dalton
Newby East
Halton Lea Gate
Stonehouse
Bearsbridge
Whitley
Little Corby
Hayton
Talkin

36
37
38
39
40
77
A
B
C
D
E
F
G
0 2 4 6 8 10 miles
0 2 4 6 8 10 km
South Hazelrigg
East Horton
Warenton
Bellshill
Adderstone
Bradford
Spindlestone
Burton
Seahouses
North Sunderland
Elford
Newham Hall
West Fleetham
Beadnell
Benthall
Beadnell Bay
Greendykes
Twizell House
Warenford
Newham
Newstead
Swinhoe
Wandon
Chatton
Chillingham
CHILLINGHAM PARK
Rosebrough
Chathill
Tughall
Ellingham
High Newton by-the-Sea
Snook Point
Preston
Newtown
Lilburn Tower
Hepburn
Wandylaw
Brunton
Newton Haven
Low Newton-by-the-Sea
Embleton Bay
Cateran Hill
Brownieside
Middle Moor
Christon Bank
East Lilburn
Old Bewick
Bewick Moor
North Charlton
Embleton
DUNSTANBURGH (NT)
New Bewick
West Ditchburn
South Charlton
Dunstan
Craster
Rock
Rennington
Stamford
Cullernose Point
Eglingham
Beanley
HOWICK HALL
Howick
Howick Haven
Brandon
Powburn
East Bolton
Shipley
Littlehoughton
Branton
HULNE PRIORY
Hulne Park
Longhoughton Steel
Glanton
Bolton
ALNWICK ABBEY
Alnwick
Denwick
Longhoughton
Boulmer
Boulmer Haven
Abberwick
Hawkhill
Whittingham
Broome Wood
Lesbury
Thrunton
CALLALY CASTLE
Alnmouth Sta.
Bilton
Alnmouth
Alnmouth Bay
Alnwick Moor
Callaly
Thrunton Wood
Edlingham
Shilbottle
High Buston
Lorbottle Hall
Long Crag
Bigges' Pillar
Birling
Lorbottle
Eastfield Hall
Warkworth
Cartington
Newton-on-the-Moor
Coquet Island
Gloster Hill
Amble
Guyzance
Snitter
Shirlaw Pike
Swarland
Morwick Hall
Hauxley
Forest
CRAGSIDE (NT)
Nelly's Moss Lakes
Old Swarland
North Togston
Hauxley Haven
Acklington
Radcliffe
Rothbury
North End
Togston
Whitton
Longframlington
Felton
Broomhill
Hadston Carrs
Tosson
Pauperhaugh
South Broomhill
Chevington Drift
East Thirston
Red Row
BRINKBURN
Low Hesleyhurst
Eshott
Druridge Bay
West Chevington
Forestburn Gate
Widdrington
Causey Park
Coldrife
Wingates
Longhorsley
Earsdon Moor
The Scars
Widdrington Sta.
Cresswell
R L A N D
Fontburn Resr
Fenrother
Tritlington
Ulgham
Snab Point
Ellington
Espley Hall
Lynemouth
Ewesley Burn
Stanton
Netherwitton
Hebron
Todd Hill
Longhirst
Beacon Point
Woodhorn
Longwitton
QUEEN ELIZABETH II
Rothley
Pigdon
Pegswood
ASHINGTON
Newbiggin-by-the-Sea
Hart Burn
Bothal
Hirst
Scots' Gap
Hartburn
Throphill
Mitford
Morpeth
Sheepwash
North Seaton
NEWMINSTER
Shadfen
Stakeford
Middleton
Guide Post
Cambois
Scotland Gate
Wansbeck
Middleton Bank Top
Meldon
Tranwell
Hepscott
Clifton
East Sleekburn
BOLAM LAKE
West Edington
Bedlington
BLYTH
Whalton
Nedderton
PLESSEY WOODS
Cowpen
Bebside
Saltwick
Newsham
East Hartford
Belsay
BELSAY HALL
Ogle
Stannington
Shankhouse
Nelson Village
New Hartley
Cramlington
Seaton Sluice
Hartley
Seaton Delaval
Black Heddon
Westgate
New Horton Grange
Higham Dykes
Milbourne
St Mary's or Bait Island
Ingoe
Berwick Hill
Brenkley
Danger Zone
Seaton Burn
Dudley
Seghill
Dinnington
Heugh
Prestwick
Wide Open
Burradon
Backworth
Earsdon
WHITLEY BAY
Fenwick
Ponteland
Stamfordham
Dalton
Hazlerigg
Monkseaton
Hawkwell
Darras Hall
Camperdown
Newcastle (Woolsington)
Killingworth
Shiremoor
New York
Cullercoats
Marden
High Callerton
Ouston
Forest Hall
Benton Square
Preston
TYNEMOUTH
Fawdon
Callerton Lane End
Black Callerton
Longbenton
North Shields
Harlow Hill
Gosforth
Willington
SOUTH SHIELDS
Vallum
Rudchester
Heddon-on-the-Wall
Wallsend
Kenton
Jesmond
Blakelaw
Wallbottle
Horsley
Throckley
NEWCASTLE UPON TYNE
Heaton
Hebburn
Jarrow
Harton
Marsden Bay
Marsden
Newburn
Lemington
STEPHENSON'S BIRTHPLACE
Wylam
Walker
Byker
Newton
Ryton
Ovingham
Monkton
Stella
Crawcrook
Cleadon
Whitburn
Danger Zone
Prudhoe
Blaydon
Swalwell
Dunston
Pelaw
East Boldon
Mickley Square
Winlaton
FELLING
West Boldon
Stocksfield
Greenside
WHICKHAM
GATESHEAD
BOLDON
Whitburn Bay
Coalburns
Barlow
Winlaton Mill
Team Valley
Painshawfield
High Spen
Rowlands Gill
Roker
Hedley on the Hill
Wrekenton
Southwick
Fulwell
Monkwearmouth
Marley Hill
Sunniside
Lamesley
Springwell
Chopwell
Castletown
SUNDERLAND
South Hylton
TYNE & WEAR
Stavanger, Haugesund & Bergen
Göteborg (summer only)
Esbjerg (summer only)
Hamburg (summer only)
Ijmuiden (summer only)
A1
A697
A1068
A189
A197
A196
A192
A193
A1061
A190
A186
A191
A1056
A696
A69
A167
A1058
A187
A167(M)
A6085
A186
A695
A184
A185
A194
A194(M)
A1300
A1018
A183
A692
A195
A1290
B6341
B6346
B6347
B6348
B6349
B1340
B1339
B6345
B6344
B1337
B6343
B6524
B1331
B6318
B6528
B6309
B1318
B1326
B1325
B6316

8
9
10
11
12
A
B
C
D
E
F
G
Eilean Dubh
Balnahard
Kiloran Bay
Oban
Port Ceann a'Gharraidh
COLONSAY
Kiloran
Colonsay
Upper Kilchattan
Lower Kilchattan
L. Fada
Scalasaig
Machrins
Port Lotha
B8086
B8085
B8087
Loch Staosnaig
Balerominmdubh
Rubha Dubh
Sguide Loinne
Garvard
Balerominmore
Eilean Mhucaig
Rubha Ban
PRIORY
Dubh Eilean
Oronsay
Eilean nan Ron
Caolas Mor
Eilean Ghaoideamal
Beinn nan Capull
Cruach na Seil
Glengarrisdale Bay
Bagh Gleann Speireig
Glengarrisdale
Glendebadel Bay
Ben Garrisdale
365
Lussa
Cruach lonnastail
Corpach Bay
Beinn Bhreac
467
Lealt
Lealt Burn
Dubh Bheinn
Tramaig Bay
J U R A
Ardlussa
Rainberg Mor
453
Cruach Sganadail
Inverlussa
Lussa Point
Shian Bay
Lussagiven
Eilean an Rubha
A846
Gleann Dorch
Gleann Aoistail
Beinn Sgaillinish
Loch Righ Mor
Sgeir Mhor a'Bhrein-phuirt
Rubh' an t-Sailein
Tarbert
Loch Tarbert
Tarbert Bay
Rubh' a'Chrois-aoinidh
Creag Nam Fiadh Mor
Keillmor
Glenbatrick
Lagg
Scrinadle
Beinn Bhreac
439
Rubh' a'Chamais
Gatehouse
Rubh' a'Mhail
Rubha Bholsa
Beinn Tarsuinn
Achamore
Danna Island
Sgarbh Breac
364
Jura Forest
Nave Island
Na Peilleirean
Margadale Hill
Beinn an Oir
785
Beinn Shiantaidh
755
Eilean Mor
EILEAN MOR CHAPEL
Ardnave Point
Bunnahabhainn Bay
Loch a'Chnuic Bhric
734
Paps of Jura
Loch an t-Siob
Ardmenish
Gortantaoid Point
Kilmory
Ardnave
Killinallan Point
Bunnahabhainn
Beinn a'Chaolais
Corran
An Dunan
Ardnave Loch
Giur-bheinn
316
Rubh 'an Leim
Ton Mhor
Carraig Bhan
Tayovullin
Killinallan
Ardnahoe
Gleann Asdale
Knockrome
Lowlandman's Bay
Point of
Beinn Bhreac
286
Loch Staoisha
Leargybreck
Sron Garbh
Sanaigmore
Kilnave
Loch Gruinart
Loch na Mile
Rubh 'an Leanachais
Glas Bheinn
561
Eilean Mor
Balulive
Feolin
Eilean Bhride
Leckgruinart
Port Askaig
Feolin Ferry
Braigo
Rubha Lamanais
B8018
Keills
Keils
Small Isles
Smaull
Aoradh
Dubh Bheinn
Loch Finlaggan
Craigens
Craighouse
Ballinaby
Carnduncan
B8017
A846
Eilean nan Gabhar
Grainel
Gruinart Flats
Loch Cam
Ballygrant
Loch Ballygrant
Crackaig
Rubha na Caillich
342
Brat Bheinn
Loch Gorm
I S L A Y
Coul Point
Machir
Aruadh
Foreland
Lyrabus
Moin'a'choire
Esknish
Loch Lossit
Cabrach
Na Cuiltean
Rockside
Redhouses
Sannaig
Kilberry
Ardfin
Jura Ho.
Machir Bay
Kilchoman
Blackrock
A847
Islay Ho.
Beinn Dubh
Rubha na Traille
Conisby
Bridgend
Am Fraoch Eilean
Brosdale Island
Bruichladdich
Cachlaidh Mhor
Sgorr nam Faoileann
Kilchiaran
Bowmore
Neriby
Barr
Beinn na Caillich
Kilchiaran Bay
Loch Indaal
Gartnatra
Cattadale
McArthur's Head
Gearach
Port Charlotte
Cruach
Glas Bheinn
471
Tormisdale
Gartbreck
Ronnachmore
Cluanach
Kilennan
Proaig
Beinn Tart a'Mhill
232
Carn
Lossit
Laggan
Beinn Bhan
471
Beinn Bheigeir
491
Port Mor
Lossit Bay
Rinns of Islay
Nereabolls
Ardtalla
Rubha Liath
Duich
B8016
Beinn Uraraidh
454
West Tarbert Bay
East Tarbert Bay
Easter Ellister
Loch Uraraidh
Claggain Bay
Portnahaven
A847
Trudernish
Tarbert
Port Wemyss
Laggan Bay
A846
Islay (Port Ellen)
Kintour
Creag Bhan
100
Druimyeon Bay
Orsay
Rinns Point
Glenegedale
Sgorr Bhogachain
Loch Uigeadail
Ardmore Point
Ardailly
Rhunahaorine Point
Machrie
KILDALTON CH & CROSSES
Ardmore
Gigha Island
Machrie
Leorin
Beinn Sholum
347
Ardminish
Rubha Mor
Kintra
Leorin Lochs
Eilean a'Chuirn
Craro Island
Cornabus
Ardbeg
Eilean Bhride
ACHAMORE GARDENS
Maol Buidhe
165
Lagavulin
Rubha na Gainmhich
Grob Bagh
Carnmore
A846
Port Ellen
Laphroaig
Cara Island
The Oa
Caolas an Eilein
The Ard
Mull of Cara
Lower Killeyan
Risabus
Texa
Port Chubaird
Loch Kinnabus
Inerval
Mull Of Oa
Rubha nan Leacan
Glenacardoch Point
Bellochantuy
Glenbarr
Bellochantuy Bay
Bellochantuy
Killocraw
Tangy Loch
0
2
4
6
8
10 miles
0
2
4
6
8
10 km

STRATHCLYDE
ARGYLL FOREST PARK
KNAPDALE
KINTYRE
ARRAN
BUTE
LOCH FYNE
KILBRANNAN SOUND
SOUND OF BUTE
FIRTH OF CLYDE
Great Cumbrae
Little Cumbrae
Holy Island
Inchmarnock
Lochgilphead
Ardrishaig
Tarbert
Kennacraig
Whitehouse
Redhouse
Skipness
Claonaig
Carradale
Saddell
Dunoon
Gourock
Kilcreggan
Rosneath
Cove
Garelochhead
Strone
Kilmun
Sandbank
Ardnadam
Hunter's Quay
Kirn
Innellan
Toward
Rothesay
Port Bannatyne
Ardbeg
Craigmore
Kingarth
Kilchattan
Millport
Largs
Skelmorlie
Wemyss Bay
Inverkip
Fairlie
West Kilbride
Seamill
Ardrossan
Saltcoats
Horse Isle
Brodick
Lamlash
Kingscross
Corrie
Lochranza
Pirnmill
Imachar
Blackwaterfoot
Shiskine
Machrie
Dougarie
Kilmartin
Crinan
Bellanoch
Cairnbaan
Kilmichael Glassary
Minard
Furnace
Strachur
Portavadie
Tighnabruaich
Colintraive
Kames
Millhouse
Otter Ferry
Tayvallich
Achahoish
Clachan
Ronachan
Ballochroy
Grogport
Torrisdale
Bunlarie
Glen Chalmadale
Goat Fell 874
Caisteal Abhail 859
Cock of Arran
Garroch Head
Cloch Point
Toward Point
Kames Bay
A83
A886
A815
A880
A885
A8003
A8015
A844
A841
A78
A760
A770
B8024
B8025
B8000
B842
B880
B881
B7048
(summer only)
Douglas, Isle of Man (summer only)
A
B
C
D
E
F
G
13
14
15
16
17
66
74
80

LOCH LOMOND
LOMOND
REGIONAL
PARK
QUEEN ELIZABETH FOREST PARK
Loch Ard
Forest
CENTRAL
FIRTH OF CLYDE
CUNNINGHAME
STRATHCLYDE
KYLE
CAMPSIE FELLS
Kilpatrick Hills
Lennox Forest
Loch Lomond
Lochgoilhead
Ardgoil Estate
The Brack
Ardgartan Forest
Arrochar
Stuckgowan
Ardmay
Coilessan
Tullich Hill
Ben Lomond 974
Ben Reoch 661
Beinn Bhreac 681
Rowardennan Lodge
Glen Douglas
Doune
Inverbeg
Ross Point
Culag
Luss
Glen Luss
Camstraddan
Aldochlay
Rossdhu House
Inchmurrin
Inchconnachan
Inchtavannach
Inchcruin
Inchfad
Inchmoan
Inchcailloch
Torrinch
Balmaha
Pass of Balmaha
Milton
Cashel
Milarrochy
Garadhban Forest
Buchanan Castle
Drymen
Ross Priory
Gartocharn
Duncryne
Caldarvan
Kinlochard
Ledard
Pass of Aberfoyle
Blairhullichan
Aberfoyle
Achray Forest
Dukes Pass
Milton
Duchray
Baleich
Cobleland
Gartmore
Dalmary
Kelty Water
Beinn Uird 596
Beinn Bhreac 578
Port of Menteith
Malling
Lake of Menteith
Inchmahome Priory
Torrie Forest
Blairhoyle
Easter Jand
Thornhill
Tamavoid
Dykehead
Flanders Moss
Easter Poldar
Arnprior
Arngomery
Cauldhame
Kippen
Gargunnock
Garden
Buchlyvie
Arngibbon
Gartachoil
Wrightpark
Balafark
Balfron
Balfron Station
Boquhan
Killearn
Ling Hill
Fintry Hills
Loup of Fintry
Culcreuch
Craigton
Fintry
Gonachan
Gartness
Craighat
Dumgoyne
Baptiston
Blairquhosh
Strathblane
Strathblane Hills
Earl's Seat 578
Dumgoyne Hill
Hart Hill
Fin Glen
Meikle Bin 570
Carron Valley Res
Lecket Hill
Blanefield
Clachan of Campsie
Haughhead
Lennoxtown
Milton of Campsie
Kilsyth
Carbeth
Finnich Glen
Queen's View
Dumbarton Muir
Mugdock
Milngavie
Baldernock
Dougalston
Kinkell
Torrance
Kirkintilloch
Balmore
Cadder
Lenzie
Bearsden
Drumchapel
Bishopbriggs
Auchinloch
Moodiesburn
Maryhill
Springburn
Stepps
Partick
Govan
GLASGOW
Shettleston
Tollcross
RUTHERGLEN
Carmyle
Cambuslang
Uddingston
Castlemilk
Flemington
Pollokshaws
Thornliebank
Giffnock
Clarkston
Carmunnock
Busby
Newton Mearns
Waterfoot
Mearns
Thorntonhall
EAST KILBRIDE
Jackton
Eaglesham
Polnoon
Auldhouse
Rutherend
Chapelton
Torrance
Crutherland
Nerston
Lymekilns
Stonefield
Dechmont Hill
Ardochrig
Corse Hill 376
Laird's Seat
Hareshaw
Caldermill
Drumclog
Dungavel
Mill Rig
Glengavel Reservoir
Strathaven
Lochgoin
Lochgoin Reservoir
Kingswell
Melowther Hill
Dunwan Dam
Ballageich Hill 330
Bennan Loch
Kingsford
Fenwick
Waterside
Tayburn
Pley Moss
Polbaith Burn
Moscow
Newmilns
Darvel
Priestland
Greenholm
Galston
Changue Hill
Sornhill
Distinkhorn
Auchmannoch Muir
Milrig
Middleyard
Wedder Hill
Mid Hill 434
Dun Rig
Middlefield
Netherwood
Crosshands
Mauchline
Mossgiel
Hurlford
Crookedholm
Crossroads
Boydston
Craigie
KILMARNOCK
Kilmaurs
Rowallan
Stewarton
Riccarton
Knockentiber
Springside
Crosshouse
Gatehead
Drybridge
Dundonald
Coodham
Bogend
Whitelees
Symington
Loans
Troon
Barassie
Lady Isle
Monkton
Prestwick
Rosemount
Adamhill
Fail
Irvine
Irvine Bay
Dreghorn
Perceton
Scottish Maritime Museum
Cunninghamhead
Montgreenan
Kilwinning
Eglinton
Stevenston
Saltcoats
Ardrossan
Horse Isle
Brodick
Douglas (summer only)
Dalgarven
Auchentiber
Dunlop
Burnhouse
Barrmill
Lugton
Caldwell
Uplawmoor
Neilston
Malletsheugh
Barrhead
Caplaw
Gleniffer Braes
Howwood
Lochwinnoch
Castle Semple
Kilbirnie
Beith
Glengarnock
Gateside
Highfield
The Den
Dalry
Blair
Giffordland
Munnoch
West Kilbride
Seamill
Portencross
Farland Head
Ardneil Bay
Hunterston
Inner Brigurd Point
Crosbie
Kaim Hill 387
Knockendon Resr
South Hourat
Whitehill
Blairpark
Cock Law
Kelburn Country Centre
Fairlie
Largs
Skelmorlie Aisle
Netherhall
Routenburn
Noddsdale
Rowantree Hill
Hill of Stake 522
Misty Law
Slaty Law
Irish Law 484
Black Law
Muirshiel
Kilbarchan
Johnstone
Milliken Park
Elderslie
Johnstone Castle
PAISLEY
Linwood
Crosslee
Bridge of Weir
Quarrier's Village
Houston
Duchal
Duchal Moor
Carruthmuir
Kilmacolm
Georgetown
Renfrew
Glasgow
Inchinnan
Southbar
Erskine
Bishopton
Langbank
Auchenbothie
Yoker
CLYDEBANK
Duntocher
Old Kilpatrick
Bowling
Cochno
Milton
DUMBARTON
Townend
Crosslet
Renton
Bonhill
Alexandria
Jamestown
Balloch
Cardross
Keppoch
Colgrain
Camis Eskan
Craigendoran
Helensburgh
Cameron
Arden
Daligan
Dumfin
Inverlauren
Blarglas
Shantron
Auchinvennal
Blairnairn
Glen Fruin
Balernock
Shandon
Blairvadach
Rhu
Stroul
Clynder
Rosneath
Camsail
Kilcreggan
Rosneath Point
Cove
Meikle Rahane
Faslane
Mambeg
Glenarn
Garelochhead
Portincaple
Finnart
Glenmallan
Danger Zone
Beinn Eich 702
Edentaggart
Beinn Chaorach 713
Beinn Ruisg 593
Beinn Tharsuinn
Doune Hill 734
Craggan Hill
Argyll's Bowling Green
Loch Long
Stuckbeg
The Lodge
Corrow
Beinn Lochain
Beinn Bheula 779
Cruach nam Miseag
Culimuich
Sgurr a'Choinnich
Carrick
Ardnahein
Corran
Cruach a'Bhuic
Creachan Mor 657
Glen Finart
Barnacabber
Coylet
Ardentinny
Stronchullin Hill 548
Coulport
Ardpeaton
Cnoc a'Mhadaidh 470
Uig
Ardbeg
Orchard
Kilmun
Blairmore
Strone
Strone Point
Holy Loch
Sandbank
Ardnadam
Hunter's Quay
Kirn
Dunloskin
Dunoon
Gourock
GREENOCK
Ardmore
PORT GLASGOW
Cloch Point
Castle Levan
Chrisswell
Lunderston Bay
Ardgowan
Inverkip
Loch Thom
Lurg Moor
Gryfe Reservoirs
Strath Gryfe
Garvock
Auchenfoyle
Cairncurran Hill
Cairncurran
Leap Moor
Corkney Top
Creuch Hill 441
Dunan
Wemyss Point
Wemyss Bay
Innellan
Upper Skelmorlie
Skelmorlie
Bullwood
Toward Point
Meigle
North Burnt Hill
Black Fell
Peat Hill
Queenside Muir
Tomont End
Great Cumbrae
Ballochmartin
Millport
Millport Bay
A82
A811
A81
A821
A873
A875
A809
A891
A803
A807
A879
A814
A813
A815
A880
A885
A8
A78
A770
A761
A737
A726
A736
A760
A735
A77
A71
A719
A759
A76
A724
A725
A749
A89
A74
A73
M8
M80
M898
B835
B822
B818
B834
B821
B8050
B812
B806
B829
B839
B833
B831
B788
B789
B790
B786
B775
B774
B773
B769
B764
B767
B759
B761
B762
B780
B781
B7048
B7047
B707
B706
B777
B778
B785
B751
B7038
B7081
B7064
B708
B730
B744
B7073
B7037
B745
B743
B8032
B826
B8034
B8037
B885
B7036
73
80
81
67
18
19
20
21
22
A
B
C
D
E
F
G

75
23
24
25
81
26
27
Doune
Dunblane
Bridge of Allan
Menstrie
Alva
Tillicoultry
Dollar
Kinross
Loch Leven
Scotlandwell
Auchmuirbridge
Kinglassie
Lochore
Ballingry
Auchterderran
Cardenden
Lochgelly
Cowdenbeath
Kelty
Cleish Hills
Saline
Blairadam Forest
Stirling
Cambusbarron
St Ninians
Bannockburn
Fallin
Cowie
Clackmannan
Alloa
Tullibody
Cambuskenneth
New Sauchie
Kincardine
Airth
Dunmore
Kennet
F I F E
Oakley
Carnock
Dunfermline
Crossford
Cairneyhill
Culross
Torryburn
Valleyfield
Rosyth
Inverkeithing
Charlestown
Limekilns
Aberdour
Burntisland
Dalgety Bay
Inchcolm
North Queensferry
Forth Road Bridge
Forth Bridge
Firth of Forth
Bo'ness
Carriden
Blackness
South Queensferry
Dalmeny
Cramond
EDINBURGH
Kirkliston
Edinburgh (Turnhouse)
Corstorphine
Gogar
Ratho
Hermiston
Juniper Green
Currie
Colinton
Balerno
Fairmilehead
Grangemouth
Falkirk
Larbert
Stenhousemuir
Denny
Dunipace
Bonnybridge
Polmont
Laurieston
Linlithgow
Philpstoun
Winchburgh
Broxburn
Uphall
Livingston
Mid Calder
East Calder
Kirknewton
Bathgate
Armadale
Whitburn
Blackburn
West Calder
Torphichen
Westfield
Avonbridge
Slamannan
Cumbernauld
Caldercruix
Blackridge
Harthill
Fauldhouse
Breich
Stoneyburn
Addiewell
Loganlea
Shotts
Salsburgh
Airdrie
Chapelhall
Calderbank
Holytown
Newhouse
Bellshill
Mossend
Motherwell
Newarthill
Cleland
Newmains
Wishaw
Cambusnethan
Morningside
Overtown
Waterloo
Carluke
Law
Larkhall
Kilncadzow
Braidwood
Crossford
Lanark
New Lanark
Carstairs
Carstairs Junction
Ravenstruther
Carnwath
Newbigging
Dunsyre
Dolphinton
West Linton
Carlops
Penicuik
Pentland Hills Regional Park
L O T H I A N
76
Blyth Bridge
Romannobridge
Lamancha
Leadburn
Kirkdean
Elsrickle
Walston
Libberton
Biggar
Skirling
Broughton
Drumelzier
Coulter
Symington
Thankerton
Covington
Pettinain
Hyndford Bridge
Lesmahagow
Kirkmuirhill
Blackwood
Stonehouse
Coalburn
Douglas
Douglas Water
Rigside
Uddington
Abington
Lamington
Wiston
Roberton
C L Y D E
Tweeddale
68
69
M9
M8
M90
M80
M876
M74
M73
A70
A71
A72
A73
A702
A701
A706
A721
A723

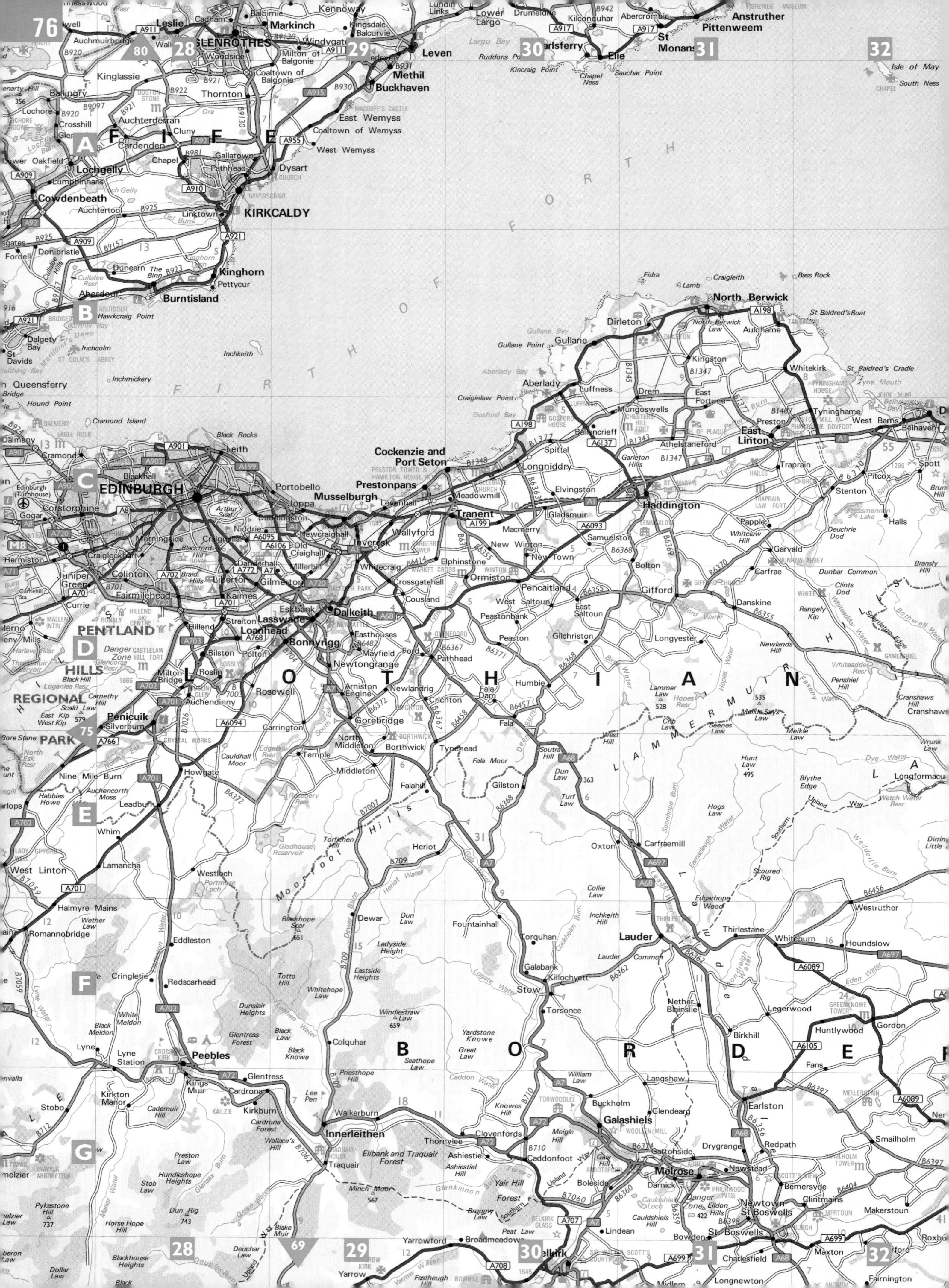

Leslie
GLENROTHES
Markinch
Kennoway
Kingsdale
Balcurvie
Windygates
Milton of Balgonie
Woodside
Coaltown of Balgonie
Auchmuirbridge
Leven
Methil
Buckhaven
Lundin Links
Lower Largo
Largo Bay
Drumeldrie
Kilconquhar
Abercrombie
Anstruther
Pittenweem
St Monans
Elie
Earlsferry
Ruddons Point
Kincraig Point
Chapel Ness
Sauchar Point
Isle of May
South Ness
CHAPEL
Kinglassie
Ballingry
Lochore
Crosshill
Auchterderran
Cluny
Cardenden
Thornton
Chapel
Gallatown
Pathhead
Dysart
RAVENSCRAIG
Lochgelly
Lumphinnans
Lower Oakfield
Cowdenbeath
Auchtertool
Linktown
KIRKCALDY
MACDUFF'S CASTLE
East Wemyss
Coaltown of Wemyss
West Wemyss
F I F E
FIRTH OF FORTH
Donibristle
Fordell
Dunearn
The Binn
Kinghorn
Pettycur
Burntisland
Aberdour
ABERDOUR
Hawkcraig Point
Dalgety Bay
St Davids
Inchcolm
ST COLM'S ABBEY
Inchkeith
Inchmickery
Queensferry
Hound Point
Cramond Island
DALMENY
EAGLE ROCK
Dalmeny
Cramond
Black Rocks
Leith
Fidra
Lamb
Craigleith
Bass Rock
North Berwick
North Berwick Law
St Baldred's Boat
Dirleton
Gullane Bay
Gullane Point
Gullane
Auldhame
Kingston
Whitekirk
St. Baldred's Cradle
Tyne Mouth
Aberlady Bay
Aberlady
Luffness
Drem
East Fortune
Craigielaw Point
Gosford Bay
Mungoswells
Tyninghame
West Barns
Belhaven
GOSFORD HOUSE
Ballencrieff
Athelstaneford
Preston
East Linton
Spittal
Cockenzie and Port Seton
Longniddry
Traprain
Pitcox
Spott
Prestonpans
Musselburgh
Portobello
Joppa
EDINBURGH
Blackhall
Corstorphine
Gogar
Edinburgh (Turnhouse)
Elvingston
Haddington
Stenton
Meadowmill
Tranent
Gladsmuir
Levenhall
Wallyford
Inveresk
Macmerry
Samuelston
Papple
Halls
Deuchrie Dod
Whitelaw Hill
Garvald
NUNRAW ABBEY
Morningside
Craigmillar
Niddrie
Newcraighall
Craighall
New Winton
Elphinstone
New Town
Bolton
Carfrae
Dunbar Common
Bransly Hill
Hermiston
Craiglockhart
Juniper Green
Colinton
Currie
Liberton
Danderhall
Gilmerton
Whitecraig
Crossgatehall
Ormiston
Pencaitland
Gifford
Clints Dod
Fairmilehead
Kaimes
Eskbank
Dalkeith
Cousland
West Saltoun
East Saltoun
Danskine
Rangely Kip
PENTLAND HILLS REGIONAL PARK
Hillend
Straiton
Lasswade
Loanhead
Bonnyrigg
Peastonbank
Peaston
Gilchriston
Longyester
Newlands Hill
Bilston
Polton
Easthouses
Mayfield
Newtongrange
Ford
Pathhead
Penshiel Hill
Whiteadder Resr
Roslin
Milton Bridge
Humbie
L O T H I A N
Auchendinny
Rosewell
Arniston Engine
Newlandrig
Crichton
Fala Dam
Lammer Law
Hopes Resr
Meikle Says Law
Crib Law
Seenes Law
Meikle Law
Cranshaws Hill
Cranshaws
Penicuik
Silverburn
Carrington
Gorebridge
Fala
Scald Law
East Kip
West Kip
Bore Stane
North Middleton
Borthwick
Tynehead
Soutra Hill
West Hill
L A M M E R M U I R
Wrunk Law
Cauldhall Moor
Temple
Middleton
Fala Moor
Dun Law
Hunt Law
Blythe Edge
Longformacus
Nine Mile Burn
Howgate
Falahill
Gilston
Turf Law
Watch Water Resr
Habbies Howe
Auchencorth Moss
Leadburn
Hogs Law
Whim
Torfichen Hill
Heriot
Oxton
Carfraemill
Dirrington Little
Gladhouse Reservoir
West Linton
Lamancha
Westloch
Portmore Loch
Moorfoot Hills
Collie Law
Scoured Rig
Halmyre Mains
Blackhope Scar
Dewar
Dun Law
Fountainhall
Inchkeith Hill
Edgarhope Wood
Westruther
Romannobridge
Eddleston
Ladyside Height
Torquhan
Lauder
Thirlestane
Whiteburn
Houndslow
Lauder Common
Cringletie
Redscarhead
Totto Hill
Eastside Heights
Whitehope Law
Galabank
Killochyett
Stow
Torsonce
Nether Blainslie
Legerwood
GREENKNOWE TOWER
Gordon
White Meldon
Black Meldon
Dunslair Heights
Windlestraw Law
Huntlywood
Birkhill
Glentress Forest
Black Law
Yardstone Knowe
Great Law
Lyne
Lyne Station
Peebles
Black Knowe
Colquhar
Seathope Law
B O R D E R S
Glentress
Kings Muir
Cardrona
Kirkton Manor
Stobo
Priesthope Hill
Caddon Water
William Law
Langshaw
Fans
Cademuir Hill
KAILZIE
Kirkburn
Cardrona Forest
Lee Pen
Walkerburn
Knowes Hill
TORWOODLEE
Buckholm
Glendearg
Earlston
MELLERSTAIN
Smailholm
Innerleithen
Wallace's Hill
Thornylee
Clovenfords
Ashiestiel
Ashiestiel Hill
Galashiels
WOOLLEN MILL
Meigle Hill
Caddonfoot
Gattonside
Drygrange
Redpath
Traquair
TRAQUAIR HOUSE
Elibank and Traquair Forest
Preston Law
DAWYCK ARBORETUM
Hundleshope Heights
Stob Law
Minch Moor
Yair Hill Forest
Gala Hill
ABBOTSFORD
Boleside
Melrose
Newstead
Bemersyde
Darnick
Cauldshiel Loch
Eildon Hills
PRIORWOOD
Newtown St Boswells
Clintmains
Makerstoun
Pykestone Hill
Dun Rig
Horse Hope Hill
Broomy Law
Peat Law
Cauldshiels Hill
Lindean
Bowden
St Boswells
Maxton
Blake Muir
Yarrowford
Broadmeadows
Deuchar Law
Blackhouse Heights
Selkirk
Charlesfield
Yarrow
Dollar Law
Fastheugh Hill
Midlem
Longnewton
Fairnington
SIR WALTER SCOTT'S COURTROOM

33
34
35
36
37
A
B
C
D
E
F
G
0 2 4 6 8 10 miles
0 2 4 6 8 10 km
Barns Ness
Skateraw
Skateraw Harbour
Thorntonloch
Bilsdean
Reed Point
Cove
DUNGLASS CHURCH
Cockburnspath
Siccar Point
Wheat Stack
Telegraph Hill
St Abb's Head (NTS)
Lumsdaine
Coldingham Loch
Meikle Black Law
A1107
Cross Law
Coldingham Moor
Northfield
St Abbs
Coldingham Bay
Ecclaw
Ecclaw Hill
A1
Grantshouse
Coldingham
PRIORY
Way Blackburn Rig
Southern Upland
Heart Law
Laughing Law
Houndwood
Eye Water
Ale Water
Eyemouth
MUS
Cairncross
ABBEY ST TROUT FARM
Horseley Hill
Reston
Abbey St Bathans
Drakemire
Marygold
B6438
Auchencrow
Ayton
Burnmouth
Cockburn Law
EDIN'S HALL BROCH
B6355
Millerton Hill
Ayton Hill
Hilton Bay
Lamberton Beach
A6112
Lintlaw
Lamberton
TITHE BARN
Preston
Chirnsidebridge
Chirnside
Foulden
Mordington
Halidon Hill
Needles Eye
EDROM NORMAN ARCH
Edrom
MANDERSTON
A6105
Whiteadder Water
Clappers
Sharper's Head
RAVENSDOWNE BARRACKS
Berwick-upon-Tweed
DUNS
Duns
Cheeklaw
Allanton
Hutton
Paxton
Tweedmouth
Spittal
Gavinton
Blackadder
B6460
Whitelaw
Sunwick
Choicelee
A6112
B6437
UNION BRIDGE
A698
East Ord
Redshin Cove
Polwarth
Whitsome
Fishwick
Longridge Towers
Sinclair's Hill
Horncliffe
Scremerston
Fogo
Horndean
Thornton Park
Murton
Blackadder Water
NORHAM
Fogorig
Ladykirk
Thornton
Swinton
B6461
B6470
Norham
Cheswick Black Rocks
Allerdean Burn
Shoreswood
West Allerdean
Swintonmill
Upsettlington
Shoresdean
Cheswick
Goswick
Simprim
Grindon
Ancroft
Purves Hall
Leitholm
Felkington
B6354
Berrington
Emmanuel Head
Holy Island or Lindisfarne
LINDISFARNE (NT)
Castle Point
Easter Howlaws
Orange Lane
Duddo
West Mains
Beal
Holy Island Sands
PRIORY
THE HIRSEL GROUNDS & DUNDOCK WOOD
A6112
Bowsden
B6525
Humehall
Eccles
A697
Lennel
Castle Heaton
West Kyloe
Guile Point
Burrows Hole
Legars
A698
Barmoor Lane End
Fenwick
Fenham Flats
Coldstream
Cornhill on Tweed
Pallinsburn House
Etal
B6353
Kyloe Hills
Lowick
Longstone
Birgham
Wark
Crookham
Buckton
Farne Islands
Staple Sound
Ednam
Carham
Branxton
Ford
Elwick
Ross
Budle Bay
Budle Point
Bamburgh
Farne Island
A698
Detchant
Hendersyde Park
Hadden
East Learmouth
FLODDEN FIELD 1513
Holburn
Middleton
Easington
GRACE DARLING MUSEUM
Pressen
NORTHUMBERLAND
Kimmerston
Cockenheugh
Waren Mill
Budle
B1340
Sprouston
B6396
Downham
Howtel
B6352
Flodden
Belford
Rocks
House
Kelso
Mindrum
Pawston
Milfield
Fenton
Doddington
North Hazelrigg
B1342
Spindlestone
Glororum
Seahouses
Burton
Maxwellheugh
Lempitlaw
Kilham
Housedon Hill
A697
Nesbit
Roman Road
South Hazelrigg
Bradford
Swinhoe Burn
North Sunderland
Elford
Heiton
Blakelaw
Kilham Hill
Ewart Newtown
West Horton
East Horton
Warenton
Bellshill
B1341
Newham
Beadnell
B6352
Shotton
Westnewton
Lanton
Coupland
B6349
Adderstone
Lucker
Vencken Hill
B6351
Glen
HOMILDON HILL 1402
Twizell House
West Weetham
Bowmont Forest
Linton Hill
Town Yetholm
Kirk Yetholm
Hethpool
Kirknewton
Yeavering Bell
B6348
Wooler
Humbleton
Wandon
Chatton
Newham
Newstead
Swinhoe
Chathill
Tughall
Newton
Haugh
CHILLINGHAM
70
71

5
6
7
8
9
A
B
C
D
E
F
G
Lochboisdale
Castlebay
Point of Ard
Eag na Maoile
Eilean Mor
Rubha Mor
Bousd
Rubha Sgor-Innis
Sorisdale
Rubh' a'Bhinnein
Torastan
Loch Fada
Bagh na Coille
Cliad Bay
B8072
Grishipoll Bay
Grishipoll
Arnabost
B8071
73
Clabhach
Ballyhaugh
Ben Hogh
104
Hogh Bay
Loch Cliad
B8071
Arinagour
Totamore
Totronald
C O L L
B8070
Loch Eatharna
Feall Bay
Port Mine
Arileod
Uig
Acha
Eilean Ornsay
Calgary Point
Crossapol
Gorton
Caolas Ban
Crossapol Bay
Port na Eatha
Friesland Bay
Gunna
Breachacha
Loch Breachacha
Rubha Fasachd
Port a'Mhurain
Soa
Urvaig
Miodar
Salum Bay
Balephetrish Bay
Sgeir Bharrach
Vaul
Rubha Dubh
Caolas
Balephetrish Hill
Ruaig
The Green
B8069
Brock
Port Ban
Rubha Liath
Hough Bay
B8068
Gott Bay
T I R E E
Soa
Scarinish
Kilkenneth
Moss
Tiree
B8068
Heanish
Saundaig
Heylipoll
Crossapoll
Baugh
Barrapoll
B8065
Hynish Bay
B8067
Balemartine
Balephuil
Mannel
Rinn Thorbhais
Hynish
B8066
SKERRYVORE MUSEUM
Qu
Port na B
Caliach Point
Sunipol
Langamu
Mornish
Cruach Sleibhe
166
Rubha nan Oirean
Calgar
Calgary Bay
B8073
Ensay
Treshnish Point
Treshnish
Beinn Duill
191
Rubh' a'Chaoil
Tost
Rubh' an t-Suibhein
Cairn na Burgh More
Cairn na Burgh Beg
Fladda
Loch Tua
Sgeir a Chaisteil
Eilean Dioghlum
Gometra Ho.
Rubha Maol na Mine
Lunga
Gometra
Treshnish Isles
Maisgeir
Bac Mor or Dutchman's Cap
Bac Beag
Little Colonsay
Staffa
Eilean Dubh
STAFFA (NTS)
Fingal's Cave
Erisgeir
Aird na
Mhi
Reidh Eilean
Eilean Chalbha
MACLEAN'S CROSS
Rubha nan Cearc
Dun
IONA ABBEY
Kintra
Port an Duine Mhairbh
IONA (NTS)
Beinn Chladan
Eorabus
Ruanaich
Fionnphort
Loch na Lathaich
Stac an Aoineidh
Iona
Sound of Iona
Aridhglas
A849
Rubha na Carraig-geire
Fidden
Bunessa
R O S S
Knockvologan
Soa Island
Ardalanish
Erraid
Torr Fada
Ardchiava
Eilean Dubh
Aird Mor
Port Mor
Eilean a'Chalmain
Eilean Mor
Rubh' Ardala
Dearg Sgeir
Torran Rocks
Ruadh Sgeir
West Reef
Na Torrain
McPhail's Anvil
Torran Sgoilte
Sgeir Ghobhlach
Otter Rock
0
2
4
6
8
10 miles
0
2
4
6
8
10 km
Dubh Artach
COLONS
72
Kiloran
Loch an Sgoltaire

Bailetonach
Brunery Hill
Glen Forslan
Gaskan
Scamodale
Meall Mor
759
Rubha Aird Druimnich
Kinlochmoidart
Moidart
Shiel
Gorstanvorran
Mhic Bhuidhe
721
10
11
12
13
14
86
Ockle Point
Ockle
Carn Mor
Beinn Bhreac
240
Ardmolich
Glen
Ghaill
371
Sgurr Ghiubhsachain
497
Resourie
Sanna Point
Sanna
Fascadale
Kilmory
Achateny
Swordle
Ardtoe
Newton of Ardtoe
Shielfoot
Kentra
Kentra Bay
Cliff
Dalnabreck
Dalelia
Carn na Nathrach
786
Glen
Tighnacomaire
Sanna Bay
Achnaha
Meall nan Con
437
Branault
Beinn Bhreac
357
Gorteneorn
Arivegaig
B8044
Acharacle
Clash Moss
Polloch
Glenhurich
Glen Hurich
Druim Garbh
Sgurr Dhomhnuill
888
Portuairk
Achosnich
Beinn an Leathaid
Ardshealach
Achnanellan
Kinlochan
Grigadale
B8007
Meall an Tarmachain
404
313
Loch Mudle
A R D N A M U R C H A N
S U N A R T
A R D G
Sgorr a' Chaorachain
477
Leac Shoilleir
440
Beinn Resipol
845
A
Glen Gour
Beinn na Seilg
342
Kilchoan
Beinn nan Losgann
Camphouse
Lochan nam Fiann
Salen
Resipole
Sgurr nan Cnamh
701
Ormsaigmore
Mingary
Ben Hiant
528
Loch Laga
Tarbert
Strontian
Scotstown
Kilchoan Bay
23
Beinn Bhuidhe
278
Glenbeg
Natural History Centre
Ben Laga
512
B8007
A861
Ardery
Anaheilt
Drumnatorran
Garbh Bheinn
885
Sron Bheag
Ardslignish
Sunart
Ranachan
Strontian
Achnalea
Gearradh
Maclean's Nose
Eilean Mor
Glenborrodale
Laga
Gearr Chreag
340
Woodend
Ardnastang
25
A861
Glen Tarbert
Oronsay
Risga
Carna
Loch
Meall a' Bhroin
Glencripesdale
Eilean Mor
Liddesdale
Achleek
Meall a' Choirein Luachraich
Ardmore Bay
Ardmore Point
Auliston Point
H I G H L A N D
Creach Bheinn
853
Maol Odhar
Bloody Bay
Beinn Ghormaig
452
Taobh Dubh
352
Glas Bheinn
620
765
Meall nan Each
591
B8043
Point
Meall an Inbhire
Tobermory Bay
Rahoy
Beinn Iadain
571
Meall a' Chaise
522
Achagavel
Lochuisge
Fuar Bheinn
B
Mishnish
Tobermory
Calve Island
Barr
Kinloch
Loch Uisge
B8043
Quinish
Achleanan
Ardantiobairt
Gleann Dubh
A884
Beinn Chlaonleud
475
Beach
Meall a' Chaorainn
Loch Uisge
Sgurr Shalachain
Beinn Na Cille
651
Glengalmadale
Rubha na h-Airde Uinnsinn
Camasnacroise
S'Airdhe Beinn
Drimnin
Beinn Bhuidhe
451
Beinn na h-Uamha
464
M O R V E R N
Clounlaid
Mishnish Lochs
Dervaig
Achnadrish
Aros
Durinemast
Sidhean na Raplaich
550
Gleann Geal
Beinn Mheadhoin
739
Loch a' Choire
Ceanna Mor
Shuna Island
Rhemore
Loch Arienas
Claggan
Alltachonaich
Caol Lochan
Speinne Mor
A848
Beinn an t-Sruthain
Creag Bhan Ard
339
Beinn Bhan
400
Ardtornish
Braigh na Glaice Moire
Meall Damh
Sgurr a' Bhuic
569
Cruachan Ceann a' Ghairbh
261
Lettermore
Ardnacross
Killundine
B849
Larachbeg
Kinlochaline
Ardtornish
Beinn a'Chaisil
437
Loch Laich
Clach-corra
315
Achnacraig
Salen Forest
Meall na Caoraich
Fiunary Forest
A884
Glensanda
Ledmore
Fiunary
Rannoch
Loch Tearnait
Loch nan Clach
Eilean Ramsay
Eilean Loch Oscair
Ardtur
Tynribbie
Kinloch
Druim an Fhraoich Mhin
318
Glen Aros
Eilean an Glasa
Tighachnoic
Port Ramsay
Port Appin
Cnoc an da Chinn
390
Tenga
Achnaha
C
Beinn Bhuidhe
387
Meall an Fhiar Mhaim
309
Salen Bay
Fishnish Point
Lochaline
Meall a' Chaorainn
481
462
513
Appin Rocks
North Shian
Ballygown
Kilbrenan
Beinn na Drise
424
Salen
A849
Glais Bheinn
479
Mam a' Chullaich
An Sleaghach
Eignaig
Bachuil
Clachan
Eriska
Pennygown
Inninbeg
Ardtornish Point
Eilean Dubh
South Shian
Ballygown Bay
19
Beinn nan Carn
333
Killichronan
Cruach Torran Lochain
Killbeg
Fishnish
Inninmore Bay
Lismore
Achnacroish
Lynn
Rubha nan Gall
Laggan Bay
Lagganulva
Kellan
Bailemeonach
Garmony
Lynn of Morven
Baligrundle
80
Culcharan
Achronich
B8073
Gruline
Beinn Bhuidhe
412
Glen Forsa
Beinn Chreagach Mhor
579
Rubha an Ridire
Morven
Bernera
Kilcheran
Kiel Crofts
A828
BEN
Killiemor
Gaodhail
Salen Forest
Scallastle Bay
Loch Fiart
Eilean Dubh
Balure
Benderloch
A'Chrannag
Knock
Na Binneinean
Beinn Mheadhon
637
Scallastle
Craignure Bay
Ledaig
Eorsa
Loch Ba
Beinn na Duatharach
Craignure
Isle of Mull Railway
Pladda Island
South Ledaig
Beinn a'Ghraig
591
18
Dun da Ghaoithe
766
Maol nan Uan
Rubha Garbh-aird
Ardmucknish Bay
Samalan Island
Inch Kenneth
Beinn Fhada
702
M U L L
Torosay Castle
Duart Bay
Duart
Duart Point
Eilean Musdile
Eilean Mor
D
Achnacairn
Clachandhu
Dishig
Beinn Talaidh
761
Sgurr Dearg
741
Lady's Rock
Dunstaffnage
Connel
Balnahard
Gortenbuie
Lochdon
Culnadalloch
Ben More
966
Cruachan Dearg
704
Beinn Chaisgidle
504
Oakbank
Ganavan Bay
Dunbeg
Cuil-uaine
Balmeanach
Coirc Bheinn
561
Corra-bheinn
704
Gorten
Maiden Island
Pennyfuir
Ardchonnel
Fearnoch Forest
Guibean Uluvailt
Cruach Choireadail
Ishriff
Ardachoil
Ardnadrochet
Loch Don
Rubh' a'Bhearnaig
Eilean nan Gamhna
Black Lochs
A85
Beinn na Sreine
519
Maol na Coille Moire
Dererach
Uluvalt
A849
Craig
Glen More
Ardura
Grass Point
Ruba na Lice
Ardantrive
Glencruitten
Strontoiller
B8035
Balevulin
15
Beinn Fhada
Cruach Ardura
Auchnacraig
Barr-nam-boc Bay
Oban Bay
Oban
Beinn Bheinn
491
Gib Bheinn
Aird of Kinloch
Creag na h-Iolaire
Loch Airdeglais
Glas Bheinn
Carn Ban
Port Donain
Kerrera
Balliemore
Soroba
Glenamachrie
Ardmeanach
Kilfinichen Bay
698
Fellonmore
Upper Gylen
Bearraich
Burg (NTS)
Port na Croise
Cruach nan Con
Ben Buie
717
Creach Beinn
Croggan
Rubha na Faoilinn
Ardmore
A816
Loch Scridain
Maol nan Uan
Loch Fuaron
Loch Spelve
Dalnaha
Portfield
Bach Island
Gallanach
Cleigh
Beinn na Croise
503
Kinlochspelve
Rubha Seanach
Lerags
Kilbride
E
Killunaig
Pennyghael
Lochbuie
Loch Uisg
Dubh Sgeir
Dunach
Loch Nell
Port an Aird Fhada
Creag nam Fitheach
Maol Ban
Ardentallan
Loch Feochan
Glenfeochan
20
Brolass
Leidle
Minard Point
Barnacarry Bay
Druim Fada
405
Barnacarry
Knipoch
A'Chruach
368
Cruachan Min
376
Beinn Chreagach
376
Carsaig
S T R A T H C L Y D E
Kilninver
Musdale
Loch Buie
Eilean Duin
Beinn a'Bhainne
Rubha Dubh
Duachy
Scamadale
Bragleenbeg
MULL
Carsaig Bay
Nun's Pass
Port Ohirnie
Rubha Garbh Airde
Ardencaple
Glen Euchar
Shellachan
Loch Scamadale
Beinn Chapull
515
Creachan Mor
Frank Lockwood's Island
Insh Island
Ardfad
Seil
Clachan-Seil
B844
Scoor
Malcolm's Point
Sound of Insh
Ardshellach
28
Rubha nam Braithrean
An Cala Garden
Dun-Mor
Corrielorne
Loch na Sreinge
Easdale
Easdale
Folk Museum
F I R T H
Balvicar
B8003
Cruach nam Fearna
332
F
Drissaig
Henderson's Rock
Cuan Sound
Caddletown
Loch Tralaig
Naddsidhe
Pass of Melfort
Loch a' Phearsain
Melfort
Ardanstur
Garvellachs
Isles of the Sea
Cullipool
Torsay Island
Kilchoan
Kilmelford
Degnish
Maolachy
Garbh Eileach
Belnahua
Glas Eilean
Ardinamar
Degnish Point
Melfort
Tullich
Lagalochan
A'Chuli
Luing
Eilean Gamhna
Loch Melfort
43
Kames
Eilean Dubh Mor
Arduaine
Arduaine Garden
Tom Soilleir
365
Carn Duchan
491
Eileach an Naoimh
Monastery (ruin)
Asknish Bay
Lochan a'Bhruic
Inverliever Forest
Kilmaha
Lunga
Black Mill Bay
Toberonochy
Craobh Haven
Barravullin
Carn Loch
Guirasdeal
Shuna
Eilean Arsa
Lunga
Gleann Domhain
A816
Cruach an Eachlaich
Arichamish
Shuna Sound
Shuna Point
Gemmil
Kintraw
Inverliever
G
Cruach Scarba
449
Ardfern
Torran
B840
Barrackan
Bagh Ban
Eilean Mhic Chrion
Ford
Fincharn
Fincharn Loch
Colonsay
S c a r b a
Bagh Gleann a'Mhaoil
Corranmore
Tibertich
Loch Ederline
Rubha Righinn
Str. of Corryvreckan
Craignish
B8002
Eilean Righ
Old Poltalloch
Carnassarie
Reisa Mhic Phaidean
Kirkton
Sculptured Stones
Carnassarie
73
Eurach
Loch Gainneamhach
Balnahard Bay
Rubh' a' Geodha
Island Macaskin
Bhan
Barmolloch
Balnahard
10
11
Beinn
12
Capull
Kinuachdrach
Reisa an t-Sruith
13
Stone Circle
Slockavullin
14
Kilmartin
Loch Leathan
Craignish Point
Kinuachdrach Harbour
Gleann Garrisdale Bay
Cruach na Seilcheig
Ri Cruin Cairn
Baluachraig
Knockalava

HIGHLAND
STRATHCLYDE
ARDGOUR
BENDERLOCH
LORN
LOCH LOMOND REGIONAL PARK
Rannoch Moor
Black Mount
Royal Forest
Nevis Forest
Mamore Forest
Glenrigh Forest
Glenduror Forest
Inverliever Forest
Eredine Forest
Inverinan Forest
Fearnoch Forest
Ben Nevis 1344
Ben Cruachan 1126
Ben Lui 1130
Ben Oss 1028
Ben More
Ben Vorlich 943
Bidean Nam Bian 1150
Buachaille Etive Mor
Buachaille Etive Beag
Aonach Eagach
The Three Sisters
Pass of Glencoe
Pass of Brander
Loch Linnhe
Loch Leven
Loch Etive
Loch Awe
Loch Fyne
Loch Lomond
Blackwater Reservoir
Strath of Appin
Strath of Orchy
Strath Fillan
Glen Coe
Glen Etive
Glen Orchy
Glen Lochy
Glen Kinglass
Glen Aray
Glen Shira
Glen Fyne
Glen Falloch
Glen Croe
Glen Douglas
Glen Tarbert
Glen Gour
Glen Duror
Glen Creran
Glen Noe
Glen Strae
West Highland Way
Old Military Road
Fort William
Corran
Onich
North Ballachulish
South Ballachulish
Ballachulish
Glencoe
Kinlochleven
Kinlochmore
Kingshouse Hotel
Altnafeadh
Dalness
Kentallen
Duror
Dalnatrat
Lurignich
Appin Ho.
Portnacroish
Port Appin
Creagan
South Creagan
Barcaldine
Benderloch
Ledaig
Connel
Dunbeg
Oban
Soroba
Kilbride
Glenfeochan
Kilmelford
Taynuilt
Bonawe
Lochawe
Dalmally
Stronmilchan
Tyndrum
Clifton
Crianlarich
Bridge of Orchy
Inveroran Hotel
Forest Lodge
Kilchrenan
Portsonachan
Cladich
Inveraray
Furnace
Strachur
Cairndow
Arrochar
Tarbet
Ardlui
Inverarnan
Inveruglas
Succoth
Lochgoilhead
Ardgartan
Dalavich
Ford
Kilmaha
Inverchorachan
Ardchonnel
Achnalea
Inversanda
Kilmalieu
Glengalmadale
Corrlarach
Resourie
Druimarbin
Blarmachfoldach
Lundavra
Achriabhach
Polldubh
Corrour Sta.
Luibeilt
Black Corries Lodge
Achallader
Auch
Arrivain
Duiletter
Achnafalnich
Auchtertyre
Auchreoch
Inverherive
Cononish
A82
A828
A85
A819
A83
A815
A814
A861
A886
B863
B8043
B8074
B8077
B845
B840
B839
B828
15
16
17
18
19
73
74
79
86
87
A
B
C
D
E
F
G

ATHOLL
TAY FOREST
TAY FOREST PARK
TAYSIDE
BREADALBANE
CENTRAL
QUEEN ELIZABETH FOREST PARK
Glen Garry
Calvine
Pitagowan
Struan
Blair Atholl
Dalchalloch
Trinafour
Killiecrankie
Pass of Killiecrankie
The Soldier's Leap
Tulach Hill
Tressait
Loch Tummel
Queen's View
Port na Craig
Pitlochry
Loch Errochty
Glen Errochty
Craig nan Caisean
Balliemore
Dunalastair
Tummel Bridge
Kinloch Rannoch
Loch Rannoch
Bridge of Gaur
Bridge of Ericht
Killichonan
Talla Bheith
Aulich
Finnart
Camghouran
Rannoch School
Carie
Inverhadden
Tempar
Lassintullich
Braes of Foss
Foss
Schiehallion
Beinn Eagagach
Farragon Hill
Pitnacree
Grandtully
Little Ballinluig
Edradynate
Weem Hill
Camserney
Weem
Aberfeldy
Dull
Coshieville
Keltneyburn
Strath of Appin
Bolfracks
Gatehouse
Stix
Kenmore
Fortingall
Drummond Hill
Fearnan
Woodend
Balintyre
Invervar
Camusvrachan
Glen Lyon
Innerwick
Bridge of Balgie
Meall Garbh
Carn Mairg
Creag Mhor
Carn Gorm
Beinn Dearg
Meall Buidhe
Cam Chreag
Meall Cruinn
Kenknock
Moar
Pubil
Cashlie
Lubreoch
Meall Greigh
Ben Lawers
Meall Corranaich
Beinn Ghlas
Ben Lawers (NTS)
Lawers
Cragganruar
Ardradnaig
Remony
Acharn
Ardtalnaig
Creag an Sgliata
Beinn Bhreac
Loch Tay
Carie
Kiltyre
Milton Morenish
Morenish
Tullich
Duncroist
Glen Lochay
Boreland
Murlaganmore
Finlarig
Killin
Kinnell
Achmore
Craignavie
Bovain
Mid Lix
Auchlyne
Ardchyle
Glen Dochart
Auchessan
Suie Lodge Hotel
Ledcharrie
Batavaime
Camusurich
Cloichran
Ardeonaig
Tullich Hill
Creag Uchdag
Ben Chonzie
Glen Almond
Auchnafree
Dalriech
Newton
Amulree
Achnafauld
Corrymuckloch
Garrow
Auchnacloich
Milton
Aldville
Scotston
Glen Cochill
Loch Freuchie
Meall nam Fuaran
Buchanty
Logiealmond
Glen Turret
Loch Turret Resr
Invergeldie
Carroglen
Glen Lednock
Glen Ogle
Lochearnhead
Glenbeich
Ardveich
Dalveich
Derry
St Fillans
Loch Earn
Auchraw
Edinample
Ardvorlich
Ardtrostan
Edinchip
Dunira
Comrie
Tullybannocher
Ross
Dalginross
Strath Earn
Lawers
Ochtertyre
Hosh
Quoig
Crieff
Monzie
Gilmerton
Madderty
Lochlane
Cultybraggan Camp
Mill of Fortune
Balloch
Culloch
Craggan
Ochtermuthill
Muthill
Tighnablair
Dalchruin
Findhuglen
Auchinner
Glen Artney
Forest of Glenartney
Ben Vorlich
Stuc a'Chroin
Langside
Westerton
Greenscares
Glenlichorn
Auchterarder
Muirtown
Gleneagles Hotel
Garrick
Braco
Blackford
Greenloaning
Strathallan
Kinbuck
Balhaldie
Quoigs
Glassingall
Ashfield
Sheriff Muir
Balquhidder
Auchtoo
Kingshouse
Craigruie
Monachylemore
Stronvar
Strathyre Forest
Strathyre
Inverlochlarig
Ballimore
Immeroin
Kipp
Runacraig
Ardchullarie More
Laggan
Ben Vane
Ben Ledi
Braeleny
Anie
Pass of Leny
Kilmahog
Callander
Bochastle
Coilantogle
Easter Dullater
West Dullater
Drummond
Loch Venachar
Brig o'Turk
Lendrick
Duncraggan
Milton
The Trossachs
Loch Katrine
Glasahoile
Strone
Edra
Blairuskinmore
Kinlochard
Ledard
Achray Forest
Menteith Hills
Invertrossachs
Aberfoyle
Blairhullichan
Duchray
Balleich
Braeval
Cobleland
Loch Ard
Port of Menteith
Malling
Blairhoyle
Ruskie
Easter Borland
Torrie Forest
Thornhill
Tamavoid
Dykehead
Flanders Moss
Easter Poldar
Drumvaich
Burn of Cambus
Argaty
Deanston
Doune
Stockbridge
Dunblane
Inverardoch Mains
Gartincaper
Keir
Pisgah
Kippenross Ho
Cauldhame
Sunnylaw
Bridge of Allan
Ochtertyre
Nyadd
Menstrie
Tillicoultry
Braes of Ogilvie
Glen Eagles
Glen Devon
Blairdenon Hill
Ben Cleuch
Craighorn
King's Seat Hill
20
21
22
23
24
75
81
82
88
89
A
B
C
D
E
F
G

T A Y S I D E
F I F E
PERTH
DUNDEE
Pitlochry
Blair Atholl
Killiecrankie
Pass of Killiecrankie
Aberfeldy
Dunkeld
Birnam
Blairgowrie
Rattray
Alyth
Coupar Angus
Kirriemuir
Crieff
Auchterarder
Kinross
Milnathort
Glenrothes
Leslie
Markinch
Falkland
Auchtermuchty
Newburgh
Cupar
Ladybank
Methven
Stanley
Scone
New Scone
Old Scone
Bridge of Earn
Glenfarg
Dunning
Muthill
Gleneagles
Blackford
Dollar
Tillicoultry
Glendevon
Spittal of Glenshee
Kirkmichael
Bridge of Cally
Meigle
Errol
Longforgan
Invergowrie
Kirkton of Glenisla
Glenshee
Methil
Buckhaven
Kennoway
Kingskettle
Freuchie
Strathmiglo
Abernethy
Amulree
Kenmore
Strathbraan
Logiealmond
Forest of Alyth
Forest of Clunie
Carse of Gowrie
Sidlaw Hills
Lomond Hills
Glen Devon
Glen Eagles
Loch Leven
FIRTH OF TAY
A9
A93
A94
A85
A90
A91
A92
A822
A823
A824
A912
A913
A914
A923
A924
A926
A977
A984
M90
89
81
75
25
26
27
28
29
A
B
C
D
E
F
G

30
31
32
33
34
90
91
A
B
C
D
E
F
G
Inverbervie
Woodtown
Thornyhill
The Burn
Dalbog
Meikle Strath
Mains of Thornton
Laurencekirk
Gannochy
Inch
Arnhall
Sauchieburn
Edzell
Feus of Caldhame
Luthermuir
Johnston Mains
Redford
Dykelands
Benholm
Johnshaven
Gourdon
Bervie Bay
Knox Hill
Hill of Formal
Hill of Glansie
Burn of Calletar
Balfield
Bridgend
Dunlappie
Hill of Garbet
Peat Hill
Tillyarblet
BROWN CATERTHUN
WHITE CATERTHUN
Hill of Menmuir
Kirkton of Menmuir
Tigerton
Inchbare
Stracathro
Pert
Gallery
Marykirk
Kirktonhill
Ecclesgreig
Craigo
Lochside
St Cyrus
Milton Ness
Naked Tam
Pinderachy
Tullo Hill
Redheugh
Glenogil
Auchnacree
Mains of Balhall
Balnamoon
Bellichill
Newtonmill
Keithock
Logie Pert
Logie
Morphie
Pathhead
Ogil
Falls of Drumly Harry
Deuchar Hill
Fern
Noranside
Little Brechin
Templewood
Muirton of Ballochy
Trinity
Hillside
Newmill of Inshewan
West Muir
Brechin
Dun's Dish
HOUSE OF DUN
Kirkhill
Memus
Careston
Noran Water
Dun
Tayock
Tannadice
A935
Arrat
Bridge of Dun
CALEDONIAN RLY
Montrose Basin
Montrose
MONTROSE MUSEUM & ART GALLERY
Scurdie Ness
Murthill
Finavon
Marcus
Netherton
Middle Drums
Barnhead
Inchbraoch
Mains of Melgund
Ferryden
Oathlaw
Aberlemno
SCULPTURED STONES
Carcary
Farnell
Bonnyton
Maryton
Kirkton of Craig
Parkford
Hill of Finavon
Montreathmont Forest
Montreathmont Moor
Fishtown of Usan
Pitkennedy
Rossie Moor
Westerton
Long Craig
Turin Hill
Wuddy Law
Boddin Point
Mosside
Turin
Rossie Farm School
Lunanhead
Rescobie
Dubton
Braehead
Padanaram
RESTENNETH
Rescobie Loch
Balgavies
Glasterlaw
Bolshan
Lunan
Reswallie
Lunan Bay
Forfar
Milldens
Guthrie
Kinnell
Redcastle
Burnside
Balmadies
Friockheim
Boysack
Kingsmuir
Letham
Pitmuies
Inverkeilor
Dunnichen
Middleton
Chapelton
Lang Craig
Caldhame
Lownie Moor
Inchock
Red Head
Idvies
Leysmill
Cauldcots
Ethie Mains
Kinnettles
Craichie
Cononsyth
Kinblethmont
Lour
Drunkendub
Fothringham Hill
Tulloes
Colliston
Parkhill
Inverarity
Whigstreet
Lochlair
Mosston
Redford
Auchmithie
Kirkbuddo
Greystone
Marywell
Meg's Craig
Carmyllie
St Vigeans
Denhead
Carlingheugh Bay
Hayhillock
Carrot
Guynd
The Deil's Heid
Elliot Water
Arbirlot
Carrot Hill
Crombie Mill
Arbroath
Todhills
Greenburn
Bonnington
Easter Knox
Wormiehills
Affleck
Kirkton of Monikie
Newbigging
Monikie
Salmond's Muir
Craigton
Wellbank
East March
Muirdrum
Bucklerheads
East Haven
Kellas
Drumsturdy
Upper Victoria
Panbride
Burnside of Duntrune
Murroes
Laws
Mains of Ardestie
Barry
Carnoustie
Baldovie
Douglas and Angus
Monifieth
Buddon
Danger Zone
Barry Links
Broughty Ferry
Buddon Ness
DISCOVERY
BROUGHTY
TAY
Tayport
Tentsmuir Point
Newport-on-Tay
Tentsmuir Forest
Inchcape or Bell Rock
Pickletillem
Carrick
Leuchars
EARLSHALL
Eden Mouth
Guardbridge
Out Head
St Andrews Bay
Kincaple
St Andrews
BRITISH GOLF MUSEUM
Strathkinness
Kinkell Ness
Blebocraigs
Buddo Ness
Magus Muir
Brownhills
Boarhills
Babbet Ness
Dura
Prior Muir
Pitscottie
Denhead
Cambo Ness
Kenly Burn
Baldinnie
Cameron Resr
Stravithie
Kingsbarns
North Carr
Lathockar
Kinaldy
Dunino
Tullybothy Craigs
Peat Inn
Craighead
Falfield
West Lingo
Wormistone
Fife Ness
Lathones
Lochty
Airdrie
Backmuir of New Gilston
Largoward
Crail
West Ness
Balhousie
Lathallan Mill
Carnbee
Spalefield
Kellie Law
Arncroach
Wester Newburn
KELLIE
Inverkeillor
Kilrenny
Cellardyke
Upper Largo
Lahill
Colinsburgh
Grangemuir
SCOTTISH FISHERIES MUSEUM
Lower Largo
Drumeldrie
Kilconquhar
Abercrombie
Anstruther
Pittenweem
St Monans
Earlsferry
Elie
Ruddons Point
Chapel Ness
Sauchar Point
North Ness
Isle of May
South Ness
0 2 4 6 8 10 miles
0 2 4 6 8 10 km

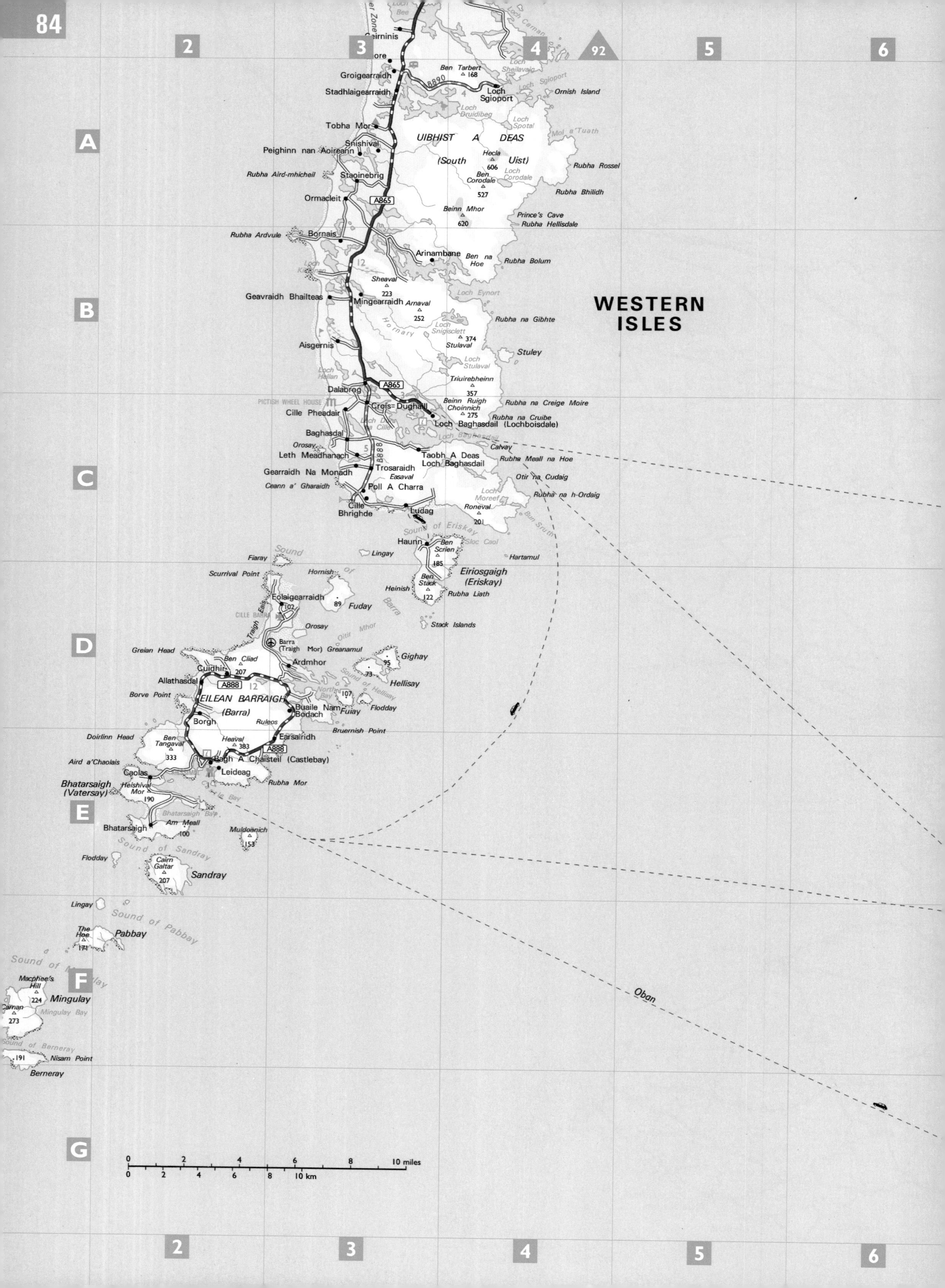

92
WESTERN ISLES
UIBHIST A DEAS (South Uist)
Cairinis
Groigearraidh
Stadhlaigearraidh
Ben Tarbert 168
B890
Loch Sgioport
Ornish Island
Loch Druidibeg
Loch Spotal
Mol a' Tuath
Tobha Mor
Snishival
Peighinn nan Aoireann
Hecla 606
Ben Corodale 527
Loch Corodale
Rubha Rossel
Rubha Aird-mhicheil
Staoinebrig
Rubha Bhilidh
Ormacleit
A865
Beinn Mhor 620
Prince's Cave
Rubha Hellisdale
Rubha Ardvule
Bornais
Arinambane
Ben na Hoe
Rubha Bolum
Loch Kildonan
Sheaval 223
Loch Eynort
Geavraidh Bhailteas
Mingearraidh
Arnaval 252
Hornary
Rubha na Gibhte
Loch Snigisclett
374 Stulaval
Aisgernis
Stuley
Loch Stulaval
Loch Hellan
Triuirebheinn 357
Dalabrog
PICTISH WHEEL HOUSE
Cille Pheadair
Crois Dughaill
Beinn Ruigh Choinnich 275
Rubha na Creige Moire
Rubha na Cruibe
Loch Baghasdail (Lochboisdale)
Baghasdal
Orosay
Leth Meadhanach
B888
Taobh A Deas Loch Baghasdail
Calvay
Rubha Meall na Hoe
Gearraidh Na Monadh
Trosaraidh
Easaval
Otir na Cudaig
Ceann a' Gharaidh
Poll A Charra
Rubha na h-Ordaig
Cille Bhrighde
Ludag
Loch Moreef
Roneval 201
Ban Sruth
Sound of Eriskay
Haunn
Ben Scrien 185
Sloc Caol
Hartamul
Fiaray
Lingay
Eiriosgaigh (Eriskay)
Scurrival Point
Hornish
Ben Stack 122
Heinish
Rubha Liath
Sound of Barra
Eolaigearraidh
102
89 Fuday
CILLE BARRA
Traigh Eais
Orosay
Stack Islands
Oitir Mhor
Barra (Traigh Mor)
Greanamul
Greian Head
Gighay 95
Ben Cliad 207
Ardmhor
73
Hellisay
Cuidhir
Allathasdal
A888
Borve Point
EILEAN BARRAIGH (Barra)
North Bay
107
Sound of Hellisay
Flodday
Buaile Nam Bodach
Fuiay
Borgh
Ruleos
Bruernish Point
Doirlinn Head
Ben Tangaval 333
Heaval 383
Earsairidh
Aird a'Chaolais
Bagh A Chaisteil (Castlebay)
Caolas
Leideag
Bhatarsaigh (Vatersay)
Heishival Mor 190
Rubha Mor
Vatersay Bay
Bhatarsaigh Bay
Bhatarsaigh
Am Meall 100
Muldoanich 153
Sound of Sandray
Flodday
Cairn Galtar 207
Sandray
Lingay
Sound of Pabbay
The Hoe 171
Pabbay
Sound of Mingulay
Macphee's Hill 224
Mingulay
Carnan 273
Mingulay Bay
Sound of Berneray
191
Nisam Point
Berneray
Oban
0 2 4 6 8 10 miles
0 2 4 6 8 10 km
2 3 4 5 6
A B C D E F G

RAASAY
SKYE
MINGINISH
Cuillin Hills
CUILLIN SOUND
CANNA
Sanday
RUM (RHUM)
NATIONAL NATURE RESERVE
EIGG
Muck
Soay
Scalpay
SEA OF THE HEBRIDES
Sound of Canna
SOUND OF RUM
Sound of Eigg
Mallaig (summer only)
Oban
The Hoe
Lorgill
Healabhal Bheag
Macleod's Table South
Balmore
Harlosh
Ose
Glen Ose
Beinn na Cloiche
Am Maol
Beinn na Greine
Penifiler
Glame
Ben Connan
Beinn na Boineid
Ben Idrigill
Harlosh Point
Harlosh Island
Loch Bracadale
MacLeod's Maidens
Idrigill Point
An Dubh Sgeir
Wiay
Tarner Island
Ullinish
Struan
Bracadale
Coillore
DUN BEAG
Loch Duagrich
Ben Duagrich
Mugeary
Stroc-bheinn
Glenmore
Camastianavaig
Ben Tianava
Balach
Dun Caan
Holoman Bay
Oskaig Point
Oskaig
Rubha na' Leac
Beinn na' Leac
Clachan
Inverarish
East Suisnish
Suisnish Point
Narrows of Raasay
Lower Ollach
Upper Ollach
Meall an Fhuarain
Glen Varragill
Beinn Totaig
Roineval
Ardtreck Point
Oronsay
Portnalong
Fernilea
Rubha nan Clach
Loch Harport
Ben Lee
The Braes
Peinchorran
Broc-bheinn
Kyle More
Rubh' an Lochain
Arnaval
Carbost
Drynoch
Glen Drynoch
Loch Sligachan
Sconser
Meall a' Mhaoil
Glamaig
Sligachan
Mullach na Carn
Camas Fisteod
Talisker Bay
Gleann Oraid
Talisker
Stockval
Glen Eynort
Beinn Bhreac
Allt Dearg Mor
Glen Sligachan
Loch Ainort
Luib
Dunan
Caolas Scalpay
Biod Mor
Eynort
Beinn Dearg
Blackhill
Glas Bheinn Mhor
Strath Mor
Am Basteir
Sgurr nan Gillean
Bruach na Frithe
Marsco
Beinn a'Bhraghad
Sgurr Thuilm
Harta Corrie
Belig
Beinn na Caillich
Corry
Broadford
Harrapool
Loch Eynort
Beinn Staic
Sgurr a'Mhadaidh
Sgurr a'Ghreadaidh
Garbh-bheinn
Beinn Dearg Mhor
Strath Suardal
An Cruachan
Sgurr na Banachdich
Sgurr Dearg (Inaccessible Pinnacle)
Bla Bheinn (Blaven)
Torrin
Loch Cill Chriosd
Glenbrittle
Bualintur
Sgurr Mhic Choinnich
Sgurr Alasdair
Sgurr Dubh Mor
Druim Hain
Beinn an Eoin
Culnamean
Loch Coruisk
Loch na Creitheach
Strathaird
Kilbride
Ben Suardal
Sgurr nan Eag
Sgurr na Stri
Camasunary
Loch Slapin
Rubha Thearna Sgurr
Loch Brittle
Gars-bheinn
Beinn nan Carn
Kirkibost
Kilmarie
Ben Meabost
Beinn Bhuidhe
Ceann na Beinne
Rubh' an Dunain
Soay Sound
Beinn Bhreac
Loch Scavaig
Camas Fhionnairigh
Rubha Suisnish
Leac nam Faoileann
Mol-chlach
Camas nan Gall
Drinan
Elgol
Loch Eishort
Ord
Prince Charles's Cave
Spar Cave
Glasnakille
Rubha na h-Easgainne
DUNSGAITH
Tokavaig
Tarskavaig
Sgurr na h-Iolaire
Tarskavaig Bay
Achnacloich
Loch Uamh
Sgurr Breac
Kilmore
Loch a' Ghlinne
Inver Dalavil
Gleann Meadhonach
Armadale
Ardvasar
Calligarry
Sgurr nan Caorach
Geur Rubha
Aird of Sleat
Ard Thurinish
Point of Sleat
Camas Tharbernish
Carn a' Ghaill
Compass Hill
Garrisdale Point
(NTS)
Sron Ruail
A'Chill
Tarbert Bay
Canna Harbour
Rubha Shamhnan Insir
Kilmory
Sgaorishal
Mullach Mor
Bloodstone Hill
Humla
A' Bhrideanach
Rubha na Roinne
Kinloch
KINLOCH
Orval
Sgor Reidh
Barkeval
Bagh na h-Uamha
An Dornabac
Hallival
Askival
Harris
Garbh Sgeir
Oigh-sgeir
Ainshval
Ruinsival
Sgurr nan Gillean
Rubha Sgor an t-Snidhe
Rubha nam Meirleach
Cleadale
Bay of Laig
An Cruachan
Rubha an Fhasaidh
Laig
Beinn Tighe
Kildonnan
An Sgurr
Galmisdale
Eilean nan Each
Godag
Rubh' Leam na Laraich
Beinn Airein
Port Mor
Portnalucha
Eilean Ighe
Luinga Mhor
Rhumach
Cruach Doire 'n Dobhrain
Sound of
Samalaman Is
Smirisary
Shona
Baileтonach
Rubha Aird Druimnich
Ockle Point
Ockle
Kilmory
Sanna Point
Fascadale
Achateny
Sanna Bay
Achnaha
Branault
Meall nan Con
Beinn an Leathaid
Beinn Bhreac
Carn Mor
Ardtoe
Gorteneorn
Portuairk
A850
(A87)
A863
B8009
B883
B885
B8083
85
93
86
79
A
B
C
D
E
F
G
7
8
9
10
11

Penifiler
Ben Tianavaig 413
Glame 385
RAASAY
Balachuirn
Camusteel
Camasterach
Culduie
Russel
Ardarroch
Lochcarron
Strathcarron Sta.
Achintee
A896
A890
Glenmore
Stroc-bheinn 400
Camastianavaig
B883
Holoman Bay
Dun Caan 443
Rubha na' Leac
Toscaig
Loch Kishorn
Achintraid
An Sgurr 392
Sgeir Fhada
Attadale
Lower Ollach
Oskaig Point
Oskaig
Upper Ollach
Beinn na' Leac 319
Clachan
Meall Loch Airigh Alasdair 352
Airigh-drishaig
Bad a'Chreamha 395
Stromemore
Carn nan Iomairean 485
Meall an Fhuarain
A850
(A87)
Glen Varragill
The Braes
Ben Lee 445
Inverarish
East Suisnish
Suisnish Point
Crowlin Islands
Eilean Meadhonach
Eilean Mor
Caolas Mor
Uags
Ardaneaskan
L. Reraig
STROME (NTS)
Ardnarff
Stromeferry
Peinchorran
Rubh' an Lochain
Kyle More
Plockton
Achmore
Strath Ascaig
Glen Ling
Drynoch
Sconser
Meall a'Mhaoil 284
Scalpay
Loch Sligachan
Longay
Bagh an t-Srathaird
Beinn Raimh 447
Sallachy
Ben Killilan
Sgumain Coinntich 879
Sligachan
Glamaig 775
Mullach na Carn 396
Drumbuie
Duirinish
Killilan
Glen Sligachan
BALMACARRA ESTATE
Erbusaig
Auchtertyre Hill 452
Allt-na-subh
Long
Allt Dearg Mor
Camas na Fisteodh
Badicaul
Camus-luinie
Beinn Dearg
Loch Ainort
Conchra
Coille-rig
Luib
Dunan
Pabay
Kyle of Lochalsh
Kirkton
Balmacara
Nostie
Ardelve
Bundalloch
Am Basteir 935
Sgurr nan Gillean 965
Blackhill
Glas Bheinn Mhor 570
Caolas Scalpay
Toll
A87
Kyleakin
CAISTAL MAOL
Loch Alsh
Dornie
Boc Mor 631
Loch nan Eun
Bruach na Frithe 958
Marsco 736
Belig
SKYE
Broadford Bay
Corry
Broadford
Harrapool
Lower Breakish
Upper Breakish
L. na Beiste
Ardintoul Point
Glas Eilean
EILEAN DONAN
Keppoch
Sgurr an Airgid 841
Dorusduain
Harta Corrie
Sgurr a'Ghreadaidh
Sgurr na Banachdich
Sgurr (Inaccessible Pinnacle)
Sgurr Mhic Choinnich
Sgurr Alasdair
Sgurr Dubh Mor 944
Garbh-bheinn 806
Beinn Dearg Mhor 709
Beinn na Caillich 732
Strath Mor
Bla Bheinn (Blaven) 928
Torrin
Loch Cill Chriosd
Strath Suardal
Skulamus
A851
Glen Arroch
Cnoc Glac na Luachrach
Beinn na Caillich
Sgurr na Coinnich 739
Kylerhea
Ardintoul
Letterfearn
Glas Bheinn 394
Beinn a'Chuirn 603
Inverinate
Lienassie
Morvich
Loch Duich
Druim Hain
Loch Coruisk
Loch na Creitheach
Strathaird
Kilbride
B8083
Ben Suardal 283
Bernera
Galltair
Scallasaig
Ault a'chruinn
Inverhiel
Shiel Bridge
Eag 924
Gars-bheinn 895
Sgurr na Stri 497
Camasunary
Loch Slapin
Beinn nan Carn 301
Ben Aslak 610
Glenelg Bay
BERNERA BARRACKS
Glenelg
Beinn a'Chaoinich 408
Sgurr Mhic Bharraich 781
Sgurr na Moraich 876
Camas Fhionnairigh
Kilmarie
Ben Meabost 346
Kirkibost
Beinn Bhuidhe 277
Heast
Beinn na Seamraig 561
Beinn Bhreac 436
Port a'Gharaidh
Eilanreach
Glen More
Balvraid
Sgurr a'Gharg Gharaidh 681
Beinn Bhreac 141
Camas nan Gall
Rubha Suisnish
Eilean Heast
Drumfearn
GLENELG BROCH'S
Beinn a'Chapuill 742
Gleann Beag
Drinan
Elgol
Spar Cave
Glasnakille
Rubha na h-Easgainne
Prince Charles's Cave
Loch Eishort
Ord
Sgorach Breac 299
Duisdealmor
Eilean Iarmain (Isleornsay)
Isle Ornsay
Ardnameacan
Sandaig Islands
Sandaig
Meall Buidhe 486
Beinn Mhialairigh 548
Beinn Sgritheall 981
Beinn nan Caorach 773
Beinn Aoidhdailean 633
The Saddle 1010
Spidean Dhomhuill Bhric 940
Sgurr na Sgine 945
DUNSGAITH
Tokavaig
Camascross
Camus Croise
Tarskavaig
Sgurr na h-Iolaire 292
Teangue
KNOCK
Knock Bay
LOCH HOURN
Arnisdale
Beinn Clachach 617
Corran
Glen Arnisdale
Druim Fada 614 713
Buidhe Bheinn 879
Tarskavaig Bay
Achnacloich
Loch nam Uamh
Rubh Ard Slisneach
SOUND OF SLEAT
Kilmore
Sgurr Breac 249
Na Cruachan 583
Beinn na Caillich 785
Kinloch Hourn
Inverguseran
Loch a' Ghlinne
Inver Dalavil
Gleann Meadhonach
Kilbeg
CLAN DONALD CENTRE
Armadale Bay
Airor
Meall Gaothar 422
Druim Cluain-airighe 518
Gleann Guiserein
Barrisdale Bay
Barrisdale
Carn Mairi 502
Meall nan Eun 666
Sgurr Sgiath Airigh 881
Ladhar Bheinn 1020
Aonach Sgoilte 849
Glen Barrisdale
Slat Bheinn 701
Sgurr a'Chlaidheimh
CUILLIN SOUND
Sgurr nan Caorach 280
Armadale
Ardvasar
Calligarry
Roinn na Beinne 441
Sandaig
KNOYDART
Sgurr Coire na Coinnich 796
Luinne Bheinn 939
Sgurr a'Choire-bheithe 913
Gleann Cosaidh
Druim Chosaidh
Geur Rubha
Aird of Sleat
Sandaig Bay
Aultvoulin
Inverie
Ard Thurinish
Inverie Bay
Point of Sleat
Rubha Raonuill
Gleann Meadail
Loch an Dubh-Lochain
Meall Buidhe 946
Ben Aden 885
Sgurr Mor 1003
Lochboisdale (summer only)
Mallaigvaig
Mallaigmore
Sron Raineach
A'Chruach 395
Carn a' Ghobhaur 547
Sgurr an Eilein Ghiubhais 522
Loch an Nostarie
Mallaig
Glasnacardoch
B8008
Beinn Bhuidhe 865
Sgurr Coire nan Gobhar 739
Sgurr na Ciche 1040
Garbh Chioch Mhor 1013
Sgurr nan Coireachan 953
Druim a'Chuirn 817
Camusrory
Loch Nevis
A830
Loch a'Ghille Ghobaich
Sgurr Bhuidhe 440
Stoul
Kylesknoydart
Kylesmorar
Morar
Bracora
Bracorina
Eilean a'Phidhir
NORTH MORAR
Tarbet
Swordland
Sgurr na h-Aide 859
Sgurr Breac
Kinlochmorar
Upper Glendessarry
Glen Dessarry
Monadh Gorm 470
Kinlocharkaig
Carn Mor 829
Glen Pean
Castlebay (summer only)
Cleadale
Bay of Laig
Laig
An Cruachan 299
Lettermorar
LOCH MORAR
Portnaluchaig
Carn a'Mhadaidh ruaidh 503
Druim a' Chuirn
An Stac 718
Sgurr an Ursainn 817
Sgurr nan Coireachan 956
Sgurr Thuilm 963
Eilean Ighe
Back of Keppoch
Loch a'Choire Riabhaich
SOUTH MORAR
Meith Bheinn 710
Meoble
Braigh nan Uamhachan 765
EIGG
Sgurr
An Sgurr 393
Galmisdale
Luinga Mhor
Arisaig
Sidhean Mor 599
Beinn nan Cabar 574
Streap 909
Stob Coire nan Cearc 887
Rhumach
Morroch
Glen Beasdale
Loch Beoraid
Kinlochbeoraid
Rubh' Arisaig
Cruach Doire 'n Dobhrain 103
Druimindarroch
CAIRN
ARISAIG
Sron Thoraraidh 383
Arnipol
Ariensklll
Glas-charn 633
Sgurr an Utha 796
Sgurr a' Mhuidhe
Beinn an Tuim 810
Na h-Uamhachan 691
Loch Beag
Ardnish
Lochailort
Loch nan Uamh
Loch Doir a'Ghearrain
Inverailort
Loch Eilt
Ranochan
Rubha Chaolais
Eilean nan Gobhar
Sgurr na Paite
Glenfinnan
GLENFINNAN MONUMENT (NTS)
Sound of Arisaig
Beinn Odhar Mhor 870
Meall a' Bhainne 559
Drumfern
A861
Garvan
Samalaman Island
Glenuig Bay
Roshven
Smirisary
An Stac
Druim Fiaclach 869
Beinn Odhar Bheag 882
Cruach Bhrochdadail 357
Glenuig Hill
Rios Bheinn 882
Croit Bheinn 663
Sgurr Dhomhnuill Mor 713
Loch Shiel
Sgorr Craobh a'Chaorainn 775
Sgurr Ghiubhsachain
Glen Garvan
Sron an t-Sluichd 367
Eilean Shona
Shona Beag 265
Kylesbeg
MOIDART
Beinn Gaire 666
Glenaladale
Meall nan Damh 723
Meall an Fheidh 423
Baileonach
Rubha Aird Druimnich
Brunery Hill
Glen Forslan
Kinlochmoidart
Gaskan
Scamodale
Meall Mor 759
Meall an Shleagha 407
Ockle Point
Carn Mor
Beinn Bhreac 240
TIORAM
Glen Moidart
Ardmolich
Gorstanvorran
Sgurr an Tarmachain 756
Stob a'Bheathain 721
Corrlarach
Glen Cona
Kilmory
Ockle
Ardtoe
Newton of Ardtoe
Cruach a' Ghaill
Sgurr na Greine 497
Resourie
Fascadale
Achateny
Sanna
Branault
Beinn Bhreac 357
Gorteneorn
Kentra Bay
Kentra
Cliff
Dalnabreck
Polloch
Carn na Nathrach 786
Glenhurich
Tighnacomaire
Scaddle
Achnaha
Meall nan Con 437
Arivegaig
Acharacle
Claish Moss
Achnanellan
Sgurr Dhomhnuill
A
B
C
D
E
F
G
H
11
12
13
14
15
94
85
79

West Monar Forest
East Monar Forest
Loch Monar
Crask of Aigas
Oldtown of Aigas
Culligran
Kiltarlity
Culburnie
Sgurr na Muice
Sgurr a'Choire Ghlais
Carn Ban
16
17
18
19
20
95
Struy
Erchless Castle
Eskadale
Camault Muir
Druimkinnerras
Foxhole
Lurg Mhor
Loch Calavie
Meallan Odhar
Inchvuilt
Ardchuilk
Glen Strathfarrar
Uisge Misgeach
Loch Beannacharan
Culligran Falls
Stuy Forest
Mauld
Loch Neaty
Boblainy Forest
Beinn Dronaig
Beinn Bheag
Meallan Buidhe
Loch a'Mhuillidh
Crelevan
Carnoch
Ardblair
An Cruachan
Sgurr na Lapaich
Meallan Odhar
Sgor na Diollaid
Carn a' Mhuilt
Carn Gorm
Glassburn
Meall nan Caorach
Carn Mor
Meall Gorm
Abriachan
Balchragg
Carn na Sean Luibe
Loch Cruoshie
An Riabhachan
Carn nan Gobhar
Creag Dubh
Glencannich Forest
A831
Strathglass
Carn nam Bad
Lochan an Tairt
Muchrachd
Balmore
Liatrie
An Socach
Braigh a'Choire Bhig
Loch Carrie
Millness
Buntait
Balbeg
Gartally
Achmony
A833
Meall na h-Eilrig
Creag Nay
Forest
Aonach Buidhe
Loch Mhoicean
Fasnakyle Forest
Cannich
Grange
Chambered Cairn
Bearnock
Glen Urquhart
A831
Milton
Drumnadrochit
Loch Mullardoch
Glen Cannich
Mony's Stone
Corrimony
Balnain
Loch Meiklie
Glenurquhart Forest
Loch Ness Monster Exhibition Centre
Lewiston
Strone
Urquhart
Loch na Leitreach
Beinn Fhionnlaidh
Coire Lochan
Tom a'Choinich
Toll Creagach
Doire Tana
Fasnakyle
Carn Macsna
Lenie
Suidhe Ghuirmain
Falls of Glomach
Mullach na Dheiragain
Carn Eighe
Knockfin
Tomich
Enrick
Coiltie
Gleann Sithidh
Gleann nam Fiadh
Beinn a'Mheadhoin
Beinn Mhor
Balmacaan Forest
Bunloit
Mam Sodhail
Sgurr na Lapaich
Loch Beinn a'Mheadhoin
Divach Burn
General Wades Military Road
B
Balbeg
Grotaig
Inverfarigaig
Sgurr nan Ceathreamhnan
An Socach
Plodda Falls
Glen Affric
Guisachan Forest
Loch ma Stac
Meall a'Chrathaich
Loch nam Meur
Loch nam Breac Dearga
Meal Fuar-mhonaidh
Easter Boleskine
Dhuhallow
Ault
Loch Gaorsaic
Loch a'Bhealaich
Loch Affric
Cougie
Creag nan Caiman
Loch nan Eun
Loch a'Chrathaich
Foyers
Lyne
Alltbeithe
Gleann Gniomhaidh
Allt Garbh
Allt Riabhach
Loch na Beinne Baine
Carn Mhic an Toisich
Allt Bhlaraidh
Levishie Forest
Alltsigh
Lochgarthside
B862
Aonach Shasuinn
Carn a'Chaochain
Meallan Odhar
Carn a'Choire Bhuidhe
Levishie
Dundreggan Forest
A82
Invermoriston
Loch Mhor
Bailebeag
Ciste Dhubh
Mullach Fraoch-choire
Meall Cuileig
A887
Portclair Forest
Loch Kemp
Glen Mor
Foyers
Sail Chaorainn
A'Chralaig
Beinn an t-Sidhein
Dundreggan
Whitebridge
Easter Drummond
Stratherrick
C
Sgurr a'Bhealaich Dheirg
Aonach Meadhoin
Sgurr nan Conbhairean
Ceannacroc Forest
Burach
Torgyle
Moriston
Dalchreichart
Inverwick Forest
Carn Ghluasaid
Carn nam Feuaich
Tomchrasky
Doe
Loch Ness
Carn Fliuch
Beinn a'Bhacaidh
Glen Albyn
Lundie
A87
A887
Glen Moriston
Inchnacardoch Hotel
Loch Tarff
Killin
88
Sgurr an Doire Leathain
Glen Cluanie
Cluanie Forest
Loch Cluanie
Roderick Mackenzie's Memorial
Great Glen Exhibition Centre
Fort Augustus
B862
Glendoebeg
Maol Chinn-dearg
Aonach air Chrith
Druim Shionnach
Creag a'Mhaim
Druim nan Cnamh
Bunloinn Forest
Bun Loyne
Ceann a'Mhaim
Carn Mhic Raonuill
St. Benedict's Abbey
Glen Doe
Allt Doe
Glen Brein
Coire Odhar
Beinn Loinne
Meall Dubh
Glen Loyne
Beinneun Forest
Loch Oich
Caledonian Canal
Cairn Vungie
Carn Easgann Bana
Lochan na Staime
Gleouraich
Spidean Mialach
Glenquoich Forest
Mullach Coire Ardachaidh
Loch a'Bhainne
Glen More
Glendoe Forest
D
Loch Fearna
Druim na h-Achlaise
Cnocan Dubh
Munerigie
Loch Lundie
Newtown
Aberchalder
Carn a'Chuilinn
Glen Tarff
Coille Mhorgil
Tomdoun
Inchlaggan
Loch Garry
Invergarry
Loch na h-Aisre
Meall na h-Aisre
Gearr Garry
Glen Garry
Greenfield
A87
Mandally
Invergarry
Laggan Swing Bridge
Beinn Bheag
Gairich
Glengarry Forest
Culachy Forest
Corrieyairack Hill
G
H
L
A
N
D
Glen Kingie
Glas Bheinn
Ben Tee
Laggan
Gairbeinn
Carn Leac
Corrieyairack Forest
Creag Mhor
Meall Tarsuinn
Meall Coire nan Saobhaidh
Allt a'Choire Ghlais
Kilfinnan
Carn Dearg
Corrieyairack Pass
Melgarve
Lochan Dubh
Meall a'Bhlair
Sgurr Choinich
Geal Charn
Sron a'Choire Ghairbh
Leacann Doire Bainneir
Spey
E
Loch a'Bhlair
Beinn Chraoibh
Glas Bheinn
Gleann Cia-Aig
Meall na Teanga
Leckroy
Turret
Murlaggan
Loch Arkaig
Ardachvie
Loch Lochy
Letter Finlay
Glen Gloy
Beinn Iaruinn
Turret Bridge
Glen Roy
Carn Liath
Comra
Kinloch Laggan
Mullach Choire nan Geur-oirean
Achnasaul
Altura
Stob Poite Coire Ardair
Coille Coire Chrannaig
Locheil Forest
Inver Mallie
Clunes
A82
Invergloy
Leana Mhor
Carn Dearg
Loch Sguadaig
Creag Meagaidh
Aberarder
Ardverikie
Glen Mallie
Bunarkaig
B8005
Coire Ceirsle Hill
Beinn Bhan
Meall a'Phubuill
Druim Gleann Laoigh
Rathliesbeag
Stronenaba
Bohuntine Hill
Beinn Teallach
Beinn a'Chaorainn
An Cearcallach
Loch Laggan
F
Glen Loy
Gairlochy
Bohuntine
Moy Forest
Moy
Binnein Shuas
Lochan na h-Earba
Suileag
Coille Mhor
Stob a'Ghrianain
Moy
Strone
Brackletter
B8004
Spean Bridge
Tirindrish
Commando Memorial
Inverroy
Roybridge
Bohenie
Creag Dhubh
Roughburn
Craigbeg
Creag Pitridh
Geal Charn
Druim Fada
Cruim Leacainn
A82
Killiechanate
Spean
A86
Murlaggan
Braes o' Lochaber
Tulloch Sta.
Ardverikie Forest
Glen Spean
Meall Bhanabhie
Torcastle
Tom an Tseine
Leanachan Forest
Aonach Mhor Mountain Gondola Lift & Nevis Range Ski Centre
Beinn Chlianaig
Meall Liath Mhor
Fassfern
A830
Loch Eil Centre
Loch Eil
Corpach
Banavie
Neptune's Staircase
Torlundy
Fersit
Beinn a'Chlachair
Blaich
Achaphubuil
Camusnagaul
Trislaig
Caol
Sgurr Finnisg-aig
An Lairig
Carn Dearg
Ben Alder Forest
Allt a'Chaoil Reidhe
Fort William
Claggan
Achintee Ho
West Highland Mus.
Killiechonate Forest
Stob Choire Claurigh
Stob a'Choire Mheadhoin
Stob Coire Sgriodain
Chno Dearg
Loch Guilbinn
Aonach Beag
Geal Charn
G
Ceann Caol
Meall an t-Slamain
Aonach Mor
Carn Mor Dearg
Aonach Beag
Stob Coire an Laoigh
Stob Ban
Stob Coire Easain
Lairig Leacach
Loch Treig
Strath Ossian
Beinn Eibhinn
Loch a'Bhealaich Bheithe
Goirtean a'Chladaich
A861
Ben Nevis
Sgurr Choinnich Mor
Meall a'Bhuiridh
Garbh Bheinn
Ben Alder
Beinn Bheoil
Beinn a'Chumhainn
Glen Nevis
Carn an Daimh
Carn Dearg
Druimarbin
Nevis Forest
Blarmachfoldach
Water of Nevis
Abhainn Rath
Corrour Shooting Lodge
Bealach
Prince Charlie's Cave
Stob an Aonaich Mhoir
16
17
18
19
80
20
Achriabhach
West Highland Way
Binnein Beag
Luibelt
Corrour Forest
Sgor Gaibhre
Ben Alder Cottage
Loch Ossian
G R A M P I A N
L O C H A B E R
M O N A D H L I A T H

Crask of Aigas
Oldtown of Aigas
Culligran
Struy
Erchless Castle
Kiltarlity
Belladrum
Tomnacross
Moniack
The Aird
Lagnalean
Dochgarroch
Kirkton
Lochend
Dores
Scaniport
Essich
Newton of Leys
Drummossie Muir
Bogbain
Castletown
Craggie
Daviot
Mains of Faillie
Scatraig
Ardchuilk
Glen Strathfarrar
Mauld
Crelevan
Carnoch
Glassburn
Strathglass
Eskadale
Culburnie
Camault Muir
Druimkinnerras
Boblainy Forest
Foxhole
Glen Convinth
Ardblair
Abriachan
Balchraggan
Brachla
Muchrachd
Balmore
Cannich
Fasnakyle Forest
Millness
Buntait
Grange
Corrimony
Bearnock
Balnain
Glen Urquhart
Balbeg
Gartally
Achmony
Milton
Drumnadrochit
Lewiston
Strone
Urquhart
Glenurquhart Forest
Fasnakyle
Tomich
Knockfin
Balmacaan Forest
Lenie
Bunloit
Grotaig
Ashie Moor
Achnabat
Whitefield
Torness
Abersky
Tullich
Brinmore
East Croachy
Balnafoich
Tombreck
Dalvourn
Tordarroch
Farr
Gaick
Strathnairn
Moy
Corrievorrie
Aberarder Ho.
Daltomach
Inverfarigaig
Aultnagoire
Errogie
Farraline
Dhuhallow
Easter Boleskine
Foyers
Lyne of Gorthleck
Wester Aberchalder
Lochgarthside
Bailebeag
Glen Mazeran
Dalmigavie
Strath Dearn
Levishie Forest
Levishie
Alltsigh
Invermoriston
Dundreggan Forest
Portclair Forest
Dundreggan
Torgyle
Dalchreichart
Glen Moriston
Inverwick Forest
Loch Ness
Glen Mor
Whitebridge
Easter Drummond
Stratherrick
Glen Albyn
Inchnacardoch Hotel
Fort Augustus
Glendoebeg
Glen Doe
Glendoe Forest
Monadhliath Mountains
Highland
Coignafearn Forest
Newtown
Aberchalder
Munerigie
Invergarry
Mandally
Laggan Swing Bridge
Glen Garry
Laggan
Kilfinnan
Culachy Forest
Corrieyairack Forest
Corrieyairack Pass
Melgarve
Garvamore
Crathie
Sherramore
Blargie
Laggan
Balgowan
Dalballoch
Glen Banchor
Bialaid
Newtonmore
Kingussie
Ruthven
Highland Folk Mus
Clan Macpherson House & Mus
Phones
Etteridge
Falls of Truim
Lynaberack
Leckroy
Turret Bridge
Letterfinlay
Glen Gloy
Glen Roy
Comra
Kinloch Laggan
Ardverikie
Aberarder
Loch Laggan
Creag Meagaidh
Dalwhinnie
Gaick Lodge
Gaick Forest
Bohuntine
Bohenie
Roybridge
Murlaggan
Roughburn
Craigbeg
Moy
Moy Forest
Tulloch Sta.
Glen Spean
Fersit
Ardverikie Forest
Ben Alder Lodge
Ben Alder Forest
Loch Ericht
Ben Alder
Glen Truim
Drumochter
Dalnacardoch Forest
Sronphadruig Lodge
Dalnamein Forest
Forest of Atholl
Badnambiast
Grampian Mountains
Corrour Shooting Lodge
Corrour Forest
Strath Ossian
Loch Treig
Prince Charlie's Cave
Ben Alder Cottage
Craiganour Forest
Glen Garry
Loch Garry
Boar of Badenoch (An Torc)
Pass of Drumochter
Sow of Atholl
Beinn Udlamain
A82
A831
A833
A887
A86
A889
A9
B862
B852
B851
B861
B9154
96
87
80
19
20
21
22
23
A
B
C
D
E
F
G

Dulsie
Carn Sgumain
Carnoch
Banchor
Milltown
Aitnoch
Duhie
Knock of Braemoray
Sliabh Bainneach
Larig Hill
Carn Kitty
Carn Shalag
Roy's Hill
Paul's Hill
Knockando
KNOCKANDO DISTILLERY
Carron
Daugh of Kinermony
Speyview
Milltown of Edinvillie
Dufftown
BALVENIE CASTLE
MORTLACH CHURCH
Daless
Strathdearn
Carn na Sguabaich
Lochindorb
Dava
Dava Moor
Carn Bad na Caorach
Ruighe an Uain
Carne na Loine
Glen Tulchan
Scootmore Forest
Marypark
Daugh of Carron
GLENFARCLAS DISTILLERY
Sheandow
Meikle Conval
Gallow Hill
Lynemore
Bellehiglash
Baby's Hill
Beatshach
Laggan
Brigehaugh
Bridge of Avon
Ben Rinnes
Carn Ruigh Charrach
Anaboard
Upper Derraid
Auchnagallin
Knock of Auchnahannet
Advie
Toremore
Craigroy Farm
Dalchirach
Favillar
Achnastank
Carn an t-Sean-liathanaich
Glaschoil
Camerory
Cottartown
Tomvaich
Dellefure
Lettoch
Duiar
Craggan
Cairnacay
GLENLIVET DISTILLERY & VISITOR CENTRE
Creag an Tarmachain
Drumin
Tervieside
Hill of Achmore
Glen Fiddich Forest
Balvraid
Inverbrough
Creag Liath
Carn a' Choire Mhoir
Carn Glas-choire
Achnahannet
Beinn Mhor
Glenbeg
Cromdale
Charn a' Ghille Chear
Shenval
Auchbreck
Carn a' Bhodaich
Corryhabbie Hill
Glenlivet
Carn Eachie
Carn Liath
Cairn Muldonich
Cook's Cairn
Tullochgribban High
Dulnain Bridge
Gaich
Grantown-on-Spey
Congash
Speybridge
Haughs of Cromdale
Hills of Cromdale
Tomnavoulin DISTILLERY
Carn an t-Suidhe
Blackwater Forest
Carn nam-Bain Tighearna
Slochd
Duthil
Skye of Curr
Carn Tuairneir
Creagan a' Chaise
Lynemore
Carn Daimh
Knockandhu
Cairn Ellick
Glenconglass
Clashnoir
Braes of Glenlivet
Chapeltown
Round Hill
Geal Charn
Letterach
Cairnbrallan
Hill of Three Stones
Carrbridge
LANDMARK VISITOR CENTRE & SCULPTURE PARK
Bogroy
Sluggan
Carn na Loinne
Sgor Gaoithe
Fodderletter
Drumuillie
Boat of Garten
Cullachie
Nethy Bridge
Sliemore
Dirdhu
Bridge of Brown
Tomintoul
Findron
Lagganvoulin
Breac Leathad
Carn Mor
Moss Hill
Ladder Hills
Dalnahaitnach
Beinn Ghuilbin
Kinveachy
Loch Garten
Loch Mallachie
Dell Lodge
Lettoch
Baddoch
Lainchoil
Tom an t-suidhe Mhor
Carn Meadhonach
Delnabo
VISITOR CENTRE
Badnafrave
Blairnamarrow
Monadh Fergie
Ladylea Hill
Torra
Carn Sleamhuinn
Avielochan
Abernethy Forest
Tore Hill
Braes of Abernethy
Carn Tuadhan
Delavorar
Carn Liath
The Socach
Granish
Auchgourish
Aundorach
Tulloch
Carn na h-Ailig
Carn na Farraidh
LECHT SKI CENTRE
Beinn a' Chruinnich
Breagach Hill
Carn Dearg Mor
Craiggowrie
Loch Pityoulish
GLENMORE FOREST PARK
Geal Charn
Torbain
Aviemore
Meall a' Bhuachaille
Carn Bheadhair
Carn Ealasaid
Cairn Vachich
Geal Charn
Strathdon
Geal-charn Mor
An Sguabach
Inverdruie
The Queen's Forest
Dalestie
Craig Veann
Chaochan Aitinn
Doune
Coylumbridge
REINDEER HOUSE
Glenmore Lodge
An Lurg
Cock Bridge
Colnabaichin
Fleuchats
Alvie
Polchar
Loch Morlich
VISITOR CENTRE & FOREST TRAIL
Mam Suim
Big Garvoun
CORGARFF
Corgarff
Tornahaish
Kinrara
CASTLE (RUINS)
Rothiemurchus
Loch an Eilein
CAIRNGORM MOUNTAINS
Carn na Feannaige
Inchrory
Loch Gamhna
Castle Hill
Bynack More
Carn Leac Saighdeir
Cairn Mona Gowan
Kincraig
Carn Eilrig
The Bruach
Feshiebridge
CAIRNGORM CHAIRLIFT & SKI CENTRE
Creag Dhubh
Cairn Gorm
Forest of Glenavon
Brown Cow Hill
Carn a' Bhacain
Balnespick
Loch Avon
Stob an t-Sluichd
Loch Builg
Farr
Beinn Mheadhoin
Beinn a' Chaorainn
Leabaidh an Daimh Bhuidhe
Gairnshiel Lodge
Inshriach Forest
Sgoran Dubh Mor
Shelter Stone
Loch Etchachan
North Top
Ben Avon
Daldownie
Rinloan
Dalfad
Lary
Braeriach
Pools of Dee
Ben Macdui
Beinn a' Bhuird
Carn Eas
Culardoch
Braenaloin
Torbeg
Tolvah
Loch Einich
Sgor Gaoith
Cairngorms
Derry Cairngorm
South Top
Creag an Dail Bheag
Geallaig Hill
Culsh
Achlean
Baileguish
Carn Ban Mor
Cairn Toul
Nature Reserve
Beinn Bhreac
Carn Liath
Bush
Crathie
Greystone
Carn Crom
GRAMPIAN
The Devil's Point
Carn a' Mhaim
Invercauld Forest
BALMORAL
Meall Dubhag
Monadh Mor
Glen Quoich
Meall Gorm
Crathie
Easter Balmoral
Clachanturn
Birkhall
Mullach Clach a' Bhlair
Beinn Bhrotain
Carn na Drochaide
Inver
Invergelder
Glen Feshie
Sgor Mor
Mar Forest
Linn of Quoich
Braemar
INVERCAULD BRIDGE
Creag nan Gall
The Coyles of Muick
Carn Dearg Mor
Glenfeshie Forest
Allanaquoich
Creag Bhalg
Mar Lodge
KINDROCHIT
Bridge of Dee
Linn of Dee
Muir
Inverey
Morrone Hill
Falls of Garbh Allt
Auchallater
Ballochbuie Forest
Linn
Cairn Geldie
Linn of Corriemulzie
Balmoral Forest
Inchnabobart
Carn an Fhidhleir Lorgaidh
Carn Liath
The Colonel's Bed
Conachcraig
Newbigging
Lochnagar
Cac Carn Beag
Carn an t-Sagairt Mor
Carn a' Coire Bhoidheach
Fasheilach
Carn an Fhidhleir (Carn Ealar)
An Sgarsoch
Glen Ey Forest
Creag nan Gabhar
White Mounth
Dubh Loch
Loch Muick
Beinn Bhreac
Carn Bhac
An Socach
Sgor Mor
Cairn Bannoch
Broad Cairn
Black Hill of Mark
Tarf Water
Falls of Tarf
Beinn Iutharn Mhor
Beinn Iutharn Bheag
Carn an Tuirc
Tolmount
Cairn of Claise
Tom Buidhe
Loch Mhairc
Braigh Sron Ghorm
An Sligearnach
Carn Aosda
Craig Mellon
Lair of Aldararie
Beinn Dearg
Carn an Righ
Glas Tulaichean
The Cairnwell
Carn a' Gheoidh
Devil's Elbow
GLENSHEE CHAIRLIFTS & SKI CENTRE
Glas Maol
Glendoll Lodge
Glen Doll
Carn a' Chlamain
Loch Loch
Creag Leacach
Monega Hill
Caenlochan Forest
Braedownie
Beinn a' Chait
Finalty Hill
Mayar
Driesh
Hill of Strone
Clova
Forest Lodge
Carn nan Gabhar
Braigh Coire Chruinn-bhalgain
Carn Aig
Ben Gulabin
Hunt Hill
Cairn of Barns
Beinn a' Ghlo
Meall a' Choire Bhuidhe
Dalmunzie Hotel
Carn an Daimh
Monamenach
Mount Bouie
Meall Reamhar
Carn Liath
Ben Vuirich
Spittal of Glenshee
Auchavan
Mid Hill
Cairn Baddoch
Croftmore
Meall Breac
Ben Earb
Meall Uaine
Mealna Letter
Badandun Hill
Cairn Daunie
Runtaleave
Balnaboth
A939
A940
A95
A941
A938
A9
B9152
B9153
B970
B9102
B9007
B9136
B9008
B9009
B9138
A944
B976
A93
24
25
26
27
28
97
90
82
A
B
C
D
E
F
G

G R A M P I A N
T A Y S I D E
Grantown-on-Spey
Cromdale
Hills of Cromdale
Dellefure
Congash
Lynemore
Dirdhu
Lainchoil
Braes of Abernethy
Bridge of Brown
Fodderletter
Glenlivet
Drumin
Tomintoul
Findron
Lagganvoulin
Delnabo
Delavorar
Badnafrave
Blairnamarrow
Torbain
Dalestie
Inchrory
Knockandhu
Glenconglass
Tomnavoulin
Auchbreck
Shenval
Tervie
Clashnoir
Chapeltown
Braes of Glenlivet
Ladder Hills
Conglass Water
Lecht Ski Centre
Cock Bridge
Corgarff
Colnabaichin
Tornahaish
Bridgend
Inverharroch
Auchmair
Aldunie
Aldivalloch
Cabrach
Bracklach
Elrick
Longlands
Craik
Rhynie
Wheedlemont
Kennethmont
Clashindarroch Forest
Clashindarroch
Kirkney
Gartly
Newnoth
The Buck
Clova
Lumsden
Mossat
Kildrummy
Edinbanchory
Bridge of Alford
Alford
Badenyon
Dulax
Torrancroy
Kirkton of Glenbuchat
Mains of Glenbuchat
Rinmore
Glencuie
Milltown
Bellabeg
Forbestown
Strathdon
Waterside
Heugh-head
Glenkindie
Towie
Sinnahard
Milltown of Towie
Hillockhead
Boultenstone
Bogston
Fleuchats
Tillypronie
Migvie
Coynach
Logie Coldstone
Corrachree
Tarland
Davan
Ordie
Leys
Coull
Cromar
Dinnet
Cambus o' May
Milton of Tullich
Ballater
Bridge of Gairn
Culsh
Candacraig
Lary
Dalfad
Torbeg
Gairnshiel Lodge
Rinloan
Daldownie
Braenaloin
Bush
Crathie
Greystone
Balmoral
Easter Balmoral
Clachanturn
Strathgirnock
Birkhall
Bridgend
Inver
Invergelder
Braemar
Allanaquoich
Bridge of Dee
Inverey
Mar Lodge
Auchallater
Ballochbuie Forest
Balmoral Forest
Inchnabobart
Lochnagar
White Mounth
Loch Muick
Spittal of Glenmuick
Linn of Muick Cottage
Aucholzie
Glascorrie
Deecastle
Ballaterach
Glen Tanar
Forest of Glentanar
Oldhall
Heugh-head
Aboyne
Birsemore
Rosehill
Glencat
Forest of Birse
Ballochan
Mount Keen
Glen Mark
Water of Mark
Glen Lee
Monawee
Glenlee
Inchgrundle
Auchronie
Tarfside
Glen Esk
Mid Caircross
Fernybank
Newbigging
Glen Clunie
Glen Callater
Glenshee Ski Centre
The Cairnwell
Devil's Elbow
Glen Doll
Glendoll Lodge
Braedownie
Clova
Glen Clova
Wheen
Rottal
The Drums
Runtaleave
Balnaboth
Glenprosen
Clachnabrain
Glenarm
Spittal of Glenshee
Dalmunzie Hotel
Auchavan
Finegand
Dalnaglar Castle
Forter
Cray
Folda
Alrick
Bridge of Brewlands
Kirkton of Glenisla
Glenisla Forest
Glenhead Farm
Blacklunans
Enochdhu
Kirkmichael
Ballinluig
Bellaty
Dykends
Dykehead
Cortachy
Memus
Tannadice
Glenmoy
Glenogil
Newmill of Inshewan
Noranside
Fern
Careston
Brechin
Kirkton of Menmuir
Tigerton
Balnamoon
Bridgend
Tillyarblet
Balfield
Witton
Dunlappie
27
28
29
30
31
98
89
82
A
B
C
D
E
F
G
A939
A944
A97
A93
A941
A980
B9008
B9136
B9002
B976
B9119
B9094
B955
B951
B950

FORMARTINE
GARIOCH
HOWE OF THE MEARNS
ABERDEEN
Ellon
Oldmeldrum
Inverurie
Kintore
Dyce
Westhill
Banchory
Peterculter
Stonehaven
Inverbervie
Laurencekirk
Montrose
Insch
Kemnay
Newburgh
Balmedie
Bridge of Don
Old Aberdeen
Cults
Portlethen
Newtonhill
Muchalls
Johnshaven
St Cyrus
Gourdon
Fordoun
Auchenblae
Marykirk
Luthermuir
Echt
Collieston
Pitmedden
Udny Green
Udny Station
Potterton
Blackdog
Cove Bay
Altens
Nigg
Torry
Kincorth
Culter
Drumoak
Crathes
Durris
Chapelton
Catterline
Kinneff
Arbuthnott
Girdle Ness
Nigg Bay
Garron Point
Todhead Point
Milton Ness
Scurdie Ness
Newburgh Bar
Danger Zone
Stromness, Lerwick & Torshavn
Bergen (Summer only)
A90
A92
A93
A96
A944
A947
A920
A957
A980
A937
A935
A956
A975
B9077
B979
B977
B993
B9119
B9125
B974
B966
B967
B9120
32
33
34
35
36
99
83
A
B
C
D
E
F
G
0 2 4 6 8 10 miles
0 2 4 6 8 10 km

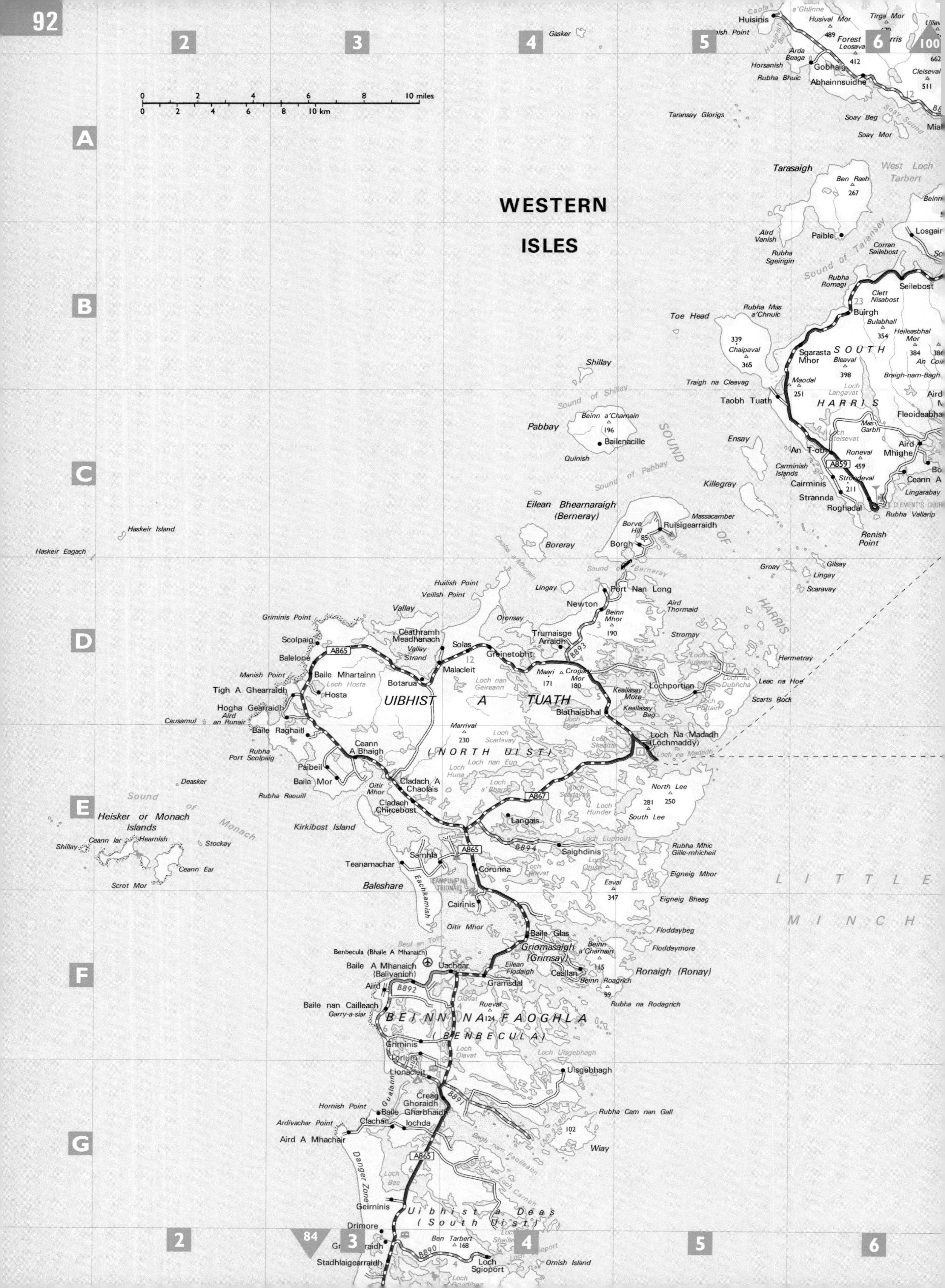
WESTERN
ISLES
0 2 4 6 8 10 miles
0 2 4 6 8 10 km
Gasker
Huisinis
Husival Mor
Tirga Mor
Forest
Leosavat
Arda Beaga
Gobhaig
Horsanish
Rubha Bhuic
Abhainnsuidhe
Cleiseval
Taransay Glorigs
Soay Beg
Soay Mor
Soay Sound
Tarasaigh
Ben Raah
267
West Loch Tarbert
Aird Vanish
Paible
Losgair
Corran Seilebost
Rubha Sgeirigin
Sound of Taransay
Rubha Romagi
Seilebost
Clett Nisabost
Toe Head
Rubha Mas a'Chnuic
Buirgh
Bulabhall
Heileasbhal Mor
339
Chaipaval
365
Sgarasta Mhor
SOUTH
Bleaval
398
HARRIS
Braigh-nam-Bagh
Shillay
Traigh na Cleavag
Maodal
Loch Langavat
Taobh Tuath
Sound of Shillay
Beinn a'Charnain
196
Pabbay
Bailenacille
Fleoideabhagh
Mas Garbh
Ensay
Aird Mhighe
An T-ob
A859
Roneval
459
Carminish Islands
Cairminis
Strondeval
211
Ceann A
Lingarabay
Quinish
Sound of Pabbay
Killegray
Strannda
Roghadal
ST CLEMENT'S CHURCH
Rubha Vallarip
Eilean Bhearnaraigh (Berneray)
Borve Hill
Ruisigearraidh
Massacamber
Renish Point
Haskeir Island
Boreray
Borgh
Haskeir Eagach
Sound of Berneray
Groay
Gilsay
Lingay
Scaravay
Lingay
Port Nan Long
Huilish Point
Veilish Point
Newton
Aird Thormaid
Vallay
Griminis Point
Oronsay
Beinn Mhor
190
Stromay
Scolpaig
Ceathramh Meadhanach
Trumaisge Arraidh
Balelone
A865
Vallay Strand
Solas
Greinetobht
B893
Hermetray
Manish Point
Baile Mhartainn
Botarua
Malacleit
Maari
171
Crogary Mor
180
Lochportian
Leac na Hoe
Tigh A Ghearraidh
Loch Hosta
Hosta
UIBHIST A TUATH
Loch nan Geireann
Keallasay More
Keallasay Beg
Scarts Rock
Hogha Gearraidh
Blathaisbhal
Causamul
Aird an Runair
Baile Raghaill
Marrival
230
Loch Scadavay
Loch Na Madadh (Lochmaddy)
Rubha Port Scolpaig
Ceann A Bhaigh
(NORTH UIST)
Loch nan Eun
Paibeil
Baile Mor
Deasker
Cladach A Chaolais
North Lee
281
250
South Lee
Sound of Monach
Rubha Raouill
Oitir Mhor
A867
Heisker or Monach Islands
Cladach Chircebost
Langais
Kirkibost Island
Shillay
Ceann Iar
Hearnish
Stockay
A865
B894
Saighdinis
Rubha Mhic Gille-mhicheil
Teanamachar
Samhla
Ceann Ear
Corunna
Eigneig Mhor
Scrot Mor
Baleshare
TEAMPULL NA TRIONAID
Eval
347
LITTLE
Eachkamish
Cairinis
Eigneig Bheag
MINCH
Oitir Mhor
Floddaybeg
Baile Glas
Beul an Toim
Beinn a'Charnain
Floddaymore
Benbecula (Bhaile A Mhanaich)
Griomasaigh (Grimsay)
Baile A Mhanaich (Balivanich)
Uachdar
Eilean Flodaigh
115
Ronaigh (Ronay)
Ceallan
Aird
B892
Gramsdal
Beinn Roagrich
99
Rubha na Rodagrich
Baile nan Cailleach
Garry-a-siar
Rueval
124
BEINN NA FAOGHLA
(BENBECULA)
Griminis
Loch Olavat
Loch Uisgebhagh
Torlum
Lionacleit
Uisgebhagh
Creag Ghoraidh
Gualann
B891
Hornish Point
Baile Gharbhaidh
Rubha Cam nan Gall
Ardivachar Point
Clachan
Iochda
102
Aird A Mhachair
Wiay
Bagh nam Faoileann
A865
Danger Zone
Loch Bee
Loch Carnan
Geirninis
Uibhist a Deas
(South Uist)
Drimore
Ben Tarbert
168
Stadhlaigearraidh
B890
Loch Sgioport
Ornish Island
A
B
C
D
E
F
G
2
3
4
5
6
84
100

EILEAN HEARADH
Park
(HARRIS)
Athlinne
Seaforth Island
Aird A Mhulaidh
Clett Ard
Mullach a' Ruisg
Stulaval
Mulla-fo-dheas
Clisham
Beinn na h-Uamha
Eisgean
Loch Seaforth
Kenmore
Maruig
Bun Abhainn Eadarra
Sgaoth Aird
Straiaval
Toddun
Laxadale Lochs
Caiteshal
Aird Asaig
Reinigeadal
Corlabhadh
Crionaig
Uisenis
Mulhagery
Tathas Mhor
Mol Truisg
Loch Claidh
Loch Bhrollum
Bhalamus
Rubha Bhrollum
Gob Rubh'Uisenis
Rubh'a'Bhaird
Sgeir na h-Eigheach
Eilean Mor A'Bhaigh
Eilean Iubhard
Leumrabhagh
Gob na Milaid
Srianach
Caolas Luath
Loch Shell
Tairbeart (Tarbert)
Taoth Siar
Ceann Reamhar
Urgha
Beinn a'Chaolais
Uiesval
Carragrich
Sgeotasaigh
Caolas Scalpaigh
Scalpay
Ben Scoravick
Kennavay
Eilaen Scalpaigh (Scalpay)
Meall Challibost
Loch Ceann Dibig
East Loch Tarbert
Meabhag
East Rocklett
Greosabhagh
Leac A Li
Scadabhagh
Loch Grosebay
Rubha Bocaig
Cluer
Rubha Cluer
Ard Manish
Quidnish
Braigh Mor
SOUND OF SHIANT
Garbh Eilean
Eilean Mhuire
Shiant Islands
Eilean an Tighe
Fladda-chuain
Gaeilavore Island
Gearran Island
Eilean Trodday
Rubha Hunish
Loch Hunish
Lub a'Sgiathain
Rubha na h-Aiseig
The Aird
Kilmaluag Bay
Duntulm Bay
Tulm Island
Duntulm
Kilmaluag
Galta Mor
Score Bay
SKYE COTTAGE MUSEUM
Sgeir Eirin
Flodigarry
Eilean Flodigarry
Ru Bornaskitaig
Hunglader
Kilmuir
Camas Mor
Loch Sheosdal
Meall na Suiramach
Digg
Staffin Island
Kilvaxter
Balgown
Suidh' a'Mhinn
The Needle
Staffin Bay
Rubha Garbhaig
Staffin
Monkstadt
Stenscholl
Bioda Buidhe
Loch Cleap
Elishader
Vaternish Point
Linicro
Kilbride Point
Stack of Skudiburgh
Maligar
Ben Gorm
L. Mealt
Idrigil
Uig
Ascrib Islands
South Ascrib
Rubha Idrigil
Uig Bay
Marishader
Rubha nam Brathairean
Garros
Beinn Edra
Balnaknock
Culnaknock
Rubha Chorachan
Earlish
Loch a' Bhraige
Sron Ocrhulan
Ben Geary
Geary
Trumpan
TROTTERNISH
Lealt
LOCH SNIZORT
Halistra
Gillen
Stac a' Bhothain
Poll na h-Ealaidh
Cuidrach
Glenuachdarach
Creag a'Lain
Baca Ruadh
Ardmore Point
Hallin
Peinlich
Hinnisdal
Leac Tressirnish
Dry Harbour
RONA
Isay Island
Mingay Island
Biod nan Laogh
Lyndale Point
Rigg
Dunvegan Head
Rubha Maol
Stein
Lusta
Greshornish Point
Kingsburgh
Beinn a'Sga
Hartaval
Lampay Islands
Loch Bay
Ben Diubaig
Lynedale
Greshornish
Romesdal
The Storr
Eilean Tigh
Galtrigill
Claigan
Beinn Bhreac
Treaslane
Borreraig
Ben Skriaig
Flashader
The Aird
Lon Mor
Bearreraig Bay
Loch a'Sguirr
Uig
Beinn Chreagach
Eyre
Eilean Fladday
Husabost
Kensaleyre
Haultin
Loch Leathan
Feriniquarrie
Edinbain
Ben Horneval
Bernisdale
Ben Dearg
Beinn na h-Iolaire
Milovaig
Totaig
Tote
Borve
Torran
Black House
Colbost
Skinidin
Uiginish
Dunvegan
Ben Uigshader
Skeabost
Carbost
Loch Fada
Prince Charles's Cave
Manish Point
Loch Arnish
Arnish
Oisgill Bay
Loch Mor
Beinn na Creiche
Waterstein Head
Kilmuir
Lonmore
Ben Sca
Cruachan Beinn a'Chearcaill
Drumuie
Sithean Bhealaich Chumhaing
Brochel
Point
Moonen Bay
Glen Dale
Ben Aketil
Uigshader
Beinn a'Ghlinne Bhig
Ben Corkeval
Healabhal Mhor Macleod's Table North
Roskhill
Glengrasco
Torvaig
Ramasaig
Roag
Vatten
SKYE
Loch Connan
Portree
Ramasaig Bay
Hoe Rape
Orbost
Loch Portree
Glame
The Hoe
Lorgill
Healabhal Bheag Macleod's Table South
Harlosh
Glen Ose
Beinn na Cloiche
Am Maol
Beinn na Greine
Penifiler
Ben Tianavaig
RAASAY
Balmore
Ose
Loch Duagrich
Ben Connan
Harlosh Point
Glenmore
Balachuirn
Dun Caan
Beinn na Boine
Ben Idrigill
Harlosh Island
Tarner Island
Ullinish
Bracadale
Struan
Coillore
Ben Duagrich
Mugeary
Camastianavaig
Oskaig Point
Oskaig
Rubha na' Leac
Loch Bracadale
Lower Ollach
Fada
SOUND OF RAASAY
A850
A855
A856
A863
A87
B886
B884
B885
B8036
B883

11
12
13
14
15
A
B
C
D
E
F
G
H
I
93
85
86
0 2 4 6 8 10 miles
0 2 4 6 8 10 km
THE MINCH
Stornoway
Eilean Mullagrach
Glas-leac Mor
Summer Isles
Tanera Beg
Glas-leac Beag
Priest Island
Bottle Island
Greenstone Point
Cailleach Head
Obinan
Leac Mhor
Rubha Beag
Rubha Mor
Mellon Udrigle
Static Point
Gruinard Island
Badluarchrach
Slaggan Bay
Gruinard Bay
Achgarve
Mungasdale
Eilean Furadh Mor
Rubha Reidh
Camas Mor
Cove
Laide
Mellon Charles
Ormiscaig
First Coast
Second Coast
Loch an Draing
Bualnaluib
Aultbea
Little Gruinard
Drumchork
An Cuaidh
296
Isle of Ewe
LOCH EWE
Loch Sguod
Melvaig
Aultgrishan
Inverasdale
Midtown
A832
Creag-mheall Beag
347
Cnoc Breac
293
Loch Thurnaig
Tuirnaig
Peterburn
Naast
B8021
B8057
INVEREWE (NTS)
Londubh
Meall na Meine
251
Beinn a'Chaisgein Beag
680
North Erradale
Boor
Poolewe
Fisherfield
Big Sand
Mial
Longa Island
Carn Dearg
Gairloch
Auchtercairn
349
Meall A'irigh Mhic Craidh
GAIRLOCH HERITAGE MUSEUM
Strath Bay
Gair Loch
Eilean Horrisdale
Charlestown
Loch Airigh a' Phuill
Beinn Airigh Charr
791
Meall Mheannaidh
Port Henderson
Badachro
Kerrysdale
Opinan
B8056
Shieldaig
Meall Aundrary
329
Eilean Ruairidh Mor
Slattadale
Eilean Suthainn
Beinn Lair
860
South Erradale
Letterewe
Furnace
Loch Bad an Sgalaig
VICTORIA FALLS
Talladale
Dubh Loch
Redpoint
Maol Ruadh
Mullach nan Cadhaichean
294
Red Point
Staffin Island
Digg
The Needle
Stenscholl
Staffin
Rubha Garbhaig
Elishader
Maligar
Marishader
Garros
Culnaknock
Rubha nam Brathairean
Lealt
Leac Tressirnish
Rigg
Hartaval
Eilean Trodday
Galta Mor
Sgeir Eirin
Eilean Flodigarry
Loch a' Bhraige
Rona
Dry Harbour
125
Eilean Tigh
Kyle Rona
Eilean Fladday
Beinn na h-Iolaire
254
Torran
Arnish
Brochel
Manish Point
SOUND OF RAASAY
INNER SOUND
RAASAY
Glame
385
Balachuirn
Dun Caan
443
Oskaig
Oskaig Point
Rubha na' Leac
SKYE
A855
A850
A87
Ben Dearg
552
Prince Charles's Cave
Sithean Bhealaich Chumhaing
392
Portree
Penifiler
Ben Tianavaig
413
Camastianavaig
B883
Lower Ollach
Borve
Meall na h-Uamha
288
Baosbheinn
875
Beinn an Eoin
855
Shieldaig Forest
Beinn Bhreac
624
Craig
Loch a'Bhealaich
Beinn a'Chearcaill
Meall a' Ghiubhais
LOCH TORRIDON
Rubha na Fearn
Lower Diabaig
Upper Diabaig
Ruadh-mheallan
672
Sgurr Mhor
985
Beinn Dearg
914
922
Beinn Alligin
Ruadh-stac Mor
1010
Sail Mhor
981
Beinn Eighe
TORRIDON ESTATE (NTS)
Fearnmore
Fearnbeg
Arinacrinachd
Cuaig
Kenmore
Alligin Shuas
Inveralligan
Mullach an Rathain
1023
Spidean a'Choire Leith
1054
Liathach
UPPER LOCH TORRIDON
Fasag
Torridon
Ardheslaig
Inverbain
Shieldaig Island
Shieldaig
Rubha na Feola
Balgy
A896
Annat
436
Seana Mheallan
Kalnakill
Lonbain
An Garbh-mheall
493
Croic-bheinn
493
Ben Shieldaig
516
Ben-damph Forest
737
Beinn na h-Eaglaise
Meall na Fhuaid
518
An Fur
387
Glenshieldaig
Forest
Beinn Damh
902
Maol Chean-dearg
933
Sgorr Ruadh
960
Fuar Tholl
907
626
An Staonach
513
Meall na Saobhaidhe
368
An Ruadh-stac
892
Applecross Forest
Hartfield
Applecross
Milton
Camusteel
Camasterach
Culduie
Toscaig
646
Beinn Bhan
896
Sgurr a'Chaorachain
776
792
Bealach na Ba
710
Meall Gorm
Russel
Sgurr a Gharaidh
730
Balnacra
Coulags
A890
Strathcarron Sta.
Achintee
Lochcarron
Sgeir Fhada
Attadale
Achintraid
Loch Kishorn
Sron na h-Airde Baine
Carn Geuradainn
594
Stroc-bheinn
400
Beinn na Greine
417
719
Strath Lungard
Fionn Loch
Coulin Forest
Sgurr Dubh
782
Kishorn

Ledmore
Elphin
Knockan
Inverpolly Forest
Stac Pollaidh
Cul Mor
849
Drumrunie Forest
Aird of Coigach
Loch Osgaig
16
101
17
18
19
20
102
Beinn Sgeireach
476
Badintagairt
Bo Maola
424
Allt a' Bhunn
Colaboll
Sallachy
Loch na Caillich
Achiltibuie
Polglass
Loch Bad a' Ghaill
Loch Lurgainn
Cul Beag
769
A835
A837
Cnoc na Glas Choille
307
An Stuc
364
Beinn an Eoin
544
Glen Oykel
Glen Cassley
An t-Sail
490
Beinn na Eoin
618
Achvraie
Crom Allt
Cromalt Hills
516
Drumrunie
Loch Craggie
Fionn Bheinn Mhor
330
Loch na Fuaralaich
Grudie Burn
Cnoc
A
Claonel
Ben Mor Coigach
743
C O I G A C H
Achduart
Culnacraig
Geodha Mor
Strathkanaird
Kanaird
Rappach
Strath nan Lon
Meall an Fhuarain
578
Coire a' Chonachair
Lubcroy
Oykel Bridge
Langwell
Strath
Brae
Doune
Invercassley
Glenrossal
Oykel Forest
Rosehall
Aucharrigill
Altass
Auchintoul
A839
Shin
Cnoc Ceann nam Bad
Camas Mor
Na Dromannan
408
Loch Maoile
Tutim Burn
1408
Birchfield
Achnahanat
Lins
A837
Isle Martin
Cul a' Bhogha
Loch Canaird
Ardmair
Rhue
Allt Beinn Donuill
Rappach Water
Glen Einig
Einig
Rhidorroch Forest
Meall Liath Choire
548
Knockdamph
Abhainn Poiblidh
Beinn Ulbhaidh
493
Rheloe
Kyle of Sutherland
Achmore
Annat Bay
Rhireavach
Morefield
Ullapool
Rhidorroch
Creag Loisgte
412
Lubachoinnich
Breac-Bheinn
Beinn Ghobhlach
635
Braes of Ullapool
Loch Achall
Glen Achall
Loch an Daimh
Strath Mulzie
Meall Dheirgidh
507
B
Cnoc a' Bhaid-rallaich
545
Allt na h-Airbhe
Beinn Eilideach
558
Carn a' Choin Deirg
701
Sgodachail
Strathcarron
Croick
Wester Gruinards
The Craigs
Badrallach
Loch Broom
A832
Blarnalevoch
Loggie
Rhiroy
Ardindrean
Leckmelm
Ardcharnich
Meall Dubh
642
Glen Douchary
Meall nam Bradhan
677
Amat Forest
Bodach Mor
822
Freevater Forest
Alladale
Allt a' Ghlinne
Ardessie
Camusnagaul
Sail Mhor
Eilean Darach
Dundonnell
Letters
Loch a' Choire Mhoir
Seana Bhraigh
927
Carn Ban
Sron Gun Aran
Gleann Mor
Carn Bhrain
635
Gruinard Forest
Dundonnell House
Strath Beag
Inverlael Forest
Carn Mor
649
Glencalvie Forest
Glen Calvie
Strathnasheallag Forest
Bidein a' Ghlas Thuill
1062
An Teallach
Sgurr Fiona
1059
Inverlael
Eididh nan Clach Geala
928
Glenbeg
Gleann Beag
Abhainn a' Ghlinne Bhig
Dunan Liath
691
Diebidale Forest
C
Carn Chuinneag
838
Meall Bheni
532
Dundonnell Forest
Inverbroom
Auchlunachan
Glackour
Strath More
Meall nan Ceapraichean
977
Meall a' Chuaille
628
Crom Loch
Beinn Tharsuinn
714
Creag Ruadh
671
Carn Cas nan Gabhar
602
Strath na Sealga
Beinn Deargh Mhor
908
Auchindrean
Fasagrianach
Beinn Enaiglair
889
Beinn Dearg
1084
Cona' Mheall
980
Tollomuick Forest
Inchbae Forest
Abhainn na Glasa
Loch a' Chaorainn
96
Braemore
Fain
Corrieshalloch Gorge (NTS)
Am Faochagach
954
Strathvaich Forest
Kildermorie Forest
Kildermorie Lodge
Loch Magharaidh
Loch Morie
Beinn a' Chlaidheimh
914
Meall an t-Sithe
601
Dirrie More
Meall Leacachain
618
Loch Coire Lair
Loch Vaich
Loch a' Gharbhrain
Ruadh Stac Mor
918
Sgurr Ban
989
Creag Rainich
807
Creag Dhubh
522
Lochdrum
Tom Ban Mor
742
Beinn nan Eun
742
Strathrannoch
Strath Vaich
Strath Rannoch
Wyvis Lodge
D
Meall an Tuirc
625
Loch Glass
Mullach Coire Mhic Fhearchair
1019
Beinn Tarsuinn
936
Loch a' Bhraoin
Meall a' Chrasgaidh
934
Beinn Liath Bheag
665
Loch Droma
Loch Glascarnoch
Loch a' Mhadaidh
Sgurr Mor
1110
954
Beinn Liath Mhor Fannaich
Beinn Liath Mhor a' Ghiubhais Li
766
Abhainn a' Ghiubhais Li
Loch Bealach Cuiaidh
Queen's Cairn
Carn Mor
Wyvis Forest
Beinn Bheag
Groban
748
A' Chailleach
999
Sgurr Breac
1000
Sgurr nan Clach Geala
1093
Sgurr nan Each
923
Meall Gorm
949
Allt a' Choire Mhoir
Loch Gorm
Kinlochluichart Forest
Aultguish Inn
20
Lubfearn
A835
Meall na Drochaide
Kinlochmore
Meallan Chuaich
Fannich Forest
Beinn Dearg
687
An Coileachan
923
Meall Mhic Iomhair
607
Carn na Dubh Choille
479
Garbat Forest
Garbat
Glas Leathad Mor
1046
Ben Wyvis
An Cabar
Meall na Speireig
Allt nan Caorach
Gleann na Muice
Gleann Tanagaidh
Abhainn a' Chadh Bhuidhe
Corriemoillie Forest
Black Water
W E S T E R R O S S
Beinn a' Mhuinidh
692
Kinlochewe Forest
Heights of Kinlochewe
Beinn nan Ramh
711
Loch Fannich
Grudie
Loch nam Fiadh
Beinn a' Bhric
442
Achnaclerach
Little Wyvis
764
E
Cloch Mhor
482
Strath Sgitheach
Taagan
Leckie
Strath Chrombuill
Bruachaig
Lochrosque Forest
An Cabar
558
Carn na Beiste
518
Carn Daraich
465
Lochluichart
A832
Strathgarve Forest
Carn Gorm
556
Glensgaich
Allt Dearg
G H L A N D
Kinlochewe
Fionn Bheinn
933
Knockban
Loch Luichart
Gorstan
Garve
Mountrich
Bottacks
Heights of Brae
Fodderty
Carn a' Ghlinne
539
Meall a' Chaorainn
705
Loch Achanalt
Loch a' Chuilinn
Strath Bran
Carn Chaiseachain
312
Loch Bhad Ghaineamhaich
Sgurr Marcasaidh
Loch Garve
Rogie Burn
Auchterneed
Castle Leod
Strath Peffer
Dingwall
A834
A896
Glen Docherty
Badavanich
Loch a' Chroisg
A832
Achnasheen
Carn na Cre
461
Falls of Conon
Tarvie
Rogie Falls
Strathpeffer
Lubmore
An Liathanach
A890
Carn Loisgte
Creag Loch nan Dearcag
536
Little Scatwell
Loch Achilty
Loch Kinellan
Loch Ussie
Maryburgh
Abhainn Dubh
Loch an Fhiarlaid
Ledgowan Forest
Carn Beag
550
Loch Gowan
Sgurr a' Ghlas Leathaid
844
Sgurr a' Mhuilinn
879
Milltown
Loch Meig
Torrachilty Wood
Jamestown
Contin
Lochussie
Conon Bridge
Loch Coulin
Meallan nan Uan
840
Porin
Meig
Loch Achonachie
A835
F
Carn Breac
678
Cnoc an t-Sidhein
372
Carn Mhartuin
538
Carn an Leanaidh
574
Gleann Meinich
Meall na Faochaig
680
Glenmeanie
Carn na Cloiche Moire
591
Meall nan Damh
671
Strathconon
Marybank
Urray
A862
Balvaird
55
Loch Sgamhain
Scardroy
Loch Beannachan
Carnoch
Inverchoran
Meall Giubhais
662
Carn na Coinnich
Sron nan Saobhaidh
408
Falls of Orrin
Orrin
A832
Faebait
Muir of Ord
Craig
Carron
Moruisg
928
Carn Liath
857
875
Carn Gorm
Glencarron and Glenuig Forest
Bac an Eich
849
Strathconon Forest
Glen Orrin
Orrin Reservoir
Gleann Goibhre
Loch nan Eun
Ardnagrask
Windhill
Allt a' Chonais
Sgurr nan Ceannaichean
915
Gleann Fhiodhaig
Corriehallie Forest
Allt Goibhre
Loch nam Bonnach
Cnoc Eille Mor
Rheindown
A862
Beauly
Achnashellach Forest
Loch a' Chlaidheimh
Sgurr Coire nan Eun
789
Loch na Caoidhe
Beinn nam Fitheach
494
Urchany and Farley Forest
Ruilick
Maoile Lunndaidh
1007
Sgurr na Cairbe
Erchless Forest
Sgurr a' Phollain
854
G
Achnagairn
Sgurr na Feartaig
862
Sgurr Choinnich
999
Sgurr a' Chaorachain
1053
An Gorm Loch
Sgurr Fhuar-thuill
1049
Carn nan Gobhar
992
Meallan Buidhe
766
Cluanie Deer Park Farm
A831
Kilmorack
A862
Balchraggan
Beinn Tharsuinn
863
Carn Eiteige
882
1083
Sgurr na Ruaidhe
993
Beinn a' Bha'ach Ard
862
Lochan Fada
Crask of Aigas
A833
Belladrum
West Monar Forest
Loch Mhuilich
East Monar Forest
Sgurr a' Choire Ghlais
Oldtown of Aigas
Kiltarlity
Loch an Laoigh
945
Sgurr na Muice
891
Carn Ban
736
Neaty Burn
Culligran
Craigdhu
Culburnie
Tomnacross
Bidean a' Choire Sheasgaich
986
Lurg Mhor
Loch Monar
Struy
Erchless Castle
87
Eskadale
Camault Muir
Druimkinnerras
Foxhole
16
17
Meallan Odhar
18
Ardchuilk
Glen Strathfarrar
Loch Beannacharan
19
Culligran Falls
Struy Forest
20
Boblainy Forest
An Gead Loch
Uisge Misgeach
Inchvuilt
Mauld
Loch Neaty
Loch Bruicheach
Loch an Tachdaidh
Meallan Buidhe
Beinn Bheag
Beinn Dronaig
Loch a' Mhuillidh
Carn a' Mhuilt
Crelevan

H I G H L A N D
E A S T E R R O S S
Loch Borralan
A837
Glen Oykel
An Stuc
364
Beinn an Eoin
544
Badintagairt
Glen Cassley
Beinn Sgeireach
476
Bo Maola
424
Loch Sgeireach
Achnairn
Colchork
A836
Loch Beannach
Sithean Achadh nan Eun
Loch Gaineimh
Cnoc Leamhnachd
Grumby Rock
102
Strath Brora
Scibercross
Tannachy
Rhilochan
West Langwell
East Langwell
Farlary
Cnoc na Glas Choille
307
Loch Craggie
Fionn Bheinn Mhor
330
Loch na Claise Moire
Loch na Fuaralaich
Cnoc a'Choire
402
Loch na Caillich
Sallachy
Savalmore
Savalbeg
Lairg Lo.
Meall Dola
323
Loch Craggie
Lairg
Balchraggan
Tomich
Torroble
Lairg Sta.
Rhaoine
Muie
Strath Fleet
Ardochu
Little Rogart
Blairmore
Rogart
Rogart Sta.
Pittentrail
A839
Morvich
Aberscross
Mound Rock
Allt a'Chaoruinn
Meall an Fhuarain
578
Glenrossal
Oykel Forest
Claonel
Gruids
Achany Glen
Braemore
Shin Forest
Achany
Cnoc Ceann nam Bad
Creagan Glas
813
Loch Cracail Mor
Strath Tollaidh
Lubcroy
Oykel Bridge
Langwell
Strath Oykel
Brae
Doune
Invercassley
Rosehall
Aucharrigill
Altass
Auchintoul
A837
SHIN FALLS
Linsidemore
B864
Achinduich
Loch Laro
Loch Buidhe
Torboll
Dalnamain
Little Torboll
Glen Einig
Rappach Water
Meoir Langwell
Birchfield
Achnahanat
Invershin
Invershin Sta.
Rhelonie
Sron Ach' a'Bhacaidh
Beinn Domhnaill
349
Loch Laoigh
Ardshave
Knockdamph
Creag Loisgte
412
Beinn Ulbhaidh
493
Lubachoinnich
Kyle of Sutherland
Breac-Bheinn
462
Clashban
Loch an Lagain
CARBISDALE
Culrain
Achvaich
Achosnich
Badninish
Strath Mulzie
Corriemulzie
Meall Dheirgidh
507
Balblair
Meall Moraig
Clashcoig
Rearquhar
Creagan Asdale
Evelix
Birichen
Carn a'Choin Deirg
701
Sgodachail
Strathcarron
Tulloch
Migdale
Croick
Wester Gruinards
The Craigs
Soyal
Lower Gledfield
A836
Bonar Bridge
Kyloag
Gablon
Clashmore Wood
Evelix
Meall nam Bradhan
677
Glen Douchary
Amat Forest
Dounie
Ardgay
Kincardine
Ardchronie
Loch Migdale
Little Creich
Spinningdale
A949
Clashmore
Carmore
A9
Whiteface
SKIBO
Pulrossie
CRAFT CENTRE
Lonemore
Dornoch Sands
Cuthill
Loch a'Choire Mhoir
Freevater Forest
Bodach Mor
822
Carn Ban
Alladale
Sron Gun Aran
Gleann Mor
Carron
Glen Calvie
Allt a'Ghlinne
Carn Bhrain
635
Glencalvie Forest
Seana Bhraigh
927
Douchary
Coire Bog
Wester Fearn Burn
Easter Fearn
Struie Hill
Dounie
Ardmore
Cambuscurry Bay
DORNOCH FIRTH
Ardjachie Point
Eididh nan Clach Geala
928
Meall nan Ceapraichean
977
Cona' Mheall
980
Beinn Dearg
1084
Dunan Liath
691
Beinn Tharsuinn
714
Diebidale Forest
Carn Chuinneag
838
Glen Diebidale
Creag Ruadh
671
Meall Bhenneit
532
Beinn Clach an Fheadain
477
Struie
371
Edderton
A836
Glenbeg
Gleann Beag
Abhainn a'Ghlinne Bhig
Meall a' Chuaille
628
Crom Loch
Carn Cas nan Gabhar
602
Abhainn Glac an t-Seilich
Cnoc Muigh-bhlaraidh
B9176
Aultnamain Inn
Easter Fearn Burn
Morangie
Tain
Morangie Forest
Lairgs of Tain
Glen Aldie
Aldie
95
Tollomuick Forest
Inchbae Forest
Loch a'Chuorainn
Abhainn na Glasa
Beinn Tharsuinn
692
Cnoc an t-Sabhail
Strathvaich Forest
Loch Vaich
Loch Coire Lair
Kildermorie Forest
Loch Magharaidh
Kildermorie Lodge
Braeantra
Strath Rusdale
Loch Morie
Black Water
Strath Rory
Lamington
Newfield
Logie Hill
Lochdrum
Loch a' Gharbhrain
Tom Ban Mor
742
Beinn nan Eun
742
Cnoc Corr Guinie
Scotsburn
Torran
Inchlumpie
Balnagown Castle
Kildary
Strathrannoch
Strath Rannoch
Strath Vaich
Loch Droma
Loch Glascarnoch
Meall Mor
738
Wyvis Lodge
Loch Bealach Culaidh
Loch Glass
Meall an Tuirc
625
Boath
Easter Ardross
Inchindown
Stittenham
Dalnavie
Averon or Alness
Tullich Muir
Milton
Wester Lonvine
Kilmuir
Beinn Liath Mhor a'Ghiubhais Li
766
Aultguish Inn
A835
Lubfearn
Queen's Cairn
Carn Mor
Wyvis Forest
Bendcallt
Wester Lealty
Cnoc Ceislein
523
Contullich
Achandunie
Balnaguisich
Achnagarron
Rhicullen
Delny
Barbaraville
Tomich
Balintraid
Nigg Bay
Kinlochluichart Forest
Meall na Drochaide
Kinloch
Glen Glass
Alness
Rosskeen
Saltburn
Balnabruaich
Balnapaling
Glas Leathad Mor
1046
Garbat Forest
Garbat
Ben Wyvis
An Cabar
Beinn Dearg
687
Meall Mhic Iomhair
607
Corriemoillie Forest
Carn na Dubh Choille
479
B817
B9176
Dalmore
Invergordon
Cromarty
Redburn
BLACK ROCK GORGE
Alness Bay
Balblair
Newhall Point
Cromarty Bay
Meall na Speireig
Allt nan Caorach
Achnaclerach
Little Wyvis
764
Loch nam Fiadh
Beinn a'Bhric
442
Carn na Beiste
518
An Cabar
558
Swordale
Evanton
Drummond
Balconie Point
CROMARTY FIRTH
Resolis
Newmills
Udale Bay
Shoremill
Jemimaville
B9163
Lochluichart
Lochluichart Sta.
A832
Strathgarve Forest
Carn Gorm
556
Cloich Mhor
482
Strath Sgitheach
Ardullie
Cullicudden
The Den
Poyntzfield
Muirton
Gorstan
Garve
Loch Luichart
Glensgaich
Bottacks
Mountgerald
Shoretown
Easter Brae
Glenurquhart
B9160
Upper Eathie
Craighead
BRAN
Loch Bhad Ghaineamhaich
Sgurr Marcasaidh
Loch Garve
Rogie Burn
Auchterneed
Heights of Brae
Fodderty
A862
Findon Mains
Culbo
Millbuie
Forest
187
A832
Carn na Cre
461
A835
ROGIE FALLS
Castle Leod
Strathpeffer
Strath Peffer
A834
Dingwall
TOWN HOUSE
Urquhart
Danger Zone
B9163
Culbokie
Mount Eagle
256
Balmungie
Janefield
Rosemarkie Bay
Danger Area
Creag Loch nan Dearcag
536
Falls of Conon
Tarvie
Loch Achilty
Loch Kinellan
Knock Ussie
Maryburgh
Alcaig
BLACK ISLE
Killen
Rosemarkie
Fort George
Sgurr a'Mhuilinn
879
Little Scatwell
Milltown
Loch Meig
Torrachilty Wood
Jamestown
Lochussie
Contin
Duncanston
Belmaduthy
Easter Suddie
Fortrose
Chanonry Point
Ardersier
Meallan nan Uan
840
Porin
Meig
Strathconon
Loch Achonachie
Conon Bridge
Corntown
Bogbuie
Easter Kinkell
Knockbain
Avoch
Avoch Bay
Meall na Faochaig
680
Glenmeanie
Carn na Cloiche Moire
591
Meall nan Damh
671
Marybank
Urray
Leanaig
A835
Shantullich
Munlochy
Munlochy Bay
Moray Firth
B9039
Carnoch
Carn na Coinnich
Sron nan Saobhaidh
408
A862
Balvaird
Tore
Drumderfit
Inverchoran
Meall Giubhais
662
Orrin
Falls of Orrin
A832
Kilcoy
Newton
Bogallan
Fisherton
Orrin Reservoir
Glen Orrin
Faebait
Muir of Ord
A832
Redcastle
Kilmuir
Alturlie Point
Castle Stuart
Tornagrain
Strathconon Forest
Corriehallie Forest
Gleann Goibhre
Allt Goibhre
Loch nan Eun
Cnoc Eille Mor
Ardnagrask
Loch nam Bonnach
Windhill
Milton
North Kessock
Craigton Point
Newton
Dalcross
Beinn nam Fitheach
494
Urchany and Farley Forest
Rheindown
Ruilick
A862
Beauly
Beauly Firth
Charlestown
South Kessock
Longman Point
A96
Cantraywood
Balloch
Culloden Forest
Sgurr na Cairbe
Erchless Forest
PRIORY
B9164
Kirkhill
Rhindouie
Clachnaharry
A862
INVERNESS
Smithtown
Culloden
Culloden Muir
CULLODEN 1746
CUMBERLAND'S STONE
Carn nan Gobhar
992
1083
Sgurr na Ruaidhe
993
Sgurr a'Choire Ghlais
Meallan Buidhe
766
Beinn a'Bha'ach Ard
862
Sgurr a'Phollain
854
CLUANIE DEER PARK FARM
Lochan Fada
A831
Kilmorack
Achnagairn
A862
Drumchardine
Bunchrew
Leachkin
Culcabock
B9006
Westhill
Leanach
Dalroy
CLAVA CAIRNS
Crask of Aigas
Balchraggan
Easter Moniack
The Aird
Carn Ban
736
Oldtown of Aigas
Craigdhu
Kiltarlity
A833
Belladrum
Culburnie
Tomnacross
Cnoc na Moine
316
An Leacainn
Lagnalean
KNOCKNAGAEL BOAR STONE
Bogbain
Castletown
B851
Culligran
Neaty Burn
Caledonian Canal
Drummossie Muir
Beinn Bhuidhe
Struy
Erchless Castle
Camault Muir
Foxhole
Dochgarroch
B862
Newton of Leys
Culligran Falls
Eskadale
Drumnadrochit
Balnacarras
Dores
Scaniport
B861
Daviot
Craggie
Ardchuilk
Glen Strathfarrar
Struy Forest
Loch Bunacharan
Mauld
Boblainy Forest
Kirkton
Lochend
Mains of Faillie
Loch a'Mhuillidh
Crelevan
Loch Neaty
Loch Bruicheach
Carn a' Mhuilt
501
Carn
Scatraig
A82
19
20
21
22
23
88
A
B
C
D
E
F
G

24
25
26
27
28
103
A
B
C
D
E
F
G
98
89
0 2 4 6 8 10 miles
0 2 4 6 8 10 km
Portgower
Lothmore
Culgower
Kilmote
Lothbeg
Lothbeg Point
Creag a' Chrionaich
394
Col-bheinn
538
Gordonbush
Kilbraur Hill
323
Carrol Rock
Killin
Carrol
Killin Rock
Kintradwell
Achrimsdale
Greenhill
West Clyne
Dalchalm
Clynelish
East Brora
Brora
Doll
Cagar Feosaig
Backies
Dunrobin Sta.
DUNROBIN CASTLE
Golspie
Embo
Street
Danger Zone
FIRTH
Tarbat Ness
Port Mor
Wilkhaven
Whiteness Sands
Innis Mhor
Hilton
Portmahomack
Innis Bheag
Bindal
Balcherry
Inver
Rockfield
Balnagall
Tarrel
Lochslin
Rhynie
Balaldie
Hill of Fearn
Geanies Ho.
Fearn
Cadboll
Tullich
Hilton of Cadboll
FEARN ABBEY
Clay of Allan
Balintore
Shandwick
Chapelhill
Hill of Nigg
Castlecraig
North Sutor
Sutor Stacks
Blue Head
MORAY FIRTH
Halliman Skerries
Covesea Skerries
LOSSIEMOUTH FISHERIES & COMMUNITIES MUS
Stotfield
Branderburgh
Lossiemouth
Clashach Point
Covesea
BURGHEAD WELL
Hopeman
Burghead
Gordonstoun
Cummingstown
Roseisle
Duffus
DUFFUS
Oakenhead
Salterhill
Lossie Forest
Boar's Head Rock
Danger Zone
Innes Links
Burghead Bay
Roseisle Forest
Findrassie
Buthill
Innes Canal
Kingston
Findhorn
Hempriggs
Quarrywood
PALACE OF SPYNIE
INNES HOUSE
Bishopmill
Coltfield
Ardgye
Muirhead
Miltonhill
OLD MILLS
Elgin
Urquhart
Muir of Lochs
Newton
Bogmoor
Culbin Forest
Welhill
Kintessack
Findhorn Bay
Kinloss
Alves
Pittendreich
Palmerscross
Lhanbryde
Inverene
Grange Hall
Cloves
Miltonduff
New Elgin
Moss of Barmuckity
Moy House
Springfield
Toreduff
Hillside
Mosstodloch
Fochabers
The Bar
Forres
Mains of Burgie
Monaughty Forest
Paddockhaugh
Dipple
Dyke
Longmorn
Orbliston
Heldon Hill
234
PLUSCARDEN PRIORY
Cloddach
Blackhills
Nairn
Kingsteps
Macbeth's Hillock
Newton of Dalvey
Blervie Castle
Califer
Barnhill
Auchtertyre
Altonside
Hilton of Delnies
Thomshill
Whitewreath
Tradespark
Househill
Rafford
Tulloch
Crofts of Buinach
Inchberry
Auldearn
AULDEARN 1645
Boghole Fm
Dallas Forest
Kellas
Leanoch
Teindland Forest
Findlay's Seat
262
Edinvale
Hill of the Wangie
319
Glenlatterach
Whitemire
Bardon
Briach
Moss-side
Laiken Forest
Conicavel
Altyre Woods
Newtyle Forest
Branchill
Craigend
Glenlatterach Resr
Wood of Dundurcas
Muir of the Clans
Milton
Mains of Sluie
Phorp
Dallas
Brylach Hill
325
Kirkhill
Boat o' Brig
Torrich
Darnaway Forest
Mill Buie
355
Pikey Hill
355
Auchinroath
Piperhill
Regoul
Presley
Romach Hill
313
Ardoch
Cairn Uish
365
Glen of Rothes
Clephanton
Cawdor
Fornighty
Logie
Tomnamoon
Drumine Forest
Mill Buie
371
Meikle Hill
The Kettles
Culcharry
Littlemill
Lethen Bar
Craigroy
Knock More
356
Hill of Tomechole
344
Rothes
Urchany
GRAMPIAN
Ben Aigan
471
Dallaschyle
Relugas
Carn na Cailliche
404
Easter Galcantray
Achindown
Redburn
Loch Dallas
Hill of Stob
Cairn Cattoch
369
Dandaleith
Kirkton of Barevan
Clunas
Bruachmary
Carnachie
359
Hunt Hill
Whiteacen
Maggieknockater
ARDCLACH BELL TOWER
Mount
Carn Ghiubhais
430
Elchies Forest
Ringorm
Balmore
Ferness
Tomdow
Archiestown
Robertstown
Charlestown of Aberlour
Daltra
Burn of Cowlatt
Cardow
Tullich
Carn a'Chrasgie
401
Cairn Duhie
Carn Kitty
483
521
Carn Shalag
470
Upper Knockando
Knockando
Speyview
Dulsie
Carron
Daugh of Kinermony
Milltown of Edinvillie
Carn Sgumain
456
Sliabh Bainneach
KNOCKANDO DISTILLERY
Speyside Way
Milltown
Larig Hill
545
Roy's Hill
516
Carnoch
Knock of Braemoray
Paul's Hill
BALVENIE
Banchor
Hill of Aitnoch
Aitnoch
Dufftown
Carn nan Tri-tighearnan
615
Glen Tulchan
Glen Gheallaidh
Scootmore Forest
Daugh Marypark
552
Dalness
Dava
Carn an Uain
546
Ruighe
GLENFARCLAS DISTILLERY
MORTLACH CHURCH
Meikle Conval
Streens
Lochindorb
Dava Moor
Gallow Hill
Lynemore
Bellehiglash
Baby's Hill
Beatshach
Laggan
A9
A96
A939
A940
A941
A95
B9012
B9040
B9013
B9089
B9011
B9135
B9010
B9103
B9015
B9092
B9091
B9090
B9101
B9007
B9102
B9138
B9165
B9166

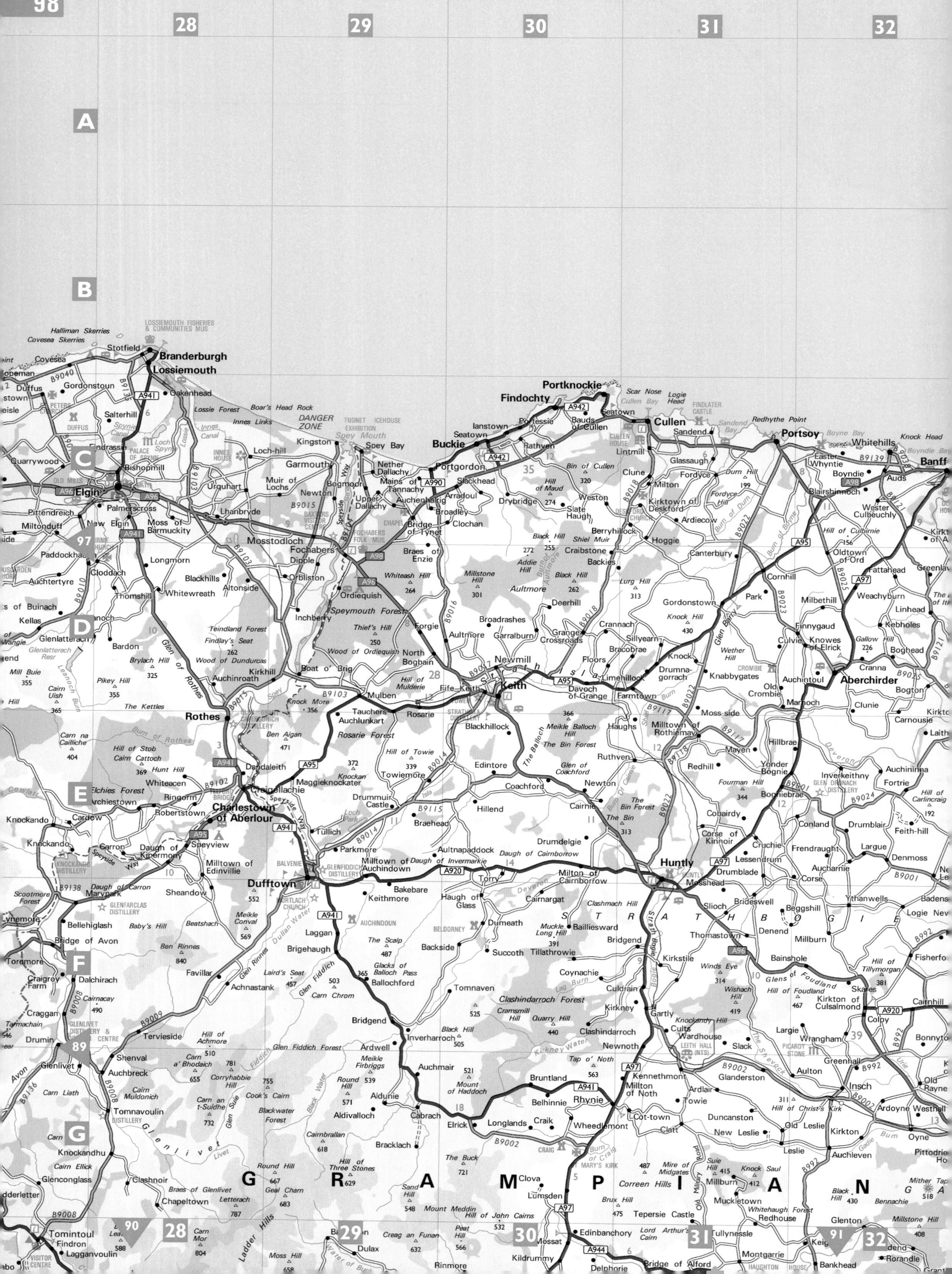

28
29
30
31
32
A
B
C
D
E
F
G
Halliman Skerries
Covesea Skerries
LOSSIEMOUTH FISHERIES & COMMUNITIES MUS
Stotfield
Branderburgh
Lossiemouth
Covesea
Duffus
Gordonstoun
Oakenhead
Salterhill
Lossie Forest
Boar's Head Rock
Innes Links
DANGER ZONE
TUGNET ICEHOUSE EXHIBITION
Spey Mouth
Spey Bay
Kingston
Loch-hill
Garmouth
Findrassie
PALACE OF SPYNIE
Quarrywood
Bishopmill
Urquhart
Muir of Lochs
Newton
OLD MILLS
Elgin
Pittendreich
Palmerscross
Lhanbryde
Miltonduff
New Elgin
Moss of Barmuckity
Mosstodloch
Fochabers
Dipple
Orbliston
Paddockhaugh
Cloddach
Longmorn
Blackhills
Altonside
Auchtertyre
Thomshill
Whitewreath
Kellas
Glenlatterach
Bardon
Teindland Forest
Findlay's Seat
262
Wood of Dundurcas
Brylach Hill
325
Mill Buie
355
Pikey Hill
Cairn Uish
365
The Kettles
Glen of Rothes
Kirkhill
Auchinroath
Rothes
Carn na Cailliche
404
Hill of Stob Cairn Cattoch
369
Hunt Hill
Whiteacen
Dandaleith
Craigellachie
Elchies Forest
Archiestown
Ringorm
Robertstown
Charlestown of Aberlour
Knockando
Cardow
Carron
Daugh of Kinermony
Speyview
Milltown of Edinvillie
Sheandow
Marypark
Daugh of Carron
GLENFARCLAS DISTILLERY
Scootmore Forest
Bellehiglash
Baby's Hill
Bridge of Avon
Ben Rinnes
840
Toremore
Dalchirach
Craigroy Farm
Cairnacay
490
Craggan
Favillar
Achnastank
Tervieside
Drumin
Glenlivet
Shenval
Auchbreck
Tomnavoulin
Knockandhu
Cairn Ellick
Glenconglass
Clashnoir
Chapeltown
Braes of Glenlivet
Letterach
787
Tomintoul
Findron
Lagganvoulin
VISITOR CENTRE
Ladder Hills
Carn Mor
804
Moss Hill
Findochty
Portknockie
Scar Nose
Logie Head
FINDLATER CASTLE
Cullen Bay
Portessie
Ianstown
Seatown
Bauds of Cullen
Buckie
Rathven
Cullen
Sandend
Redhythe Point
Portsoy
Boyne Bay
Whitehills
Knock Head
Banff
Portgordon
Nether Dallachy
Mains of Tannachy
Bogmoor
Upper Dallachy
Auchenhalrig
Arradoul
Slackhead
Broadley
Clochan
Bridge of Tynet
Braes of Enzie
Drybridge
Hill of Maud
Bin of Cullen
320
Lintmill
Clune
Milton
Glassaugh
Fordyce
Durn Hill
199
Kirktown of Deskford
Ardiecow
Slate Haugh
Weston
Berryhillock
Hoggie
Black Hill
Shiel Muir
Craibstone
Backies
Canterbury
Whitheash Hill
264
Millstone Hill
301
Aultmore
Black Hill
262
Ordiequish
Speymouth Forest
Inchberry
Thief's Hill
250
Wood of Ordiequish
Forgie
North Bogbain
Boat o' Brig
Hill of Mulderie
Mulben
Tauchers
Auchlunkart
Rosarie
Rosarie Forest
Knock More
356
Ben Aigan
471
Hill of Towie
339
Towiemore
Maggieknockater
Drummuir Castle
Tullich
Braehead
Parkmore
Aultnapaddock
Daugh of Invermarkie
Milltown of Auchindown
Dufftown
552
Bakebare
Keithmore
Meikle Conval
569
Laggan
Brigehaugh
Glen Fiddich
Ballochford
Bridgend
Ardwell
Inverharroch
Auchmair
Aldunie
Aldivalloch
Cabrach
Elrick
Bracklach
Broadrashes
Garralburn
Newmill
Keith
Fife Keith
Blackhillock
Edintore
Coachford
Hillend
Drumdelgie
Torry
Haugh of Glass
Dumeath
Backside
Succoth
Tomnaven
Deerhill
Grange Crossroads
Crannach
Sillyearn
Bracobrae
Floors
Knock
Drumnagorrach
Limehillock
Davoch of Grange
Farmtown
Haughs
Milltown of Rothiemay
Ruthven
Newton
Cairnie
The Bin
313
Milton of Cairnborrow
Cairnargat
Huntly
Clashmach Hill
Bailliesward
Tillathrowie
Bridgend
Kirkstile
Coynachie
Culdrain
Kirkney
Gartly
Clashindarroch Forest
Clashindarroch
Newnoth
Kennethmont
Rhynie
Bruntland
Belhinnie
Craik
Longlands
Wheedlemont
Cot-town
Clatt
Clova
Lumsden
Correen Hills
Tap o' Noth
563
Edinbanchory
Kildrummy
Mossat
Tullynessle
Montgarrie
Bridge of Alford
Cornhill
Park
Gordonstown
Milbethill
Knowes of Elrick
Culvie
Aberchirder
Crombie
Knabbygates
Auchintoul
Marnoch
Clunie
Bogton
Carnousie
Moss-side
Hillbrae
Mayen
Redhill
Yonder Bognie
Inverkeithny
Auchininna
Fortrie
Bogniebrae
Cobairdy
Conland
Drumblair
Feith-hill
Corse of Kinnoir
Cruchie
Lessendrum
Frendraught
Largue
Denmoss
Drumblade
Auchamie
Corse
Messhead
Brideswell
Slioch
Beggshill
Ythanwells
Logie Newton
Denend
Thomastown
Millburn
Bainshole
Fisherford
Glens of Foudland
Skares
Kirkton of Culsalmond
Colpy
Largie
Wrangham
Greenhall
Insch
Cults
Wardhouse
Slack
Aulton
Glanderston
Ardlair
Towie
Duncanston
New Leslie
Old Leslie
Kirkton
Leslie
Auchleven
Oyne
Westhall
Ardoyne
Knock Saul
Millburn
Mucklestown
Redhouse
Glenton
Keig
Bankhead
Boyndie
Auds
Blairshinnoch
Wester Culbeuchly
Hill of Culbirnie
Oldtown of Ord
Fattahead
Greenlaw
Weachyburn
Linhead
Finnygaud
Kebholes
Boghead
Cranna
G
R
A
M
P
I
A
N
S
T
R
A
T
H
B
O
G
I
E
89
90
91
97
A96
A941
A942
A990
A98
A95
A920
A97
A944
B9040
B9015
B9103
B9016
B9018
B9022
B9023
B9025
B9139
B9117
B9014
B9115
B9102
B9138
B9008
B9009
B9002
B992
B9001
B9024

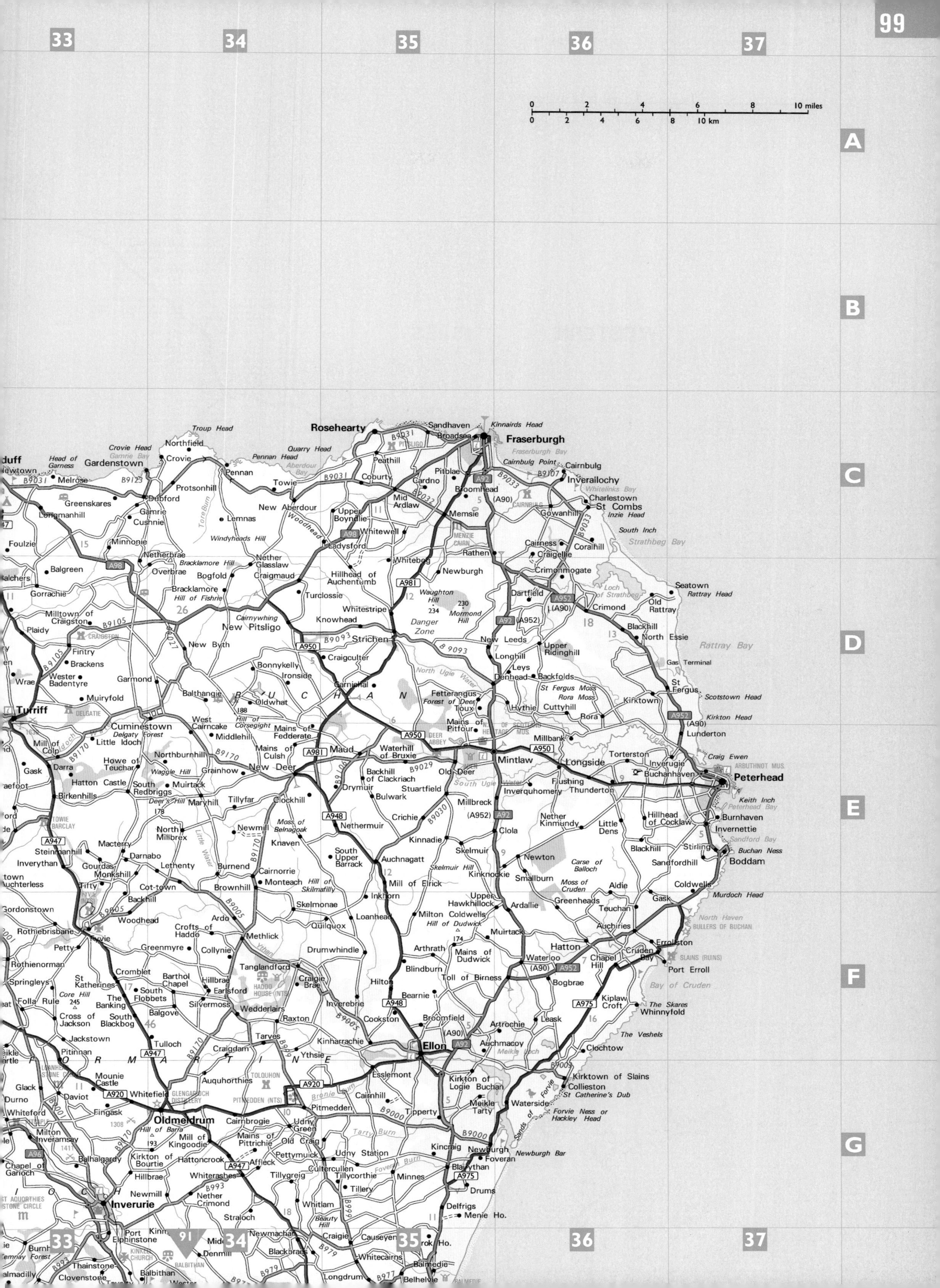
33
34
35
36
37
A
B
C
D
E
F
G
0
2
4
6
8
10 miles
0
2
4
6
8
10 km
Troup Head
Rosehearty
Sandhaven
Kinnairds Head
Broadsea
Fraserburgh
Fraserburgh Bay
Cairnbulg Point
Cairnbulg
Inverallochy
Whitelinks Bay
Charlestown
St Combs
Inzie Head
South Inch
Strathbeg Bay
Coralhill
Crovie Head
Gamrie Bay
Northfield
Quarry Head
Pennan Head
Aberdour Bay
Head of Garness
Gardenstown
Crovie
Pennan
Macduff
Melrose
Towie
Peathill
Pitsligo
Coburty
Pitblae
Cardno
Broomhead
(A90)
Protsonhill
Dubford
Greenskares
Gamrie
Cushnie
Longmanhill
New Aberdour
Lemnas
Upper Boyndlie
Mid Ardlaw
Memsie
Gowanhill
Cairness
Craigellie
Crimonmogate
Windyheads Hill
Whitewell
Ladysford
Whitebog
Rathen
Minnonie
Foulzie
Netherbrae
Overbrae
Balgreen
Bracklamore Hill
Nether Glasslaw
Bogfold
Craigmaud
Hillhead of Auchentumb
Newburgh
Gorrachie
Bracklamore
Hill of Fishrie
Turclossie
Whitestripe
Waughton Hill
Mormond Hill
Dartfield
Loch of Strathbeg
Seatown
Rattray Head
Old Rattray
Crimond
Milltown of Craigston
Cairnywhing
New Pitsligo
Knowhead
Danger Zone
Strichen
Plaidy
Craigston
Fintry
Brackens
New Byth
Leeds
Upper Ridinghill
Blackhill
North Essie
Rattray Bay
Gas Terminal
Bonnykelly
Ironside
Craigculter
Longhill
Leys
Denhead
Backfolds
Wester Badentyre
Garmond
Carnichal
North Ugie Water
St Fergus Moss
Rora Moss
St Fergus
Scotstown Head
Wrae
Muiryfold
Balthangie
Oldwhat
Fetterangus
Forest of Deer
Toux
Cuttyhill
Kirktown
Rora
Kirkton Head
Turriff
Delgatie
Cuminestown
West Cairncake
Hill of Corsegight
Mains of Fedderate
Mains of Pitfour
Lunderton
Delgaty Forest
Little Idoch
Middlehill
Waterhill of Bruxie
Deer Abbey
Millbank
Mill of Colp
Mains of Culsh
Maud
Mintlaw
Longside
Torterston
Inverugie
Craig Ewen
Buchanhaven
Peterhead
Gask
Darra
Howe of Teuchar
Northburnhill
Waggle Hill
Grainhow
New Deer
Backhill of Clackriach
Old Deer
Flushing
Thunderton
Hatton Castle
South Redbriggs
Muirtack
Drymuir
Stuartfield
Inverquhomery
Keith Inch
Peterhead Bay
Birkenhills
Deer's Hill
Maryhill
Tillyfar
Clockhill
Bulwark
Millbreck
South Ugie Water
Hillhead of Cocklaw
Burnhaven
Towie Barclay
North Millbrex
Newmill
Moss of Belnagoak
Nethermuir
Crichie
(A952)
Clola
Nether Kinmundy
Little Dens
Invernettie
Sandford Bay
Knaven
Kinnadie
Stirling
Buchan Ness
Macterry
Steinmanhill
Darnabo
Inverythan
South Upper Barrack
Auchnagatt
Skelmuir
Newton
Blackhill
Boddam
Gourdas
Monkshill
Lethenty
Burnend
Cairnorrie
Skelmuir Hill
Kinknockie
Carse of Balloch
Sandfordhill
Auchterless
Tifty
Monteach
Hill of Skilmafilly
Mill of Elrick
Smallburn
Moss of Cruden
Aldie
Coldwells
Murdoch Head
Fyvie
Cot-town
Backhill
Brownhill
Inkhorn
Upper Hawkhillock
Greenheads
Gask
Gordonstown
Woodhead
Skelmonae
Ardo
Loanhead
Milton
Coldwells
Hill of Dudwick
Ardallie
Teuchan
North Haven
Bullers of Buchan
Rothiebrisbane
Crofts of Haddo
Quilquox
Muirtack
Auchiries
Methlick
Erroll
Petty
Greenmyre
Collynie
Drumwhindle
Arthrath
Mains of Dudwick
Hatton
Chapel Hill
Cruden Bay
Slains (Ruins)
Rothienorman
Crombie
Barthol Chapel
Tanglandford
Blindburn
Waterloo
Port Erroll
Springleys
St Katherines
South Flobbets
Hillbrae
Earlsford
Haddo House (NTS)
Craigie Brae
Hilton
Toll of Birness
Bogbrae
Bay of Cruden
Folla Rule
Core Hill
The Banking
Silvermoss
Wedderlairs
Inverebrie
Bearnie
Kiplaw Croft
The Skares
Whinnyfold
Cross of Jackson
South Blackbog
Balgove
Raxton
Cookston
Broomfield
Artrochie
Leask
Jackstown
Tulloch
Tarves
Kinharrachie
Ellon
Auchmacoy
Meikle Loch
The Veshels
Pitinnan
Craigdam
Ythsie
Clochtow
Formartine
Mounie Castle
Auquhorthies
Tolquhon
Esslemont
Kirkton of Logie Buchan
Kirktown of Slains
Collieston
St Catherine's Dub
Glack
Daviot
Whiteford
Glengarioch Distillery
Pitmedden (NTS)
Cairnhill
Tipperty
Meikle Tarty
Waterside
Sands of Forvie
Forvie Ness or Hackley Head
Durno
Fingask
Oldmeldrum
Cairnbrogie
Udny Green
Pitmedden
Tarty Burn
Milton
Inveramsay
Hill of Barra
Mill of Kingoodie
Mains of Pittrichie
Old Craig
Kincraig
Newburgh
Foveran
Newburgh Bar
Chapel of Garioch
Balhalgardy
Kirkton of Bourtie
Hattoncrook
Affleck
Pettymuick
Udny Station
Culterculen
Tillycorthie
Foveran Burn
Blairythan
Hillbrae
Whiterashes
Tillygreig
Minnes
Tillery
Drums
Inverurie
Newmill
Nether Crimond
Whitlam
Delfrigs
East Aquhorthies Stone Circle
Garioch
Straloch
Beauty Hill
Menie Ho.
Port Elphinstone
Kinmuck
Middleton
Newmachar
Craigie
Causeyend
Burnhervie
Kemnay Forest
Kinkell Church
Denmill
Blackbraes
Whitecairns
Balbithan
Thainstone
Balmedie
Clovenstone
Balbithan
Longdrum
Belhelvie
Balmedie
91
A98
A947
A920
A96
A981
A950
A952
A92
A948
A975
A90
B9031
B9123
B9032
B9033
B9107
B9105
B9027
B9093
B9170
B9029
B9106
B9030
B9005
B9000
B999
B993
B977
B979
B9170
B9170
B9001
B9003
B9031
188
178
174
230
234
245
1308
193
1411
1658

6
7
8
9
10
0 2 4 6 8 10 miles
0 2 4 6 8 10 km
A
B
C
D
E
F
G
WESTERN ISLES
EILEAN LEODHAIS
(LEWIS)
Bad an
Aird Dhail
Dail Bho Dheas
Toa Galson
Gabhsunn Bho Dheas
Gabhsunn Bho Thuath
A857
Mealabost
BROCH
Roinn a' Bhuic
Coig Peighinnean
Borve
South Galson
Airighean Loch Breihav
Rubha Leathann
Siadar Uarach
Siadar Iarach
STEINACLEIT CAIRN & STANDING STONES
Baile an Truiseil
Diaval
Glen Shader
Goile Chroic
Danger Area
Loch Mor Bharabhais
Loch Gress
Rinn Druim Tallig
BLACK HOUSE
Barabhas
Aird Mhor Bragair
Port Arnol
Labost
Bru
Torray
Muirnea
248
Rubh'an Dunain
Fibhig
Bragar
Arnol
26
Loch Mor Sandavit
Gleann Mor Bharabhais
Loch Urrahag
Loch Casgro
Bagh Dail Beag
Siabost
A857
Loch an Tobair
Grials
Dail Beag
Aird Mhor
Dail Mor
Glen Bragar
Gleann Bragar
Loch Breivat
Gearrannan
Mullach Charlabhaigh
A858
Beinn Bragar
261
Beinn Choinnich
210
Bhruthadail
11
Craigeam
20
Borghastan
Carlabhagh
Beinn Rahacleit
248
Roishal Mor
174
Col
Loch Carlabhagh
Creag Mhor
Cirbhig
Little Bernera
CARLOWAY BROCH
Loch na Scaravat
Bac
Col
West Loch Roag
Gallan Head
Tobson
Pabaidh Mor
Camas Sandig
Great Bernera
East Loch Roag
Tolastadh a Chaolais
Beinn Mholach
292
Loch Mor an Stairr
Col Sands
B895
Aird Uige
Bhaltos
Breacleit
Vacsay
Stacashal
216
Loch nam Breac
Loch nan Stearnag
Tunga
Aird Thun
Geodha Nasavig
Forsnaval
205
Nisa Mhor
Laxdale
Newmarket
Sron Ruadh
Flavig Bagh
Vuia Mor
Barraglom
Breascleit
Laxdale
Melbost Sands
Aird Mhor Mangersta
Miabhig
Uigen
Tacleit
Kirkibost
Loch Vatandip
Stornoway
East
Melbost
Camas Uig
Timsgearraidh
Vuia Beag
Crulabhig
Eilean Kearstay
Calanais
Loch an Tairbeart
Loch Airigh nan Sloc
Loch Uraval
LEWS CASTLE
Melbost
Cradhlastadh
Floday
STANDING STONES
A858
Sandwick
Cairisiadar
Ben Drovinish
Beinn nan Surrag
Creed
Stornoway Harbour
Branahuie Banks
Mangurstadh
Eadar Dha Fhadhail
Geisiadar
Linsiadar
Loch Sean Thulabhig
Gearraidh Na H-Aibhne
13
Suarda
Loch Sgaslabhat
Suainaval
429
B8011
B8059
Eitshal
200
223
Beinn a' Bhuna
Arnish Moor
Arnish Pt
Loch Croistean
Teahaval
256
Griomarstaidh
B8011
Loch ne Gainmhich
Acha Mor
Aird Fenish
Loch Suainaval
Loch Tungavat
Loch Thota Bridein
A859
Loch Orasay
Rubh a'Bhaigh Uaine
Loch Raonasgail
Loch Grunavat
Einacleit
Aird Brenish
Islibhig
Mealisval
574
16
Scealascro
Loch Cleit Steirmeis
Loch nam Falcag
Tahaval
515
Gisla
Loch an Fhir Mhaoil
Liurbost
Grimsiadar
Breanais
Cracaval
514
Skeun
265
Giosla
Loch Nisreaval
Loch Grimshader
Calltraiseal Bheag
Beinn Mohal
207
Crosbost
Raerinish Point
Mealasta
467
Loch Dibadale
Beinn Mheadhonach
397
226
Loch Fadagoa
Loch Fada
Tamanaisval
Coduinn
241
Calltraiseal Mhor
228
Loch Airigh na h-Airde
Tabhaigh Mhor
Caolas an Eilein
Loch Trealaval
Laxay
12
Mealasta Island
Maghannan
Lacasaigh
Ceos
Eilean Chalum Chille
Orasaigh
Griomaval
Loch na Craobhaig
Loch Morsgail
Roineval
281
37
Loch Erisort
Gleann Ghrabhair
Loch Coirigerod
Cabharstadh
Baile Ailein
Cearsiadar
Gearraidh Bhaird
Torraigh
Liongam
Loch Tamanavay
Loch Beinnsval
Loch Strandavat
Tabost
Aird Bheag
Loch Bodavat
Scalaval Sandig
Sleiteachal Mhor
248
Kintarvie
B8060
13
Marthig
Loch Thealasbhaidh
Morsgail Forest
Loch Langavat
172 Malasgair
Loch Sgibacleit
Calbost
Kearstay
Aird Mhor
Resort
Gob na h-Airde Moire
Beinn a'Bhoth
308
Airidh A Bhruaich
Rubha Iosal
Ceann Loch Shiophoirt
Glen Ouirn
Sron Romul
308
Kearnaval
378
Aird an Troim
Grabhair
Feirihisval
326
Loch Cravadale
Mas a'Chnoic-chuairtich
386
Uladale
295
Loch Shanndabhat
Tom an Fhuadain
Loch Odhairn
Kebock Head
Sidhean an Airgid
381
401
Sgianait
425
Mullach na Reidheachd
Loch Voshimid
Rapaire
453
Liuthaid
492
Beinn a Mhuil
370
A859
Mor Mhonadh
Loch a'Ghlinne
Tirga Mor
679
473
Mullach a' Ruisg
18
Beinn na h-Uamha
424
389
Leumrabhagh
Caolas an Scarp
Huisinis
Husival Mor
489
Ullaval
659
579
Stulaval
Langadale
Vig a dale
Athlinne
Eisgean
Gob na Milaid
Huisinish Point
Huisinish Bay
Forest of Harris
Leosaval
412
Oreval
662
Seaforth Island
Muaithabhal
Loch Shell
Caolas Tuath
Arda Beaga
Aird A Mhulaidh
Beinn Mhor
572
Beannan Mor
242
Srianach
Horsanish
Gobhaig
Sgaladal
Eilean Iubhard
Rubha Bhuic
Abhainnsuidhe
Cleiseval
511
Uisgnaval Mor
729
Mulla-fo-dheas
743
799
Clisham
Clett Ard
Corlabhadh
12
P a r k
Uisenis
371
Glorigs
Soay Beg
Soay Sound
B887
Maruig
Kenmore
Crionaig
470
Mulhagery
Miabhag
Loch Seaforth
Mol Truisg
Soay Mor
Bun Abhainn Eadarra
Caiteshal
449
Loch Claidh
Tathas Mhor
G
Tarasaigh
WEST LOCH TARBERT
Sgaoth Aird
559
Straiaval
389
Toddun
528
Loch Bhrollum
Gob Rubh'Uisenis
Ben Raah
267
Aird Asaig
Laxadale Lochs
3
Reinigeadal
Bhalamus
Rubha Bhrollum
SHIANT
Beinn Dhubh
506
Taoth Siar
Tairbeart (Tarbert)
Rubh'a'Bhaird
Beesdale
Ceann Reamhar
467
Eilean Mor A'Bhaigh
Sgeir na h-Eigheach
OF
Aird Vanish
Paible
6
Losgaintir
Corran Seilebost
7
Urgha
Beinn a'Chaolais
93
8
9
10
Rubha Sgeirigin
Sound of Taransay
South Harris Forest
287
Carragrich
Sgeotasaigh
334
Caolas Scalpaigh
Loch Ceann Dibig
SOUND
Garbh Eilean
Eilean Mhuire
161
Shiant Islands
Rubha

11
12
13
18
19
A
B
C
D
E
F
G
15
16
17
18
19
102
95
Cape Wrath
Duslic
Stack Clo Kearvaig
An Garbh-eilean
Kearvaig
Sgribhis-bheinn
371
A'Gholl
Faraid Head
Geodha Ruadh na Fola
Danger Zone
Cnoc a'Ghiubhais
297
Inshore
Maovally
299
Loch Inshore
Danger Zone
Balnakeil
Balnakeil Bay
Sango Bay
Durness
Pocan Smoo
Leirinmore
Bay of Keisgaig
Loch Keisgaig
Fashven
457
Achiemore
Loch Airigh na Beinne
Keoldale
Sangobeg
Kyle of Durness
Beinn Dearg
423
Beinn an Amair
278
Am Balg
Sandwood Bay
Am Buachaille
Sandwood Loch
Creag Riabhach
485
Sarsgrum
Loch Meadaidh
Beinn Ceannabeinne
383
Meall Meadhonach
422
Rubh' an Fhir Leithe
An Grianan
467
Meall na Moine
464
Strath Shinary
Grudie
Ghlas-bheinn
332
Drochaid Mhor
Sheigra
Balchrick
Blairmore
Loch na Gainimh
Oldshore Beg
Oldshore More
Beinn a'Chraisg
257
Abhainnan t-Srathain
Farrmheall
521
Meall a'Chraidh
490
Portnancon
Loch Eriboll
Laid
Eilean Choraidh
Eilean an Roin Mor
An Socach
358
Beinn Spionnaidh
772
Rubha na Leacaig
Kinlochbervie
Loch Clash
Loch na Gainimh
B801
Badcall
Achriesgill
Loch Tarbhaidh
Cranstackie
802
Strath Dionard
Polla
A838
Eriboll
Bagh Loch an Roinn
Loch Inchard
Loch Crocach
Achlyness
Strath Beag
An Lean-charn
521
Loch Dughaill
Ardmore Point
Ceathramh Garbh
Rhiconich
Loch na Claise Carnaich
Conamheall
482
Rubha Ruadh
Loch na h-Ula
Foinaven
915
Loch Uidh an Tuim
Loch Dionard
Fanagmore
Tarbet
A838
867
Creag Dionard
778
Loch Crocach
Handa Island
Foindle
Loch Laxford
Loch nam Breac
Laxford Bridge
Loch na Tuadh
Loch a'Gharbh Bhaid Mhoir
Feinne-Bheinn Mhor
465
Loch an Laig Aird
A894
Badnabay
Loch an Easain Uaine
Arkle
787
Alltnacaillich
Scourie Bay
Sound of Handa
Meall a'Chuirn
777
Sabhal Mor
703
Sabhal Beag
729
Scourie More
Scourie
Gorm Loch
Rubh' Aird an t-Sionnaich
Loch Stack
A838
721
Ben Stack
Abhainnan Loin
Strath Dionard
Glen Golly
Badcall
A894
Badcall Bay
Ben Auskaird
386
Reay Forest
Achfary
Strath Stack
Ben Screavie
322
801
Carn Dearg
796
759
Carn an Tionail
Meallan Liath Coire Mhic Dhughaill
Eilean a'Bhreitheimh
52
Loch Crocach
Loch More
Rubh' a'Mhucard
Meall Mor
10
Allt nan Ramh
Meall Beag
Calbha Beag
Calbha Mor
Loch na Creige Duibhe
Strath na Caran
Ben Strome
426
Loch an Leathaid Bhuain
Beinn a'Bhutha
547
Beinn Lice
470
Aultanrynie
Allt Beithe
Loch ant-Seilg
Sgeir nan Gall
Oldany Island
Eddrachillis Bay
Point of Stoer
Rubha nan Cosan
Loch a'Chairn Bhain
Kylestrome
Glendhu Forest
Kinloch
Ben Hee
873
Meallan Liath Mor
683
Ardvar
161
Eilean Chrona
Culkein
Loch Glendhu
Unapool
Gleann Dubh
Meall na Leitreach
566
Raffin
Cluas Deas
Achnacarnin
Clashnessie Bay
Drumbeg
Loch Nedd
Nedd
B869
Newton
Beinn Aird da Loch
530
Meall a Fheur Loch
613
Loch Merkland
24
Loch Glencoul
Balchladich
Clashnessie
Loch Poll
Gleann Leireag
Sail Gorm
776
Beinn Leoid
792
Meallan a'Chuail
750
Loch Flag
Rubh' a' Mhill Dheirg
Loch Poll Dhaidh
Loch an Leothaid
Quinag
808
Spidean Coinich
764
Loch na Gainmhich
Loch Dubh a'Chuail
Bay of Stoer
Stoer
Loch Crocach
A894
Clachtoll
Loch Beanach
10
Glas Bheinn
776
Eas a Chual Aluinn (Waterfall)
Loch an Eircill
Loch a'Ghriama
Cnoc a'Ghriama
Rubha Leumair
B869
Little Assynt
A837
Beinn Uidhe
740
Corrykinloch
Abhainn a'Choire
Achmelvich Bay
Rhicarn
Loch Assynt
Gorm Loch Mor
Achmelvich
A837
Inver
Allt an t-Sluagaich
Ardvreck (Ruins)
Fionn Loch Mor
Overscaig Hotel
37
Ardroe
Rubha Rodha
Baddidarach
Lochinver
Loch Feith an Leothaid
Beinn Gharbh
540
Inchnadamph
Inchnadamph Forest
Soyea Island
Loch Inver
Loch Culag
Gleann Dubh
Traligill
Maovally
512
Kirkaig Point
Badnaban
Strathan
Conival
987
Ben More Assynt
998
A'Chleit
Loch Kirkaig
Inverkirkaig
Glencanisp Forest
Stronechrubie
Cnoc a' Bhaid Bhain
367
Rubha na Breige
Loch na Gainimh
Canisp
846
Dubh Loch Mor
Suilven
731
Fionn Loch
9
Duchally
Rubha Coigeach
Eilean Mor
Falls of Kirkaig
715
Strath an Loin
Feochag Bay
Lochan Fada
A837
Dubh Loch Beag
Enard Bay
Rhegreanoch
Loch Awe
Loanan
Breabag
814
Benmore Forest
Leathad Dail nan Cliabh
329
Beinn Sgreamhaidh
435
Camas Coille
Camas Eilean Ghlais
Rubh' a'Choin
Polly Bay
Loch Veyatie
Cam Loch
Meall a Bhraghaid
688
Rubha Mor
Reiff
H I G H L A N D
Ledbeg
Ledmore
Glenmuick
Loch Langwell
Loch an Alltain Duibh
Alltan Dubh
Loch Sionascaig
Cul Mor
849
Eilean Mullagrach
Loch Osgaig
Aird of Coigach
Inverpolly Forest
Stac Polly
613
Loch an Doire Dhuibh
Drumrunie Forest
Elphin
Knockan
Loch Borralan
Loch Ailsh
Glen Cassley
Badintagairt
Isle Ristol
Polbain
Loch Bad a'Ghaill
Cul Beag
769
A837
364
Oykel
Glas-leac Mor
Summer Isles
Achiltibuie
Polglass
Ardnagoine
Badentarbat Bay
A835
Cnoc na Glas Choille
307
Beinn an Eoin
544
Tanera Beg
An t-Sail
Beinn
Rubha Robhanais (Butt of Lewis)
Port a'Stoth
Teampull Mholuidh
Coig Peighinnean
Port Nis
Eorodal
Port Skigersta
Sgiogarstaigh
Meall Geal
Port Alasdair
Laimhrig
Cellar Head
Loch Langavat
Port Geiraha
Tolastadh Ur
Tolastadh
Tolsta Head
Port nam Bothag
Gleann Tholastaidh
Port Bun a'Ghlinne
Creag Fhraoich
Tiumpan Head
Port Nan Giuran
Rubha Deas
Siulaisiadar
Seisiadar
A866
An Rubha (Eye Peninsula)
Rubha na Greine
Rubha na Bearnaich
Pabil Uarach
Bagh Phabail
Pabil Iarach
Ullapool

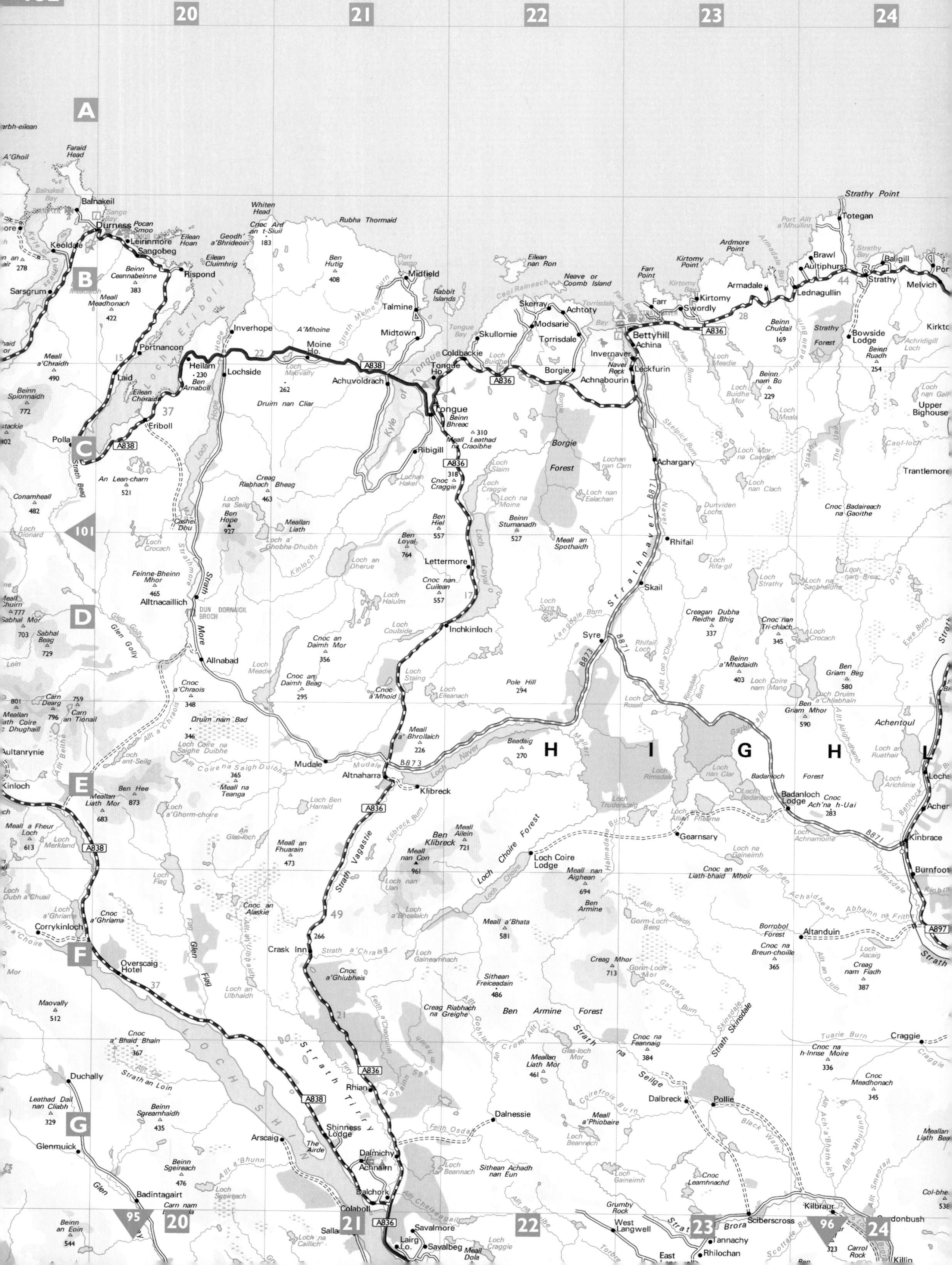
20
21
22
23
24
A
B
C
D
E
F
G
Faraid Head
A'Ghoil
Balnakeil Bay
Balnakeil
Durness
Pocan Smoo
Leirinmore
Sangobeg
Keoldale
Eilean Hoan
Geodh' a'Bhrideoin
Cnoc Ard an t-Siuil
183
Whiten Head
Rubha Thormaid
Eilean Cluimhrig
Rispond
Beinn Ceannabeinne
383
Sarsgrum
Meall Meadhonach
422
Ben Hutig
408
Port Vasgo
Midfield
Rabbit Islands
Talmine
Eilean nan Ron
Neave or Coomb Island
Farr Point
Kirtomy Point
Ardmore Point
Port Allt a'Mhuillinn
Strathy Point
Totegan
Brawl
Aultiphurst
Strathy Bay
Baligill
Strathy
Melvich
Armadale
Lednagullin
Kirtomy
Swordly
Farr
Skerray
Achtoty
Modsarie
Torrisdale
Bettyhill
Achina
Invernaver
Naver Rock
Leckfurin
Borgie
Achnabourin
Skullomie
Coldbackie
Tongue Bay
Tongue Ho.
Tongue
Moine Ho.
A'Mhoine
Midtown
Inverhope
Portnancon
Loch Eriboll
Heilam
230
Ben Arnaboll
Lochside
Laid
Eilean Choraidh
Eriboll
Polla
A838
A836
B871
B873
A897
Meall a'Chraidh
490
Beinn Spionnaidh
772
Druim nan Cliar
262
Achuvoldrach
Kyle of Tongue
Ribigill
Beinn Bhreac
310 Leathad
Meall na Craoibhe
318
Cnoc Craggie
Strath Beag
An Lean-charn
521
Creag Riabhach Bheag
463
Conamheall
482
Loch na Seilg
Ben Hope
927
Meallan Liath
Cashel Dhu
Loch Dionard
Loch Crocach
Loch a' Ghobha-Dhuibh
Ben Hiel
557
Ben Loyal
764
Loch an Dherue
Lettermore
Loch Loyal
Beinn Stumanadh
527
Borgie Forest
Lochan nan Carn
Loch nan Ealachan
Meall an Spothaidh
Achargary
Rhifail
Dunviden Lochs
Strathnaver
Feinne-Bheinn Mhor
465
Alltnacaillich
Dun Dornaigil Broch
Strath More
Cnoc nan Cuilean
557
Loch Halulm
Loch Coulside
Inchkinloch
Skail
Loch Syre
Langdale Burn
Syre
Creagan Dubha Reidhe Bhig
337
Cnoc nan Tri-chlach
345
Loch Crocach
Glen Golly
Allnabad
Cnoc an Daimh Mor
356
Loch Meadie
Cnoc an Daimh Beag
295
Cnoc a'Mhoid
Loch Staing
Loch Eileanach
Pole Hill
294
Beinn a'Mhadaidh
403
Loch Coire nam Mang
Ben Griam Beg
580
Loch Druim a'Chliabhain
Ben Griam Mhor
590
Achentoul
Cnoc a'Chraois
348
Druim nam Bad
346
Loch Coire na Saighe Duibhe
Meall a'Bhrollaich
226
Mudale
Altnaharra
Loch Naver
Klibreck
Beadaig
270
H I G H L
Loch Rimsdale
Loch nan Clar
Badanloch Forest
Badanloch Lodge
Cnoc Ach'na h-Uai
283
Kinloch
Ben Hee
873
Meall na Teanga
365
Meallan Liath Mor
683
Loch Ben Harrald
Loch a'Ghorm-choire
Meall a Fheur Loch
613
Loch Merkland
Meall an Fhuarain
473
Ben Klibreck
Meall nan Con
961
Meall Ailein
721
Loch Choire Forest
Loch Coire Lodge
Gearnsary
Kinbrace
Burnfoot
Meall nan Aighean
694
Ben Armine
Cnoc an Liath-bhaid Mhoir
Corrykinloch
Cnoc a'Ghriama
Cnoc an Alaskie
Glen Fiag
Strath Vagastie
49
266
Crask Inn
Meall a'Bhata
581
Gorm-Loch Beag
Borrobol Forest
Altanduin
Cnoc na Breun-choille
365
Creag nam Fiadh
387
Overscaig Hotel
37
Cnoc a'Ghiubhais
Loch an Ulbhaidh
Sithean Freiceadain
486
Creag Mhor
713
Maovally
512
Creag Riabhach na Greighe
Ben Armine Forest
Cnoc a'Bhaid Bhain
367
Strath Tirry
Loch Shin
Meallan Liath Mor
461
Cnoc na Feannaig
384
Strath na Seilge
Strath Skinsdale
Tuarie Burn
Craggie
Cnoc na h-Innse Moire
336
Cnoc Meadhonach
345
Duchally
Leathad Dail nan Cliabh
329
Beinn Sgreamhaidh
435
Rhian
Dalnessie
Dalbreck
Pollie
Meall a'Phiobaire
Glenmuick
Arscaig
Shinness Lodge
The Airde
Dalmichy
Achnairn
Beinn Sgeireach
476
Sithean Achadh nan Eun
Cnoc Leamhnachd
Meallan Liath Beag
Badintagairt
Carn nam
Dalchork
Colaboll
Kilbraur
Grumby Rock
West Langwell
Sciberscross
Strath Brora
Tannachy
Rhilochan
Col-bheinn
538
95
96
Beinn an Eoin
544
Savalmore
Lairg
Savalbeg
Meall Dola
Loch Craggie
East
323
Carrol Rock
Killin
Loch Beannach
Loch Gaineimh
Loch Caillich

PENTLAND FIRTH
25
26
27
28
29
105
Langaton Point
Island of Stroma
Nethertown
Red Head
Uppertown
Mell Head
St John's Point
Men of Mey
Inner Sound
Boars of Duncansby
Ness of Duncansby
Dunnet Head
Easter Head
Stromness
Scarfskerry Point
Tang Head
Head of Crees
Scarfskerry
Harrow
East Mey
Gills Bay
Ham
Rattar
Gills
A836
Duncansby Head
Huna
John 'o' Groats
Stacks of Duncansby
Dunnet Hill
121
Brough
Hunspow
St John's Loch
Loch of Mey
Castle of Mey
B855
The Thirl
West Dunnet
Dwarwick Head
Whitebridge
Mey
Upper Gills
Canisbay
Hill of Crogodale
Barrock
Dunnet
Dunnet Bay
Warth Hill
124
Wife Geo
Brims Ness
Port of Brims
Ness of Litter
Spear Head
Clett
Holborn Head
Scrabster
Thurso Bay
Clardon Head
The Spur
Murkle Bay
Links of Dunnet
Inkstack
Brabster
Everley
Crosskirk Bay
St Marys Chapel
Crosskirk
Lybster
Thurso
Clardon
Murkle
Greenland
Loch Heilen
Lochend
Gill Burn
Tofts
Skirza
Skirza Head
Freswick Bay
Freswick
Ness Head
Red Point
Sandside Head
Dounreay
Fresgoe
Sandside Bay
Bridge of Forss
Viewfield
Ormwe
Haimer
Castletown
Thurdistoft
Slickly
Achreamie
Buldoo
Lythmore
Janetstown
Tain
Auckengill
Isauld
Reay
Sandside House
A836
Drum Hollistan
Achvarasdal
Newlands of Geise
Glengolly
A882
(A9)
Olrig House
Hayfield
Lochside
Alterwall
Reaster
Shalmstry
Hilliclay
Weydale
Durran
Bowermadden
Sortat
Nybster
Kirk Burn
Shebster
Westfield
Buckies
Carsgoe
Hoy
Lyth
Forsie
Lieurary
Aimster
Achingills
Brough Head
Beinn Ratha
242
Skinnet
Sordale
Stemster
Bowertower
B876
Howe
Keiss
Loch Calder
Braal Castle
Knockdee
Tister
Hastigrow
Stain
Tang Head
Loch Akran
Broubster
Calder Mains
Gerston
Halkirk
Roadside
Stemster House
Corsback
Gillock
Halcro
Mireland
Loch na Seilge
Georgemas Junc. Sta.
Clayock
A882
Loch Scarmclate
North Watten
Kirk
Loch of Wester
Shurrery
Brawlbin
Loch Olgrey
Lynegar
Quoys of Reiss
Sinclair's Bay
Killimster
Shurrery Lodge
Bloody Moss
Scotscalder Sta
B870
Spittal Hill
Loch Watten
Mains of Watten
B874
Ackergill Tower
Girnigoe
Noss Head
Sinclair
Reiss
Winless
Loch of Winless
Wick
Watten
Ben Dorrery
244
Olgrinmore
Harpsdale
Achies
A895
Dunn
Oldhall
Houstry of Dunn
Newton
Loch Scye
Loch Shurrery
Beinn nam Bad Mor
Dorrery
Cnoc an Fhuarain Bhain
243
Spital
Mybster
Backlass
Whitefield
Bilbster
Sibster
Ackergill
(A836)
Staxigoe
Loch Tuim Ghlais
Loch Caluim
Thurso
Loch of Toftingall
Burn of Acharole
Strath Burn
Strath
Thuster
Haster
Stirkoke House
Milton
North Head
Wick Bay
South Head
Westerdale
Tormsdale
Cnoc Cloisgte Water
Newton
Whiterow
(A836)
Northfield
Badlipster
Castle of Old Wick
Pulldagon
Tannach
Loch Hempriggs
Hempriggs House
Lochan Dubh nan Geodh
Loch Meadie
Loch Eileanach
Little
Camster Burn
Achairn Burn
Sletill Hill
280
Loch Sletill
Altnabreac Sta
Tacher
Lower Camster
Toftcarl
Ires Geo
Loch More
Stemster
Grey Cairns of Camster
145
Ballharn Hill
Thrumster
Lochdhu Hotel
Loch of Yarrows
Corbiegoe
Sarclet
Sarclet Head
Cnoc nan Gall
275
Loch a'Mhuilinn
Loch Ruard
Achavanich
213
Hill of Yarrows
Whiteleen
Loch Stemster
248
Loch Thulachan
Loch Rangag
Stemster Hill
Upper Camster
Cairn of Get
Cnoc an Earrannaiche
Ulbster
Stack of Ulbester
Rumsdale Water
Dalganachan
Loch Sand
Whaligoe
Coire na Beinne
226
Sheppardstown
Roster
East Clyth
Bruan
Cnoc Cromuillt
365
Ben Alisky
349
Crofts of Benachielt
Ben-a-chielt
Rumster Forest
Reisgill Burn
Upper Lybster
Prehistoric Stones
Mid Clyth
A
N
D
Cnocan Conachreag
269
Reisgill
Occumster
Blackness
Glutt Water
Cnoc na Saobhaidhe
290
Burn of Houstry
A895
(A9)
Swiney
Knockfin Heights
438
Houstry
Nottingham
Lybster
Gillivoan
A9
(A836)
Forse
Dunbeath Water
Achnaclyth
Smerral
Latheron
Feith Gaineimh Mhor
Badnagie
Latheronwheel
Laidhay Croft Museum
Cnoc Coire na Fearna
437
Gobernuisgeach
Berriedale Water
Braemore
Achorn
Toremore
Dunbeath
Inver
Maiden Pap
484
Knockally
Dunbeath Bay
Dunbeath
Cnoc an Eireannaich
517
Morven
706
Scaraben
626
Meall na Caorach
Ramscraigs
Wag
A9
Borgue
Loch Scalabsdale
Garvery Hill
333
Langwell
Forest
20
Newport
Cnoc Salisiade
483
555
Creag Scalabsdale
Aultibea
Ceann Leathad nam Bo
Kildonan Burn
Kildonan Lodge
330
Mid Hill
312
Langwell Water
Langwell House
Berriedale
Blar a'Ghille Dhomhnaich
422
Braigh na h-Eaglaise
Beinn Dubhain
414
Torrish Burn
Ousdale
Duible
Kilphedir
Creag Thoraraidh
Badbea
Torrish
A897
Caen
Ord of Caithness
Ben Uarie
Eldrable Hill
Marrel
Navidale
Beinn Mhealaich
592
Beinn Dhorain
628
West Helmsdale
East Helmsdale
Helmsdale
Gartymore
Glen Sletdale
Glen Loth
Portgower
A9
Lothmore
Culgower
Creag a' Chrionaich
394
Kilmote
Lothbeg
97
0 2 4 6 8 10 miles
0 2 4 6 8 10 km
A
B
C
D
E
F
G

ORKNEY
27
28
29
30
31
32
33
A
B
C
D
E
0 2 4 6 8 10 miles
0 2 4 6 8 10 km
NORTH RONALDSAY
Point of Sinsoss
Tor Ness
Linklet Bay
Hollandstoun
Bride's Ness
South Bay
Strom Ness
NORTH RONALDSAY FIRTH
Tafts Ness
Whitemill Point
Sandquoy
Scuthvie Bay
Start Point
Bay of Lopness
Newark
SANDAY
Scar
Burness
Otters Wick
North Bay
Broughtown
Roadside
Sanday
Cata Sand
Overbister
Bay of Newark
Kettletoft
Sty Wick
Quoy Ness
QUOYNESS CHAMBERED CAIRN
Els Ness
Tres Ness
B9069
B9068
B9070
Holms of Ire
THE NORTH SOUND
Braeswick
Stove
Loth
Spur Ness
SANDAY SOUND
Calf of Eday
Grey Head
Red Head
Calfsound
VINQUOY CHAMBERED CAIRN
STONE OF SETTER
Guith
Millbounds
Eday
EDAY
B9063
Backaland
Veness
War Ness
Geo Luon
Fall of Warness
Sound of Faray
Eday Sound
Faray
Rusk Holm
Fers Ness
Point of Huro
Rapness Sound
Holm of Huip
Huip Ness
Papa Stronsay
Links Ness
Odie
Stronsay
Whitehall
STRONSAY
B9062
B9060
B9061
Mill Bay
Odness
Linga Holm
St Catherine's Bay
Aith
Everbay
Kirbister
Odin Bay
Grobister
Bay of Bomasty
Rothiesholm
Bay of Holland
Dishes
Holland
Burgh Head
Bay of Houseby
Lamb Head
Rothiesholm Head
Greenli Ness
Tor Ness
Ingale Skerry
Auskerry Sound
Auskerry
STRONSAY FIRTH
PAPA WESTRAY
Mull Head
The Bore
Papa Sound
BONIFACE CHURCH
Holm of Papa
CHAMBERED CAIRN
KNAP OF HOWAR
Holland
ST TREDWELLS CHAPEL
Backaskaill
Head of Moclett
Bow Head
Aikerness
Westray
Rackwick
NOLTLAND
Ouse Ness
LADY KIRK
Noup Head
Gentlemens' Cave
Monivey
Bis Geos
Pierowall
Broughton
Braehead
WESTRAY
B9066
B9067
Spo Ness
Skelwick
Midbea
Bay of Tuquoy
WESTSIDE CHURCH
Inga Ness
Langskaill
Berst Ness
Stanger Head
Rapness
Twiness
Skea Skerries
WESTRAY FIRTH
ROUSAY
Sacquoy Head
Saviskaill Head
Saviskaill Bay
Bring Head
Faraclett Head
Wasbister
B9064
Sourin
Muckle Water
Blotchnie Fiold
250
MIDHOWE BROCH
KNOWE OF YARSO CHAMBERED CAIRN
Westness
Brinyan
Rousay Sound
Kili Holm
Mae Ness
ST MAGNUS CHURCH
Egilsay
Wyre Sound
ST MARYS CHAPEL
Wyre
CUBBIE ROO'S CASTLE
Muckle Green Holm
Gairsay Sound
Sweyn Holm
Gairsay
Costa Head
Skea
Eynhallow
Costa
Eynhallow Sound
Brough Head
EARLS PALACE
BROUGH OF BIRSAY
Birsay Bay
Birsay
Abune-the-Hill
STANDING STONES
Loch of Boardhouse
Loch of Swannay
Loch of Hundland
A966
A967
A986
Evie
Aiker Ness
GURNESS BROCH
Redland
Woodwick
Marwick Head
KITCHENER'S MONUMENT
Marwick
Twatt
Kirbuster
B9057
Burn of Hillside
CLICK MILL
Beaquoy
Tingwall
Lerwick
Outshore Point
B9056
Isbister
Quoyloo
Northdyke
Skeabrae
Dounby
Mirbister
Milldoe
221
Hackland
CORRIGALL FARM MUSEUM
Settiscarth
Gorseness
Tor Ness
Bay of Skaill
SKARA BRAE
Skaill
Row Head
Aith
Brough
Isbister
Bay of Isbister
Broad Taing
Loch of Skaill
Netherbrough
Bimbister
B9055
Ness of Tenston
Loch of Harray
Yesnaby
Voy
Wide Firth
Hill of Miffia
158
Nebak Point
Quholm
Loch of Stenness
RING OF BRODGAR
MAES HOWE
STONES OF STENNESS
Finstown
Bay of Firth
Damsay
Heddle
CHAMBERED CAIRN
A965
Clouston
RENNIBISTER EARTH HOUSE
GRAIN EARTH HOUSE
225
Bay of Kirkwall
Kirkwall
Work
Car Ness
Head of Holland
Rerwick Head
The Galt
Veantrow Bay
Bay of Furrowend
Ness of Ork
Edmonstone
B9058
B9059
Bay of Linton
SHAPINSAY
BALFOUR CASTLE
Balfour
Helliar Holm
The Foot
Sandgarth
Haco's Ness
Shapinsay Sound

A
B
C
D
E
27
28
29
30
31
32
33
103
SCAPA FLOW
PENTLAND FIRTH
HOY
FLOTTA
BURRAY
SOUTH RONALDSAY
HIGHLAND
Island of Stroma
DUNNET HEAD
DUNCANSBY HEAD
Pentland Skerries
Muckle Skerry
Swona
Copinsay
Graemsay
Cava
Fara
Switha
Hunda
Aberdeen
Stromness
Hoy Sound
Clestrain Sound
Bring Deeps
Holm Sound
Water Sound
Echnaloch Bay
Widewall Bay
Sound of Hoxa
Inner Sound
Sinclair's Bay
Thurso Bay
Dunnet Bay
Murkle Bay
Freswick Bay
Gills Bay
Kame of Hoy
St John's Head
The Sow
Old Man of Hoy
Rora Head
Sneuk Head
Rack Wick
Little Rack Wick
Heldale Water
Knap of Trowieglen
Ward Hill
479
433
399
354
Cuilags
Murra
Linksness
Rackwick
DWARFIE STANE
Lyrawa Burn
Pegal Burn
Burn of Ore
Green Head
Rysa Little
Lyness
Rinnigill
Crock Ness
SCAPA FLOW VISITOR CENTRE
Longhope
North Bay
Melsetter
Hurliness
Hackness
MARTELLO TOWER
Brims Ness
Tor Ness
Garth Head
Cantick Head
South Walls
Oil Terminal
Pan
Bow
Calf of Flotta
Roan Head
Barrel of Butter
Houton Head
Houton
Midland Ness
Clestrain
Kirbister
Ward Hill
268
Hobbister
Greenigo
Gyre
Swanbister Bay
Waulkmill Bay
Ve Ness
ST NICHOLAS CHURCH AND EARLS BU
PIER ARTS CENTRE
Tradespark
Kirkwall
Long Geo
Scapa Bay
Bay of Sandoyne
St Mary's
Lamb Holm
ITALIAN CHAPEL
Glimps Holm
North Dawn
Foubister
Toab
Deer Sound
Mirkady Point
Upper Sanday
Braehead
Cornquoy
Carny
Rose Ness
Gritley
Skaill
Marka Ber
Roana Bay
Newark Bay
Point of Ayre
Corn Holm
South Nevi
A964
A961
A960
B9053
B9052
B9051
B9050
B9047
B9045
B9043
B9044
B9042
B9041
Northtown
Southtown
Hoxa
Quindry
St Margaret's Hope
Grimness
Grim Ness
Eastside
Herston
Herston Head
Widewall
Aikers
Lythes
Ward Hill
Linklater
Halcro Head
Barth Head
The North Head
The Tails of Tarf
Burwick
Cleat
Liddel
Old Head
Brough Ness
Langaton Point
Nethertown
Red Head
Uppertown
Mell Head
St John's Point
Men of Mey
Head of Crees
Boars of Duncansby
Ness of Duncansby
Bay of Sannick
Easter Head
Dunnet Hill
121
Brough
The Thirl
Hunspow
West Dunnet
Dwarwick Head
Scarfskerry Point
Tang Head
Scarfskerry
Harrow
East Mey
Ham
Rattar
St John's Loch
Loch of Mey
Whitebridge
Mey
Barrock
Gills
A836
Huna
John 'o' Groats
Stacks of Duncansby
Canisbay
Hill of Crogodale
Upper Gills
Warth Hill
124
Wife Geo
Everley
Skirza Head
Skirza
Tofts
Freswick
Ness Head
Brabster
Gill Burn
Dunnet
Links of Dunnet
Inkstack
Lochend
Loch Heilen
Slickly
Alterwall
Ness of Litter
Spear Head
Clett
Holborn Head
Scrabster
Clardon Head
The Spur
Thurso
Clardon
Murkle
Ormwe
Haimer
Castletown
Thurdistoft
Greenland
Olrig House
Hayfield
Tain
Lochside
Reaster
Bowermadden
Auckengill
Kirk Burn
A9
(A836)
Nybster
Brough Head
Shalmstry
A882
(A9)
Hilliclay
Durran
Weydale
Carsgoe
Achingills
Hoy
Lyth
Sortat
Burn of Lyth
Howe
Keiss
Stain
Tang Head
B876
Buckies
Aimster
Lieurary
Sordale
Stemster
Bowertower
Knockdee
Tister
Hastigrow
Skinnet
Braal Castle
Stemster House
Corsback
Halcro
Mireland
Gillock
Loch Scarmclate
Loch of Wester
Calder Mains
Gerston
Halkirk
Clayock
B874
Lynegar
Quoys of Reiss
Killimster
B870
Bloody Moss
Scotscalder Sta
(A9)
A895
Spittal Hill
Harpsdale
Achies
Olgrinmore
Dunn
Oldhall
Loch Watten
Houstry
Mains of Watten
Wick
ACKERGILL TOWER
GIRNIGOE
Noss Head

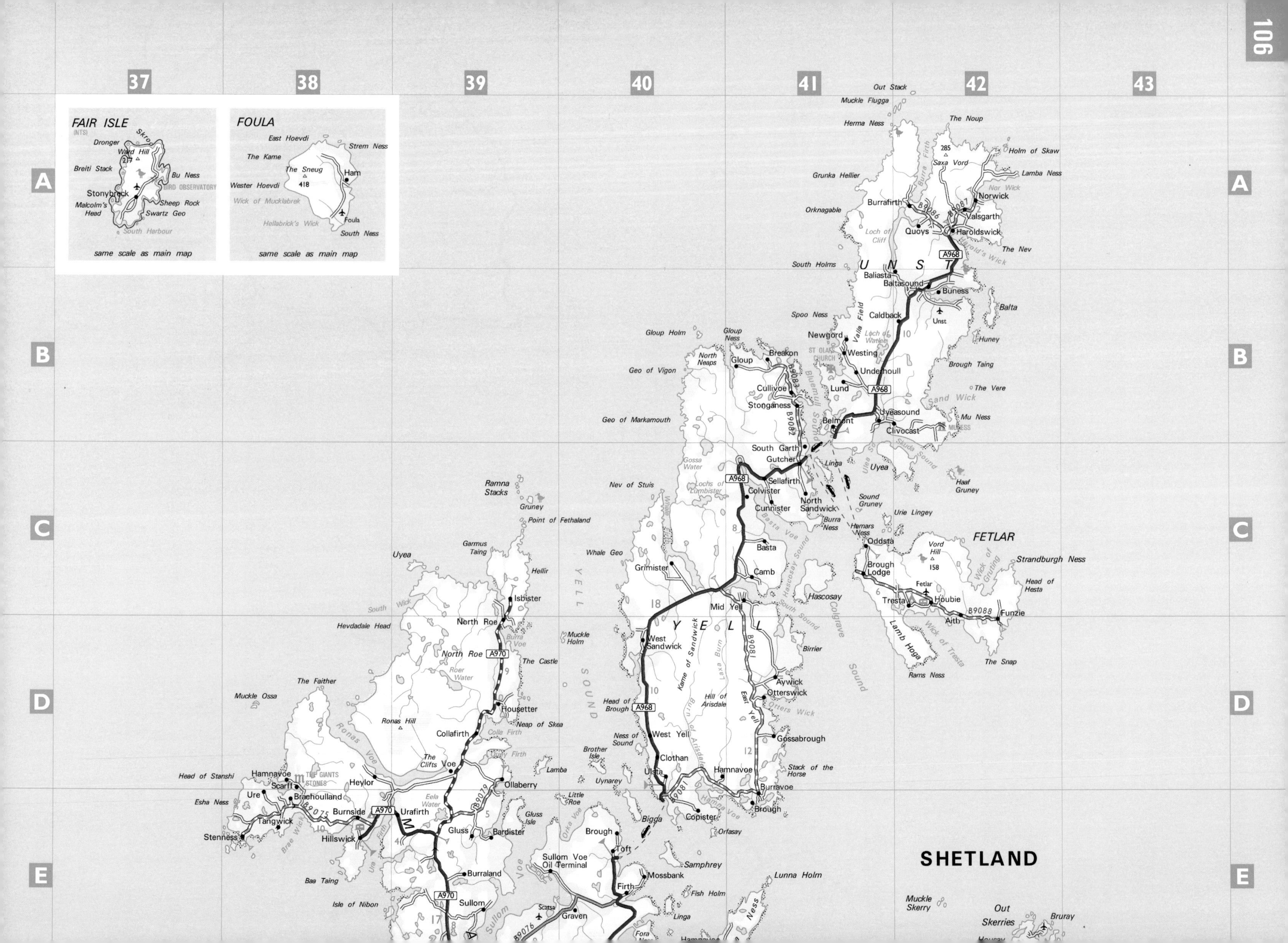
SHETLAND
FAIR ISLE
(NTS)
Dronger
Ward Hill
217
Breiti Stack
Bu Ness
BIRD OBSERVATORY
Stonybreck
Malcolm's Head
Sheep Rock
Swartz Geo
South Harbour
same scale as main map
FOULA
East Hoevdi
Strem Ness
The Kame
The Sneug
418
Ham
Wester Hoevdi
Wick of Mucklabrek
Hellabrick's Wick
Foula
South Ness
same scale as main map
Out Stack
Muckle Flugga
Herma Ness
The Noup
Saxa Vord
285
Holm of Skaw
Lamba Ness
Grunka Hellier
Nor Wick
Norwick
Burrafirth
B9086
B9087
Valsgarth
Orknagable
Loch of Cliff
Quoys
Haroldswick
A968
The Nev
Harold's Wick
South Holms
UNST
Baliasta
Baltasound
Buness
Spoo Ness
Caldback
Balta
Unst
Gloup Holm
Gloup Ness
Valla Field
Newgord
Loch of Watlee
Huney
North Neaps
Gloup
Breakon
ST OLAF'S CHURCH
Westing
Brough Taing
Geo of Vigon
B9083
Underhoull
Cullivoe
Lund
The Vere
Bluemull Sound
Stonganess
B9082
Sand Wick
Uyeasound
Mu Ness
Geo of Markamouth
Belmont
Clivocast
MUNESS
South Garth
Gutcher
Gossa Water
Linga
Uyea
Skuda Sound
Uyea Sound
Lochs of Lumbister
Sellafirth
Haaf Gruney
Nev of Stuis
Colvister
Ramna Stacks
Gruney
Cunnister
North Sandwick
Sound Gruney
Urie Lingey
Point of Fethaland
Burra Ness
Hamars Ness
Oddsta
FETLAR
Basta Voe
Basta
Vord Hill
158
Strandburgh Ness
Garmus Taing
Whale Geo
Uyea
Hellir
Grimister
Camb
Brough Lodge
Wick of Gruting
Hascosay Sound
Head of Hesta
Fetlar
Isbister
Hascosay
Tresta
Houbie
South Wick
Mid Yell
18
Aith
B9088
Funzie
Colgrave Sound
North Roe
Hevdadale Head
YELL
Muckle Holm
West Sandwick
Lamb Hoga
Wick of Tresta
Burra Voe
North Roe
A970
Kame of Sandwick
Laxa Burn
B9081
The Castle
Birrier
The Snap
Roer Water
YELL SOUND
Rams Ness
The Faither
Aywick
Otterswick
Muckle Ossa
Head of Brough
A968
Hill of Arisdale
East Yell
Otters Wick
Housetter
Ronas Hill
Neap of Skea
Burn of Arisdale
Ronas Voe
Collafirth
Colla Firth
Ness of Sound
West Yell
Gossabrough
Brother Isle
Dales Voe
The Clifts
Voe
Clothan
Stack of the Horse
Head of Stanshi
Hamnavoe
THE GIANTS STONES
Lamba
Uynarey
Ulsta
Hamnavoe
Heylor
Ollaberry
Burravoe
Scarff
Braehoulland
Ure
Eela Water
B9079
Little Roe
Hamna Voe
Esha Ness
Burnside
Urafirth
Gluss Isle
Copister
Brough
Tangwick
Bigga
Orfasay
Stenness
Hillswick
Gluss
Bardister
Brough
Brae Wick
Orka Voe
Toft
Samphrey
SHETLAND
Baa Taing
Sullom Voe Oil Terminal
Burraland
Mossbank
Lunna Holm
Firth
Fish Holm
Muckle Skerry
Isle of Nibon
A970
Sullom
Scatsta
Graven
Linga
Out Skerries
Bruray
B9076
Sullom Voe
Ness
Fora Ness
Housay
37
38
39
40
41
42
43
A
B
C
D
E

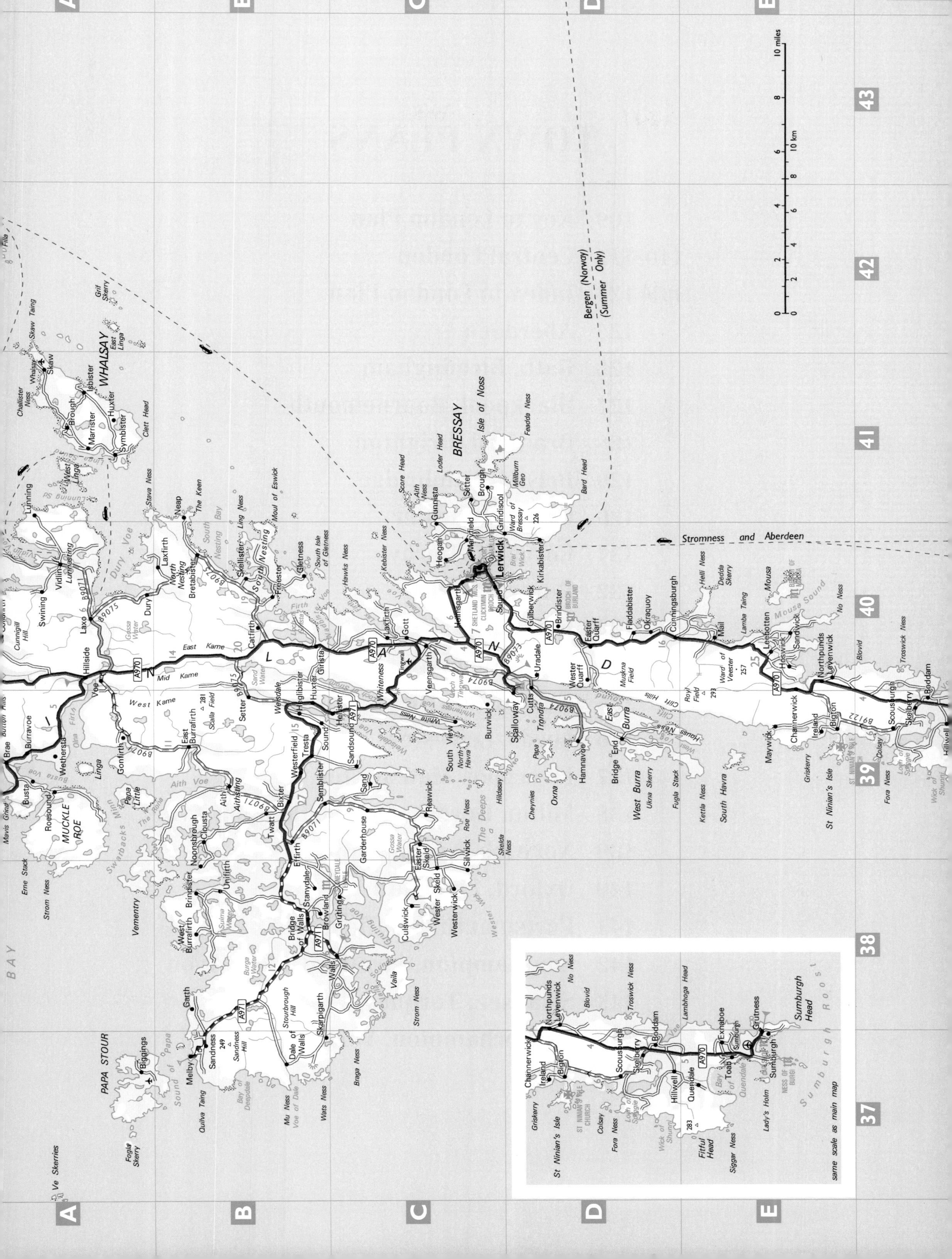

PAPA STOUR
MUCKLE ROE
WHALSAY
BRESSAY
Isle of Noss
Lerwick
Scalloway
Walls
Aith
Voe
Brae
Sandness
Bixter
Tresta
Whiteness
Gott
Laxfirth
Cunningsburgh
Sandwick
Levenwick
Boddam
Sumburgh
Sumburgh Head
West Burra
East Burra
Hamnavoe
Vaila
Vementry
Stromness and Aberdeen
Bergen (Norway) (Summer Only)
St Ninian's Isle
Fitful Head
Mousa
Fair Isle
same scale as main map
10 miles
10 km

TOWN PLANS

109 Key to London Plan
110-117 Central London
118-124 Index to London Plan
125 Aberdeen
126 Bath, Birmingham
127 Blackpool, Bournemouth
128 Bradford, Brighton
129 Bristol, Cambridge
130 Cardiff, Chester
131 Coventry, Derby
132 Dover, Dundee
133 Edinburgh, Exeter
134 Folkestone, Glasgow
135 Gloucester, Hull
136 Leeds, Leicester
137 Liverpool, Manchester
138 Milton Keynes, Newcastle upon Tyne
139 Norwich, Nottingham
140 Oxford, Plymouth
141 Portsmouth, Sheffield
142 Southampton, Stratford-upon-Avon
143 Swansea, Torquay
144 Wolverhampton, York

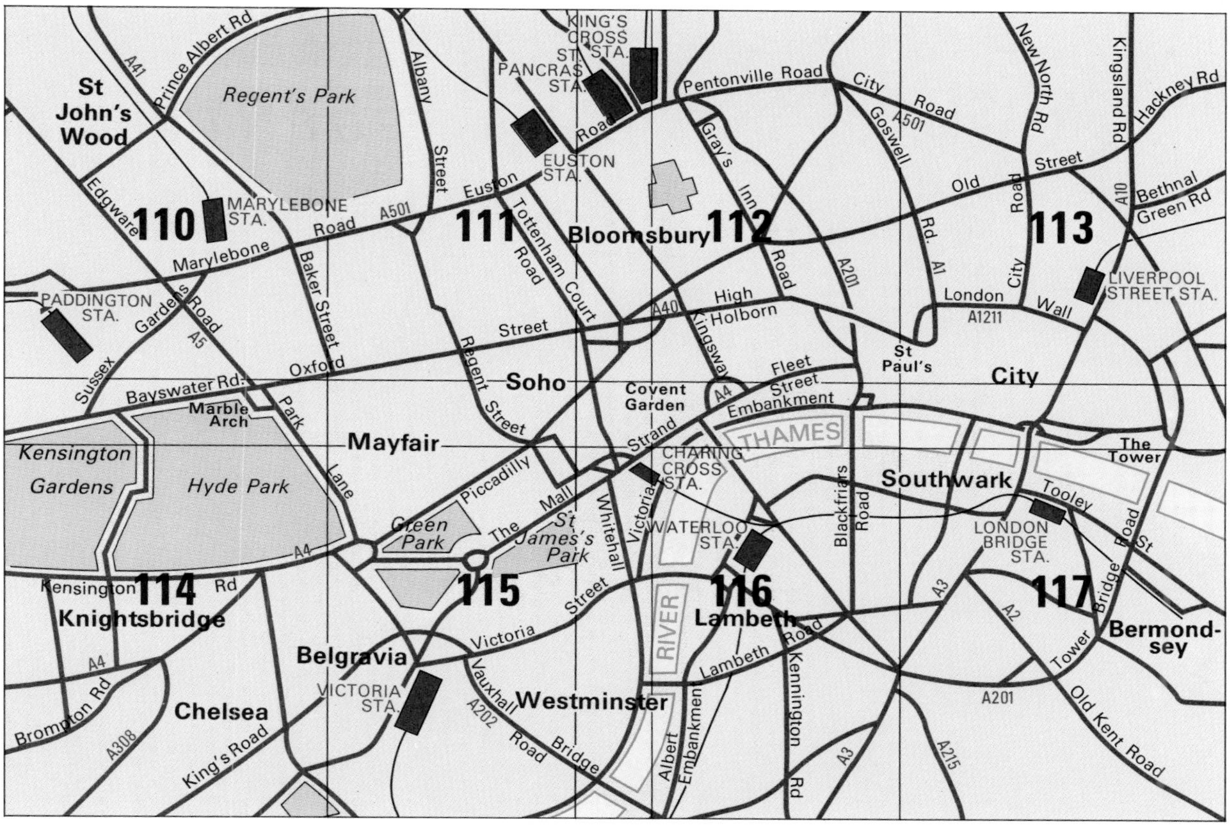

KEY TO MAP SYMBOLS

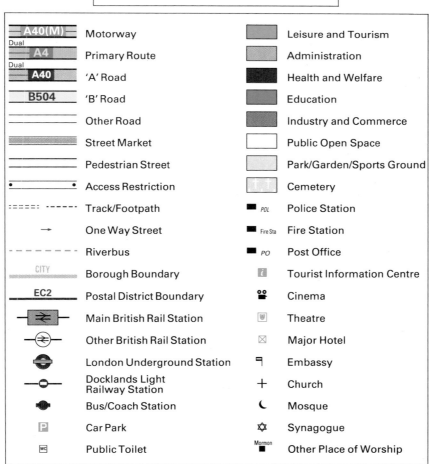

A40(M)	Motorway		Leisure and Tourism
Dual A4	Primary Route		Administration
Dual A40	'A' Road		Health and Welfare
B504	'B' Road		Education
	Other Road		Industry and Commerce
	Street Market		Public Open Space
	Pedestrian Street		Park/Garden/Sports Ground
	Access Restriction		Cemetery
	Track/Footpath	POL	Police Station
	One Way Street	Fire Sta	Fire Station
	Riverbus	PO	Post Office
CITY	Borough Boundary		Tourist Information Centre
EC2	Postal District Boundary		Cinema
	Main British Rail Station		Theatre
	Other British Rail Station		Major Hotel
	London Underground Station		Embassy
	Docklands Light Railway Station		Church
	Bus/Coach Station		Mosque
	Car Park		Synagogue
WC	Public Toilet	Mormon	Other Place of Worship

Scale 1:10,000 (6.3 inches to 1 mile)

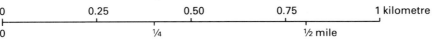

0 — 0.25 — 0.50 — 0.75 — 1 kilometre

0 — ¼ — ½ mile

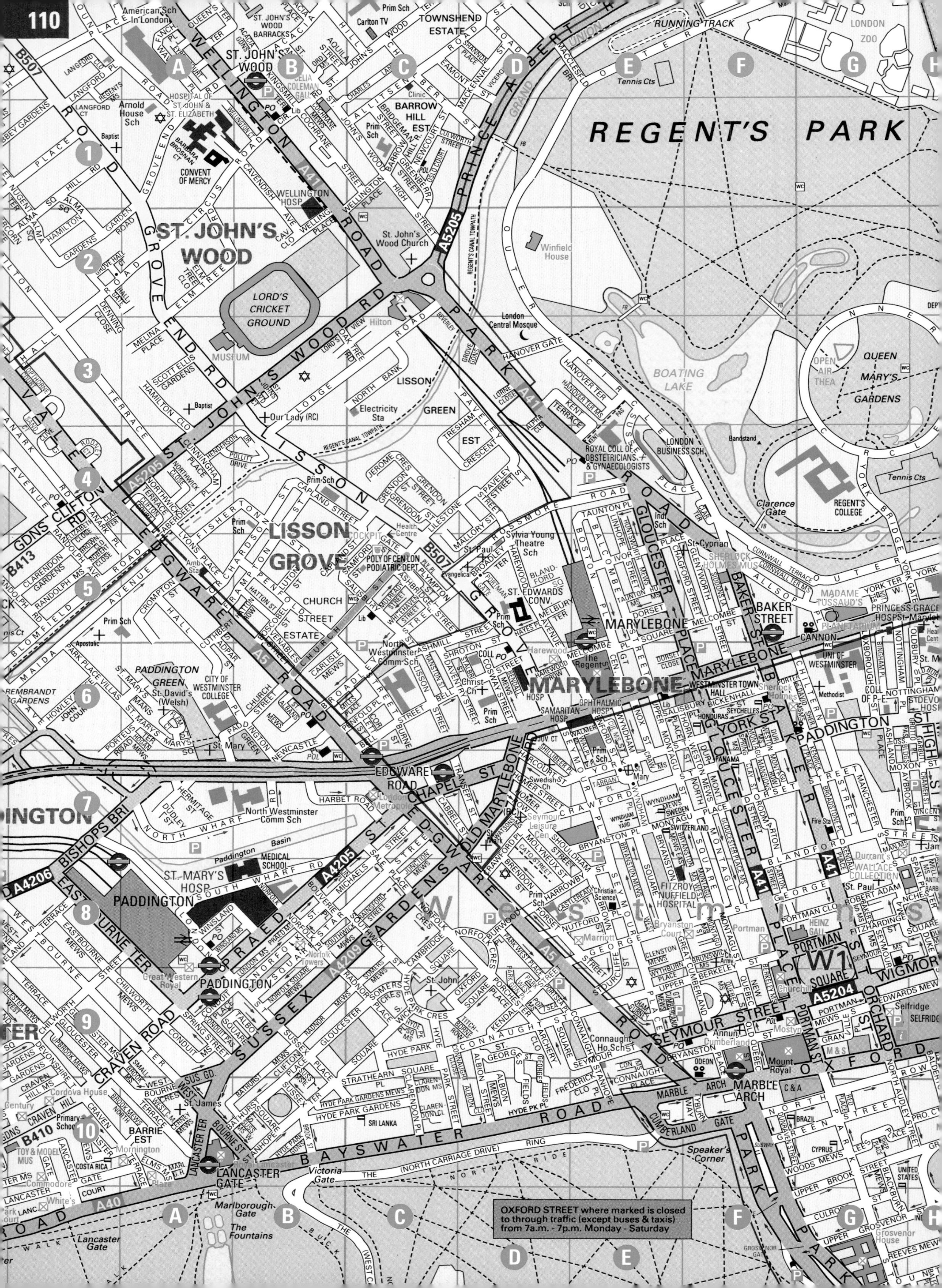
REGENT'S PARK
ST. JOHN'S WOOD
LORD'S CRICKET GROUND
LISSON GROVE
MARYLEBONE
PADDINGTON
LONDON ZOO
QUEEN MARY'S GARDENS
BOATING LAKE
OPEN AIR THEA
Winfield House
London Central Mosque
LONDON BUSINESS SCH
ROYAL COLL OF OBSTETRICIANS & GYNAECOLOGISTS
REGENT'S COLLEGE
Clarence Gate
Hanover Gate
RUNNING TRACK
TOWNSHEND ESTATE
BARROW HILL EST
ST. JOHN'S WOOD
St. John's Wood Church
WELLINGTON HOSP
HOSPITAL OF ST. JOHN & ST. ELIZABETH
CONVENT OF MERCY
American Sch In London
Arnold House Sch
MUSEUM
CHURCH STREET ESTATE
PADDINGTON GREEN
CITY OF WESTMINSTER COLLEGE
North Westminster Comm Sch
ST. MARY'S HOSP
MEDICAL SCHOOL
Paddington Basin
EDGWARE ROAD
BAKER STREET
MARYLEBONE
MADAME TUSSAUD'S
PLANETARIUM
SHERLOCK HOLMES MUS
Sylvia Young Theatre Sch
ST. EDWARDS CONV.
WESTMINSTER TOWN HALL
UNI OF WESTMINSTER
FITZROY NUFFIELD HOSPITAL
WALLACE COLLECTION
Durrant's
HEINZ GALL
W1
PORTMAN SQUARE
MARBLE ARCH
Mount Royal
Selfridge
SELFRIDGES
Speaker's Corner
LANCASTER GATE
Victoria Gate
Marlborough Gate
The Fountains
Lancaster Gate
BAYSWATER ROAD
THE RING
(NORTH CARRIAGE DRIVE)
OXFORD STREET
SEYMOUR STREET
EDGWARE ROAD
SUSSEX GARDENS
PRAED ST
MARYLEBONE ROAD
GLOUCESTER PLACE
BAKER ST
PRINCE ALBERT ROAD
WELLINGTON ROAD
ST. JOHN'S WOOD RD
PARK ROAD
OUTER CIRCLE
INNER CIRCLE
GROVE END RD
MAIDA VALE
CLIFTON GDNS
CRAVEN ROAD
BISHOPS BRI
GROSVENOR
Grosvenor House
TOY & MODEL MUS
BARRIE EST
A41
A5
A40
A5205
A4205
A4209
A5204
A4206
B507
B413
B410
OXFORD STREET where marked is closed to through traffic (except buses & taxis) from 7a.m. - 7p.m. Monday - Saturday

NW1
REGENT'S PARK
SOMERS TOWN
KING'S CROSS
ST. PANCRAS
EUSTON
Camden
UNIVERSITY COLLEGE LONDON
UNIVERSITY OF LONDON
BLOOMSBURY
THE BRITISH MUSEUM AND BRITISH LIBRARY
MIDDLESEX HOSP
OXFORD CIRCUS
TOTTENHAM COURT ROAD
SOHO
COVENT GARDEN
LEICESTER SQ
STRAND
WC2
MAYFAIR
NATIONAL GALLERY
EUSTON ROAD
OXFORD ST
REGENT STREET
GOWER ST
HAMPSTEAD ROAD
ALBANY STREET
GT. PORTLAND ST
BOND ST
PICCADILLY CIR.
CHARING CROSS ROAD
SHAFTESBURY AVE
HIGH HOLBORN
SOUTHAMPTON ROW
WOBURN PLACE
PANCRAS ROAD
GRAY'S INN ROAD
A501
A4200
A400
A40
A4201
A5202
A401
B406
B506
B504
B402
B401
1
2
3
4
5
6
7
8
9
10
H
J
K
L
M
N
P
Q

KING'S CROSS
ST. PANCRAS
PENTONVILLE
FINSBURY
CLERKENWELL
ST. PANCRAS
WC1
BLOOMSBURY
HOLBORN
LINCOLN'S INN FIELDS
COVENT GARDEN
STRAND
WC2
EC4
BLACKFRIARS
ANGEL
FARRINGDON
CHANCERY LANE
TEMPLE
VICTORIA EMBANKMENT
RIVER THAMES
KING'S REACH
HMS PRESIDENT
PENTONVILLE RD
CITY ROAD
GOSWELL ROAD
GRAY'S INN ROAD
FARRINGDON RD
CLERKENWELL RD
THEOBALD'S ROAD
HIGH HOLBORN
HOLBORN VIADUCT
FLEET STREET
KINGSWAY
SOUTHAMPTON ROW
CALEDONIAN RD
ROSEBERY AVE
KING'S CROSS RD
NEW OXFORD ST
SHAFTESBURY AVE
BLOOMSBURY WAY
CORAM'S FIELDS
GRAY'S INN GDNS
MOUNT PLEASANT POST OFFICE
THE BRITISH MUSEUM
ROYAL COURTS OF JUSTICE
PUBLIC RECORD OFFICE
SOMERSET HOUSE
ST. BARTHOLOMEW'S HOSPITAL
CENTRAL CRIMINAL COURT (Old Bailey)
THAMESLINK
CITY THAMESLINK
A B C D E F G H
1 2 3 4 5 6 7 8 9 10

SHOREDITCH PARK
HOXTON
HAGGERSTON PARK
SPORTS GROUND
Haggerston City Farm
Haggerston Sec School
GEFFRYE MUSEUM
HACKNEY ROAD
A1208
COLUMBIA ROAD
GOSSET ST
Daneford Secondary School
BETHNAL GREEN COLLEGE (Adult Ed)
BETHNAL GREEN ROAD
A1209
CHESHIRE ST
SCLATER ST
SHOREDITCH
B135
BRICK LANE
B134
QUAKER STREET
HANBURY STREET
Site of Old Spitalfields Market
COMMERCIAL STREET
A1202
SHOREDITCH HIGH ST
KINGSLAND ROAD
A10
OLD STREET
A5201
GREAT EASTERN ST
CITY ROAD
EAST RD
NEW NORTH RD
B101
MOORFIELDS EYE HOSPITAL
ST. LUKE'S
EC1
BUNHILL FIELDS
BUNHILL ROW
B144
A501
CHISWELL STREET
B100
BARBICAN
MOORGATE
EC2
BROADGATE
LIVERPOOL STREET
BISHOPSGATE
HOUNDSDITCH
MIDDLESEX ST
A1210
ALDGATE
ALDGATE EAST
WHITECHAPEL HIGH ST
WHITECHAPEL ART GALL
LONDON WALL
A1211
Bank of England
BANK
Stock Exch
MANSION HOUSE
ST. PAUL'S CATHEDRAL
CHEAPSIDE
CANNON ST
MONUMENT
Lloyds of London
FENCHURCH ST
EC3
TOWER HILL
TOWER GATEWAY
ROYAL MINT ST
B126
LEMAN STREET
PRESCOT ST
MANSELL ST
MINORIES
THE TOWER
EAST SMITHFIELD
A1203
LOWER THAMES ST
Custom House
Site of Old Billingsgate Mkt
Swan Lane Pier
Southwark Bridge Steps
London Commodity Exchange
E1
WHITECHAPEL
H J K L M N P Q
1 2 3 4 5 6 7 8 9 10

HYDE PARK
KENSINGTON GARDENS
OXFORD STREET where marked is closed to through traffic (except buses & taxis) from 7a.m. - 7p.m. Monday - Saturday
BAYSWATER ROAD
LANCASTER GATE
Victoria Gate
Marlborough Gate
The Fountains
THE LONG WATER
THE SERPENTINE
The Lido
Pier
Speaker's Corner
MARBLE ARCH
PARK LANE
ROTTEN ROW
Albert Memorial
Alexandra Gate
Queen's Gate
Prince of Wales Gate
Rutland Gate
Edinburgh Gate
Albert Gate
HYDE PARK CORNER
KNIGHTSBRIDGE
KENSINGTON GORE
ROYAL ALBERT HALL
ROYAL COLL OF ART
IMPERIAL COLLEGE
SCIENCE MUSEUM
NATURAL HISTORY MUSEUM
GEOLOGICAL MUSEUM
VICTORIA & ALBERT MUSEUM
BROMPTON
Brompton Oratory
SW7
HARRODS
SLOANE STREET
CROMWELL RD
SOUTH KENSINGTON
BROMPTON ROAD
SW3
ROYAL MARSDEN HOSP
BROMPTON HOSP
KING'S ROAD
SLOANE SQUARE
DUKE OF YORK'S HEADQUARTERS
ROYAL HOSPITAL MUSEUM
RANELAGH GARDENS
PIMLICO
CHELSEA BR
FULHAM ROAD
Chelsea Sports Centre
OLD TOWN HALL
SUTTON ESTATE
SAMUEL LEWIS TRUST DWELLINGS
CHELSEA CLOISTERS
A40
A315
A4
A3216
A3217
A3218
A308
B304
B302
B319
B310
A4202
Kensington
Chelsea

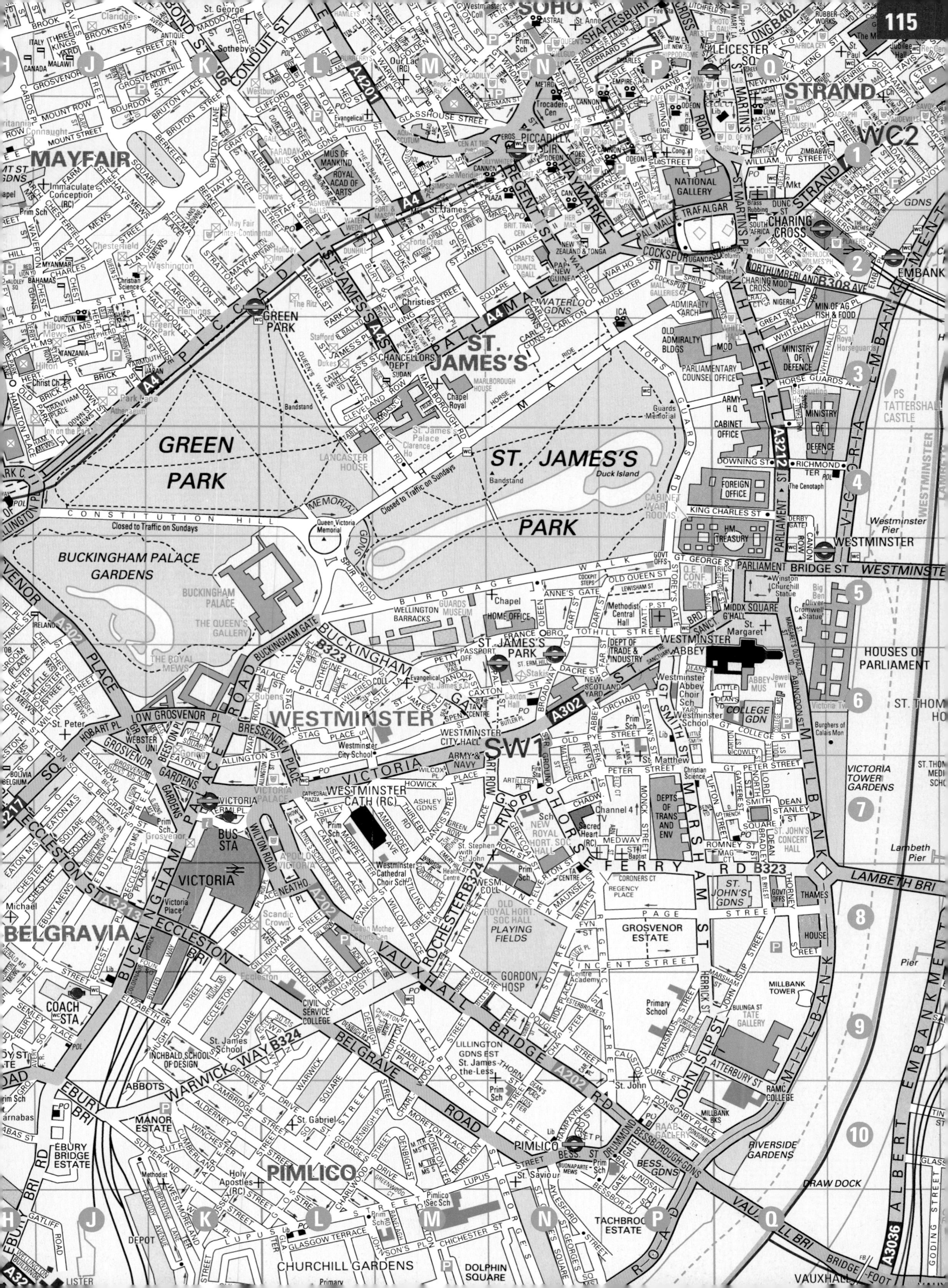
MAYFAIR
SOHO
STRAND
WC2
GREEN PARK
ST. JAMES'S
ST. JAMES'S PARK
BUCKINGHAM PALACE GARDENS
BUCKINGHAM PALACE
THE QUEEN'S GALLERY
THE ROYAL MEWS
WESTMINSTER
SW1
BELGRAVIA
PIMLICO
VICTORIA
HOUSES OF PARLIAMENT
VICTORIA TOWER GARDENS
NATIONAL GALLERY
TRAFALGAR SQ
CHARING CROSS
PICCADILLY CIR.
LEICESTER SQ
EMBANKMENT
WESTMINSTER ABBEY
WESTMINSTER CATH (RC)
TATE GALLERY
MILLBANK TOWER
ROYAL ACAD OF ARTS
MUS OF MANKIND
FOREIGN OFFICE
HM TREASURY
MINISTRY OF DEFENCE
CABINET OFFICE
DOWNING ST
HOME OFFICE
NEW SCOTLAND YARD
WELLINGTON BARRACKS
GUARDS MUSEUM
ST. JAMES'S PALACE
LANCASTER HOUSE
MARLBOROUGH HOUSE
CONSTITUTION HILL
Closed to Traffic on Sundays
PICCADILLY
PALL MALL
THE MALL
BIRDCAGE WALK
HORSE GUARDS RD
WHITEHALL
PARLIAMENT ST
MILLBANK
VICTORIA EMBANKMENT
ALBERT EMBANKMENT
LAMBETH BRI
VAUXHALL BRI
VAUXHALL BRIDGE RD
VICTORIA ST
BUCKINGHAM PALACE RD
GROSVENOR PL
BELGRAVE ROAD
REGENT ST
HAYMARKET
COACH STA
BUS STA
GROSVENOR ESTATE
CHURCHILL GARDENS
DOLPHIN SQUARE
RIVERSIDE GARDENS
PS TATTERSHALL CASTLE
Westminster Pier
Lambeth Pier
DRAW DOCK
A4
A4201
A302
A3212
A3213
A202
A3036
B323
B324
B402
B308
1
2
3
4
5
6
7
8
9
10
H
J
K
L
M
N
P
Q

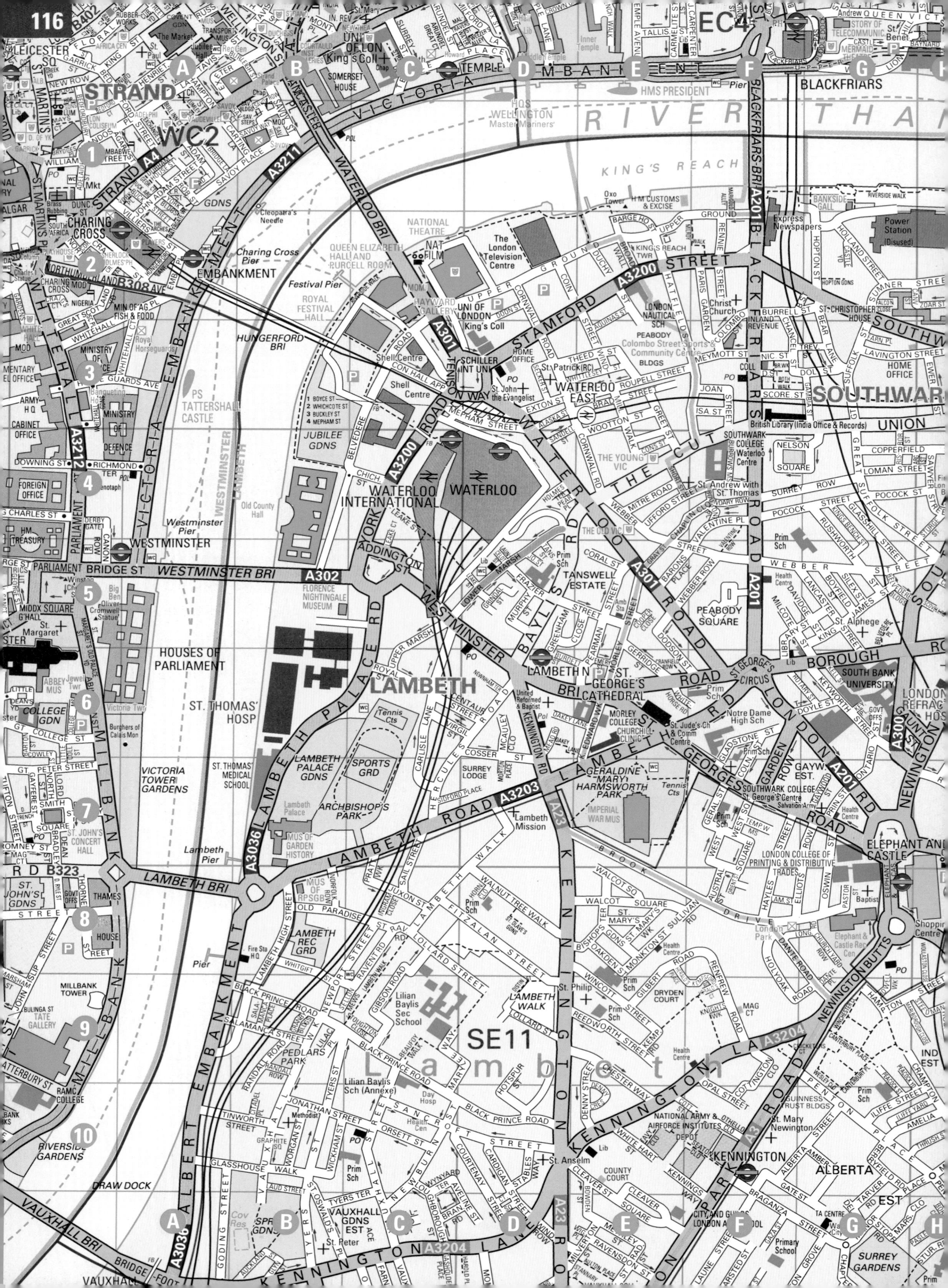

STRAND
WC2
EC4
CHARING CROSS
EMBANKMENT
TEMPLE
BLACKFRIARS
RIVER THAMES
KING'S REACH
VICTORIA EMBANKMENT
WATERLOO BRI
HUNGERFORD BRI
WESTMINSTER BRI
LAMBETH BRI
VAUXHALL BRI
NATIONAL THEATRE
QUEEN ELIZABETH HALL AND PURCELL ROOM
ROYAL FESTIVAL HALL
HAYWARD GALLERY
The London Television Centre
Shell Centre
JUBILEE GDNS
WATERLOO INTERNATIONAL
WATERLOO
WATERLOO EAST
THE OLD VIC
THE YOUNG VIC
STAMFORD STREET
THE CUT
BLACKFRIARS ROAD
UNION
SOUTHWARK
Southwark College Waterloo Centre
British Library (India Office & Records)
SOUTH BANK UNIVERSITY
BOROUGH ROAD
ST. GEORGE'S CIRCUS
ST. GEORGE'S CATHEDRAL
IMPERIAL WAR MUS
GERALDINE MARY HARMSWORTH PARK
ELEPHANT AND CASTLE
NEW KENT ROAD
LONDON COLLEGE OF PRINTING & DISTRIBUTIVE TRADES
WESTMINSTER
HOUSES OF PARLIAMENT
Big Ben
ABBEY
Victoria Twr
VICTORIA TOWER GARDENS
MINISTRY OF DEFENCE
FOREIGN OFFICE
HM TREASURY
CABINET OFFICE
WHITEHALL
DOWNING ST
HORSE GUARDS AVE
PARLIAMENT SQUARE
ST. THOMAS' HOSP
LAMBETH
LAMBETH PALACE GDNS
Lambeth Palace
ARCHBISHOP'S PARK
LAMBETH PALACE RD
LAMBETH ROAD
LAMBETH NORTH
WESTMINSTER BRIDGE ROAD
KENNINGTON ROAD
KENNINGTON LANE
KENNINGTON
SE11
Lambeth
MILLBANK
MILLBANK TOWER
TATE GALLERY
RIVERSIDE GARDENS
ALBERT EMBANKMENT
VAUXHALL GDNS EST
NEWINGTON BUTTS
ALBERTA EST
SURREY GARDENS

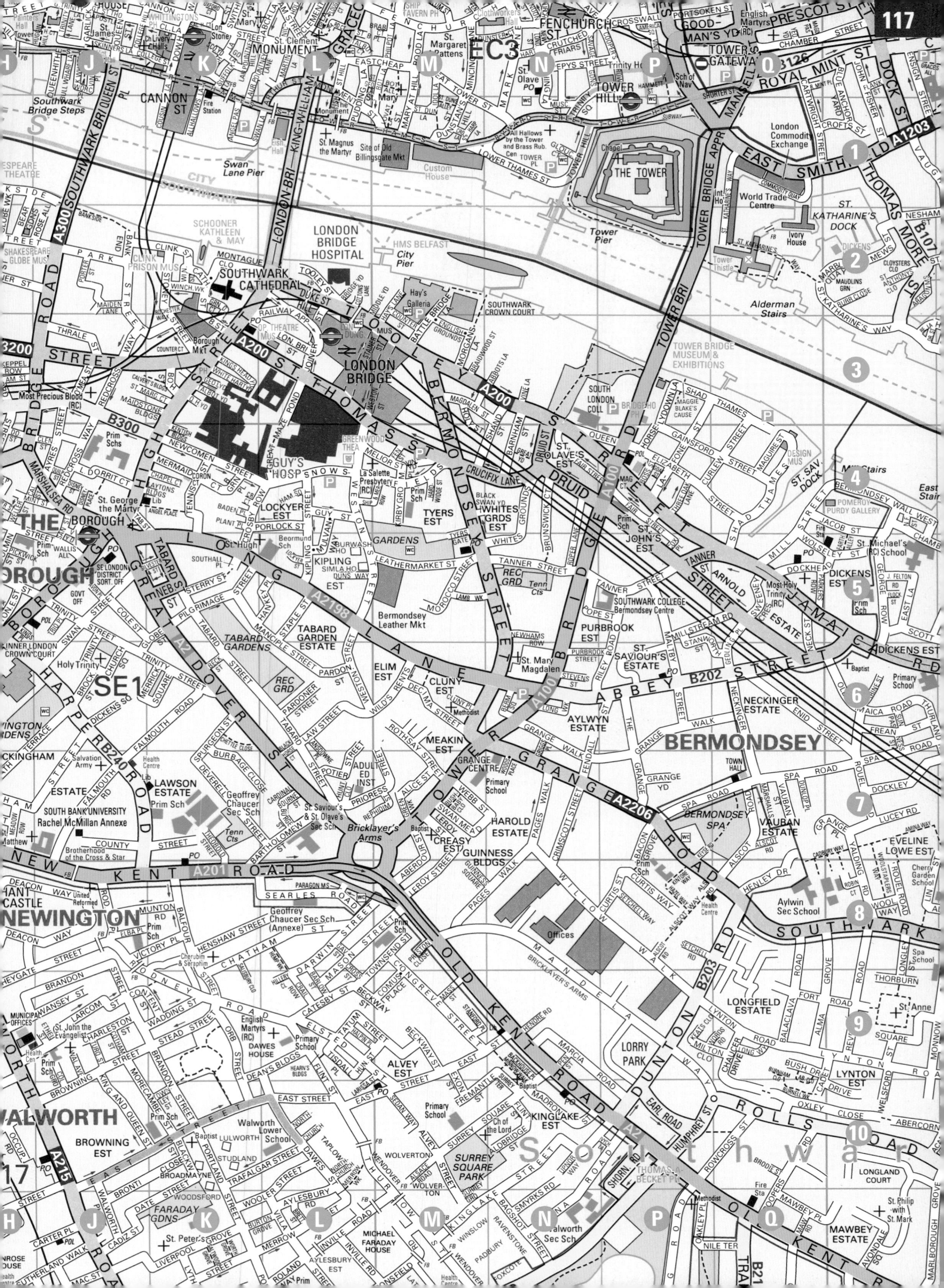
EC3
FENCHURCH ST
MONUMENT
CANNON ST
TOWER HILL
TOWER GATEWAY
ROYAL MINT ST
PRESCOT ST
DOCK ST
EAST SMITHFIELD
A1203
London Commodity Exchange
World Trade Centre
THE TOWER
Tower Pier
ST. KATHARINE'S DOCK
Ivory House
Alderman Stairs
ST. KATHARINE'S WAY
TOWER BRIDGE APPR
TOWER BRI
TOWER BRIDGE MUSEUM & EXHIBITIONS
LONDON BRIDGE HOSPITAL
HMS BELFAST
City Pier
SOUTHWARK CROWN COURT
Hay's Galleria
SOUTHWARK CATHEDRAL
Southwark Bridge Steps
Swan Lane Pier
St. Magnus the Martyr
Site of Old Billingsgate Mkt
Custom House
SCHOONER KATHLEEN & MAY
CLINK PRISON MUS
SHAKESPEARE GLOBE MUS
SOUTHWARK BRI
QUEEN ST
LONDON BRI
KING WILLIAM ST
A300
A200
LONDON BRIDGE
TOOLEY ST
BERMONDSEY ST
CRUCIFIX LANE
DRUID ST
GUY'S HOSP
Borough Mkt
ST THOMAS ST
SOUTH LONDON COLL
DESIGN MUS
ST. SAV. DOCK
Mill Stairs
POMEROY PURDY GALLERY
JAMAICA ROAD
DICKENS EST
St. Michael's (RC) School
THE BOROUGH
BOROUGH
SE LONDON DISTRICT SORT. OFF
LONG LANE
A2198
TABARD GARDEN ESTATE
TABARD GARDENS
Bermondsey Leather Mkt
TYERS EST
WHITES GRDS EST
ST. JOHN'S EST
ST. OLAVE'S EST
SOUTHWARK COLLEGE Bermondsey Centre
PURBROOK EST
ST. SAVIOUR'S ESTATE
St. Mary Magdalen
ABBEY STREET
B202
NECKINGER ESTATE
BERMONDSEY
AYLWYN ESTATE
GRANGE WALK
GRANGE ROAD
A2206
BERMONDSEY SPA
VAUBAN ESTATE
EVELINE LOWE EST
Aylwin Sec School
SOUTHWARK PARK ROAD
SE1
Holy Trinity
GREAT DOVER ST
A2
LAWSON ESTATE
Geoffrey Chaucer Sec Sch
SOUTH BANK UNIVERSITY Rachel McMillan Annexe
Bricklayer's Arms
HAROLD ESTATE
GUINNESS BLDGS
MEAKIN EST
NEW KENT ROAD
A201
NEWINGTON
HEYGATE STREET
OLD KENT ROAD
MANDELA WAY
Offices
LORRY PARK
LONGFIELD ESTATE
LYNTON EST
St. Anne
DUNTON ROAD
B203
ROLLS ROAD
ALVEY EST
KINGLAKE EST
SURREY SQUARE PARK
WALWORTH
BROWNING EST
A215
EAST STREET
FARADAY GDNS
Walworth Lower School
Walworth Sec Sch
MICHAEL FARADAY HOUSE
AYLESBURY EST
MAWBEY ESTATE
LONGLAND COURT
St. Philip with St. Mark
Southwark

London Index

Abbey Orchard St. SW1 115 P6
Abbey St. SE1 117 N6
Abbots La. SE1 117 N3
Abbots Manor Est. SW1 115 J10
Abchurch La. EC4 113 L10
Abchurch Yd. EC4 113 K10
Aberdeen Pl. NW8 110 A4
Aberdour St. SE1 117 M8
Abingdon Clo. SE1 117 Q9
Abingdon St. SW1 115 Q6
Achilles Way W1 114 H3
Acton St. WC1 112 B3
Adam & Eve Ct. W1 111 M8
Adam St. WC2 116 A1
Adams Ct. EC2 113 L8
Adams Row W1 114 H1
Addington St. SE1 116 C5
Addle Hill EC4 112 G9
Addle St. EC2 113 J7
Adelaide St. WC2 115 Q1
Adeline Pl. WC1 111 P7
Adelphi Ter. WC2 116 A1
Adpar St. W2 110 A6
Affleck St. N1 112 C1
Agar St. WC2 115 Q1
Agdon St. EC1 112 F4
Air St. W1 115 M1
Alaska St. SE1 116 D3
Albany, The W1 115 L1
Albany Ctyd. W1 115 M1
Albemarle St. W1 115 L1
Albemarle Way EC1 112 F5
Albert Ct. SW7 114 A5
Albert Hall Mans. SW7 114 A5
Alberta Est. SE17 116 G10
Alberta St. SE17 116 F10
Albion Clo. W2 110 D10
Albion Ms. W2 110 D10
Albion Pl. EC1 112 F6
Albion Pl. EC2 113 L7
Albion St. W2 110 D9
Albion Way EC1 112 H7
Aldbridge St. SE17 117 N10
Aldenham St. NW1 111 M1
Aldermanbury EC2 113 J8
Aldermanbury Sq. EC2 113 J7
Alderman's Wk. EC2 113 M7
Alderney St. SW1 115 K10
Aldersgate St. EC1 112 H6
Aldford St. W1 114 G2
Aldgate EC3 113 P9
Aldgate Ave. E1 113 P8
Aldgate High St. EC3 113 P9
Aldwych WC2 112 B10
Alexander Pl. SW7 114 C8
Alexander Sq. SW3 114 C8
Alford Pl. N1 113 J1
Alfred Ms. W1 111 N6
Alfred Pl. WC1 111 N6
Alice St. SE1 117 M7
Alie St. E1 113 Q9
All Souls Pl. W1 111 K7
Allgood St. E2 113 Q1
Allhallows La. EC4 117 K1
Allington St. SW1 115 K7
Allitsen Rd. NW8 110 C1
Allsop Pl. NW1 110 F5
Alma Gro. SE1 117 Q9
Alpha Clo. NW1 110 D3
Alsace Rd. SE17 117 M10
Alscot Rd. SE1 117 Q8
Alscot Way SE1 117 P8
Alvey Est. SE17 117 M9
Alvey St. SE17 117 M10
Ambassador's Ct. SW1 115 M3
Ambergate St. SE17 116 G10
Ambrosden Ave. SW1 115 M7
Amelia St. SE17 116 H10
Amen Cor. EC4 112 G9
Amen Ct. EC4 112 G8
America Sq. EC3 113 P10
America St. SE1 116 H3
Ampthill Sq. Est. NW1 111 M1
Ampton Pl. WC1 112 B3
Ampton St. WC1 112 B3
Amwell St. EC1 112 D2
Anchor Yd. EC1 113 J4
Anderson St. SW3 114 E10
Andrew Borde St. WC2 111 P8
Andrews Crosse WC2 112 D9
Angel All. E1 113 Q8
Angel Ct. EC2 113 L8
Angel Ct. SW1 115 M3
Angel Ms. N1 112 E1
Angel Pas. EC4 117 K1
Angel Pl. SE1 117 K4
Angel St. EC1 112 H8
Anning St. EC2 113 N4
Ann's Clo. SW1 114 F5
Ann's Pl. E1 113 P7
Apothecary St. EC4 112 F9
Apple Tree Yd. SW1 115 M2
Appleby St. E2 113 P1
Appold St. EC2 113 M6
Aquinas St. SE1 116 E3
Arcade, The EC2 113 M7
Arch St. SE1 116 H7
Archer St. W1 111 N10
Archery Clo. W2 110 D9
Arches, The WC2 116 A2
Archibald Ms. W1 115 J1
Arden Est. N1 113 M1
Argent St. SE1 116 G4
Argyle Sq. WC1 112 A2
Argyle St. WC1 111 Q2
Argyle Wk. WC1 111 Q3
Argyll St. W1 111 L9
Arlington St. SW1 115 L2
Arlington Way EC1 112 E2
Armstrong Rd. SW7 114 A7
Arne St. WC2 112 A9
Arneway St. SW1 115 P7
Arnold Circ. E2 113 P3
Arnold Est. SE1 117 Q5
Arthur St. EC4 113 L10
Artillery La. E1 113 N7
Artillery Pas. E1 113 N7
Artillery Pl. SW1 115 N7
Artillery Row SW1 115 N7
Artizan St. E1 113 N8
Arundel Great Ct. WC2 112 C10
Arundel St. WC2 112 C10
Ashbridge St. NW8 110 C5
Ashby St. EC1 112 G3
Ashford St. N1 113 M2
Ashland Pl. W1 110 G6
Ashley Gdns. SW1 115 M7
Ashley Pl. SW1 115 L7
Ashmill St. NW1 110 C6
Aske St. N1 113 M2
Astell St. SW3 114 D10
Atterbury St. SW1 115 Q9
Attneave St. WC1 112 D3
Audley Sq. W1 114 H2
Augustus St. NW1 111 K1
Austin Friars EC2 113 L8
Austin Friars Pas. EC2 113 L8
Austin Friars Sq. EC2 113 L8
Austin St. E2 113 P3
Austral St. SE11 116 F8
Ave Maria La. EC4 112 G9
Avery Fm. Row SW1 115 J9
Avery Row W1 111 K10
Avon Pl. SE1 117 J5
Avonmouth St. SE1 116 H6
Aybrook St. W1 110 G7
Aylesbury St. EC1 112 F5
Aylwyn Est. SE1 117 N6
Ayres St. SE1 117 J4
Ayrton Rd. SW7 114 A6

B

Babmaes St. SW1 115 N2
Bacchus Wk. N1 113 M1
Baches St. N1 113 L3
Back Hill EC1 112 D5
Backhouse Pl. SE17 117 N9
Bacon Gro. SE1 117 P7
Bacon St. E1 113 Q4
Bacon St. E2 113 Q4
Baden Pl. SE1 117 K4
Bainbridge St. WC1 111 P8
Baird St. EC1 113 J4
Baker St. NW1 110 F5
Baker St. W1 110 F6
Baker's Ms. W1 110 G8
Baker's Rents E2 113 P3
Baker's Row EC1 112 D5
Balaclava Rd. SE1 117 Q9
Balcombe St. NW1 110 E4
Balderton St. W1 110 H9
Baldwin St. EC1 113 K3
Baldwin's Gdns. EC1 112 D6
Balfe St. N1 112 A1
Balfour Ms. W1 114 H2
Balfour Pl. W1 114 H1
Balfour St. SE17 117 K8
Balniel Gate SW1 115 P10
Baltic St. EC1 112 H5
Banbury Ct. WC2 111 Q10
Bank End SE1 117 J2
Bankside SE1 116 H1
Barbara Brosnan Ct. NW8 110 A1
Barbican, The EC2 112 H6
Barbon Clo. WC1 112 A6
Barge Ho. St. SE1 116 E2
Barley Mow Pas. EC1 112 G7
Barlow Pl. W1 115 K1
Barlow St. SE17 117 L9
Barnard's Inn EC1 112 D8
Barnby St. NW1 111 M2
Barnham St. SE1 117 N4
Baron St. N1 112 D1
Baroness Rd. E2 113 Q2
Barons Pl. SE1 116 E5
Barrett St. W1 110 H9
Barrie Est. W2 110 A10
Barrow Hill Est. NW8 110 C1
Barrow Hill Rd. NW8 110 C1
Barter St. WC1 112 A7
Bartholomew Clo. EC1 112 H7
Bartholomew La. EC2 113 L9
Bartholomew Pl. EC1 112 H7
Bartholomew Sq. EC1 113 J4
Bartholomew St. SE1 117 L7
Bartlett Ct. EC4 112 E8
Barton St. SW1 115 Q6
Basil St. SW3 114 E6
Basing Ho. Yd. E2 113 N2
Basing Pl. E2 113 N2
Basinghall Ave. EC2 113 K7
Basinghall St. EC2 113 K8
Bastwick St. EC1 112 H4
Bateman St. W1 111 N9
Bateman's Bldgs. W1 111 N9
Bateman's Row EC2 113 N4
Bath Ct. EC1 112 D5
Bath St. EC1 113 J3
Bath Ter. SE1 116 H7
Bathurst Ms. W2 110 B10
Bathurst St. W2 110 B10
Battle Bri. La. SE1 117 M3
Battle Bri. Rd. NW1 111 Q1
Bayley St. WC1 111 N7
Baylis Rd. SE1 116 D5
Beak St. W1 111 M10
Bear All. EC4 112 F8
Bear Gdns. SE1 116 H2
Bear La. SE1 116 G3
Bear St. WC2 111 P10
Beauchamp Pl. SW3 114 D6
Beaufort Gdns. SW3 114 D6
Beaufoy Wk. SE11 116 C9
Beaumont Ms. W1 110 H6
Beaumont Pl. W1 111 M4
Beaumont St. W1 110 H6
Becket St. SE1 117 K6
Beckway St. SE17 117 M9
Bedale St. SE1 117 K3
Bedford Ave. WC1 111 P7
Bedford Ct. WC2 115 Q1
Bedford Pl. WC1 111 Q6
Bedford Row WC1 112 C6
Bedford Sq. WC1 111 P7
Bedford St. WC2 111 Q10
Bedford Way WC1 111 P5
Bedfordbury WC2 115 Q1
Beech St. EC2 112 H6
Beehive Pas. EC3 113 M9
Beeston Pl. SW1 115 K7
Belgrave Ms. N. SW1 114 G5
Belgrave Ms. S. SW1 114 H6
Belgrave Ms. W. SW1 114 G6
Belgrave Pl. SW1 114 H6
Belgrave Rd. SW1 115 L9
Belgrave Sq. SW1 114 G6
Belgrave Yd. SW1 115 J7
Belgrove St. WC1 112 A2
Bell Inn Yd. EC3 113 L9
Bell La. E1 113 P7
Bell St. NW1 110 C6
Bell Yd. WC2 112 D9
Belvedere Bldgs. SE1 116 G5
Belvedere Pl. SE1 116 G5
Belvedere Rd. SE1 116 C4
Bendall Ms. NW1 110 D6
Benjamin St. EC1 112 F6
Bennet's Hill EC4 112 G10
Bennett St. SW1 115 L2
Bennetts Yd. SW1 115 P7
Bentinck Ms. W1 110 H8
Bentinck St. W1 110 H8
Berkeley Ms. W1 110 F9
Berkeley Sq. W1 115 K1
Berkeley St. W1 115 K2
Bermondsey Sq. SE1 117 N6
Bermondsey St. SE1 117 M3
Bernard St. WC1 111 Q5
Berners Ms. W1 111 M7
Berners Pl. W1 111 M8
Berners St. W1 111 M7
Berry Pl. EC1 112 G3
Berry St. EC1 112 G4
Berryfield Rd. SE17 116 G10
Berwick St. W1 111 M8
Bessborough Gdns. SW1 115 P10
Bessborough Pl. SW1 115 N10
Bessborough St. SW1 115 N10
Bethnal Grn. Rd. E1 113 P4
Betterton St. WC2 111 Q9
Bevenden St. N1 113 L2
Beverley Way NW8 110 C3
Bevin Way WC1 112 D2
Bevis Marks EC3 113 N8
Bickenhall St. W1 110 F6
Bidborough St. WC1 111 Q3
Billiter Sq. EC3 113 N9
Billiter St. EC3 113 N9
Bingham Pl. W1 110 G6
Binney St. W1 110 H9
Birchin La. EC3 113 L9
Bird St. W1 110 H9
Birdcage Wk. SW1 115 M5
Birkenhead St. WC1 112 A2
Bishop's Ct. EC4 112 F8
Bishop's Ct. WC2 112 D8
Bishops Ter. SE11 116 E8
Bishopsgate EC2 113 N7
Bishopsgate Chyd. EC2 113 M8
Bittern St. SE1 116 H5
Black Friars Ct. EC4 112 F10
Black Friars La. EC4 112 F10
Black Horse Ct. SE1 117 L6
Black Prince Rd. SE1 116 A9
Black Prince Rd. SE11 116 C9
Black Swan Yd. SE1 117 M4
Blackall St. EC2 113 M4
Blackbird Yd. E2 113 Q2
Blackburnes Ms. W1 110 G10
Blackfriars Pas. EC4 112 F10
Blackfriars Rd. SE1 116 F2
Blackland Ter. SW3 114 E9
Blackwood St. SE17 117 K10
Blandford Sq. NW1 110 D5
Blandford St. W1 110 F8
Bleeding Heart Yd. EC1 112 E7
Blenheim St. W1 111 J9
Bletchley Ct. N1 113 K1
Bletchley St. N1 113 J1
Blomfield St. EC2 113 L7
Bloomburg St. SW1 115 M9
Bloomfield Pl. W1 111 K10
Bloomfield Ter. SW1 114 H10
Bloomsbury Ct. WC1 112 A7
Bloomsbury Pl. WC1 112 A6
Bloomsbury Sq. WC1 112 A7
Bloomsbury St. WC1 111 P7
Bloomsbury Way WC1 111 Q8
Blore Ct. W1 111 N10
Blossom St. E1 113 N5
Blue Ball Yd. SW1 115 L3
Bolsover St. W1 111 K5
Bolt Ct. EC4 112 E9
Bolton St. W1 115 K2
Bond Ct. EC4 113 K9
Bonhill St. EC2 113 L5
Book Ms. WC2 111 P9
Boot St. N1 113 M3
Booth's Pl. W1 111 M7
Boreas Wk. N1 112 G1
Borer's Pas. E1 113 N8
Borough High St. SE1 117 J5
Borough Rd. SE1 116 G6
Borough Sq. SE1 116 H5
Boscobel Pl. SW1 114 H8
Boscobel St. NW8 110 B5
Boss St. SE1 117 P4
Boston Pl. NW1 110 E5
Boswell Ct. WC1 112 A6
Boswell St. WC1 112 A6
Botolph All. EC3 117 M1
Botolph La. EC3 117 M1
Boundary Pas. E2 113 P4
Boundary Row SE1 116 F4
Boundary St. E2 113 P3
Bourchier St. W1 111 N10
Bourdon Pl. W1 111 K10
Bourdon St. W1 115 J1
Bourlet Clo. W1 111 L7
Bourne Est. EC1 112 D6
Bourne St. SW1 114 G9
Bouverie Pl. W2 110 B8
Bouverie St. EC4 112 E9
Bow Chyd. EC4 113 J9
Bow La. EC4 113 J9
Bow St. WC2 112 A9
Bowden St. SE11 116 E10
Bowland Yd. SW1 114 F5
Bowling Grn. Ct. EC2 113 N5
Bowling Grn. La. EC1 112 E4
Bowling Grn. Pl. SE1 117 K4
Bowling Grn. Wk. N1 113 M2
Boyce St. SE1 116 D3
Boyfield St. SE1 116 G5
Boyle St. W1 111 L10
Brabant Ct. EC3 113 M10
Brackley St. EC1 113 J6
Brad St. SE1 116 E3
Braham St. E1 113 Q9
Braidwood St. SE1 117 M3
Brandon St. SE17 117 J9
Bray Pl. SW3 114 E9
Bread St. EC4 113 J10
Bream's Bldgs. EC4 112 D8
Brendon St. W1 110 D8
Bressenden Pl. SW1 115 K6
Brewer St. W1 111 M10
Brewer's Grn. SW1 115 M6
Brewhouse Yd. EC1 112 F4
Brick Ct. EC4 112 D9
Brick La. E1 113 Q3
Brick La. E2 113 Q5
Brick St. W1 115 J3
Bricklayer's Arms SE1 117 N8
Bride Ct. EC4 112 F9
Bride La. EC4 112 F9
Bridewell Pl. EC4 112 F9
Bridford Ms. W1 111 K6
Bridge Pl. SW1 115 K8
Bridge St. SW1 115 Q5
Bridge Yd. SE1 117 L2
Bridgeman St. NW8 110 C1
Bridgewater Sq. EC2 112 H6
Bridgewater St. EC2 112 H6
Bridgeway St. NW1 111 M1
Bridle La. W1 111 M10
Brill Pl. NW1 111 P1
Brinton Wk. SE1 116 F3
Briset St. EC1 112 F6
Britannia St. WC1 112 B2
Britannia Wk. N1 113 K2
Britton St. EC1 112 F5
Broad Ct. WC2 112 A9
Broad Sanctuary SW1 115 P5
Broad St. Ave. EC2 113 M7
Broad St. Pl. EC2 113 L7
Broad Wk. W1 114 G2
Broad Yd. EC1 112 F5
Broadbent St. W1 111 J10
Broadgate Circle EC2 113 M6
Broadley St. NW8 110 B6
Broadley Ter. NW1 110 D5
Broadmayne SE17 117 K10
Broadstone Pl. W1 110 G7
Broadwall SE1 116 E2
Broadway SW1 115 N6
Broadwick St. W1 111 M10
Brockham St. SE1 117 J6
Brodie St. SE1 117 Q10
Bromley Pl. W1 111 L6
Brompton Arc. SW3 114 E5
Brompton Pl. SW3 114 D6
Brompton Rd. SW1 114 E5
Brompton Rd. SW3 114 C8
Brompton Rd. SW7 114 C7
Brompton Sq. SW3 114 C6
Brook Dr. SE11 116 E7
Brook Gate W1 114 F1
Brook St. W1 111 J10
Brook St. W2 110 B10
Brooke St. EC1 112 D7
Brooke's Ct. EC1 112 D6
Brook's Ms. W1 111 J10
Brown Hart Gdns. W1 110 H10
Brown St. W1 110 E8
Browning Est. SE17 117 J10
Browning Ms. W1 110 H7
Browning St. SE17 117 J10
Brownlow Ms. WC1 112 C5
Brownlow St. WC1 112 C7
Brown's Bldgs. EC3 113 N9
Brune St. E1 113 P7
Brunswick Cen. WC1 111 Q4
Brunswick Ct. SE1 117 N4
Brunswick Ms. W1 110 F8
Brunswick Pl. N1 113 L3
Brunswick Sq. WC1 112 A4
Brushfield St. E1 113 N6
Bruton La. W1 115 K1
Bruton Pl. W1 115 K1
Bruton St. W1 115 K1
Bryanston Ms. E. W1 110 E7
Bryanston Ms. W. W1 110 E7
Bryanston Pl. W1 110 E7
Bryanston Sq. W1 110 E7
Bryanston St. W1 110 E9
Brydges Pl. WC2 115 Q1
Buck Hill Wk. W2 114 B1
Buckingham Arc. WC2 116 A1
Buckingham Gate SW1 115 L5
Buckingham Ms. SW1 115 L6
Buckingham Palace Rd. SW1 115 J9
Buckingham Pl. SW1 115 L6
Buckingham St. WC2 116 A1
Buckland St. N1 113 L1
Buckle St. E1 113 Q8
Bucklersbury EC4 113 K9
Buckley St. SE1 116 D3
Bucknall St. WC2 111 P8
Budge Row EC4 113 K10
Bulinga St. SW1 115 Q9
Bull Inn Ct. WC2 116 A1
Bull Wf. La. EC4 113 J10
Bullied Way SW1 115 K9
Bulls Gdns. SW3 114 D8
Bull's Head Pas. EC3 113 M9
Bulstrode Pl. W1 110 H7
Bulstrode St. W1 110 H8
Bunhill Row EC1 113 K4
Bunhouse Pl. SW1 114 G10
Buonaparte Ms. SW1 115 N10
Burbage Clo. SE1 117 K7
Burdett St. SE1 116 D6
Burge St. SE1 117 L7
Burgon St. EC4 112 G9
Burleigh St. WC2 112 A10
Burlington Arc. W1 115 L1
Burlington Gdns. W1 115 L1
Burne St. NW1 110 C6
Burnell Wk. SE1 117 Q10
Burnham Clo. SE1 117 Q9
Burnsall St. SW3 114 D10
Burrell St. SE1 116 F2
Burrows Ms. SE1 116 F4
Burton Ms. SW1 114 H9
Burton Pl. WC1 111 P3
Burton St. WC1 111 P3
Burwash Ho. SE1 117 L5
Burwood Pl. W2 110 D8
Bury Ct. EC3 113 N8
Bury Pl. WC1 111 Q7
Bury St. EC3 113 N9
Bury St. SW1 115 M2
Bury Wk. SW3 114 C9
Busby St. E2 113 Q4
Bush La. EC4 113 K10
Bushbaby Clo. SE1 117 M7
Bushwood Dr. SE1 117 Q9
Bute St. SW7 114 A8
Butler Pl. SW1 115 N6
Buttesland St. N1 113 L2
Buxton Ct. N1 113 J2
Buxton St. E1 113 Q5
Byng Pl. WC1 111 N5
Byward St. EC3 117 N1
Bywater St. SW3 114 E10
Bywell Pl. W1 111 L7

C

Cabbell St. NW1 110 C7
Cadbury Way SE16 117 Q7
Cadell Clo. E2 113 Q1
Cadet Dr. SE1 117 Q10
Cadogan Gdns. SW3 114 F8
Cadogan Gate SW1 114 F8
Cadogan La. SW1 114 G7
Cadogan Pl. SW1 114 F6

Cadogan Sq. SW1 **114 F7**
Cadogan St. SW3 **114 E9**
Cahill St. EC1 **113 J5**
Cale St. SW3 **114 C10**
Caleb St. SE1 **116 H4**
Caledonia St. N1 **112 A1**
Caledonian Rd. N1 **112 A1**
Callendar Rd. SW7 **114 A6**
Calthorpe St. WC1 **112 C4**
Calvert Ave. E2 **113 N3**
Calvert's Bldgs. SE1 **117 K3**
Calvin St. E1 **113 P5**
Cambridge Gate NW1 **111 K4**
Cambridge Gate Ms. NW1 **111 K4**
Cambridge Sq. W2 **110 C8**
Cambridge St. SW1 **115 K10**
Cambridge Ter. NW1 **111 J3**
Cambridge Ter. Ms. NW1 **111 K3**
Camlet St. E2 **113 P4**
Camomile St. EC3 **113 M8**
Camperdown St. E1 **113 Q9**
Candover St. W1 **111 L7**
Cannon St. EC4 **112 H9**
Canon Row SW1 **115 Q5**
Canterbury Pl. SE17 **116 G9**
Canvey St. SE1 **116 G2**
Capel Ct. EC2 **113 L9**
Capener's Clo. SW1 **114 G5**
Capland St. NW8 **110 B4**
Capper St. WC1 **111 M5**
Carburton St. W1 **111 K6**
Cardigan St. SE11 **116 D10**
Cardinal Bourne St. SE1 **117 L7**
Cardington St. NW1 **111 M2**
Carey La. EC2 **112 H8**
Carey Pl. SW1 **115 N9**
Carey St. WC2 **112 C9**
Carlisle Ave. EC3 **113 P9**
Carlisle La. SE1 **116 C7**
Carlisle Ms. NW8 **110 B6**
Carlisle Pl. SW1 **115 L7**
Carlisle St. W1 **111 N9**
Carlos Pl. W1 **110 H10**
Carlton Gdns. SW1 **115 N3**
Carlton Ho. Ter. SW1 **115 N3**
Carlton St. SW1 **115 N1**
Carlton Twr. Pl. SW1 **114 F6**
Carmelite St. EC4 **112 E10**
Carnaby St. W1 **111 L9**
Caroline Gdns. E2 **113 N2**
Caroline Ter. SW1 **114 G9**
Carpenter St. W1 **115 J1**
Carrington St. W1 **115 J3**
Carter La. EC4 **112 G9**
Carteret St. SW1 **115 N5**
Carthusian St. EC1 **112 H6**
Carting La. WC2 **116 A1**
Carton St. W1 **110 F8**
Cartwright Gdns. WC1 **111 Q3**
Cartwright St. E1 **117 Q1**
Castle Baynard St. EC4 **112 G10**
Castle Ct. EC3 **113 L9**
Castle La. SW1 **115 L6**
Castle Yd. SE1 **116 G2**
Castlereagh St. W1 **110 D8**
Catesby St. SE17 **117 L9**
Cathedral Pl. EC4 **112 H9**
Cathedral St. SE1 **117 K2**
Catherine Griffiths Ct. EC1 **112 E4**
Catherine Pl. SW1 **115 L6**
Catherine St. WC2 **112 B10**
Catherine Wheel All. E1 **113 N7**
Catherine Wheel Yd. SW1 **115 L3**
Cato St. W1 **110 D7**
Catton St. WC1 **112 B7**
Causton St. SW1 **115 P9**
Cavendish Ave. NW8 **110 A1**
Cavendish Clo. NW8 **110 B2**
Cavendish Ct. EC3 **113 N8**
Cavendish Ms. N. W1 **111 K6**
Cavendish Ms. S. W1 **111 K7**
Cavendish Pl. W1 **111 K8**
Cavendish Sq. W1 **111 K8**
Cavendish St. N1 **113 K1**
Caxton St. SW1 **115 M6**
Cayton Pl. EC1 **113 K3**
Cayton St. EC1 **113 K3**
Cecil Ct. WC2 **115 Q1**
Centaur St. SE1 **116 C6**
Central Mkts. EC1 **112 G7**
Central St. EC1 **112 H2**
Cerney Ms. W2 **110 A10**
Chadwell St. EC1 **112 E2**
Chadwick St. SW1 **115 N7**
Chagford St. NW1 **110 E5**
Chamber St. E1 **113 Q10**
Chambord St. E2 **113 Q3**
Chance St. E1 **113 P4**
Chancel St. SE1 **116 F3**
Chancery La. WC2 **112 D8**
Chandos Pl. WC2 **115 Q1**
Chandos St. W1 **111 K7**
Change All. EC3 **113 L9**
Chapel Ct. SE1 **117 K4**
Chapel Pl. EC2 **113 M3**
Chapel Pl. W1 **111 J9**
Chapel St. NW1 **110 C7**
Chapel St. SW1 **114 H5**
Chaplin Clo. SE1 **116 E4**
Chapone Pl. W1 **111 N9**
Chapter Ho. Ct. EC4 **112 G9**
Chapter St. SW1 **115 N9**
Charing Cross WC2 **115 Q2**
Charing Cross Rd. WC2 **111 P9**
Charles Pl. NW1 **111 M3**
Charles II St. SW1 **115 N2**
Charles Sq. N1 **113 L3**
Charles St. W1 **115 J2**
Charleston St. SE17 **117 J9**
Charlotte Ms. W1 **111 M6**
Charlotte Pl. SW1 **115 L9**
Charlotte Pl. W1 **111 M7**
Charlotte Rd. EC2 **113 M3**
Charlotte St. W1 **111 M6**
Charlwood Pl. SW1 **115 M9**
Charlwood St. SW1 **115 M10**
Chart St. N1 **113 L2**
Charterhouse Bldgs. EC1 **112 G5**
Charterhouse Sq. EC1 **112 G6**
Charterhouse St. EC1 **112 F6**
Chatham St. SE17 **117 K8**
Chaucer Dr. SE1 **117 Q9**
Cheapside EC2 **112 H9**
Chelsea Bri. Rd. SW1 **114 G10**
Chelsea Cloisters SW3 **114 D9**
Chelsea Sq. SW3 **114 B10**
Cheltenham Ter. SW3 **114 F10**
Cheney Rd. NW1 **111 Q1**
Chenies Ms. WC1 **111 N5**
Chenies St. WC1 **111 N6**
Chequer St. EC1 **113 J5**
Cherbury St. N1 **113 L1**
Chesham Clo. SW1 **114 G7**
Chesham Ms. SW1 **114 G6**
Chesham Pl. SW1 **114 G7**
Chesham St. SW1 **114 G7**
Cheshire St. E2 **113 Q4**
Chester Clo. SW1 **115 J5**
Chester Clo. N. NW1 **111 K2**
Chester Clo. S. NW1 **111 K3**
Chester Cotts. SW1 **114 G9**
Chester Ct. NW1 **111 K2**
Chester Gate NW1 **111 J3**
Chester Ms. SW1 **115 J6**
Chester Pl. NW1 **111 J2**
Chester Rd. NW1 **110 H3**
Chester Row SW1 **114 G9**
Chester Sq. SW1 **114 H8**
Chester Sq. Ms. SW1 **115 J7**
Chester St. SW1 **114 H6**
Chester Ter. NW1 **111 J2**
Chester Way SE11 **116 E9**
Chesterfield Gdns. W1 **115 J2**
Chesterfield Hill W1 **115 J2**
Chesterfield St. W1 **115 J2**
Chettle Clo. SE1 **117 K6**
Cheval Pl. SW7 **114 D6**
Chicheley St. SE1 **116 C4**
Chichester Rents WC2 **112 D8**
Chicksand St. E1 **113 Q7**
Chiltern St. W1 **110 G6**
Chilton St. E2 **113 Q4**
Chilworth Ms. W2 **110 A9**
Ching Ct. WC2 **111 Q9**
Chiswell St. EC1 **113 K6**
Chitty St. W1 **111 M6**
Christina St. EC2 **113 M4**
Christopher Pl. NW1 **111 P3**
Christopher St. EC2 **113 L5**
Church Pl. SW1 **115 M1**
Church St. NW8 **110 B6**
Church St. W2 **110 B6**
Church St. Est. NW8 **110 B5**
Church Yd. Row SE11 **116 G8**
Churchway NW1 **111 P2**
Churton Pl. SW1 **115 M9**
Churton St. SW1 **115 M9**
Circus Ms. W1 **110 E6**
Circus Pl. EC2 **113 L7**
Circus Rd. NW8 **110 A2**
Citadel Pl. SE11 **116 B10**
City Gdn. Row N1 **112 G1**
City Rd. EC1 **112 F1**
Clabon Ms. SW1 **114 E7**
Clare Mkt. WC2 **112 B9**
Claremont Clo. N1 **112 D1**
Claremont Sq. N1 **112 D1**
Clarence Gdns. NW1 **111 K3**
Clarence Pas. NW1 **111 Q1**
Clarence Ter. NW1 **110 F4**
Clarendon Clo. W2 **110 C10**
Clarendon Gro. NW1 **111 N2**
Clarendon Ms. W2 **110 C10**
Clarendon Pl. W2 **110 C10**
Clarendon St. SW1 **115 K10**
Clarges Ms. W1 **115 J2**
Clarges St. W1 **115 K2**
Clarke's Ms. W1 **110 H6**
Clarks Pl. EC2 **113 M8**
Clay St. W1 **110 F7**
Cleaver Sq. SE11 **116 E10**
Cleaver St. SE11 **116 E10**
Clement's Inn WC2 **112 C9**
Clement's Inn Pas. WC2 **112 C9**
Clements La. EC4 **113 L10**
Clenham St. SE1 **117 J4**
Clenston Ms. W1 **110 E8**
Clere St. EC2 **113 L4**
Clerkenwell Clo. EC1 **112 E4**
Clerkenwell Grn. EC1 **112 E5**
Clerkenwell Rd. EC1 **112 D5**
Cleveland Ms. W1 **111 L6**
Cleveland Pl. SW1 **115 M2**
Cleveland Row SW1 **115 L3**
Cleveland St. W1 **111 K5**
Clifford St. W1 **115 L1**
Clifton Ct. NW8 **110 A4**
Clifton Pl. W2 **110 B9**
Clifton St. EC2 **113 M6**
Clink St. SE1 **117 K2**
Clipstone Ms. W1 **111 L5**
Clipstone St. W1 **111 K6**
Cliveden Pl. SW1 **114 G8**
Cloak La. EC4 **113 K10**
Cloth Ct. EC1 **112 G7**
Cloth Fair EC1 **112 G7**
Cloth St. EC1 **112 H6**
Club Row E1 **113 P4**
Club Row E2 **113 P4**
Clunbury St. N1 **113 L1**
Cluny Est. SE1 **117 M6**
Cluny Pl. SE1 **117 M6**
Coach & Horses Yd. W1 **111 L10**
Cobb St. E1 **113 P7**
Cobourg St. NW1 **111 M3**
Coburg Clo. SW1 **115 M8**
Cochrane Ms. NW8 **110 B1**
Cochrane St. NW8 **110 B1**
Cock Hill E1 **113 N7**
Cock La. EC1 **112 F7**
Cockpit Steps SW1 **115 P5**
Cockpit Yd. WC1 **112 C6**
Cockspur Ct. SW1 **115 P2**
Cockspur St. SW1 **115 P2**
Code St. E1 **113 Q5**
Coin St. SE1 **116 D2**
Colchester St. E1 **113 Q8**
Coldbath Sq. EC1 **112 D4**
Cole St. SE1 **117 J5**
Colebrooke Row N1 **112 F1**
Coleman St. EC2 **113 K8**
Coley St. WC1 **112 C5**
College Hill EC4 **113 J10**
College Ms. SW1 **115 Q6**
College St. EC4 **113 K10**
Collier St. N1 **112 B1**
Collinson St. SE1 **116 H5**
Collinson Wk. SE1 **116 H5**
Colnbrook St. SE1 **116 F7**
Colombo St. SE1 **116 F3**
Colonade Wk. SW1 **115 J9**
Colonnade WC1 **112 A5**
Columbia Rd. E2 **113 P2**
Colville Pl. W1 **111 M7**
Colworth Gro. SE17 **117 J9**
Commercial St. E1 **113 P5**
Commodity Quay E1 **117 Q1**
Compton Clo. NW1 **111 K3**
Compton Pas. EC1 **112 G4**
Compton Pl. WC1 **111 Q4**
Compton St. EC1 **112 F4**
Comus Pl. SE17 **117 M9**
Concert Hall App. SE1 **116 C3**
Conduit Ct. WC2 **111 Q10**
Conduit Ms. W2 **110 A9**
Conduit Pas. W2 **110 A9**
Conduit Pl. W2 **110 A9**
Conduit St. W1 **111 K10**
Congreve St. SE17 **117 M9**
Connaught Clo. W2 **110 C9**
Connaught Ms. W2 **110 E9**
Connaught Pl. W2 **110 E9**
Connaught Sq. W2 **110 E9**
Connaught St. W2 **110 D9**
Cons St. SE1 **116 E4**
Constitution Hill SW1 **115 J4**
Content St. SE17 **117 J9**
Conway Ms. W1 **111 L5**
Conway St. W1 **111 L5**
Coombs St. N1 **112 G1**
Cooper Clo. SE1 **116 E5**
Coopers La. NW1 **111 P1**
Cooper's Row EC3 **113 P10**
Copperfield St. SE1 **116 G4**
Copthall Ave. EC2 **113 L8**
Copthall Bldgs. EC2 **113 L8**
Copthall Clo. EC2 **113 K8**
Copthall Ct. EC2 **113 L8**
Coptic St. WC1 **111 Q7**
Coral St. SE1 **116 E5**
Coram St. WC1 **111 Q5**
Corbet Ct. EC3 **113 L9**
Corbet Pl. E1 **113 P6**
Cork St. W1 **115 L1**
Cork St. Ms. W1 **115 L1**
Corlett St. NW1 **110 C6**
Corner Ho. St. WC2 **115 Q2**
Cornhill EC3 **113 L9**
Cornwall Rd. SE1 **116 D2**
Cornwall Ter. NW1 **110 F5**
Cornwall Ter. Ms. NW1 **110 F5**
Coronet St. N1 **113 M3**
Corporation Row EC1 **112 E4**
Corsham St. N1 **113 L3**
Cosmo Pl. WC1 **112 A6**
Cosser St. SE1 **116 D6**
Cosway St. NW1 **110 D6**
Cotham St. SE17 **117 J9**
Cottage Pl. SW3 **114 C7**
Cottington Clo. SE11 **116 F9**
Cottington St. SE11 **116 E10**
Cottons Gdns. E2 **113 N2**
Cottons La. SE1 **117 L2**
Coulson St. SW3 **114 E10**
Counter Ct. SE1 **117 K3**
Counter St. SE1 **117 M3**
County St. SE1 **117 J7**
Courtenay St. SE11 **116 D10**
Cousin La. EC4 **117 K1**
Covent Gdn. WC2 **112 A10**
Coventry St. W1 **115 N1**
Cowcross St. EC1 **112 F6**
Cowley St. SW1 **115 Q6**
Cowper St. EC2 **113 L4**
Coxson Pl. SE1 **117 P5**
Crace St. NW1 **111 N2**
Craigs Ct. SW1 **115 Q2**
Crail Row SE17 **117 L9**
Cramer St. W1 **110 H7**
Crampton St. SE17 **116 H10**
Cranbourn All. WC2 **111 P10**
Cranbourn St. WC2 **111 P10**
Crane Ct. EC4 **112 E9**
Cranfield Row SE1 **116 E6**
Cranleigh St. NW1 **111 M1**
Cranley Pl. SW7 **114 A9**
Cranmer Ct. SW3 **114 D9**
Cranston Est. N1 **113 L1**
Cranwood St. EC1 **113 L3**
Craven Pas. WC2 **115 Q2**
Craven St. WC2 **115 Q2**
Crawford Ms. W1 **110 E7**
Crawford Pas. EC1 **112 D5**
Crawford Pl. W1 **110 D8**
Crawford St. W1 **110 D7**
Creasy Est. SE1 **117 M7**
Creechurch La. EC3 **113 N9**
Creechurch Pl. EC3 **113 N9**
Creed La. EC4 **112 G9**
Cremer St. E2 **113 P1**
Crescent, The EC3 **113 P10**
Crescent Pl. SW3 **114 C8**
Crescent Row EC1 **112 H5**
Crestfield St. WC1 **112 A2**
Cricketers Ct. SE11 **116 F9**
Crimscott St. SE1 **117 N7**
Cripplegate St. EC2 **112 H6**
Crispin St. E1 **113 P7**
Cromer St. WC1 **112 A3**
Crompton St. W2 **110 A5**
Cromwell Gdns. SW7 **114 B7**
Cromwell Ms. SW7 **114 B8**
Cromwell Pl. SW7 **114 B8**
Cromwell Rd. SW7 **114 A8**
Crondall St. N1 **113 M1**
Crosby Ct. SE1 **117 K4**
Crosby Row SE1 **117 K4**
Crosby Sq. EC3 **113 M9**
Cross Keys Clo. W1 **110 H7**
Cross La. EC3 **117 M1**
Crosslet St. SE17 **117 L8**
Crosswall EC3 **113 P10**
Crown Ct. EC2 **113 J9**
Crown Ct. WC2 **112 A9**
Crown Office Row EC4 **112 D10**
Crown Pas. SW1 **115 M3**
Crucifix La. SE1 **117 M4**
Cruikshank St. WC1 **112 D2**
Crutched Friars EC3 **113 N10**
Cubitt St. WC1 **112 C3**
Cubitts Yd. WC2 **112 A10**
Cuff Pt. E2 **113 P2**
Culford Gdns. SW3 **114 F9**
Cullum St. EC3 **113 M10**
Culross St. W1 **114 G1**
Culworth St. NW8 **110 C1**
Cumberland Gdns. WC1 **112 C2**
Cumberland Gate W1 **110 E10**
Cumberland Mkt. NW1 **111 K2**
Cumberland Mkt. Est. NW1 **111 K2**
Cumberland Pl. NW1 **111 J2**
Cumberland St. SW1 **115 K10**
Cumberland Ter. NW1 **111 J1**
Cumberland Ter. Ms. NW1 **111 J1**
Cumming St. N1 **112 C1**
Cunard Pl. EC3 **113 N9**
Cundy St. SW1 **114 H9**
Cundy St. Est. SW1 **114 H9**
Cunningham Pl. NW8 **110 A4**
Cureton St. SW1 **115 P9**
Curlew St. SE1 **117 P4**
Cursitor St. EC4 **112 D8**
Curtain Rd. EC2 **113 N3**
Curtis St. SE1 **117 P8**
Curtis Way SE1 **117 P8**
Curzon Gate W1 **114 H3**
Curzon Pl. W1 **114 H3**
Curzon St. W1 **114 H3**
Cut, The SE1 **116 E4**
Cuthbert St. W2 **110 A6**
Cutler St. E1 **113 N8**
Cutlers Gdns. E1 **113 N8**
Cygnet St. E1 **113 Q4**
Cynthia St. N1 **112 C1**
Cypress Pl. W1 **111 M5**
Cyrus St. EC1 **112 G4**

D

Dacre St. SW1 **115 N6**
Dalehead NW1 **111 L1**
Dallington St. EC1 **112 G4**
Dane St. WC1 **112 B7**
Dansey Pl. W1 **111 N10**
Dante Pl. SE11 **116 G9**
Dante Rd. SE11 **116 F8**
Danube St. SW3 **114 D10**
D'Arblay St. W1 **111 M9**
Dartmouth St. SW1 **115 P5**
Darwin St. SE17 **117 L8**
Daventry St. NW1 **110 C6**
David Ms. W1 **110 G6**
Davidge St. SE1 **116 G5**
Davies Ms. W1 **111 J10**
Davies St. W1 **111 J10**
Dawes Ho. SE17 **117 K9**
Dawes St. SE17 **117 L10**
Dawson St. E2 **113 Q1**
De Walden St. W1 **110 H7**
Deacon Way SE17 **116 H8**
Dean Bradley St. SW1 **115 Q7**
Dean Farrar St. SW1 **115 P6**
Dean Ryle St. SW1 **115 Q8**
Dean Stanley St. SW1 **115 Q7**
Dean St. W1 **111 N8**
Dean Trench St. SW1 **115 Q7**
Deanery Ms. W1 **114 H2**
Deanery St. W1 **114 H2**
Deans Bldgs. SE17 **117 L9**
Dean's Ct. EC4 **112 G9**
Deans Ms. W1 **111 K8**
Dean's Pl. SW1 **115 N10**
Dean's Yd. SW1 **115 P6**
Decima St. SE1 **117 M6**
Dell's Ms. SW1 **115 M9**
Denbigh Ms. SW1 **115 L9**
Denbigh Pl. SW1 **115 L10**
Denbigh St. SW1 **115 L9**
Denman St. W1 **115 N1**
Denmark Pl. WC2 **111 P8**
Denmark St. WC2 **111 P9**
Denny Cres. SE11 **116 E10**
Denny St. SE11 **116 E10**
Denyer St. SW3 **114 D9**
Derby Gate SW1 **115 Q4**
Derby St. W1 **114 H3**
Dereham Pl. EC2 **113 N3**
Dering St. W1 **111 J9**
Deverell St. SE1 **117 K7**
Devereux Ct. WC2 **112 D9**
Devonshire Clo. W1 **111 J6**
Devonshire Ms. N. W1 **111 J6**
Devonshire Ms. S. W1 **111 J6**
Devonshire Ms. W. W1 **111 J5**
Devonshire Pl. W1 **110 H5**
Devonshire Pl. Ms. W1 **110 H5**
Devonshire Row EC2 **113 N7**
Devonshire Row Ms. W1 **111 K5**
Devonshire Sq. EC2 **113 N7**
Devonshire St. W1 **110 H6**
Diadem Ct. W1 **111 N9**
Diana Pl. NW1 **111 K4**
Dickens Sq. SE1 **117 J6**
Dingley Pl. EC1 **113 J3**
Dingley Rd. EC1 **112 H3**
Disney Pl. SE1 **117 J4**
Disney St. SE1 **117 J4**
Diss St. E2 **113 P2**
Distaff La. EC4 **112 H10**
Distin St. SE11 **116 D9**
Dockhead SE1 **117 Q5**
Dodson St. SE1 **116 E5**
Dolben St. SE1 **116 G3**
Dombey St. WC1 **112 B6**
Domingo St. EC1 **112 H4**
Dominion St. EC2 **113 L6**
Donegal St. N1 **112 C1**
Donne Pl. SW3 **114 D8**
Doon St. SE1 **116 D2**
Doric Way NW1 **111 N2**
Dorrington St. EC1 **112 D6**
Dorset Bldgs. EC4 **112 F9**
Dorset Clo. NW1 **110 E6**
Dorset Est. E2 **113 Q2**
Dorset Ms. SW1 **115 J6**
Dorset Pl. SW1 **115 N10**
Dorset Ri. EC4 **112 F9**
Dorset Sq. NW1 **110 E5**
Dorset St. W1 **110 F7**
Doughty Ms. WC1 **112 B5**
Doughty St. WC1 **112 B4**
Douglas St. SW1 **115 N9**
Dove Ct. EC2 **113 K9**
Dove Wk. SW1 **114 G10**
Dovehouse St. SW3 **114 C10**
Dover St. W1 **115 K1**
Dover Yd. W1 **115 K2**
Dowgate Hill EC4 **113 K10**
Down St. W1 **115 J3**
Down St. Ms. W1 **115 J3**
Downing St. SW1 **115 Q4**
Doyce St. SE1 **116 H4**
D'Oyley St. SW1 **114 G8**
Drake St. WC1 **112 B7**
Draycott Ave. SW3 **114 D8**
Draycott Pl. SW3 **114 E9**
Draycott Ter. SW3 **114 F9**
Druid St. SE1 **117 N4**
Drum St. E1 **113 Q8**
Drummond Cres. NW1 **111 N2**
Drummond Gate SW1 **115 P10**
Drummond St. NW1 **111 L4**
Drury La. WC2 **112 A8**
Dryden Ct. SE11 **116 E9**
Dryden St. WC2 **112 A9**
Drysdale Pl. N1 **113 N2**
Drysdale St. N1 **113 N2**
Ducal St. E2 **113 Q3**

Duchess Ms. W1 **111 K7**
Duchess St. W1 **111 K7**
Duchy St. SE1 **116 E2**
Duck La. W1 **111 N9**
Dudley St. W2 **110 A7**
Dudmaston Ms. SW3 **114 B10**
Dufferin Ave. EC1 **113 K5**
Dufferin St. EC1 **113 J5**
Dufour's Pl. W1 **111 M9**
Duke of Wellington Pl. SW1 **114 H4**
Duke of York St. SW1 **115 M2**
Duke St. SW1 **115 M2**
Duke St. W1 **110 H8**
Duke St. Hill SE1 **117 L2**
Duke's Ms. W1 **110 H8**
Dukes Pl. EC3 **113 N9**
Duke's Rd. WC1 **111 P3**
Duke's Yd. W1 **110 H10**
Duncan Ter. N1 **112 F1**
Duncannon St. WC2 **115 Q1**
Dunloe St. E2 **113 Q1**
Dunlop Pl. SE16 **117 Q7**
Dunmore Pt. E2 **113 P3**
Dunns Pas. WC1 **112 A8**
Dunraven St. W1 **110 F10**
Dunstable Ms. W1 **110 H6**
Dunster Ct. EC3 **113 M10**
Dunsterville Way SE1 **117 L5**
Dunton Rd. SE1 **117 P9**
Duplex Ride SW1 **114 F5**
Durham Ho. St. WC2 **116 A1**
Durweston Ms. W1 **110 F6**
Durweston St. W1 **110 F7**
Dyer's Bldgs. EC1 **112 D7**
Dyott St. WC1 **111 P8**
Dysart St. EC2 **113 M5**

E

Eagle Ct. EC1 **112 F6**
Eagle Pl. SW1 **115 M1**
Eagle St. WC1 **112 B7**
Earl Rd. SE1 **117 P10**
Earl St. EC2 **113 L6**
Earlham St. WC2 **111 P9**
Earlstoke St. EC1 **112 F2**
Earnshaw St. WC2 **111 P8**
Easley's Ms. W1 **110 H8**
East Harding St. EC4 **112 E8**
East Pas. EC1 **112 H6**
East Poultry Ave. EC1 **112 F7**
East Rd. N1 **113 L2**
East Smithfield E1 **117 Q1**
East St. SE17 **117 J10**
East Tenter St. E1 **113 Q9**
Eastcastle St. W1 **111 L8**
Eastcheap EC3 **113 L10**
Easton St. WC1 **112 D3**
Eaton Clo. SW1 **114 G9**
Eaton Gate SW1 **114 G8**
Eaton La. SW1 **115 K7**
Eaton Ms. N. SW1 **114 G7**
Eaton Ms. S. SW1 **115 J7**
Eaton Ms. W. SW1 **114 H8**
Eaton Pl. SW1 **114 G7**
Eaton Row SW1 **115 J7**
Eaton Sq. SW1 **114 H8**
Eaton Ter. SW1 **114 G8**
Eaton Ter. Ms. SW1 **114 G8**
Ebenezer St. N1 **113 K2**
Ebor St. E1 **113 P4**
Ebury Bri. SW1 **115 J10**
Ebury Bri. Est. SW1 **115 J10**
Ebury Ms. SW1 **115 J8**
Ebury Ms. E. SW1 **115 J7**
Ebury Sq. SW1 **114 H9**
Ebury St. SW1 **114 H9**
Eccleston Bri. SW1 **115 K8**
Eccleston Ms. SW1 **114 H7**
Eccleston Pl. SW1 **115 J8**
Eccleston Sq. SW1 **115 K9**
Eccleston Sq. Ms. SW1 **115 K9**
Eccleston St. SW1 **114 H7**
Edgware Rd. W2 **110 A5**
Edinburgh Gate SW1 **114 E5**
Edward Ms. NW1 **111 K1**
Edwards Ms. W1 **110 G9**
Egerton Cres. SW3 **114 D8**
Egerton Gdns. SW3 **114 C7**
Egerton Gdns. Ms. SW3 **114 D7**
Egerton Pl. SW3 **114 D7**
Egerton Ter. SW3 **114 D7**
Elba Pl. SE17 **117 J8**
Elder St. E1 **113 P5**
Eldon St. EC2 **113 L7**
Elephant & Castle SE1 **116 G8**
Elephant Rd. SE17 **116 H8**
Elia Ms. N1 **112 F1**
Elia St. N1 **112 F1**
Elim Est. SE1 **117 M6**
Elizabeth Bri. SW1 **115 J9**
Elizabeth Ct. SW1 **115 P7**
Elizabeth St. SW1 **114 H8**
Elliotts Row SE11 **116 F8**
Ellis St. SW1 **114 F8**
Elm Ct. EC4 **112 D10**
Elm Pl. SW7 **114 A10**
Elm St. WC1 **112 C5**
Elm Tree Clo. NW8 **110 A2**
Elm Tree Rd. NW8 **110 A2**
Elms Ms. W2 **110 A10**
Elsted St. SE17 **117 L9**
Elverton St. SW1 **115 N8**
Ely Ct. EC1 **112 E7**
Ely Pl. EC1 **112 E7**
Elystan Pl. SW3 **114 D10**
Elystan St. SW3 **114 C9**
Embankment Pl. WC2 **116 A2**
Emerald St. WC1 **112 B6**
Emerson St. SE1 **116 H2**
Emery Hill St. SW1 **115 M7**
Emery St. SE1 **116 E6**
Endell St. WC2 **111 Q8**
Endsleigh Gdns. WC1 **111 N4**
Endsleigh Pl. WC1 **111 P4**
Endsleigh St. WC1 **111 P4**
Enford St. W1 **110 E6**
English Grds. SE1 **117 M3**
Enid St. SE16 **117 Q6**
Ennismore Gdns. SW7 **114 C6**
Ennismore Gdns. Ms. SW7 **114 C6**
Ennismore Ms. SW7 **114 C6**
Ennismore St. SW7 **114 C6**
Ensor Ms. SW7 **114 A10**
Epworth St. EC2 **113 L5**
Erasmus St. SW1 **115 P9**
Errol St. EC1 **113 J5**
Essex Ct. EC4 **112 D9**
Essex St. WC2 **112 D10**
Esterbrooke St. SW1 **115 N9**
Ethel St. SE17 **117 J9**
Europa Pl. EC1 **112 H3**
Euston Gro. NW1 **111 N3**
Euston Rd. NW1 **111 K5**
Euston Sq. NW1 **111 N3**
Euston Sta. Colonnade NW1 **111 N3**
Euston St. NW1 **111 M3**
Evelyn Ct. N1 **113 K1**
Evelyn Wk. N1 **113 K1**
Evelyn Yd. W1 **111 N8**
Everton Bldgs. NW1 **111 L3**
Ewer St. SE1 **116 H3**
Excel Ct. WC2 **115 P1**
Exchange Arc. EC2 **113 N6**
Exchange Ct. WC2 **116 A1**
Exchange Pl. EC2 **113 M6**
Exeter St. WC2 **112 A10**
Exhibition Rd. SW7 **114 B6**
Exmouth Mkt. EC1 **112 D4**
Exmouth Ms. NW1 **111 M3**
Exon St. SE17 **117 M9**
Exton St. SE1 **116 D3**
Eyre St. Hill EC1 **112 D5**
Ezra St. E2 **113 Q2**

F

Fair St. SE1 **117 N4**
Fairchild Pl. EC2 **113 N5**
Fairchild St. EC2 **113 N5**
Fairholt St. SW7 **114 D6**
Falcon Clo. SE1 **116 G2**
Falconberg Ct. W1 **111 P8**
Falconberg Ms. W1 **111 N8**
Falkirk St. N1 **113 N1**
Falmouth Rd. SE1 **117 J7**
Fann St. EC1 **112 H5**
Fanshaw St. N1 **113 M2**
Fareham St. W1 **111 N8**
Farm St. W1 **115 J1**
Farnham Pl. SE1 **116 G3**
Farringdon La. EC1 **112 E5**
Farringdon St. EC4 **112 F8**
Fashion St. E1 **113 Q7**
Faulkner's All. EC1 **112 F6**
Featherstone St. EC1 **113 K4**
Fellows Ct. E2 **113 P1**
Fen Ct. EC3 **113 M10**
Fenchurch Ave. EC3 **113 M9**
Fenchurch Bldgs. EC3 **113 N9**
Fenchurch Pl. EC3 **113 N10**
Fenchurch St. EC3 **113 M10**
Fendall St. SE1 **117 N7**
Fenning St. SE1 **117 M4**
Fernsbury St. WC1 **112 D3**
Fetter La. EC4 **112 E9**
Field Ct. WC1 **112 C7**
Field St. WC1 **112 B2**
Finch La. EC3 **113 L9**
Finsbury Ave. EC2 **113 L7**
Finsbury Circ. EC2 **113 L7**
Finsbury Est. EC1 **112 E3**
Finsbury Mkt. EC2 **113 M5**
Finsbury Pavement EC2 **113 L6**
Finsbury Sq. EC2 **113 L5**
Finsbury St. EC2 **113 K6**
First St. SW3 **114 D8**
Fish St. Hill EC3 **117 L1**
Fisher St. WC1 **112 B7**
Fisherton St. NW8 **110 A4**
Fitzalan St. SE11 **116 D8**
Fitzhardinge St. W1 **110 G8**
Fitzmaurice Pl. W1 **115 K2**
Fitzroy Ct. W1 **111 M5**
Fitzroy Ms. W1 **111 L5**
Fitzroy Sq. W1 **111 L5**
Fitzroy St. W1 **111 L5**
Flaxman Ct. W1 **111 N9**
Flaxman Ter. WC1 **111 P3**
Fleet La. EC4 **112 F8**
Fleet Sq. WC1 **112 C3**
Fleet St. EC4 **112 E9**
Fleming Ct. W2 **110 A6**
Fleur de Lis St. E1 **113 N5**
Flint St. SE17 **117 L9**
Flinton St. SE17 **117 N10**
Flitcroft St. WC2 **111 P9**
Floral St. WC2 **111 Q10**
Flower & Dean Wk. E1 **113 Q7**
Foley St. W1 **111 L7**
Folgate St. E1 **113 N6**
Fore St. EC2 **113 J7**
Fore St. Ave. EC2 **113 K7**
Forset St. W1 **110 D8**
Fort Rd. SE1 **117 Q9**
Fort St. E1 **113 N7**
Fortune St. EC1 **113 J5**
Foster La. EC2 **112 H8**
Foubert's Pl. W1 **111 L9**
Foulis Ter. SW7 **114 B10**
Founders Ct. EC2 **113 K8**
Foundry Ms. NW1 **111 M4**
Fountain Ct. EC4 **112 D10**
Fountain Sq. SW1 **115 J8**
Fournier St. E1 **113 Q6**
Fox and Knot St. EC1 **112 G6**
Frampton St. NW8 **110 B5**
Francis St. SW1 **115 L8**
Frankland Rd. SW7 **114 A7**
Franklin's Row SW3 **114 F10**
Frazier St. SE1 **116 D5**
Frederic Ms. SW1 **114 F5**
Frederick Clo. W2 **110 D10**
Frederick St. WC1 **112 B3**
Frederick's Pl. EC2 **113 K9**
Frederick's Row EC1 **112 F2**
Fremantle St. SE17 **117 M10**
French Pl. E1 **113 N4**
Friar St. EC4 **112 G9**
Friary Ct. SW1 **115 M3**
Friday St. EC4 **112 H10**
Friend St. EC1 **112 F2**
Frith St. W1 **111 N9**
Frying Pan All. E1 **113 P7**
Fullwoods Ms. N1 **113 L2**
Fulwood Pl. WC1 **112 C7**
Furnival St. EC4 **112 D8**
Fynes St. SW1 **115 N8**

G

Gage St. WC1 **112 A6**
Gainsford St. SE1 **117 P4**
Galen Pl. WC1 **112 A7**
Galway St. EC1 **113 J3**
Gambia St. SE1 **116 G3**
Ganton St. W1 **111 L10**
Garbutt Pl. W1 **110 H6**
Gard St. EC1 **112 G2**
Garden Ct. EC4 **112 D10**
Garden Row SE1 **116 F7**
Garden Ter. SW1 **115 N10**
Garden Wk. EC2 **113 M3**
Garlick Hill EC4 **113 J10**
Garnault Ms. EC1 **112 E3**
Garnault Pl. EC1 **112 E3**
Garrett St. EC1 **113 J4**
Garrick St. WC2 **111 Q10**
Gascoigne Pl. E2 **113 P2**
Gate Ms. SW7 **114 D5**
Gate St. WC2 **112 B8**
Gateforth St. NW8 **110 C5**
Gatesborough St. EC2 **113 M4**
Gateways, The SW3 **114 D9**
Gaunt St. SE1 **116 G6**
Gavel St. SE17 **117 L8**
Gayfere St. SW1 **115 Q7**
Gaywood Est. SE1 **116 G7**
Gaywood St. SE1 **116 G7**
Gedling Pl. SE1 **117 Q6**
Gee St. EC1 **112 H4**
Gees Ct. W1 **110 H9**
Geffrye Ct. N1 **113 N1**
Geffrye St. E2 **113 P1**
George Ct. WC2 **116 A1**
George Inn Yd. SE1 **117 K3**
George Loveless Ho. E2 **113 Q2**
George Ms. NW1 **111 L3**
George St. EC4 **113 K9**
George St. W1 **110 E8**
George Yd. EC3 **113 L9**
George Yd. W1 **110 H10**
Georgina Gdns. E2 **113 Q2**
Gerald Ms. SW1 **114 H8**
Gerald Rd. SW1 **114 H8**
Geraldine St. SE11 **116 F7**
Gerrard Pl. W1 **111 P10**
Gerrard St. W1 **111 P10**
Gerridge St. SE1 **116 E6**
Gibraltar Wk. E2 **113 Q3**
Gibson Rd. SE11 **116 C9**
Gilbert Pl. WC1 **111 Q7**
Gilbert Rd. SE11 **116 E9**
Gilbert St. W1 **110 H9**
Gildea St. W1 **111 K7**
Gillfoot NW1 **111 L1**
Gillingham Ms. SW1 **115 L8**
Gillingham Row SW1 **115 L8**
Gillingham St. SW1 **115 K8**
Giltspur St. EC1 **112 G8**
Gladstone St. SE1 **116 F6**
Glasshill St. SE1 **116 G4**
Glasshouse All. EC4 **112 E9**
Glasshouse St. W1 **115 M1**
Glasshouse Wk. SE11 **116 A10**
Glasshouse Yd. EC1 **112 H5**
Glendower Pl. SW7 **114 A8**
Glentworth St. NW1 **110 F5**
Globe St. SE1 **117 K5**
Globe Yd. W1 **111 J9**
Gloucester Ct. EC3 **117 N1**
Gloucester Pl. NW1 **110 E4**
Gloucester Pl. W1 **110 F6**
Gloucester Pl. Ms. W1 **110 F7**
Gloucester Sq. W2 **110 B9**
Gloucester Way EC1 **112 E3**
Glynde Ms. SW3 **114 D7**
Godfrey St. SW3 **114 D10**
Godliman St. EC4 **112 H9**
Golden La. EC1 **112 H5**
Golden La. Est. EC1 **112 H5**
Golden Sq. W1 **111 M10**
Goldsmith St. EC2 **113 J8**
Goodge Pl. W1 **111 M7**
Goodge St. W1 **111 M7**
Goodmans Yd. E1 **113 P10**
Goodwins Ct. WC2 **111 Q10**
Gophir La. EC4 **113 K10**
Gordon Sq. WC1 **111 N4**
Gordon St. WC1 **111 N4**
Goring St. EC3 **113 N8**
Gorsuch Pl. E2 **113 P2**
Gorsuch St. E2 **113 P2**
Gosfield St. W1 **111 L6**
Goslett Yd. WC2 **111 P9**
Gosset St. E2 **113 Q3**
Goswell Rd. EC1 **112 F1**
Gough Sq. EC4 **112 E8**
Gough St. WC1 **112 C4**
Goulston St. E1 **113 P8**
Gower Ct. WC1 **111 N4**
Gower Ms. WC1 **111 P7**
Gower Pl. WC1 **111 M4**
Gower St. WC1 **111 N5**
Gracechurch St. EC3 **113 L10**
Grafton Ms. W1 **111 L5**
Grafton Pl. NW1 **111 N3**
Grafton St. W1 **115 K1**
Grafton Way W1 **111 L5**
Grafton Way WC1 **111 M5**
Graham St. N1 **112 G1**
Graham Ter. SW1 **114 G9**
Granby Bldgs. SE11 **116 B9**
Granby Ter. NW1 **111 L1**
Grand Ave. EC1 **112 G6**
Grange, The SE1 **117 P6**
Grange Ct. WC2 **112 C9**
Grange Rd. SE1 **117 N7**
Grange Wk. SE1 **117 N6**
Grange Yd. SE1 **117 P7**
Grantham Pl. W1 **115 J3**
Granville Pl. W1 **110 G9**
Granville Sq. WC1 **112 C3**
Granville St. WC1 **112 C3**
Grape St. WC2 **111 Q8**
Graphite Sq. SE11 **116 B10**
Gravel La. E1 **113 P8**
Gray St. SE1 **116 E5**
Gray's Inn Pl. WC1 **112 C7**
Gray's Inn Rd. WC1 **112 A2**
Gray's Inn Sq. WC1 **112 D6**
Gray's Yd. W1 **110 H8**
Great Bell All. EC2 **113 K8**
Great Castle St. W1 **111 K8**
Great Cen. St. NW1 **110 E6**
Great Chapel St. W1 **111 N8**
Great College St. SW1 **115 Q6**
Great Cumberland Ms. W1 **110 E9**
Great Cumberland Pl. W1 **110 F8**
Great Dover St. SE1 **117 K5**
Great Eastern St. EC2 **113 M3**
Great Eastern Wk. EC2 **113 M7**
Great George St. SW1 **115 P5**
Great Guildford St. SE1 **116 H3**
Great James St. WC1 **112 B6**
Great Marlborough St. W1 **111 L9**
Great Maze Pond SE1 **117 L4**
Great New St. EC4 **112 E8**
Great Newport St. WC2 **111 P10**
Great Ormond St. WC1 **112 A6**
Great Percy St. WC1 **112 C2**
Great Peter St. SW1 **115 N7**
Great Portland St. W1 **111 K6**
Great Pulteney St. W1 **111 M10**
Great Queen St. WC2 **112 A9**
Great Russell St. WC1 **111 P8**
Great St. Helens EC3 **113 M8**
Great St. Thomas Apostle EC4 **113 J10**
Great Scotland Yd. SW1 **115 Q2**
Great Smith St. SW1 **115 P6**
Great Suffolk St. SE1 **116 G3**
Great Sutton St. EC1 **112 G5**
Great Swan All. EC2 **113 K8**
Great Titchfield St. W1 **111 L6**
Great Twr. St. EC3 **113 M10**
Great Trinity La. EC4 **113 J10**
Great Turnstile WC1 **112 C7**
Great Winchester St. EC2 **113 L8**
Great Windmill St. W1 **111 N10**
Great Yd. SE1 **117 N4**
Greek Ct. W1 **111 P9**
Greek St. W1 **111 P9**
Greek Yd. WC2 **111 Q10**
Green Arbour Ct. EC1 **112 F8**
Green Dragon Ct. SE1 **117 K2**
Green St. W1 **110 F10**
Green Wk. SE1 **117 M7**
Greenberry St. NW8 **110 C1**
Greencoat Pl. SW1 **115 M8**
Greencoat Row SW1 **115 M7**
Greenham Clo. SE1 **116 D5**
Greenhill's Rents EC1 **112 F6**
Green's Ct. W1 **111 N10**
Greenwell St. W1 **111 K5**
Greet St. SE1 **116 E3**
Grendon St. NW8 **110 C4**
Grenville St. WC1 **112 A5**
Gresham St. EC2 **113 J8**
Gresse St. W1 **111 N8**
Greville St. EC1 **112 E7**
Grey Eagle St. E1 **113 Q5**
Greycoat Pl. SW1 **115 N7**
Greycoat St. SW1 **115 N7**
Greyfriars Pas. EC1 **112 G8**
Greystoke Pl. EC4 **112 D8**
Griggs Pl. SE1 **117 N6**
Grimsby St. E2 **113 Q5**
Grindal St. SE1 **116 D5**
Grocer's Hall Ct. EC2 **113 K9**
Groom Pl. SW1 **114 H6**
Grosvenor Cotts. SW1 **114 G8**
Grosvenor Cres. SW1 **114 H5**
Grosvenor Cres. Ms. SW1 **114 G5**
Grosvenor Est. SW1 **115 P8**
Grosvenor Gdns. SW1 **115 K7**
Grosvenor Gdns. Ms. E. SW1 **115 K6**
Grosvenor Gdns. Ms. N. SW1 **115 J7**
Grosvenor Gdns. Ms. S. SW1 **115 K7**
Grosvenor Gate W1 **114 F1**
Grosvenor Hill W1 **111 J10**
Grosvenor Pl. SW1 **114 H5**
Grosvenor Sq. W1 **110 H10**
Grosvenor St. W1 **111 J10**
Grotto Pas. W1 **110 H6**
Grove End Rd. NW8 **110 A2**
Grove Gdns. NW8 **110 D3**
Groveland Ct. EC4 **113 J9**
Guildhall Bldgs. EC2 **113 K8**
Guildhouse St. SW1 **115 L8**
Guilford Pl. WC1 **112 B5**
Guilford St. WC1 **112 A5**
Guinness Bldgs. SE1 **117 M7**
Guinness Sq. SE1 **117 M8**
Guinness Trust Bldgs. SE11 **116 F10**
Guinness Trust Bldgs. SW3 **114 E9**
Gun St. E1 **113 P7**
Gunpowder Sq. EC4 **112 E8**
Gunthorpe St. E1 **113 Q7**
Guthrie St. SW3 **114 C10**
Gutter La. EC2 **113 J8**
Guy St. SE1 **117 L4**
Gwynne Pl. WC1 **112 C3**

H

Haberdasher Pl. N1 **113 L2**
Haberdasher St. N1 **113 L2**
Hackney Rd. E2 **113 P2**
Half Moon Ct. EC1 **112 H7**
Half Moon Pas. E1 **113 Q9**
Half Moon St. W1 **115 K2**
Halkin Arc. SW1 **114 G6**
Halkin Ms. SW1 **114 G6**
Halkin Pl. SW1 **114 G6**
Halkin St. SW1 **114 H5**
Hall Pl. W2 **110 A5**
Hall St. EC1 **112 G2**
Hallam Ms. W1 **111 K6**
Hallam St. W1 **111 K5**
Halpin Pl. SE17 **117 L9**
Halsey Ms. SW3 **114 E8**
Halsey St. SW3 **114 E8**
Halstead Ct. N1 **113 L1**
Ham Yd. W1 **111 N10**
Hamilton Clo. NW8 **110 A3**
Hamilton Ms. W1 **115 J4**
Hamilton Pl. W1 **114 H3**
Hamilton Sq. SE1 **117 L4**
Hammett St. EC3 **113 P10**
Hampden Clo. NW1 **111 P1**
Hampden Gurney St. W1 **110 E9**
Hampstead Rd. NW1 **111 L1**
Hampton St. SE1 **116 G9**
Hampton St. SE17 **116 G9**
Hanbury St. E1 **113 Q6**
Hand Ct. WC1 **112 C7**
Handel St. WC1 **111 Q4**
Hankey Pl. SE1 **117 L5**
Hanover Gate NW1 **110 D3**
Hanover Pl. WC2 **112 A9**
Hanover Sq. W1 **111 K9**
Hanover St. W1 **111 K9**
Hanover Ter. NW1 **110 D3**
Hanover Ter. Ms. NW1 **110 D3**
Hans Cres. SW1 **114 E6**
Hans Pl. SW1 **114 F6**
Hans Rd. SW3 **114 E6**
Hans St. SW1 **114 F7**
Hanson St. W1 **111 L6**
Hanway Pl. W1 **111 N8**
Hanway St. W1 **111 N8**

Harbet Rd. W2 **110 B7**
Harcourt St. W1 **110 D7**
Hardwick St. EC1 **112 E3**
Hardwidge St. SE1 **117 M4**
Hare Ct. EC4 **112 D9**
Hare Pl. EC4 **112 E9**
Hare Wk. N1 **113 N1**
Harewood Ave. NW1 **110 D5**
Harewood Pl. W1 **111 K9**
Harewood Row NW1 **110 D6**
Harley Pl. W1 **111 J7**
Harley St. W1 **111 J5**
Harold Est. SE1 **117 N7**
Harp All. EC4 **112 F8**
Harp La. EC3 **117 M1**
Harper Rd. SE1 **117 J6**
Harpur Ms. WC1 **112 B6**
Harpur St. WC1 **112 B6**
Harriet St. SW1 **114 F5**
Harriet Wk. SW1 **114 F5**
Harrington Rd. SW7 **114 B8**
Harrington Sq. NW1 **111 L1**
Harrington St. NW1 **111 L1**
Harrison St. WC1 **112 A3**
Harrow Pl. E1 **113 P8**
Harrowby St. W1 **110 D8**
Hart St. EC3 **113 N10**
Hartshorn All. EC3 **113 N9**
Harwich La. EC2 **113 N6**
Hasker St. SW3 **114 D8**
Hassard St. E2 **113 Q1**
Hastings St. WC1 **111 Q3**
Hat and Mitre Ct. EC1 **112 G5**
Hatfields SE1 **116 E2**
Hatherley St. SW1 **115 M9**
Hatton Gdn. EC1 **112 E6**
Hatton Row NW8 **110 B5**
Hatton St. NW8 **110 B5**
Hatton Wall EC1 **112 D6**
Haunch of Venison Yd. W1 **111 J9**
Haverstock St. N1 **112 G1**
Hay Hill W1 **115 K1**
Haydon St. EC3 **113 P10**
Haydon Wk. E1 **113 Q10**
Hayes Pl. NW1 **110 D5**
Hayles St. SE11 **116 F8**
Haymarket SW1 **115 N1**
Haymarket Arc. SW1 **115 N1**
Hayne St. EC1 **112 G6**
Hay's La. SE1 **117 M3**
Hay's Ms. W1 **115 J2**
Hayward's Pl. EC1 **112 F5**
Hazel Way SE1 **117 P8**
Headfort Pl. SW1 **114 H5**
Hearn St. EC2 **113 N5**
Hearn's Bldgs. SE17 **117 L9**
Heathcote St. WC1 **112 B4**
Heddon St. W1 **111 L10**
Helmet Row EC1 **113 J4**
Hemp Wk. SE17 **117 L8**
Henderson Dr. NW8 **110 A4**
Hendre Rd. SE1 **117 N9**
Heneage La. EC3 **113 N9**
Heneage St. E1 **113 Q6**
Henley Dr. SE1 **117 Q8**
Henrietta Ms. WC1 **112 A4**
Henrietta Pl. W1 **111 J8**
Henrietta St. WC2 **112 A10**
Henshaw St. SE17 **117 K8**
Herald's Ct. SE11 **116 F9**
Herald's Pl. SE11 **116 E8**
Herbal Hill EC1 **112 E5**
Herbert Cres. SW1 **114 F6**
Herbrand St. WC1 **111 Q4**
Hercules Rd. SE1 **116 C7**
Hermes St. N1 **112 D1**
Hermit St. EC1 **112 F2**
Hermitage St. W2 **110 A7**
Herrick St. SW1 **115 P9**
Hertford Pl. W1 **111 L5**
Hertford St. W1 **114 H3**
Hewett St. EC2 **113 N5**
Heygate St. SE17 **116 H9**
Hide Pl. SW1 **115 N9**
High Holborn WC1 **111 Q8**
Hill St. W1 **114 H2**
Hillery Clo. SE17 **117 L9**
Hills Pl. W1 **111 L9**
Hind Ct. EC4 **112 E9**
Hinde St. W1 **110 H8**
Hobart Pl. SW1 **115 J6**
Hocker St. E2 **113 P3**
Hogans Ms. W2 **110 A6**
Hogarth Ct. EC3 **113 N10**
Holbein Ms. SW1 **114 G10**
Holbein Pl. SW1 **114 G9**
Holborn EC1 **112 D7**
Holborn Circ. EC1 **112 E7**
Holborn Pl. WC1 **112 B7**
Holborn Viaduct EC1 **112 E7**
Holford Pl. WC1 **112 C2**
Holford St. WC1 **112 D2**
Holland St. SE1 **116 G2**
Hollen St. W1 **111 M8**
Holles St. W1 **111 K8**
Holmes Ter. SE1 **116 D4**
Holsworthy Sq. WC1 **112 C5**
Holyoak Rd. SE11 **116 F8**
Holyrood St. SE1 **117 M3**
Holywell La. EC2 **113 N4**
Holywell Row EC2 **113 M5**
Homefield St. N1 **113 M1**
Homer Row W1 **110 D7**
Homer St. W1 **110 D7**
Honduras St. EC1 **112 H4**
Honey La. EC2 **113 J9**
Hood Ct. EC4 **112 E9**
Hooper's Ct. SW3 **114 E5**
Hop Gdns. WC2 **115 Q1**
Hopetown St. E1 **113 Q7**
Hopkins St. W1 **111 M9**
Hopton Gdns. SE1 **116 G2**
Hopton St. SE1 **116 G2**
Horatio St. E2 **113 Q1**
Hornbeam Clo. SE11 **116 D8**
Horse and Dolphin Yd. W1 **111 P10**
Horse Guards Ave. SW1 **115 Q3**
Horse Guards Rd. SW1 **115 P3**
Horse Ride SW1 **115 N3**
Horse Shoe Yd. W1 **111 K10**
Horseferry Rd. SW1 **115 N7**
Horselydown La. SE1 **117 P4**
Hosier La. EC1 **112 F7**
Hotspur St. SE11 **116 D10**
Houghton St. WC2 **112 C9**
Houndsditch EC3 **113 N8**
Howard Pl. SW1 **115 L7**
Howell Wk. SE1 **116 G9**
Howick Pl. SW1 **115 M7**
Howland Ms. E. W1 **111 M6**
Howland St. W1 **111 L6**
Hoxton Mkt. N1 **113 M3**
Hoxton Sq. N1 **113 M3**
Hudson's Pl. SW1 **115 L8**
Huggin Ct. EC4 **113 J10**
Huggin Hill EC4 **113 J10**
Hugh Ms. SW1 **115 K9**
Hugh Pl. SW1 **115 N8**
Hugh St. SW1 **115 K9**
Hull St. EC1 **112 H3**
Humphrey St. SE1 **117 P10**
Hungerford Bri. SE1 **116 B3**
Hungerford Bri. WC2 **116 B3**
Hungerford La. WC2 **116 A2**
Hunter Clo. SE1 **117 L7**
Hunter St. WC1 **112 A4**
Huntley St. WC1 **111 M5**
Hunt's Ct. WC2 **115 P1**
Huntsman St. SE17 **117 L9**
Huntsworth Ms. NW1 **110 E5**
Hutton St. EC4 **112 E9**
Hyde Pk. W2 **114 C2**
Hyde Pk. Cor. W1 **114 H4**
Hyde Pk. Cres. W2 **110 C9**
Hyde Pk. Gdns. W2 **110 B10**
Hyde Pk. Gdns. Ms. W2 **110 B10**
Hyde Pk. Pl. W2 **110 D10**
Hyde Pk. Sq. W2 **110 C9**
Hyde Pk. Sq. Ms. W2 **110 C9**
Hyde Pk. St. W2 **110 C9**

I

Idol La. EC3 **117 M1**
Iliffe St. SE17 **116 G10**
Iliffe Yd. SE17 **116 G10**
Imperial College Rd. SW7 **114 A6**
India St. EC3 **113 P9**
Ingestre Pl. W1 **111 M9**
Inglebert St. EC1 **112 D2**
Ingram Clo. SE11 **116 C8**
Inigo Pl. WC2 **111 Q10**
Inner Circle NW1 **110 G3**
Inner Temple La. EC4 **112 D9**
Insurance St. WC1 **112 D3**
Ireland Yd. EC4 **112 G9**
Ironmonger La. EC2 **113 K9**
Ironmonger Pas. EC1 **113 J3**
Ironmonger Row EC1 **113 J3**
Irving St. WC2 **115 P1**
Isabella St. SE1 **116 F3**
Ives St. SW3 **114 D8**
Ivor Pl. NW1 **110 E5**
Ivybridge La. WC2 **116 A1**
Ivychurch La. SE17 **117 N10**
Ixworth Pl. SW3 **114 C10**

J

Jacob's Well Ms. W1 **110 H8**
Jamaica Rd. SE1 **117 Q5**
James Hammett Ho. E2 **113 Q2**
James St. W1 **110 H8**
James St. WC2 **112 A10**
Jasper Wk. N1 **113 K1**
Jermyn St. SW1 **115 M2**
Jerome Cres. NW8 **110 C4**
Jerome St. E1 **113 P5**
Jerrard St. N1 **113 N1**
Jerusalem Pas. EC1 **112 F5**
Jervis Ct. W1 **111 K9**
Jewry St. EC3 **113 P9**
Joan St. SE1 **116 F3**
Jockey's Flds. WC1 **112 C6**
Johanna St. SE1 **116 D5**
John Adam St. WC2 **116 A1**
John Carpenter St. EC4 **112 E10**
John Islip St. SW1 **115 P10**
John Princes St. W1 **111 K8**
John St. WC1 **112 C5**
John's Ms. WC1 **112 C5**
Joiner St. SE1 **117 L3**
Jonathan St. SE11 **116 B10**
Jones St. W1 **115 J1**
Jubilee Pl. SW3 **114 D10**
Judd St. WC1 **111 Q3**
Junction Ms. W2 **110 C8**
Junction Pl. W2 **110 B8**
Junction Wf. N1 **112 H1**
Juxon St. SE11 **116 C8**

K

Kean St. WC2 **112 B9**
Keats Clo. SE1 **117 P9**
Keats Pl. EC2 **113 K7**
Keeley St. WC2 **112 B9**
Kell St. SE1 **116 G6**
Kemble St. WC2 **112 B9**
Kemp's Ct. W1 **111 M9**
Kempsford Rd. SE11 **116 F9**
Kendal St. W2 **110 D9**
Kendall Pl. W1 **110 G7**
Kendrick Ms. SW7 **114 A8**
Kendrick Pl. SW7 **114 A9**
Kennet Wf. La. EC4 **113 J10**
Kennings Way SE11 **116 F10**
Kennington Rd. SE1 **116 D6**
Kennington Rd. SE11 **116 D8**
Kenrick Pl. W1 **110 G7**
Kensington Gore SW7 **114 A5**
Kent Pas. NW1 **110 E4**
Kent Ter. NW1 **113 Q3**
Kent Yd. SW7 **114 D5**
Kentish Bldgs. SE1 **117 K4**
Kenton St. WC1 **111 Q4**
Keppel Row SE1 **116 H3**
Keppel St. WC1 **111 P6**
Kestrel Ho. EC1 **112 H2**
Keyse Rd. SE1 **117 P7**
Keystone Cres. N1 **112 A1**
Keyworth Pl. SE1 **116 G6**
Keyworth St. SE1 **116 G6**
Kiffen St. EC2 **113 L4**
Kimbolton Row SW3 **114 C9**
King & Queen St. SE17 **117 J10**
King Charles St. SW1 **115 Q4**
King Edward St. EC1 **112 H8**
King Edward Wk. SE1 **116 E6**
King James St. SE1 **116 G5**
King John Ct. EC2 **113 N4**
King Sq. EC1 **112 H3**
King St. EC2 **113 J9**
King St. SW1 **115 M3**
King St. WC2 **111 Q10**
King William St. EC4 **117 L1**
Kinghorn St. EC1 **112 H7**
Kinglake Est. SE17 **117 N10**
Kingly Ct. W1 **111 M10**
Kingly St. W1 **111 L10**
Kings Arms Yd. EC2 **113 K8**
Kings Bench St. SE1 **116 G4**
Kings Bench Wk. EC4 **112 E9**
King's Cross Rd. WC1 **112 B2**
Kings Head Yd. SE1 **117 K3**
King's Ms. WC1 **112 C5**
Kings Pl. SE1 **116 H5**
King's Reach Twr. SE1 **116 E2**
King's Rd. SW1 **114 H8**
King's Scholars' Pas. SW1 **115 L7**
Kingscote St. EC4 **112 F10**
Kingsland Rd. E2 **113 N2**
Kingsway WC2 **112 B8**
Kinnerton Pl. N. SW1 **114 F5**
Kinnerton Pl. S. SW1 **114 F5**
Kinnerton St. SW1 **114 G5**
Kinnerton Yd. SW1 **114 F5**
Kintore Way SE1 **117 P8**
Kipling Est. SE1 **117 L5**
Kipling St. SE1 **117 L5**
Kirby Gro. SE1 **117 M4**
Kirby St. EC1 **112 E6**
Kirkman Pl. W1 **111 N7**
Kirton Gdns. E2 **113 Q3**
Knightrider St. EC4 **112 G10**
Knights Arc. SW1 **114 E5**
Knights Wk. SE11 **116 F9**
Knightsbridge SW1 **114 F4**
Knightsbridge SW7 **114 D5**
Knightsbridge Grn. SW1 **114 E5**
Knox St. W1 **110 E6**

L

Lackington St. EC2 **113 L6**
Lafone St. SE1 **117 P4**
Lamb St. E1 **113 P6**
Lamb Wk. SE1 **117 M5**
Lambeth Bri. SE1 **116 A8**
Lambeth Bri. SW1 **116 A8**
Lambeth High St. SE1 **116 B8**
Lambeth Hill EC4 **112 H10**
Lambeth Palace Rd. SE1 **116 B7**
Lambeth Rd. SE1 **116 D7**
Lambeth Wk. SE11 **116 C8**
Lamb's Bldgs. EC1 **113 K5**
Lambs Conduit Pas. WC1 **112 B6**
Lamb's Conduit St. WC1 **112 B5**
Lamb's Pas. EC1 **113 K6**
Lamlash St. SE11 **116 F8**
Lancashire Ct. W1 **111 K10**
Lancaster Pl. WC2 **112 B10**
Lancaster St. SE1 **116 G5**
Lancaster Ter. W2 **110 A10**
Lancelot Pl. SW7 **114 E5**
Lancing St. NW1 **111 N3**
Landon Pl. SW1 **114 E6**
Langham Pl. W1 **111 K7**
Langham St. W1 **111 K7**
Langley Ct. WC2 **111 Q10**
Langley St. WC2 **111 Q9**
Langthorn Ct. EC2 **113 L8**
Langton Clo. WC1 **112 C4**
Lansdowne Pl. SE1 **117 L6**
Lansdowne Row W1 **115 K2**
Lansdowne Ter. WC1 **112 A5**
Lant St. SE1 **116 H4**
Larcom St. SE17 **117 J9**
Larissa St. SE17 **117 L10**
Laud St. SE11 **116 B10**
Launcelot St. SE1 **116 D5**
Laurence Pountney Hill EC4 **113 K10**
Laurence Pountney La. EC4 **113 K10**
Lavington St. SE1 **116 G3**
Law St. SE1 **117 L6**
Lawrence La. EC2 **113 J9**
Lawson Est. SE1 **117 K7**
Laxton Pl. NW1 **111 K4**
Laystall St. EC1 **112 D5**
Laytons Bldgs. SE1 **117 K4**
Leadenhall Mkt. EC3 **113 M9**
Leadenhall Pl. EC3 **113 M9**
Leadenhall St. EC3 **113 M9**
Leake Ct. SE1 **116 C4**
Leake St. SE1 **116 C4**
Leather La. EC1 **112 D6**
Leathermarket St. SE1 **117 M5**
Lecky St. SW7 **114 A10**
Leeke St. WC1 **112 B2**
Lees Pl. W1 **110 G10**
Leicester Ct. WC2 **111 P10**
Leicester Pl. WC2 **111 P10**
Leicester Sq. WC2 **115 P1**
Leicester St. WC2 **111 P10**
Leigh Hunt St. SE1 **116 H4**
Leigh St. WC1 **111 Q4**
Leman St. E1 **113 Q9**
Lennox Gdns. SW1 **114 E7**
Lennox Gdns. Ms. SW1 **114 E7**
Leo Yd. EC1 **112 G5**
Leonard St. EC2 **113 L4**
Leopards Ct. EC1 **112 D6**
Leroy St. SE1 **117 M7**
Lever St. EC1 **112 G3**
Leverett St. SW3 **114 D8**
Lewisham St. SW1 **115 P5**
Lexington St. W1 **111 M10**
Leyden St. E1 **113 P7**
Library St. SE1 **116 F5**
Lidlington Pl. NW1 **111 M1**
Ligonier St. E2 **113 P4**
Lilac Pl. SE11 **116 B9**
Lilestone St. NW8 **110 C4**
Lillington Gdns. Est. SW1 **115 M9**
Lily Pl. EC1 **112 E6**
Lime St. EC3 **113 M10**
Lime St. Pas. EC3 **113 M10**
Lincoln St. SW3 **114 E9**
Lincoln's Inn Flds. WC2 **112 B8**
Lindsey St. EC1 **112 G6**
Linhope St. NW1 **110 E4**
Lisle St. WC2 **111 P10**
Lisson Grn. Est. NW8 **110 C3**
Lisson Gro. NW1 **110 D5**
Lisson Gro. NW8 **110 B4**
Lisson St. NW1 **110 C6**
Litchfield St. WC2 **111 P10**
Little Albany St. NW1 **111 K3**
Little Argyll St. W1 **111 L9**
Little Britain EC1 **112 G7**
Little Chester St. SW1 **115 J6**
Little College St. SW1 **115 Q6**
Little Dean's Yd. SW1 **115 Q6**
Little Dorrit Ct. SE1 **117 J4**
Little Edward St. NW1 **111 K2**
Little Essex St. WC2 **112 D10**
Little George St. SW1 **115 Q5**
Little Marlborough St. W1 **111 L9**
Little New St. EC4 **112 E8**
Little Newport St. WC2 **111 P10**
Little Portland St. W1 **111 K8**
Little Russell St. WC1 **111 Q7**
Little St. James's St. SW1 **115 L3**
Little Sanctuary SW1 **115 P5**
Little Smith St. SW1 **115 P6**
Little Somerset St. E1 **113 P9**
Little Titchfield St. W1 **111 L7**
Little Trinity La. EC4 **113 J10**
Little Turnstile WC1 **112 B7**
Liverpool St. EC2 **113 M7**
Livonia St. W1 **111 M9**
Lizard St. EC1 **113 J3**
Lloyd Baker St. WC1 **112 C3**
Lloyd Sq. WC1 **112 D2**
Lloyd St. WC1 **112 D2**
Lloyd's Ave. EC3 **113 N9**
Lloyd's Row EC1 **112 F3**
Lockyer Est. SE1 **117 L4**
Lockyer St. SE1 **117 L5**
Lodge Rd. NW8 **110 B3**
Lolesworth Clo. E1 **113 Q7**
Lollard St. SE11 **116 C8**
Loman St. SE1 **116 G4**
Lombard Ct. EC3 **113 L10**
Lombard La. EC4 **112 E9**
Lombard St. EC3 **113 L9**
London Bri. EC4 **117 L2**
London Bri. SE1 **117 L2**
London Bri. St. SE1 **117 L3**
London Ms. W2 **110 B9**
London Rd. SE1 **116 F6**
London St. EC3 **113 N10**
London St. W2 **110 A8**
London Wall EC2 **113 J7**
Long Acre WC2 **111 Q10**
Long Ct. WC2 **115 P1**
Long La. EC1 **112 G6**
Long La. SE1 **117 K5**
Long St. E2 **113 P2**
Long Wk. SE1 **117 N6**
Long Yd. WC1 **112 B5**
Longfellow Way SE1 **117 Q9**
Longfield Est. SE1 **117 Q9**
Longford St. NW1 **111 K4**
Longmoore St. SW1 **115 L9**
Longville Rd. SE11 **116 G8**
Lord N. St. SW1 **115 Q7**
Lords Vw. NW8 **110 C3**
Lorenzo St. WC1 **112 B1**
Lorne Clo. NW8 **110 D3**
Lothbury EC2 **113 K8**
Lovat La. EC3 **117 M1**
Love La. EC2 **113 J8**
Lover's Wk. W1 **114 G2**
Lower Belgrave St. SW1 **115 J7**
Lower Grosvenor Pl. SW1 **115 J6**
Lower James St. W1 **111 M10**
Lower John St. W1 **111 M10**
Lower Marsh SE1 **116 D5**
Lower Robert St. WC2 **116 A1**
Lower Sloane St. SW1 **114 G9**
Lower Thames St. EC3 **117 L1**
Lowndes Clo. SW1 **114 H7**
Lowndes Pl. SW1 **114 G7**
Lowndes Sq. SW1 **114 F5**
Lowndes St. SW1 **114 F6**
Lowther Gdns. SW7 **114 A5**
Loxham St. WC1 **112 A3**
Lucan Pl. SW3 **114 C9**
Ludgate Bdy. EC4 **112 F9**
Ludgate Circ. EC4 **112 F9**
Ludgate Ct. EC4 **112 F9**
Ludgate Hill EC4 **112 F9**
Ludgate Sq. EC4 **112 G9**
Ludlow St. EC1 **112 H4**
Luke St. EC2 **113 M4**
Lulworth SE17 **117 K10**
Lumley Ct. WC2 **116 A1**
Lumley St. W1 **110 H9**
Luton St. NW8 **110 B5**
Luxborough St. W1 **110 G5**
Lyall Ms. SW1 **114 G7**
Lyall Ms. W. SW1 **114 G7**
Lyall St. SW1 **114 G7**
Lygon Pl. SW1 **115 J7**
Lynton Rd. SE1 **117 Q9**
Lyons Pl. NW8 **110 A5**

M

Mabledon Pl. WC1 **111 P3**
Macclesfield Rd. EC1 **112 H2**
Macclesfield St. W1 **111 P10**
Macfarren Pl. NW1 **110 H5**
Macklin St. WC2 **112 A8**
Mackworth St. NW1 **111 L2**
Maddox St. W1 **111 K10**
Madron St. SE17 **117 N10**
Magdalen Pas. E1 **113 Q10**
Magdalen St. SE1 **117 M3**
Maggie Blake's Cause SE1 **117 P3**
Magpie All. EC4 **112 E9**
Maguire St. SE1 **117 Q4**
Maiden La. SE1 **117 J2**
Maiden La. WC2 **112 A10**
Maidstone Bldgs. SE1 **117 K3**
Mail Coach Yd. N1 **113 N2**
Makins St. SW3 **114 D9**
Malet Pl. WC1 **111 N5**
Malet St. WC1 **111 N5**
Mall, The SW1 **115 M4**
Mallory St. NW8 **110 C5**
Mallow St. EC1 **113 K4**
Malta St. EC1 **112 G4**
Maltby St. SE1 **117 P5**
Maltravers St. WC2 **112 C10**
Malvern Ct. SW7 **114 B8**
Manchester Ms. W1 **110 G7**
Manchester Sq. W1 **110 G8**
Manchester St. W1 **110 G7**
Manciple St. SE1 **117 L5**
Mandela Way SE1 **117 N8**
Mandeville Pl. W1 **110 H8**
Manette St. W1 **111 P9**
Manningford Clo. EC1 **112 F2**
Manor Pl. SE17 **116 H10**
Mansell St. E1 **113 Q9**
Mansfield Ms. W1 **111 J7**
Mansfield St. W1 **111 J7**
Mansion Ho. Pl. EC4 **113 K9**
Manson Ms. SW7 **114 A9**
Manson Pl. SW7 **114 A9**
Maple Pl. W1 **111 M5**
Maple St. W1 **111 L6**
Marble Arch W1 **110 E10**
Marchmont St. WC1 **111 Q4**
Marcia Rd. SE1 **117 N9**

Margaret Ct. W1 **111 L8**
Margaret St. W1 **111 K8**
Margery St. WC1 **112 D3**
Marigold All. SE1 **116 F1**
Mark La. EC3 **113 N10**
Mark St. EC2 **113 M4**
Market Ct. W1 **111 L8**
Market Ms. W1 **115 J3**
Market Pl. W1 **111 L8**
Markham Pl. SW3 **114 E10**
Markham Sq. SW3 **114 E10**
Markham St. SW3 **114 D10**
Marlborough Bldgs. SW3 **114 D8**
Marlborough Clo. SE17 **116 H9**
Marlborough Gate Ho. W2 **110 A10**
Marlborough Rd. SW1 **115 M3**
Marlborough St. SW3 **114 C9**
Marshall St. W1 **111 M9**
Marshalls Pl. SE16 **117 Q7**
Marshalsea Rd. SE1 **117 J4**
Marsham St. SW1 **115 P7**
Mart St. WC2 **112 A10**
Martin La. EC4 **113 L10**
Martlett Ct. WC2 **112 A9**
Marylebone Flyover NW1 **110 C7**
Marylebone Flyover W2 **110 B7**
Marylebone High St. W1 **110 H6**
Marylebone La. W1 **110 H8**
Marylebone Ms. W1 **111 J7**
Marylebone Pas. W1 **111 M8**
Marylebone Rd. NW1 **110 F6**
Marylebone St. W1 **110 H7**
Marylee Way SE11 **116 C10**
Mason St. SE17 **117 L8**
Masons Arms Ms. W1 **111 K10**
Masons Ave. EC2 **113 K8**
Mason's Pl. EC1 **112 H2**
Mason's Yd. SW1 **115 M2**
Massinger St. SE17 **117 M9**
Matthew Parker St. SW1 **115 P5**
Matthews Yd. WC2 **111 Q9**
Maunsel St. SW1 **115 N8**
Mayfair Pl. W1 **115 K2**
Mays Ct. WC2 **115 Q1**
McAuley Clo. SE1 **116 D6**
McCoid Way SE1 **116 H5**
Mead Row SE1 **116 D6**
Meadow Row SE1 **116 H7**
Meakin Est. SE1 **117 M6**
Meard St. W1 **111 N9**
Mecklenburgh Pl. WC1 **112 B4**
Mecklenburgh Sq. WC1 **112 B4**
Mecklenburgh St. WC1 **112 B4**
Medway St. SW1 **115 P7**
Melbourne Pl. WC2 **112 C9**
Melbury Ter. NW1 **110 D5**
Melcombe Pl. NW1 **110 E6**
Melcombe St. NW1 **110 F5**
Melina Pl. NW8 **110 A3**
Melior Pl. SE1 **117 M4**
Melior St. SE1 **117 M4**
Melton Ct. SW7 **114 B9**
Melton St. NW1 **111 M3**
Memel Ct. EC1 **112 H5**
Memel St. EC1 **112 H5**
Mepham St. SE1 **116 D3**
Mercer St. WC2 **111 Q9**
Meredith St. EC1 **112 F3**
Merlin St. WC1 **112 D3**
Mermaid Ct. SE1 **117 K4**
Merrick Sq. SE1 **117 K6**
Merrow Wk. SE17 **117 L10**
Meymott St. SE1 **116 F3**
Micawber St. N1 **113 J2**
Middle St. EC1 **112 H6**
Middle Temple La. EC4 **112 D9**
Middle Yd. SE1 **117 M2**
Middlesex Pas. EC1 **112 G7**
Middlesex St. E1 **113 N7**
Middleton Bldgs. W1 **111 L7**
Midford Pl. W1 **111 M5**
Midhope St. WC1 **112 A3**
Midland Rd. NW1 **111 P1**
Milcote St. SE1 **116 F5**
Miles Pl. NW1 **110 C6**
Milford La. WC2 **112 D10**
Milk St. EC2 **113 J8**
Mill St. SE1 **117 Q5**
Mill St. W1 **111 L10**
Millbank SW1 **115 Q6**
Millbank Twr. SW1 **115 Q9**
Millman Ms. WC1 **112 B5**
Millman St. WC1 **112 B5**
Mills Ct. EC2 **113 M4**
Millstream Rd. SE1 **117 P5**
Milner St. SW3 **114 E8**
Milroy Wk. SE1 **116 F2**
Milton Clo. SE1 **117 P9**
Milton Ct. EC2 **113 K6**
Milton St. EC2 **113 K6**
Mincing La. EC3 **113 M10**
Minera Ms. SW1 **114 H8**
Minnow Wk. SE17 **117 N9**
Minories EC3 **113 P9**
Mint St. SE1 **116 H4**
Mitchell St. EC1 **112 H4**
Mitre Ct. EC2 **113 J8**
Mitre Ct. EC4 **112 E9**
Mitre Rd. SE1 **116 E4**
Mitre Sq. EC3 **113 N9**
Mitre St. EC3 **113 N9**
Molyneux St. W1 **110 D7**
Monck St. SW1 **115 P7**
Moncorvo Clo. SW7 **114 C5**
Monkton St. SE11 **116 E8**
Monkwell Sq. EC2 **113 J7**
Monmouth St. WC2 **111 Q10**
Montagu Mans. W1 **110 F6**
Montagu Ms. N. W1 **110 F7**
Montagu Ms. S. W1 **110 F8**
Montagu Ms. W. W1 **110 F8**
Montagu Pl. W1 **110 E7**
Montagu Row W1 **110 F7**
Montagu Sq. W1 **110 F7**
Montagu St. W1 **110 F8**
Montague Clo. SE1 **117 K2**
Montague Pl. WC1 **111 P6**
Montague St. EC1 **112 H7**
Montague St. WC1 **111 Q6**
Montclare St. E2 **113 P4**
Montpelier Ms. SW7 **114 D6**
Montpelier Pl. SW7 **114 D6**
Montpelier Sq. SW7 **114 D6**
Montpelier St. SW7 **114 D5**
Montpelier Ter. SW7 **114 D5**
Montpelier Wk. SW7 **114 C6**
Montreal Pl. WC2 **112 B10**
Montrose Ct. SW7 **114 B5**
Montrose Pl. SW1 **114 H5**
Monument St. EC3 **113 L10**
Moor La. EC2 **113 K7**
Moor Pl. EC2 **113 K7**
Moor St. W1 **111 P9**
Moore St. SW3 **114 E8**
Moorfields EC2 **113 K7**
Moorgate EC2 **113 K7**
Moorgate Pl. EC2 **113 K8**
Mora St. EC1 **113 J3**
Morecambe St. SE17 **117 J9**
Moreland St. EC1 **112 G2**
Moreton Pl. SW1 **115 M10**
Moreton St. SW1 **115 M10**
Moreton Ter. SW1 **115 M10**
Moreton Ter. Ms. N. SW1 **115 M10**
Moreton Ter. Ms. S. SW1 **115 M10**
Morgans La. SE1 **117 M3**
Morley St. SE1 **116 E6**
Morocco St. SE1 **117 M5**
Morpeth Ter. SW1 **115 L7**
Mortimer Mkt. WC1 **111 M5**
Mortimer St. W1 **111 L8**
Morton Pl. SE1 **116 D7**
Morwell St. WC1 **111 P7**
Mossop St. SW3 **114 D8**
Motcomb St. SW1 **114 F6**
Mount Mills EC1 **112 G3**
Mount Pleasant WC1 **112 D5**
Mount Row W1 **115 J1**
Mount St. W1 **114 G1**
Moxon St. W1 **110 G7**
Mozart Ter. SW1 **114 H9**
Mulready St. NW8 **110 C5**
Mulvaney Way SE1 **117 L5**
Mumford Ct. EC2 **113 J8**
Mundy St. N1 **113 N2**
Munster Sq. NW1 **111 K3**
Munton Rd. SE17 **117 J8**
Murphy St. SE1 **116 D5**
Murray Gro. N1 **113 J1**
Muscovy St. EC3 **117 N1**
Museum St. WC1 **111 Q7**
Myddelton Pas. EC1 **112 E2**
Myddelton Sq. EC1 **112 E2**
Myddelton St. EC1 **112 E3**
Mylne St. EC1 **112 D2**
Myrtle Wk. N1 **113 M1**

N

Nag's Head Ct. EC1 **113 J5**
Nantes Pas. E1 **113 P6**
Nash St. NW1 **111 K2**
Nassau St. W1 **111 L7**
Nathaniel Clo. E1 **113 Q7**
Navarre St. E2 **113 P4**
Nazrul St. E2 **113 P2**
Neal St. WC2 **111 Q9**
Neal's Yd. WC2 **111 Q9**
Neathouse Pl. SW1 **115 L8**
Nebraska St. SE1 **117 K5**
Neckinger SE16 **117 Q6**
Neckinger Est. SE16 **117 Q6**
Neckinger St. SE1 **117 Q6**
Nelson Pas. EC1 **113 J3**
Nelson Pl. N1 **112 G1**
Nelson Sq. SE1 **116 F4**
Nelson Ter. N1 **112 G1**
Netley St. NW1 **111 L3**
Neville Clo. NW1 **111 P1**
Neville St. SW7 **114 A10**
Neville Ter. SW7 **114 A10**
New Bond St. W1 **111 J9**
New Bri. St. EC4 **112 F9**
New Broad St. EC2 **113 M7**
New Burlington Ms. W1 **111 L10**
New Burlington Pl. W1 **111 L10**
New Burlington St. W1 **111 L10**
New Cavendish St. W1 **110 H7**
New Change EC4 **112 H9**
New Charles St. EC1 **112 G2**
New Compton St. WC2 **111 P9**
New Ct. EC4 **112 D10**
New Coventry St. W1 **115 P1**
New Fetter La. EC4 **112 E8**
New Goulston St. E1 **113 P8**
New Inn Bdy. EC2 **113 N4**
New Inn Pas. WC2 **112 C9**
New Inn St. EC2 **113 N4**
New Inn Yd. EC2 **113 N4**
New Kent Rd. SE1 **116 H7**
New London St. EC3 **113 N10**
New N. Pl. EC2 **113 M5**
New N. St. WC1 **112 B6**
New Oxford St. WC1 **111 P8**
New Quebec St. W1 **110 F9**
New Ride SW7 **114 C4**
New Row WC2 **111 Q10**
New Sq. WC2 **112 C8**
New St. EC2 **113 N7**
New St. Sq. EC4 **112 E8**
New Turnstile WC1 **112 B7**
New Union St. EC2 **113 K7**
Newburgh St. W1 **111 L9**
Newbury St. EC1 **112 H6**
Newcastle Clo. EC4 **112 F8**
Newcastle Pl. W2 **110 B7**
Newcastle Row EC1 **112 E5**
Newcomen St. SE1 **117 K4**
Newcourt St. NW8 **110 C1**
Newgate St. EC1 **112 G8**
Newhams Row SE1 **117 N5**
Newington Butts SE1 **116 G9**
Newington Butts SE11 **116 G9**
Newington Causeway SE1 **116 G7**
Newman Pas. W1 **111 M7**
Newman St. W1 **111 M7**
Newman Yd. W1 **111 M8**
Newman's Ct. EC3 **113 L9**
Newman's Row WC2 **112 C7**
Newnham Ter. SE1 **116 D6**
Newport Ct. WC2 **111 P10**
Newport Pl. WC2 **111 P10**
Newport St. SE11 **116 B9**
Newton St. WC2 **112 A8**
Nicholas La. EC4 **113 L10**
Nicholson St. SE1 **116 F3**
Nile St. N1 **113 J2**
Noble St. EC2 **112 H8**
Noel St. W1 **111 M9**
Norfolk Cres. W2 **110 C8**
Norfolk Pl. W2 **110 B8**
Norfolk Row SE1 **116 B8**
Norfolk Sq. W2 **110 B9**
Norfolk Sq. Ms. W2 **110 B9**
Norman St. EC1 **112 H3**
Norris St. SW1 **115 N1**
North Audley St. W1 **110 G9**
North Bank NW8 **110 C3**
North Carriage Dr. W2 **110 C10**
North Ct. W1 **111 M6**
North Cres. WC1 **111 N6**
North Gower St. NW1 **111 M3**
North Ms. WC1 **112 C5**
North Ride W2 **114 C1**
North Row W1 **110 F10**
North Tenter St. E1 **113 Q9**
North Ter. SW3 **114 C7**
North Wf. Rd. W2 **110 A7**
Northampton Rd. EC1 **112 E4**
Northampton Sq. EC1 **112 F3**
Northburgh St. EC1 **112 G5**
Northchurch SE17 **117 L10**
Northington St. WC1 **112 C5**
Northumberland All. EC3 **113 N9**
Northumberland Ave. WC2 **115 Q2**
Northumberland St. WC2 **115 Q2**
Northwick Clo. NW8 **110 A4**
Northwick Ter. NW8 **110 A4**
Norton Folgate E1 **113 N6**
Norwich St. EC4 **112 D8**
Nottingham Ct. WC2 **111 Q9**
Nottingham Pl. W1 **110 G5**
Nottingham St. W1 **110 G6**
Nottingham Ter. NW1 **110 G5**
Nun Ct. EC2 **113 K8**
Nutford Pl. W1 **110 D8**

O

Oak Tree Rd. NW8 **110 B3**
Oakden St. SE11 **116 E8**
Oakey La. SE1 **116 D6**
Oakley Cres. EC1 **112 G1**
Oat La. EC2 **113 J8**
Occupation Rd. SE17 **116 H10**
Octagon Arc. EC2 **113 M7**
Odhams Wk. WC2 **111 Q9**
Ogle St. W1 **111 L6**
Old Bailey EC4 **112 G9**
Old Barge Ho. All. SE1 **116 E2**
Old Barrack Yd. SW1 **114 G5**
Old Bond St. W1 **115 L1**
Old Brewers Yd. WC2 **111 Q9**
Old Broad St. EC2 **113 L9**
Old Bldgs. WC2 **112 D8**
Old Burlington St. W1 **111 L10**
Old Castle St. E1 **113 P8**
Old Cavendish St. W1 **111 J8**
Old Compton St. W1 **111 N10**
Old Fish St. Hill EC4 **112 H10**
Old Gloucester St. WC1 **112 A6**
Old Jewry EC2 **113 K9**
Old Kent Rd. SE1 **117 M8**
Old Marylebone Rd. NW1 **110 D7**
Old Nichol St. E2 **113 P4**
Old N. St. WC1 **112 B6**
Old Palace Yd. SW1 **115 Q6**
Old Paradise St. SE11 **116 B8**
Old Pk. La. W1 **114 H3**
Old Pye St. SW1 **115 N6**
Old Quebec St. W1 **110 F9**
Old Queen St. SW1 **115 P5**
Old Seacoal La. EC4 **112 F9**
Old Sq. WC2 **112 C8**
Old St. EC1 **112 H5**
Oldbury Pl. W1 **110 H6**
Olivers Yd. EC1 **113 L4**
O'Meara St. SE1 **117 J3**
Omega Pl. N1 **112 A1**
Onslow Gdns. SW7 **114 A10**
Onslow Ms. E. SW7 **114 A9**
Onslow Ms. W. SW7 **114 A9**
Onslow Sq. SW7 **114 B9**
Onslow St. EC1 **112 E5**
Ontario St. SE1 **116 G7**
Opal St. SE11 **116 F10**
Orange St. WC2 **115 P1**
Orange Yd. W1 **111 P9**
Oratory La. SW3 **114 B10**
Orb St. SE17 **117 K9**
Orchard St. W1 **110 G9**
Orchardson St. NW8 **110 A5**
Orde Hall St. WC1 **112 B6**
Orient St. SE11 **116 F8**
Ormond Clo. WC1 **112 A6**
Ormond Ms. WC1 **112 A5**
Ormond Yd. SW1 **115 M2**
Ormonde Pl. SW1 **114 G9**
Ormsby St. E2 **113 P1**
Orsett St. SE11 **116 C10**
Osbert St. SW1 **115 N9**
Osborn St. E1 **113 Q7**
Oslo Ct. NW8 **110 C1**
Osnaburgh St. NW1 **111 K4**
Osnaburgh Ter. NW1 **111 K4**
Osric Path N1 **113 M1**
Ossington Bldgs. W1 **110 G6**
Ossulston St. NW1 **111 N1**
Oswin St. SE11 **116 G8**
Othello Clo. SE11 **116 F10**
Outwich St. EC3 **113 N8**
Ovington Gdns. SW3 **114 D7**
Ovington Ms. SW3 **114 D7**
Ovington Sq. SW3 **114 D7**
Ovington St. SW3 **114 D7**
Owen St. EC1 **112 E1**
Owen's Ct. EC1 **112 F2**
Owen's Row EC1 **112 F2**
Oxendon St. SW1 **115 N1**
Oxenholme NW1 **111 M1**
Oxford Circ. Ave. W1 **111 L9**
Oxford Ct. EC4 **113 K10**
Oxford Sq. W2 **110 D9**
Oxford St. W1 **110 G9**
Oxley Clo. SE1 **117 Q10**

P

Padbury Ct. E2 **113 Q3**
Paddington Grn. W2 **110 B6**
Paddington St. W1 **110 G6**
Page St. SW1 **115 P8**
Pages Wk. SE1 **117 M8**
Paget St. EC1 **112 F2**
Pakenham St. WC1 **112 C3**
Palace Ms. SW1 **114 H9**
Palace Pl. SW1 **115 L6**
Palace St. SW1 **115 L6**
Palissy St. E2 **113 P3**
Pall Mall SW1 **115 M3**
Pall Mall E. SW1 **115 P2**
Pall Mall Pl. SW1 **115 M3**
Palmer St. SW1 **115 N6**
Pancras La. EC4 **113 J9**
Panton St. SW1 **115 N1**
Panyer All. EC4 **112 H8**
Paragon Ms. SE1 **117 L8**
Pardon St. EC1 **112 G4**
Pardoner St. SE1 **117 L6**
Paris Gdn. SE1 **116 F2**
Park Clo. SW1 **114 E5**
Park Cres. W1 **111 J5**
Park Cres. Ms. E. W1 **111 K5**
Park Cres. Ms. W. W1 **111 J5**
Park Gdn. Pl. W2 **110 B9**
Park La. W1 **110 F10**
Park Pl. SW1 **115 L3**
Park Rd. NW1 **110 E4**
Park Rd. NW8 **110 C2**
Park Sq. E. NW1 **111 J4**
Park Sq. Ms. NW1 **111 J5**
Park Sq. W. NW1 **111 J4**
Park St. SE1 **116 H2**
Park St. W1 **110 G10**
Park W. W2 **110 B9**
Park W. Pl. W2 **110 D8**
Parker Ms. WC2 **112 A8**
Parker St. WC2 **112 A8**
Parkers Row SE1 **117 Q5**
Parliament Sq. SW1 **115 Q5**
Parliament St. SW1 **115 Q5**
Passing All. EC1 **112 F5**
Passmore St. SW1 **114 G9**
Pastor St. SE11 **116 G8**
Paternoster Row EC4 **112 H9**
Paternoster Sq. EC4 **112 G8**
Paton St. EC1 **112 H3**
Paul St. EC2 **113 L5**
Paveley St. NW8 **110 D3**
Pavilion Rd. SW1 **114 F5**
Pavilion St. SW1 **114 F7**
Peabody Dws. WC1 **111 Q4**
Peabody Est. EC1 **113 J5**
Peabody Sq. SE1 **116 F5**
Peacock St. SE17 **116 G9**
Peacock Yd. SE17 **116 G9**
Pear Pl. SE1 **116 D4**
Pear Tree Ct. EC1 **112 E5**
Pear Tree St. EC1 **112 G4**
Pearman St. SE1 **116 E6**
Pedley St. E1 **113 Q5**
Peerless St. EC1 **113 K3**
Pelham Cres. SW7 **114 C9**
Pelham Pl. SW7 **114 C8**
Pelham St. SW7 **114 B8**
Pelter St. E2 **113 P2**
Pemberton Row EC4 **112 E8**
Pembroke Clo. SW1 **114 H5**
Penfold Pl. NW1 **110 C6**
Penfold St. NW1 **110 C6**
Penfold St. NW8 **110 B5**
Penry St. SE1 **117 N9**
Penton Gro. N1 **112 D1**
Penton Pl. SE17 **116 G10**
Penton Ri. WC1 **112 C2**
Penton St. N1 **112 D1**
Pentonville Rd. N1 **112 B1**
Pepper St. SE1 **116 H4**
Pepys St. EC3 **113 N10**
Percival St. EC1 **112 F4**
Percy Circ. WC1 **112 C2**
Percy Ms. W1 **111 N7**
Percy Pas. W1 **111 M7**
Percy St. W1 **111 N7**
Percy Yd. WC1 **112 C2**
Peregrine Ho. EC1 **112 G2**
Perkin's Rents SW1 **115 N6**
Perrys Pl. W1 **111 N8**
Peter St. W1 **111 N10**
Peters Hill EC4 **112 H10**
Peters La. EC1 **112 F6**
Peto Pl. NW1 **111 K4**
Petticoat Sq. E1 **113 P8**
Petty France SW1 **115 M6**
Petyward SW3 **114 D9**
Philpot La. EC3 **113 M10**
Phipp St. EC2 **113 M4**
Phipp's Ms. SW1 **115 J7**
Phoenix Pl. WC1 **112 C4**
Phoenix Rd. NW1 **111 N2**
Phoenix St. WC2 **111 P9**
Piccadilly W1 **115 K3**
Piccadilly Arc. SW1 **115 L2**
Piccadilly Circ. W1 **115 N1**
Piccadilly Pl. W1 **115 M1**
Pickard St. EC1 **112 G2**
Pickering Pl. SW1 **115 M3**
Pickford Wf. N1 **112 H1**
Pickwick St. SE1 **116 H5**
Picton Pl. W1 **110 H9**
Pilgrim St. EC4 **112 F9**
Pilgrimage St. SE1 **117 K5**
Pimlico Rd. SW1 **114 G10**
Pimlico Wk. N1 **113 M2**
Pindar St. EC2 **113 M6**
Pine St. EC1 **112 D4**
Pineapple Ct. SW1 **115 L6**
Pitfield Est. N1 **113 M2**
Pitfield St. N1 **113 M3**
Pitt's Head Ms. W1 **114 H3**
Plantain Pl. SE1 **117 K4**
Platina St. EC2 **113 L4**
Playhouse Yd. EC4 **112 F9**
Pleydell St. EC4 **112 E9**
Plough Ct. EC3 **113 L10**
Plough Pl. EC4 **112 E8**
Plough Yd. EC2 **113 N5**
Plumtree Ct. EC4 **112 F8**
Plympton Pl. NW8 **110 C5**
Plympton St. NW8 **110 C5**
Pocock St. SE1 **116 F4**
Poland St. W1 **111 M8**
Pollen St. W1 **111 L9**
Pollitt Dr. NW8 **110 B4**
Polygon Rd. NW1 **111 N1**
Pomell Way E1 **113 Q8**
Pond Pl. SW3 **114 C9**
Ponsonby Pl. SW1 **115 P10**
Ponsonby Ter. SW1 **115 P10**
Pont St. SW1 **114 E7**
Pont St. Ms. SW1 **114 E7**
Pontypool Pl. SE1 **116 F4**
Pooles Bldgs. EC1 **112 D5**
Pope St. SE1 **117 N5**
Poppins Ct. EC4 **112 F9**
Porchester Pl. W2 **110 D9**
Porlock St. SE1 **117 L4**
Porter St. SE1 **117 J2**
Porter St. W1 **110 F6**
Portland Ms. W1 **111 M9**
Portland Pl. W1 **111 J5**
Portland St. SE17 **117 K10**
Portman Clo. W1 **110 F8**
Portman Ms. S. W1 **110 G9**
Portman Sq. W1 **110 G8**
Portman St. W1 **110 G9**

Portpool La. EC1 **112 D6**
Portsea Ms. W2 **110 D9**
Portsea Pl. W2 **110 D9**
Portsmouth St. WC2 **112 B9**
Portsoken St. E1 **113 P10**
Portugal St. WC2 **112 B9**
Post Office Ct. EC3 **113 L9**
Potier St. SE1 **117 L7**
Poultry EC2 **113 K9**
Powis Pl. WC1 **112 A5**
Praed Ms. W2 **110 B8**
Praed St. W2 **110 B8**
Pratt Wk. SE11 **116 C8**
Prescot St. E1 **113 Q10**
President St. EC1 **112 H2**
Preston Clo. SE1 **117 M8**
Prestwood St. N1 **113 J1**
Price's St. SE1 **116 G3**
Prideaux Pl. WC1 **112 C2**
Priest Ct. EC2 **112 H8**
Primrose Hill EC4 **112 E9**
Primrose St. EC2 **113 M6**
Prince Albert Rd. NW1 **110 D1**
Prince Albert Rd. NW8 **110 D1**
Prince Consort Rd. SW7 **114 A6**
Prince of Wales Gate SW7 **114 C5**
Prince of Wales Pas. NW1 **111 L3**
Princelet St. E1 **113 Q6**
Prince's Arc. SW1 **115 M2**
Princes Gdns. SW7 **114 B6**
Princes Gate SW7 **114 B5**
Princes Gate Ct. SW7 **114 B5**
Princes Gate Ms. SW7 **114 B6**
Princes Pl. SW1 **115 M2**
Princes St. EC2 **113 K9**
Princes St. W1 **111 K9**
Princess St. SE1 **116 G7**
Princeton St. WC1 **112 B7**
Printer St. EC4 **112 E8**
Printing Ho. Yd. E2 **113 N3**
Prioress St. SE1 **117 L7**
Procter St. WC1 **112 B7**
Providence Ct. W1 **110 H10**
Providence Row N1 **112 B1**
Provost Est. N1 **113 K2**
Provost St. N1 **113 K1**
Prudent Pas. EC2 **113 K8**
Pudding La. EC3 **117 L1**
Puddle Dock EC4 **112 G10**
Puma Ct. E1 **113 P6**
Pump Ct. EC4 **112 D9**
Purbrook Est. SE1 **117 N5**
Purbrook St. SE1 **117 N6**

Q

Quadrant Arc. W1 **115 M1**
Quaker St. E1 **113 P5**
Quality Ct. WC2 **112 D8**
Quebec Ms. W1 **110 F9**
Queen Anne Ms. W1 **111 K7**
Queen Anne St. W1 **111 J8**
Queen Anne's Gate SW1 **115 N5**
Queen Anne's Wk. WC1 **112 A5**
Queen Elizabeth St. SE1 **117 P4**
Queen Sq. WC1 **112 A6**
Queen Sq. Pl. WC1 **112 A5**
Queen St. EC4 **113 J10**
Queen St. W1 **115 J2**
Queen St. Pl. EC4 **117 J1**
Queen Victoria St. EC4 **112 G10**
Queenhithe EC4 **113 J10**
Queens Head Yd. SE1 **117 K3**
Queen's Wk. SW1 **115 L3**
Queens Yd. WC1 **111 M5**
Queensberry Ms. W. SW7 **114 A8**
Queensberry Pl. SW7 **114 A8**
Queensberry Way SW7 **114 A8**
Queensbridge Rd. E2 **113 Q1**
Quick St. N1 **112 G1**
Quilp St. SE1 **116 H4**

R

Radnor Ms. W2 **110 B9**
Radnor Pl. W2 **110 C9**
Radnor St. EC1 **113 J3**
Railway App. SE1 **117 L3**
Railway St. N1 **112 A1**
Rainsford St. W2 **110 C8**
Ramillies Pl. W1 **111 L9**
Ramillies St. W1 **111 L9**
Rampayne St. SW1 **115 N10**
Randall Rd. SE11 **116 B9**
Randall Row SE11 **116 B9**
Ranelagh Gro. SW1 **114 H10**
Ranston St. NW1 **110 C6**
Raphael St. SW7 **114 E5**
Rathbone Pl. W1 **111 N7**
Rathbone St. W1 **111 M7**
Ravenscroft St. E2 **113 Q1**
Ravent Rd. SE11 **116 C8**
Ravey St. EC2 **113 M4**
Rawlings St. SW3 **114 E8**
Rawstorne Pl. EC1 **112 F2**
Rawstorne St. EC1 **112 F2**
Ray St. EC1 **112 E5**
Ray St. Bri. EC1 **112 E5**
Raymond Bldgs. WC1 **112 C6**
Red Lion Ct. EC4 **112 E9**
Red Lion Sq. WC1 **112 B7**
Red Lion St. WC1 **112 B6**
Red Lion Yd. W1 **114 H2**
Red Pl. W1 **110 G10**
Redchurch St. E2 **113 P4**
Redcross Way SE1 **117 J4**
Redhill St. NW1 **111 K2**
Redvers St. N1 **113 N2**
Reece Ms. SW7 **114 A8**
Reedworth St. SE11 **116 E9**
Reeves Ms. W1 **114 G1**
Regan Way N1 **113 M1**
Regency Pl. SW1 **115 P8**
Regency St. SW1 **115 P8**
Regent Pl. W1 **111 M10**
Regent Sq. WC1 **112 A3**
Regent St. SW1 **115 N1**
Regent St. W1 **111 K8**
Regents Pk. NW1 **110 E1**
Regents Pk. Est. NW1 **111 L3**
Regnart Bldgs. NW1 **111 M4**
Relton Ms. SW7 **114 D6**
Rembrandt Clo. SW1 **114 G9**
Remington St. N1 **112 G1**
Remnant St. WC2 **112 B8**
Renfrew Rd. SE11 **116 F8**
Rennie St. SE1 **116 F2**
Rephidim St. SE1 **117 L7**
Retford St. N1 **113 N1**
Rex Pl. W1 **114 H1**
Rhoda St. E2 **113 Q4**
Richards Pl. SW3 **114 D8**
Richardson's Ms. W1 **111 L5**
Richbell Pl. WC1 **112 B6**
Richmond Bldgs. W1 **111 N9**
Richmond Ms. W1 **111 N9**
Richmond Ter. SW1 **115 Q4**
Ridgmount Gdns. WC1 **111 N6**
Ridgmount Pl. WC1 **111 N6**
Ridgmount St. WC1 **111 N6**
Riding Ho. St. W1 **111 K7**
Riley Rd. SE1 **117 P6**
Ring, The W2 **110 C10**
Risborough St. SE1 **116 G4**
Rising Sun Ct. EC1 **112 G7**
River St. EC1 **112 D2**
Riverside Wk. SE1 **116 C2**
Rivington Pl. EC2 **113 N3**
Rivington St. EC2 **113 M3**
Robert Adam St. W1 **110 G8**
Robert Dashwood Way SE17
116 H9
Robert St. NW1 **111 K3**
Robert St. WC2 **116 A1**
Roberts Ms. SW1 **114 G7**
Robert's Pl. EC1 **112 E4**
Rochelle St. E2 **113 P3**
Rochester Row SW1 **115 M8**
Rochester St. SW1 **115 N7**
Rochester Wk. SE1 **117 K2**
Rockingham Est. SE1 **116 H7**
Rockingham St. SE1 **116 H7**
Rocliffe St. N1 **112 G1**
Rodmarton St. W1 **110 F7**
Rodney Pl. SE17 **117 J8**
Rodney Rd. SE17 **117 J8**
Roger St. WC1 **112 C5**
Rolls Bldgs. EC4 **112 D8**
Rolls Pas. EC4 **112 D8**
Rolls Rd. SE1 **117 Q10**
Romilly St. W1 **111 N10**
Romney St. SW1 **115 Q7**
Rood La. EC3 **113 M10**
Ropemaker St. EC2 **113 K6**
Roper La. SE1 **117 N5**
Roscoe St. EC1 **113 J5**
Rose All. SE1 **117 J2**
Rose & Crown Ct. EC2 **112 H8**
Rose & Crown Yd. SW1 **115 M2**
Rose St. WC2 **111 Q10**
Rosebery Ave. EC1 **112 D4**
Rosebery Sq. EC1 **112 D5**
Rosemoor St. SW3 **114 E9**
Rosoman Pl. EC1 **112 E4**
Rosoman St. EC1 **112 E3**
Rossmore Rd. NW1 **110 D5**
Rotary St. SE1 **116 F6**
Rotherham Wk. SE1 **116 F3**
Rothsay St. SE1 **117 M6**
Rotten Row SW1 **114 E4**
Rotten Row SW7 **114 D4**
Roupell St. SE1 **116 E3**
Rowcross St. SE1 **117 Q10**
Royal Arc. W1 **115 L1**
Royal Ave. SW3 **114 E10**
Royal Ex. EC3 **113 L9**
Royal Ex. Ave. EC3 **113 L9**
Royal Ex. Bldgs. EC3 **113 L9**
Royal Mint Pl. E1 **113 Q10**
Royal Mint St. E1 **113 Q10**
Royal Opera Arc. SW1 **115 N2**
Royal St. SE1 **116 C6**
Royalty Ms. W1 **111 N9**
Rufus St. N1 **113 M3**
Rugby St. WC1 **112 B5**
Rupert Ct. W1 **111 N10**
Rupert St. W1 **111 N10**
Rushworth St. SE1 **116 G4**
Russell Ct. SW1 **115 M3**
Russell Sq. WC1 **111 Q5**
Russell St. WC2 **112 A10**
Russia Ct. EC2 **113 J9**
Russia Row EC2 **113 J9**
Rutherford St. SW1 **115 N8**
Rutland Gdns. SW7 **114 D5**
Rutland Gdns. Ms. SW7 **114 D5**
Rutland Gate SW7 **114 D5**
Rutland Gate Ms. SW7 **114 C5**
Rutland Ms. E. SW7 **114 C6**
Rutland Ms. S. SW7 **114 C6**
Rutland Pl. EC1 **112 G6**
Rutland St. SW7 **114 D6**
Ryder Ct. SW1 **115 M2**
Ryder St. SW1 **115 M2**
Ryder Yd. SW1 **115 M2**
Rysbrack St. SW3 **114 E6**

S

Sackville St. W1 **115 M1**
Saffron Hill EC1 **112 E6**
Saffron St. EC1 **112 E6**
Sage Way WC1 **112 B3**
Sail St. SE11 **116 C8**
St. Albans Ms. W2 **110 B6**
St. Albans St. SW1 **115 N1**
St. Alphage Gdns. EC2 **113 J7**
St. Andrew St. EC4 **112 E7**
St. Andrew's Hill EC4 **112 G10**
St. Andrews Pl. NW1 **111 K4**
St. Anne's Ct. W1 **111 N9**
St. Ann's La. SW1 **115 P6**
St. Ann's St. SW1 **115 P6**
St. Anselms Pl. W1 **111 J9**
St. Barnabas St. SW1 **114 H10**
St. Benet's Pl. EC3 **113 L10**
St. Botolph Row EC3 **113 P9**
St. Botolph St. EC3 **113 P8**
St. Bride St. EC4 **112 F8**
St. Bride's Pas. EC4 **112 F9**
St. Catherine's Ms. SW3 **114 E8**
St. Chad's Pl. WC1 **112 A2**
St. Chad's St. WC1 **112 A2**
St. Christopher's Pl. W1 **110 H8**
St. Clare St. EC3 **113 P9**
St. Clement's La. WC2 **112 C9**
St. Cross St. EC1 **112 E6**
St. Dunstan's All. EC3 **117 M1**
St. Dunstan's Hill EC3 **117 M1**
St. Dunstan's La. EC3 **117 M1**
St. Ermin's Hill SW1 **115 N6**
St. George St. W1 **111 K10**
St. Georges Circ. SE1 **116 F6**
St. George's Dr. SW1 **115 K9**
St. Georges Flds. W2 **110 D9**
St. Georges La. EC3 **113 L10**
St. Georges Rd. SE1 **116 E6**
St. Giles High St. WC2 **111 P8**
St. Giles Pas. WC2 **111 P9**
St. Helena St. WC1 **112 D3**
St. Helens Pl. EC3 **113 M8**
St. James's Ct. SW1 **115 M6**
St. James's Mkt. SW1 **115 N1**
St. James's Pk. SW1 **115 N6**
St. James's Pas. EC3 **113 N9**
St. James's Pl. SW1 **115 L3**
St. James's Row EC1 **112 F4**
St. James's Sq. SW1 **115 M2**
St. James's St. SW1 **115 L2**
St. James's Wk. EC1 **112 F4**
St. John St. EC1 **112 F2**
St. Johns Est. N1 **113 L1**
St. John's Est. SE1 **117 P5**
St. John's La. EC1 **112 F5**
St. John's Path EC1 **112 F5**
St. John's Pl. EC1 **112 F5**
St. John's Sq. EC1 **112 F5**
St. John's Wd. Ct. NW8 **110 B3**
St. John's Wd. High St. NW8
110 B1
St. John's Wd. Rd. NW8 **110 A4**
St. John's Wd. Ter. NW8 **110 B1**
St. Katharine's Way E1 **117 Q2**
St. Katherine's Row EC3 **113 N10**
St. Leonards Ct. N1 **113 L2**
St. Luke's Est. EC1 **113 K3**
St. Luke's St. SW3 **114 D10**
St. Margaret's Ct. SE1 **117 K3**
St. Margaret's St. SW1 **115 Q5**
St. Mark St. E1 **113 Q9**
St. Martin's Ct. WC2 **111 Q10**
St. Martin's La. WC2 **111 Q10**
St. Martin's le Grand EC1 **112 H8**
St. Martin's Pl. WC2 **115 Q1**
St. Martin's St. WC2 **115 P1**
St. Mary at Hill EC3 **117 M1**
St. Mary Axe EC3 **113 M9**
St. Mary's Gdns. SE11 **116 E8**
St. Marys Mans. W2 **110 A6**
St. Marys Sq. W2 **110 A6**
St. Marys Ter. W2 **110 A6**
St. Mary's Wk. SE11 **116 E8**
St. Matthew St. SW1 **115 N7**
St. Michael's All. EC3 **113 L9**
St. Michaels St. W2 **110 B8**
St. Mildred's Ct. EC2 **113 K9**
St. Olaves Ct. EC2 **113 K9**
St. Olave's Est. SE1 **117 N4**
St. Olaves Gdns. SE11 **116 D8**
St. Oswulf St. SW1 **115 P9**
St. Paul's Chyd. EC4 **112 G9**
St. Peter's All. EC3 **113 L9**
St. Saviour's Est. SE1 **117 P6**
St. Stephens Row EC4 **113 K10**
St. Swithin's La. EC4 **113 K10**
St. Thomas St. SE1 **117 L3**
St. Vincent St. W1 **110 H7**
Salamanca Pl. SE11 **116 B9**
Salamanca St. SE11 **116 B9**
Sale Pl. W2 **110 C7**
Salisbury Clo. SE17 **117 K8**
Salisbury Ct. EC4 **112 E9**
Salisbury Pl. W1 **110 E6**
Salisbury Sq. EC4 **112 E9**
Salisbury St. NW8 **110 C5**
Salters Hall Ct. EC4 **113 K10**
Samford St. NW8 **110 C5**
Samuel Lewis Trust Dws. SW3
114 C9
Sancroft St. SE11 **116 C10**
Sanctuary, The SW1 **115 P6**
Sanctuary St. SE1 **117 J5**
Sandell St. SE1 **116 D4**
Sandland St. WC1 **112 C7**
Sandwich St. WC1 **111 Q3**
Sandys Row E1 **113 N7**
Sans Wk. EC1 **112 E4**
Saracen's Head Yd. EC3 **113 P9**
Sarah St. N1 **113 N2**
Sardinia St. WC2 **112 B9**
Satchwell Rd. E2 **113 Q3**
Satchwell St. E2 **113 Q3**
Savage Gdns. EC3 **113 N10**
Savile Row W1 **111 L10**
Savoy Bldgs. WC2 **116 B1**
Savoy Ct. WC2 **116 A1**
Savoy Hill WC2 **116 B1**
Savoy Pl. WC2 **116 A1**
Savoy Row WC2 **116 B1**
Savoy Steps WC2 **116 B1**
Savoy St. WC2 **116 B1**
Savoy Way WC2 **116 B1**
Sawyer St. SE1 **116 H4**
Scala St. W1 **111 M6**
Scarborough St. E1 **113 Q9**
Scawfell St. E2 **113 Q1**
Sclater St. E1 **113 P4**
Scoresby St. SE1 **116 F3**
Scotland Pl. SW1 **115 Q3**
Scotswood St. EC1 **112 E4**
Scott Ellis Gdns. NW8 **110 A3**
Scott's Yd EC4 **113 K10**
Scovell Cres. SE1 **116 H5**
Scovell Rd. SE1 **116 H5**
Scrutton St. EC2 **113 M5**
Seacoal La. EC4 **112 F9**
Seaford St. WC1 **112 A3**
Seaforth Pl. SW1 **115 M6**
Searles Rd. SE1 **117 L8**
Seaton Clo. SE11 **116 E10**
Seaton Pl. NW1 **111 L4**
Sebastian St. EC1 **112 G3**
Secker St. SE1 **116 D3**
Sedan Way SE17 **117 M10**
Sedding St. SW1 **114 G8**
Seddon St. WC1 **112 C3**
Sedley Pl. W1 **111 J9**
Seething La. EC3 **113 N10**
Sekforde St. EC1 **112 F5**
Sellon Ms. SE11 **116 C9**
Selwood Pl. SW7 **114 A10**
Selwood Ter. SW7 **114 A10**
Semley Pl. SW1 **114 H9**
Serjeants Inn EC4 **112 E9**
Serle St. WC2 **112 C8**
Serpentine Rd. W2 **114 E3**
Setchell Rd. SE1 **117 P8**
Setchell Way SE1 **117 P8**
Seville St. SW1 **114 F5**
Seward St. EC1 **112 G3**
Seymour Ms. W1 **110 G8**
Seymour Pl. W1 **110 D6**
Seymour St. W1 **110 E9**
Seymour St. W2 **110 E9**
Shacklewell St. E2 **113 Q4**
Shad Thames SE1 **117 P3**
Shaftesbury Ave. W1 **111 N10**
Shaftesbury Ave. WC2 **115 N1**
Shaftesbury St. N1 **113 J1**
Shafto Ms. SW1 **114 E7**
Shand St. SE1 **117 N3**
Shavers Pl. SW1 **115 N1**
Sheffield St. WC2 **112 B9**
Shelton St. WC2 **111 Q9**
Shenfield St. N1 **113 N1**
Shepherd Mkt. W1 **115 J3**
Shepherd St. W1 **115 J3**
Shepherdess Pl. N1 **113 J2**
Shepherdess Wk. N1 **113 J1**
Shepherds Pl. W1 **110 G10**
Sheraton St. W1 **111 N9**
Sherborne La. EC4 **113 K10**
Sherlock Ms. W1 **110 G6**
Sherwood St. W1 **111 M10**
Shillibeer Pl. W1 **110 D7**
Ship and Mermaid Row SE1
117 L4
Ship Tavern Pas. EC3 **113 M10**
Shipton St. E2 **113 Q2**
Shoe La. EC4 **112 E8**
Shoreditch High St. E1 **113 N5**
Shorncliffe Rd. SE1 **117 P10**
Short St. SE1 **116 E4**
Shorter St. E1 **113 Q10**
Shorts Gdns. WC2 **111 Q9**
Shouldham St. W1 **110 D7**
Shropshire Pl. WC1 **111 M5**
Shroton St. NW1 **110 C6**
Sicilian Ave. WC1 **112 A7**
Siddons La. NW1 **110 F5**
Sidford Pl. SE1 **116 C7**
Sidmouth St. WC1 **112 A3**
Sidney Gro. EC1 **112 F1**
Silbury St. N1 **113 K2**
Silex St. SE1 **116 G5**
Silk St. EC2 **113 J6**
Silver Pl. W1 **111 M10**
Silvester St. SE1 **117 K5**
Simla Ho. SE1 **117 L5**
Singer St. EC2 **113 L3**
Sise La. EC4 **113 K9**
Sivill Ho. E2 **113 Q2**
Skinner Pl. SW1 **114 G9**
Skinner St. EC1 **112 E3**
Skinners La. EC4 **113 J10**
Skipton St. SE1 **116 G7**
Slingsby Pl. WC2 **111 Q10**
Sloane Ave. SW3 **114 D9**
Sloane Ct. E. SW3 **114 G10**
Sloane Ct. W. SW3 **114 G10**
Sloane Gdns. SW1 **114 G9**
Sloane Sq. SW1 **114 F9**
Sloane St. SW1 **114 F6**
Sloane Ter. SW1 **114 F8**
Smallbrook Ms. W2 **110 A9**
Smart's Pl. WC2 **112 A8**
Smith Sq. SW1 **115 Q7**
Smith St. SW3 **114 E10**
Smithfield St. EC1 **112 F7**
Smith's Ct. W1 **111 M10**
Snow Hill EC1 **112 F7**
Snow Hill Ct. EC1 **112 G8**
Snowden St. EC2 **113 M5**
Snowsfields SE1 **117 L4**
Soho Sq. W1 **111 N8**
Soho St. W1 **111 N8**
Soley Ms. WC1 **112 D2**
Somers Cres. W2 **110 C9**
Somers Ms. W2 **110 C9**
South Audley St. W1 **114 H1**
South Carriage Dr. SW7 **114 C4**
South Cres. WC1 **111 N7**
South Eaton Pl. SW1 **114 H8**
South Molton La. W1 **111 J9**
South Molton St. W1 **111 J9**
South Par. SW3 **114 B10**
South Pl. EC2 **113 L7**
South Pl. Ms. EC2 **113 L7**
South Sq. WC1 **112 D7**
South St. W1 **114 H2**
South Tenter St. E1 **113 Q9**
South Ter. SW7 **114 C8**
South Wf. Rd. W2 **110 A8**
Southall Pl. SE1 **117 K5**
Southampton Bldgs. WC2 **112 D7**
Southampton Pl. WC1 **112 A7**
Southampton Row WC1 **112 A6**
Southampton St. WC2 **112 A10**
Southwark Bri. EC4 **117 J1**
Southwark Bri. SE1 **117 J1**
Southwark Bri. Rd. SE1 **116 H5**
Southwark Gro. SE1 **116 H3**
Southwark Pk. Rd. SE16 **117 Q8**
Southwark St. SE1 **116 G2**
Southwick Ms. W2 **110 B8**
Southwick Pl. W2 **110 C9**
Southwick St. W2 **110 C8**
Spa Grn. Est. EC1 **112 E2**
Spa Rd. SE16 **117 P7**
Spafield St. EC1 **112 D4**
Spanish Pl. W1 **110 H8**
Speedy Pl. WC1 **111 Q3**
Spencer St. EC1 **112 F3**
Spenser St. SW1 **115 M6**
Spital Sq. E1 **113 N6**
Spital Yd. E1 **113 N6**
Spitalfields Mkt. E1 **113 P6**
Sprimont Pl. SW3 **114 E10**
Spring Gdns. SW1 **115 P2**
Spring Ms. W1 **110 F6**
Spring St. W2 **110 A9**
Spur Rd. SW1 **115 L5**
Spurgeon St. SE1 **117 K7**
Stable Yd. SW1 **115 L4**
Stable Yd. Rd. SW1 **115 M4**
Stables Way SE11 **116 D10**
Stacey St. WC2 **111 P9**
Stackhouse St. SW3 **114 E6**
Staff St. EC1 **113 L3**
Stafford Pl. SW1 **115 L6**
Stafford St. W1 **115 L2**
Stag Pl. SW1 **115 L6**
Stainer St. SE1 **117 L3**
Staining La. EC2 **113 J8**
Stalbridge St. NW1 **110 D6**
Stamford St. SE1 **116 D3**
Stamp Pl. E2 **113 P2**
Standard Pl. EC2 **113 N3**
Stanford Pl. SE17 **117 M9**
Stanford St. SW1 **115 N9**
Stanhope Gate W1 **114 H2**
Stanhope Par. NW1 **111 L2**
Stanhope Pl. W2 **110 E9**
Stanhope Row W1 **115 J3**
Stanhope St. NW1 **111 L2**
Stanhope Ter. W2 **110 B10**
Stanley Pas. NW1 **111 Q1**
Stanworth St. SE1 **117 P5**
Staple Inn Bldgs. WC1 **112 D7**
Staple St. SE1 **117 L5**

Star St. W2 **110 B8**
Star Yd. WC2 **112 D8**
Starcross St. NW1 **111 M3**
Stead St. SE17 **117 K9**
Stedham Pl. WC1 **111 Q8**
Steedman St. SE17 **116 H9**
Stephen Ms. W1 **111 N7**
Stephen St. W1 **111 N7**
Stephenson Way NW1 **111 M4**
Sterling St. SW7 **114 D5**
Sterry St. SE1 **117 K5**
Stevens St. SE1 **117 N6**
Steward St. E1 **113 N6**
Stewart's Gro. SW3 **114 C10**
Stillington St. SW1 **115 M8**
Stone Bldgs. WC2 **112 C7**
Stone Ho. Ct. EC3 **113 N8**
Stonecutter St. EC4 **112 F8**
Stones End St. SE1 **116 H5**
Stoney La. E1 **113 P8**
Stoney St. SE1 **117 K2**
Store St. WC1 **111 N7**
Storey's Gate SW1 **115 P5**
Stothard Pl. EC2 **113 N6**
Stoughton Clo. SE11 **116 C9**
Stourcliffe St. W1 **110 E9**
Strand WC2 **115 Q1**
Strand La. WC2 **112 C10**
Stratford Pl. W1 **111 J9**
Strathearn Pl. W2 **110 C10**
Stratton St. W1 **115 K2**
Streatham St. WC1 **111 Q8**
Strouts Pl. E2 **113 P2**
Strutton Grd. SW1 **115 N6**
Strype St. E1 **113 P7**
Studio Pl. SW1 **114 F5**
Studland SE17 **117 K10**
Stukeley St. WC2 **112 A8**
Sturge St. SE1 **116 H4**
Sturt St. N1 **113 J1**
Sudeley St. N1 **112 G1**
Sudrey St. SE1 **116 H5**
Suffolk La. EC4 **113 K10**
Suffolk Pl. SW1 **115 P2**
Suffolk St. SW1 **115 P1**
Sugar Bakers Ct. EC3 **113 N9**
Sullivan Rd. SE11 **116 E8**
Summers St. EC1 **112 D5**
Sumner Pl. SW7 **114 B9**
Sumner Pl. Ms. SW7 **114 B9**
Sumner St. SE1 **116 G2**
Sun Ct. EC3 **113 L9**
Sun St. EC2 **113 L6**
Sun St. Pas. EC2 **113 M7**
Surrey Lo. SE1 **116 D7**
Surrey Row SE1 **116 F4**
Surrey Sq. SE17 **117 M10**
Surrey St. WC2 **112 C10**
Surrey Ter. SE17 **117 N10**
Sussex Gdns. W2 **110 A10**
Sussex Ms. E. W2 **110 B9**
Sussex Ms. W. W2 **110 B10**
Sussex Pl. NW1 **110 E3**
Sussex Pl. W2 **110 B9**
Sussex Sq. W2 **110 B10**
Sutherland Row SW1 **115 K10**
Sutherland St. SW1 **115 J10**
Sutton Est. SW3 **114 D10**
Sutton Row W1 **111 P8**
Sutton's Way EC1 **113 J5**
Swallow Pas. W1 **111 K9**
Swallow Pl. W1 **111 K9**
Swallow St. W1 **115 M1**
Swan La. EC4 **117 K1**
Swan Mead SE1 **117 M7**
Swan St. SE1 **117 J6**
Swanfield St. E2 **113 P3**
Sweeney Cres. SE1 **117 Q5**
Swinton Pl. WC1 **112 B2**
Swinton St. WC1 **112 B2**
Sycamore St. EC1 **112 H5**
Sydney Clo. SW3 **114 B9**
Sydney Ms. SW3 **114 B9**
Sydney Pl. SW7 **114 B9**
Sydney St. SW3 **114 C10**
Symons St. SW3 **114 F9**

T

Tabard Gdn. Est. SE1 **117 L5**
Tabard St. SE1 **117 K5**
Tabernacle St. EC2 **113 L5**
Tachbrook Ms. SW1 **115 L8**
Tachbrook St. SW1 **115 M9**
Talbot Ct. EC3 **113 L10**
Talbot Sq. W2 **110 B9**
Talbot Yd. SE1 **117 K3**
Tallis St. EC4 **112 E10**
Tankerton St. WC1 **112 A3**
Tanner St. SE1 **117 N5**
Tanswell Est. SE1 **116 E5**
Tanswell St. SE1 **116 D5**
Taplow SE17 **117 L10**
Taplow St. N1 **113 J1**
Tarn St. SE1 **116 H7**
Tarrant Pl. W1 **110 E7**
Tatum St. SE17 **117 L9**
Taunton Ms. NW1 **110 E5**
Taunton Pl. NW1 **110 E4**
Tavistock Pl. WC1 **111 Q4**
Tavistock Sq. WC1 **111 P4**
Tavistock St. WC2 **112 A10**
Taviton St. WC1 **111 N4**
Tavy Clo. SE11 **116 E10**
Telegraph St. EC2 **113 K8**
Temple EC4 **112 D10**
Temple Ave. EC4 **112 E10**
Temple La. EC4 **112 E9**
Temple Pl. WC2 **112 C10**
Temple W. Ms. SE11 **116 F7**
Tenison Ct. W1 **111 L10**
Tenison Way SE1 **116 C3**
Tennis St. SE1 **117 K4**
Tenter Grd. E1 **113 P7**
Tenterden St. W1 **111 K9**
Terminus Pl. SW1 **115 K7**
Thanet St. WC1 **111 Q3**
Thavies Inn EC1 **112 E8**
Thayer St. W1 **110 H7**
Theed St. SE1 **116 E3**
Theobald St. SE1 **117 K7**
Theobald's Rd. WC1 **112 A7**
Theseus Wk. N1 **112 G1**
Thirleby Rd. SW1 **115 M7**
Thomas Doyle St. SE1 **116 G6**
Thoresby St. N1 **113 J2**
Thorndike St. SW1 **115 N9**
Thorney St. SW1 **115 Q8**
Thornhaugh Ms. WC1 **111 P5**
Thornhaugh St. WC1 **111 P6**
Thornton Pl. W1 **110 E6**
Thrale St. SE1 **117 J3**
Thrawl St. E1 **113 Q7**
Threadneedle St. EC2 **113 L9**
Three Cups Yd. WC1 **112 C7**
Three Kings Yd. W1 **111 J10**
Three Oak La. SE1 **117 P4**
Throgmorton Ave. EC2 **113 L8**
Throgmorton St. EC2 **113 L8**
Thrush St. SE17 **116 H10**
Thurloe Clo. SW7 **114 C8**
Thurloe Pl. SW7 **114 B8**
Thurloe Pl. Ms. SW7 **114 B8**
Thurloe Sq. SW7 **114 C8**
Thurloe St. SW7 **114 B8**
Thurlow St. SE17 **117 L10**
Tilney Ct. EC1 **113 J4**
Tilney St. W1 **114 H2**
Timber St. EC1 **112 H4**
Tinworth St. SE11 **116 A10**
Tisbury Ct. W1 **111 N10**
Tisdall Pl. SE17 **117 L9**
Titchborne Row W2 **110 D9**
Tiverton St. SE1 **116 H6**
Tokenhouse Yd. EC2 **113 K8**
Tolmers Sq. NW1 **111 M4**
Tomlinson Clo. E2 **113 Q3**
Tompion St. EC1 **112 F3**
Tonbridge St. WC1 **111 Q2**
Tonbridge Wk. WC1 **111 Q2**
Took's Ct. EC4 **112 D8**
Tooley St. SE1 **117 L2**
Topham St. EC1 **112 D4**
Torrens St. N1 **112 E1**
Torrington Pl. WC1 **111 M6**
Torrington Sq. WC1 **111 P5**
Tothill St. SW1 **115 N5**
Tottenham Ct. Rd. W1 **111 M5**
Tottenham Ms. W1 **111 M6**
Tottenham St. W1 **111 M7**
Toulmin St. SE1 **116 H5**
Tower Bri. E1 **117 P3**
Tower Bri. SE1 **117 P3**
Tower Bri. App. E1 **117 P2**
Tower Bri. Rd. SE1 **117 M7**
Tower Ct. WC2 **111 Q9**
Tower Hill EC3 **117 P1**
Tower Pl. EC3 **117 N1**
Tower Royal EC4 **113 J10**
Tower St. WC2 **111 P9**
Townley St. SE17 **117 K10**
Townsend St. SE17 **117 M8**
Toynbee St. E1 **113 P7**
Trafalgar Sq. WC2 **115 P2**
Trafalgar St. SE17 **117 K10**
Transept St. NW1 **110 D7**
Trebeck St. W1 **115 J2**
Tresham Cres. NW8 **110 C4**
Treveris St. SE1 **116 G3**
Trevor Pl. SW7 **114 D5**
Trevor Sq. SW7 **114 E5**
Trevor St. SW7 **114 D5**
Trinity Ch. Sq. SE1 **117 J6**
Trinity Sq. EC3 **117 N1**
Trinity St. SE1 **117 J5**
Trio Pl. SE1 **117 J5**
Triton Sq. NW1 **111 L4**
Trump St. EC2 **113 J9**
Trundle St. SE1 **116 H4**
Tryon St. SW3 **114 E10**
Tudor Pl. W1 **111 N8**
Tudor St. EC4 **112 E10**
Tufton St. SW1 **116 A7**
Turk's Head Yd. EC1 **112 F6**
Turks Row SW3 **114 F10**
Turnagain La. EC4 **112 F8**
Turnmill St. EC1 **112 E5**
Turnpike Ho. EC1 **112 G3**
Turquand St. SE17 **117 J9**
Turville St. E2 **113 Q4**
Tweezer's All. WC2 **112 D10**
Twyford Pl. WC2 **112 B8**
Tyburn Way W1 **110 F10**
Tyers Est. SE1 **117 M4**
Tyers Gate SE1 **117 M5**
Tyler's Ct. W1 **111 N9**
Tyne St. E1 **113 Q8**
Tysoe St. EC1 **112 D3**
Tyssen St. N1 **113 N1**

U

Udall St. SW1 **115 M9**
Ufford St. SE1 **116 E4**
Ulster Pl. NW1 **111 J5**
Ulster Ter. NW1 **111 J4**
Undershaft EC3 **113 M9**
Underwood Row N1 **113 J2**
Underwood St. N1 **113 J2**
Union Ct. EC2 **113 M8**
Union St. SE1 **116 G3**
Union Wk. E2 **113 N2**
University St. WC1 **111 M5**
Unwin Rd. SW7 **114 A6**
Upnor Way SE17 **117 N10**
Upper Belgrave St. SW1 **114 H6**
Upper Berkeley St. W1 **110 E9**
Upper Brook St. W1 **114 G1**
Upper Grosvenor St. W1 **114 G1**
Upper Grd. SE1 **116 D2**
Upper Harley St. NW1 **110 H5**
Upper James St. W1 **111 M10**
Upper John St. W1 **111 M10**
Upper Marsh SE1 **116 C6**
Upper Montagu St. W1 **110 E6**
Upper St. Martin's La. WC2 **111 Q10**
Upper Tachbrook St. SW1 **115 M8**
Upper Thames St. EC4 **112 G10**
Upper Wimpole St. W1 **110 H6**
Upper Woburn Pl. WC1 **111 P3**

V

Valentine Pl. SE1 **116 F4**
Valentine Row SE1 **116 F5**
Vandon Pas. SW1 **115 M6**
Vandon St. SW1 **115 M6**
Vandy St. EC2 **113 M5**
Vane St. SW1 **115 M8**
Varndell St. NW1 **111 L2**
Vauban Est. SE16 **117 Q7**
Vauban St. SE16 **117 Q7**
Vauxhall Bri. Rd. SW1 **115 M8**
Vauxhall Wk. SE11 **116 B10**
Venables St. NW8 **110 B5**
Vere St. W1 **111 J9**
Vernon Pl. WC1 **112 A7**
Vernon Ri. WC1 **112 C2**
Vernon Sq. WC1 **112 C2**
Verulam Bldgs. WC1 **112 C6**
Verulam St. WC1 **112 D6**
Vestry St. N1 **113 K2**
Victoria Ave. EC2 **113 N7**
Victoria Embk. EC4 **112 D10**
Victoria Embk. SW1 **116 A4**
Victoria Embk. WC2 **116 C1**
Victoria Sq. SW1 **115 K6**
Victoria Sta. SW1 **115 K8**
Victoria St. SW1 **115 L7**
Victory Pl. SE17 **117 J8**
Vigo St. W1 **115 L1**
Villiers St. WC2 **116 A2**
Vince St. EC1 **113 L3**
Vincent Sq. SW1 **115 N8**
Vincent St. SW1 **115 N8**
Vine Hill EC1 **112 D5**
Vine La. SE1 **117 N3**
Vine St. EC3 **113 P9**
Vine St. W1 **115 M1**
Vine St. Bri. EC1 **112 E5**
Vine Yd. SE1 **117 J5**
Vinegar Yd. SE1 **117 M4**
Vineyard Wk. EC1 **112 D4**
Vintners Pl. EC4 **113 J10**
Virgil Pl. W1 **110 E7**
Virgil St. SE1 **116 C6**
Virginia Rd. E2 **113 P3**
Viscount St. EC1 **112 H6**

W

Wadding St. SE17 **117 K9**
Waithman St. EC4 **112 F9**
Wakefield Ms. WC1 **112 A3**
Wakefield St. WC1 **112 A3**
Wakley St. EC1 **112 F2**
Walbrook EC4 **113 K10**
Walcorde Ave. SE17 **117 J9**
Walcot Sq. SE11 **116 E8**
Walcott St. SW1 **115 M8**
Walkers Ct. W1 **111 N10**
Wallis All. SE1 **117 J5**
Walmer Pl. W1 **110 E6**
Walmer St. W1 **110 E6**
Walnut Tree Wk. SE11 **116 D8**
Walpole St. SW3 **114 E10**
Walton Pl. SW3 **114 E6**
Walton St. SW3 **114 D8**
Walworth Rd. SE1 **116 H9**
Walworth Rd. SE17 **116 H9**
Wansey St. SE17 **117 J9**
Wardens Gro. SE1 **116 H3**
Wardour Ms. W1 **111 M9**
Wardour St. W1 **111 M8**
Wardrobe Pl. EC4 **112 G9**
Wardrobe Ter. EC4 **112 G10**
Warner St. EC1 **112 D5**
Warner Yd. EC1 **112 D5**
Warren Ms. W1 **111 L5**
Warren St. W1 **111 K5**
Warwick Ct. WC1 **112 C7**
Warwick Ho. St. SW1 **115 P2**
Warwick La. EC4 **112 G9**
Warwick Pl. N. SW1 **115 L9**
Warwick Row SW1 **115 K6**
Warwick Sq. EC4 **112 G8**
Warwick Sq. SW1 **115 L10**
Warwick Sq. Ms. SW1 **115 N9**
Warwick St. W1 **111 M10**
Warwick Way SW1 **115 K10**
Warwick Yd. EC2 **113 J5**
Water St. WC2 **112 C10**
Watergate EC4 **112 F10**
Watergate Wk. WC2 **116 A1**
Waterloo Bri. SE1 **116 B1**
Waterloo Bri. WC2 **116 B1**
Waterloo Pl. SW1 **115 N2**
Waterloo Rd. SE1 **116 D4**
Waterson St. E2 **113 N2**
Watling Ct. EC4 **113 J9**
Watling St. EC4 **112 H9**
Watson Ms. W1 **110 D7**
Watts Way SW7 **114 B6**
Waverton St. W1 **115 J2**
Webb St. SE1 **117 M7**
Webber Row SE1 **116 E5**
Webber St. SE1 **116 F5**
Wedgwood Ms. W1 **111 P9**
Weighouse St. W1 **110 H9**
Weir's Pas. NW1 **111 P2**
Welbeck St. W1 **110 H7**
Welbeck Way W1 **111 J8**
Well Ct. EC4 **113 J9**
Weller St. SE1 **116 H4**
Wellers Ct NW1 **111 Q1**
Wellesley Pl. NW1 **111 N3**
Wellesley Ter. N1 **113 J2**
Wellington Ct. NW8 **110 A1**
Wellington Pl. NW8 **110 B2**
Wellington Row E2 **113 Q2**
Wellington Sq. SW3 **114 E10**
Wellington St. WC2 **112 A10**
Wells Ms. W1 **111 M7**
Wells Sq. WC1 **112 B3**
Wells St. W1 **111 L7**
Wells Way SW7 **114 A6**
Wendover SE17 **117 M10**
Wenlock Ct. N1 **113 L1**
Wenlock Rd. N1 **112 H1**
Wenlock St. N1 **113 J1**
Wentworth St. E1 **113 P8**
Werrington St. NW1 **111 M1**
Wesley Clo. SE17 **116 G9**
Wesley St. W1 **110 H7**
West Carriage Dr. W2 **114 C1**
West Cen. St. WC1 **111 Q8**
West Eaton Pl. SW1 **114 G8**
West Eaton Pl. Ms. SW1 **114 G7**
West Halkin St. SW1 **114 G6**
West Harding St. EC4 **112 E8**
West Ms. SW1 **115 L9**
West Poultry Ave. EC1 **112 F7**
West Smithfield EC1 **112 F7**
West Sq. SE11 **116 F7**
West St. WC2 **111 P10**
West Tenter St. E1 **113 Q9**
West Warwick Pl. SW1 **115 L9**
Westbourne Cres. W2 **110 A10**
Westbourne Cres. Ms. W2 **110 A10**
Westbourne St. W2 **110 A10**
Westland Pl. N1 **113 K2**
Westminster Bri. SE1 **116 A5**
Westminster Bri. SW1 **116 A5**
Westminster Bri. Rd. SE1 **116 C5**
Westminster Cathedral Piazza SW1 **115 L7**
Westmoreland St. W1 **110 H7**
Weston Ri. WC1 **112 C1**
Weston St. SE1 **117 L4**
Weymouth Ms. W1 **111 J6**
Weymouth St. W1 **110 H7**
Whalebone Ct. EC2 **113 L8**
Wharf Rd. N1 **112 H1**
Wharton St. WC1 **112 C3**
Wheatley St. W1 **110 H7**
Wheler St. E1 **113 P5**
Whetstone Pk. WC2 **112 B8**
Whichcote St. SE1 **116 B3**
Whidborne St. WC1 **112 A3**
Whiskin St. EC1 **112 F3**
Whitby St. E1 **113 P4**
Whitcomb St. WC2 **115 P1**
White Hart St. SE11 **116 E10**
White Hart Yd. SE1 **117 K3**
White Horse St. W1 **115 K3**
White Kennet St. E1 **113 N8**
White Lion Ct. EC3 **113 M9**
White Lion Hill EC4 **112 G10**
White Lion St. N1 **112 D1**
White Lion Yd. W1 **111 J10**
Whitechapel High St. E1 **113 Q8**
Whitecross Pl. EC2 **113 L6**
Whitecross St. EC1 **113 J4**
Whitecross St. EC2 **113 J6**
Whitefriars St. EC4 **112 E9**
Whitehall SW1 **115 Q2**
Whitehall Ct. SW1 **116 A3**
Whitehall Gdns. SW1 **115 Q3**
Whitehall Pl. E7 **115 Q3**
Whitehaven St. NW8 **110 C5**
Whitehead's Gro. SW3 **114 D10**
Whitehorse Rd. SE1 **116 E6**
Whites Grds. SE1 **117 N5**
Whites Grds. Est. SE1 **117 N4**
White's Row E1 **113 P7**
Whitfield Pl. W1 **111 L5**
Whitfield St. W1 **111 L5**
Whitgift St. SE11 **116 B8**
Whittaker St. SW1 **114 G9**
Whittington Ave. EC3 **113 M9**
Whittlesey St. SE1 **116 E3**
Wickham St. SE11 **116 B10**
Wicklow St. WC1 **112 B2**
Widegate St. E1 **113 N7**
Wigmore Pl. W1 **111 J8**
Wigmore St. W1 **110 G9**
Wilbraham Pl. SW1 **114 F8**
Wilcox Pl. SW1 **115 M7**
Wild Ct. WC2 **112 B8**
Wild St. WC2 **112 A9**
Wild's Rents SE1 **117 M6**
Wilfred St. SW1 **115 L6**
Wilkes St. E1 **113 Q6**
Wilks Pl. N1 **113 N1**
William IV St. WC2 **115 Q1**
William Ms. SW1 **114 F5**
William Rd. NW1 **111 L3**
William St. SW1 **114 F5**
Willoughby St. WC1 **111 Q7**
Willow Pl. SW1 **115 M8**
Willow St. EC2 **113 M4**
Willow Wk. SE1 **117 N8**
Wilmington Sq. WC1 **112 D3**
Wilmington St. WC1 **112 D3**
Wilson St. EC2 **113 L6**
Wilton Cres. SW1 **114 G5**
Wilton Ms. SW1 **114 H6**
Wilton Pl. SW1 **114 G5**
Wilton Rd. SW1 **115 K7**
Wilton Row SW1 **114 G5**
Wilton St. SW1 **115 J6**
Wilton Ter. SW1 **114 G6**
Wiltshire Clo. SW3 **114 E9**
Wimpole Ms. W1 **111 J6**
Wimpole St. W1 **111 J7**
Winchester Clo. SE17 **116 G9**
Winchester Sq. SE1 **117 K2**
Winchester St. SW1 **115 K10**
Winchester Wk. SE1 **117 K2**
Wincott St. SE11 **116 E9**
Windmill St. W1 **111 N7**
Windmill Wk. SE1 **116 E3**
Windsor Pl. SW1 **115 M7**
Windsor Ter. N1 **113 J2**
Wine Office Ct. EC4 **112 E9**
Winnett St. W1 **111 N10**
Winsland Ms. W2 **110 A8**
Winsland St. W2 **110 A8**
Winsley St. W1 **111 L8**
Woburn Pl. WC1 **111 P4**
Woburn Sq. WC1 **111 P5**
Woburn Wk. WC1 **111 P3**
Wollaston Clo. SE1 **116 H8**
Wolseley St. SE1 **117 Q5**
Wolverton SE17 **117 M10**
Wood St. EC2 **113 J9**
Woodbridge St. EC1 **112 F4**
Woods Ms. W1 **110 G10**
Woods Pl. SE1 **117 N7**
Woodseer St. E1 **113 Q6**
Woodstock Ms. W1 **110 H7**
Woodstock St. W1 **111 J9**
Wootton St. SE1 **116 E3**
Worcester Pl. EC4 **113 J10**
Wordsworth Rd. SE1 **117 P9**
Worgan St. SE11 **116 B10**
World Trade Cen. E1 **117 Q1**
Wormwood St. EC2 **113 M8**
Worship St. EC2 **113 L5**
Wren St. WC1 **112 C4**
Wybert St. NW1 **111 L4**
Wyclif St. EC1 **112 F3**
Wyndham Ms. W1 **110 E7**
Wyndham Pl. W1 **110 E7**
Wyndham St. W1 **110 E6**
Wyndham Yd. W1 **110 E7**
Wynyard Ter. SE11 **116 C10**
Wynyatt St. EC1 **112 F3**
Wythburn Pl. W1 **110 E9**

Y

Yardley St. WC1 **112 D3**
Yarmouth Pl. W1 **115 J3**
Yeoman's Row SW3 **114 D7**
Yeomans Yd. E1 **113 Q10**
York Bri. NW1 **110 G4**
York Bldgs. WC2 **116 A1**
York Gate NW1 **110 G5**
York Pl. WC2 **116 A1**
York Rd. SE1 **116 C4**
York St. W1 **110 E7**
York Ter. E. NW1 **110 H5**
York Ter. W. NW1 **110 G5**
Yorkshire Grey Yd. WC1 **112 B7**
Young's Bldgs. EC1 **113 J4**

Z

Zoar St. SE1 **116 H2**

Aberdeen 125
Bath 126
Birmingham.......126
Blackpool 127
Bournemouth 127
Bradford 128
Brighton.............128
Bristol 129
Cambridge 129
Cardiff...............130
Chester...............130
Coventry............131
Derby 131
Dover 132
Dundee..............132
Edinburgh..........133
Exeter 133
Folkestone..........134
Glasgow 134
Gloucester..........135
Hull 135
Leeds.................136
Leicester 136
Liverpool............136
Manchester 137
Milton Keynes 138
Newcastle...........138
Norwich 139
Nottingham 139
Oxford 140
Plymouth...........140
Portsmouth 141
Sheffield............141
Southampton......142
Stratford 142
Swansea 143
Torquay 143
Wolverhampton .144
York 144

Motorways
Throughroutes
Other Roads
One-way
Restricted Roads
Pedestrian Roads
Footpaths
Shopping Area
Car Park (covered)
Car Park (open)
Tourist Information Centre
Abbey/Cathedral
Church
Public Convenience
Metro

ABERDEEN

Academy Street B3
Affleck Street B4
Albert Quay D4
Albury Road A4
Back Wynd B2
Baker Street A1
Bath Street B3
Beach Boulevard D1
Belmont Street B2
Berry Street C1
Blackfriars Street B1/2
Blaikies Quay D3
Bon Accord Cres. A4/B4
Bon Accord Square A3
Bon Accord Street B3/4
Bon Accord Terrace A3
Bridge Street B3
Broad Street C2
Caledonian Place A4
Castle Terrace D2
Correction Wynd C2
Chapel Street A3
Charlotte Street B1
Clyde Street D4
College Street B3
Commerce Street D2
Commercial Quay D3
Constitution Street D1
Cragie Street B1
Craibstone Lane A4/B3
Crimon Place A2
Crooked Lane B1
Crown Street B3/4
Crown Terrace B3
Dee Place B4
Dee Street B3
Denburn Road B1/2
Diamond Street B2
East Green C2
East North Street D1
Exchange Street C3
Farmers Hall A1
Ferryhill Terrace B4
Flourmill Lane C2
Forbes Street A1
Frederick Street D1
Gallowgate C1
George Street B1
Gilcomston Park A1
Golden Square B2
Gordon Street B3
Green, The C2/3
Guild Street C3
Hanover Street D1/2
Hardgate A4
Harriet Street B2
Hill Street A1
Huntly Street A2/3
Jacks Brae A2
James Street D2
Jamieson's Quay C3/D3
John Street B1
Jopps Lane B1
Justice Mill Lane A3
Justice Street D2
Kidd Street A2
King Street C1/2
Kintore Place A1
Langstane Place B3
Leadside Road A2
Lemon Street D1
Littlejohn Street C1
Loch Street B1
Maberley Street A1/B1
Marischal Street C2/D2
Market Street C2/C3/D4
Marywell Street B4
Meal Market Street C1
Mearns Street D2
Mount Street A1
North Esp'de East D4
North Esp'de West C3
North Silver Street B2
Palmerston Road C4
Park Place D1
Park Road D1
Portland Street B4/C4
Poynernook Road C4
Princes Street D1
Queen Street C2
Raeburn Place A1
Raik Road C4
Regent Quay D2
Regent Road D3
Rennies Wynd C3
Richmond Street A1
Rose Street A2/3
Rosebank Place A4
Rosebank Terrace B4
Rosemount Place A1
Rosemount Viaduct A2
Russell Road C4
St Andrew Street B1
St Mary's Place B3
Schoolhill B2
Shiprow C2
Skene Square A1
Skene Street A2/B2
Skene Terrace A2
South College Street C4
South Constitution St D1
South Mount Street A1
Spa Street B1/2
Springbank Street B4
Springbank Terrace B4
Stell Road C4
Stirling Street C3
Summer Street A2/3
Summerfield Terrace D1
Thistle Street A3
Trinity Quay C3
Union Glen A4
Union Row A3
Union Street A3/C2
Union Terrace B2
Upper Denburn A2
Upper Kirkgate C2
Virginia Street C2
Wales Street D1
Waterloo Quay D2
Wellington Place B4
West North Street C1
White House Street A2
Willowbank Road A4
Windmill Brae B3

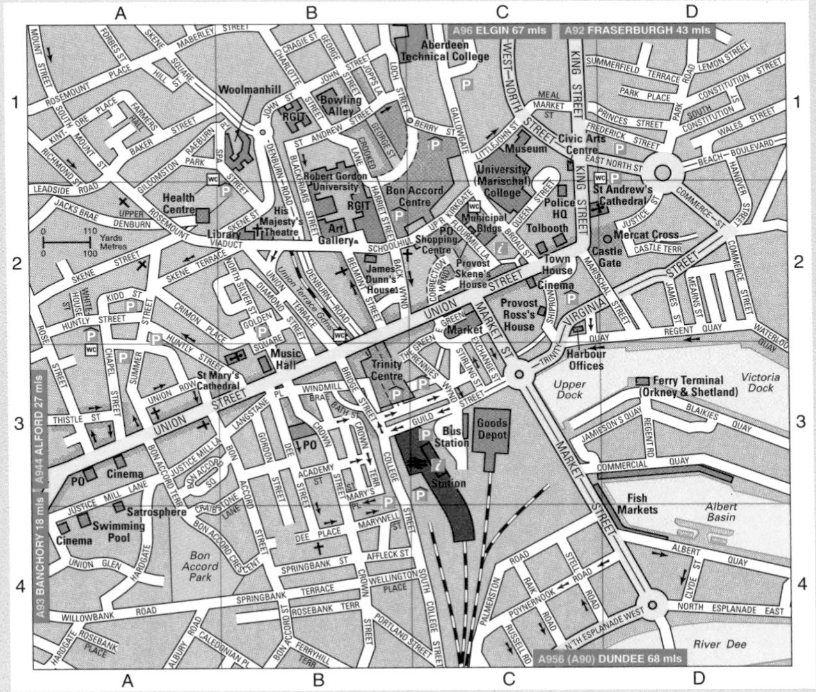

BATH

Abbey Green C3
Abbeygate Street C3
Alfred Street B1
Ambury Street B4
Amery Lane B3
Archway Street D4
Argyle Street C2
Avon Street B3
Bartlett Street B1
Barton Street B2
Bath Street B3
Bathwick Street D1
Beau Street B3
Beaufort Square B2
Bennett Street B1
Bilbury Lane B3
Bridge Street C2
Bristol Road A4
Broad Quay B4
Broad Street B2
Broadway D4
Brock Street A1
Catherine Place A1
Chapel Row A2
Charles Street A3
Charlotte Street A2
Cheap Street C3
Circus, The B1
Circus Mews B1
Claverton Street C4
Corn Street B4
Corridor, The C3
Crescent Gardens A2
Crescent Lane A1
Daniel Street D1
Dorchester Street C4
Duke Street C3
Edward Street D2
Excelsior Street D4
Ferry Lane D3
Gay Street B2
George Street B2
Grand Parade C2
Great Pulteney Street D2
Green Park A3
Green Park Road A3
Green Street B2
Grove Street C2
Guinea Lane B1
Hatfield Buildings D4
Henrietta Gardens D1
Henrietta Mews C2
Henrietta Street C1/2
Henry Street C3
High Street C2
Hot Bath Street B3
James Street West A3
John Street B2
Johnstone Street C2
Julian Road B1
Kingsmead North A3
Kingsmead Terrace B3
Kingsmead West A3
Lansdown Road B1
Laura Place C2
Lower Borough Walls B3
Mall, The C4
Manvers Street C3/4
Midland Br. Road A3
Miles's Buildings B2
Milk Street B3
Milsom Street B2
Monmouth Place A2
Monmouth Street A2
Northgate Street C2
N'thumberland Place B2
Newark Street C4
New Bond Street B2
New King Street A2
New Orchard Street C3
Norfolk Buildings A2
North Pde. Buildings C3
North Pde. Street C3/D3
Oak Street A4
Old Bond Street B2
Old King Street B2
Orange Grove C3
Orchard Street C3
Palace Yard Mews A2
Paragon C1
Pierrepont Street C3
Prince's Buildings D4
Princes Street B2
Pulteney Mews D2
Pulteney Road D2/3/4
Queen Square B2
Queen Street B2
Queens Parade A2
Queens Parade Place B2
Quiet Street B2
Railway Place C4
Railway Street C4
Rivers Street A1/B2
Rossiter Road D4
Royal Avenue A1/2
Royal Cresent A1
Russel Street B1
St Andrew's Ter. B1
St James's Pde. B4
St Johns Road C1
St Mark's Road C4
St Michael's Pl. B3
Saracen Street B2
Saville Row B1
Saw Close B3
Somerset Street B4
Southgate C4
South Parade C3
Spring Crescent D3
Spring Gardens D4
Stall Street B3
Stanier Road A3
Sutton Street D1
Swallow Street C3
Sydney Mews D2
Sydney Place D1
Thornbank Villas A4
Trim Street B2
Trinity Street B3
Union Street B2
Upper Borough Walls B2
Upper Church Street A1
Walcot Street C1/2
Wells Road A4
Westgate Buildings B3
Westgate Street B3
Widcombe Hill D4
William Street D2
Wood Street B2
York Street C3

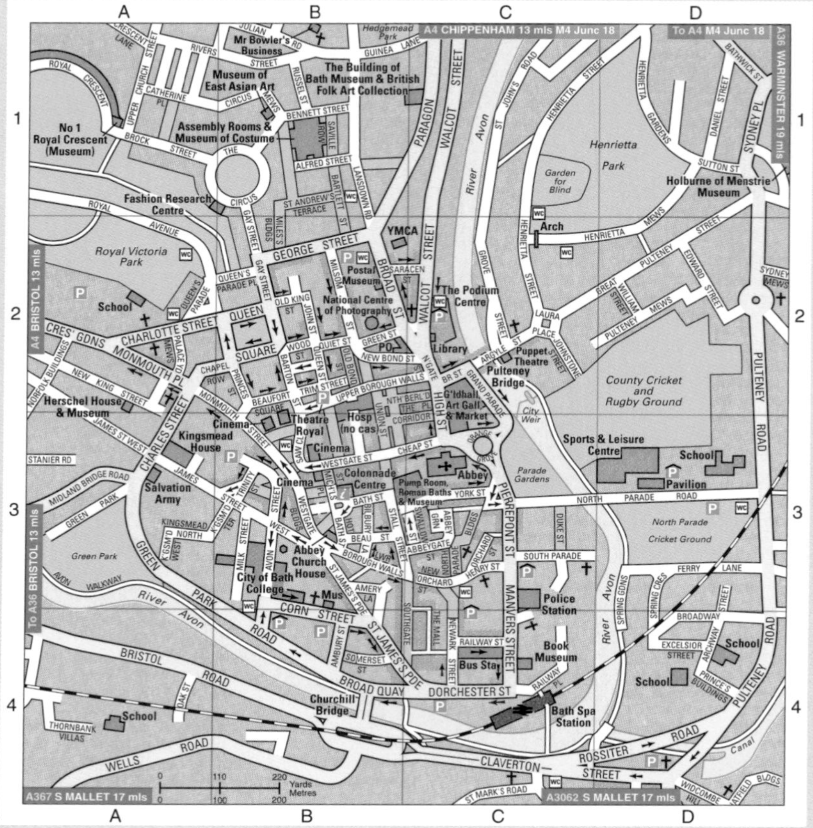

BIRMINGHAM

Albert Street C3/D4
Alison Street D4
Aston Road D1
Aston Street D2
Bagot Street C1
Banbury Street D3
Barford Street D5
Barr Street A1
Bartholomew Street D3
Barwick Street B3
Bath Row A5
Bath Street C2
Bennetts Hill B3/4
Birchall Street D5
Blews Street C1
Blucher Street B5
Bordesley Street D4
Bow Street B5
Bradford Street D5
Branston Street A1
Brearley Street B1
Brewery Street C1
Bridge Street A4
Brindley Drive A3
Bristol Street B5
Broad Street A4
Bromsgrove St. B5/C5
Brook Street A2
Buckingham St. A1/B1
Bull Street C3
Bullring C4
Cambridge Street A4
Cannon Street B4
Caroline Street A2
Carrs Lane C4
Cecil Street C1
Chapel Street D3
Charlotte Street A3
Cheapside D5
Cherry Street C3
Church Street B3
Colmore Circus C3
Colmore Row B3
Commercial Street A5
Cornwall Street B3
Corporation St. C4-D1
Coventry Street D4
Cox Street A2
Cregoe Street A5
Curzon Street D3
Digbeth D5
Edgbaston Street C4
Edmund Street B3
Ellis Street B5
Ernest Street B5
Essex Street B5
Fazeley Street D3/4
Fleet Street A3
Florence Street B5
Fox Street D3
Gas Street A4
George Street A3
Gloucester Street C4/5
Gough Street B5
Graham Street A2
Granville Street A5
Gt Charles St. Q'way B3
Great Hampton Row A1
Great Hampton St. A1
Grosvenor Street D3
Hall Street A1/2
Hampton Street B1/2
Hanley Street B1/C2
Hatchett Street B1/C1
Henrietta Street B2
High Street C4
Hill Street B4
High Street (Deritend) D5
Hinkley Street B4
Hockley Street A1
Holland Street A3
Holliday Street A4/5
Holloway Head A5/B5
Holt Street D2
Hospital Street B1
Howard Street A2
Hurst Street C5
Inge Street B5
Irving Street B5
James Street A2
James Watt Q'way D3
Jennens Road D3
Kenyon Street A2
Ladywell Walk C5
Lancaster Circus C2
Lionel Street A3/B3
Lister Street D2
Livery Street A2/B2/3
Love Lane D1
Lower Loveday St. B2/C2
Lower Tower St. B1/C1
Marshall Street A5
Masshouse Circus C3/D3
Meriden Street D4
Milk Street D5
Moor Street Q'way C4
Moseley Street D5
Mott Street A1/B1
Navigation Street B4
Needles Alley B4
New Street B4
New Bartholomew St. D4
New Canal Street D4/3
New John Street C1/D1
New Meeting Street D4
Newhall Street A3/B3
Newton Street C3
Northwood Street A2
Nova Scotia Street D3
Old Snow Hill B2
Old Square C3
Oxford Street D4
Paradise Circus A3/4
Park Street D4
Pershore Street C5
Pickford Street D4
Pinfold Street B4
Price Street C2
Princip Street C2
Printing House St. C2/3
Priory Q'way C3
Pritchett Street C1/D1
Rea Street D5
Regent Place A2
St Chad's Circus B2
St Chad's Q'way C2
St George's Street B1
St Martin's Circus C4
St Paul's Square A2
St Phillip's Pl. B3
Severn Street B4
Shadwell Street B2/C2
Sherlock Street C5
Smallbrook Q'way B5
Smith Street A1
Snowhill Q'way B3
Spencer Street A1/2
Stanforth Street C1/2
Station Street B4
Steelhouse Lane C3
Stephenson Street B4
Suffolk St. Q'way A4/B4
Summer Lane B1/2
Summer Row A3
Sutton Street A5
Temple Row B3
Temple Row West B3
Temple Street B4
Thorp Street B5
Tower Street B1
Trent Street D4
Unett Street A1
Union Pass C4
Union Street C4
Upper Gough Street A5
Uxbridge Street B1
Vesey Street C2
Warstone Lane A2
Water Street B2
Waterloo Street B4
Weaman Street C2/3
Whittall Street C2
William Street North B1
Woodcock Street D2

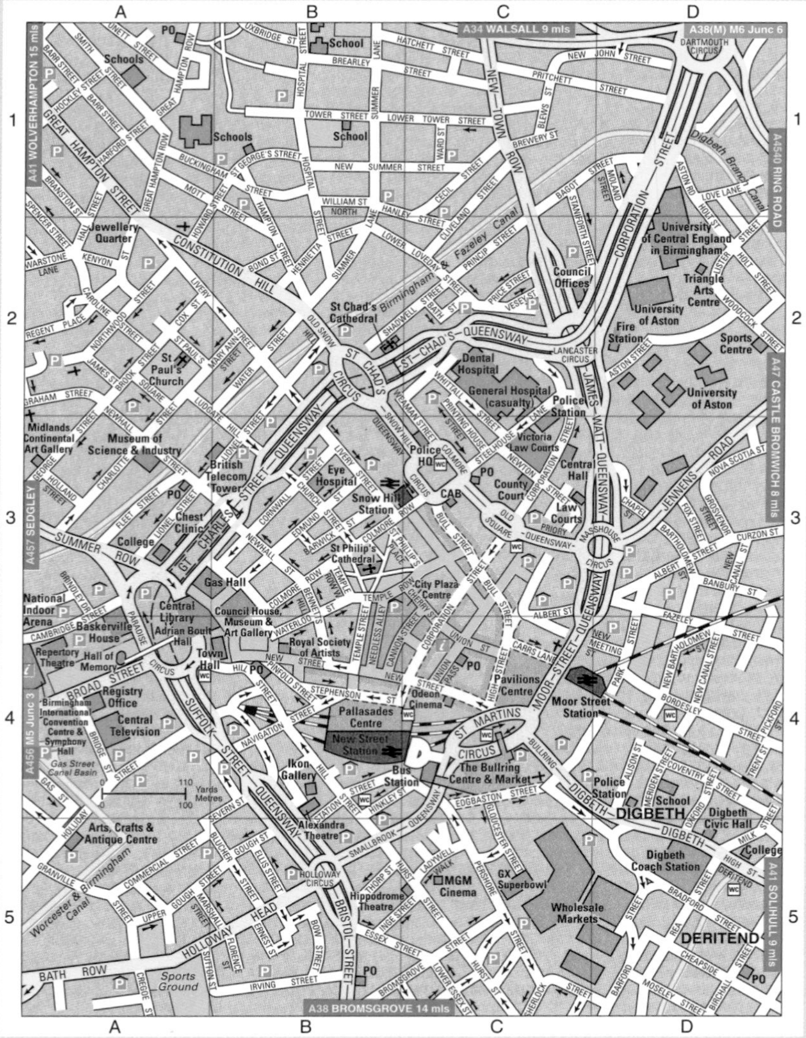

BLACKPOOL

Abingdon Street B2
Addison Crescent D1
Adelaide Street B3
Albert Road B3
Alfred Street B3
Ascot Road D2
Ashton Road C4
Back Church Street B3
Back Lord Street B1
Back Read's Road C4
Bank Hey Street B3
Banks Street B1
Belmont Avenue C4
Birley Street B2
Blenheim Avenue C4
Bonny Street B4
Boothley Road C1
Breck Road D3
Bryan Road D2
Buchanan Street C2
Butler Street C1
Cambridge Road D2
Caunce Street C2/D1
Central Drive B4
Central Car Park Link Road B4
Chapel Street B4
Charles Street C2
Charnley Road B3
Cheapside B2
Church Street B3/C2
Clifton Street B2
Clinton Avenue C4
Cocker Street B1
Coleridge Road C1
Collingwood Ave. D1/2
Cookson Street B2
Coronation Street B3
Corporation Street B2
Cross Street B1
Cumberland Avenue D4
Deansgate B2
Devonshire Road D1/2
Devonshire Square D2
Dickson Road B1
Durham Road C2
Dutton Road D2
East Topping Street B2
Edward Street B2
Elizabeth Street C1/2
Exchange Street B1
Fenton Road C1
Forest Gate D3
Gainsborough Road D3
General Street B1
George Street B2/C1
Gloucester Avenue D4
Gorse Road D4
Gorton Street C1
Granville Road C2
Grosvenor Street C2
Harrison Street C4
High Street B1/2
Hornby Road B3/ C3
Hull Road B3
Kensington Road D3
Kent Road B4
King Street B2
Lark Hill Street C2
Laycock Gate D1
Leamington Road C3
Leeds Road C3/D3
Leicester Road C3
Leopold Grove B3
Lewtas Street B1
Lily Street C2
Lincoln Road C3
Livingstone Road B4
London Road D2
Longton Road C3
Manchester Road D2
Manor Road D3/4
Marlborough Road D3
Mather Street D1
Mere Road D3
Milbourne Street C2
New Bonny Street B4
Newcastle Avenue D3
Newton Drive D2
Olive Grove D3
Oxford Road D2
Palatine Road C4/D3
Park Road C3/4
Peter Street C2
Pleasant Street B1
Portland Road D4
Princess Parade A2
Promenade A1/2/3/4
Queen Street B2
Raikes Parade C3
Read's Avenue B4/C3/D3
Regent Road C3
Regent Road East C3
Ribble Road C4
Ripon Road D4
St Alban's Road D4
Salisbury Road D4
Seed Street C2
Selbourne Road C1
South King Street B3/C3
Springfield Road B2
Stirling Road D1
Swanson Street B2
Talbot Road B2/C1
Topping Street B2
Vance Road B4
Victoria Street B3
Victory Road C1
Walker Street B2
Wayman Road D2
Westmorland Ave. D4
Whitegate Drive D3/4
Woolman Road C4

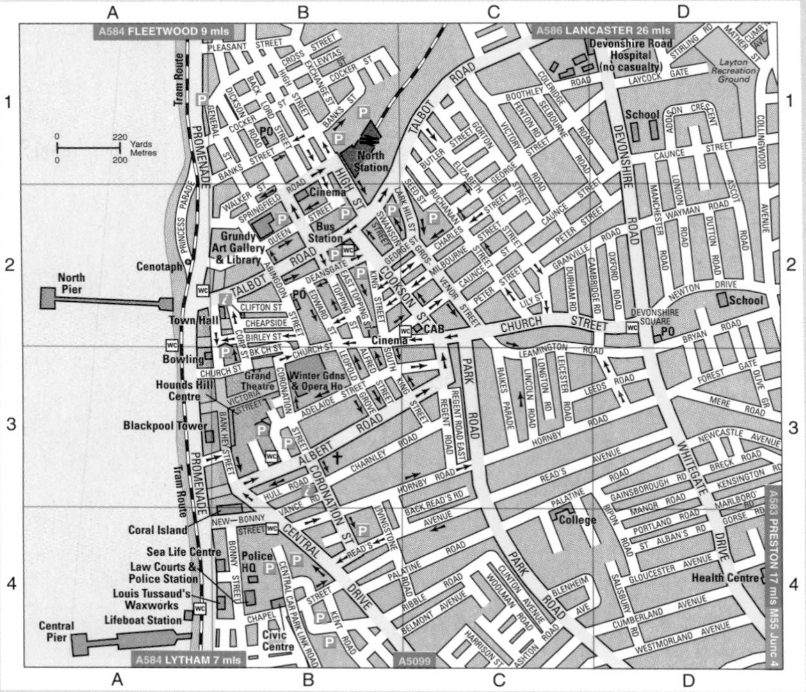

BOURNEMOUTH

Albert Road B2
Avenue Lane A3
Avenue Road A2
Bath Road B4/D3
Beacon Road B4
Bodorgon Road B1
Bourne Avenue A2
Bradburn Road A2
Braidley Road B1/2
Branksome Wood Rd. A1
Cavendish Road C1
Central Drive A1
Christchurch Road D2
Commercial Road A3
Cranborne Road A3
Crescent Road A2
Cumnor Road C2
Dean Park Crescent C2
Dean Park Road C1
Durley Promenade A4
Durley Road A3
Durrant Road A2
East Cliff Promenade C4
East Overcliff Drive D4
Exeter Crescent B3
Exeter Lane B3
Exeter Park Road B3
Exeter Road B3
Fir Vale Road C2
Gervis Place B3
Gervis Road D3
Glen Fern Road C2
Grove Road D3
Hinton Road B3
Holdenhurst Road D2
Lansdowne Road D1/2
Lorne Park Road C2
Madeira Road C2
Merlewood Close B1
Meyrick Road D3
Norwich Avenue A2
Norwich Road A2
Old Christchurch Road B2/D2
Orchard Street A3
Oxford Road D2
Park Road D1
Parsonage Road C3
Pier Approach B4
Poole Hill A3
Post Office Road B3
Priory Road A4
Purbeck Road A3
Richmond Gardens B2
Richmond Hill B2
Richmond Hill Drive B2
Russell-Cotes Road C3
St Michael's Road A3/4
St Paul's Lane D1
St Paul's Road D1
St Peter's Road C3
St Peter's Walk B3
St Stephen's Road A2
St Stephen's Way B2
South View Place A3
Square, The B3
Stafford Road D2
Suffolk Road A2
Terrace Road A3
Tregonwell Road A3
Triangle, The A3
Trinity Road C2
Undercliff Drive C/D4
Upper Hinton Road C3
Upper Norwich Road A3
Upper Terrace Road A3
Verulam Place B2
Wessex Way A2/D1
West Cliff Gardens A4
West Cliff Prom. A/B4
West Cliff Road A4
West Hill Road A3/4
West Promenade A/B4
Westover Road B3
Wimborne Road B1
Wootton Gardens C2
Wootton Mount D2
Wychwood Close B1
Yelverton Road B2

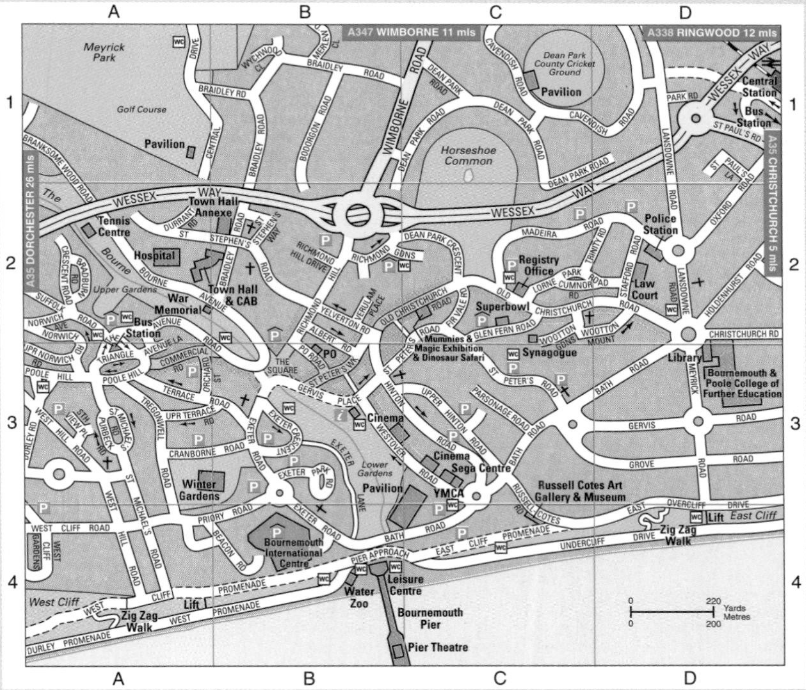

Think before you park

If you are parking on a road, remember not to cause an obstruction, nor to park in such a way as to endanger other road users. Even where there are no road markings, you should not park near a road junction, a school entrance, a bus stop, or a taxi rank, nor on the approach to a level crossing. It is always safer to get out of your car on the side next to the kerb, but do watch out for pedestrians.

BRADFORD

Aldermanbury B3
Ann Place A4
Ash Grove A4
Bank Street B3
Baptist Place A2
Barkerend Road D2
Barry Street A3
Bolling Road C4
Bolton Road C1/2
Bolton Street D2
Bridge Street B3
Britannia Street C4
Broadway B3
Brookfield Road D1
Buck Street D4
Burnett Street C2
Butler Street West D1
Caledonia Street B4
Canal Road C1
Carlton Street A3
Chain Street A2
Channing Way B3
Chapel Street C3
Charles Street B3
Cheapside B2
Church Bank C2
Claremont A4
Croft Street B4
Dale Street B2
Darley Street B2
Drake Street C3
Drewton Road A2
Dryden Street C4
Dyson Street A2
East Parade C3
Eastbrook Lane C3
Edderthorpe Street D3
Edmund Street A4
Edward Street C4
Eldon Place A1
Essex Street D4
Filey Street D3
Forster Square C2
Fullerton Street D3
Fulton Street A3
Garnett Street D2
George Street C3
Godwin Street B2/3
Goit Side A3
Grammar School St. B2
Grattan Road A2
Great Horton Road A3
Greenway, The D1
Guy Street C4
Hallfield Road A1
Hallings B3
Hammerton Street D3
Hammstrasse B1
Hanover Square A1
Harris Street D2
Head Lane D2
Heaton Street D4
Hillside Road D2
Holdsworth Street C2
Howard Street A4
Humboldt Street D2
Ivegate B3
John Street A2
Joseph Street D3
Kirkgate B3
Lansdowne Place A4
Leeds Road C/D3
Little Horton Lane A4/B3
Longside Lane A3
Lumb Lane A1
Manchester Road B4
Manningham Lane A1
Manor Row B2
Manville Terrace A4
Market Street B3
Maudsley Street D2
Melbourne Place A4
Mill Street C2
Morley Street A4
Neal Street A4
Nelson Street B4
New Otley Road D1
North Brook Street B1
North Parade B2
North Street C2
North Wing C1
Nuttall Road D2
Otley Road D2
Paradise Street A2
Peckover Street C2
Peel Street C3
Petergate C3
Piccadilly B2
Pit Lane D2
Portland Street B4
Princes Way B3
Rawson Road A2
Rebecca Street A2
Richmond Road A3
Russell Street A4
St Thomas Road A2
Salem Street B2
Sawrey Place A4
Senior Way B4
Sharpe Street B4
Shipley-Airdale Rd. C1/2
Simes Street A2
Smith Street A3
Snowden Street B1
Southgate A3
Spring Gardens A1
Stott Street C2
Sunbridge Road A2/B3
Tetley Street A3
Thornton Road A3
Trafalgar Street A1
Tumbling Hill Street A3
Tyrls, The B3
Upper Parkgate C2
Valley Road B1
Valley Street B2
Ventnor Street D3
Vicar Lane C2/3
Wakefield Road C4
Wapping Road C1
Water Lane A2
Well Street C3
Wellington Street C2
Westgate A2
Wharf Street C1
White Abbey Road A1
Wigan Street A2
William Street B4
Wilton Street A4

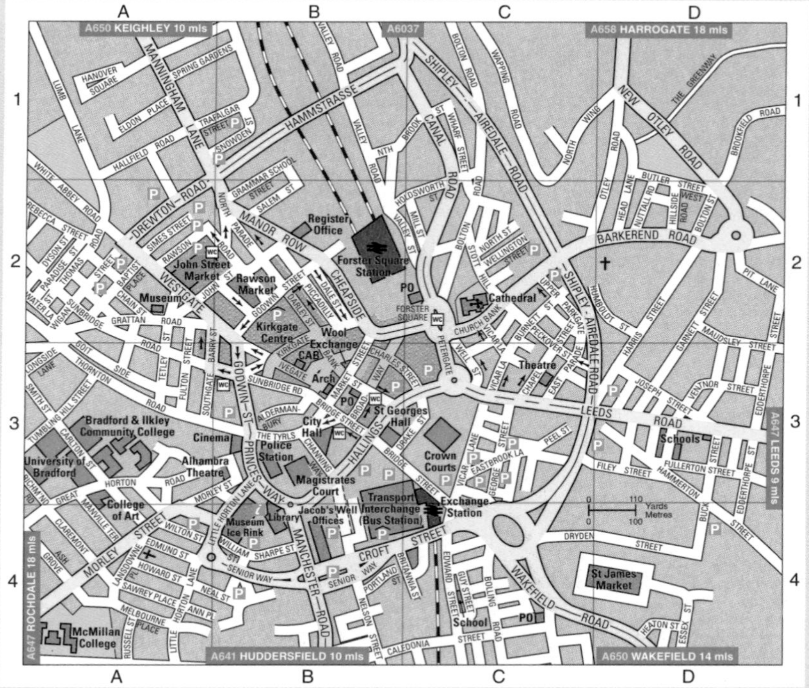

BRIGHTON

Albert Road B1
Albion Hill D1
Albion Street D1
Alexandra Views B1
Alfred Road B1
Ashton Rise D2
Bath Street A1
Belgrave Street D1
Black Lion Street C4
Bond Street C3
Broad Street D4
Buckingham Road B1
Buckingham Street B1
Camelford Street D4
Cannon Place A3
Carlton Hill D3
Castle Square C3
Castle Street A3
Centurion Road B2
Chapel Street D3
Cheapside C1
Cheltenham Place C2
Church Street B2/C2
Circus Street D2
Clarence Square A3
Clifton Hill A1
Clifton Passage B1
Clifton Place A2
Clifton Road A1
Clifton Street B1
Clifton Terrace A2
Compton Avenue B1
Crown Street A3
Dean Street A3
Denmark Terrace A1
Dorset Gardens D3
Duke Street B3
Dukes Lane B3
Dyke Road A1/B2
East Street C3/4
Edward Street D3
Elmore Road D2
Foundry Street C2
Frederick Gardens C2
Frederick Place C1
Frederick Street C2
Gardner Street C2
George Street D3
Gloucester Place D2
Gloucester Road C2
Gloucester Street C2
Grand Junction Road C4
Grand Parade D2
Grove Hill D1
Guildford Road B1
Guildford Street B1
Hampton Place A2
High Street D3
Jersey Street D1
John Street D2/3
Kemp Street C1
Kensington Place C1
Kensington Street C2
Kew Street B2
King Place C3
King's Road A3/B4
Lanes, The C3
Leopold Road B2
Lewes Road D1
Lewes Street D1
Little Preston Street A3
Madeira Drive D4
Madeira Place D4
Marine Parade D4
Market Street C3
Marlborough Mews A3
Marlborough Place C2
Marlborough Street A3
Michell Street D3
Middle Street B4
Montpelier Crescent A1
Montpelier Road A2
Montpelier Street A2
Montpelier Terrace A2
Montpelier Views A2
Morley Street D2
New Dorset Street B2
New Road C3
Newark Place D1
Newhaven Street D1
North Gardens B2
North Place C2
North Road C2
North Street C3
Old Steine C4
Over Street C1
Pelham Square C1
Pelham Street C1
Phoenix Place D1
Portland Street B3
Powis Grove A2
Powis Road A2
Powis Square A1
Powis Villas A2
Preston Street A3
Princess Street D3
Queen Square B3
Queens Gardens C2
Queens Road B2
Redcar Street C1
Regency Road B3
Regency Square A3
Regent Hill B3
Regent Street C2
Richmond Street D2
Robert Street C2
Russell Road B3
Russell Square A3
St James Street D4
St Michael's Place A1
St Nicholas Road B2
St Peter's Place D1
Ship Street B4
Sillwood Road A3
South Street B4
Spring Gardens C2
Spring Street A2
Station Street C1
Steine Street D4
Stone Street A3
Surrey Street B1
Sussex Street D2
Sydney Street C2
Terminus Road B1
Tichborne Street C2
Tidy Street C1
Trafalgar Lane C1
Trafalgar Street C1
Upper Gardner Street C2
Upper North Street A2
Vernon Terrace A1
Victoria Road A2
Victoria Street A2
Vine Place A2
Vine Street C2
Wentworth Street D4
West Hill Road B1
West Hill Street B1
West Street B3
Western Road A2/B3
White Street D3
Whitecross Street C1
William Street D3
Windlesham Gardens A1
Windlesham Road A1
Windsor Street B3
York Place C1

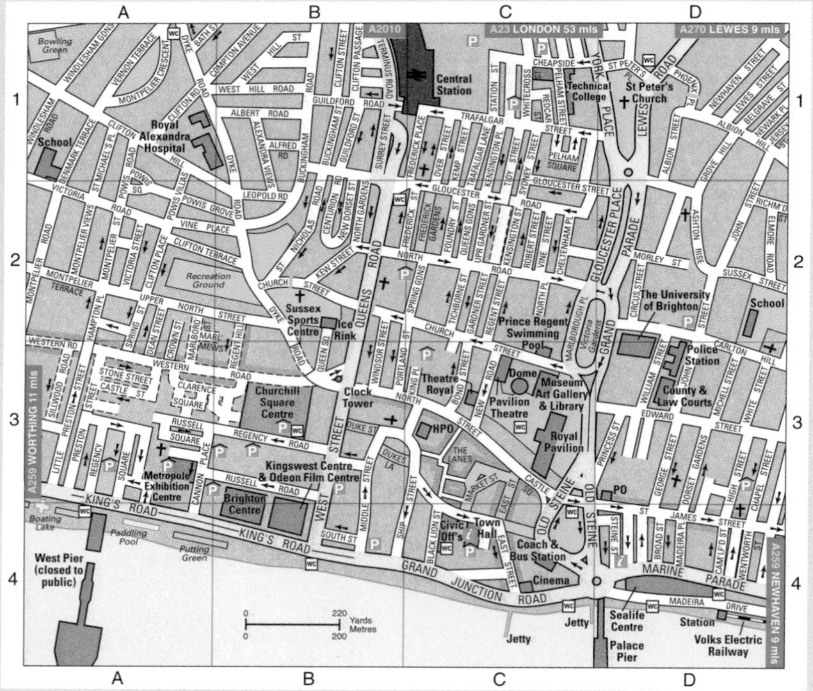

BRISTOL

Anchor Road A3
Approach Road D4
Avon Street D3
Baldwin Street B3
Bond Street C1
Broad Quay B3
Broad Street B2
Broadmead C1
Broad Weir C2
Butts Road A4
Canon's Road A3
Canon's Way A4
Castle Street C2
Cattle Market Road D4
Church Lane C3
College Green A3
College Street A3
Colston Avenue B2
Colston Street B2
Counterslip C3
Dale Street D1
Denmark Street A2/3
Frogmore Street A2
Great George Street D1
Guinea Street B4
Haymarket C1
Hill Street A2
Horfield Road A1
Houlton Street D1
Jacob Street D2
Jubilee Place B4
King Street B3
Lewins Mead B1
Lwr Castle Street C2/D2
Marlborough Street B1
Marsh Street B3
Merchant Street C1
Midland Road D2
Mitchell Lane C3
Narrow Quay B3
Nelson Street B2
New Street D1
Newfoundland Street D1
Newgate C2
Old Bread Street D3
Old Market Street D2
Park Row A2
Park Street A2
Passage Street C2
Penn Street C1
Perry Road A2
Pipe Lane A2
Pipe Lane (Redcliffe) D4
Pithay B2
Portwall Lane C4
Prewett Street C4
Prince Street B3
Pritchard Street D1
Pump Lane C4
Quakers Friars C1/2
Queen Charlotte St. B3
Queen Square C3/4
Queen Street C2
Redcliffe Hill C4
Redcliffe Mead Lane C4
Redcliffe Parade B4
Redcliffe Street C3
Redcliffe Way B3/C4
Redcross Street D2
Rose Street D4
Rupert Street B1
St Augustine's Pde. A2/3
St James Barton C1
St Matthias Park D1/2
St Michael's Rd. A1
St Nicholas Street B2
St Paul's Street D1
St Stephen's St. B2
St Thomas Street C3
Small Street B2
Strait Street D2
Stratton Street D1
Temple Back C3
Temple Gate D4
Temple Way D3
The Grove B4
The Horsefair C1
Tower Hill C2
Tyndall Avenue A1
Union Street C2
Unity Street D2
University Walk A1
Upper Maudlin Street B1
Victoria Street C3
Wade Street D1
Wapping Road B4
Wellington Road D1
Welsh Back B3
Whitson Street B1
Wine Street B2
Woodland Road A1

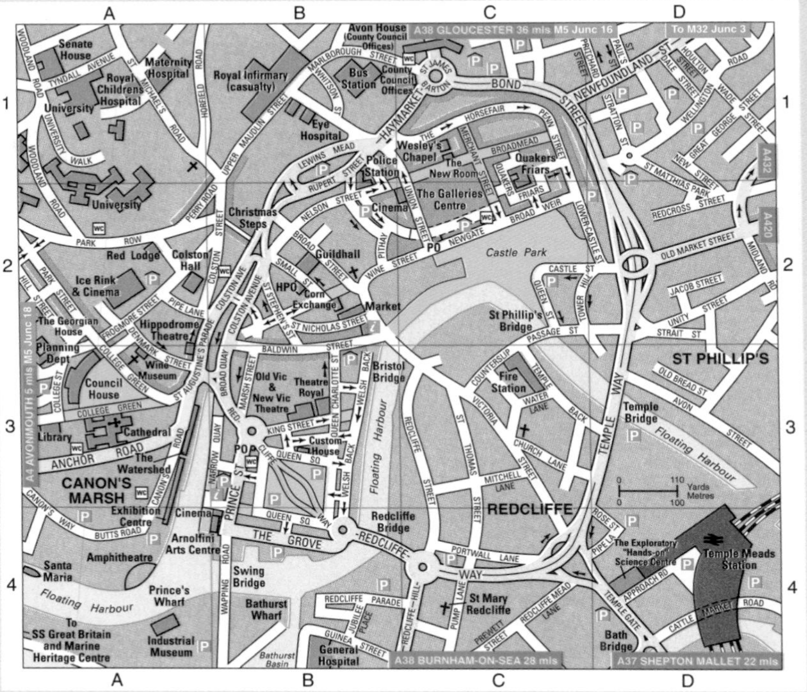

CAMBRIDGE

Acrefield Drive D1
Adam & Eve Street D3
Albert Street B1
Albion Row A1
Alpha Road A1
Auckland Road D2
Aylestone Road C1
Backway C2
Belvoir Road D1
Benet Street B3
Bradmore Street D3
Brandon Place D3
Bridge Street B2
Broad Street D3
Brunswick Gardens C2
Brunswick Terrace C2
Burleigh Street D2
Cambridge Place C4/D4
Carlyle Road A1/B1
Castle Street A1
Chesterton Lane A1
Chesterton Road B1
City Road C3/D2
Clare Street A1
Clarendon Street C3
Collier Road D3
Corn Exchange St. B3
Covent Garden D4
Cross Street D4
De Freville Avenue C1
Downing Place B3
Downing Street B3
Drummer Street B3/C3
Earl Street C3
East Road D2/3
Eden Street C2/3
Elizabeth Way D1
Elm Street C2/3
Emery Street D3
Emmanuel Road C2/3
Emmanuel Street B3/C3
Fen Causeway A4/B4
Fisher Street A1/B1
Fitzroy Street C2/D2
Fitzwilliam Street B4
Glisson Road D4
Gloucester Street A1
Gonville Place C4
Grafton Street D3
Green Street B2
Grenta Place A4
Gresham Road D4
Guest Road D3
Hale Street A1
Hamilton Road C1
Harvey Road C4
Hertford Street A1
Hilda Street A1
Hills Road C4
Hobson Street B2
Holland Street B1
Humberstone Rd. D1
Jesus Lane B2
John Street D3
Kimberley Road C1
King Street B2/C2
Kings Parade B3
Lensfield Road C4
Little St Mary's Lane B4
Lower Park Street B2
Lyndewode Road D4
Mackenzie Road D3
Magdalene Street A2
Magrath Avenue A1
Maids Causeway C2
Malcolm Street B2
Malting Lane A4
Manhattan Drive D1
Market Street B2/3
Mawson Road D4
Mill Lane B3
Mill Road D3/4
Mill Street D4
Montague Road D1
Mortimer Road D3
New Park Street B2
New Square C2
New Street D2
Newmarket Road D2
Newnham Walk A4
Newnham Road A4
Norfolk Street D3
Norfolk Terrace D3
Northampton Street A2
Orchard Street C3
Panton Street C4
Paradise Street D3
Park Parade B1/2
Park Street B2
Park Terrace C3
Parker Street C3
Parkside C3
Pembroke Street B3
Perowne Street D3/4
Petty Cury B3
Pretoria Road C1
Prospect Row C3
Queen's Lane A3
Queen's Road A2/3
Regent Street C3/4
Regent Terrace C3/4
Ridley Hall Road A4
St Andrews Road D1
St Andrew's St. B3
St Barnabas Rd. D4
St John's Street B2
St Luke's Street A1
St Mary's Street B3
St Matthew's St. D2
St Paul's Rd. C4/D4
St Peter's Street A1
St Tibb's Row B3
Saxon Road B4/C4
Searle Street A1
Severn Place D2
Short Street C2
Sidgwick Avenue A4
Sidney Street B2
Silver Street A3/4
Staffordshire Street D2/3
Tenison Road D4
Tennis Court Road B3/4
Tennis Court Terrace B4
Thompson's Lane B1/2
Trafalgar Road C1
Trinity Lane A2/3
Trinity Street B2/3
Trumpington St. B3/4
Union Road C4
Victoria Avenue C1/2
Victoria Road B1
Victoria Street C3
Warkworth Street C3/D3
West Road A3
Willow Walk C2
Willis Road D3
Wordsworth Grove A4

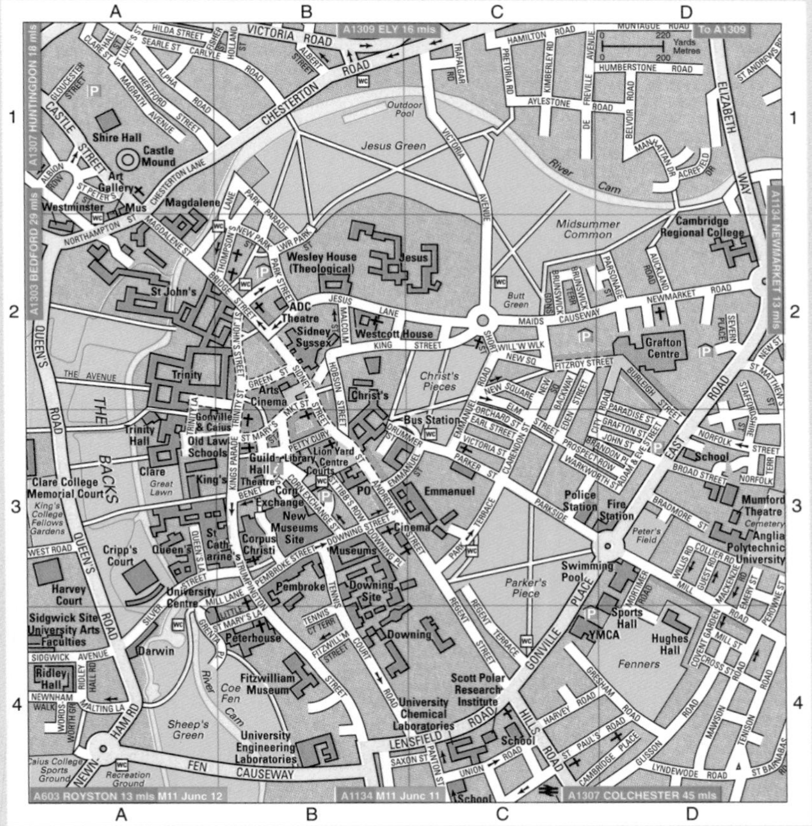

Town Plans

CARDIFF

Adam Street D4
Allerton Street A4
Beauchamp Street A4
Bedford Street D1
Blvd. de Nantes C2
Bridge Street C3/D3
Brook Street A3
Bute Street C4/D4
Bute Terrace D4
Caroline Street C4
Castle Street B3
Cathedral Road A2/3
Central Square B4/C4
Charles Street C3/D3
Church Street C3
Churchill Way D3
City Hall Road B2
City Road D1
Clare Road A4
Clare Street A4
Coburn Street C1
Coldstream Terrace A3
College Road B1
Colum Road B1
Corbett Road B1
Court Road A4
Cowbridge Road East A3
Craddock Street A4
Cranbrook Street D1
Crichton Street C4
Crockherbtown Lane C2
Custom House Street C4
David Street D3
De Burgh Street A3
Despenser Place A4
Despenser Street A3
Duke Street B3
Dumfries Place D2
East Canal Wharf C4
Ellen Street D4
Fitzhamon Emb. B4
Friary, The C2/3
Gloucester Street A4
Glynrhondda Street C1
Gordon Road D1/2
Gorsedd Gdns Road C2
Great Western Lane C4
Green Street A3
Greyfriars Road C2
Hayes, The C3
Hayes Bridge Road C4
Herbert Street D4
High Street B3
Hill's Street C3
King Edward VII Avenue B1/2
Kingsway C3
Knox Road D3
Lower Cathedral RD. A3
Lowther Road D1
Machen Place A3/4
Mark Street A3
Mary Ann Street D3/4
Mill Lane C4
Miskin Street C1
Monmouth Street A4
Museum Avenue B1/C2
Museum Place C2
Neville Street A3
Newport Road D2
North Road A1/B1/B2
Northcote Lane D1
Northcote Street D1
Parade, The D2
Park Lane C2
Park Place B1/C1/C2
Park Street B4
Pendyris Street A4/B4
Plantagenet Street A3/4
Queen Street C3
Rawden Place A3
Rhymney Street D1
Richmond Road D1
Russell Street D1
St Andrews Place C2
St Mary Street C3/4
St Peter's Street D2
Salisbury Road C1/D1
Sandon Road D3
Sandon Street D3
Senghennydd Road C1
Station Terrace D3
Stuttgart Strasse C2
Thesiger Street C1
Trinity Street C3
Tudor Close A4
Tudor Street A4
Walk, The D2
Wedmore Road A4
Wesley Lane D3
West Canal Wharf C4
West Grove D2
Westgate Street B3
Wharf Street C4
Wharton Street C3
Windsor Place D2
Womanby Street B3
Wood Street B4
Working Street C3
Wyeverne Road C1

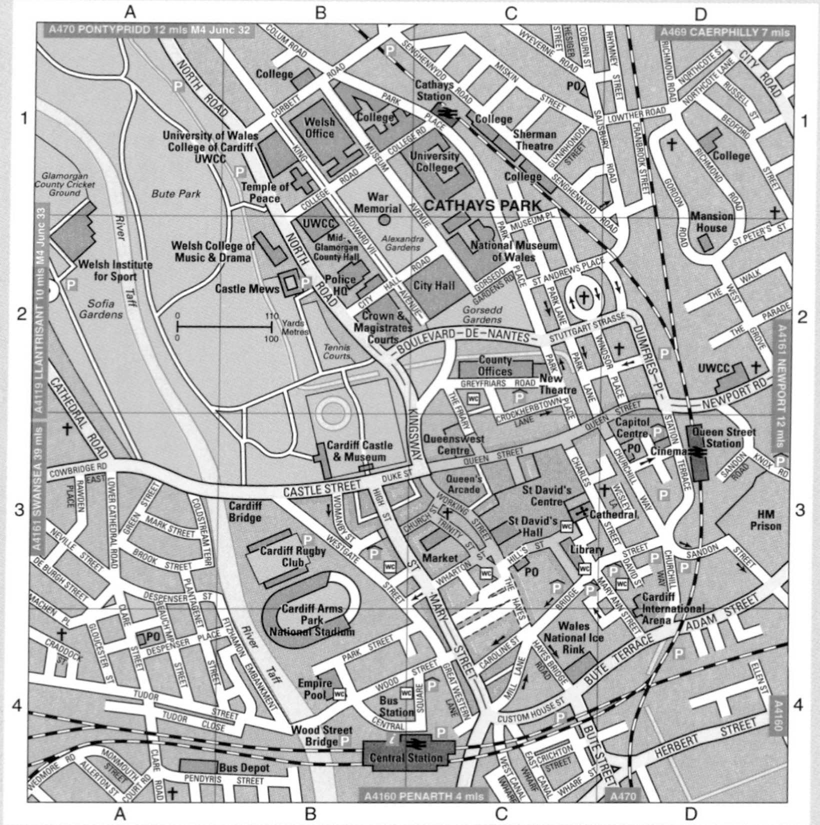

CHESTER

Abbey Square B2
Abbey Street B2
Albion Street B3/C3
Andrew Crescent D4
Anne's Way D3
Bars, The D2
Bath Street D2
Beaconsfield Street D2
Bedward Row A2
Black Friars A3
Boughton D2
Bridge Street B3
Brook Street C1
Canal Side C2/D2
Castle Drive B4
Castle Street B3
Charles Street C1
Chichester Street A1
City Road D1/2
City Walls Road A2
Commonhall Street B3
Crewe Street D1
Cross Heys D4
Cuppin Street B3
Dee Hills Park D2
Dee Lane D2
Delamere Street B1
Deva Terrace D2
Duke Street B3/C3
Eastgate Street B2
East Pathway D4
Edinburgh Way D4
Egerton Street C1
Elizabeth Crescent D3
Foregate Street C2
Forest Street C2
Francis Street C1/D1
Frodsham Street C2
Garden Lane A1
Garden Terrace A1
George Street B1
Gorse Stacks B1/C1
Greenway Street B4
Grey Friars A3
Grosvenor Road A4
Grosvenor Street B3
Groves, The C3
Groves Road D3
Hamilton Place B2
Handbridge C4
Hoole Way C1
Hunter Street B2
King Street A2/B2
Leadworks Lane D1
Lorne Street A1
Louise Street A1
Love Street C2
Lower Bridge Street B3
Lower Park Road D3
Lyon Street C1
Meadow's Lane D4
Mill Street C4
Milton Street C1
New Crane Street A3
Nicholas Street A3
Nicholas Street Mews A3
Nicholas St. Viaduct A1
Northern Path D4
Northgate Street B2
Nuns Road A3
Park Street C3
Pepper Street B3
Princes Avenue D1
Princess Street A2
Queen Street C2
Queens Avenue D1
Queens Drive D3
Queens Road D1
Queen's Park Road C4
Queen's Park View C4
Raymond Street A1/2
Russell Street D2
St Anne Street B1/C1
St George's Cres. D4
St John Street C2/3
St John's Road D4
St Martins Way A2
St Mary's Hill B3/4
St Oswalds Way B1-C2
St Werburgh Street B2
Seller Street C1/D2
Sibell Street D1
Souters Lane C3
South Crescent Road D3
South View Road A2
Stanley Street A2
Station Road D1
Steam Mill Street D2
Tower Road A2
Tower Wharf A1
Trafford Street B1
Trinity Street A2
Union Street C2/D2
Vicar's Lane C3
Victoria Crescent C3/D3
Victoria Path D4
Victoria Road B1
Water Tower Street A2
Watergate Street A3/B3
Weaver Street B3
West Lorne Street A1
White Friars B3
York Street C2

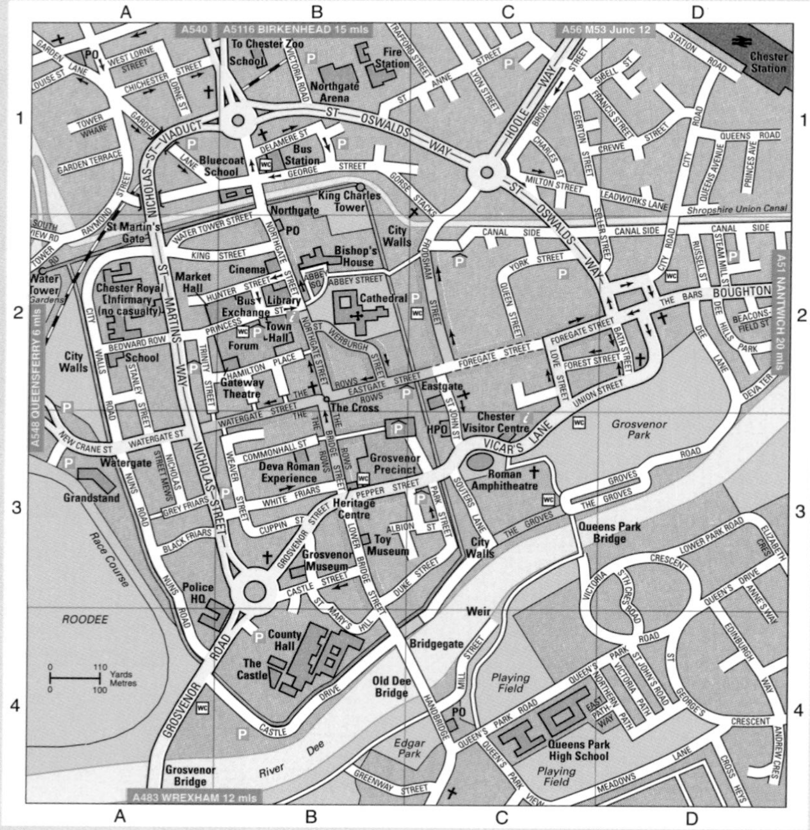

COVENTRY

Abbotts Lane A1
Acacia Avenue D4
Albany Road A3
Albert Street D1
Alma Street D2
Barras Lane A2
Bayley Lane C2
Bishop Street B1
Bond Street B2
Broadgate B2
Burges B2
Butts Road A3
Canterbury Street D1
Chapel Street B2
Charles Street D1
Chauntry Place C2
Chester Street A1
Clifton Street D1
Colchester Street D1
Cornwall Road D4
Corporation Street B2
Coundon Road A1
Coundon Street A1
Cox Street C3
Croft Road A3/B3
Earl Street C3
Eaton Road B4
Fairfax Street C2
Ford Street D2
Friars Road B4
Gloucester Street A2
Gordon Street A4
Gosford Street D3
Greyfriars Lane B3/C3
Greyfriars Road B3
Grosvenor Road B4
Gulson Road D3
Hales Street C2
Harper Road D3
Hertford Place A3
Hertford Street B3
High Street C3
Hill Street B2
Holyhead Road A2
Hood Street D2
Jordan Well C3
King William Street D1
Lamb Street B1
Leicester Row B1
Little Park Street C3
London Road D4
Lower Ford Street D2
Lower Holyhead Road A2/B2
Lower Precinct B2
Manor House Drive B3
Market Way B3
Meadow Street A2/3
Meriden Street A1/2
Middleborough Road A1
Mile Lane C4
Mill Street B1
Minster Road A2
Much Park Street C3
New Buildings C2
New Union Street B3/C3
Norfolk Street A2
Park Road B4/C4
Parkside C4/D4
Precinct, The B2
Primrose Hill Street D1
Priory Row C2
Priory Street C2
Puma Road C4/D4
Quarryfield Lane D4
Queen Victoria Road B3
Quinton Road C4
Radford Road B1
Raglan Street D2
Regent Street A3/4
Ringway Hill Cross A2
Ringway Queens A3/B3
Ringway Rudge A2/3
Ringway St John's C3
Ringway St Patrick's B4/C4
Ringway St Nicholas B1
Ringway Swanswell C1/2
Ringway Whitefriars D2/3
St Columba's Cl. B1
St Nicholas Street B1
St Patrick's Road B4/C4
Salt Lane C3
Seagrove Road D4
Silver Street C1
Smithford Way B2
Spon Street A2/B2
Starley Road B3
Stoney Road B4/C4
Stoney Stanton Road C1
Strathmore Avenue D3/4
Swansell Street C1
Tower Street B1/C1
Trinity Street C2
Upper Hill Street A2
Upper Spon Street A2
Upper Well Street B2
Upper York Street A3/4
Victoria Street D1
Vine Street D1/2
Warwick Road B3/4
Waveley Road A2
Well Street B2
Westminster Road A4
White Street C1
Whitefriars Street C3
Winchester Street D2
Windsor Street A2/3
Yardley Street D1

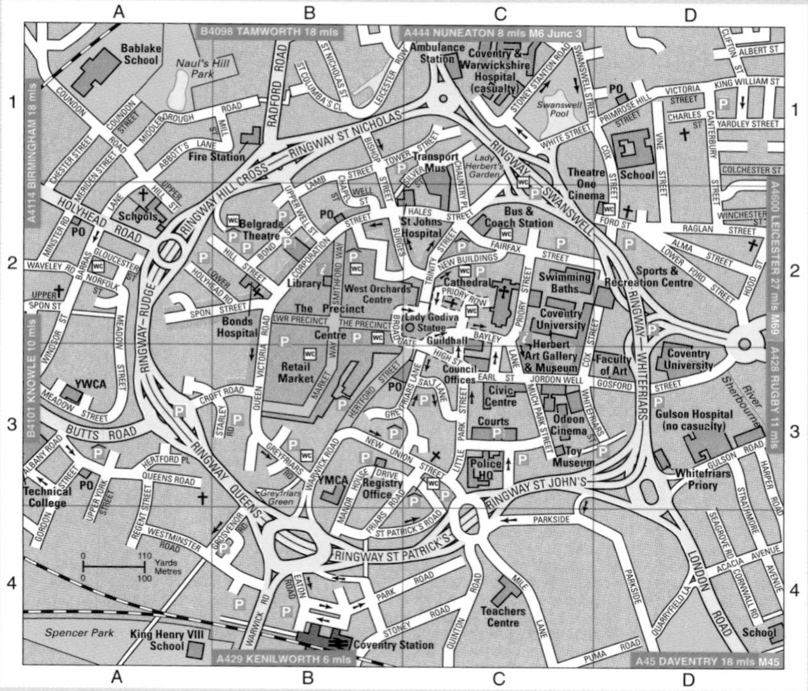

DERBY

Abbey Street A3/4
Albert Street B3
Albion Street B/C3
Alice Street C1
Arthur Street A1
Ashlyn Road D3
Babington Lane B4
Becket Street A3
Becketwell Lane B3
Bold Lane A2
Bradshaw Way C4
Bridge Street A1
Brook Street A2
Burrows Walk B4
Burton Road A4
Calvert Street D4
Canal Street D4
Cathedral Road A2
Chapel Street A2
Chequers Road D2
City Road B1
Clarke Street C1
Cock Pit, The C3
Colyear Street A3
Copeland Street C3
Cornmarket B3
Corporation Street B2
Cranmer Road D2
Crompton Street A3
Crown Walk B3
Curzon Street A3
Darley Lane B1
Darwin Place C2
Derwent Street B2
Drewry Lane A3
Duffield Road A1
Duke Street B1
Dunton Close D3
East Street B3
Eastgate D2
Edward Street A1
Exeter Street B2
Ford Street A2
Forester Street A4
Fox Street C1
Friar Gate A2
Friary Street A3
Full Street B2
George Street A2
Gerard Street A3/4
Gower Street B3
Green Lane B3/4
Handyside Street B1
Hansard Gate D2
Harcourt Street A4
Henry Street A1
Hope Street C4
Irongate B2
John Street C4
Jury Street A2
Keys Street C1
King Street A1
Leopold Street B4
Liversage Road C4
Liversage Street C4
Lodge Lane A1
London Road B/C4
Macklin Street A3
Mansfield Road B1
Market Place B2
Meadow Road C2
Midland Place D4
Monk Street A3
Moreledge B3
Newland Street A3
Normanton Road B4
North Parade A1
North Street A1
Nottingham Road C2
Osmaston Road B4
Park Street D4
Pentagon, The D2
Phoenix Street B2
Queen Street B2
Railway Terrace D4
River Street B1
Sacheverel Street B4
Sadlergate B2
Siddals Road C3
Sir Frank Whittle Rd. D1
Sitwell Street B4
Sowter Road B2
Spot, The B4
St Alkmund's Way B1/C2
St Helens Street A1
St Mary's Court B1
St Mary's Gate A2
St Michael's Lane B2
St Peter's Ch. Yard B3
St Peter's Street B3
Stafford Street A3
Station Approach C3
Stores Road C1
Strand, The B3
Stuart Street B2
Traffic Street C4
Trinity Street C4
Victoria Street B3
Wardwick, The A3
Webster Street A4
Werburgh Street A4
West Avenue A1
Willow Row A2
Wilmot Street B4
Wilson Street A4
Wood Street B1
Woods Lane A4

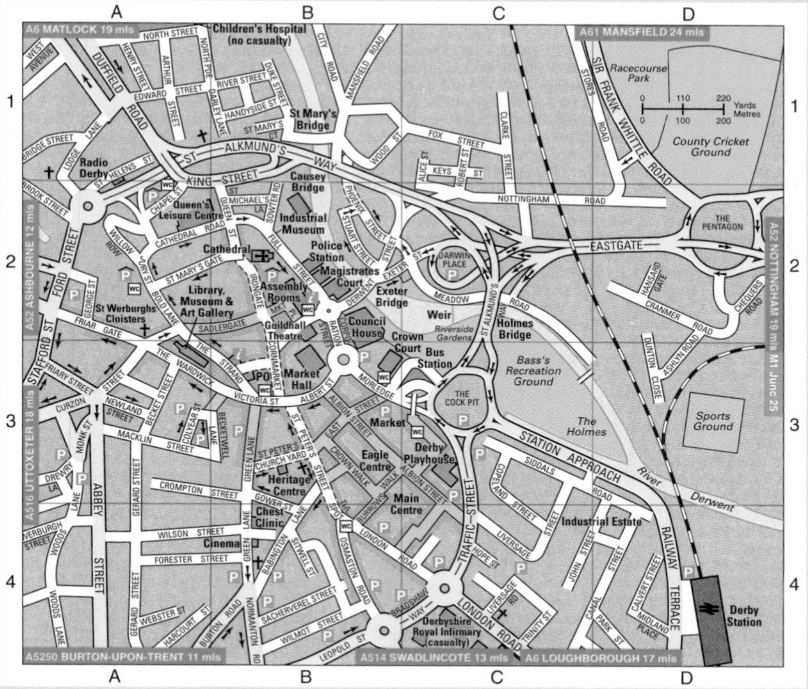

Seat belts save lives

It is the driver's responsibility to ensure that passengers under the age of 14 are wearing seat belts. Children under the age of 11 should wear the appropriate child restraint. Remember, in the event of an accident at 30mph, a child in the rear seat could be thrown forward with the force equivalent to the weight of a baby elephant.

Town Plans

DOVER

Adrian Street B2
Albany Place B2
Archcliffe Road A4
Biggin Street B1
Cambridge Road B3
Camden Crescent B2
Canons Gate Road C1
Castle Hill Road B1
Castle Street B2
Castlemount Road B1
Centre Road A3
Channel View Road A4
Chapel Street B2
Church Street B2
Citadel Road A3
Clarendon Place A2
Clarendon Road A2
Constable Road C1
Dolphin Lane B2
Dour Street A1
Drop Redoubt Road A2
Durham Hill A2
East Cliff C2
East Norman Road C1
East Roman Ditch C1
Effingham Street A1
Elizabeth Street A3
Esplanade B3
Folkestone Road A2
Gateway, The B2
Godwyne Close B1
Godwyne Road B1
Goodwin Road C1
Harold Street B1
Harolds Road C1
High Street A1
Jubilee Way D1/2
King Street B2
Knights Road C1
Knights Templars A3
Ladywell Place A1
Laureston Place B1
Leyburne Road B1
Limekiln Street A3
Lord Warden Square A4
Maison Dieu Road B1
Malvern Road A2
Marine Parade B2/C2
Military Road A2
North Military Road A2
Park Street B1
Pencester Road B1
Priory Gate Road A1
Priory Hill A1
Priory Road A1
Queen Elizabeth Rd. C1
Russell Street B2
St Johns Road A2
Snargate Street A3
Strond Street A3
Taswell Street B1
Tower Hamlets Road A1
Tower Street A1
Townwall Street B2
Union Street A3
Upper Road C1/D1
Viaduct, The A4
Victoria Park B1
Waterloo Crescent B3
West Norman Road C1
West Roman Ditch C1
Woolcomber Street B2
York Street B2

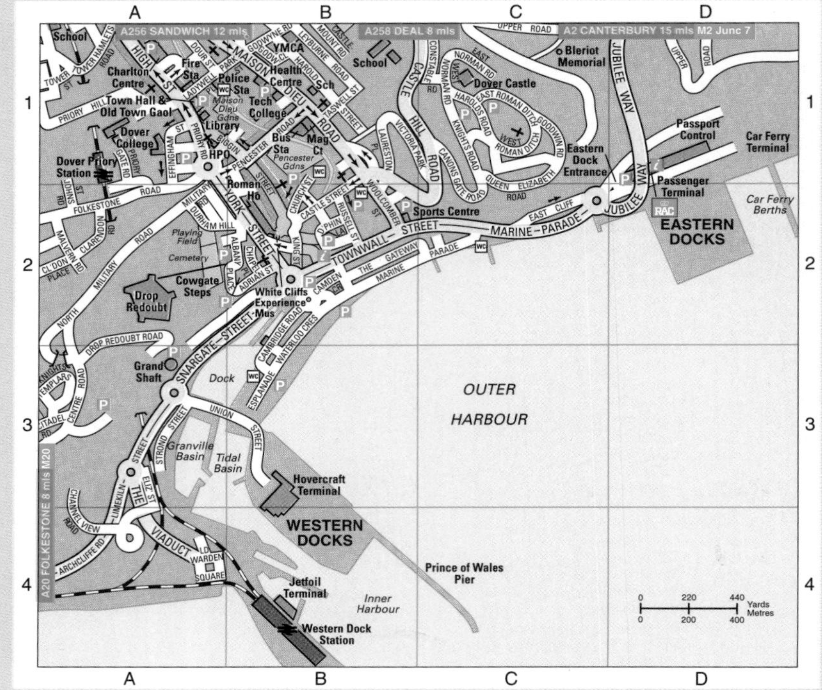

DUNDEE

Ann Street B1
Arthur Street B1
Bank Street B3
Barrack Road A2
Barrack Street B3
Bell Street B2
Blackscroft D1
Bonnybank Road C1
Brown Street A2/3
Camperdown Street D3
Candle Lane C3
Castle Street C3
City Square C3
Commercial Street C3
Constable Street D1
Constitution Road A1/B2
Constitution Street A1
Court House Square A3
Cowgate C2
Crescent Lane D1
Crescent Street D1
Crichton Street B3
Dens Brae D1
Dock Street C3
Dudhope Street B2
Dudhope Terrace A1
Eadies Road C1
East Dock Street D2
East Henderson's Wynd A3
East Marketgait D2
Euclid Crescent B2
Exchange Street C3
Forebank Road B1
Foundry Lane D2
Gellatly Street C3
Guthrie Street A3
Hawk Hill A3
High Street B3
Hilltown B1
Hilltown Terrace B1
Johnston Street A3
King Street C2
Ladywell Lane C1
Laurel Bank A1
Lindsay Street A3
Market Gait A2/3
Mary Ann Lane C2
McDonald Street B1
Meadowside B2/3
Murraygate C2
Nelson Street C1
Nethergate B4
Nicoll Street B3
North Marketgait A2/B2
Panmure Street B2
Park Place A4
Perth Road A4
Powrie Road B1
Princes Street D1
Prospect Place A1
Queens Street C2
Reform Street B3
Riverside Drive C4
Rosebank Road A1
Rosebank Street B1
St Andrews Street C2
Seagate C2/3
Session Street A3
South Marketgait C4
South Victoria Dock Road D3
South Ward Road A3
Southay Street A4
Tay Road Bridge D4
Trades Lane C2
Union Street B4
Union Terrace A1
Victoria Road C1
Victoria Street D1
Ward Road A3
Wellington Street C1
West Bell Street A2
West Marketgait A4/B4
Westport A3
Whitehall Crescent C4
Whitehall Street B3
William Street C1
Willison Street B3

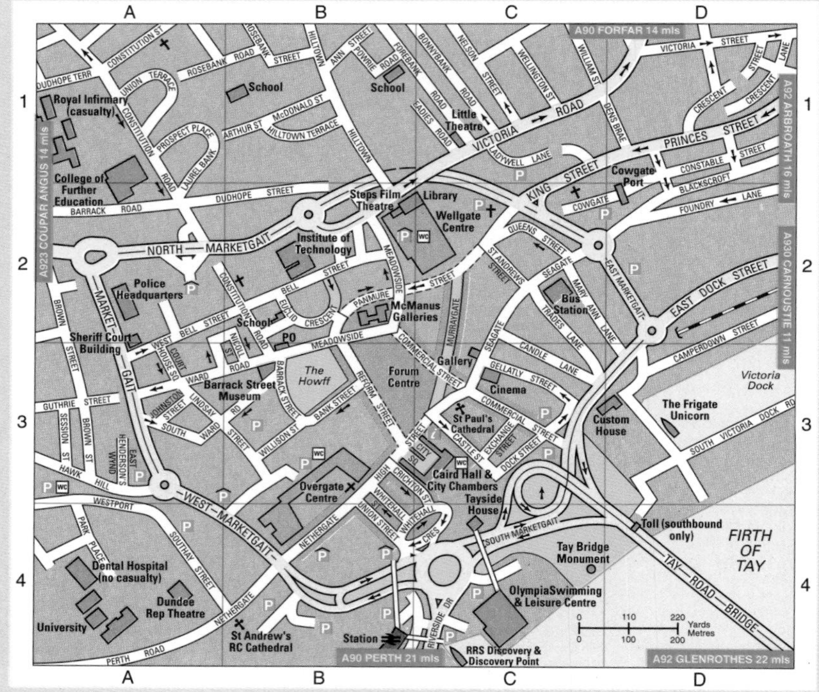

What to carry in your car

Don't be at a loss if you break down or are involved in an accident. The following items can be easily stored in your vehicle and will prove useful - torch, hazard warning triangle, jump leads, tow rope, first aid kit, and a blanket. In winter, always carry warm clothing and a pair of wellington boots.

EDINBURGH

Abercrombie Place B1
Adam Street D3
Albany Street C1
Argyle Place C4
Bank Street B2
Beaumont Place D3
Bernard Terrace D4
Bread Street A3
Bristo Place C3
Brougham Street A3/B4
Broughton Street C1
Bruntsfield Place A4
Buccleuch Place C4
Buccleugh Street D4
Calton Hill C1
Calton Road C2/D2
Candlemaker Row C3
Canongate D2
Castle Hill B2
Castle Street A1/2
Castle Terrace A2/3
Chalmers Street B3/4
Chambers Street C3
Chapel Street C3
Charles Street C3
Charlotte Square A2
Circus Lane A1
Clerk Street D4
Clyde Street C1
Cockburn Street C2
College Street C3
Coronation Walk B4
Cowgate C2
Cross Causeway D3
Davie Street D3
Dean Street A1
Doune Terrace A1
Drummond Street C3/D3
Dublin Street B1/C1
Dumbiedykes Road D2/3
Dundas Street B1
Earl Grey Street A3
East Market Street C2/3
East Prenton Street D4
Elder Street C1
Forrest Road C3
Forth Street C1
Fountainbridge A3
Frederick Street B1/2
George Square C3
George Street A2/B1
George IV Bridge C2/3
Gillespie Crescent A4
Gilmore Place A4
Gladstone Terrace C4
Glen Street A3
Glengyle Terrace A4
Gloucester Lane A1
Gloucester Street A1
Grassmarket B3
Great King Street B1
Grindlay Street A3
Gullan's Close D2
Hanover Street B1
Herriot Row A1/B1
High Riggs A3
High Street C2
Hill Place D3
Hill Street A1
Hillside Crescent D1
Holyrood Road D2
Home Street A4
Hope Park Terrace D4
Hope Street A2
Howe Street A1/B1
India Place A1
India Street A1
Infirmary Street C3
Jawbone Walk B4/C4
Jeffrey Street C2
Johnston Terrace B3
Kerr Street A1
Kier Street B3
King's Stables Rd. A2/B3
Lady Lawson Street B3
Lauriston Gardens B3/4
Lauriston Place B3
Lauriston Street B3
Lawn Market B2
Leamington Terrace A4
Leith Street C1
Leven Street A4
Leven Terrace B4
Lochrin Place A4
London Road D1
Lonsdale Terrace B4
Lothian Road A2/3
Lothian Street C3
Lower Gilmore Place A4
Lutton Place D4
Marchmont Crescent B4
Marchmont Road B4
Market Street C2
Meadow Lane C4
Melville Drive B4/C4
Melville Terrace C4
Meuse Lane C1/2
Moncrieff Terrace D4
Montague Street D4
Moray Place A1
Morrison Street A3
Mound, The B2
Nelson Street B1
New Circus Place A1
New Street D2
Nice Square C3
Nicolson Street C3/D3
North Bridge C2
North Lane A1
Northumberland St. B1
Old Tolbooth Wynd D2
Oxford Street D4
Panmure Place B4
Parkside Street D4
Pleasance Street D3
Ponton Street A3
Potter Row C3
Princes Street A2/B2
Queen Street A1/B1
Queen's Drive D3
Rankeillor Street D4
Regent Road D1/D2
Regent Terrace D1
Richmond Lane D3
Richmond Place D3
Rose Street A2/B2
Rosen Terrace C4
Roxburgh Place D3
Royal Circus A1
Royal Terrace D1
Rutland Street A2
St John Street D2
St Leonard's Hill D3
St Leonard's Lane D4
St Leonard's St. D3/4
St Mary's Street D2
St Vincent Street A1
Sciennes D4
Semple Street A3
Simon Square D3
South Bridge C2/3
South Clerk Street D4
South Charlotte St. A2
South Lane A1
Spittal Street A3
Summerhall D4
Sylvan Place C4
Tarvit Street A4
Teviot Place C3
Thistle Street B1
Union Street C1
Upper Gilmore Place A4
Valleyfield Street A4
Victoria Street B2/3
Warrender Park Rd. B4
Warrender Park Ter. B4
Waterloo Place C1
Waverley Bridge C2
Wemyss Place A1
West Approach Road A3
West End A2
West Port B3
West Preston Street D4
West Register Street C1
West Richmond St. D3
West Tolcross A3
York Lane C1
York Place C1
Young Street A2

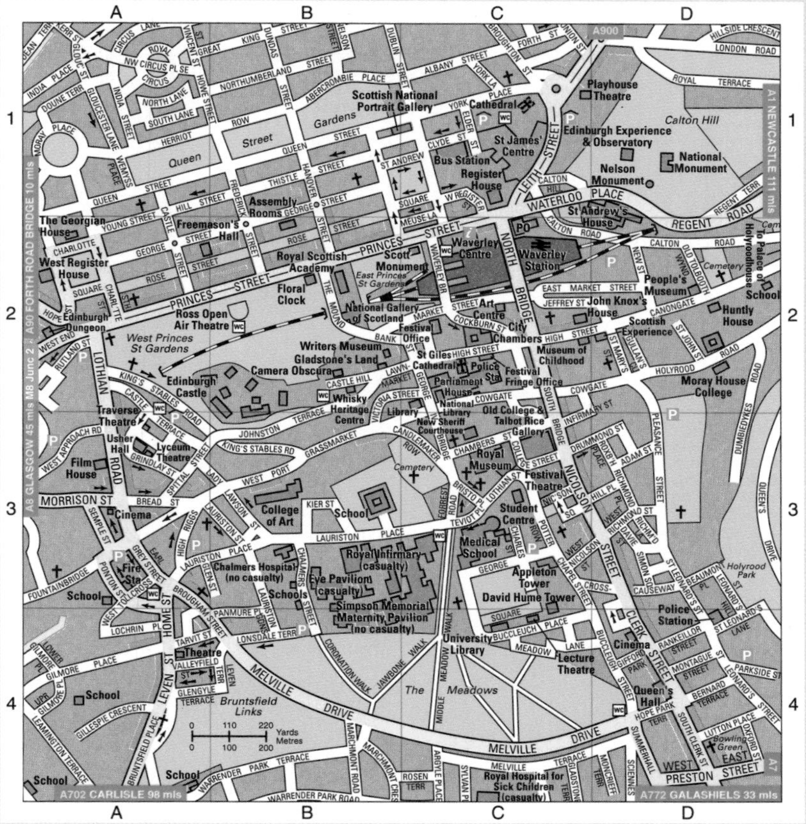

EXETER

Archibald Road D2
Athelstan Road D2
Auckland Road D1
Bailey Street C2
Bampfylde Street D1
Barbican Steps A3
Barnfield Cres. C2/D2
Barnfield Road C2/D2
Bartholomew St East B2
Bartholomew St West A3
Bartholomew Ter. A3
Bear Street B3
Bedford Street C2
Belgrave Road D1
Bernado Road D4
Bonhay Road A2/3
Bude Street C1/D1
Bull Meadow Road C4
Castle Street C1/2
Cathedral Close C2/3
Cathedral Yard B2
Catherine Street C2
Cedars Road D4
Chapel Street C2
Cheeke Street D1
Colleton Crescent C4
Commercial Road B4
Coombe Street B3
Cowick Street A4
Dean Street D4
Denmark Road D2/3
Dinham Crescent A2
Dinham Road A2
Dix's Field C2/D2
East Grove Road D4
Exe Bridge North A4
Exe Bridge South A4
Exe Street A2/3
Fairpark Road D3/4
Fore Street B3
Friars Walk C4
Friars Gate C4
Frog Street A4
Gandy Street B2
George Street B3
Haldon Road A2
Haven Road B4
Hele Road A1
High Street B2/C2
Holloway Street C4
Iron Bridge A2/B2
King Street B3
King William St. C1/D1
Little Silver A1
Longbrook Street C1
Longbrook Terrace C1
Lower North Street A2
Lucky Lane C4
Magdalen Road D3
Magdalen Street C3
Market Street B3
Mary Arches Street B2/3
Melbourne Place C4
Melbourne Street C4
Musgrave Row B2/C2
Napier Terrace A2
New Bridge Street A3/4
New North Road B1/C1
North Street B2
Northernhay Street B2
Okehampton Place A4
Okehampton Street A4
Palace Gate C3
Paris Street 2/D2
Paul Street B2
Post Office Street C2
Preston Street B3
Princes Way C2
Quay, The C4
Quay Hill B4
Queen Street B1/2
Queens Terrace A1
Radford Road D4
Red Lion Lane D1
Richmond Road A1
Roberts Road C4/D4
St David's Hill A1/2
St Leonards Rd. D4
Sidwell Street D1
South Street B3
Southernay East C2/3
Southernay West C2/3
Southgate C4
Spicer Road D3
Stepcote Hill B3
Summerland Street D1
Temple Road C4/D4
Topsham Road C4
Tudor Court A4
Tudor Street A3
Verney Street D1
West Grove Road D4
Western Way B3/4
Western Way D1/2/3
Westgate C4
Wonford Road D4

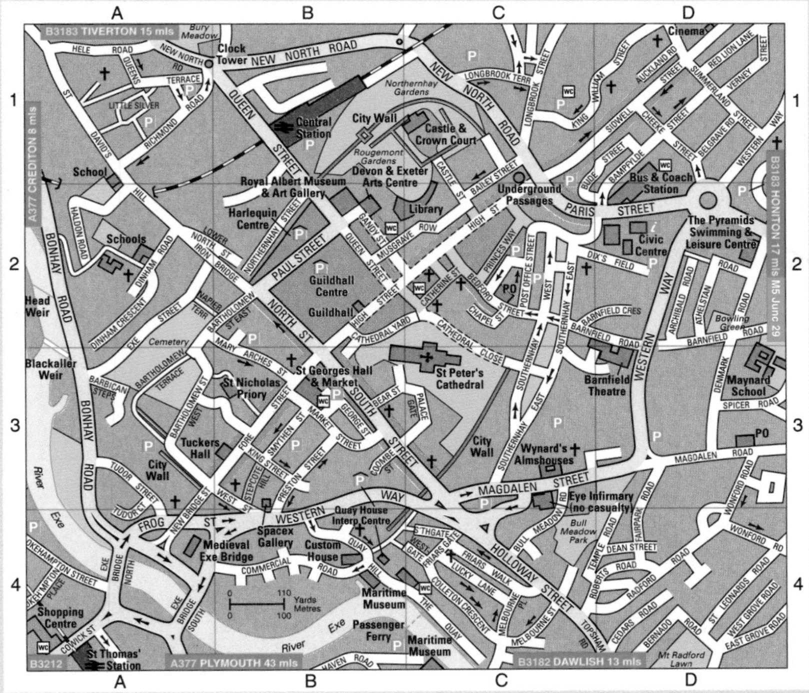

Town Plans

FOLKESTONE

Abbott Road C2
Albert Road B1/C1
Albion Road C1
Albion Villas B4
Alexandra Grove B3
Alexandra Street D1
Archer Road C1
Bellevue Street C2
Black Bull Road C1
Bolton Road C1
Boscombe Road B1
Bournemouth Gdns. B1
Bournemouth Road B1/2
Bouverie Place B3
Bouverie Road East B3
Bouverie Road West A3
Bradstone Avenue C1/2
Bradstone Road C2
Bridge Street D1
Broadmead Road A2/B2
Brockman Road A2
Cambridge Gardens B2
Canterbury Road D1
Castle Hill Avenue A3
Charlotte Street C2
Cheriton Gardens A3
Cheriton Place B3
Cheriton Road A1/B3
Christchurch Road A3
Church Street C3
Claremont Road A2
Clarence Street C2
Connaught Road B3
Coolinge Road B2
Copt Hall B3
Darby Road B2
Dawson Road C1
Denmark Street D1
Dover Road C2/D2
Dudley Road D3
East Cliff Gardens D3
East Cliff D3
Eastfields C2
Fern Bank Crescent C1
Folly Road D2
Foord Road B2
Foresters Way B3
Garden Road C1
Gladstone Road D1
Grace Hill B2/C3
Grove Road D2
Guildhall Street B2/B3
Harbour Street C3
Harbour Way C3
Harvey Street C2
Ingles Road A3
Jesmond Street B1
Kingsnorth Gardens A2
Leas, The A4/B4
Lennard Road D2
Linden Crescent C1
Lower Sandgate Road A4/B4
Manor Road A3
Marine Crescent B4
Marine Place B4/C4
Marine Terrace C4
Martello Road D2
Mill Field B3
Morrison Road D2
North Dyke Road D3
Old High Street, The C3
Parade, The C3
Park Farm Road B1
Pavillion Road B1
Penfold Road D2
Peter Street C2
Princess Street D1
Priory Grove C4
Queen Street C2
Radnor Bridge Road D3
Radnor Park Avenue A1
Radnor Park Cres. B2
Radnor Park Road A1/B1
Radnor Park West A1
Rendezvous Street B3
Rd of Rememberance B4
Rossendale Road D2
Russell Road B1
Ryland Place D2
St John's Church Rd. B1
St John's Street C2
St Michaels Street C3
Sandgate Road A3/B3
Shakespeare Terrace A4
Shellons Street B3
Shepway Close C1
Ship Street B2
Shorncliffe Road A2
Sidney Street D1
Stade, The D3
Tontine Street C3
Tram Road, The D3
Victoria Road B2
Victorian Grove B3
Walton Road C1
Watkin Road B1
West Terrace B4
Wiltie Gardens A2
Wilton Road A1

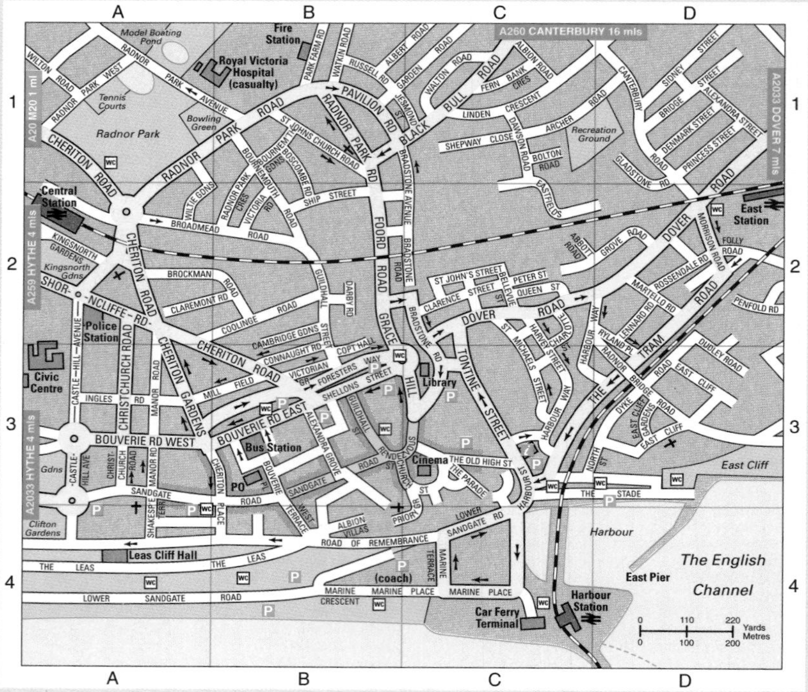

GLASGOW

Albert Bridge C4
Albion Street D3
Argyle Arcade C3
Argyle Street A3/B3
Baird Street D1
Ballater Street C4
Bath Street A2/B2
Bell Street D3
Blackfriars Street D3
Black Street D1
Blythswood Street A2/B2
Bothwell Street A2/B2
Bridgegate C4
Bridge Street B4
Broomielaw A3/B3
Brown Street A3
Brunswick Street C3
Buccleuch Street A1/B1
Buchanan Street C2/C3
Cadogan Street A3/B3
Calgary Street C1
Cambridge Street B1
Canal Street C1
Candleriggs D3
Carlton Place B4
Carnoustie Street A4
Carrick Street A3
Cathedral Street C2/D2
Centre Street B4
Charlotte Street D4
Cheapside Street A3
Clyde Place B4
Clyde Street C4
Coburg Street B4
Cochrane Street C3
College Street D3
Collins Street D2
Commerce Street B4
Cook Street A4/B4
Cooper Street D1
Cowcaddens Road B1/C1
Crimea Street A3
Dalhouse Street B1
Dobbie's Loan B1/C1
Douglas Street A2
Drury Street B2
Dunlop Street C3/4
Eglinton Street B4
Elmbank Street A2
Frederick Street C2/3
Fox Street B3/C3
Gallowgate D3/4
Garnet Hill Street A1
Garnet Street A1
Garscube Road B1
George V Bridge B3/4
George Square C2
George Street C2/D3
Glasgow Bridge B3/4
Glassford Street C3
Glebe Court D1
Glebe Street D2
Gloucester Street A4
Gorbals Street C4
Gordon Street B3
Grafton Street C2
Grant Street A1
Greendyke Street D4
Hill Street A1/B1
Holland Street A2
Holm Street A3/B3
Hope Street B2/B3
Howard Street B3/C3
Hutcheson Street C3
India Street A2
Ingram Street C3/D3
Jamaica Street B3
James Watt Street A3
Kennedy Street D1
Killermont Street C2
King Street C3/4
Kingston Bridge A3
Kingston Street A4/B4
Kinning Street A4
Kyle Street C1/D1
Laidlaw Street A4
Lanark Street D4
Lister Street D1
London Road D4
McAlpine Street A3
McAslin Court D2
McPhater Street B1
Martha Street C2
Miller Street C3
Milton Street B1/C1
Mitchell Street B3
Moir Street D4
Molendinar Street D3
Montrose Street D2/3
Morrison Street A4
Nelson Street A4/B4
New Wynd C3
Newton Street A1/2
Nicholson Street B4
Norfolk Court B4
Norfolk Street B4
North Street A2
North Hanover Street C2
North Wallace Street D1
Old Wynd C3
Osborne Street C3
Oswald Street B3
Oxford Street B4
Paisley Road A4
Parnie Street C3/D3
Paterson Street A4
Pinkston Road D1
Pitt Street A2
Port Dundas Road C1
Queen Street C3
Renfield Street B2
Renfrew Street A1/B1
Renton Street C1
Richmond Street D2
Robertson Street B3
Rose Street B1/2
Rottenrow D2
Royal Exchange Sq. C3
St Andrew's Sq. D4
St Andrew's St. D4
St Enoch Square B3
St George's Road A1
St James Road D2
St Mungo Ave. D2
St Mungo Place D2
St Vincent Place C2
St Vincent St. A2/B2
Saltmkt. High St. C4/D3
Sauchiehall Street A1/B2
Scott Street A1
Shamrock Street A1/B1
Shuttle Street D3
South Portland Street B4
Steel Street D4
Stewart Street B1
Stirling Road D2
Stockwell Street C3/4
Suspension Bridge B4
Taylor Street D2
Tradeston Street A4
Trongate C3
Turnbull Street D4
Tyndrum Street C1
Union Street B3
Victoria Bridge C4
Virginia Street C3
Wallace Street A4
Washington Street A3
Waterloo Street A2/B3
Watson Street D3
Wellington Street B2/B3
West Street A4
West Campbell St. B2/3
West George Street A2/B2/C2
West Graham St. A1/B1
West Nile Street B2/C2
West Regent St. A2/B2
William Street A2
Wilson Street C3
York Street B3

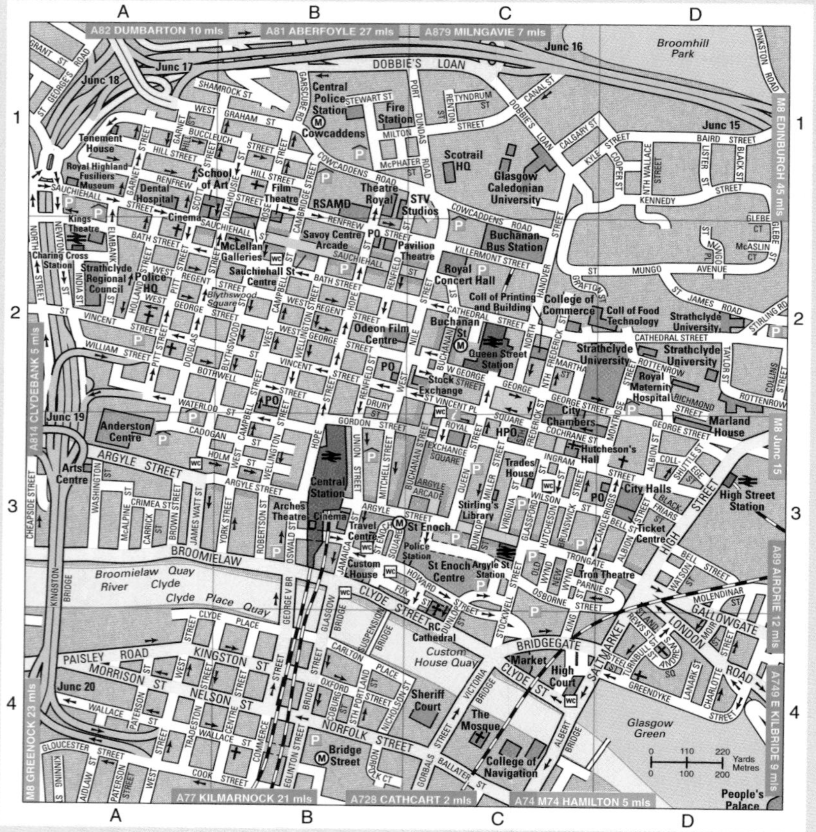

GLOUCESTER

Albert Street D3
Albion Street B4
All Saints Road C4
Alvin Street C1
Archdeacon Street B2
Archibald Street C4
Arthur Street C4
Baker Street A4
Barbican Road B3
Barbican Way A3
Barton Street D4
Bearland B2
Belgrave Road C4
Berkeley Street B2
Black Dog Way C2
Blackfriars B3
Blenheim Road D4
Bristol Road A4
Brunswick Road B3/B4
Brunswick Square B4
Bruton Way C3
Bull Lane B3
Church Street A4
Clare Street A1
Claremont Road D2
Clarence Street C3
College Court B2
College Street B2
Columbia Close C1
Commercial Road A3/B3
Cromwell Street C4
Crosskeys Lane B3
Dean's Walk B1
Dean's Way B1
Denmark Road D1
Eastgate Street B3/C3
Firs, The D1
Goodyere Street C4
Gouda Way B1
Great Western Road D2
Greyfriars B3
Guinea Street C1
Heathville Road D1
Henry Road D1
Henry Street D1
High Orchards A4
Honyatt Road D1
Jersey Road D4
Kings Barton Street C3/4
King's Square C2
Kingsholm Road C1
Lady Bellegate Street B3
Llanthony Road A4
London Road D2
Longsmith Street B3
Lower Westgate St. A1
Magdala Street D4
Market Parade C2
Merchants Road A4
Mercia Road B1
Metz Way D3
Midland Road C4
Mill Street D4
Millbrook Street D4
Montpelier B4
Mount Street B1
Napier Street D4
Nettleton Road C3
New Inn Lane B3
Norfolk Street B4
Northgate Street B2/C2
Old Tram Road B4
Oxbode, The C2
Oxford Road D1
Oxford Street D2
Park Road C4
Park Street C2
Parliament Street B3
Pembroke Street C4
Pitt Street B2
Prince Street C3
Priory Road B1
Quay, The A2
Quay Street A2
Royal Oak Road A1/2
Russell Street C3
St Aldate Street C2
St Catherine St. B1/C1
St John's Lane B2
St Lukes Street A4
St Mary's Square B2
St Michael's Sq. C3/B4
St Oswald's Street A1/B1
Serlo Road B1
Severn Road A3
Sherborne Street D1
Skinner Street C1
Somerset Place B4
Southgate Street B3
Spa Road B4
Station Road C3
Stratton Road D4
Swan Road C1
Sweetbriar Street C1
Three Cocks Lane B2
Trier Way C4
Union Street C1
Vauxhall Street D4
Victoria Street D4
Wellington Pde. C2/D2
Wellington Street C4
Westgate Street A2/B2
Widden Street D4
Worcester Parade C1
Worcester Street C2

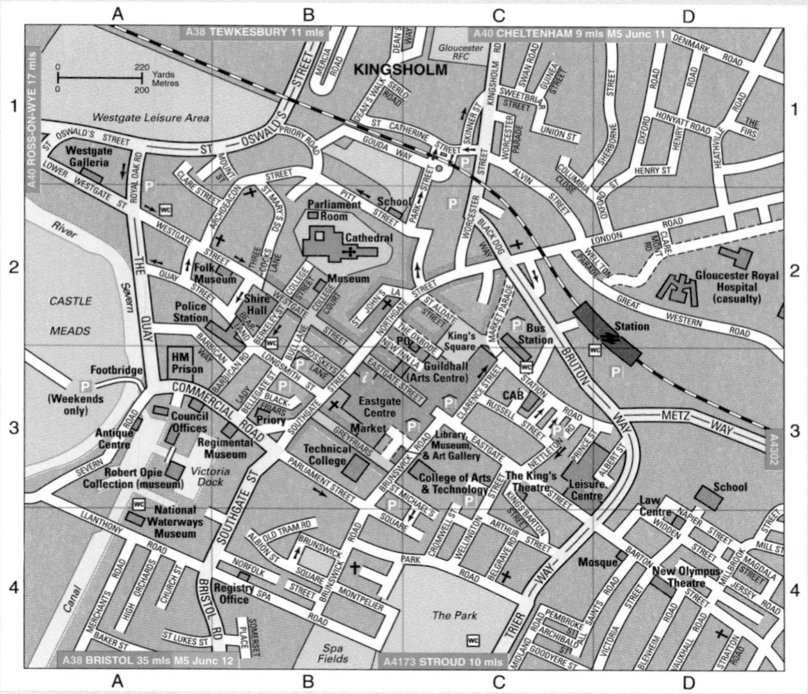

HULL

Adelaide Street A3
Albion Street B2
Aldbrough Street B1
Alfred Gelder Street C2
Alma Street D2
Anlaby Road A3
Baker Street B2
Beverley Road A1
Bishop Lane C3
Blackfriar Gate C3
Blake Close A1
Blanket Row C4
Bourne Street C1
Bridlington Avenue B1
Brook Street A2
Canning Street A2
Caroline Place B1
Caroline Street B1
Carr Lane B3
Carr Street B1
Castle Street B3
Chapel Lane C2
Charles Street B1
Charter House Lane C1
Church Street D2
Citadel Way D3
Clarence Street D2
Clifton Street A1
Coelus Street D1
Collier Street A2
Colonial Street A2
Commercial Road B4
Dagger Lane B3
Dansom Lane D1
Davis Street B2
Dock Avenue C2
Dock Street B2
Drypool Bridge C2/D2
Durban Street C1
Egton Street C1
English Street A4
Ferensway A2/3
Fish Street B3
Francis Street C1
Freetown Way A1/C1
Garrison Road C3/D3
George Street B2
Great Passage Street A3
Great Thornton St. A3
Great Union Street D2
Grey Street A1
Grimston Street B2
Guildhall Road B2
Hall Street A1
Hanover Square C2
Hedon Road D2
Hessle Road A4
High Street C2/3
Hodgson Street C1
Holborn Street D1
Humber Dock St. B3/4
Humber Street C4
Hyperion Street D2
Jameson Street B2
Jarratt Street B2
John Street B1
Kilburn Avenue B1
King Edward Street B2
King Street C3
Kingston Street B4
Liberty Lane C3
Liddel Street B1
Lime Street C1
Lister Street A4
Lockwood Street B1
Lombard Street A2
Low Gate C3
Manor House Street B4
Manor Street C3
Market Place C3
Marlborough Terrace A1
Marvel Street D2
Melville Street A3
Midland Street A3
Mill Street A2
Minerva Terrace C4
Myton Street B3
Nelson Street C4
New Cleveland Street C1
New Garden Street B2
New George Street B1/C1
Norfolk Street A1
North Church Side C3
North Street A2
Osborne Street A3/B3
Paragon Street B2
Pearson Street A2
Pease Street A3
Pemberton Street D1
Pennington Street D1
Percy Street B2
Pier Street C4
Popple Street D2
Porter Street A3/4
Portland Street A2
Postern Gate B3
Prince's Dock Street B3
Princess Street C1
Prospect Street A2
Queen Street C4
Railway Street B4
Raywell Street B1
Reform Street B1
Roper Street B3
Russell Street A1
St James Square A4
St James Street A4
St Luke's Street A3
St Peters Street D2
Salthouse Lane C2
Saville Street B2
Scale Lane C3
Scott Street B1
Silvester Street B2
South Bridge Road D3
South Church Side C3
Spring Bank A1
Spring Street A2
Spyvee Street C1/D1
Stephens Square A2
Story Street B2
Sykes Street B1
Tower Street C3
Trafalgar Street A1
Tynem Street B1/2
Upper Union Street A3
Vane Street A1
Waltham Street B2
Waterhouse Lane B3
Waverley Street A4
Wellington Street B4
West Street A2
Whitefriargate B3
Wilberforce Drive C2
William Street A4
Wilton Street D1
Wincolmlee C1
Witham D1
Wright Street A1

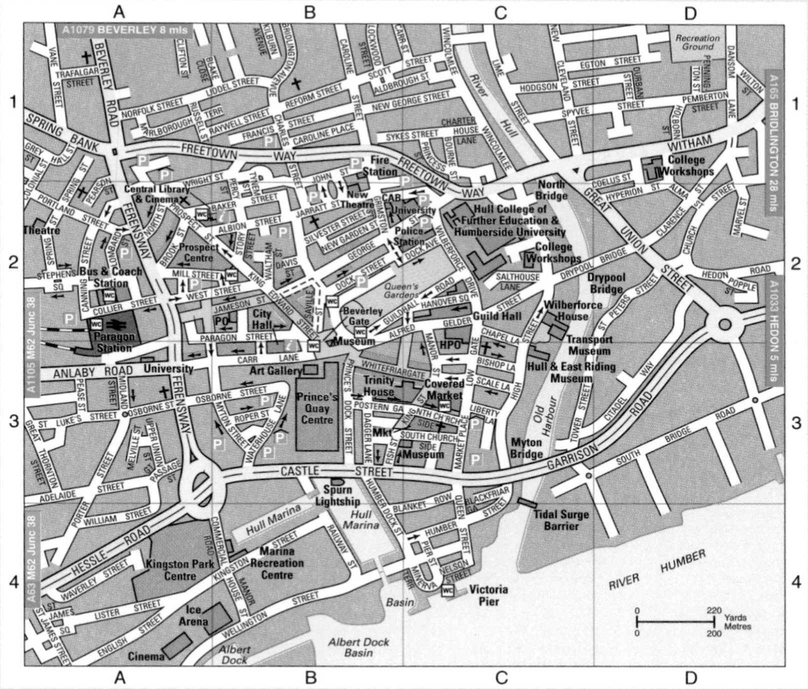

LEEDS

Aire Street B4
Albion Place C3
Albion Street C2/3
Bedford Street B3
Beech Grove Terrace A1
Belgrave Street C2
Blenheim Walk B1
Blundell Street A2
Boar Lane C4
Bond Street B3
Bowman Lane D4
Bridge End C4
Bridge Street D2
Briggate C3
Brunswick Terrace C1
Byron Street D2
Call Lane C4
Calls, The D4
Calverley Street A1/B2
Carlton Carr C1
Carlton Gate C1
Carlton Street B1
City Square B3/B4
Clay Pit Lane B2/C1
Cockbridge Street B2
Commercial Street C3
Crown Point Road D4
Dock Street D4
Dortmund Square C2
Duncan Street C3/D3
Dyer Street D3
East Parade B3
Eastgate C3/D3/D2
Elmwood Road C1
Fenton Street A2
George Street D3
Gower Street D2
Grafton Street D1
Great George Street A2/B2
Greek Street B3
Harewood Street D3
Harper Street D3
Harrison Street C2
Headrow, The B3/C3
High Court D4
Hillary Place A1
Hunslet Road D4
Infirmary Street B3
Inner Ring Road B1/C1/D2
Kendal Street D4
King Street B3
King Edward Street C3
Kirkgate C3/D3
Lands Lane C3
Leylands Road D1/2
Little Queen Street A3
Lovell Park Road C1
Lower Basinghall St. B3
Mark Lane C2
Merrion Street C2
Merrion Way C2
Mill Hill C4
Neville Street B4
New Briggate C2
New Market Street C3/D3
New Station Street B4/C4
New York Street D3
Nile Street D2
North Street D1/2
Northern Street A4
Oxford Place B2
Oxford Row B2
Park Cross Street B3
Park Place A3/B3
Park Row B3
Park Square East B3
Park Square North A3
Park Square South A3
Park Square West A3
Park Street A2
Portland Crescent B2
Portland Street B2
Portland Way B1/2
Quebec Street B3
Queen Square B1
Queen Street A3
Rossington Street B2
St Ann Street B2
St Pauls Street A3/B3
Sheepscar Grove D1
Sheepscar Street Sth D1
Skinner Lane D1
South Parade B3
Sovereign Street C4
Swinegate C4
Templar Lane D2
Templar Place D2
Templar Street D2
Thoresby Place A2
Trafalgar Street D2
Union Street D3
Upper Basinghall St. B3
Vicar Lane D2/3
Victoria Quarter C3
Wade Lane C2
Waterloo Street D4
Wellington Street A4
Westgate A3/B3
Westgate Tunnel A2
Wharf Street D4
Whitehall Road A4
Willow Terrace Road A1
Woodhouse Lane B1/2
York Place A3

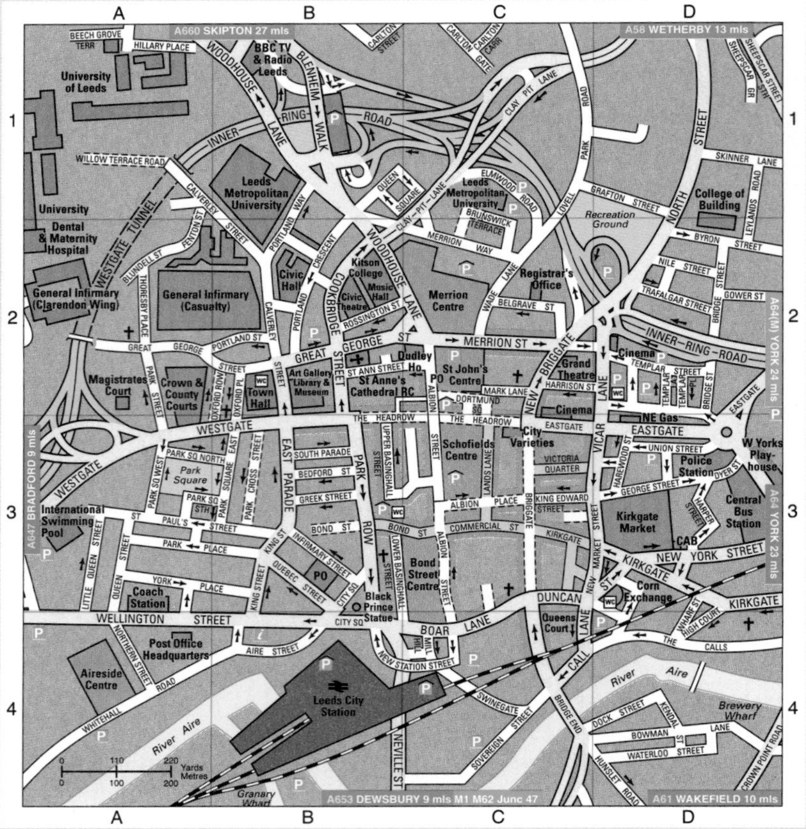

LEICESTER

Abbey Street C1
Albion Street C3
All Saints Road A2
Baron Street D2
Bath Lane A2/3
Bedford Street South C1
Belgrave Gate C1
Belvoir Street C3
Blackfriars Street A2
Bowling Green Street C3
Braunstone Gate A4
Brown Street C4
Burgess Street B1
Burleys Way B1
Burton Street D2
Campbell Street D3
Cank Street C2
Carlton Street C4
Castle Street B3
Charles Street C2/D3
Chatham Street C3
Church Gate B1/C2
Clarence Street C2
Clyde Street D1
Colton Street D3
Conduit Street D4
Crafton Street West D1
Craven Street B1
De Montfort Street D4
Dover Street C3
Dryden Street C1
Duke Street C4
Duns Lane A3
East Street D3
Eastbond Street B1
Fox Street D3
Freeschool Lane B2
Friar Lane B3
Gallowtree Gate C2
Gateway Street B4
Granby Street C3
Grange Lane B4
Grasmere Street B4
Gravel Street C1
Great Central St. A1/2
Greyfriars B3
Guildhall Lane B2
Halford Street C2
Haymarket C2
High Cross Street B1/B2
High Street B2
Horsefair Street C3
Hotel Street C3
Humberstone Gate C2/D2
Jarvis Street A1
King Street C4
Lee Street C1
London Road D4
Manitoba Road D1
Mansfield Street C1
Market Place C2
Market Place C3
Market Street C3
Midland Street D2
Mill Lane B4
Millstone Lane B3
Moreledge Street D2
Nelson Street D4
New Walk C4
Newarke, The B4
Newarke Street B3
Newpark Street A3
Nichols Street D2
Northgate Street A1
Orchard Street C1
Ottawa Road D1
Oxford Street B4
Peacock Lane B3
Pocklingtons Walk C3
Princess Road West C4
Queen Street D2
Regent Road C4
Regent Street D4
Rutland Street D2
St George Street D3
St George's Way D3
St Johns Walk D3
St Margaret's Way B1
St Martins B3
St Mathews Way D1
St Nicholas Circle B2/3
St Peters Lane B2
Sanvey Gate B1
Silver Street B2
Soar Lane A1
South Albion Street D4
Southampton Street D2
Southgates B3
Station Street D3
Swain Street D3
Tower Street C4
Upper King Street C4
Vaughan Way B1
Waterloo Way D3/D4
Welford Road C4
Wellington Street C4
West Bridge A3
Western Blvd. A3/A4
Western Road A4
Wharf Street North D1
Wharf Street South D1
Wimbledon Street D2
Yeoman Street C2
York Road B4

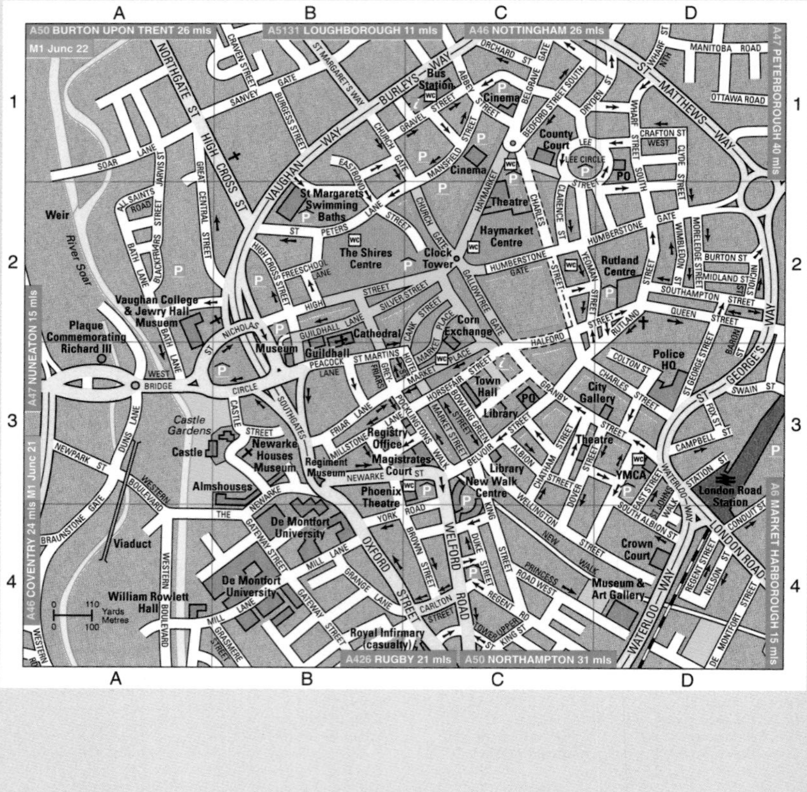

LIVERPOOL

Addison Street B2/C2
Bath Street A2
Berry Street D4
Birkett Street C1
Bixteth Street B2
Blackstock Street B1
Bold Street C3
Bond Street B1
Brownlow Hill D3
Brunswick Street A3/B3
Bryom Street C2
Burlington Street B1
Bute Street D1
Caldedonia Street D4
Canning Place B3
Canning Street D4
Canterbury Street D2
Carlton Street A1
Carruthers Street B1
Carver Street D2
Castle Street B3
Catherine Street D4
Chapel Street A3/B2
Cheapside B2
Chisenhale Street B1
Church Street C3
Churchill Way South C2
Clarence Street D3
Clegg Street C1
College Lane B3
College Way D1
Colquitt Street C4
Comus Street C1
Cook Street B3
Copperas Hill C3/D3
Corn Hill B4
Cornwallis Street C4
Cotton Street A1
Covent Garden A3
Cropper Street C3
Crosshall Street B2/3
Dale Street B2/3
Dawson Street C3
Douro Street D1
Drury Lane B3
Duke Street C4
East Street A2
Eaton Street B1
Edmund Street A2/B2
Eldon Street B1
Eldonian Way B1
Everton Brow D1
Everton Terrace D1
Falkland Street D2
Falkner Street D4
Fenwick Street B3

LIVERPOOL

continued from page 136

Fleet Street C3/4
Fontenoy Street C2
Forrest Street C4
Fox Street C1
Fraser Street C2
Freemasons Row B2
Gardners Row C1
Gascoyne Street B2
Gill Street D3
Gradwell Street C3/4
Great Crosshall St. B2/C2
Great George Street C4
Great Homer Street C1
Great Howard Street A1
Great Newton Street D3
Grenville Street Sth. C4
Haigh Street D1
Hanover Street B3/C3
Hardman Street D4
Harrington Street B3
Hart Street D2
Hatton Garden B2
Hawke Street C3
Haymarket C2
Henry Street C4
Highfield Street B2
Hood Street C3
Hope Street D4
Iliad Street C1
Islington C2/D2
James Street B3
Kempston Street D2
Kent Street C4
King Edward Street A2
Kingsway A1
Langdale Street D2
Leece Street D4
Leeds Street A2/B2
Lime Street C2/3
Limekiln Lane C1
London Road C2/D2
Lord Street B3
Lord Nelson Street C2/D3
Love Lane A1
Lydia Ann Street C4
Manchester Street C2
Mann Island A3
Mansfield Street C2/D1
Marybone B2
Maryland Street D4
Midghall Street B2
Moorfields B2
Mount Pleasant D3
Myrtle Street D4
Naylor Street B1/2
Nelson Street C4
Netherfield Road Sth. D1
New Islington C2/D2
New Quay A2/3
North Street B2
Oil Street A1
Old Hall Street A2
Oriel Street B1
Pall Mall A1/A2/B2
Paradise Street B3/4
Park Lane B4/C4
Parker Street C3
Parr Street C4
Paul Street B1
Pembroke Place D2/3
Pembroke Street D3
Pilgrim Street D4
Porter Street A1
Prince Edwin St. C1/D1
Queensway Tunnel A3/4
Ranelagh Street C3
Redcross Street B3
Regent Street A1
Renshaw Street C3
Richmond Row C1
Roberts Street A2
Rodney Street D4
Roe Street C3
Roscoe Street D4
Rose Hill C1
Rose Place C1
Russell Street D3
St Andrew Street D3
St Anne Street C1/2
St Nicholas Place A3
Salisbury Street D1
School Lane B3/C3
Scotland Road C1/C2
Seel Street C3/4
Seymour Street D2/3
Shaw Street D1
Shaw's Alley B4
Sir Thomas Street B3
Skelhorne Street C3
Slater Street C4
Soho Street D2
South John Street B3
Sparling Street C4
Springfield Street D2
Stafford Street D2
Stanley Street B3
Strand Street B3/4
Suffolk Street C4
Tabley Street B4
Tarleton Street C3
Temple Street B3
Titchfield Street B1
Tithebarn Street B2
Upper Duke Street D4
Upper Frederick St. C4
Upper Hope Place D4
Vandries Street A1
Vauxhall Road B1/B2
Vernon Street B2
Victoria Street B3
Village Street D1
Vulcan Street A1
Wapping B4
Water Street A3/B3
Waterloo Road A1/2
Whitechapel B3
William Brown St. C2
William Henry St. D1
Wood Street C3/4
York Street C4

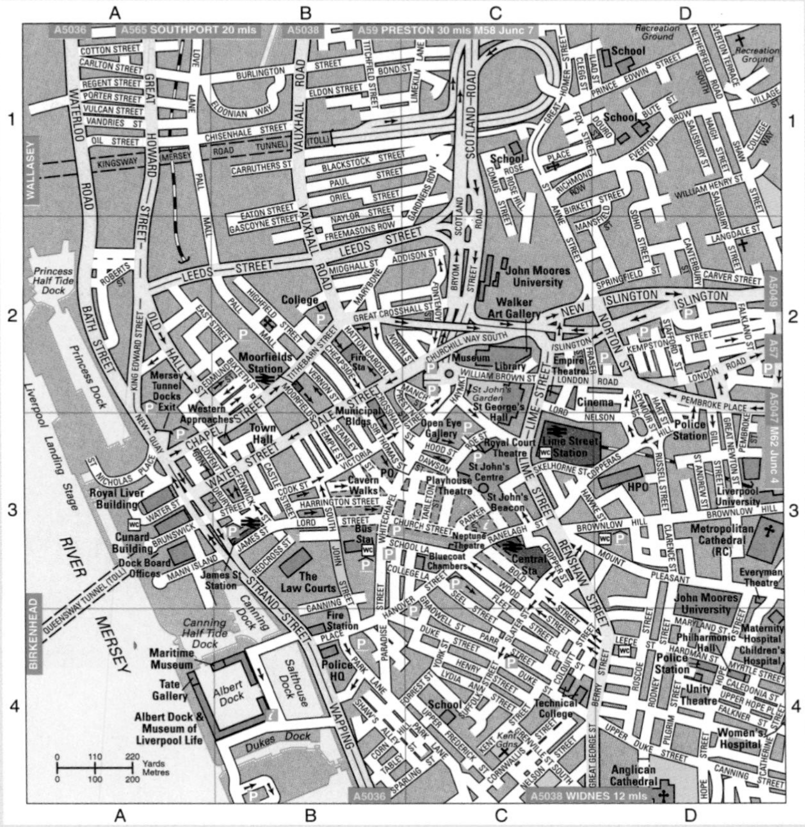

MANCHESTER

Addington Street D2
Albert Square B3
Albion Street B4/5
Angel Street C1
Aytoun Street D3/4
Back Piccadilly C3/D3
Balloon Street C2
Bendix Street D2
Blackfriars Road A1/2
Blackfriars Street B2
Bloom Street C4
Bombay Street C4
Booth Street A2
Booth Street B3/C3
Bootle Street B4
Bound Street A2
Bradshaw Street C2
Brazenose Street B3
Bridge Street A3
Bridgwater Viaduct A5
Brook Street D5
Brown Street B3/C3
Brown Street A2
Bury Street A2
Byrom Street A3/4
Cable Street D2
Calder Street B4
Cambridge Street B5
Camp Street A4
Cannon Street C2
Castle Street A5
Cateaton Street B2
Chapel Street A2/B2
Charles Street C5/D4
Charlotte Street C3
Chepstow Street B4
Chester Road A5
Chester Street B5/C5
China Lane D3
Chorlton Street C4/D4
Church Street C2
City Road B5
Clowes Street A2
College Land B3
Commercial Street A5
Cook Street A2
Corporation St. B2/C2
Cray Walk D5
Cross Street B3
Crown Street A5
Dale Street D3
Dantzic Street C1/2
Dean Street D3
Deansgate A4/B3/B2
Dickinson Street B4/C4
Ducie Street D3
Duke Place A4
Duke Street A4
East Street B4
Fairfield Street D4
Fennel Street B2
Fountain Street C3
Garden Lane A2
Garden Street C2
Gartside Street A3
George Leigh Street D2
George Street B3/4
Goadsby Street C2/D2
Goulden Street D2
Granby Row D4
Grape Street A4
Gravel Lane B2
Great Ancoats Street D2
Great Bridgewater Street A4/B4
Great Jackson Street A5
Greengate A1/B2
Grosvenor Street C5/D5
Hall Street B4
Hanover Street C2
Hardman Street A3
Henry Street D2
Hewitt Street A5/B5
High Street C3/C2
Hilton Street D2/3
Houldsworth Street D2
Hulme Street B5
Jackson Crescent A5
John Dalton Street B3
Jordan Street A5
Kennedy Street B3
Kincardine Road D5
King Street A2
King Street B3
King Street West A3/B3
Lever Street D2/3
Little Peter Street A5/B5
Liverpool Road A4
Lloyd Street B3
London Road D4
Long Millgate B2/C2
Longworth Street A4
Lower Byrom Street A4
Lower Mosley Street B4
Major Street C3/C4
Mancunian Way A5-D5
Marble Street C3
Market Street C3
Marsden Street B3
Marshall Street D2
Medlock Street B5
Miller Street C2
Minshull Street C3/D4
Mosley Street C3
Mount Street B4
New Bailey Street A3
New Bridge Street B1
New Quay Street A3
Newcastle Street B5
Newton Street D3
Nicholas Street C3
Oak Street D2
Oldham Road D2/C4
Oldham Street C3/D2
Oxford Road C5
Oxford Street B4/C4
Pall Mall B3
Parker Street C3
Peter Street B4
Piccadilly D3
Port Street D3
Portland Street C3/4
Princess Street B3/C4/C5
Pritchard Street C5
Quay Street A2/A3
Queen Street A2
Queen Street B3
Rice Street A4
Richmond Street C4
River Street B5
Rochdale Road D1
Sackville Street C4/D4
St Ann's Square B3
St Ann's Street B3
St James Street C4
St John's Street A4
St Mary's Gate B2
St Mary's Parsonage A3/B3
St Peter's Square B4
Salford Approach B2
Shude Hill C2
South King Street B3
Southmill Street B4
Spear Street D2/3
Spring Gardens C3
Stanley Street A3
Station Approach B2/C2
Store Street D3/4
Swan Street D2
Tariff Street D3
Thomas Street C2
Thompson Street D1/2
Tib Lane B3
Tib Street C3/D2
Tonman Street A4
Trafford Street A4/B4
Trinity Way A2

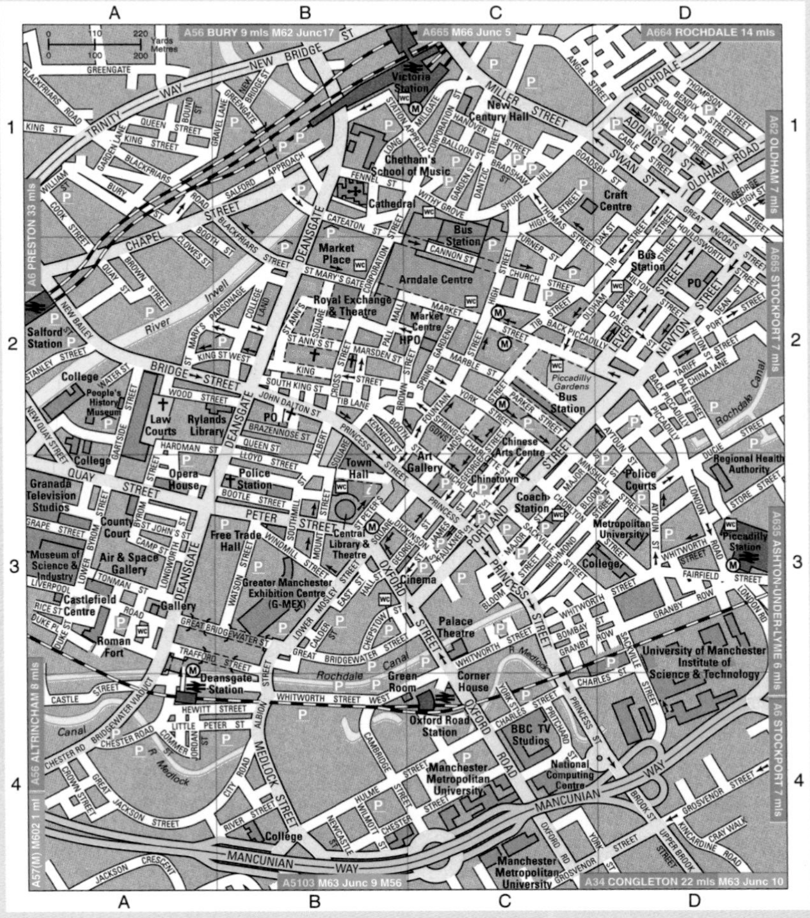

Turner Street C2
Upper Brook Street D5
Water Street A3
Watson Street B4
Whitworth Street C4/D4
Whitworth St. West B4
William Street A2
Wilmot Street B5
Windmill Street B4
Withy Grove C2
Wood Street A3
York Street C3
York Street C4/5
York Street C5/D5

MILTON KEYNES

Adelphi Street C1
Albion Place D2
Arbrook Avenue A2
Arlott Crescent C4
Avebury Blvd. A4/D1
Blairmont Street C1
Booker Avenue A1
Bossiney Place C3
Boycott Avenue B4/C3
Bradwell Common Boulevard A2
Boundary, The C4
Brill Place A2
Burnham Drive A1
Carlina Place B1
Century Avenue C4
Chaffron Way (H7) D4
Childs Way (H6) A4/D2
Cleavers Avenue B1
Coleshill Place A1
Colgrain Street D1
Coltsfoot Place B1
Columbia Place D2
Conniburrow Blvd. B1
Cranesbill Place B1
Craven, The A1
Dalgin Place D2
Dansteed Way (H4) A1
Dexter Avenue C4
Douglas Place B4
Edrich Avenue C4
Eelbrook Avenue A2
Elder Gate A3/A4
Enmore Gate D2
Evans Gate B4
Falcon Avenue D2
Falmouth Place C3
Fennel Drive B1
Fishermead Blvd. C3/D3
Forrabury Avenue A2
Germander Place B1
Gibsons Green A1
Grace Avenue B4
Grafton Gate (V6) A3/A4
Grafton Street (V6) A2
Grafton Street (V6) B4
Great Denson D4
Gurnards Avenue D3
Hadley Place A2
Hampstead Gate A2
Harrier Drive D4
Helford Place D3
Hutton Avenue C4
Ibstone Avenue A1
Kellan Drive D3
Kenwood Gate D2
Kernow Crescent D3
Kirkstall Place B4
Larwood Place C4
Lower 2nd Street A3
Lower 3rd Street B3
Lower 4th Street B3
Lower 8th Street C3
Lower 9th Street C2
Lower 10th Street C2
Lower 12th Street C2
Mallow Gate B1
Marigold Place B1
Marjoram Place B1
Marlborough Gate C1
Marlborough Street (V8) C1/D2/D3
Mayditch Place A2
Midsummer Boulevard A3/B3/C2
Milburn Avenue B4
Mullion Place D3
Newlyn Place D3
North 2nd Street A3
North 3rd Street A3
North 4th Street A3
North 5th Street B2
North 6th Street B2
North 7th Street B2
North 8th Street B2
North 9th Street B2
North 10th Street B2
North 11th Street C1
North 12th Street C1
North 13th Street C1
North Row A3/B2/C1
Oldbrook Boulevard B4
Padstow Avenue C3
Pencarrow Place C3/D3
Penryn Avenue D3
Pentewan Gate C3
Perran Avenue C4/D4
Plumstead Avenue B2
Polruan Place D4
Porthleven Place D3
Portway (H5) A3/B2/C1
Ramsons Avenue C1
Ravensbourne Place D2
Saxon Gate (V7) B2/C3
Saxon Street (V7) B1
Saxon Street (V7) C4
Secklow Gate C2/C3
Shackleton Place C4
Silbury Boulevard A3/D1
Skeldon Gate D1
Smithsons Place D2
South 5th Street B3
South 6th Street B3
South 7th Street B3
South 8th Street C3
South 9th Street C3
South 10th Street C3
South Row B3/C3
Speedwell Place C1
Stainton Drive A1
Statham Place C4
Stokenchurch Place A1
Stonecrop Place B1
Streatham Place A2
Strudwick Drive C4
Sutcliffe Avenue B4
Talland Avenue C3
Taymouth Place D1
Tolcarne Avenue D3
Towan Avenue D4
Trueman Place C4
Tylers Green A1
Ulyett Place C4
Upper 2nd Street A3
Upper 3rd Street A3
Upper 4th Street B3
Upper 5th Street B3
Vellan Avenue D4
Veryan Place D3
Wandsworth Place A2
Wardle Place B4
Wealdstone Place D2
Wimbledon Place A2
Wisley Avenue B2
Witan Gate A3/B3
Woodruff Avenue B1
Yarrow Place C1

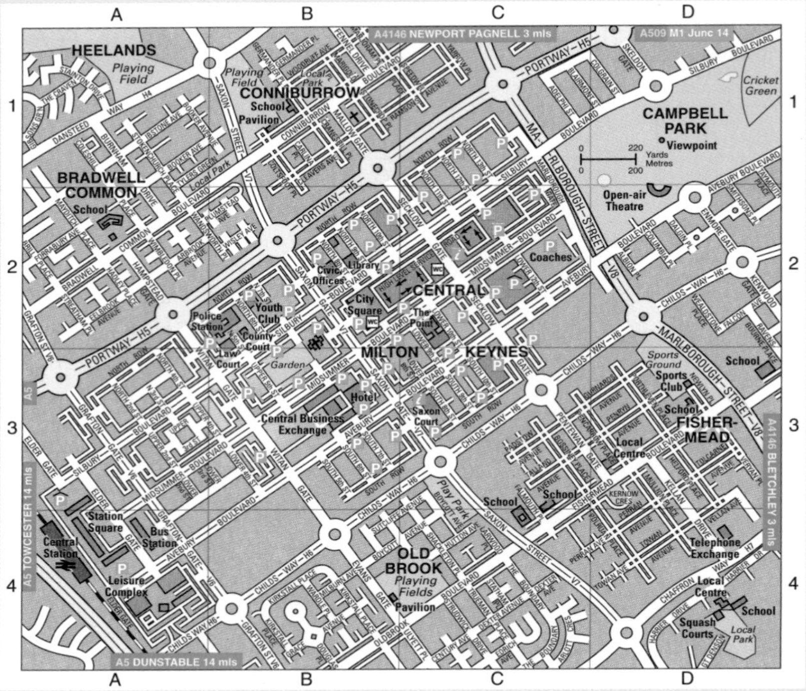

NEWCASTLE

Abbot's Road D4
Argyle Street D2
Bath Lane A3
Bells Court C3
Bewick Street A3/4
Bigg Market B3
Blackett Street B2
Bridge Street D4
Broad Chare D3
Byron Street D1
Camden Street D1
Carliol Square C2
Carliol Street C2
City Road D3
Clayton Street A3/B2/B3
Clayton Street West A3/4
Close, The B4/C4
Cloth Market B3
College Street C1
Collingwood Street B3
Corporation Street A2
Cross Street A3
Durant Road C1/2
Eldon Square B2
Ellison Place C1/D1
Falconar Street D1
Fenkle Street A3
Forth Banks A4
Forth Street A4/B4
Friar Street A3
Gallowgate A2
Garth Heads D3
Grainger Street B3
Grey Street B2/C3
Groat Market B3
Hanover Square B4
Hanover Street B4
Haymarket B1
High Bridge B3/C3
Hillgate D4
Hood Street B2/C2
John Dobson Street C1
Killingworth Place A2
King Street D4
Leazes Crescent A1
Leazes Lane A1/2
Leazes Park Road A1/2
Leazes Terrace A1
Low Friar Street A3
Manor Chare C3/D3
Market Street B2/C2
Melbourne Street D3
Monk Street A3
Morden Street B1
Mosley Street C3
Napier Street D1
Nelson Street B2
Neville Street A4/B3
New Bridge Street C2/D2
Newgate Street A2/B3
Northumberland Rd. C1
Northumberland Street B1/C2
Nun Street B3
Oakwellgate D4
Orchard Street B4
Pandon D3
Pandon Bank D3
Percy Street B1/2
Pilgrim Street C2/3
Pink Lane A3
Prudhoe Place B1
Prudhoe Street B1
Pudding Chare B3
Quayside D3/4
Queen Street D4
Ridley Place B1/C1
Rock Terrace D1
St Andrew's Street A2
St James Street A2
St John's Street B3
St Mary's Place B1/C1
St Nicholas Street C3/4
St Thomas Crescent A1/B1
St Thomas Street. A1/B1
Sandhill C4
Sandyford Road C1
Saville Row C2
Scotswood Road A4
Side C3
Simpson Terrace D2
South Street B4
Stepney Lane D2
Stowell Street A2/3
Strawberry Lane A2
Strawberry Place A2
Sunderland Street A3/4
Swing Bridge C4
Terrace Place A1
Tower Street D3
Tyne Bridge C3/D4
Vine Lane B1/C1
Waterloo Street A3/4
West Walls A3
Westgate Road A3/B3
Worswick Street C2

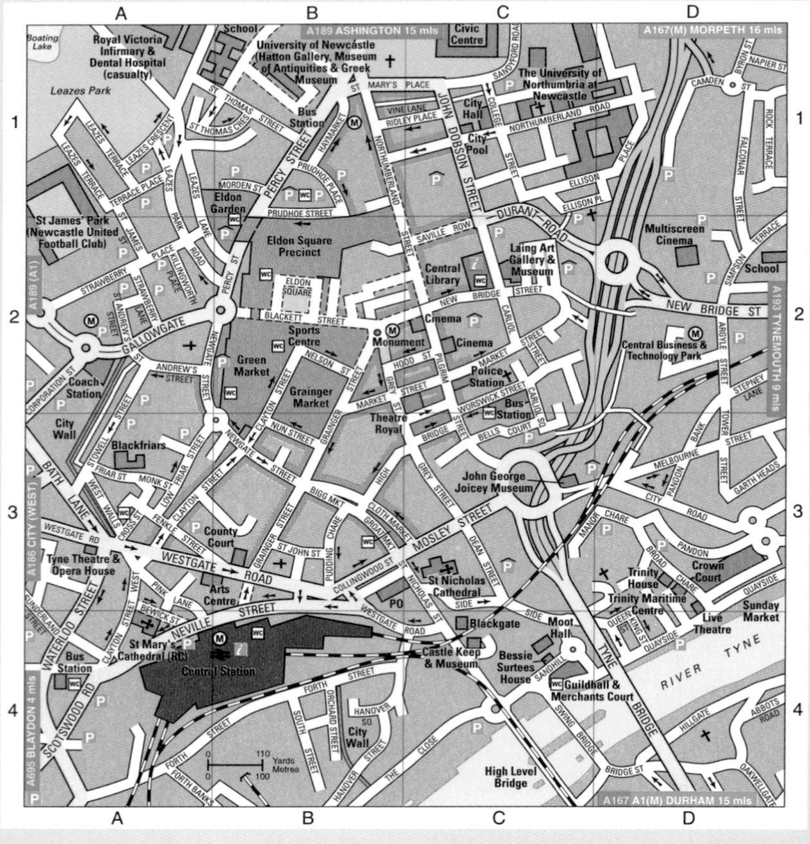

NORWICH

All Saints Green B4
Aspland Road D3
Bank Plain C2
Barker Street A1
Barn Road A1
Barrack Street D1
Bedford Street B2
Ber Street C4
Bethel Street A3
Bishop Bridge Road D1
Bishopgate C1/D2
Blackfriars Street C1
Botolph Street B1
Brazengate B4
Brigg Street B3
Bull Lane B4
Calvert Street B1
Carrow Road D4
Castle Meadow B3
Cathedral Street C2
Cattle Market Street C3
Chalk Hill Road D3
Chantry Road B3
Chapel Field Road A3
Chapel Loke C4
Chapelfield East A3
Chapelfield North A3
Charing Cross B2
Chatham Street B1
Cleveland Road A3
Colegate B1
Convent Road A3
Coslany Street B1/2
Cow Hill A2
Cowgate C1
Crooks Place A4
Derby Street A1
Duke Street B1/2
Ella Road D3
Elm Hill C2
Ely Street A1
Farmers Avenue B3
Fishergate C1
Fishers Lane A2
Fye Bridge C1/2
Gaol Hill B3
Gas Hill D2
Gentleman's Walk B3
Golden Ball Street C3
Golden Dog Lane B1
Golding Place A2
Grapes Hill A2
Gurney Road D1
Heigham Street A1
Horns Lane C4
James Close D1
King Street C2-D4
London Street B2
Lothian Street A1/2
Lower Clarence Road D3
Lower Close C2
Magdalen Street B1
Malthouse Road B3/4
Mariners Lane C4
Market Avenue C3
Mountergate C3
Mousehold Street D1
Music House Lane C4
Muspole Street B1
New Mills Yard A1
Norfolk Street A4
Oak Street A1/B1
Old Barge Lane C3/4
Opie Street B2
Orchard Street A1
Palace Street C2
Pitt Street B1
Pottergate A2/B2
Prince of Wales Road C2/D3
Prince's Street C2
Quay Side C1/2
Queen Street C2
Queen's Road B4
Rampant Horse Street B3
Recorder Road D2/3
Red Lion Street B3
Riverside Road D2
Riverside D3/4
Rosary Road D2/3
Rose Lane C3
Rouen Road C3/4
Sayer's Street A1
St Andrews Street B2
St Ann Lane C3
St Benedicts Street A2
St Crispins Road A1/B1
St Faiths Lane C2
St Georges Street B1/2
St Giles Street A2/B2
St Julian's Alley C4
St Leonards Road D2
St Martin at Palace Plain C1
St Mary's Plain B1
St Peters Street B3
St Saviours Lane C1
St Stephens Road A4
St Stephens Square A4
St Stephens Street B3/4
St Swithins Road A2
Surrey Street B4/C4
Theatre Street B3
Thorn Lane C4
Thorpe Road D3
Timber Hill B3
Trory Street A3
Union Street A4
Unthank Road A3
Upper Close C2
Upper Goat Lane B2
Upper King Street C2
Upper St Giles Street A2
Vauxhall Street A3/4
Victoria Street B4
Walpole Street A3
Wellington Lane A2
Wensum Street C2
Wessex Street A4
Westlegate B3
White Lion Street B3
Whitefriars C1
Willis Street C1
Wingate Way A1

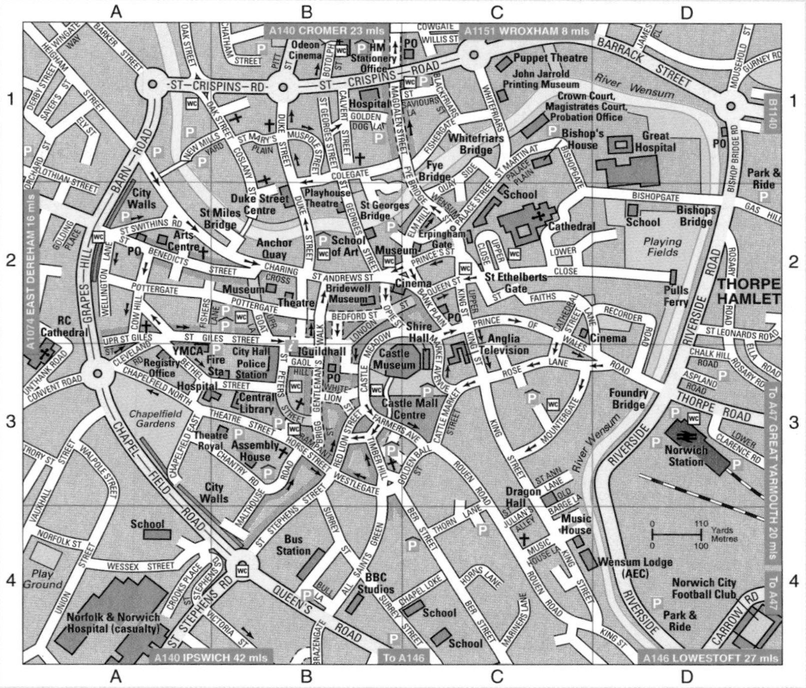

NOTTINGHAM

Alfred Street B3
Angel Row A2/B2
Barker Gate D3
Bath Street D1
Beast Market Hill B2
Beck Street D1/2
Bellar Gate D3
Belward Street D2
Bottle Lane C2
Bridgesmith Gate C3
Broad Street C2
Broadway C3
Bromley Place A2/3
Brook Street D2
Burton Street B1/2
Byard Lane C3
Cairns Street C1
Canal Street B4/C4
Carlton Street C2
Carrington Street C4
Castle Boulevard A4/B4
Castle Gate B3
Castle Road A4/B4
Castle Road B3/4
Chaucer Street A1
Cheapside B2
Clarendon Street A1
Cliff Road C3/D3
Clumber Street C2
Collin Street B4/C4
Convent Street C2
Cranbrook Street D2
Cumberland Place A3
Curzon Place C1
Curzon Street C1
Dean Street D3
Derby Road A2
East Circus Street A2
East Street C2
Exchange Walk B3
Fishergate D3
Fletcher Gate C2/3
Forman Street B2
Friar Lane A3/B3
Gedling Street D2
George Street C2
Glasshouse Street C1
Goldsmith Street A1
Goose Gate D2
Hamilton Drive A4
Hampden Street A1
Hanley Street A2
Heathcote Street C2
High Pavement C3
Hockley Street D2
Hollowstone D3
Hope Drive A4
Hounds Gate B3
Howard Street C1
Huntingdon Street C1/D2
Hurts Yard B2
Kayes Walk C3/D3
Kent Street C1
King Edward Street C1/2
King Street B2
Lamartine Street D1
Lenton Road A3
Lincoln Street C2
Lister Gate B3
London Road D4
Long Row B2
Low Pavement B3/C3
Lower Parliament Street C2/D2
Maid Marian Way A2-B3
Maiden Lane D2
Mansfield Road B1
Market Street B2
Middle Hill C3
Mid Pavement C3
Milton Street B1
Mount Street A2/3
Mowbray Court D1
North Church Street B1
North Sherwood St. B1
Park Row A3
Park Terrace A3
Park Valley A3
Peck Lane B2/3
Peel Street A1
Pelham Street C2
Pemberton Street D3
Perth Street C1
Peveril Drive A4
Pilcher Gate C3
Plantagenet Street D1
Plumptre Street D3
Popham Street C3/4
Queen Street B2
Regent Street A3
Rick Street C1
Ropewalk, The A3
St Ann's Street C1
St Ann's Well Road D1
St James's Street A3/B3
St James's Terrace A3
St Mark's Street C1
St Mary's Gate C3
St Peter's Gate B3/C3
St Peter's Ch. Walk C3
Shakespeare St. A1/B1
Shakespeare Villas A1/B1
Shelton Street C1/D1
Smithy Row B2
South Parade B2
South Sherwood St. B1
Spaniel Row B3
Standard Hill A3
Stanford Street B3
Station Street C4/D4
Stoney Street D3
Talbot Street A2
Thurland Street C2
Toll House Hill A2
Trent Street C4
Trinity Row B1/2
Trinity Walk B2
Trinity Square B1/2
Union Road B1
Union Road C1
Upper Parliament Street A2/B2
Vernon Street A2
Victoria Street C2
Warser Gate C2
Waverley Street A1
Weekday Cross C3
Wellington Circus A2
Wheeler Gate B3
Wilford Road B4
Wilford Street B4
Wollaton Street A2
Woolpack Lane D2
York Street B1

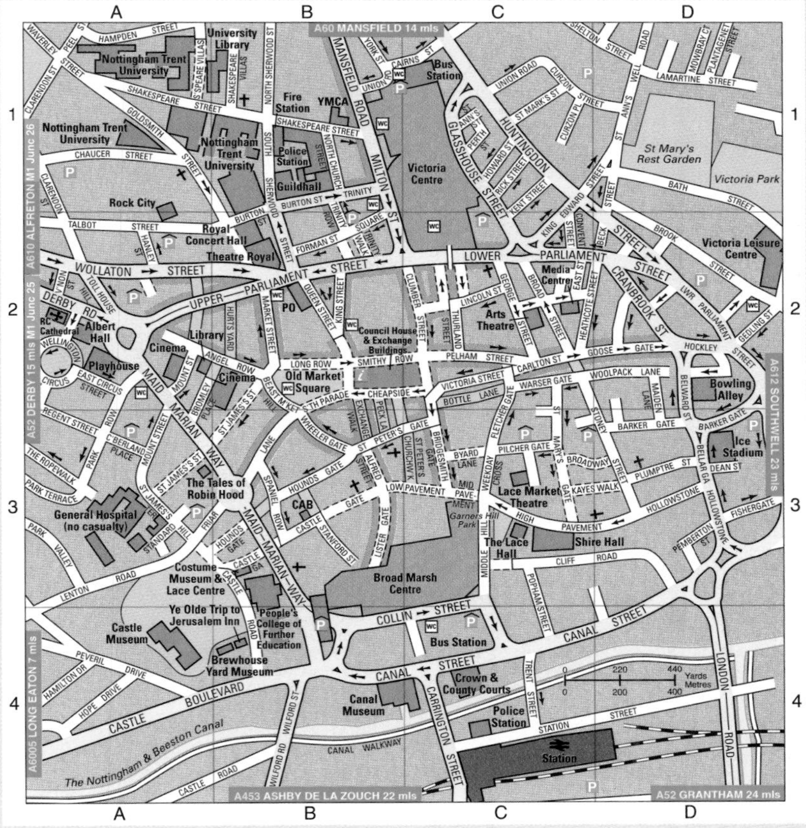

OXFORD

Adelaide Street A1
Albert Street A1/2
Banbury Road B1
Beaumont Buildings B2
Beaumont Street B2
Becket Street A3
Blackfriars Road B4
Blackhall Road B1/2
Brewer Street B3/4
Broad Street B3/C3
Broad Walk C4
Canal Street A1/2
Cardigan Street A1/2
Castle Street B3
Catte Street C3
Cobden Crescent B4
Cornmarket Street B3
Cowley Place D4
Cowley Road D4
Cranham Street A1
Dale Close A4/B4
Deadman's Walk C3
Floyds Row B4
Friars Wharf B4
George Street B3
Gibbs Crescent A4
Great Clarendon Street A1/2
Hart Street A1
High Street C3
Hollybush Row A3
Holywell Street C2
Hythe Bridge Street A3
Iffley Road D4
Jericho Street A1
Jowett Walk C2/D2
Juxon Street A1
Keble Road B1
King Street A1
Little Clarendon St. B2
Littlegate Street B4
Longwall Street D3
Love Lane C2
Magdalen Bridge D3
Manor Place D2
Manor Road D2
Mansfield Road C2
Marlborough Road B4
Merton Street C3
Museum Road B2/C2
Nelson Street A2
New Inn Hall Street B3
New Road B3
Norfolk Street B3/4
Observatory Street A1/B1
Old Greyfriars Street B4
Osney Lane A3
Oxpens Road A3/4
Paradise Street A3/B3
Park End Street A3
Parks Road B1/C2
Pembroke Street B3
Pusey Street B2
Queen Street B3
Rewley Road A2/3
Richmond Road A2
Rose Lane D3
St Aldates B3/B4
St Bernard's Road A1
St Cross Road D2
St Giles B2
St John Street B2
St Michael's Street B3
St Thomas' Street A3
Saville Road C2
Ship Street B3
South Parks Road C2
Speedwell Street B4
Thames Street B4
Trinity Street B4
Turl Street C3
Walton Crescent A2
Walton Lane B2
Walton Street A1/B2
Walton Well Road A1
Wellington Square B2
Wellington Street A2
Woodstock Road B1
Worcester Place A2
Worcester Street A3/B2

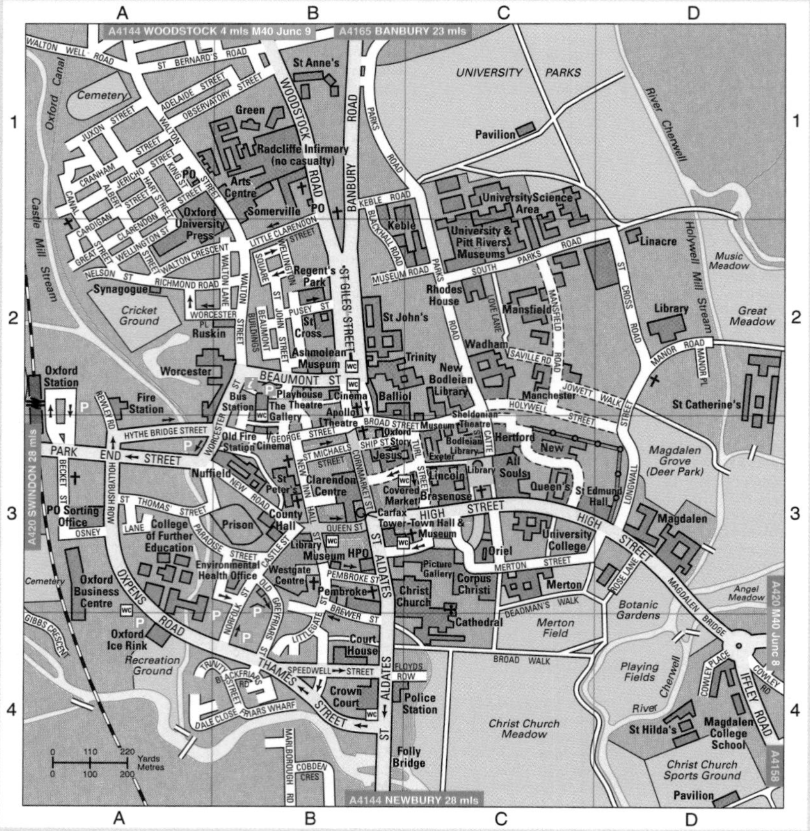

PLYMOUTH

Alfred Street B3
Alice Street A2
Anstis Street A1/2
Anthenaeum Street B3
Armada Street D1
Armada Way B1/2
Armada Way B3/C3
Barbican, The D3
Baring Street D1
Bath Street A3
Beaumont Road D2
Beaumont Street D1
Blenheim Road C1
Bretonside C2/D2
Buckwell Street C2
Camden Street D1
Castle Street D3
Chapel Street C1
Charles Cross C2
Charles Street C2
Citadel Road B3/C3
Citadel Road East C3
Claremont Street B1
Cliff Road A4/B4
Cobourg Street B1
Cornwall Street B2/C2
Crescent, The B3
Crescent Avenue B3
Derry's Cross B2
Drake Circus C1
Eastlake Street C2
Ebrington Street C2
Elliot Street B3
Endsleigh Place C1
Eton Avenue B1
Eton Place B1
Exeter Street C2/D2
Flora Cottages A2
Flora Court A2
Gasking Street D2
Gibbons Lane C1
Gibbons Street C1
Gilwell Street C1
Grand Parade B4
Great Western Road A4
Greenbank Road D1
Harbour Avenue D2
Harwell Street A1
Hastings Street A1
Hastings Terrace A1
Hetling Close A2
Hoe Approach C3
Hoe Road B4/C3
Hoe Street C3
Hoegate Street C3
Howe Street C2
Ilbert Street A1
King Street A2
Lambhay Hill C3/D3
Leigham Street B4
Lipson Road D1
Lockyer Street B3
Looe Street C2
Madeira Road C4/D4
Manor Street A2
Market Avenue B2
Marlborough Road C1
Martin Street A3
May Terrace D1
Mayflower Street B1
Millbay Road A3
Mount Street D1
Neswick Street A1
New George Street B2/C2
New Street D3
North Cross B1
North Hill C1
North Street D1
North Road West A1/B1
Notte Street B3
Octagon Street A2
Oxford Place B1
Oxford Street B1
Parade Quay C3
Penrose Street A1
Phoenix Street A3
Pier Street B4
Plym Street D1
Portland Square C1
Portland Villas B1
Princess Street B3
Prospect Place A3
Prospect Street D1
Prynne Close A2
Radford Road A4/B4
Radnor Place D1
Radnor Street D1
Regent Street C1
Rendle Street A2
Royal Parade B2
Sawrey Street A3
Southside Street C3
St Andrews Cross C2
St Barnabus Terrace A1
St James Place B3
Sussex Street C3
Sutton Road D2
Sydney Street B1
Tavistock Place C1
Tothill Avenue D1
Trafalgar Street D1
Union Street A3/B3
Vauxhall Street C2
Walker Terrace A4
Well Gardens A2
West Hoe Road A4
Western Approach A2
White Friars Lane D2
Wyndham Street East A1
Zion Street C3

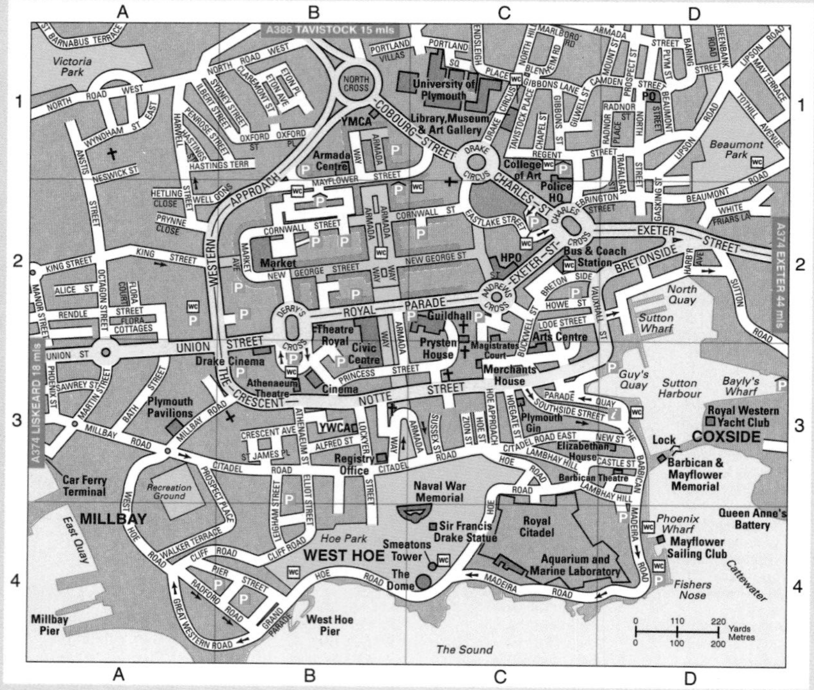

PORTSMOUTH

Admiralty Road B2
Alec Rose Lane C3
Alfred Road C2
Angelsea Road C2/3
Armory Lane B3/4
Arundel Street D2
Astley Street C4
Aylward Street B2
Bath Square A4
Belmont Street D4
Bishop Street B2
Broad Street A4
Brougham Road D4
Burnaby Road B3/C3
Bush Street East C4
Cambridge Road B4/C3
Cascades Approach C1
Castle Road C4
Charlotte Street D2
Church Path North D2
College Street B3
Commercial Road D1
Cottage Grove D4
Crasswell Street D2
Cross Street B2
Cumberland Street B2
Curzon Howe Road B2
Dunsmore Close D4
Earlsdon Street C3
East Street A4
Edinburgh Road C2
Elm Grove D4
Flint Street C4
Green Road D4
Grosvenor Street D3/4
Guildhall Walk C3
Gunwharf Road B3/4
Hampshire Terrace C3/4
Havant Street B2
Hawke Street B2
Hay Street B2
High Street B4
Hyde Park Road D3
Isambard Brunel Road C2/D3
Jacob's Street D1/2
Kent Street B2
King Henry I Street C3
King Street C4/D4
King William Street B2
Kings Road C4
Kings Terrace C4
Landport Terrace C4
Lansdowne Street C3/4
Lion Terrace B3
Lower Church Path D2
Marketway D1
Middle Street C3/4
Museum Road C4
North Street B2
Paradise Street D2
Park Road B3/C3
Park Street C4
Penny Street B4
Prince George Street B2
Quay A4
Queen Street B2/C2
Radnor Street D3/4
St George's Road B3/4
St James Road D3/4
St James Street B2
St Michael's Road C3
St Paul's Road C3/4
St Thomas's St. B4
Sackville Street C4/D4
Somers Road D4
Stanhope Road C2
Station Street D2
Stone Street C4
Temple Street D2
The Hard A2/B3
Waltham Street C3
Warblington Street B4
Warwick Crescent D4
Waterloo Street D3
Wellington Street D3
White Swan Road C3
Whitehart Road A4/B4
Wiltshire Street C3
York Place B2
Yorke Street C4

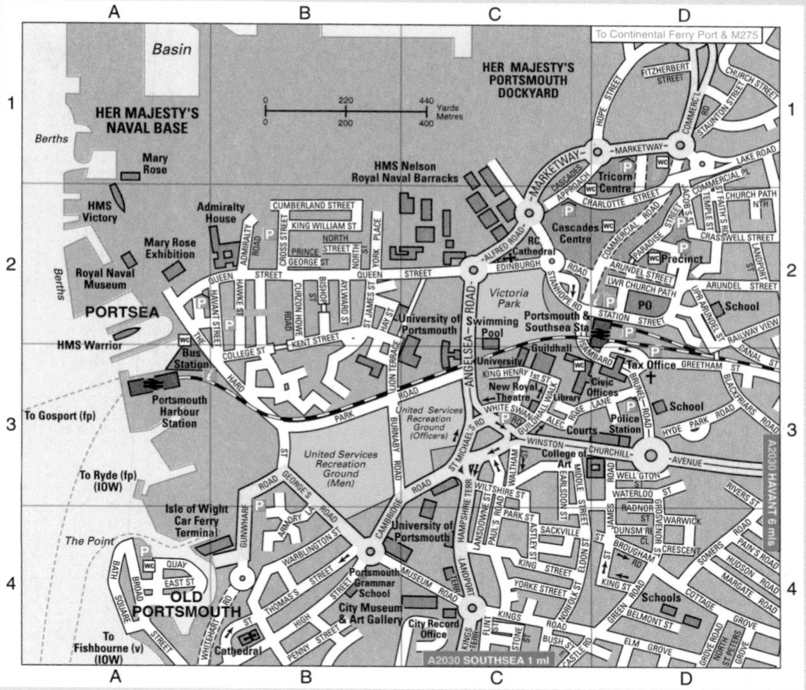

SHEFFIELD

Acorn Street B1
Allen Street B1
Alma Street C1
Angel Street C2
Arundel Gate C2/3
Arundel Street C3/4
Bailey Lane B2
Bailey Street B2
Balm Green B2/3
Bank Street C2
Barkers Place B3
Best Street A2
Bishop Street B4
Blonk Street D1
Bolton Street A3
Boston Street B4
Bower Street C1
Bowling Green B1
Bramwell Street A1/2
Bridge Street C1
Broad Lane A2/B2
Broad Street D2
Brocco Street A1/B2
Brook Hill A2
Broomhall Place A4
Broomhall Street A4
Brown Street C3
Brunswick Road C1
Burlington Street A1
Cambridge Street B3
Campo Lane C2
Carver Lane B2/3
Carver Street B2/3
Castlegate D1
Castle Street B1
Castle Street C2
Cavendish Street A3
Cemetery Road B4
Chapel Walk C2
Charles Street C3
Charlotte Road C4
Charter Row B3
Church Street C2
Clarence Lane A4
Clough Road C4
Commercial Street D2
Copper Street B1
Corporation Street C1
Cotton Street C1
Cross Smithfield B1
Daisy Way A2
Devonshire Street A3
Division Street B3
Dixon Lane D2
Dover Street A1
Duchess Road C4
Dun Street B1
Earl Street B4/C4
Earl Way B4/C3
Ecclesall Road A4
Edmund Road C4
Edward Street A2/B1
Egerton Street A3/4
Eldon Street B3
Ellin Street B4
Ellis Street B1
Exchange Street D2
Exeter Road A4
Eyre Street B4
Fargate C2
Farm Road D4
Fawcett Street A1
Fitzalan Square C2/D2
Fitzwilliam Street A3/B3
Fornham Street C4/D4
Furnace Street B1
Furnival Road D1
Furnival Street B3/C3
Garden Street B2
Gell Street A3
George Street C2
Gibraltar Street B1/C1
Glossop Road A3
Granville Road D4
Granville Street D3
Green Lane B1
Hanover Square A4
Hanover Way A3/4
Harmer Lane D3
Harrow Street A4
Harts Head C2
Hawley Street B2
Haymarket D2
Headford Street A3/4
Henry Street A1
Hereford Street B4
High Street C2
Hillsands C1
Hodgson Street A4/B4
Holland Street B2
Hollis Croft B2
Holly Street B2
Howard Street C3
Hoyle Street A1/B1
Jericho Street A1
Jessop Street B4
Johnson Street C1/D1
King Street C2
Lambert Street B1/C1
Leadmill Road C4
Leavygreave Road A2
Leicester Walk A2
Leopold Street C2
London Road B4
Love Lane C1
Love Street C1
Malinda Street A1
Mapping Street A2
Margaret Street C4
Mary Street C4
Matilda Street B3/C4
Meadow Street A1/B1
Midland Street C4
Milton Street A4/B3
Moor, The B3/4
Moore Street A4/B4
Moorfields B1
Mulberry Street C2
Napier Road A4
Netherthorpe Place A1
Netherthorpe Road A1/2
Netherthorpe Street A1
Norfolk Road D3
Norfolk Street C2
Nursery Lane C1/D1
Nursery Street C1
Park Square D2
Paternoster Row C3
Pinstone Street C3
Pitt Street A2/3
Pond Hill D2
Pond Street C3/D2
Portobello Street A2/B2
Queen Street C2
Queen's Road D4
Radford Street A2
Regent Street A2/3
Regent Terrace A2/3
Renton Street A4
Rockingham Lane B3
Rockingham Street B2/3
Rockingham Way B3
Roscoe Road B1
Russell Street B1/C1
St George's Close A2
St Mary's Gate B4/C4
St Mary's Road C4
St Philip's Road A1
Savile Street D1
Scotland Street B1
Shales Moor B1
Sheaf Gardens C4/D4
Sheaf Street D2/3
Sheldon Row D1
Shepherd Street B1
Shoreham Street C4
Shrewsbury Road D3/4
Silver Street C2
Smithfield Lane B1
Snig Hill C2
Snow Lane B1
Solly Street A2/B2
South Lane B4
South Parade B1
South Street D2/3
Spring Lane A3
Spring Street C1
Stanley Street D1
Suffolk Road C3/D4
Surrey Street C2/3
Sydney Street C4
Sylvester Street C4
Talbot Street D3
Tenter Street B2
Thomas Street B3/4
Townhead Street B2

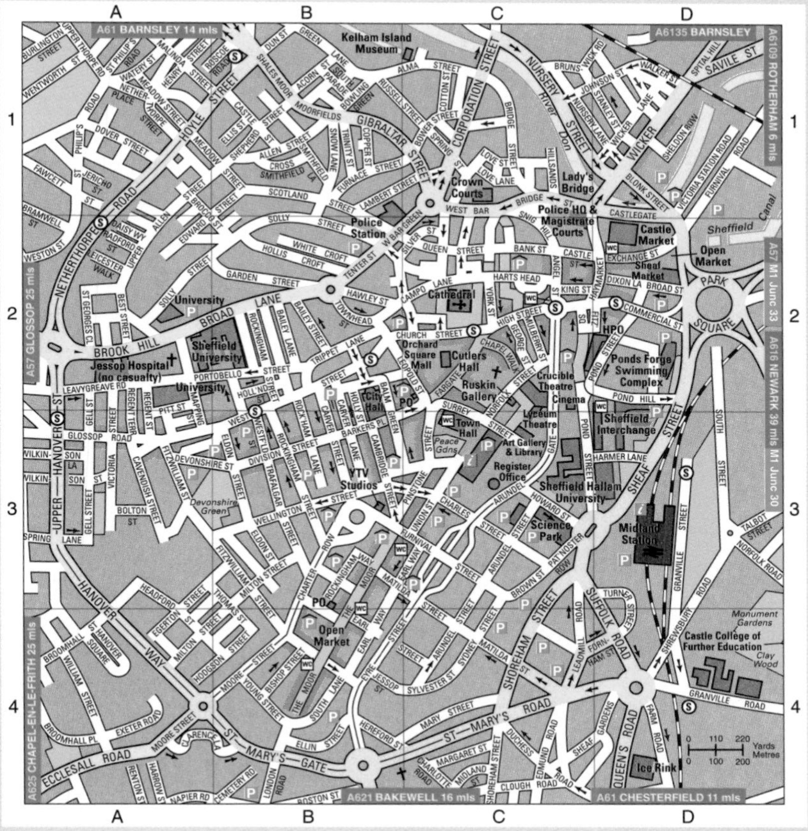

Trafalgar Street B3
Trinity Street B1
Trippet Lane B2
Turner Street D3
Union Street C3
Upper Allen Street A1/2
Upper Hanover St. A3
Upper Thorpe Road A1
Victoria Station Road D1
Victoria Street A3
Walker Street D1
Watery Street A1
Wellington Street B3
Wentworth Street A1
West Bar C1
West Bar Green B2/C2
West Street B2/3
Westfield Street B3
Weston Street A2
White Croft B2
Wicker Lane D1
Wicker Spital Hill D1
Wilkinson Lane A3
Wilkinson Street A3
William Street A4
York Street C2
Young Street B4

SOUTHAMPTON

Above Bar Street B2
Albert Road North D3/4
Albert Road South D4
Anderson's Road D3/4
Argyle Road C1
Back of The Walls B3/4
Bedford Place B1
Belvidere Road D2
Bernard Street B4/C4
Blechynden Terrace A2
Boundary Road C4
Bridge Terrace D4
Brinton's Road C1
Britannia Road D1
Briton Street B4
Broad Green C2
Brunswick Place B1
Bugle Street B4
Cable Street D1
Canal Walk B3/C3
Canute Road C4/D4
Castle Way B3
Central Bridge D4
Channel Road D4
Channel Way D4
Chantry Road D4
Chapel Road C3/D3
Chapel Street C3
Civic Centre Road B2
Clovelly Road C1
Coleman Street C3
College Street C4
Commercial Road A1/B1
Cook Street C3
Craven Walk C2
Crosshouse Road D4
Cumberland Place B1
Derby Road D1
Devonshire Road A1
Duke Street C3
Durnford Road D1
East Park Terrace B1
East Road D4
East Street B3
Eastgate Street B3
Elm Street D3
Endle Street D3
Evans Street C3
Floating Bridge Road D4
French Street B4
Glebe Road D3
Golden Grove C2
Graham Road C1
Granville Street D3
Grosvenor Square B1
Grove Street D3
Handel Road A1
Handel Terrace A1
Hanover Buildings B3
Hartington Road D1
Havelock Road B1
Herbert Walker Avenue A3
High Street B3/B4
Houndwell Place C3
Itchen Bridge D4
James Street C2
John Street C4
Johnson Street C2
Kent Street D1
King Street C3
Kingsway C2
Latimer Street C4
Lime Street C3
Lower Canal Walk B4
Marine Parade D2/3
Marsh Lane C3
Melbourne Street D3
Morris Road A1
New Road B2/C2
Newcombe Road A1
North Front C2
Northam Road C2/D1
Northbrook Road C1
Northumberland Rd. D1
Ogle Road B2
Orchard Lane C3
Orchard Place C4
Oriental Terrace B4
Oxford Avenue C1
Oxford Street C4
Page Street D3
Palmerston Road C2
Park Walk B2
Peel Street D1
Platform Road C4
Polygon, The A1
Portland Terrace B2
Pound Tree Road B2
Queens Terrace C4
Queens Way C3/4
Radcliffe Road D1
Richmond Street C4
Rochester Street D1
Royal Crescent Road D4
Ryde Terrace D4
St Alban's Road D1
St Andrews Road C1
St Mary Street C2/3
St Mary's Place C2/3
St Mary's Road C1
Solent Road A3
South Bridge Road A2
South Front C2
Spa Road B3
Terminus Terrace C4
Threefield Lane C4
Town Quay B4
Upper Bugle Street B3
West Marlands Road B1
West Park Road A2
West Quay Road A3
West Road C4
Western Esplanade A2/B3
Wilson Street D1
Wolverton Road D1
York Walk B3

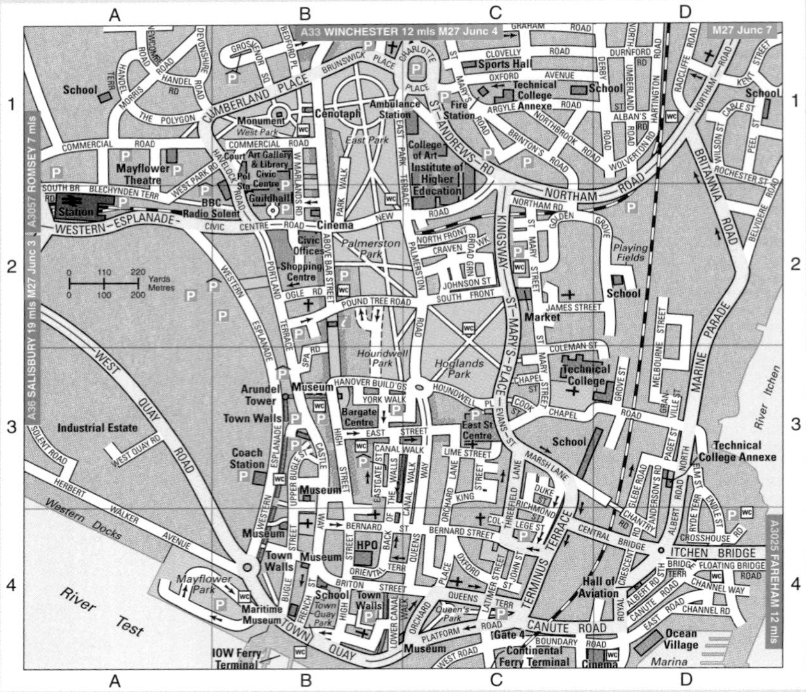

STRATFORD-UPON-AVON

Albany Road A2
Alcester Road A2
Arden Street B1/2
Bancroft Place D2
Bell Court B2
Birmingham Road B1
Brewery Street B1
Bridge Foot D2
Bridge Street C2
Bridgeway D2
Broad Street B3
Broad Walk B3
Bull Street B4
Chapel Lane C3
Chapel Street C3
Cherry Orchard A4
Cherry Street B4
Chestnut Walk B3
Church Street B3
Clopton Bridge D3
Clopton Road B1
College Lane B4
College Street B4
Ely Street B2
Evesham Place B3
Evesham Road A4
Great William Street C1
Greenhill Street B2
Grove Road B3
Guild Street C2
Henley Street B2/C2
High Street C2
Holtom Street B4
John Street C2
Kendall Avenue C1
Mansell Street B2
Meer Street B2
Mill Lane B4
Mulberry Street C1
Narrow Lane B4
New Broad Street B4
New Street B4
Old Town B4
Old Tramway Walk D4
Orchard Way A4
Payton Street C2
Rother Street B3
Ryland Street B4
St Andrew's Crescent A3
St Gregory's Road C1
St Johns Close A4
St Martin's Close A2
Sanctus Drive B4
Sanctus Road A4
Sanctus Street A4
Sandfield Road A4
Scholar's Lane B3
Seven Meadow Road A4
Shakespeare Street B1
Sheep Street C3
Shipston Road D4
Shottery Road A3
Southern Lane C3/4
Swan's Nest Lane D3
Tiddington Road D3
Trinity Street B4
Tyler Street C1
Union Street C2
Warwick Court C1
Warwick Crescent D1
Warwick Road C2/D1
Waterside C3
Welcombe Road D1
Wellesbourne Grove A2
West Street B4
Western Road A1
Windsor Street B2
Wood Street B2

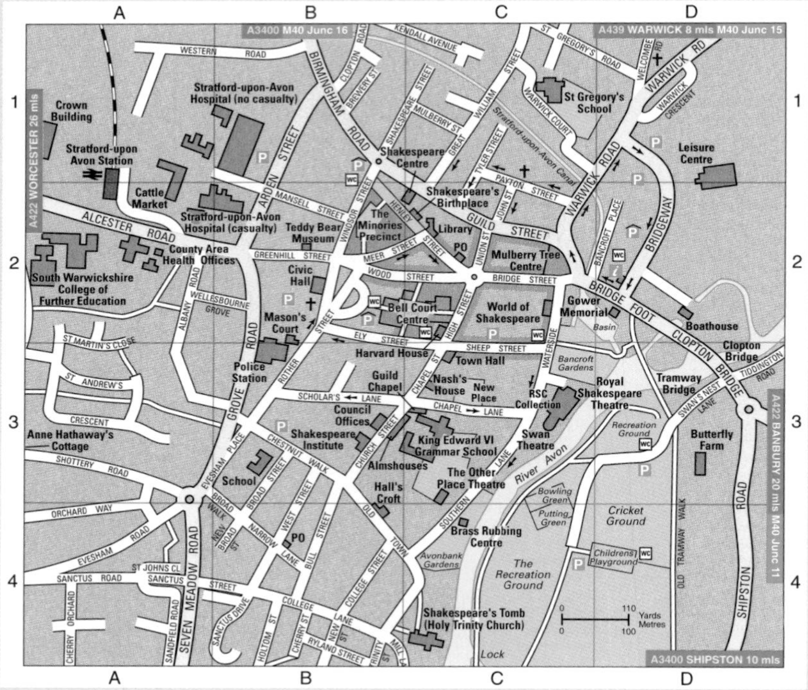

SWANSEA

Adelaide Street D3
Albert Row C3
Alexandra Road C1
Argyle Street B3
Bathurst Street B3/4
Beach Street A3
Bellevue Way C2
Berwick Terrace C1
Bond Street A3
Brooklands Terrace A2
Brunswick Street A2
Bryn-Syfi Terrace B1
Bryn-y-Mor Road A3
Bullin's Lane A2
Burman Street A2
Burrows Place D3
Burrows Road B3
Cadfan Road A1
Cambrian Place D3
Carlton Terrace B2
Castle Street C2
Catherine Street A3
Chaddesley Terrace B2
Clifton Hill C1
Constitution Hill A1/2
Craig Terrace C1
Crole Street A2
Cromwell Street B2
Dilwyn Street B3
Duke Street A2
Dyfatty Street C1
Dyfed Avenue A1
East Burrows Road D3
Ebenezer Street C1
Elfed Road A1
Evans Terrace C1
Fabian Way D2
Fairfield Terrace A1
Ferry Side D3
Ffynone Close A2
Ffynone Drive A2
Ffynone Road A2
Firm Street C1
Fleet Street A3
Fullers Row C1
George Street B2
Glamorgan Street B3
Glyndwr Place A1
Grove Place C2
Guildhall Rd Sth. A3
Hanover Lane A2
Hanover Street A2/B2
Harcourt Street B1
Harries Street B1
Heathfield Road B2
Henrietta Street A2
Hewson Street B1
High Street C1
Hill Street C1
Hump Street A2
Islwyn Road A1
Jockey Street D1
John Street D1
Jones Terrace C1
Kilvey Terrace D1
King's Road D2
Kingsway, The B2/C2
Madoc Street B3
Mansel Street B2
Milton Terrace C1
Montpellier Terrace A2
Morfa Street D1
Mount Pleasant B1
New Cut Road D1/2
New Street C1
Nicander Parade B1
Nicholl Street B2
Norfolk Street B1
North Hill Road C1
Northampton Lane B2
Orchard Street C2
Oxford Street A3/B2
Oystermouth Road A4/C3
Page Street B2
Pant-y-Celyn Road A1
Paxton Drive C4
Paxton Street B3
Pen-y-Craig Road A1
Penmaen Terrace A1
Pentre Guinea Road D1/2
Phillips Parade A3
Pier Street D3
Pleasant View Ter. C1
Portia Terrace B1
Portland Street C2
Prince of Wales Road D1
Princess Way C2/3
Promenade B2
Quay Parade D2
Rhianfa Lane A1/2
Rhondda Street B1
Richard Street B3
Rodney Street A3/A4
Rosehill A2
Rosehill Terrace A2
Russell Street A2/3
St Davids Square C3
St Helens Avenue A3
St Helens Road A3
St James's Crescent A2
St Mary's Square C3
Short Street C1
Somerset Place D3
Stanley Place B1
Stanley Terrace B1
Strand C2
Swan Street C1
Taliesyn Road A1
Tan-y-Marian Road B1
Teilo Crescent A1
Terrace Road A1/B1
Tontine Street C1
Trawler Road C4
Union Street C2
Victoria Road D3
Vincent Street A3
Walter Road A2
Watkin Street C1
Wellington Street C3
West Way B3
Westbury Street A3
Western Street A3/B3
White Street A2
William Street B3
Wind Street C3
Windmill Terrace D1
Winston Street C1
Woodlands Terrace A2
York Street C3

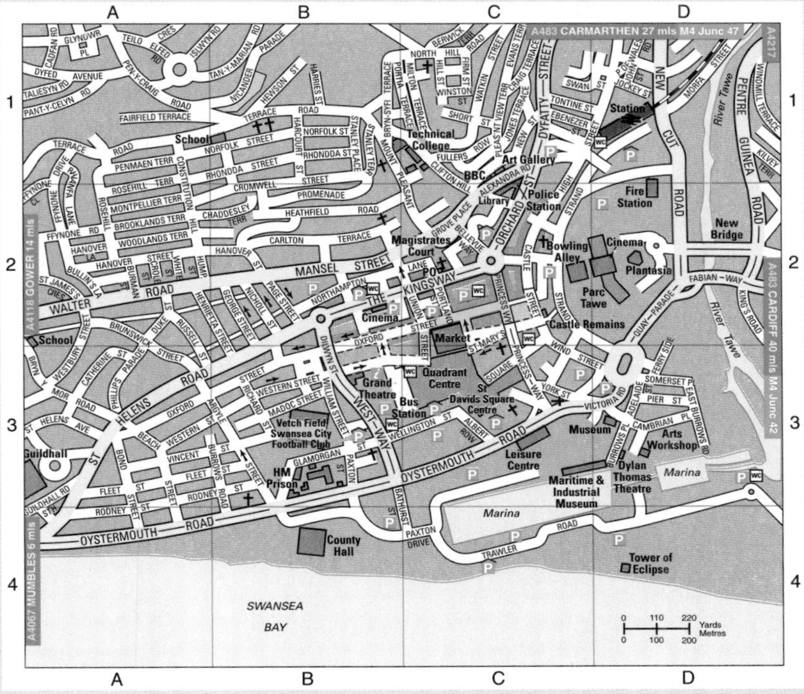

TORQUAY

Abbey Road B2
Alexandra Lane C1
Alexandra Road C1
Alpine Road C2
Ash Hill Road B1
Babbacombe Road D3
Bampfylde Road A2
Bath Lane A2
Beacon Quay D4
Belgrave Road A1/A2
Braddons Hill Rd East C2
Braddons Hill Rd West C3
Braddons Street C2
Bridge Road A1
Camden Road C1
Cary Parade C3
Castle Road C1
Cavern Road C1
Chatsworth Road C1
Chestnut Avenue A2
Church Street A1
Croft Hill B2
Croft Road B2
East Street A1
Egerton Road D1
Ellacombe Road C1
Falkland Road A2
Fleet Street C3
Grafton Road D2
Grange Road D1
Higher Union Lane B1
Higher Warberry Rd. D1
Hillesdon Road C2
Hoxton Road C1
Hunsdon Road D2
King's Drive, The A3
Laburnham Street A1
Lime Avenue A2
Lower Ellacombe Church Road D1
Lower Union Avenue B2
Lower Warberry Rd. D2
Lucius Street A2
Lymington Road B1
Magdalene Road A1
Market Street C2
Meadfoot Lane D4
Meadfoot Road D3
Middle Warberry Rd. D2
Mill Lane A1
Montpellier Road C3
Morgan Avenue B1
Museum Road D3
Newton Road A1
Parkhill Road D4
Parkhill Road D4
Pennsylvania Road C1
Pimlico C2
Potters Hill C1
Princes Road East D1
Princes Road West C1
Princes Road C1/D1
Queen Street C2
Rathmore Road A3
Rillage Lane A1
Rock Road C3
Rock Walk B3
Rosehill Road D1
Rowdens Road A2
St Efrides Road A1
St Luke's Road North B2
St Luke's Road South B2
St Luke's Road B2
St Marychurch Road B1
Scarborough Road A2
Shedden Hill B3
South Hill Road D3
South Street A1
Stitchill Road D2
Strand C3
Sutherland Road D2
Temperence Street B2
Terrace, The D3
Tor Church Road A2
Tor Hill Road A1/B1
Torbay Road A4/B3
Torwood Gdns. Road D3
Torwood Street D3
Trematon Avenue B1
Union Street B1
Upper Braddons Hill D2
Vane Hill Road D4
Vansittart Road A1
Victoria Parade C4
Victoria Road C1
Warberry Road West C1
Warren Road B3/C2
Wellington Road C1
Woodside Close D2

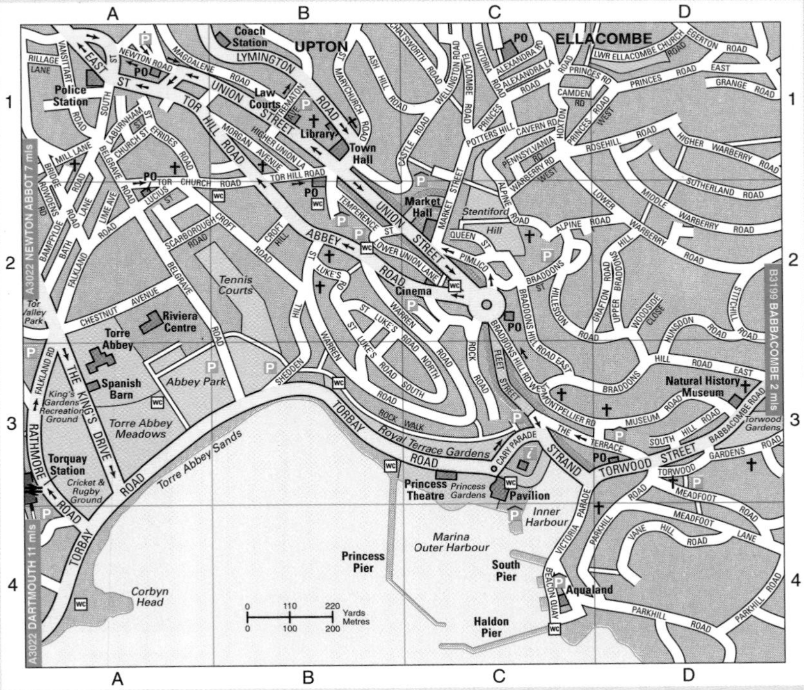

WOLVERHAMPTON

Ablow Street B4
Albion Street D2
Alexandra Street A3
Bath Avenue A1
Bath Road A2
Bell Street B3
Berry Street C2
Bilston Road D3
Bilston Street C3
Birch Street A2
Birmingham Road C4
Bloomsbury Street B4
Bond Street B3
Broad Street C2
Burton Crescent D1
Burton Road D1
Castle Street C2
Chapel Ash A3
Cheapside B2
Church Lane B4
Church Street B4
Clarence Road A2
Clarence Street B2
Cleveland Road C3
Cleveland Street B3
Commercial Road D3
Corn Hill D2
Corn Hill Street D2
Corporation Street B2
Culwell Street C1/D1
Dale Street A4
Darlington Street B2
Dartmouth Street D4
Drummond Street A1
Dudley Road C4
Dudley Street B2
Dunkley Street A1
Fold Street B3
Frederick Street B4
Fryer Street C2
Garrick Street C3
Gordon Street D4
Graiseley Street A4
Great Brick Kiln St. A3
Great Western Street C1
Grimstone Street C1
Herbert Street C1
Herrick Street A3
Horseley Fields D2
Howard Street C4
Jeddo Street B4
Jenner Street D4
King Street C2
Lansdowne Road A1
Lever Street C4
Lichfield Street B2/C2
Littles Lane C1
Lock Street C1
Long Street C2
Lord Street A3
Lower Walsall Street D3
Maltings, The C1
Mander Street A4
Market Street C2
Melbourne Street C4
Merridale Street A4
Merridale St. West A4
Middle Cross D3
Mitre Field B2
Molineux Alley B1
New Hampton Road East A1
North Street B2
Old Hall Street C3
Oxford Street D3
Paget Street A1
Park Avenue A1
Park Crescent A2
Park Road East A1
Paul Street B4
Peel Street A3
Penn Road A4
Pipers Row C2
Pitt Street B3
Pool Street B4
Powlett Street C4
Princess Street C2
Queen Square B2
Queen Street C2
Raby Street C4
Raglan Street A3
Railway Drive C2
Red Lion Street B2
Retreat Street A4
Ring Road A2/C4
Russell Street A4
St Georges Parade C3
St James's Street D3
St John's Square B4
St Mark's Road A3
St Mark's Street A3
Salisbury Street A4
Salop Street B3
School Street B3
Sharrocks Street D3
Skinner Street B3
Snow Hill C3
Stafford Street C1/2
Steelhouse Lane D4
Stephenson Street A3
Stewart Street B4
Summer Row B3
Summerfield Road A2
Sun Street D1
Sutherland Place D4
Tempest Street C3
Temple Street B3
Thomas Street B4
Thornley Street C2
Tower Street C3
Union Mill Street D2
Union Street D3
Upper Zoar Street A4
Vicarage Road C4
Victoria Street B3
Walsall Street D3
Warwick Street D3
Waterloo Road B1/B2
Wednesfield Road D1
Wharf Street D3
Williamson Street A4
Worcester Street B3
Wulfruna Street B2
York Street D3
Zoar Street A4

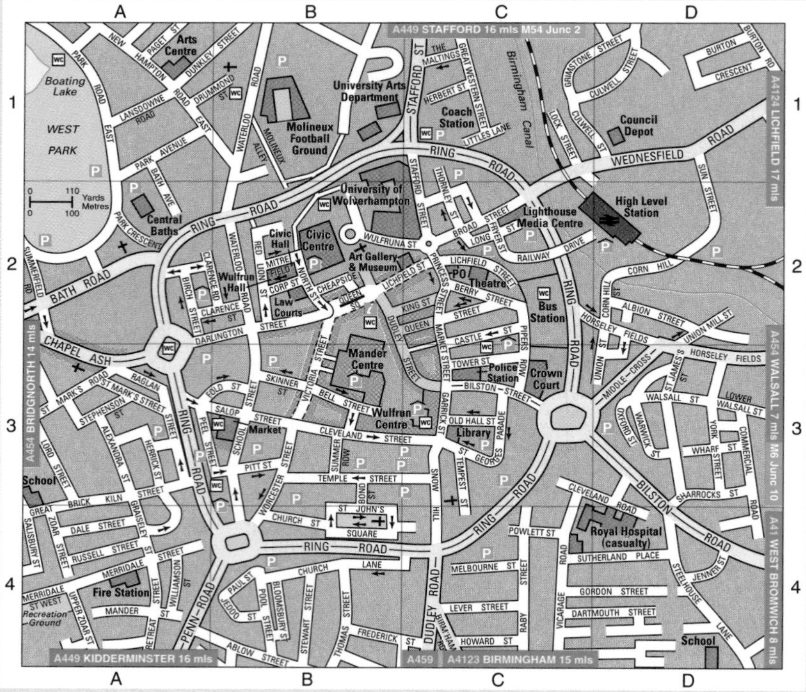

YORK

Aldwark C2
Barbican Road D4
Bishopgate Street B4
Bishophill B3
Bishophill Jnr. B3
Blake Street B2
Blossom Street A4
Bootham B1
Bootham Row B1
Bootham Terrace A1
Bridge Street B3
Buckingham Street B3
Carmelite Street C3
Castlegate C3
Church Street C2
Cinder Lane A2
Clementhorpe B4/C4
Clifford Street C3
Colliergate C2
Coney Street B2
Coppergate C3
Crescent, The A4
Cromwell Road B4
Dale Street A4/B4
Darnborough Street B4/C4
Davygate B2
Deangate C2
Dennis Street C3
Dewsbury Terrace A3/B4
Duncombe Place B2
Dundas Street C2/D2
East Mount Road A4
Esplanade, The A2/B2
Fairfax Street B4
Fawcett Street D4
Fetter Lane B3
Fishergate C4
Foss Bank D1
Foss Islands Road D2/3
Fossgate C3
Frederick Street A2
Garden Place C3
George Street D4
George Hudson St. B3
Gillygate B1
Goodramgate C2
Gordon Street D4
Hallfield Road D1
Hampden Street B4
Heslington Road D4
High Ousegate C3
High Petergate B1/2
Hope Street D4
Jewbury C2/D2
Kent Street D4
King Street B3
Kyme Street B4
Layerthorpe D1
Lead Mill Street C4
Leeman Road A2
Lendal B2
Long Close Lane D4
Longfield Terrace A1/2
Lord Mayor's Walk C1
Low Petergate C2
Lower Priory Street B4
Mansfield Street D2
Margaret Street D3/4
Market Street B3/C2
Marygate A2/B1
Micklegate A3/B3
Mill Street C4
Minster Yard B2/C2
Monkgate C1
Moss Street A4
Mount, The A4
Museum Street B2
Navigation Road D3
New Street B2
Newton Terrace B4
North Parade A1
North Street B3
Nunnery Lane A4/B4
Nunthorpe Road A4/B4
Palmer Lane C2
Paragon Street D4
Park Street A4
Parliament Street C2/3
Pavement C3
Peasholme Green D2
Penley's Grove Street C1
Percy's Lane D3
Piccadilly C3
Portland Street B1
Price's Lane B4
Priory Street A3/B3
Queen Anne's Road A1
Queen's Staith B3
Redeness Street D1/2
Rougier Street B2/3
St Andrewgate C2
St Benedict Road B4
St Deny's Road C3
St John Street C1
St Leonard's Place B1/2
St Martin's Lane B3
St Maurice's Road C1/2
St Mary's A1
St Saviourgate C2
St Saviourgate Place C2
Scarcroft Road A4
Shambles C2
Shaws Terrace A4
Skelder Gate Bridge C4
Skeldergate B3/4
South Parade A4
Spen Lane C2
Spurrier Gate B3
Station Avenue A2
Station Road A3/B2
Stonebow, The C2
Stonegate B2
Swann Street B4
Swine Gate C2
Sycamore Terrace A1
Tanner Row B3
Terry Avenue C4
Toft Green A3
Tower Street C3/C4
Trinity Lane B3
Victor Street B4
Walmgate D3
Wellington Row B2
Wellington Street D4
Willis Street D4

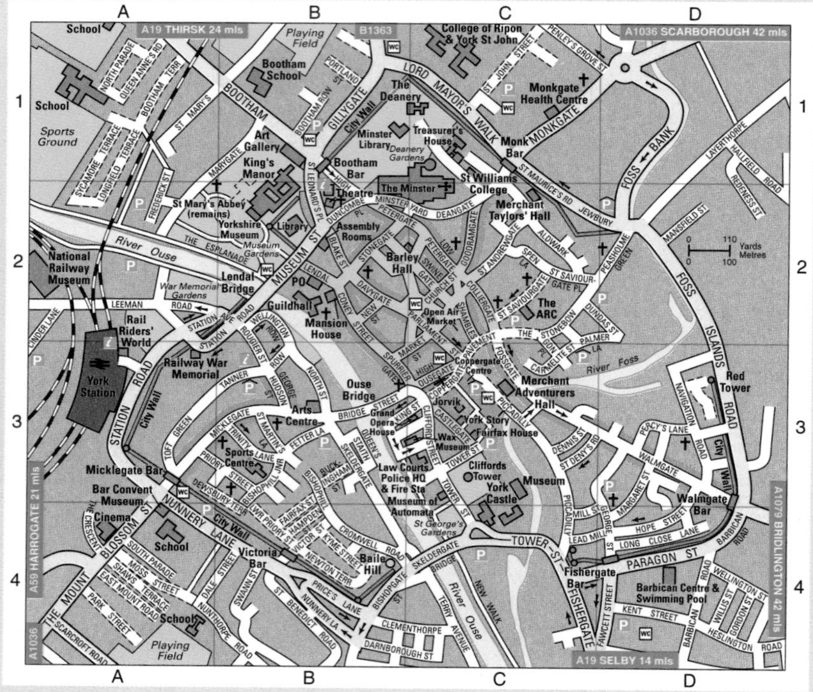

Key to Ireland Map Section

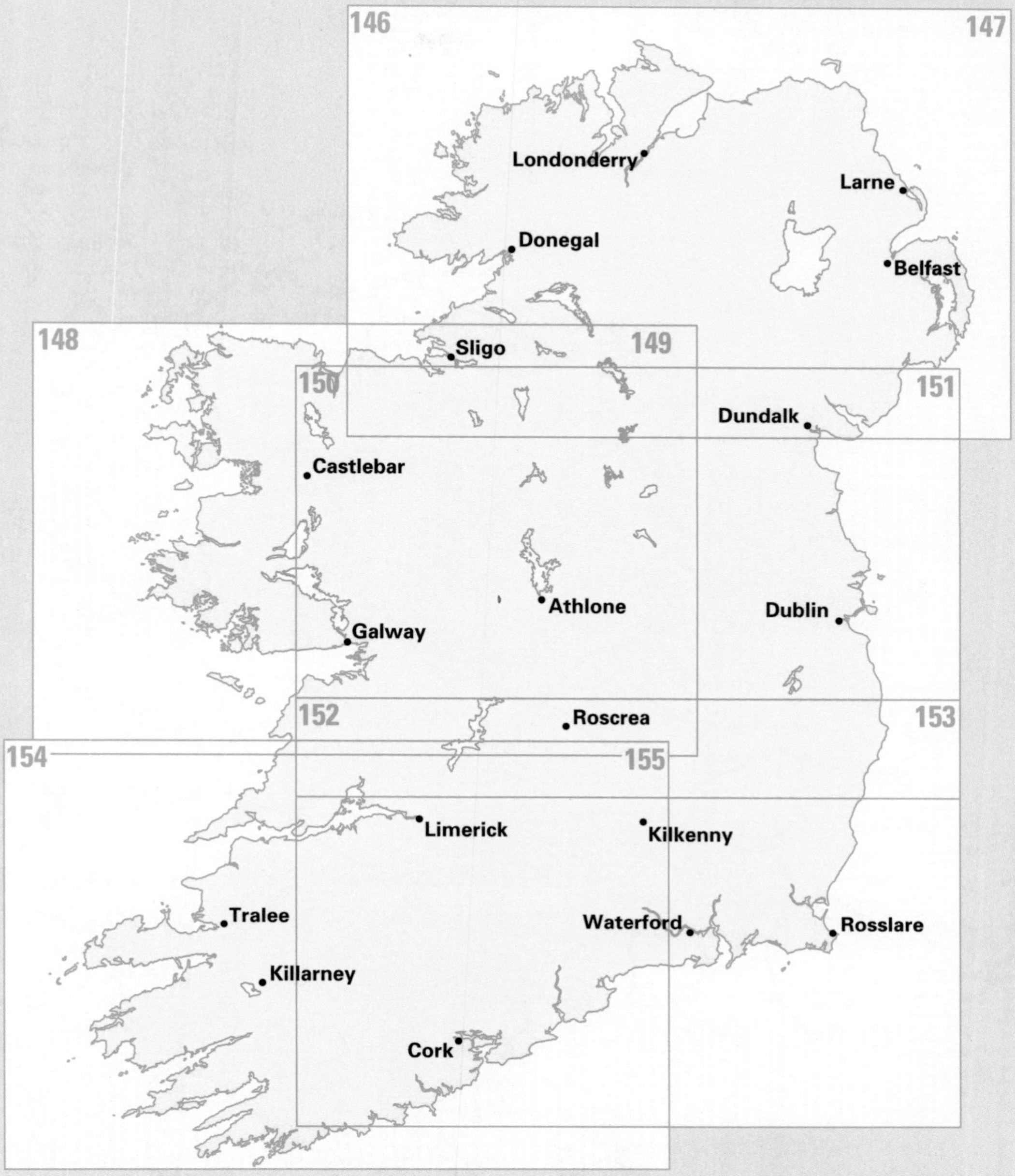

KEY TO SYMBOLS

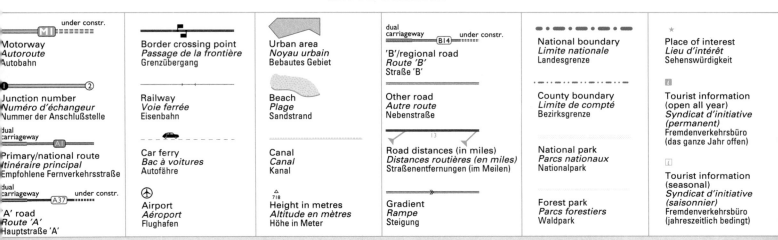

under constr.
Motorway
Autoroute
Autobahn

Junction number
Numéro d'échangeur
Nummer der Anschlußstelle

dual carriageway
Primary/national route
Itinéraire principal
Empfohlene Fernverkehrsstraße

dual carriageway — under constr.
'A' road
Route 'A'
Hauptstraße 'A'

Border crossing point
Passage de la frontière
Grenzübergang

Railway
Voie ferrée
Eisenbahn

Car ferry
Bac à voitures
Autofähre

Airport
Aéroport
Flughafen

Urban area
Noyau urbain
Bebautes Gebiet

Beach
Plage
Sandstrand

Canal
Canal
Kanal

718
Height in metres
Altitude en mètres
Höhe in Meter

dual carriageway — under constr.
'B'/regional road
Route 'B'
Straße 'B'

Other road
Autre route
Nebenstraße

13
Road distances (in miles)
Distances routières (en miles)
Straßenentfernungen (im Meilen)

Gradient
Rampe
Steigung

National boundary
Limite nationale
Landesgrenze

County boundary
Limite de compté
Bezirksgrenze

National park
Parcs nationaux
Nationalpark

Forest park
Parcs forestiers
Waldpark

Place of interest
Lieu d'intérêt
Sehenswürdigkeit

Tourist information (open all year)
Syndicat d'initiative (permanent)
Fremdenverkehrsbüro (das ganze Jahr offen)

Tourist information (seasonal)
Syndicat d'initiative (saisonnier)
Fremdenverkehrsbüro (jahreszeitlich bedingt)

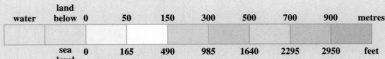

water	land below sea level	0	50	150	300	500	700	900	metres
		0	165	490	985	1640	2295	2950	feet

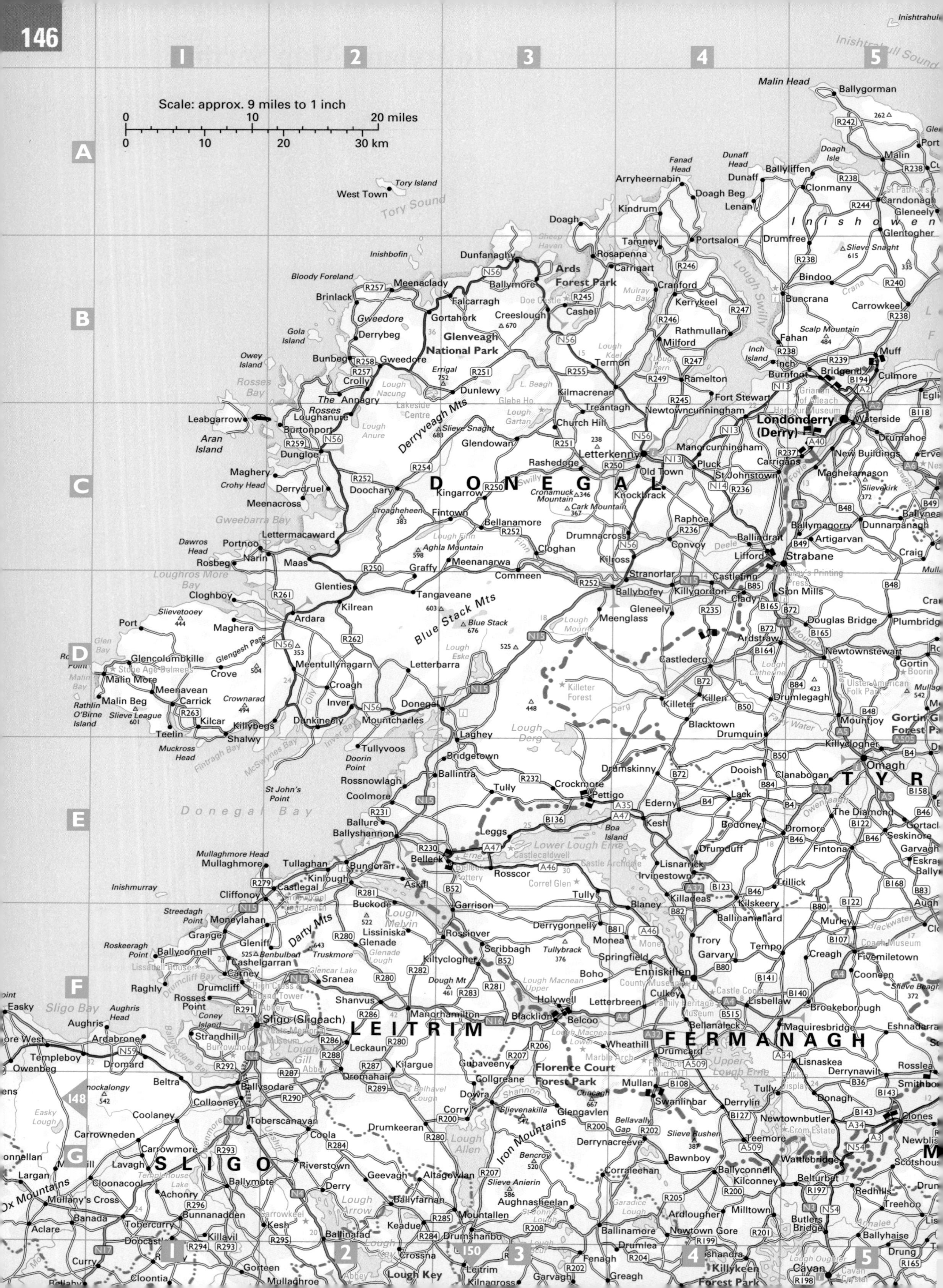
1
2
3
4
5
A
B
C
D
E
F
G
Scale: approx. 9 miles to 1 inch
0
10
20 miles
0
10
20
30 km
Inishtrahull
Inishtrahull Sound
Malin Head
Ballygorman
Tory Island
West Town
Tory Sound
Fanad Head
Dunaff Head
Doagh Isle
Malin
Arryheernabin
Ballyliffen
Dunaff
Clonmany
Doagh Beg
Lenan
Carndonagh
Kindrum
Gleneely
Inishowen
Glentogher
Doagh
Drumfree
Slieve Snaght
Sheep Haven
Tamney
Portsalon
Rosapenna
Inishbofin
Dunfanaghy
Carrigart
Bloody Foreland
Ards Forest Park
Ballymore
Meenaclady
Brinlack
Falcarragh
Mulroy Bay
Cranford
Bindoo
Buncrana
Kerrykeel
Carrowkeel
Gweedore
Gortahork
Creeslough
Doe Castle
Cashel
Lough Swilly
Gola Island
Derrybeg
Glenveagh National Park
Rathmullan
Fahan
Scalp Mountain
Owey Island
Bunbeg
Gweedore
Errigal
Lough Keel
Milford
Termon
Inch Island
Inch
Muff
Crolly
Dunlewy
Burnfoot
Bridgend
Culmore
Rosses Bay
Lough Nacung
L. Beagh
Ramelton
Grianan of Aileach
The Annagry
The Rosses
Lakeside Centre
Glebe Ho.
Kilmacrenan
Fort Stewart
Leabgarrow
Loughanure
Derryveagh Mts
Lough Gartan
Treantagh
Newtowncunningham
Harbour Museum
Burtonport
Slieve Snaght
Church Hill
Londonderry (Derry)
Waterside
Aran Island
Dungloe
Lough Anure
Glendowan
Letterkenny
Manorcunningham
Drumahoe
Carrigans
New Buildings
Rashedoge
Pluck
Maghery
Old Town
St Johnstown
Magheramason
Crohy Head
Derrydruel
Doochary
DONEGAL
Kingarrow
Cronamuck Mountain
Knockbrack
Slievekirk
Meenacross
Cark Mountain
Croaghaneen
Fintown
Raphoe
Gweebarra Bay
Bellanamore
Ballymagorry
Dunnamanagh
Lettermacaward
Lough Finn
Drumnacross
Artigarvan
Dawros Head
Portnoo
Aghla Mountain
Cloghan
Convoy
Ballindrait
Craig
Narin
Maas
Kilross
Lifford
Strabane
Rosbeg
Meenanarwa
Graffy
Stranorlar
Castlefinn
Loughros More Bay
Commeen
Glenties
Ballybofey
Killygordon
Sion Mills
Cloghboy
Tangaveane
Clady
Kilrean
Blue Stack Mts
Gleneely
Douglas Bridge
Plumbridge
Slievetooey
Ardara
Meenglass
Port
Maghera
Blue Stack
Lough Mourne
Ardstraw
Glen Bay
Glengesh Pass
Lough Eske
Newtownstewart
Gortin
Glencolumbkille
Castlederg
Stone Age Dolmens
Crove
Meentullynagarn
Letterbarra
Lough Catherine
Malin More
Killeter Forest
Malin Bay
Croagh
Ulster American Folk Park
Meenavean
Killen
Drumlegagh
Rathlin O'Birne Island
Malin Beg
Carrick
Crownarad
Inver
Donegal
Killeter
Slieve League
Kilcar
Dunkineely
Mountcharles
Blacktown
Mountjoy
Gortin Glen Forest Park
Teelin
Killybegs
Inver Bay
Drumquin
Fairy Water
Shalwy
Laghey
Lough Derg
Killyclogher
Muckross Head
Tullyvoos
Fintragh Bay
McSwynes Bay
Doorin Point
Bridgetown
Omagh
Ballintra
Drumskinny
Dooish
Clanabogan
TYR
Rossnowlagh
Tully
Crockmore
Pettigo
Lack
St John's Point
Coolmore
Ederny
The Diamond
Donegal Bay
Ballure
Kesh
Bodoney
Dromore
Gortaclare
Ballyshannon
Leggs
Boa Island
Seskinore
Lower Lough Erne
Fintona
Garvagh
Mullaghmore Head
Mullaghmore
Tullaghan
Bundoran
Belleek
Castlecaldwell
Drumduff
Castle Archdale
Lisnarrick
Irvinestown
Kinlough
Belleek Pottery
Rosscor
Inishmurray
Cliffoney
Castlegal
Askill
Correl Glen
Tully
Trillick
Buckode
Garrison
Blaney
Killadeas
Kilskeery
Streedagh Point
Moneylahan
Lough Melvin
Derrygonnelly
Ballinamallard
Murley
Grange
Darty Mts
Lissiniska
Glenade
Rossinver
Monea
Trory
Blackwater
Coach Museum
Roskeeragh Point
Ballyconnell
Gleniff
Benbulben
Truskmore
Glenade Lough
Kiltyclogher
Scribbagh
Tullybrack
Springfield
Garvary
Tempo
Creagh
Fivemiletown
Lissadell House
Carney
Cashelgarran
Glencar Lake
Boho
Enniskillen
Cooneen
Drumcliff Bay
High Cross & Round Tower
Sranea
Dough Mt
Lough Macnean Upper
County Museum
Castle Coole
Slieve Beagh
Raghly
Drumcliff
Drumcliff
Shanvus
Holywell
Letterbreen
Culkey
Lisbellaw
Brookeborough
Easky
Sligo Bay
Aughris Head
Rosses Point
Coney Island
Manorhamilton
Blacklion
Belcoo
Family Heritage Museum
Aughris
Ardabrone
Sligo (Sligeach)
LEITRIM
Lough Macnean Lower
Bellanaleck
Maguiresbridge
Eshnadarragh
Strandhill
Yeats Memorial Museum
Leckaun
FERMANAGH
Templeboy
Owenbeg
Dromard
Ballysodare Bay
Lough Gill
Abbey
Kilargue
Gubaveeny
Marble Arch
Wheathill
Drumcard
Lisnaskea
Rosslea
Florence Court Forest Park
Florence Court (NT)
Upper Lough Erne
Derrynawilt
Beltra
Ballysodare
Dromahair
Collgreane
Cuncagh
Mullan
Tully
Smithboro
Folklife Display
Collooney
Belhavel Lough
Dowra
Swanlinbar
Derrylin
Donagh
Easky Lough
Coolaney
Shannon
Corry
Slievenakilla
Glengavlen
Newtownbutler
Clones
Toberscanavan
Coola
Drumkeeran
Iron Mountains
Bellavally Gap
Slieve Rushen
Crom Estate
Carrowneden
Lough Allen
Derrynacreeve
Teemore
Newbliss
Carrowmore
Riverstown
Bencroy
Bawnboy
Wattlebridge
Scotshouse
Lavagh
SLIGO
Templehouse Lake
Geevagh
Altagowlan
Corraleehan
Ballyconnell
Kilconey
Belturbet
Largan
Cloonacool
Ballymote
Slieve Anierin
Redhills
Ox Mountains
Mullany's Cross
Achonry
Derry
Lough Arrow
Ballyfarnan
Aughnasheelan
Garadice Lough
Ardlougher
Milltown
Treehoo
Banada
Bunnanadden
Carrowkeel
Mountallen
St John's Lough
Butlers Bridge
Aclare
Tobercurry
Kesh
Keadue
Ballinamore
Newtown Gore
Annalee
Killavil
Ballinafad
Drumshanbo
Drumlea
Ballyhaise
Doocastle
Curry
Lough Key
Crossna
Fenagh
Killykeen Forest Park
Cavan
Cloontia
Gorteen
Mullaghroe
Leitrim
Kilnagross
Garvagh
Greagh
Lough Oughter
N56
N15
N13
N14
N16
N17
N59
N4
N3
N54
A2
A5
A6
A32
A35
A46
A47
A4
A34
A509
A505
A3
148
150

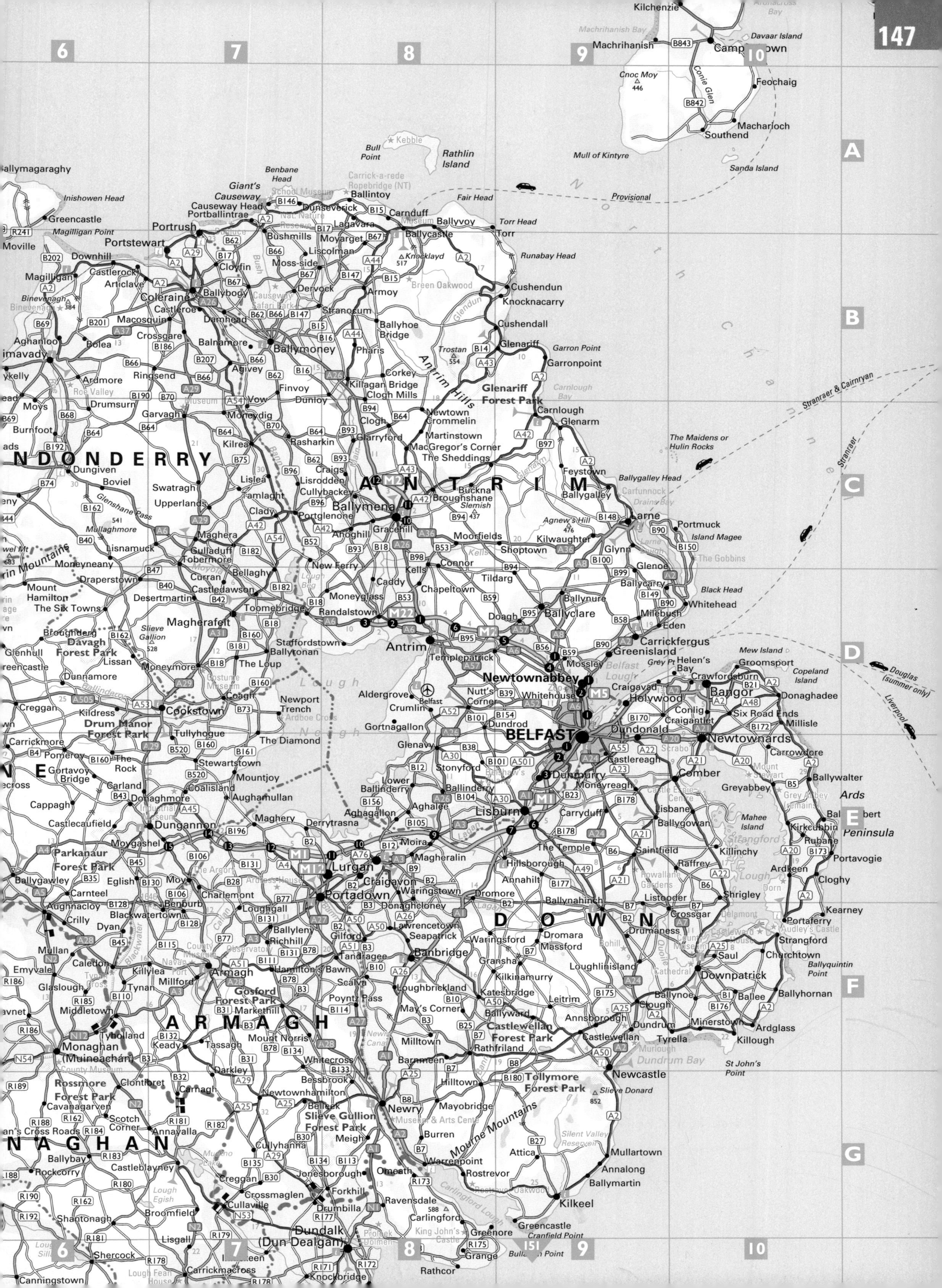
6
7
8
9
10
A
B
C
D
E
F
G
Kilchenzie
Machrihanish Bay
Machrihanish
Campbeltown
Davaar Island
Cnoc Moy
446
Conie Glen
Feochaig
Macharioch
Southend
Mull of Kintyre
Sanda Island
Provisional
North Channel
Kebble
Bull Point
Rathlin Island
Benbane Head
Giant's Causeway
Causeway Head
Portballintrae
Carrick-a-rede Ropebridge (NT)
Ballintoy
Dunseverick
Carnduff
Fair Head
Ballyvoy
Torr Head
Torr
Ballycastle
Runabay Head
Portrush
Portstewart
Bushmills
Moyarget
Liscolman
Moss-side
Knocklayd
517
Breen Oakwood
Cushendun
Knocknacarry
Cushendall
Glenariff
Garron Point
Garronpoint
Trostan
554
Antrim Hills
Glenariff Forest Park
Carnlough Bay
Carnlough
Glenarm
Inishowen Head
Greencastle
Magilligan Point
Moville
Downhill
Magilligan
Castlerock
Articlave
Coleraine
Ballybogy
Castleroe
Damhead
Causeway Safari Park
Dervock
Armoy
Stranocum
Ballyhoe Bridge
Binevenagh
384
Macosquin
Crossgare
Aghanloo
Bolea
Limavady
Balnamore
Ballymoney
Pharis
Corkey
Killagan Bridge
Clogh Mills
Agivey
Ringsend
Ardmore
Roe Valley
Finvoy
Dunloy
Vow
Moneydig
Drumsurn
Garvagh
Moys
Burnfoot
Newtown Crommelin
Martinstown
MacGregor's Corner
The Sheddings
Cloagh
Glarryford
Rasharkin
Kilrea
LONDONDERRY
Dungiven
Boviel
Craigs
Lisrodden
Cullybackey
Lislea
Tamlaght
Swatragh
Upperlands
ANTRIM
Buckna
Broughshane
Slemish
437
Feystown
Ballygalley Head
Carfunnock
Ballygalley
Drains Bay
Larne
Portmuck
Island Magee
The Gobbins
Glenshane Pass
541
Mullaghmore
Clady
Portglenone
Ballymena
Gracehill
Ahoghill
Agnew's Hill
476
Kilwaughter
Moorfields
Shoptown
Kells
Glynn
Glenoe
Ballycarry
Black Head
Whitehead
Maghera
Gulladuff
Tobermore
Lisnamuck
Moneyneany
Draperstown
Mount Hamilton
The Six Towns
Curran
Castledawson
Bellaghy
New Ferry
Connor
Tildarg
Caddy
Chapeltown
Moneyglass
Desertmartin
Magherafelt
Toomebridge
Randalstown
Ballyclare
Ballynure
Doagh
Milebush
Eden
Carrickfergus
Greenisland
The Maidens or Hulin Rocks
Stranraer & Cairnryan
Stranraer
Mew Island
Copeland Island
Groomsport
Helen's Bay
Grey Pt
Crawfordsburn
Bangor
Donaghadee
Douglas (summer only)
Liverpool
Slieve Gallion
528
Broughderg
Davagh Forest Park
Lissan
Moneymore
Staffordstown
Ballyronan
The Loup
Antrim
Templepatrick
Mossley
Belfast Lough
Newtownabbey
Whitehouse
Holywood
Craigavad
Glenhull
Dunnamore
Costume Museum
Coagh
Newport Trench
Ardboe Cross
Lough Neagh
Aldergrove
Belfast
Nutt's Corner
Crumlin
Dundrod
BELFAST
Conlig
Craigantlet
Six Road Ends
Millisle
Dundonald
Newtownards
Creggan
Kildress
Cookstown
Drum Manor Forest Park
Tullyhogue
Gortnagallon
Glenavy
Carrickmore
Pomeroy
The Rock
Stewartstown
The Diamond
Scrabo
Castlereagh
Carrowdore
Ballywalter
Gortavoy Bridge
Mountjoy
Coalisland
Stonyford
Belshaw's
Dunmurry
Comber
Mount Stewart
Greyabbey
Grey Abbey (remains)
Ards Peninsula
Cappagh
Carland
Donaghmore
Aughamullan
Lower Ballinderry
Ballinderry
Moneyreagh
Castle Espie Centre
Ballyhalbert
Castlecaulfield
Dungannon
Maghery
Derrytrasna
Aghagallon
Aghalee
Lisburn
Carryduff
Lisbane
Ballygowan
Mahee Island
Kirkcubbin
Rubane
Moygashel
Moira
The Temple
Saintfield
Strangford Lough
Killinchy
Portavogie
Parkanaur Forest Park
Magheralin
Hillsborough
Raffrey
Ardkeen
Cloghy
Ballygawley
Eglish
Moy
The Argory
Charlemont
Ardress House
Lurgan
Craigavon
Portadown
Waringstown
Annahilt
Rowallane Gardens
Shrigley
Dromore
Ballynahinch
Listooder
Crossgar
Kearney
Carnteel
Aughnacloy
Crilly
Benburb
Blackwatertown
Loughgall
Ballyleny
Richhill
Donaghcloney
Lawrencetown
Seapatrick
DOWN
Dromara
Drumaness
Portaferry
Audley's Castle
Castleward House
Strangford
Dyan
Mullan
Caledon
Emyvale
Glaslough
Tynan
Killylea
Navan Fort
County Museum
Observatory
Armagh
Millford
Hamilton's Bawn
Gilford
Tandragee
Banbridge
Waringsford
Massford
Gransha
Kilkinamurry
Loughinisland
County Museum
Cathedral
Saul
Downpatrick
Churchtown
Ballyquintin Point
Middletown
Tyholland
Gosford Forest Park
Markethill
Scarva
Poyntz Pass
Loughbrickland
Katesbridge
Leitrim
Ballynoe
Ballee
Ballyhornan
Monaghan (Muineachán)
Keady
ARMAGH
Mount Norris
Tassagh
May's Corner
Ballyward
Castlewellan Forest Park
Annsborough
Clough
Dundrum
Minerstown
Ardglass
Killough
Tyrella
Milltown
Rathfriland
Castlewellan
Murlough
Dundrum Bay
St John's Point
County Museum
Darkley
Whitecross
Barnmeen
Bessbrook
Hilltown
Tollymore Forest Park
Slieve Donard
852
Newcastle
Rossmore Forest Park
Clontibret
Carnagh
Newtownhamilton
Newry
Museum & Arts Centre
Mayobridge
Cavanagarven
Scotch Corner
Annayalla
Belleek
Slieve Gullion Forest Park
Mourne Mountains
Silent Valley Reservoir
Cullyhanna
Burren
Meigh
Attica
Mullartown
Annalong
Ballybay
Castleblayney
Rockcorry
Creggan
Jonesborough
Omeath
Warrenpoint
Rostrevor
Ballymartin
Lough Egish
Crossmaglen
Forkhill
Cullaville
Drumbilla
Ravensdale
588
Carlingford
Rostrevor Oakwood
Carlingford Lough
Kilkeel
Broomfield
Shantonagh
Lisgall
Dundalk (Dun-Dealgan)
Proleek Dolmen
King John's Castle
Greenore
Greencastle
Cranfield Point
Shercock
Carrickmacross
Inniskeen
Grange
Bullan Point
Lough Fea House
Knockbridge
Rathcor
Cannington
151
M1
M2
M5
M12
M22
A1
A2
A29
A6
A26

1
2
3
4
5
A
B
C
D
E
F
G
Stags of Broad Haven
Benwee Head
Portacloy
Stonefield
Porturlin
Belderg
Downpatrick Head
Ceide Fields
Ballycastle
Rathlackan
Kilcummin
Lenadoon Point
Aghadoon
Broad Haven
Doonamo Fort
Corclogh
Pollatomish
Bunalty
R314
Glenamoy
Maumakeogh 380
Killala Bay
Rathlee
Dromore
Belmullet
Knocknalina
Barnatra
Glenamoy
R315
R314
Creevagh
R297
Bartragh I.
Binghamstown
R313
R314
Bunnahowen
Trawmore Bay
Kincon
Killala
Inniscrone
N59
Culleens
The Mullet
R313
Carrowmore Lake
Sheskin
Inishkea North
Attavalley
Bangor Erris
Doobehy
Belville
Castleconor
Corbally
Owenmore
N59
Lough Dahybaun
R314
Crockets Town
Inishkea South
Aghleam
Gweensalia
Bellacorick
Crossmolina
N59
Bunnyconnellan
Fallmore
Ballina (Béal an Átha)
R294
Duvillaun More
Doohooma
N59
Moylaw
Srahnamanragh Bridge
Slieve Car 772
Deel
Blacksod Bay
Doona
R316
Castlehill
R310
Attymass
Keenagh
R312
Lahardaun
Nephin Beg 629
Ballycroy
N57
Valley
Slieve More 672
Nephin 806
Knockmore
Slieve Gamph or Ox
Doogort
Nephin Beg Range
R315
Lough Conn
Corlee
Croaghaun 668
Keel
Derreen
Birreencorragh 700
Cullin
Achill Head
Dooagh
Bunacurry
Annagh Island
Claggan
R318
N57
Levally Lough
Foxford
Cushcamcarragh 714
Srahmore
Pontoon
Lough Cullin
Achill Island
R319
Achill
Lough Feeagh
M A Y O
R310
Kilmore
Dooega
R317
Beltra
N58
Beltra Lough
Strade Franciscan Friary
R321
Furnace Lough
Corraun Peninsula
Mulrany
Burren
Bellavary
Barnacahy
Rosturk
Newport
Turlough
N5
Bohola
Cloughmore
Corraun
Dooghbeg
N59
R311
R312
Round Tower
R320
Achillbeg Island
Kilmeena
Clogher
Castlebar Lough
Castlebar (Caisleán an Bharraigh)
Kiltimagh
Islandeady Lough
Clare Island
Westport House
Manulla
Ballytoohy
Cloonkeen
R324
R323
Clew Bay
N60
Balla
R320
Westport Quay
Westport
Ballyhean
Church & Basilica
Ballycarra
R335
N60
Ballyfarnon
Louisburgh
Roonah Quay
Mullagh
Croagh Patrick 765
Aghagower
Abbey
Mayo
Caher Island
Liscarney
R330
Ballintober
Ballyglass
Cordarragh
N84
Lough Carra
Claremorris
Murrisk
Srahmee
Megalithic Tomb
Inishturk
Killadoon
Srah
Cregganbaun
Carrowkennedy
Partry
Culmore
N17
Kinnadoohy
R335
R331
Robe
N59
Tourmakeady
Hollymount
Inishbofin
Benbury 795
Roundfort
Lough
Killary Harbour
Bengorm 702
Inishark
Mweelrea 819
Aasleagh
Partry Mts
Ballinrobe
Castleville
Cashleen
Glennagevlagh
650
Benwee 682
Trean
Ballynakill Bay
Rinvyle
Devil's Mother
Mask
R334
Tully Cross
Salruck
Leenane
Kilmaine
R332
Lough Fee
Kylemore Abbey
R336
Joyce's Country
Finny
Neale
Aughrus More
Letterfrack
N59
Cleggan
Connemara National Park
Abbey
R345
N84
Ballyhear
Moyard
Maumturk Mts
Clonbur
Cong
R346
Cross
Omey Island
Benbaun 730
667
Maam
Lough Inagh
Shrule
Clifden
The Twelve Pins
Derrylea
Bencorr 712
R336
R345
Cornamona
R334
Mannin Bay
R334
613
Lough
Curraun
R333
Connemara
Recess
Greenfield
Ballinaboy
Derryneen
Maam Cross
Corrib
Headford
Doonloughan
R341
Ballynahinch
N59
Ballyconneely
R342
R340
49
Ballyhale
Cummer
Toombeola
Oughterard
Slyne Head
Cashel
Derryerglinna
Killarone
Aughanure
Roundstone
R336
N59
G A L W
Ballyconneely Bay
R341
Derryrush
Gortmore
Annaghdown
Bertraghboy Bay
Pearse's Cottage
Screeb
Rosscahill
Cloonboo
Glinsk
R340
Rosmuck
Iar Connaght
Laghtgeorge
Moyrus
Garrivinnagh
Carna
Kilkieran
Kinvarra
Owenboliska
Moycullen
Glencmurrin Lough
Ard
Ardmore
Ballindooly
N17
Mweenish Island
Lettercallow
Costelloe
Menlough
Galway (Gaillimh)
Cathedral
N6
R343
Rossaveel
Spanish Arch Museum
Lettermullen
Gorumna Island
Carraloe
Spiddal
R336
Salthill
Barna
Inveran
Golam Head
Kilcaimin
Tawin Island
Claribridge
North Sound
Galway Bay
Carrowmore
Eddy Island
Onaght
Inismore
Newtownlynch
Black Head
Parkmore
Dun Aengus Fort
Burren
Murroogh
N67
Kilronan
Ballyvaughan
Bealaclugga
Fanore
Formoyle
Aillwee Cave
Killeany
Inishmaan
Slieve Elva 345
Turlough
Aran Islands
R477
Burren
Megalithic Tombs
Gleninsheen Megalithic Tombs
Inisheer
N67
Scale: approx. 9 miles to 1 inch
0
10
20 miles
0
10
20
30 km
South Sound
R479
Lisdoonvarna
R480
Carran
Doolin Point
Roadford
R476
Noughaval
Castletown
Aughrim
Kilshanny
Kilfenora
Burren Display Centre
R460
Cliffs of Moher
R478
O'Brien's Tower
R481
Lickeen Lough
Inchiquin Lough
Killinaboy
Lough George
Kilconnell
Hag's Head
Liscannor
Ennistymon
Corofin
Lough Atedaun
Lahinch
Willbrook
Ruan
Liscannor Bay
N67
Cullenagh
Dysert O'Dea
R476
Mauricemills
Binneen
154
C L

SLIGO
LEITRIM
FERMANAGH
MON
CAVAN
ROSCOMMON
LONGFORD
WESTMEATH
OFFALY
LAOIS
Sligo (Sligeach)
Enniskillen
Cavan
Carrick-on-Shannon
Longford
Mullingar (An Muileann gCearr)
Athlone (Baile Átha Luain)
Ballinasloe (Béal Átha na Sluaighe)
Tullamore (Tulach Mhór)
Portlaoise
Roscommon
Boyle
Birr
Loughrea
Tuam
Clones
Florence Court Forest Park
Lough Key Forest Park
Portumna Forest Park
Iron Mountains
Slieve Bloom Mts
Slieve Aughty Mts
Upper Lough Erne
Lough Allen
Lough Ree
Lough Derg
146
147
151
152

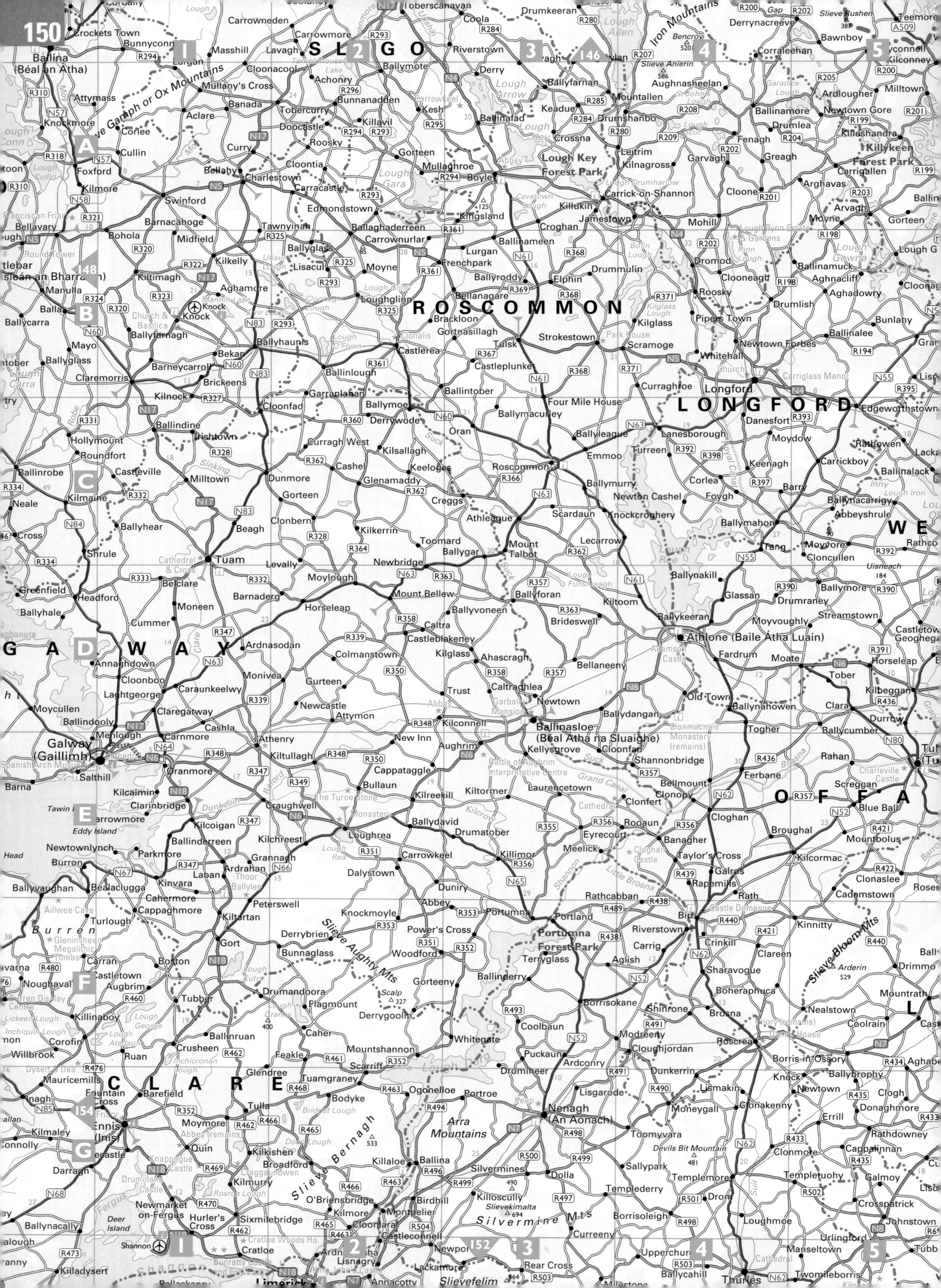
SLIGO
ROSCOMMON
LONGFORD
GALWAY
CLARE
OFFALY
Ballina (Béal an Atha)
Ox Mountains
Castlebar (Caisleán an Bharraigh)
Claremorris
Knock
Charlestown
Swinford
Boyle
Lough Key Forest Park
Carrick-on-Shannon
Drumshanbo
Lough Allen
Iron Mountains
Longford
Strokestown
Castlerea
Roscommon
Tuam
Athlone (Baile Átha Luain)
Ballinasloe (Béal Átha na Sluaighe)
Galway (Gaillimh)
Athenry
Oranmore
Loughrea
Gort
Portumna
Portumna Forest Park
Birr
Tullamore
Slieve Bloom Mts
Slieve Aughty Mts
Lough Derg
Nenagh (An Aonach)
Arra Mountains
Ennis (Inis)
Killaloe
Ballina
Slieve Bernagh
Silvermine Mts
Shannon
Limerick
Thurles
Roscrea
Burren
Lough Ree
Devils Bit Mountain
Ballinrobe
Headford
Ballyvaughan
Kinvara
Shannonbridge
Clonmacnois
Banagher
Borrisokane
Templemore
Newmarket on-Fergus
Sixmilebridge
146
148
152
154

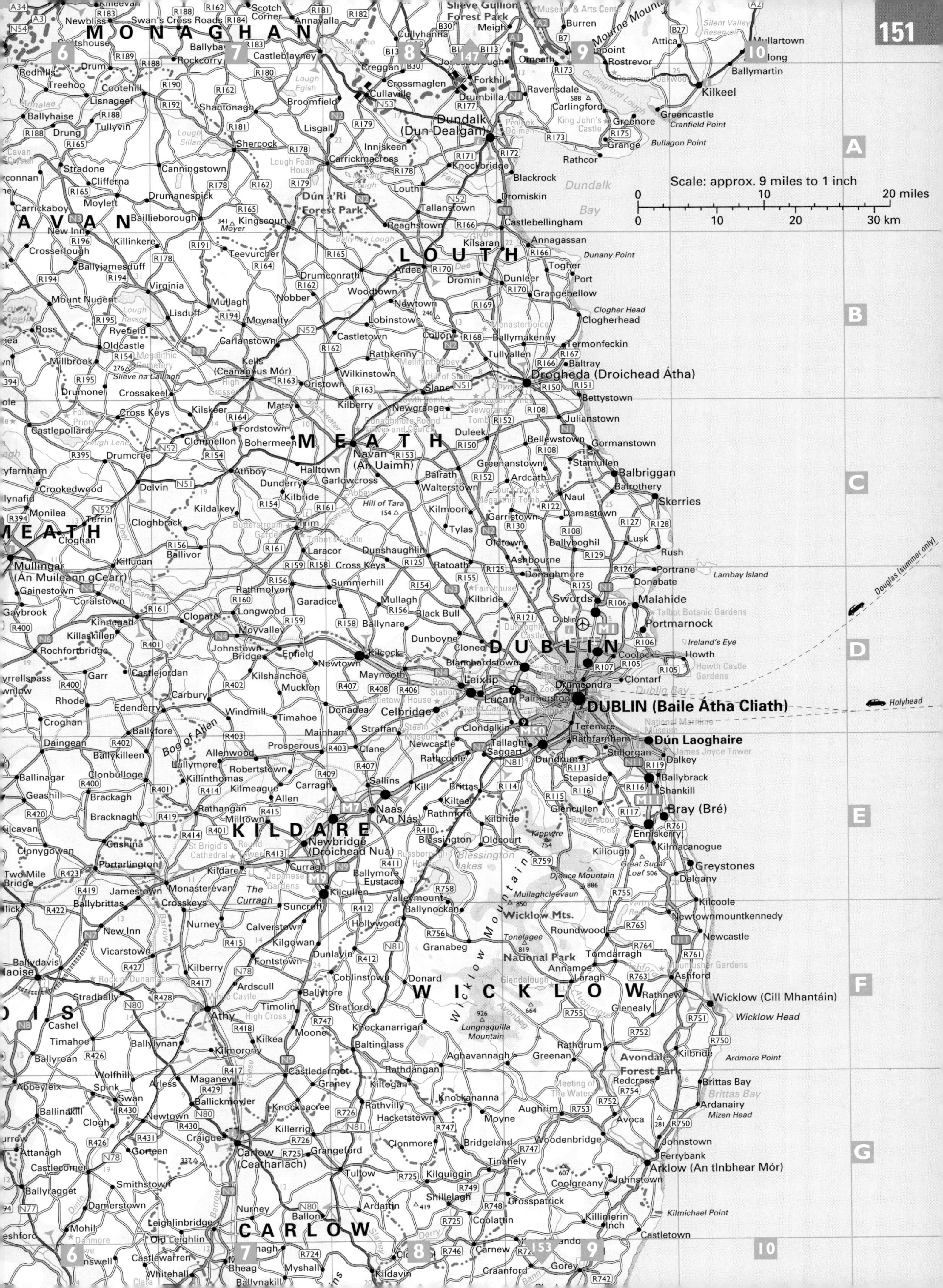
Scale: approx. 9 miles to 1 inch
0
10
20 miles
0
10
20
30 km
MONAGHAN
LOUTH
MEATH
DUBLIN
KILDARE
WICKLOW
CARLOW
Dundalk (Dun Dealgan)
Drogheda (Droichead Átha)
Navan (An Uaimh)
Kells (Ceanannus Mór)
Mullingar (An Muileann gCearr)
DUBLIN (Baile Átha Cliath)
Dún Laoghaire
Naas (An Nás)
Newbridge (Droichead Nua)
Bray (Bré)
Wicklow (Cill Mhantáin)
Arklow (An tInbhear Mór)
Carlow (Ceatharlach)
Athy
Kilkeel
Carlingford
Castleblayney
Carrickmacross
Ardee
Balbriggan
Skerries
Swords
Malahide
Howth
Maynooth
Leixlip
Lucan
Celbridge
Kilcock
Trim
Greystones
Blessington
Rathdrum
Tullow
Gorey
Dundalk Bay
Dublin Bay
Wicklow Mts.
Wicklow Mountains
Lambay Island
Ireland's Eye
Wicklow Head
Holyhead
Douglas (summer only)
A
B
C
D
E
F
G
6
7
8
9
10
147
153

CLARE
LIMERICK
TIPPERARY
CORK
WATERF
Castletown
Augbrim
Tubber
Drumandoora
Flagmount
Gorteeny
Ballinderry
Borrisokane
Shinrone
Boheraphuca
Brosna
Mountrath
Nealstown
Killinaboy
Corofin
Crusheen
Ballinruan
Caher
Mountshannon
Whitegate
Puckaun
Modreeny
Cloughjordan
Roscrea
Borris-in-Ossory
Willbrook
Ruan
Feakle
Scarriff
Lough Derg
Dromineer
Ardcony
Dunkerrin
Knock
Ballybrophy
Mauricemills
Fountain Cross
Barefield
Glendree
Tuamgraney
Bodyke
Ogonelloe
Portroe
Lisgarode
Lismakin
Newtown
Clogh
Inagh
Ennis (Inis)
Tulla
Moymore
Nenagh (An Aonach)
Moneygall
Clonakenny
Donaghmore
Errill
Kilmaley
Arra Mountains
Toomyvara
Rathdowney
Connolly
Clarecastle
Quin
Kilkishen
Slieve Bernagh
Killaloe
Ballina
Devils Bit Mountain
Clonmore
Cappalinnan
Darragh
Broadford
Silvermines
Dolla
Sallypark
Templemore
Templetuohy
Galmoy
Kilmurry
O'Briensbridge
Birdhill
Killoscully
Templederry
Drom
Crosspatrick
Newmarket on-Fergus
Hurler's Cross
Sixmilebridge
Kilmore
Montpelier
Silvermine Mts
Borrisoleigh
Loughmoe
Johnstown
Ballynacally
Cloonlara
Castleconnell
Curreeny
Urlingford
Shannon
Cratloe
Ardnacrusha
Lisnagry
Newport
Upperchurch
Manseltown
Tubb
Killadysert
Lackamore
Rear Cross
Ballycahill
Thurles (Durlas)
Twomileborris
Ballysteen
Pallaskenry
Limerick (Luimneach)
Annacotty
Slievefelim Mountains
Milestone
Drumbane
Coolmeen
Holycross
Littleton
Foynes
Curraghchase Forest Park
New Kildimo
Mungret
Abington
Hollyford
Loghill
Askeaton
Patrickswell
Ballyneety
Boher
Cappamore
Doon
Clonoulty
New Birmingham
Kilmana
Shanagolden
Caherconlish
Cappawhite
Ballynunty
Ballingarry
Ballyhahill
Newbridge
Adare
Crecora
Ballybroad
Pallas Green
Annacarty
Dundrum
Ballinure
Killenaule
Cappagh
Fedamore
Croagh
Rathkeale
Donohill
Dually
Reens
Croom
Kilfinny
Herbertstown
Kilteely
Oola
Rock of Cashel
Golden
Cashel
Drangan
Mullin
Ardagh
Bruff
Hospital
Cullen
Knockbrit
Cloneen
Ballingarry
Kilcolman
Ballinleeny
Emly
Tipperary
Rosegreen
Fethard
Ninemilehouse
Newcastle West
Mahoonagh
Athlacca
Knocklong
Newinn
Bruree
Rockhill
Kilross
Slievenamuck
Bansha
Slievenamon
Kilmeedy
Elton
Newtown
Lisronagh
Strand
Feonanagh
Ballyagran
Kilmallock
Martinstown
Galbally
Poulnamucky
Ashford
Kilfinnane
Ballylanders
Galtymore
Galtee Mountains
Cahir
Rathkeevin
Clonmel (Cluain Meala)
Broadford
Drumcollogher
Rathluirc (Charleville)
Ardpatrick
Kilcommon
Carrick
Mullaghareirk Mts
Milford
Ballyhaght
Cullane
Ardfinnan
Kilmanahan
Dromina
Newtown
Ballyhoura Mts
Kilbeheny
Comeragh Mts
Knockanaffrin
Freemount
Knockanevin
Knockacummer
Meelin
Churchtown
Liscarroll
Mitchelstown
Ballyporeen
Clogheen
Newcastle
Ballymacarbery
Bawn Cross Roads
Kildorrey
Taur
Buttevant
Glenduff
Monavullagh Mountains
Newmarket
Rockmills
Kilworth Camp
Knockmealdown Mts
Seefin
Castlecor
Doneraile
Araglin
Ballinamult
Kishkeam
Kanturk
Ballyclough
Castletownroche
Glanworth
Kilworth
Kilbrien
Boherboy
Mallow (Mala)
Ballyhooly
Lyrenaglogh
Ballyduff
Cappoquin
Cloonbannin
Killavullen
Clondulane
Millstreet
Lemybrien
Dernagree
Banteer
Nagles Mts
Fermoy
Lismore
Rathcool
Burnfoot
Knocknaskagh
Whitechurch
Ballymacmague
Drommahane
Castlelyons
Duncannon Bridge
Lyre
Nad
Ballynamona
Rathcormac
Curraglass
Tallow
Villierstown
Dungarvan (Dún Garbhán)
Boggeragh Mts
Crean's Cross Roads
Bottlehill
Aghern
Aglish
Britway
Glenville
Ballynoe
Dunmoon
Helvick Head
Musheramore
Donoughmore
Watergrasshill
The Pike
Gorteen
Ringville
Kilmona
Killeagh
Ardglass
Loskeran
Clashmore
Mine Head
Carriganimmy
Rylane Cross
Lisgoold
Leamlara
Grange
Ballynagree
Whitechurch
Dungourney
Kinsalebeg
Reanaclogheen
Ballyvourney
Aghabullogue
Matehy
Knockraha
Ardmore
Blarney Castle
Blarney
Youghal (Eochaill)
Ardmore Bay
Garrane
Tower
Riverstown
Mogeely
St Declan
Coachford
Dripsey
Cork (Corcaigh)
Glanmire
Glounthaune
Midleton
Castlemartyr
Ballymadog
Ballyvoge
Macroom
Ovens
Ballincollig
Carrigtwohill
Ladysbridge
Ballymacoda
Toames
Douglas
Great Island
Bawnard
Knockadoon Head
Inchigeelagh
Teerelton
Aherla
Waterfall
Passage West
Cloyne
Garryvoe
Kilmichael
Crookstown
Raheen
Cobh (An Cobh)
Shanagarry
Bealnablath
Ballinhassig
Ringaskiddy
Rostellan
Churchtown
Ballycotton
Shanacrane
Coppeen
Cross Barry
Halfway
Carrigaline
Whitegate
Newcestown
Gyleen
Crosshaven
Power Head
Castletown
Innishannon
Youghal Bay
Ballineen
Enniskean
Bandon
Ballyfeard
Minane Bridge
Dunmanway
Kilcolman
Belgooly
Swansea (summer only)
Ballynacarriga
Ballinadee
Nohoval
Kinsale
Ballingurteen
Knocks
Ballinascarthy
Kilbrittain
Oysterhaven
Le Havre, St Malo & Roscoff
Drinagh
Timoleague
Ballinspittle
Kinsale Harbour
Old Head
Clonakilty
Courtmacsherry
Lispatrick
North Ring
Old Head of Kinsale
Ross Carbery
Butlerstown
Castlefrek
Seven Heads
Glandore
Clonakilty Bay
Castletownshend
Galley Head

WICKLOW
CARLOW
KILKENNY
WEXFORD
Wicklow (Cill Mhantáin)
Wicklow Head
Arklow (An tInbhear Mór)
Carlow (Ceatharlach)
Kilkenny (Cill Chainnigh)
Enniscorthy (Inis Córthaidh)
Wexford (Loch Garman)
Waterford (Port Láirge)
Tramore (Trá Mhór)
New Ross
Gorey
Athy
Tullow
Bunclody
Ferns
Rosslare
Rosslare Harbour
Kilmore Quay
Saltee Islands
Carnsore Point
Hook Head
Wexford Bay
Ballyteige Bay
Tramore Bay
Blackstairs Mountains
Mount Leinster
Brittas Bay
Avondale Forest Park
Fishguard
Pembroke Dock
Cherbourg & Le Havre
Roscoff (summer only)
Scale: approx. 9 miles to 1 inch
0
10
20 miles
0
10
20
30 km
A
B
C
D
E
F
G
6
7
8
9
10

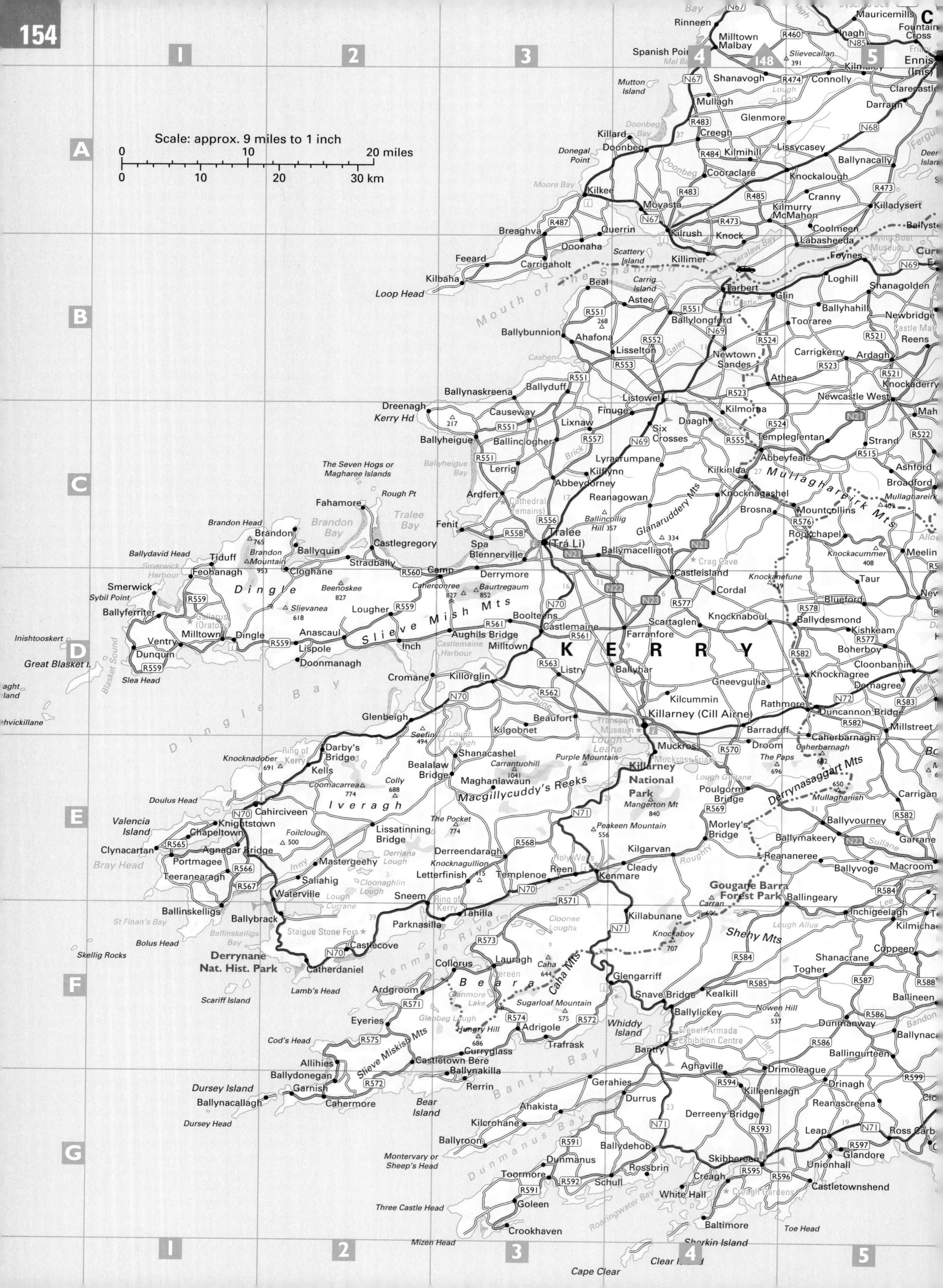
Scale: approx. 9 miles to 1 inch
0 10 20 miles
0 10 20 30 km
1
2
3
4
5
A
B
C
D
E
F
G
C
KERRY
Bay
Rinneen
Milltown Malbay
Spanish Point
Mal Bay
Mauricemills
Fountain Cross
Inagh
Ennis (Inis)
148
Slievecallan 391
Shanavogh
Connolly
Clarecastle
Mutton Island
Mullagh
Darragh
Glenmore
Doonbeg Bay
Killard
Creegh
Donegal Point
Doonbeg
Kilmihill
Lissycasey
Ballynacally
Cooraclare
Knockalough
Moore Bay
Kilkee
Cranny
Moyasta
Kilmurry McMahon
Killadysert
Coolmeen
Breaghva
Querrin
Kilrush
Knock
Labasheeda
Doonaha
Scattery Island
Killimer
Foynes
Feeard
Carrigaholt
Kilbaha
Loop Head
Beal
Carrig Island
Tarbert
Glin
Loghill
Shanagolden
Mouth of the Shannon
Astee
Glin Castle
Ballyhahill
Newbridge
Ballylongford
Tooraree
Ballybunnion
Ahafona
Lisselton
Newtown Sandes
Carrigkerry
Ardagh
Reens
Cashen
Athea
Knockaderry
Ballynaskreena
Ballyduff
Listowel
Newcastle West
Dreenagh
Kerry Hd
Causeway
Finuge
Kilmorna
Lixnaw
Duagh
Ballyheigue
Ballinclogher
Six Crosses
Templeglentan
Strand
Lyracrumpane
Abbeyfeale
Ballyheigue Bay
Lerrig
Kilflynn
Kilkinlea
Ashford
The Seven Hogs or Magharee Islands
Abbeydorney
Broadford
Mullaghareirk Mts
Rough Pt
Ardfert
Reanagowan
Knocknagashel
Mullaghareirk 409
Fahamore
Cathedral (remains)
Brosna
Mountcollins
Tralee Bay
Brandon Head
Brandon Bay
Fenit
Ballincollig Hill 357
Glanaruddery Mts
Brandon 765
Rockchapel
Castlegregory
Tralee (Trá Li)
334
Knockacummer 408
Meelin
Ballydavid Head
Brandon Mountain 953
Ballyquin
Spa
Blennerville
Ballymacelligott
Tiduff
Smerwick Harbour
Stradbally
Crag Cave
Feohanagh
Cloghane
Camp
Derrymore
Castleisland
Knockanefune 439
Smerwick
Beenoskee 827
Caherconree 827
Baurtregaum 852
Cordal
Taur
Sybil Point
Dingle
Slievanea 618
Lougher
Slieve Mish Mts
Blueford
Ballyferriter
Gallarus (Oratory)
Boolteens
Knocknaboul
Ballydesmond
Milltown
Dingle
Anascaul
Aughils Bridge
Castlemaine
Scartaglen
Kishkeam
Inishtooskert
Ventry
Lispole
Inch
Castlemaine Harbour
Milltown
Farranfore
Boherboy
Dunquin
Great Blasket I.
Blasket Sound
Doonmanagh
Listry
Ballyhar
Cloonbanin
Slea Head
Cromane
Killorglin
Knocknagree
Gneevgullia
Dernagree
Dingle Bay
Kilcummin
Rathmore
Laune
Beaufort
Killarney (Cill Airne)
Duncannon Bridge
Glenbeigh
Transport Museum
Barraduff
Millstreet
Seefin 494
Kilgobnet
Lough Caragh
Lough Leane
Caherbarnagh
Muckross
Droom
Ring of Kerry
Darby's Bridge
Shanacashel
Muckross Friary
Caherbarnagh 682
Knocknadober 691
Carrantuohill 1041
Purple Mountain
Killarney National Park
The Paps 696
Derrynasaggart Mts
Kells
Bealalaw Bridge
Maghanlawaun
Lough Guitane
Poulgorm Bridge
650
Colly 688
Coomacarrea 774
Mullaghanish
Carrigan
Macgillycuddy's Reeks
Mangerton Mt 840
Doulus Head
Iveragh
Cahirciveen
The Pocket 774
Peakeen Mountain 556
Morley's Bridge
Ballyvourney
Valencia Island
Knightstown
Chapeltown
Foilclough 500
Lissatinning Bridge
Ballymakeery
Sullane
Garrane
Clynacartan
Kilgarvan
Portmagee
Agnagar Bridge
Derreendaragh
Roughty
Reananeree
Bray Head
Mastergeehy
Derriana Lough
Knocknagullion 415
Holy Wells
Cleady
Ballyvoge
Macroom
Teeranearagh
Saliahig
Inny
Letterfinish
Templenoe
Reen
Kenmare
Gougane Barra Forest Park
Cloonaghlin Lough
Waterville
Lough Currane
Sneem
Ballingeary
Ballinskelligs
Ring of Kerry
Tahilla
Carran 606
St Finan's Bay
Ballybrack
Parknasilla
Killabunane
Inchigeelagh
Ballinskelligs Bay
Cloonee Loughs
Lough Allua
Bolus Head
Staigue Stone Fort
Kenmare River
Knockaboy 707
Shehy Mts
Skellig Rocks
Derrynane Nat. Hist. Park
Castlecove
Lauragh
Caha 644
Caha Mts
Shanacrane
Coppeen
Catherdaniel
Collorus
Tooreen
Glengarriff
Togher
Lamb's Head
Beara
Ardgroom
Glanmore Lake
Snave Bridge
Kealkill
Scariff Island
Sugarloaf Mountain 575
Nowen Hill 537
Ballineen
Eyeries
Glenbeg Lough
Whiddy Island
Ballylickey
Dunmanway
Hungry Hill 686
Adrigole
French Armada Exhibition Centre
Bandon
Cod's Head
Slieve Miskish Mts
Trafrask
Ilen
Curryglass
Bantry
Ballingurteen
Allihies
Castletown Bere
Bantry Bay
Aghaville
Drimoleague
Ballydonegan
Ballynakilla
Gerahies
Drinagh
Garnish
Rerrin
Durrus
Killeenleagh
Dursey Island
Bear Island
Reanascreena
Ballynacallagh
Cahermore
Ahakista
Derreeny Bridge
Dursey Head
Kilcrohane
Leap
Ross Carbery
Dunmanus Bay
Montervary or Sheep's Head
Ballyroon
Ballydehob
Glandore
Dunmanus
Skibbereen
Unionhall
Rossbrin
Toormore
Schull
Creagh
Castletownshend
White Hall
Creagh Gardens
Goleen
Roaringwater Bay
Three Castle Head
Crookhaven
Baltimore
Toe Head
Mizen Head
Sherkin Island
Cape Clear
Clear Island
N67
R460
N85
R474
R483
R484
N68
R473
R485
R487
N67
N69
R551
R552
R553
R524
R521
R523
R557
N69
R555
R515
R522
R556
R558
N21
R560
R559
N22
N23
N70
R577
R578
R561
R563
R562
R582
N72
R583
R570
R569
N71
R568
R565
R566
R567
N70
R571
N22
R584
R573
N71
R585
R587
R588
R571
R574
R572
R586
R575
R572
R594
R599
R593
R591
R592
R597
R595
R596

6
7
8
9
10
150
Nenagh (An Aonach)
Lisgarode
Portroe
Ogonelloe
Bodyke
Tulla
Moymore
Arra Mountains
Slieve Bernagh
Lismakin
Clonakenny
Moneygall
Toomyvara
Devils Bit Mountain
Newtown
Errill
Clogh
Donaghmore
Ballycolla
Rathdowney
Durrow
Abbeyleix
Ballina
Quin
Kilkishen
Broadford
Killaloe
Ballina
Silvermines
Dolla
Sallypark
Templemore
Clonmore
Cappalinnan
Templetuohy
Galmoy
Cullahill
Attanagh
Castlecomer
Ballyragget
Lisdowney
Kilmurry
O'Briensbridge
Birdhill
Killoscully
Slievekimalta
Templederry
Drom
Crosspatrick
Johnstown
Freshford
Mohil
Dunmore Cave
Damerstown
Hurler's Cross
Sixmilebridge
Kilmore
Montpelier
Silvermine Mts
Borrisoleigh
Loughmoe
Urlingford
Tubbrid
Johnswell
Cratloe
Cratloe Woods Ho.
Bunratty Castle and Folk Park
Ardnacrusha
Lisnagry
Castleconnell
Newport
Curreeny
Upperchurch
Manseltown
Cathedral
Lackamore
Rear Cross
Slievefelim Mountains
Ballycahill
Thurles (Durlas)
Twomileborris
Kilcooley Abbey
Slieveardagh Hills
Tullaroan
Limerick (Luimneach)
Annacotty
Hunt Museum
King John's Castle
Milestone
Drumbane
Holycross
Abbey
Littleton
Kilkenny (Cill Chainnigh)
Rothe House
Ballaskenry
New Kildimo
Mungret
Abington
Hollyford
Cathedral
New Birmingham
Ballycallan
Kilmanagh
Grevine
Patrickswell
Boher
Cappamore
Doon
Clonoulty
TIPPERARY
Grange
Ballingarry
Ballymack
Ballynunty
Burnchurch
Adare
Manor
Crecora
Fedamore
Ballyneety
Caherconlish
Cappawhite
Dundrum
Cappamurra
Ballinure
Killenaule
Callan
KILKENNY
Stoneyford
Kells
LIMERICK
Croom
Kilfinny
Ballybroad
Pallas Green
Annacarty
Donohill
Lough Gur
Stone Age Centre
Kilteely
Herbertstown
Oola
Rock of Cashel
Cashel
Dually
Drangan
Mullinahone
Knockbrit
Golden
Cullen
Athassel Abbey
GPA-Bolton Library
Cloneen
Dunnamaggan
Knocktopher
Bruff
Hospital
Emly
Tipperary
Rosegreen
Fethard
Killamerry
Ninemilehouse
Newmarket
Windgap
Kilmaganny
Ballinleeny
Athlacca
Knocklong
Kilross
Slievenamuck
Bansha
Newinn
Lisronagh
Slievenamon
Boolyglass
Rockhill
Bruree
Elton
Newtown
Aherlow
Ahenny
Lukeswell
Kilmallock
Ballyagran
Martinstown
Galbally
Galtymore
Poulnamucky
Ballylanders
Galtee Mountains
Rathkeevin
Cahir
Clonmel (Cluain Meala)
County Museum
St Mary's Church
High Crosses
Booley Hills
Carrick-on-Suir (Carraig na Siuire)
Kilfinnane
Kilcommon
Ormond Castle
Carrickbeg
Piltown
Fiddown
Rathluirc (Charleville)
Milford
Dromina
Ardpatrick
Ballyhaght
Cullane
Ardfinnan
Kilmanahan
Comeragh Mts
Rathgormuck
Mothel
Mooncoin
Granny Castle
Newtown
Ballyhoura Mts
Knockanevin
Kilbeheny
Mitchelstown Caves
Knockanaffrin
Clonea
Portlaw
Freemount
Churchtown
Ballyporeen
Clogheen
Ballymacarberry
Croughaun Hill
Liscarroll
Kildorrery
Mitchelstown
Newcastle
Monavullagh Mountains
Fews
Waterford (Port Láirge)
Bawn Cross Roads
Buttevant
Doneraile
Glenduff
Kilworth Camp
Knockmealdown Mts
Seefin
Reginald's Tower
Rockmills
Araglin
Ballinamult
Furraleigh
Kilmacthomas
Lisnakill
Castlecor
Annes Grove Gardens
Glanworth
Kilworth
Castletownroche
WATERFORD
Kilbrien
Lemybrien
Ballymorris
Ballyclough
Lyrenaglogh
Ballyduff
Cappoquin
Ballylaneen
Kill
Annestown
Tramore (Trá Mhór)
Mallow (Mala)
Killavullen
Ballyhooly
Clondulane
Millstreet
Bunmahon
Stradbally
Banteer
Nagles Mts
Knocknaskagh
Fermoy
Blackwater
Castle Gardens
Lismore
Whitechurch
Ballymacmague
Ballyvoyle
King John's Castle
Dromahane
Burnfoot
Castlelyons
Tallow
Villierstown
Dungarvan (Dún Garbhán)
Nad
Ballynamona
Rathcormac
Curraglass
Aglish
Aghern
Helvick Head
Crean's Cross Roads
Bottlehill
Britway
Ballynoe
Dunmoon
Gorteen
Ringville
CORK
Glenville
Watergrasshill
The Pike
Loskeran
Donoughmore
Kilmona
Killeagh
Ardglass
Clashmore
Mine Head
Rylane Cross
Grange
Whitechurch
Leamlara
Lisgoold
Kinsalebeg
Reanaclogheen
Knockraha
Dungourney
Ardmore Bay
Ardmore
Matehy
Blarney Castle and Stone
Blarney
Tower
Riverstown House
Riverstown
Collegiate Church of St Mary
Youghal (Eochaill)
St Declan
Coachford
Dripsey
Inniscarra Reservoir
Cork (Corcaigh)
Glanmire
Glounthaune
Midleton
Mogeely
Castlemartyr
Ballymadog
Carrigtwohill
Cathedral
Fota
Great Island
Ladysbridge
Ballymacoda
Carrigadrohid Reservoir
Ovens
Ballincollig
Douglas
Passage West
Bawnard
Cloyne
Garryvoe
Knockadoon Head
Aherla
Waterfall
Cobh (An Cobh)
Shanagarry
Crookstown
Raheen
Cork
Ringaskiddy
Rostellan
Churchtown
Ballycotton
Cross Barry
Ballinhassig
Carrigaline
Whitegate
Newcestown
Halfway
Crosshaven
Gyleen
Power Head
Innishannon
Youghal Bay
Ballyfeard
Minane Bridge
Bandon
Kilcolman
Belgooly
Desmond Castle
Nohoval
Swansea (summer only)
Ballinadee
Kinsale
Oysterhaven
Le Havre, St.Malo & Roscoff
Ballinascarthy
Kilbrittain
Kinsale Harbour
Castle Gardens
Ballinspittle
Timoleague
Old Head
Courtmacsherry
Courtmacsherry Bay
Lispatrick
North Ring
Old Head of Kinsale
Butlerstown
Clonakilty Bay
Seven Heads
A
B
C
D
E
F
G
153
N7
N8
N18
N20
N22
N24
N25
N62
N71
N72
N73
N74
N76
N77
N10
R463
R468
R490
R494
R500
R499
R497
R501
R502
R503
R504
R505
R507
R511
R512
R513
R514
R515
R516
R518
R519
R522
R576
R578
R579
R580
R581
R586
R589
R590
R600
R601
R602
R603
R605
R606
R607
R609
R610
R611
R612
R613
R614
R617
R618
R619
R624
R626
R627
R628
R629
R630
R632
R633
R634
R660
R661
R662
R663
R665
R666
R668
R669
R670
R671
R672
R673
R674
R675
R676
R677
R681
R682
R687
R688
R689
R690
R691
R692
R693
R694
R695
R697
R698
R699
R700
R701
R706
R426
R433
R435
R462
R465
R466
R469
R470
R496
R498
R498
Slievenamon
719
755
728
793
392
320
370
517
429
238
464
490
694
481
533
1690

INDEX TO IRELAND SECTION

A

Aasleagh 148 D3
Abbey 149 G7
Abbeydorney 154 C3
Abbeyfeale 154 C4
Abbeyleix 151 G6
Abbeyshrule 149 D9
Abington 152 B2
Achill 148 B3
Achonry 149 B6
Aclare 150 A1
Adamstown 153 C8
Adare 155 B6
Adrigole 154 F3
Aghaboe 152 A5
Aghabullogue 152 F1
Aghadoon 148 A2
Aghadowry 149 C9
Aghagallon 147 E8
Aghagower 148 C4
Aghalee 147 E8
Aghamore 150 B1
Aghanloo 147 B6
Aghavannagh 153 A9
Aghaville 154 G4
Aghern 152 E3
Aghleam 148 A2
Aghnacliff 149 C9
Agivey 147 B7
Aglish *Tipperary* 149 G8
Aglish *Waterford* 152 E4
Agnagar Bridge 154 E1
Ahafona 154 B3
Ahakista 154 G3
Ahascragh 150 D3
Ahenny 155 C10
Aherla 152 F1
Ahoghill 147 C8
Aldergrove 147 D8
Allen 151 E7
Allenwood 151 E7
Allihies 154 G2
Altagowlan 149 B8
Anascaul 154 D2
Annacarty 155 B8
Annacotty 152 B2
Annagassan 151 B9
Annaghdown 150 D1
Annagry 146 C2
Annahilt 147 E9
Annalong 147 G9
Annamoe 151 F9
Annayalla 147 G7
Annestown 153 E6
Annsborough 147 F9
Antrim 147 D8
Araglin 155 D8
Ard 148 F2
Ardabrone 146 F1
Ardagh 154 B5
Ardanairy 151 G10
Ardara 146 D2
Ardattin 153 B8
Ardcath 151 C9
Ardconry 152 A3
Ardee 151 B8
Ardfert 154 C3
Ardfinnan 155 C9
Ardglass *Down* 147 F10
Ardglass *Cork* 155 E8
Ardgroom 154 F2
Ardkeen 147 E10
Ardlougher 149 B9
Ardmore *Londonderry* 147 B6
Ardmore *Galway* 148 F3
Ardmore *Waterford* 155 E9
Ardnacrusha 152 B2
Ardnasodan 149 E6
Ardpatrick 152 D2
Ardrahan 150 E1
Ardscull 151 F7
Ardstraw 146 D5
Arghavas 149 B9
Arklow (An tinbhear Mór) 151 G9
Arless 151 G7
Armagh 147 F7
Armoy 147 B8
Arryheernabin 146 A4
Arthurstown 153 D7
Articlave 147 B7
Artigarvan 146 C5
Arvagh 149 C9
Ashbourne 151 C9
Ashford *Wicklow* 151 F10
Ashford *Limerick* 154 C5
Askeaton 152 B1
Askill 146 E2
Astee 154 B4
Athboy 151 C7
Athea 154 B4
Athenry 149 F6
Athlacca 152 C2
Athleague 149 D7
Athlone (Baile Átha Luain) 150 D4
Athy 151 F7
Attanagh 151 G6
Attavalley 148 A3
Attica 147 G9
Attymass 148 B5
Attymon 150 D2
Augbrim 148 G5
Aughamullan 147 E7
Augher 146 F5
Aughils Bridge 154 D3
Aughnacloy 147 F6
Aughnasheelan 146 G3
Aughrim *Galway* 150 E3
Aughrim *Wicklow* 151 G9
Aughris 149 A6
Aughrus More 148 D2
Avoca 151 G9
Abbey 150 F3

B

Baillieborough 151 A7
Balbriggan 151 C9
Balla 148 C5
Ballaghaderreen 149 C6
Ballaghkeen 153 C9
Ballee 147 F10
Ballickmoyler 151 G7
Ballina (Béal an Átha) 148 B5
Ballina *Tipperary* 155 A7
Ballinaboy 148 E2
Ballinadee 152 G2
Ballinafad 149 B7
Ballinagar 149 F10
Ballinagh 149 B10
Ballinagore 149 E10
Ballinakill 151 G6
Ballinalack 150 C5
Ballinalee 149 C9
Ballinamallard 146 F4
Ballinameen 150 B3
Ballinamore 149 B9
Ballinamuck 149 C9
Ballinamult 155 D9
Ballinascarthy 155 F6
Ballinasloe
(Béal Átha na Sluaighe) 149 F8
Ballinclogher 154 C3
Ballincollig 152 F2
Ballincrea 153 D7
Ballinderreen 150 E1
Ballinderry *Antrim* 147 E8
Ballinderry Tipperary 150 F3
Ballindine 150 C1
Ballindooly 148 F5
Ballindrait 146 C4
Ballineen 154 F5
Ballingarry *Limerick* 152 C1
Ballingarry *Tipperary* 152 B5
Ballingeary 154 F5
Ballingurteen 154 F5
Ballinhassig 152 F2
Ballinleeny 152 C1
Ballinlough 150 B2
Ballinrobe 148 D5
Ballinruan 150 F1
Ballinskelligs 154 F1
Ballinspittle 152 G2
Ballintober *Mayo* 148 C4
Ballintober *Roscommon* 149 D7
Ballintoy 147 A8
Ballintra 146 E3
Ballinure 155 B9
Ballisodare 149 A7
Ballivor 151 C7
Ballon 153 B7
Ballure 146 E2
Ballyagran 152 C1
Ballybay 147 G6
Ballybofey 146 D4
Ballyboghil 151 C9
Ballybogy 147 B7
Ballybrack *Dublin* 151 E9
Ballybrack *Kerry* 154 F2
Ballybrittas 151 F6
Ballybroad 155 B7
Ballybrophy 150 G5
Ballybunnion 154 B3
Ballycahill 152 B4
Ballycallan 155 B10
Ballycanew 153 B9
Ballycarney 153 B8
Ballycarra 148 C5
Ballycarry 147 D10
Ballycastle *Antrim* 147 B8
Ballycastle *Mayo* 148 A4
Ballyclare 147 D9
Ballyclough 155 D6
Ballycolla 152 A5
Ballyconneely 148 E2
Ballyconnell *Sligo* 146 F1
Ballyconnell *Cavan* 146 G4
Ballycotton 152 F4
Ballycroy 148 B3
Ballycumber 150 E5
Ballydangan 149 F8
Ballydavid 149 F7
Ballydavis 151 F6
Ballydehob 154 G4
Ballydesmond 154 D5
Ballydonegan 154 G2
Ballyduff *Waterford* 152 E4
Ballyduff *Kerry* 154 B3
Ballyfarnagh 148 C5
Ballyfarnan 149 B8
Ballyfasy 153 C7
Ballyfeard 155 F7
Ballyferriter 154 D1
Ballyfin 149 G10
Ballyforan 150 D3
Ballyfore 151 E6
Ballygalley 147 C9
Ballygar 149 E7
Ballygarrett 153 B9
Ballygawley 147 E6
Ballyglass *Mayo* 148 C5
Ballyglass *Mayo* 149 C6
Ballygorman 146 A5
Ballygowan 147 E9
Ballyhack 153 D7
Ballyhaght 152 D2
Ballyhahill 154 B5
Ballyhaise 151 A6
Ballyhalbert 147 E10
Ballyhale *Galway* 148 E5
Ballyhale *Kilkenny* 153 C6
Ballyhar 154 D4
Ballyhaunis 149 C6
Ballyhean 148 C4
Ballyhear 148 D5
Ballyheigue 154 C3
Ballyhoe Bridge 147 B8
Ballyhooly 155 D7
Ballyhornan 147 F10
Ballyjamesduff 151 B6
Ballykeeran 149 E9
Ballykelly 147 B6
Ballykilleen 151 E6
Ballylanders 152 C3
Ballylaneen 155 D10
Ballyleague 149 D8
Ballyleny 147 F7
Ballylickey 154 F4
Ballyliffen 146 A5
Ballylongford 154 B4
Ballylynan 151 F7
Ballymacarberry 152 D5
Ballymacelligott 154 C4
Ballymack 153 B6
Ballymackilroy 147 E6
Ballymacmague 152 E5
Ballymacoda 155 E9
Ballymacurley 150 C3
Ballymadog 155 E9
Ballymagaraghy 147 A6
Ballymagorry 146 C5
Ballymahon 149 D9
Ballymakeery 154 E5
Ballymakenny 151 B9
Ballymartin 147 G9
Ballymena 147 C8
Ballymoe 149 D7
Ballymoe 150 C2
Ballymoney 147 B7
Ballymore Eustace 151 E8
Ballymore *Donegal* 146 B3
Ballymore *Westmeath* 149 E9
Ballymorris 153 D6
Ballymote 149 B7
Ballymurphy 153 B7
Ballymurry 149 D8
Ballynabola 153 C7
Ballynacallagh 154 G2
Ballynacally 154 A5
Ballynacarriga 154 F5
Ballynacarrigy 149 D10
Ballynafid 151 C6
Ballynagree 155 E6
Ballynahinch *Down* 147 F9
Ballynahinch *Galway* 148 E3
Ballynahowen 150 D4
Ballynakill *Westmeath* 150 D4
Ballynakill *Carlow* 153 B7
Ballynakilla 154 G3
Ballynamona 152 E2
Ballynare 151 D8
Ballynaskreena 154 C3
Ballynastraw 153 C8
Ballyneaner 146 C5
Ballyneety 152 B2
Ballynockan 151 F8
Ballynoe *Down* 147 F10
Ballynoe *Cork* 155 E8
Ballynunty 152 B5
Ballynure 147 D9
Ballyporeen 152 D3
Ballyquin 154 C2
Ballyragget 151 G6
Ballyroan 151 F6
Ballyroddy 149 C7
Ballyroebuck 153 B8
Ballyronan 147 D7
Ballyroon 154 G3
Ballyshannon 146 E2
Ballysimon 153 C8
Ballysteen 152 B1
Ballytoohy 148 C2
Ballytore 151 F7
Ballyvaldon 153 C9
Ballyvaughan 148 G5
Ballyvoge 154 E5
Ballyvoneen 149 E7
Ballyvourney 154 E5
Ballyvoy 147 B8
Ballyvoyle 155 D10
Ballywalter 147 E10
Ballyward 147 F9
Ballywilliam 153 C7
Balnamore 147 B7
Balrath 151 C8
Balrothery 151 C9
Baltimore 154 G4
Baltinglass 151 F8
Baltray 151 B9
Banada 149 B6
Banagher 150 E4
Banbridge 147 F8
Bandon 155 F6
Bangor Erris 148 A3
Bangor 147 D10
Bannow 153 D7
Bansha 155 C8
Banteer 152 E1
Bantry 154 F4
Barefield 152 A1
Barna 148 F5
Barnacahoge 150 B1
Barnaderg 149 E6
Barnatra 148 A3
Barneycarroll 150 B1
Barnmeen 147 G8
Barraduff 154 D4
Barry 149 D9
Bawn Cross Roads 152 D1
Bawnard 152 F3
Bawnboy 146 G4
Beagh 149 D6
Beal 154 B3
Bealaclugga 148 G5
Bealalaw Bridge 154 E3
Bealnablath 152 F1
Beaufort 154 D3
Bekan 149 C6
Belclare 150 D1
Belcoo 149 A9
Belderg 148 A4
Belfast 147 E9
Belgooly 155 F7
Bellacorick 148 B3
Bellaghy 147 D7
Bellahy 149 B6
Bellanagare 149 C7
Bellanaleck 146 F4
Bellanamore 146 C3
Bellaneeny 149 E8
Bellavary 148 C5
Belleek *Fermanagh* 146 E3
Belleek *Armagh* 147 G7
Bellewstown 151 C9
Bellmount 150 E4
Belmullet 148 A2
Beltra *Sligo* 146 G1
Beltra *Mayo* 148 B4
Belturbet 149 B10
Belville 148 A4
Benburb 147 F7
Bennettsbridge 153 B6
Beragh 146 E5
Bessbrook 147 G8
Bettystown 151 C9
Bindoo 146 B5
Binghamstown 148 A2
Birdhill 152 A2
Birr 150 F4
Black Bull 151 D8
Blacklion 146 F3
Blackrock 151 A9
Blacktown 146 D4
Blackwater 153 C9
Blackwatertown 147 F7
Blanchardstown 151 D9
Blaney 146 F4
Blarney 152 F2
Blennerville 154 C3
Blessington 151 E8
Blue Ball 150 E5
Blueford 154 D5
Bodoney 146 E4
Bodyke 152 A2
Boher 152 B2
Boheraphuca 150 F4
Boherboy 154 D5
Bohermeen 151 C7
Boho 146 F4
Bohola 148 C5
Bolea 147 B6
Boolteens 154 D3
Boolyglass 153 C6
Borris-in-Ossory 152 A5
Borris 153 B7
Borrisokane 149 G8
Borrisoleigh 152 B4
Boston 150 F1
Bottlehill 152 E2
Boviel 147 C6
Boyle 150 A3
Brackagh 151 E6
Brackloon 149 C7
Bracknagh 151 E6
Brandon 154 C2
Bray (Bré) 151 E10
Breaghva 154 B3
Breen 153 C8
Brickeens 149 D6
Brideswell 149 E8
Bridgeland 151 G8
Bridgend 146 B5
Bridgetown *Donegal* 146 E3
Bridgetown *Wexford* 153 D8
Brinlack 146 B2
Brittas Bay 151 G10
Brittas 151 E8
Britway 152 E3
Broadford *Limerick* 154 C5
Broadford *Clare* 155 A6
Broadway 153 D9
Brookeborough 146 F5
Broomfield 151 A8
Brosna Offaly 150 F4
Brosna Kerry 154 C4
Broughal 149 F9
Broughderg 147 D6
Broughshane 147 C8
Brownstown 153 E6
Bruff 152 C2
Bruree 152 C2
Buckna 147 C8
Buckode 146 F2
Bullaun 150 E2
Bunacurry 148 B2
Bunalty 148 A3
Bunbeg 146 B2
Bunclody 153 B8
Buncrana 146 B5
Bundoran 146 E2
Bunlahy 150 B5
Bunmahon 155 D10
Bunnaglass 149 G6
Bunnahowen 148 A2
Bunnanadden 146 G1
Bunnyconnellan 148 B5
Burnchurch 153 B6
Burnfoot *Donegal* 146 B5
Burnfoot *Londonderry* 147 C6
Burnfoot *Cork* 155 D7
Burren *Down* 147 G8
Burren *Mayo* 148 C4
Burron 148 F5
Burtonport 146 C2
Bushmills 147 B7
Butlers Bridge 149 B10
Butlerstown 155 G6
Buttevant 152 D2

C

Cahir 152 C4
Cadamstown 149 G9
Caddy 147 D8
Caher 150 F2
Caherbarnagh 154 E5
Caherconlish 155 B7
Cahermore *Galway* 150 F1
Cahermore *Cork* 154 G2
Cahir 155 C9
Cahirciveen 154 E2
Caledon 147 F6
Callan 155 B10
Caltra 149 E7
Caltraghlea 149 E7
Calverstown 151 F7
Camaross 153 C8
Camolin 153 B9
Camp 154 D3
Campile 153 D7

Canningstown **151 A7**
Cappagh *Tyrone* **147 E6**
Cappagh *Limerick* **152 C1**
Cappaghmore **150 F1**
Cappalinnan **152 A5**
Cappamore **155 B7**
Cappataggle **149 F7**
Cappawhite **155 B8**
Cappoquin **155 D9**
Caraunkeelwy **150 D1**
Carbury **151 D7**
Carland **147 E7**
Carlanstown **151 B7**
Carlingford **151 A9**
Carlow (Ceatharlach) **151 G7**
Carna **148 F3**
Carnagh **147 G7**
Carnanreagh **146 C5**
Carndonagh **146 A5**
Carnduff **147 A8**
Carnew **153 B8**
Carney **146 F1**
Carnlough **147 C9**
Carnmore **150 E1**
Carnteel **147 E6**
Carracastle **149 B6**
Carragh **151 E8**
Carraloe **148 F3**
Carran **148 G5**
Carrick-on-Shannon **149 B8**
Carrick-on-Suir (Carraig na Siuire) **153 D6**
Carrick *Donegal* **146 D1**
Carrick *Wexford* **153 D8**
Carrickaboy **151 A6**
Carrickbeg **152 D5**
Carrickboy **149 D9**
Carrickfergus **147 D9**
Carrickmacross **151 A8**
Carrickmore **147 E6**
Carrig **149 G8**
Carrigaholt **154 B3**
Carrigaline **152 F2**
Carrigallen **149 B9**
Carriganimmy **154 E5**
Carrigans **146 C5**
Carrigart **146 B4**
Carrigkerry **154 B5**
Carrigtwohill **152 F3**
Carrowdore **147 E10**
Carrowkeel *Donegal* **146 B5**
Carrowkeel *Galway* **149 F7**
Carrowkennedy **148 D4**
Carrowmore *Galway* **148 F5**
Carrowmore *Sligo* **149 B6**
Carrowneden **149 A6**
Carrownurlar **149 C7**
Carryduff **147 E9**
Cashel *Donegal* **146 B3**
Cashel *Galway* **148 E3**
Cashel *Laois* **149 G10**
Cashel *Galway* **149 D6**
Cashel *Tipperary* **152 C4**
Cashelgarran **146 F1**
Cashla **150 E1**
Cashleen **148 D2**
Castlebar (Calsléan an Bharraigh) **148 C4**
Castlebellingham **151 B9**
Castleblakeney **149 E7**
Castleblayney **147 G7**
Castlebridge **153 C9**
Castlecaufield **147 E6**
Castlecomer **151 G6**
Castleconnell **152 B2**
Castleconor **148 A5**
Castlecor **152 D1**
Castlecove **154 F2**
Castledawson **147 D7**
Castlederg **146 D4**
Castledermot **151 G7**
Castleellis **153 C9**
Castlefinn **146 D4**
Castlefreke **154 G5**
Castlegal **146 E2**
Castlegregory **154 C2**
Castlehill **148 B4**
Castleisland **154 D4**
Castlejordan **151 D6**
Castlelyons **152 E3**
Castlemaine **154 D3**
Castlemartyr **152 F4**
Castleplunket **150 B3**
Castlepollard **151 C6**
Castlerea **149 C7**
Castlereagh **147 E9**
Castlerock **147 B6**
Castleroe **147 B7**
Castletown Bere **154 G2**
Castletown Geoghegan **149 E10**
Castletown *Clare* **148 G5**
Castletown *Westmeath* **149 C10**
Castletown *Laois* **149 G10**
Castletown *Meath* **151 B8**
Castletown *Cork* **152 G1**
Castletown *Wexford* **153 B9**
Castletownroche **155 D7**
Castletownshend **154 G5**
Castleville **148 D5**
Castlewarren **153 B6**
Castlewellan **147 F9**
Catherdaniel **154 F2**
Causeway Head **147 A7**
Causeway **154 C3**
Cavan **149 B10**
Cavanagarven **147 G6**
Celbridge **151 D8**
Chapeltown *Antrim* **147 D8**
Chapeltown *Kerry* **154 E1**
Charlemont **147 E7**
Charlestown **150 A1**
Cheekpoint **153 D7**
Church Hill **146 C3**
Churchtown *Down* **147 F10**
Churchtown *Cork* **152 D1**
Churchtown *Cork* **152 F3**
Churchtown *Wexford* **153 E7**
Churchtown *Wexford* **153 D9**
Clady *Tyrone* **146 D4**
Clady *Londonderry* **147 C7**
Claggan **148 B3**
Clanabogan **146 E5**
Clane **151 E8**
Clara **150 D5**
Clarecastle **154 A5**
Clareen **149 G9**
Claregatway **150 D1**
Claremorris **148 D5**
Clarinbridge **150 E1**
Clashmore **152 E4**
Claudy **146 C5**
Cleady **154 E4**
Cleggan **148 D2**
Clifden **148 E2**
Clifferna **151 A6**
Cliffonoy **146 E2**
Clogh Mills **147 C8**
Clogh *Antrim* **147 C8**
Clogh *Laois* **150 G5**
Clogh *Kilkenny* **151 G6**
Clogh *Wexford* **153 B9**
Cloghan *Donegal* **146 C3**
Cloghan *Offaly* **149 F9**
Cloghan *Westmeath* **151 C6**
Cloghane **154 D2**
Cloghboy **146 D1**
Cloghbrack **151 C7**
Clogheen **152 D5**
Clogher *Tyrone* **146 F5**
Clogher *Mayo* **148 C4**
Clogherhead **151 B9**
Cloghy **147 E10**
Clohamon **153 B8**
Clohernagh **153 D7**
Clonakenny **150 G4**
Clonakilty **152 G1**
Clonare **151 D7**
Clonaslee **150 E5**
Clonbern **149 D6**
Clonbulloge **151 E6**
Clonbur **148 E4**
Cloncullen **149 E9**
Clondalkin **151 D9**
Clondulane **152 E3**
Clonea **155 C10**
Clonee **151 D8**
Cloneen **152 C5**
Clonegal **153 B8**
Clones **146 G5**
Clonfert **149 F8**
Clonmany **146 A5**
Clonmel (Cluain Meala) **152 D5**
Clonmellon **151 C7**
Clonmore *Tipperary* **150 G4**
Clonmore *Carlow* **151 G8**
Clonopy **150 E4**
Clonoulty **152 B4**
Clonroche **153 C8**
Clontarf **151 D9**
Clontibret **147 G6**
Clonygowan **151 E6**
Cloonacool **149 B6**
Cloonagh **150 B5**
Cloonbannin **154 D5**
Cloonboo **148 E5**
Cloone **149 B9**
Clooneagh **149 C9**
Cloonfad *Roscommon* **149 D6**
Cloonfad *Roscommon* **149 F8**
Cloonkeen **148 C4**
Cloonlara **152 B2**
Cloontia **150 A2**
Clough **147 F9**
Cloughjordan **152 A4**
Cloughmore **148 C2**
Cloyfin **147 B7**
Cloyne **152 F3**
Clynacartan **154 E1**
Coachford **152 F1**
Coagh **147 D7**
Coalisland **147 E7**
Cobh (An Cóbh) **152 F3**
Coblinstown **151 F8**
Coleraine **147 B7**
Collgreane **146 G3**
Collon **151 B8**
Collooney **146 G1**
Collorus **154 F3**
Colmanstown **150 D2**
Comber **147 E10**
Commeen **146 D3**
Cong **148 E4**
Conlig **147 D10**
Connolly **154 A5**
Connor **147 D8**
Convoy **146 C4**
Cookstown **147 D7**
Coola **146 G2**
Coolaney **146 G1**
Coolattin **153 B8**
Coolbaun **150 F3**
Coole **149 D10**
Coolgrange **153 B6**
Coolgreany **151 G9**
Coolmeen **154 B5**
Coolmore **146 E2**
Coolock **151 D9**
Coolrain **150 F5**
Coolroebeg **153 C6**
Cooneen **146 F5**
Cooraclare **154 A4**
Cootehill **151 A7**
Coppeen **152 F1**
Coralstown **151 D6**
Corbally **148 A5**
Corclogh **148 A2**
Cordal **154 D4**
Cordarragh **148 D4**
Cork (Corcaigh) **152 F2**
Corkey **147 B8**
Corlea **150 C4**
Corlee **148 B5**
Cornamona **148 E4**
Corraleehan **149 B9**
Corraun **148 C2**
Corry **146 G3**
Costelloe **148 F3**
Courtmacsherry **152 G1**
Courtown **153 B9**
Craanford **153 B9**
Craig **146 C5**
Craigantlet **147 D10**
Craigavad **147 D9**
Craigavon **147 E8**
Craigs **147 C8**
Craigue **151 G7**
Cranagh **147 D6**
Cranford **146 B4**
Cranny **154 A5**
Cratloe **152 B1**
Craughwell **149 F6**
Crawfordsburn **147 D10**
Creagh *Fermanagh* **146 F5**
Creagh *Cork* **154 G4**
Crean's Cross Roads **152 E1**
Crecora **152 B2**
Creegh **154 A4**
Creeslough **146 B3**
Creevagh **148 A4**
Creggan *Tyrone* **147 D6**
Creggan *Armagh* **147 G7**
Cregganbaun **148 D3**
Creggs **149 D7**
Crilly **147 F6**
Crinkill **150 F4**
Croagh *Donegal* **146 D2**
Croagh *Limerick* **152 C1**
Crockets Town **148 B5**
Crockmore **146 E3**
Croghan *Offaly* **149 F10**
Croghan *Roscommon* **149 C8**
Crolly **146 B2**
Cromane **154 D3**
Crookedwood **151 C6**
Crookhaven **154 G3**
Crookstown **152 F1**
Croom **152 C1**
Cross Barry **152 F2**
Cross Keys *Meath* **151 C6**
Cross Keys *Meath* **151 D8**
Cross **148 E5**
Crossakeel **151 C7**
Crossdoney **149 B10**
Crosserlough **151 B6**
Crossgar **147 F10**
Crossgare **147 B7**
Crosshaven **152 F3**
Crosskeys **151 F7**
Crossmaglen **147 G7**
Crossmolina **148 B4**
Crossna **149 B8**
Crosspatrick *Kilkenny* **150 G5**
Crosspatrick *Wicklow* **151 G9**
Crove **146 D1**
Crumlin **147 D8**
Crusheen **150 F1**
Cuilmore **148 D3**
Culdaff **146 A5**
Culkey **146 F4**
Cullahill **155 A10**
Cullane **152 D3**
Cullaville **147 G7**
Culleens **148 A5**
Cullen **152 C3**
Cullin **148 B5**
Cullybackey **147 C8**
Cullyhanna **147 G7**
Culmore **146 B5**
Cummer **148 E5**
Curracloe **153 C9**
Curragh West **149 D6**
Curragh **151 E7**
Curraghroe **149 D8**
Curraglass **155 D8**
Curran **147 D7**
Curraun **148 E4**
Curreeny **152 B3**
Curry **149 B6**
Curryglass **154 F3**
Cushendall **147 B9**
Cushendun **147 B9**
Cushina **151 E6**

D

Daingean **151 E6**
Dalkey **151 E10**
Dalystown **150 E2**
Damastown **151 C9**
Damerstown **151 G6**
Damhead **147 B7**
Danesfort **149 D9**
Darby's Bridge **154 E2**
Darkley **147 G7**
Darragh **154 A5**
Davidstown **153 C8**
Delgany **151 E10**
Delvin **151 C6**
Dernagree **154 D5**
Derreen **148 B4**
Derreendaragh **154 E3**
Derreeny Bridge **154 G4**
Derry **149 B7**
Derrybeg **146 B2**
Derrybrien **149 G6**
Derrydruel **146 C2**
Derryerglinna **148 E4**
Derrygonnelly **146 F3**
Derrygoolin **149 G7**
Derrylea **148 E2**
Derrylin **146 G4**
Derrymore **154 D3**
Derrynacreeve **146 G4**
Derrynawilt **149 A10**
Derryneen **148 E3**
Derryrush **148 E3**
Derrytrasna **147 E7**
Derrywode **149 D7**
Dervock **147 B7**
Desertmartin **147 D7**
Dingle **154 D1**
Doagh Beg **146 A4**
Doagh *Donegal* **146 A3**
Doagh *Antrim* **147 D9**
Dolla **152 A3**
Donabate **151 D9**
Donadea **151 D8**
Donagh **146 G5**
Donaghadee **147 D10**
Donaghcloney **147 F8**
Donaghmore *Tyrone* **147 E6**
Donaghmore *Laois* **150 G5**
Donaghmore *Meath* **151 D9**
Donard **151 F8**
Donegal **146 D3**
Doneraile **152 D2**
Donohill **152 C3**
Donoughmore **152 E1**
Dooagh **148 B2**
Doobehy **148 A4**
Doocastle **149 B6**
Doochary **146 C2**
Dooega **148 C2**
Dooghbeg **148 C3**
Doogort **148 B2**
Doohooma **148 B2**
Dooish **146 E4**
Doon **152 B3**
Doona **148 B3**
Doonaha **154 B3**
Doonbeg **154 A4**
Doonloughan **148 E2**
Doonmanagh **154 D2**
Douglas Bridge **146 D5**
Douglas **152 F2**
Downhill **147 B6**
Downpatrick **147 F10**
Dowra **146 G3**
Drangan **152 C5**
Draperstown **147 D6**
Dreenagh **154 C2**
Drimmo **149 G10**
Drimoleague **154 G4**
Drinagh **154 G5**
Dripsey **152 F1**
Drogheda (Droichead Átha) **151 B9**
Droichead Nua (Newbridge) **151 E7**
Drom **155 A9**
Dromahair **146 G2**
Dromara **147 F9**
Dromard **149 A6**
Dromin **151 B8**
Dromina **152 D1**
Dromineer **150 G3**
Dromineer **152 A3**
Dromiskin **151 A9**
Drommahane **155 D6**
Dromod **150 B4**
Dromore West **149 A6**
Dromore *Tyrone* **146 E5**
Dromore *Down* **147 F8**
Droom **154 E4**
Drum **146 G5**
Drumahoe **146 C5**
Drumandoora **149 G6**
Drumanespick **151 A7**
Drumaness **147 F9**
Drumatober **149 F7**
Drumbane **152 B4**
Drumbilla **151 A8**
Drumcard **146 F4**
Drumcliff **146 F1**
Drumcollogher **152 D1**
Drumcondra **151 D9**
Drumconrath **151 B8**
Drumcree **151 C6**
Drumduff **146 E4**
Drumfea **153 B7**
Drumfree **146 B5**
Drumkeeran **146 G2**
Drumlea **149 B9**
Drumlegagh **146 D4**
Drumlish **149 C9**
Drummin **153 C7**
Drummulin **149 C8**
Drumnacross **146 C4**
Drumnakilly **146 E5**
Drumone **151 B6**
Drumquin **146 E4**
Drumraney **149 E9**
Drumshanbo **149 B8**
Drumskinny **146 E4**
Drumsurn **147 C6**
Drung **151 A6**
Duagh **154 C4**
Dually **152 C4**
Dublin (Baile Átha Cliath) **151 D9**
Duleek **151 C8**
Dun Laoghaire **151 E9**
Dunaff **146 A4**
Dunbell **153 B6**
Dunboyne **151 D8**
Duncannon Bridge **154 D5**
Duncannon **153 D7**
Duncormick **153 D8**
Dundalk (Dun Dealgan) **151 A8**
Dunderry **151 C7**
Dundonald **147 E9**
Dundrod **147 D9**
Dundrum *Down* **147 F9**
Dundrum *Tipperary* **152 C4**
Dunfanaghy **146 B3**
Dungannon **147 E7**
Dungarvan (Dún Garbhán) *Waterford* **152 E5**
Dungarvan *Kilkenny* **153 B6**
Dungiven **147 C6**
Dungloe **146 C2**
Dungourney **152 F3**
Duniry **149 G7**
Dunkerrin **152 A4**
Dunkineely **146 D2**
Dunkitt **153 D6**
Dunlavin **151 F8**
Dunleer **151 B9**
Dunlewy **146 B3**
Dunloy **147 C8**
Dunmanus **154 G3**
Dunmanway **154 F5**
Dunmoon **152 E4**
Dunmore East **153 E7**
Dunmore **149 D6**
Dunmurry **147 E9**
Dunnamaggan **153 C6**
Dunnamanagh **146 C5**
Dunnamore **147 D6**
Dunquin **154 D1**
Dunseverick **147 A7**
Dunshaughlin **151 C8**
Durrow *Offaly* **150 D5**
Durrow *Laois* **153 A6**
Durrus **154 G4**
Dyan **147 F6**

E

Easky **148 A5**
Eden **147 D10**
Edenderry **151 D7**
Ederny **146 E4**
Edgeworthstown **149 D9**
Edmondstown **149 C7**
Eglinton **146 B5**
Eglish **147 E6**
Elphin **149 C8**
Elton **152 C2**
Emly **152 C3**
Emmoo **149 D8**

Emyvale **147 F6**
Enfield **151 D7**
Ennis (Inis) **150 G1**
Enniscorthy (Inis Córthaidh) **153 C8**
Enniskean **152 G1**
Enniskerry **151 E9**
Enniskillen **146 F4**
Errill **152 A5**
Ervey Cross Roads **146 C5**
Eshnadarragh **149 A10**
Eskragh **146 E5**
Eyeries **154 F2**
Eyrecourt **149 F8**

F

Fahamore **154 C2**
Fahan **146 B5**
Falcarragh **146 B3**
Fallmore **148 B2**
Fanore **148 G4**
Fardrum **149 E9**
Farranfore **154 D4**
Feakle **152 A2**
Fedamore **152 C2**
Feeard **154 B3**
Feeny **147 C6**
Fenagh *Leitrim* **149 B9**
Fenagh *Carlow* **153 B7**
Fenit **154 C3**
Feohanagh *Kerry* **154 D1**
Feonanagh *Limerick* **152 C1**
Ferbane **149 F9**
Fermoy **152 E3**
Ferns **153 B8**
Ferrybank **151 G9**
Ferrycarrig **153 D8**
Fethard *Tipperary* **152 C5**
Fethard *Wexford* **153 D7**
Fews **152 D5**
Feystown **147 C9**
Fiddown **153 D6**
Finnea **149 C10**
Finny **148 D4**
Fintona **146 E5**
Fintown **146 C3**
Finuge **154 C4**
Finvoy **147 C7**
Fivemiletown **146 F5**
Flagmount **149 G6**
Fontstown **151 F7**
Ford **153 C9**
Fordstown **151 C7**
Forkhill **147 G8**
Formoyle **148 G4**
Fort Stewart **146 C4**
Foulkesmill **153 D8**
Fountain Cross **152 A1**
Four Mile House **149 D8**
Foxford **148 B5**
Foygh **149 D9**
Foynes **154 B5**
Freemount **152 D1**
Frenchpark **149 C7**
Freshford **153 B6**
Furraleigh **152 D5**

G

Gainestown **151 D6**
Galbally *Limerick* **152 C3**
Galbally *Wexford* **153 C8**
Galmoy **152 A5**
Galros **150 E4**
Galway (Gaillimh) **148 F5**
Garadice **151 D8**
Garlowcross **151 C8**
Garnish **154 G2**
Garr **151 D6**
Garrane **154 E5**
Garranlahan **149 D6**
Garrison **146 F3**
Garristown **151 C9**
Garrivinnagh **148 F3**
Garronpoint **147 B9**
Garryvoe **152 F4**
Garvagh *Londonderry* **147 C7**
Garvagh *Leitrim* **149 B9**
Garvaghy **146 E5**
Garvary **146 F4**
Gaybrook **149 E10**
Geashill **149 F10**
Geevagh **149 B7**
Gerahies **154 G3**
Gilford **147 F8**
Glandore **154 G5**
Glanmire **155 E7**
Glanworth **155 D7**
Glarryford **147 C8**
Glaslough **147 F6**
Glassan **149 E9**
Glenade **146 F2**
Glenamaddy **149 D7**
Glenamoy **148 A3**
Glenariff **147 B9**
Glenarm **147 C9**
Glenavy **147 E8**
Glenbeigh **154 D2**
Glencolumbkille **146 D1**
Glencullen **151 E9**
Glendowan **146 C3**
Glendree **152 A1**
Glenduff **152 D3**
Glenealy **151 F9**
Gleneely *Donegal* **146 D4**
Gleneely *Donegal* **146 A5**
Glengarriff **154 F4**
Glengavlen **149 A9**
Glenhead **147 C6**
Glenhull **147 D6**
Gleniff **146 F2**
Glenmore *Kilkenny* **153 D7**
Glenmore *Clare* **154 A5**
Glennagevlagh **148 D3**
Glenoe **147 D9**
Glenties **146 D2**
Glentogher **146 B5**
Glenville **152 E2**
Glin **154 B5**
Glinsk **148 E3**
Glounthaune **152 F3**
Glynn *Antrim* **147 C9**
Glynn *Carlow* **153 C7**
Gneevgullia **154 D4**
Golden **152 C4**
Goleen **154 G3**
Goresbridge **153 B7**
Gorey **153 B9**
Gormanstown **151 C9**
Gort **149 G6**
Gortaclare **146 E5**
Gortahork **146 B2**
Gortavoy Bridge **147 E6**
Gorteen *Cavan* **149 C10**
Gorteen *Galway* **149 D6**
Gorteen *Sligo* **149 B7**
Gorteen *Waterford* **152 E5**
Gorteen *Kilkenny* **153 A6**
Gorteeny **149 G7**
Gortin **146 D5**
Gortmore **148 E3**
Gortnagallon **147 D8**
Gortnasillagh **149 C7**
Gowran **153 B7**
Gracehill **147 C8**
Graffy **146 D2**
Graiguenamanagh **153 C7**
Granabeg **151 F8**
Granard **149 C10**
Graney **151 G7**
Grange *Sligo* **146 F1**
Grange *Louth* **151 A9**
Grange *Waterford* **152 E4**
Grange *Kilkenny* **153 B6**
Grangebellow **151 B9**
Grangeford **151 G7**
Grannagh **150 E1**
Gransha **147 F9**
Greagh **149 B9**
Greenan **151 F9**
Greenanstown **151 C9**
Greencastle *Donegal* **147 A6**
Greencastle *Tyrone* **147 D6**
Greencastle *Down* **147 G9**
Greenfield **148 E5**
Greenisland **147 D9**
Greenore **151 A9**
Grevine **153 B6**
Greyabbey **147 E10**
Greystones **151 E10**
Groomsport **147 D10**
Gubaveeny **149 A8**
Gulladuff **147 C7**
Gurteen **149 E6**
Gweedore **146 B2**
Gweensalia **148 B2**
Gyleen **152 F3**

H

Hacketstown **151 G8**
Halfway **152 F2**
Halltown **151 C7**
Hamilton's Bawn **147 F7**
Headford **148 E5**
Helen's Bay **147 D10**
Herbertstown **152 C2**
Hillsborough **147 E9**
Hilltown **147 G8**
Hollyford **152 B3**
Hollymount **148 D5**
Hollywood **151 F8**
Holycross **152 B4**
Holywell **146 F3**
Holywood **147 D9**
Horseleap **149 E6**
Horseleap **149 E9**
Hospital **152 C2**
Howth **151 D10**
Hurler's Cross **152 B1**

I

Inch *Donegal* **146 B4**
Inch *Wexford* **153 B9**
Inch *Kerry* **154 D2**
Inchigeelagh **154 F5**
Inistioge **153 C7**
Inniscrone **148 A5**
Innishannon **152 G2**
Inniskeen **151 A8**
Inver **146 D2**
Inveran **148 F4**
Irishtown **149 D6**
Irvinestown **146 E4**

J

Jamestown *Roscommon* **149 C8**
Jamestown *Laois* **151 E6**
Johnstown Bridge **151 D7**
Johnstown *Wicklow* **151 G9**
Johnstown *Kilkenny* **152 B5**
Johnswell **153 B6**
Jonesborough **147 G8**
Julianstown **151 C9**

K

Kanturk **152 D1**
Katesbridge **147 F8**
Keadue **149 B8**
Keady **147 F7**
Kealkill **154 F4**
Kearney **147 F10**
Keel **148 B2**
Keeloges **149 D7**
Keenagh *Mayo* **148 B4**
Keenagh *Kilkenny* **149 D9**
Kells (Ceanannus Mór) **151 B7**
Kells *Antrim* **147 D8**
Kells *Kilkenny* **153 C6**
Kells *Kerry* **154 E2**
Kellysgrove **149 F7**
Kenmare **154 E4**
Kerrykeel **146 B4**
Kesh *Fermanagh* **146 E4**
Kesh *Sligo* **149 B7**
Kilargue **149 A8**
Kilbaha **154 B3**
Kilbeggan **149 E10**
Kilbeheny **152 D3**
Kilberry *Kildare* **151 F7**
Kilberry *Meath* **151 C8**
Kilbride *Wicklow* **151 F10**
Kilbride *Meath* **151 C7**
Kilbride *Wicklow* **151 E8**
Kilbride *Meath* **151 D9**
Kilbrien **152 D5**
Kilbrittain **152 G2**
Kilcaimin **148 F5**
Kilcar **146 D1**
Kilcavan **151 E6**
Kilchreest **149 F6**
Kilcock **151 D8**
Kilcoigan **149 F6**
Kilcolman **152 G1**
Kilcommon **152 D4**
Kilconnel **148 G4**
Kilconnell **149 F7**
Kilconney **149 B10**
Kilcoole **151 F10**
Kilcormac **149 F9**
Kilcrohane **154 G3**
Kilcullen **151 E8**
Kilcummin *Mayo* **148 A5**
Kilcummin *Kerry* **154 D4**
Kildalkey **151 C7**
Kildare **151 E7**
Kildavin **153 B8**
Kildorrey **152 D2**
Kildress **147 D6**
Kilfenora **148 G4**
Kilfinnane **152 D2**
Kilfinny **152 C1**
Kilflynn **154 C3**
Kilgarvan **154 E4**
Kilglass *Galway* **149 E7**
Kilglass *Roscommon* **149 C8**
Kilgobnet **154 D3**
Kilgowan **151 F7**
Kilkea **151 F7**
Kilkee **154 A3**
Kilkeel **147 G9**
Kilkelly **149 C6**
Kilkenny (Cill Chainnigh) **153 B6**
Kilkerrin **150 C2**
Kilkieran **148 F3**
Kilkinamurry **147 F9**
Kilkinlea **154 C4**
Kilkishen **155 A6**
Kill *Kildare* **151 E8**
Kill *Waterford* **153 D6**
Killabunane **154 F4**
Killadeas **146 E4**
Killadoon **148 D2**
Killadysert **154 A5**
Killagan Bridge **147 B8**
Killala **148 A5**
Killaloe **150 G2**
Killamerry **155 B10**
Killann **153 C8**
Killard **154 A4**
Killarney (Cill Airne) **154 D4**
Killarone **148 E4**
Killaskillen **151 D6**
Killavil **150 A2**
Killavullen **152 E2**
Killeagh **152 E2**
Killeany **148 G3**
Killedmond **153 B7**
Killeenleagh **154 G4**
Killeevan **146 G5**
Killeigh **149 F10**
Killen **146 D4**
Killena **153 B9**
Killenaule **152 B5**
Killerrig **151 G7**
Killeshandra **150 A5**
Killeter **146 D4**
Killimer **154 B4**
Killimor **149 F7**
Killinaboy **148 G5**
Killinchy **147 E10**
Killinick **153 D8**
Killinierin **153 B9**
Killinkere **151 B7**
Killinthomas **151 E7**
Killorglin **154 D3**
Killoscully **152 A3**
Killough *Down* **147 F10**
Killough *Wicklow* **151 E9**
Killucan **151 C6**
Killukin **149 C8**
Killurin **153 C8**
Killybegs **146 D2**
Killyclogher **146 E5**
Killyconnan **149 B10**
Killygordon **146 D4**
Killylea **147 F7**
Kilmacanogue **151 E9**
Kilmacrenan **146 B4**
Kilmacthomas **155 D10**
Kilmaganny **153 C6**
Kilmaine **148 D5**
Kilmaley **154 A5**
Kilmallock **152 C2**
Kilmanagh **152 B5**
Kilmanahan **152 D4**
Kilmeague **151 E7**
Kilmeedy **152 C1**
Kilmeena **148 C3**
Kilmichael **154 F5**
Kilmihill **154 A4**
Kilmona **152 E2**
Kilmoon **151 C8**
Kilmore Quay **153 D8**
Kilmore *Mayo* **148 B5**
Kilmore *Clare* **152 B2**
Kilmore *Wexford* **153 D8**
Kilmorna **154 C4**
Kilmorony **151 F7**
Kilmurry Mcmahon **154 A4**
Kilmurry **152 A1**
Kilmyshall **153 B8**
Kilnagross **149 B8**
Kilnaleck **149 C10**
Kilnamanagh **153 C9**
Kilnock **150 C1**
Kilquiggin **151 G8**
Kilrane **153 D9**
Kilrea **147 C7**
Kilrean **146 D2**
Kilreekill **149 F7**
Kilronan **148 G3**
Kilross *Donegal* **146 C4**
Kilross *Tipperary* **152 C3**
Kilrush **154 B4**
Kilsallagh **149 D7**
Kilsaran **151 B9**
Kilshanchoe **151 D7**
Kilshanny **148 G4**
Kilskeer **151 C7**
Kilskeery **146 F4**
Kiltartan **149 G6**
Kilteely **153 B8**
Kilteel **151 E8**
Kilteely **155 B7**
Kiltimagh **150 B1**
Kiltogan **151 G8**
Kiltoom **149 E8**
Kiltormer **149 F7**
Kiltullagh **149 F6**
Kiltyclogher **146 F3**
Kilwaughter **147 C9**
Kilworth Camp **152 D3**
Kilworth **152 D3**
Kincon **148 A4**
Kindrum **146 A4**
Kingarrow **146 C3**
Kingscourt **151 B7**
Kingsland **149 C7**
Kinlough **146 E2**
Kinnadoohy **148 D2**
Kinnegad **151 D6**
Kinnitty **149 G9**
Kinsale **152 G2**
Kinsalebeg **155 E9**
Kinvara *Galway* **150 E1**
Kinvarra *Galway* **148 F4**
Kirkcubbin **147 E10**
Kishkeam **154 D5**
Knightstown **154 E1**
Knock *Mayo* **150 B1**
Knock *Tipperary* **152 A5**
Knock *Clare* **154 B4**
Knockaderry **154 B5**
Knockalough **154 A5**
Knockananna **151 G8**
Knockanarrigan **151 F8**
Knockanevin **152 D3**
Knockbrack **146 C4**
Knockbrandon **153 B9**
Knockbridge **151 A8**
Knockbrit **152 C4**
Knockcroghery **149 D8**
Knocklong **152 C2**
Knockmore **148 B5**
Knockmoyle **149 G7**
Knocknaboul **154 D4**
Knocknacarry **147 B9**
Knocknacree **151 G7**
Knocknagashel **154 C4**
Knocknagree **154 D5**
Knocknalina **148 A3**
Knockraha **152 F3**
Knocks **152 G1**
Knocktopher **153 C6**

L

Laban **149 G6**
Labasheeda **154 B5**
Lack **146 E4**
Lackamore **155 A7**
Lackan **149 D10**
Ladysbridge **155 E8**
Lagavara **147 B8**
Laghey **146 E3**
Laghtgeorge **150 D1**
Lahardaun **148 B4**
Lanesborough **149 D8**
Laracor **151 C7**
Laragh **151 F9**
Largan **150 A1**
Larne **147 C9**
Lauragh **154 F3**
Laurencetown **149 F8**
Lavagh **149 B6**
Lawrencetown **147 F8**
Leabgarrow **146 C1**
Leamlara **152 E3**
Leap **154 G5**
Lecarrow **149 E8**
Leckaun **146 F2**
Leenane **148 D3**
Leggs **146 E3**
Leighlinbridge **153 B7**
Leitrim *Down* **147 F9**
Leitrim *Leitrim* **149 B8**
Leixlip **151 D8**
Lemybrien **152 E5**
Lenan **146 A4**
Lerrig **154 C3**
Letterbarra **146 D2**
Letterbreen **146 F4**
Lettercallow **148 F3**
Letterfinish **154 E3**
Letterfrack **148 D2**
Letterkenny **146 C4**
Lettermacaward **146 C2**
Lettermullen **148 F3**
Levally **149 E6**
Lifford **146 C4**
Limavady **147 B6**
Limerick (Luimneach) **152 B2**
Lisacul **149 C6**
Lisbane **147 E10**
Lisbellaw **146 F4**
Lisburn **147 E9**
Liscarney **148 D4**
Liscarroll **152 D1**
Liscolman **147 B7**
Lisdoonvarna **148 G4**
Lisdowney **155 A10**
Lisduff **151 B7**
Lisgall **151 A8**
Lisgarode **152 A3**
Lisgoold **152 E3**
Lislea **147 C7**
Lismakin **152 A4**
Lismore **152 E4**
Lisnageer **146 G5**
Lisnageer **151 A6**
Lisnagry **152 B2**
Lisnakill **153 D6**
Lisnamuck **147 C7**
Lisnarrick **146 E4**
Lisnaskea **146 F5**
Lispatrick **152 G2**
Lispole **154 D2**
Lisrodden **147 C7**
Lisronagh **152 C5**
Lisryan **149 D10**
Lissan **147 D6**
Lissatinning Bridge **154 E2**
Lisselton **154 B4**
Lissiniska **146 F2**
Lissycasey **154 A5**

Listerlin **153 C7**
Listooder **147 F9**
Listowel **154 C4**
Listry **154 D3**
Littleton **155 B9**
Lixnaw **154 C3**
Lobinstown **151 B8**
Loghill **154 B5**
Londonderry (Derry) **146 C4**
Longford **149 D9**
Longwood **151 D7**
Loskeran **152 E5**
Lough Gowna **149 C10**
Loughanure **146 C2**
Loughbrickland **147 F8**
Lougher **154 D2**
Loughgall **147 F7**
Loughglinn **150 B2**
Loughlinisland **147 F9**
Loughmoe **152 B4**
Loughrea **149 F6**
Louisburgh **148 C3**
Louth **151 A8**
Lower Ballinderry **147 E8**
Lucan **151 D8**
Lukeswell **153 C6**
Lullymore **151 E7**
Lurgan *Armagh* **147 E8**
Lurgan *Roscommon* **149 C7**
Lusk **151 C9**
Lyracrumpane **154 C4**
Lyre **152 E1**
Lyrenaglogh **152 E3**

M

Maam Cross **148 E4**
Maam **148 E3**
Maas **146 C2**
Macgregor's Corner **147 C8**
Macosquin **147 B7**
Macroom **152 F1**
Maganey **151 G7**
Maghanlawaun **154 E3**
Maghera *Donegal* **146 D1**
Maghera *Londonderry* **147 C7**
Magherafelt **147 D7**
Magheralin **147 E8**
Magheramason **146 C5**
Maghery *Donegal* **146 C2**
Maghery *Armagh* **147 E7**
Magilligan **147 B6**
Maguiresbridge **146 F5**
Mahoonagh **152 C1**
Mainham **151 E8**
Malahide **151 D9**
Malin Beg **146 D1**
Malin More **146 D1**
Malin **146 A5**
Mallow (Mala) **152 E2**
Manorcunningham **146 C4**
Manorhamilton **149 A8**
Manseltown **152 B4**
Manulla **148 C5**
Markethill **147 F7**
Marshalstown **153 C8**
Martinstown *Antrim* **147 C8**
Martinstown *Limerick* **152 C2**
Massford **147 F9**
Masshill **149 B6**
Mastergeehy **154 E2**
Matehy **152 F2**
Matry **151 C7**
May's Corner **147 F8**
Maynooth **151 D8**
Mayo **148 C5**
Mayobridge **147 G8**
Meelick **149 F8**
Meelin **154 C5**
Meenaclady **146 B2**
Meenacross **146 C2**
Meenanarwa **146 C3**
Meenavean **146 D1**
Meenglass **146 D3**
Meentullynagarn **146 D2**
Meigh **147 G8**
Menlough **148 F5**
Middletown **147 F6**
Midfield **150 B1**
Midleton **152 F3**
Mile House **153 C8**
Milebush **147 D9**
Milestone **152 B3**
Milford *Donegal* **146 B4**
Milford *Cork* **152 D1**
Millbrook **151 B6**
Millford **147 F7**
Millisle **147 D10**
Millstreet *Waterford* **152 E4**
Millstreet *Cork* **154 E5**
Milltown *Tyrone* **147 E6**
Milltown *Down* **147 F8**
Milltown *Cavan* **149 B10**
Milltown *Galway* **150 C1**
Milltown *Kildare* **151 E7**
Milltown *Kerry* **154 D1**
Milltown *Kerry* **154 D3**
Minane Bridge **152 G3**
Mine Head **152 E5**
Minerstown **147 F10**
Mitchelstown **152 D3**
Moate **149 E9**
Modreeny **150 F4**
Mogeely **152 F4**
Mohil *Kilkenny* **153 B6**
Mohill *Leitrim* **149 C9**
Moira **147 E8**
Monaghan (Muineachán) **147 F6**
Monamolin **153 C9**
Monasterevan **151 E7**
Monea **146 F4**
Moneen **150 D1**
Moneydig **147 C7**
Moneygall **152 A4**
Moneyglass **147 D8**
Moneylahan **146 F2**
Moneymore **147 D7**
Moneyneany **147 D6**
Moneyreagh **147 E9**
Monilea **149 D10**
Monivea **149 E6**
Montpelier **152 B2**
Mooncoin **153 D6**
Moone **151 F7**
Moorfields **147 C8**
Morley's Bridge **154 E4**
Moss-side **147 B8**
Mossley **147 D9**
Mothel **152 D5**
Mount Bellew **149 E7**
Mount Hamilton **147 D6**
Mount Norris **147 F7**
Mount Nugent **151 B6**
Mount Talbot **149 E7**
Mountallen **149 B8**
Mountbolus **149 F9**
Mountcharles **146 D2**
Mountcollins **154 C5**
Mountfield **146 D5**
Mountjoy *Tyrone* **146 D5**
Mountjoy *Tyrone* **147 E7**
Mountmellick **149 G10**
Mountrath **149 G10**
Mountshannon **152 A2**
Moville **147 B6**
Moy **147 E7**
Moyard **148 D2**
Moyarget **147 B8**
Moyasta **154 A4**
Moycullen **148 F5**
Moydow **149 D9**
Moygashel **147 E7**
Moylaw **148 B4**
Moylett **151 A6**
Moylough **149 E6**
Moymore **152 A1**
Moynalty **151 B7**
Moyne *Roscommon* **149 C7**
Moyne *Longford* **149 C9**
Moyne *Wicklow* **151 G8**
Moyrus **148 E3**
Moys **147 C6**
Moyvalley **151 D7**
Moyvore **149 E9**
Moyvoughly **149 E9**
Mucklon **151 D7**
Muckross **154 E4**
Muff **146 B5**
Muine Bheag **153 B7**
Mullagh *Mayo* **148 C3**
Mullagh *Cavan* **151 B7**
Mullagh *Meath* **151 D8**
Mullagh *Clare* **154 A4**
Mullaghmore **146 E2**
Mullaghroe **149 B7**
Mullan *Monaghan* **147 F6**
Mullan *Fermanagh* **149 A9**
Mullany's Cross **149 B6**
Mullartown **147 G9**
Mullinahone **155 B10**
Mullinavat **153 D6**
Mullingar (Án Muileann gcearr) **151 D6**
Mulrany **148 C3**
Multyfarnham **149 D10**
Mungret **155 B6**
Murley **146 F5**
Murntown **153 D8**
Murroogh **148 G4**
Myshall **153 B7**

N

Naas (An Nás) **151 E8**
Nad **152 E1**
Narin **146 C2**
Naul **151 C9**
Navan (Án Uaimh) **151 C8**
Neale **148 D4**
Nealstown **149 G9**
Nenagh (An Aonach) **152 A3**
New Birmingham **152 B5**
New Buildings **146 C5**
New Ferry **147 D7**
New Inn *Galway* **149 F7**
New Inn *Cavan* **151 B6**
New Inn *Laois* **151 F6**
New Kildimo **152 B1**
New Ross **153 C7**
Newbawn **153 D7**
Newbliss **146 G5**
Newbridge *Galway* **149 E7**
Newbridge *Limerick* **154 B5**
Newcastle West **154 C5**
Newcastle *Down* **147 G9**
Newcastle *Galway* **150 D2**
Newcastle *Wicklow* **151 F10**
Newcastle *Dublin* **151 E8**
Newcastle *Tipperary* **152 D4**
Newcestown **152 F1**
Newgrange **151 C8**
Newinn **152 C4**
Newmarket on-Fergus **152 B1**
Newmarket *Cork* **152 D1**
Newmarket *Kilkenny* **153 C6**
Newport Trench **147 D7**
Newport *Mayo* **148 C4**
Newport *Tipperary* **155 A7**
Newry **147 G8**
Newton Cashel **149 D8**
Newtown Crommelin **147 C8**
Newtown Forbes **149 C9**
Newtown Gore **149 B9**
Newtown Sandes **154 B4**
Newtown *Roscommon* **150 D3**
Newtown *Laois* **151 G6**
Newtown *Meath* **151 B8**
Newtown *Kildare* **151 D8**
Newtown *Cork* **152 D2**
Newtown *Tipperary* **152 C3**
Newtown *Tipperary* **152 A5**
Newtown *Waterford* **153 D6**
Newtownabbey **147 D9**
Newtownards **147 E10**
Newtownbutler **146 G5**
Newtowncunningham **146 C4**
Newtownhamilton **147 G7**
Newtownlow **149 E10**
Newtownlynch **148 F5**
Newtownmountkennedy **151 F10**
Newtownstewart **146 D5**
Ninemilehouse **152 C5**
Nobber **151 B7**
Nohoval **155 F7**
North Ring **152 G1**
Noughaval **148 G5**
Nurney *Kildare* **151 F7**
Nurney *Carlow* **151 G7**
Nutt's Corner **147 D8**

O

O'Briensbridge **155 A7**
Ogonelloe **150 G2**
Oilgate **153 C8**
Old Head **152 G2**
Old Leighlin **153 B7**
Old Ross **153 C7**
Old Town **150 D4**
Oldcastle **151 B6**
Oldcourt **151 E8**
Oldtown **151 C9**
Omagh **146 E5**
Omeath **147 G8**
Onaght **148 F3**
Oola **152 C3**
Oran **149 D7**
Oranmore **150 E1**
Oristown **151 B7**
Oughterard **148 E4**
Oulart **153 C9**
Ovens **155 E6**
Owenbeg **148 A5**
Oysterhaven **155 F7**

P

Pallas Green **155 B7**
Pallaskenry **152 B1**
Palmerston **151 D9**
Park **147 C6**
Parkmore **148 F5**
Parknasilla **154 F3**
Partry **148 D4**
Passage East **153 D7**
Passage West **152 F3**
Patrickswell **152 B2**
Peterswell **149 G6**
Peterswell **150 F1**
Pettigo **146 E3**
Pharis **147 B8**
Pipers Town **150 B4**
Pluck **146 C4**
Plumbridge **146 D5**
Pollatomish **148 A3**
Pomeroy **147 E6**
Pontoon **148 B5**
Port *Donegal* **146 D1**
Port *Louth* **151 B9**
Portadown **147 F8**
Portaferry **147 F10**
Portaleen **146 A5**
Portarlington **151 E6**
Portavogie **147 E10**
Portballintrae **147 A7**
Portglenone **147 C7**
Portland **149 G8**
Portlaoise **151 F6**
Portlaw **153 D6**
Portmagee **154 E1**
Portmarnock **151 D9**
Portmuck **147 C10**
Portnoo **146 C2**
Portrane **151 D9**
Portroe **152 A3**
Portrush **147 B7**
Portsalon **146 B4**
Portstewart **147 B7**
Portumna **150 F3**
Porturlin **148 A3**
Poulgorm Bridge **154 E4**
Poulnamucky **155 C9**
Power's Cross **149 G7**
Poyntz Pass **147 F8**
Priesthaggard **153 D7**
Prosperous **151 E8**
Puckaun **152 A3**

Q

Querrin **154 B3**
Quin **152 A1**

R

Raffrey **147 E10**
Raghly **146 F1**
Rahan **149 F9**
Raheen **152 F2**
Ramelton **146 B4**
Randalstown **147 D8**
Rapemills **150 E4**
Raphoe **146 C4**
Rasharkin **147 C7**
Rashedoge **146 C3**
Rath **149 G9**
Rathangan **151 E7**
Rathcabban **149 G8**
Rathconrath **149 E10**
Rathcool **152 E1**
Rathcoole **151 E8**
Rathcor **151 A9**
Rathcormac **152 E3**
Rathdangan **151 G8**
Rathdowney **152 A5**
Rathdrum **151 F9**
Rathfarnham **151 E9**
Rathfriland **147 F8**
Rathgormuck **155 C10**
Rathkeale **152 C1**
Rathkeevin **155 C9**
Rathkenny **151 B8**
Rathlackan **148 A4**
Rathlee **148 A5**
Rathluirc (Charleville) **152 D2**
Rathmolyon **151 D7**
Rathmore *Kildare* **151 E8**
Rathmore *Kerry* **154 D5**
Rathmullan **146 B4**
Rathnew **151 F10**
Rathnure **153 C7**
Rathowen **150 C5**
Rathumney **153 D7**
Rathvilly **151 G8**
Ratoath **151 D8**
Ravensdale **151 A9**
Reaghstown **151 B8**
Reanaclogheen **155 E10**
Reanagowan **154 C4**
Reananeree **154 E5**
Reanascreena **154 G5**
Rear Cross **152 B3**
Recess **148 E3**
Redcastle **146 B5**
Redcross **151 G9**
Redhills **151 A6**
Reen **154 E3**
Reens **154 B5**
Rerrin **154 G3**
Rhode **151 D6**
Richhill **147 F7**
Ringaskiddy **155 F7**
Ringsend **147 B7**
Ringville **152 E5**
Rinvyle **148 D2**
Riverchapel **153 B9**
Riverstown *Sligo* **149 B7**
Riverstown *Tipperary* **149 G8**
Riverstown *Cork* **152 F2**
Roadford **148 G4**
Robertstown **151 E7**
Rochestown **153 D7**
Rochfortbridge **151 D6**
Rockcorry **151 A7**
Rockhill **155 C6**
Rockmills **155 D7**
Rooaun **149 F8**
Rookchapel **154 C5**
Roonah Quay **148 C2**
Roosky *Mayo* **149 B6**
Roosky *Roscommon* **149 C8**
Rosapenna **146 B3**
Rosbeg **146 D1**
Rosbercon **153 C7**
Roscommon **149 D8**
Roscrea **150 F4**
Rosegreen **152 C4**
Rosenallis **149 G10**
Rosmuck **148 E3**
Ross Carbery **154 G5**
Ross **151 B6**
Rossaveel **148 F4**
Rossbrin **154 G4**
Rosscahill **148 E4**
Rosscor **146 E3**
Rosses Point **146 F1**
Rossinver **146 F3**
Rosslare Harbour **153 D9**
Rosslare **153 D9**
Rosslea **146 F5**
Rossnowlagh **146 E2**
Rostellan **152 F3**
Rostrevor **147 G8**
Rosturk **148 C3**
Roundfort **148 D5**
Roundstone **148 E2**
Roundwood **151 F9**
Rousky **146 D5**
Ruan **152 A1**
Rubane **147 E10**
Rush **151 C9**
Ryefield **151 B7**
Rylane Cross **152 E1**

S

Saggart **151 E8**
Saintfield **147 E9**
Saliahig **154 E2**
Sallins **151 E8**
Sallypark **152 A4**
Salruck **148 D3**
Salthill **148 F5**
Saul **147 F10**
Scalva **147 F8**
Scardaun **149 D8**
Scarriff **152 A2**
Scartaglen **154 D4**
Schull **154 G4**
Scotch Corner **147 G6**
Scotch Town **146 D5**
Scotshouse **146 G5**
Scotstown **147 F6**
Scramoge **149 C8**
Screeb **148 E4**
Screen **153 C9**
Screggan **149 F9**
Scribbagh **146 F3**
Seapatrick **147 F8**
Seskinore **146 E5**
Shalwy **146 E1**
Shanacashel **154 E3**
Shanacrane **154 F5**
Shanagarry **152 F4**
Shanagolden **154 B5**
Shanavogh **154 A4**
Shankill **151 E9**
Shannonbridge **149 F8**
Shantonagh **151 A7**
Shanvus **146 F2**
Sharavogue **150 F4**
Shercock **151 A7**
Sheskin **148 A3**
Shillelagh **151 G8**
Shinrone **149 G8**
Shoptown **147 C9**
Shrigley **147 F10**
Shrule **148 E5**
Silvermines **152 A3**
Sion Mills **146 D5**
Six Crosses **154 C4**
Six Road Ends **147 D10**
Sixmilebridge **155 A6**
Sixmilecross **147 E6**
Skerries **151 C9**
Skibbereen **154 G4**
Slane **151 C8**
Sligo (Sligeach) **146 F2**
Smerwick **154 D1**
Smithborough **147 G6**
Smithstown **151 G6**
Sneem **154 F3**
Spa **154 C3**
Spiddal **148 F4**
Spink **151 G6**
Springfield **146 F4**
Srah **148 D4**
Srahmore **148 B4**
Srahnamanragh Bridge **148 B3**
Sranea **146 F2**
St Johnstown **146 C5**
Staffordstown **147 D8**
Stamullen **151 C9**
Stepaside **151 E9**
Stewartstown **147 E7**
Stillorgan **151 E9**
Stonefield **148 A3**
Stoneyford **153 C6**
Stonyford **147 E8**
Strabane **146 C5**

Stradbally *Laois* **151 F6**
Stradbally *Kerry* **154 C2**
Stradbally *Waterford* **155 D10**
Stradone **151 A6**
Straffan **151 E8**
Strand **154 C5**
Strandhill **146 F1**
Strangford **147 F10**
Stranocum **147 B8**
Stranorlar **146 D4**
Stratford **151 F8**
Streamstown **149 E9**
Strokestown **149 C8**
Summerhill **151 D8**
Suncroft **151 F7**
Swan's Cross Roads **147 G6**
Swan **151 G6**
Swanlinbar **146 G4**
Swatragh **147 C7**
Swinford **150 A1**
Swords **151 D9**

T

Taghmon **153 D8**
Tahilla **154 F3**
Tallaght **151 E9**
Tallanstown **151 A8**
Tallow **152 E4**
Tamlaght **147 C7**
Tamney **146 B4**
Tandragee **147 F8**
Tang **149 E9**
Tangaveane **146 D2**
Tarbert **154 B4**
Tassagh **147 F7**
Taur **154 D5**
Tawnyinah **149 C6**
Taylor's Cross **149 F8**
Teelin **146 E1**
Teemore **146 G4**
Teeranearagh **154 E1**
Teerelton **152 F1**
Teevurcher **151 B7**
Templeboy **146 F1**
Templederry **152 A3**
Templeglentan **154 C5**
Templemore **152 A4**
Templenoe **154 E3**
Templepatrick **147 D9**
Templetown **153 D7**
Templetuohy **150 G5**
Tempo **146 F5**
Terenure **151 E9**
Termon **146 B3**
Termonfeckin **151 B9**
Terrin **151 C6**
Terryglass **150 F3**
The Diamond *Tyrone* **146 E5**
The Diamond *Tyrone* **147 E7**
The Harrow **153 B9**
The Loup **147 D7**
The Pike **152 E4**
The Rock **147 E6**
The Sheddings **147 C9**
The Six Towns **147 D6**
The Temple **147 E9**
Thomastown **153 C6**
Thurles (Durlas) **152 B4**
Tiduff **154 D1**
Tildarg **147 D9**
Timahoe *Laois* **151 F6**
Timahoe *Kildare* **151 D7**
Timoleague **152 G1**
Timolin **151 F7**
Tinahely **151 G8**
Tipperary **152 C3**
Toames **152 F1**
Tober **149 E9**
Tobercurry **149 B6**
Tobermore **147 D7**
Toberscanavan **149 A7**
Togher *Offaly* **149 F9**
Togher *Louth* **151 B9**
Togher *Cork* **154 F5**
Tomdarragh **151 F9**
Toomard **149 E7**
Toombeola **148 E3**
Toomebridge **147 D7**
Toomyvara **152 A4**
Tooraree **154 B5**
Toormore **154 G3**
Torr **147 B9**
Tourmakeady **148 D4**
Tower **152 F2**
Trafrask **154 F3**
Tralee (Trá Li) **154 C3**
Tramore (Trá Mhór) **153 E6**
Trean **148 D4**
Treantagh **146 C3**
Treehoo **146 G5**
Trillick **146 E5**
Trim **151 C7**
Trory **146 F4**
Trust **149 E7**
Tuam **149 E6**
Tuamgraney **152 A2**
Tubber **150 F1**
Tubbrid **155 A10**
Tulla **152 A1**
Tullaghan **146 E2**
Tullamore (Tulach Mhór) **149 F10**
Tullaroan **155 A10**
Tullogher **153 C7**
Tullow **151 G8**
Tully Cross **148 D2**
Tully **146 E3**
Tully **146 E3**
Tully **149 A10**
Tullyallen **151 B8**
Tullycanna **153 D8**
Tullyhogue **147 E7**
Tullyvin **151 A6**
Tullyvoos **146 E2**
Tulsk **149 C7**
Turlough *Mayo* **148 C5**
Turlough *Clare* **148 G5**
Turreen **149 D8**
Two Mile Bridge **151 E6**
Twomileborris **152 B5**
Tydavnet **147 F6**
Tyholland **147 F6**
Tylas **151 C8**
Tynan **147 F6**
Tyrella **147 F10**
Tyrrellspass **151 D6**

U

Unionhall **154 G5**
Upperchurch **152 B4**
Upperlands **147 C7**
Urlingford **152 B5**

V

Valley **148 B2**
Valleymount **151 F8**
Ventry **154 D1**
Vicarstown **151 F7**
Villierstown **152 E4**
Virginia **151 B7**
Vow **147 C7**

W

Waddingtown **153 D8**
Walterstown **151 C8**
Waringsford **147 F9**
Waringstown **147 F8**
Warrenpoint **147 G8**
Waterfall **152 F2**
Waterford (Port Láirgé) **153 D6**
Watergrasshill **152 E3**
Waterside **146 C5**
Waterville **154 F2**
Wattlebridge **146 G5**
Wellington Bridge **153 D8**
West Town **146 A2**
Westport Quay **148 C4**
Westport **148 C4**
Wexford (Loch Garman) **153 D8**
Wheathill **146 F4**
White Hall **154 G4**
Whitechurch *Cork* **152 E2**
Whitechurch *Waterford* **152 E4**
Whitecross **147 G7**
Whitegate *Clare* **150 F3**
Whitegate *Clare* **152 F3**
Whitehall *Roscommon* **150 B4**
Whitehall *Kilkenny* **153 B7**
Whitehead **147 D10**
Whitehouse **147 D9**
Wicklow (Cill Mhantáin) **151 F10**
Wilkinstown **151 B8**
Windgap **155 B10**
Windmill **151 D7**
Wolfhill **151 G6**
Woodenbridge **151 G9**
Woodford **149 G7**
Woodstown **153 D7**
Woodtown **151 B8**

Y

Youghal (Eochaill) **155 E9**

INDEX

Abbreviations

Bfd.	Bedfordshire
Bkh.	Buckinghamshire
Bor.	Borders
Brk.	Berkshire
Cbs.	Cambridge
Cen.	Central
Che.	Cheshire
C.I.	Channel Islands
Cle.	Cleveland
Clw.	Clwyd
Cnw.	Cornwall
Cum.	Cumbria
Dby.	Derbyshire
Dev.	Devon
D.&G.	Dumfries & Galloway
Dor.	Dorset
Drm	Durham
Dyf.	Dyfed
E.S.	East Sussex
Esx	Essex
G.L.	Greater London
Glo.	Gloucestershire
G.M.	Greater Manchester
Grm.	Grampian
Gwe.	Gwent
Gwy.	Gwynedd
Ham.	Hampshire
Hfs.	Hertfordshire
Hgh.	Highland
Hum.	Humberside
H.&W.	Hereford & Worcester
I.o.M.	Isle of Man
I.o.S.	Isles of Scilly
I.o.W.	Isle of Wight
Lan.	Lancashire
Lcn.	Lincolnshire
Lei.	Leicestershire
Ltn	Lothian
Mer.	Merseyside
M.G.	Mid Glamorgan
Nfk	Norfolk
Nmp.	Northamptonshire
Nor.	Northumberland
Not.	Nottinghamshire
N.Y.	North Yorkshire
Ork.	Orkney
Oxf.	Oxfordshire
Pow.	Powys
Sfk	Suffolk
S.G.	South Glamorgan
She.	Shetland
Shr.	Shropshire
Som.	Somerset
Sry	Surrey
Stf.	Staffordshire
Str.	Strathclyde
S.Y.	South Yorkshire
Tay.	Tayside
T.&W.	Tyne & Wear
War.	Warwickshire
W.G.	West Glamorgan
W.I.	Western Isles
W.M.	West Midlands
W.S.	West Sussex
Wts.	Wiltshire
W.Y.	West Yorkshire

A

Abbas Combe **9 B32**
Abberley **29 B33**
Abberton *H.&W.* **29 C35**
Abberton *Esx* **34 G56**
Abberwick **71 B37**
Abbess Roding **33 G51**
Abbeycwmhir **27 A26**
Abbey Dore **28 E29**
Abbey Hulton **40 A35**
Abbey St Bathans **77 D33**
Abbeystead **55 D31**
Abbeytown **60 A27**
Abbey Wood **23 D50**
Abbotrule **70 B31**
Abbots Bickington **6 D19**
Abbots Bromley **40 C36**
Abbotsbury **8 F31**
Abbotsham **6 C19**
Abbotskerswell **5 D24**
Abbots Langley **22 A46**
Abbots Leigh **19 D31**
Abbotsley **33 C48**
Abbots Morton **30 C36**
Abbots Ripton **32 A47**
Abbot's Salford **30 C36**
Abbotts Ann **21 G39**
Abbottswood **10 B39**
Abdon **38 G31**
Aber *Gwy.* **36 B18**
Aber *Dyf.* **26 D20**
Aber *Gwy.* **46 E22**
Aber *M.G.* **18 B25**
Aberaeron **26 B20**
Aberaman **18 A25**
Aberangell **37 E24**
Aberarad **17 A18**
Aberarder **88 F20**
Aberarder Ho. **88 B22**
Aberargie **82 F27**
Aberarth **26 B20**
Aberavon **18 B23**
Aber-banc **26 D19**
Aber Bargoed **18 A27**
Aberbeeg **18 A27**
Aber Bowlan **17 A22**
Abercanaid **18 A26**
Abercarn **18 B27**
Abercastle **16 A14**
Abercegir **37 E23**
Aberchalder **88 D19**
Aberchirder **98 D31**
Abercorn **75 C26**
Abercraf **27 G24**
Abercrombie **83 G30**
Abercrychan **27 E23**
Abercwmboi **18 A25**
Abercych **26 D18**
Abercynafon **27 G26**
Abercynon **18 B26**
Aber-cywarch **37 D24**
Aberdalgie **82 E26**
Aberdare **18 A25**
Aberdaron **36 C17**
Aberdeen **91 C35**
Aberdesach **46 G20**
Aberdour **75 B27**
Aberduhonw **27 C26**
Aberdulais **18 B23**
Aberdyfi **36 F21**
Aberedw **27 D26**
Abereiddy **16 A13**
Abererch **36 B19**
Aberfan **18 A26**
Aberfeldy **81 C24**
Aberffraw **46 F19**
Aberffrwd **27 A22**
Aberford **57 F40**
Aberfoyle **81 G21**
Abergarw **18 C25**
Abergavenny **28 G28**
Abergele **47 E25**
Abergiar **26 D20**
Abergorlech **17 A21**
Abergwesyn **27 C24**
Abergwili **17 B20**
Abergwydol **37 E23**
Abergwynant **37 D22**
Abergwynfi **18 B24**
Abergynolwyn **37 E22**
Aberhafesp **37 F26**
Aberhosan **37 F23**
Aberkenfig **18 C24**
Aberlady **76 B30**
Aberlemno **83 B30**
Aberllefenni **37 E23**
Aber-llia **27 G25**
Abermad **26 A21**
Abermeurig **26 C21**
Abermule **38 F27**
Aber-Naint **38 C27**
Aber-nant **18 A25**
Abernant **17 B19**
Abernethy **82 F27**
Abernyte **82 D28**
Aber-pergwm **18 A24**
Aberporth **26 C18**
Aberriw (Berriew) **38 E27**
Aberscross **96 A23**
Abersky **88 B21**
Abersoch **36 C18**
Abersychan **19 A28**
Aberthin **18 D26**
Abertillery **18 A27**
Abertridwr *M.G.* **18 C26**
Abertridwr *Pow.* **37 D26**
Abertysswg **18 A27**
Aberuthven **82 F25**
Aberyscir **27 F25**
Aberystwyth **36 G21**
Abhainnsuidhe **100 G6**
Abingdon **21 B40**
Abinger Common **22 G47**
Abinger Hammer **22 G46**
Abington **68 A25**
Abington Pigotts **33 D48**
Abingworth **12 E47**
Ab Kettleby **41 C42**
Ablington **20 A36**
Abney **50 E37**
Aboyne **90 D31**
Abram **49 B32**
Abriachan **88 A21**
Abridge **23 B50**
Abson **19 D32**
Abthorpe **31 D42**
Abune-the-Hill **104 D28**
Aby **53 E50**
Acaster Malbis **58 E41**
Acaster Selby **58 E41**
Accrington **56 G33**
Accurrach **80 E16**
Acha **78 B7**
Achacha **80 C15**
Achadacaie **73 D14**
Achadh-chaorrunn **73 E13**
Achadunan **80 F17**
Achagavel **79 B13**
Achaglass **72 F12**
Achahoish **73 C13**
Achalader **82 C27**
Achallader **80 C19**
Acha Mor **100 E9**
Achamore **72 C11**
Achanamara **73 B13**
Achandunie **96 D22**
Achany **96 A21**
Achaphubuil **87 G16**
Acharacle **79 A12**
Achargary **102 C22**
Acharn *Tay.* **81 C23**
Acharn *Str.* **80 D17**
Acharosson **73 C15**
Achateny **79 A11**
Achath **91 B33**
Achavanich **103 D27**
Achduart **95 A16**
Achentoul **102 E24**
Achfary **101 D18**
Achgarve **94 B14**
Achiemore *Hgh.* **101 B19**
Achiemore *Hgh.* **102 C24**
Achies **103 C27**
A'Chill **85 D8**
Achiltibuie **94 A15**
Achina **102 B22**
Achindown **97 G24**
Achinduich **96 A21**
Achingills **103 B27**
Achintee **94 G15**
Achintee Ho **87 G17**
Achintraid **86 A14**
Achlean **89 E24**
Achleanan **79 B11**
Achleek **79 B13**
Achlian **80 E17**
Achlyness **101 C18**
Achmelvich **101 F16**
Achmony **88 A20**
Achmore *Hgh.* **86 A14**
Achmore *Hgh.* **95 B16**
Achmore *Cen.* **81 D21**
Achnaba **73 B14**
Achnabat **88 A21**
Achnabourin **102 C22**
Achnacairn **80 D15**
Achnacarnin **101 E16**
Achnaclerach **96 E19**
Achnaclioch **80 D15**
Achnacloich **86 D11**
Achnaclyth **103 E26**
Achnacraig **79 C10**
Achnacroish **79 C14**
Achnadrish **79 B10**
Achnafalnich **80 E17**
Achnafauld **81 D24**
Achnagairn **96 G21**
Achnagarron **96 D22**
Achnaha *Hgh.* **79 C12**
Achnaha *Hgh.* **79 A10**
Achnahanat **96 B20**
Achnahannet **89 B25**
Achnairn **102 G21**
Achnalea **79 A14**
Achnanellan **79 A13**
Achnasaul **87 F17**
Achnasheen **95 F17**
Achnashelloch **73 A14**
Achnastank **98 F28**
Achorn **103 E27**
Achosnich *Hgh.* **79 A10**
Achosnich *Hgh.* **96 B22**
Achreamie **103 B25**
Achriabhach **80 A17**
Achriesgill **101 C18**
Achrimsdale **97 A24**
Achronich **79 D10**
Achtoty **102 B22**
Achurch **42 G46**
Achuvoldrach **102 C21**
Achvaich **96 B22**
Achvarasdal **103 B25**
Achvlair **80 B15**
Achvraie **95 A16**
Ackergill **103 C29**
Acklam *Cle.* **62 E40**
Acklam *N.Y.* **58 C43**
Ackleton **39 F33**
Acklington **71 C38**
Ackton **57 G40**
Ackworth Moor Top **51 A40**
Acle **45 D59**
Acock's Green **40 G36**
Acol **25 E58**
Acomb *N.Y.* **58 D41**
Acomb *Nor.* **70 G35**
Aconbury **28 E30**
Acre **56 G33**
Acrefair **38 A28**
Acrise Place **15 C57**
Acton *Shr.* **38 G28**
Acton *H.&W.* **29 B34**
Acton *G.L.* **22 C47**
Acton *Sfk* **34 D54**
Acton *Che.* **49 G32**
Acton Beauchamp **29 C32**
Acton Bridge **48 E31**
Acton Burnell **38 E31**
Acton Green **29 D32**
Acton Pigott **38 E31**
Acton Round **39 F32**
Acton Scott **38 G30**
Acton Trussell **40 D35**
Acton Turville **20 C34**
Adamhill **74 G20**
Adbaston **39 C33**
Adber **8 B31**
Adderbury **31 E40**
Adderley **39 B32**
Adderstone **77 G37**
Addiewell **75 D25**
Addingham **57 E36**
Addington *Bkh.* **31 F43**
Addington *Kent* **23 F52**
Addington *G.L.* **23 E49**
Addlestone **22 E46**
Addlethorpe **53 F51**
Adel **57 F38**
Adeney **39 D32**
Adfa **37 E26**
Adforton **28 A29**
Adisham **15 B57**
Adlestrop **30 F38**
Adlingfleet **58 G44**
Adlington *Che.* **49 D35**
Adlington *Lan.* **48 A31**
Admaston *Shr.* **39 D32**
Admaston *Stf.* **40 C36**
Admington **30 D37**
Adsborough **8 B28**
Adstock **31 E43**
Adstone **31 C41**
Adversane **12 D46**
Adwalton **57 G38**
Adwell **21 B42**
Adwick le Street **51 B41**
Adwick upon Dearne **51 B40**
Ae Village **68 E25**
Affleck *Tay.* **83 D30**
Affleck *Grm.* **91 A34**
Affpuddle **9 E33**
Afon-wen **47 E27**
Afton Bridgend **68 B22**
Agglethorpe **57 A36**
Aigburth **48 D29**
Aignis **100 D10**
Aike **59 E46**
Aikerness **104 A30**
Aikers **105 B30**
Aiketgate **61 B30**
Aikshaw **60 B27**
Aikton **60 A28**
Aikwood Tower **69 A30**
Ailey **28 D29**
Ailsworth **42 F47**
Aimster **103 B27**
Ainderby Quernhow **57 A39**
Ainderby Steeple **62 G39**
Aingers Green **35 G57**
Ainsdale **48 A29**
Ainstable **61 B31**
Ainsworth **49 A33**
Ainthorpe **63 F42**
Aintree **48 C29**
Aird **92 F3**
Aird a'Chaolais **84 E2**
Aird A Mhachair **92 G3**
Aird A Mhulaidh **100 F7**
Aird Asaig **100 G7**
Aird Dhail **100 A10**
Aird Leimhe **92 C6**
Aird Mhige **92 B6**
Aird Mhighe **92 C6**
Aird of Sleat **86 D11**
Airdrie *Fife* **83 G31**
Airdrie *Str.* **75 D23**
Aird Thunga **100 D10**
Aird Uige **100 D6**
Airidh A Bhruaich **100 F8**
Airieland **65 E23**
Airigh-drishaig **86 A13**
Airmyn **58 G43**
Airntully **82 D26**
Airor **86 D13**
Airth **75 B24**
Airton **56 D35**
Airyhassen **64 F19**
Aisby *Lcn.* **42 B46**
Aisby *Lcn.* **52 C44**
Aisgernis **84 B3**
Aiskew **57 A38**
Aislaby *N.Y.* **58 A43**
Aislaby *N.Y.* **63 F44**
Aislaby *Cle.* **62 E39**
Aisthorpe **52 D45**
Aith *Ork.* **104 E28**
Aith *She.* **106 D42**
Aith *She.* **107 B39**
Aith *Ork.* **104 D32**
Aitnoch **89 A25**
Akeld **70 A35**
Akeley **31 E42**
Akenham **35 D57**
Albaston **4 C20**
Alberbury **38 D29**
Albourne **13 E48**
Albrighton *Shr.* **39 E33**
Albrighton *Shr.* **38 D30**
Alburgh **45 G58**
Albury *Sry* **22 G46**
Albury *Hfs.* **33 F50**
Albury Heath **22 G46**
Alby Hill **45 B57**
Alcaig **96 F21**
Alcaston **38 G30**
Alcester **30 C36**
Alciston **13 F50**
Alcombe **7 A25**
Alconbury **32 A47**
Alconbury Hill **32 A47**
Alconbury Weston **32 A47**
Aldborough *Nfk* **45 B57**
Aldborough *N.Y.* **57 C40**
Aldbourne **21 D38**
Aldbrough **59 F48**
Aldbrough St John **62 E37**
Aldburgh **57 B38**
Aldbury **32 G45**
Aldclune **81 A24**

Aldeburgh 35 C60
Aldeby 45 F60
Aldenham 22 B47
Alderbury 10 B37
Alderford 45 D57
Alderholt 10 C37
Alderley 20 B33
Alderley Edge 49 E34
Alderman's Green 41 G39
Aldermaston 21 E41
Aldermaston Soke 21 E41
Aldermaston Wharf 21 E42
Alderminster 30 D38
Aldersey Green 48 G30
Aldershot 22 F43
Alderton *Wts.* 20 C34
Alderton *Shr.* 38 C30
Alderton *Sfk* 35 D59
Alderton *Nmp.* 31 D43
Alderton *Glo.* 29 E35
Alderwasley 50 G38
Aldfield 57 C38
Aldford 48 G29
Aldham *Esx* 34 F55
Aldham *Sfk* 34 D56
Aldie *Grm.* 99 E36
Aldie *Hgh.* 96 C23
Aldingbourne 12 F44
Aldingham 55 B28
Aldington *H.&W.* 30 D36
Aldington *Kent* 15 D56
Aldivalloch 90 A29
Aldochlay 74 A19
Aldons 67 E17
Aldreth 33 A50
Aldridge 40 E36
Aldringham 35 B60
Aldro 58 C44
Aldsworth 20 A37
Aldunie 90 A29
Aldville 82 D25
Aldwark *N.Y.* 57 C40
Aldwark *Dby.* 50 G38
Aldwick 12 G45
Aldwincle 42 G45
Aldworth 21 D41
Alexandria 74 C19
Alfardisworthy 6 D18
Alfington 7 F27
Alfold 12 C46
Alfold Crossways 12 C46
Alford *Grm.* 90 B31
Alford *Som.* 9 A32
Alford *Lcn.* 53 E50
Alfreton 51 G39
Alfrick 29 C33
Alfriston 13 F50
Algarkirk 43 B48
Alhampton 9 A32
Alkborough 58 G44
Alkerton 30 D39
Alkham 15 C58
Alkington 38 B31
Alkmonton 40 B37
Allaleigh 5 E24
Allanaquoich 89 E26
Allancreich 90 D31
Allangillfoot 69 D28
Allanton *D.&G.* 68 E24
Allanton *Bor.* 77 E34
Allanton *Str.* 75 E24
Allanton *Str.* 75 E23
Allardice 91 F33
Allathasdal 84 D2
All Cannings 20 E36
Allendale Town 61 A34
Allenheads 61 B34
Allensford 62 A36
Allen's Green 33 G50
Allensmore 28 E30
Aller 8 B29
Allerby 60 C26
Allerford *Dev.* 6 G20
Allerford *Som.* 7 A25
Allerston 58 A44
Allerthorpe 58 E43
Allerton *W.Y.* 57 F37
Allerton *Mer.* 48 D30
Allerton Bywater 57 G39
Allesley 40 G38
Allestree 41 B39
Allexton 42 E44
Allgreave 49 F35
Allhallows 24 D54
Alligin Shuas 94 F13
Allimore Green 40 D34
Allington *Wts.* 10 A38
Allington *Wts.* 20 E36
Allington *Lcn.* 42 A44
Allithwaite 55 B29
Allnabad 102 D20
Alloa 75 A24
Allonby 60 B26
Alloway 67 B19
All Saints South Elmham 45 G59
Allscot 39 F33
All Stretton 38 F30
Alltachonaich 79 B13
Alltan Dubh 101 G15
Alltbeithe 87 B16
Alltforgan 37 C25
Alltmawr 27 D26
Alltnacaillich 102 D20
Allt na h-Airbhe 95 B16
Allt-na-subh 86 B14
Alltsigh 88 C20
Alltwalis 17 A20
Alltwen 18 A23
Alltyblaca 26 D21
Allweston 9 C32
Almeley 28 C29
Almer 9 E34
Almington 39 B33
Almiston Cross 6 C19
Almondbank 82 E26
Almondbury 50 A37
Almondsbury 19 C31
Alne 57 C40
Alness 96 E22
Alnham 70 B35
Alnmouth 71 B38
Alnwick 71 B37
Alphamstone 34 E54
Alpheton 34 C54
Alphington 7 G25
Alpington 45 E58
Alport 50 F38
Alpraham 48 G31
Alresford 34 F56
Alrewas 40 D37
Alrick 82 A27
Alsager 49 G33
Alsagers Bank 40 A34
Alsop en le Dale 50 G37
Alston *Dev.* 8 D29
Alston *Cum.* 61 B33
Alstone 29 E35
Alstonefield 50 G36
Alswear 6 C22
Altanduin 102 F23
Altarnun 4 B18
Altass 96 A20
Altens 91 C35
Alterwall 103 B28
Altham 56 F33
Althorne 25 B55
Althorpe 52 B44
Alticry 64 E18
Altnafeadh 80 B17
Altnaharra 102 E21
Altofts 57 G39
Alton *Ham.* 22 G43
Alton *Dby.* 51 F39
Alton *Stf.* 40 A36
Alton Barnes 20 E37
Alton Pancras 9 D32
Alton Priors 20 E37
Altonside 98 D28
Altrincham 49 D33
Altura 87 E18
Alva 75 A24
Alvanley 48 E30
Alvaston 41 B39
Alvechurch 30 A36
Alvecote 40 E38
Alvediston 9 B35
Alveley 39 G33
Alverdiscott 6 C21
Alverstoke 11 E42
Alverstone 11 F41
Alverton 42 A43
Alves 97 E27
Alvescot 21 A38
Alveston *War.* 30 C38
Alveston *Avon* 19 C32
Alvie 89 D24
Alvingham 53 C49
Alvington 19 A31
Alwalton 42 F47
Alwinton 70 C34
Alwoodley Gates 57 E39
Alyth 82 C28
Amalebra 2 E10
Ambergate 51 G39
Amber Hill 43 A48
Amberley *Glo.* 20 A34
Amberley *W.S.* 12 E46
Amble 71 C38
Amblecote 40 G34
Ambleside 60 F29
Ambleston 16 B15
Ambrismore 73 E16
Ambrosden 31 G41
Amcotts 52 A44
Amersham 22 B45
Amesbury 20 G37
Amington 40 E38
Amisfield Town 68 E25
Amlwch 46 C20
Amlwch Port 46 C20
Ammanford 17 C21
Amotherby 58 B43
Ampfield 10 B39
Ampleforth 58 B41
Ampleforth College 58 B41
Ampney Crucis 20 A36
Ampney St Mary 20 A36
Ampney St Peter 20 A36
Amport 21 G38
Ampthill 32 E46
Ampton 34 A54
Amroth 16 D17
Amulree 81 D24
Anaboard 89 A25
Anaheilt 79 A14
Ancaster 42 A45
Anchor 38 G27
Ancroft 77 F35
Ancrum 70 A32
Ancton 12 F45
Anderby 53 E51
Anderson 9 E34
Anderton 49 E32
Andover 21 G38
Andover Down 21 G39
Andoversford 29 G35
Andreas 54 D25
Anelog 36 C17
Angarrack 2 E11
Angersleigh 7 D27
Angerton 60 A28
Angle 16 D14
Angler's Retreat 37 F23
Angmering 12 F46
Angram 57 E40
Anie 81 F21
Ankerville 96 D23
Anlaby 59 G46
Anmer 44 C53
Annan 69 G27
Annaside 54 A26
Annat *Str.* 80 E16
Annat *Hgh.* 94 F14
Anna Valley 21 G39
Annbank 67 A20
Annesley 51 G40
Annesley Woodhouse 51 G40
Annfield Plain 62 A37
Annscroft 38 E30
Ansdell 55 G29
Ansford 9 A32
Ansley 40 F38
Anslow 40 C37
Anslow Gate 40 C37
Anstey *Lei.* 41 E41
Anstey *Hfs.* 33 E50
Anstruther 83 G31
Ansty *W.S.* 13 D48
Ansty *Wts.* 9 B35
Ansty *War.* 41 G39
Anthill Common 11 C42
Anthorn 60 A27
Antingham 45 B58
An T-ob 92 C5
Antony 4 E20
Antrobus 49 E32
Anvil Corner 6 E19
Anwick 52 G47
Anwoth 65 E21
Aoradh 72 D8
Apes Hall 43 G51
Apethorpe 42 F46
Apley 52 E46
Apperknowle 51 E39
Apperley 29 F34
Appin Ho. 80 C15
Appleby 52 A45
Appleby Magna 41 D39
Appleby Parva 41 E39
Applecross 94 G12
Appledore *Kent* 14 E55
Appledore *Dev.* 7 D26
Appledore *Dev.* 6 B20
Appledore Heath 14 D55
Appleford 21 B41
Appleshaw 21 G39
Applethwaite 60 D28
Appleton 21 A40
Appleton-le-Moors 58 A43
Appleton-le-Street 58 B43
Appleton Roebuck 58 E41
Appleton Thorn 49 D32
Appleton Wiske 62 F39
Appletreehall 69 B30
Appletreewick 57 C36
Appley 7 C26
Appley Bridge 48 A31
Apse Heath 11 F41
Apsley 22 A46
Apsley End 32 E47
Apuldram 12 F44
Arbirlot 83 C31
Arborfield 22 E43
Arborfield Cross 22 E43
Arborfield Garrison 22 E43
Arbroath 83 D32
Arbuthnott 91 F33
Archdeacon Newton 62 E38
Archiestown 97 G27
Arclid 49 F33
Ard a'Chapuill 73 C16
Ardacheranbeg 73 B16
Ardacheranmor 73 B16
Ardachoil 79 D12
Ardachvie 87 E17
Ardailly 72 F12
Ardalanish 78 F9
Ardanaiseig 80 E16
Ardaneaskan 86 A14
Ardanstur 79 F14
Ardantiobairt 79 B12
Ardantrive 79 E14
Ardarroch 86 A14
Ardbeg *Str.* 73 D16
Ardbeg *Str.* 73 B17
Ardbeg *Str.* 72 F10
Ardblair 88 A20
Ardbrecknish 80 E16
Ardcharnich 95 C17
Ardchiavaig 78 F9
Ardchonnel 79 D14
Ardchonnell 80 F15
Ardchrishnish 78 E9
Ardchronie 96 C21
Ardchuilk 87 A18
Ardchullarie More 81 F21
Ardchyle 81 E21
Arddlin 38 D28
Ardeley 33 F48
Ardelve 86 B14
Arden 74 B19
Ardencaple 79 F13
Ardens Grafton 30 C37
Ardentallan 79 E14
Ardentinny 73 B17
Ardeonaig 81 D22
Ardersier 96 F23
Ardery 79 A13
Ardessie 95 C16
Ardfad 79 F13
Ardfern 79 G13
Ardfin 72 D10
Ardgartan 80 G18
Ardgay 96 B21
Ardgenavan 80 F17
Ardgowan 73 C17
Ardgowse 90 B31
Ardgye 97 E27
Ardhallow 73 C17
Ardheslaig 94 F13
Ardiecow 98 C31
Ardinamar 79 F13
Ardindrean 95 C17
Ardingly 13 D49
Ardington 21 C40
Ardintoul 86 B14
Ardkinglas Ho 80 G17
Ardlair 90 A31
Ardlamont 73 D15
Ardleigh 34 F56
Ardleish 80 F19
Ardler 82 C28
Ardley 31 F41
Ardlui 80 F19
Ardlussa 72 B12
Ardmaddy 80 D16
Ardmair 95 B16
Ardmaleish 73 D16
Ardmay 80 G18
Ardmenish 72 C11
Ardmhor 84 D3
Ardminish 72 F12
Ardmolich 86 G13
Ardmore *Str.* 79 E13
Ardmore *Str.* 74 C19
Ardmore *Str.* 72 F10
Ardmore *Hgh.* 96 C23
Ardnackaig 73 A13
Ardnacross 79 C11
Ardnadam 73 C17
Ardnadrochet 79 D12
Ardnagoine 94 A15
Ardnagowan 80 G16
Ardnagrask 96 G20
Ardnahein 73 A17
Ardnahoe 72 C10
Ardnarff 86 A14
Ardnastang 79 A13
Ardnave 72 C8
Ardno 80 G17
Ardo 99 F34
Ardoch *Grm.* 97 F27
Ardoch *D.&G.* 68 C24
Ardoch *Tay.* 82 D26
Ardochrig 74 F22
Ardochu 96 A22
Ardoyne 91 A32
Ardpatrick 73 D13
Ardpeaton 73 B17
Ardradnaig 81 C22
Ardrishaig 73 B14
Ardroe 101 F16
Ardrossan 73 F17
Ardscalpsie 73 E16
Ardshave 96 B23
Ardshealach 79 A12
Ardshellach 79 F13
Ardsley 51 B39
Ardslignish 79 A11
Ardtalla 72 E10
Ardtalnaig 81 D22
Ardtarig 73 B16
Ardteatle 80 E17
Ardtoe 86 G12
Ardtornish 79 C12
Ardtrostan 81 E22
Ardtur 80 C15
Arduaine 79 F13
Ardullie 96 E21
Ardura 79 D12
Ardvar 101 E17
Ardvasar 86 D12
Ardveich 81 E22
Ardverikie 88 F20
Ardvorlich *Tay.* 81 E22
Ardvorlich *Str.* 80 F19
Ardwall 65 E21
Ardwell *Str.* 67 D17
Ardwell *D.&G.* 64 F17
Ardwell *Grm.* 98 F29
Areley Kings 29 A33
Arford 12 C44
Argaty 81 G23
Argoed 18 B27
Argoed Mill 27 B25
Argrennan 65 E22
Arichamish 79 G14
Arichastlich 80 D18
Arichonan 73 A13
Aridhglas 78 E9
Arienskill 86 F13
Arileod 78 B7
Arinacrinachd 94 F13
Arinafad Beg 73 B13
Arinagour 78 B8
Arinambane 84 B3
Arisaig 86 F12
Arivegaig 79 A12
Arkendale 57 C39
Arkesden 33 E50
Arkholme 55 B31
Arkleby 60 B27
Arkleside 57 A36
Arkleton 69 D29
Arkley 23 B48
Arksey 51 B41
Arkwright Town 51 F40
Arlary 82 G27
Arlecdon 60 E26
Arlesey 32 E47
Arleston 39 D32
Arley 49 D32
Arlingham 29 G32
Arlington *Dev.* 6 A22
Arlington *Glo.* 20 A36
Arlington *E.S.* 13 F51
Arlington Beccott 6 A22
Armadale *Ltn* 75 D25
Armadale *Hgh.* 102 B23
Armadale *Hgh.* 86 D12
Armathwaite 61 B30
Arminghall 45 E58
Armitage 40 D36
Armscote 30 D38
Armston 42 G46
Armthorpe 51 B42
Arnabost 78 B7
Arncliffe 56 B35
Arncliffe Cote 56 B35
Arncroach 83 G30
Arne 9 F35
Arnesby 41 F42
Arngask 82 F27
Arngibbon 74 A22
Arngomery 74 A22
Arnhall 83 A31
Arnicle 73 G13
Arnipol 86 F13
Arnisdale 86 C14
Arnish 94 G12
Arniston Engine 76 D29
Arnol 100 C8
Arnold 41 A41
Arnprior 74 A21
Arnside 55 B30
Arowry 38 B30
Arrad Foot 55 A29
Arradoul 98 C30
Arram 59 E46
Arrat 83 B32
Arrathorne 62 G37
Arreton 11 F41
Arrington 33 C49
Arrivain 80 D18
Arrochar 80 G18
Arrow 30 C36
Arscaig 102 G20
Arthington 57 E38
Arthingworth 42 G43

Arthog 37 D22
Arthrath 99 F35
Arthurstone 82 C28
Artrochie 99 F35
Aruadh 72 D8
Arundel 12 F46
Aryhoulan 80 A15
Asby 60 D26
Ascog 73 D17
Ascot 22 E45
Ascott 30 E39
Ascott-under-Wychwood 30 G39
Ascreavie 82 B29
Asenby 57 B39
Asfordby 41 D42
Asfordby Hill 42 D43
Asgarby *Lcn.* 42 A47
Asgarby *Lcn.* 53 F49
Ash *Som.* 8 B30
Ash *Dev.* 6 E21
Ash *Kent* 15 B58
Ash *Kent* 23 E51
Ash *Sry* 22 F44
Ashampstead 21 D41
Ashbocking 35 C57
Ashbourne 40 A37
Ashbrittle 7 C26
Ash Bullayne 7 E23
Ashburnham Place 13 E52
Ashburton 5 C23
Ashbury *Dev.* 6 F21
Ashbury *Oxf.* 21 C38
Ashby 52 B45
Ashby by Partney 53 F50
Ashby cum Fenby 53 B48
Ashby de la Launde 52 G46
Ashby de la Zouch 41 D39
Ashby Folville 42 D43
Ashby Magna 41 F41
Ashby Parva 41 G41
Ashby Puerorum 53 E49
Ashby St Ledgers 31 B41
Ashby St Mary 45 E59
Ashchurch 29 E35
Ashcombe 5 C25
Ashcott 8 A30
Ashdon 33 D51
Ashe 21 G41
Asheldham 25 A55
Ashen 34 D53
Ashenden 14 D54
Ashendon 31 G42
Ashens 73 C14
Ashfield *Str.* 73 B13
Ashfield *Cen.* 81 G23
Ashfield *Sfk* 35 B57
Ashfield Green 35 A58
Ashfold Crossways 13 D48
Ashford *Kent* 14 C55
Ashford *Sry* 22 D46
Ashford *Dev.* 6 B21
Ashford *Dev.* 5 F22
Ashford *Ham.* 10 C37
Ashford Bowdler 28 A30
Ashford Carbonel 28 A31
Ashford Hill 21 E41
Ashford in the Water 50 E37
Ashgill 75 E23
Ashiestiel 76 G30
Ashill *Dev.* 7 D26
Ashill *Som.* 8 C29
Ashill *Nfk* 44 E54
Ashingdon 24 B54
Ashington *W.S.* 12 E47
Ashington *Som.* 8 B31
Ashington *Nor.* 71 E38
Ashkirk 69 A30
Ashleworth 29 F33
Ashley *Cbs.* 33 B52
Ashley *Stf.* 39 B33
Ashley *Nmp.* 42 F43
Ashley *Ham.* 10 A39
Ashley *Wts.* 20 E33
Ashley *Glo.* 20 B35
Ashley *Che.* 49 D33
Ashley *Dev.* 6 D22
Ashley *Ham.* 10 E38
Ashley *Kent* 15 C58
Ashley Green 22 A45
Ashley Heath 10 D37
Ash Magna 38 B31
Ashmanhaugh 45 C59
Ashmansworth 21 F40
Ashmansworthy 6 D18
Ash Mill 7 C23
Ashmore *Dor.* 9 C35
Ashmore *Tay.* 82 B27
Ashorne 30 C38
Ashover 51 F39
Ashow 30 A38
Ashperton 29 D32
Ashprington 5 E23
Ash Priors 7 C27
Ashreigney 6 D21
Ashtead 22 F47
Ash Thomas 7 D26
Ashton *Che.* 48 F30
Ashton *Nmp.* 31 C43
Ashton *Nmp.* 42 G46
Ashton *H.&W.* 28 B31
Ashton *Cnw.* 2 F11
Ashton *Cnw.* 4 D19
Ashton Common 20 F34
Ashton-in-Makerfield 48 C31
Ashton Keynes 20 B36
Ashton under Hill 29 E35
Ashton-under-Lyne 49 C35
Ashton upon Mersey 49 C33
Ashurst *Ham.* 10 C39
Ashurst *E.S.* 13 C50
Ashurst *W.S.* 12 E47
Ashurstwood 13 C50
Ash Vale 22 F44
Ashwater 6 F19
Ashwell *Lei.* 42 D44
Ashwell *Hfs.* 33 E48
Ashwellthorpe 45 F57
Ashwick 19 G32
Ashwicken 44 D53
Ashybank 70 B31
Askam in Furness 55 B28
Askern 51 A41
Askerswell 8 E31
Askett 22 A44
Askham *Not.* 51 E43
Askham *Cum.* 61 D30
Askham Bryan 58 E41
Askham Richard 58 E41
Asknish 73 A15
Askrigg 61 G35
Askwith 57 E37
Aslackby 42 B46
Aslacton 45 F57
Aslockton 42 A43
Asloun 90 B31
Aspall 35 B57
Aspatria 60 B27
Aspenden 33 F49
Aspley Guise 32 E45
Aspull 49 B32
Asselby 58 G42
Assington 34 E55
Astbury 49 F34
Astcote 31 C42
Asterby 53 E48
Asterley 38 E29
Asterton 38 F29
Asthall 30 G38
Asthall Leigh 30 G38
Astley *H.&W.* 29 B33
Astley *Shr.* 38 D31
Astley *War.* 41 G39
Astley Abbotts 39 F33
Astley Bridge 49 A33
Astley Cross 29 A33
Astley Green 49 C32
Aston *Dby.* 50 D37
Aston *Che.* 48 E31
Aston *Clw.* 48 F29
Aston *Oxf.* 21 A39
Aston *W.M.* 40 G36
Aston *Shr.* 39 E32
Aston *S.Y.* 51 D40
Aston *Stf.* 39 A33
Aston *Shr.* 38 C31
Aston *Che.* 38 A31
Aston *Hfs.* 33 F48
Aston *H.&W.* 28 A30
Aston *Bkh.* 22 C43
Aston Abbotts 32 F44
Aston Botterell 39 G32
Aston-by-Stone 40 B34
Aston Cantlow 30 B37
Aston Clinton 32 G44
Aston Crews 29 F32
Aston Cross 29 E35
Aston End 33 F48
Aston Eyre 39 F32
Aston Fields 29 B35
Aston Flamville 41 F40
Aston Ingham 29 F32
Aston juxta Mondrum 49 G32
Aston le Walls 31 C40
Aston Magna 30 E37
Aston Munslow 38 G31
Aston on Clun 38 G29
Aston on Trent 41 B40
Aston Rogers 38 E29
Aston Rowant 22 B43
Aston Sandford 22 A43
Aston Somerville 30 E36
Aston Subedge 30 D37
Aston Tirrold 21 C41
Aston Upthorpe 21 C41
Astwick 33 E48
Astwood 32 D45
Astwood Bank 30 B36
Aswarby 42 A46
Aswardby 53 E49
Aswick Grange 43 D48
Atcham 38 E31
Atch Lench 30 C36
Athelington 35 A58
Athelney 8 B29
Athelstaneford 76 C30
Atherington 6 C21
Atherstone 40 F38
Atherstone on Stour 30 C38
Atherton 49 B32
Athlinne 100 F7
Atlow 40 A38
Attadale 86 A15
Attenborough 41 B40
Atterby 52 C45
Attleborough *War.* 41 F39
Attleborough *Nfk* 44 F56
Attlebridge 45 D57
Atwick 59 D47
Atworth 20 E34
Aubourn 52 F45
Auch 80 D19
Auchachenna 80 E15
Auchairne 66 E16
Auchallater 90 E27
Auchameanach 73 E14
Aucharnie 98 E32
Aucharrigill 96 A20
Auchattie 91 D32
Auchavan 82 A27
Auchbraad 73 B14
Auchbreck 90 A27
Auchenblae 91 F33
Auchenbothie 74 C19
Auchenbrack 68 D23
Auchenbreck 73 B16
Auchencairn 65 E23
Auchencrow 77 D34
Auchendinny 76 D28
Auchendolly 65 D23
Auchenfoyle 74 C19
Auchengray 75 E25
Auchenhalrig 98 C29
Auchenheath 75 F24
Auchenhessnane 68 D23
Auchenlochan 73 C15
Auchenmalg 64 E18
Auchenrivock 69 E29
Auchentiber 74 F19
Auchessan 81 E20
Auchgourish 89 C25
Auchinafaud 72 E12
Auchincruive 67 A19
Auchindarrach 73 B14
Auchindarroch 80 B15
Auchindrain 80 G16
Auchindrean 95 C17
Auchininna 98 E32
Auchinleck 67 A21
Auchinloch 74 C22
Auchinner 81 F22
Auchinroath 98 D28
Auchintoul *Grm.* 98 D31
Auchintoul *Grm.* 90 B31
Auchintoul *Hgh.* 96 A21
Auchinvennal 74 B18
Auchiries 99 F36
Auchleven 91 A32
Auchlochan 75 G23
Auchlunachan 95 C17
Auchlunies 91 D34
Auchlunkart 98 E29
Auchlyne 81 E20
Auchmacoy 99 F35
Auchmair 90 A29
Auchmantle 64 D17
Auchmithie 83 C32
Auchmuirbridge 82 G27
Auchmull 90 F31
Auchnabony 65 F23
Auchnabreac 80 G16
Auchnacloich 81 D24
Auchnacraig 79 E13
Auchnacree 83 A30
Auchnafree 81 D23
Auchnagallin 89 A26
Auchnagatt 99 E35
Auchnaha 73 B15
Auchnangoul 80 G16
Aucholzie 90 D29
Auchorrie 91 C32
Auchraw 81 E21
Auchreoch 80 E19
Auchronie 90 E30
Auchterarder 82 F25
Auchtercairn 94 D14
Auchterderran 75 A27
Auchterhouse 82 D28
Auchtermuchty 82 F28
Auchterneed 96 E20
Auchtertool 75 A27
Auchtertyre *Tay.* 82 C28
Auchtertyre *Cen.* 80 E19
Auchtertyre *Grm.* 97 F27
Auchtoo 81 E21
Auckengill 103 B29
Auckley 51 B42
Audenshaw 49 C35
Audlem 39 A32
Audley 49 G33
Audley End 33 E50
Auds 98 C32
Aughton *Lan.* 48 B29
Aughton *Lan.* 55 C31
Aughton *S.Y.* 51 D40
Aughton *Hum.* 58 F42
Aughton Park 48 B29
Auldearn 97 F25
Aulden 28 C30
Auldhame 76 B31
Auldhouse 74 E21
Aulich 81 B21
Ault a'chruinn 86 C15
Aultanrynie 101 E19
Aultbea 94 C14
Aultgrishan 94 C13
Aultguish Inn 96 D19
Ault Hucknall 51 F40
Aultibea 103 F26
Aultiphurst 102 B23
Aultmore 98 D29
Aultnagoire 88 B21
Aultnamain Inn 96 C22
Aultnapaddock 98 E29
Aulton 90 A31
Aultvoulin 86 D13
Aundorach 89 C25
Aunk 7 E26
Aunsby 42 B46
Auquhorthies 91 A34
Aust 19 C31
Austerfield 51 C42
Austonley 50 B37
Austrey 40 E38
Austwick 56 C33
Authorpe 53 D49
Authorpe Row 53 E51
Avebury 20 D36
Aveley 23 D51
Avening 20 B34
Averham 51 G43
Aveton Gifford 5 F22
Avielochan 89 C24
Aviemore 89 C24
Avington *Ham.* 11 A41
Avington *Brk.* 21 E39
Avoch 96 F22
Avon 10 E37
Avonbridge 75 C25
Avon Dassett 31 C40
Avonmouth 19 D30
Avonwick 5 E23
Awbridge 10 B39
Awhirk 64 E16
Awkley 19 C31
Awliscombe 7 E27
Awre 19 A32
Awsworth 41 A40
Axbridge 19 F29
Axford *Ham.* 21 G42
Axford *Wts.* 21 D38
Axminster 8 E29
Axmouth 8 E28
Aycliffe 62 D38
Aydon 71 G36
Aylburton 19 A31
Ayle 61 B33
Aylesbeare 7 F26
Aylesbury 31 G43
Aylesby 53 B48
Aylesford 14 B53
Aylesham 15 B58
Aylestone 41 E41
Aylmerton 45 B57
Aylsham 45 C57
Aylton 29 E32
Aymestrey 28 B29
Aynho 31 E40
Ayot St Lawrence 32 G47
Ayot St Peter 32 G47
Ayr 67 A19
Aysgarth 56 A35
Ayshford 7 D26
Ayside 55 A29
Ayston 42 E44
Aythorpe Roding 33 G51
Ayton *Tay.* 82 F27
Ayton *Bor.* 77 D35
Aywick 106 D41
Azerley 57 B38

B

Babbacombe 5 D25
Babbinswood 38 B29
Babcary 8 B31
Babel 27 E24
Babell 47 E27
Babeny 5 C22
Babraham 33 C50
Babworth 51 D42
Bac 100 C10
Backaland 104 C31
Backaskaill 104 A30
Backbarrow 55 A29
Backburn 98 F32
Backfolds 99 D36
Backford 48 E29
Backhill *Grm.* 99 F33
Backhill *Grm.* 99 F36
Backhill of Clackriach 99 E35
Backhill of Trustach 91 D32
Backies *Grm.* 98 D30
Backies *Hgh.* 97 A24
Backlass 103 C27
Backmuir of New Gilston 83 G30
Back of Keppoch 86 F12
Backside 98 F29
Backwell 19 E30
Backworth 71 F38
Bacon End 33 G51
Baconsthorpe 45 B57
Bacton *Nfk* 45 B59
Bacton *H.&W.* 28 E29
Bacton *Sfk* 34 B56
Bacup 56 G34
Badachro 94 D13
Badanloch Lodge 102 E23
Badavanich 95 F16
Badbea 103 G26
Badbury 20 C37
Badby 31 C41
Badcall *Hgh.* 101 C18
Badcall *Hgh.* 101 D17
Badcaul 94 B15
Baddeley Green 49 G35
Badden 73 B14
Baddesley Ensor 40 F38
Baddidarach 101 F16
Badenscoth 98 F32
Badenyon 90 B29
Badger 39 F33
Badgerbank 49 E34
Badgers Mount 23 E50
Badgeworth 29 G34
Badgworth 19 F29
Badicaul 86 B13
Badingham 35 B59
Badintagairt 102 G20
Badlesmere 14 B55
Badley 34 C56
Badlipster 103 D28
Badluarchrach 94 B15
Badminton 20 C34
Badnaban 101 F16
Badnabay 101 D17
Badnafrave 90 B27
Badnagie 103 E27
Badnambiast 88 G22
Badninish 96 B23
Badrallach 95 B16
Badsey 30 D36
Badshot Lea 22 G44
Badsworth 51 A40
Badwell Ash 34 B55
Badyo 82 A25
Bagby 57 A40
Bag Enderby 53 E49
Bagendon 20 A35
Baggrave Hall 41 E42
Baggrow 60 B27
Bagh A Chaisteil (Castlebay) 84 E2
Baghasdal 84 C3
Bagillt 48 E28
Baginton 30 A39
Baglan 18 B23
Bagley 38 C30
Bagnall 49 G35
Bagnor 21 E40
Bagshot *Sry* 22 E44
Bagshot *Wts.* 21 E39
Bagstone 19 C32
Bagthorpe 51 G40
Baguley 49 D33
Bagworth 41 E40
Bagwyllydiart 28 F30
Baildon 57 F37
Baile Ailein 100 E8
Baile A Mhanaich (Balivanich) 92 F3
Baile an Truiseil 100 B9
Bailebeag 88 C20
Baile Boidheach 73 C13
Baile Gharbhaidh 92 G3
Baile Glas 92 F4
Baileguish 89 E24
Bailemeonach 79 C12
Baile Mhartainn 92 D3
Baile Mor 92 E3
Bailenacille 92 C4
Baile nan Cailleach 92 F3
Baile Raghaill 92 E2
Bailetonach 86 G12
Bailliesward 98 F30
Bainbridge 61 G35
Bainsford 75 B24
Bainshole 98 F31
Bainton *Cbs.* 42 E47

Bainton Hum. 59 D45
Bairnkine 70 B32
Bakebare 98 F29
Baker's End 33 G49
Baker Street 24 C52
Bakewell 50 F37
Bala 37 B25
Balachuirn 94 G11
Balafark 74 A22
Balaldie 97 D24
Balameanach 73 A14
Balavil 88 D23
Balbeg Hgh. 88 A20
Balbeg Hgh. 88 B20
Balbeggie 82 E27
Balbirnie 82 G28
Balbithan 91 B33
Balblair Hgh. 96 B21
Balblair Hgh. 96 E22
Balcharn 96 A21
Balcherry 96 C23
Balchers 98 D32
Balchladich 101 E16
Balchraggan Hgh. 96 G21
Balchraggan Hgh. 88 A21
Balchrick 101 B17
Balcombe 13 C49
Balcurvie 82 G29
Baldernock 74 C21
Baldersby 57 B39
Balderstone 56 F32
Balderton 52 G44
Baldhu 2 D13
Baldinnie 83 F30
Baldock 33 E48
Baldovie Tay. 82 B29
Baldovie Tay. 83 D30
Baldrine 54 E26
Baldslow 14 F54
Baldwin 54 E25
Baldwinholme 60 A29
Baldwin's Gate 39 A33
Bale 44 B56
Balelone 92 D3
Balemartine 78 C5
Balendoch 82 C28
Balephuil 78 C5
Balerno 75 D27
Balernock 74 B18
Baleromindubh 72 A9
Balerominmore 72 A9
Balevulin 79 E10
Balfield 83 A31
Balfour Grm. 90 D31
Balfour Ork. 104 E30
Balfron 74 B21
Balfron Station 74 B21
Balgavies 83 B31
Balgedie 82 G27
Balgonar 75 A25
Balgove 99 F34
Balgowan D.&G. 64 F17
Balgowan Hgh. 88 E22
Balgown 93 E9
Balgray 82 D29
Balgreen 99 D33
Balgreggan 64 E16
Balgy 94 F14
Balhaldie 81 G23
Balhalgardy 91 A33
Balhary 82 C28
Balhelvie 82 E28
Balhousie 83 G30
Baliasta 106 B41
Baligill 102 B24
Baligrundle 79 D14
Balindore 80 D15
Balintore 97 D24
Balintraid 96 D23
Balintyre 81 C22
Balivanich (Baile A Mhanaich) 92 F3
Balkeerie 82 C29
Balkholme 58 G43
Balkissock 67 E17
Ball 38 C29
Ballabeg 54 F24
Ballacannell 54 E26
Ballacarnane Beg 54 E24
Ballachulish 80 B16
Balladoole 54 G24
Ballafesson 54 F23
Ballagyr 54 E24
Ballajora 54 D26
Ballakilpheric 54 F24
Ballamodha 54 F24
Ballantrae 66 E16
Ballards Gore 25 B55
Ballasalla I.o.M. 54 D25
Ballasalla I.o.M. 54 F24
Ballater 90 D29
Ballaterach 90 D29
Ballaugh 54 D25
Ballaveare 54 F25
Ballechin 82 B25
Balleich 81 G20
Ballencrieff 76 C30
Ball Haye Green 49 G35
Ball Hill 21 E40
Ballidon 50 G37
Balliekine 73 G14
Balliemeanoch 80 G16
Balliemore Tay. 81 B23
Balliemore Str. 73 A16
Balliemore Str. 79 E14
Ballig 54 E24
Ballimeanoch 80 F15
Ballimore Cen. 81 F21
Ballimore Str. 73 B15
Ballinaby 72 D8
Ballindean 82 E28
Ballingdon 34 D54
Ballinger Common 22 A44
Ballingham 28 E31
Ballingry 75 A27
Ballinlick 82 C25
Ballinluig Tay. 82 B25
Ballinluig Tay. 82 B26
Ballintuim 82 B26
Balloch Tay. 82 B29
Balloch Tay. 81 F24
Balloch Hgh. 96 G23
Balloch Str. 74 B19
Ballochan 90 D31
Ballochandrain 73 B15
Ballochford 98 F29
Ballochgair 66 A13
Ballochmartin 73 E17
Ballochmorrie 5 F17
Ballochmyle 67 A21
Ballochroy 73 E13
Ballogie 90 D31
Balls Cross 12 D45
Ballyaurgan 73 C13
Ballygown 79 C10
Ballygrant 72 D9
Ballyhaugh 78 B7
Ballymichael 73 G14
Balmacara 86 B13
Balmaclellan 65 C22
Balmacneil 82 B25
Balmadies 83 C31
Balmae 65 F22
Balmaha 74 A20
Balmalcolm 82 G28
Balmeanach 79 D10
Balmedie 91 B35
Balmerino 82 E29
Balmerlawn 10 D39
Balminnoch 64 D18
Balmore Hgh. 97 G24
Balmore Str. 74 C22
Balmore Hgh. 88 A19
BalmoreHgh. 93 G8
Balmullo 83 E30
Balmungie 96 F23
Balmyle 82 B26
Balnaboth 82 A28
Balnabruaich 96 D23
Balnacra 94 G15
Balnafoich 88 A22
Balnagall 97 C24
Balnagown Castle 96 D23
Balnaguard 82 B25
Balnaguisich 96 D22
Balnahard Str. 79 D10
Balnahard Str. 72 A10
Balnain 88 A20
Balnakeil 101 B19
Balnaknock 93 E10
Balnamoon 83 A31
Balnapaling 96 E23
Balnespick 89 D24
Balquhidder 81 E21
Balsall 30 A38
Balsall Common 30 A38
Balscote 30 D39
Balsham 33 C51
Baltasound 106 B41
Balterley 39 A33
Baltersan 64 D20
Balthangie 99 D34
Balthayock 82 E27
Baltonsborough 8 A31
Baluachraig 73 A14
Balulive 72 D9
Balure Str. 80 D16
Balure Str. 79 D14
Balvaird 96 F21
Balvarran 82 A26
Balvicar 79 F13
Balvraid Hgh. 86 C14
Balvraid Hgh. 89 A24
Bamber Bridge 55 G31
Bamber's Green 33 F51
Bamburgh 77 G37
Bamff 82 B28
Bamford 50 D37
Bampton Oxf. 21 A38
Bampton Cum. 61 E30
Bampton Dev. 7 C25
Banavie 87 G16
Banbury 31 D40
Bancffosfelen 17 C20
Banchor 97 G24
Banchory 91 D32
Banchory-Devenick 91 C35
Bancyfelin 17 C18
Banc-y-ffordd 17 A19
Bandon 82 G28
Banff 98 C32
Bangor 46 E21
Bangor-is-y-coed 38 A29
Bangor Teifi 26 D19
Banham 44 G56
Bank 10 D38
Bankend Str. 75 G24
Bank End 54 A27
Bankend D.&G. 69 G26
Bankfoot 82 D26
Bankhead Grm. 91 C32
Bankhead Grm. 91 C34
Bankhead Grm. 91 B32
Bankhead D.&G. 65 F23
Bank Newton 56 D35
Banknock 75 C23
Banks Cum. 70 G31
Banks Lan. 55 G29
Bankshill 69 E27
Bank Street 29 B32
Banningham 45 C58
Bannister Green 33 F52
Bannockburn 75 A24
Banstead 23 F48
Bantham 5 F22
Banton 75 C23
Banwell 19 F29
Bapchild 25 E55
Baptiston 74 B21
Barabhas 100 B9
Barachander 80 E16
Barassie 74 G18
Barbaraville 96 D23
Barber Booth 50 D37
Barbon 56 A32
Barbrook 7 A23
Barby 31 A41
Barcaldine 80 C15
Barcaple 65 E22
Barcheston 30 D38
Barcombe 13 E50
Barcombe Cross 13 E50
Barden 62 G37
Bardennoch 67 D21
Bardfield End Green 33 E52
Bardfield Saling 33 F52
Bardister 106 E39
Bardney 52 F47
Bardon Lei. 41 D40
Bardon Grm. 97 F28
Bardon Mill 70 G33
Bardsea 55 B29
Bardsey 57 E39
Bardsley 49 B35
Bardwell 34 A55
Barewood 28 C29
Barfad 73 D14
Barford War. 30 B38
Barford Nfk 45 E57
Barford St John 31 E40
Barford St Martin 10 A36
Barford St Michael 30 E39
Barfreston 15 B58
Bargaly 64 D20
Bargany 67 C18
Bargoed 18 B27
Bargrennan 64 C19
Barham Cbs. 32 A47
Barham Sfk 35 C57
Barham Kent 15 B57
Barharrow 65 E21
Bar Hill 33 B49
Barholm Lcn. 42 D46
Barholm D.&G. 64 E20
Barkby 41 E42
Barkby Thorpe 41 E42
Barkestone-le-Vale 42 B43
Barkham 22 E43
Barking G.L. 23 C50
Barking Sfk 34 C56
Barking & Dagenham 23 C50
Barkingside 23 C50
Barkisland 50 A36
Barkston Lcn. 42 A45
Barkston N.Y. 57 F40
Barkway 33 E49
Barlae 64 D18
Barlaston 40 B34
Barlavington 12 E45
Barlay 65 E21
Barlborough 51 E40
Barlby 58 F42
Barlestone 41 E40
Barley Hfs. 33 E49
Barley Lan. 56 E34
Barleycroft End 33 F49
Barleyhill 62 A36
Barleythorpe 42 E44
Barling 25 C55
Barlings 52 E46
Barlow Dby. 51 E39
Barlow T.&W. 71 G37
Barlow N.Y. 58 G42
Barmby Moor 58 E43
Barmby on the Marsh 58 G42
Barmolloch 73 A14
Barmoor Lane End 77 F35
Barmouth 36 D21
Barmpton 62 E38
Barmston 59 D47
Barnacabber 73 B17
Barnacarry 73 A16
Barnack 42 E46
Barnacle 41 G39
Barnamuc 80 C16
Barnard Castle 62 E36
Barnard Gate 31 G40
Barnardiston 33 D52
Barnard's Green 29 D33
Barnbarroch D.&G. 65 E24
Barnbarroch D.&G. 64 E19
Barnburgh 51 B40
Barnby 45 F60
Barnby Dun 51 B41
Barnby in the Willows 52 G44
Barnby Moor 51 D42
Barndennoch 68 E24
Barnes 23 D48
Barnet 23 B48
Barnetby le Wold 52 B46
Barney 44 B55
Barnham W.S. 12 F45
Barnham Sfk 34 A54
Barnham Broom 44 E56
Barnhead 83 B32
Barnhill 97 F27
Barningham Sfk 34 A55
Barningham Drm 62 E36
Barnoldby le Beck 53 B48
Barnoldswick 56 E34
Barns Green 12 D47
Barnsley S.Y. 51 B39
Barnsley Glo. 20 A36
Barnstaple 6 B21
Barnston Mer. 48 D28
Barnston Esx 33 G52
Barnstone 42 B43
Barnt Green 30 A36
Barnton 49 E32
Barnwell All Saints 42 G46
Barnwell St Andrew 42 G46
Barnwood 29 G34
Barr Str. 72 D9
Barr Hgh. 79 B12
Barr Str. 67 D18
Barrackan 79 G13
Barraer 64 D19
Barraglom 100 D7
Barrahormid 72 B12
Barran 80 E17
Barrapoll 78 C5
Barrasford 70 F34
Barra (Traigh Mor) Airport 84 D3
Barravullin 79 G13
Barregarrow 54 E24
Barr Hall 34 E53
Barrhead 74 E21
Barrhill 67 E18
Barrington Som. 8 C29
Barrington Cbs. 33 D49
Barripper 2 E12
Barrisdale 86 D14
Barrmill 74 E19
Barrnacarry 79 E13
Barrock 103 A28
Barrow Sfk 34 B53
Barrow Shr. 39 E32
Barrow Lei. 42 D44
Barrow Lan. 56 F33
Barrow Som. 9 A33
Barrowby 42 B44
Barrowden 42 E45
Barrowford 56 F34
Barrow Gurney 19 E31
Barrow Haven 59 G46
Barrow-in-Furness 54 B27
Barrow Nook 48 B30
Barrow Street 9 A34
Barrow upon Humber 59 G46
Barrow upon Soar 41 D41
Barrow upon Trent 41 C39
Barry S.G. 18 E27
Barry Tay. 83 D31
Barsby 41 D42
Barsham 45 F59
Barskimming 67 A20
Barsloisnoch 73 A13
Barston 30 A37
Bartestree 28 D31
Barthol Chapel 99 F34
Barthomley 49 G33
Bartley 10 C39
Bartlow 33 D51
Barton Glo. 30 F36
Barton War. 30 C37
Barton Lan. 48 B29
Barton Che. 48 G30
Barton Dev. 5 D25
Barton N.Y. 62 F38
Barton Cbs. 33 C49
Barton Lan. 55 F30
Barton Bendish 44 E53
Barton Common 45 C59
Barton End 20 B34
Barton Hartshorn 31 E42
Barton in Fabis 41 B41
Barton in the Beans 41 E40
Barton-le-Clay 32 E46
Barton-le-Street 58 B43
Barton-le-Willows 58 C43
Barton Mills 34 A53
Barton on Sea 10 E38
Barton-on-the-Heath 30 E38
Barton Seagrave 32 A44
Barton Stacey 21 G40
Barton Stacey Camp 21 G40
Barton St David 8 A31
Barton Turf 45 C59
Barton-under-Needwood 40 D37
Barton-upon-Humber 59 G45
Barway 33 A51
Barwell 41 F40
Barwhinnock 65 E22
Barwick 8 C31
Barwick in Elmet 57 F39
Barwinnock 64 F19
Baschurch 38 C29
Bascote 30 B39
Basford Green 49 G35
Bashall Eaves 56 E32
Bashall Town 56 E32
Bashley 10 E38
Basildon Esx 24 C53
Basildon Brk. 21 D42
Basingstoke 21 F41
Baslow 50 E38
Bason Bridge 19 G29
Bassaleg 19 C28
Bassenthwaite 60 C27
Bassett 11 C40
Bassett's Cross 6 E21
Bassingbourn 33 D48
Bassingfield 41 B42
Bassingham 52 F44
Bassingthorpe 42 C45
Basta 106 C41
Baston 42 D47
Bastwick 45 D60
Batavaime 81 D20
Batchworth 22 B46
Batchworth Heath 22 B46
Batcombe Som. 9 A32
Batcombe Dor. 9 D32
Bate Heath 49 E32
Bath 20 E33
Bathampton 20 E33
Bathealton 7 C26
Batheaston 20 E33
Bathford 20 E33
Bathgate 75 D25
Bathley 51 G43
Bathpool Cnw. 4 C18
Bathpool Som. 8 B28
Batley 57 G38
Batsford 30 E37
Battersby 63 F41
Battersea 23 D48
Battisborough Cross 5 F22
Battisford 34 C56
Battisford Tye 34 C56
Battle Pow. 27 E25
Battle E.S. 14 F53
Battlefield 38 D31
Battlesbridge 24 B53
Battlesden 32 F45
Battleton 7 C24
Battramsley 10 E38
Batt's Corner 22 G44
Bauds of Cullen 98 C30
Baugh 78 C6
Baughton 29 D34
Baughurst 21 F41
Baulds 90 D31
Baulking 21 B39
Baumber 53 E48
Baunton 20 A36
Baveney Wood 29 A32
Baverstock 10 A36
Bawburgh 45 E57
Bawdeswell 44 C56
Bawdrip 8 A29
Bawdsey 35 D59
Bawtry 51 C42
Baxenden 56 G33
Baxterley 40 F38
Baycliff 55 B28
Baydon 21 D38
Bayford Bfd. 23 A48

Bayford *Som.* 9 B33
Bayfordbury 33 G48
Bayham Abbey 13 C52
Bayles 61 B32
Baylham 34 C56
Baynards Green 31 F41
Baysham 28 F31
Bayston Hill 38 E30
Baythorn End 34 D53
Bayton 29 A32
Beach 79 B13
Beachampton 31 E43
Beacharr 72 F12
Beachborough 15 D57
Beachley 19 B31
Beacon 7 E27
Beacon End 34 F55
Beacon Hill 12 C44
Beacon's Bottom 22 B43
Beaconsfield 22 B45
Beadlam 58 A42
Beadnell 71 A38
Beaford 6 D21
Beal *Nor.* 77 F36
Beal *N.Y.* 58 G41
Bealach 80 B15
Beambridge 49 G32
Beamhurst 40 B36
Beaminster 8 D30
Beamish 62 A38
Beamsley 57 D36
Bean 23 D51
Beanacre 20 E34
Beanley 71 B36
Beaquoy 104 D28
Beardon 6 G21
Beare Green 22 G47
Bearley 30 B37
Bearnie 99 F35
Bearnock 88 A19
Bearnus 78 C9
Bearpark 62 B38
Bearsbridge 61 A33
Bearsden 74 C21
Bearsted 14 B53
Bearwood 10 E36
Beattock 69 C26
Beauchamp Roding 33 G51
Beauchief 51 D39
Beaudesert 30 B37
Beaufort 28 G27
Beaulieu 10 D39
Beauly 96 G21
Beaumaris 46 E21
Beaumont *Esx* 35 F57
Beaumont *Cum.* 60 A29
Beausale 30 A38
Beauworth 11 B41
Beaworthy 6 F20
Beazley End 34 F53
Bebington 48 D29
Bebside 71 E38
Beccles 45 F60
Becconsall 55 G30
Beckbury 39 E33
Beckenham 23 E49
Beckermet 60 F25
Beck Foot 61 G32
Beckfoot *Cum.* 60 B26
Beckfoot *Cum.* 60 F27
Beckford 29 E35
Beckhampton 20 E36
Beck Hole 63 F44
Beckingham *Lcn.* 52 G44
Beckingham *Not.* 51 C43
Beckington 20 F33
Beckley *E.S.* 14 E54
Beckley *Oxf.* 31 G41
Beck Row 33 A52
Beck Side 55 A28
Beckton 23 C50
Beckwithshaw 57 D38
Becontree 23 C50
Bedale 57 A38
Bedburn 62 C36
Bedchester 9 C34
Beddau 18 C26
Beddgelert 36 A21
Beddingham 13 F50
Beddington 23 E48
Beddington Corner 23 E48
Bedfield 35 B57
Bedford 32 C46
Bedgebury Cross 13 C52
Bedhampton 11 D43
Bedingfield 35 B57
Bedlington 71 E38
Bedlinog 18 A26
Bedmond 22 A46
Bednall 40 D35
Bedol 48 E28
Bedrule 70 B31
Bedstone 28 A29
Bedwas 18 C27
Bedwellty 18 A27
Bedworth 41 G39
Beeby 41 E42
Beech *Stf.* 40 B34
Beech *Ham.* 11 A42
Beechamwell 44 E53
Beech Hill 21 E42
Beechingstoke 20 F36
Beedon 21 D40
Beeford 59 D47
Beeley 50 F38
Beelsby 53 B48
Beenham 21 E41
Beer 8 F28
Beercrocombe 8 B29
Beer Hackett 9 C32
Beesands 5 F24
Beesby 53 D50
Beeson 5 F23
Beeston *Che.* 48 G31
Beeston *Not.* 41 B41
Beeston *Bfd.* 32 D47
Beeston *W.Y.* 57 F38
Beeston *Nfk* 44 D55
Beeston Regis 45 A57
Beeston St Lawrence 45 C59
Beeswing 65 D24
Beetham 55 B30
Beetley 44 D55
Began 19 C28
Begbroke 31 G40
Begelly 16 D17
Beggshill 98 F31
Beguildy 28 A27
Beighton *Dby.* 51 D40
Beighton *Nfk* 45 E59
Beith 74 E19
Bekesbourne 15 B57
Belaugh 45 D58
Belbroughton 29 A34
Belchamp Otten 34 D54
Belchamp St Paul 34 D53
Belchamp Walter 34 D54
Belchford 53 E48
Belford 77 G36
Belgrave 41 E41
Belhaven 76 C32
Belhelvie 91 B35
Belhinnie 90 A30
Bellabeg 90 B29
Belladrum 96 G21
Bellanoch 73 A13
Bellasize 58 G44
Bellaty 82 B28
Bell Bar 23 A48
Bell Busk 56 D35
Belleau 53 E49
Bell End 29 A35
Bellerby 62 G37
Bellever 5 C22
Belliehill 83 A31
Bellingdon 22 A45
Bellingham 70 E34
Belloch 72 G12
Bellochantuy 72 G12
Bellsdyke 75 B25
Bellshill *Nor.* 77 G37
Bellshill *Str.* 75 E23
Bellside 75 E24
Bellspool 75 G27
Bellsquarry 75 D26
Bells Yew Green 13 C52
Belluton 19 E31
Belmaduthy 96 F22
Belmesthorpe 42 D46
Belmont *She.* 106 B41
Belmont *Lan.* 49 A32
Belmont *G.L.* 23 E48
Belowda 3 B15
Belper 41 A39
Belper Lane End 51 G39
Belsay 71 F36
Belsford 5 E23
Belstead 35 D57
Belston 67 A19
Belstone 6 F21
Belstone Corner 6 F22
Belsyde 75 C25
Belthorn 56 G33
Beltinge 25 E57
Beltoft 52 B44
Belton *Hum.* 51 B43
Belton *Lei.* 42 E44
Belton *Lei.* 41 C40
Belton *Lcn.* 42 B45
Belton *Nfk* 45 E60
Beltring 23 G52
Belvedere 23 D50
Belvoir 42 B44
Bembridge 11 F42
Bemersyde 76 G31
Bempton 59 B47
Benacre 45 G61
Ben Alder Cottage 81 A20
Ben Alder Lodge 88 G21
Benbecula (Bhaile A Mhanaich) Airport 92 F3
Benbuie 68 D22
Benderloch 79 D14
Bendish 32 F47
Benenden 14 D54
Benfield 64 D19
Bengate 45 C58
Bengeo 33 G49
Benholm 91 G34
Beningbrough 58 D41
Benington *Hfs.* 33 F48
Benington *Lcn.* 43 A49
Benington Sea End 43 A50
Benllech 46 D20
Benmore *Str.* 73 B17
Benmore *Cen.* 81 E20
Bennacott 4 A18
Bennan 65 C22
Benniworth 53 D48
Benover 14 C53
Benson 21 B42
Benthall *Nor.* 71 A38
Benthall *Shr.* 39 E32
Bentham 29 G35
Benthoul 91 C33
Bentley *Ham.* 22 G43
Bentley *Hum.* 59 F46
Bentley *War.* 40 F38
Bentley *S.Y.* 51 B41
Bentley Heath 30 A37
Benton 6 B22
Benton Square 71 G39
Bentpath 69 D28
Bentworth 21 G42
Benvie 82 D29
Benville Lane 8 D31
Benwick 43 G49
Beoley 30 B36
Bepton 12 E44
Berden 33 F50
Berea 16 B13
Bere Alston 4 D20
Bere Ferrers 4 D20
Berepper 2 F12
Bere Regis 9 E34
Bergh Apton 45 E59
Berinsfield 21 B41
Berkeley 19 B32
Berkhamsted 22 A45
Berkley 20 G33
Berkswell 30 A38
Bermondsey 23 D49
Bernera 86 B14
Berners Roding 24 A52
Bernice 73 A17
Bernisdale 93 F9
Berrick Salome 21 B42
Berriedale 103 F26
Berriew (Aberriw) 38 E27
Berrington *Shr.* 38 E31
Berrington *Nor.* 77 F35
Berrow 19 F28
Berrow Green 29 C33
Berry Down Cross 6 A21
Berry Hill *Dyf.* 16 A16
Berry Hill *Glo.* 28 G31
Berryhillock 98 C30
Berrynarbor 6 A21
Berry Pomeroy 5 D24
Bersham 38 A28
Berstane 104 E30
Berwick 13 F50
Berwick Bassett 20 D36
Berwick Hill 71 F37
Berwick St James 10 A36
Berwick St John 9 B35
Berwick St Leonard 9 A35
Berwick-upon-Tweed 77 E35
Bescar 48 A29
Besford *Shr.* 38 C31
Besford *H.&W.* 29 D35
Bessacarr 51 B41
Bessels Leigh 21 A40
Bessingby 59 C47
Bessingham 45 B57
Best Beech Hill 13 C52
Besthorpe *Nfk* 44 F56
Besthorpe *Not.* 52 F44
Beswick 59 E46
Betchworth 23 F48
Bethania *Dyf.* 26 B21
Bethania *Gwy.* 37 A22
Bethel *Gwy.* 37 A25
Bethel *Gwy.* 46 F21
Bethel *Gwy.* 46 E19
Bethersden 14 D55
Bethesda *Gwy.* 46 F21
Bethesda *Dyf.* 16 C16
Bethlehem 17 B22
Bethnal Green 23 C49
Betley 39 A33
Betsham 24 D52
Betteshanger 15 B58
Bettiscombe 8 E29
Bettisfield 38 B30
Betton *Shr.* 38 E29
Betton *Shr.* 39 B32
Bettws 19 B28
Bettws Bledrws 26 C21
Bettws Cedewain 38 F27
Bettws Evan 26 D18
Bettws Gwerfil Goch 37 A26
Bettws-Newydd 19 A29
Bettws-y-crwyn 38 G27
Bettyhill 102 B22
Betws *M.G.* 18 C24
Betws *Dyf.* 17 C22
Betws Disserth 27 C26
Betws Garmon 46 G21
Betws-y-coed 47 G23
Betws-yn-Rhos 47 E24
Beulah *Pow.* 27 C25
Beulah *Dyf.* 26 D18
Bevendean 13 F49
Bevercotes 51 E42
Beverley 59 F46
Beverstone 20 B34
Bevington 19 B32
Bewaldeth 60 C27
Bewcastle 70 F31
Bewdley 29 A33
Bewerley 57 C37
Bewholme 59 E47
Bewley Common 20 E35
Bexhill 14 G53
Bexley 23 D50
Bexleyheath 23 D50
Bexwell 44 E52
Beyton 34 B55
Beyton Green 34 B55
Bhalamus 100 G8
Bhaltos 100 D6
Bhatarsaigh 84 E2
Biallaid 88 E22
Bibury 20 A37
Bicester 31 F41
Bickenhall 8 C28
Bickenhill 40 G37
Bicker 43 B48
Bickerstaffe 48 B30
Bickerton *Che.* 48 G30
Bickerton *N.Y.* 57 D40
Bickford 40 D34
Bickham Bridge 5 E23
Bickham House 7 G25
Bickington *Dev.* 6 B21
Bickington *Dev.* 5 C23
Bickleigh *Dev.* 7 E25
Bickleigh *Dev.* 5 D21
Bickleton 6 B21
Bickley 23 E50
Bickley Moss 38 A31
Bickley Town 38 A31
Bicknacre 24 A53
Bicknoller 7 B26
Bicknor 14 B54
Bickton 10 C37
Bicton *Shr.* 38 G28
Bicton *Shr.* 38 D30
Bicton Heath 38 D30
Bidborough 23 G51
Biddenden 14 D54
Biddenham 32 D46
Biddestone 20 D34
Biddisham 19 F29
Biddlesden 31 D42
Biddlestone 70 C35
Biddulph 49 G34
Biddulph Moor 49 G35
Bideford 6 C20
Bidford-on-Avon 30 C36
Bidston 48 C28
Bielby 58 E43
Bieldside 91 C34
Bierley *I.o.W.* 11 G40
Bierley *W.Y.* 57 G37
Bierton 32 G44
Bigbury 5 F22
Bigbury-on-Sea 5 F21
Bigby 52 B46
Bigert Mire 60 G27
Biggar *Cum.* 54 C27
Biggar *Str.* 75 G26
Biggin *Dby.* 50 G37
Biggin *Dby.* 40 A38
Biggin *N.Y.* 58 F41
Biggings 107 A37
Biggin Hill 23 F50
Biggleswade 32 D47
Bigholms 69 E29
Bighouse 102 B24
Bighton 11 A42
Biglands 60 A28
Bignor 12 E45
Bigrigg 60 E25
Big Sand 94 D13
Bigton 107 E39
Bilberry 4 E16
Bilborough 41 A41
Bilbrook *Stf.* 40 E34
Bilbrook *Som.* 7 A26
Bilbrough 58 E41
Bilbster 103 C28
Bildershaw 62 D37
Bildeston 34 D55
Billericay 24 B52
Billesdon 42 E43
Billesley 30 C37
Billholm 69 D28
Billingborough 42 B47
Billinge 48 B31
Billingford *Nfk* 35 A57
Billingford *Nfk* 44 C55
Billingham 62 D40
Billinghay 52 G47
Billingley 51 B40
Billingshurst 12 D46
Billingsley 39 G32
Billington *Bfd.* 32 F45
Billington *Lan.* 56 F32
Billockby 45 D60
Billy Row 62 C37
Bilsborrow 55 E30
Bilsby 53 E50
Bilsdean 77 C33
Bilsham 12 F45
Bilsington 15 D56
Bilsthorpe 51 F42
Bilston *W.M.* 40 F35
Bilston *Ltn* 76 D28
Bilstone 41 E39
Bilting 15 C56
Bilton *Hum.* 59 F47
Bilton *N.Y.* 57 D39
Bilton *N.Y.* 57 D40
Bilton *War.* 31 A40
Bilton *Nor.* 71 B38
Bimbister 104 E29
Binbrook 53 C48
Bincombe 9 F32
Bindal 97 C25
Binegar 19 G31
Bines Green 12 E47
Binfield 22 D44
Binfield Heath 22 D43
Bingfield 70 F35
Bingham 41 B42
Bingham's Melcombe 9 D33
Bingley 57 F37
Binham 44 B55
Binley *Ham.* 21 F40
Binley *War.* 30 A39
Binniehill 75 C24
Binsness 97 E26
Binsoe 57 A38
Binstead 11 E41
Binsted *W.S.* 12 F45
Binsted *Ham.* 22 G43
Binton 30 C37
Bintree 44 C56
Binweston 38 E28
Birch *Esx* 34 G55
Birch *G.M.* 49 B34
Birchanger 33 F50
Bircher 28 B30
Birchfield 96 B20
Birchgrove *W.G.* 18 B23
Birchgrove *S.G.* 18 C27
Birch Heath 48 F31
Birchington 25 E58
Birchover 50 F38
Birch Vale 50 D36
Bircotes 51 C42
Birdbrook 33 D52
Bird End 40 F36
Birdfield 73 A15
Birdham 12 G44
Birdingbury 31 B40
Birdlip 29 G35
Birdsall 58 C44
Birdsgreen 39 G33
Birdsmoor Gate 8 D29
Birdwell 51 B39
Birdwood 29 G33
Birgham 77 G33
Birichen 96 B23
Birkby 62 F39
Birkdale *Mer.* 48 A29
Birkdale *N.Y.* 61 F34
Birkenhead 48 D28
Birkenhills 99 E33
Birkenshaw 57 G37
Birkhall 90 D29
Birkhill *Tay.* 82 D29
Birkhill *Bor.* 69 B27
Birkhill *Bor.* 76 F31
Birkin 58 G41
Birkwood 75 G23
Birley 28 C30
Birley Carr 51 C39
Birling *Nor.* 71 C38
Birling *Kent* 24 E52
Birling Gap 13 G51
Birlingham 29 D35
Birmingham 40 G36
Birmingham Airport 40 G37
Birnam 82 C26
Birsay 104 D28
Birse 90 D31
Birsemore 90 D31

Birstall 41 E41
Birstall Smithies 57 G38
Birstwith 57 D38
Birthorpe 42 B46
Birtley *Drm* 62 A38
Birtley *H.&W.* 28 B29
Birtley *Nor.* 70 F34
Birts Street 29 E33
Bisbrooke 42 F44
Bisham 22 C44
Bishampton 29 C35
Bish Mill 7 C23
Bishop Auckland 62 D38
Bishopbridge 52 C46
Bishopbriggs 74 C21
Bishop Burton 59 F45
Bishop Middleham 62 C39
Bishopmill 97 E27
Bishop Monkton 57 C39
Bishop Norton 52 C45
Bishopsbourne 15 B57
Bishops Cannings 20 E36
Bishop's Castle 38 G28
Bishop's Caundle 9 C32
Bishop's Cleeve 29 F35
Bishop's Frome 29 D32
Bishop's Green 33 G52
Bishop's Hull 7 C27
Bishop's Itchington 30 C39
Bishop's Lydeard 7 C27
Bishop's Nympton 7 C23
Bishop's Offley 39 C33
Bishop's Stortford 33 F50
Bishop's Sutton 11 A42
Bishop's Tachbrook 30 B39
Bishop's Tawton 6 B21
Bishopsteignton 5 C25
Bishopstoke 11 C40
Bishopston 17 F21
Bishopstone *Wts.* 21 C38
Bishopstone *E.S.* 13 F50
Bishopstone *H.&W.* 28 D29
Bishopstone *Bkh.* 31 G43
Bishopstone *Wts.* 10 B36
Bishopstrow 20 G34
Bishop Sutton 19 F31
Bishop's Waltham 11 C41
Bishop's Wood 40 E34
Bishopswood 8 C28
Bishopsworth 19 E31
Bishop Thornton 57 C38
Bishopthorpe 58 E41
Bishopton *Str.* 74 C20
Bishopton *Drm* 62 D39
Bishop Wilton 58 D43
Bishton 19 C29
Bisley *Glo.* 20 A35
Bisley *Sry* 22 F45
Bispham 55 E28
Bissoe 2 D13
Bisterne 10 D37
Bisterne Close 10 D38
Bitchfield 42 C45
Bittadon 6 A21
Bittaford 5 E22
Bittering 44 D55
Bitterley 28 A31
Bitterne 11 C40
Bitteswell 41 G41
Bitton 19 E32
Bix 22 C43
Bixter 107 B39
Blaby 41 F41
Blackacre 69 D26
Blackadder 77 E34
Blackawton 5 E23
Blackborough 7 E26
Blackborough End 44 D52
Black Bourton 21 A38
Blackboys 13 D51
Blackbraes *Grm.* 91 B34
Blackbraes *Cen.* 75 C24
Blackbrook 39 B33
Blackburn *Ltn* 75 D25
Blackburn *Lan.* 56 G32
Blackburn *Grm.* 91 B34
Black Callerton 71 G37
Blackcastle 97 F24
Blackchambers 91 B33
Black Clauchrie 67 E18
Black Corries Lodge 80 B18
Blackcraig *D.&G.* 68 E22
Blackcraig *D.&G.* 64 D20
Black Cross 3 B14
Blackden Heath 49 E33
Black Dog 7 E24
Blackdog 91 B35
Blackdown *Dor.* 8 D29
Blackdown *Dev.* 5 C21
Blackfield 11 D40
Blackford *Som.* 9 B32
Blackford *Tay.* 81 G24
Blackford *Cum.* 69 G29
Blackford *Grm.* 98 F32
Blackford *Som.* 19 G29
Blackfordby 41 D39
Blackgang 11 G40
Blackhall 76 C28
Blackhall Colliery 62 B40
Blackhall Rocks 62 C40
Blackham 13 C51
Blackheath *Sry* 22 G46
Blackheath *W.M.* 40 G35
Blackheath *Sfk* 35 A59
Blackheath *Esx* 34 F55
Black Heddon 71 F36
Blackhill *Hgh.* 86 B11
Blackhill *Grm.* 99 D36
Blackhill *Grm.* 99 E36
Blackhillock 98 E30
Blackhills 98 D28
Blackland 20 E35
Blacklunans 82 A27
Black Marsh 38 F29
Blackmill 18 C25
Blackmoor *Som.* 7 D27
Blackmoor *Ham.* 11 A43
Blackmoor Gate 6 A22
Blackmore 23 A51
Blackmore End *Hfs.* 32 G47
Blackmore End *Esx* 34 E53
Black Mount 80 C18
Blackness *Cen.* 75 C26
Blackness *Hgh.* 103 E28
Blackness *Grm.* 91 D32
Blacknest 22 G43
Black Notley 34 F53
Blacko 56 E34
Black Pill 17 F22
Blackpool 55 F28
Blackpool Airport 55 F29
Blackpool Gate 69 F30
Blackridge 75 D24
Blackrock *Gwe.* 28 G27
Blackrock *Str.* 72 D8
Blackrod 48 A31
Blackshaw 69 G26
Blackshaw Head 56 G35
Blacksmith's Corner 34 E56
Blackstone 13 E48
Blackthorn 31 G41
Blackthorpe 34 B54
Blacktoft 58 G44
Blacktop 91 C34
Black Torrington 6 E20
Blacktown 19 C28
Blackwater *Cnw.* 2 D12
Blackwater *Sfk* 35 A60
Blackwater *I.o.W.* 11 F41
Blackwater *Ham.* 22 F44
Blackwaterfoot 66 A14
Blackwell *Dby.* 50 E37
Blackwell *Drm* 62 E38
Blackwell *War.* 30 D38
Blackwell *H.&W.* 29 A35
Blackwell *Dby.* 51 G40
Blackwells End 29 F33
Blackwood *Str.* 75 F23
Blackwood *D.&G.* 68 E24
Blackwood *Gwe.* 18 B27
Blackwood Hill 49 G35
Blacon 48 F29
Bladbean 15 C57
Blades 62 G35
Bladnoch 64 E20
Bladon 31 G40
Blaenannerch 26 D18
Blaenau Dolwyddelan 46 G22
Blaenau Ffestiniog 37 A23
Blaenavon 19 A28
Blaenawey 28 G28
Blaencwm 18 A24
Blaen Dyryn 27 E25
Blaenffos 16 A17
Blaengarw 18 B24
Blaengweche 17 C22
Blaengwrach 18 A24
Blaengwynfi 18 B24
Blaenos 27 E23
Blaenpennal 27 B22
Blaenplwyf 26 A21
Blaenporth 26 D18
Blaenrhondda 18 A25
Blaenwaun 17 B18
Blaen-y-coed 17 B19
Blagdon *Avon* 19 F30
Blagdon *Dev.* 5 D24
Blagdon Hill 8 C28
Blaich 87 G16
Blaina 18 A27
Blair 74 F18
Blairannaich 80 G18
Blair Atholl 81 A24
Blairbuie 73 C16
Blair Drummond 75 A23
Blairgowrie 82 C27
Blairhall 75 B25
Blairhoyle 81 G21
Blairhullichan 81 G20
Blairingone 75 A25
Blairkip 74 G21
Blairlogie 75 A24
Blairmore *Hgh.* 101 B17
Blairmore *Str.* 73 B17
Blairmore *Hgh.* 96 A23
Blairnairn 74 B19
Blairnamarrow 90 B27
Blairpark 74 E18
Blairquhan 67 C19
Blairquhosh 74 B21
Blair's Ferry 73 D15
Blairshinnoch 98 C32
Blairuskinmore 81 G20
Blairvadach 74 B18
Blairydryne 91 D33
Blairythan 91 A35
Blaisdon 29 G32
Blakebrook 29 A33
Blakedown 29 A34
Blake End 33 F52
Blakelaw *Bor.* 77 G33
Blakelaw *T.&W.* 71 G38
Blakemere 28 D29
Blakeney *Nfk* 44 A56
Blakeney *Glo.* 19 A32
Blakenhall *Che.* 39 A33
Blakenhall *Stf.* 40 F34
Blakeshall 40 G34
Blakesley 31 C42
Blanchland 61 A35
Blandford Camp 9 D35
Blandford Forum 9 D34
Blandford St Mary 9 D34
Bland Hill 57 D38
Blanefield 74 C21
Blankney 52 F46
Blar a'Chaorainn 80 A16
Blargie 88 E21
Blarglas 74 B19
Blarmachfoldach 80 A16
Blarnalevoch 95 B17
Blashford 10 D37
Blaston 42 F43
Blathaisbhal 92 D4
Blatherwycke 42 F45
Blawith 55 A28
Blaxhall 35 C59
Blaxton 51 B42
Blaydon 71 G37
Bleadney 19 G30
Bleadon 19 F29
Bleak Hey Nook 49 B35
Blean 25 E57
Bleasby 42 A43
Bleatarn 61 E33
Blebocraigs 83 F30
Bleddfa 28 B27
Bledington 30 F38
Bledlow 22 A43
Bledlow Ridge 22 B43
Blencarn 61 C32
Blencogo 60 B27
Blencow 60 C30
Blendworth 11 C43
Blennerhasset 60 B27
Blervie Castle 97 F26
Bletchingdon 31 G40
Bletchingley 23 F49
Bletchley *Bkh.* 32 E44
Bletchley *Shr.* 39 B32
Bletherston 16 B16
Bletsoe 32 C46
Blewbury 21 C41
Blickling 45 C57
Blidworth 51 G41
Blindburn *Grm.* 99 F35
Blindburn *Nor.* 70 B34
Blindcrake 60 C27
Blindley Heath 23 G49
Blisland 4 C17
Blissford 10 C37
Bliss Gate 29 A33
Blisworth 31 C43
Blithbury 40 C36
Blitterlees 60 A26
Blockley 30 E37
Blofield 45 E59
Blo Norton 34 A56
Blore 40 A37
Blossomfield 30 A37
Blount's Green 40 B36
Bloxham 31 E40
Bloxholm 52 G46
Bloxwich 40 E36
Bloxworth 9 E34
Blubberhouses 57 D37
Blue Anchor *Cnw.* 3 C15
Blue Anchor *Som.* 7 A26
Blue Bell Hill 24 E53
Blundeston 45 F60
Blunham 32 C47
Blunsdon St Andrew 20 B37
Bluntisham 33 A49
Blunts 4 D19
Blyborough 52 C45
Blyford 35 A60
Blymhill 40 D34
Blyth *Not.* 51 D42
Blyth *Nor.* 71 E39
Blyth Bridge 75 F27
Blythburgh 35 A60
Blythe Bridge 40 A35
Blythe Marsh 40 A35
Blyton 52 C44
Boarhills 83 F31
Boarhunt 11 D41
Boarshead 13 C51
Boars Hill 21 A40
Boarstall 31 G42
Boarzell 14 E53
Boasley Cross 6 F20
Boath 96 D21
Boat o' Brig 98 D28
Boat of Garten 89 C25
Bobbing 24 E54
Bobbington 39 F33
Bobbingworth 23 A51
Bocaddon 4 E17
Bochastle 81 G21
Bockhampton 21 D39
Bocking 34 F53
Bocking Churchstreet 34 F53
Boconnoc 4 D17
Boddam *She.* 107 D37
Boddam *Grm.* 99 E37
Boddington 29 F34
Bodedern 46 D19
Bodelwyddan 47 E26
Bodenham *Wts.* 10 B37
Bodenham *H.&W.* 28 C31
Bodenham Moor 28 C31
Bodesbeck 69 C27
Bodewryd 46 C19
Bodfari 47 E26
Bodffordd 46 E20
Bodfuan 36 B19
Bodham Street 45 A57
Bodiam 14 E53
Bodicote 31 E40
Bodieve 3 A15
Bodinnick 4 E17
Bodior 46 E18
Bodle Street Green 13 E52
Bodmin 4 D16
Bodney 44 F54
Bodorgan 46 F19
Bodsham Green 15 C56
Bodwen 4 D16
Bogallan 96 F22
Bogbain 96 G22
Bogbrae 99 F36
Bogbuie 96 F21
Bogend 74 G19
Bogfern 90 C31
Bogfields 90 C31
Bogfold 99 D34
Boghead *Str.* 75 F23
Boghead *Grm.* 98 D32
Boghead *Str.* 68 A22
Boghole Fm 97 F25
Bogmoor 98 C29
Bogniebrae 98 E31
Bognor Regis 12 G45
Bograxie 91 B32
Bogroy 89 B24
Bogside 75 A25
Bogston 90 C29
Bogton 98 D32
Bogue 68 E22
Bohenie 87 F18
Bohortha 3 E14
Bohuntine 87 F18
Boirseam 92 C6
Bojewyan 2 E9
Bolam 62 D37
Bolberry 5 G22
Bolderwood 10 D38
Bold Heath 48 D31
Boldon 71 G39
Boldre 10 E38
Boldron 62 E36
Bole 51 D43
Bolehill 50 G38
Boleigh 2 F10
Boleside 76 G30
Bolfracks 81 C23
Bolgoed 17 D21
Bolham 7 D25
Bolham Water 7 D27
Bolingey 2 C13
Bollington *Che.* 49 E35
Bollington *Che.* 49 D33
Bolney 13 D48
Bolnhurst 32 C46
Bolshan 83 B32
Bolsover 51 E40
Bolsterstone 50 C38
Bolstone 28 E31
Boltby 57 A40
Bolter End 22 B43
Bolton *Cum.* 61 D32
Bolton *Hum.* 58 D43
Bolton *G.M.* 49 B32
Bolton *Ltn* 76 C31
Bolton *Nor.* 71 B36
Bolton Abbey 57 D36
Bolton Bridge 57 D36
Bolton by Bowland 56 E33
Boltonfellend 69 G30
Boltongate 60 B28
Bolton-le-Sands 55 C30
Bolton Low Houses 60 B28
Bolton-on-Swale 62 G38
Bolton Percy 58 E41
Bolton upon Dearne 51 B40
Bolventor 4 C17
Bombie 65 F23
Bomere Heath 38 D30
Bonar Bridge 96 B21
Bonawe 80 D15
Bonawe Quarries 80 D16
Bonby 52 A46
Boncath 16 A17
Bonchester Bridge 70 B31
Bonchurch 11 G41
Bondleigh 6 E22
Bonehill 40 E37
Bo'ness 75 B25
Bonhill 74 C19
Boningale 39 E33
Bonjedward 70 A32
Bonkle 75 E24
Bonnington *Kent* 15 D56
Bonnington *Tay.* 83 D31
Bonnybank 82 G29
Bonnybridge 75 B24
Bonnykelly 99 D34
Bonnyrigg 76 D28
Bonnyton *Grm.* 98 F32
Bonnyton *Tay.* 82 D29
Bonnyton *Tay.* 83 B32
Bonsall 50 G38
Bont 28 G29
Bontddu 37 D22
Bont dolgadfan 37 F24
Bont-goch (Elerch) 37 G22
Bont Newydd 37 C23
Bontnewydd 46 F20
Bontuchel 47 G26
Bonvilston 18 D26
Bon-y-maen 17 E22
Boohay 5 E25
Booker 22 B44
Booley 38 C31
Boor 94 C14
Boosbeck 63 E42
Boot 60 F27
Boothby Graffoe 52 G45
Boothby Pagnell 42 B45
Boothstown 49 B33
Boothtown 57 G36
Boothville 31 B43
Booth Wood 50 A36
Bootle *Mer.* 48 C29
Bootle *Cum.* 54 A27
Booton 45 C57
Boquhan 74 B21
Boraston 28 A31
Bordeaux 3 E17
Borden 24 E54
Bordley 56 C35
Bordon 11 A43
Boreham *Esx* 24 A53
Boreham *Wts.* 20 G34
Boreham Street 13 E52
Borehamwood 22 B47
Boreland *Cen.* 81 D21
Boreland *D.&G.* 69 D27
Boreland *D.&G.* 64 D19
Boreraig 93 F7
Borgh *W.I.* 84 D2
Borgh *W.I.* 92 C4
Borghastan 100 C7
Borgie 102 C22
Borgue *D.&G.* 65 F22
Borgue *Hgh.* 103 F27
Borley 34 D54
Bornais 84 B3
Borness 65 F22
Boroughbridge 57 C39
Borough Green 23 F51
Borras Head 48 G29
Borrowash 41 B39
Borrowby *N.Y.* 63 E43
Borrowby *N.Y.* 57 A40
Borrowdale 60 E28
Borrowfield 91 D34
Borstal 24 E53
Borth 36 G21
Borthwick 76 E29
Borthwickbrae 69 B29
Borthwickshiels 69 B30
Borth-y-Gest 36 B21
Borve 93 G10
Borwick 55 B31
Bosavern 2 E9
Bosbury 29 D32
Boscastle 4 A16
Boscombe *Wts.* 10 A37
Boscombe *Dor.* 10 E37

Boscoppa 4 E16
Bosham 12 F44
Bosherston 16 E15
Bosley 49 F35
Bossa I 58 C43
Bossiney 4 B16
Bossingham 15 C57
Bossington *Ham.* 10 A39
Bossington *Som.* 7 A24
Bostock Green 49 F32
Boston 43 A48
Boston Spa 57 E40
Boswinger 3 D15
Botallack 2 E9
Botany Bay 23 B49
Botarua 92 D3
Botcheston 41 E40
Botesdale 34 A56
Bothal 71 E38
Bothamsall 51 E42
Bothel 60 C27
Bothenhampton 8 E30
Bothwell 75 E23
Botley *Oxf.* 21 A40
Botley *Ham.* 11 C41
Botley *Bkh.* 22 A45
Botloe's Green 29 F32
Botolph 44 E56
Botolph Claydon 31 F43
Botolphs 12 F47
Bottacks 96 E20
Bottesford *Hum.* 52 B45
Bottesford *Lei.* 42 B43
Bottisham 33 B51
Bottomcraig 82 E29
Bottom Head 56 C32
Botusfleming 4 D19
Botwnnog 36 B18
Bough Beech 23 G50
Boughrood 28 E27
Boughspring 19 B31
Boughton *Nmp.* 31 B43
Boughton *Not.* 51 F42
Boughton *Nfk* 44 E52
Boughton Aluph 14 C55
Boughton Green 14 B53
Boughton Lees 15 C56
Boughton Malherbe 14 C54
Boughton Street 15 B56
Boulby 63 E43
Bouldon 38 G31
Boulmer 71 B38
Boulston 16 C15
Boultenstone 90 B29
Boultham 52 F45
Bourn 33 C49
Bournbrook 40 G36
Bourne 42 C47
Bournebridge 23 B51
Bourne End *Bkh.* 22 C44
Bourne End *Hfs.* 22 A46
Bourne End *Bfd.* 32 D45
Bournemouth 10 F36
Bournemouth (Hurn) Airport 10 E37
Bournes Green 20 A35
Bournheath 29 A35
Bournmoor 62 A38
Bournville 40 G36
Bourton *Oxf.* 21 C38
Bourton *Shr.* 38 F31
Bourton *Avon* 19 E29
Bourton *Dor.* 9 A33
Bourton on Dunsmore 31 A40
Bourton-on-the-Hill 30 E37
Bourton-on-the-Water 30 F37
Bousd 78 A8
Boustead Hill 60 A28
Bouth 55 A29
Bouthwaite 57 B37
Bovain 81 D21
Boveney 22 D45
Boveridge 10 C36
Boverton 18 E25
Bovey Tracey 5 C24
Bovingdon 22 A45
Bovinger 23 A51
Bovington Camp 9 F34
Bow *Ork.* 105 B29
Bow *Dev.* 7 E23
Bowbank 61 D35
Bow Brickhill 32 E45
Bowburn 62 C38
Bowcombe 11 F40
Bowd 7 G27
Bowden *Dev.* 5 F24
Bowden *Bor.* 76 G31
Bowden Hill 20 E35
Bowdon 49 D33
Bower 70 E33
Bowerchalke 10 B36
Bower Hinton 8 C30
Bowermadden 103 B28
Bowers Gifford 24 C53
Bowershall 75 A26
Bowertower 103 B28
Bowes 62 E35
Bowgreave 55 E30
Bowland Bridge 55 A30
Bowley 28 C31
Bowlhead Green 12 C45
Bowling 74 C20
Bowling Bank 38 A29
Bowlish 19 G31
Bowmanstead 60 G29
Bowmore 72 E8
Bowness-on-Solway 69 G27
Bowness-on-Windermere 60 G30
Bow of Fife 82 F29
Bowsden 77 F35
Bowside Lodge 102 B24
Bow Street 37 G22
Bowthorpe 45 E57
Bowtrees 75 B24
Box *Wts.* 20 E34
Box *Glo.* 20 A34
Boxbush 29 G33
Box End 32 D45
Boxford *Sfk* 34 D55
Boxford *Brk.* 21 D40
Boxgrove 12 F45
Boxley 14 B53
Boxmoor 22 A46
Boxted *Esx* 34 E55
Boxted *Sfk* 34 C54
Boxted Cross 34 E55
Boxworth 33 B49
Boxworth End 33 B49
Boyden Gate 25 E58
Boydston 74 G20
Boylestone 40 B37
Boyndie 98 C32
Boynton 59 C47
Boysack 83 C31
Boyton *Wts.* 9 A35
Boyton *Cnw.* 6 F19
Boyton *Sfk* 35 D59
Boyton Cross 24 A52
Bozeat 32 C44
Braaid 54 F25
Braal Castle 103 B27
Brabling Green 35 B58
Brabourne 15 C56
Brabourne Lees 15 C56
Brabster 103 B28
Bracadale 85 A9
Braceborough 42 D46
Bracebridge 52 F45
Bracebridge Heath 52 F45
Braceby 42 B46
Bracewell 56 E34
Brachla 88 A21
Brackenber 61 D32
Brackenfield 51 G39
Brackens 99 D33
Bracklach 90 A29
Bracklamore 99 D34
Brackletter 87 F17
Brackley *Nmp.* 31 E41
Brackley *Hgh.* 97 F24
Brackly 73 B14
Bracknell 22 E44
Braco 81 G24
Bracobrae 98 D30
Bracon Ash 45 F57
Bracora 86 E13
Bracorina 86 E13
Bradbourne 50 G37
Bradbury 62 D38
Bradda 54 F23
Bradda East 54 F23
Bradden 31 D42
Bradenham 22 B44
Bradenstoke 20 D35
Bradfield *Dev.* 7 E26
Bradfield *Esx* 35 E57
Bradfield *Nfk* 45 B58
Bradfield *Brk.* 21 D42
Bradfield Combust 34 C54
Bradfield Green 49 G32
Bradfield Heath 35 F57
Bradfield St Clare 34 C55
Bradfield St George 34 C55
Bradford *Dev.* 6 E20
Bradford *Nor.* 77 G37
Bradford *N.Y.* 57 F37
Bradford Abbas 8 C31
Bradford Leigh 20 E34
Bradford-on-Avon 20 E33
Bradford-on-Tone 7 C27
Bradford Peverell 9 E32
Brading 11 F42
Bradley *Hum.* 53 B48
Bradley *Ham.* 21 G42
Bradley *N.Y.* 57 A36
Bradley *W.M.* 40 F35
Bradley *Dby.* 40 A38
Bradley *Stf.* 40 D34
Bradley Green 29 B35
Bradley in the Moors 40 A36
Bradley Stoke 19 C32
Bradmore *Not.* 41 B41
Bradmore *W.M.* 40 F34
Bradninch 7 E25
Bradnop 49 G35
Bradpole 8 E30
Bradshaw 49 A33
Bradstone 6 G19
Bradwall Green 49 F33
Bradwell *Dby.* 50 D37
Bradwell *Bkh.* 32 E44
Bradwell *Esx* 34 F53
Bradwell *Nfk* 45 E60
Bradwell Grove 20 A37
Bradwell-on-Sea 25 A55
Bradwell Waterside 25 A55
Bradworthy 6 D19
Brae *D.&G.* 65 C24
Brae *She.* 107 A39
Brae *Hgh.* 96 A20
Braeantra 96 D21
Braedownie 90 F28
Braefoot 98 E32
Braegrum 82 E25
Braehead *Tay.* 83 B32
Braehead *Ork.* 105 A31
Braehead *Grm.* 98 E29
Braehead *Ork.* 104 B30
Braehead *Str.* 75 E25
Braehead *Str.* 75 G24
Braehoulland 106 E38
Braeleny 81 F22
Braemar 90 D27
Braemore *Hgh.* 95 D17
Braemore *Hgh.* 96 A21
Braemore *Hgh.* 103 E26
Braenaloin 90 D28
Braes of Enzie 98 D29
Braes of Foss 81 B23
Braes of Ullapool 95 B17
Braeswick 104 C31
Braeval 81 G21
Brafferton *N.Y.* 57 B40
Brafferton *Drm* 62 D38
Brafield-on-the-Green 32 C44
Bragar 100 C8
Bragbury End 33 F48
Bragleenbeg 79 E14
Braichmelyn 46 F21
Braides 55 D30
Braidwood 75 F24
Braigo 72 D8
Brailsford 40 A38
Braintree 34 F53
Braiseworth 35 A57
Braishfield 10 B39
Braithwaite *S.Y.* 51 A42
Braithwaite *Cum.* 60 D28
Braithwell 51 C41
Bramber 12 E47
Brambletye 13 C49
Bramcote 41 B40
Bramdean 11 B42
Bramerton 45 E58
Bramfield *Sfk* 35 A59
Bramfield *Hfs.* 33 G48
Bramford 34 D56
Bramhall 49 D34
Bramham 57 E40
Bramhope 57 E38
Bramley *Sry* 22 G46
Bramley *Ham.* 21 F42
Bramley *S.Y.* 51 C40
Bramling 15 B58
Brampford Speke 7 F25
Brampton *Lcn.* 52 D44
Brampton *S.Y.* 51 B39
Brampton *Dby.* 51 E39
Brampton *Cbs.* 32 A47
Brampton *Sfk* 45 G60
Brampton *Cum.* 70 G31
Brampton *Nfk* 45 C58
Brampton Abbotts 28 F31
Brampton Ash 42 G43
Brampton Bryan 28 A29
Brampton-en-le-Morthen 51 D40
Bramshall 40 B36
Bramshaw 10 C38
Bramshill 22 E43
Bramshott 12 C44
Bramwell 8 B30
Branault 79 A11
Brancaster 44 A53
Brancepeth 62 C37
Branchill 97 F26
Branderburgh 98 B28
Brandesburton 59 E47
Brandeston 35 B58
Brand Green 29 F33
Brandis Corner 6 E20
Brandiston 45 C57
Brandon *Sfk* 44 G53
Brandon *Drm* 62 C38
Brandon *War.* 30 A39
Brandon *Lcn.* 42 A44
Brandon *Nor.* 71 B36
Brandon Bank 43 G51
Brandon Creek 44 F52
Brandon Parva 44 E56
Brandsby 58 B41
Brandy Wharf 52 C45
Brane 2 F9
Bran End 33 F52
Branksome 10 E36
Branksome Park 10 E36
Bransby 52 E44
Branscombe 7 G27
Bransford 29 C33
Bransford Bridge 29 C34
Bransgore 10 E37
Branson's Cross 30 A36
Branston *Lcn.* 52 F46
Branston *Lei.* 42 C43
Branston *Stf.* 40 C38
Branston Booths 52 F46
Branstone 11 F41
Brant Broughton 52 G44
Brantham 35 E57
Branthwaite *Cum.* 60 C28
Branthwaite *Cum.* 60 D26
Brantingham 59 G45
Branton *S.Y.* 51 B42
Branton *Nor.* 71 B36
Brantwood 60 G29
Branxholm Bridgend 69 B30
Branxholme 69 B30
Branxton 77 G34
Brassington 50 G38
Brasted 23 F50
Brasted Chart 23 F50
Brathens 91 D32
Bratoft 53 F50
Brattleby 52 D45
Bratton 20 F34
Bratton Clovelly 6 F20
Bratton Fleming 6 B22
Bratton Seymour 9 B32
Braughing 33 F49
Braunston *Nmp.* 31 B41
Braunston *Lei.* 42 E44
Braunstone 41 E41
Braunton 6 B20
Brawby 58 B43
Brawdy 16 B14
Brawl 102 B23
Brawlbin 103 C26
Bray 22 D45
Braybrooke 42 G43
Brayford 6 B22
Brayshaw 56 D33
Bray Shop 4 C19
Brayton 58 F41
Bray Wick 22 C44
Brazacott 4 A18
Breach 15 C57
Breachwood Green 32 F47
Breacleit 100 D7
Breadsall 41 A39
Breadstone 19 A32
Breage 2 F12
Breakon 106 B41
Bream 19 A31
Breamore 10 C37
Brean 19 F28
Breanais 100 E6
Brearton 57 C39
Breascleit 100 D8
Breaston 41 B40
Brechfa 17 A21
Brechin 83 A31
Brecklate 66 B12
Breckles 44 F55
Breckonside 68 C23
Brecon 27 F26
Bredbury 49 C35
Brede 14 F54
Bredenbury 28 C31
Bredfield 35 C58
Bredgar 24 E54
Bredhurst 24 E53
Bredicot 29 C34
Bredon 29 E35
Bredon's Hardwick 29 E34
Bredon's Norton 29 E34
Bredwardine 28 D29
Breedon on the Hill 41 C39
Breibhig 100 D10
Breich 75 D25
Breighton 58 F43
Breinton 28 E30
Bremhill 20 D35
Brenachoil 80 G15
Brenchley 23 G52
Brendon *Dev.* 7 A23
Brendon *Dev.* 6 D19
Brenkley 71 F37
Brent 22 C47
Brent Eleigh 34 D55
Brentford 22 D47
Brentingby 42 D43
Brent Knoll 19 F29
Brent Pelham 33 E49
Brentwood 24 B52
Brenzett 14 E55
Breoch 65 E23
Brereton 40 D36
Brereton Green 49 F33
Brereton Heath 49 F34
Bressingham 44 G56
Bretabister 107 B40
Bretby 40 C38
Bretford 31 A40
Bretforton 30 D36
Bretherdale Head 61 F31
Bretherton 55 G30
Brettenham *Nfk* 44 G55
Brettenham *Sfk* 34 C55
Bretton 48 F29
Brewood 40 E34
Briach 97 F26
Briantspuddle 9 E33
Bricket Wood 22 A47
Bricklehampton 29 D35
Bride 54 C26
Bridekirk 60 C26
Bridell 26 D17
Bridestones 49 F35
Bridestowe 6 G20
Brideswell 98 F31
Bridford 7 G23
Bridge *Cnw.* 2 D12
Bridge *Kent* 15 B57
Bridge End *Bfd.* 32 C45
Bridge End *Lcn.* 42 B47
Bridge End *She.* 107 D39
Bridgefoot *Cum.* 60 D26
Bridgefoot *Cbs.* 33 D50
Bridgehampton 8 B31
Bridge Hewick 57 B39
Bridgemary 11 D41
Bridgemere 39 A32
Bridgend *Str.* 73 A14
Bridgend *Str.* 72 D9
Bridgend *Ltn* 75 C26
Bridgend *M.G.* 18 D25
Bridgend *Grm.* 98 F29
Bridgend *Grm.* 98 F30
Bridgend *Tay.* 82 E27
Bridgend *Tay.* 83 A31
Bridgend *Grm.* 90 D29
Bridgend *Fife* 82 F29
Bridgend *Cum.* 60 E29
Bridgend *Cnw.* 4 E17
Bridgend of Lintrathen 82 B28
Bridge of Alford 90 B31
Bridge of Allan 75 A23
Bridge of Balgie 81 C21
Bridge of Bogendreip 91 D32
Bridge of Brewlands 82 A27
Bridge of Brown 89 B26
Bridge of Cally 82 B27
Bridge of Canny 91 D32
Bridge of Craigisla 82 B28
Bridge of Dee *Grm.* 90 D27
Bridge of Dee *Grm.* 91 D32
Bridge of Dee *D.&G.* 65 D23
Bridge of Don 91 C35
Bridge of Dun 83 B32
Bridge of Dye 91 E32
Bridge of Earn 82 F26
Bridge of Ericht 81 B20
Bridge of Ess 90 D30
Bridge of Feugh 91 D32
Bridge of Forss 103 B26
Bridge of Gairn 90 D29
Bridge of Gaur 81 B20
Bridge of Muchalls 91 D34
Bridge of Orchy 80 D18
Bridge of Tilt 81 A24
Bridge of Tynet 98 C29
Bridge of Walls 107 B38
Bridge of Weir 74 D19
Bridgerule 6 E18
Bridges 38 F29
Bridge Sollers 28 D30
Bridge Street 34 D54
Bridgeton 90 B31
Bridgetown *Som.* 7 B25
Bridgetown *Cnw.* 6 G19
Bridge Trafford 48 E30
Bridgeyate 19 D32
Bridgham 44 G55
Bridgnorth 39 F32
Bridgtown 40 E35
Bridgwater 8 A28
Bridlington 59 C47
Bridport 8 E30
Bridstow 28 F31
Brierfield 56 F34
Brierley *S.Y.* 51 A40
Brierley *H.&W.* 28 C30
Brierley *Glo.* 29 G32
Brierley Hill 40 G34
Brierton 62 D40
Brigehaugh 98 F29
Brigg 52 B46
Brigham *Cum.* 60 C26
Brigham *Hum.* 59 D46

Brighouse 57 G37
Brighstone 10 F39
Brightgate 50 G38
Brighthampton 21 A39
Brightling 13 D52
Brightlingsea 34 G56
Brighton *Cnw.* 3 C14
Brighton *E.S.* 13 F49
Brightons 75 C24
Brightwalton 21 D39
Brightwell *Sfk* 35 D58
Brightwell *Oxf.* 21 B41
Brightwell Baldwin 21 B42
Brignall 62 E36
Brig o'Turk 81 G21
Brigsley 53 B48
Brigsteer 55 A30
Brigstock 42 G45
Brill *Bkh.* 31 G42
Brill *Cnw.* 2 F13
Brilley 28 D28
Brilley Mountain 28 C28
Brimfield 28 B31
Brimington 51 E39
Brimington Common 51 E39
Brimley 5 C23
Brimpsfield 29 G35
Brimpton 21 E41
Brimstage 48 D28
Brind 58 F43
Brindister *She.* 107 D40
Brindister *She.* 107 B38
Brindle 55 G31
Brindley Ford 49 G34
Brineton 40 D34
Bringhurst 42 F44
Brington 32 A46
Brinington 44 B56
Brinkhill 53 E49
Brinkley 33 C51
Brinklow 31 A40
Brinkworth 20 C36
Brinmore 88 B22
Brinscall 56 G32
Brinsley 41 A40
Brinsop 28 D30
Brinsworth 51 D39
Brinton 44 B56
Brinyan 104 D30
Brisco 60 A30
Brisley 44 C55
Brislington 19 D31
Bristol 19 D31
Bristol (Lulsgate) Airport 19 E30
Briston 44 B56
Britannia 56 G34
Britford 10 B37
Brithdir 37 D23
Brithem Bottom 7 D26
Briton Ferry 18 B23
Britwell Salome 21 B42
Brixham 5 E25
Brixton 5 E21
Brixton Deverill 9 A34
Brixworth 31 A43
Brize Norton 21 A38
Broad Blunsdon 20 B37
Broadbottom 49 C35
Broadbridge 11 D43
Broadbridge Heath 12 C47
Broad Campden 30 E37
Broad Chalke 10 B36
Broad Clyst 7 F25
Broadford 86 B12
Broadford Bridge 12 D46
Broadgate 54 A27
Broad Green *Bfd.* 32 D45
Broad Green *H.&W.* 29 C33
Broad Green *Esx* 34 F54
Broadgroves 33 G52
Broadhaugh 69 C30
Broad Haven 16 C14
Broadheath 49 D33
Broad Heath 29 B32
Broadhembury 7 E26
Broadhempston 5 D23
Broad Hill 33 A51
Broad Hinton 20 D36
Broadholme 52 E44
Broadland Row 14 F54
Broadlay 17 D19
Broad Laying 21 E40
Broadley *Lan.* 49 A34
Broadley *Grm.* 98 C29
Broadley Common 23 A50
Broad Marston 30 D37
Broadmayne 9 F33
Broadmeadows 76 G29
Broadmere 21 G42
Broadnymet 7 E23
Broadoak *Dor.* 8 E30
Broad Oak *H.&W.* 28 F30
Broadoak *Kent* 25 E57
Broad Oak *E.S.* 14 E54
Broadoak *E.S.* 13 D52
Broad Oak *Cum.* 60 G27
Broadoak *Dyf.* 17 B21
Broadrashes 98 D29
Broadsea 99 C35
Broadstairs 25 E59
Broadstone *Dor.* 9 E35
Broadstone *Shr.* 38 G31
Broad Street 14 B54
Broadstreet Common 19 C29
Broad Street Green 24 A54
Broad Town 20 D36
Broadwas 29 C33
Broadwater *Hfs.* 33 F48
Broadwater *W.S.* 12 F47
Broadway *Dyf.* 17 D19
Broadway *Dyf.* 17 C18
Broadway *Dyf.* 16 C14
Broadway *Sfk* 35 A59
Broadway *H.&W.* 30 E36
Broadway *Som.* 8 C28
Broadwell *Oxf.* 21 A38
Broadwell *War.* 31 B40
Broadwell *Glo.* 30 F37
Broadwell *Glo.* 28 G31
Broadwell House 61 A34
Broadwey 9 F32
Broadwindsor 8 D30
Broadwood Kelly 6 E22
Broadwoodwidger 6 G20
Brobury 28 D29
Brochel 94 G11
Brochloch 67 D21
Brock 78 C6
Brockbridge 11 C42
Brockdish 35 A58
Brockenhurst 10 D38
Brockfield 58 D42
Brockford Street 34 B56
Brockhall 31 B42
Brockham 22 G47
Brockhampton 28 E31
Brockholes 50 A37
Brockhurst 13 C50
Brocklebank 60 B28
Brocklesby 52 A47
Brockley 19 E30
Brockley Green 34 C54
Brockton *Shr.* 38 G29
Brockton *Shr.* 38 F31
Brockton *Shr.* 38 E28
Brockton *Shr.* 39 E33
Brockweir 19 A31
Brockwood Park 11 B42
Brockworth 29 G34
Brocton 40 D35
Brodick 73 G16
Brodsworth 51 B40
Brogborough 32 E45
Brogyntyn 38 B28
Brokenborough 20 C34
Broken Cross *Che.* 49 E34
Broken Cross *Che.* 49 E32
Bromborough 48 D29
Brome 35 A57
Brome Street 35 A57
Bromeswell 35 C58
Bromfield *Cum.* 60 B27
Bromfield *Shr.* 28 A30
Bromham *Bfd.* 32 C45
Bromham *Wts.* 20 E35
Bromley 23 E50
Bromley Green 14 D55
Brompton *N.Y.* 59 A45
Brompton *Kent* 24 E53
Brompton *N.Y.* 62 G39
Brompton on Swale 62 F37
Brompton Ralph 7 B26
Brompton Regis 7 B25
Bromsash 29 F32
Bromsberrow Heath 29 E33
Bromsgrove 29 A35
Bromstead Heath 40 D34
Bromyard 29 C32
Bromyard Downs 29 C32
Bronaber 37 B22
Brongest 26 D19
Bronington 38 B30
Bronllys 28 E27
Bronnant 27 B22
Bronydd 28 D28
Bron-y-Gaer 17 C18
Bronygarth 38 B28
Brook *Dyf.* 17 D18
Brook *Kent* 15 C56
Brook *Sry* 12 C45
Brook *I.o.W.* 10 F39
Brook *Ham.* 10 C38
Brook *Ham.* 10 B39
Brooke *Lei.* 42 E44
Brooke *Nfk* 45 F58
Brookend 19 B31
Brookhouse 55 C31
Brookhouse Green 49 F33
Brookland 14 E55
Brooklands 65 C23
Brookmans Park 23 A48
Brooks 38 F27
Brooksby 41 D42
Brooks Green 12 D47
Brook Street *W.S.* 13 D48
Brook Street *Esx* 23 B51
Brook Street *Kent* 14 D55
Brook Street *Sfk* 34 D54
Brookthorpe 29 G34
Brookwood 22 F45
Broom *Bfd.* 32 D47
Broom *War.* 30 C36
Broomcroft 38 E31
Broome *Shr.* 38 G29
Broome *H.&W.* 29 A34
Broome *Nfk* 45 F59
Broomedge 49 D33
Broomer's Corner 12 D47
Broome Wood 71 B37
Broomfield *Kent* 25 E57
Broomfield *Esx* 24 A52
Broomfield *Kent* 14 B54
Broomfield *Som.* 7 B27
Broomfield *Grm.* 99 F35
Broomfleet 58 G44
Broomhaugh 71 G36
Broomhead 99 C35
Broomhill 71 C38
Broom Hill 10 D36
Broom of Dalreach 82 F25
Broom's Green 29 E32
Brora 97 A24
Broseley 39 E32
Brotherlee 61 C35
Brothertoft 43 A48
Brotherton 57 G40
Brotton 63 D42
Broubster 103 B26
Brough *Ork.* 104 E29
Brough *Dby.* 50 D37
Brough *She.* 106 E40
Brough *She.* 106 E41
Brough *She.* 107 C41
Brough *Not.* 52 G44
Brough *Cum.* 61 E33
Brough *Hum.* 59 G45
Brough *She.* 107 A41
Broughall 38 A31
Brougham 61 D31
Brough Lodge 106 C41
Brough Sowerby 61 E33
Broughton *N.Y.* 58 B43
Broughton *Lan.* 55 F31
Broughton *N.Y.* 56 D35
Broughton *Lcn.* 52 B45
Broughton *Cbs.* 33 A48
Broughton *Bkh.* 32 D44
Broughton *Oxf.* 31 E40
Broughton *Nmp.* 32 A44
Broughton *G.M.* 49 C34
Broughton *Clw.* 48 F29
Broughton *M.G.* 18 D24
Broughton *Bor.* 75 G26
Broughton *Ork.* 104 B30
Broughton *Ham.* 10 A39
Broughton Astley 41 F41
Broughton Beck 55 A28
Broughton Gifford 20 E34
Broughton Hackett 29 C35
Broughton in Furness 55 A28
Broughton Mills 60 G27
Broughton Moor 60 C26
Broughton Poggs 21 A38
Broughtown 104 B32
Broughty Ferry 83 D30
Browland 107 B38
Brown Candover 11 A41
Brown Edge *Stf.* 49 G35
Brown Edge *Lan.* 48 A29
Brownhill 99 E34
Brownhills *W.M.* 40 E36
Brownhills *Fife* 83 F31
Browniesside 71 A37
Brown Lees 49 G34
Brownlow Heath 49 F34
Brownshill Green 40 G38
Brownston 5 E22
Broxa 63 G45
Broxbourne 23 A49
Broxburn *Ltn* 75 C26
Broxburn *Ltn* 76 C32
Broxholme 52 E44
Broxted 33 F51
Broxton 48 G30
Broxwood 28 C29
Bru 100 C9
Bruachmary 97 G24
Bruan 103 E28
Bruera 48 F30
Bruichladdich 72 D8
Bruisyard 35 B59
Bruisyard Street 35 B59
Brund 50 F36
Brundall 45 E59
Brundish 35 B58
Brundish Street 35 A58
Bruntingthorpe 41 G41
Bruntland 90 A30
Brunton *Fife* 82 E29
Brunton *Nor.* 71 A37
Brushford 7 C24
Brushford Barton 6 E22
Bruton 9 A32
Bryanston 9 D34
Brydekirk 69 F27
Brymbo 48 G28
Bryn *G.M.* 48 B31
Bryn *Shr.* 38 G28
Bryn *W.G.* 18 B24
Bryn *Dyf.* 17 D21
Brynamman 17 C22
Brynberian 16 A16
Bryncae 18 C25
Bryncethin 18 C25
Bryncir 36 A20
Bryn-Coch 18 B23
Bryncroes 36 B17
Bryncrug 36 E21
Bryneglwys 38 A27
Brynford 47 E27
Bryn Gates 48 B31
Bryngwran 46 E19
Bryngwyn *Gwe.* 19 A29
Bryngwyn *Pow.* 28 D27
Bryn-henllan 16 A15
Brynhoffnant 26 C19
Brynmawr 28 G27
Brynmelyn 28 A27
Brynmenyn 18 C25
Brynna 18 C25
Brynog 26 C21
Brynrefail *Gwy.* 46 D20
Brynrefail *Gwy.* 46 F21
Brynsadler 18 D25
Brynsiencyn 46 F20
Brynteg 46 D20
Bryn-y-maen 47 E24
Buaile Nam Bodach 84 D3
Bualintur 85 B9
Bualnaluib 94 C14
Bubbenhall 30 A39
Bubwith 58 F42
Buccleuch 69 B29
Buchan 65 D23
Buchanan Castle 74 B20
Buchanhaven 99 E36
Buchanty 82 E25
Buchlyvie 74 A21
Buckabank 60 B29
Buckby Wharf 31 B41
Buckden *Cbs.* 32 B47
Buckden *N.Y.* 56 B35
Buckenham 45 E59
Buckerell 7 E27
Buckfast 5 D23
Buckfastleigh 5 D22
Buckhaven 76 A29
Buckholm 76 G30
Buckhorn Weston 9 B33
Buckhurst Hill 23 B50
Buckie 98 C29
Buckies 103 B26
Buckingham 31 E42
Buckland *Bkh.* 32 G44
Buckland *Glo.* 30 E36
Buckland *Dev.* 5 F22
Buckland *Sry* 23 F48
Buckland *Oxf.* 21 B39
Buckland *Hfs.* 33 E49
Buckland *Kent* 15 C58
Buckland Brewer 6 C20
Buckland Common 22 A45
Buckland Dinham 20 F33
Buckland Filleigh 6 E20
Buckland in the Moor 5 C23
Buckland Monachorum 4 D20
Buckland Newton 9 D32
Buckland St Mary 8 C28
Buckland-tout-Saints 5 F23
Bucklebury 21 D41
Bucklerheads 83 D30
Bucklers Hard 10 D39
Bucklesham 35 D58
Buckley 48 F28
Buckman Corner 12 D46
Buckminster 42 C44
Bucknall *Stf.* 40 A35
Bucknall *Lcn.* 52 F47
Bucknell *Oxf.* 31 F41
Bucknell *Shr.* 28 A29
Bucksburn 91 C34
Buck's Cross 6 C19
Bucks Green 12 C46
Bucks Hill 22 A46
Bucks Horn Oak 22 G44
Buck's Mills 6 C19
Buckspool 16 E15
Buckton *H.&W.* 28 A29
Buckton *Hum.* 59 B47
Buckton *Nor.* 77 G36
Buckworth 32 A47
Budbrooke 30 B38
Budby 51 F42
Buddon 83 D31
Bude 6 E18
Budlake 7 E25
Budle 77 G37
Budleigh Salterton 7 G26
Budock Water 2 E13
Buerton 39 A32
Bugbrooke 31 C42
Bugle 3 C15
Bugthorpe 58 D43
Buildwas 39 E32
Builth Road 27 C26
Builth Wells 27 D26
Buirgh 92 B6
Bulby 42 C46
Buldoo 103 B25
Bulford 20 G37
Bulford Camp 20 G37
Bulkeley 48 G31
Bulkington *Wts.* 20 F35
Bulkington *War.* 41 G39
Bulkworthy 6 D19
Bull Bay 46 C20
Bulley 29 F33
Bull Green 14 D55
Bullington 21 G40
Bullpot Farm 56 A32
Bull's Green 33 G48
Bullwood 73 C17
Bulmer *Esx* 34 D54
Bulmer *N.Y.* 58 C42
Bulmer Tye 34 E54
Bulphan 24 C52
Bulverhythe 14 G53
Bulwark 99 E35
Bulwell 41 A41
Bulwick 42 F45
Bumble's Green 23 A50
Bun Abhainn Eadarra 100 G7
Bunarkaig 87 F17
Bunbury 48 G31
Bunchrew 96 G22
Bundalloch 86 B14
Buness 106 B42
Bunessan 78 E9
Bungay 45 G59
Bunlarie 73 G13
Bunloit 88 B20
Bun Loyne 87 D17
Bunnahabhainn 72 C9
Bunny 41 C41
Buntait 88 A19
Buntingford 33 F49
Bunwell 45 F57
Bunwell Street 45 F57
Burbage *Wts.* 21 E38
Burbage *Lei.* 41 F40
Burbage *Dby.* 50 E36
Burchett's Green 22 C44
Burcombe 10 A36
Burcot 21 B41
Burcott 32 F44
Burdale 58 C44
Burdocks 12 D46
Bures 34 E54
Bures Green 34 E54
Burford 30 G38
Burgate 34 A56
Burgess Hill 13 E49
Burgh 35 C58
Burgh by Sands 60 A29
Burgh Castle 45 E60
Burghclere 21 E40
Burghead 97 E26
Burghfield 21 E42
Burghfield Common 21 E42
Burghfield Hill 21 E42
Burgh Heath 23 F48
Burghill 28 D30
Burgh le Marsh 53 F51
Burgh next Aylsham 45 C58
Burgh on Bain 53 D48
Burgh St Margaret 45 D59
Burgh St Peter 45 F60
Burghwallis 51 A41
Burham 24 E53
Buriton 11 B43
Burland 48 G31
Burlawn 3 A15
Burleigh 22 D45
Burlescombe 7 D26
Burleston 9 E33
Burley *Ham.* 10 D37
Burley *Lei.* 42 D44
Burleydam 39 A32
Burley Gate 28 D31
Burley in Wharfedale 57 E37
Burley Street 10 D38
Burlingjobb 28 C28
Burlow 13 E51
Burlton 38 C30
Burmarsh 15 D56
Burmington 30 E38
Burn 58 G41
Burnage 49 C34
Burnaston 40 B38
Burnby 58 E44

Burndell 12 F45
Burnend 99 E34
Burneside 61 G31
Burness 104 B32
Burneston 57 A39
Burnett 19 E32
Burnfoot *Bor.* 69 B30
Burnfoot *Bor.* 69 B30
Burnfoot *Hgh.* 102 E24
Burnfoot *Tay.* 82 G25
Burnham *Bkh.* 22 C45
Burnham *Hum.* 52 A46
Burnham Deepdale 44 A54
Burnham Green 33 G48
Burnham Market 44 A53
Burnham Norton 44 A54
Burnham-on-Crouch 25 B55
Burnham-on-Sea 19 G28
Burnham Overy 44 A54
Burnham Thorpe 44 A54
Burnhaven 99 E37
Burnhead *D.&G.* 68 D24
Burnhead *D.&G.* 67 E21
Burnhervie 91 B33
Burnhill Green 39 E33
Burnhope 62 B37
Burnhouse 74 E19
Burniston 63 G46
Burnley 56 F34
Burnmouth 77 D35
Burn Naze 55 E29
Burn of Cambus 81 G23
Burnopfield 62 A37
Burnsall 57 C36
Burnside *Grm.* 91 B33
Burnside *Fife* 82 G27
Burnside *Tay.* 83 C30
Burnside *Str.* 67 B21
Burnside *Ltn* 75 C26
Burnside *She.* 106 E38
Burnside of Duntrune 83 D30
Burnstones 61 A32
Burnswark 69 F27
Burntcliff Top 49 F35
Burnt Houses 62 D37
Burntisland 76 B28
Burnton *Str.* 67 C20
Burnton *Str.* 67 B20
Burntwood 40 D36
Burntwood Green 40 E36
Burnt Yates 57 C38
Burpham *W.S.* 12 F46
Burpham *Sry* 22 F46
Burradon *T.&W.* 71 F38
Burradon *Nor.* 70 C35
Burrafirth 106 A41
Burraland 106 E39
Burras 2 E12
Burravoe *She.* 107 A39
Burravoe *She.* 106 D41
Burrells 61 E32
Burrelton 82 D27
Burridge 11 C41
Burrill 57 A38
Burringham 52 B44
Burrington *Som.* 19 F30
Burrington *Dev.* 6 D21
Burrington *H.&W.* 28 A30
Burrough End 33 C52
Burrough Green 33 C52
Burrough on the Hill 42 D43
Burrow Bridge 8 B29
Burrowhill 22 E45
Burry Port 17 D20
Burscough 48 A30
Burscough Bridge 48 A30
Bursea 58 F44
Burshill 59 E46
Bursledon 11 D40
Burslem 40 A34
Burstall 34 D56
Burstock 8 D30
Burston *Stf.* 40 B35
Burston *Nfk* 45 G57
Burstow 23 G49
Burstwick 59 G48
Burtersett 56 A34
Burtle 19 G29
Burton *Wts.* 20 D34
Burton *Nor.* 77 G37
Burton *Som.* 7 A27
Burton *Mer.* 48 E29
Burton *Che.* 48 F30
Burton *Lcn.* 52 E45
Burton *Dyf.* 16 D15
Burton *Dor.* 10 E37
Burton *Dor.* 9 E32
Burton Agnes 59 C47
Burton Bradstock 8 F30
Burton Coggles 42 C45
Burton Green *Clw.* 48 G29
Burton Green *W.M.* 30 A38
Burton Hastings 41 F40
Burton-in-Kendal 55 B31
Burton in Lonsdale 56 B32
Burton Joyce 41 A42
Burton Latimer 32 A44
Burton Lazars 42 D43
Burton Leonard 57 C39
Burton on the Wolds 41 C41
Burton Overy 41 F42
Burton Pedwardine 42 A47
Burton Pidsea 59 F48
Burton Salmon 57 G40
Burton upon Stather 52 A44
Burton upon Trent 40 C38
Burtonwood 48 C31
Burwardsley 48 G30
Burwarton 38 G31
Burwash 13 D52
Burwash Common 13 D52
Burwash Weald 13 D52
Burwell *Lcn.* 53 E49
Burwell *Cbs.* 33 B51
Burwen 46 C20
Burwick *Ork.* 105 C30
Burwick *She.* 107 C39
Bury *Som.* 7 C25
Bury *G.M.* 49 A33
Bury *W.S.* 12 E46
Bury *Cbs.* 43 G48
Buryas Bridge 2 F10
Bury Green 33 F50
Bury St Edmunds 34 B54
Burythorpe 58 C43
Busbridge 22 G45
Busby *Tay.* 82 E26
Busby *Str.* 74 E21
Buscot 21 B38
Bush Bank 28 C30
Bushbury 40 E35
Bushby 41 E42
Bush Crathie 90 D28
Bushey 22 B46
Bushey Heath 22 B47
Bush Green 45 G58
Bushley 29 E34
Bushton 20 D36
Bussage 20 A34
Busta 107 A39
Butcher's Cross 13 D51
Butcher's Pasture 33 F52
Butcombe 19 E30
Buthill 97 E27
Butleigh 8 A31
Butleigh Wootton 8 A31
Butler's Cross 22 A44
Butler's Hill 41 A41
Butlers Marston 30 C38
Butley 35 C59
Butsfield 62 B36
Butterburn 70 F32
Buttercrambe 58 D43
Butterknowle 62 D36
Butterleigh 7 E25
Butterley 51 G39
Buttermere *Wts.* 21 E39
Buttermere *Cum.* 60 E27
Butters Green 49 G34
Buttershaw 57 G37
Butterstone 82 C26
Butterton 50 G36
Butterwick *Lcn.* 43 A49
Butterwick *N.Y.* 59 B45
Butterwick *N.Y.* 58 B43
Butt Green 49 G32
Buttington 38 E28
Butt Lane 49 G34
Buttonoak 29 A33
Buxhall 34 C55
Buxted 13 D50
Buxton *Nfk* 45 C58
Buxton *Dby.* 50 E36
Buxton Heath 45 C57
Bwlch 28 F27
Bwlch-clawdd 17 A19
Bwlch Derwin 36 A20
Bwlchgwyn 48 G28
Bwlch-llan 26 C21
Bwlchnewydd 17 B18
Bwlchtocyn 36 C18
Bwlch-y-cibau 38 D27
Bwlch-y-ddar 38 C27
Bwlch-y-ffridd 37 F26
Bwlch-y-groes 17 A18
Bwlch-y-sarnau 27 A25
Byers Green 62 C38
Byfield 31 C41
Byfleet 22 E46
Byford 28 D29
Bygrave 33 E48
Byker 71 G38
Bylane End 4 E18
Bylchau 47 F25
Byley 49 F33
Bynea 17 E21
Byrness 70 C33
Bythorn 32 A46
Byton 28 B29
Byworth 12 D45

C

Cabharstadh 100 E9
Cabourne 52 B47
Cabrach *Str.* 72 D10
Cabrach *Grm.* 90 A29
Cackle Street 14 F54
Cacrabank 69 B28
Cadboll 97 D24
Cadbury 7 E25
Cadbury Barton 6 D22
Cadbury Heath 19 D32
Cadder 74 C21
Cadderlie 80 D16
Caddington 32 G46
Caddletown 79 F13
Caddonfoot 76 G30
Cadeby *S.Y.* 51 B41
Cadeby *Lei.* 41 E40
Cadeleigh 7 E24
Cade Street 13 D51
Cadgwith 2 G13
Cadham 82 G28
Cadishead 49 C32
Cadle 17 E22
Cadley 21 E38
Cadmore End 22 B43
Cadnam 10 C39
Cadney 52 B46
Cadole 48 F28
Cadover Bridge 5 D21
Cadoxton *S.G.* 18 E27
Cadoxton *W.G.* 18 B23
Caeathro 46 F20
Cae Ddafydd 36 A21
Caehopkin 27 G23
Caen 103 G26
Caenby 52 D46
Caenby Corner 52 D45
Caeo 17 A22
Caerau *M.G.* 18 B24
Caerau *S.G.* 18 D27
Caerdeon 37 D22
Caer Farchell 16 B13
Caergeiliog 46 E18
Caergwrle 48 G29
Caerhun 47 E23
Caer-Lan 27 G23
Caerleon 19 B29
Caer Llan 19 A30
Caernarfon 46 F20
Caerphilly 18 C27
Caersws 37 F26
Caerwent 19 B30
Caerwys 47 E27
Caethle 36 F21
Caggan 89 C24
Cairinis 92 F4
Cairisiadar 100 D6
Cairminis 92 C5
Cairnargat 98 F30
Cairnbaan 73 A14
Cairnbeathie 90 C31
Cairnbrogie 91 A34
Cairnbulg 99 C36
Cairncross 77 D34
Cairncurran 74 D19
Cairndoon 64 G19
Cairndow 80 F17
Cairne 91 C33
Cairness 99 C36
Cairneyhill 75 B26
Cairney Lodge 82 F29
Cairnhill *Grm.* 91 A35
Cairnhill *Grm.* 98 F32
Cairnie 98 E30
Cairnorrie 99 E34
Cairnryan 64 D16
Cairnsmore 64 D20
Caister-on-Sea 45 D61
Caistor 52 B46
Caistor St Edmund 45 E58
Caistron 70 C35
Cake Street 44 F56
Calanais 100 D8
Calbost 100 F10
Calbourne 11 F40
Calcot 21 D42
Calcott 25 E57
Caldarvan 74 B20
Caldback 106 B41
Caldbeck 60 C29
Caldbergh 57 A36
Caldecote *Cbs.* 42 G47
Caldecote *Cbs.* 33 C49
Caldecote *Hfs.* 33 E48
Caldecote *War.* 41 F39
Caldecott *Lei.* 42 F44
Caldecott *Nmp.* 32 B45
Calderbank 75 D23
Calder Bridge 60 F26
Calderbrook 49 A35
Caldercruix 75 D23
Calderglen 74 E22
Calder Mains 103 C26
Caldermill 74 F22
Calder Vale 55 E31
Caldhame 83 C30
Caldicot 19 C30
Caldwell *Str.* 74 E19
Caldwell *N.Y.* 62 E37
Caldwell *Dby.* 40 D38
Caldy 48 D28
Caledrhydiau 26 C20
Calfsound 104 C31
Calgary 78 B9
Califer 97 F26
California *Cen.* 75 C24
California *Nfk* 45 D61
Calke 41 C39
Callaly 71 C36
Callander 81 G22
Callerton Lane End 71 G37
Callestick 2 C13
Calligarry 86 D12
Callington 4 D19
Callisterhall 69 E28
Callow 28 E30
Callow End 29 D34
Callow Hill *H.&W.* 29 A33
Callow Hill *Wts.* 20 C36
Callows Grave 28 B31
Callyburn 66 A13
Calmore 10 C39
Calmsden 20 A36
Calne 20 D35
Calow 51 E40
Calrossie 96 D23
Calshot 11 D40
Calstock 4 D20
Calstone Wellington 20 E36
Calthorpe 45 B57
Calthwaite 60 B30
Calton *Stf.* 50 G36
Calton *N.Y.* 56 D35
Calveley 48 G31
Calver 50 E38
Calverhall 39 B32
Calver Hill 28 D29
Calverleigh 7 D24
Calverley 57 F37
Calvert 31 F42
Calverton *Bkh.* 31 E43
Calverton *Not.* 41 A41
Calvine 81 A23
Calvo 60 A27
Cam 20 B33
Camasnacroise 79 B14
Camasterach 94 G13
Camastianavaig 85 A10
Camasunary 86 C11
Camault Muir 96 G20
Camb 106 C41
Camber 14 F55
Camberley 22 E44
Camberwell 23 D49
Camblesforth 58 G42
Cambo 71 E36
Cambois 71 E38
Camborne 2 E12
Cambridge *Cbs.* 33 C50
Cambridge *Glo.* 20 A33
Cambridge Airport 33 C50
Cambus 75 A24
Cambusbarron 75 A23
Cambuskenneth 75 A24
Cambuslang 74 D22
Cambusnethan 75 E23
Cambus o'May 90 D29
Camchuart 73 B15
Camden 23 C48
Cameley 19 F31
Camelford 4 B17
Camelon 75 B24
Camelsdale 12 C44
Camer 24 E52
Cameron 74 B19
Camerory 89 A25
Camer's Green 29 E33
Camerton *Som.* 19 F32
Camerton *Cum.* 60 C26
Camghouran 81 B21
Camis Eskan 74 B19
Cammachmore 91 D34
Cammeringham 52 D45
Campbeltown 66 A12
Camperdown 71 F38
Camphouse 79 A10
Campmuir 82 D27
Campsall 51 A41
Camps End 33 D51
Campsey Ash 35 C59
Camps Heath 45 F60
Campton 32 E47
Camptown 70 B32
Camrose 16 C14
Camsail 74 B18
Camserney 81 C23
Camstraddan 74 A19
Camus Croise 86 C12
Camus-luinie 86 B15
Camusnagaul *Hgh.* 87 G16
Camusnagaul *Hgh.* 95 C16
Camusrory 86 E14
Camusteel 94 G13
Camusurich 81 D22
Camusvrachan 81 C21
Canada 10 C38
Candacraig 90 D29
Candlesby 53 F50
Candy Mill 75 F26
Cane End 21 D42
Canewdon 24 B54
Canford Bottom 10 D36
Canford Cliffs 10 F36
Canford Magna 10 E36
Canisbay 103 A29
Cann 9 B34
Cannard's Grave 19 G32
Cann Common 9 B34
Cannich 88 A19
Cannington 8 A28
Cannock 40 D35
Cannock Wood 40 D36
Cannop 28 G31
Canonbie 69 F29
Canon Bridge 28 D30
Canon Frome 29 D32
Canon Pyon 28 D30
Canons Ashby 31 C41
Canon's Town 2 E10
Canterbury *Kent* 15 B57
Canterbury *Grm.* 98 D31
Cantley *S.Y.* 51 B42
Cantley *Nfk* 45 E59
Cantlop 38 E31
Canton 18 D27
Cantray 96 G23
Cantraydoune 96 G23
Cantraywood 96 G23
Cantsfield 56 B32
Canvey Island 24 C53
Canwell Hall 40 E37
Canwick 52 F45
Canworthy Water 4 A17
Caol 87 G16
Caolas 78 C6
Caolasnacon 80 A17
Caolas Scalpaigh 93 B8
Capel *Kent* 23 G52
Capel *Sry* 22 G47
Capel Bangor 37 G22
Capel Betws Lleucu 27 C22
Capel Carmel 36 C17
Capel Coch 46 D20
Capel Curig 46 G22
Capel Cynon 26 D19
Capel Dewi *Dyf.* 26 D20
Capel Dewi *Dyf.* 17 B20
Capel Dewi *Dyf.* 37 G22
Capel Garmon 47 G24
Capel Gwyn *Gwy.* 46 E19
Capel Gwyn *Dyf.* 17 B20
Capel Gwynfe 27 F23
Capel Hendre 17 C21
Capel Isaac 17 B21
Capel Iwan 17 A18
Capel le Ferne 15 D58
Capel Parc 46 D20
Capel Seion 37 G22
Capel St Andrew 35 D59
Capel St Mary 34 E56
Capel St Silin 26 C21
Capel Tygwydd 26 D18
Capeluchaf 36 A19
Capelulo 47 E23
Capel-y-ffin 28 E28
Capenhurst 48 E29
Capernwray 55 B31
Capheaton 71 E36
Caplaw 74 E20
Cappercleuch 69 A28
Capplegill 69 C27
Capstone 24 E53
Capton 5 E24
Caputh 82 C26
Carbellow 68 A22
Carbeth 74 C21
Carbis Bay 2 E11
Carbost *Hgh.* 85 A9
Carbost *Hgh.* 93 G10
Carbrooke 44 E55
Carburton 51 E41
Carcary 83 B32
Carclew 2 E13
Carco 68 B23
Car Colston 42 A43
Carcroft 51 B41
Cardenden 76 A28
Cardeston 38 D29
Cardiff 18 D27
Cardiff Airport 18 E26
Cardigan 26 D17
Cardington *Shr.* 38 F30
Cardington *Bfd.* 32 D46
Cardinham 4 D16
Cardno 99 C35
Cardoness 65 E21

Cardow 97 G27
Cardrona 76 G28
Cardross 74 C19
Cardurnock 60 A27
Careby 42 D46
Careston 83 B31
Carew 16 D16
Carew Cheriton 16 D16
Carew Newton 16 D16
Carey 28 E31
Carfrae 76 D31
Cargen 65 C25
Cargenbridge 65 C25
Cargill 82 D27
Cargo 60 A29
Cargo Fleet 63 D41
Cargreen 4 D20
Carham 77 G33
Carhampton 7 A25
Carharrack 2 D13
Carie *Tay.* 81 D22
Carie *Tay.* 81 B22
Carines 2 C13
Carisbrooke 11 F40
Cark 55 B29
Carkeel 4 D20
Carlabhagh 100 C8
Carland Cross 3 C14
Carlby 42 D46
Carlecotes 50 B37
Carleton *Cum.* 60 A30
Carleton *W.Y.* 57 G40
Carleton *N.Y.* 56 E35
Carleton *Lan.* 55 E29
Carleton Fishery 66 E16
Carleton Forehoe 44 E56
Carleton Rode 44 F56
Carlingcott 19 F32
Carlin How 63 E42
Carlisle 60 A29
Carlops 75 E27
Carlton *Drm* 62 D39
Carlton *Lei.* 41 E39
Carlton *Not.* 41 A41
Carlton *S.Y.* 51 B39
Carlton *Sfk* 35 B59
Carlton *Cbs.* 33 C52
Carlton *Bfd.* 32 C45
Carlton *N.Y.* 58 G42
Carlton *W.Y.* 57 G39
Carlton *N.Y.* 57 A36
Carlton *N.Y.* 58 A42
Carlton Colville 45 G61
Carlton Curlieu 41 F42
Carlton Husthwaite 57 B40
Carlton in Cleveland 63 F41
Carlton in Lindrick 51 D41
Carlton-le-Moorland 52 G44
Carlton Miniott 57 A39
Carlton-on-Trent 51 F43
Carlton Scroop 42 A45
Carluke 75 E24
Carlyon Bay 4 E16
Carmacoup 68 A23
Carmarthen 17 B19
Carmel *Dyf.* 17 C21
Carmel *Clw.* 47 E27
Carmel *Gwy.* 46 D19
Carmel *Gwy.* 46 G20
Carmont 91 E33
Carmore 96 B23
Carmunnock 74 E22
Carmyle 74 D22
Carmyllie 83 C31
Carn 72 E8
Carnaby 59 C47
Carnach 87 B16
Carnassarie 79 G14
Carnbee 83 G31
Carnbo 82 G26
Carn Brea 2 D12
Carn Dearg 94 D13
Carnduncan 72 D8
Carne 3 E15
Carnforth 55 B30
Carnhell Green 2 E12
Carnichal 99 D35
Carnmore 72 F9
Carno 37 F25
Carnoch *Hgh.* 97 G24
Carnoch *Hgh.* 88 A19
Carnoch *Hgh.* 95 F18
Carnock 75 B26
Carnon Downs 3 D14
Carnousie 98 D32
Carnoustie 83 D31
Carnwath 75 F25
Carnyorth 2 E9
Carperby 62 G36
Carradale 73 G13
Carragrich 93 B7
Carrbridge 89 B24
Carrefour Selous 3 G17
Carreglefn 46 D19
Carrick *Str.* 73 B14
Carrick *Str.* 73 A17
Carrick *Fife* 83 E30
Carriden 75 B25
Carrine 66 C12
Carrington *G.M.* 49 C33
Carrington *Lcn.* 53 G49
Carrington *Ltn* 76 D28
Carroch 68 D22
Carrog 38 A27
Carroglen 81 E23
Carrol 97 A24
Carron *Grm.* 98 E28
Carron *Cen.* 75 B24
Carron *Str.* 73 A15
Carron Bridge 75 B23
Carronbridge 68 D24
Carronshore 75 B24
Carrot 83 C30
Carr Shield 61 B33
Carrutherstown 69 F26
Carruthmuir 74 D19
Carr Vale 51 F40
Carrville 62 B38
Carry 73 D15
Carsaig 79 E11
Carscreugh 64 D18
Carse 73 D13
Carsegowan 64 E19
Carse of Ardesier 97 F24
Carseriggan 64 D18
Carsethorn 65 E25
Carsgoe 103 B27
Carshalton 23 E48
Carsington 50 G38
Carsluith 64 E20
Carsphairn 67 D21
Carstairs 75 F25
Carstairs Junction 75 F25
Carswell Marsh 21 B39
Carter's Clay 10 B38
Carterton 21 A38
Carterway Heads 62 A36
Carthew 3 C15
Carthorpe 57 A38
Cartington 71 C36
Cartmel 55 B29
Cartmel Fell 55 A30
Carway 17 D20
Cascob 28 B28
Cashel 74 A20
Cashlie 81 C20
Cashmoor 9 C35
Cassencarie 64 E20
Cassington 31 G40
Cassop 62 C39
Castellau 18 C26
Castell Gorfod 17 B18
Castell Howell 26 D20
Castell-y-bwch 19 B28
Casterton 56 A32
Castle Acre 44 D54
Castle Ashby 32 C44
Castle Bank 40 C35
Castlebay (Bagh A Chaisteil) 84 E2
Castle Bolton 62 G35
Castle Bromwich 40 G37
Castle Bytham 42 D45
Castlebythe 16 B16
Castle Caereinion 38 E27
Castle Camps 33 D52
Castle Carrock 61 A31
Castle Cary 9 A32
Castlecary 75 C23
Castle Combe 20 D34
Castlecraig *Hgh.* 97 E24
Castlecraig *Bor.* 75 F27
Castle Donington 41 C40
Castle Douglas 65 D23
Castle Eaton 20 B37
Castle Eden 62 C40
Castle End 30 A38
Castlefairn 68 E23
Castleford 57 G40
Castle Frome 29 D32
Castle Gresley 40 D38
Castle Heaton 77 F35
Castle Hedingham 34 E53
Castle Hill 35 D57
Castle Kennedy 64 E16
Castle Leod 96 F20
Castle Levan 74 C18
Castle Madoc 27 E25
Castlemartin 16 E15
Castlemilk *Str.* 74 E21
Castlemilk *D.&G.* 69 F27
Castle Morris 16 A14
Castlemorton 29 E33
Castle O'er 69 D28
Castle Rising 44 C52
Castleside 62 B36
Castle Stuart 96 F23
Castlethorpe 31 D43
Castleton *Dby.* 50 D37
Castleton *Str.* 73 B14
Castleton *N.Y.* 63 F42
Castleton *Grm.* 98 D32
Castleton *Gwe.* 19 C28
Castleton *Lan.* 49 A34
Castleton *Bor.* 70 D31
Castleton *Tay.* 82 C29
Castletown *Drm* 62 A39
Castletown *Hgh.* 96 G23
Castletown *Hgh.* 103 B27
Castletown *I.o.M.* 54 G24
Castleweary 69 C29
Castlewigg 64 F20
Caston 44 F55
Castor 42 F47
Castramont 65 D21
Cat and Fiddle Inn 49 E35
Catbrain 19 C31
Catchall 2 F10
Catcleugh 70 C33
Catcliffe 51 D40
Catcott 8 A29
Caterham 23 F49
Catesby 31 C41
Catfield 45 C59
Catfirth 107 B40
Catford 23 D49
Catforth 55 F30
Cathedine 28 F27
Catherington 11 C42
Catherton 29 A32
Catlow 56 F34
Catlowdy 69 F30
Catmore 21 D40
Caton *Lan.* 55 C31
Caton *Dev.* 5 C23
Cator Court 5 C22
Catrine 67 A21
Catsfield 14 F53
Catshill 29 A35
Cattadale 72 E9
Cattal 57 D40
Cattawade 35 E57
Catterall 55 E30
Catterick 62 G38
Catterick Camp 62 G37
Catterlen 61 C30
Catterline 91 F34
Catterton 57 E40
Catthorpe 31 A41
Cattistock 8 D31
Catton *Nor.* 61 A34
Catton *Nfk* 45 D58
Catton *N.Y.* 57 B39
Catton Hall 40 D38
Catwick 59 E47
Catworth 32 A46
Caudworthy 4 A18
Caulcott 31 F40
Cauldcots 83 C32
Cauldhame *Cen.* 81 G24
Cauldhame *Cen.* 74 A22
Cauldon 40 A36
Cauldside 69 E30
Caulkerbush 65 E25
Caundle Marsh 9 C32
Caunsall 40 G34
Caunton 51 F43
Causeway End *D.&G.* 64 D19
Causeway End *Esx* 33 G52
Causewayhead *Cen.* 75 A24
Causewayhead *Cum.* 60 A26
Causeyend 91 B35
Causey Park 71 D37
Cautley 61 G32
Cavendish 34 D53
Cavenham 34 B53
Cavens 65 E25
Caversfield 31 F41
Caversham 22 D43
Caverswall 40 A35
Cawdor 97 F24
Cawkwell 53 D48
Cawood 58 F41
Cawsand 4 F20
Cawston 45 C57
Cawthorne 50 B38
Cawthorpe 42 C46
Cawton 58 B42
Caxton 33 C48
Caxton Gibbet 33 C48
Caynham 28 A31
Caythorpe *Lcn.* 42 A45
Caythorpe *Not.* 41 A42
Cayton 59 A46
Ceallan 92 F4
Ceann A Bhaigh *W.I.* 92 C6
Ceann A Bhaigh *W.I.* 92 E3
Ceann Loch Shiophoirt 100 F8
Cearsiadar 100 E9
Ceathramh Meadhanach 92 D3
Cedig 37 C25
Cefn-brith 47 G25
Cefn-caer-Ferch 36 A19
Cefn Cantref 27 F26
Cefn Coch 47 G27
Cefn-coch 37 C26
Cefn-coed-y-cymmer 18 A26
Cefn Cribwr 18 C24
Cefn Cross 18 C24
Cefn-ddwysarn 37 B25
Cefndeuddwr 37 C23
Cefn Einion 38 G28
Cefneithin 17 C21
Cefn-gorwydd 27 D24
Cefn-gwyn 38 G27
Cefn Hengoed 18 B27
Cefn-mawr 38 A28
Cefn-y-bedd 48 G29
Cefn-y-pant 16 B17
Ceidio 46 D19
Ceidio Fawr 36 B18
Ceint 46 E20
Cellan 27 D22
Cellardyke 83 G31
Cellarhead 40 A35
Cemaes 46 C19
Cemmaes 37 E24
Cenarth 26 D18
Cennin 36 A20
Ceos 100 E9
Ceres 82 F29
Cerne Abbas 9 D32
Cerney Wick 20 B36
Cerrigceinwen 46 E19
Cerrigydrudion 37 A25
Cessford 70 A33
Chaceley 29 E34
Chacewater 2 D13
Chackmore 31 E42
Chacombe 31 D40
Chadderton 49 B34
Chaddesden 41 B39
Chaddesley Corbett 29 A34
Chaddleworth 21 D40
Chadlington 30 F38
Chadshunt 30 C39
Chad Valley 40 G36
Chadwell 42 C43
Chadwell St Mary 24 D52
Chadwick End 30 A38
Chaffcombe 8 D29
Chagford 7 G23
Chailey 13 E49
Chainhurst 14 C53
Chalbury Common 10 D36
Chaldon 23 F49
Chaldon Herring or East Chaldon 9 F33
Chale 11 G40
Chale Green 11 F40
Chalfont Common 22 B46
Chalfont St Giles 22 B45
Chalfont St Peter 22 B46
Chalford 20 A34
Chalgrove 21 B42
Chalk 24 D52
Challacombe 6 A22
Challoch 64 D19
Challock 14 B55
Chalmington 8 D31
Chalton *Bfd.* 32 F46
Chalton *Ham.* 11 C43
Chalvington 13 F51
Champany 75 C26
Chandler's Cross 22 B46
Chandler's Ford 11 B40
Channerwick 107 E39
Chantry *Sfk* 35 D57
Chantry *Som.* 20 G33
Chapel 76 A28
Chapel Allerton *Som.* 19 F29
Chapel Allerton *W.Y.* 57 F39
Chapel Amble 3 A15
Chapelbank 82 F25
Chapel Brampton 31 B43
Chapel Chorlton 39 B33
Chapel Cross 13 D52
Chapeldonan 67 C17
Chapel End 41 F39
Chapel-en-le-Frith 50 D36
Chapel Fields 30 A39
Chapelgate 43 C50
Chapel Haddlesey 58 G41
Chapelhall 75 D23
Chapel Hill *Gwe.* 19 B31
Chapelhill *Hgh.* 97 D24
Chapel Hill *Grm.* 99 F36
Chapel Hill *Lcn.* 52 G47
Chapelhill *Tay.* 82 D26
Chapelhill *Tay.* 82 F28
Chapelknowe 69 F28
Chapel Lawn 28 A29
Chapel-le-Dale 56 B33
Chapel of Garioch 91 A33
Chapel Rossan 64 F16
Chapel Row 21 E41
Chapel Stile 60 F29
Chapel St Leonards 53 E51
Chapelton *Tay.* 83 C32
Chapelton *Grm.* 91 E34
Chapelton *Str.* 74 F22
Chapeltown *Lan.* 49 A33
Chapeltown *Cum.* 69 F30
Chapeltown *S.Y.* 51 C39
Chapeltown *Grm.* 90 A28
Chapel Town 3 C14
Chapmanslade 20 G33
Chapman's Well 6 F19
Chapmore End 33 G49
Chappel 34 F54
Chard 8 D29
Chard Junction 8 D29
Chardstock 8 D28
Charfield 19 B32
Charing 14 C55
Charing Heath 14 C55
Charingworth 30 D37
Charlbury 30 G39
Charlcombe 20 E33
Charlcutt 20 D35
Charlecote 30 C38
Charles 6 B22
Charleshill 22 G44
Charleston 82 C29
Charlestown *Dor.* 9 G32
Charlestown *Grm.* 91 C35
Charlestown *Hgh.* 94 D14
Charlestown *Fife* 75 B26
Charlestown *Hgh.* 96 G22
Charlestown *Cnw.* 4 E16
Charlestown *Grm.* 99 C36
Charlestown of Aberlour 98 E28
Charles Tye 34 C55
Charlesworth 49 C35
Charlinch 8 A28
Charlton *Nor.* 70 E33
Charlton *Wts.* 20 F37
Charlton *Som.* 19 F32
Charlton *Wts.* 20 C35
Charlton *Hfs.* 32 F47
Charlton *H.&W.* 29 D36
Charlton *Nmp.* 31 E41
Charlton *G.L.* 23 D50
Charlton *Oxf.* 21 C40
Charlton *Ham.* 21 G39
Charlton *W.S.* 12 E44
Charlton *Wts.* 9 B34
Charlton Abbots 30 F36
Charlton Adam 8 B31
Charlton-All-Saints 10 B37
Charlton Horethorne 9 B32
Charlton Kings 29 F35
Charlton Mackrell 8 B31
Charlton Marshall 9 D34
Charlton Musgrove 9 A33
Charlton-on-Otmoor 31 G41
Charlwood 23 G48
Charminster 9 E32
Charmouth 8 E29
Charndon 31 F42
Charney Bassett 21 B39
Charnock Richard 48 A31
Charsfield 35 C58
Chart Corner 14 C53
Charter Alley 21 F41
Charterhouse 19 F30
Charterville Allotments 30 G39
Chartham 15 B56
Chartham Hatch 15 B56
Chartridge 22 A45
Chart Sutton 14 C53
Charwelton 31 C41
Chase End Street 29 E33
Chase Terrace 40 D36
Chasetown 40 E36
Chastleton 30 F38
Chasty 6 E19
Chatburn 56 E33
Chatcull 39 B33
Chatham 24 E53
Chathill 71 A37
Chattenden 24 D53
Chatteris 43 G49
Chattisham 34 D56
Chatto 70 B33
Chatton 71 A36
Chawleigh 7 D23
Chawley 21 A40
Chawston 32 C47
Chawton 11 A43
Cheadle *Stf.* 40 A35
Cheadle *G.M.* 49 D34
Cheadle Hulme 49 D34
Cheam 23 E48
Cheapside 22 E45
Chearsley 21 A42
Chebsey 40 C34
Checkendon 21 C42
Checkley *Stf.* 40 B36
Checkley *Che.* 39 A33
Checkley *H.&W.* 28 E31
Chedburgh 34 C53
Cheddar 19 F30
Cheddington 32 G44
Cheddleton 49 G35
Cheddon Fitzpaine 8 B28
Chedglow 20 B35
Chedgrave 45 F59
Chedington 8 D30
Chediston 35 A59

Chedworth 30 G36
Chedzoy 8 A29
Cheeklaw 77 E33
Cheesden 49 A34
Cheeseman's Green 15 D56
Cheetham Hill 49 B34
Cheldon 7 D23
Chelford 49 E34
Chellaston 41 B39
Chellington 32 C45
Chelmarsh 39 G32
Chelmondiston 35 E58
Chelmorton 50 F36
Chelmsford 24 A52
Chelsfield 23 E50
Chelsham 23 F49
Chelsworth 34 D55
Cheltenham 29 F35
Chelveston 32 B45
Chelvey 19 E30
Chelwood 19 E32
Chelwood Gate 13 D49
Chelworth 20 B35
Cheney Longville 38 G29
Chenies 22 B46
Chepstow 19 B31
Cherhill 20 D36
Cherington *Glo.* 20 B34
Cherington *War.* 30 E38
Cheriton *Dev.* 7 A23
Cheriton *W.G.* 17 E20
Cheriton *Kent* 15 D57
Cheriton *Dyf.* 16 E15
Cheriton *Ham.* 11 B41
Cheriton Bishop 7 F23
Cheriton Cross 7 F23
Cheriton Fitzpaine 7 E24
Cherrington 39 D32
Cherry Burton 59 E45
Cherry Hinton 33 C50
Cherry Willingham 52 E46
Chertsey 22 E46
Cheselbourne 9 E33
Chesham 22 A45
Chesham Bois 22 B45
Cheshunt 23 A49
Cheslyn Hay 40 E35
Chessington 22 E47
Chester 48 F29
Chesterblade 19 G32
Chesterfield *Dby.* 51 E39
Chesterfield *Stf.* 40 E36
Chester-le-Street 62 A38
Chesters *Bor.* 70 B32
Chesters *Bor.* 70 A31
Chesterton *Shr.* 39 F33
Chesterton *Oxf.* 31 F41
Chesterton *Cbs.* 42 F47
Chesterton *Stf.* 40 A34
Chesterton *Cbs.* 33 C50
Chesterton Green 30 C39
Chestfield 25 E57
Cheswardine 39 C33
Cheswick 77 F36
Chetnole 8 D31
Chettiscombe 7 D25
Chettisham 43 G51
Chettle 9 C35
Chetton 39 F32
Chetwode 31 F42
Chetwynd Aston 39 D33
Cheveley 33 B52
Chevening 23 F50
Cheverell's Green 32 G46
Chevington 34 C53
Chevington Drift 71 D38
Chevithorne 7 D25
Chew Magna 19 E31
Chew Stoke 19 E31
Chewton Keynsham 19 E32
Chewton Mendip 19 F31
Chicheley 32 D44
Chichester 11 D43
Chickerell 9 F32
Chickering 35 A58
Chicklade 9 A34
Chickney 33 F51
Chicksands 32 E47
Chidden 11 C42
Chiddingfold 12 C45
Chiddingly 13 E51
Chiddingstone 23 G50
Chiddingstone Causeway 23 G51
Chiddingstone Hoath 23 G51
Chideock 8 E29
Chidham 11 D43
Chieveley 21 D40
Chignall Smealy 33 G52
Chignall St James 33 G52
Chigwell 23 B50
Chigwell Row 23 B50
Chilbolton 21 G39
Chilcomb 11 B40
Chilcombe 8 E31
Chilcompton 19 F32
Chilcote 40 D38
Childerditch 24 C52
Childer Thornton 48 E29
Child Okeford 9 C34
Childrey 21 C39
Child's Ercall 39 C32
Childswickham 30 E36
Childwall 48 D30
Childwick Green 32 G47
Chilfrome 8 E31
Chilgrove 12 E44
Chilham 15 B56
Chillaton 6 G20
Chillenden 15 B58
Chillerton 11 F40
Chillesford 35 C59
Chillingham 71 A36
Chillington *Dev.* 5 F23
Chillington *Som.* 8 C29
Chilmark 9 A35
Chilson 30 G39
Chilsworthy *Cnw.* 4 C20
Chilsworthy *Dev.* 6 E19
Chilthorne Domer 8 C31
Chilton *Drm* 62 C38
Chilton *Bkh.* 31 G42
Chilton *Oxf.* 21 C40
Chilton Candover 11 A41
Chilton Cantelo 8 B31
Chilton Foliat 21 D39
Chilton Polden 8 A29
Chilton Street 34 D53
Chilton Trinity 8 A28
Chilvers Coton 41 F39
Chilworth *Sry* 22 G46
Chilworth *Ham.* 11 C40
Chimney 21 A39
Chineham 21 F42
Chingford 23 B49
Chinley 50 D36
Chinley Head 50 D36
Chinnor 22 A43
Chipchase Castle 70 F34
Chipley Park 7 C27
Chipnall 39 B33
Chippenham *Cbs.* 33 B52
Chippenham *Wts.* 20 D34
Chipperfield 22 A46
Chipping *Lan.* 56 E32
Chipping *Hfs.* 33 E49
Chipping Campden 30 E37
Chipping Hill 34 G53
Chipping Norton 30 F39
Chipping Ongar 23 A51
Chipping Sodbury 20 C33
Chipping Warden 31 D40
Chipstable 7 C26
Chipstead *Sry* 23 F48
Chipstead *Kent* 23 F50
Chirbury 38 F28
Chirk 38 B28
Chirmorrie 64 C17
Chirnside 77 E34
Chirnsidebridge 77 E34
Chirton 20 F36
Chisbury 21 E38
Chiscan 66 B12
Chiselborough 8 C30
Chiseldon 20 D37
Chislehampton 21 B41
Chislehurst 23 D50
Chislet 25 E57
Chiswell Green 22 A47
Chiswick 23 D48
Chisworth 49 C35
Chithurst 12 D44
Chittering 33 B50
Chitterne 20 G35
Chittlehamholt 6 C22
Chittlehampton 6 C22
Chittoe 20 E35
Chivelstone 5 G23
Chobham 22 E45
Choicelee 77 E33
Cholderton 21 G38
Cholesbury 22 A45
Chollerton 70 F35
Cholsey 21 C41
Cholstrey 28 C30
Cholwell *Dev.* 4 C20
Cholwell *Avon* 19 F32
Chop Gate 63 F41
Chopwell 62 A36
Chorley *Che.* 48 G31
Chorley *Lan.* 48 A31
Chorley *Stf.* 40 D36
Chorley *Shr.* 39 G32
Chorleywood 22 B45
Chorlton 49 G33
Chorlton-cum-Hardy 49 C34
Chorlton Lane 38 A30
Chowley 48 G30
Chrishall 33 E50
Chrishall Grange 33 D50
Chrisswell 74 C18
Christchurch *Gwe.* 19 C29
Christchurch *Glo.* 28 G31
Christchurch *Dor.* 10 E37
Christchurch *Cbs.* 43 F50
Christian Malford 20 D35
Christleton 48 F30
Christmas Common 22 B43
Christon 19 F29
Christon Bank 71 A37
Christow 7 G23
Chryston 74 C22
Chudleigh 5 C24
Chudleigh Knighton 5 C24
Chulmleigh 6 D22
Chunal 50 C36
Church 56 G33
Churcham 29 G33
Church Aston 39 D33
Church Brampton 31 B43
Church Broughton 40 B37
Church Common 35 C59
Church Crookham 22 F43
Churchdown 29 F34
Church Eaton 40 D34
Churchend *Avon* 20 B33
Church End *Ham.* 21 F42
Churchend *Esx* 25 B55
Church End *Hum.* 59 D46
Church End *Cbs.* 33 A49
Church End *Hfs.* 32 G47
Church End *Bfd.* 32 F45
Church End *Bfd.* 32 E47
Churchend *Esx* 33 F51
Church End *Esx* 33 F52
Church End *Cbs.* 33 C50
Church End *Esx* 33 D51
Church End *Cbs.* 43 E49
Church End *Lcn.* 43 B48
Church End *War.* 40 F38
Church End *Lcn.* 53 C50
Church End *Wts.* 20 D36
Church Enstone 30 F39
Church Fenton 58 F41
Churchgate 23 A49
Churchgate Street 33 G50
Church Green 7 F27
Church Gresley 40 D38
Church Hanborough 31 G40
Church Houses 63 G42
Churchill *Avon* 19 F30
Churchill *Oxf.* 30 F38
Churchill *H.&W.* 29 A34
Churchill *H.&W.* 29 C35
Churchingford 7 D27
Church Knowle 9 F35
Church Langton 42 F43
Church Lawford 31 A40
Church Lawton 49 G34
Church Leigh 40 B36
Church Lench 30 C36
Church Minshull 49 F32
Church Norton 12 G44
Churchover 41 G40
Church Preen 38 F31
Church Pulverbatch 38 E30
Churchstanton 7 D27
Church Stoke 38 F28
Churchstow 5 F23
Church Stowe 31 C42
Church Street 24 D53
Church Stretton 38 F30
Churchthorpe 53 C49
Churchtown *I.o.M.* 54 D25
Churchtown *Dev.* 6 A22
Churchtown *Mer.* 48 A29
Churchtown *Lan.* 55 E30
Church Village 18 C26
Church Warsop 51 F41
Churnsike Lodge 70 F32
Churston Ferrers 5 E24
Churt 12 C44
Churton 48 G30
Churwell 57 G38
Chute Cadley 21 F39
Chute Standen 21 F39
Chwilog 36 B20
Chyandour 2 E10
Cilan Uchaf 36 C18
Cilcain 47 F27
Cilcennin 26 B21
Cilfrew 18 A23
Cilgerran 26 D17
Cilgwyn *Dyf.* 27 F23
Cilgwyn *Dyf.* 16 A16
Ciliau-Aeron 26 C20
Cille Bhrighde 84 C3
Cille Pheadair 84 C3
Cilmery 27 C25
Cilrhedyn 17 A18
Cilrhedyn Bridge 16 A15
Ciltalgarth 37 A24
Cilwendeg 17 A18
Cilybebyll 18 A23
Cilycwm 27 D23
Cinderford 29 G32
Cippyn 26 D17
Cirbhig 100 C7
Cirencester 20 A35
City Dulas 46 D20
City of London 23 D49
City of Westminster 23 C48
Clabhach 78 B7
Clachaig 73 B17
Clachan *Str.* 73 E13
Clachan *W.I.* 92 G3
Clachan *Hgh.* 86 A11
Clachan *Str.* 80 F17
Clachan *Str.* 79 C14
Clachandhu 79 D10
Clachaneasy 64 C19
Clachanmore 64 F16
Clachan of Campsie 74 C21
Clachan of Glendaruel 73 B15
Clachan-Seil 79 F13
Clachanturn 90 D28
Clach-bhreac 73 C13
Clachnabrain 82 A29
Clachnaharry 96 G22
Clachtoll 101 F16
Clackmannan 75 A24
Clacton-on-Sea 35 G57
Cladach A Chaolais 92 E3
Cladach Chircebost 92 E3
Cladich 80 E16
Claggan *Hgh.* 87 G17
Claggan *Hgh.* 79 C12
Claigan 93 F8
Claines 29 C34
Clandown 19 F32
Clanfield *Ham.* 11 C42
Clanfield *Oxf.* 21 A38
Clannaborough Barton 7 E23
Clanville 21 G38
Claonaig 73 E14
Claonairigh 80 G16
Claonel 96 A21
Clapgate 10 D36
Clap Gate 57 E39
Clapham *N.Y.* 56 C33
Clapham *Bfd.* 32 C46
Clapham *W.S.* 12 F46
Clapham *G.L.* 23 D48
Clapham Hill 25 E56
Clappers 77 E35
Clappersgate 60 F29
Clapton 8 D29
Clapton-in -Gordano 19 D30
Clapton-on-the-Hill 30 G37
Clapworthy 6 C22
Clarbeston 16 B16
Clarbeston Road 16 B16
Clarborough 51 D43
Clardon 103 B27
Clare 34 D53
Clarebrand 65 D23
Clarencefield 69 G26
Clareton 57 D39
Clarilaw 70 B31
Clarkston 74 E21
Clashban 96 B22
Clashcoig 96 B22
Clashgour 80 C18
Clashindarroch 98 F30
Clashmore 96 B23
Clashnessie 101 E16
Clashnoir 90 A28
Clathy 82 E25
Clatt 90 A31
Clatter 37 F25
Clatterford End 23 A51
Clatterin Brig 91 F32
Clatteringshaws 65 C21
Clatworthy 7 B26
Claughton *Lan.* 55 C31
Claughton *Lan.* 55 E31
Claverdon 30 B37
Claverham 19 E30
Clavering 33 E50
Claverley 39 F33
Claverton 20 E33
Clawdd-newydd 47 G26
Clawfin 67 C21
Clawthorpe 55 B31
Clawton 6 F19
Claxby *Lcn.* 52 C47
Claxby *Lcn.* 53 E50
Claxby Pluckacre 53 F48
Claxton *N.Y.* 58 C42
Claxton *Nfk* 45 E59
Claybrooke Magna 41 G40
Claybrooke Parva 41 G40
Clay Common 45 G60
Clay Coton 31 A41
Clay Cross 51 F39
Claydene 23 G50
Claydon *Oxf.* 31 C40
Claydon *Sfk* 35 D57
Claygate *Kent* 14 C52
Claygate *Sry* 22 E47
Claygate Cross 23 F51
Clayhanger *W.M.* 40 E36
Clayhanger *Dev.* 7 C25
Clayhidon 7 D27
Clayock 103 C27
Clay of Allan 97 D24
Claypole 42 A44
Claythorpe 53 E50
Clayton *S.Y.* 51 B40
Clayton *Stf.* 40 A34
Clayton *W.S.* 13 E48
Clayton *W.Y.* 57 F37
Clayton-le-Moors 56 F32
Clayton-le-Woods 55 G31
Clayton West 50 A38
Clayworth 51 D43
Cleadale 85 F10
Cleadon 71 G39
Clearbrook 5 D21
Clearwell 19 A31
Cleasby 62 E38
Cleat 105 C30
Cleatlam 62 E36
Cleatop 56 C34
Cleator 60 E26
Cleator Moor 60 E26
Cleckheaton 57 G37
Cleedownton 38 G31
Cleehill 28 A31
Clee St Margaret 38 G31
Cleethorpes 53 B49
Cleeton St Mary 29 A32
Cleeve *Avon* 19 E30
Cleeve *Oxf.* 21 C42
Cleeve Hill 29 F35
Cleeve Prior 30 D36
Cleghorn 75 F24
Clehonger 28 E30
Cleigh 79 E14
Cleish 75 A26
Cleland 75 E23
Clench Common 20 E37
Clenchwarton 43 C51
Clent 40 G35
Cleobury Mortimer 29 A32
Cleobury North 39 G32
Clephanton 96 F23
Clerklands 69 A30
Clestrain 105 A28
Cleuchbrae 69 F26
Cleuch Head 70 C31
Clevancy 20 D36
Clevedon 19 D29
Cleveland Tontine 62 G40
Cleveleys 55 E28
Clevelode 29 D34
Cleverton 20 C35
Clewer 19 F30
Clewer Village 22 D45
Cley next the Sea 44 A56
Cliburn 61 D31
Cliddesden 21 G42
Cliff *Dyf.* 17 D19
Cliff *Hgh.* 79 A12
Cliffe *N.Y.* 58 F42
Cliffe *Kent* 24 D53
Cliff End 14 F54
Cliffe Woods 24 D53
Clifford *H.&W.* 28 D28
Clifford *W.Y.* 57 E40
Clifford Chambers 30 C37
Clifford's Mesne 29 F33
Cliffs End 25 E59
Clifton *Cum.* 61 D31
Clifton *Lan.* 55 F30
Clifton *Bfd.* 32 E47
Clifton *Oxf.* 31 E40
Clifton *H.&W.* 29 D34
Clifton *Not.* 41 B41
Clifton *Dby.* 40 A37
Clifton *Nor.* 71 E37
Clifton *Avon* 19 D31
Clifton *Cen.* 80 D19
Clifton Campville 40 D38
Clifton Hampden 21 B41
Clifton Reynes 32 C45
Clifton upon Dunsmore 31 A41
Clifton upon Teme 29 B33
Cliftonville 25 D59
Clifynydd 18 B26
Climping 12 F46
Climpy 75 E25
Clint 57 C38
Clinterty 91 B34
Clint Green 44 D56
Clintmains 76 G31
Clippesby 45 D60
Clipsham 42 D45
Clipston *Nmp.* 41 G42
Clipston *Not.* 41 B42
Clipstone 51 F41
Clitheroe 56 E33
Clive 38 C30
Clivocast 106 B41
Clocaenog 47 G26
Clochan 98 C29
Clochtow 99 F36
Clock Face 48 C31
Clockhill 99 E34
Cloddach 97 F27

Clodock 28 F29
Cloford 20 G33
Cloichran 81 D22
Clola 99 E36
Clonrae 68 D24
Clophill 32 E46
Clopton 42 G46
Clopton Green 34 C53
Closeburn 68 D24
Close Clark 54 F24
Closworth 8 C31
Clothall 33 E48
Clothan 106 D40
Clotton 48 F31
Clough *G.M.* 49 A35
Clough *Cum.* 61 G33
Clough Foot 56 G34
Cloughton 63 G46
Cloughton Newlands 63 G46
Clounlaid 79 B13
Clousta 107 B38
Clouston 104 E28
Clova *Grm.* 90 A30
Clova *Tay.* 90 F29
Clovelly 6 C19
Clovelly Cross 6 C19
Clove Lodge 61 E35
Clovenfords 76 G30
Clovenstone 91 B33
Cloverhill 91 B35
Cloves 97 E27
Clovullin 80 A15
Clowne 51 E40
Clows Top 29 A32
Cloyntie 67 C19
Cluanach 72 E9
Clubworthy 4 A18
Cluer 93 B7
Clun 38 G28
Clunas 97 G24
Clunbury 38 G29
Clune *Grm.* 98 C31
Clune *Hgh.* 88 B23
Clunes 87 F17
Clungunford 28 A29
Clunie *Tay.* 82 C27
Clunie *Grm.* 98 D32
Clunton 38 G29
Cluny 76 A28
Clutton *Che.* 48 G30
Clutton *Avon* 19 F32
Clwt-y-bont 46 F21
Clydach *W.G.* 17 D22
Clydach *Gwe.* 28 G28
Clydach Vale 18 B25
Clydebank 74 D21
Clydey 17 A18
Clyffe Pypard 20 D36
Clynder 74 B18
Clynderwen 16 C16
Clynelish 97 A24
Clynfyw 17 A18
Clynnog-fawr 36 A19
Clyro 28 D28
Clyst Honiton 7 F25
Clyst Hydon 7 E26
Clyst St George 7 G25
Clyst St Lawrence 7 E26
Clyst St Mary 7 F25
Cnewr 27 F24
Cnoc 100 D10
Cnoc nan Sltheag 81 G20
Cnwch Coch 27 A22
Coachford 98 E30
Coad's Green 4 C18
Coal Aston 51 D39
Coalbrookdale 39 E32
Coalbrookvale 18 A27
Coalburn 75 G23
Coalburns 71 G37
Coalcleugh 61 B33
Coaley 20 A33
Coalpit Heath 19 C32
Coalpit Hill 49 G33
Coalport 39 E32
Coalsnaughton 75 A25
Coaltown of Balgonie 76 A28
Coaltown of Wemyss 76 A29
Coalville 41 D40
Coat 8 B30
Coatbridge 74 D22
Coate *Wts.* 20 E36
Coate *Wts.* 20 C37
Coates *Glo.* 20 A35
Coates *Cbs.* 43 F48
Coates *W.S.* 12 E45
Coatham 63 D41
Coatham Mundeville 62 D38
Cobairdy 98 E31
Cobbaton 6 C22
Coberley 29 G35
Cobham *Kent* 24 E52
Cobham *Sry* 22 F47
Cobleland 74 A20
Cobler's Green 33 G52
Cobnash 28 B30
Coburty 99 C35
Cochno 74 C20
Cock Alley 51 E40
Cockayne 63 G42
Cockayne Hatley 33 D48
Cock Bridge 90 C28
Cockburnspath 77 C33
Cock Clarks 24 A53
Cockenzie and Port Seton 76 C29
Cockerham 55 D30
Cockermouth 60 C26
Cockernhoe 32 F47
Cockett 17 E22
Cockfield *Drm* 62 D37
Cockfield *Sfk* 34 C54
Cockfosters 23 B48
Cocking 12 E44
Cockington 5 D24
Cocklake 19 G30
Cockley Beck 60 F28
Cockley Cley 44 E53
Cockpole Green 22 C43
Cockshutt 38 C30
Cockthorpe 44 A55
Cockwood 7 G25
Codda 4 C17
Coddenham 35 C57
Coddington *H.&W.* 29 D33
Coddington *Not.* 52 G44
Coddington *Che.* 48 G30
Codford St Mary 20 G35
Codford St Peter 20 G35
Codicote 32 G47
Codmore Hill 12 D46
Codnor 41 A40
Codrington 19 D32
Codsall 40 E34
Codsall Wood 40 E34
Coedcae 19 A28
Coedely 18 C26
Coedkernew 19 C28
Coed Morgan 28 G29
Coedpoeth 48 G28
Coed-y-paen 19 B29
Coed-yr-ynys 28 F27
Coed Ystumgwern 36 C21
Coelbren 27 G24
Cofcott Green 6 F19
Coffinswell 5 D24
Cofton Hackett 30 A36
Cogan 18 D27
Cogenhoe 32 C44
Coggeshall 34 F54
Coggeshall Hamlet 34 F54
Coggins Mill 13 D51
Coig Peighinnean *W.I.* 101 A11
Coig Peighinnean *W.I.* 100 B9
Coilantogle 81 G21
Coileitir 80 C17
Coilesan 80 G18
Coillaig 80 E16
Coille Mhorgil 87 D16
Coille -righ 86 B15
Coillore 85 A9
Coity 18 C25
Col 100 C10
Colaboll 102 G21
Colan 3 B14
Colaton Raleigh 7 G26
Colbost 93 G7
Colbury 10 C39
Colby *Nfk* 45 B58
Colby *Cum.* 61 D32
Colby *I.o.M.* 54 F24
Colchester 34 F55
Colcot 18 D27
Cold Ash 21 E41
Cold Ashby 31 A42
Cold Ashton 20 D33
Cold Aston 30 F37
Coldbackie 102 B21
Coldblow 23 D50
Cold Blow 16 C17
Cold Brayfield 32 C45
Cold Chapel 68 A25
Coldean 13 F49
Coldeast 5 C23
Colden Common 11 B40
Coldfair Green 35 B60
Coldham 43 E50
Cold Hanworth 52 D46
Coldharbour 22 G47
Coldhayes 11 B43
Cold Hesledon 62 B39
Cold Higham 31 C42
Coldingham 77 D34
Cold Kirby 58 A41
Cold Newton 42 E43
Cold Norton 24 B54
Cold Overton 42 E43
Coldrain 82 G26
Coldred 15 C58
Coldrey 22 G43
Coldridge 6 E22
Coldrife 71 D36
Coldstream 77 G34
Coldwaltham 12 E46
Coldwells 99 E37
Cole 9 A32
Colebatch 38 G28
Colebrook 7 E25
Coleby *Lcn.* 52 F45
Coleby *Hum.* 52 A45
Coleford *Glo.* 28 G31
Coleford *Som.* 19 G32
Coleford *Dev.* 7 E23
Cole Green 33 G48
Colehill 10 D36
Coleman's Hatch 13 C50
Colemere 38 B30
Colemore 11 A43
Colenden 82 E26
Coleorton 41 D39
Colerne 20 D33
Colesbourne 29 G35
Cole's Cross 5 F23
Colesden 32 C47
Coleshill *War.* 40 G37
Coleshill *Bkh.* 22 B45
Coleshill *Oxf.* 21 B38
Colestocks 7 E26
Colfin 64 E16
Colgate 13 C48
Colgrain 74 B19
Colinsburgh 83 G30
Colinton 76 D28
Colintraive 73 C16
Colkirk 44 C55
Collace 82 D27
Collafirth *She.* 107 A40
Collafirth *She.* 106 D39
Collamoor Head 4 A17
Collaton St Mary 5 E24
Collessie 82 F28
Colleton Mills 6 D22
Collett's Green 29 C33
Collier Row 23 B50
Collier's End 33 F49
Collier Street 14 C53
Colliery Row 62 B39
Collieston 91 A36
Collin 69 F26
Collingbourne Ducis 21 F38
Collingbourne Kingston 21 F38
Collingham *S.Y.* 57 E39
Collingham *Not.* 52 F44
Collington 29 B32
Collingtree 31 C43
Collins Green 48 C31
Colliston 83 C31
Colliton 7 E26
Collmuir 90 C31
Collycroft 41 G39
Collynie 99 F34
Collyweston 42 E46
Colmonell 67 E17
Colmworth 32 C46
Coln 30 G36
Colnabaichin 90 C28
Colnbrook 22 D46
Colne *Lan.* 56 F34
Colne *Cbs.* 33 A49
Colne Engaine 34 E54
Colney 45 E57
Colney Heath 22 A47
Colney Street 22 A47
Coln Rogers 20 A36
Coln St Aldwyns 20 A37
Colonsay 72 A9
Colpy 98 F32
Colquhar 76 F29
Colsterdale 57 A37
Colsterworth 42 C45
Colston Bassett 41 B42
Coltfield 97 E26
Coltishall 45 C58
Colton *Nfk* 45 D57
Colton *N.Y.* 58 E41
Colton *Stf.* 40 C36
Colton *Cum.* 55 A29
Colva 28 C27
Colvend 65 E24
Colvister 106 C40
Colwall Green 29 D33
Colwall Stone 29 D33
Colwell 70 F35
Colwich 40 C35
Colwick 41 A41
Colwinston 18 D25
Colworth 12 F45
Colwyn Bay 47 E24
Colyford 8 E28
Colyton 8 E28
Combe *Brk.* 21 E39
Combe *Oxf.* 30 G39
Combe *H.&W.* 28 B29
Combe Cross 5 C23
Combe Down 20 E33
Combe Florey 7 B27
Combe Hay 20 E33
Combeinteignhead 5 C25
Combe Martin 6 A21
Combe Moor 28 B29
Combe Raleigh 7 E27
Comberbach 49 E32
Comberford 40 E37
Comberton *H.&W.* 28 B30
Comberton *Cbs.* 33 C49
Combe St Nicholas 8 C29
Combpyne 8 E28
Combrook 30 C38
Combs *Sfk* 34 C56
Combs *Dby.* 50 E36
Combs Ford 34 C56
Combwich 19 G28
Comer 80 G19
Comers 91 C32
Commercial End 33 B51
Commins Coch 37 E24
Commondale 63 E42
Common Edge 55 F29
Common Moor 4 D18
Commonside 40 A38
Common Side 51 E39
Compstall 49 C35
Compton *Dev.* 5 D24
Compton *W.S.* 11 C43
Compton *Ham.* 11 B40
Compton *Sry* 22 G45
Compton *Brk.* 21 D41
Compton Abbas 9 C34
Compton Abdale 30 G36
Compton Bassett 20 D36
Compton Beauchamp 21 C38
Compton Bishop 19 F29
Compton Chamberlayne 10 B36
Compton Dando 19 E32
Compton Dundon 8 A30
Compton Martin 19 F31
Compton Pauncefoot 9 B32
Compton Valence 8 E31
Comra 88 E21
Comrie 81 E23
Conchra *Hgh.* 86 B14
Conchra *Str.* 73 B16
Concraigie 82 C26
Conder Green 55 D30
Conderton 29 E35
Condicote 30 F37
Condorrat 75 C23
Condover 38 E30
Coneyhurst Common 12 D47
Coneysthorpe 58 B43
Coneythorpe 57 D39
Coney Weston 34 A55
Conford 12 C44
Congash 89 B26
Congdon's Shop 4 C18
Congerstone 41 E39
Congham 44 C52
Congleton 49 F34
Congresbury 19 E30
Conicavel 97 F25
Coningsby 53 G48
Conington *Cbs.* 42 G47
Conington *Cbs.* 33 B49
Conisbrough 51 C40
Conisby 72 D8
Conisholme 53 C49
Coniston *Cum.* 60 G28
Coniston *Hum.* 59 F47
Coniston Cold 56 D34
Conistone 56 C35
Conland 98 E31
Connah's Quay 48 F28
Connel 80 D15
Connel Park 67 B21
Connor Downs 2 E11
Conon Bridge 96 F21
Cononish 80 E18
Cononley 56 E35
Cononsyth 83 C31
Consall 40 A35
Consett 62 A36
Constable Burton 62 G37
Constantine 2 F13
Contin 96 F20
Contlaw 91 C34
Contullich 96 D22
Conwy 47 E23
Conyer 25 E55
Cooden 13 F52
Coodham 74 G19
Cookbury 6 E19
Cookham 22 C44
Cookham Dean 22 C44
Cookham Rise 22 C44
Cookhill 30 C36
Cookley *Sfk* 35 A59
Cookley *H.&W.* 40 G34
Cookley Green 21 C42
Cookney 91 D34
Cooksbridge 13 E50
Cookshill 40 A35
Cooksmill Green 24 A52
Cookston 99 F35
Coolham 12 D47
Cooling 24 D53
Coombe *Cnw.* 2 D12
Coombe *Cnw.* 3 C15
Coombe *Dev.* 7 G24
Coombe *Cnw.* 6 D18
Coombe *Dev.* 5 F23
Coombe Bissett 10 B37
Coombe Hill 29 F34
Coombe Keynes 9 F34
Coombes 12 F47
Coopersale Common 23 A50
Cooper's Corner *E.S.* 14 E53
Cooper's Corner *Kent* 23 G50
Cooper's Hill 22 D45
Cootham 12 E46
Copdock 35 D57
Copford Green 34 F55
Copgrove 57 C39
Copister 106 E40
Cople 32 D46
Copley 62 D36
Coplow Dale 50 E37
Copmanthorpe 58 E41
Coppathorne 6 E18
Coppenhall 40 D34
Coppenhall Moss 49 G33
Coppingford 32 A47
Coppleridge 9 B34
Copplestone 7 E23
Coppull 48 A31
Coppull Moor 48 A31
Copsale 12 D47
Copster Green 56 F32
Copston Magna 41 G40
Cop Street 15 B58
Copt Heath 30 A37
Copt Hewick 57 B39
Copthorne 13 C49
Copt Oak 41 D40
Copy Lake 6 D22
Copythorne 10 C39
Coralhill 99 C36
Corbiegoe 103 D29
Corbridge 70 G35
Corby 42 G44
Corby Glen 42 C46
Cordach 90 D31
Coreley 29 A32
Corfe 8 C28
Corfe Castle 9 F35
Corfe Mullen 9 E35
Corfton 38 G30
Corgarff 90 C28
Corhampton 11 B42
Corley 40 G38
Corley Ash 40 G38
Corley Moor 40 G38
Cornabus 72 F9
Corney 60 G27
Cornforth 62 C38
Cornhill 98 D31
Cornhill on Tweed 77 G34
Cornholme 56 G35
Cornish Hall End 33 E52
Cornquoy 105 A30
Cornriggs 61 B34
Cornsay 62 B37
Cornsay Colliery 62 B37
Corntown *Hgh.* 96 F21
Corntown *M.G.* 18 D25
Cornwell 30 F38
Cornwood 5 E22
Cornworthy 5 E24
Corpach 87 G16
Corpusty 45 C57
Corrachree 90 C30
Corran *Hgh.* 86 D14
Corran *Hgh.* 80 A15
Corran *Str.* 74 A18
Corranbuie 73 D14
Corranmore 79 G13
Corrany 54 E26
Corrie 73 F16
Corriechrevie 73 E13
Corrie Common 69 E28
Corriecravie 66 A14
Corriedoo 68 E22
Corrielorne 79 F14
Corrievorrie 88 B23
Corrimony 88 A19
Corringham *Lcn.* 52 C44
Corringham *Esx* 24 C53
Corris 37 E23
Corris Uchaf 37 E23
Corrlarach 86 G15
Corrour Shooting Lodge 80 A19
Corrow 80 G17
Corry 86 B12
Corrychurrachan 80 A16
Corrykinloch 101 F19
Corrylach 72 G12
Corrymuckloch 81 D24
Corsback 103 B27
Corscombe 8 D30
Corse 98 E31
Corsebank 68 B23

Corsehill 69 E27
Corse Lawn 29 E34
Corsemalzie 64 E19
Corse of Kinnoir 98 E31
Corsewall 64 D16
Corsham 20 D34
Corsindae 91 C32
Corsley 20 G34
Corsley Heath 20 G34
Corsock 65 C23
Corston *Wts.* 20 C35
Corston *Avon* 19 E32
Corstorphine 75 C27
Cortachy 82 B29
Corton *Wts.* 20 G35
Corton *Sfk* 45 F61
Corton Denham 9 B32
Corunna 92 E4
Corwar House 67 E18
Corwen 37 A26
Coryton *Dev.* 6 G20
Coryton *Esx* 24 C53
Cosby 41 F41
Coseley 40 F35
Cosford 39 E33
Cosgrove 31 D43
Cosham 11 D42
Cosheston 16 D15
Coshieville 81 C23
Cossall 41 A40
Cossington *Lei.* 41 D41
Cossington *Som.* 19 G29
Costa 104 D29
Costessey 45 D57
Costock 41 C41
Coston *Lei.* 42 C44
Coston *Nfk* 44 E56
Cote *Oxf.* 21 A39
Cote *Som.* 19 G29
Cotebrook 48 F31
Cotehill 61 A30
Cotes *Lei.* 41 C41
Cotes *Stf.* 40 B34
Cotes *Cum.* 55 A30
Cotesbach 41 G41
Cotgrave 41 B42
Cothall 91 B34
Cotham 42 A43
Cothelstone 7 B27
Cothercott 38 E30
Cotheridge 29 C33
Cotherstone 62 E35
Cothill 21 B40
Cotleigh 7 E27
Coton *Cbs.* 33 C49
Coton *Stf.* 40 E37
Coton *Stf.* 40 B35
Coton *Nmp.* 31 A42
Coton Clanford 40 C34
Coton in the Clay 40 C37
Coton in the Elms 40 D38
Cottam *Not.* 52 D44
Cottam *Hum.* 59 C45
Cottam *Lan.* 55 F30
Cottartown 89 A26
Cottenham 33 B50
Cotterdale 61 G34
Cottered 33 F49
Cotteridge 40 G36
Cotterstock 42 F46
Cottesbrooke 31 A42
Cottesmore 42 D44
Cottingham *Nmp.* 42 F44
Cottingham *Hum.* 59 F46
Cottisford 31 E41
Cotton 34 B56
Cotton End 32 D46
Cot-town *Grm.* 99 E33
Cot-town *Grm.* 90 A31
Cottown 91 B33
Cotwalton 40 B35
Couch's Mill 4 E17
Coughton *War.* 30 B36
Coughton *H.&W.* 28 F31
Cougie 87 B18
Coulaghailtro 72 D12
Coulags 94 G15
Coulby Newham 63 E41
Coull 90 C31
Coulport 73 B17
Coulsdon 23 F48
Coulston 20 F35
Coulter 75 G26
Coultershaw Bridge 12 E45
Coultings 19 G28
Coulton 58 B42
Coultra 82 E29
Cound 38 E31
Coundon 62 C38
Coundon Grange 62 D37
Countersett 56 A35
Countess 20 G37
Countess Wear 7 F25
Countesthorpe 41 F41
Countisbury 7 A23
County Oak 13 C48
Coupar Angus 82 C28
Coupland *Cum.* 61 E32
Coupland *Nor.* 77 G35
Cour 73 F14
Court-at-Street 15 D56
Court Barton 7 F23
Courteenhall 31 C43
Court Henry 17 B21
Court House Green 41 G39
Courtsend 25 B56
Courtway 7 B27
Cousland 76 D29
Cousley Wood 13 C52
Coustonn 73 C16
Cove *Dev.* 7 D25
Cove *Str.* 74 B18
Cove *Hgh.* 94 B14
Cove *Ham.* 22 F44
Cove Bay 91 C35
Covehithe 45 G61
Coven 40 E34
Coveney 43 G50
Covenham St Bartholomew 53 C49
Covenham St Mary 53 C49
Coventry 30 A39
Coventry Airport 30 A39
Coverack 2 G13
Coverham 57 A36
Covesea 97 D27
Covington *Str.* 75 G25
Covington *Cbs.* 32 A46
Cowan Bridge 56 B32
Cowbeech 13 E52
Cowbit 43 D48
Cowbridge 18 D25
Cowden 23 G50
Cowdenbeath 75 A27
Cowden Pound 23 G50
Cowes 11 E40
Cowesby 62 G40
Cowfold 13 D48
Cowgill 56 A33
Cowie *Grm.* 91 E34
Cowie *Cen.* 75 B24
Cowlam Manor 59 C45
Cowley *G.L.* 22 C46
Cowley *Oxf.* 21 A41
Cowley *Glo.* 29 G35
Cowley *Dev.* 7 F24
Cowling *N.Y.* 57 A38
Cowling *N.Y.* 56 E35
Cowlinge 33 C52
Cowmes 50 A37
Cowpen 71 E38
Cowpen Bewley 62 D40
Cowplain 11 C42
Cowshill 61 B34
Cowthorpe 57 D40
Coxbank 39 A32
Coxbench 41 A39
Cox Common 45 G59
Coxheath 14 B53
Coxhoe 62 C38
Coxley 19 G31
Coxtie Green 23 B51
Coxwold 58 B41
Coychurch 18 D25
Coylet 73 B17
Coylton 67 B20
Coylumbridge 89 C24
Coynach 90 C30
Coynachie 98 F30
Coytrahen 18 C24
Crabbet Park 13 C49
Crabbs Cross 30 B36
Crabtree *Dev.* 4 E20
Crabtree *W.S.* 12 D47
Crackaig 72 D11
Crackenthorpe 61 D32
Crackington 4 A17
Crackington Haven 4 A16
Crackleybank 39 D33
Crackpot 62 G35
Cracoe 56 C35
Craddock 7 D26
Cradhlastadh 100 D6
Cradley *W.M.* 40 G35
Cradley *H.&W.* 29 D33
Crafthole 4 E19
Cragg 56 G35
Craggan 81 F23
Cragganruar 81 C22
Craggie *Hgh.* 88 A23
Craggie *Hgh.* 102 F24
Craghead 62 A37
Craibstone *Grm.* 91 B34
Craibstone *Grm.* 98 D30
Craichie 83 C30
Craig *Str.* 67 C19
Craig *D.&G.* 65 D22
Craig *Str.* 80 D16
Craig *Str.* 79 E11
Craig *Hgh.* 95 G16
Craig *Hgh.* 94 E13
Craigandaive 73 B16
Craigans 73 A14
Craigbeg 88 F19
Craigcefnparc 17 D22
Craigcleuch 69 E29
Craigculter 99 D34
Craigdallie 82 E28
Craigdam 99 F34
Craigdarroch *D.&G.* 68 D23
Craigdarroch *Str.* 68 C22
Craigdhu *D.&G.* 64 F19
Craigdhu *Hgh.* 96 G20
Craigearn 91 B32
Craigellachie 98 E28
Craigellie 99 C36
Craigencallie 64 C20
Craigend *Grm.* 97 F27
Craigend *Tay.* 82 F26
Craigendoran 74 B19
Craigengillan 67 C20
Craigenputtock 68 E23
Craigens 72 D8
Craigglass 73 B14
Craighall 82 F29
Craighat 74 B20
Craighead *Fife* 83 G32
Craighead *Hgh.* 96 E23
Craighlaw 64 D18
Craighouse 72 D11
Craigie *Str.* 74 G20
Craigie *Tay.* 82 C27
Craigie *Grm.* 91 B35
Craigie Brae 99 F34
Craigieburn 69 C26
Craigieholm 82 D27
Craiglockhart 75 C27
Craiglug 91 D33
Craigmaud 99 D34
Craigmillar 76 C28
Craigmore 73 D17
Craigmyle Ho. 91 C32
Craignafeich 73 C15
Craignant 38 B28
Craignavie 81 D21
Craigneil 67 E17
Craignure 79 D13
Craigo 91 G32
Craigoch 67 C19
Craigow 82 G26
Craig Penllyn 18 D25
Craigrothie 82 F29
Craigroy 97 F27
Craigruie 81 E20
Craigsanquhar 82 F29
Craigton *Grm.* 91 C34
Craigton *Cen.* 74 B22
Craigton *Tay.* 82 B29
Craigton *Tay.* 83 D31
Craigtown 102 C24
Craig-y-nos 27 G24
Craik *Grm.* 90 A30
Craik *Bor.* 69 C29
Crail 83 G32
Crailing 70 A32
Crailinghall 70 A32
Craiselound 51 C43
Crakehill 57 B40
Crambe 58 C43
Cramlington 71 F38
Cramond 75 C27
Cranage 49 F33
Cranberry 39 B33
Cranborne 10 C36
Cranbourne 22 D45
Cranbrook 14 D53
Cranbrook Common 14 D53
Cranfield 32 D45
Cranford *Dev.* 6 C19
Cranford *G.L.* 22 D47
Cranford St Andrew 32 A45
Cranford St John 32 A45
Cranham *Glo.* 29 G34
Cranham *Esx* 23 C51
Crank 48 B30
Cranleigh 12 C46
Cranmer Green 34 A56
Cranmore *Som.* 19 G32
Cranmore *I.o.W.* 10 E39
Cranna 98 D32
Crannach 98 D30
Cranoe 42 F43
Cransford 35 B59
Cranshaws 76 D32
Cranstal 54 C26
Crantock 2 B13
Cranwell 52 G46
Cranwich 44 F53
Cranworth 44 E55
Craobh Haven 79 G13
Crapstone 4 D20
Crarae 73 A15
Crask Inn 102 F21
Craskins 90 C30
Crask of Aigas 96 G20
Craster 71 A38
Craswall 28 E28
Cratfield 35 A59
Crathes 91 D33
Crathie *Grm.* 90 D28
Crathie *Hgh.* 88 E21
Crathorne 62 F40
Craven Arms 38 G30
Craw 73 F14
Crawcrook 71 G37
Crawford *Lan.* 48 B31
Crawford *Str.* 68 A25
Crawfordjohn 68 A24
Crawfordton 68 D23
Crawick 68 B23
Crawley *Oxf.* 30 G39
Crawley *W.S.* 13 C48
Crawley *Ham.* 11 A40
Crawley Down 13 C49
Crawleyside 62 B35
Crawshawbooth 56 G33
Crawton 91 F34
Crawyn 54 D25
Cray *Tay.* 82 A27
Cray *Pow.* 27 F24
Cray *N.Y.* 56 B35
Crayford 23 D51
Crayke 58 B41
Crays Hill 24 B53
Cray's Pond 21 C42
Crazies Hill 22 D43
Creacombe 7 D24
Creagbheitheachain 80 A15
Creag Ghoraidh 92 G3
Creaton 31 A42
Creca 69 F28
Credenhill 28 D30
Crediton 7 E24
Creech St Michael 8 B28
Creed 3 D15
Creedy Park 7 E24
Creekmouth 23 C50
Creeting St Mary 34 C56
Creeton 42 C46
Creetown 64 E20
Creggans 80 G16
Cregneish 54 G23
Cregrina 28 C27
Creich 82 E29
Creigiau 18 C26
Crelevan 88 A19
Cremyll 4 E20
Cressage 38 E31
Cresselly 16 D16
Cressing 34 F53
Cresswell *Stf.* 40 B35
Cresswell *Nor.* 71 D38
Cresswell *Dyf.* 16 D16
Creswell 51 E41
Cretingham 35 B58
Cretshengan 72 D12
Crewe *Che.* 48 G30
Crewe *Che.* 49 G33
Crewgreen 38 D29
Crewkerne 8 D30
Crewton 41 B39
Crianlarich 80 E19
Cribyn 26 C21
Criccieth 36 B20
Crich 51 G39
Crich Carr 51 G39
Crichie 99 E35
Crichton 76 D29
Crick *Gwe.* 19 C30
Crick *Nmp.* 31 A41
Crickadarn 27 D26
Cricket Malherbie 8 C29
Cricket St Thomas 8 D29
Crickheath 38 C28
Crickhowell 28 G27
Cricklade 20 B36
Cridling Stubbs 58 G41
Crieff 81 E24
Criggion 38 D28
Crigglestone 51 A39
Crimdon Park 62 C40
Crimond 99 D36
Crimonmogate 99 D36
Crimplesham 44 E52
Crinan 73 A13
Cringleford 45 E57
Cringletie 76 F28
Crinow 16 C17
Cripplesease 2 E10
Cripp's Corner 14 E53
Crix 34 G53
Croalchapel 68 D24
Croasdale 60 E26
Crockenhill 23 E50
Crockernwell 7 F23
Crockerton 20 G34
Crocketford or Ninemile Bar 65 C24
Crockey Hill 58 E42
Crockham Hill 23 F50
Crockhurst Street 23 G52
Crockleford Heath 34 F56
Crock Street 8 C29
Croesau Bach 38 C28
Croeserw 18 B24
Croesgoch 16 B14
Croes Hywel 28 G29
Croes-lan 26 D19
Croesor 37 A22
Croespenmaen 18 B27
Croesyceiliog *Gwe.* 19 B29
Croesyceiliog *Dyf.* 17 C20
Croes-y-mwyalch 19 B28
Croes y pant 19 A28
Croft *Che.* 49 C32
Croft *Lcn.* 53 F51
Croft *Lei.* 41 F41
Crofthead 69 F29
Croftmore 81 A24
Crofton *W.Y.* 51 A39
Crofton *Wts.* 21 E38
Croft-on-Tees 62 E38
Crofts 65 C23
Crofts of Benachielt 103 E27
Crofts of Buinach 97 F27
Crofts of Haddo 99 F34
Crofty 17 E21
Crogen 37 B26
Croggan 79 E12
Croglin 61 B31
Croick *Hgh.* 102 C24
Croick *Hgh.* 96 B20
Croig 78 B9
Crois Dughaill 84 C3
Croit e Caley 54 G24
Cromarty 96 E23
Crombie Mill 83 C31
Cromblet 99 F33
Cromdale 89 B26
Cromer *Nfk* 45 A58
Cromer *Hfs.* 33 F48
Cromer Hyde 32 G47
Cromford 50 G38
Cromhall 19 B32
Cromhall Common 19 C32
Crompton Fold 49 B35
Cromwell 51 F43
Cronberry 67 A21
Crondall 22 G43
Cronk-y-Voddy 54 E24
Cronton 48 D30
Crook *Drm* 62 C37
Crook *Cum.* 61 G30
Crookedholm 74 G20
Crookham *Nor.* 77 G34
Crookham *Brk.* 21 E41
Crookham Village 22 F43
Crooklands 55 A31
Crook of Devon 82 G26
Cropredy 31 D40
Cropston 41 D41
Cropthorne 29 D35
Cropton 58 A43
Cropwell Bishop 41 B42
Cropwell Butler 41 B42
Cros 101 A11
Crosbie 74 F18
Crosbost 100 E9
Crosby *I.o.M.* 54 F24
Crosby *Cum.* 60 C26
Crosby *Mer.* 48 B28
Crosby *Hum.* 52 A44
Crosby Court 62 G39
Crosby Garrett 61 F33
Crosby Ravensworth 61 E32
Croscombe 19 G31
Cross 19 F29
Crossaig 73 E14
Crossapol 78 B7
Crossapoll 78 C5
Cross Ash 28 F29
Cross-at-Hand 14 C53
Cross Bush 12 F46
Crosscanonby 60 C26
Crossdale Street 45 B58
Crossens 55 G29
Crossford *D.&G.* 68 E24
Crossford *Str.* 75 F24
Crossford *Fife* 75 B26
Cross Foxes Inn 37 D23
Crossgate 43 C48
Crossgatehall 76 D29
Crossgates *Tay.* 82 E26
Cross Gates 57 F39
Crossgates *Pow.* 27 B26
Crossgates *Fife* 75 B27
Crossgill 55 C31
Cross Green *Sfk* 34 C55
Cross Green *Sfk* 34 C54
Cross Green *Cnw.* 6 G19
Crosshands 74 G20
Cross Hands *Dyf.* 16 C16
Cross Hands *Dyf.* 17 C21
Cross Hill 41 A39
Crosshill *Fife* 75 A27
Crosshill *Str.* 67 C19
Crosshouse 74 G19
Cross Houses 38 E31
Cross in Hand 13 D51
Cross Inn *Dyf.* 26 B21

Cross Inn *Dyf.* 26 C19
Cross Inn *M.G.* 18 C26
Cross Keys 20 D34
Crosskeys 18 B27
Crosskirk 103 A26
Cross Lane Head 39 F32
Crosslanes *Shr.* 38 D29
Cross Lanes *N.Y.* 58 C41
Crosslanes *Cnw.* 2 F12
Cross Lanes *Cnw.* 2 D13
Crosslee *Str.* 74 D20
Crosslee *Bor.* 69 B28
Crosslet 74 C20
Crossmichael 65 D23
Crossmoor 55 F30
Cross of Jackson 99 F33
Cross o' the Hands 40 A38
Crossroads *Str.* 74 G20
Crossroads *Grm.* 91 D33
Cross Street 35 A57
Crossway *Gwe.* 28 G30
Crossway *Pow.* 27 C26
Crossway Green 29 B34
Crossways 28 G31
Crosswell 16 A17
Crosthwaite 60 G30
Croston 48 A30
Crostwick 45 D58
Crostwight 45 C59
Crouch 23 F52
Crouch Hill 9 C32
Croughton 31 E41
Crovie 99 C33
Crow 10 D37
Crowan 2 E12
Crowborough 13 C51
Crowcombe 7 B27
Crowdecote 50 F36
Crowdhill 11 B40
Crowfield *Sfk* 35 C57
Crowfield *Nmp.* 31 D41
Crow Hill 29 F32
Crowhurst *E.S.* 14 F53
Crowhurst *Sry* 23 G49
Crowhurst Lane End 23 G49
Crowland *Sfk* 34 A56
Crowland *Lcn.* 43 D48
Crowlas 2 E11
Crowle *H.&W.* 29 C35
Crowle *Hum.* 51 A43
Crowle Green 29 C34
Crowmarsh Gifford 21 C42
Crownhill 4 E20
Crownthorpe 44 E56
Crowntown 2 E12
Crows-an-wra 2 F9
Crowthorne 22 E44
Crowton 48 E31
Croxall 40 D37
Croxdale 62 C38
Croxden 40 B36
Croxley Green 22 B46
Croxton *Cbs.* 33 C48
Croxton *Nfk* 44 G54
Croxton *Stf.* 39 B33
Croxton *Hum.* 52 A47
Croxtonbank 39 B33
Croxton Green 48 G31
Croxton Kerrial 42 C44
Croy *Str.* 75 C23
Croy *Hgh.* 96 G23
Croyde 6 B20
Croydon *Cbs.* 33 D48
Croydon *Sry* 23 E49
Cruach 72 E9
Cruchie 98 E31
Cruckmeole 38 E30
Cruckton 38 D30
Cruden Bay 99 F36
Crudgington 39 D32
Crudwell 20 B35
Crug 28 A27
Crugmeer 3 A15
Crugybar 17 A22
Crulabhig 100 D7
Crumlin 18 B27
Crundale *Dyf.* 16 C15
Crundale *Kent* 15 C56
Crutherland 74 E22
Cruwys Morchard 7 D24
Crux Easton 21 F40
Crwbin 17 C20
Cryers Hill 22 B44
Crymlyn 46 E22
Crymych 16 A17
Crynant 18 A23
Crystal Palace 23 D49
Cuaig 94 F13
Cubbington 30 B39
Cubert 2 C13
Cublington 32 F44
Cuckfield 13 D49
Cucklington 9 B33
Cuckney 51 E41
Cuckoo's Nest 48 F29
Cuddesdon 21 A41
Cuddington *Che.* 48 E31
Cuddington *Bkh.* 31 G43
Cuddington Heath 38 A30
Cuddy Hill 55 F30
Cudham 23 F50
Cudliptown 5 C21
Cudworth *S.Y.* 51 B39
Cudworth *Som.* 8 C29
Cuffley 23 A48
Cuidhaseadair 101 B11
Cuidhir 84 D2
Cuidhtinis 92 C6
Cuidrach 93 F9
Cuilmuich 73 A17
Cuil-uaine 79 D14
Culag 74 A19
Culbo 96 E22
Culbokie 96 F21
Culbone 7 A24
Culburnie 96 G20
Culcabock 96 G22
Culcharan 79 D14
Culcharry 97 F24
Culcheth 49 C32
Culdrain 98 F30
Culduie 94 G13
Culford 34 B54
Culgaith 61 D31
Culgower 103 G25
Culham 21 B41
Culindrach 73 E14
Culkein 101 E16
Culkerton 20 B35
Cullachie 89 B25
Cullen 98 C31
Cullercoats 71 F39
Cullicudden 96 E22
Culligran 96 G19
Cullingworth 57 F36
Cullipool 79 F13
Cullivoe 106 B41
Culloch 81 F23
Culloden 96 G23
Cullompton 7 E25
Culmaily 96 B23
Culmington 38 G30
Culmstock 7 D26
Culnacraig 95 A16
Culnadalloch 80 D15
Culnaknock 94 E11
Culnamean 85 B10
Culpho 35 D57
Culquhirk 64 E20
Culrain 96 B21
Culross 75 B25
Culroy 67 B19
Culsh 90 D29
Culshabbin 64 E18
Culswick 107 C38
Culter Allers Farm 75 G26
Cultercullen 91 A34
Cults *Grm.* 91 C34
Cults *D.&G.* 64 F20
Cults *Grm.* 98 F31
Cultybraggan Camp 81 E23
Culverstone Green 24 E52
Culverthorpe 42 A45
Culvie 98 D31
Culworth 31 D41
Cumberhead 75 G23
Cumbernauld 75 C23
Cumberworth 53 E50
Cuminestown 99 D33
Cumloden 64 D20
Cummersdale 60 A29
Cummertrees 69 G27
Cummingstown 97 E26
Cumnock 67 B21
Cumnor 21 A40
Cumrew 61 A31
Cumrue 69 E26
Cumstoun 65 E22
Cumwhinton 60 A30
Cumwhitton 61 A30
Cundall 57 B40
Cunninghamhead 74 F19
Cunnister 106 C41
Cunnoquhie 82 F28
Cupar 82 F29
Cupar Muir 82 F29
Curbar 50 E38
Curbridge *Oxf.* 21 A39
Curbridge *Ham.* 11 C41
Curdridge 11 C41
Curdworth 40 F37
Curland 8 C28
Curload 8 B29
Curridge 21 D40
Currie 75 D27
Curry Mallet 8 B29
Curry Rivel 8 B29
Curteis' Corner 14 D54
Curtisden Green 14 C53
Cury 2 F12
Cushnie 99 C33
Cushuish 7 B27
Cusop 28 D28
Cutcloy 64 G20
Cutcombe 7 B25
Cuthill 96 C23
Cutiau 37 D22
Cutnall Green 29 B34
Cutsdean 30 E36
Cutthorpe 51 E39
Cutts 107 D39
Cuttyhill 99 D36
Cuxham 21 B42
Cuxton 24 E52
Cuxwold 52 B47
Cwm *Clw.* 47 E26
Cwm *W.G.* 17 E22
Cwm *Gwe.* 18 A27
Cwmafan 18 B23
Cwmaman 18 B25
Cwmann 26 D21
Cwmbach *Pow.* 27 C26
Cwmbach *Dyf.* 17 B18
Cwmbach *M.G.* 18 A25
Cwmbach *Pow.* 28 D27
Cwmbelan 37 G25
Cwmbran 19 B28
Cwmbrwyno 37 G22
Cwmcarn 18 B27
Cwmcarvan 19 A30
Cwm-Cewydd 37 D24
Cwmcoy 26 D18
Cwmdare 18 A25
Cwmdu *Pow.* 28 F27
Cwmdu *Dyf.* 17 A22
Cwmduad 17 A19
Cwmfelin Boeth 16 C17
Cwmfelinfach 18 B27
Cwmfelin Mynach 16 B17
Cwmffrwd 17 C20
Cwm Frrwd-oer 19 A28
Cwmgiedd 27 G23
Cwmgors 17 C22
Cwmgwrach 18 A24
Cwm Irfon 27 D24
Cwmisfael 17 C20
Cwm-Llinau 37 E24
Cwmllyfri 17 C19
Cwmllynfell 27 G23
Cwm-Morgan 17 A18
Cwm Owen 27 D25
Cwm-parc 18 B25
Cwmpengraig 17 A19
Cwmsychbant 26 D20
Cwmsymlog 37 G22
Cwmtillery 18 A27
Cwm-twrch Isaf 27 G23
Cwm-y-glo 46 F21
Cwmyoy 28 F28
Cwmystwyth 27 A23
Cwrt 37 E22
Cwrt-newydd 26 D20
Cwrt-y-gollen 28 G28
Cydwelli (Kidwelly) 17 D20
Cyffylliog 47 G26
Cymmer *M.G.* 18 B26
Cymmer *W.G.* 18 B24
Cynghordy 27 E23
Cynheidre 17 D20
Cynwyd 37 A26
Cynwyl Elfed 17 B19

D

Dabton 68 D24
Daccombe 5 D24
Dacre *Cum.* 60 D30
Dacre *N.Y.* 57 C37
Dacre Banks 57 C37
Daddry Shield 61 C34
Dadford 31 E42
Dadlington 41 F39
Dafen 17 D21
Daffy Green 44 E55
Dagenham 23 C51
Daggons 10 C36
Daglingworth 20 A35
Dagnall 32 G45
Dail 80 D16
Dail Beag 100 C8
Dail Bho Dheas 100 A10
Dail Bho Thuath 100 A10
Dailly 67 C18
Dail Mor 100 C7
Dailnamac 80 D15
Dairsie or Osnaburgh 82 F29
Dalabrog 84 B3
Dalavich 80 F15
Dalballoch 88 E22
Dalbeattie 65 D24
Dalblair 68 B22
Dalbog 90 F31
Dalbreck 102 G23
Dalbury 40 B38
Dalby 54 F24
Dalcairnie 67 C20
Dalchalloch 81 A23
Dalchalm 97 A24
Dalchenna 80 G16
Dalchork 102 G21
Dalchreichart 87 C18
Dalchruin 81 F22
Dalcross 96 G23
Dalderby 53 F48
Daldownie 90 C28
Dale *Dyf.* 16 D14
Dale *Dby.* 41 B40
Dale *She.* 107 B37
Dale Head 60 E30
Dalehouse 63 E43
Dalelia 79 A13
Dale Park 12 F45
Daless 89 A24
Dalestie 90 B27
Dalfad 90 C29
Dalganachan 103 D25
Dalgarven 74 F18
Dalgety Bay 75 B27
Dalgig 67 B21
Dalginross 81 E23
Dalgonar 68 C22
Dalguise 82 C25
Dalhalvaig 102 C24
Dalham 34 B53
Daligan 74 B18
Dalivaddy 66 B12
Daljarrock 67 E17
Dalkeith 76 D29
Dallas 97 F27
Dallaschyle 96 G23
Dallash 64 D20
Dallinghoo 35 C58
Dallington *E.S.* 13 E52
Dallington *Nmp.* 31 B43
Dalmadilly 91 B33
Dalmally 80 E17
Dalmarnock 82 C25
Dalmary 74 A21
Dalmellington 67 C20
Dalmeny 75 C27
Dalmichy 102 G21
Dalmigavie 88 C23
Dalmore 96 E22
Dalmunzie Hotel 89 G26
Dalnabreck 79 A12
Dalnacarn 82 A25
Dalnaglar Castle 82 A27
Dalnaha 79 E12
Dalnahaitnach 89 C24
Dalnamain 96 B23
Dalnatrat 80 B15
Dalnavie 96 D22
Dalness 80 B17
Dalnessie 102 G22
Dalnigap 64 C17
Dalqueich 82 G26
Dalreoch 67 E17
Dalriech 81 D23
Dalroy 96 G23
Dalrulzian 82 B27
Dalry 74 F18
Dalrymple 67 B19
Dalserf 75 E24
Dalshangan 67 E21
Dalskairth 65 C25
Dalston 60 A29
Dalswinton 68 E25
Daltomach 88 B23
Dalton *D.&G.* 69 F26
Dalton *N.Y.* 62 F36
Dalton *Nor.* 61 A35
Dalton *Lan.* 48 B30
Dalton *Nor.* 71 F36
Dalton *S.Y.* 51 C40
Dalton *N.Y.* 57 B40
Dalton-in-Furness 54 B27
Dalton-le-Dale 62 B39
Dalton-on-Tees 62 F38
Dalton Piercy 62 C40
Daltot 73 B13
Daltra 97 G25
Dalveich 81 E22
Dalvennan 67 B19
Dalvourn 88 A22
Dalwhinnie 88 F22
Dalwood 8 D28
Damerham 10 C37
Damgate 45 E60
Damnaglaur 64 G16
Damside 82 F25
Danbury 24 A53
Danby 63 F42
Danby Wiske 62 G39
Dandaleith 98 E28
Danderhall 76 D28
Danebridge 49 F35
Dane End 33 F49
Danehill 13 D50
Dane Hills 41 E41
Danesmoor 51 F39
Danestone 91 B34
Danskine 76 D31
Darby Green 22 E44
Darenth 23 D51
Daresbury 48 D31
Darfield 51 B39
Dargate 25 E56
Dargues 70 D34
Darite 4 D18
Darlaston 40 F35
Darley 57 D38
Darley Dale 50 F38
Darlingscott 30 D38
Darlington 62 E38
Darliston 38 B31
Darlton 51 E43
Darnabo 99 E33
Darnall 51 D39
Darnconner 67 A21
Darnford 91 D33
Darngarroch 65 D22
Darnick 76 G31
Darowen 37 E24
Darra 99 E33
Darras Hall 71 F37
Darrington 51 A40
Darsham 35 B60
Dartfield 99 D36
Dartford 23 D51
Dartington 5 D23
Dartmeet 5 C22
Dartmouth 5 E24
Darton 51 B39
Darvel 74 G21
Darwell 14 E53
Darwen 56 G32
Datchet 22 D45
Datchworth 33 G48
Datchworth Green 33 G48
Daubhill 49 B33
Daugh of Kinermony 98 E28
Dauntsey 20 C35
Dava 89 A25
Davaar 66 B13
Davan 90 C30
Davenham 49 E32
Daventry 31 B41
Davidstow 4 B17
Davington 69 C28
Daviot *Hgh.* 88 A23
Daviot *Hgh.* 91 A33
Davoch of Grange 98 D30
Dawley 39 E32
Dawlish 5 C25
Dawn 47 E24
Daws Heath 24 C54
Dawsmere 43 B50
Daylesford 30 F38
Ddol 47 E27
Deadwaters 75 F23
Deal 15 B59
Deal Hall 25 B55
Dean *Ham.* 11 C41
Dean *Dor.* 9 C35
Dean *Dev.* 5 D23
Dean *Cum.* 60 D26
Dean *Som.* 19 G32
Dean *Oxf.* 30 F39
Dean Bank 62 C38
Deanburnhaugh 69 B29
Deane 21 F41
Deanland 9 C35
Dean Prior 5 D22
Dean Row 49 D34
Deanscales 60 D26
Deanshanger 31 D43
Deanston 81 G22
Dean Street 14 B53
Dearham 60 C26
Debach 35 C58
Debate 69 E28
Debden 33 E51
Debden Green 33 E51
Debenham 35 B57
Dechmont 75 C26
Deddington 31 E40
Dedham 34 E56
Deecastle 90 D30
Deene 42 F45
Deenethorpe 42 F45
Deepcar 50 C38
Deepcut 22 F45
Deepdale *Cum.* 56 A33
Deepdale *N.Y.* 56 A34
Deeping Gate 42 E47
Deeping St James 42 D47
Deeping St Nicholas 43 D48
Deerhill 98 D30
Deerhurst 29 E34
Defford 29 D35
Defynnog 27 F25
Deganwy 47 E23
Degnish 79 F13
Deighton *N.Y.* 62 F39
Deighton *N.Y.* 58 E42
Deiniolen 46 F21
Delabole 4 B16
Delamere 48 F31
Delavorar 90 B27
Delfrigs 91 A35

Delliefure 89 A26
Dell Lodge 89 C25
Delnabo 90 B27
Delny 96 D23
Delph 49 B35
Delphorie 90 B30
Delves 62 A37
Delvine 82 C27
Dembleby 42 B46
Denaby 51 C40
Denaby Main 51 C40
Denbigh 47 F26
Denbury 5 D23
Denby 41 A39
Denby Dale 50 B38
Denchworth 21 B39
Dendron 55 B28
Denend 98 F31
Denford 32 A45
Dengie 25 A55
Denham *Bkh.* 22 C46
Denham *Sfk* 35 A57
Denham *Sfk* 34 B53
Denham Green 22 C46
Denhead *Grm.* 91 B33
Denhead *Grm.* 99 D36
Denhead *Tay.* 82 D29
Denhead *Tay.* 83 C31
Denhead *Fife* 83 F30
Denholm 70 B31
Denholme 57 F36
Denholme Clough 57 F36
Denio 36 B19
Denmead 11 C42
Denmill 91 B34
Denmoss 98 E32
Dennington 35 B58
Denny 75 B24
Dennyloanhead 75 B23
Denshaw 49 A35
Denside 91 D33
Densole 15 C57
Denston 34 C53
Denstone 40 A36
Dent 56 A32
Denton *N.Y.* 57 E37
Denton *Kent* 15 C57
Denton *E.S.* 13 F50
Denton *Cbs.* 42 G47
Denton *Lcn.* 42 B44
Denton *Nmp.* 32 C44
Denton *G.M.* 49 C35
Denton *Nfk* 45 G58
Denton *Oxf.* 21 A41
Denton *Drm* 62 E37
Denver 43 E51
Denvilles 11 D43
Denwick 71 B37
Deopham 44 E56
Deopham Green 44 F56
Depden 34 C53
Deptford *Wts.* 10 A36
Deptford *G.L.* 23 D49
Derby 41 B39
Derbyhaven 54 G24
Dererach 79 E10
Deri 18 A27
Derringstone 15 C57
Derrington 40 C34
Derry 81 E22
Derry Hill 20 D35
Derrythorpe 52 B44
Dervaig 79 B10
Derwen 47 G26
Derwenlas 37 F22
Derwydd 17 C21
Derybruich 73 C15
Desborough 42 G43
Desford 41 E40
Detchant 77 G36
Detling 14 B53
Deuddwr 38 D28
Deunant 47 F25
Deuxhill 39 G32
Devauden 19 B30
Devil's Bridge 27 A23
Devizes 20 E36
Devonport 4 E20
Devonside 75 A25
Devoran 2 E13
Dewar 76 F29
Dewlish 9 E33
Dewsall Court 28 E30
Dewsbury 57 G38
Dhoon 54 E26
Dhoor 54 D26
Dhowin 54 C25
Dhuhallow 88 B21
Dial Post 12 E47
Dibden 11 D40
Dibden Purlieu 10 D39
Dickleburgh 45 G57
Didbrook 30 E36
Didcot 21 C41
Diddington 32 B47
Diddlebury 38 G30
Didley 28 E30
Didling 12 E44
Didmarton 20 C33
Didsbury 49 C34
Didworthy 5 D22
Digby 52 G46
Digg 93 E10
Diggle 50 B36
Digmoor 48 B30
Digswell 33 G48
Dihewyd 26 C20
Dildawn 65 E23
Dilham 45 C59
Dilhorne 40 A35
Dilston 70 G35
Dilton Marsh 20 G34
Dilwyn 28 C29
Dilwyn Common 28 C30
Dinas *Dyf.* 17 B18
Dinas *Dyf.* 16 A16
Dinas *Gwy.* 36 B18
Dinas *Gwy.* 46 G20
Dinas-Mawddwy 37 D24
Dinas Powys 18 D27
Dinder 19 G31
Dinedor 28 E31
Dingestow 28 G30
Dingley 42 G43
Dingwall 96 F21
Dinlabyre 70 D31
Dinnet 90 D30
Dinnington *Som.* 8 C29
Dinnington *S.Y.* 51 D41
Dinnington *T.&W.* 71 F37
Dinorwic 46 F21
Dinton *Bkh.* 31 G43
Dinton *Wts.* 10 A36
Dinwoodie Mains 69 D26
Dinworthy 6 D19
Dippen 73 G13
Dippenhall 22 G43
Dippin 66 A16
Dipple *Grm.* 98 D29
Dipple *Str.* 67 C18
Diptford 5 E23
Dipton 62 A37
Dirdhu 89 B26
Dirleton 76 B30
Discoed 28 B28
Diseworth 41 C40
Dishes 104 D32
Dishforth 57 B39
Dishig 79 D10
Disley 49 D35
Diss 45 G57
Disserth 27 C26
Distington 60 D25
Ditcheat 9 A32
Ditchingham 45 F59
Ditchley 30 F39
Ditchling 13 E49
Ditteridge 20 E33
Dittisham 5 E24
Ditton *Che.* 48 D30
Ditton *Kent* 23 F52
Ditton Green 33 C52
Ditton Priors 39 G32
Dixton *Glo.* 29 E35
Dixton *H.&W.* 28 G31
Dobwalls 4 D18
Doccombe 7 G23
Dochgarroch 96 G21
Docklow 28 C31
Dockray 60 D29
Doddinghurst 23 B51
Doddington *Cbs.* 43 G49
Doddington *Shr.* 28 A31
Doddington *Kent* 14 B55
Doddington *Nor.* 77 G35
Doddington *Lcn.* 52 E44
Doddiscombsleigh 7 G24
Dodford *Nmp.* 31 B42
Dodford *H.&W.* 29 A35
Dodington *Som.* 7 A27
Dodington *Avon* 20 C33
Dodington Ash 20 D33
Dodleston 48 F29
Dodworth 50 B38
Doe Lea 51 F40
Dogdyke 52 G47
Dogmersfield 22 F43
Dog Village 7 F25
Dolanog 37 D26
Dolau 28 B27
Dolau Honddu 27 D25
Dolbenmaen 36 A20
Dolfach 27 A24
Dol Fawr 37 E24
Dolfor 37 G26
Dolgarreg 27 E23
Dolgarrog 47 F23
Dolgellau 37 D23
Dolgoch 37 E22
Dol-gran 17 A20
Doll 97 A24
Dollar 75 A25
Dollarbeg 75 A25
Dolleycanney 28 D27
Dolphinholme 55 D31
Dolphinton 75 F26
Dolton 6 D21
Dolwen *Clw.* 47 E24
Dolwen *Pow.* 37 E25
Dolwyddelan 47 G23
Dolybont 37 G22
Dolyhir 28 C28
Dolywern 38 B28
Domgay 38 D28
Doncaster 51 B41
Donhead St Andrew 9 B35
Donhead St Mary 9 B34
Donibristle 75 B27
Doniford 7 A26
Donington 43 B48
Donington le Heath 41 D40
Donington on Bain 53 D48
Donisthorpe 40 D38
Donkey Town 22 E45
Donnington *Brk.* 21 E40
Donnington *W.S.* 12 F44
Donnington *Shr.* 38 E31
Donnington *Shr.* 39 D33
Donnington *Glo.* 30 F37
Donnington *H.&W.* 29 E33
Donyatt 8 C29
Dorchester *Dor.* 9 E32
Dorchester *Oxf.* 21 B41
Dordon 40 E38
Dore 50 D38
Dores 88 A21
Dorket Head 41 A41
Dorking 22 G47
Dormansland 23 G50
Dormans Park 23 G49
Dormanstown 63 D41
Dormington 28 D31
Dorney 22 D45
Dornie 86 B14
Dornoch 96 C23
Dornock 69 G28
Dorrery 103 C26
Dorridge 30 A37
Dorrington *Lcn.* 52 G46
Dorrington *Shr.* 38 E30
Dorsell 90 B31
Dorsington 30 C37
Dorstone 28 D28
Dorton 31 G42
Dorusduain 86 B15
Dosthill 40 F38
Dotland 61 A35
Dottery 8 E30
Doublebois 4 D17
Dougalston 74 C21
Dougarie 73 G14
Doughton 20 B34
Douglas *Str.* 75 G24
Douglas *I.o.M.* 54 F25
Douglas and Angus 83 D30
Douglas Hall 65 E24
Douglas Hill 46 F22
Douglastown 82 C29
Douglas Water 75 G24
Doulting 19 G32
Dounby 104 D28
Doune *Str.* 81 G23
Doune *Str.* 80 F19
Doune *Str.* 74 A18
Doune *Hgh.* 89 C24
Doune *Hgh.* 96 A20
Doune Park 98 C32
Douneside 90 C30
Dounie *Hgh.* 96 B21
Dounie *Hgh.* 96 C22
Dounreay 103 B25
Dousland 5 D21
Dovaston 38 C29
Dove Holes 50 E36
Dovenby 60 C26
Dover 15 C59
Doverdale 29 B34
Doveridge 40 B36
Doversgreen 23 G48
Dowally 82 C25
Dowdeswell 29 F35
Dowhill 67 C18
Dowland 6 D21
Dowlands 8 E28
Dowlish Wake 8 C29
Down Ampney 20 B37
Downderry 4 E18
Downe 23 E50
Downend *Brk.* 21 D40
Downend *I.o.W.* 11 F41
Downend *Avon* 19 D32
Down End 19 G28
Downfield 82 D29
Down Field 33 A51
Downgate 4 C19
Downham *Nor.* 77 G34
Downham *Lan.* 56 E33
Downham *Esx* 24 B53
Downham Market 44 E52
Down Hatherley 29 F34
Downhead *Cnw.* 4 B18
Downhead *Som.* 19 G32
Downholland Cross 48 B29
Downholme 62 G37
Downies 91 D35
Downing 47 E27
Downley 22 B44
Downside *Sry* 22 F47
Downside *Som.* 19 G32
Downside *Avon* 19 E30
Down St Mary 7 E23
Down Thomas 5 F21
Downton *Dby.* 6 G21
Downton *Dev.* 5 E24
Downton *Ham.* 10 E38
Downton *Wts.* 10 B37
Downton on the Rock 28 A30
Dowsby 42 B47
Dowthwaitehead 60 D29
Doynton 19 D32
Draethen 18 C27
Draffan 75 F23
Drakeland Corner 5 E21
Drakes Broughton 29 D34
Drakes Cross 30 A36
Drambuie 68 B23
Draughton *Nmp.* 31 A43
Draughton *N.Y.* 57 D36
Drax 58 G42
Draycote 31 A40
Draycott *Glo.* 30 E37
Draycott *Dby.* 41 B40
Draycott *Som.* 19 F30
Draycott *H.&W.* 29 D34
Draycott in the Clay 40 C37
Draycott in the Moors 40 A35
Drayton *Ham.* 11 D42
Drayton *Nfk* 45 D57
Drayton *Lcn.* 43 B48
Drayton *Lei.* 42 F44
Drayton *Oxf.* 31 D40
Drayton *H.&W.* 29 A35
Drayton *Oxf.* 21 B40
Drayton *Som.* 8 B29
Drayton Bassett 40 E37
Drayton Beauchamp 32 G45
Drayton Parslow 32 F44
Drayton St Leonard 21 B41
Drebley 57 D36
Dreemskerry 54 D26
Dreenhill 16 C14
Dre-fach 26 D20
Drefach *Dyf.* 17 C21
Drefach *Dyf.* 17 A19
Dreghorn 74 G19
Drellingore 15 C58
Drem 76 B30
Drewsteignton 7 F23
Driby 53 E49
Driffield 20 B36
Drigg 60 G26
Drighlington 57 G37
Drimfern 80 F16
Drimlee 80 F17
Drimnin 79 B11
Drimore 92 G3
Drimpton 8 D29
Drimsynie 80 G17
Drimvore 73 A14
Drinan 86 C11
Drinkstone 34 B55
Drinkstone Green 34 C55
Drishaig 80 F17
Drissaig 80 F15
Drointon 40 C36
Droitwich 29 B34
Dron 82 F27
Dronfield 51 E39
Dronfield Woodhouse 51 E39
Drongan 67 B20
Dronley 82 D29
Dropmore 22 C45
Droxford 11 C41
Droylsden 49 C34
Druid 37 A26
Druidston 16 C14
Druimarbin 87 G16
Druimavuic 80 C15
Druimdrishaig 73 C13
Druimindarroch 86 F12
Druimkinnerras 88 A20
Drum *Str.* 73 C15
Drum *Tay.* 82 G26
Drumachloy 73 D16
Drumbeg 101 E17
Drumblade 98 E31
Drumblair 98 E32
Drumbuie 86 A13
Drumburgh 60 A28
Drumchapel 74 C21
Drumchardine 96 G21
Drumchork 94 C14
Drumclog 74 G22
Drumdelgie 98 E30
Drumderfit 96 F22
Drumeldrie 83 G30
Drumelzier 75 G27
Drumfearn 86 C12
Drumfern 86 G15
Drumgarve 66 A13
Drumgley 82 B29
Drumguish 88 E23
Drumhead 90 D31
Drumine 96 F23
Drumjohn 67 D21
Drumlamford Ho. 64 C18
Drumlasie 91 C32
Drumlemble 66 B12
Drumlithie 91 E33
Drummond *Hgh.* 96 E22
Drummond *Cen.* 81 G22
Drummore 64 G17
Drummuir Castle 98 E29
Drumnadrochit 88 A20
Drumna-gorrach 98 D31
Drumnatorran 79 A13
Drumoak 91 D33
Drumore 66 A12
Drumour 82 C25
Drumrash 65 C22
Drumrunie 95 A17
Drums 91 A35
Drumsturdy 83 D30
Drumuie 93 G10
Drumuillie 89 B25
Drumvaich 81 G22
Drumwhindle 99 F34
Drumwhirn 68 E23
Drunkendub 83 C32
Drury 48 F28
Drybeck 61 E32
Drybridge *Grm.* 98 C30
Drybridge *Str.* 74 G19
Drybrook 29 G32
Dry Doddington 42 A44
Dry Drayton 33 B49
Drygrange 76 G31
Dry Harbour 94 F11
Dryhope 69 A28
Drymen 74 B20
Drymuir 99 E34
Drynoch 85 A9
Dry Sandford 21 B40
Dryslwyn 17 B21
Dry Street 24 C52
Dryton 38 E31
Duachy 79 E13
Dubford 99 C33
Dubhchladach 73 D14
Dubheads 82 E25
Dubton 83 B31
Duchal 74 D19
Duchally 101 G19
Duchray 74 A20
Duck End 33 F52
Duckington 48 G30
Ducklington 21 A39
Duck's Cross 32 C47
Duddenhoe End 33 E50
Duddingston 76 C28
Duddington 42 E45
Duddleswell 13 D50
Duddo 77 F35
Duddon 48 F30
Duddon Bridge 54 A27
Dudleston Heath 38 B29
Dudley *W.M.* 40 F35
Dudley *T.&W.* 71 F38
Dudley Hill 57 F37
Dudley Port 40 F35
Dudsbury 10 E36
Duffield 41 A39
Duffryn 18 B24
Dufftown 98 E28
Duffus 97 E27
Dufton 61 D32
Duggleby 58 C44
Duible 103 F25
Duiletter 80 E17
Duinish 81 A21
Duirinish 86 A13
Duisdealmor 86 C12
Duisky 86 G15
Dukestown 28 G27
Dukinfield 49 C35
Dulas 46 D20
Dulax 90 B29
Dulcote 19 G31
Dulford 7 E26
Dull 81 C23
Dullatur 75 C23
Dullingham 33 C51
Dulnain Bridge 89 B25
Duloe *Cnw.* 4 E18
Duloe *Bfd.* 32 B47
Dulsie 97 G25
Dulverton 7 C24
Dulwich 23 D49
Dumbarton 74 C20
Dumbleton 29 E35

Dumcrieff 69 C26
Dumeath 98 F30
Dumfin 74 B19
Dumfries 65 C25
Dumgoyne 74 B21
Dummer 21 G41
Dun 83 B32
Dunach 79 E14
Dunalastair 81 B22
Dunan *Str.* 73 C17
Dunan *Hgh.* 86 B11
Dunans 73 A16
Dunball 19 G28
Dunbar 76 C32
Dunbeath 103 F27
Dunbeg 79 D14
Dunblane 81 G23
Dunbog 82 F28
Duncanston *Grm.* 90 A31
Duncanston *Hgh.* 96 F21
Dunchideock 7 G24
Dunchurch 31 A40
Duncote 31 C42
Duncow 68 E25
Duncraggan 81 G21
Duncrievie 82 G27
Duncroist 81 D21
Duncrub 82 F25
Duncryne 74 B20
Duncton 12 E45
Dundee 82 D29
Dundee Airport 82 E29
Dundon 8 A30
Dundonald 74 G19
Dundonnell 95 C16
Dundraw 60 B27
Dundreggan 88 C19
Dundrennan 65 F23
Dundry 19 E31
Dunearn 75 B27
Dunecht 91 C33
Dunfermline 75 B26
Dunfield 20 B37
Dunford Bridge 50 B37
Dungavel 74 G22
Dunham 51 E43
Dunham-on-the-Hill 48 E30
Dunhampton 29 B34
Dunham Town 49 D33
Dunholme 52 E46
Dunino 83 F31
Dunipace 75 B24
Dunira 81 E23
Dunkeld 82 C26
Dunkerton 19 F32
Dunkeswell 7 E27
Dunkeswick 57 E39
Dunkirk 15 B56
Dunk's Green 23 F52
Dunlappie 83 A31
Dunley 29 B33
Dunlop 74 F19
Dunloskin 73 C17
Dunmere 4 D16
Dunmore *Str.* 73 D13
Dunmore *Cen.* 75 B24
Dunn 103 C27
Dunnabie 69 E28
Dunnet 103 A28
Dunnichen 83 C30
Dunning 82 F26
Dunnington *N.Y.* 58 D42
Dunnington *War.* 30 C36
Dunnington *Hum.* 59 D47
Dunnockshaw 56 G33
Dunoon 73 C17
Dunragit 64 E17
Dunrostan 73 B13
Duns 77 E33
Dunsby 42 C47
Dunscore 68 E24
Dunscroft 51 B42
Dunsdale 63 E41
Dunsden Green 22 D43
Dunsfold 12 C46
Dunsford 7 G23
Dunshelt 82 F28
Dunsinnan 82 D27
Dunsland Cross 6 E20
Dunsley 63 E44
Dunsmore 22 A44
Dunsop Bridge 56 E32
Dunstable 32 F45
Dunstall 40 C37
Dunstall Green 34 B53
Dunstan 71 A38
Dunster 7 A25
Duns Tew 31 F40
Dunston *Stf.* 40 D35
Dunston *Lcn.* 52 F46
Dunston *T.&W.* 71 G38
Dunston *Nfk* 45 E58
Dunstone *Dev.* 5 F23
Dunstone *Dev.* 5 E21
Dunstone *Dev.* 5 C23
Dunsville 51 B42
Dunswell 59 F46
Dunsyre 75 F26
Dunterton 4 C19
Duntisbourne Abbots 20 A35
Duntisbourne Leer 20 A35
Duntisbourne Rouse 20 A35
Duntish 9 D32
Duntocher 74 C20
Dunton *Bfd.* 33 D48
Dunton *Bkh.* 32 F44
Dunton Bassett 41 F41
Dunton Green 23 F51
Dunton Wayletts 24 B52
Duntulm 93 D9
Dunure 67 B18
Dunure Mains 67 B18
Dunvant 17 E21
Dunvegan 93 G8
Dunwich 35 A60
Dura 83 F30
Durdar 60 A29
Durgates 13 C52
Durham 62 B38
Durinemast 79 B12
Durisdeer 68 C24
Durleigh 8 A28
Durley *Ham.* 11 C41
Durley *Wts.* 21 E38
Durnamuck 94 B15
Durness 101 B19
Durno 91 A33
Duror 80 B15
Durran *Str.* 80 G15
Durran *Hgh.* 103 B27
Durrington *Wts.* 20 G37
Durrington *W.S.* 12 F46
Dursley 20 B33
Durston 8 B28
Durweston 9 D34
Dury 107 A40
Duston 31 B43
Duthil 89 B25
Dutlas 28 A27
Duton Hill 33 F51
Dutton 48 E31
Duxford 33 D50
Dwygyfylchi 47 E23
Dwyran 46 F20
Dyce 91 B34
Dyfatty 17 D20
Dyffryn *M.G.* 18 B24
Dyffryn *Dyf.* 16 A15
Dyffryn Ardudwy 36 C21
Dyffryn Castell 37 G23
Dyffryn Ceidrych 17 B22
Dyffryn Cellwen 18 A24
Dyke *Grm.* 97 F25
Dyke *Dev.* 6 C19
Dyke *Lcn.* 42 C47
Dykehead *Str.* 75 E24
Dykehead *Tay.* 82 A29
Dykehead *Cen.* 74 A22
Dykelands 91 G33
Dykends 82 B28
Dykeside 99 E33
Dylife 37 F24
Dymchurch 15 E56
Dymock 29 E32
Dyrham 20 D33
Dysart 76 A28
Dyserth 47 E26

E

Eadar Dha Fhadhail 100 D6
Eagland Hill 55 E30
Eagle 52 F44
Eaglescliffe 62 E39
Eaglesfield *D.&G.* 69 F28
Eaglesfield *Cum.* 60 D26
Eaglesham 74 E21
Eaglethorpe 42 F46
Eagley 49 A33
Eairy 54 F24
Eakley 32 C44
Eakring 51 F42
Ealand 51 A43
Ealing 22 C47
Eamont Bridge 61 D30
Earby 56 E35
Earcroft 56 G32
Eardington 39 F32
Eardisland 28 C29
Eardisley 28 D28
Eardiston *H.&W.* 29 B32
Eardiston *Shr.* 38 C29
Earith 33 A49
Earle 70 A35
Earlestown 48 C31
Earlham 45 E57
Earlish 93 E9
Earls Barton 32 B44
Earls Colne 34 F54
Earl's Common 29 B35
Earl's Croome 29 D34
Earlsdon 30 A38
Earlsferry 83 G30
Earlsford 99 F34
Earl's Green 34 B56
Earl Shilton 41 F40
Earl Soham 35 B58
Earl Sterndale 50 F36
Earlston 76 G31
Earl Stonham 35 C57
Earlswood *War.* 30 A36
Earlswood *Gwe.* 19 B30
Earnley 12 G44
Earsairidh 84 E3
Earsdon 71 F39
Earsdon Moor 71 D37
Earsham 45 G59
Earswick 58 D42
Eartham 12 F45
Earthcote Green 19 C32
Easby 63 F41
Eascairt 73 E14
Easdale 79 F13
Easebourne 12 D44
Easenhall 41 G40
Eashing 22 G45
Easington *Oxf.* 21 B42
Easington *Hum.* 53 A50
Easington *Cle.* 63 E43
Easington *Nor.* 77 G36
Easington *Bkh.* 21 A42
Easington *Drm* 62 B39
Easington Colliery 62 B39
Easington Lane 62 B39
Easingwold 58 C41
Easole Street 15 B58
Eassie and Nevay 82 C29
East Aberthaw 18 E26
East Allington 5 F23
East Anstey 7 C24
East Appleton 62 G38
East Ardsley 57 G38
East Ashey 11 F41
East Ashling 12 F44
East Auchronie 91 C33
East Ayton 59 A45
East Barkwith 52 D47
East Barming 14 B53
East Barnby 63 E44
East Barnet 23 B48
East Barsham 44 B55
East Beckham 45 B57
East Bedfont 22 D46
East Bergholt 34 E56
East Bilney 44 C55
East Blatchington 13 F50
East Boldon 71 G39
East Boldre 10 D39
East Bolton 71 B37
Eastbourne *Drm* 62 E38
Eastbourne *E.S.* 13 G52
East Bradenham 44 E55
East Brent 19 F29
East Bridge 35 B60
East Bridgford 41 A42
East Brora 97 A24
East Buckland 6 B22
East Budleigh 7 G26
Eastburn 59 D45
East Burrafirth 107 B39
East Burton 9 F34
Eastbury *G.L.* 22 B47
Eastbury *Brk.* 21 D39
Eastby 57 D36
East Cairnbeg 91 F32
East Calder 75 D26
East Carleton 45 E57
East Carlton 42 G44
East Challow 21 C39
East Charleton 5 F23
East Chelborough 8 D31
East Chiltington 13 E49
East Chinnock 8 C30
East Chisenbury 20 F37
Eastchurch 25 D55
East Clandon 22 F46
East Claydon 31 F43
East Clyth 103 E28
East Coker 8 C31
Eastcombe 20 A34
East Combe 7 B27
East Cornworthy 5 E23
Eastcote *G.L.* 22 C47
Eastcote *Nmp.* 31 C42
Eastcote *W.M.* 30 A37
Eastcott *Cnw.* 6 D18
Eastcott *Wts.* 20 F36
East Cottingwith 58 E43
Eastcourt 20 B35
East Cowes 11 E41
East Cowick 58 G42
East Cowton 62 F39
East Cranmore 19 G32
East Creech 9 F35
East Croachy 88 B22
East Darlochan 66 A12
East Davoch 90 C30
East Dean *E.S.* 13 G51
East Dean *Ham.* 10 B38
East Dean *W.S.* 12 E45
East Dereham 44 D55
East Down 6 A21
East Drayton 51 E43
East End *Kent* 14 D54
East End *Ham.* 10 E39
East End *Ham.* 21 E40
East End *Avon* 19 D30
East End *Dor.* 9 E35
East End *Oxf.* 30 G39
Eastend 30 F39
East End *Sfk* 35 E57
East End *Cbs.* 33 F50
Easter Ardross 96 D22
Easter Balmoral 90 D28
Easter Boleskine 88 B21
Easter Borland 81 G22
Easter Brae 96 E22
Easter Buckieburn 75 B23
Easter Compton 19 C31
Easter Drummond 88 C20
Easter Dullater 81 G21
Easter Ellister 72 E8
Easter Fearn 96 C22
Easter Galcantray 97 G24
Eastergate 12 F45
Easter Howlaws 77 F33
Easter Kinkell 96 F21
Easter Knox 83 D31
Easter Lednathie 82 A29
Easter Moniack 96 G21
Easter Ord 91 C34
Easter Poldar 74 A22
Easter Quarff 107 D40
Easter Skeld 107 C38
Easter Suddie 96 F22
Easterton 20 F35
Eastertown 19 F29
Easter Tulloch 91 F33
Easter Whyntie 98 C32
East Farleigh 14 B53
East Farndon 42 G43
East Ferry 51 C43
Eastfield *Str.* 75 D24
Eastfield *N.Y.* 59 A46
Eastfield Hall 71 C38
East Fortune 76 B31
East Garston 21 D39
Eastgate *Drm* 61 C35
Eastgate *Nfk* 45 C57
Eastgate *Lcn.* 42 D47
East Ginge 21 C40
East Goscote 41 D42
East Grafton 21 E38
East Grimstead 10 B38
East Grinstead 13 C49
East Guldeford 14 E55
East Haddon 31 B42
East Hagbourne 21 C41
East Halton 52 A47
East Ham 23 C50
Eastham 48 D29
Easthampstead 22 E44
East Hanney 21 B40
East Hanningfield 24 A53
East Hardwick 51 A40
East Harling 44 G55
East Harlsey 62 F40
East Harptree 19 F31
East Hartford 71 F38
East Harting 12 E44
East Hatch 9 B35
East Hatley 33 C48
East Hauxwell 62 G37
East Haven 83 D31
Eastheath 22 E44
East Heckington 42 A47
East Hedleyhope 62 B37
East Helmsdale 103 G26
East Hendred 21 C40
East Heslerton 59 B45
East Hoathly 13 E51
Easthope 38 F31
East Horndon 24 C52
Easthorpe *Lei.* 42 B43
Easthorpe *Not.* 51 G43
Easthorpe *Esx* 34 F55
East Horrington 19 G31
East Horsley 22 F46
East Horton 77 G36
Easthouses 76 D29
East Huntspill 19 G29
East Hyde 32 G47
East Ilsley 21 C40
Eastington *Glo.* 20 A33
Eastington *Dev.* 7 E23
Eastington *Glo.* 30 G37
East Keal 53 F49
East Kennett 20 E37
East Keswick 57 E39
East Kilbride 74 E22
East Kirkby 53 F49
East Knapton 58 B44
East Knighton 9 F34
East Knoyle 9 A34
East Lambrook 8 C30
East Langdon 15 C59
East Langton 42 F43
East Langwell 96 A23
East Lavant 12 F44
East Lavington 12 E45
East Layton 62 E37
Eastleach Martin 21 A38
Eastleach Turville 20 A37
East Leake 41 C41
East Learmouth 77 G34
East Learney 91 C32
Eastleigh *Ham.* 11 C40
Eastleigh *Dev.* 6 C20
East Leigh 7 E23
East Lexham 44 D54
East Lilburn 71 A36
Eastling 14 B55
East Linton 76 C31
East Liss 11 B43
East Looe 4 E18
East Lound 51 C43
East Lulworth 9 F34
East Lutton 59 C45
East Lydford 8 A31
East Mains 91 D32
East Malling 14 B53
East March 83 D30
East Marden 12 E44
East Markham 51 E43
East Marton 56 D34
East Meon 11 B42
East Mere 7 D25
East Mersea 34 G56
East Mey 103 A28
East Midlands Airport 41 C40
East Molesey 22 E47
East Morden 9 E34
East Morton 57 E36
East Ness 58 B42
Eastney 11 E42
Eastnor 29 E33
East Norton 42 E43
East Oakley 21 G41
Eastoft 51 A43
East Ogwell 5 D24
Eastoke 11 E43
Easton *Ham.* 11 A41
Easton *I.o.W.* 10 F39
Easton *Wts.* 20 D34
Easton *Nfk* 45 D57
Easton *Cum.* 60 A28
Easton *Som.* 19 G30
Easton *Dev.* 9 G32
Easton *Dev.* 7 G23
Easton *Cum.* 69 F30
Easton *Lcn.* 42 C45
Easton *Cbs.* 32 A47
Easton *Sfk* 35 C58
Easton Grey 20 C34
Easton-in -Gordano 19 D31
Easton Maudit 32 C44
Easton on the Hill 42 E46
Easton Royal 21 E38
East Orchard 9 C34
East Ord 77 E35
East Panson 6 F19
East Peckham 23 G52
East Pennard 8 A31
East Poringland 45 E58
East Portlemouth 5 G23
East Prawle 5 G23
East Preston 12 F46
East Putford 6 D19
East Quantoxhead 7 A27
East Rainton 62 B39
East Ravendale 53 C48
East Raynham 44 C54
Eastrea 43 F48
East Retford (Retford) 51 D42
Eastriggs 69 G28
East Rigton 57 E39
Eastrington 58 F43
East Rolstone 19 E29
East Rounton 62 F40
East Rudham 44 C54
East Runton 45 A57
East Ruston 45 C59
Eastry 15 B58
East Saltoun 76 D30
East Shefford 21 D39
Eastside 105 B30
East Sleekburn 71 E38
East Somerton 45 C60
East Stockwith 51 C43
East Stoke *Not.* 42 A43
East Stoke *Dor.* 9 F34
East Stour 9 B33
East Stourmouth 25 E58
East Stratton 11 A41
East Studdal 15 B59
East Suisnish 86 A11
East Taphouse 4 D17
East-the-Water 6 C20
East Thirston 71 D37
East Tilbury 24 D52

East Tisted 11 A43
East Torrington 52 D47
East Tuddenham 44 D56
East Tytherley 10 B39
East Tytherton 20 D35
East Village 7 E24
Eastville 53 G50
East Wall 38 F31
East Walton 44 D53
Eastwell 42 C43
East Wellow 10 B39
East Wemyss 76 A29
East Whitburn 75 D25
Eastwick 33 G50
East Wickham 23 D50
East Williamston 16 D16
East Winch 44 D52
East Wittering 11 E43
East Witton 57 A37
Eastwood W.Y. 56 G35
Eastwood Esx 24 C54
Eastwood Not. 41 A40
East Woodhay 21 E39
East Worldham 11 A43
East Worlington 7 D23
Eathorpe 30 B39
Eaton Lei. 42 C43
Eaton Shr. 38 F31
Eaton Shr. 38 G29
Eaton Not. 51 E42
Eaton Oxf. 21 A40
Eaton Che. 49 F34
Eaton Nfk 45 E58
Eaton Che. 48 F31
Eaton Bishop 28 E30
Eaton Bray 32 F45
Eaton Constantine 39 E32
Eaton Ford 32 C47
Eaton Green 32 F45
Eaton Hall 48 F30
Eaton Hastings 21 B38
Eaton Socon 32 C47
Eaton upon Tern 39 C32
Eavestone 57 C37
Ebberston 58 A44
Ebbesborne Wake 9 B35
Ebbw Vale 18 A27
Ebchester 62 A36
Ebford 7 G25
Ebrington 30 D37
Ecchinswell 21 F40
Ecclaw 77 D33
Ecclefechan 69 F27
Eccles Bor. 77 F33
Eccles G.M. 49 C33
Eccles Kent 24 E53
Ecclesfield 51 C39
Ecclesgreig 83 A33
Ecclesgrieg 91 G33
Eccleshall 40 C34
Ecclesmachan 75 C26
Eccles Road 44 F56
Eccleston Che. 48 F30
Eccleston Mer. 48 C30
Eccleston Lan. 48 A30
Eccup 57 E38
Echt 91 C33
Eckford 70 A32
Eckington Dby. 51 E40
Eckington H.&W. 29 D35
Ecton Nmp. 32 B44
Ecton Stf. 50 G37
Edale 50 D37
Eday Airport 104 C31
Edburton 13 E48
Edderside 60 B26
Edderton 96 C22
Eddington 21 E39
Eddleston 76 F28
Eddlewood 75 E23
Edenbridge 23 G50
Edendonich 80 E17
Edenfield 49 A34
Edenhall 61 C31
Edenham 42 C46
Eden Park 23 E49
Edensor 50 F38
Edentaggart 74 A18
Edenthorpe 51 B42
Edern 36 B18
Edgarley 8 A30
Edgbaston 40 G36
Edgcott 31 F42
Edgcumbe 2 E13
Edge Shr. 38 E29
Edge Glo. 20 A34
Edgebolton 38 C31
Edge End 28 G31
Edgefield 45 B57
Edgeley 38 A31
Edgerley 38 D29
Edgeworth 20 A34
Edginswell 5 D24
Edgmond 39 D32
Edgmond Marsh 39 C33
Edgton 38 G29
Edgware 22 B47
Edgworth 49 A33
Edial 40 E36
Edinample 81 E21
Edinbain 93 F9
Edinbanchory 90 B30
Edinbarnet 74 C21
Edinburgh 76 C28
Edinburgh (Turnhouse) Airport 75 C27
Edinchip 81 E21
Edingale 40 D37
Edingley 51 G42
Edingthorpe 45 B59
Edington Som. 8 A29
Edington Wts. 20 F35
Edintore 98 E30
Edinvale 97 F26
Edistone 6 C18
Edithmead 19 G29
Edith Weston 42 E45
Edlaston 40 A37
Edlesborough 32 G45
Edlingham 71 C36
Edlington 53 E48
Edmondsham 10 C36
Edmondsley 62 B38
Edmondthorpe 42 D44
Edmonstone 104 D31
Edmonton 23 B49
Edmundbyres 62 A36
Ednam 77 G33
Ednaston 40 A38
Edney Common 24 A52
Edra 81 F20
Edradynate 81 B24
Edrom 77 E34
Edstaston 38 B31
Edstone 30 B37
Edvin Loach 29 C32
Edwalton 41 B41
Edwardstone 34 D55
Edwinsford 17 A22
Edwinstowe 51 F41
Edworth 33 D48
Edwyn Ralph 29 C32
Edzell 83 A31
Efail Isaf 18 C26
Efailnewydd 36 B19
Efailwen 16 B17
Efenechtyd 47 G26
Effingham 22 F46
Effirth 107 B38
Efford 7 E24
Egbury 21 F40
Egdean 12 D45
Egerton Kent 14 C55
Egerton G.M. 49 A33
Egerton Forstal 14 C54
Egerton Green 48 G31
Egg Buckland 5 E21
Eggerness 64 F20
Eggesford Barton 6 D22
Eggington 32 F45
Egginton 40 C38
Egglescliffe 62 E39
Eggleston 62 D35
Egham 22 D46
Egleton 42 E44
Eglingham 71 B36
Egloshayle 4 C16
Egloskerry 4 B18
Eglwysbach 47 E23
Eglwys-Brewis 18 E25
Eglwys Cross 38 A30
Eglwys Fach 37 F22
Eglwyswrw 16 A17
Egmanton 51 F43
Egremont 60 E25
Egton 63 F43
Egton Bridge 63 F44
Egypt 21 G40
Eight Ash Green 34 F55
Eignaig 79 C13
Eil 89 C24
Eilanreach 86 C14
Eilean Darach 95 C16
Eilean Iarmain (Isleornsay) 86 C12
Einacleit 100 E7
Eisgean 100 F9
Eisingrug 36 B21
Eisteddfa Gurig 37 G23
Elan Village 27 B25
Elberton 19 C31
Elburton 5 E21
Elcho 82 E27
Elcombe 20 C36
Eldernell 43 F48
Eldersfield 29 E33
Elderslie 74 D20
Eldrick 67 E18
Eldroth 56 C33
Eldwick 57 E37
Elerch (Bont-goch) 37 G22
Elford Stf. 40 D37
Elford Nor. 77 G37
Elgin 97 E27
Elgol 86 C11
Elham 15 C57
Elie 83 G30
Elilaw 70 C35
Elim 46 D19
Eling 10 C39
Eliock 68 C23
Elishader 94 E11
Elishaw 70 D34
Elkesley 51 E42
Elkstone 29 G35
Elland 57 G36
Ellary 73 C13
Ellastone 40 A36
Ellemford 77 D33
Ellenborough 60 C26
Ellenhall 40 C34
Ellen's Green 12 C47
Ellerbeck 62 G40
Ellerby 63 E43
Ellerdine Heath 39 C32
Elleric 80 C16
Ellerker 59 G45
Ellerton Hum. 58 E42
Ellerton N.Y. 62 G38
Ellerton Shr. 39 C33
Ellesborough 22 A44
Ellesmere 38 B29
Ellesmere Port 48 E30
Ellingham Nfk 45 F59
Ellingham Nor. 71 A37
Ellingham Ham. 10 D36
Ellingstring 57 A37
Ellington Nor. 71 D38
Ellington Cbs. 32 A47
Ellisfield 21 G42
Ellistown 41 D40
Ellon 99 F35
Ellonby 60 C30
Ellough 45 G60
Elloughton 59 G45
Ellwood 19 A31
Elm 43 E50
Elmbridge 29 B34
Elmdon Esx 33 E50
Elmdon W.M. 40 G37
Elmdon Heath 40 G37
Elmesthorpe 41 F40
Elmhurst 40 D36
Elmley Castle 29 D35
Elmley Lovett 29 B34
Elmore 29 G33
Elmore Back 29 G33
Elm Park 23 C51
Elmscott 6 C18
Elmsett 34 D56
Elmstead Market 34 F56
Elmstone 25 E58
Elmstone Hardwicke 29 F35
Elmswell Sfk 34 B55
Elmswell Hum. 59 D45
Elmton 51 E40
Elphin 101 G18
Elphinstone 76 C29
Elrick Grm. 90 A30
Elrick Grm. 91 C34
Elrig 64 F19
Elrigbeag 80 F17
Elsdon 70 D35
Elsecar 51 C39
Elsenham 33 F51
Elsfield 21 A41
Elsham 52 A46
Elsing 44 D56
Elslack 56 E35
Elson 38 B29
Elsrickle 75 F26
Elstead 22 G44
Elsted 12 E44
Elsthorpe 42 C46
Elstob 62 D39
Elston Not. 42 A43
Elston Lan. 55 F31
Elstone 6 D22
Elstow 32 D46
Elstree 22 B47
Elstronwick 59 F48
Elswick 55 F30
Elsworth 33 B48
Elterwater 60 F29
Eltham 23 D50
Eltisley 33 C48
Elton Glo. 29 G33
Elton H.&W. 28 A30
Elton Cbs. 42 F46
Elton Dby. 50 F38
Elton Che. 48 E30
Elton Cle. 62 E39
Elton Not. 42 B43
Elvanfoot 68 B25
Elvaston 41 B39
Elveden 34 A54
Elvingston 76 C30
Elvington N.Y. 58 E43
Elvington Kent 15 B58
Elwick Nor. 77 G36
Elwick Cle. 62 C40
Elworth 49 F33
Elworthy 7 B26
Ely S.G. 18 D27
Ely Cbs. 33 A51
Emberton 32 D44
Embleton Nor. 71 A38
Embleton Cum. 60 C27
Embo 97 B24
Emborough 19 F31
Embo Street 96 B23
Embsay 56 D35
Emery Down 10 D38
Emley 50 A38
Emmer Green 22 D43
Emmington 22 A43
Emneth 43 E50
Emneth Hungate 43 E51
Empingham 42 E45
Empshott 11 A43
Emsworth 11 D43
Enborne 21 E40
Enchmarsh 38 F30
Enderby 41 F41
Endmoor 55 A31
Endon 49 G35
Enfield 23 B49
Enford 20 F37
Engine Common 19 C32
Englefield 21 D42
Englefield Green 22 D45
Englesea-brook 49 G33
English Bicknor 28 G31
Englishcombe 19 E32
English Frankton 38 B30
Enham Alamein 21 F39
Enmore 8 A28
Ennerdale Bridge 60 E26
Enochdu 82 A26
Ensay 78 C9
Ensdon 38 D29
Ensis 6 C21
Enstone 30 F39
Enterkinfoot 68 C24
Enterpen 62 F40
Enville 40 G34
Eolaigearraidh 84 D3
Eorabus 78 E9
Eorodal 101 A11
Eoropaidh 100 A10
Epperstone 41 A42
Epping 23 A50
Epping Green Esx 23 A50
Epping Green Hfs. 23 A48
Epping Upland 23 A50
Eppleby 62 E37
Eppleworth 59 F46
Epsom 22 E47
Epwell 30 D39
Epworth 51 B43
Erbistock 38 A29
Erbusaig 86 B13
Erchless Castle 96 G20
Erdington 40 F36
Eredine 80 G15
Eriboll 102 C20
Ericstane 69 B26
Eridge Green 13 C51
Eriff 67 C21
Erines 73 C14
Eriswell 33 A52
Erith 23 D50
Erlestoke 20 F35
Ermington 5 E22
Erpingham 45 B57
Errogie 88 B21
Errol 82 E28
Errollston 99 F36
Erskine 74 C20
Erwarton 35 E58
Erwood 27 D26
Eryholme 62 F39
Eryrys 48 G28
Escart 73 D14
Escrick 58 E42
Esgair 17 B19
Esgairgeiliog 37 E23
Esh 62 B37
Esher 22 E47
Eshott 71 D37
Eshton 56 D35
Esh Winning 62 B37
Eskadale 88 A20
Eskbank 76 D29
Eskdale Green 60 F27
Eskdalemuir 69 D28
Eskham 53 C49
Esknish 72 D9
Espley Hall 71 D37
Esprick 55 F30
Essendine 42 D46
Essendon 23 A48
Essich 88 A22
Essington 40 E35
Esslemont 91 A35
Eston 63 E41
Etal 77 G35
Etchilhampton 20 E36
Etchingham 13 D52
Etchinghill Kent 15 D57
Etchinghill Stf. 40 D35
Ethie Mains 83 C32
Eton 22 D45
Eton Wick 22 D45
Etteridge 88 E22
Ettingshall 40 F35
Ettington 30 D38
Etton Cbs. 42 E47
Etton Hum. 59 E45
Ettrick 69 B28
Ettrickbridge 69 A29
Ettrickhill 69 B28
Etwall 40 B38
Eurach 79 G14
Euston 34 A54
Euxton 55 G31
Evanton 96 E21
Evedon 42 A46
Evelix 96 B23
Evenjobb 28 B28
Evenley 31 E41
Evenlode 30 F37
Evenwood 62 D37
Everbay 104 D32
Evercreech 9 A32
Everdon 31 C41
Everingham 58 E44
Everleigh 20 F37
Everley N.Y. 59 A45
Everley Hgh. 103 B29
Eversholt 32 E45
Evershot 8 D31
Eversley 22 E43
Eversley Cross 22 E43
Everthorpe 58 F44
Everton Bfd. 32 C47
Everton Not. 51 C42
Everton Ham. 10 E38
Evertown 69 F29
Evesbatch 29 D32
Evesham 30 D36
Evie 104 D29
Evington 41 E42
Ewart Newtown 77 G35
Ewden Village 50 C38
Ewell 22 E47
Ewell Minnis 15 C58
Ewelme 21 B42
Ewen 20 B36
Ewenny 18 D24
Ewerby 42 A47
Ewerby Thorpe 42 A47
Ewhurst Sry 22 G46
Ewhurst E.S. 14 E53
Ewhurst Green 12 C46
Ewloe 48 F28
Ewood 56 G32
Eworthy 6 F20
Ewshot 22 G44
Ewyas Harold 28 F29
Exbourne 6 E22
Exbury 11 D40
Exebridge 7 C24
Exelby 57 A38
Exeter 7 F24
Exford 7 B24
Exfords Green 38 E30
Exhall 30 C36
Exlade Street 21 C42
Exminster 7 G25
Exmouth 7 G25
Exnaboe 107 E37
Exning 33 B51
Exton Lei. 42 D45
Exton Dev. 7 G25
Exton Som. 7 B25
Exton Ham. 11 B41
Exwick 7 F24
Eyam 50 E38
Eydon 31 C41
Eye H.&W. 28 B30
Eye Sfk 35 A57
Eye Cbs. 43 E48
Eye Green 43 E48
Eyemouth 77 D35
Eyeworth 33 D48
Eyhorne Street 14 B54
Eyke 35 C59
Eynesbury 32 C47
Eynort 85 B9
Eynsford 23 E51
Eynsham 21 A40
Eype 8 E30
Eyre 93 F10
Eythorne 15 C58
Eyton H.&W. 28 B30
Eyton Clw. 38 A29
Eyton Shr. 38 G29
Eyton upon the Weald Moors 39 D32

Eywood 28 C28

F

Faccombe 21 F39
Faceby 62 F40
Fachwen 46 F21
Faddiley 48 G31
Fadmoor 58 A42
Faebait 96 F20
Faifley 74 C21
Fail 67 A20
Failand 19 D30
Failford 67 A20
Failsworth 49 B34
Fain 95 D17
Fairbourne 36 D21
Fairburn 57 G40
Fairfield *Dby.* 50 E36
Fairfield *H.&W.* 29 A35
Fairford 20 A37
Fairgirth 65 E24
Fairholm 75 E23
Fairley 91 C34
Fairlie 73 E17
Fairlight 14 F54
Fairlight Cove 14 F54
Fairmile 7 F26
Fairmilehead 76 D28
Fairnington 70 A32
Fairoak 39 B33
Fair Oak *Ham.* 11 C40
Fair Oak *Ham.* 21 E41
Fairseat 24 E52
Fairstead *Esx* 34 G53
Fairstead *Nfk* 45 C58
Fairwarp 13 D50
Fairy Cross 6 C19
Fairyhill 17 E20
Fakenham 44 C55
Fala 76 D30
Fala Dam 76 D30
Falahill 76 E29
Faldingworth 52 D46
Falfield *Avon* 19 B32
Falfield *Fife* 83 G30
Falkenham 35 E58
Falkirk 75 B24
Falkland 82 G28
Falla 70 B32
Fallgate 51 F39
Fallin 75 A24
Falmer 13 F49
Falmouth 2 E13
Falsgrave 59 A46
Falstone 70 E33
Fanagmore 101 C17
Fanans 80 E16
Fancott 32 F46
Fangdale Beck 63 G41
Fangfoss 58 D43
Fanmore 79 C10
Fans 76 F32
Farcet 42 F47
Far Cotton 31 C43
Farden 28 A31
Fareham 11 D41
Farewell 40 D36
Far Forest 29 A33
Farforth 53 E49
Far Gearstones 56 A33
Faringdon 21 B38
Farington 55 G31
Farlam 61 A31
Farlary 96 A23
Farleigh *Sry* 23 E49
Farleigh *Avon* 19 E30
Farleigh Hungerford 20 F33
Farleigh Wallop 21 G42
Farlesthorpe 53 E50
Farleton 55 A31
Farley *Stf.* 40 A36
Farley *Shr.* 38 E29
Farley *Wts.* 10 B38
Farley Green 22 G46
Farley Hill 22 E43
Farleys End 29 G33
Farlington 58 C42
Farlow 39 G32
Farmborough 19 E32
Farmcote 30 F36
Farmington 30 G37
Farmoor 21 A40
Farmtown 98 D30
Farnborough *Ham.* 22 F43
Farnborough *War.* 31 C40
Farnborough *Sry* 23 E50
Farnborough *Brk.* 21 C40
Farnborough Green 22 F44
Farncombe 22 G45
Farndish 32 B45
Farndon *Not.* 51 G43
Farndon *Che.* 48 G30
Farnell 83 B32
Farnham *Sfk* 35 C59
Farnham *Esx* 33 F50
Farnham *Sry* 22 G44
Farnham *N.Y.* 57 C39
Farnham *Dor.* 9 C35
Farnham Common 22 C45
Farnham Green 33 F50
Farnham Royal 22 C45
Farningham 23 E51
Farnley 57 E37
Farnley Tyas 50 A37
Farnsfield 51 G42
Farnworth *G.M.* 49 B33
Farnworth *Che.* 48 D31
Farr *Hgh.* 88 A22
Farr *Hgh.* 89 D24
Farr *Hgh.* 102 B23
Farraline 88 B21
Farr Ho. 88 A22
Farringdon 7 F26
Farrington Gurney 19 F32
Farsley 57 F38
Farthinghoe 31 E41
Farthingloe 15 D58
Farthingstone 31 C41
Farway 7 F27
Fasag 94 F14
Fasagrianach 95 C17
Fascadale 79 A10
Faslane 74 B18
Fasnacloich 80 C16
Fasnakyle 87 B18
Fassfern 87 G16
Fatfield 62 A38
Fattahead 98 D32
Faugh 61 A30
Fauldhouse 75 D24
Faulkbourne 34 G53
Faulkland 20 F33
Fauls 38 B31
Faversham 25 E55
Favillar 98 F28
Fawdington 57 B40
Fawdon 71 G38
Fawfieldhead 50 F36
Fawkham Green 23 E51
Fawler 30 G39
Fawley *Bkh.* 22 C43
Fawley *Brk.* 21 C39
Fawley *Ham.* 11 D40
Fawley Chapel 28 F31
Fawsyde 91 F34
Faxfleet 58 G44
Faxton 31 A43
Faygate 12 C47
Fazeley 40 E37
Fearby 57 A37
Fearn 97 D24
Fearnach 73 C16
Fearnan 81 C23
Fearnbeg 94 F13
Fearnhead 49 C32
Fearnmore 94 E13
Fearnoch 73 B15
Featherstone *W.Y.* 57 G39
Featherstone *Stf.* 40 E35
Featherstone Castle 70 G32
Feckenham 29 B35
Feering 34 F54
Feetham 62 G35
Feith-hill 98 E32
Feizor 56 C33
Felbridge 13 C49
Felbrigg 45 B58
Felcourt 23 G49
Felden 22 A46
Felindre *Dyf.* 17 B21
Felindre *Dyf.* 27 F23
Felindre *Dyf.* 17 A19
Felindre *Pow.* 38 G27
Felindre *W.G.* 17 D22
Felinfach 27 E26
Felinfoel 17 D21
Felingwmuchaf 17 B20
Felixkirk 57 A40
Felixstowe 35 E59
Felixstoweferry 35 E59
Felkington 77 F35
Felldownhead 6 G19
Felling 71 G38
Fellonmore 79 E12
Felmersham 32 C45
Felmingham 45 C58
Felpham 12 G45
Felsham 34 C55
Felsted 33 F52
Feltham 22 D46
Felthorpe 45 D57
Felton *Avon* 19 E31
Felton *H.&W.* 28 D31
Felton *Nor.* 71 C37
Felton Butler 38 D29
Feltwell 44 G52
Fence 56 F34
Fence Houses 62 A38
Fencott 31 G41
Fendike Corner 53 F50
Fen Ditton 33 C50
Fen Drayton 33 B49
Fen End 30 A38
Fenhouses 43 A48
Feniscowles 56 G32
Feniton 7 F26
Fenny Bentley 40 A37
Fenny Bridges 7 F26
Fenny Compton 31 C40
Fenny Drayton 41 F39
Fenny Stratford 32 E44
Fenrother 71 D37
Fenstanton 33 B49
Fen Street 34 A55
Fenton *Cbs.* 33 A49
Fenton *Stf.* 40 A34
Fenton *Lcn.* 52 G44
Fenton *Lcn.* 52 E44
Fenton *Nor.* 77 G35
Fenwick *Nor.* 77 F36
Fenwick *Str.* 74 F20
Fenwick *S.Y.* 51 A41
Fenwick *Nor.* 71 F36
Feochaig 66 B13
Feock 3 E14
Feolin 72 D11
Feolin Ferry 72 D10
Feorlan 66 C12
Feorlin 73 A15
Feriniquarrie 93 F7
Fern 83 A30
Ferndale 18 B25
Ferndown 10 D36
Ferness 97 G25
Fernham 21 B38
Fernhill Heath 29 C34
Fernhurst 12 D44
Fernie 82 F29
Fernilea 85 A9
Fernilee 49 E35
Fernybank 90 F31
Ferrensby 57 C39
Ferring 12 F46
Ferrybridge 57 G40
Ferryden 83 B32
Ferryhill 62 C38
Ferryside 17 C19
Fersfield 44 G56
Fersit 88 G19
Feshiebridge 89 D24
Fetcham 22 F47
Fetterangus 99 D35
Fettercairn 91 F32
Fetternear Ho. 91 B32
Feus of Caldhame 91 G32
Fewcott 31 F41
Fewston 57 D37
Ffairfach 17 B22
Ffair-Rhos 27 B23
Ffarmers 27 D22
Ffawyddog 28 G27
Ffestiniog 37 A22
Ffordd-las 47 F27
Fforest 17 D21
Fforest-fach 17 E21
Ffostrasol 26 D19
Ffos-y-ffin 26 B20
Ffridd Uchaf 46 G21
Ffrith 48 G28
Ffrwdgrech 27 F26
Ffynnon-ddrain 17 B19
Ffynnongroyw 47 D27
Fibhig 100 C8
Fichlie 90 B30
Fidden 78 E8
Fiddington *Som.* 19 G28
Fiddington *Glo.* 29 E34
Fiddler's Green 28 E31
Fiddlers Hamlet 23 A50
Field 40 B36
Field Broughton 55 A29
Field Dalling 44 B56
Field Head 41 E40
Fifehead Magdalen 9 B33
Fifehead Neville 9 C33
Fife Keith 98 D29
Fifield *Brk.* 22 D45
Fifield *Oxf.* 30 G38
Fifield Bavant 10 B36
Figheldean 20 G37
Filby 45 D60
Filey 59 B47
Filgrave 32 D44
Filkins 21 A38
Filleigh *Dev.* 6 C22
Filleigh *Dev.* 7 D23
Fillingham 52 D45
Fillongley 40 G38
Filmore Hill 11 B42
Filton 19 D31
Fimber 58 C44
Finavon 83 B30
Fincham 44 E52
Finchampstead 22 E43
Finchdean 11 C43
Finchingfield 33 E52
Finchley 23 B48
Findern 40 B38
Findhorn 97 E26
Findhorn Bridge 88 B23
Findhuglen 81 F23
Findochty 98 C30
Findo Gask 82 E26
Findon *W.S.* 12 F47
Findon *Grm.* 91 D35
Findon Mains 96 E21
Findrassie 97 E27
Findron 90 B27
Finedon 32 A45
Finegand 82 A27
Fingal Street 35 A58
Fingask 91 A33
Fingerpost 29 A33
Fingest 22 B43
Finghall 57 A37
Fingland *Cum.* 60 A28
Fingland *D.&G.* 69 C28
Fingland *D.&G.* 68 B23
Finglesham 15 B58
Fingringhoe 34 G56
Finlarig 81 D21
Finmere 31 E42
Finnart *Tay.* 81 B21
Finnart *Str.* 74 A18
Finningham 34 B56
Finningly 51 C42
Finnygaud 98 D31
Finsbury 23 C48
Finstall 29 A35
Finsthwaite 55 A29
Finstock 30 G39
Finstown 104 E29
Fintry *Cen.* 74 B21
Fintry *Grm.* 99 D33
Finzean 90 D31
Fionnphort 78 E8
Firbank 61 G32
Firbeck 51 D41
Firgrove 49 A35
Firsby 53 F50
Firs Road 10 A38
First Coast 94 B14
Firth 106 E40
Fir Tree 62 C37
Fir Vale 51 D39
Fishbourne *W.S.* 12 F44
Fishbourne *I.o.W.* 11 E41
Fishburn 62 C39
Fisherford 98 F32
Fisher's Pond 11 B40
Fisher's Row 55 E30
Fisherstreet 12 C45
Fisherton *Hgh.* 96 F23
Fisherton *Str.* 67 B18
Fisherton de la Mere 20 G35
Fishguard 16 A15
Fishlake 51 A42
Fishley Barton 6 C21
Fishpond Bottom 8 E29
Fishponds 19 D32
Fishpool 49 B33
Fishtoft 43 A49
Fishtoft Drove 43 A48
Fishtown of Usan 83 B32
Fishwick *Bor.* 77 E34
Fishwick *Lan.* 55 F31
Fiskerton *Lcn.* 52 E46
Fiskerton *Not.* 51 G43
Fittleton 20 F37
Fittleworth 12 E46
Fitton End 43 D50
Fitz 38 D30
Fitzhead 7 C27
Fitzwilliam 51 A39
Fiunary 79 C12
Five Ash Down 13 D50
Five Ashes 13 D51
Five Bridges 29 D32
Fivehead 8 B29
Fivelanes 4 B17
Five Oak Green 23 G52
Five Oaks *W.S.* 12 D46
Five Oaks *C.I.* 3 G17
Five Roads 17 D20
Five Turnings 28 A28
Five Wents 14 B53
Flackwell Heath 22 C44
Fladbury 29 D35
Fladdabister 107 D40
Flagg 50 F37
Flamborough 59 B47
Flamstead 32 G46
Flamstead End 23 A49
Flansham 12 F45
Flasby 56 D35
Flash 50 F36
Flashader 93 F9
Flask Inn 63 F45
Flaunden 22 A46
Flawborough 42 A43
Flawith 57 C40
Flax Bourton 19 E30
Flaxby 57 D39
Flaxley 29 G32
Flaxpool 7 B27
Flaxton 58 C42
Fleckney 41 F42
Flecknoe 31 B40
Fleet *Lcn.* 43 C49
Fleet *Ham.* 22 F43
Fleet Hargate 43 C49
Fleetwood 55 E28
Flemingston 18 E25
Flemington 74 E22
Flempton 34 B53
Fleoideabhagh 92 C6
Fletchertown 60 B27
Fletching 13 D50
Flete 5 E22
Fleuchats 90 C29
Fleur-de-lis 18 B27
Flexbury 6 E18
Flexford 22 F45
Flimby 60 C26
Flimwell 14 D53
Flint 48 E28
Flint Cross 33 D49
Flintham 42 A43
Flint Mountain 48 E28
Flinton 59 F48
Flishinghurst 14 D53
Flitcham 44 C53
Flitton 32 E46
Flitwick 32 E46
Flixborough 52 A44
Flixton *G.M.* 49 C33
Flixton *Sfk* 45 G59
Flockton 50 A38
Flockton Green 50 A38
Flodden 77 G34
Flodigarry 93 D10
Flookburgh 55 B29
Floors 98 D30
Flordon 45 F57
Flore 31 B42
Flotterton 70 C35
Flowton 34 D56
Flushing *Grm.* 99 E36
Flushing *Cnw.* 3 E14
Flyford Flavell 29 C35
Fobbing 24 C53
Fochabers 98 D29
Fochriw 18 A26
Fockerby 52 A44
Fodderletter 90 A27
Fodderty 96 E20
Foel 37 D25
Foffarty 82 C29
Foggathorpe 58 F43
Fogo 77 F33
Fogorig 77 F33
Foindle 101 D17
Folda 82 A27
Fole 40 B36
Foleshill 41 G39
Folke 9 C32
Folkestone 15 D58
Folkingham 42 B46
Folkington 13 F51
Folksworth 42 G47
Folla Rule 99 F33
Follifoot 57 D39
Folly *Dyf.* 16 B15
Folly *Dor.* 9 D33
Folly Gate 6 F21
Fonthill Bishop 9 A35
Fonthill Gifford 9 A35
Fontmell Magna 9 C34
Fontwell 12 F45
Foolow 50 E37
Foots Cray 23 D50
Forbestown 90 B29
Force Forge 60 G29
Forcett 62 E37
Forches Cross 7 E23
Ford *Str.* 79 G14
Ford *Dev.* 5 E22
Ford *Dev.* 6 C20
Ford *Mer.* 48 B29
Ford *Dev.* 5 F23
Ford *Ltn* 76 D29
Ford *Wts.* 20 D34
Ford *Nor.* 77 G35
Ford *Shr.* 38 D30
Ford *Glo.* 30 F36
Ford *Som.* 7 C26
Ford *Dyf.* 16 B15
Ford *Bkh.* 22 A43
Ford *W.S.* 12 F45
Fordcombe 23 G51
Fordell 75 B27
Forden 38 E28
Ford End 33 G52
Forder Green 5 D23
Fordham *Esx* 34 F55
Fordham *Cbs.* 33 A52
Fordham *Nfk* 43 F51
Fordham Abbey 33 B52
Fordingbridge 10 C37

Fordoun 91 F33
Fordstreet 34 F54
Ford Street 7 D27
Fordwells 30 G38
Fordwich 15 B57
Fordyce 98 C31
Forebrae 82 E25
Foreland 72 D8
Forestburn Gate 71 D36
Forest Gate 23 C50
Forest Green 22 G46
Forest Hall *Cum.* 61 F31
Forest Hall *T.&W.* 71 G38
Forest Head 61 A31
Forest Hill 21 A41
Forest-in-Teesdale 61 D34
Forest Lodge *Str.* 80 C18
Forest Lodge *Tay.* 89 G25
Forest Mill 75 A25
Forest Row 13 C50
Forestside 11 C43
Forest Town 51 F41
Forfar 83 C30
Forgandenny 82 F26
Forgie 98 D29
Formby 48 B28
Forncett End 45 F57
Forncett St Mary 45 F57
Forncett St Peter 45 F57
Forneth 82 C26
Fornham All Saints 34 B53
Fornham St Martin 34 B54
Fornighty 97 F25
Forres 97 F26
Forrest 75 D24
Forrest Lodge 67 E21
Forsbrook 40 A35
Forse 103 E28
Forsie 103 B26
Forsinain 102 D24
Forsinard 102 D24
Forston 9 E32
Fort Augustus 88 D19
Forter 82 A27
Forteviot 82 F26
Fort George 96 F23
Forth 75 E25
Forthampton 29 E34
Fortingall 81 C23
Forton *Som.* 8 D29
Forton *Stf.* 39 C33
Forton *Shr.* 38 D30
Forton *Ham.* 21 G40
Forton *Lan.* 55 D30
Fortrie 98 E32
Fortrose 96 F23
Fortuneswell 9 G32
Fort William 87 G16
Forty Green 22 B45
Forty Hill 23 B49
Forward Green 34 C56
Fosbury 21 F39
Foscot 30 F38
Fosdyke 43 B49
Foss 81 B23
Foss Cross 30 G36
Fossdale 61 G34
Fossebridge 30 G36
Foster's Booth 31 C42
Foster Street 23 A50
Foston *N.Y.* 58 C42
Foston *Lcn.* 42 A44
Foston *Dby.* 40 B37
Foston on the Wolds 59 D47
Fotherby 53 C48
Fotheringhay 42 F46
Foubister 105 A31
Foulbog 69 C28
Foulden *Bor.* 77 E35
Foulden *Nfk* 44 F53
Foul Mile 13 E52
Foulridge 56 E34
Foulsham 44 C56
Foulzie 99 C33
Fountainhall 76 F30
Four Ashes *Sfk* 34 A55
Four Ashes *Stf.* 40 E35
Four Crosses *Stf.* 40 E35
Four Crosses *Pow.* 38 D28
Four Crosses *Clw.* 37 A26
Four Crosses *Pow.* 37 E26
Four Elms 23 G50
Four Forks 8 A28
Four Gotes 43 D50
Fourlane Ends 51 G39
Four Lanes 2 E12
Fourlanes End 49 G34
Four Marks 11 A42
Four Mile Bridge 46 E18
Four Oaks *W.M.* 40 G38
Four Oaks *W.M.* 40 F36
Four Oaks *E.S.* 14 E54
Fourpenny 96 B23
Four Roads 17 D20
Fourstones 70 G34
Four Throws 14 E53
Fovant 10 B36
Foveran 91 A35
Fowey 4 E16
Fowlis 82 D29
Fowlis Wester 82 E25
Fowlmere 33 D49
Fownhope 28 E31
Foxcote 29 G35
Foxdale 54 F24
Foxearth 34 D54
Foxfield 55 A28
Foxham 20 D35
Foxhole *Hgh.* 88 A21
Foxhole *Cnw.* 3 C15
Foxhunt Green 13 E51
Fox Lane 22 F44
Foxley *Wts.* 20 C34
Foxley *Nmp.* 31 C42
Foxley *H.&W.* 28 D30
Foxley *Nfk* 44 C56
Fox Street 34 F56
Foxt 40 A36
Foxton *Cbs.* 33 D49
Foxton *Lei.* 41 G43
Foxton *N.Y.* 62 D39
Foxup 56 B34
Foxwist Green 49 F32
Foy 28 F31
Foyers 88 B20
Frachadil 78 B9
Fraddam 2 E11
Fraddon 3 C15
Fradley 40 D37
Fradswell 40 B35
Fraisthorpe 59 C47
Framfield 13 D50
Framingham Earl 45 E58
Framingham Pigot 45 E58
Framlingham 35 B58
Frampton *Lcn.* 43 B49
Frampton *Dor.* 9 E32
Frampton Cotterell 19 C32
Frampton Mansell 20 A34
Frampton on Severn 20 A33
Frampton West End 43 A49
Framsden 35 C58
Framwellgate Moor 62 B38
Franche 29 A34
Frankby 48 D28
Frankley 40 G35
Frankton 31 A40
Frant 13 C51
Fraserburgh 99 C35
Frating Green 34 F56
Fratton 11 D42
Freathy 4 E19
Freckenham 33 A52
Freckleton 55 G30
Freeby 42 C43
Freefolk 21 G40
Freeland 30 G39
Freemantle 11 C40
Freester 107 B40
Freethorpe 45 E60
Freethorpe Common 45 E59
Freiston *Lcn.* 43 A49
Freiston *Lcn.* 42 A45
Freiston Shore 43 A50
Fremington *Dev.* 6 B21
Fremington *N.Y.* 62 G36
Frenchay 19 D32
Frenchbeer 6 G22
Frendraught 98 E31
Frenich 80 G19
Frensham 22 G44
Fresgoe 103 B25
Freshfield 48 B28
Freshford 20 F33
Freshwater 10 F39
Freshwater East 16 E16
Fressingfield 35 A58
Freston 35 E57
Freswick 103 B29
Frettenham 45 D58
Freuchie 82 G28
Freystrop Cross 16 C15
Friars Carse 68 E25
Friar's Gate 13 C50
Friarton 82 E26
Friday Bridge 43 E50
Friday Street *E.S.* 13 F52
Friday Street *Sry* 22 G47
Fridaythorpe 58 D44
Friern Barnet 23 B48
Friesthorpe 52 D46
Frieth 22 B43
Frilford 21 B40
Frilsham 21 D41
Frimley 22 F44
Frimley Green 22 F44
Frindsbury 24 E53
Fringford 31 F41
Frinsted 14 B54
Frinton-on-Sea 35 G58
Friockheim 83 C31
Friog 37 D22
Frisby on the Wreake 41 D42
Friskney 53 G50
Friskney Eaudike 53 G50
Friston *E.S.* 13 G51
Friston *Sfk* 35 C60
Fritchley 51 G39
Frith 14 B55
Fritham 10 C38
Frith Bank 43 A49
Frith Common 29 A32
Frithelstock 6 D20
Frithelstock Stone 6 D20
Frithville 53 G49
Frittenden 14 C53
Fritton *Nfk* 45 E60
Fritton *Nfk* 45 F58
Fritwell 31 F41
Frizington 60 E26
Frocester 20 A33
Frochas 38 E28
Frodesley 38 E30
Frodingham 52 A44
Frodsham 48 E31
Frogden 70 A33
Frog End 33 C50
Froggatt 50 E38
Froghall 40 A36
Frogham 10 C37
Frogmore *Ham.* 22 F44
Frogmore *Hfs.* 22 A47
Frogmore *Dev.* 5 F23
Frog Pool 29 B33
Frolesworth 41 F40
Frome 20 G33
Fromes Hill 29 D32
Frome St Quentin 8 D31
Fron *Pow.* 38 E28
Fron *Gwy.* 36 B19
Fron *Pow.* 27 B26
Froncysyllte 38 A28
Fron-goch 37 B24
Frostenden 45 G60
Frosterley 62 C36
Froxfield 21 E38
Froxfield Green 11 B43
Fryerning 24 A52
Fryton 58 B42
Fugglestone St Peter 10 A37
Fulbeck 52 G45
Fulbourn 33 C50
Fulbrook 30 G38
Fulford *Stf.* 40 B35
Fulford *Som.* 7 C27
Fulford *N.Y.* 58 E42
Fulham 23 D48
Fulking 13 E48
Fuller's Moor 48 G30
Fuller Street 34 G53
Fullerton 10 A39
Fulletby 53 E48
Full Sutton 58 D43
Fullwood 74 F20
Fulmer 22 C45
Fulmodeston 44 B55
Fulnetby 52 E47
Fulready 30 D38
Fulstow 53 C49
Fulwell *Oxf.* 30 F39
Fulwell *T.&W.* 62 A39
Fulwood *S.Y.* 51 D39
Fulwood *Lan.* 55 F31
Fundenhall 45 F57
Funtington 11 D43
Funtley 11 D41
Funzie 106 C42
Furley 8 D28
Furnace *Str.* 80 G16
Furnace *Dyf.* 37 F22
Furnace *Hgh.* 94 D15
Furneux Pelham 33 F50
Furzehill 7 A23
Furze Platt 22 C44
Fyfett 8 C28
Fyfield *Oxf.* 21 B40
Fyfield *Wts.* 20 E37
Fyfield *Glo.* 21 A38
Fyfield *Esx* 23 A51
Fyfield *Ham.* 21 G38
Fylingthorpe 63 F45
Fyvie 99 F33

G

Gabhsunn Bho Dheas 100 A10
Gabhsunn Bho Thuath 100 B10
Gablon 96 B22
Gabroc Hill 74 E20
Gaddesby 41 D42
Gaddesden Row 32 G46
Gaer 28 F27
Gaerllwyd 19 B30
Gaerwen 46 E20
Gagingwell 30 F39
Gaich 89 B26
Gaick 88 A22
Gaick Lodge 88 F23
Gailey 40 D34
Gainford 62 E37
Gainsborough 51 C43
Gairloch 94 D13
Gairlochy 87 F17
Gairney Bank 75 A27
Gairnshiel Lodge 90 C28
Gaitsgill 60 B29
Galabank 76 F30
Galashiels 76 G30
Galby 41 E42
Galdenoch 64 D17
Galgate 55 D30
Galhampton 9 B32
Gallanach 79 E14
Gallantry Bank 48 G31
Gallatown 76 A28
Gallchoille 73 B13
Gallery 91 G32
Galley Common 41 F39
Galleyend 24 A52
Galleywood 24 A52
Gallowfauld 83 C30
Gallowstree Common 21 C42
Gallowstree Elm 39 G33
Galltair 86 C14
Galmisdale 85 F10
Galmpton *Dev.* 5 E24
Galmpton *Dev.* 5 F22
Galphay 57 B38
Galston 74 G21
Galtrigill 93 F7
Gamblesby 61 C31
Gamble's Green 34 G53
Gamelsby 60 A28
Gamlingay 33 C48
Gammaton Moor 6 C20
Gammersgill 57 A36
Gamrie 99 C33
Gamston *Not.* 41 B41
Gamston *Not.* 51 E42
Ganarew 28 G31
Ganllwyd 37 C23
Gannochy 90 F31
Ganstead 59 F47
Ganthorpe 58 B42
Ganton 59 B45
Gaodhail 79 D11
Garabal 80 F18
Gara Bridge 5 E23
Garadheancal 94 A15
Garbat 96 E20
Garbhallt 73 A16
Garboldisham 44 G56
Garden 74 A21
Garden City 48 F29
Gardenstown 99 C33
Garderhouse 107 C38
Gardham 59 E45
Gare Hill 20 G33
Garelochhead 73 A17
Garford 21 B40
Garforth 57 F40
Gargrave 56 D35
Gargunnock 74 A22
Gariob 73 B13
Garlies Castle 64 D20
Garlieston 64 F20
Garlogie 91 C33
Garmond 99 D33
Garmony 79 C12
Garmouth 98 C28
Garn 36 B18
Garnant 17 C22
Garn-Dolbenmaen 36 A20
Garneddwen 37 E23
Garnett Bridge 61 G31
Garnswllt 17 D22
Garrabost 100 D10
Garrachra 73 B16
Garralburn 98 D30
Garras 2 F12
Garreg 36 A21
Garreg Bank 38 D28
Garrick 81 F24
Garrigill 61 B33
Garroch 67 E21
Garrochty 73 E16
Garros 93 E10
Garrow 81 D24
Garryhorn 67 D21
Garsdale Head 61 G33
Garsdon 20 C35
Garshall Green 40 B35
Garsington 21 A41
Garstang 55 E30
Garston 48 D29
Garswood 48 C31
Gartachoil 74 A21
Gartally 88 A20
Gartavaich 73 E14
Gartbreck 72 E8
Gartcosh 74 D22
Garth *M.G.* 18 B24
Garth *Gwy.* 46 E21
Garth *I.o.M.* 54 F25
Garth *She.* 107 B38
Garth *Clw.* 38 A28
Garth *Pow.* 27 D25
Garthbrengy 27 E26
Gartheli 26 C21
Garthmyl 38 F27
Garthorpe *Lei.* 42 C44
Garthorpe *Hum.* 52 A44
Garths 61 G31
Garthynty 27 D22
Gartincaper 81 G22
Gartly 98 F31
Gartmore 74 A20
Gartnagrenach 73 E13
Gartnatra 72 E9
Gartness 74 B20
Gartocharn 74 B19
Garton 59 F48
Garton-on-the-Wolds 59 C45
Gartymore 103 G25
Garvald 76 C31
Garvamore 88 E21
Garvan 86 G15
Garvard 72 A9
Garve 96 E19
Garveld 66 C12
Garvestone 44 E55
Garvie 73 B16
Garvock *Str.* 74 C18
Garvock *Tay.* 82 F26
Garvock *Grm.* 91 F33
Garwald 69 C28
Garwaldwaterfoot 69 C28
Garway 28 F30
Garway Hill 28 F30
Gask *Grm.* 99 E33
Gask *Grm.* 99 F36
Gask *Tay.* 82 F25
Gaskan 86 G13
Gass 67 C20
Gastard 20 E34
Gasthorpe 44 G55
Gatcombe 11 F40
Gateacre 48 D30
Gatebeck 55 A31
Gate Burton 52 D44
Gateford 51 D41
Gateforth 58 G41
Gatehead 74 G19
Gate Helmsley 58 D42
Gatehouse *Tay.* 81 C24
Gatehouse *Str.* 72 C11
Gatehouse of Fleet 65 E22
Gatelawbridge 68 D24
Gateley 44 C55
Gatenby 57 A39
Gateshaw 70 A33
Gateshead 71 G38
Gatesheath 48 F30
Gateside *Str.* 74 E19
Gateside *Fife* 82 G27
Gateside *Tay.* 83 C30
Gateside *Grm.* 91 B32
Gateslack 68 C24
Gathurst 48 B31
Gatley 49 D34
Gattonside 76 G31
Gatwick (London) Airport 23 G48
Gaufron 27 B25
Gauldry 82 E29
Gaunt's Common 10 D36
Gautby 52 E47
Gavinton 77 E33
Gawber 51 B39
Gawcott 31 E42
Gawsworth 49 E34
Gawthrop 56 A32
Gawthwaite 55 A28
Gaydon 30 C39
Gayhurst 32 D44
Gayles 62 F37
Gay Street 12 D46
Gayton *Nfk* 44 D53
Gayton *Mer.* 48 D28
Gayton *Nmp.* 31 C42
Gayton *Stf.* 40 C35
Gayton le Marsh 53 D50
Gayton le Wold 53 D48
Gayton Thorpe 44 D53
Gaywood 44 C52
Gazeley 34 B53
Geanies Ho. 97 D24
Gearach 72 E8
Gearnsary 102 E23
Gearradh 80 A15
Gearraidh Bhaird 100 F9
Gearraidh Na H-Aibhne 100 D8
Gearraidh Na Monadh 84 C2
Gearrannan 100 C7
Geary 93 E8
Geavraidh Bhailteas 84 B2
Gedding 34 C55
Geddington 42 G44
Gedgrave Hall 35 D60
Gedling 41 A42

Gedney 43 C49
Gedney Broadgate 43 C49
Gedney Drove End 43 C50
Gedney Dyke 43 C50
Gedney Hill 43 D49
Gee Cross 49 C35
Geirninis 92 G3
Geisiadar 100 D7
Geldeston 45 F59
Gell *Clw.* 47 F24
Gell *Gwy.* 36 B20
Gelligaer 18 B26
Gelli Gynan 47 G27
Gellilydan 37 B22
Gellioedd 37 A25
Gelly 16 C16
Gellyburn 82 D26
Gellywen 17 B18
Gelston 65 E23
Gembling 59 D47
Gemmil 79 G13
Genoch 64 E17
Genoch Square 64 E17
Gentleshaw 40 D36
George Green 22 C46
Georgeham 6 B20
George Nympton 7 C23
Georgetown 74 D20
Gerlan 46 F22
Germansweek 6 F19
Germoe 2 F11
Gerrans 3 E14
Gerrards Cross 22 C45
Gerston 103 C27
Gestingthorpe 34 E53
Geuffordd 38 D28
Geufron 37 G24
Gibbshill 65 C23
Gibraltar 53 G51
Gidea Park 23 C51
Gidleigh 6 G22
Giffnock 74 E21
Gifford 76 D31
Giffordland 74 F18
Giggleswick 56 C33
Gilberdyke 58 G44
Gilchriston 76 D30
Gilcrux 60 C27
Gildersome 57 G38
Gildingwells 51 D41
Gileston 18 E25
Gilfach 18 B27
Gilfach Goch 18 C25
Gilfachrheda 26 C19
Gilgarran 60 D26
Gillamoor 63 G42
Gillen 93 F8
Gillenbie 69 E27
Gillfoot 65 C25
Gilling East 58 B42
Gillingham *Nfk* 45 F60
Gillingham *Dor.* 9 B33
Gillingham *Kent* 24 E53
Gilling West 62 F37
Gillivoan 103 E27
Gillock 103 C27
Gillow Heath 49 G34
Gills 103 A29
Gill's Green 14 D53
Gilmanscleuch 69 A29
Gilmerton *Tay.* 81 E24
Gilmerton *Ltn* 76 D28
Gilmilnscroft 67 A21
Gilmonby 62 E35
Gilmorton 41 G41
Gilsland 70 G32
Gilsland Spa 70 G32
Gilston 76 E30
Gilston Park 33 G50
Gilwern 28 G28
Gimingham 45 B58
Giosla 100 E7
Gipping 34 B56
Gipsey Bridge 53 G48
Girlsta 107 B40
Girsby 62 F39
Girtford 32 D47
Girthon 65 E21
Girton *Cbs.* 33 B50
Girton *Not.* 52 F44
Girvan 67 D17
Gisburn 56 E34
Gisleham 45 G60
Gislingham 34 A56
Gissing 45 G57
Gittisham 7 F27
Givons Grove 22 F47
Glack 91 A33
Glackour 95 C17
Gladestry 28 C28
Gladsmuir 76 C30
Glaic 73 C16
Glais 17 D22
Glaisdale 63 F43
Glaister 73 G15
Glame 94 G11
Glamis 82 C29
Glanaber Terrace 37 A23
Glan Adda 46 E21
Glanaman 17 C22
Glanbran 27 E23
Glan-Conwy 47 G24
Glanderston 90 A31
Glandford 44 A56
Glandwr *Gwe.* 19 A28
Glandwr *Dyf.* 16 B17
Glan-Dwyfach 36 A20
Glangrwyne 28 G28
Glan Honddu 27 E25
Glan-llynfi 18 B24
Glanmule 38 G27
Glanrhyd 26 D17
Glanton 71 B36
Glantwymyn 37 E23
Glanvilles Wootton 9 D32
Glan-y-don 47 E27
Glan-y-llyn 18 C27
Glan-yr-afon *Clw.* 37 A26
Glan-yr-afon *Gwy.* 37 A25
Glapthorn 42 G46
Glapwell 51 F40
Glasahoile 81 G20
Glasbury 28 E27
Glaschoil 89 A26
Glascoed 19 A29
Glascorrie 90 D29
Glascote 40 E38
Glascwm 28 C27
Glasdrum 80 C15
Glasfryn 47 G25
Glasgow 74 D21
Glasgow Airport 74 D20
Glashmore 91 C33
Glasinfryn 46 F21
Glasnacardoch 86 E12
Glasnakille 86 C11
Glaspant 17 A18
Glaspwll 37 F23
Glassaugh 98 C31
Glassburn 88 A19
Glassel 91 D32
Glassenbury 14 D53
Glasserton 64 G19
Glassford 75 F23
Glasshouse Hill 29 F33
Glasshouses 57 C37
Glassingall 81 G23
Glasslie 82 G28
Glasson *Cum.* 69 G28
Glasson *Lan.* 55 D30
Glassonby 61 C31
Glasterlaw 83 B31
Glaston 42 E44
Glastonbury 8 A30
Glatton 42 G47
Glazebury 49 C32
Glazeley 39 G32
Gleadless 51 D39
Gleadsmoss 49 F34
Gleann Ghrabhair 100 E10
Gleann Tholastaidh 101 C11
Gleaston 55 B28
Glecknabae 73 D16
Gledhow 57 F39
Gledrid 38 B28
Glemsford 34 D54
Glen *D.&G.* 65 E21
Glen *D.&G.* 65 C24
Glenae 68 E25
Glenaladale 86 G14
Glenald 74 A18
Glenamachrie 79 E14
Glenapp Castle 66 E16
Glenarm 82 A29
Glen Auldyn 54 D26
Glenbarr 72 G12
Glenbatrick 72 C10
Glenbeg *Hgh.* 79 A11
Glenbeg *Hgh.* 89 B25
Glenbeg *Hgh.* 95 C18
Glenbeich 81 E21
Glenbervie *Grm.* 91 E33
Glenbervie *Cen.* 75 B24
Glenboig 75 D23
Glenborrodale 79 A11
Glenbranter 73 A16
Glenbreck 69 A26
Glenbrittle 85 B9
Glenbuck 68 A23
Glenbyre 79 E11
Glencaird 64 C19
Glencaple 65 D25
Glencarse 82 E27
Glencat 90 D31
Glenceitlein 80 C17
Glencloy 73 G15
Glencoe 80 B16
Glenconglass 90 A27
Glencraig 75 A27
Glencripesdale 79 B12
Glencrosh 68 E23
Glencruittein 79 E14
Glencuie 90 B30
Glendearg *D.&G.* 69 C28
Glendearg *Bor.* 76 G30
Glendessary 86 E15
Glendevon 82 G25
Glendoebeg 88 D19
Glendoick 82 E27
Glendoll Lodge 90 F28
Glendoune 67 D17
Glendrissaig 67 D17
Glenduckie 82 F28
Glenduisk 67 E17
Glendye Lodge 91 E32
Gleneagles 82 G25
Gleneagles Hotel 81 F24
Glenearn 82 F26
Glenegedale 72 E9
Glenelg 86 C14
Glenfarg 82 F27
Glenfeochan 79 E14
Glenfield 41 E41
Glenfinnan 86 F14
Glenfoot 82 F27
Glengalmadale 79 B14
Glengap 65 E22
Glengarnock 74 E18
Glengarrisdale 72 A12
Glengennet 67 D18
Glengolly 103 B26
Glengrasco 93 G10
Glengyle 80 F19
Glenhead 68 E24
Glenhead Farm 82 A28
Glenhurich 79 A14
Glenkerry 69 B28
Glenkiln 73 G16
Glenkin 73 C17
Glenkindie 90 B30
Glenlair 65 C23
Glenlatterach 97 F27
Glenlean 73 B16
Glenlee *D.&G.* 67 E21
Glenlee *Tay.* 90 E30
Glenlichorn 81 F23
Glenlivet 90 A27
Glenlochar 65 D23
Glenluce 64 E17
Glenmallan 74 A18
Glenmanna 68 C23
Glenmavis 75 D23
Glenmaye 54 E24
Glenmeanie 95 F18
Glenmore *Hgh.* 93 G10
Glenmore *Str.* 73 D16
Glenmore Lodge 89 D25
Glenmoy 82 A29
Glenmuick 101 G19
Glennoe 80 D16
Glenochar 68 B25
Glenogil 83 A30
Glen Parva 41 F41
Glenprosen 82 A29
Glenquiech 82 A29
Glenramskill 66 B13
Glenrazie 64 D19
Glenridding 60 E29
Glenrisdell 73 E14
Glenrossal 96 A20
Glenrothes 82 G28
Glensanda 79 C14
Glensaugh 91 F32
Glensgaich 96 E20
Glenshalg 90 C31
Glenshee 82 D25
Glenshellish 73 A16
Glensluan 73 A16
Glentaggart 68 A24
Glentham 52 C45
Glenton 91 A32
Glentress 76 G28
Glen Trool Lodge 67 E19
Glentruan 54 C26
Glentworth 52 D45
Glenuachdarach 93 F10
Glenure 80 C16
Glenurquhart 96 E23
Glen Vine 54 F25
Glenwhilly 64 C17
Glespin 68 A23
Gletness 107 B40
Glewstone 28 F31
Glinton 42 E47
Glooston 42 F43
Glororum 77 G37
Glossop 50 C36
Gloster Hill 71 C38
Gloucester 29 G33
Gloucester (Staverton) Airport 29 F34
Gloup 106 B40
Gloweth 2 D13
Glusburn 56 E35
Gluss 106 E39
Glympton 31 F40
Glyn 47 G23
Glynarthen 26 D18
Glyn Ceiriog 38 B27
Glyncoch 18 B26
Glyncorrwg 18 B24
Glyn-Cywarch 36 B21
Glynde 13 F50
Glyndebourne 13 E50
Glyndyfrdwy 38 A27
Glyn-Neath 18 A24
Glynogwr 18 C25
Glyntaff 18 C26
Glynteg 17 A19
Gnosall 40 C34
Gnosall Heath 40 D34
Goadby 42 F43
Goadby Marwood 42 C43
Goatacre 20 D36
Goatfield 80 G15
Goathill 9 C32
Goathland 63 F44
Goathurst 8 A28
Gobernuisgeach 103 E25
Gobhaig 100 G6
Gobowen 38 B29
Godalming 22 G45
Godford Cross 7 E27
Godmanchester 33 B48
Godmanstone 9 E32
Godmersham 15 B56
Godolphin Cross 2 E12
Godor 38 D27
Godre'r-graig 18 A23
Godshill *I.o.W.* 11 F41
Godshill *Ham.* 10 C37
Godstone 23 F49
Goetre 19 A29
Goff's Oak 23 A49
Gogar 75 C27
Gogarth 47 D23
Goginan 37 G22
Goirtean a'Chladaich 87 G16
Goirtein 73 B15
Golan 36 A21
Golant 4 E17
Golberdon 4 C18
Golborne 48 C31
Golcar 50 A36
Goldcliff 19 C29
Golden Cross 13 E51
Golden Green 23 G52
Golden Grove 17 C21
Goldenhill 49 G34
Golden Pot 22 G43
Golden Valley 29 F34
Golders Green 23 C48
Goldhanger 24 A54
Gold Hill 43 F51
Goldielea 65 C25
Golding 38 E31
Goldington 32 C46
Goldsborough *N.Y.* 63 E44
Goldsborough *N.Y.* 57 D39
Goldsithney 2 E11
Goldthorpe 51 B40
Goldworthy 6 C19
Gollanfield 96 F23
Golspie 97 B24
Golval 102 B24
Gomeldon 10 A37
Gomersal 57 G37
Gometra Ho. 78 C9
Gomshall 22 G46
Gonachan 74 B22
Gonalston 41 A42
Gonfirth 107 A39
Good Easter 33 G51
Gooderstone 44 E53
Goodleigh 6 B21
Goodmanham 58 E44
Goodnestone *Kent* 25 E56
Goodnestone *Kent* 15 B58
Goodrich 28 G31
Goodrington 5 E24
Goodwick 16 A15
Goodworth Clatford 21 G39
Goodyers End 41 G39
Goole 58 G43
Goonbell 2 D13
Goonhavern 2 C13
Goose Green 23 F52
Gooseham 6 D18
Goosewell 5 E21
Goosey 21 B39
Goosnargh 55 F31
Goostrey 49 F33
Gorcott Hill 30 B36
Gorddinog 46 E22
Gordon 76 F32
Gordonbush 97 A24
Gordonstoun 97 E27
Gordonstown *Grm.* 98 D31
Gordonstown *Grm.* 99 F33
Gorebridge 76 D29
Gore Cross 20 F36
Gorefield 43 D50
Gore Street 25 E58
Gorey 3 G18
Goring 21 C42
Goring-by-Sea 12 F47
Gorleston on Sea 45 E61
Gorllwyn 17 A19
Gornalwood 40 F34
Gorrachie 99 D33
Gorran Churchtown 3 D15
Gorran Haven 4 F16
Gors 27 A22
Gorsedd 47 E27
Gorseinon 17 E21
Gorseness 104 E29
Gorsgoch 26 C20
Gorslas 17 C21
Gorsley 29 F32
Gorsley Common 29 F32
Gorstan 96 E19
Gorstanvorran 86 G13
Gorten 79 D13
Gortenbuie 79 D11
Gorteneorn 79 A12
Gorton *G.M.* 49 C34
Gorton *Str.* 78 B7
Gosbeck 35 C57
Gosberton 43 B48
Goseley Dale 41 C39
Gosfield 34 F53
Gosforth *Cum.* 60 F26
Gosforth *T.&W.* 71 G38
Gosmore 32 F47
Gospel End 40 F35
Gosport 11 E41
Gossabrough 106 D41
Gossops Green 13 C48
Goswick 77 F36
Gotham 41 B41
Gotherington 29 F35
Gott 107 C40
Goudhurst 13 C52
Goulceby 53 E48
Gourdas 99 E33
Gourdon 91 F34
Gourock 74 C18
Govan 74 D21
Goveton 5 F23
Govilon 28 G28
Gowanhill 99 C36
Gowdall 58 G42
Gowerton 17 E21
Gowkhall 75 B26
Gowthorpe 58 D43
Goxhill *Hum.* 59 G47
Goxhill *Hum.* 59 E47
Goytre 18 C23
Grabhair 100 F9
Gradbach 49 F35
Grade 2 G12
Graffham 12 E45
Grafham *Sry* 22 G46
Grafham *Cbs.* 32 B47
Grafton *H.&W.* 28 E30
Grafton *H.&W.* 28 B31
Grafton *Shr.* 38 D30
Grafton *Oxf.* 21 A38
Grafton *N.Y.* 57 C39
Grafton Flyford 29 C35
Grafton Regis 31 D43
Grafton Underwood 42 G45
Grafty Green 14 C54
Graianrhyd 47 G27
Graig *Clw.* 47 E26
Graig *Gwy.* 47 E24
Graig-fechan 47 G27
Grain 24 D54
Grainel 72 D8
Grainhow 99 E34
Grainsby 53 C48
Grainthorpe 53 C49
Grampound 3 D15
Grampound Road 3 C15
Gramsdal 92 F4
Granborough 31 F43
Granby 42 B43
Grandborough 31 B40
Grandtully 81 B24
Grange *Mer.* 48 D28
Grange *Cum.* 60 E28
Grange *N.Y.* 63 G41
Grange *Tay.* 82 E28
Grange *Hgh.* 88 A19
Grange *Kent* 24 E53
Grange Crossroads 98 D30
Grange Hall 97 E26
Grange Hill 23 B50
Grangemill 50 G38
Grange Moor 50 A38
Grangemouth 75 B25
Grangemuir 83 G31
Grange of Lindores 82 F28
Grange-over-Sands 55 B30
Grangeston 67 D17
Grangetown *Cle.* 63 D41
Grangetown *S.G.* 18 D27
Grange Villa 62 A38
Granish 89 C24
Gransmoor 59 D47

Granston 16 A14
Grantchester 33 C49
Grantham 42 B44
Grantley 57 B38
Grantlodge 91 B32
Granton House 69 C26
Grantown-on-Spey 89 B25
Grantshouse 77 D33
Grappenhall 49 D32
Grasby 52 B46
Grasmere 60 F29
Grasscroft 49 B35
Grassendale 48 D29
Grassholme 61 D34
Grassington 57 C36
Grassmoor 51 F39
Grassthorpe 51 F43
Grateley 21 G38
Gratwich 40 B36
Graveley *Hfs.* 33 F48
Graveley *Cbs.* 33 B48
Gravelly Hill 40 F37
Gravels 38 F29
Graven 106 E39
Graveney 25 E56
Gravesend 24 D52
Grayingham 52 C45
Grayrigg 61 G31
Grays 24 D52
Grayshott 12 C44
Grayswood 12 C45
Grazeley 21 E42
Greasbrough 51 C39
Greasby 48 D28
Great Abington 33 D51
Great Addington 32 A45
Great Alne 30 C36
Great Altcar 48 B29
Great Amwell 33 G49
Great Asby 61 E32
Great Ashfield 34 B55
Great Ayton 63 E41
Great Baddow 24 A53
Great Bardfield 33 E52
Great Barford 32 C47
Great Barr 40 F36
Great Barrington 30 G38
Great Barrow 48 F30
Great Barton 34 B54
Great Barugh 58 B43
Great Bavington 70 E35
Great Bealings 35 D58
Great Bedwyn 21 E38
Great Bentley 35 F57
Great Billing 31 B43
Great Blakenham 34 C56
Great Bolas 39 C32
Great Bookham 22 F47
Great Bourton 31 D40
Great Bowden 42 G43
Great Bradley 33 C52
Great Braxted 34 G54
Great Bricett 34 C56
Great Brickhill 32 E45
Great Bridgeford 40 C34
Great Brington 31 B42
Great Bromley 34 F56
Great Broughton *N.Y.* 63 F41
Great Broughton *Cum.* 60 C26
Great Budworth 49 E32
Great Burdon 62 E39
Great Burstead 24 B52
Great Busby 63 F41
Great Canfield 33 G51
Great Canney 24 A53
Great Carlton 53 D50
Great Casterton 42 E46
Great Chart 14 C55
Great Chatwell 39 D33
Great Chesterford 33 D50
Great Cheverell 20 F35
Great Chishill 33 E50
Great Clacton 35 G57
Great Clifton 60 C26
Great Coates 53 B48
Great Comberton 29 D35
Great Corby 61 A30
Great Cornard 34 D54
Great Cowden 59 E48
Great Coxwell 21 B38
Great Crakehall 62 G38
Great Cransley 32 A44
Great Cressingham 44 E54
Great Crosby 48 C29
Great Cubley 40 B37
Great Dalby 42 D43
Great Doddington 32 B44
Great Driffield 59 D46
Great Dunham 44 D54
Great Dunmow 33 F52
Great Durnford 10 A37
Great Easton *Esx* 33 F51
Great Easton *Lei.* 42 F44
Great Eccleston 55 E29
Great Edstone 58 A43
Great Ellingham 44 F56
Great Elm 20 G33
Great Eversden 33 C49
Great Fencote 62 G38
Great Finborough 34 C56
Greatford 42 D46
Great Fransham 44 D54
Great Gaddesden 32 G46
Greatgate 40 A36
Great Gidding 42 G47
Great Givendale 58 D44
Great Glemham 35 B58
Great Glen 41 F42
Great Gonerby 42 B44
Great Gransden 33 C48
Great Green *Nfk* 45 F58
Great Green *Sfk* 34 C55
Great Habton 58 B43
Great Hale 42 A47
Great Hallingbury 33 G51
Greatham *Cle.* 62 D40
Greatham *W.S.* 12 E46
Greatham *Ham.* 11 A43
Great Hanwood 38 E30
Great Harrowden 32 A44
Great Harwood 56 F33
Great Haseley 21 A42
Great Hatfield 59 E47
Great Haywood 40 C35
Great Heath 41 G39
Great Heck 58 G41
Great Henny 34 E54
Great Hinton 20 F35
Great Hockham 44 F55
Great Holland 35 G58
Great Horkesley 34 E55
Great Hormead 33 F49
Great Horwood 31 E43
Great Houghton *Nmp.* 31 C43
Great Houghton *S.Y.* 51 B40
Great Hucklow 50 E37
Great Kelk 59 D47
Great Kimble 22 A43
Great Kingshill 22 B44
Great Langton 62 G38
Great Leighs 34 G53
Great Limber 52 B47
Great Linford 32 D44
Great Livermere 34 A54
Great Longstone 50 E38
Great Lumley 62 B38
Great Lyth 38 E30
Great Malvern 29 D33
Great Maplestead 34 E54
Great Marton 55 F29
Great Massingham 44 C54
Great Melton 45 E57
Great Milton 21 A42
Great Missenden 22 A44
Great Mitton 56 F33
Great Mongeham 15 B59
Great Moulton 45 F57
Great Musgrave 61 E33
Great Ness 38 D29
Great Oak 28 G29
Great Oakley *Esx* 35 F57
Great Oakley *Nmp.* 42 G44
Great Offley 32 F47
Great Ormside 61 E33
Great Orton 60 A29
Great Ouseburn 57 C40
Great Oxendon 42 G43
Great Oxney Green 24 A52
Great Palgrave 44 D54
Great Parndon 23 A50
Great Paxton 33 B48
Great Plumpton 55 F29
Great Plumstead 45 D59
Great Ponton 42 B44
Great Preston 57 G40
Great Raveley 43 G48
Great Rissington 30 G37
Great Rollright 30 E39
Great Ryburgh 44 C55
Great Ryle 71 B36
Great Ryton 38 E30
Great Saling 33 F52
Great Salkeld 61 C31
Great Sampford 33 E52
Great Sankey 48 D31
Great Saxham 34 B53
Great Shefford 21 D39
Great Shelford 33 C50
Great Smeaton 62 F39
Great Snoring 44 B55
Great Somerford 20 C35
Great Stainton 62 D39
Great Stambridge 24 B54
Great Staughton 32 B47
Great Steeping 53 F50
Great Stonar 15 B59
Greatstone-on-Sea 15 E56
Great Strickland 61 D31
Great Stukeley 33 A48
Great Sturton 53 E48
Great Sutton *Shr.* 38 G31
Great Sutton *Che.* 48 E29
Great Swinburne 70 F35
Great Tew 30 F39
Great Tey 34 F54
Great Thurlow 33 D52
Great Torrington 6 D21
Great Tosson 71 C36
Great Totham *Esx* 34 G54
Great Totham *Esx* 34 G54
Great Urswick 55 B28
Great Wakering 25 C55
Great Waldingfield 34 D55
Great Walsingham 44 B55
Great Waltham 33 G52
Great Warley 23 B51
Great Washbourne 29 E35
Great Welnetham 34 C54
Great Wenham 34 E56
Great Whittington 70 F35
Great Wigborough 34 G55
Great Wilbraham 33 C51
Great Wishford 10 A36
Great Witcombe 29 G35
Great Witley 29 B33
Great Wolford 30 E38
Great Woolstone 32 E44
Greatworth 31 D41
Great Wratting 33 D52
Great Wymondley 33 F48
Great Wyrley 40 E35
Great Wytheford 38 D31
Great Yarmouth 45 E61
Great Yeldham 34 E53
Greenburn 83 D30
Greencroft Hall 62 B37
Greendams 91 D32
Greendykes 71 A36
Green End *Hfs.* 33 F49
Green End *Bfd.* 32 C47
Greenfield *Bfd.* 32 E46
Greenfield *G.M.* 50 B36
Greenfield *Clw.* 48 E28
Greenfield *Oxf.* 22 B43
Greenfield *Hgh.* 87 D18
Greenford 22 C47
Greengairs 75 C23
Greenhalgh 55 F30
Greenhall 91 A32
Greenham *Brk.* 21 E40
Greenham *Som.* 7 C26
Green Hammerton 57 D40
Greenhaugh 70 E33
Greenhead 70 G32
Greenheads 99 F36
Greenhill *Hgh.* 97 A25
Greenhill *S.Y.* 51 D39
Greenhill *G.L.* 22 C47
Greenhithe 23 D51
Greenholm 74 G21
Greenholme 61 F31
Greenhow Hill 57 C37
Greenigo 105 A29
Greenland 103 B28
Greenlands 22 C43
Greenlaw *Grm.* 98 D32
Greenlaw *Bor.* 76 F32
Greenloaning 81 G24
Greenmount 49 A33
Greenmyre 99 F33
Greenock 74 C18
Greenodd 55 A29
Green Ore 19 F31
Greenscares 81 F23
Greenside 71 G37
Greenskares 99 C33
Greens Norton 31 C42
Greenstead Green 34 F54
Greensted 23 A51
Green Street 22 B47
Green Street Green *G.L.* 23 E50
Green Street Green *Kent* 23 D51
Green Tye 33 G50
Greenway *Som.* 8 B29
Greenway *Dyf.* 16 A16
Greenwich 23 D49
Greet 30 E36
Greete 28 A31
Greetham *Lcn.* 53 E49
Greetham *Lei.* 42 D45
Greetland 57 G36
Greinetobht 92 D4
Greinton 8 A29
Grenaby 54 F24
Grendon *War.* 40 E38
Grendon *Nmp.* 32 B44
Grendon Common 40 F38
Grendon Green 28 C31
Grendon Underwood 31 F42
Grenoside 51 C39
Greosabhagh 93 B7
Gresford 48 G29
Gresham 45 B57
Greshornish 93 F9
Gressenhall 44 D55
Gressingham 55 B31
Greta Bridge 62 E36
Gretna 69 G29
Gretna Green 69 G28
Gretton *Nmp.* 42 F44
Gretton *Shr.* 38 F31
Gretton *H.&G.* 29 E35
Grewelthorpe 57 B37
Greygarth 57 B37
Greylake 8 A29
Greys Green 22 C43
Greysouthen 60 D26
Greystoke 60 C30
Greystone *Tay.* 83 C31
Greystone *Grm.* 90 D28
Greystone *Lan.* 56 E34
Greywell 22 F43
Griais 100 C10
Gribthorpe 58 F43
Gribton 68 E25
Gridley Corner 6 F19
Griff 41 G39
Griffithstown 19 B28
Grigadale 79 A10
Grigghall 60 G30
Grimeford Village 49 A32
Grimethorpe 51 B40
Griminis 92 F3
Grimister 106 C40
Grimley 29 B34
Grimmet 67 B19
Grimness 105 B30
Grimoldby 53 D49
Grimpo 38 C29
Grimsargh 55 F31
Grimsbury 31 D40
Grimsby 53 B48
Grimscote 31 C42
Grimscott 6 E18
Grimsiadar 100 E9
Grimsthorpe 42 C46
Grimston *Lei.* 41 C42
Grimston *Nfk* 44 C53
Grimstone 9 E32
Grindale 59 B47
Grindiscol 107 C40
Grindle 39 E33
Grindleford 50 E38
Grindleton 56 E33
Grindley 40 C36
Grindlow 50 E37
Grindon *Stf.* 50 G36
Grindon *Nor.* 77 F34
Gringley on the Hill 51 C43
Grinsdale 60 A29
Grinshill 38 C31
Grinton 62 G36
Griomarstaidh 100 D7
Grishipoll 78 B7
Gristhorpe 59 A46
Griston 44 F55
Gritley 105 A31
Grittenham 20 C36
Grittleton 20 C34
Grizebeck 55 A28
Grizedale 60 G29
Grobister 104 D32
Groby 41 E41
Groes 47 F26
Groes-faen 18 C26
Groesffordd 36 B18
Groesffordd Marli 47 E26
Groeslon 46 G20
Groes-lwyd 38 D27
Grogport 73 F13
Groigearraidh 84 A3
Gromford 35 C59
Gronant 47 D26
Groombridge 13 C51
Grosmont *N.Y.* 63 F44
Grosmont *Gwe.* 28 F29
Grotaig 88 B20
Groton 34 D55
Grouville 3 G18
Grove *Dor.* 9 G32
Grove *Oxf.* 21 B39
Grove *Not.* 51 E43
Grove *Kent* 25 E58
Grove Park 23 D50
Grovesend 17 D21
Gruids 96 A21
Gruinart Flats 72 D8
Gruline 79 D11
Grundcruie 82 E26
Grundisburgh 35 C57
Gruting 107 C38
Grutness 107 E38
Gualachulain 80 C16
Guardbridge 83 F30
Guarlford 29 D33
Guay 82 C25
Gubbergill 60 G26
Guestling Green 14 F54
Guestling Thorn 14 F54
Guestwick 44 C56
Guide Post 71 E38
Guilden Morden 33 D48
Guilden Sutton 48 F30
Guildford 22 G46
Guildtown 82 D27
Guilsborough 31 A42
Guilsfield 38 D28
Guisborough 63 E41
Guiseley 57 E37
Guist 44 C55
Guith 104 C31
Guiting Power 30 F36
Gulberwick 107 D40
Gullane 76 B30
Gulval 2 E10
Gulworthy 4 C20
Gumfreston 16 D16
Gumley 41 F42
Gunby *Lcn.* 42 C45
Gunby *Hum.* 58 F43
Gundleton 11 A42
Gunn 6 B22
Gunnerside 61 G35
Gunnerton 70 F34
Gunness 52 A44
Gunnislake 4 C20
Gunnista 107 C40
Gunter's Bridge 12 D45
Gunthorpe *Nfk* 44 B56
Gunthorpe *Not.* 41 A42
Gunville 11 F40
Gunwalloe 2 F12
Gurnard 11 E40
Gurney Slade 19 G32
Gurnos 18 A23
Gussage All Saints 9 C35
Gussage St Michael 9 C35
Guston 15 C58
Gutcher 106 C41
Guthrie 83 B31
Guyhirn 43 E50
Guynd 83 C31
Guy's Head 43 C50
Guy's Marsh 9 B34
Guyzance 71 C37
Gwaelod-y-garth 18 C26
Gwaenysgor 47 D26
Gwaithla 28 C27
Gwalchmai 46 E19
Gwaun-Cae-Gurwen 27 G23
Gwaun-leision 17 C22
Gwaynynog 47 F26
Gwbert 26 C17
Gweek 2 F13
Gwehelog 19 A29
Gwenddwr 27 D26
Gwennap 2 D13
Gwenter 2 G13
Gwernaffield 47 F27
Gwernesney 19 A29
Gwernogle 17 A21
Gwernymynydd 48 F28
Gwersyllt 48 G29
Gwespyr 47 D26
Gwinear 2 E11
Gwithian 2 D11
Gwyddelwern 37 A26
Gwyddgrug 17 A20
Gwystre 27 B26
Gwytherin 47 F24
Gyfelia 38 A29
Gyffin 47 E23
Gyre 105 A29
Gyrn Goch 36 A19

H

Habberley 38 E29
Habrough 52 A47
Haccombe 5 D24
Hacconby 42 C47
Haceby 42 B46
Hacheston 35 C59
Hackenthorpe 51 D39
Hackford 44 E56
Hackforth 62 G38
Hackland 104 D29
Hackleton 31 C43
Hacklinge 15 B59
Hackness *Ork.* 105 B29
Hackness *N.Y.* 63 G45
Hackney 23 C49
Hackthorn 52 D45
Hackthorpe 61 D31
Hadden 77 G33
Haddenham *Cbs.* 33 A50
Haddenham *Bkh.* 22 A43
Haddington *Ltn.* 76 C30
Haddington *Lcn.* 52 F44
Haddiscoe 45 F60
Haddon 42 F47
Hademore 40 E37
Hadfield 50 C36
Hadham Cross 33 G50
Hadham Ford 33 F50
Hadleigh *Sfk* 34 D56
Hadleigh *Esx* 24 C54
Hadley 39 D32
Hadley End 40 C37
Hadley Wood 23 B48

Hadlow 23 G52
Hadlow Down 13 D51
Hadnall 38 C31
Hadstock 33 D51
Hadzor 29 B35
Haffenden Quarter 14 C54
Hafod-Dinbych 47 G24
Hafodunos 47 F24
Haggate 56 F34
Haggbeck 69 F30
Haggs 75 C23
Hagley *H.&W.* 28 D31
Hagley *H.&W.* 40 G34
Hagnaby 53 F49
Hagworthingham 53 F49
Haigh 49 B32
Haighton Green 55 F31
Haile 60 F26
Hailes 30 E36
Hailey *Oxf.* 30 G39
Hailey *Hfs.* 23 A49
Hailey *Oxf.* 21 C42
Hailsham 13 F51
Hail Weston 32 B47
Haimer 103 B27
Hainault 23 B50
Hainford 45 D58
Hainton 52 D47
Haisthorpe 59 C47
Halam 51 G42
Halbeath 75 B27
Halberton 7 D25
Halcro 103 B28
Hale *G.M.* 49 D33
Hale *Sry* 22 G44
Hale *Ham.* 10 C37
Hale Bank 48 D30
Halebarns 49 D33
Hales *Nfk* 45 F59
Hales *Stf.* 39 B33
Halesowen 40 G35
Hales Place 15 B57
Hale Street 23 G52
Halesworth 35 A59
Halewood 48 D30
Halford *War.* 30 D38
Halford *Shr.* 38 G30
Halfpenny Green 40 F34
Halfway *S.Y.* 51 D40
Halfway *Dyf.* 27 E24
Halfway *Brk.* 21 E39
Halfway *Dyf.* 17 A22
Halfway House 38 D29
Halfway Houses 25 D55
Half Way Inn 7 G26
Halghton Mill 38 A29
Halifax 57 G36
Halistra 93 E8
Halkirk 103 C27
Halkyn 47 E27
Hall 74 E20
Halland 13 E51
Hallaton 42 F43
Hallatrow 19 F32
Hallbankgate 61 A31
Hall Dunnerdale 60 G28
Hallen 19 C31
Hall Green 40 G37
Hallin 93 F8
Halling 24 E52
Hallington *Lcn.* 53 D48
Hallington *Nor.* 70 F35
Hall of the Forest 38 G28
Halloughton 51 G42
Hallow 29 C34
Hallow Heath 29 C34
Hallrule 70 B31
Halls 76 C32
Hallsands 5 G24
Hall's Green 33 F48
Hall's Tenement 61 A31
Halltoft End 43 A49
Hallworthy 4 B17
Halmer End 39 A33
Halmore 19 A32
Halmyre Mains 75 F27
Halnaker 12 F45
Halsall 48 A29
Halse *Nmp.* 31 D41
Halse *Som.* 7 C27
Halsetown 2 E10
Halsham 59 G48
Halsinger 6 B21
Halstead *Lei.* 42 E43
Halstead *Esx* 34 E53
Halstead *Kent* 23 E50
Halstock 8 D31
Haltham 53 F48
Halton *Lan.* 55 C31
Halton *Clw.* 38 B29
Halton *Bkh.* 32 G44
Halton *Nor.* 70 G35
Halton *Che.* 48 D31
Halton East 57 D36
Halton Gill 56 B34
Halton Holegate 53 F50
Halton Lea Gate 61 A32
Halton West 56 D34
Haltwhistle 70 G32
Halvergate 45 E60
Halwell 5 E23
Halwill 6 F19
Halwill Junction 6 F20
Ham *Glo.* 19 B32
Ham *Som.* 8 B28
Ham *Hgh.* 103 A28
Ham *She.* 106 A38
Ham *G.L.* 22 D47
Ham *Wts.* 21 E39
Ham *Kent* 15 B59
Hamble 11 D40
Hambleden 22 C43
Hambledon *Sry* 12 C45
Hambledon *Ham.* 11 C42
Hambleton *Lan.* 55 E29
Hambleton *N.Y.* 58 F41
Hambleton Moss Side 55 E29
Hambridge 8 B29
Hambrook *Avon* 19 D32
Hambrook *W.S.* 11 D43
Hameringham 53 F49
Hamerton 32 A47
Ham Green *H.&W.* 29 B35
Ham Green *Avon* 19 D31
Ham Hill 24 E52
Hamilton 74 E22
Hamlet 7 F27
Hammer 12 C44
Hammerpot 12 F46
Hammersmith & Fulham 22 D47
Hammerwich 40 E36
Hammerwood 13 C50
Hammond Street 23 A49
Hammoon 9 C33
Hamnavoe *She.* 106 E40
Hamnavoe *She.* 106 D40
Hamnavoe *She.* 107 D39
Hamnavoe *She.* 106 D38
Hampden Park 13 F52
Hampnett 30 G36
Hampole 51 B40
Hampreston 10 E36
Hampstead 23 C48
Hampstead Norreys 21 D41
Hampsthwaite 57 D38
Hampton Heath 38 A30
Hampton *H.&W.* 30 D36
Hampton *Shr.* 39 G33
Hampton *G.L.* 22 E47
Hampton Bishop 28 E31
Hampton in Arden 40 G38
Hampton Lovett 29 B34
Hampton Lucy 30 C38
Hampton on the Hill 30 B38
Hampton Poyle 31 G40
Hamptworth 10 B38
Hamsey 13 E50
Hamstall Ridware 40 D36
Hamstead *W.M.* 40 F36
Hamstead *I.o.W.* 10 E39
Hamstead Marshall 21 E39
Hamsterley *Drm* 62 C37
Hamsterley *Drm* 62 A36
Ham Street 8 A31
Hamstreet 14 D55
Hamworthy 9 E35
Hanbury *Stf.* 40 C37
Hanbury *H.&.W.* 29 B35
Hanbury Woodend 40 C37
Hanchurch 40 A34
Handbridge 48 F30
Handcross 13 D48
Handforth 49 D34
Handley 48 G30
Handsacre 40 D36
Handsworth *W.M.* 40 F36
Handsworth *S.Y.* 51 D39
Handy Cross 22 B44
Hanford 40 A34
Hanging Bridge 40 A37
Hanging Langford 9 A35
Hangingshaw 69 E26
Hangleton 13 F48
Hanham 19 D32
Hankelow 39 A32
Hankerton 20 B35
Hankham 13 F52
Hanley 40 A34
Hanley Castle 29 D34
Hanley Child 29 B32
Hanley Swan 29 D34
Hanley William 29 B32
Hanlith 56 C35
Hanmer 38 B30
Hannah 53 E51
Hannington *Nmp.* 31 A43
Hannington *Ham.* 21 F41
Hannington *Wts.* 20 B37
Hannington Wick 20 B37
Hanslope 31 D43
Hanthorpe 42 C46
Hanwell *Oxf.* 31 D40
Hanwell *G.L.* 22 D47
Hanworth *G.L.* 22 D47
Hanworth *Nfk.* 45 B57
Happisburgh 45 B59
Happisburgh Common 45 C59
Hapsford 48 E30
Hapton *Nfk.* 45 F57
Hapton *Lan.* 56 F34
Harberton 5 E23
Harbertonford 5 E23
Harbledown 15 B56
Harborne 40 G36
Harborough Magna 31 A40
Harbottle 70 C35
Harbourneford 5 D22
Harbridge 10 C37
Harbury 30 C39
Harby *Lei.* 42 B43
Harby *Not.* 52 E44
Harcombe 7 F27
Harden 57 F36
Hardenhuish 20 D34
Hardgate 91 C33
Hardham 12 E46
Hardingham 44 E56
Hardingstone 31 C43
Hardings Wood 49 G33
Hardington 20 F33
Hardington Mandeville 8 C31
Hardington Marsh 8 D31
Hardley 11 D40
Hardley Street 45 E59
Hardmead 32 D45
Hardraw 61 G34
Hardstoft 51 F40
Hardway *Ham.* 11 D41
Hardway *Som.* 9 A33
Hardwick *Cbs.* 33 C49
Hardwick *Nmp.* 32 B44
Hardwick *Bkh.* 31 G44
Hardwick *Oxf.* 31 F41
Hardwick *Nfk.* 45 F58
Hardwick *Oxf.* 21 A39
Hardwicke *Glo.* 29 F34
Hardwicke *Glo.* 29 G33
Hardwicke *H.&W.* 28 D28
Hardy's Green 34 G55
Hareby 53 F49
Hareden 56 D32
Harefield 22 B46
Hare Green 34 F56
Hare Hatch 22 D44
Harehills 57 F39
Harelaw 75 F25
Haresceugh 61 B31
Harescombe 29 G34
Haresfield 29 G33
Hareshaw 74 F22
Hare Street *Hfs.* 33 F49
Hare Street *Hfs.* 33 F49
Harewood 57 E39
Harewood End 28 F31
Harford 5 E22
Hargate 45 F57
Hargrave *Che.* 48 F30
Hargrave *Sfk* 34 C53
Hargrave *Nmp.* 32 A46
Haringey 23 C49
Harker 69 G29
Harkstead 35 E57
Harlaston 40 D37
Harlaxton 42 B44
Harlech 36 B21
Harlesden 23 C48
Harleston *Sfk* 34 C56
Harleston *Nfk* 45 G58
Harlestone 31 B42
Harle Syke 56 F34
Harley 38 E31
Harleyholm 75 G25
Harlington 32 E46
Harlosh 93 G8
Harlow 33 G50
Harlow Hill 71 G36
Harlthorpe 58 F43
Harlton 33 C49
Harman's Cross 9 F35
Harmby 62 G37
Harmer Green 33 G48
Harmer Hill 38 C30
Harmondsworth 22 D46
Harmston 52 F45
Harnham 10 B37
Harnhill 20 A36
Harold Hill 23 B51
Haroldston West 16 C14
Haroldswick 106 A42
Harold Wood 23 C51
Harome 58 A42
Harpenden 32 G47
Harpford 7 F26
Harpham 59 C47
Harpley *H.&W.* 29 B32
Harpley *Nfk* 44 C53
Harpole 31 B42
Harprigg 55 A31
Harpsdale 103 C27
Harpsden 22 C43
Harpswell 52 D45
Harpurhey 49 B34
Harpur Hill 50 E36
Harrapool 86 B12
Harrietfield 82 D25
Harrietsham 14 B54
Harrington *Nmp.* 31 A43
Harrington *Lcn.* 53 E49
Harringworth 42 F44
Harris 85 E9
Harriseahead 49 G34
Harrogate 57 D38
Harrold 32 C45
Harrow *Hgh.* 103 A28
Harrow *G.L.* 22 C47
Harrowbarrow 4 C19
Harrowden 32 D46
Harrow on the Hill 22 C47
Harrow Weald 22 B47
Harston *Cbs.* 33 C50
Harston *Lei.* 42 B44
Hart 62 C40
Hartburn *Nor.* 62 E40
Hartburn *Cle.* 71 E36
Hartest 34 C54
Hartfield *E.S.* 13 C50
Hartfield *Hgh.* 94 G13
Hartford *Cbs* 33 A48
Hartford *Che.* 49 E32
Hartfordbridge 22 F43
Hartford End 33 G52
Harthill *Che.* 48 G30
Harthill *S.Y.* 51 D40
Harthill *Ltn* 75 D25
Hartington 50 F37
Hartland 6 C18
Hartlebury 29 A34
Hartlepool 62 C40
Hartley *Kent* 14 D53
Hartley *Kent* 23 E51
Hartley *Cum.* 61 F33
Hartley *T.&W.* 71 F39
Hartley Wespall 21 F42
Hartley Wintney 22 F43
Hartlip 24 E54
Harton *T.&W.* 71 G39
Harton *N.Y.* 58 C43
Harton *Shr.* 38 G30
Hartpury 29 F33
Hartrigge 70 A32
Hartshill 41 F39
Hartshorne 40 C38
Hartsop 60 E29
Hartwell *Bkh.* 31 G43
Hartwell *Nmp.* 31 D43
Hartwell *E.S.* 13 C50
Hartwood 75 E24
Harvel 24 E52
Harvington *H.&W.* 30 D36
Harvington *H.&W.* 29 A34
Harwell 21 C40
Harwich 35 E58
Harwood *Drm* 61 C34
Harwood *G.M.* 49 A33
Harwood Dale 63 G45
Harwood on Teviot 69 C30
Harworth 51 C41
Hasbury 40 G35
Hascombe 12 C46
Haselbech 31 A42
Haselbury Plucknett 8 C30
Haseley 30 B38
Haselor 30 C37
Hasfield 29 F34
Hasguard 16 D14
Haskayne 48 B29
Hasketon 35 C58
Hasland 51 F39
Haslemere 12 C44
Haslingden 56 G33
Haslingden Grane 56 G33
Haslingfield 33 C49
Haslington 49 G33
Hassall 49 G33
Hassall Green 49 G33
Hassell Street 15 C56
Hassendean 70 A31
Hassingham 45 E59
Hassocks 13 E48
Hassop 50 E38
Haster 103 C29
Hastigrow 103 B28
Hastingleigh 15 C56
Hastings 14 G54
Hastingwood 23 A50
Hastoe 22 A45
Haswell 62 B39
Hatch *Bfd.* 32 D47
Hatch *Ham.* 21 F42
Hatch Beauchamp 8 B28
Hatch End 22 B47
Hatch Green 8 C28
Hatching Green 32 G47
Hatchmere 48 E31
Hatcliffe 53 B48
Hatfield *Hfs.* 23 A48
Hatfield *H.&W.* 28 C31
Hatfield *S.Y.* 51 B42
Hatfield Broad Oak 33 G51
Hatfield Heath 33 G50
Hatfield Hyde 33 G48
Hatfield Peverel 34 G53
Hatfield Woodhouse 51 B42
Hatford 21 B39
Hatherden 21 F39
Hatherleigh 6 E21
Hathern 41 C40
Hatherop 20 A37
Hathersage 50 D38
Hatherton *Stf.* 40 D35
Hatherton *Che.* 39 A32
Hatley St George 33 C48
Hatt 4 D19
Hattingley 11 A42
Hatton *G.L.* 22 D47
Hatton *War.* 30 B38
Hatton *Shr.* 38 F30
Hatton *Lcn.* 52 E47
Hatton *Che.* 48 D31
Hatton *Grm.* 99 F36
Hatton *Dby* 40 B37
Hatton Castle 99 E33
Hattoncrook 91 A34
Hatton Heath 48 F30
Hatton of Fintray 91 B34
Haugham 53 D49
Haugh Head 71 A36
Haughhead 74 C21
Haughley 34 B56
Haughley Green 34 B56
Haughley New Street 34 B55
Haugh of Glass 98 F29
Haugh of Urr 65 D23
Haughs 98 E30
Haughton *Not.* 51 E42
Haughton *Stf.* 40 C34
Haughton *Shr.* 38 D31
Haughton *Shr.* 38 C29
Haughton *Shr.* 39 F32
Haughton Green 49 C35
Haughton Le Skerne 62 E38
Haughton Moss 48 G31
Haultwick 33 F49
Haunn 84 C3
Haunton 40 D38
Hauxley 71 C38
Hauxton 33 C50
Havant 11 D42
Haven 28 C29
Haven Side 59 G49
Havenstreet 11 E41
Haverfordwest 16 C14
Haverhill 33 D52
Haverigg 54 B27
Havering 23 C51
Havering-atte-Bower 23 B51
Haversham 32 D44
Haverthwaite 55 A29
Haverton Hill 62 D40
Hawarden 48 F29
Hawbridge 29 D34
Hawbush Green 34 G53
Hawcoat 54 B27
Hawen 26 D19
Hawes 56 A34
Hawford 29 B34
Hawick 69 B30
Hawkchurch 8 D29
Hawkedon 34 C53
Hawkenbury 13 C51
Hawkeridge 20 F34
Hawkerland 7 G26
Hawkesbury 20 C33
Hawkesbury Upton 20 C33
Hawkes End 40 G38
Hawkhill 71 B38
Hawkhurst 14 D53
Hawkinge 15 C57
Hawkley 11 B43
Hawkridge 7 B24
Hawkshead 60 G29
Hawksland 75 G24
Hawkswick 56 B35
Hawksworth *W.Y.* 57 E37
Hawksworth *Not.* 42 A43
Hawkwell *Nor.* 71 F36
Hawkwell *Esx* 24 B54
Hawley *Ham.* 22 F44
Hawley *Kent* 23 D51
Hawling 30 F36
Hawnby 63 G41
Haworth 57 F36
Hawstead 34 C54
Hawthorn *Drm* 62 B40
Hawthorn *Wts.* 20 E34
Hawthorn Hill *Brk.* 22 D44
Hawthorn Hill *Lcn.* 53 G48
Hawthorpe 42 C46
Hawton 51 G43
Haxby 58 D42

Haxey 51 C43
Haxted 23 G50
Haydock 48 C31
Haydon 9 C32
Haydon Bridge 70 G34
Haydon Wick 20 C37
Haye 4 C19
Hayes *G.L.* 23 E49
Hayes *G.L.* 22 C46
Hayfield *Dby* 50 D36
Hayfield *Hgh.* 103 B27
Hayfield *Str.* 80 E16
Hayhillock 83 C30
Haylands 11 E41
Hayle 2 E11
Hay Mills 40 G37
Haynes 32 D46
Haynes Church End 32 D46
Hay-on-Wye 28 D28
Hayscastle 16 B14
Hayscastle Cross 16 B15
Hay Street 33 F49
Hayton *Not.* 51 D43
Hayton *Cum.* 61 A30
Hayton *Hum.* 58 E44
Hayton *Cum.* 60 B26
Hayton's Bent 38 G31
Haytor Vale 5 C23
Haywards Heath 13 D49
Haywood Oaks 51 G41
Hazelbank *Str.* 80 G17
Hazelbank *Str.* 75 F24
Hazelbury Bryan 9 D33
Hazeleigh 24 A53
Hazel End 33 F50
Hazeley 22 F43
Hazel Grove 49 D35
Hazelhead 91 C34
Hazelside 68 A23
Hazelslade 40 D36
Hazelton Walls 82 E29
Hazelwood *G.L.* 23 E50
Hazelwood *Dby* 41 A39
Hazlefield 65 F23
Hazlemere 22 B44
Hazlerigg 71 F38
Hazleton 30 G36
Headbourne Worthy 11 A40
Head Bridge 6 D22
Headcorn 14 C54
Headington 21 A41
Headlam 62 D37
Headless Cross 29 B35
Headley *Ham.* 12 C44
Headley *Sry* 22 F47
Headley *Ham.* 21 E40
Headley Down 12 C44
Headon 51 E43
Heads Nook 61 A30
Heage 51 G39
Healaugh *N.Y.* 62 G36
Healaugh *N.Y.* 57 E40
Heald Green 49 D34
Heale 6 A22
Healey *G.M.* 49 A34
Healey *Drm* 62 A36
Healey *N.Y.* 57 A37
Healeyfield 62 B36
Healing 52 A47
Heamoor 2 E10
Heanish 78 C6
Heanor 41 A40
Heanton Punchardon 6 B21
Heanton Satchville 6 D21
Heapey 56 G32
Heapham 52 D44
Hearthstane 69 A26
Heasley Mill 6 B22
Heaste 86 C12
Heath 51 F40
Heath and Reach 32 F45
Heathcot 91 C34
Heathcote *Dby* 50 F37
Heathcote *Stf.* 39 C32
Heath End *Ham.* 22 G44
Heath End *Ham.* 21 E41
Heather 41 D39
Heathfield *Dev.* 5 C23
Heathfield *Som.* 7 C27
Heathfield *E.S.* 13 D51
Heath Hayes 40 D35
Heath Hill 39 D33
Heath House 19 G30
Heathrow (London) Airport 22 D46
Heathton 39 F33
Heath Town 40 F35
Heatley 49 D32
Heaton *T.&W.* 71 G38
Heaton *Stf.* 49 F35
Heaton *Lan.* 55 C30
Heaton Moor 49 C34
Heaverham 23 F51
Heaviley 49 D34
Hebburn 71 G38
Hebden 57 C36
Hebden Bridge 56 G35
Hebden Green 49 F32
Hebing End 33 F49
Hebron *Nor.* 71 E37
Hebron *Dyf.* 16 B17
Heck 69 E26
Heckfield 22 E43
Heckfield Green 35 A57
Heckfordbridge 34 F55
Heckingham 45 F59
Heckington 42 A47
Heckmondwike 57 G38
Heddington 20 E35
Heddle 104 E29
Heddon-on-the-Wall 71 G37
Hedenham 45 F59
Hedge End 11 C40
Hedgerley 22 C45
Hedging 8 B28
Hedley on the Hill 62 A36
Hednesford 40 D35
Hedon 59 G48
Hedsor 22 C45
Heeley 51 D39
Heglibister 107 B39
Heighington *Lcn.* 52 F46
Heighington *Drm* 62 D38
Heights of Brae 96 E20
Heilam 102 B20
Heithat 69 E27
Heiton 76 G32
Hele *Dev.* 6 A21
Hele *Dev.* 7 E25
Helebridge 6 E18
Hele Bridge 6 E21
Hele Lane 7 D23
Helensburgh 74 B19
Helford 2 F13
Helhoughton 44 C54
Helions Bumpstead 33 D52
Helland 4 C16
Hellandbridge 4 C16
Hellesdon 45 D58
Hellidon 31 C40
Hellifield 56 D34
Hellingly 13 E51
Hellington 45 E59
Hellister 107 C39
Helmdon 31 D41
Helmingham 35 C57
Helmsdale 103 G26
Helmshore 56 G33
Helmsley 58 A42
Helperby 57 C40
Helperthorpe 59 B45
Helpringham 42 A47
Helpston 42 E47
Helsby 48 E30
Helston 2 F12
Helstone 4 B16
Helton 61 D30
Helwith Bridge 56 C34
Hemblington 45 D59
Hemborough Post 5 E24
Hemel Hempstead 22 A46
Hemingbrough 58 F42
Hemingby 53 E48
Hemingford Abbots 33 A48
Hemingford Grey 33 B48
Hemingstone 35 C57
Hemington *Nmp.* 42 G46
Hemington *Lei.* 41 C40
Hemington *Som.* 20 F33
Hemley 35 D58
Hemlington 62 E40
Hempholme 59 E46
Hempnall 45 F58
Hempnall Green 45 F58
Hempriggs 97 E26
Hempriggs House 103 D29
Hempstead *Nfk* 45 C60
Hempstead *Nfk* 45 B57
Hempstead *Esx* 33 E52
Hempsted 29 G33
Hempton *Oxf.* 31 E40
Hempton *Nfk* 44 C54
Hemsby 45 D60
Hemswell 52 C45
Hemsworth 51 A40
Hemyock 7 D27
Henbury *Che.* 49 E34
Henbury *Avon* 19 D31
Henderland 65 C24
Hendersyde Park 77 G33
Hendon *T.&W.* 62 A39
Hendon *G.L.* 23 C48
Hendy 17 D21
Heneglwys 46 E20
Henfield 12 E47
Henford 6 F19
Henghurst 14 D55
Hengoed *M.G.* 18 B27
Hengoed *Pow.* 28 C28
Hengoed *Clw.* 38 B28
Hengrave 34 B54
Henham 33 F51
Heniarth 37 E26
Henlade 8 B28
Henley *Som.* 8 A30
Henley *Shr.* 28 A31
Henley *Sfk* 35 C57
Henley *W.S.* 12 D44
Henley Corner 8 A30
Henley-in-Arden 30 B37
Henley-on-Thames 22 C43
Henley Park 22 F45
Henley's Down 14 F53
Henllan *Dyf.* 26 D19
Henllan *Clw.* 47 F26
Henllan Amgoed 16 B17
Henllys 19 B28
Henlow 32 E47
Hennock 7 G24
Henny Street 34 E54
Henryd 47 E23
Henry's Moat 16 B16
Hensall 58 G41
Henshaw 70 G33
Hensingham 60 E25
Henstead 45 G60
Hensting 11 B40
Henstridge 9 C32
Henstridge Ash 9 B32
Henstridge Marsh 9 B33
Henton *Oxf.* 22 A43
Henton *Som.* 19 G30
Henwick 29 C34
Henwood 4 C18
Heogan 107 C40
Heol-ddu 17 C21
Heol Lly Goden 28 F27
Heol Senni 27 F25
Heol-y-Cyw 18 C25
Hepburn 71 A36
Hepple 70 C35
Hepscott 71 E38
Heptonstall 56 G35
Hepworth *Sfk* 34 A55
Hepworth *W.Y.* 50 B37
Herbrandston 16 D14
Herdicott 6 F19
Hereford 28 E30
Heriot 76 E29
Hermiston 75 C27
Hermitage *Bor.* 69 D30
Hermitage *D.&G.* 65 D24
Hermitage *Dor.* 9 D32
Hermitage *Brk.* 21 D41
Hermitage *W.S.* 11 D43
Hermon *Dyf.* 17 A18
Hermon *Dyf.* 17 A19
Hermon *Gwy.* 46 F19
Herne 25 E57
Herne Bay 25 E57
Herne Common 25 E57
Herner 6 C21
Hernhill 25 E56
Herodsfoot 4 D17
Herongate 24 B52
Heronsgate 22 B45
Heron's Ghyll 13 D50
Herriard 21 G42
Herringfleet 45 F60
Herring's Green 32 D46
Herringswell 33 B52
Herrington 62 A39
Hersden 25 E57
Hersham *Sry* 22 E46
Hersham *Cnw.* 6 E18
Herstmonceux 13 E52
Herston *Ork.* 105 B30
Herston *Dor.* 10 G36
Hertford 33 G49
Hertford Heath 33 G49
Hertingfordbury 33 G48
Hesketh Bank 55 G30
Hesketh Lane 56 E32
Hesket Newmarket 60 C29
Heskin Green 48 A31
Hesleden 62 C40
Hesleyside 70 E33
Heslington 58 D42
Hessay 58 D41
Hessenford 4 E18
Hessett 34 B55
Hessle 59 G46
Hest Bank 55 C30
Heston 22 D47
Heswall 48 D28
Hethe 31 F41
Hetherington 70 F33
Hethersett 45 E57
Hethersgill 69 G30
Hethpool 70 A34
Hett 62 C38
Hetton 56 D35
Hetton-le-Hole 62 B39
Heugh 71 F36
Heugh-head *Grm.* 90 D30
Heugh-head *Grm.* 90 B29
Heveningham 35 A59
Hever 23 G50
Heversham 55 A30
Hevingham 45 C57
Hewas Water 3 D15
Hewell Grange 30 B36
Hewell Lane 29 B35
Hewelsfield 19 A31
Hewelsfield Common 19 A31
Hewish *Avon* 19 E29
Hewish *Som.* 8 D30
Hewton 6 F20
Hexham 70 G35
Hextable 23 D51
Hexton 32 E47
Hexworthy 5 C22
Heybridge *Esx* 24 B52
Heybridge *Esx* 24 A54
Heybridge Basin 24 A54
Heybrook Bay 4 F20
Heydon *Cbs.* 33 D50
Heydon *Nfk* 45 C57
Heydour 42 B45
Heylipoll 78 C5
Heylor 106 D38
Heysham 55 C29
Heyshaw 57 C37
Heyshott 12 E44
Heyside 49 B35
Heytesbury 20 G34
Heythrop 30 F39
Heywood *G.M.* 49 A34
Heywood *Wts.* 20 F34
Hibaldstow 52 B45
Hickleton 51 B40
Hickling *Not.* 41 C42
Hickling *Nfk* 45 C60
Hickling Green 45 C60
Hickling Heath 45 C60
Hickstead 13 D48
Hidcote Boyce 30 D37
High Ackworth 51 A40
Higham *Dby* 51 G39
Higham *Sfk* 34 E56
Higham *Sfk* 34 B53
Higham *Kent* 24 D53
Higham *Lan.* 56 F34
Higham Dykes 71 F37
Higham Ferrers 32 B45
Higham Gobion 32 E46
Higham on the Hill 41 F39
Highampton 6 E20
Higham Wood 23 G52
High Balantyre 80 F16
High Beach 23 B49
High Bentham 56 C32
High Bickington 6 C22
High Birkwith 56 B34
High Blantyre 74 E22
High Bonnybridge 75 C24
High Borgue 65 E22
High Bradfield 50 C38
High Bray 6 B22
Highbridge 19 G28
Highbrook 13 C49
High Brooms 23 G51
High Bullen 6 C20
Highburton 50 A37
High Burton 57 A38
Highbury 19 G32
Highbury Vale 41 A41
High Buston 71 C38
High Callerton 71 F37
High Catton 58 D43
Highclere 21 E40
Highcliffe 10 E38
High Cogges 21 A39
High Coniscliffe 62 E38
High Cross *Hfs.* 33 G49
High Cross *Ham.* 11 B43
High Cross Bank 40 D38
High Easter 33 G52
High Ellington 57 A37
High Entercommon 62 F39
Higher Ansty 9 D33
Higher Ashton 7 G24
Higher Ballam 55 F29
Higher Blackley 49 B34
Higher Brixham 5 E25
High Ercall 38 D31
Higher Cheriton 7 E26
Higher Gabwell 5 D25
Higher Green 49 B33
Higher Kingcombe 8 D31
Higher Tale 7 E26
Higher Thrushgill 56 C32
Higher Town 2 A11
Higher Walreddon 4 C20
Higher Walton *Che.* 49 D32
Higher Walton *Lcn.* 55 G31
Higher Whatcombe 9 D34
Higher Whitley 49 D32
Higher Wych 38 A30
High Etherley 62 D37
Highfield *T.&W.* 62 A37
Highfield *Hum.* 58 F43
Highfield *Str.* 74 E19
Highfields 33 C49
High Garrett 34 F53
High Gate 56 G35
High Grange 62 C37
High Green *Nfk* 45 E57
High Green *H.&W.* 29 D34
High Green *S.Y.* 51 C39
Highgreen Manor 70 D33
High Halden 14 D54
High Halstow 24 D53
High Ham 8 A30
High Harrington 60 D25
High Harrogate 57 D39
High Hatton 39 C32
High Hawsker 63 F44
High Heath 39 C32
High Hesket 61 B30
High Hoyland 50 B38
High Hunsley 59 F45
High Hurstwood 13 D50
High Hutton 58 C43
High Ireby 60 C28
High Kilburn 57 A40
Highlane *Dby* 51 D39
Highlane *Che.* 49 F34
High Lane *Dby* 41 A40
High Lane *H.&W.* 29 B32
High Laver 23 A51
Highlaws 60 B27
Highleadon 29 F33
High Legh 49 D33
Highleigh 12 G44
High Leven 62 E40
Highley 39 G33
High Littleton 19 F32
High Lorton 60 D27
Highmead 26 D20
High Melton 51 B41
Highmoor Cross 21 C42
Highmoor Hill 19 C30
Highnam 29 G33
High Newton 55 A30
High Newton by-the-Sea 71 A38
High Nibthwaite 60 G28
High Offley 39 C33
High Ongar 23 A51
High Onn 40 D34
High Risby 52 A45
High Roding 33 G51
High Salvington 12 F47
High Shaw 61 G34
High Spen 71 G37
Highstead 25 E57
Highsted 24 E54
High Street *Cnw.* 3 C15
High Street *Kent* 14 D53
High Street *Sfk* 35 C60
Highstreet Green 34 E53
High Street Green 34 C56
Hightae 69 F26
High Throston 62 C40
Hightown *Mer.* 48 B28
Hightown *Che.* 49 F34
High Toynton 53 F48
High Trewhitt 71 C36
Highway 20 D36
Highweek 5 C24
High Wollaston 19 B31
Highworth 20 B37
High Wray 60 G29
High Wych 33 G50
High Wycombe 22 B43
Hilborough 44 E53
Hilcott 20 F37
Hildenborough 23 G51
Hilden Park 23 G51
Hildersham 33 D51
Hilderstone 40 B35
Hilderthorpe 59 C47
Hilfield 9 D32
Hilgay 44 F52
Hill 19 B32
Hillam 58 G41
Hillbeck 61 E33
Hillberry 54 E25
Hillborough 25 E57
Hillbrae *Grm.* 98 E31
Hillbrae *Grm.* 99 F34
Hillbrae *Grm.* 91 A33
Hill Brow 11 B43
Hill Chorlton 39 B33
Hill Dyke 43 A49
Hillend *Grm.* 98 E30
Hill End *Drm* 62 C36
Hill End *N.Y.* 57 D36
Hillend *Ltn.* 76 D28
Hillend *Fife* 75 B27
Hill End *Fife* 75 A26
Hillesden 31 F42
Hillesley 20 C33
Hillfarrance 7 C27
Hillhead 5 E25
Hill Head 11 D41
Hillhead of Auchentumb 99 D35
Hillhead of Cocklaw 99 E36
Hilliard's Cross 40 D37
Hilliclay 103 B27

Hillingdon **22 C46**
Hillington **44 C53**
Hillmorton **31 A41**
Hillockhead *Grm.* **90 B30**
Hillockhead *Grm.* **90 C29**
Hill of Beath **75 A27**
Hill of Fearn **97 D24**
Hillowton **65 D23**
Hillpound **11 C41**
Hill Ridware **40 D36**
Hillsford Bridge **7 A23**
Hillside *Grm.* **97 E27**
Hillside *Tay.* **91 G32**
Hillside *She.* **107 A39**
Hillside *Grm.* **91 D35**
Hills Town **51 F40**
Hillswick **106 E38**
Hill Top *W.Y.* **51 A39**
Hill Top *Ham.* **11 D40**
Hill View **9 E35**
Hillway **11 F42**
Hillwell **107 D37**
Hilmarton **20 D36**
Hilperton **20 F34**
Hilsea **11 D42**
Hilton *Dor.* **9 D33**
Hilton *Cum.* **61 D33**
Hilton *Hgh.* **97 C25**
Hilton *Grm.* **99 F35**
Hilton *Cle.* **62 E40**
Hilton *Drm* **62 D37**
Hilton *Dby.* **40 B38**
Hilton *Shr.* **39 F33**
Hilton *Cbs.* **33 B48**
Hilton of Cadboll **97 D24**
Hilton of Delnies **97 F24**
Himbleton **29 C35**
Himley **40 F34**
Hincaster **55 A31**
Hinckley **41 F40**
Hinderclay **34 A56**
Hinderwell **63 E43**
Hindford **38 B29**
Hindhead **12 C44**
Hindley **49 B32**
Hindley Green **49 B32**
Hindlip **29 C34**
Hindolveston **44 C56**
Hindon **9 A34**
Hindringham **44 B55**
Hingham **44 E56**
Hinstock **39 C32**
Hintlesham **34 D56**
Hinton *Nmp.* **31 C41**
Hinton *H.&W.* **28 E29**
Hinton *Shr.* **38 E30**
Hinton *Avon* **20 D33**
Hinton *Ham.* **10 E38**
Hinton Admiral **10 E37**
Hinton Ampner **11 B42**
Hinton Blewett **19 F31**
Hinton Charterhouse **20 F33**
Hinton-in-the-Hedges **31 E41**
Hinton Martell **9 D35**
Hinton on the Green **29 D35**
Hinton Parva **21 C38**
Hinton St George **8 C30**
Hinton St Mary **9 C33**
Hinton Waldrist **21 B39**
Hints *Shr.* **29 A32**
Hints *Stf.* **40 E37**
Hinwick **32 B45**
Hinxhill **15 C56**
Hinxton **33 D50**
Hinxworth **33 D48**
Hipperholme **57 G37**
Hirn **91 D33**
Hirnant **37 C26**
Hirst **71 E38**
Hirst Courtney **58 G42**
Hirwaen **47 F27**
Hirwaun **18 A25**
Hiscott **6 C21**
Histon **33 B50**
Hitcham *Sfk* **34 C55**
Hitcham *Bkh.* **22 C45**
Hitchin **32 E47**
Hither Green **23 D49**
Hittisleigh **7 F23**
Hixon **40 C35**
Hoaden **15 B58**
Hoaldalbert **28 F29**
Hoar Cross **40 C37**
Hoarwithy **28 F31**
Hoath **25 E57**
Hobarris **28 A28**
Hobbister **105 A29**
Hobbs Lots Bridge **43 E49**
Hobkirk **70 B31**
Hobland Hall **45 E61**
Hobson **62 A37**
Hoby **41 D42**
Hockering **44 D56**
Hockerton **51 G42**
Hockley **24 B54**
Hockley Heath **30 A37**
Hockliffe **32 F45**
Hockwold cum Wilton **44 G53**
Hockworthy **7 D26**
Hoddesdon **23 A49**
Hoddlesden **56 G33**
Hodgeston **16 E16**
Hodnet **39 C32**
Hodthorpe **51 E41**
Hoe **44 D55**
Hoe Gate **11 C42**
Hoff **61 E32**
Hoffleet Stow **43 B48**
Hoggeston **31 F43**
Hoggie **98 C31**
Hogha Gearraidh **92 D2**
Hoghton **55 G31**
Hognaston **50 G38**
Hogsthorpe **53 E51**
Holbeach **43 C49**
Holbeach Bank **43 C49**
Holbeach Clough **43 C49**
Holbeach Drove **43 D49**
Holbeach Hurn **43 C49**
Holbeach St Johns **43 D49**
Holbeach St Marks **43 B49**
Holbeach St Matthew **43 B50**
Holbeck **51 E41**
Holberrow Green **29 B35**
Holbeton **5 F22**
Holborn **23 C49**
Holborough **24 E53**
Holbrook *Sfk* **35 E57**
Holbrook *Dby.* **41 A39**
Holburn **77 G36**
Holbury **11 D40**
Holcombe *Som.* **19 G32**
Holcombe *Dev.* **5 C25**
Holcombe Rogus **7 D26**
Holcot **31 B43**
Holden **56 E33**
Holdenby **31 B42**
Holdenhurst **10 E37**
Holdgate **38 G31**
Holdingham **42 A46**
Holditch **8 D29**
Hole-in-the-Wall **28 F31**
Hole Park **14 D54**
Hole Street **12 E47**
Holford **7 A27**
Holker **55 B29**
Holkham **44 A54**
Hollacombe **6 E19**
Holland *Ork.* **104 A30**
Holland *Ork.* **104 D32**
Holland *Sry* **23 F50**
Holland-on-Sea **35 G58**
Hollandstoun **104 A33**
Hollee **69 G28**
Hollesley **35 D59**
Hollingbourne **14 B54**
Hollingbury **13 F49**
Hollington *E.S.* **14 F53**
Hollington *Stf.* **40 B36**
Hollington *Dby.* **40 B38**
Hollingworth **49 C35**
Hollins **49 B33**
Hollinsclough **50 F36**
Hollins Green **49 C32**
Hollinswood **39 E33**
Hollinwood **38 B31**
Hollocombe **6 D21**
Holloway **51 G39**
Hollowell **31 A42**
Hollybush *H.&W.* **29 E33**
Hollybush *Gwe.* **18 A27**
Hollybush *Str.* **67 B19**
Holly End **43 E51**
Holly Green **29 D34**
Hollym **59 G49**
Holm **69 D28**
Holmbury St Mary **22 G47**
Holmbush *W.S.* **13 C48**
Holmbush *Cnw.* **4 E16**
Holme *Cbs.* **42 G47**
Holme *Cum.* **55 B31**
Holme *W.Y.* **50 B36**
Holme *Not.* **52 G44**
Holmebridge **9 F34**
Holme Chapel **56 G34**
Holme Hale **44 E54**
Holme Lacy **28 E31**
Holme Marsh **28 C29**
Holme next the Sea **44 A52**
Holme-on-Spalding-Moor **58 F43**
Holme on the Wolds **59 E45**
Holme Pierrepont **41 B42**
Holmer **28 D30**
Holmer Green **22 B45**
Holmes Chapel **49 F33**
Holmesfield **50 E38**
Holme's Hill **13 E51**
Holmeswood **48 A29**
Holmewood **51 F40**
Holmfield **57 G36**
Holmfirth **50 B37**
Holmhead *D.&G.* **68 E23**
Holmhead *Str.* **67 A21**
Holm of Drumlanrig **68 D24**
Holmpton **59 G49**
Holmrook **60 F26**
Holmsgarth **107 C40**
Holmside **62 B37**
Holmston **67 A19**
Holmwrangle **61 B30**
Holne **5 D23**
Holnest **9 D32**
Holsworthy **6 E19**
Holsworthy Beacon **6 E19**
Holt *Clw.* **48 G29**
Holt *Wts.* **20 E34**
Holt *H.&W.* **29 B34**
Holt *Nfk* **44 B56**
Holt *Dor.* **10 D36**
Holtby **58 D42**
Holt End *H.&W.* **30 B36**
Holt End *Ham.* **11 A42**
Holt Fleet **29 B34**
Holt Heath *H.&W.* **29 B34**
Holt Heath *Dor.* **10 D36**
Holton *Som.* **9 B32**
Holton *Oxf.* **21 A41**
Holton *Sfk* **35 A59**
Holton *Lcn.* **52 D47**
Holton Heath **9 E35**
Holton le Clay **53 B48**
Holton le Moor **52 C46**
Holton St Mary **34 E56**
Holtspur **22 B45**
Holtye Common **13 C50**
Holwell *Dor.* **9 C32**
Holwell *Hfs.* **32 E47**
Holwell *Lei.* **42 C43**
Holwell *Oxf.* **21 A38**
Holwell *Som.* **20 G33**
Holwick **61 D34**
Holworth **9 F33**
Holybourne **22 G43**
Holy Cross **29 A34**
Holymoorside **51 F39**
Holyport **22 D44**
Holystone **70 C35**
Holytown **75 D23**
Holywell *Cnw.* **2 C13**
Holywell *Dor.* **8 D31**
Holywell *Clw.* **47 E27**
Holywell *Cbs.* **33 A49**
Holywell *E.S.* **13 G52**
Holywell Green **50 A36**
Holywell Lake **7 D27**
Holywell Row **34 A53**
Holywood **68 E25**
Homer **39 E32**
Homersfield **45 G58**
Hom Green **28 F31**
Homington **10 B37**
Honeyborough **16 D15**
Honeybourne **30 D36**
Honeychurch **6 E22**
Honey Hill **25 E57**
Honey Tye **34 E55**
Honiley **30 A38**
Honing **45 C59**
Honingham **45 D57**
Honington *War.* **30 D38**
Honington *Sfk* **34 A54**
Honington *Lcn.* **42 A45**
Honiton **7 E27**
Honley **50 A37**
Hoo *Sfk* **35 C58**
Hoo *Kent* **24 D53**
Hooe *E.S.* **13 F52**
Hooe *Dev.* **4 E20**
Hooe Common **13 E52**
Hook *G.L.* **22 E47**
Hook *Ham.* **22 F43**
Hook *Dyf.* **16 C15**
Hook *Hum.* **58 G43**
Hook *Wts.* **20 C36**
Hook-a-Gate **38 E30**
Hooke **8 D31**
Hookgate **39 B33**
Hook Green *Kent* **24 E52**
Hook Green *Kent* **24 D52**
Hook Green *Kent* **13 C52**
Hook Norton **30 E39**
Hookway **7 F24**
Hookwood **23 G48**
Hoole **48 F30**
Hooley **23 F48**
Hooton **48 E29**
Hooton Levitt **51 C41**
Hooton Pagnell **51 B40**
Hooton Roberts **51 C40**
Hopcrofts Holt **31 F40**
Hope *Dby.* **50 D37**
Hope *Shr.* **38 E29**
Hope *Pow.* **38 E28**
Hope *Clw.* **48 G29**
Hope *Dev.* **5 G22**
Hope Bagot **28 A31**
Hope Bowdler **38 F30**
Hope End Green **33 G51**
Hopehouse **69 B28**
Hopeman **97 E27**
Hope Mansell **29 G32**
Hopesay **38 G29**
Hope's Green **24 C53**
Hope under Dinmore **28 C30**
Hopkinstown **18 B26**
Hopton *Nfk* **45 E61**
Hopton *Stf.* **40 C35**
Hopton *Shr.* **38 C31**
Hopton *Dby.* **50 G38**
Hopton *Sfk* **34 A55**
Hopton Cangeford **38 G31**
Hopton Castle **28 A29**
Hoptonheath **28 A29**
Hopton Wafers **29 A32**
Hopwas **40 E37**
Hopwood **30 A36**
Horam **13 E51**
Horbling **42 B47**
Horbury **50 A38**
Horden **62 B40**
Horderley **38 G29**
Hordle **10 E38**
Hordley **38 B29**
Horeb *Dyf.* **17 D21**
Horeb *Dyf.* **26 D19**
Horfield **19 D31**
Horham **35 A58**
Horkesley Heath **34 F55**
Horkstow **52 A45**
Horley *Oxf.* **31 D40**
Horley *W.S.* **23 G48**
Hornblotton Green **8 A31**
Hornby *N.Y.* **62 G38**
Hornby *N.Y.* **62 F39**
Hornby *Lan.* **55 C31**
Horncastle **53 F48**
Hornchurch **23 C51**
Horncliffe **77 E35**
Horndean *Bor.* **77 F34**
Horndean *Ham.* **11 C42**
Horndon **6 G21**
Horndon on the Hill **24 C52**
Horne **23 G49**
Horn Hill **22 B46**
Horniehaugh **82 A29**
Horning **45 D59**
Horninghold **42 F43**
Horninglow **40 C38**
Horningsea **33 B50**
Horningsham **20 G33**
Horningtoft **44 C55**
Horningtops **4 D18**
Hornsby **61 B30**
Hornsby Gate **61 A31**
Horns Cross *Dev.* **6 C19**
Horns Cross *E.S.* **14 E54**
Hornsea **59 E48**
Hornsey **23 C48**
Hornton **30 D39**
Horrabridge **4 D20**
Horridge **5 C23**
Horringer **34 B54**
Horsebridge *Dev.* **4 C20**
Horse Bridge **49 G35**
Horsebridge *Ham.* **10 A39**
Horsebrook **40 D34**
Horsehay **39 E32**
Horseheath **33 D51**
Horsehouse **57 A36**
Horsell **22 F45**
Horseman's Green **38 A30**
Horseway **43 G50**
Horsey **45 C60**
Horsford **45 D57**
Horsforth **57 F38**
Horsham *H.&W.* **29 C33**
Horsham *W.S.* **12 C47**
Horsham St Faith **45 D58**
Horsington *Lcn.* **52 F47**
Horsington *Som.* **9 B32**
Horsley *Dby.* **41 A39**
Horsley *Glo.* **20 B34**
Horsley *Nor.* **71 G36**
Horsley *Nor.* **70 D34**
Horsley Cross **35 F57**
Horsleycross Street **35 F57**
Horsleyhill **70 B31**
Horsley Woodhouse **41 A39**
Horsmonden **23 G52**
Horspath **21 A41**
Horstead **45 D58**
Horsted Keynes **13 D49**
Horton *Dor.* **10 D36**
Horton *Bkh.* **22 D46**
Horton *Lan.* **56 D34**
Horton *Wts.* **20 E36**
Horton *Avon* **20 C33**
Horton *W.G.* **17 F20**
Horton *Som.* **8 C29**
Horton *Stf.* **49 G35**
Horton *Bkh.* **32 G45**
Horton *Nmp.* **32 C44**
Horton Cross **8 C29**
Horton-cum-Studley **31 G41**
Horton Green **38 A30**
Horton Heath **11 C40**
Horton Inn **10 D36**
Horton in Ribblesdale **56 B34**
Horton Kirby **23 E51**
Horwich **49 A32**
Horwood **6 C21**
Hose **42 C43**
Hoses **60 G28**
Hosh **81 E24**
Hosta **92 D3**
Hoswick **107 E40**
Hotham **58 F44**
Hothfield **14 C55**
Hoton **41 C41**
Houbie **106 C42**
Hough **49 G33**
Hougham **42 A44**
Hough Green **48 D30**
Hough-on-the-Hill **42 A44**
Houghton *Cbs.* **33 A48**
Houghton *Dev.* **5 F22**
Houghton *Cum.* **60 A29**
Houghton *W.S.* **12 E45**
Houghton *Ham.* **10 A39**
Houghton *Dyf.* **16 D15**
Houghton Bank **62 D38**
Houghton Conquest **32 D46**
Houghton-le-Side **62 D38**
Houghton le Spring **62 A39**
Houghton on the Hill **41 E42**
Houghton Regis **32 F46**
Houghton St Giles **44 B55**
Houlsyke **63 F43**
Hound **11 D40**
Hound Green **22 F43**
Houndslow **76 F32**
Houndwood **77 D34**
Hounsdown **10 C39**
Hounslow **22 D47**
Hounslow Green **33 G52**
Househill **97 F24**
Housetter **106 D39**
Houston **74 D19**
Houstry **103 E27**
Houstry of Dunn **103 C27**
Houton **105 A29**
Hove **13 F48**
Hoveringham **41 A42**
Hoveton **45 D59**
Hovingham **58 B42**
How **61 A31**
How Caple **28 E31**
Howden **58 G43**
Howden-le-Wear **62 C37**
Howe *N.Y.* **57 A39**
Howe *Nfk* **45 E58**
Howe *Hgh.* **103 B29**
Howe *Cum.* **55 A30**
Howe Green **24 A53**
Howell **42 A47**
How End **32 D46**
Howe of Teuchar **99 E33**
Howe Street *Esx* **33 G52**
Howe Street *Esx* **33 E52**
Howey **27 C26**
Howgate **76 E28**
Howgill **57 D36**
Howick **71 B38**
Howle **39 C32**
Howlett End **33 E51**
Howley **8 D28**
How Man **60 F25**
Hownam **70 B33**
Hownam Mains **70 A33**
Howpasley **69 C29**
Howsham *N.Y.* **58 C43**
Howsham *Hum.* **52 B46**
Howtel **77 G34**
Howton **28 F29**
Howwood **74 D20**
Hoxa **105 B30**
Hoxne **35 A57**
Hoy **103 B28**
Hoylake **47 D27**
Hoyland **51 B39**
Hoyland Swaine **50 B38**
Hubberholme **56 B34**
Hubbert's Bridge **43 A48**
Huby *N.Y.* **58 C41**
Huby *N.Y.* **57 E38**
Hucclecote **29 G34**
Hucking **14 B54**
Hucknall **41 A41**
Huddersfield **50 A37**
Huddington **29 C35**
Hudscott **6 C22**
Hudswell **62 F37**
Huggate **58 D44**
Hugglescote **41 D40**
Hughenden Valley **22 B44**
Hughley **38 F31**
Hugh Town **2 A10**
Hugmore **48 G29**
Huish *Dev.* **6 D21**

Huish *Wts.* 20 E37
Huish Champflower 7 C26
Huish Episcopi 8 B29
Huisinis 100 F6
Hulcott 32 G44
Hulland 40 A38
Hullavington 20 C34
Hullbridge 24 B54
Hulme End 50 G37
Hulme Walfield 49 F34
Hulver Street 45 G60
Humber Court 28 C31
Humberside Airport 52 B46
Humberston 53 B49
Humberstone 41 E42
Humbie 76 D30
Humbleton *Hum.* 59 F48
Humbleton *Nor.* 70 A35
Humby 42 B46
Hume 76 F32
Humehall 76 F32
Humshaugh 70 F34
Huna 103 A29
Huncoat 56 F33
Huncote 41 F41
Hundalee 70 B32
Hunderthwaite 62 D35
Hundleby 53 F49
Hundleton 16 D15
Hundon 34 D53
Hundred Acres 11 C41
Hundred End 55 G30
Hundred House 28 C27
Hungarton 41 E42
Hungerford *Ham.* 10 C37
Hungerford *Bkh.* 21 E39
Hungerford Newtown 21 D39
Hunglader 93 D9
Hunningham 30 B39
Hunny Hill 11 F40
Hunsdon 33 G49
Hunsingore 57 D40
Hunsonby 61 C31
Hunspow 103 A27
Hunstanton 44 A52
Hunstanworth 61 B35
Hunston *Sfk* 34 B55
Hunston *W.S.* 12 F44
Hunstrete 19 E32
Hunt End 30 B36
Huntercombe End 21 C42
Hunters Forstal 25 E57
Hunter's Quay 73 C17
Hunterston 73 E17
Huntford 70 C32
Hunt House 63 G44
Huntingdon 33 A48
Huntingfield 35 A59
Huntingford 9 B33
Huntington *H.&W.* 28 C28
Huntington *N.Y.* 58 D42
Huntington *Stf.* 40 D35
Huntingtower 82 E26
Huntley 29 G33
Huntly 98 E31
Huntlywood 76 F31
Hunton *N.Y.* 62 G37
Hunton *Kent* 14 C53
Hunton *Ham.* 11 A40
Huntonbridge 22 A46
Hunt's Cross 48 D30
Huntsham 7 C25
Huntshaw Cross 6 C21
Huntspill 19 G28
Huntworth 8 A28
Hunwick 62 C37
Hunworth 44 B56
Hurdsfield 49 E35
Hurley *War.* 40 F38
Hurley *Brk.* 22 C44
Hurley Bottom 22 C44
Hurlford 74 G20
Hurliness 105 C28
Hurn 10 E37
Hursley 11 B40
Hurst *Brk.* 22 D43
Hurst *G.M.* 49 B35
Hurst *N.Y.* 62 F36
Hurstbourne Priors 21 G40
Hurstbourne Tarrant 21 F39
Hurst Green *E.S.* 14 E53
Hurst Green *Lan.* 56 F32
Hurstpierpoint 13 E48
Hurstway Common 28 D28
Hurstwood 56 F34
Hurtmore 22 G45
Hurworth-on-Tees 62 E38
Hury 61 D35
Husabost 93 F7
Husbands Bosworth 41 G42
Husborne Crawley 32 E45
Husthwaite 58 B41
Huthwaite 51 G40
Huttoft 53 E51
Hutton *Bor.* 77 E34
Hutton *Avon* 19 F29
Hutton *Cum.* 60 D30
Hutton *Esx* 24 B52
Hutton *Lan.* 55 G30
Hutton Bonville 62 F39
Hutton Buscel 59 A45
Hutton Conyers 57 B39
Hutton Cranswick 59 D46
Hutton End 60 C30
Hutton Henry 62 C40
Hutton-le-Hole 63 G42
Hutton Magna 62 E37
Hutton Roof *Cum.* 60 C29
Hutton Roof *Cum.* 55 B31
Hutton Rudby 62 F40
Hutton Sessay 57 B40
Hutton Wandesley 58 D41
Huxley 48 F31
Huxter *She.* 107 A41
Huxter *She.* 107 B39
Huyton 48 C30
Hycemoor 54 A26
Hyde *G.M.* 49 C35
Hyde *Glo.* 20 A34
Hyde Heath 22 B45
Hyde Lea 40 D34
Hydestile 22 G45
Hyndford Bridge 75 F25
Hyndlee 70 C31
Hynish 78 D5
Hyssington 38 F28
Hythe *Ham.* 11 D40
Hythe *Kent* 15 D57
Hythe End 22 D46
Hythie 99 D36
Hyton 54 A26

I

Ianstown 98 C30
Ibberton 9 D33
Ible 50 G38
Ibsley 10 D37
Ibstock 41 D39
Ibstone 22 B43
Ibthorpe 21 F39
Ibworth 21 F41
Icelton 19 E29
Ickburgh 44 F53
Ickenham 22 C46
Ickford 21 A42
Ickham 15 B57
Ickleford 32 E47
Icklesham 14 F54
Ickleton 33 D50
Icklingham 34 A53
Ickwell Green 32 D47
Icomb 30 F37
Idbury 30 F38
Iddesleigh 6 E21
Ide 7 F24
Ideford 5 C24
Ide Hill 23 F50
Iden 14 E55
Iden Green *Kent* 14 D53
Iden Green *Kent* 14 D54
Idlicote 30 D38
Idmiston 10 A38
Idridgehay 40 A38
Idrigil 93 E9
Idstone 21 C38
Idvies 83 C31
Iffley 21 A41
Ifield 13 C48
Ifieldwood 13 C48
Ifold 12 C46
Iford 13 F50
Ifton Heath 38 B29
Ightfield 38 B31
Ightham 23 F51
Iken 35 C60
Ilam 50 G37
Ilchester 8 B31
Ilderton 70 A35
Ilford 23 C50
Ilfracombe 6 A20
Ilkeston 41 A40
Ilketshall St Andrew 45 G59
Ilketshall St Lawrence 45 G59
Ilketshall St Margaret 45 G59
Ilkley 57 E36
Illey 40 G35
Illington 44 G55
Illingworth 57 G36
Illogan 2 D12
Illston on the Hill 42 F43
Ilmer 22 A43
Ilmington 30 D37
Ilminster 8 C29
Ilsington 5 C23
Ilston 17 E21
Ilton *N.Y.* 57 B37
Ilton *Som.* 8 C29
Imachar 73 F14
Immeroin 81 F21
Immingham 52 A47
Immingham Dock 53 A48
Impington 33 B50
Ince 48 E30
Ince Blundell 48 B29
Ince-in-Makerfield 48 B31
Inch 91 F32
Inchbare 83 A31
Inchberry 98 D28
Inchbraoch 83 B32
Inchgrundle 90 F29
Inchindown 96 D22
Inchinnan 74 D20
Inchkinloch 102 D21
Inchlaggan 87 D17
Inchlumpie 96 D21
Inchmarlo 91 D32
Inchnabobart 90 E28
Inchnacardoch Hotel 88 C19
Inchnadamph 101 F18
Inchock 83 C32
Inchrory 90 C27
Inchture 82 E28
Inchvuilt 87 A18
Inchyra 82 E27
Indian Queens 3 C15
Inerval 72 F9
Ingatestone 24 A52
Ingbirchworth 50 B38
Ingerthorpe 57 C38
Ingestre 40 C35
Ingham *Lcn.* 52 D45
Ingham *Sfk* 34 A54
Ingham *Nfk* 45 C59
Ingleby 41 C39
Ingleby Arncliffe 62 F40
Ingleby Barwick 62 E40
Ingleby Cross 62 F40
Ingleby Greenhow 63 F41
Inglesbatch 19 E32
Inglesham 20 B37
Ingleton *Drm.* 62 D37
Ingleton *N.Y.* 56 B32
Inglewhite 55 E31
Ingmire Hall 61 G32
Ingoe 71 F36
Ingoldmells 53 F51
Ingoldsby 42 B45
Ingon 30 C38
Ingram 70 B35
Ingrave 24 B52
Ingrow 57 F36
Ings 60 G30
Ingst 19 C31
Ingworth 45 B57
Inistrynich 80 E16
Injebreck 54 E25
Inkberrow 29 C35
Inkhorn 99 F35
Inkpen 21 E39
Inkstack 103 A28
Innellan 73 D17
Innergellie 83 G31
Innerleithen 76 G29
Innerleven 82 G29
Innermessan 64 D16
Innerwick *Tay.* 81 C21
Innerwick *Ltn.* 76 C32
Inninbeg 79 C12
Innsworth 29 F34
Insch 91 A32
Insh 89 D24
Inshore 101 A19
Inskip 55 F30
Instow 6 B20
Intake 51 D39
Intwood 45 E57
Inver *Hgh.* 97 C24
Inver *Hgh.* 103 F27
Inver *Str.* 80 C15
Inver *Tay.* 82 C26
Inver *Grm.* 90 D28
Inverailort 86 F13
Inveralligan 94 F14
Inverallochy 99 C36
Inveran 96 B21
Inveraray 80 G16
Inverardoch Mains 81 G23
Inverardran 80 E19
Inverarish 86 A11
Inverarity 83 C30
Inverarnan 80 F18
Inverasdale 94 C13
Inverbain 94 F13
Inverbeg 74 A19
Inverbervie 91 F34
Inverbroom 95 C17
Inverbrough 88 B23
Invercassley 96 A20
Inverchaolain 73 C16
Invercharnan 80 C17
Inverchorachan 80 F17
Inverchoran 95 F18
Invercreran 80 C15
Inverdruie 89 C24
Inverebrie 99 F35
Invereen 88 A23
Invererne 97 E26
Inveresk 76 C29
Inverey 89 F26
Inverfarigaig 88 B20
Invergarry 87 D18
Invergelder 90 D28
Invergeldie 81 E23
Invergloy 87 F18
Invergordon 96 E22
Invergowrie 82 D29
Inverguseran 86 D13
Inverhadden 81 B22
Inverharroch 98 F29
Inverherive 80 E19
Inverhope 102 B20
Inverie 86 D13
Inverinan 80 F15
Inverinate 86 B15
Inverkeilor 83 C32
Inverkeithing 75 B26
Inverkeithny 98 E32
Inverkip 74 C18
Inverkirkaig 101 F16
Inverlael 95 C17
Inverlauren 74 B18
Inverliever 79 G14
Inverliver 80 D16
Inverlochlarig 81 F20
Inverlochy 80 E17
Inverlussa 72 B12
Inver Mallie 87 F17
Invermay 82 F26
Invermoriston 88 C19
Invernaver 102 B22
Inverneil 73 B14
Inverness 96 G22
Inverness (Dalcross) Airport 96 F23
Invernettie 99 E37
Invernoaden 73 A17
Inveroran Hotel 80 C18
Inverquharity 82 B29
Inverquhomery 99 E36
Inverroy 87 F18
Inversanda 80 B15
Invershiel 86 C15
Inversnaid Hotel 80 G19
Invertrossachs 81 G21
Inverugie 99 E36
Inveruglas 80 G18
Inveruglass 88 D23
Inverurie 91 A33
Invervar 81 C22
Invervegain 73 C16
Invery Ho. 91 D32
Inverythan 99 E33
Inwardleigh 6 F21
Inworth 34 G54
Iochda 92 G3
Iping 12 D44
Ipplepen 5 D24
Ipsden 21 C42
Ipstones 50 G36
Ipswich 35 D57
Irby 48 D28
Irby in the Marsh 53 F50
Irby upon Humber 52 B47
Irchester 32 B45
Ireby *Cum.* 60 C28
Ireby *Lan.* 56 B32
Ireland *Ork.* 105 A29
Ireland *She.* 107 E39
Ireleth 55 B28
Ireshopeburn 61 C34
Irlam 49 C33
Irnham 42 C46
Iron Acton 19 C32
Ironbridge 39 E32
Iron Cross 30 C36
Ironside 99 D34
Ironville 51 G40
Irstead 45 C59
Irthington 69 G30
Irthlingborough 32 B45
Irton 59 A46
Irvine 74 G18
Isauld 103 B25
Isbister *Ork.* 104 D28
Isbister *Ork.* 104 E29
Isbister *She.* 107 A41
Isbister *She.* 106 C39
Isfield 13 E50
Isham 32 A44
Ishriff 79 D12
Islay Ho. 72 D9
Isle Abbotts 8 B29
Isle Brewers 8 B29
Isleham 33 A52
Isle of Dogs 23 D49
Isle of Whithorn 64 G20
Isleornsay (Eilean Iarmain) 86 C12
Islesburgh 107 A39
Isleworth 22 D47
Isley Walton 41 C40
Islibhig 100 E6
Islington 23 C48
Islip *Nmp.* 32 A45
Islip *Oxf.* 31 G41
Isombridge 38 D31
Istead Rise 24 E52
Itchen 11 C40
Itchen Abbas 11 A41
Itchen Stoke 11 A41
Itchingfield 12 D47
Itchington 19 C32
Itteringham 45 B57
Itton 6 F22
Itton Common 19 B30
Ivegill 60 B29
Ivelet 61 G35
Iver 22 C46
Iver Heath 22 C45
Iveston 62 A37
Ivinghoe 32 G45
Ivinghoe Aston 32 G45
Ivington 28 C30
Ivington Green 28 C30
Ivybridge 5 E21
Ivychurch 15 E56
Ivy Hatch 23 F51
Ivy Todd 44 E54
Iwade 25 E55
Iwerne Courtney or Shroton 9 C34
Iwerne Minster 9 C34
Ixworth 34 B55
Ixworth Thorpe 34 A54

J

Jack Hill 57 D37
Jackstown 99 F33
Jackton 74 E21
Jacobstow 4 A18
Jacobstowe 6 E21
Jameston 16 E16
Jamestown *Hgh.* 96 F20
Jamestown *Str.* 74 B19
Jamestown *D.&G.* 69 D29
Janefield 96 F23
Janetstown 103 B26
Jarrow 71 G39
Jarvis Brook 13 D51
Jasper's Green 33 F52
Jawcraig 75 C24
Jayes Park 22 G47
Jaywick 35 G57
Jedburgh 70 B32
Jeffreyston 16 D16
Jemimaville 96 E22
Jersay 75 D24
Jerviswood 75 F24
Jesmond 71 G38
Jevington 13 F51
Jodrell Bank 49 E33
Johnby 60 C30
John 'o' Groats 103 A29
John's Cross 14 E53
Johnshaven 91 G33
Johnston 16 C15
Johnstone 74 D20
Johnstonebridge 69 D26
Johnstone Castle 74 D20
Johnston Mains 91 G33
Johnstown *Clw.* 38 A29
Johnstown *Dyf.* 17 C19
Joppa *Ltn.* 76 C29
Joppa *Str.* 67 B19
Jordans 22 B45
Jordanston 16 A14
Jordanstone 82 C28
Jump 51 B39
Juniper Green 75 D27
Jura Ho. 72 D10
Jurby East 54 D25
Jurby West 54 D25

K

Kaber 61 E33
Kaimes 76 D28
Kalnakill 94 F12
Kames *Str.* 73 C15
Kames *Str.* 79 F14
Kames *Str.* 68 A22
Kea 2 D13
Keadby 52 A44
Keal Cotes 53 F49
Kearsley 49 B33
Kearstwick 55 A31
Kearton 62 G35
Kearvaig 101 A18
Keasden 56 C33
Kebholes 98 D32
Keckwick 48 D31
Keddington 53 D49
Kedington 33 D52
Kedleston 40 A38
Keelby 52 B47
Keele 40 A34
Keeley Green 32 D46
Keeres Green 33 G51

Keeston 16 C15
Keevil 20 F35
Kegworth 41 C40
Kehelland 2 D11
Keig 91 B32
Keighley 57 E36
Keil *Hgh.* 80 B15
Keil *Str.* 66 C12
Keilhill 98 D32
Keillmore 72 B12
Keillor 82 C28
Keillour 82 E25
Keills 72 D10
Keils 72 D11
Keinton Mandeville 8 A31
Keir 75 A23
Keir Mill 68 D24
Keisby 42 C46
Keisley 61 D32
Keiss 103 B29
Keith 98 D30
Keithick 82 D27
Keithmore 98 F29
Keithock 83 A31
Kelbrook 56 E35
Kelby 42 A45
Keld *N.Y.* 61 F34
Keld *Cum.* 61 E31
Keldholme 58 A43
Keldy Castle 63 G43
Kelfield *N.Y.* 58 F41
Kelfield *Hum.* 52 B44
Kelham 51 G43
Kellan 79 C11
Kellas *Grm.* 97 F27
Kellas *Tay.* 83 D30
Kellaton 5 G24
Kelleth 61 F32
Kelleythorpe 59 D46
Kelling 44 A56
Kellington 58 G41
Kelloe 62 C39
Kelloholm 68 B23
Kelly *Dev.* 6 G19
Kelly *Cnw.* 4 C16
Kelly Bray 4 C19
Kelmarsh 31 A43
Kelmscott 21 B38
Kelsale 35 B59
Kelsall 48 F31
Kelsay 72 E8
Kelshall 33 E49
Kelsick 60 A27
Kelso 77 G33
Kelstedge 51 F39
Kelstern 53 C48
Kelston 19 E32
Keltneyburn 81 C23
Kelton 65 C25
Kelty 75 A27
Kelvedon 34 G54
Kelvedon Hatch 23 B51
Kelynack 2 E9
Kemback 83 F30
Kemberton 39 E33
Kemble 20 B35
Kemerton 29 E35
Kemeys Commander 19 A29
Kemeys Inferior 19 B29
Kemnay 91 B33
Kempley 29 F32
Kempley Green 29 F32
Kempsey 29 D34
Kempsford 20 B37
Kempshott 21 G41
Kempston 32 D46
Kempston Church End 32 D46
Kempston Hardwick 32 D46
Kempton 38 G29
Kemp Town 13 F49
Kemsing 23 F51
Kemsley 24 E54
Kenardington 14 D55
Kenchester 28 D30
Kencott 21 A38
Kendal 61 G30
Kenderchurch 28 F29
Kenfig 18 C23
Kenfig Hill 18 C24
Kenilworth 30 A38
Kenknock *Cen.* 81 D20
Kenknock *Tay.* 81 C21
Kenley *Shr.* 38 E31
Kenley *G.L.* 23 F49
Kenmore *Hgh.* 94 F13
Kenmore *Tay.* 81 C23
Kenmore *Str.* 80 G16
Kenmore *W.I.* 100 G8
Kenn *Dev.* 7 G25
Kenn *Avon* 19 E30
Kennacraig 73 D14
Kennards House 4 B18
Kennavay 93 B8
Kennerleigh 7 E23
Kennerty 91 D32
Kennet 75 A25
Kennethmont 90 A31
Kennett 33 B52
Kennford 7 G25
Kenninghall 44 G56
Kennington *Oxf.* 21 A40
Kennington *Kent* 14 C55
Kennoway 82 G29
Kennyhill 33 A52
Kennythorpe 58 C43
Kensaleyre 93 F10
Kensington & Chelsea 23 D48
Kensworth 32 G46
Kensworth Common 32 G46
Kentallen 80 B15
Kentchurch 28 F29
Kentford 33 B52
Kentisbeare 7 E26
Kentisbury 6 A22
Kentisbury Ford 6 A22
Kentmere 60 F30
Kenton *T.&W.* 71 G38
Kenton *Sfk* 35 B57
Kenton *Dev.* 7 G25
Kentra 79 A12
Kents Bank 55 B30
Kent's Green 29 F33
Kent's Oak 10 B39
Kent Street *E.S.* 14 F53
Kent Street *Kent* 23 F52
Kenwick 38 B29
Kenwyn 3 D14
Kenyon 49 C32
Keoldale 101 B19
Keppanach 80 A16
Keppoch *Str.* 74 C19
Keppoch *Hgh.* 86 B15
Keprigan 66 B12
Kepwick 62 G40
Keresley 40 G38
Kerne Bridge 28 G31
Kerridge 49 E35
Kerris 2 F10
Kerry 38 G27
Kerrycroy 73 D17
Kerrysdale 94 D14
Kerry's Gate 28 E29
Kersall 51 F43
Kersey 34 D55
Kershopefoot 69 E30
Kerswell 7 E26
Kerswell Green 29 D34
Kesgrave 35 D58
Kessingland 45 G61
Kessingland Beach 45 G61
Kestle Mill 3 C14
Keston 23 E49
Keswick *Nfk* 45 E58
Keswick *Nfk* 45 B59
Keswick *Cum.* 60 D28
Ketsby 53 E49
Kettering 32 A44
Ketteringham 45 E57
Kettins 82 D28
Kettlebaston 34 D55
Kettlebridge 82 G28
Kettlebrook 40 E37
Kettleburgh 35 C58
Kettleholm 69 F27
Kettleness 63 E44
Kettleshulme 49 E35
Kettlesing 57 D37
Kettlesing Bottom 57 D38
Kettlestone 44 B55
Kettlethorpe 52 E44
Kettletoft 104 C32
Kettlewell 56 B35
Ketton 42 E45
Kew 22 D47
Kewstoke 19 E29
Kexbrough 50 B38
Kexby *Lcn.* 52 D44
Kexby *N.Y.* 58 D43
Key Green 49 F34
Keyham 41 E42
Keyhaven 10 E39
Keyingham 59 G48
Keymer 13 E49
Keynsham 19 E32
Keysoe 32 B46
Keysoe Row 32 B46
Key's Toft 53 G50
Keyston 32 A46
Keyworth 41 B41
Kibblesworth 62 A38
Kibworth Beauchamp 41 F42
Kibworth Harcourt 41 F42
Kidbrooke 23 D50
Kiddal Lane End 57 F40
Kiddemore Green 40 E34
Kidderminster 29 A33
Kiddington 30 F39
Kidlington 31 G40
Kidmore End 21 D42
Kidsdale 64 G20
Kidsgrove 49 G34
Kidstones 56 A35
Kidwelly (Cydweli) 17 D20
Kiel Crofts 79 D14
Kielder 70 D32
Kilbarchan 74 D19
Kilbeg 86 D12
Kilberry 73 D13
Kilbirnie 74 E18
Kilblaan 80 F17
Kilbraur 102 G24
Kilbrenan 79 C10
Kilbride *Hgh.* 86 B11
Kilbride *Str.* 79 E14
Kilbride *Str.* 73 D16
Kilbride Farm 73 D15
Kilbridemore 73 A15
Kilburn *Dby.* 41 A39
Kilburn *N.Y.* 57 B40
Kilby 41 F42
Kilcadzow 75 F24
Kilchattan 73 E17
Kilchenzie 66 A12
Kilcheran 79 D14
Kilchiaren 72 E8
Kilchoan *Str.* 79 A10
Kilchoan *Hgh.* 79 F13
Kilchrenan 80 E16
Kilchrist 66 B12
Kilconquhar 83 G30
Kilcot 29 F32
Kilcoy 96 F21
Kilcreggan 74 B18
Kildale 63 F41
Kildary 96 D23
Kildavie 66 B13
Kildermorie Lodge 96 D20
Kildonan 66 A16
Kildonan Lodge 103 F25
Kildonnan 85 F10
Kildrochet 64 E16
Kildrummy 90 B30
Kildwick 57 E36
Kilfinan 73 C15
Kilfinnan 87 E18
Kilgetty 16 D17
Kilgwrrwg Common 19 B30
Kilham *Hum.* 59 C46
Kilham *Nor.* 77 G34
Kilkenneth 78 C5
Kilkenny 29 G35
Kilkerran *Str.* 67 C19
Kilkerran *Str.* 66 B13
Kilkhampton 6 D18
Killamarsh 51 D40
Killay 17 E22
Killbeg 79 C11
Killean *Str.* 80 G16
Killean *Str.* 72 F12
Killearn 74 B21
Killellan 66 B12
Killen 96 F22
Killerby 62 D37
Killichonan 81 B21
Killichronan 79 C11
Killiechanate 87 F18
Killiecrankie 81 A24
Killiehuntly 88 E23
Killiemor 79 D10
Killilan 86 A15
Killimster 103 C28
Killin *Hgh.* 97 A24
Killin *Cen.* 81 D21
Killinallan 72 C8
Killinghall 57 D38
Killington 56 A32
Killingworth 71 F38
Killochyett 76 F30
Killocraw 66 A12
Killunaig 79 E10
Killundine 79 C11
Kilmacolm 74 D19
Kilmaha 80 G15
Kilmahog 81 G21
Kilmalieu 79 B14
Kilmaluag 93 D10
Kilmany 82 E29
Kilmarie 86 C11
Kilmarnock 74 G20
Kilmartin 73 A14
Kilmaurs 74 F20
Kilmelford 79 F14
Kilmersdon 19 F32
Kilmeston 11 B41
Kilmichael 66 A12
Kilmichael Glassary 73 A14
Kilmichael of Inverlussa 73 B13
Kilmington *Wts.* 9 A33
Kilmington *Dev.* 8 E28
Kilmington Street 9 A33
Kilmorack 96 G20
Kilmore *Hgh.* 86 D12
Kilmore *Str.* 79 E14
Kilmory *Hgh.* 85 D9
Kilmory *Hgh.* 86 G11
Kilmory *Str.* 73 B13
Kilmory *Str.* 72 C12
Kilmote 103 G25
Kilmuir *Hgh.* 96 G22
Kilmuir *Hgh.* 93 D9
Kilmuir *Hgh.* 96 D23
Kilmuir *Hgh.* 93 G8
Kilmun 73 B17
Kilmux 82 G29
Kilnave 72 C8
Kilndown 14 D53
Kiln Green 22 D44
Kilnhurst 51 C40
Kilninian 78 C9
Kilninver 79 E14
Kiln Pit Hill 62 A36
Kilnsea 53 A50
Kilnsey 56 C35
Kilnwick 59 E46
Kiloran 72 A9
Kilpatrick 66 A14
Kilpeck 28 E30
Kilphedir 103 G25
Kilpin 58 G43
Kilrenny 83 G31
Kilsby 31 A41
Kilspindie 82 E28
Kilstay 64 G17
Kilsyth 74 C22
Kiltarlity 96 G20
Kilton *Cle.* 63 E42
Kilton *Som.* 7 A27
Kiltyre 81 D22
Kilvaxter 93 E9
Kilve 7 A27
Kilverstone 44 G54
Kilvington 42 A43
Kilwinning 74 F18
Kimberley *Nfk* 44 E56
Kimberley *Not.* 41 A40
Kimblesworth 62 B38
Kimble Wick 22 A43
Kimbolton *H.&W.* 28 B31
Kimbolton *Cbs.* 32 B46
Kimcote 41 G41
Kimmeridge 9 F34
Kimmerston 77 G35
Kimpton *Hfs.* 32 G47
Kimpton *Ham.* 21 G38
Kinaldy 83 F30
Kinblethmont 83 C32
Kinbrace 102 E24
Kinbreack 86 E15
Kinbuck 81 G23
Kincaldrum 82 C29
Kincaple 83 F30
Kincardine *Fife* 75 B25
Kincardine *Hgh.* 96 C21
Kincardine O'Neil 90 D31
Kinclaven 82 D27
Kincorth 91 C35
Kincraig *Grm.* 91 A35
Kincraig *Hgh.* 89 D24
Kincraigie 82 C25
Kindallachan 82 C25
Kindrogan Field Centre 82 A26
Kinellar 91 B33
Kineton *Glo.* 30 F36
Kineton *War.* 30 C39
Kineton Green 40 G36
Kinfauns 82 E27
Kingarth 73 E16
Kingcoed 19 A30
Kingerby 52 C46
Kingham 30 F38
Kingholm Quay 65 C25
Kinghorn 76 B28
Kinglassie 76 A28
Kingoodie 82 E29
Kingsand 4 E20
Kingsbarns 83 F31
Kingsbridge *Dev.* 5 F23
Kingsbridge *Som.* 7 B25
King's Bromley 40 D37
Kingsburgh 93 F9
Kingsbury *G.L.* 22 C47
Kingsbury *War.* 40 F38
Kingsbury Episcopi 8 B30
Kings Caple 28 F31
Kingscavil 75 C26
Kingsclere 21 F41
King's Cliffe 42 F45
Kingscote 20 B33
Kingscott 6 D21
King's Coughton 30 C36
Kingscross 66 A16
Kingsdale 82 G29
Kingsdon 8 B30
Kingsdown 15 C59
Kingseat 75 A27
Kingsey 22 A43
Kingsfold *Dyf.* 16 E15
Kingsfold *W.S.* 12 C47
Kingsford *Grm.* 91 C34
Kingsford *Grm.* 90 B31
Kingsford *Grm.* 99 E33
Kingsford *Str.* 74 F20
Kingsford *H.&W.* 39 G33
Kingsforth 52 A46
Kingsgate 25 D59
King's Green 29 E33
Kingsheanton 6 B21
King's Heath 40 G36
King's Hill 40 F35
Kingshouse 81 E21
Kingshouse Hotel 80 B18
Kingskerswell 5 D24
Kingskettle 82 G28
Kingsland *Gwy.* 46 D18
Kingsland *H.&W.* 28 B30
Kings Langley 22 A46
Kingsley *Che.* 48 E31
Kingsley *Stf.* 40 A35
Kingsley *Ham.* 11 A43
Kingsley Green 12 C44
King's Lynn 43 C51
Kings Meaburn 61 D32
King's Mill 3 E16
Kings Muir 76 G28
Kingsmuir 83 C30
King's Newton 41 C39
Kingsnorth 14 D55
Kingsnorth Power Station 24 D54
King's Norton *Lei.* 41 E42
King's Norton *W.M.* 30 A36
King's Nympton 6 D22
King's Pyon 28 C30
Kings Ripton 33 A48
King's Somborne 10 A39
King's Stag 9 C32
King's Stanley 20 A34
King's Sutton 31 E41
Kingstanding 40 F36
Kingsteignton 5 C24
Kingsteps 97 F24
King Sterndale 50 E36
Kingsthorne 28 E30
Kingsthorpe 31 B43
Kingston *Cbs.* 33 C49
Kingston *Grm.* 98 C29
Kingston *Dor.* 9 G35
Kingston *Ltn.* 76 B31
Kingston *Dev.* 5 F22
Kingston *Dor.* 9 D33
Kingston *Ham.* 10 D37
Kingston *Kent* 15 B57
Kingston *I.o.W.* 11 F40
Kingston *W.S.* 12 F46
Kingston Bagpuize 21 B39
Kingston Blount 22 B43
Kingston by Sea 13 F48
Kingston Deverill 9 A34
Kingstone *Som.* 8 C29
Kingstone *H.&W.* 28 E30
Kingstone *Stf.* 40 C36
Kingston Lisle 21 C39
Kingston near Lewes 13 F49
Kingston on Soar 41 C40
Kingston Russell 8 E31
Kingston Seymour 19 E29
Kingston St Mary 8 B28
Kingston Upon Hull 59 G47
Kingston upon Thames 22 D47
Kingston Warren 21 C39
Kingstown 60 A29
King's Walden 32 F47
Kingswear 5 E24
Kingswell 74 F21
Kingswells 91 C34
Kingswinford 40 G34
Kingswood *Pow.* 38 E28
Kingswood *Bkh.* 31 G42
Kingswood *War.* 30 A37
Kingswood *Glo.* 20 B33
Kingswood *Avon* 19 D32
Kingswood *Kent* 14 B54
Kingswood *Sry* 23 F48
Kingswood Common 28 C28
King's Worthy 11 A40
Kingthorpe 52 E47
Kington *H.&W.* 29 C35
Kington *H.&W.* 28 C28
Kington Langley 20 D35
Kington Magna 9 B33
Kington St Michael 20 D34
Kingussie 88 D23
Kingweston 8 A31
Kinharrachie 99 F34
Kinharvie 65 D25
Kinkell 74 C22
Kinkell Bridge 82 F25
Kinknockie 99 E35
Kinlet 39 G33
Kinloch *Hgh.* 101 E19
Kinloch *Hgh.* 79 B12
Kinloch *Tay.* 82 C27
Kinloch *Fife* 82 F28
Kinloch *Hgh.* 85 E10
Kinloch *Tay.* 82 C28
Kinloch *Hgh.* 96 D21
Kinlochan 79 A14
Kinlochard 81 G20
Kinlocharkaig 86 E15
Kinlochbeoraid 86 F14

Kinlochbervie 101 C17
Kinlocheil 86 G15
Kinlochetive 80 C16
Kinlochewe 95 E16
Kinloch Hourn 86 D15
Kinloch Laggan 88 F21
Kinlochlaich 80 C15
Kinlochleven 80 A17
Kinlochmoidart 86 G12
Kinlochmorar 86 E14
Kinlochmore 80 A17
Kinloch Rannoch 81 B22
Kinlochspelve 79 E12
Kinloss 97 E26
Kinmel Bay 47 D25
Kinmuck 91 B34
Kinnadie 99 E35
Kinnaird 82 E28
Kinneff 91 F34
Kinnelhead 69 C26
Kinnell *Tay.* 83 B32
Kinnell *Cen.* 81 D21
Kinnerley 38 C29
Kinnersley *H.&W.* 29 D34
Kinnersley *H.&W.* 28 D29
Kinnerton 28 B28
Kinnesswood 82 G27
Kinnettles 83 C30
Kinninvie 62 D36
Kinnordy 82 B29
Kinoulton 41 B42
Kinrara 89 D24
Kinross 82 G26
Kinrossie 82 D27
Kinsbourne Green 32 G47
Kinsham 28 B29
Kinsley 51 A39
Kinson 10 E36
Kintarvie 100 F8
Kintbury 21 E39
Kintessack 97 E25
Kintillo 82 F27
Kintocher 90 C31
Kinton *Shr.* 38 D29
Kinton *H.&W.* 28 A30
Kintore 91 B33
Kintour 72 E10
Kintra *Str.* 72 F9
Kintra *Str.* 78 E9
Kintradwell 97 A24
Kintraw 79 G14
Kinuachdrach 72 A12
Kinveachy 89 C24
Kinver 40 G34
Kiplaw Croft 99 F36
Kiplin 62 G38
Kipp 81 F21
Kippax 57 F39
Kippen *Tay.* 82 F26
Kippen *Cen.* 74 A22
Kippenross Ho 81 G23
Kippford or Scaur 65 E24
Kipping's Cross 23 G52
Kirbister *Ork.* 105 A29
Kirbister *Ork.* 104 D32
Kirbuster 104 D28
Kirby Bedon 45 E58
Kirby Cane 45 F59
Kirby Corner 30 A38
Kirby Cross 35 F57
Kirby Grindalythe 59 C45
Kirby Hill *N.Y.* 57 C39
Kirby Hill *N.Y.* 62 F37
Kirby Knowle 57 A40
Kirby le Soken 35 F58
Kirby Misperton 58 B43
Kirby Muxloe 41 E41
Kirby Row 45 F59
Kirby Sigston 62 G39
Kirby Underdale 58 D44
Kirby Wiske 57 A39
Kirdford 12 D46
Kirk 103 C28
Kirkabister 107 D40
Kirkandrews 65 F21
Kirkandrews-upon-Eden 60 A29
Kirkbampton 60 A28
Kirkbean 65 E25
Kirk Bramwith 51 A42
Kirkbride 60 A28
Kirkbridge 62 G38
Kirkbuddo 83 C30
Kirkburn *Hum.* 59 D45
Kirkburn *Bor.* 76 G28
Kirkburton 50 A38
Kirkby *Lcn.* 52 C46
Kirkby *Mer.* 48 C30
Kirkby *N.Y.* 63 F41
Kirkby Bellars 41 D42
Kirkby Fleetham 62 G38
Kirkby Green 52 G46
Kirkby in Ashfield 51 G40
Kirkby la Thorpe 42 A47
Kirkby Lonsdale 55 B31
Kirkby Malham 56 C34
Kirkby Mallory 41 E40
Kirkby Malzeard 57 B38
Kirkby Mills 58 A43
Kirkbymoorside 58 A42
Kirkby on Bain 53 F48
Kirkby Overblow 57 E39
Kirkby Stephen 61 F33
Kirkby Thore 61 D32
Kirkby Underwood 42 C46
Kirkby Wharfe 58 E41
Kirkcaldy 76 A28
Kirkcambeck 70 G31
Kirkcolm 64 D16
Kirkconnel 68 B23
Kirkconnell 65 D25
Kirkcowan 64 D19
Kirkcudbright 65 E22
Kirkdale 65 E21
Kirkdean 75 F27
Kirk Deighton 57 D39
Kirk Ella 59 G46
Kirkfieldbank 75 F24
Kirkgunzeon 65 D24
Kirk Hallam 41 B40
Kirkham *N.Y.* 58 C43
Kirkham *Lan.* 55 F30
Kirkhamgate 57 G38
Kirk Hammerton 57 D40
Kirkharle 70 E35
Kirkhaugh 61 A32
Kirkheaton *W.Y.* 50 A37
Kirkheaton *Nor.* 71 F36
Kirkhill *Hgh.* 96 G21
Kirkhill *Grm.* 98 D28
Kirkhill *Tay.* 91 G32
Kirkhope 69 A29
Kirkibost *W.I.* 100 D7
Kirkibost *Hgh.* 86 C11
Kirkinch 82 C28
Kirkinner 64 E20
Kirkintilloch 74 C22
Kirk Ireton 50 G38
Kirkland *Cum.* 60 E26
Kirkland *D.&G.* 69 E26
Kirkland *D.&G.* 68 B23
Kirkland *D.&G.* 68 D23
Kirkland *Cum.* 61 C32
Kirkland of Longcastle 64 F19
Kirk Langley 40 B38
Kirkleatham 63 D41
Kirklevington 62 E39
Kirkley 45 F61
Kirklington *N.Y.* 57 A38
Kirklington *Not.* 51 G42
Kirklinton 69 G30
Kirkliston 75 C27
Kirkmaiden 64 G16
Kirk Merrington 62 C38
Kirkmichael *Str.* 67 C19
Kirk Michael 54 D24
Kirkmichael *Tay.* 82 A26
Kirkmuirhill 75 F23
Kirknewton *Ltn.* 75 D26
Kirknewton *Nor.* 70 A34
Kirkney 98 F30
Kirk of 75 D24
Kirkoswald *Str.* 67 C18
Kirkoswald *Cum.* 61 B31
Kirkpatrick Durham 65 C23
Kirkpatrick-Fleming 69 F28
Kirk Sandall 51 B42
Kirksanton 54 A27
Kirk Smeaton 51 A41
Kirkstall 57 F38
Kirkstead 52 F47
Kirkstile *Grm.* 98 F31
Kirkstile *D.&G.* 69 D29
Kirkton *Grm.* 91 A32
Kirkton *Hgh.* 96 B23
Kirkton *Hgh.* 96 F23
Kirkton *Grm.* 98 D32
Kirkton *Bor.* 70 B31
Kirkton *Str.* 79 G13
Kirkton *D.&G.* 68 E25
Kirkton *Hgh.* 102 B24
Kirkton *Tay.* 83 C30
Kirkton *Grm.* 91 B32
Kirkton *Hgh.* 88 A21
Kirkton *Fife* 82 E29
Kirkton *Tay.* 82 F25
Kirktonhill 91 G32
Kirkton Manor 76 G28
Kirkton of Airlie 82 B29
Kirkton of Auchterhouse 82 D29
Kirkton of Barevan 97 G24
Kirkton of Bourtie 91 A33
Kirkton of Collace 82 D27
Kirkton of Craig 83 B32
Kirkton of Culsalmond 98 F32
Kirkton of Durris 91 D33
Kirkton of Glenbuchat 90 B29
Kirkton of Glenisla 82 A28
Kirkton of Kingoldrum 82 B29
Kirkton of Lethendy 82 C27
Kirkton of Logie Buchan 91 A35
Kirkton of Maryculter 91 D34
Kirkton of Menmuir 83 A31
Kirkton of Monikie 83 D31
Kirkton of Skene 91 C33
Kirkton of Strathmartine 82 D29
Kirkton of Tealing 82 D29
Kirktown 99 D36
Kirktown of Alvah 98 C32
Kirktown of Auchterless 99 E33
Kirktown of Deskford 98 C31
Kirktown of Fetteresso 91 E34
Kirktown of Rayne 91 A32
Kirktown of Slains 91 A36
Kirkwall 104 E30
Kirkwall Airport 105 A30
Kirkwhelpington 70 E35
Kirk Yetholm 70 A33
Kirmington 52 A47
Kirmond le Mire 52 C47
Kirn 73 C17
Kirriemuir 82 B29
Kirstead Green 45 F58
Kirtlebridge 69 F28
Kirtling 33 C52
Kirtling Green 33 C52
Kirtlington 31 G40
Kirtomy 102 B23
Kirton *Lcn.* 43 B48
Kirton *Hgh.* 86 B14
Kirton *Sfk* 35 E58
Kirton *Not.* 51 F42
Kirton End 43 B48
Kirton Holme 43 A48
Kirton in Lindsey 52 C45
Kiscadale 66 A16
Kislingbury 31 C42
Kismeblon Bridge 6 D19
Kites Hardwick 31 B40
Kitley 5 E21
Kittisford 7 C26
Kitwood 11 A42
Kiveton Park 51 D40
Klibreck 102 E21
Knabbygates 98 D31
Knaith 52 D44
Knap Corner 9 B33
Knaphill 22 F45
Knapp *Som.* 8 B28
Knapp *Tay.* 82 D28
Knapton *Nfk* 45 B58
Knapton *N.Y.* 58 D41
Knapton Green 28 C30
Knapwell 33 B49
Knaresborough 57 D39
Knarsdale 61 A32
Knaven 99 E34
Knayton 57 A40
Knebworth 33 F48
Knedlington 58 G43
Kneesall 51 F42
Kneesworth 33 D49
Kneeton 41 A42
Knelston 17 F20
Knettishall 44 G55
Knightacott 6 B22
Knightcote 30 C39
Knighton *Pow.* 28 A28
Knighton *Lei.* 41 E41
Knighton *Stf.* 39 C33
Knighton *Stf.* 39 B33
Knighton *Dev.* 5 F21
Knighton *Wts.* 21 D38
Knighton *Som.* 7 A27
Knightwick 29 C33
Knill 28 B28
Knipoch 79 E14
Knipton 42 B44
Knitsley 62 B36
Kniveton 50 G37
Knock *Cum.* 61 D32
Knock *Grm.* 98 D31
Knock *Str.* 79 D11
Knockalava 73 A14
Knockally 103 F27
Knockaloe Moar 54 E24
Knockan 101 G17
Knockandhu 90 A27
Knockando 97 G27
Knockbain 96 F22
Knockban 95 E17
Knockbreck 96 C23
Knockbrex 65 F21
Knockdamph 95 B18
Knockdee 103 B27
Knockdow 73 C17
Knockdown 20 C34
Knockenkelly 66 A15
Knockentiber 74 G19
Knockfin 87 B18
Knockgray 67 D21
Knockholt 23 F50
Knockholt Pound 23 F50
Knockin 38 C29
Knocklearn 65 C23
Knocknaha 66 B12
Knocknalling 67 E21
Knock of Auchnahannet 89 A26
Knockrome 72 C11
Knocksharry 54 E24
Knockville 64 C19
Knockvologan 78 F8
Knodishall 35 B60
Knolls Green 49 E34
Knolton 38 B29
Knook 20 G35
Knossington 42 E43
Knott End-on-Sea 55 E29
Knotting 32 B45
Knotting Green 32 B46
Knottingley 57 G40
Knotty Ash 48 C30
Knotty Green 22 B45
Knowbury 28 A31
Knowe 64 C19
Knowesgate 70 E35
Knoweside 67 B18
Knowes of Elrick 98 D32
Knowetownhead 70 B31
Knowhead 99 D34
Knowle *Dev.* 7 E23
Knowle *Dev.* 7 G26
Knowle *Shr.* 28 A31
Knowle *Dev.* 6 B20
Knowle *Avon* 19 D31
Knowle *W.M.* 30 A37
Knowle Green 56 F32
Knowle Hall 19 G29
Knowl Green 34 D53
Knowl Hill 22 D44
Knowlton *Kent* 15 B58
Knowlton *Dor.* 10 C36
Knowl Wall 40 B34
Knowsley 48 C30
Knowstone 7 C24
Knucklas 28 A28
Knutsford 49 E33
Knypersley 49 G34
Kuggar 2 G13
Kyleakin 86 B13
Kyle of Lochalsh 86 B13
Kylerhea 86 B13
Kylesbeg 86 G12
Kylesknoydart 86 E13
Kylesmorar 86 E13
Kylestrome 101 E17
Kyloag 96 B22
Kynnersley 39 D32
Kyre Park 29 B32

L

Labost 100 C8
Lacasaigh 100 E9
Laceby 53 B48
Lacey Green 22 B44
Lach Dennis 49 E33
Lackford 34 A53
Lacock 20 E34
Ladbroke 31 C40
Laddingford 23 G52
Lade Bank 53 G50
Ladock 3 C14
Ladybank 82 F28
Ladycross 6 G19
Ladyfield 80 F16
Lady Hall 54 A27
Ladykirk 77 F34
Ladysford 99 C34
Lady's Green 34 C53
Laga 79 A12
Lagalochan 79 F14
Lagavulin 72 F9
Lagg *Str.* 72 C11
Lagg *Str.* 67 B18
Lagg *Str.* 66 A15
Laggan *Hgh.* 87 E18
Laggan *Hgh.* 88 E22
Laggan *Cen.* 81 F21
Laggan *Str.* 72 E8
Laggan *Grm.* 98 F29
Lagganulva 79 C10
Lagganvoulin 90 B27
Laglingarten 80 G17
Lagnalean 96 G21
Lagrae 68 B22
Laguna 82 D26
Lahill 83 G30
Laid 102 C20
Laide 94 B14
Laig 85 F10
Laight 67 B21
Lainchoil 89 C26
Laindon 24 C52
Lair 82 A27
Lairg 96 A21
Lairg Lo. 96 A21
Lairigmor 80 A16
Laithers 98 E32
Laithes 60 C30
Lake 10 A37
Lakenham 45 E58
Lakenheath 44 G52
Lakesend 43 F50
Lakeside 55 A29
Laleham 22 E46
Laleston 18 D24
Lamarsh 34 E54
Lamas 45 C58
Lamb Corner 34 E56
Lamberhurst 13 C52
Lamberhurst Quarter 13 C52
Lamberton 77 E35
Lambeth 23 D48
Lambfell Moar 54 E24
Lambley *Nor.* 61 A32
Lambley *Not.* 41 A42
Lambourn 21 D38
Lambourne End 23 B50
Lambourn Woodlands 21 D39
Lambs Green 13 C48
Lambston 16 C14
Lamellion 4 D18
Lamerton 4 C20
Lamesley 62 A38
Lamington *Str.* 75 G25
Lamington *Hgh.* 96 D23
Lamlash 73 G15
Lamloch 67 D21
Lamonby 60 C29
Lamorran 3 D14
Lampert 70 F32
Lampeter 26 D21
Lampeter Velfrey 16 C17
Lamphey 16 D15
Lamplugh 60 D26
Lamport 31 A43
Lamyatt 9 A32
Lana 6 F19
Lanark 75 F24
Lancaster 55 C30
Lanchester 62 B37
Landbeach 33 B50
Landcross 6 C20
Landerberry 91 C33
Landewednack 2 G13
Landford 10 C38
Landimore 17 E20
Landkey 6 B21
Landore 17 E22
Landrake 4 D19
Landscove 5 D23
Landshipping 16 C15
Landulph 4 D20
Landwade 33 B51
Landywood 40 E35
Laneast 4 B18
Lane-end 4 D16
Lane End *Dby.* 51 F40
Lane End *Cum.* 60 G27
Lane End *Kent* 23 D51
Lane End *Bkh.* 22 B44
Lane End *Dor.* 9 E34
Lane Green 40 E34
Laneham 51 E43
Lane Head *Dby.* 50 B37
Lane Head *G.M.* 49 C32
Lane Head *Drm.* 62 E36
Lanehead 70 E33
Laneshaw Bridge 56 E35
Langais 92 E4
Langamull 78 B9
Langar 42 B43
Langbank 74 C19
Langbar 57 D36
Langcliffe 56 C34
Langdale End 63 G45
Langdon 4 A18
Langdon Beck 61 C34
Langdon Hills 24 C52
Langdon House 5 C25
Langdyke 82 G29
Langenhoe 34 G56
Langford *Bfd.* 32 D47
Langford *Not.* 52 G44
Langford *Dev.* 7 E25
Langford *Oxf.* 21 A38
Langford *Esx* 24 A54
Langford Budville 7 C26
Langford End 32 C47
Langham *Esx* 34 E56
Langham *Sfk* 34 B55
Langham *Lei.* 42 D44
Langham *Nfk* 44 A56
Langham Moor 34 E55
Langho 56 F33
Langholm 69 E29
Langlands 65 E22
Langlee 70 B32
Langleeford 70 A35
Langley *Brk.* 22 D46
Langley *Kent* 14 B53
Langley *W.S.* 12 D44
Langley *Ham.* 11 D40
Langley *Esx* 33 E50
Langley *Hfs.* 33 F48
Langley *War.* 30 B37
Langley *Dby.* 41 A40
Langley *Che.* 49 E35
Langley Burrell 20 D35
Langley Green 40 B38

Langley Heath 14 B54
Langley Marsh 7 C26
Langley Mill 41 A40
Langley Moor 62 B38
Langley Park 62 B37
Langley Street 45 E59
Langney 13 F52
Langold 51 D41
Langore 6 G19
Langport 8 B29
Langrick 43 A48
Langridge *Dev.* 6 C21
Langridge *Avon* 20 E33
Langridgeford 6 C21
Langrigg 60 B27
Langrish 11 B42
Langriville 43 A48
Langsett 50 B38
Langshaw 76 G30
Langshawburn 69 C28
Langside 81 F23
Langskaill 104 B30
Langstone 11 D42
Langthorne 62 G38
Langthorpe 57 C39
Langthwaite 62 F35
Langtoft *Hum.* 59 C46
Langtoft *Lcn.* 42 D47
Langton *Lcn.* 53 F48
Langton *N.Y.* 58 C43
Langton *Drm* 62 E37
Langton *Lcn.* 53 E49
Langton by Wragby 52 E47
Langton Green 13 C51
Langton Herring 9 F32
Langton Long Blandford 9 D35
Langton Matravers 9 G35
Langtree 6 D20
Langwathby 61 C31
Langwell 96 A19
Langwell House 103 F26
Langworth 52 E46
Lanivet 4 D16
Lanlivery 4 E16
Lanner 2 D12
Lanreath 4 E17
Lansallos 4 E17
Lansdown 20 E33
Lanteglos 4 B16
Lanton *Nor.* 77 G35
Lanton *Bor.* 70 A32
Lapford 7 E23
Laphroaig 72 F9
Lapley 40 D34
Lapworth 30 A37
Larachbeg 79 C12
Larach na Gaibhre 73 D13
Larbert 75 B24
Larden Green 48 G31
Larg 64 C19
Largie 98 F31
Largiemore 73 B15
Largoward 83 G30
Largs 73 E17
Largue 98 E32
Largybeg 66 A16
Largymore 66 A16
Larkhall 75 E23
Lark Hall 33 C51
Larkhill 20 G37
Larling 44 G55
Larriston 70 D31
Lartington 62 E35
Lary 90 C29
Lasborough 20 B33
Lasham 21 G42
Lassington 29 F33
Lassintullich 81 B22
Lassodie 75 A27
Lasswade 76 D28
Lastingham 63 G43
Latchford 48 D31
Latchingdon 24 A54
Latchley 4 C20
Lately Common 49 C32
Lathallan Mill 83 G30
Lathbury 32 D44
Latheron 103 E27
Latheronwheel 103 E27
Lathockar 83 F30
Lathones 83 G30
Lathrisk 82 G28
Latimer 22 B46
Latteridge 19 C32
Lattiford 9 B32
Latton 20 B36
Lauchentyre 65 E21
Lauchintilly 91 B33
Lauder 76 F31
Laugharne 17 C18
Laughterton 52 E44
Laughton *Lcn.* 52 C44
Laughton *Lcn.* 42 B46
Laughton *Lei.* 41 G42
Laughton *E.S.* 13 E51
Laughton-en-le-Morthen 51 D41
Launcells 6 E18
Launcells Cross 6 E18
Launceston 6 G19
Launde Abbey 42 E44
Launton 31 F41
Laurencekirk 91 F32
Laurieston *D.&G.* 65 D22
Laurieston *Cen.* 75 C25
Lavendon 32 C44
Lavenham 34 D54
Laverhay 69 D27
Lavernock 18 E27
Laversdale 69 G30
Laverstock 10 A37
Laverstoke 21 G40
Laverton *Som.* 20 F33
Laverton *N.Y.* 57 B38
Laverton *Glo.* 30 E36
Lavister 48 G29
Law 75 E24
Lawers *Tay.* 81 E23
Lawers *Tay.* 81 D22
Lawford 34 E56
Lawhitton 6 G19
Lawkland 56 C33
Lawley 39 E32
Lawnhead 40 C34
Lawrenny 16 D15
Laws 83 D30
Lawshall 34 C54
Lawton 28 C30
Laxdale 100 D10
Laxey 54 E26
Laxfield 35 A58
Laxfirth *She.* 107 C40
Laxfirth *She.* 107 B40
Laxford Bridge 101 D18
Laxo 107 A40
Laxton *Nmp.* 42 F45
Laxton *Not.* 51 F43
Laxton *Hum.* 58 G43
Laycock 57 E36
Layer Breton 34 G55
Layer de la Haye 34 G55
Layer Marney 34 G55
Layham 34 D56
Laysters Pole 28 B31
Laytham 58 F43
Lazenby 63 D41
Lazonby 61 C31
Lea *H.&W.* 29 F32
Lea *Lcn.* 52 D44
Lea *Dby.* 51 G39
Lea *Shr.* 38 G29
Lea *Shr.* 38 E30
Lea *Wts.* 20 C35
Leac A Li 93 B7
Leachkin 96 G22
Leack 73 A16
Leadburn 76 E28
Leadenham 52 G45
Leaden Roding 33 G51
Leadgate *T.&W.* 62 A37
Leadgate *Cum.* 61 B32
Leadhills 68 B24
Leafield 30 G39
Leagrave 32 F46
Leake Common Side 53 G49
Leake Hurn's End 43 A50
Lealands 13 E51
Lealholm 63 F43
Lealt *Str.* 72 A12
Lealt *Hgh.* 93 E10
Lea Marston 40 F38
Leamington Hastings 31 B40
Leanach *Str.* 73 A16
Leanach *Hgh.* 96 G23
Leanaig 96 F21
Leanoch 97 F27
Leargybreck 72 C11
Leasgill 55 A30
Leasingham 42 A46
Leask 99 F36
Leatherhead 22 F47
Leathley 57 E38
Leaton 38 D30
Lea Town 55 F30
Leaveland 14 B55
Leavening 58 C43
Leaves Green 23 E49
Lea Yeat 56 A33
Lebberston 59 A46
Lechlade 20 B37
Lechuary 73 A14
Leck 56 B32
Leckford 10 A39
Leckfurin 102 C22
Leckgruinart 72 D8
Leckhampstead *Bkh.* 31 E42
Leckhampstead *Brk.* 21 D39
Leckhampton 29 G35
Leckie *Cen.* 74 A22
Leckie *Hgh.* 95 E16
Leckmelm 95 B17
Leckroy 88 E19
Leckwith 18 D27
Leconfield 59 E46
Ledaig 79 D14
Ledard 81 G20
Ledbeg 101 G18
Ledburn 32 F44
Ledbury 29 E32
Ledcharrie 81 E20
Ledgemoor 28 C29
Ledicot 28 B29
Ledmore *Hgh.* 101 G18
Ledmore *Str.* 79 C11
Lednagullin 102 B23
Ledsham *W.Y.* 57 F40
Ledsham *Che.* 48 E29
Ledston 57 G40
Ledwell 30 F39
Lee *Shr.* 38 B29
Lee *Dev.* 6 A20
Lee *Str.* 79 E10
Lee *Ham.* 10 C39
Lee *Lan.* 55 D31
Leebotten 107 E40
Leebotwood 38 F30
Lee Brockhurst 38 C31
Leece 55 C28
Lee Clump 22 A45
Leeds *Kent* 14 B54
Leeds *W.Y.* 57 F38
Leeds & Bradford Airport 57 E38
Leedstown 2 E12
Leeford 7 A23
Leegomery 39 D32
Leek 49 G35
Leek Wootton 30 B38
Lee Mill Bridge 5 E21
Leeming *W.Y.* 57 F36
Leeming *N.Y.* 57 A38
Leeming Bar 62 G38
Lee Moor 5 D21
Lee-on-the-Solent 11 D41
Lees *G.M.* 49 B35
Lees *Dby.* 40 B38
Leeswood 48 G28
Legars 77 F33
Legbourne 53 D49
Legerwood 76 F31
Legsby 52 D47
Leicester 41 E41
Leideag 84 E2
Leigh *Kent* 23 G51
Leigh *Wts.* 20 B36
Leigh *G.M.* 49 B32
Leigh *Shr.* 38 E29
Leigh *Glo.* 29 F34
Leigh *H.&W.* 29 C33
Leigh *Sry* 23 G48
Leigh *Dor.* 9 D32
Leigh Beck 24 C54
Leigh Common 9 A33
Leigh Delamere 20 C34
Leigh Green 14 D55
Leigh-on-Sea 24 C54
Leigh Sinton 29 C33
Leighterton 20 B33
Leighton *Som.* 20 G33
Leighton *N.Y.* 57 B37
Leighton *Shr.* 38 E31
Leighton *Pow.* 38 E28
Leighton Bromswold 32 A47
Leighton Buzzard 32 F45
Leigh upon Mendip 19 G32
Leigh Woods 19 D31
Leinthall Earls 28 B30
Leinthall Starkes 28 B30
Leintwardine 28 A29
Leire 41 G41
Leirinmore 101 B19
Leiston 35 B60
Leitfie 82 C28
Leith 76 C28
Leitholm 77 F33
Lelant 2 E11
Lelley 59 F48
Lem Hill 29 A32
Lemington 71 G37
Lemnas 99 C34
Lempitlaw 77 G33
Lemsford 32 G47
Lenchwick 30 D36
Lendalfoot 67 D17
Lendrick 81 G21
Lenham 14 B54
Lenham Heath 14 C55
Lenie 88 B21
Lenimore 73 F14
Lennel 77 F34
Lennox Plunton 65 E21
Lennoxtown 74 C22
Lenton 42 B46
Lenwade 44 D56
Lenzie 74 C22
Leoch 82 D29
Leochel-Cushnie 90 B31
Leominster 28 C30
Leonard Stanley 20 A33
Leorin 72 F9
Lepe 11 E40
Lephinchapel 73 A15
Lephinmore 73 A15
Leppington 58 C43
Lepton 50 A38
Lerags 79 E14
Lerryn 4 E17
Lerwick 107 C40
Lerwick (Tingwall) Airport 107 C40
Lesbury 71 B38
Leschangie 91 B33
Lescrow 4 E17
Leslie *Fife* 82 G28
Leslie *Grm.* 90 A31
Lesmahagow 75 G23
Lesnewth 4 A17
Lessendrum 98 E31
Lessingham 45 C59
Lessonhall 60 A27
Leswalt 64 D16
Letchmore Heath 22 B47
Letchworth 33 E48
Letcombe Bassett 21 C39
Letcombe Regis 21 C39
Letham *Fife* 82 F28
Letham *Tay.* 83 C31
Lethanhill 67 B20
Lethendy 82 E27
Lethenty 99 E33
Letheringham 35 C58
Letheringsett 44 B56
Leth Meadhanach 84 C3
Lettaford 7 G23
Letterewe 94 D15
Letterfearn 86 B14
Letter Finlay 87 E18
Lettermorar 86 E13
Lettermore *Str.* 79 C11
Lettermore *Hgh.* 102 D21
Letters 95 C17
Lettershaws 68 A24
Letterston 16 B15
Lettoch *Hgh.* 89 A26
Lettoch *Hgh.* 89 C26
Letton *H.&W.* 28 D29
Letton *H.&W.* 28 A29
Letty Green 33 G48
Letwell 51 D41
Leuchars 83 E30
Leumrabhagh 100 F9
Levedale 40 D34
Leven *Fife* 82 G29
Leven *Hum.* 59 E47
Levencorroch 66 A16
Levenhall 76 C29
Levens 55 A30
Levenshulme 49 C34
Levenwick 107 E40
Leverington 43 D50
Leverstock Green 22 A46
Leverton 43 A49
Leverton Outgate 43 A50
Levington 35 E58
Levisham 63 G44
Levishie 88 C19
Lew 21 A39
Lewannick 4 B18
Lewdown 6 G20
Lewes 13 F49
Leweston 16 B15
Lewisham 23 D49
Lewiston 88 B20
Lewknor 21 B42
Leworthy 6 B22
Lewtrenchard 6 G20
Ley *Grm.* 90 B31
Ley *Cnw.* 4 D17
Leybourne 23 F52
Leyburn 62 G37
Leycett 39 A33
Ley Green 32 F47
Leyland 55 G31
Leylodge 91 B33
Leys *Tay.* 82 D28
Leys *Grm.* 90 C30
Leys *Grm.* 99 D36
Leysdown-on-Sea 25 D55
Leysmill 83 C31
Leys of Cossans 82 C29
Leyton 23 C49
Lezant 4 C19
Lhanbryde 98 C28
Liatrie 87 A18
Libanus 27 F25
Libberton 75 F25
Liberton 76 D28
Liceasto 92 B6
Lichfield 40 E37
Lickey 29 A35
Lickey End 29 A35
Lickfold 12 D45
Liddel 105 C30
Liddesdale 79 B13
Liddington 21 C38
Lidgate *Sfk* 34 C53
Lidgate *Dby.* 50 E38
Lidlington 32 E45
Lidsing 24 E53
Lidstone 30 F39
Lienassie 86 B15
Lieurary 103 B26
Liff 82 D29
Lifton 6 G19
Liftondown 6 G19
Lighthorne 30 C39
Lightwater 22 E45
Lightwood 40 A34
Lightwood Green *Che.* 39 A32
Lightwood Green *Clw.* 38 A29
Lilbourne 31 A41
Lilburn Tower 71 A36
Lilleshall 39 D33
Lilley *Bfd.* 32 F47
Lilley *Brk.* 21 D40
Lilliesleaf 70 A31
Lillingstone Dayrell 31 E43
Lillingstone Lovell 31 D43
Lillington 9 C32
Lilliput 10 E36
Lilstock 7 A27
Limbrick 48 A31
Limbury 32 F46
Limefield 49 A33
Limehillock 98 D30
Limekilnburn 74 E22
Limekilns 75 B26
Limerigg 75 C24
Limerstone 11 F40
Limington 8 B31
Limpenhoe 45 E59
Limpley Stoke 20 E33
Limpsfield 23 F50
Linbriggs 70 C34
Linby 51 G41
Linchmere 12 C44
Lincoln 52 E45
Lincomb 29 B33
Lincombe 5 E23
Lindale 55 A29
Lindal in Furness 55 B28
Lindean 76 G30
Lindertis 82 B29
Lindfield 13 D49
Lindford 11 A43
Lindifferon 82 F28
Lindley 50 A37
Lindores 82 F28
Lindridge 29 B32
Lindsaig 73 C15
Lindsell 33 F52
Lindsey 34 D55
Linford *Ham.* 10 D37
Linford *Esx* 24 D52
Lingague 54 F24
Lingdale 63 E42
Lingen 28 B29
Lingfield 23 G49
Lingwood 45 E59
Linhead 98 D32
Linhope 69 C29
Linicro 93 E9
Linkenholt 21 F39
Linkhill 14 E54
Linkinhorne 4 C18
Linklater 105 C30
Linksness *Ork.* 104 E31
Linksness *Ork.* 105 A28
Linktown 76 A28
Linley 38 F29
Linley Green 29 C32
Linlithgow 75 C26
Linlithgow Bridge 75 C25
Linnels 70 G35
Linney 16 E14
Linn of Muick Cottage 90 E28
Linshiels 70 C34
Linsiadar 100 D7
Linsidemore 96 B21
Linslade 32 F44
Linstead Parva 35 A59
Linstock 60 A30
Linthwaite 50 A37
Lintlaw 77 E34
Lintmill 98 C30
Linton *W.Y.* 57 E39
Linton *Dby.* 40 D38
Linton *Cbs.* 33 D51
Linton *H.&W.* 29 F32
Linton *Kent* 14 C53
Linton *Bor.* 70 A33
Linton *N.Y.* 56 C35
Linton-on-Ouse 57 C40
Lintzford 62 A37
Linwood *Str.* 74 D20
Linwood *Lcn.* 52 D47
Linwood *Ham.* 10 D37
Lionacleit 92 G3
Lional 101 A11
Liphook 12 C44
Liscombe 7 B24

Liskeard 4 D18
L'Islet 3 E17
Liss 11 B43
Lissett 59 D47
Liss Forest 11 B43
Lissington 52 D46
Liston 34 D54
Lisvane 18 C27
Liswerry 19 C29
Litcham 44 D54
Litchborough 31 C42
Litchfield 21 F40
Litherland 48 C29
Litlington *Cbs.* 33 D48
Litlington *E.S.* 13 F51
Little Abington 33 D51
Little Addington 32 A45
Little Alne 30 B37
Little Amwell 33 G49
Little Assynt 101 F17
Little Aston 40 E36
Little Atherfield 10 G39
Little Ayton 63 F41
Little Baddow 24 A53
Little Badminton 20 C33
Little Ballinluig 82 B25
Little Bampton 60 A28
Little Bardfield 33 E52
Little Barford 32 C47
Little Barningham 45 B57
Little Barrington 30 G38
Little Barugh 58 A43
Little Bealings 35 D58
Littlebeck 63 F44
Little Bedwyn 21 E38
Little Bentley 35 F57
Little Berkhamsted 23 A48
Little Billing 31 B43
Little Birch 28 E31
Little Bispham 55 E28
Little Blakenham 35 D57
Little Bookham 22 F47
Littleborough *G.M.* 49 A35
Littleborough *Not.* 51 D43
Littlebourne 15 B57
Little Bowden 42 G43
Little Bradley 33 C52
Little Brampton 38 G29
Little Braxted 34 G54
Little Brechin 83 A31
Littlebredy 8 F31
Little Brickhill 32 E44
Little Bridgeford 40 C34
Little Brington 31 B42
Little Bromley 34 F56
Little Broughton 60 C26
Little Budworth 48 F31
Little Burstead 24 B52
Little Burton 59 E47
Littlebury 33 E50
Littlebury Green 33 E50
Little Bytham 42 D46
Little Carlton 53 D50
Little Casterton 42 D46
Little Catwick 59 E47
Little Cawthorpe 53 D49
Little Chalfont 22 B45
Little Chart 14 C55
Little Chesterford 33 D51
Little Cheverell 20 F35
Little Chishill 33 E50
Little Clacton 35 G57
Little Clifton 60 D26
Little Comberton 29 D35
Little Common 14 G53
Little Compton 30 E38
Little Corby 61 A30
Little Cowarne 28 C31
Little Coxwell 21 B38
Little Crakehall 62 G38
Little Creich 96 C22
Little Cressingham 44 F54
Little Crosby 48 B28
Little Cubley 40 B37
Little Dalby 42 D43
Littledean 29 G32
Little Dens 99 E36
Little Dewchurch 28 E31
Little Downham 43 G51
Little Driffield 59 D45
Little Dunham 44 D54
Little Dunkeld 82 C25
Little Dunmow 33 F52
Little Easton 33 F51
Little Eaton 41 A39
Little Ellingham 44 F56
Little End 23 A51
Little Eversden 33 C49
Little Fakenham 34 A54
Little Faringdon 20 A37
Little Fencote 62 G38
Little Fenton 58 F41
Littleferry 96 B23
Little Finborough 34 C56
Little Fransham 44 D55
Little Gaddesden 32 G45
Little Garway 28 F30
Little Gidding 42 G47
Little Glemham 35 C59
Little Gorsley 29 F32
Little Gransden 33 C48
Little Green 34 A56
Little Grimsby 53 C49
Little Gruinard 94 C15
Little Habton 58 B43
Little Hadham 33 F50
Little Hale 42 A47
Little Hallingbury 33 G50
Littleham *Dev.* 6 C20
Littleham *Dev.* 7 G26
Little Hampden 22 A44
Littlehampton 12 F46
Little Harrowden 32 A44
Little Haseley 21 A42
Little Hautbois 45 C58
Little Haven 16 C14
Little Hay 40 E36
Little Hayfield 50 D36
Little Haywood 40 C36
Little Heath 41 G39
Littlehempston 5 D24
Little Hereford 28 B31
Little Holtby 62 G38
Little Horkesley 34 E55
Little Hormead 33 F49
Little Horsted 13 E50
Little Horwood 31 E43
Little Houghton 32 C44
Littlehoughton 71 B37
Little Hucklow 50 E37
Little Hulton 49 B32
Little Hungerford 21 D41
Little Idoch 99 E33
Little Kimble 22 A44
Little Kineton 30 C39
Little Kingshill 22 B44
Little Langford 10 A36
Little Laver 23 A51
Little Lawford 31 A40
Little Leigh 48 E31
Little Leighs 34 G53
Little Lever 49 B33
Little Ley 91 B32
Little Linford 32 D44
Little London *Lcn.* 53 E49
Little London *Ham.* 21 F39
Little London *I.O.M.* 54 E25
Little London *Nfk* 44 F53
Little London *Ham.* 21 F42
Little London *E.S.* 13 E51
Little London *Nfk* 43 C51
Little London *Lcn.* 43 C48
Little London *Lcn.* 43 C50
Little Longstone 50 E37
Little Malvern 29 D33
Little Maplestead 34 E54
Little Marcle 29 E32
Little Marlow 22 C44
Little Massingham 44 C53
Little Melton 45 E57
Little Mill 19 A29
Littlemill *Hgh.* 97 F24
Littlemill *Str.* 67 B20
Little Milton 21 A41
Little Missenden 22 B45
Littlemore 21 A41
Little Musgrave 61 E33
Little Ness 38 D29
Little Neston 48 E28
Little Newcastle 16 B15
Little Newsham 62 E37
Little Oakley *Esx* 35 F58
Little Oakley *Nmp.* 42 G44
Little Orton 60 A29
Little Ouseburn 57 C40
Littleover 41 B39
Little Parndon 33 G50
Little Paxton 32 B47
Little Petherick 3 A15
Little Plumstead 45 D59
Little Ponton 42 B44
Littleport 43 G51
Little Raveley 33 A48
Little Ribston 57 D39
Little Rissington 30 G37
Little Rogart 96 A23
Little Ryburgh 44 C55
Little Ryle 70 B35
Little Salkeld 61 C31
Little Sampford 33 E52
Little Saxham 34 B53
Little Scatwell 96 F19
Little Shelford 33 C50
Little Smeaton 51 A41
Little Snoring 44 B55
Little Sodbury 20 C33
Little Somborne 10 A39
Little Somerford 20 C35
Little Stainton 62 D39
Little Stanney 48 E29
Little Staughton 32 B47
Little Steeping 53 F50
Littlestone-on-Sea 15 E56
Little Stonham 35 B57
Little Stretton *Shr.* 38 F30
Little Stretton *Lei.* 41 F42
Little Strickland 61 D31
Little Stukeley 33 A48
Little Sutton 48 E29
Little Swinburne 70 F35
Little Tew 30 F39
Little Tey 34 F54
Little Thetford 33 A51
Little Thirkleby 57 B40
Little Thorpe 62 B39
Littlethorpe 57 C39
Little Thurlow 33 C52
Little Thurrock 24 D52
Littleton *Sry* 22 E46
Littleton *Ham.* 11 A40
Littleton *Tay.* 82 D28
Littleton *Che.* 48 F30
Littleton *Som.* 8 A30
Littleton Drew 20 C34
Littleton -on-Severn 19 B31
Littleton Panell 20 F35
Little Torboll 96 B23
Little Torrington 6 D20
Little Totham 34 G54
Littletown 62 B39
Little Town 60 E28
Little Urswick 55 B28
Little Wakering 25 C55
Little Walden 33 D51
Little Waldingfield 34 D55
Little Waltham 33 G52
Little Warley 24 B52
Little Weighton 59 F45
Little Welland 29 E33
Little Welnetham 34 B54
Little Wenham 34 E56
Little Wenlock 39 E32
Little Whittingham Green
35 A58
Little Whittington 70 G35
Littlewick Green 22 D44
Little Wilbraham 33 C51
Little Witcombe 29 G35
Little Witley 29 B33
Little Wittenham 21 B41
Little Wolford 30 E38
Little Woolstone 32 E44
Littleworth *Stf.* 40 D36
Littleworth *H.&W.* 29 C34
Littleworth *Oxf.* 21 B38
Little Wratting 33 D52
Little Wymondley 33 F48
Little Wyrley 40 E36
Little Yeldham 34 D53
Littley Green 33 G52
Litton *Dby.* 50 E37
Litton *Som.* 19 F31
Litton *N.Y.* 56 B35
Litton Cheney 8 E31
Liurbost 100 E9
Liverpool 48 C29
Liversedge 57 G37
Liverton *Dev.* 5 C23
Liverton *Cle.* 63 E42
Liverton Street 14 C54
Livingston 75 D26
Livingston Village 75 D26
Lixwm 47 E27
Lizard 2 G12
Llaingoch 46 D18
Llaithddu 37 G26
Llan 37 E24
Llanaber 36 D21
Llanaelhaearn 36 A19
Llanaeron 26 B20
Llanafan 27 A22
Llanafan-fawr 27 C25
Llanafan-fechan 27 C25
Llanallgo 46 D20
Llanarmon 36 B20
Llanarmon Dyffryn Ceiriog
38 B27
Llanarmon-yn-Ial 47 G27
Llanarth *Gwe.* 28 G29
Llanarth *Dyf.* 26 C20
Llanarthney 17 B21
Llanasa 47 D27
Llanbabo 46 D19
Llanbadarn Fawr 36 G21
Llanbadarn Fynydd 27 A26
Llanbadarn-y-garreg 27 D26
Llanbadoc 19 A29
Llanbadrig 46 C19
Llanbeder 19 B29
Llanbedr *Pow.* 28 F28
Llanbedr *Pow.* 28 D27
Llanbedr *Gwy.* 36 C21
Llanbedr-Dyffryn-Clwyd 47 G27
Llanbedrgoch 46 D20
Llanbedrog 36 B19
Llanbedr-y-cennin 47 F23
Llanberis 46 F21
Llanbethery 18 E26
Llanbister 27 A26
Llanblethian 18 D25
Llanboidy 16 B17
Llanbradach 18 C27
Llanbrynmair 37 E24
Llancarfan 18 E26
Llancayo 19 A29
Llancynfelyn 37 F22
Llan-dafel 18 A27
Llandaff 18 D27
Llandaff North 18 D27
Llandanwg 36 C21
Llandawke 17 C18
Llanddaniel Fab 46 E20
Llanddarog 17 C20
Llanddeiniol 26 A21
Llanddeiniolen 46 F21
Llandderfel 37 B25
Llanddeusant *Dyf.* 27 F23
Llanddeusant *Gwy.* 46 D19
Llanddew 27 E26
Llanddewi 17 F20
Llanddewi-Brefi 27 C22
Llanddewi'r Cwm 27 D26
Llanddewi Rhydderch 28 G29
Llanddewi Velfrey 16 C17
Llanddewi Ystradenni 27 B26
Llanddoged 47 F23
Llanddona 46 E21
Llanddowror 17 C18
Llanddulas 47 E24
Llanddwywe 36 C21
Llanddyfnan 46 E20
Llandefaelog 17 C19
Llandefaelog Fach 27 E26
Llandefaelog-tre'r-graig 27 E26
Llandefalle 27 E26
Llandegai 46 E21
Llandegfan 46 E21
Llandegla 47 G27
Llandegley 28 B27
Llandegveth 19 B29
Llandegwning 36 B18
Llandeilo 17 B22
Llandeilo Abercywyn 17 C19
Llandeilo Graban 27 D26
Llandeilo'r-Fan 27 E24
Llandeloy 16 B14
Llandenny 19 A29
Llandevenny 19 C29
Llandinabo 28 F30
Llandinam 37 G26
Llandissilio 16 B16
Llandogo 19 A31
Llandough *S.G.* 18 D25
Llandough *S.G.* 18 D27
Llandovery 27 E23
Llandow 18 D25
Llandre *Dyf.* 27 D22
Llandre *Dyf.* 37 G22
Llandre *Dyf.* 16 B17
Llandrillo 37 B26
Llandrillo-yn-Rhos 47 D23
Llandrindod Wells 27 B26
Llandrinio 38 D28
Llandudno 47 D23
Llandudno Junction 47 E23
Llandwrog 46 G20
Llandybie 17 C21
Llandyfriog 26 D19
Llandyfrydog 46 D20
Llandygwydd 26 D18
Llandyrnog 47 F27
Llandyry 17 D20
Llandysilio 38 D28
Llandyssil 38 F27
Llandysul 26 D19
Llanedeyrn 18 C27
Llanegryn 36 E21
Llanegwad 17 B20
Llaneilian 46 C20
Llanelian-yn-Rhos 47 E24
Llanelidan 38 A27
Llanelieu 28 E27
Llanellen 28 G28
Llanelli 17 D20
Llanelltyd 37 D22
Llanelly 28 G28
Llanelwedd 27 C26
Llanelwy (St Asaph) 47 E26
Llanenddwyn 36 C21
Llanengan 36 C18
Llanerchymedd 46 D19
Llanerfyl 37 E26
Llanfachraeth 46 D18
Llanfachreth 37 C23
Llanfaelog 46 E19
Llanfaelrhys 36 C17
Llanfaes *Pow.* 27 F26
Llanfaes *Gwy.* 46 E21
Llanfaethlu 46 D18
Llanfaglan 46 F20
Llanfair 36 C21
Llanfair Caereinion 38 E27
Llanfair Clydogau 26 C21
Llanfair Dyffryn Clwyd 47 G27
Llanfairfechan 46 E22
Llanfair-Nant-Gwyn 16 A17
Llanfair-Orllwyn 26 D19
Llanfairpwllgwyngyll 46 E20
Llanfair Talhaiarn 47 E24
Llanfair Waterdine 28 A28
Llanfairynghornwy 46 C18
Llanfair-yn-Neubwll 46 E18
Llanfallteg 16 C17
Llanfallteg West 16 C17
Llanfaredd 27 C26
Llanfarian 26 A21
Llanfechain 38 C27
Llanfechell 46 C19
Llanfendigaid 36 E21
Llanferres 47 F27
Llanfflewyn 46 D19
Llanfigael 46 D19
Llanfihangel ar-Arth 17 A20
Llanfihangel Crucorney 28 F29
Llanfihangel Glyn Myfyr 37 A25
Llanfihangel Nant Bran 27 E25
Llanfihangel-nant-Melan 28 C27
Llanfihangel Rhydithon 28 B27
Llanfihangel Rogiet 19 C30
Llanfihangel-Tal-y-llyn 28 F27
Llanfihangel uwch-gwili 17 B20
Llanfihangel-y-Creuddyn 27 A22
Llanfihangel-yng-Ngwynfa
37 D26
Llanfihangel-y-pennant *Gwy.*
36 A21
Llanfihangel-y-pennant *Gwy.*
37 E22
Llanfihangel-y-traethau 36 B21
Llanfilo 28 E27
Llanfoist 28 G28
Llanfor 37 B25
Llanfrechfa 19 B28
Llanfrothen 36 A21
Llanfrynach 27 F26
Llanfwrog *Clw.* 47 G26
Llanfwrog *Gwy.* 46 D18
Llanfyllin 38 D27
Llanfynydd *Clw.* 48 G28
Llanfynydd *Dyf.* 17 B21
Llanfyrnach 17 A18
Llangadfan 37 D25
Llangadog 17 B22
Llangadwaladr *Gwy.* 46 F19
Llangadwaladr *Clw.* 38 B27
Llangaffo 46 F20
Llangain 17 C19
Llangammarch Wells 27 D25
Llangan 18 D25
Llangarron 28 F31
Llangasty-Talyllyn 28 F27
Llangathen 17 B21
Llangattock 28 G27
Llangattock Lingoed 28 F29
Llangattock-Vibon-Avel 28 G30
Llangedwyn 38 C27
Llangefni 46 E20
Llangeinor 18 C24
Llangeitho 26 C21
Llangeler 17 A19
Llangelynin 36 E21
Llangendeirne 17 C20
Llangennech 17 D21
Llangennith 17 E19
Llangenny 28 G28
Llangernyw 47 F24
Llangian 36 C18
Llangiwg 18 A23
Llanglydwen 16 B17
Llangoed 46 D21
Llangoedmor 26 D17
Llangollen 38 A27
Llangolman 16 B16
Llangorse 28 F27
Llangorwen 36 G21
Llangovan 19 A30
Llangower 37 B24
Llangranog 26 C18
Llangristiolus 46 E19
Llangrove 28 G31
Llangua 28 F29
Llangunllo 28 A27
Llangunnor 17 B20
Llangurig 27 A24
Llangwm *Clw.* 37 A25
Llangwm *Dyf.* 16 D15
Llangwm-isaf 19 A29
Llangwnnadl 36 B17
Llangwyfan 47 F27
Llangwyllog 46 E20
Llangwyryfon 26 A21
Llangybi *Gwy.* 36 A20
Llangybi *Gwe.* 19 B29
Llangybi *Dyf.* 26 C21
Llangyfelach 17 E22
Llangynhafal 47 F27
Llangynidr 28 G27
Llangynin 17 C18
Llangynmyd 18 C24
Llangynog *Dyf.* 17 C19

Llangynog *Pow.* 37 C26
Llanhamlach 27 F26
Llanharan 18 C25
Llanharry 18 C25
Llanhennock 19 B29
Llanhilleth 18 A27
Llanidloes 37 G25
Llaniestyn 36 B18
Llanigon 28 D27
Llanilar 27 A22
Llanilid 18 C25
Llanishen *Gwe.* 19 A30
Llanishen *S.G.* 18 C27
Llanllawddog 17 B20
Llanllechid 46 F21
Llanlleonfel 27 D25
Llanllugan 37 E26
Llanllwch 17 C19
Llanllwchaiarn 37 F26
Llanllwni 26 D20
Llanllyfni 46 G20
Llanllywel 19 B29
Llanmadoc 17 E20
Llanmaes 18 E25
Llanmartin 19 C29
Llanmerewig 38 F27
Llanmihangel 18 D25
Llanmiloe 17 D18
Llanmorlais 17 E21
Llannefydd 47 E25
Llannerch 47 E26
Llannerch-y-mor 47 E27
Llannon 17 D21
Llannor 36 B19
Llanon 26 B21
Llanover 19 A28
Llanpumsaint 17 B19
Llanreithan 16 B14
Llanrhaeadr 47 F26
Llanrhaeadr-ym-Mochnant 38 C27
Llanrhian 16 A13
Llanrhidian 17 E21
Llanrhos 47 D23
Llanrhyddlad 46 D19
Llanrhystud 26 B21
Llanrothal 28 G30
Llanrug 46 F21
Llanrumney 18 C27
Llanrwst 47 F23
Llansadurnen 17 C18
Llansadwrn *Dyf.* 17 A22
Llansadwrn *Gwy.* 46 E21
Llansaint 17 D19
Llansamlet 17 E22
Llansannan 47 F25
Llansannor 18 D25
Llansantffraed 27 F26
Llansantffraed-Cwmdeuddwr 27 B25
Llansantffraed-in-Elvel 27 C26
Llansantffraid 26 B20
Llansantffraid Glan Conwy 47 E24
Llansantffraid-ym-Mechain 38 C27
Llansawel 17 A21
Llansilin 38 C28
Llansoy 19 A30
Llanspyddid 27 F25
Llanstadwell 16 D15
Llanstephan *Dyf.* 17 C19
Llanstephan *Pow.* 28 D27
Llantarnam 19 B28
Llanteg 16 C17
Llanthony 28 F28
Llantilio Crossenny 28 G30
Llantilio Pertholey 28 G29
Llantood 26 D17
Llantrisant *M.G.* 18 C26
Llantrisant *Gwe.* 19 B29
Llantrithyd 18 D26
Llantwit Fardre 18 C26
Llantwit Major 18 E25
Llantysilio 38 A27
Llanuwchllyn 37 B24
Llanvaches 19 B30
Llanvair-Discoed 19 B30
Llanvapley 28 G29
Llanvetherine 28 G29
Llanveynoe 28 E28
Llanvihangel Gobion 19 A29
Llanvihangel-Ystern-Llewern 28 G30
Llanwarne 28 F30
Llanwddyn 37 D25
Llanwenog 26 D20
Llanwern 19 C29
Llanwinio 17 B18
Llanwnda *Dyf.* 16 A15
Llanwnda *Gwy.* 46 G20
Llanwnen 26 D21
Llanwnog 37 F25
Llanwonno 18 B26
Llanwrda 17 A22
Llanwrin 37 E23
Llanwrthwl 27 B25
Llanwrtyd 27 D24
Llanwrtyd Wells 27 D24
Llanwyddelan 37 E26
Llanyblodwel 38 C28
Llanybri 17 C19
Llanybydder 26 D21
Llanycefn 16 B16
Llanychaer Bridge 16 A15
Llanycil 37 B24
Llanycrwys 27 D22
Llanymawddwy 37 D24
Llanymynech 38 C28
Llanynghenedl 46 D18
Llanynys 47 F27
Llan-y-pwll 48 G29
Llanyre 27 B26
Llanystumdwy 36 B20
Llanywern 27 F26
Llawhaden 16 C16
Llawnt 38 B28
Llawr-y-dref 36 C18
Llawryglyn 37 F25
Llay 48 G29
Llechcynfarwy 46 D19
Llechfaen 27 F26
Llechryd *Dyf.* 26 D17
Llechryd *M.G.* 18 A26
Llechrydau 38 B27
Lledrod *Clw.* 38 C28
Lledrod *Dyf.* 27 A22
Llethr 16 B14
Llidiadnenog 17 A21
Llidiardau 37 B24
Llithfaen 36 A19
Lloc 47 E27
Llong 48 F28
Llowes 28 D27
Lloyney 28 A28
Llwyd 27 C25
Llwydcoed 18 A25
Llwydiarth 37 D26
Llwyn 38 G28
Llwyncelyn 26 C20
Llwyndafydd 26 C19
Llwynderw 38 E27
Llwyndyrys 36 A19
Llwyngwril 36 E21
Llwynhendy 17 E21
Llwyn-Madoc 27 C24
Llwynmawr 38 B28
Llwyn-onn 26 C19
Llwyn-y-brain *Dyf.* 27 E23
Llwyn-y-brain *Dyf.* 16 C17
Llwynypia 18 B25
Llynclys 38 C28
Llynfaes 46 E19
Llysfaen 47 E24
Llyswen 28 E27
Llysworney 18 D25
Llys-y-fran 16 B16
Llywel 27 E24
Loandhu 96 D23
Loanhead *Ltn* 76 D28
Loanhead *Grm.* 99 F35
Loans 74 G19
Lochailort 86 F13
Lochaline 79 C12
Lochans 64 E16
Locharbriggs 68 E25
Lochawe 80 E17
Loch Baghasdail (Lochboisdale) 84 C3
Lochboisdale 84 C3
Lochbuie 79 E11
Lochcarron 86 A14
Loch Coire Lodge 102 E22
Lochdhu Hotel 103 D25
Lochdon 79 D13
Lochdrum 95 D18
Lochearnhead 81 E21
Lochee 82 D29
Loch Eil Centre 87 G16
Lochend *Hgh.* 88 A21
Lochend *Hgh.* 103 B28
Lochfoot 65 C24
Lochgair 73 A15
Lochgarthside 88 C20
Lochgelly 75 A27
Lochgilphead 73 B14
Lochgoilhead 80 G17
Lochgoin 74 F20
Loch Head *D.&G.* 64 F19
Loch Head *D.&G.* 67 D20
Lochhill 68 B22
Loch-hill 98 C28
Lochinch Castle 64 D16
Lochinver 101 F16
Lochlair 83 C31
Lochlane 81 E24
Lochlea 67 A20
Lochluichart 96 E19
Lochmaben 69 E26
Lochmaddy 92 E5
Loch Na Madadh (Lochmaddy) 92 E5
Lochore 75 A27
Lochportian 92 D5
Lochranza 73 F15
Loch Sgioport 84 A4
Lochside *Grm.* 91 G33
Lochside *Hgh.* 102 C20
Lochside *Hgh.* 102 E24
Lochside *Hgh.* 103 B28
Lochslin 97 C24
Lochton 67 E18
Lochty 83 G31
Lochuisge 79 B13
Lochurr 68 E23
Lochussie 96 F20
Lochwinnoch 74 E19
Lockengate 4 D16
Lockerbie 69 E27
Lockeridge 20 E37
Lockerley 10 B38
Locking 19 F29
Lockington *Hum.* 59 E45
Lockington *Lei.* 41 C40
Lockleywood 39 C32
Locksbottom 23 E50
Locks Heath 11 D41
Lockton 63 G44
Loddington *Nmp.* 31 A43
Loddington *Lei.* 42 E43
Loddiswell 5 F22
Loddon 45 F59
Lode 33 B51
Loders 8 E30
Lodsworth 12 D45
Lofthouse *W.Y.* 57 G39
Lofthouse *N.Y.* 57 B36
Loftus 63 E43
Logan *Str.* 67 A21
Logan *D.&G.* 64 F16
Loganlea 75 D25
Loggerheads 39 B33
Loggie 95 B17
Logie *Grm.* 97 F25
Logie *Tay.* 82 B29
Logie *Fife* 83 E30
Logie *Tay.* 91 G32
Logie Coldstone 90 C29
Logie Hill 96 D23
Logie Newton 98 F32
Logie Pert 91 G32
Logierait 82 B25
Login 16 B17
Lolworth 33 B49
Lonbain 94 F12
Londesborough 58 E44
London Beach 14 D54
London City Airport 23 C50
London Colney 22 A47
Londonderry 57 A38
Londonthorpe 42 B45
Londubh 94 C14
Lonemore 96 C23
Long Ashton 19 D31
Long Bennington 42 A44
Longbenton 71 G38
Longborough 30 E37
Long Bredy 8 E31
Longbridge *War.* 30 B38
Longbridge *W.M.* 29 A35
Longbridge Deverill 20 G34
Long Buckby 31 B42
Longburgh 60 A28
Longburton 9 C32
Long Clawson 42 C43
Longcliffe 50 G38
Long Common 11 C41
Long Compton *Stf.* 40 C34
Long Compton *War.* 30 E38
Longcot 21 B38
Long Crendon 21 A42
Long Crichel 9 C35
Longcross *Sry* 22 E45
Longcross *Dev.* 4 C20
Longden 38 E30
Long Ditton 22 E47
Longdon *H.&W.* 29 E34
Longdon *Stf.* 40 D36
Longdon upon Tern 38 D31
Longdown 7 F24
Long Downs 2 E13
Long Drax 58 G42
Longdrum 91 B35
Long Duckmanton 51 E40
Long Eaton 41 B40
Longfield 24 E52
Longfield Hill 24 E52
Longfleet 10 E36
Longford *G.L.* 22 D46
Longford *W.M.* 41 G39
Longford *Dby.* 40 B37
Longford *Shr.* 39 D33
Longford *Shr.* 39 B32
Longford *Glo.* 29 F34
Longforgan 82 D28
Longformacus 76 E32
Longframlington 71 C36
Long Gill 56 D33
Longham *Dor.* 10 E36
Longham *Nfk* 44 D55
Long Hanborough 31 G40
Longhill 99 D35
Longhirst 71 E38
Longhope *Glo.* 29 G32
Longhope *Ork.* 105 B28
Longhorsley 71 D37
Longhoughton 71 B38
Long Itchington 31 B40
Longlands *Cum.* 60 C28
Longlands *Grm.* 90 A30
Longlane *Dby.* 40 B38
Longlane *Brk.* 21 D41
Long Lawford 31 A40
Longley Green 29 C32
Long Load 8 B30
Longmanhill 99 C33
Long Marston *N.Y.* 57 D40
Long Marston *War.* 30 D37
Long Marston *Hfs.* 32 G44
Long Marton 61 D32
Long Melford 34 D54
Longmoor Camp 11 A43
Longmorn 98 D28
Long Newnton 20 B35
Longnewton *Bor.* 70 A31
Longnewton *Cle.* 62 E39
Longney 29 G33
Longniddry 76 C30
Longnor *Shr.* 38 E30
Longnor *Stf.* 50 F36
Longparish 21 G40
Long Preston 56 D34
Longridge *Lan.* 56 F32
Longridge *Ltn* 75 D25
Longridge Towers 77 E35
Longriggend 75 C24
Long Riston 59 E47
Longrock 2 E11
Longsdon 49 G35
Longside 99 E36
Longslow 39 B32
Longstanton 33 B49
Longstock 10 A39
Longstowe 33 C48
Long Stratton 45 F57
Longstreet 20 F37
Long Street 31 D43
Long Sutton *Lcn.* 43 C50
Long Sutton *Ham.* 22 G43
Long Sutton *Som.* 8 B30
Longthorpe 42 F47
Long Thurlow 34 B56
Longton *Stf.* 40 A34
Longton *Lan.* 55 G30
Longtown *Cum.* 69 G29
Longtown *H.&W.* 28 F29
Longville in the Dale 38 F31
Long Waste 39 D32
Longwell Green 19 D32
Long Whatton 41 C40
Longwick 22 A43
Long Wittenham 21 B41
Longwitton 71 E36
Longwood 39 E32
Longworth 21 B39
Longyester 76 D31
Lonmore 93 G8
Loose 14 B53
Loosegate 43 C48
Loosley Row 22 A44
Lopcombe Corner 10 A38
Lopen 8 C30
Loppington 38 C30
Lorbottle 71 C36
Lorbottle Hall 71 C36
Lorgill 93 G7
Lorn 74 B19
Lornty 82 C27
Loscoe 41 A40
Losgaintir 92 B6
Lossiemouth 98 B28
Lossit 72 E8
Lostock Gralam 49 E32
Lostock Green 49 E33
Lostock Junction 49 B32
Lostwithiel 4 E16
Lothbeg 103 G25
Lothersdale 56 E35
Lothmore 103 G25
Loudwater 22 B44
Loughborough 41 C40
Loughor 17 E21
Loughton *Bkh.* 32 E44
Loughton *Shr.* 39 G32
Loughton *Esx* 23 B50
Lound *Lcn.* 42 D46
Lound *Not.* 51 D42
Lound *Sfk* 45 F61
Lount 41 D39
Lour 83 C30
Louth 53 D49
Loveacott 6 C21
Love Clough 56 G34
Lovedean 11 C42
Lover 10 B38
Loversall 51 C41
Loves Green 24 A52
Loveston 16 D16
Lovington 8 A31
Low 55 A30
Low Ballivain 66 A12
Low Bentham 56 C32
Low Bolton 62 G36
Low Bradfield 50 C38
Low Bradley 57 E36
Low Braithwaite 60 B30
Low Brunton 70 F34
Low Burnham 51 B43
Low Burton 57 A38
Low Catton 58 D42
Low Coniscliffe 62 E38
Low Craighead 67 C18
Low Crosby 69 G30
Lowdham 41 A42
Low Dinsdale 62 E39
Low Eggborough 58 G41
Low Entercommon 62 F39
Lower Aisholt 8 A28
Lower Apperley 29 F34
Lower Ashton 7 G24
Lower Assendon 22 C43
Lower Auchalick 73 C15
Lower Barewood 28 C29
Lower Beeding 13 D48
Lower Benefield 42 G45
Lower Berry Hill 28 G31
Lower Bockhampton 9 E33
Lower Boddington 31 C40
Lower Boscaswell 2 E9
Lower Bourne 22 G44
Lower Brailes 30 E38
Lower Breakish 86 B12
Lower Broadheath 29 C34
Lower Brynamman 27 G23
Lower Bullingham 28 E31
Lower Burgate 10 C37
Lower Caldecote 32 D47
Lower Cam 20 A33
Lower Camster 103 D28
Lower Chapel 27 E25
Lower Chute 21 F38
Lower Crossings 50 D36
Lower Darwen 56 G32
Lower Dean 32 B46
Lower Diabaig 94 E13
Lower Dicker 13 E51
Lower Dinchope 38 G30
Lower Down 38 G29
Lower Drift 2 F10
Lower Dunsforth 57 C40
Lower Egleton 28 D31
Lower End 32 B44
Lower Everleigh 20 F37
Lower Failand 19 D31
Lower Farringdon 11 A43
Lower Freystrop 16 C15
Lower Froyle 22 G43
Lower Gabwell 5 D25
Lower Gledfield 96 B21
Lower Godney 19 G30
Lower Green *Nfk* 44 B55
Lower Green *Stf.* 40 E34
Lower Green *Kent* 23 G52
Lower Green Bank 55 D31
Lower Halstow 24 E54
Lower Hardres 15 B57
Lower Hawthwaite 55 A28
Lower Hayton 38 G30
Lower Hergest 28 C28
Lower Heyford 31 F40
Lower Higham 24 D53
Lower Holbrook 35 E57
Lower Hordley 38 C29
Lower Horsebridge 13 E51
Lower Kilchattan 72 A9
Lower Killeyan 72 F8
Lower Kingcombe 8 E31
Lower Kinnerton 48 F29
Lower Langford 19 E30
Lower Largo 83 G30
Lower Lemington 30 E38
Lower Lydbrook 28 G31
Lower Lye 28 B29
Lower Machen 18 C27
Lower Maes-coed 28 E29
Lower Moor 29 D35
Lower Nazeing 23 A49
Lower Oakfield 75 A27
Lower Oddington 30 F38
Lower Ollach 85 A10
Lower Penarth 18 D27
Lower Penn 40 F34
Lower Pennington 10 E39
Lower Peover 49 E33
Lower Quinton 30 D37
Lower Seagry 20 C35
Lower Shelton 32 D45
Lower Shiplake 22 D43
Lower Shuckburgh 31 B40
Lower Slaughter 30 F37

Lower Stanton St Quintin 20 C35
Lower Stoke 24 D54
Lower Stondon 32 E47
Lower Street 13 E52
Lower Sundon 32 F46
Lower Swanwick 11 D40
Lower Swell 30 F37
Lower Tean 40 B35
Lower Thurlton 45 F60
Lower Thurnham 55 D30
Lower Town *Dyf.* 16 A15
Lower Town *I.o.S.* 2 A11
Lower Tysoe 30 D39
Lower Upham 11 C41
Lower Vexford 7 B27
Lower Wallop 38 E29
Lower Walton 48 D31
Lower Weare 19 F30
Lower Welson 28 C28
Lower Whitley 49 E32
Lower Wield 21 G42
Lower Winchendon 31 G43
Lower Withington 49 F34
Lower Woodend 22 C44
Lower Woodford 10 A37
Lower Wraxall 8 D31
Lower Wyche 29 D33
Lowesby 42 E43
Lowestoft 45 F61
Lowestoft End 45 F61
Loweswater 60 D27
Low Etherley 62 D37
Lowfield Heath 13 C48
Low Gate 70 G35
Lowgill *Cum.* 61 G32
Lowgill *Lan.* 56 C32
Low Habberley 29 A33
Low Ham 8 B30
Low Hawkser 63 F45
Low Haygarth 61 G32
Low Hesket 60 B30
Low Hesleyhurst 71 D36
Low Hutton 58 C43
Lowick *Nor.* 77 G35
Lowick *Cum.* 55 A28
Lowick *Nmp.* 42 G45
Low Laithe 57 C37
Low Leighton 49 D35
Low Marishes 58 B44
Low Mill 63 G42
Low Moor 56 E32
Low Newton-by-the-Sea 71 A38
Lownie Moor 83 C30
Low Redford 62 C36
Low Risby 52 A45
Low Row *Cum.* 70 G31
Low Row *N.Y.* 62 G35
Low Santon 52 A45
Lowsonford 30 B37
Low Stillaig 73 D15
Low Street 45 C59
Lowther 61 D31
Lowther Castle 61 D31
Lowthorpe 59 D46
Lowton 48 C31
Lowton Common 49 C32
Low Torry 75 B26
Low Toynton 53 E48
Low Waters 75 E23
Low Wood 55 A29
Low Worsall 62 E39
Loxbeare 7 D24
Loxhill 12 C46
Loxhore 6 B22
Loxley 30 C38
Loxton 19 F29
Loxwood 12 C46
Lubachoinnich 96 B19
Lubcroy 96 A19
Lubenham 42 G43
Lubfearn 96 D19
Lubmore 95 F16
Lubreoch 81 C20
Luccombe 7 A25
Luccombe Village 11 G41
Lucker 77 G37
Luckett 4 C19
Luckington 20 C34
Lucklawhill 82 E29
Luckwell Bridge 7 B24
Lucton 28 B30
Ludag 84 C3
Ludborough 53 C48
Ludchurch 16 C17
Luddenden 57 G36
Luddenham Court 25 E55
Luddesdown 24 E52
Luddington *Hum.* 52 A44
Luddington *War.* 30 C37
Luddington in the Brook 42 G46
Ludford 28 A31
Ludford Magna 53 D48
Ludford Parva 52 D47
Ludgershall *Bkh.* 31 G42
Ludgershall *Wts.* 21 F38
Ludgvan 2 E10
Ludham 45 D59
Ludlow 28 A30
Ludney 53 C49
Ludstock 29 E32
Ludwell 9 B34
Ludworth 62 B39
Luffincott 4 A18
Luffness 76 B30
Lugar 67 A21
Luggiebank 75 C23
Lugton 74 E20
Lugwardine 28 D31
Luib 86 B11
Luibeilt 80 A18
Lulham 28 D29
Lullington *Som.* 20 F33
Lullington *Dby.* 40 D38
Lulsgate Bottom 19 E30
Lulsley 29 C33
Lulworth Camp 9 F34
Lumb 57 G36
Lumbutts 56 G35
Lumby 57 F40
Lumphanan 90 C31
Lumphinnans 75 A27
Lumsdaine 77 D34
Lumsden 90 A30
Lunan 83 B32
Lunanhead 83 B30
Luncarty 82 E26
Lund *Hum.* 59 E45
Lund *N.Y.* 58 F42
Lund *She.* 106 B41
Lundavra 80 A16
Lunderton 99 E37
Lundie *Tay.* 82 D28
Lundie *Hgh.* 87 C17
Lundin Links 82 G29
Lunga 79 G13
Lunna 107 A40
Lunning 107 A41
Lunsford's Cross 14 F53
Lunt 48 B29
Luntley 28 C29
Luppitt 7 E27
Lupton 55 A31
Lurgashall 12 D45
Lurignich 80 B15
Lusby 53 F49
Luss 74 A19
Lussagiven 72 B12
Lusta 93 F8
Lustleigh 7 G23
Luston 28 B30
Luthermuir 91 G32
Luthrie 82 F29
Luton *Dev.* 7 E26
Luton *Bfd.* 32 F46
Luton *Kent* 24 E53
Luton *Dev.* 5 C24
Luton Airport 32 F47
Lutterworth 41 G41
Lutton *Lcn.* 43 C50
Lutton *Nmp.* 42 G47
Lutton *Dev.* 5 E21
Luxborough 7 B25
Luxulyan 4 E16
Lybster *Hgh.* 103 B26
Lybster *Hgh.* 103 E28
Lydacott 6 E20
Lydbury North 38 G29
Lydcott 6 B22
Lydd 15 E56
Lydd Airport 15 E56
Lydden 15 C58
Lyddington 42 F44
Lydd-on-Sea 15 E56
Lydeard St Lawrence 7 B27
Lydford 6 G20
Lydford-on-Fosse 8 A31
Lydgate 56 G35
Lydham 38 F29
Lydiard Millicent 20 C36
Lydiate 48 B29
Lydlinch 9 C33
Lydney 19 A32
Lydstep 16 E16
Lye 40 G35
Lye Green 22 A45
Lyford 21 B39
Lymbridge Green 15 C56
Lymekilns 74 E22
Lyme Regis 8 E29
Lyminge 15 C57
Lymington 10 E38
Lyminster 12 F45
Lymm 49 D32
Lymore 10 E39
Lympne 15 D57
Lympsham 19 F29
Lympstone 7 G25
Lynaberack 88 E23
Lynchat 88 D23
Lyndhurst 10 D39
Lyndon 42 E44
Lyne *Sry* 22 E45
Lyne *Grm.* 91 C33
Lyneal 38 B30
Lynedale Ho 93 F9
Lynegar 103 C28
Lyneham *Wts.* 20 C36
Lyneham *Oxf.* 30 F38
Lyneholmeford 69 F30
Lynemore 89 B26
Lynemouth 71 D38
Lyne of Gorthleck 88 B20
Lyne of Skene 91 B33
Lyness 105 B28
Lynford 44 F54
Lyng *Nfk* 44 D56
Lyng *Som.* 8 B29
Lynmouth 7 A23
Lynsted 25 E55
Lynton 7 A23
Lyon's Gate 9 D32
Lyonshall 28 C29
Lyrabus 72 D8
Lytchett Matravers 9 E35
Lytchett Minster 9 E35
Lyth 103 B28
Lytham 55 G29
Lytham St Anne's 55 G28
Lythe 63 E44
Lythe Hill 12 C45
Lythes 105 C30
Lythmore 103 B26

M

Mabe Burnthouse 2 E13
Mabie 65 C25
Mablethorpe 53 D51
Macclesfield 49 E35
Macclesfield Forest 49 E35
Macduff 98 C32
Machan 75 E23
Machany 81 F24
Macharioch 66 C13
Machen 18 C27
Machrie *Str.* 73 G14
Machrie *Str.* 72 F9
Machrihanish 66 A12
Machrins 72 A9
Machynlleth 37 E23
Mackworth 40 B38
Macmerry 76 C30
Macterry 99 E33
Madderty 82 E25
Maddiston 75 C25
Madehurst 12 E45
Madeley *Shr.* 39 E33
Madeley *Stf.* 39 A33
Madeley Heath 39 A33
Madford 7 D27
Madingley 33 C49
Madjeston 9 B34
Madley 28 E30
Madresfield 29 D33
Madron 2 E10
Maenaddwyn 46 D20
Maenclochog 16 B16
Maendy 18 D25
Maentwrog 37 A22
Maer 39 B33
Maerdy *Clw.* 37 A26
Maerdy *Gwe.* 19 A29
Maerdy *M.G.* 18 B25
Maerdy *Dyf.* 17 B22
Maerdy *Dyf.* 17 B22
Maesbrook 38 C28
Maesbury Marsh 38 C28
Maes-glas 19 C28
Maesgwynne 16 B17
Maeshafn 47 F27
Maesllyn 26 D19
Maesmynis 27 D25
Maesteg 18 B24
Maes-Treylow 28 B28
Maesybont 17 C21
Maesycrugiau 26 D20
Maes-y-cwmmer 18 B27
Magdalen Laver 23 A51
Maggieknockater 98 E28
Magham Down 13 E51
Maghull 48 B29
Magor 19 C30
Maiden Bradley 9 A34
Maidencombe 5 D25
Maidenhead 22 C44
Maiden Law 62 A37
Maiden Newton 8 E31
Maidens 67 C17
Maiden's Green 22 D45
Maidenwell *Cnw.* 4 C17
Maidenwell *Lcn.* 53 E49
Maiden Wells 16 E15
Maidford 31 C41
Maids' Moreton 31 E43
Maidstone 14 B53
Maidwell 31 A43
Mail 107 E40
Mains of Ardestie 83 D31
Mains of Balhall 83 A30
Mains of Ballindarg 82 B29
Mains of Burgie 97 F26
Mains of Culsh 99 E34
Mains of Dillavaird 91 E33
Mains of Drum 91 C34
Mains of Dudwick 99 F35
Mains of Faillie 88 A22
Mains of Fedderate 99 E34
Mains of Glenbuchat 90 B29
Mains of Linton 91 C32
Mains of Melgund 83 B31
Mains of Pitfour 99 E35
Mains of Pittrichie 91 A34
Mains of Sluie 97 F25
Mains of Tannachy 98 C29
Mains of Thornton 91 F32
Mains of Tig 66 E16
Mains of Watten 103 C28
Mainsriddle 65 E25
Mainstone 38 G28
Maisemore 29 F33
Makendon 70 C33
Makerstoun 76 G32
Malacleit 92 D3
Malborough 5 G23
Malden 23 E48
Malden Rushett 22 E47
Maldon 24 A54
Malham 56 C34
Maligar 93 E10
Mallaig 86 E12
Mallaigmore 86 E12
Mallaigvaig 86 E12
Malleny Mills 75 D27
Malletsheugh 74 E20
Malling 81 G21
Malltraeth 46 F19
Mallwyd 37 D24
Malmesbury 20 C35
Malmsmead 7 A23
Malpas *Gwe.* 19 B28
Malpas *Che.* 38 A30
Malpas *Cnw.* 3 D14
Maltby *S.Y.* 51 C41
Maltby *Cle.* 62 E40
Maltby le Marsh 53 D50
Maltman's Hill 14 C54
Malton 58 B43
Malvern Link 29 D33
Malvern Wells 29 D33
Mambeg 74 B18
Mamble 29 A32
Mamhead 7 G25
Manaccan 2 F13
Manafon 38 E27
Manais 92 C6
Manaton 7 G23
Manby 53 D50
Mancetter 40 F38
Manchester 49 C34
Mancot Royal 48 F29
Mandally 87 D18
Manea 43 G50
Maneight 67 C21
Manfield 62 E37
Mangaster 106 E39
Mangotsfield 19 D32
Mangurstadh 100 D6
Mankinholes 56 G35
Manley 48 E30
Manmoel 18 A27
Mannel 78 C5
Manningford Abbots 20 F37
Manningford Bohune 20 F37
Manningford Bruce 20 E37
Mannings Heath 13 D48
Mannington 10 D36
Manningtree 34 E56
Mannofield 91 C34
Manorbier 16 E16
Manordeifi 26 D18
Manordeilo 17 B22
Manorowen 16 A14
Mansell Gamage 28 D29
Mansell Lacy 28 D30
Mansergh 55 A31
Mansfield 51 F41
Mansfield Woodhouse 51 F41
Mansriggs 55 A28
Manston *Kent* 25 E59
Manston *Dor.* 9 C33
Manston Airport 25 E59
Manswood 9 D35
Manthorpe *Lcn.* 42 D46
Manthorpe *Lcn.* 42 B45
Manton *Hum.* 52 B45
Manton *Wts.* 20 E37
Manton *Lei.* 42 E44
Manuden 33 F50
Maolachy 79 F14
Maperton 9 B32
Maplebeck 51 F42
Maple Cross 22 B46
Mapledurham 21 D42
Mapledurwell 21 F42
Maplehurst 12 D47
Mapleton 40 A37
Mapperley 41 A40
Mapperton 8 E30
Mappleborough Green 30 B36
Mappleton 59 E48
Mapplewell 51 B39
Mappowder 9 D33
Marazion 2 E11
Marbury 38 A31
March 43 F50
Marcham 21 B40
Marchamley 38 C31
Marchington 40 B37
Marchington Woodlands 40 C37
Marchwiel 38 A29
Marchwood 10 C39
Marcross 18 E24
Marcus 83 B30
Marden *H.&W.* 28 D31
Marden *Wts.* 20 F36
Marden *T.&W.* 71 F39
Marden *Kent* 14 C53
Marden Beech 14 C53
Marden Thorn 14 C53
Mardy 28 G28
Marefield 42 E43
Mare Green 8 B29
Mareham le Fen 53 F48
Mareham on the Hill 53 F48
Maresfield 13 D50
Marfleet 59 G47
Marford 48 G29
Margam 18 C23
Margaret Marsh 9 C34
Margaret Roding 33 G51
Margaretting 24 A52
Margate 25 D59
Margnaheglish 73 G16
Margreig 65 C24
Margrove Park 63 E42
Marham 44 E53
Marhamchurch 6 E18
Marholm 42 E47
Marian Cwm 47 E26
Marian-glas 46 D20
Mariansleigh 7 C23
Marishader 93 E10
Maristow 4 D20
Mark 19 G29
Markbeech 23 G50
Markby 53 E50
Mark Causeway 19 G29
Mark Cross 13 C51
Markdhu 64 C17
Market Bosworth 41 E39
Market Deeping 42 D47
Market Drayton 39 B32
Market Harborough 42 G43
Markethill 82 D28
Market Lavington 20 F36
Market Overton 42 D44
Market Rasen 52 D47
Market Stainton 53 D48
Market Street 45 C58
Market Weighton 58 E44
Market Weston 34 A55
Markfield 41 D40
Markham 18 A27
Markham Moor 51 E42
Markinch 82 G28
Markington 57 C38
Marksbury 19 E32
Marks Gate 23 B50
Marks Tey 34 F54
Markwell 4 E19
Markyate 32 G46
Marlborough 20 D37
Marldon 5 D24
Marlesford 35 C59
Marley Green 38 A31
Marley Hill 62 A37
Marlingford 45 E57
Mar Lodge 89 E26
Marloes 16 D13
Marlow 22 C44
Marlpit Hill 23 G50
Marlpool 41 A40
Marnhull 9 C33
Marnoch 98 D31
Marple 49 D35
Marr 51 B41
Marrel 103 G26
Marrick 62 G36
Marrister 107 A41
Marros 16 D17
Marsden *T.&W.* 71 G39
Marsden *W.Y.* 50 A36
Marsett 56 A34
Marsh 8 C28
Marshall's Heath 32 G47
Marshalsea 8 D29
Marsham 45 C57
Marshaw 55 D31
Marsh Baldon 21 B41

Marshborough 15 B58
Marshbrook 38 G30
Marsh Chapel 53 C49
Marshfield *Avon* 20 D33
Marshfield *Gwe.* 19 C28
Marshgate 4 A17
Marsh Gibbon 31 F42
Marsh Green *Shr.* 39 D32
Marsh Green *Kent* 23 G50
Marsh Green *Dev.* 7 F26
Marsh Lane 51 E39
Marshside 48 A29
Marsh Street 7 A25
Marshwood 8 E29
Marske 62 F36
Marske-by-the-Sea 63 D41
Marston *H.&W.* 28 C29
Marston *Che.* 49 E32
Marston *War.* 40 F38
Marston *Stf.* 40 D34
Marston *Stf.* 40 C35
Marston *Oxf.* 21 A41
Marston *Wts.* 20 F35
Marston *Lcn.* 42 A44
Marston Green 40 G37
Marston Magna 8 B31
Marston Meysey 20 B37
Marston Montgomery 40 B37
Marston Moretaine 32 D45
Marston on Dove 40 B38
Marston Stannett 28 C31
Marston St Lawrence 31 D41
Marston Trussell 41 G42
Marstow 28 G31
Marsworth 32 G44
Marten 21 E38
Marthall 49 E34
Martham 45 D60
Marthig 100 F10
Martin *Lcn.* 52 F47
Martin *Ham.* 10 C36
Martin Drove End 10 B36
Martinhoe 6 A22
Martin Hussingtree 29 B34
Martinscroft 49 D32
Martinstown 9 F32
Martlesham 35 D58
Martlesham Heath 35 D58
Martletwy 16 C16
Martley 29 B33
Martock 8 C30
Marton *Hum.* 59 F47
Marton *N.Y.* 58 A43
Marton *N.Y.* 57 C40
Marton *War.* 31 B40
Marton *Cle.* 63 E41
Marton *Shr.* 38 E28
Marton *Cum.* 55 B28
Marton *Che.* 49 F34
Marton *Lcn.* 52 D44
Marton Abbey 58 C41
Marton-le-Moor 57 B39
Martyr's Green 22 F46
Martyr Worthy 11 A41
Maruig 100 G7
Marwick 104 D28
Marwood 6 B21
Marybank 96 F20
Maryburgh 96 F21
Maryfield 107 C40
Marygold 77 D33
Maryhill *Grm.* 99 E34
Maryhill *Str.* 74 D21
Marykirk 91 G32
Marylebone *G.M.* 48 B31
Marylebone *G.L.* 23 C48
Maryport *Cum.* 60 C26
Maryport *D.&G.* 64 G17
Marystow 6 G20
Mary Tavy 4 C20
Maryton 83 B32
Marywell *Tay.* 83 C32
Marywell *Grm.* 90 D31
Marywell *Grm.* 91 D35
Masham 57 A38
Mashbury 33 G52
Mastrick 91 C34
Matching 33 G51
Matching Green 33 G51
Matching Tye 33 G51
Matfen 71 F36
Matfield 23 G52
Mathern 19 B31
Mathon 29 D33
Mathry 16 A14
Matlaske 45 B57
Matlock 50 F38
Matlock Bank 50 F38
Matlock Bath 50 G38
Matson 29 G34
Matterdale End 60 D29
Mattersey 51 D42
Mattingley 22 F43
Mattishall 44 D56
Mattishall Burgh 44 D56
Mauchline 67 A20
Maud 99 E35
Maufant 3 G18
Maugersbury 30 F37
Maughold 54 D26
Mauld 88 A19
Maulden 32 E46
Maulds Meaburn 61 E32
Maunby 57 A39
Maund Bryan 28 C31
Maundown 7 C26
Mautby 45 D60
Mavesyn Ridware 40 D36
Mavis Enderby 53 F49
Mawbray 60 B26
Mawdesley 48 A30
Mawdlam 18 C23
Mawgan 2 F12
Maw Green 40 F36
Mawla 2 D12
Mawnan 2 F13
Mawnan Smith 2 F13
Maxey 42 E47
Maxstoke 40 G38
Maxton *Kent* 15 C58
Maxton *Bor.* 70 A31
Maxwellheugh 76 G32
Maxwelltown 65 C25
Maxworthy 4 A18
Maybole 67 C19
Mayen 98 E31
Mayfield *Ltn* 76 D29
Mayfield *Stf.* 40 A37
Mayfield *E.S.* 13 D51
Mayford 22 F45
Mayland 24 A54
Maylandsea 24 A54
Maynard's Green 13 E51
Maypole *Kent* 25 E57
Maypole *I.o.S.* 2 A11
Maypole Green 45 F60
Maywick 107 E39
Meabhag 93 B7
Mead End 10 B36
Meadle 22 A43
Meadowmill 76 C29
Meadowtown 38 E28
Mealabost 100 B9
Mealasta 100 E6
Meal Bank 61 G31
Meals 53 C50
Mealsgate 60 B27
Meanley 56 D33
Mearbeck 56 C34
Meare 19 G30
Mearns 74 E21
Mears Ashby 32 B44
Measham 41 D39
Meathop 55 A30
Meavy 5 D21
Medbourne 42 F43
Meddon 6 D18
Meden Vale 51 F41
Medmenham 22 C44
Medomsley 62 A37
Medstead 11 A42
Meerbrook 49 F35
Meer End 30 A38
Meesden 33 E50
Meeth 6 E21
Meggethead 69 A27
Meidrim 17 B18
Meifod *Clw.* 47 G26
Meifod *Pow.* 38 D27
Meigle 82 C28
Meikle Earnock 74 E22
Meikle Grenach 73 D16
Meikle Kilmory 73 D16
Meikleour 82 D27
Meikle Rahane 74 B18
Meikle Strath 91 F32
Meikle Tarty 91 A35
Meikle Wartle 99 F33
Meinciau 17 C20
Meir 40 A35
Meirheath 40 B35
Melbost 100 D10
Melbourn 33 D49
Melbourne *Hum.* 58 E43
Melbourne *Dby.* 41 C39
Melbury 6 D19
Melbury Abbas 9 C34
Melbury Bubb 8 D31
Melbury Osmond 8 D31
Melbury Sampford 8 D31
Melby 107 B37
Melchbourne 32 B46
Melchet Court 10 B38
Melcombe Bingham 9 D33
Melcombe Regis 9 F32
Meldon *Dev.* 6 F21
Meldon *Nor.* 71 E37
Meldreth 33 D49
Melfort 79 F14
Melgarve 88 E20
Melgum 90 C30
Meliden 47 D26
Melincourt 18 A23
Melincryddan 18 B23
Melin-y-coed 47 F23
Melin-y-ddol 37 E26
Melin-y-grug 37 E26
Melin-y-Wig 37 A26
Melkinthorpe 61 D31
Melkridge 70 G33
Melksham 20 E34
Melksham Forest 20 E35
Melldalloch 73 C15
Melling *Mer.* 48 B29
Melling *Lan.* 55 B31
Melling Mount 48 B30
Mellis 34 A56
Mellon Charles 94 B14
Mellon Udrigle 94 B14
Mellor *G.M.* 49 D35
Mellor *Lan.* 56 F32
Mellor Brook 56 F32
Mells 20 G33
Melmerby *Cum.* 61 C32
Melmerby *N.Y.* 57 B39
Melmerby *N.Y.* 57 A36
Melplash 8 E30
Melrose *Grm.* 99 C33
Melrose *Bor.* 76 G31
Melsetter 105 C28
Melsonby 62 F37
Meltham 50 A37
Melton 35 C58
Meltonby 58 D43
Melton Constable 44 B56
Melton Mowbray 42 D43
Melton Ross 52 B46
Melvaig 94 C13
Melverley 38 D29
Melverley Green 38 D29
Melvich 102 B24
Membury 8 D28
Memsie 99 C35
Memus 83 B30
Menabilly 4 E16
Menai Bridge 46 E21
Mendham 45 G58
Mendlesham 34 B56
Mendlesham Green 34 B56
Menethorpe 58 C43
Menheniot 4 D18
Menie Ho. 91 A35
Mennock 68 C24
Menston 57 E37
Menstrie 75 A24
Mentmore 32 G44
Meoble 86 F13
Meole Brace 38 D30
Meon 11 D41
Meonstoke 11 C42
Meopham 24 E52
Meopham Green 24 E52
Mepal 43 G50
Meppershall 32 E47
Merbach 28 D28
Mercaston 40 A38
Mere *Che.* 49 D33
Mere *Wts.* 9 A34
Mere Brow 48 A30
Mere Green 40 F36
Mereworth 23 F52
Mergie 91 E33
Meriden 40 G38
Merkland 65 C23
Merlin's Bridge 16 C15
Merridge 7 B27
Merrifield 5 F24
Merrington 38 C30
Merrion 16 E15
Merriott 8 C30
Merrivale 5 C21
Merrow 22 F46
Merry Hill 22 B47
Merrymeet 4 D18
Mersham 15 D56
Merstham 23 F48
Merston 12 F44
Merstone 11 F40
Merther 3 D14
Merthyr 17 B19
Merthyr Cynog 27 E25
Merthyr Dyfan 18 E26
Merthyr Mawr 18 D24
Merthyr Tydfil 18 A26
Merthyr Vale 18 B26
Merton *G.L.* 23 E48
Merton *Dev.* 6 D21
Merton *Nfk* 44 F54
Merton *Oxf.* 31 G41
Mertyn 47 E27
Mervinslaw 70 B32
Meshaw 7 D23
Messing 34 G54
Messingham 52 B44
Metfield 45 G58
Metheringham 52 F46
Methil 76 A29
Methlem 36 B17
Methley 57 G39
Methlick 99 F34
Methven 82 E26
Methwold 44 F53
Methwold Hythe 44 F53
Mettingham 45 G59
Metton 45 B57
Mevagissey 4 F16
Mexborough 51 C40
Mey 103 A28
Meysey Hampton 20 B36
Miabhag 100 G6
Miabhig 100 D6
Mial 94 D13
Michaelchurch 28 F31
Michaelchurch Escley 28 E28
Michaelchurch-on-Arrow 28 C28
Michaelston-le-Pit 18 D27
Michaelston-y-Fedw 19 C28
Michaelstow 4 C16
Micheldever 11 A41
Michelmersh 10 B39
Mickfield 35 B57
Mickleby 63 E43
Mickleham 22 F47
Micklehurst 49 B35
Mickleover 40 B38
Micklethwaite 60 A28
Mickleton *Drm* 61 D35
Mickleton *Glo.* 30 D37
Mickletown 57 G39
Mickle Trafford 48 F30
Mickley 57 B38
Mickley Square 71 G36
Mid Ardlaw 99 C35
Midbea 104 B30
Mid Beltie 90 C31
Mid Cairncross 90 F30
Mid Calder 75 D26
Mid Clyth 103 E28
Middle Assendon 22 C43
Middle Aston 31 F40
Middle Barton 31 F40
Middlebie 69 F27
Middle Claydon 31 F43
Middle Drums 83 B31
Middleham 57 A36
Middle Handley 51 E40
Middle Harling 44 G55
Middlehill *Cnw.* 4 D18
Middlehill *Grm.* 99 E34
Middlehope 38 G30
Middle Kames 73 B14
Middle Littleton 30 D36
Middle Maes-coed 28 E29
Middlemarsh 9 D32
Middle Mill 16 B14
Middle Rasen 52 D46
Middle Rigg 82 G26
Middle Salter 56 C32
Middlesbrough 62 D40
Middleshaw 55 A31
Middlesmoor 57 B36
Middlestone Moor 62 C38
Middlestown 50 A38
Middleton *Lan.* 55 D30
Middleton *G.M.* 49 B34
Middleton *Dby.* 50 F38
Middleton *Dby.* 50 G38
Middleton *War.* 40 F37
Middleton *Sfk* 35 B60
Middleton *Shr.* 38 C29
Middleton *Nor.* 77 G36
Middleton *Shr.* 28 A31
Middleton *Esx* 34 E54
Middleton *Cle.* 63 C41
Middleton *Tay.* 82 C27
Middleton *Grm.* 91 B34
Middleton *Tay.* 83 C31
Middleton *Tay.* 82 G27
Middleton *Shr.* 38 F28
Middleton *N.Y.* 58 A43
Middleton *W.Y.* 57 G39
Middleton *Nfk* 44 D52
Middleton *Ltn* 76 E29
Middleton *Nor.* 71 E36
Middleton *Cum.* 56 A32
Middleton *W.G.* 17 F20
Middleton *W.Y.* 57 E37
Middleton *Nmp.* 42 G44
Middleton *Ham.* 21 G40
Middleton Bank Top 71 E36
Middleton Cheney 31 D40
Middleton Green 40 B35
Middleton Hall 70 A35
Middleton-in-Teesdale 61 D34
Middleton of Potterton 91 B35
Middleton One Row 62 E39
Middleton-on-Leven 62 E40
Middleton-on-Sea 12 G45
Middleton on the Hill 28 B31
Middleton-on -the-Wolds 59 D45
Middleton Park 91 B34
Middleton Priors 39 F32
Middleton Quernhow 57 B39
Middleton Scriven 39 G32
Middleton St George 62 E39
Middleton Stoney 31 F41
Middleton Tyas 62 F37
Middle Town 2 A11
Middletown *Pow.* 38 D28
Middletown *Cum.* 60 F25
Middle Tysoe 30 D39
Middle Wallop 10 A38
Middlewich 49 F33
Middle Winterslow 10 A38
Middlewood 49 D35
Middle Woodford 10 A37
Middlewood Green 34 B56
Middleyard 74 G21
Middlezoy 8 A29
Middridge 62 D38
Midfield 102 B21
Midford 20 E33
Midge Hall 55 G31
Midgeholme 61 A32
Midgham 21 E41
Midgley *W.Y.* 57 G36
Midgley *W.Y.* 50 A38
Midhopestones 50 C38
Midhurst 12 D44
Mid Lavant 12 F44
Midlem 70 A31
Mid Letter 80 G16
Mid Lix 81 E21
Mid Mossdale 61 G34
Midpark 73 E15
Mid Sannox 73 F16
Midsomer Norton 19 F32
Midtown *Hgh.* 102 B21
Midtown *Hgh.* 94 C13
Midtown of Barras 91 E34
Midville 53 G49
Mid Yell 106 C40
Migdale 96 B22
Migvie 90 C30
Milarrochy 74 A20
Milber 5 C24
Milbethill 98 D31
Milborne Port 9 C32
Milborne St Andrew 9 E34
Milborne Wick 9 B32
Milbourne 71 F36
Milburn 61 D32
Milbury Heath 19 C32
Milcombe 30 E39
Milden 34 D55
Mildenhall *Sfk* 34 A52
Mildenhall *Wts.* 21 D38
Milebrook 28 A28
Milebush 14 C53
Mile Elm 20 E35
Mile End *Glo.* 28 G31
Mile End *Esx* 34 F55
Mileham 44 D55
Milesmark 75 B26
Milfield 77 G35
Milford *Dev.* 6 C18
Milford *Stf.* 40 C35
Milford *Shr.* 38 C30
Milford *Dby.* 41 A39
Milford *Sry* 22 G45
Milford Haven 16 D15
Milford on Sea 10 E38
Milkwall 19 A31
Milland Marsh 12 D44
Mill Bank 57 G36
Millbank 99 E36
Millbeck 60 D28
Millbounds 104 C31
Millbreck 99 E35
Millbridge 22 G44
Millbrook *Cnw.* 4 E19
Millbrook *Bfd.* 32 E45
Millbrook *Ham.* 10 C39
Millburn *Grm.* 90 A31
Millburn *Grm.* 98 F32
Millcombe 5 F24
Millcorner 14 E54
Millden 91 B35
Milldens 83 B31
Millearn 82 F25
Mill End *Hfs.* 33 E49
Mill End *Bkh.* 22 C43
Mill End Green 33 F52
Millenheath 38 B31
Millerhill 76 D29
Miller's Dale 50 E37
Mill Green *Shr.* 39 C32
Mill Green *Esx* 24 A52
Mill Hill 23 B48
Millholme 61 G31
Millhouse *Cum.* 60 C29
Millhouse *Str.* 73 D15
Millhousebridge 69 E26
Mill Houses 56 C32
Millikenpark 74 D19
Millington 58 D44
Mill Lane 22 F43
Millmeece 40 B34
Millness 88 A19

Mill of Colp 99 E33
Mill of Elrick 99 E35
Mill of Fortune 81 F23
Mill of Kingoodie 91 A34
Mill of Monquich 91 D34
Mill of Uras 91 E34
Millom 54 A27
Millport 73 E17
Mill Street 44 D56
Millthrop 61 G32
Milltimber 91 C34
Millton of Noth 90 A31
Milltown *Grm.* 90 B30
Milltown *Hgh.* 97 G25
Milltown *D.&G.* 69 F29
Milltown *Dev.* 6 B21
Milltown *Dby.* 51 F39
Milltown *Hgh.* 95 F19
Milltown of Aberdalgie 82 E26
Milltown of Auchindown 98 E29
Milltown of Campfield 91 C32
Milltown of Craigston 99 D33
Milltown of Edinville 98 E28
Milltown of Rothiemay 98 E31
Milltown of Towie 90 B30
Milnathort 82 G26
Milngavie 74 C21
Milnrow 49 A35
Milnsbridge 50 A37
Milnthorpe 55 A30
Milovaig 93 F7
Milrig 74 G21
Milson 29 A32
Milstead 14 B54
Milston 20 G37
Milton *Oxf.* 21 B40
Milton *Dyf.* 16 D16
Milton *Gwe.* 19 C29
Milton *Cen.* 81 G20
Milton *Str.* 74 C20
Milton *Cen.* 74 A20
Milton *Cen.* 81 G21
Milton *Tay.* 82 C29
Milton *Tay.* 82 D25
Milton *Hgh.* 88 A20
Milton *Avon* 19 E29
Milton *Hgh.* 96 G21
Milton *Hgh.* 103 C29
Milton *Grm.* 98 C31
Milton *Hgh.* 97 F25
Milton *D.&G.* 65 C24
Milton *Cbs.* 33 B50
Milton *Oxf.* 31 E40
Milton *Not.* 51 E42
Milton *Stf.* 49 G35
Milton *Cum.* 70 G31
Milton *D.&G.* 68 E24
Milton *Dby.* 41 C39
Milton *Hgh.* 94 G12
Milton *Hgh.* 96 D23
Milton Abbas 9 D34
Milton Abbot 4 C19
Milton Bridge 76 D28
Milton Bryan 32 E45
Milton Clevedon 9 A32
Milton Coldwells 99 F35
Milton Combe 4 D20
Milton Damerel 6 D19
Miltonduff 97 E27
Milton Ernest 32 C46
Milton Green 48 G30
Milton Hill 21 B40
Miltonhill 97 E26
Milton Inveramsay 91 A33
Miltonise 64 C17
Milton Keynes 32 E44
Milton Keynes Village 32 E44
Milton Lilbourne 20 E37
Milton Lockhart 75 F24
Milton Malsor 31 C43
Milton Morenish 81 D21
Milton of Auchinhove 90 C31
Milton of Balgonie 82 G29
Milton of Cairnborrow 98 E30
Milton of Campsie 74 C22
Milton of Cullerlie 91 C33
Milton of Cushnie 90 B30
Milton of Dalcapon 82 B25
Milton of Tullich 90 D29
Milton on Stour 9 B33
Milton Regis 24 E54
Milton-under-Wychwood 30 G38
Milverton 7 C27
Milwich 40 B35
Minard 73 A15
Minard Castle 73 A15
Minchington 9 C35
Minchinhampton 20 A34
Mindrum 77 G34
Minehead 7 A25
Minera 48 G28
Minety 20 B36
Minffordd *Gwy.* 37 D23
Minffordd *Gwy.* 36 B21
Mingearraidh 84 B3
Miningsby 53 F49
Minions 4 C18
Minishant 67 B19
Minley Manor 22 F43
Minllyn 37 D24
Minnes 91 A35
Minnigaff 64 D19
Minnonie 99 C33
Minskip 57 C39
Minstead 10 C38
Minster *Kent* 25 E58
Minster *Kent* 25 D55
Minsterley 38 E29
Minster Lovell 30 G38
Minsterworth 29 G33
Minterne Magna 9 D32
Minting 52 E47
Mintlaw 99 E36
Minto 70 A31
Minton 38 F30
Minwear 16 C16
Minworth 40 F37
Miodar 78 C6
Mirbister 104 D28
Mireland 103 B28
Mirfield 57 G38
Miserden 20 A35
Miskin *M.G.* 18 C26
Miskin *M.G.* 18 B26
Misson 51 C42
Misterton *Not.* 51 C43
Misterton *Som.* 8 D30
Misterton *Lei.* 41 G41
Mitcham 23 E48
Mitcheldean 29 G32
Mitchell 3 C14
Mitchelland 60 G30
Mitchel Troy 19 A30
Mitcheltroy Common 19 A30
Mitford 71 E37
Mithian 2 C13
Mitton 40 D34
Mixbury 31 E41
Moar 81 C21
Moat 69 F29
Mobberley 49 E33
Moccas 28 D29
Mochdre *Pow.* 37 G26
Mochdre *Clw.* 47 E24
Mochrum 64 F19
Mockbeggar 14 C53
Mockerkin 60 D26
Modbury 5 E22
Moddershall 40 B35
Modsarie 102 B22
Moelfre *Gwy.* 46 D20
Moelfre *Clw.* 38 C27
Moffat 69 C26
Mogerhanger 32 D47
Moin'a'choire 72 D9
Moine Ho. 102 B21
Moira 41 D39
Molash 15 B56
Mol-chlach 85 C10
Mold 48 F28
Molehill Green 33 F51
Molescroft 59 E46
Molesworth 32 A46
Mollacott Cross 6 A21
Mollance 65 D23
Molland 7 C24
Mollington *Che.* 48 F29
Mollington *Oxf.* 31 D40
Mollinsburn 75 C23
Monachty 26 B20
Monachylemore 81 F20
Moncreiffe 82 F27
Monevechadan 80 G17
Monewden 35 C58
Moneydie 82 E26
Moniaive 68 D23
Monifieth 83 D30
Monikie 83 D30
Monimail 82 F28
Monington 26 D17
Monken Hadley 23 B48
Monk Fryston 58 F41
Monkhill 60 A29
Monkhopton 39 F32
Monkland 28 C30
Monkleigh 6 C20
Monknash 18 D24
Monkokehampton 6 E21
Monkseaton 71 F39
Monks Eleigh 34 D55
Monk's Gate 12 D47
Monks' Heath 49 E34
Monk Sherborne 21 F41
Monkshill 99 E33
Monksilver 7 B26
Monks Kirby 41 G40
Monk Soham 35 B58
Monks Risborough 22 A43
Monkstadt 93 E9
Monk Street 33 F51
Monkswood 19 A29
Monkton *T.&W.* 71 G39
Monkton *Str.* 67 A19
Monkton *Kent* 25 E58
Monkton *Dev.* 7 E27
Monkton Combe 20 E33
Monkton Deverill 9 A34
Monkton Farleigh 20 E33
Monkton Heathfield 8 B28
Monkton Up Wimborne 10 C36
Monkwearmouth 62 A39
Monkwood 11 A42
Monmore Green 40 F35
Monmouth (Trefynwy) 28 G30
Monnington on Wye 28 D29
Monreith 64 F19
Monsale 25 B55
Montacute 8 C30
Monteach 99 E34
Montford 38 D29
Montford Bridge 38 D30
Montgarrie 90 B31
Montgomery (Trefaldwyn) 38 F28
Montgreenan 74 F19
Montrave 82 G29
Montrose 83 B33
Monxton 21 G39
Monyash 50 F37
Monymusk 91 B32
Monzie 81 E24
Moodiesburn 74 C22
Moonzie 82 F29
Moor Allerton 57 F39
Moorby 53 F48
Moor Cock 56 C32
Moorcot 28 C29
Moor Crichel 9 D35
Moordown 10 E36
Moore 48 D31
Moor End *Hum.* 58 F44
Moor End *Cum.* 55 B31
Moorends 51 A42
Moorgate 55 C31
Moorgreen 41 A40
Moorhall 50 E38
Moorhampton 28 D29
Moorhouse *Cum.* 60 A29
Moorhouse *Not.* 51 F43
Moorlinch 8 A29
Moor Monkton 58 D41
Moor Nook 56 F32
Moorsholm 63 E42
Moor Side 53 G48
Moorside 49 B35
Moortown *Lcn.* 52 C46
Moortown *I.o.W.* 11 F40
Morangie 96 C23
Morar 86 E12
Morborne 42 F47
Morchard Bishop 7 E23
Morcombelake 8 E30
Morcott 42 E45
Morda 38 C28
Morden *Dor.* 9 E34
Morden *G.L.* 23 E48
Mordiford 28 E31
Mordington 77 E35
Mordon 62 D39
More 38 F29
Morebath 7 C25
Morebattle 70 A33
Morecambe 55 C29
Morefield 95 B16
Moreleigh 5 E23
Morenish 81 D21
Moresby 60 D25
Morestead 11 B41
Moreton *Esx* 23 A51
Moreton *Mer.* 48 D28
Moreton *Oxf.* 21 A42
Moreton *Dor.* 9 F34
Moreton *H.&W.* 28 B30
Moreton Corbet 38 C31
Moretonhampstead 6 G22
Moreton-in-Marsh 30 E38
Moreton Jeffries 29 D32
Moreton Morrell 30 C38
Moreton on Lugg 28 D31
Moreton Pinkney 31 D41
Moreton Say 39 B32
Moreton Valence 29 G33
Morewellham 4 D20
Morfa Bychan 36 B21
Morfa Glas 18 A24
Morfa Nefyn 36 A18
Morgan's Vale 10 B37
Mork 19 A31
Morland 61 D31
Morley *Drm* 62 D37
Morley *Dby.* 41 A39
Morley *W.Y.* 57 G38
Morley Green 49 D34
Morley St 44 E56
Morningside *Ltn* 76 C28
Morningside *Str.* 75 E24
Morningthorpe 45 F58
Morpeth 71 E37
Morphie 91 G33
Morrey 40 D37
Morriston *W.G.* 17 E22
Morriston *Str.* 67 C18
Morroch 86 F12
Morston 44 A55
Mortehoe 6 A20
Mortimer 21 E42
Mortimer's Cross 28 B29
Mortimer West End 21 E42
Mortlake 22 D47
Morton *Lcn.* 42 C47
Morton *Shr.* 38 C28
Morton *Not.* 51 G43
Morton *Lcn.* 51 C43
Morton *Dby.* 51 G39
Morton *Nfk* 45 D57
Morton *Avon* 19 B32
Morton Bagot 30 B37
Morton-on-Swale 62 G39
Morvah 2 E9
Morval 4 E18
Morvich *Hgh.* 96 A23
Morvich *Hgh.* 86 B15
Morvil 16 A16
Morville 39 F32
Morwenstow 6 D18
Morwick Hall 71 C38
Mosborough 51 D40
Moscow 74 F20
Mosedale 60 C29
Moselden Height 50 A36
Moseley *H.&W.* 29 C34
Moseley *W.M.* 40 G36
Moss *S.Y.* 51 A41
Moss *Clw.* 48 G28
Moss *Str.* 78 C5
Mossat 90 B30
Moss Bank 48 C31
Mossbank 106 E40
Mossblown 67 A19
Mossburnford 70 B32
Mossdale 65 C22
Mossend 75 E23
Mossgiel 67 A20
Mosshead 98 F31
Mosside 83 B30
Mossley 49 B35
Mossley Hill 48 D29
Moss Nook 49 D34
Moss of Barmuckity 98 C28
Mosspaul Hotel 69 D30
Moss-side *Hgh.* 97 F24
Moss-side *Grm.* 98 D31
Moss Side 55 F29
Mosstodloch 98 D28
Mosston 83 C31
Mosterton 8 D30
Mostyn 47 D27
Motcombe 9 B34
Motherby 60 D30
Motherwell 75 E23
Mottingham 23 D50
Mottisfont 10 B39
Mottistone 11 F40
Mottram in Longdendale 49 C35
Mottram St Andrew 49 E34
Mouldsworth 48 E30
Moulin 82 B25
Moulsecoomb 13 F49
Moulsford 21 C41
Moulsham 24 A52
Moulsoe 32 D44
Moulton *Sfk* 33 B52
Moulton *Nmp.* 31 B43
Moulton *Che.* 49 F32
Moulton *N.Y.* 62 F38
Moulton *Lcn.* 43 C48
Moulton Chapel 43 D48
Moulton Seas End 43 C49
Moulton St Mary 45 E59
Mounie Castle 91 A33
Mount *Hgh.* 97 G25
Mount *Cnw.* 2 C13
Mount *Cnw.* 4 D17
Mountain Ash 18 B26
Mountain Cross 75 F27
Mountain Water 16 B14
Mountbenger 69 A28
Mountblairy 98 D32
Mount Bures 34 E54
Mount Edgcumbe 4 E20
Mountfield 14 E53
Mountgerald 96 E21
Mount Hawke 2 D12
Mountjoy 3 B14
Mount Manisty 48 E29
Mountnessing 23 B51
Mount Oliphant 67 B19
Mounton 19 B30
Mount Pleasant *Dby.* 41 A39
Mount Pleasant *Sfk* 35 A60
Mountsorrel 41 D41
Mountstuart 73 E17
Mount Tabor 57 G36
Mousehole 2 F10
Mouswald 69 F26
Mow Cop 49 G34
Mowden 62 E38
Mowhaugh 70 A33
Mowsley 41 G42
Mowtie 91 E34
Moxley 40 F35
Moy *Hgh.* 87 F17
Moy *Hgh.* 88 A23
Moy *Hgh.* 88 F20
Moy House 97 E25
Moyles Court 10 D37
Moylgrove 16 A17
Muasdale 72 F12
Muchalls 91 D34
Much Birch 28 E30
Much Cowarne 29 D32
Much Dewchurch 28 E30
Muchelney 8 B30
Much Hadham 33 G50
Much Hoole 55 G30
Muchlarnick 4 E17
Much Marcle 29 E32
Muchra 69 B28
Muchrachd 87 A18
Much Wenlock 39 F32
Mucking 24 C52
Mucklestone 39 B33
Muckleton 38 C31
Muckletown 90 A31
Muckton 53 D49
Mudale 102 E21
Muddiford 6 B21
Muddles Green 13 E51
Muddleswood 13 E48
Mudeford 10 E37
Mudford 8 C31
Mudgley 19 G30
Mugeary 85 A10
Mugginton 40 A38
Muggleswick 62 A36
Muie 96 A22
Muir 89 F26
Muirden 98 D32
Muirdrum 83 D31
Muirhead *Tay.* 82 D29
Muirhead *Fife* 82 G28
Muirhead *Grm.* 90 B31
Muirhead *Grm.* 97 E26
Muirhead *Str.* 74 D22
Muirhouses 75 B25
Muirkirk 68 A22
Muirmill 75 B23
Muir of Fowlis 90 B31
Muir of Lochs 98 C28
Muir of Ord 96 F20
Muirskie 91 D34
Muirtack *Grm.* 99 E34
Muirtack *Grm.* 99 F35
Muirton 96 E23
Muirton of Ardblair 82 C27
Muirton of Ballochy 91 G32
Muirtown 82 F25
Muiryfold 99 D33
Muker 61 G34
Mulbarton 45 E57
Mulben 98 D29
Mulhagery 100 G9
Mullach Charlabhaigh 100 C7
Mullion 2 G12
Mumby 53 E51
Munderfield Row 29 C32
Munderfield Stocks 29 C32
Mundesley 45 B59
Mundford 44 F53
Mundham 45 F59
Mundon 24 A54
Mundurno 91 B35
Munerigie 87 D18
Mungasdale 94 B15
Mungoswells 76 C30
Mungrisdale 60 C29
Munlochy 96 F22
Munnoch 74 F18
Munsley 29 D32
Munslow 38 G30
Murchington 6 G22
Murcott 31 G41
Murdostoun 75 E24
Murkle 103 B27
Murlaganmore 81 D21
Murlaggan *Hgh.* 87 E16
Murlaggan *Hgh.* 87 F19
Murra 105 A28
Murroes 83 D30
Murrow 43 E49
Mursley 32 F44
Murston 25 E55
Murthill 83 B30
Murthly 82 D26
Murton *Drm* 62 B39
Murton *Nor.* 77 F35
Murton *Cum.* 61 D33
Murton *N.Y.* 58 D42
Musbury 8 E28

Muscoates 58 A42
Musdale 80 E15
Musselburgh 76 C29
Muston 42 B44
Mustow Green 29 A34
Mutford 45 G60
Muthill 81 F24
Mutterton 7 E26
Mybster 103 C27
Myddfai 27 E23
Myddle 38 C30
Myddlewood 38 C30
Mydroilyn 26 C20
Mylor 3 E14
Mylor Bridge 2 E13
Mynachlog-ddu 16 A17
Myndtown 38 G29
Mynydd-bach 19 B30
Mynytho 36 B18
Myrebird 91 D33
Mytchett 22 F44
Mytholm 56 G35
Mytholmroyd 56 G35
Myton-on-Swale 57 C40

N

Naast 94 C14
Naburn 58 E42
Nackington 15 B57
Nacton 35 D58
Nafferton 59 D46
Nailbridge 29 G32
Nailsea 19 D30
Nailstone 41 E39
Nailsworth 20 B34
Nairn 97 F24
Nancegollan 2 E12
Nancledre 2 E10
Nanhoron 36 B18
Nannau 37 C23
Nannerch 47 F27
Nanpantan 41 D40
Nanpean 3 C15
Nanstallon 4 D16
Nant-ddu 27 G25
Nanternis 26 C19
Nantgaredig 17 B20
Nantgarw 18 C27
Nant-glas 27 B25
Nantglyn 47 F25
Nantlle 46 G20
Nantmawr 38 C28
Nantmel 27 B26
Nantmor 36 A21
Nant Peris 46 G21
Nantwich 49 G32
Nantycaws 17 C20
Nant-y -derry 19 A29
Nant-y-dugoed 37 D24
Nantyffyllon 18 B24
Nantyglo 28 G27
Nant-y-groes 27 B26
Nant-y-moel 18 B25
Nant y Pandy 46 E22
Naphill 22 B44
Nappa 56 D34
Napton on the Hill 31 B40
Narberth 16 C16
Narborough *Nfk* 44 D53
Narborough *Lei.* 41 F41
Narrachan 79 F14
Nasareth 46 G20
Naseby 31 A42
Nash *Bkh.* 31 E43
Nash *Shr.* 28 A31
Nash *Gwe.* 19 C29
Nash *S.G.* 18 D25
Nash *H.&W.* 28 B29
Nash Lee 22 A44
Nassington 42 F46
Nasty 33 F49
Nateby *Cum.* 61 F33
Nateby *Lan.* 55 E30
Nately Scures 21 F42
Natland 55 A31
Naughton 34 D56
Naunton *Glo.* 30 F36
Naunton *H.&W.* 29 E34
Naunton Beauchamp 29 C35
Navenby 52 G45
Navestock 23 B51
Navestock Side 23 B51
Navidale 103 G26
Navity 96 E23
Nawton 58 A42
Nayland 34 E55
Nazeing 23 A49
Neacroft 10 E37
Neal's Green 41 G39
Neap 107 B40
Near Cotton 40 A36
Near Sawrey 60 G29
Neasham 62 E39
Neath 18 B23
Neatham 22 G43
Neatishead 45 C59
Nebo *Gwy.* 47 G24
Nebo *Gwy.* 46 G20
Nebo *Gwy.* 46 C20
Nebo *Dyf.* 26 B21
Necton 44 E54
Nedd 101 E17
Nedderton 71 E38
Nedging Tye 34 D56
Needham 45 G58
Needham Market 34 C56
Needingworth 33 A49
Neen Savage 29 A32
Neen Sollars 29 A32
Neenton 39 G32
Nefyn 36 A18
Neilston 74 E20
Nelson *M.G.* 18 B26
Nelson *Lan.* 56 F34
Nelson Village 71 F38
Nemphlar 75 F24
Nempnett Thrubwell 19 E31
Nenthall 61 B33
Nenthead 61 B33
Nenthorn 76 G32
Nercwys 48 F28
Nereabolls 72 E8
Neriby 72 D9
Nerston 74 E22
Nesbit 77 G35
Ness 48 E29
Nesscliffe 38 D29
Ness of Tenston 104 E28
Neston *Che.* 48 E28
Neston *Wts.* 20 E34
Nether Alderley 49 E34
Nether Auchendrane 67 B19
Netheravon 20 G37
Nether Barr 64 D20
Nether Blainslie 76 F31
Netherbrae 99 D33
Netherbrough 104 E28
Nether Broughton 41 C42
Netherburn 75 F23
Nether Burrow 56 B32
Netherbury 8 E30
Netherby *Cum.* 69 F29
Netherby *N.Y.* 57 E39
Nether Cerne 9 E32
Nether Compton 8 C31
Nethercott 31 F40
Nether Crimond 91 A34
Nether Dalgliesh 69 C28
Nether Dallachy 98 C29
Netherend 19 B31
Nether End 50 E38
Nether Exe 7 F25
Netherfield *Str.* 75 F23
Netherfield *E.S.* 14 F53
Netherfield *Not.* 41 A42
Nether Glasslaw 99 D34
Netherhall 74 D18
Netherhampton 10 A36
Nether Handwick 82 C29
Nether Haugh 51 C40
Nether Headon 51 E43
Nether Hesleden 56 B34
Nether Heyford 31 C42
Nether Kellet 55 C31
Nether Kinmundy 99 E36
Nether Langwith 51 F41
Nether Lenshie 98 E32
Netherley 91 D34
Nethermill 69 E26
Nether Moor 51 F39
Nethermuir 99 E34
Nether Padley 50 E38
Nether Pitforthie 91 F34
Nether Poppleton 58 D41
Netherseal 40 D38
Nethershield 67 A21
Nether Silton 62 G40
Nether Stowey 7 B27
Netherstreet 20 E35
Netherthird *D.&G.* 65 E23
Netherthird *Str.* 67 B21
Netherthong 50 B37
Netherthorpe 51 D41
Netherton *Dev.* 5 C24
Netherton *W.M.* 40 G35
Netherton *W.Y.* 50 A38
Netherton *H.&W.* 29 D35
Netherton *Nor.* 70 C35
Netherton *Tay.* 82 B27
Netherton *Tay.* 83 B31
Netherton *Oxf.* 21 B40
Netherton *Str.* 75 E25
Netherton *Che.* 48 E31
Netherton *Mer.* 48 B29
Nethertown *Hgh.* 103 A29
Nethertown *Cum.* 60 F25
Nether Urquhart 82 G27
Nether Wallop 10 A39
Nether Wasdale 60 F27
Nether Wellwood 68 A22
Nether Whitacre 40 F38
Netherwitton 71 E36
Netherwood *D.&G.* 65 C25
Netherwood *Str.* 68 A22
Nether Woodburn 7 C24
Nether Worton 31 E40
Nethy Bridge 89 C26
Netley 11 D40
Netley Marsh 10 C39
Nettlebed 21 C42
Nettlebridge 19 G32
Nettlecombe *Dor.* 8 E31
Nettlecombe *Som.* 7 B26
Nettleden 32 G46
Nettleham 52 E46
Nettlestead *Sfk* 34 D56
Nettlestead *Kent* 23 F52
Nettlestead Green 23 F52
Nettlestone 11 E42
Nettleton *Wts.* 20 D33
Nettleton *Lcn.* 52 B47
Netton *Dev.* 5 F21
Netton *Wts.* 10 A37
Neuadd *Gwy.* 46 C19
Neuadd *Dyf.* 27 D25
Neuadd *Dyf.* 26 C20
Nevendon 24 B53
Nevern 16 A16
Nevill Holt 42 F43
New Abbey 65 D25
New Aberdour 99 C34
New Addington 23 E49
New Alresford 11 A41
New Alyth 82 C28
Newark *Ork.* 104 B33
Newark *Cbs.* 43 E48
Newark-on-Trent 51 G43
New Arley 40 G38
Newarthill 75 E23
New Ash Green 24 E52
New Barn 24 E52
Newbarn 15 C57
New Barnet 23 B48
Newbarns 55 B28
New Belses 70 A31
New Bewick 71 A36
Newbiggin *Nor.* 70 G35
Newbiggin *Cum.* 61 D32
Newbiggin *Drm* 61 D35
Newbiggin *N.Y.* 57 A36
Newbiggin *Cum.* 61 B31
Newbiggin *Cum.* 60 D30
Newbiggin *N.Y.* 62 G35
Newbiggin *Cum.* 55 C28
Newbiggin-by-the-Sea 71 E38
Newbigging *Str.* 75 F25
Newbigging *Tay.* 82 C28
Newbigging *Grm.* 91 D34
Newbigging *Grm.* 90 E27
Newbigging *Tay.* 83 D30
Newbigging *Tay.* 83 D30
Newbiggin-on-Lune 61 F32
Newbold *Dby.* 51 E39
Newbold *Lei.* 41 D40
Newbold on Avon 31 A40
Newbold on Stour 30 D38
Newbold Pacey 30 C38
Newbold Verdon 41 E40
New Bolingbroke 53 G49
Newborough *Stf.* 40 C36
Newborough *Cbs.* 42 E47
Newborough (Niwbwrch) 46 F19
Newbottle 31 E41
Newbourne 35 D58
New Bradwell 32 D44
Newbridge *Cnw.* 4 D19
Newbridge *Clw.* 38 A28
New Bridge 65 C25
Newbridge *Ltn* 75 C26
Newbridge *Oxf.* 21 A39
Newbridge *Gwe.* 19 B28
Newbridge *Dyf.* 16 A15
Newbridge *Cnw.* 2 E10
Newbridge *I.o.W.* 11 F40
Newbridge *Ham.* 10 C38
Newbridge-on-Usk 19 B29
Newbridge on Wye 27 C25
New Brighton *Mer.* 48 C29
New Brighton *Ham.* 11 D43
New Brinsley 41 A40
Newbrough 70 G34
New Broughton 48 G29
New Buckenham 44 F56
Newburgh *Lan.* 48 A30
Newburgh *Grm.* 91 A35
Newburgh *Grm.* 99 C35
Newburgh *Fife* 82 F28
Newburgh *Bor.* 69 B29
Newburn 71 G37
Newbury 21 E40
Newby *N.Y.* 62 E40
Newby *Cum.* 61 D31
Newby *Lan.* 56 E34
Newby *N.Y.* 56 B33
Newby Bridge 55 A29
Newby East 61 A30
New Byth 99 D34
Newby West 60 A29
Newby Wiske 57 A39
Newcastle *M.G.* 18 D24
Newcastle *Shr.* 38 G28
Newcastle *Gwe.* 28 G30
Newcastle Emlyn 26 D18
Newcastleton 69 E30
Newcastle-under-Lyme 40 A34
Newcastle upon Tyne 71 G38
Newcastle (Woolsington) Airport 71 F38
Newchapel *Stf.* 49 G34
Newchapel *Dyf.* 16 A17
Newchapel *Sry* 23 G49
New Cheriton 11 B41
Newchurch *I.o.W.* 11 F41
Newchurch *Gwe.* 19 B30
Newchurch *Kent* 15 D56
Newchurch *Lan.* 56 G34
Newchurch *Lan.* 56 F34
Newchurch *Dyf.* 17 B19
Newchurch *Pow.* 28 C27
New Clipstone 51 F41
New Costessey 45 D57
Newcott 8 D28
Newcraighall 76 C28
New Cross 27 A22
New Cumnock 68 B22
New Deer 99 E34
Newdigate 22 G47
New Duston 31 B43
New Earswick 58 D42
New Edlington 51 C41
New Elgin 97 E27
New Ellerby 59 F47
Newell Green 22 D44
New Eltham 23 D50
New End 30 C36
Newenden 14 E54
New England 42 E47
Newent 29 F33
Newerne 19 A32
New Farnley 57 F38
New Ferry 48 D29
Newfield *Drm* 62 C37
Newfield *Drm* 62 A38
Newfield *Hgh.* 96 D23
New Fryston 57 G40
Newgale 16 B14
New Galloway 65 C21
Newgate 44 A56
Newgate Street 23 A48
New Gilston 83 G30
Newgord 106 B41
New Grimsby 2 A10
Newhall *Dby.* 40 C38
Newhall *Che.* 39 A32
Newham *Nor.* 71 A37
Newham *G.L.* 23 C49
Newham Hall 77 G37
New Hartley 71 F38
Newhaven 13 F50
New Haw 22 E46
New Hedges 16 D17
Newhey 49 A35
New Holland 59 G46
Newholm 63 E44
New Horton Grange 71 F37
New Houghton *Nfk* 44 C53
New Houghton *Dby.* 51 F41
Newhouse 75 D23
New Houses 56 B34
New Hutton 61 G31
New Hythe 14 B53
Newick 13 D50
Newington *Oxf.* 21 B42
Newington *Kent* 24 E54
Newington *Kent* 15 D57
Newington Bagpath 20 B33
New Inn *Gwe.* 19 A30
New Inn *Dyf.* 17 A20
New Inn *Gwe.* 19 B29
New Inn *Fife* 82 G28
New Invention *W.M.* 40 E35
New Invention *Shr.* 28 A28
New Lanark 75 F24
Newland *Glo.* 19 A31
Newland *N.Y.* 58 G42
Newland *H.&W.* 29 D33
Newlandrig 76 D29
Newlands *Nor.* 62 A36
Newlands *Nor.* 70 D31
Newland's Corner 22 G46
Newlands of Geise 103 B26
New Lane 48 A30
New Leake 53 G49
New Leeds 99 D35
New Leslie 90 A31
New Longton 55 G31
New Luce 64 D17
Newlyn 2 F10
Newlyn East 3 C14
Newmachar 91 B34
New Mains 75 G24
Newmains 75 E24
New Mains of Ury 91 E34
New Malden 23 E48
Newmarket *W.I.* 100 D10
Newmarket *Sfk* 33 B52
New Marske 63 D42
New Marton 38 B29
New Mill *W.Y.* 50 B37
New Mill *Hfs.* 32 G45
Newmill *Bor.* 69 B30
Newmill *Grm.* 98 D30
Newmill *Grm.* 99 E34
Newmill *Grm.* 91 A33
New Mill *Grm.* 91 E33
New Mill *Cnw.* 2 E10
New Mill End 32 G47
Newmill of Inshewan 83 A30
New Mills *Pow.* 37 E26
New Mills *Gwe.* 19 A31
New Mills *Dby.* 50 D36
New Mills *Cnw.* 3 C15
Newmills 96 E22
Newmiln *Tay.* 82 D27
Newmiln *Tay.* 82 E25
Newmilns 74 G21
New Milton 10 E38
New Mistley 35 E57
New Moat 16 B16
Newnham *Hfs.* 33 E48
Newnham *Nmp.* 31 C41
Newnham *Glo.* 29 G32
Newnham *H.&W.* 29 B32
Newnham *Ham.* 21 F42
Newnham *Kent* 14 B55
Newnham Paddox 41 G40
Newnoth 98 F30
New Orleans 66 B13
New Park 4 B17
New Pitsligo 99 D34
New Polzeath 3 A14
Newport *Glo.* 19 B32
Newport *Dyf.* 16 A16
Newport *Cnw.* 6 G19
Newport *Nfk* 45 D61
Newport *Dev.* 6 B21
Newport *Hum.* 58 F44
Newport *Hgh.* 103 F27
Newport *Gwe.* 19 C29
Newport *Esx* 33 E51
Newport *Shr.* 39 D33
Newport *I.o.W.* 11 F41
Newport-on-Tay 83 E30
Newport Pagnell 32 D44
Newpound Common 12 D46
New Prestwick 67 A18
New Quay 26 C19
Newquay 2 B13
Newquay (St Mawgan) Airport 3 B14
New Rackheath 45 D58
New Radnor 28 B27
New Rent 61 C30
New Road Side 56 E35
New Romney 15 E56
New Rossington 51 C42
New Row 56 F32
New Sauchie 75 A24
New Sawley 41 B40
New Scone 82 E27
Newseat 98 F32
Newsham *N.Y.* 62 E37
Newsham *N.Y.* 57 A39
Newsham *Nor.* 71 E38
Newsham *Lan.* 55 F31
Newsholme *Hum.* 58 G43
Newsholme *Lan.* 56 D34
New Silksworth 62 A39
Newstead *Bor.* 76 G31
Newstead *Nor.* 71 A37
Newstead *Not.* 51 G40
Newthorpe 57 F40
Newton *W.Y.* 57 G40
Newton *Che.* 48 E31
Newton *Nfk* 44 D54
Newton *Tay.* 81 D24
Newton *Str.* 73 A16
Newton *Str.* 73 E15
Newton *Ltn* 75 C26
Newton *Str.* 75 G25
Newton *M.G.* 18 D24
Newton *Dyf.* 16 B14
Newton *Dyf.* 16 D15
Newton *W.G.* 17 F21
Newton *Hgh.* 96 G23
Newton *Hgh.* 103 C28
Newton *Hgh.* 101 E18
Newton *Grm.* 99 E36
Newton *Grm.* 98 E30
Newton *Grm.* 98 C29
Newton *Cum.* 55 B28
Newton *Lan.* 55 B31
Newton *G.M.* 49 C35
Newton *Che.* 48 G30
Newton *Stf.* 40 C36
Newton *H.&W.* 28 B29
Newton *Nor.* 71 G36
Newton *Sfk* 34 D55

Newton *Cbs.* **33 D50**
Newton *War.* **31 A41**
Newton *Hgh.* **103 D29**
Newton *Bor.* **70 A31**
Newton *D.&G.* **69 D27**
Newton *Bor.* **69 B30**
Newton *Lan.* **56 D32**
Newton *Nfk* **43 D50**
Newton *Nmp.* **42 G44**
Newton *Lcn.* **42 B46**
Newton *Not.* **41 A42**
Newton *Ham.* **10 B38**
Newton *W.I.* **92 D4**
Newton *Hgh.* **96 E23**
Newton *Hgh.* **96 F21**
Newton Abbot **5 C24**
Newtonairds **68 E24**
Newton Arlosh **60 A27**
Newton Aycliffe **62 D38**
Newton Bewley **62 D40**
Newton Blossomville **32 C45**
Newton Bromswold **32 B46**
Newton Burgoland **41 E39**
Newton by Toft **52 D46**
Newton Ferrers **5 F21**
Newton Flotman **45 F57**
Newtongrange **76 D29**
Newton Harcourt **41 F42**
Newtonhill **91 D34**
Newton Kyme **57 E40**
Newton-le-Willows **48 C31**
Newton-le-Willows **62 G37**
Newton Longville **32 E44**
Newton Mearns **74 E21**
Newtonmill **83 A31**
Newtonmore **88 E22**
Newton Morrell **62 F38**
Newton Mountain **16 D15**
Newton Mulgrave **63 E43**
Newton of Ardtoe **86 G12**
Newton of Balcanquhal **82 F27**
Newton of Dalvey **97 F25**
Newton of Falkland **82 G28**
Newton of Leys **96 G22**
Newton-on-Ouse **58 C41**
Newton-on-Rawcliffe **63 G43**
Newton-on-the-Moor **71 C37**
Newton on Trent **51 E43**
Newton Poppleford **7 G26**
Newton Purcell **31 E42**
Newton Regis **40 E38**
Newton Reigny **61 C30**
Newton Solney **40 C38**
Newton Stacey **21 G40**
Newton St Cyres **7 F24**
Newton Stewart **64 D19**
Newton St Faith **45 D58**
Newton St Loe **19 E32**
Newton St Petrock **6 D20**
Newton Tony **21 G38**
Newton Tracey **6 C21**
Newton under Roseberry **63 E41**
Newton upon Derwent **58 E42**
Newton Valence **11 A43**
Newtown *Ham.* **11 C41**
Newtown *Ham.* **10 C38**
Newtown *Wts.* **10 B38**
Newtown *Dor.* **10 E36**
Newtown *Ham.* **11 C41**
Newtown *I.o.W.* **11 E40**
Newtown *Brk.* **21 E40**
Newtown *Hgh.* **88 D19**
Newtown *Wts.* **9 B34**
New Town *E.S.* **13 D50**
New Town *Ltn* **76 C30**
Newtown *Nor.* **71 A36**
Newtown *Nor.* **71 C36**
Newtown *Grm.* **99 C33**
Newtown *I.o.M.* **54 F25**
Newtown *Bkh.* **22 A45**
New Town *Glo.* **30 E36**
Newtown *H.&W.* **29 E32**
Newtown *Gwe.* **28 G27**
Newtown *H.&W.* **29 D32**
Newtown (Y Drenewydd) **38 F27**
Newtown *Shr.* **38 B30**
Newtown *Stf.* **50 F36**
Newtown *Che.* **48 G30**
Newtown *Stf.* **49 F35**
Newtown *Che.* **49 D35**
Newtown *Cum.* **69 G30**
Newtown in St Martin **2 F13**
Newtown Linford **41 E41**
Newtown St Boswells **76 G31**
Newtown Unthank **41 E40**
New Tredegar **18 A27**
Newtyle **82 C28**
New Ulva **73 B13**
New Walsoken **43 E50**
New Waltham **53 B48**
New Wimpole **33 D49**
New Winton *Ltn* **76 C30**
New Yatt **30 G39**
New York *Lcn.* **53 G48**
New York *T.&W.* **71 F39**
Neyland **16 D15**
Nibley *Avon* **19 C32**
Nibley *Glo.* **19 A32**
Nicholashayne **7 D26**
Nicholaston **17 F21**
Nidd **57 C39**
Niddrie **76 C28**
Nigg *Grm.* **91 C35**
Nigg *Hgh.* **97 D24**
Nightcott **7 C24**
Nilig **47 G26**
Nine Ashes **23 A51**
Ninebanks **61 A33**
Nine Elms **20 C37**
Nine Mile Burn **75 E27**
Ninfield **14 F53**
Ningwood **11 F40**
Nisbet **70 A32**
Niton **11 G40**
Nitshill **74 D20**
Niwbwrch (Newborough) **46 F19**
Nizels **23 F51**
Noak Hill **23 B51**
Noblehill **65 C25**
Nobottle **31 B42**
Nocton **52 F46**
Noddsdale **74 D18**
Noke **31 G41**
Nolton **16 C14**
No Man's Heath *War.* **40 E38**
No Man's Heath *Che.* **38 A31**
Nomansland *Dev.* **7 D24**
Nomansland *Ham.* **10 C38**
Noneley **38 C30**
Nonington **15 B58**
Nook *Cum.* **55 A31**
Nook *Cum.* **69 F30**
Noonsbrough **107 B38**
Noranside **83 A30**
Norbiton **22 E47**
Norbreck **55 E28**
Norbury *Dby.* **40 A37**
Norbury *Che.* **38 A31**
Norbury *Shr.* **38 F29**
Norbury *Stf.* **39 C33**
Norchard **29 B34**
Nordelph **43 E51**
Norden **9 F35**
Nordley **39 F32**
Norham **77 F34**
Norland Town **57 G36**
Norley **48 E31**
Norleywood **10 E39**
Normanby *N.Y.* **58 A43**
Normanby *Cle.* **63 E41**
Normanby *Hum.* **52 A44**
Normanby by Spital **52 D46**
Normanby le Wold **52 C47**
Norman Cross **42 F47**
Normandy **22 F45**
Normann's Ruh **79 C10**
Norman's Bay **13 F52**
Norman's Green **7 E26**
Normanton *Lei.* **42 E45**
Normanton *Dby.* **41 B39**
Normanton *Lei.* **42 A44**
Normanton *Lcn.* **42 A45**
Normanton *W.Y.* **57 G39**
Normanton *Not.* **51 G43**
Normanton le Heath **41 D39**
Normanton on Soar **41 C41**
Normanton on the Wolds **41 B42**
Normanton on Trent **51 F43**
Normoss **55 F29**
Norrington Common **20 E34**
Norris Hill **41 D39**
Northacre **44 F55**
Northallerton **62 G39**
Northall Green **44 D56**
Northam *Dev.* **6 C20**
Northam *Ham.* **11 C40**
Northampton **31 B43**
North Anston **51 D41**
North Ascot **22 E44**
North Aston **31 F40**
Northaw **23 A48**
Northay **8 C28**
North Baddesley **10 B39**
North Ballachulish **80 A16**
North Balloch **67 D19**
North Barrow **9 B32**
North Benfleet **24 C53**
North Bersted **12 F45**
North Berwick **76 B31**
North Boarhunt **11 D41**
North Bogbain **98 D29**
Northborough **42 E47**
Northbourne **15 B58**
North Bovey **7 G23**
North Bradley **20 F34**
North Brentor **6 G20**
North Brewham **9 A33**
Northbrook **31 F40**
North Buckland **6 A20**
North Burlingham **45 D59**
Northburnhill **99 E33**
North Cadbury **9 B32**
North Carlton **52 E45**
North Cave **58 F44**
North Cerney **20 A36**
North Chailey **13 D49**
Northchapel **12 D45**
North Charford **10 B38**
North Charlton **71 A37**
North Cheriton **9 B32**
Northchurch **22 A45**
North Cliffe **58 F44**
North Clifton **52 E44**
North Cockerington **53 C49**
North Coker **8 C31**
North Cornelly **18 C24**
Northcote Manor **6 D22**
North Cotes **53 B49**
Northcott **6 F19**
North Cove **45 G60**
North Cowton **62 F38**
North Crawley **32 D45**
North Cray **23 D50**
North Curry **8 B29**
North Dallens **80 C15**
North Dalton **59 D45**
North Dawn **105 A30**
North Deighton **57 D39**
North Duffield **58 F42**
Northdyke **104 D28**
North Elkington **53 C48**
North Elmham **44 C55**
North Elmsall **51 A40**
North End *Esx* **33 G52**
North End *Bkh.* **32 F44**
Northend *War.* **30 C39**
Northend *Avon* **20 E33**
North End *Avon* **19 E30**
North End *Nor.* **71 C37**
North End *Nfk* **44 F56**
North End *W.S.* **12 E47**
Northend *Bkh.* **22 B43**
North End *Ham.* **21 E40**
North End *Ham.* **11 D42**
North Erradale **94 C12**
North Essie **99 D36**
North Ferriby **59 G45**
Northfield *Bor.* **77 D34**
Northfield *Grm.* **99 C34**
Northfield *Hgh.* **103 D29**
Northfield *W.M.* **30 A36**
Northfield *Grm.* **91 C34**
Northfleet **24 D52**
North Frodingham **59 D47**
North Gorley **10 C37**
North Green **45 G58**
North Grimston **58 C44**
North Hayling **11 D43**
North Hazelrigg **77 G36**
North Heasley **7 B23**
North Heath **12 D46**
North Hill **4 C18**
North Hinksey **21 A40**
North Holmwood **22 G47**
Northhouse **69 C30**
North Huish **5 E23**
North Hykeham **52 F45**
Northiam **14 E54**
Northill **32 D47**
Northington **11 A41**
North Johnston **16 C15**
North Kelsey **52 B46**
North Kessock **96 G22**
North Killingholme **52 A47**
North Kilvington **57 A40**
North Kilworth **41 G42**
North Kyme **52 G47**
North Lancing **12 F47**
Northlands **53 G49**
Northleach **30 G36**
North Lee **22 A44**
Northleigh *Dev.* **7 F27**
Northleigh *Dev.* **6 B22**
North Leigh **30 G39**
North Leverton with Habblesthorpe **51 D43**
Northlew **6 F21**
North Littleton **30 D36**
North Lopham **44 G56**
North Luffenham **42 E45**
North Marden **12 E44**
North Marston **31 F43**
North Middleton **76 E29**
North Millbrex **99 E34**
North Molton **7 C23**
Northmoor **21 A40**
Northmoor Green or Moorland **8 A28**
North Moreton **21 C41**
Northmuir **82 B29**
North Mundham **12 F44**
North Muskham **51 G43**
North Newbald **59 F45**
North Newington **30 E39**
North Newnton **20 F37**
North Newton **8 A28**
Northney **11 D43**
North Nibley **20 B33**
North Oakley **21 F41**
North Ockendon **23 C51**
Northolt **22 C47**
Northop **48 F28**
Northop Hall **48 F28**
North Ormesby **63 E41**
North Ormsby **53 C48**
Northorpe *Lcn.* **52 C44**
Northorpe *Lcn.* **42 D46**
Northorpe *Lcn.* **42 B47**
North Otterington **62 G39**
Northover **8 B30**
North Owersby **52 C46**
Northowram **57 G37**
North Perrott **8 D30**
North Petherton **8 A28**
North Petherwin **4 B18**
North Pickenham **44 E54**
North Piddle **29 C35**
North Poorton **8 E31**
North Port **80 E16**
Northpunds **107 E40**
North Queensferry **75 B27**
North Radworthy **7 B23**
North Rauceby **42 A46**
Northrepps **45 B58**
North Reston **53 D49**
North Rigton **57 E38**
North Rode **49 F34**
North Roe **106 D39**
North Runcton **44 D52**
North Sandwick **106 C41**
North Scale **54 C27**
North Scarle **52 F44**
North Seaton **71 E38**
North Shian **79 C14**
North Shields **71 G39**
North Shoebury **25 C55**
North Side **43 F48**
North Skelton **63 E42**
North Somercotes **53 C50**
North Stainley **57 B38**
North Stainmore **61 E34**
North Stifford **23 C51**
North Stoke *W.S.* **12 E46**
North Stoke *Avon* **19 E32**
North Stoke *Oxf.* **21 C42**
North Stoneham **11 C40**
North Street *Ham.* **11 A42**
North Street *Kent* **15 B56**
North Street *Brk.* **21 D42**
North Sunderland **77 G37**
North Tamerton **4 A18**
North Tarbothill **91 B35**
North Tawton **6 E22**
North Third **75 A23**
North Thoresby **53 C48**
North Tidworth **21 G38**
North Togston **71 C38**
North Town *Dev.* **6 E20**
Northtown **105 B30**
North Town *Ham.* **22 F44**
North Tuddenham **44 D56**
North Walsham **45 B58**
North Waltham **21 G41**
North Warnborough **22 F43**
North Watten **103 C28**
Northway **29 E34**
North Weald Bassett **23 A50**
North Wheatley **51 D43**
North Whilborough **5 D24**
Northwich **49 E32**
North Wick **19 E31**
Northwick **19 C31**
North Widcombe **19 F31**
North Willingham **52 D47**
North Wingfield **51 F39**
North Witham **42 C44**
Northwold **44 F53**
Northwood *Shr.* **38 B30**
Northwood *G.L.* **22 B46**
Northwood *I.o.W.* **11 E40**
Northwood Green **29 G33**
North Wootton *Nfk* **44 C52**
North Wootton *Som.* **19 G31**
North Wootton *Dor.* **9 C32**
North Wraxall **20 D34**
North Wroughton **20 C37**
North Yardhope **70 C34**
Norton *I.o.W.* **10 F39**
Norton *W.S.* **12 G44**
Norton *W.S.* **12 F45**
Norton *W.M.* **40 G34**
Norton *Wts.* **20 C34**
Norton *N.Y.* **58 B43**
Norton *Shr.* **38 G30**
Norton *Che.* **48 D31**
Norton *Cle.* **62 D40**
Norton *H.&W.* **30 D36**
Norton *Glo.* **29 F34**
Norton *Pow.* **28 B28**
Norton *H.&W.* **29 C34**
Norton *Sfk* **34 B55**
Norton *Nmp.* **31 B41**
Norton *Hfs.* **33 E48**
Norton *Shr.* **39 E33**
Norton *Shr.* **38 E31**
Norton *Not.* **51 E41**
Norton *S.Y.* **51 D39**
Norton *S.Y.* **51 A41**
Norton Bavant **20 G35**
Norton Bridge **40 B34**
Norton Canes **40 E36**
Norton Canon **28 D29**
Norton Disney **52 G44**
Norton Ferris **9 A33**
Norton Fitzwarren **7 C27**
Norton Green **10 F39**
Norton Hawkfield **19 E31**
Norton Heath **24 A52**
Norton in Hales **39 B32**
Norton in the Moors **49 G34**
Norton-Juxta-Twycross **40 E38**
Norton-le-Clay **57 B39**
Norton Lindsey **30 B38**
Norton Malreward **19 E32**
Norton Mandeville **23 A51**
Norton St Philip **20 F33**
Norton Subcourse **45 F59**
Norton sub Hamdon **8 C30**
Norton Wood **28 D29**
Norwell **51 F43**
Norwell Woodhouse **51 F43**
Norwich **45 E58**
Norwich Airport **45 D58**
Norwick **106 A42**
Norwood Green **22 D47**
Norwood Hill **23 G48**
Noseley **42 F43**
Noss Mayo **5 F21**
Nosterfield **57 A38**
Nostie **86 B14**
Notgrove **30 F36**
Nottage **18 D23**
Nottingham *Hgh.* **103 E27**
Nottingham *Not.* **41 A41**
Notton *Wts.* **20 E34**
Notton *W.Y.* **51 A39**
Nounsley **24 A53**
Noutard's Green **29 B33**
Nowton **34 B54**
Nox **38 D30**
Noyadd Trefawr **26 D18**
Nuffield **21 C42**
Nunburnholme **58 E44**
Nuneaton **41 F39**
Nuneham Courtenay **21 B41**
Nun Monkton **57 D40**
Nunney **20 G33**
Nunnington **58 B42**
Nunnington Park **7 C26**
Nunthorpe **63 E41**
Nunton **10 B37**
Nunwick *N.Y.* **57 B39**
Nunwick *Nor.* **70 F34**
Nup End *Glo.* **29 F33**
Nup End *Bkh.* **32 G44**
Nursling **10 C39**
Nursted **11 B43**
Nurton **40 F34**
Nutbourne *W.S.* **11 D43**
Nutbourne *W.S.* **12 E46**
Nutfield **23 F48**
Nuthall **41 A41**
Nuthampstead **33 E49**
Nuthurst *War.* **30 A37**
Nuthurst *W.S.* **12 D47**
Nutley *E.S.* **13 D50**
Nutley *Ham.* **21 G42**
Nutwell **51 B42**
Nyadd **75 A23**
Nybster **103 B29**
Nyetimber **12 G44**
Nyewood **12 D44**
Nymet Rowland **6 E22**
Nymet Tracey **7 E23**
Nympsfield **20 A33**
Nynehead **7 C27**
Nythe **8 A30**
Nyton **12 F45**

O

Oadby **41 E42**
Oad Street **24 E54**
Oakamoor **40 A36**
Oakbank *Ltn* **75 D26**
Oakbank *Str.* **79 D13**
Oak Cross **6 F21**
Oakdale **18 B27**
Oake **7 C27**
Oaken **40 E34**
Oakenclough **55 E31**
Oakengates **39 D32**
Oakenhead **98 C28**
Oakenshaw *Drm* **62 C37**
Oakenshaw *W.Y.* **57 G37**
Oakford *Dev.* **7 C24**
Oakford *Dyf.* **26 C20**

Oakfordbridge 7 C25
Oakgrove 49 F35
Oakham 42 E44
Oakhanger 11 A43
Oakhill 19 G32
Oakington 33 B49
Oaklands *Hfs.* 33 G48
Oaklands *Clw.* 47 G24
Oakle Street 29 G33
Oakley *Fife* 75 B26
Oakley *Bfd.* 32 C46
Oakley *Bkh.* 31 G42
Oakley *Sfk* 35 A57
Oakley *Ham.* 21 F41
Oakley Green 22 D45
Oakley Park 37 G25
Oakridge 20 A34
Oaks 38 E30
Oaksey 20 B35
Oakshaw Ford 70 F31
Oakthorpe 41 D39
Oaktree Hill 62 G39
Oakwoodhill 12 C47
Oakworth 57 F36
Oalinlongart 73 B17
Oare *Wts.* 20 E37
Oare *Som.* 7 A24
Oare *Kent* 25 E55
Oasby 42 B45
Oatfield 66 B12
Oathlaw 83 B30
Oban 79 E14
Obinan 94 B14
Obley 28 A29
Oborne 9 C32
Occlestone Green 49 F32
Occold 35 A57
Occumster 103 E28
Ochiltree 67 A20
Ochr-y-Mynydd 18 A25
Ochtermuthill 81 F24
Ochtertyre *Tay.* 81 E24
Ochtertyre *Cen.* 75 A23
Ockbrook 41 B40
Ockham 22 F46
Ockle 86 G11
Ockley 12 C47
Ocle Pychard 28 D31
Octon 59 C46
Odcombe 8 C30
Odd Down 20 E33
Oddingley 29 C34
Oddington 31 G41
Oddsta 106 C41
Odell 32 C45
Odie 104 D32
Odiham 22 F43
Odstock 10 B37
Odstone 41 E39
Offchurch 30 B39
Offenham 30 D36
Offerton 49 D35
Offham *E.S.* 13 E49
Offham *Kent* 23 F52
Offord Cluny 32 B47
Offord D'Arcy 32 B47
Offton 34 D56
Offwell 7 F27
Ogbourne Maizey 20 D37
Ogbourne St Andrew 20 D37
Ogbourne St George 20 D37
Ogden 57 F36
Ogil 83 A30
Ogle 71 F37
Ogmore 18 D24
Ogmore-by-Sea 18 D24
Ogmore Vale 18 B25
Oil Terminal 105 B29
Okeford Fitzpaine 9 C34
Okehampton 6 F21
Okehampton Camp 6 F21
Okraquoy 107 D40
Old 31 A43
Old Aberdeen 91 C35
Old Alresford 11 A41
Old Arley 40 F38
Old Basford 41 A41
Old Basing 21 F42
Old Belses 70 A31
Oldberrow 30 B36
Old Bewick 71 A36
Old Bolingbroke 53 F49
Oldborough 7 E23
Old Brampton 51 E39
Old Bridge of Urr 65 D23
Old Buckenham 44 F56
Old Burghclere 21 F40
Oldbury *Kent* 23 F51
Oldbury *W.M.* 40 F35
Oldbury *War.* 41 F39
Oldbury *Shr.* 39 F32
Oldbury Naite 19 B32
Oldbury -on-Severn 19 B32
Oldbury on the Hill 20 C33
Old Byland 58 A41
Oldcastle 28 F29
Oldcastle Heath 38 A30
Old Cleeve 7 A26
Old Colwyn 47 E24
Oldcotes 51 D41
Old Craig 91 A34
Old Craighall 76 C29
Old Crombie 98 D31
Old Dailly 67 D18
Old Dalby 41 C42
Old Deer 99 E35
Old Ellerby 59 F47
Old Felixstowe 35 E59
Oldfield *W.Y.* 56 F35
Oldfield *H.&W.* 29 B34
Old Fletton 42 F47
Oldford 20 F33
Old Glossop 50 C36
Old Goginan 37 G22
Old Goole 58 G43
Old Gore 29 F32
Old Grimsby 2 A10
Oldhall *Hgh.* 103 C27
Oldhall *Grm.* 90 D30
Old Hall 53 A48
Oldham 49 B35
Oldhamstocks 77 C33
Old Heath 34 F56
Old Hill 40 G35
Oldhurst 33 A48
Old Hutton 55 A31
Old Kea 3 D14
Old Kilpatrick 74 C20
Old Kinnernie 91 C33
Old Knebworth 33 G48
Oldland 19 D32
Old Leake 43 A49
Old Leslie 90 A31
Old Malton 58 B44
Oldmeldrum 91 A33
Old Micklefield 57 F40
Oldmill 90 C31
Old Milverton 30 B38
Old Netley 11 C40
Old Newton 34 B56
Oldpark 39 E32
Old Philpstoun 75 C26
Old Poltalloch 79 G14
Old Portlethen 91 D35
Old Radnor 28 C28
Old Rattray 99 D36
Old Rayne 91 A32
Oldridge 7 F24
Old Romney 15 E56
Old Scone 82 E26
Old Shields 75 C24
Oldshore Beg 101 C17
Oldshore More 101 C18
Old Sodbury 20 C33
Old Somerby 42 B45
Oldstead 58 A41
Old Stratford 31 D43
Old Sunderlandwick 59 D46
Old Swarland 71 C37
Old Swinford 40 G34
Old Town *Cnw.* 2 A11
Old Town *Cum.* 55 A31
Old Town *Nor.* 70 D34
Oldtown of Aigas 96 G20
Oldtown of Ord 98 D32
Oldwalls 17 E20
Old Warden 32 D47
Oldways End 7 C24
Old Weston 32 A46
Oldwhat 99 D34
Old Windsor 22 D45
Old Wives Lees 15 B56
Old Woking 22 F46
Old Wolverton 32 D44
Old Woods 38 C30
Olgrinmore 103 C26
Oliver 69 A26
Oliver's Battery 11 B40
Ollaberry 106 D39
Ollerton *Shr.* 39 C32
Ollerton *Not.* 51 F42
Ollerton *Che.* 49 E33
Olmstead Green 33 D52
Olney *Bkh.* 32 C44
Olney *Nmp.* 31 D42
Olrig House 103 B27
Olton 40 G37
Olveston 19 C31
Ombersley 29 B34
Ompton 51 F42
Onchan 54 F25
Onecote 50 G36
Ongar Hill 43 C51
Ongar Street 28 B29
Onibury 28 A30
Onich 80 A16
Onllwyn 27 G24
Onneley 39 A33
Onslow Village 22 G45
Opinan 94 D13
Orange Lane 77 F33
Orbliston 98 D28
Orbost 93 G8
Orby 53 F50
Orcadia 73 D17
Orchard 73 B17
Orchard Portman 8 B28
Orchard Wyndham 7 B26
Orcheston 20 G36
Orcop 28 F30
Orcop Hill 28 F30
Ord 86 C12
Ordhead 91 B32
Ordie 90 C30
Ordiequish 98 D29
Ordsall 51 E42
Ore 14 F54
Oreham Common 12 E47
Oreston 5 E21
Oreton 39 G32
Orford *Sfk* 35 D60
Orford *Che.* 49 C32
Orgreave 40 D37
Orleton *H.&W.* 29 B32
Orleton *H.&W.* 28 B30
Orleton Common 28 B30
Orlingbury 32 A44
Ormacleit 84 A3
Ormesby 63 E41
Ormesby St Margaret 45 D60
Ormesby St Michael 45 D60
Ormiscaig 94 B14
Ormiston 76 D29
Ormsaigmore 79 A10
Ormsdale 73 B16
Ormskirk 48 B29
Ormwe 103 B26
Orpington 23 E50
Orrell 48 B31
Orrisdale 54 D25
Orrok Ho. 91 B35
Orroland 65 F23
Orsett 24 C52
Orslow 40 D34
Orston 42 A43
Orton *Nmp.* 31 A44
Orton *Cum.* 61 F32
Orton Longueville 42 F47
Orton-on-the-Hill 40 E38
Orton Waterville 42 F47
Orwell 33 C49
Osbaldeston 56 F32
Osbaldwick 58 D42
Osbaston *Shr.* 38 D31
Osbaston *Lei.* 41 E40
Osborne 11 E40
Osbournby 42 B46
Oscroft 48 F30
Ose 93 G9
Osgathorpe 41 D40
Osgodby *Lcn.* 52 C46
Osgodby *N.Y.* 59 A46
Osgodby *N.Y.* 58 F42
Oskaig 86 A11
Osmaston *Dby.* 40 A37
Osmaston *Dby.* 41 B39
Osmington 9 F33
Osmington Mills 9 F33
Osmotherley 62 G40
Osney 21 A40
Ossett 57 G38
Ossington 51 F43
Ostend 25 B55
Osterley 22 D47
Oswaldkirk 58 B42
Oswaldtwistle 56 G32
Oswestry 38 C28
Otford 23 F51
Otham 14 B53
Othery 8 A29
Otley *Sfk* 35 C58
Otley *W.Y.* 57 E37
Otter 73 C15
Otterbourne 11 B40
Otterburn *N.Y.* 56 D34
Otterburn *Nor.* 70 D34
Otterburn Camp 70 D34
Otterden Place 14 B55
Otter Ferry 73 B15
Otterham 4 A17
Otterhampton 19 G28
Ottershaw 22 E45
Otterswick 106 D41
Otterton 7 G26
Ottery St Mary 7 F27
Ottinge 15 C57
Ottringham 59 G48
Oughterby 60 A28
Oughtershaw 56 A34
Oughtibridge 50 C38
Oulston 58 B41
Oulton *Cum.* 60 A28
Oulton *W.Y.* 57 G39
Oulton *Sfk* 45 F61
Oulton *Nfk* 45 C57
Oulton *Stf.* 40 B34
Oulton Broad 45 F60
Oulton Street 45 C57
Oundle 42 G46
Ousby 61 C32
Ousdale 103 F26
Ousden 34 C53
Ousefleet 58 G44
Ouston *Drm* 62 A38
Ouston *Nor.* 71 F36
Outertown 104 E28
Outgate 60 G29
Outhgill 61 F33
Outlands 39 C33
Outlane 50 A36
Out Newton 59 G49
Out Rawcliffe 55 E30
Outwell 43 E50
Outwood *Sry* 23 G49
Outwood *W.Y.* 57 G39
Oval The 20 E33
Ovenden 57 G36
Over *Avon* 19 C31
Over *Che.* 49 F32
Over *Cbs.* 33 B49
Overbister 104 B32
Overbrae 99 D33
Overbury 29 E35
Overcombe 9 F32
Over Compton 8 C31
Over End 50 E38
Over Haddon 50 F38
Over Kellet 55 B31
Over Kiddington 30 F39
Overleigh 8 A30
Over Norton 30 F39
Over Peover 49 E33
Overpool 48 E29
Over Rankeilour 82 F29
Overscaig Hotel 102 F20
Overseal 40 D38
Over Silton 62 G40
Oversland 15 B56
Oversley Green 30 C36
Overstone 31 B43
Over Stowey 7 B27
Overstrand 45 A58
Over Stratton 8 C30
Over Tabley 49 D33
Overton *Lan.* 55 D30
Overton *Grm.* 91 B32
Overton *Shr.* 28 A30
Overton *Clw.* 38 A29
Overton *Ham.* 21 G41
Overton *Grm.* 91 B34
Overton *N.Y.* 58 D41
Overton *W.G.* 17 F20
Overtown 75 E24
Over Wallop 10 A38
Over Whitacre 40 F38
Over Worton 31 F40
Overy Staithe 44 A54
Oving *Bkh.* 31 F43
Oving *W.S.* 12 F44
Ovingdean 13 F49
Ovingham 71 G36
Ovington *Nor.* 71 G36
Ovington *Nfk* 44 E55
Ovington *Drm* 62 E37
Ovington *Esx* 34 D53
Ovington *Ham.* 11 A41
Ower 10 C39
Owermoigne 9 F33
Owlswick 22 A43
Owmby 52 B46
Owmby by Spital 52 D46
Owslebury 11 B41
Owston 42 E43
Owston Ferry 51 B43
Owstwick 59 F48
Owthorpe 41 B42
Oxborough 44 E53
Oxcliffe Hill 55 C30
Oxcombe 53 E49
Oxen End 33 F52
Oxenholme 61 G31
Oxenhope 57 F36
Oxen Park 55 A28
Oxenton 29 E35
Oxenwood 21 F39
Oxford 21 A41
Oxhill 30 D39
Oxley 40 E34
Oxley Green 34 G55
Oxley's Green 13 D52
Oxnam 70 B32
Oxnead 45 C58
Oxnop Ghyll 61 G35
Oxshott 22 E47
Oxspring 50 B38
Oxted 23 F49
Oxton *Not.* 51 G42
Oxton *Mer.* 48 D28
Oxton *Bor.* 76 E30
Oxwich 17 F20
Oxwich Green 17 F21
Oxwick 44 C55
Oykel Bridge 96 A19
Oyne 91 A32
Ozleworth 20 B33

P

Packington 41 D39
Padanaram 82 B29
Padbury 31 E43
Paddington 23 C48
Paddlesworth 15 C57
Paddockhaugh 97 F27
Paddockhole 69 E28
Paddock Wood 23 G52
Paddolgreen 38 B30
Padeswood 48 F28
Padiham 56 F33
Padside 57 D37
Padstow 3 A15
Padworth 21 E42
Pagham 12 G44
Paglesham Churchend 25 B55
Paglesham Eastend 25 B55
Paibeil 92 E3
Paible 92 B6
Paignton 5 D24
Pailton 41 G40
Painscastle 28 D27
Painshawfield 71 G36
Painswick 20 A34
Paisley 74 D20
Pakefield 45 F61
Pakenham 34 B54
Pale 37 B25
Palestine 21 G38
Paley Street 22 D44
Palgowan 67 E19
Palgrave 34 A56
Pallinsburn House 77 G34
Palmerscross 97 E27
Palmerstown 18 E27
Palnackie 65 E24
Palnure 64 D20
Palterton 51 F40
Pamber End 21 F41
Pamber Green 21 F41
Pamber Heath 21 E42
Pamington 29 E35
Pamphill 9 D35
Pampisford 33 D50
Pan 105 B29
Panborough 19 G30
Panbride 83 D31
Pancrasweek 6 E19
Pandy *Clw.* 38 B27
Pandy *Pow.* 37 E25
Pandy *Gwy.* 37 E22
Pandy *Gwe.* 28 F29
Pandy Tudur 47 F24
Panfield 34 F53
Pangbourne 21 D42
Pannal 57 D38
Panpunton 28 A28
Pant *Shr.* 38 C28
Pant *Clw.* 38 A28
Pantasaph 47 E27
Pantglas 37 F23
Pant-glas 36 A20
Pant Gwyn 37 C24
Pantgwyn 26 D18
Pant-lasau 17 D22
Pant Mawr 37 G24
Panton 52 E47
Pant-pastynog 47 F26
Pantperthog 37 E23
Pant-y-dwr 27 A25
Pantyffordd 48 G28
Pant-y-ffridd 38 E27
Pantyffynnon 17 C22
Panxworth 45 D59
Papcastle 60 C26
Papple 76 C31
Papplewick 51 G41
Papworth Everard 33 B48
Papworth St Agnes 33 B48
Par 4 E16
Parbold 48 A30
Parbrook 8 A31
Parc 37 B24
Parcllyn 26 C18
Parcrhydderch 26 C21
Pardshaw 60 D26
Parham 35 B59
Parish Holm 68 A23
Park 98 D31
Park Corner 21 C42
Parkend *Glo.* 19 A31
Parkend *Cum.* 60 C28
Park End 70 F34
Parkeston 35 E58
Parkford 83 B30
Parkgate *Che.* 48 E28
Parkgate *S.Y.* 51 C40
Parkgate *Sry* 23 G48
Park Gate 11 D41
Parkham 6 C19
Parkham Ash 6 C19
Parkhill *Tay.* 82 C27

Parkhill *Tay.* 83 C32
Parkhouse 19 A30
Parkhurst 11 E40
Park Lane 38 B30
Parkmill 17 F21
Parkmore 98 E29
Parkneuk 91 F33
Parkstone 10 E36
Park Street 22 A47
Parley Cross 10 E36
Parracombe 6 A22
Parrog 16 A16
Parsonby 60 C27
Parson Drove 43 E49
Partick 74 D21
Partington 49 C33
Partney 53 F50
Parton *D.&G.* 65 D22
Parton *Cum.* 60 D25
Partridge Green 12 E47
Parwich 50 G37
Passenham 31 D43
Passfield 12 C44
Passingford Bridge 23 B50
Paston 45 B59
Patcham 13 F49
Patching 12 F46
Patchole 6 A21
Patchway 19 C31
Pateley Bridge 57 C37
Pathe 8 A29
Pathhead *Ltn* 76 D29
Pathhead *Fife* 76 A28
Pathhead *Grm.* 91 G33
Pathhead *Str.* 68 B22
Path of Condie 82 F26
Patmore Heath 33 F50
Patna 67 B19
Patney 20 F36
Patrick 54 E24
Patrick Brompton 62 G38
Patrington 59 G48
Patrishow 28 F28
Patrixbourne 15 B57
Patterdale 60 E29
Pattingham 40 F34
Pattishall 31 C42
Pattiswick 34 F53
Paul 2 F10
Paulerspury 31 D42
Paull 59 G47
Paulton 19 F32
Pauperhaugh 71 D36
Pavenham 32 C45
Pawlett 19 G28
Pawston 77 G34
Paxford 30 E37
Paxhill Park 13 D49
Paxton 77 E35
Payhembury 7 E26
Paynes Hall 33 G49
Paythorne 56 D34
Peacehaven 13 F49
Peacemarsh 9 B33
Peachley 29 C33
Peak Dale 50 E36
Peak Forest 50 E36
Peakirk 42 E47
Pean Hill 25 E56
Pearsie 82 B29
Peasedown St John 20 F33
Peasemore 21 D40
Peasenhall 35 B59
Pease Pottage 13 C48
Peaslake 22 G46
Peasmarsh 14 E54
Peaston 76 D30
Peastonbank 76 D30
Peathill 99 C35
Peat Inn 83 G30
Peatling Magna 41 F41
Peatling Parva 41 G41
Peaton 38 G31
Pebble Coombe 23 F48
Pebmarsh 34 E54
Pebworth 30 D37
Pecket Well 56 G35
Peckforton 48 G31
Peckleton 41 E40
Pedmore 40 G34
Pedwell 8 A30
Peebles 76 F28
Peel 54 E24
Pegswood 71 E38
Peighinn nan Aoireann 84 A2
Peinchorran 85 A10
Peinlich 93 F9
Pelaw 71 G38
Pelcomb Bridge 16 C15
Pelcomb Cross 16 C14
Peldon 34 G55
Pelsall 40 E36
Pelton 62 A38
Pelutho 60 B26
Pelynt 4 E18
Pembrey 17 D20
Pembridge 28 C29
Pembroke 16 D15
Pembroke Dock 16 D15
Pembury 23 G52
Penallt 28 G31
Penally 16 E17
Penalt 28 F31
Penare 3 E15
Penarth 18 D27
Pen-bont Rhydybeddau 37 G22
Penboyr 17 A19
Penbryn 26 C18
Pencader 17 A20
Pencaenewydd 36 A19
Pencaitland 76 D30
Pencarreg 26 D21
Pencelli 27 F26
Pen-clawdd 17 E21
Pencoed 18 C25
Pencombe 28 C31
Pencoyd 28 F31
Pencraig *H.&W.* 28 F31
Pencraig *Pow.* 37 C26
Pendeen 2 E9
Penderyn 18 A25
Pendine 17 D18
Pendlebury 49 B33
Pendleton 56 F33
Pendock 29 E33
Pendoggett 4 C16
Pendomer 8 C31
Pendoylan 18 D26
Penegoes 37 E23
Pen-ffordd 16 B16
Penffordd-Las (Staylittle) 37 F24
Pengam 18 B27
Penge 23 D49
Pengenffordd 28 E27
Pengorffwysfa 46 C20
Pengover Green 4 D18
Pen-groes-oped 19 A28
Pengwern 47 E25
Penhale 2 G12
Penhallow 2 C13
Penhalvean 2 E12
Penhow 19 B30
Penhurst 13 E52
Peniarth 36 E21
Penicuik 76 D28
Penifiler 93 G10
Peninver 66 A13
Penisarcwn 37 D26
Penisar Waun 46 F21
Penistone 50 B38
Penjerrick 2 E13
Penketh 48 D31
Penkill 67 D18
Penkridge 40 D34
Penley 38 A30
Penllech 36 B17
Penllergaer 17 E21
Penllyn 18 D25
Pen-llyn 46 D19
Penmachno 47 G23
Penmaen 17 F21
Penmaenmawr 46 E22
Penmaenpool 37 D22
Penmark 18 E26
Penmon 46 D22
Penmorfa 36 A21
Penmynydd 46 E20
Penn *W.M.* 40 F34
Penn *Bkh.* 22 B45
Pennal 37 E22
Pennan 99 C34
Pennance 2 D13
Pennant *Pow.* 37 F24
Pennant *Dyf.* 26 B21
Pennant Melangell 37 C26
Pennard 17 F21
Pennerley 38 F29
Penninghame 64 D19
Pennington 55 B28
Penn Street 22 B45
Pennsylvania 20 D33
Penny Bridge 55 A28
Pennyfuir 79 D14
Pennyghael 79 E10
Pennyglen 67 B18
Pennygown 79 C11
Pennymoor 7 D24
Penparc 26 D17
Penparcau 36 G21
Penparo 16 A14
Penperlleni 19 A29
Penpillick 4 E16
Penpol 2 E13
Penpoll 4 E17
Penpont *Pow.* 27 F25
Penpont *D.&G.* 68 D24
Penrherber 17 A18
Penrhiwceiber 18 B26
Penrhiwgoch 17 C21
Penrhiw-llan 26 D19
Penrhiw-pal 26 D19
Penrhos *Pow.* 27 G23
Penrhos *Gwy.* 36 B19
Penrhos *Gwy.* 46 D18
Penrhos *Gwe.* 28 G29
Penrhos-garnedd 46 E21
Penrhyn Bay 47 D23
Penrhyn-coch 37 G22
Penrhyndeudraeth 36 B21
Penrhyn-side 47 D23
Penrhys 18 B25
Penrice 17 F20
Penrith 61 C30
Penrose 3 A14
Penruddock 60 D29
Penryn 2 E13
Pensarn *Clw.* 47 E25
Pensarn *Dyf.* 17 C20
Pen-sarn *Gwy.* 36 C21
Pen-sarn *Gwy.* 36 A20
Pensax 29 B33
Pensby 48 D28
Penselwood 9 A33
Pensford 19 E31
Pensham 29 D35
Penshaw 62 A39
Penshurst 23 G51
Pensilva 4 C18
Pensnett 40 G34
Pentewan 4 F16
Pentir 46 F21
Pentire 2 B13
Pentireglaze 3 A15
Pentlepoir 16 D16
Pentlow 34 D53
Pentney 44 D53
Penton Mewsey 21 G39
Pentraeth 46 E21
Pentre *M.G.* 18 B25
Pentre *Pow.* 28 B28
Pentre *Pow.* 38 F28
Pentre *Clw.* 38 A28
Pentre *Pow.* 37 G26
Pentre *Pow.* 37 C26
Pentre *Shr.* 38 D29
Pentre-bach 27 E24
Pentrebach *M.G.* 18 A26
Pentrebach *W.G.* 17 D22
Pentre Berw 46 E20
Pentre-bont 47 G23
Pentre-bwlch 38 A27
Pentrecagal 26 D19
Pentre-celyn 37 E24
Pentre-celyn 47 G27
Pentre-chwyth 17 E22
Pentreclwydau 18 A24
Pentre-cwrt 17 A19
Pentre Dolau 27 D25
Pentredwr 38 A27
Pentre-Dwr 17 E22
Pentrefelin *Dyf.* 17 B21
Pentrefelin *Gwy.* 47 E24
Pentrefelin *Clw.* 38 C27
Pentrefelin *Gwy.* 36 B21
Pentrefelin *Dyf.* 27 D22
Pentrefoelas 47 G24
Pentre-galar 16 A17
Pentregat 26 C19
Pentre Gwenlais 17 C22
Pentre Gwynfryn 36 C21
Pentre Halkyn 47 E27
Pentreheyling 38 F28
Pentre Isaf 47 F24
Pentre Llanrhaeadr 47 F26
Pentre-llwyn-llwyd 27 C25
Pentre Maelor 38 A29
Pentre-piod 37 B24
Pentre-poeth 19 C28
Pentre'r beirdd 38 D27
Pentre'r-felin 27 E24
Pentre Saron 47 F26
Pentre-tafarn-y-fedw 47 F23
Pentre-ty-gwyn 27 E24
Pentrich 51 G39
Pentridge 10 C36
Pen-twyn 19 A31
Pentwyn 18 C27
Pentyrch 18 C26
Penuwch 26 B21
Penwithick 4 E16
Penwortham 55 G30
Penwyllt 27 G24
Pen-y-banc 17 B21
Pen-y-bont *Dyf.* 27 E23
Penybont 27 B26
Pen-y-bont *Clw.* 38 C27
Pen-y-bont *Pow.* 37 D26
Penybontfawr 37 C26
Pen-y-bryn 37 D22
Penybryn 18 B27
Penycae 38 A28
Pen-y-cae 27 G24
Pen-y-cae-mawr 19 B30
Pen-y-cefn 47 E27
Pen-y-clawdd 19 A30
Pen-y-coedcae 18 C26
Penycwm 16 B14
Pen-y-fai 18 C24
Penyffordd 48 F29
Pen-y-garn 17 A21
Penygarnedd 37 C26
Pen-y-garreg 27 D25
Penygraig 18 B25
Penygroes *Dyf.* 17 C21
Penygroes *Gwy.* 46 G20
Pen-y-Gwryd Hotel 46 G22
Pen-y-Park 28 D28
Pen-yr-hoel 28 G29
Penysarn 46 C20
Pen-y-stryt 47 G27
Penywaun 18 A25
Penzance 2 E10
Penzance Heliport 2 E10
Peopleton 29 C35
Peover Heath 49 E33
Peper Harow 22 G45
Peplow 39 C32
Perceton 74 F19
Percie 90 D31
Perham Down 21 G38
Perivale 22 C47
Perkhill 90 C31
Perkins Beach 38 E29
Perlethorpe 51 E42
Perranarworthal 2 E13
Perranporth 2 C13
Perranuthnoe 2 F11
Perranzabuloe 2 C13
Perry Barr 40 F36
Perry Green 33 G50
Perry Street 24 D52
Persey 82 B27
Pershall 40 C34
Pershore 29 D35
Pert 91 G32
Pertenhall 32 B46
Perth 82 E26
Perthy 38 B29
Perton 40 F34
Peterborough 42 F47
Peterburn 94 C13
Peterchurch 28 E29
Peterculter 91 C34
Peterhead 99 E37
Peterlee 62 B40
Petersfield 11 B43
Peter's Green 32 G47
Peters Marland 6 D20
Peterstone Wentlooge 19 D28
Peterston-super-Ely 18 D26
Peterstow 28 F31
Peter Tavy 5 C21
Petham 15 B57
Petrockstow 6 E21
Pett 14 F54
Pettaugh 35 C57
Pettinain 75 F25
Pettistree 35 C58
Petton *Shr.* 38 C30
Petton *Dev.* 7 C26
Petty 99 F33
Pettycur 76 B28
Pettymuick 91 A34
Petworth 12 D45
Pevensey 13 F52
Pevensey Bay 13 F52
Pewsey 20 E37
Phesdo 91 F32
Philham 6 C18
Philiphaugh 69 A30
Phillack 2 E11
Philleigh 3 E14
Philpstoun 75 C26
Phoenix Green 22 F43
Phones 88 E22
Phorp 97 F26
Piabil Iarach 101 D11
Piabil Uarach 101 D11
Pibsbury 8 B30
Pica 60 D26
Piccadilly Corner 45 G58
Piccotts End 22 A46
Pickerells 23 A51
Pickering 58 A43
Picket Piece 21 G39
Picket Post 10 D37
Pickford Green 40 G38
Pickhill 57 A39
Picklescott 38 F30
Pickletillem 83 E30
Pickmere 49 E32
Pickstock 39 C33
Pickston 82 E25
Pickwell *Lei.* 42 D43
Pickwell *Dev.* 6 A20
Pickworth *Lei.* 42 D45
Pickworth *Lcn.* 42 B46
Picton *N.Y.* 62 F39
Picton *Che.* 48 E30
Piddinghoe 13 F50
Piddington *Oxf.* 31 G42
Piddington *Nmp.* 31 C43
Piddlehinton 9 E32
Piddletrenthide 9 E32
Pidley 33 A49
Piercebridge 62 E37
Pierowall 104 B30
Pigdon 71 E37
Pikehall 50 G37
Pilgrims Hatch 23 B51
Pilham 52 C44
Pill 19 D31
Pillaton 4 D19
Pillerton Hersey 30 D38
Pillerton Priors 30 D38
Pilleth 28 B28
Pilley *Glo.* 29 G35
Pilley *S.Y.* 51 B39
Pilley *Ham.* 10 E39
Pilling 55 E29
Pilling Lane 55 E29
Pillowell 19 A32
Pilning 19 C31
Pilsbury 50 F37
Pilsdon 8 E30
Pilsgate 42 E46
Pilsley *Dby.* 51 F40
Pilsley *Dby.* 50 E38
Piltdown 13 D50
Pilton *Nmp.* 42 G46
Pilton *Lei.* 42 E45
Pilton *Som.* 19 G31
Pilton *Dev.* 6 B21
Pimperne 9 D34
Pinchbeck 43 C48
Pinchbeck Bars 42 C47
Pinchbeck West 43 C48
Pinchinthorpe 63 E41
Pinfold 48 A29
Pinhay 8 E29
Pinhoe 7 F25
Pinkneys Green 22 C44
Pinley Green 30 B37
Pinminnoch 67 D17
Pinmore 67 D17
Pinn 7 G26
Pinner 22 C47
Pinner Green 22 B47
Pinvin 29 D35
Pinwherry 67 E17
Pinxton 51 G40
Pipe and Lyde 28 D30
Pipe Gate 39 A33
Piperhall 73 E17
Piperhill 97 F24
Pipe Ridware 40 D36
Piper's Pool 4 B18
Pipewell 42 G44
Pippacott 6 B20
Pipton 28 E27
Pirbright 22 F45
Pirnmill 73 F14
Pirton *H.&W.* 29 D34
Pirton *Hfs.* 32 E47
Pisgah 81 G23
Pishill 22 C43
Pistyll 36 A19
Pitagowan 81 A24
Pitblae 99 C35
Pitcairngreen 82 E26
Pitcairns 82 F26
Pitcaple 91 A33
Pitchcombe 20 A34
Pitchcott 31 G43
Pitchford 38 E31
Pitch Green 22 A43
Pitch Place 22 F45
Pitcombe 9 A32
Pitcot 18 D25
Pitcox 76 C32
Pitcur 82 D28
Pitfichie 91 B32
Pitgrudy 96 B23
Pitinnan 99 F33
Pitkennedy 83 B31
Pitkevy 82 G28
Pitlessie 82 G29
Pitlochry 82 B25
Pitmedden 91 A34
Pitminster 7 D27
Pitmuies 83 C31
Pitmunie 91 B32
Pitnacree 82 B25
Pitney 8 B30
Pitroddie 82 E27
Pitscottie 83 F30
Pitsea 24 C53
Pitsford 31 B43
Pitsford Hill 7 B26
Pitstone 32 G45
Pitstone Green 32 G45
Pitt *Dev.* 7 D26
Pitt *Ham.* 11 B40
Pittendreich 97 E27
Pittentrail 96 A23
Pittenweem 83 G31
Pittington 62 B39
Pittodrie Ho. 91 A32
Pitton 10 A37
Pity Me 62 B38

Pityme 3 A15
Pixey Green 35 A58
Place Newton 58 B44
Plaidy 99 D33
Plains 75 D23
Plaish 38 F31
Plaistow 12 C45
Plaitford 10 C38
Plas 17 B20
Plas Gogerddan 37 G22
Plas Gwynant 46 G22
Plasisaf 47 F25
Plas Isaf 37 A26
Plas Llwyd 47 E25
Plas Llwyngwern 37 E23
Plas Llysyn 37 F25
Plas Nantyr 38 B27
Plas-rhiw-Saeson 37 E24
Plastow Green 21 E41
Plas-yn-Cefn 47 E25
Platt 23 F52
Platt Lane 38 B31
Plawsworth 62 B38
Plaxtol 23 F51
Playden 14 E55
Playford 35 D57
Play Hatch 22 D43
Playing Place 3 D14
Plealey 38 E30
Plean 75 B24
Pleasance 82 F28
Pleasington 56 G32
Pleasley 51 F40
Plenmeller 70 G32
Pleshey 33 G52
Plockton 86 A13
Ploughfield 28 D29
Plowden 38 G29
Ploxgreen 38 E29
Pluckley 14 C55
Pluckley Thorne 14 C55
Plumbland 60 C27
Plumley 49 E33
Plumpton *Cum.* 61 C30
Plumpton *E.S.* 13 E49
Plumpton End 31 D42
Plumpton Green 13 E49
Plumpton Head 61 C31
Plumstead *Nfk* 45 B57
Plumstead *G.L.* 23 D50
Plumtree 41 B41
Plungar 42 B43
Plush 9 D33
Plwmp 26 C19
Plym Bridge 5 E21
Plymouth 5 E21
Plympton 5 E21
Plymstock 5 E21
Plymtree 7 E26
Pockley 58 A42
Pocklington 58 E44
Pocombe Bridge 7 F24
Pode Hole 43 C48
Podimore 8 B31
Podington 32 B45
Podmore 39 B33
Poffley End 30 G39
Pointon 42 B47
Pokesdown 10 E37
Polanach 80 B15
Polapit Tamar 4 B18
Polbae 64 C18
Polbain 101 G15
Polbathic 4 E19
Polbeth 75 D26
Polchar 89 D24
Poldean 69 D26
Polebrook 42 G46
Polegate 13 F51
Pole Moor 50 A36
Poles 96 B23
Polesworth 40 E38
Polglass 95 A16
Polgooth 3 C15
Polgown 68 C22
Poling 12 F46
Poling Corner 12 F46
Polkerris 4 E16
Polla 101 C19
Poll A Charra 84 C3
Polldubh 80 A17
Pollie 102 G23
Pollington 51 A42
Polloch 79 A13
Pollokshaws 74 D21
Polmassick 3 D15
Polmont 75 C25
Polnoon 74 E21
Polperro 4 E18
Polruan 4 E17
Polsham 19 G30
Polstead 34 E55
Poltalloch 73 A13
Poltimore 7 F25
Polton 76 D28
Polwarth 77 E33
Polyphant 4 B18
Polzeath 3 A15
Pondersbridge 43 F48
Ponders End 23 B49
Pond Street 33 E50
Ponsanooth 2 E13
Ponsonby 60 F26
Ponsworthy 5 C23
Pont Aber 27 F23
Pont Aber Glaslyn 36 A21
Pontamman 17 C22
Pontantwn 17 C20
Pontardawe 17 D22
Pontardulais 17 D21
Pontargothi 17 B20
Pontarsais 17 B20
Pontblyddyn 48 F28
Pontbren llwyd 18 A25
Pont Ceri 26 D18
Pont Crugnant 37 F24
Pont Cyfyng 47 G23
Pont Dolgarrog 47 F23
Pontefract 57 G40
Ponteland 71 F37
Ponterwyd 37 G23
Pontesbury 38 E29
Pontesford 38 E29
Pontfadog 38 B28
Pont-faen 27 E25
Pontfaen 16 A16
Pont-Henri 17 D20
Ponthir 19 B29
Ponthirwaun 26 D18
Pontllanfraith 18 B27
Pontlliw 17 D21
Pontllyfni 46 G20
Pontlottyn 18 A26
Pont Nedd Fechan 18 A24
Pontnewydd 19 B28
Pontnewynydd 19 A28
Pont Pen-y-benglog 46 G22
Pontrhydfendigaid 27 B22
Pont Rhyd-sarn 37 C24
Pont Rhyd-y-cyff 18 C24
Pont-rhyd-y-fen 18 B23
Pont-rhyd-y-groes 27 A23
Pontrhydyrun 19 B28
Pontrilas 28 F29
Pontrobert 38 D27
Pont-rug 46 F20
Ponts Green 13 E52
Pontshaen 26 D20
Pontshill 29 F32
Pontsticill 27 G26
Pont Walby 18 A24
Pontwelly 17 A19
Pontyates 17 D20
Pontyberem 17 C20
Pontybodkin 48 G28
Pontyclun 18 C26
Pontycymer 18 B24
Pont y gwaith 18 B25
Pontymister 19 B28
Pont-y-pant 47 G23
Pontypool 19 A28
Pontypridd 18 B26
Pont yr Alwen 47 G25
Pontywaun 18 B27
Pooksgreen 10 C39
Pool *W.Y.* 57 E38
Pool *Cnw.* 2 D12
Pool Bank 55 A30
Poole 9 E35
Poole Keynes 20 B35
Poolewe 94 C14
Pooley Bridge 61 D30
Poolhill 29 F33
Pool of Muckhart 82 G26
Pool Quay 38 D28
Pool Street 34 E53
Pope Hill 16 C15
Popeswood 22 E44
Popham 21 G41
Poplar 23 C49
Porchfield 11 E40
Porin 96 F19
Porkellis 2 E12
Porlock 7 A24
Porlock Weir 7 A24
Portachoillan 73 E13
Port Allen 82 E28
Port Appin 79 C14
Port Askaig 72 D10
Portavadie 73 D15
Port Bannatyne 73 D16
Portbury 19 D30
Port Carlisle 69 G28
Port Charlotte 72 E8
Portchester 11 D41
Port Clarence 62 D40
Port Driseach 73 C15
Port Ellen 72 F9
Port Elphinstone 91 B33
Portencross 73 F17
Port Erin 54 G23
Port Erroll 99 F37
Portesham 9 F32
Portessie 98 C30
Port e Vullen 54 D26
Port Eynon 17 F20
Portfield 79 E13
Portfield Gate 16 C15
Portgate 6 G19
Port Gaverne 4 B16
Port Glasgow 74 C19
Portgordon 98 C29
Portgower 103 G25
Porth *M.G.* 18 B26
Porth *Cnw.* 3 B14
Porthallow *Cnw.* 4 E18
Porthallow *Cnw.* 2 F13
Porthcawl 18 D23
Porth Colmon 36 B17
Porthcothan 3 A14
Porthcurno 2 F9
Port Henderson 94 D13
Porthgain 16 A13
Porthkerry 18 E26
Porthleven 2 F11
Porthmadog 36 B21
Porth Mellin 2 G12
Porthmeor 2 E9
Porth Navas 2 F13
Portholland 3 D15
Porthoustock 3 F14
Porthpean 4 E16
Porthtowan 2 D12
Porthyrhyd *Dyf.* 17 C21
Porthyrhyd *Dyf.* 17 A22
Porth-y-waen 38 C28
Portincaple 73 A17
Portington 58 F43
Portinnisherrich 80 F15
Portinscale 60 D28
Port Isaac 3 A15
Portishead 19 D30
Portknockie 98 C30
Portlethen 91 D35
Portloe 3 E15
Port Logan 64 F16
Portmahomack 97 C24
Portmeirion 36 B21
Port Mor 85 G10
Portmore 10 E39
Port Mulgrave 63 E43
Port na Craig 82 B25
Portnacroish 80 C15
Portnahaven 72 E8
Portnalong 85 A9
Portnaluchaig 86 F12
Portnancon 102 B20
Port Nan Giuran 101 D11
Port Nan Long 92 D4
Port Nis 101 A11
Portobello 76 C28
Port of Menteith 81 G21
Porton 10 A37
Port o' Warren 65 E24
Port Penrhyn 46 E21
Portquin 3 A15
Port Ramsay 79 C14
Portreath 2 D12
Portree 93 G10
Portscatho 3 E14
Portsea 11 D42
Portskerra 102 B24
Portskewett 19 C30
Portslade 13 F48
Portslade-by-Sea 13 F48
Portsmouth 11 E42
Portsoy 98 C31
Port St Mary 54 G24
Port Sunlight 48 D29
Portswood 11 C40
Port Talbot 18 C23
Portuairk 79 A10
Portway *War.* 30 A36
Portway *H.&W.* 28 D29
Port Wemyss 72 E8
Port William 64 F19
Portwrinkle 4 E19
Portyerrock 64 G20
Poslingford 34 D53
Postbridge 5 C22
Postcombe 22 B43
Postling 15 D57
Postwick 45 E58
Potarch 90 D31
Potsgrove 32 F45
Potten End 22 A46
Potterhanworth 52 F46
Potterhanworth Booths 52 F46
Potter Heigham 45 C60
Potterne 20 F35
Potterne Wick 20 F35
Potters Bar 23 A48
Potter's Cross 40 G34
Potters Crouch 22 A47
Potterspury 31 D43
Potter Street 23 A50
Potterton 91 B35
Potto 62 F40
Potton 33 D48
Pott Row 44 C53
Pott Shrigley 49 E35
Poughill *Cnw.* 6 E18
Poughill *Dev.* 7 E24
Poulner 10 D37
Poulshot 20 E35
Poulton 20 A36
Poulton-le-Fylde 55 F29
Pound Bank 29 A33
Poundffald 17 E21
Poundgate 13 D50
Pound Green 13 D51
Pound Hill 13 C48
Poundland 67 E17
Poundon 31 F42
Poundsbridge 23 G51
Poundsgate 5 C23
Poundstock 4 A17
Povey Cross 23 G48
Powburn 71 B36
Powderham 7 G25
Powerstock 8 E31
Powfoot 69 G27
Pow Green 29 D32
Powick 29 C34
Powler's Piece 6 D19
Powmill 75 A26
Poxwell 9 F33
Poyle 22 D46
Poynings 13 E48
Poyntington 9 C32
Poynton *Che.* 49 D35
Poynton *Shr.* 38 D31
Poynton Green 38 D31
Poyntzfield 96 E22
Poys Street 35 A59
Poyston Cross 16 C15
Poystreet Green 34 C55
Praa Sands 2 F11
Pratis 82 G29
Pratt's Bottom 23 E50
Praze-an-Beeble 2 E12
Predannack Wollas 2 G11
Prees 38 B31
Preesall 55 E29
Prees Green 38 B31
Preesgweene 38 B28
Prees Higher Heath 38 B31
Prenbrigog 48 F28
Prendergast 16 C15
Prendwick 70 B35
Pren-gwyn 26 D20
Prenteg 36 A21
Prenton 48 D28
Prescot 48 C30
Prescott 38 C30
Presley 97 F25
Pressen 77 G34
Prestatyn 47 D26
Prestbury *Che.* 49 E35
Prestbury *Glo.* 29 F35
Presteigne 28 B28
Presthope 38 F31
Prestleigh 19 G32
Prestolee 49 B33
Preston *H.&W.* 29 E32
Preston *Kent* 25 E58
Preston *Kent* 25 E56
Preston *T.&W.* 71 G39
Preston *Sfk* 34 C55
Preston *Hfs.* 32 F47
Preston *Bor.* 77 E33
Preston *Wts.* 20 D36
Preston *Ltn* 76 C31
Preston *Nor.* 71 A37
Preston *Hum.* 59 F47
Preston *Lan.* 55 G31
Preston *Glo.* 20 A36
Preston *Dev.* 9 F33
Preston *E.S.* 13 F49
Preston *Dev.* 5 C24
Preston *Lei.* 42 E44
Preston Bagot 30 B37
Preston Bissett 31 F42
Preston Brockhurst 38 C31
Preston Brook 48 D31
Preston Candover 21 G41
Preston Capes 31 C41
Preston Deanery 31 C43
Preston Gubbals 38 D30
Preston on Stour 30 D37
Preston on the Hill 48 D31
Preston on Wye 28 D29
Prestonpans 76 C29
Preston Plucknett 8 C31
Preston-under-Scar 62 G36
Preston upon the Weald Moors 39 D32
Preston Wynne 28 D31
Prestwich 49 B33
Prestwick *Str.* 67 A19
Prestwick *T.&W.* 71 F37
Prestwick Airport 67 A19
Prestwold 41 C41
Prestwood 22 A44
Price Town 18 B25
Prickwillow 43 G51
Priddy 19 F31
Priest Hill 55 F31
Priest Hutton 55 B31
Priestland 74 G21
Priestweston 38 F28
Primethorpe 41 F40
Primrose Green 44 D56
Princes End 40 F35
Princes Gate 16 C17
Princes Risborough 22 A43
Princethorpe 30 A39
Princetown *M.G.* 27 G26
Princetown *Dev.* 5 C21
Prior Muir 83 F31
Prior's Frome 28 E31
Priors Hardwick 31 C40
Priors Marston 31 C40
Priory Wood 28 D28
Priston 19 E32
Prittlewell 24 C54
Privett 11 B42
Prixford 6 B21
Proaig 72 E10
Probus 3 D14
Protsonhill 99 C33
Prudhoe 71 G36
Pubil 81 C20
Publow 19 E32
Puckeridge 33 F49
Puckington 8 C29
Pucklechurch 19 D32
Puddinglake 49 E32
Puddington *Dev.* 7 D23
Puddington *Che.* 48 E28
Puddlebrook 29 G32
Puddledock 44 F56
Puddletown 9 E33
Pudleston 28 C31
Pudsey 57 F38
Pulborough 12 E46
Puldagon 103 D28
Puleston 39 C33
Pulford 48 G29
Pulham 9 D32
Pulham Market 45 G57
Pulham St Mary 45 G58
Pulloxhill 32 E46
Pulrossie 96 C23
Pulverbatch 38 E30
Pumpherston 75 D26
Pumsaint 27 D22
Puncheston 16 B15
Puncknowle 8 F31
Punnett's Town 13 D52
Purbrook 11 D42
Purfleet 23 D51
Puriton 19 G29
Purleigh 24 A54
Purley 23 E49
Purley on Thames 21 D42
Purlogue 28 A28
Purls Bridge 43 G50
Purse Caundle 9 C32
Purslow 38 G29
Purston Jaglin 57 G40
Purton *Wts.* 20 C36
Purton *Glo.* 19 A32
Purton Stoke 20 B36
Purves Hall 77 F33
Pury End 31 D43
Pusey 21 B39
Putley 29 E32
Putloe 20 A33
Putney 23 D48
Puttenham *Sry* 22 G45
Puttenham *Hfs.* 32 G44
Puttock End 34 D53
Putts Corner 7 F27
Puxton 19 E29
Pwll 17 D20
Pwllcrochan 16 D14
Pwlldefaid 36 C17
Pwllgloyw 27 E26
Pwllheli 36 B19
Pwllmeyric 19 B30
Pwll Trap 17 C18
Pwll-y-glaw 18 B23
Pyecombe 13 E48
Pye Corner *Gwe.* 19 C29
Pye Corner *Hfs.* 33 G50
Pye Green 40 D35
Pyle *M.G.* 18 C24
Pyle *I.o.W.* 11 G40
Pylle 8 A31
Pymore 43 G50
Pyrford 22 F46
Pyrton 21 B42
Pytchley 32 A44
Pyworthy 6 E19

Q

Quabbs 38 G27
Quadring 43 B48

Quadring Eaudike 43 B48
Quainton 31 G43
Quarley 21 G38
Quarndon 41 A39
Quarr Hill 11 E41
Quarrier's Village 74 D19
Quarrington 42 A46
Quarrington Hill 62 C39
Quarry Bank 40 G35
Quarrybank 48 F31
Quarrywood 97 E27
Quarter 75 E23
Quatford 39 F33
Quatt 39 G33
Quebec 62 B37
Quedgeley 29 G33
Queen Adelaide 43 G51
Queenborough 24 D54
Queen Camel 8 B31
Queen Charlton 19 E32
Queensbury 57 F36
Queensferry 48 F29
Queen's Head 38 C29
Queen Street 23 G52
Queenzieburn 74 C22
Quemerford 20 D35
Quendale 107 E37
Quendon 33 E50
Queniborough 41 D42
Quenington 20 A37
Quernmore 55 C31
Queslett 40 F36
Quethiock 4 D19
Quholm 104 E28
Quidenham 44 G56
Quidhampton *Wts.* 10 A37
Quidhampton *Ham.* 21 F40
Quilquox 99 F34
Quina Brook 38 B31
Quindry 105 B30
Quine's Hill 54 F25
Quinhill 73 E13
Quinton *Nmp.* 31 C43
Quinton *W.M.* 40 G35
Quintrell Downs 3 C14
Quoditch 6 F19
Quoig 81 E24
Quoigs 81 G24
Quorn 41 D41
Quothquan 75 G25
Quoyloo 104 D28
Quoys 106 A42
Quoys of Reiss 103 C29

R

Raby 48 E29
Rachub 46 F22
Rackenford 7 D24
Rackham 12 E46
Rackheath 45 D58
Racks 69 F26
Rackwick *Ork.* 105 B28
Rackwick *Ork.* 104 A30
Radbourne 40 B38
Radcliffe *Nor.* 71 C38
Radcliffe *G.M.* 49 B33
Radcliffe on Trent 41 B42
Radclive 31 E42
Radcot 21 B38
Radford *Oxf.* 31 F40
Radford *W.M.* 41 G39
Radford Semele 30 B39
Radipole 9 F32
Radlett 22 A47
Radley 21 B41
Radstock 19 F32
Radstone 31 D41
Radway 30 D39
Radway Green 49 G33
Radwell *Bfd.* 32 C46
Radwell *Hfs.* 33 E48
Radwinter 33 E51
Radyr 18 C27
Raechester 70 E35
Raemoir Ho. 91 D32
Raffin 101 E16
Rafford 97 F26
Ragdale 41 C42
Raglan 19 A29
Ragnall 51 E43
Rahoy 79 B12
Rainford 48 B30
Rainham *Kent* 24 E54
Rainham *Esx* 23 C51
Rainhill 48 C30
Rainhill Stoops 48 C30
Rainow 49 E35
Rainton 57 B39
Rainworth 51 G41
Raisbeck 61 F32
Raise 61 B33
Rait 82 E28
Raithby *Lcn.* 53 F49
Raithby *Lcn.* 53 D48
Rake 12 D44
Raleigh's Cross 7 B26
Ram 26 D21
Ramasaig 93 G7
Rame *Cnw.* 2 E13
Rame *Cnw.* 4 F20
Ram Lane 14 C55
Rampisham 8 D31
Rampside 55 C28
Rampton *Not.* 51 E43
Rampton *Cbs.* 33 B50
Ramsbottom 49 A33
Ramsbury 21 D38
Ramscraigs 103 F27
Ramsdean 11 B43
Ramsdell 21 F41
Ramsden 30 G39
Ramsden Bellhouse 24 B53
Ramsden Heath 24 B52
Ramsey *Esx* 35 F57
Ramsey *I.o.M.* 54 D26
Ramsey *Cbs.* 43 G48
Ramsey Forty Foot 43 G49
Ramsey Heights 43 G48
Ramsey Island 25 A55
Ramsey Mereside 43 G48
Ramsey St Mary's 43 G48
Ramsgate 25 E59
Ramsgate Street 45 B57
Ramsgill 57 B36
Ramsholt 35 D59
Ramshorn 40 A36
Ramsnest Common 12 C45
Ranachan 79 A13
Ranby *Lcn.* 53 E48
Ranby *Not.* 51 D42
Rand 52 E47
Randwick 20 A34
Rangemore 40 C37
Rangeworthy 19 C32
Rankinston 67 B20
Rank's Green 34 G53
Rannoch School 81 B21
Ranochan 86 F14
Ranskill 51 D42
Ranton 40 C34
Ranworth 45 D59
Rapness 104 B30
Rascarrel 65 F23
Raskelf 57 B40
Rassau 28 G27
Rastrick 57 G37
Ratby 41 E40
Ratcliffe Culey 41 F39
Ratcliffe on Soar 41 C40
Ratcliffe on the Wreake 41 D42
Ratford Bridge 16 C15
Rathen 99 C35
Rathillet 82 E29
Rathliesbeag 87 F17
Rathmell 56 C33
Ratho 75 C27
Ratho Station 75 C27
Rathven 98 C30
Ratley 30 D39
Ratlinghope 38 F29
Rattar 103 A28
Ratten Row 55 E30
Rattery 5 D23
Rattlesden 34 C55
Rattray 82 C27
Raughton Head 60 B29
Raunds 32 A45
Ravenfield 51 C40
Ravenglass 60 G26
Raveningham 45 F59
Ravenscar 63 F45
Ravensdale 54 D25
Ravensden 32 C46
Ravenshaw 56 E35
Ravenshayes 7 E25
Ravenshead 51 G41
Ravensmoor 49 G32
Ravensthorpe *W.Y.* 50 A38
Ravensthorpe *Nmp.* 31 A42
Ravenstone *Bkh.* 32 C44
Ravenstone *Lei.* 41 D39
Ravenstonedale 61 F32
Ravenstruther 75 F24
Ravensworth 62 F37
Raw 63 F45
Rawcliffe *Hum.* 58 G42
Rawcliffe *N.Y.* 58 D41
Rawcliffe Bridge 58 G42
Rawdon 57 F38
Rawmarsh 51 C40
Rawreth 24 B53
Rawridge 7 E27
Rawtenstall 56 G34
Rawyards 75 D23
Raxton 99 F34
Raydon 34 E56
Raylees 70 D35
Rayleigh 24 B54
Raymond's Hill 8 E29
Rayne 34 F53
Reach 33 B51
Read 56 F33
Reading 21 D42
Reading Street 14 E55
Reagill 61 E31
Rearquhar 96 B23
Rearsby 41 D42
Rease Heath 49 G32
Reaster 103 B28
Reaveley 70 B35
Reawick 107 C39
Reay 103 B25
Reculver 25 E58
Redberth 16 D16
Redbourn 32 G46
Redbourne 52 B45
Redbridge 23 C50
Redbrook 19 A31
Redbrook Street 14 D55
Redburn *Hgh.* 96 E21
Redburn *Hgh.* 97 G25
Redcar 63 D42
Redcastle *Hgh.* 96 G21
Redcastle *Tay.* 83 C32
Redcliff Bay 19 D30
Redcloak 91 E34
Red Dial 60 B28
Reddish 49 C34
Redditch 30 B36
Rede 34 C53
Redenhall 45 G58
Redesmouth 70 E34
Redford *Tay.* 83 C31
Redford *Grm.* 91 G33
Redford *W.S.* 12 D44
Redgrave 34 A56
Redheugh 83 A30
Redhill *Grm.* 91 C33
Redhill *Grm.* 98 E31
Redhill *Grm.* 98 F32
Redhill *Avon* 19 E30
Red Hill *War.* 30 C37
Redhill *Shr.* 39 D33
Redhill *Not.* 41 A41
Red Hill *Ham.* 11 C43
Redhill *Sry* 23 F48
Redhill Aerodrome & Heliport 23 G48
Redhouse *Grm.* 90 A31
Redhouse *Str.* 73 D14
Redhouses 72 D9
Redisham 45 G60
Redland *Avon* 19 D31
Redland *Ork.* 104 D29
Redlingfield 35 A57
Red Lodge 33 A52
Redlynch *Som.* 9 A32
Redlynch *Wts.* 10 B38
Redmarley D'Abitot 29 E33
Redmarshall 62 D39
Redmile 42 B43
Redmire 62 G36
Redmoor 4 D16
Rednal *W.M.* 29 A35
Rednal *Shr.* 38 C29
Red Oaks Hill 33 D51
Redpath 76 G31
Redpoint 94 E13
Red Post *Cnw.* 6 E18
Red Post *Dev.* 5 D24
Red Rock 48 A31
Red Roses 16 C17
Red Row 71 D38
Redruth 2 D13
Redscarhead 76 F28
Redshaw 68 A24
Redstone Bank 16 C16
Red Street 49 G34
Red Wharf Bay 46 D20
Redwick *Gwe.* 19 C30
Redwick *Avon* 19 C31
Redworth 62 D38
Reed 33 E49
Reedham 45 E60
Reedness 58 G43
Reepham *Nfk* 44 C56
Reepham *Lcn.* 52 E46
Reeth 62 G36
Regaby 54 D26
Regil 19 E31
Regoul 97 F24
Reiff 101 G15
Reigate 23 G48
Reighton 59 B47
Reinigeadal 100 G8
Reisgill 103 E28
Reiss 103 C29
Rejerrah 3 C14
Relubbus 2 E11
Relugas 97 G25
Remenham 22 C43
Remenham Hill 22 C43
Remony 81 C23
Rempstone 41 C41
Rendcomb 29 G35
Rendham 35 B59
Rendlesham 35 C59
Renfrew 74 D20
Renhold 32 C46
Renishaw 51 E40
Rennington 71 B37
Renton 74 C19
Renwick 61 B31
Repps 45 D60
Repton 40 C38
Rescobie 83 B30
Resipole 79 A13
Resolis 96 E22
Resolven 18 A24
Resourie 86 G14
Reston 77 D34
Reswallie 83 B30
Retew 3 C15
Retford (East Retford) 51 D42
Rettendon 24 B53
Rettendon Place 24 B53
Retyn 3 C14
Revesby 53 F49
Rew 5 C23
Rewe 7 F25
Reydon 35 A60
Reymerston 44 E55
Reynalton 16 D16
Reynoldston 17 F20
Rezare 4 C19
Rhandirmwyn 27 D23
Rhaoine 96 A22
Rhayader 27 B25
Rhedyn 36 B18
Rhegreanoch 101 G16
Rheindown 96 G21
Rhelonie 96 B21
Rhemore 79 B11
Rhes-y-cae 47 F27
Rhewl *Clw.* 47 F27
Rhewl *Shr.* 38 B29
Rhewl *Clw.* 38 A27
Rhian 102 G21
Rhicarn 101 F16
Rhiconich 101 C18
Rhicullen 96 D22
Rhidorroch 95 B17
Rhifail 102 D23
Rhigos 18 A25
Rhilochan 96 A23
Rhinduie 96 G21
Rhireavach 95 B16
Rhiroy 95 C17
Rhiw 36 C18
Rhiwargor 37 C25
Rhiwbryfdir 37 A22
Rhiwderin 19 C28
Rhiwlas *Gwy.* 46 F21
Rhiwlas *Clw.* 38 B27
Rhiwlas *Gwy.* 37 B25
Rhodesia 51 E41
Rhodes Minnis 15 C57
Rhodiad 16 B13
Rhodmad 26 A21
Rhonadale 73 G13
Rhonehouse or Kelton Hill 65 E23
Rhoose 18 E26
Rhos *Dyf.* 17 A19
Rhos *W.G.* 18 A23
Rhos-berse 48 G28
Rhoscolyn 46 E18
Rhoscrowther 16 D15
Rhos-ddu 48 G29
Rhosesmor 47 F27
Rhos-fawr 36 B19
Rhosgadfan 46 G20
Rhosgoch *Gwy.* 46 D20
Rhosgoch *Pow.* 28 D27
Rhos Hill 26 D17
Rhoshirwaun 36 C17
Rhoslan 36 A20
Rhoslefain 36 E21
Rhosllanerchrugog 38 A28
Rhosmaen 17 B22
Rhosmeirch 46 E20
Rhosneigr 46 E18
Rhosnesni 48 G29
Rhos-on-Sea 47 D24
Rhossili 17 F19
Rhosson 16 B13
Rhostryfan 46 G20
Rhostyllen 38 A29
Rhosybol 46 D20
Rhos-y-brwyner 48 F29
Rhos-y-garth 27 A22
Rhos-y-gwaliau 37 B25
Rhos-y-llan 36 B18
Rhos-y-mawn 47 F24
Rhos-y-Meirch 28 B28
Rhu 74 B18
Rhuallt 47 E26
Rhubodach 73 C15
Rhuddlan 47 E26
Rhue 95 B16
Rhulen 28 C27
Rhumach 86 F12
Rhunahaorine 72 F12
Rhyd *Pow.* 37 E25
Rhyd *Gwy.* 37 A22
Rhydargaeau 17 B20
Rhydcymerau 17 A21
Rhydd 29 D34
Rhyd-Ddu 46 G21
Rhydding 18 B23
Rhydlanfair 47 G24
Rhydlewis 26 D19
Rhydlios 36 C17
Rhydlydan *Pow.* 37 F26
Rhydlydan *Clw.* 47 G24
Rhydolion 36 C18
Rhydowen 26 D20
Rhyd-rosser 26 B21
Rhydspence 28 D28
Rhydtalog 48 G28
Rhyd-uchaf 37 B24
Rhydwyn 46 D18
Rhyd-y-clafdy 36 B18
Rhydycroesau 38 B28
Rhydyfelin *M.G.* 18 C26
Rhydyfelin *Dyf.* 26 A21
Rhyd-y-foel 47 E24
Rhyd-y-fro 17 D22
Rhydymain 37 C23
Rhyd-y-meirch 19 A28
Rhydymwyn 48 F28
Rhyd-yr-onnen 36 E21
Rhydywrach 16 B17
Rhyl 47 D25
Rhymney 18 A26
Rhyn 38 B29
Rhynd 82 E27
Rhynie *Grm.* 90 A30
Rhynie *Hgh.* 97 D24
Ribbesford 29 A33
Ribbleton 55 F31
Ribchester 56 F32
Ribigill 102 C21
Riby 52 B47
Riccall 58 F42
Riccarton 74 G19
Richard's Castle 28 B30
Richings Park 22 D46
Richmond 62 F37
Richmond upon Thames 22 D47
Rickarton 91 E33
Rickford 19 F30
Rickinghall 34 A56
Rickling 33 E50
Rickling Green 33 F50
Rickmansworth 22 B46
Riddell 69 A30
Riddings 51 G40
Riddlecombe 6 D21
Riddlesden 57 E36
Ridge *Wts.* 9 A35
Ridge *Dor.* 9 F35
Ridge *Hfs.* 23 A48
Ridgebourne 27 C26
Ridge Green 23 G48
Ridge Lane 40 F38
Ridgeway 51 D39
Ridgeway Cross 29 D33
Ridgewell 34 D53
Ridgewood 13 E50
Ridgmont 32 E45
Riding Mill 71 G36
Ridley 24 E52
Ridleywood 48 G29
Ridlington *Nfk* 45 B59
Ridlington *Lei.* 42 E44
Ridsdale 70 E34
Riechip 82 C26
Rievaulx 58 A41
Rigg *D.&G.* 69 G28
Rigg *Hgh.* 94 F11
Riggend 75 D23
Rigmaden Park 56 A32
Rigsby 53 E50
Rigside 75 G24
Rileyhill 40 D37
Rilla Mill 4 C18
Rillington 58 B44
Rimington 56 E33
Rimpton 8 B31
Rimswell 59 G49
Rinaston 16 B15
Ringford 65 E22
Ringland 45 D57
Ringles Cross 13 D50
Ringmer 13 E50
Ringmore 5 F22
Ringorm 98 E28
Ring's End 43 E50
Ringsfield 45 G59
Ringsfield Corner 45 G60
Ringshall *Sfk* 34 C56
Ringshall *Hfs.* 32 G45
Ringshall Stocks 34 C56
Ringstead *Nmp.* 32 A45
Ringstead *Nfk* 44 A53
Ringwood 10 D37
Ringwould 15 C59
Rinloan 90 C28

Rinmore 90 B29
Rinnigill 105 B29
Rinsey 2 F11
Ripe 13 F51
Ripley *N.Y.* 57 C38
Ripley *Dby.* 51 G39
Ripley *Ham.* 10 E37
Ripley *Sry* 22 F46
Riplingham 59 F45
Ripon 57 B38
Rippingale 42 C46
Ripple *Kent* 15 B59
Ripple *H.&W.* 29 E34
Ripponden 50 A36
Risabus 72 F9
Risbury 28 C31
Risby 34 B53
Risca 19 B28
Rise 59 E47
Risegate 42 B47
Riseley *Brk.* 22 E43
Riseley *Bfd.* 32 B46
Rishangles 35 B57
Rishton 56 F33
Rishworth 50 A36
Risley 41 B40
Risplith 57 C38
Rispond 102 B20
Rivar 21 E39
Rivenhall 34 G54
Rivenhall End 34 G54
River 12 D45
River Bank 33 B51
River Bridge 19 G29
Riverford Bridge 5 D23
Riverhead 23 F51
Rivington 49 A32
Roade 31 C43
Roadhead 69 F30
Roadside *Hgh.* 103 B27
Roadside *Ork.* 104 B32
Roadside of Kinneff 91 F34
Roadwater 7 B26
Roag 93 G8
Roa Island 55 C28
Roath 18 D27
Roberton *Bor.* 69 B30
Roberton *Str.* 68 A25
Robertsbridge 14 E53
Robertstown 98 E28
Roberttown 57 G37
Robeston Cross 16 D14
Robeston Wathen 16 C16
Robin Hood *W.Y.* 57 G39
Robin Hood *Dby.* 50 E38
Robin Hood's Bay 63 F45
Robins 12 D44
Roborough *Dev.* 6 D21
Roborough *Dev.* 4 D20
Roby 48 C30
Roby Mill 48 B31
Rocester 40 B36
Roch 16 B14
Rochallie 82 B27
Rochdale 49 A34
Roche 3 B15
Rochester *Kent* 24 E53
Rochester *Nor.* 70 D34
Rochford *H.&W.* 29 B32
Rochford *Esx* 24 B54
Rock *Cnw.* 3 A15
Rock *H.&W.* 29 A33
Rock *Gwe.* 18 B27
Rock *Nor.* 71 A37
Rockbeare 7 F26
Rockbourne 10 C36
Rockcliffe *Cum.* 69 G29
Rockcliffe *D.&G.* 65 E24
Rock Ferry 48 D29
Rockfield *Str.* 73 E14
Rockfield *Hgh.* 97 C25
Rockfield *Gwe.* 28 G30
Rockhampton 19 B32
Rockhead 4 B16
Rockingham 42 F44
Rockland All Saints 44 F55
Rockland St Mary 45 E59
Rockland St Peter 44 F55
Rockley 20 D37
Rockside 72 D8
Rockwell End 22 C43
Rockwell Green 7 D27
Rodborough 20 A34
Rodbourne 20 C35
Rodbridge Corner 34 D54
Rodd 28 B29
Roddam 71 A36
Rodden 9 F32
Rode 20 F33
Rode Heath 49 G33
Rodeheath 49 F34
Roden 38 D31
Rodhuish 7 B25
Rodington 38 D31
Rodley 29 G33
Rodmarton 20 B35
Rodmell 13 F50
Rodmersham 25 E55
Rodney Stoke 19 F30
Rodsley 40 A37
Rodway 19 G28
Roecliffe 57 C39
Roe Green 33 E48
Roehampton 23 D48
Roesound 107 A39
Roewen 47 E23
Roffey 12 C47
Rogart 96 A23
Rogate 12 D44
Rogerstone 19 C28
Roghadal 92 C6
Rogiet 19 C30
Roker 62 A39
Rollesby 45 D60
Rolleston *Stf.* 40 C38
Rolleston *Not.* 51 G43
Rolleston *Lei.* 42 E43
Rollestone 20 G36
Rolston 59 E48
Rolvenden 14 D54
Rolvenden Layne 14 D54
Romaldkirk 62 D35
Romanby 62 G39
Romannobridge 75 F27
Romansleigh 6 C22
Romford *Dor.* 10 C36
Romford *Esx* 23 C51
Romiley 49 C35
Romney Street 23 E51
Romsey 10 B39
Romsley *H.&W.* 40 G35
Romsley *Shr.* 39 G33
Ronachan 73 E13
Ronague 54 F24
Ronnachmore 72 E8
Rookhope 61 B35
Rookley 11 F40
Rooks Bridge 19 F29
Rookwith 57 A37
Roos 59 F48
Roosecote 55 C28
Rootpark 75 E25
Ropley 11 A42
Ropley Dean 11 A42
Ropley Soke 11 A42
Ropsley 42 B45
Rora 99 D36
Rorandle 91 B32
Rorrington 38 E29
Rosarie 98 D29
Rose 2 C13
Roseacre 55 F30
Rose Ash 7 C23
Rosebank 75 F24
Rosebrough 71 A37
Rosebush 16 B16
Rosedale Abbey 63 G43
Roseden 71 A36
Rose Green 34 F54
Rosehall 96 A20
Rosehearty 99 C34
Rosehill *Grm.* 90 D31
Rosehill *Shr.* 39 B32
Roseisle 97 E27
Rosemarket 16 D15
Rosemarkie 96 F23
Rosemary Lane 7 D27
Rosemount *Str.* 67 A19
Rosemount *Tay.* 82 C27
Rosepool 16 C14
Rosewarne 2 E12
Rosewell 76 D28
Roseworthy 2 E11
Rosgill 61 E31
Roshven 86 G12
Roskhill 93 G8
Rosley 60 B29
Roslin 76 D28
Rosliston 40 D38
Rosneath 74 B18
Ross *Tay.* 81 E23
Ross *Nor.* 77 G37
Ross *D.&G.* 65 F22
Rossett 48 G29
Rossie Farm School 83 B32
Rossie Ochill 82 F26
Rossie Priory 82 D28
Rossington 51 C42
Rosskeen 96 D22
Ross-on-Wye 28 F31
Ross Priory 74 B20
Roster 103 E28
Rostherne 49 D33
Rosthwaite *Cum.* 55 A28
Rosthwaite *Cum.* 60 E28
Roston 40 A37
Rosyth 75 B26
Rothbury 71 C36
Rotherby 41 D42
Rotherfield 13 D51
Rotherfield Greys 22 C43
Rotherfield Peppard 21 C42
Rotherham 51 C39
Rothersthorpe 31 C42
Rotherwick 21 F42
Rothes 98 E28
Rothesay 73 D16
Rothiebrisbane 99 F33
Rothienorman 98 F32
Rothiesholm 104 D31
Rothley *Nor.* 71 E36
Rothley *Lei.* 41 D41
Rothwell *Nmp.* 42 G43
Rothwell *W.Y.* 57 G39
Rothwell *Lcn.* 52 C47
Rotsea 59 D46
Rottal 82 A29
Rottingdean 13 F49
Rottington 60 E25
Roud 11 F41
Roudham 44 G55
Rougham *Nfk.* 44 C54
Rougham *Sfk* 34 B55
Rougham Green 34 B54
Roughburn 88 F19
Rough Close 40 B35
Rough Common 15 B56
Roughlee 56 E34
Roughley 40 F37
Roughton *Nfk* 45 B58
Roughton *Shr.* 39 F33
Roughton *Lcn.* 53 F48
Roundhay 57 F39
Roundstreet Common 12 D46
Roundway 20 E36
Rousdon 8 E28
Rousham 31 F40
Rousham Gap 31 F40
Rous Lench 30 C36
Routenburn 74 D18
Routh 59 E46
Row *Cum.* 61 C32
Row *Cnw.* 4 C16
Row *Cum.* 55 A30
Rowanburn 69 F29
Rowardennan Lodge 74 A19
Rowberrow 19 F30
Rowchoish 80 G19
Rowde 20 E35
Rowfoot 70 G32
Row Heath 35 G57
Rowhedge 34 F56
Rowhook 12 C46
Rowington 30 B37
Rowington Green 30 A38
Rowland 50 E37
Rowland's Castle 11 C43
Rowlands Gill 62 A37
Rowledge 22 G44
Rowley *Drm* 62 B36
Rowley *Hum.* 59 F45
Rowley *Dev.* 7 D23
Rowley *Shr.* 38 E29
Rowley Regis 40 G35
Rowlstone 28 F29
Rowly 22 G46
Rowner 11 D41
Rowney Green 30 A36
Rownhams 10 C39
Rowrah 60 E26
Rowsham 32 G44
Rowsley 50 F38
Rowstock 21 C40
Rowston 52 G46
Rowthorne 51 F40
Rowton *Che.* 48 F30
Rowton *Shr.* 39 D32
Rowton *Shr.* 38 D29
Row Town 22 E46
Roxburgh 76 G32
Roxby *Cle.* 63 E43
Roxby *Hum.* 52 A45
Roxton 32 C47
Roxwell 24 A52
Royal British Legion Village 14 B53
Royal Leamington Spa 30 B39
Royal Tunbridge Wells 23 G51
Roybridge 87 F18
Roydon *Nfk* 44 G56
Roydon *Nfk* 44 C52
Roydon *Esx* 23 A50
Roydon Hamlet 23 A49
Royston *S.Y.* 51 A39
Royston *Hfs.* 33 D49
Royton 49 B35
Ruabon 38 A29
Ruaig 78 C6
Ruanaich 78 E8
Ruan Lanihorne 3 D14
Ruan Major 2 G12
Ruan Minor 2 G13
Ruardean 29 G32
Ruardean Woodside 29 G32
Rubery 29 A35
Ruckcroft 61 B31
Ruckinge 15 D56
Ruckland 53 E49
Ruckley 38 F31
Rudbaxton 16 B15
Rudby 62 F40
Rudchester 71 G37
Ruddington 41 B41
Ruddlemoor 4 E16
Rudford 29 F33
Rudge 20 F34
Rudgeway 19 C32
Rudgwick 12 C46
Rudhall 29 F32
Rudheath 49 E32
Rudley Green 24 A54
Rudry 18 C27
Rudston 59 C46
Rudyard 49 G35
Rufford 48 A30
Rufforth 58 D41
Ruffside 62 A35
Rugby 31 A40
Rugeley 40 D36
Ruilick 96 G20
Ruishton 8 B28
Ruisigearraidh 92 C5
Ruislip 22 C46
Rumbling Bridge 75 A26
Rumburgh 45 G59
Rumford 3 A15
Rumney 19 D28
Rumwell 7 C27
Runacraig 81 F21
Runcorn 48 D30
Runcton 12 F44
Runcton Holme 44 E52
Rundlestone 5 C21
Runfold 22 G44
Runhall 44 E56
Runham 45 D60
Runnington 7 C26
Runsell Green 24 A53
Runswick 63 E43
Runtaleave 82 A28
Runwell 24 B53
Ruscombe 22 D44
Rushall *W.M.* 40 E36
Rushall *Wts.* 20 F37
Rushall *Nfk* 45 G57
Rushall *H.&W.* 29 E32
Rushbrooke 34 B54
Rushbury 38 F30
Rushden *Hfs.* 33 E48
Rushden *Nmp.* 32 B45
Rushford 44 G55
Rush Green 23 C51
Rushlake Green 13 E52
Rushmere 45 G60
Rushmere St Andrew 35 D58
Rushmoor *Shr.* 39 D32
Rushmoor *Sry* 22 G44
Rushock 29 A34
Rusholm 49 C34
Rushton *Che.* 48 F31
Rushton *Shr.* 39 E32
Rushton *Nmp.* 42 G44
Rushton Spencer 49 F35
Rushwick 29 C33
Rushyford 62 D38
Ruskie 81 G22
Ruskington 52 G46
Rusko 65 E21
Rusland 55 A29
Rusper 13 C48
Ruspidge 29 G32
Russel 94 G14
Russell's Water 21 C42
Rusthall 23 G51
Rustington 12 F46
Ruston 59 A45
Ruston Parva 59 C46
Ruswarp 63 F44
Rutherend 74 E22
Rutherford 70 A32
Rutherglen 74 D21
Ruthernbridge 3 B15
Ruthin 47 G27
Ruthrieston 91 C35
Ruthven *Tay.* 82 C28
Ruthven *Hgh.* 88 E23
Ruthven *Grm.* 98 E30
Ruthven *Hgh.* 88 A23
Ruthvoes 3 B15
Ruthwaite 60 C28
Ruthwell 69 G26
Ruyton-XI-Towns 38 C29
Ryal 71 F36
Ryal Fold 56 G32
Ryall 8 E30
Ryarsh 23 F52
Rydal 60 F29
Ryde 11 E42
Rydon 6 E19
Rye 14 E55
Rye Foreign 14 E54
Rye Harbour 14 F55
Rye Park 23 A49
Ryhall 42 D46
Ryhill 51 A39
Ryhope 62 A39
Ryland 52 D46
Rylstone 56 D35
Ryme Intrinseca 8 C31
Ryther 58 F41
Ryton *N.Y.* 58 B43
Ryton *T.&W.* 71 G37
Ryton *Shr.* 39 E33
Ryton *Glo.* 29 E33
Ryton-on-Dunsmore 30 A39

S

Sabden 56 F33
Sackers Green 34 E55
Sacombe 33 G49
Sacriston 62 B38
Sadberge 62 E39
Saddell 73 G13
Saddington 41 F42
Saddle Bow 43 D51
Sadgill 61 F30
Saffron Walden 33 E50
Sageston 16 D16
Saham Toney 44 E54
Saighdinis 92 E4
Saighton 48 F30
St Abbs 77 D35
St Agnes 2 C12
St Albans 22 A47
St Allen 3 C14
St Andrews 83 F30
St Andrews Major 18 D27
St Anne 3 D17
St Anne's 55 G29
St Ann's 69 D26
St Ann's Chapel 4 C19
St Ann's Chapel 5 F22
St Anthony 2 F13
St Anthony 3 E14
St Arvans 19 B31
St Asaph (Llanelwy) 47 E26
St Athan 18 E25
St Aubin 3 G17
St Audries 7 A26
St Austell 3 C15
St Bees 60 E25
St Blazey 4 E16
St Blazey Gate 4 E16
St Boswells 76 G31
St Brelade 3 G17
St Breock 3 A15
St Breward 4 C17
St Briavels 19 A31
St Brides 16 C14
St Brides Major 18 D24
St Brides Netherwent 19 C30
St Bride's-super-Ely 18 D26
St Brides Wentlooge 19 C28
St Budeaux 4 E20
Saintbury 30 E36
St Buryan 2 F10
St Catherine 20 D34
St Catherines 80 G16
St Clears 17 C18
St Cleer 4 D18
St Clement 3 D14
St Clether 4 B17
St Columb Major 3 B15
St Columb Minor 3 B14
St Columb Road 3 C15
St Combs 99 C36
St Cross South Elmham 45 G58
St Cyrus 91 G33
St David's 82 E25
St Davids 75 B27
St David's 16 B13
St Day 2 D12
St Decumans 7 A26
St Dennis 3 C15
St Dennis 30 G36
St Dogmaels 26 D17
St Dogwells 16 B15
St Dominick 4 D20
St Donats 18 E24
St Edith's Marsh 20 E35
St Endellion 3 A15
St Enoder 3 C14
St Erme 3 D14
St Erth 2 E11
St Erth Praze 2 E11
St Ervan 3 A14
St Eval 3 B14
St Ewe 3 D15
St Fagans 18 D26
St Fergus 99 D37
St Fillans 81 E22
St Florence 16 D16
St Gennys 4 A17
St George 47 E25
St Georges 19 E29
St George's 18 D26
St Germans 4 E19
St Giles in the Wood 6 D21
St Giles on the Heath 4 A18

St Harmon 27 A25
St Helena 45 D57
St Helen Auckland 62 D37
St Helens *Mer.* 48 C31
St Helen's 14 F54
St Helens *I.o.W.* 11 F42
St Helier 3 G17
St Hilary *S.G.* 18 D25
St Hilary *Cnw.* 2 E11
Saint Hill 13 C49
St Illtyd 19 A28
St Ippollitts 32 F47
St Ishmael 17 D19
St Ishmael's 16 D14
St Issey 3 A15
St Ive 4 D18
St Ives *Cbs.* 33 A48
St Ives 2 D11
St Ives *Dor.* 10 D36
St James South Elmham 45 G59
St John *Cnw.* 4 E19
St John *C.I.* 3 F17
St John's *H.&W.* 29 C34
St John's 54 E24
St John's *Drm* 62 C36
St John's *Sry* 22 F45
St John's Chapel 61 C34
St John's Chapel 6 C21
St John's Fen End 43 D51
St John's Highway 43 D51
St John's Kirk 75 G25
St John's Town of Dalry 68 E22
St Judes 54 D25
St Just 2 E9
St Just in Roseland 3 E14
St Katherines 99 F33
St Keverne 2 F13
St Kew 3 A15
St Kew Highway 4 C16
St Keyne 4 D18
St Lawrence *Esx* 25 A55
St Lawrence 3 B15
St Lawrence *I.o.W.* 11 G41
St Leonards *Dor.* 10 D36
St Leonards *E.S.* 14 G53
St Leonards *Bkh.* 22 A44
St Leonards Grange 11 E40
St Leonard's Street 23 F52
St Levan 2 F9
St Lythans 18 D27
St Mabyn 4 C16
St Margarets 28 E29
St Margarets 33 G49
St Margaret's at Cliffe 15 C59
St Margaret's Hope 105 B30
St Margaret South Elmham 45 G58
St Mark's 54 F25
St Martin *C.I.* 3 G18
St Martin 4 E18
St Martin *Cnw.* 2 F13
St Martin *C.I.* 3 F17
St Martin's 38 B29
St Martins 82 D27
St Mary Bourne 21 F40
St Mary Church 18 D26
St Marychurch 5 D25
St Mary Cray 23 E50
St Mary Hill 18 D25
St Mary in the Marsh 15 E56
St Mary's 105 A30
St Mary's Bay 15 E56
St Mary's Croft 64 D16
St Mary's Grove 19 E30
St Mary's Hoo 24 D53
St Mawes 3 E14
St Mawgan 3 B14
St Mellion 4 D19
St Mellons 19 C28
St Merryn 3 A14
St Mewan 3 C15
St Michael Caerhays 3 D15
St Michael Penkevil 3 D14
St Michaels 28 B31
St Michaels 14 D54
St Michael's on Wyre 55 E30
St Michael South Elmham 45 G59
St Minver 3 A15
St Monans 83 G31
St Neot 4 D17
St Neots 32 B47
St Nicholas *S.G.* 18 D26
St Nicholas *Dyf.* 16 A14
St Nicholas at Wade 25 E58
St Ninians 75 A23
St Osyth 35 G57
St Ouen 3 F17
St Owen's Cross 28 F31
St Paul's Cray 23 E50
St Paul's Walden 32 F47
St Peter 3 G17
St Peter Port 3 E17
St Peter's 25 E59
St Petrox 16 E15
St Pinnock 4 D18
St Quivox 67 A19
St Sampson 3 E17
St Saviour 3 E16
St Stephen 3 C15
St Stephen's 4 E19
St Stephens *Cnw.* 6 G19
St Stephens *Hfs.* 22 A47
St Teath 4 B16
St Tudy 4 C16
St Twynnells 16 E15
St Veep 4 E17
St Vigeans 83 C32
St Wenn 3 B15
St Weonards 28 F30
Salachail 80 B16
Salcombe 5 G23
Salcombe Regis 7 G27
Salcott 34 G55
Sale 49 C33
Saleby 53 E50
Sale Green 29 C35
Salehurst 14 E53
Salem *Dyf.* 37 G22
Salem *Dyf.* 17 B22
Salem *Gwy.* 46 G21
Salen *Hgh.* 79 A12
Salen *Str.* 79 C11
Salesbury 56 F32
Salford *G.M.* 49 C33
Salford *Bfd.* 32 E45
Salford *Oxf.* 30 F38
Salford Priors 30 C36
Salfords 23 G48
Salhouse 45 D59
Saline 75 A26
Salisbury 10 A37
Salkeld Dykes 61 C31
Sall 45 C57
Sallachan 80 A15
Sallachry 80 F16
Sallachy *Hgh.* 86 A14
Sallachy *Hgh.* 96 A21
Salmonby 53 E49
Salmond's Muir 83 D31
Salperton 30 F36
Salph End 32 C46
Salsburgh 75 D24
Salt 40 C35
Saltash 4 E19
Saltburn 96 E23
Saltburn-by-the-Sea 63 D42
Saltby 42 C44
Saltcoats 74 F18
Saltcotes 55 G29
Saltdean 13 F49
Salterforth 56 E34
Salterhill 97 E27
Salterswall 48 F31
Saltfleet 53 C50
Saltfleetby All Saints 53 C50
Saltfleetby St Clements 53 C50
Saltfleetby St Peter 53 D50
Saltford 19 E32
Salthaugh Grange 59 G48
Salt Hill 22 C45
Salthouse 44 A56
Saltley 40 G36
Saltmarshe 58 G43
Saltney 48 F29
Salton 58 A43
Saltwick 71 E37
Saltwood 15 D57
Salvington 12 F47
Salwarpe 29 B34
Salwayash 8 E30
Sambourne 30 B36
Sambrook 39 C33
Samhla 92 E3
Samlesbury 55 F31
Samlesbury Bottoms 56 G32
Sampford Arundel 7 D26
Sampford Brett 7 A26
Sampford Courtenay 6 E22
Sampford Peverell 7 D26
Sampford Spiney 5 C21
Samuelston 76 C30
Sanaigmore 72 C8
Sancreed 2 F9
Sancton 59 F45
Sand 107 C39
Sandaig *Hgh.* 86 C13
Sandaig *Hgh.* 86 D12
Sanday Airport 104 B32
Sandbach 49 F33
Sandbank 73 B17
Sandbanks 10 F36
Sandend 98 C31
Sanderstead 23 E49
Sandford *I.o.W.* 11 F41
Sandford *Dev.* 7 E23
Sandford *Str.* 75 F23
Sandford *Avon* 19 F29
Sandford *Cum.* 61 E33
Sandford *Dor.* 9 F34
Sandfordhill 99 E36
Sandford-on-Thames 21 A41
Sandford Orcas 9 B32
Sandford St Martin 30 F39
Sandgarth 104 E31
Sandgate 15 D57
Sandgreen 65 E21
Sandhaven 99 C35
Sandhead 64 E16
Sandhills *Dor.* 9 C32
Sandhills *Sry* 12 C45
Sandhoe 70 G35
Sand Hole 58 F44
Sandholme *Hum.* 58 F44
Sandholme *Lcn.* 43 B49
Sandhurst *Kent* 14 E53
Sandhurst *Brk.* 22 E44
Sandhurst *Glo.* 29 F34
Sand Hutton 58 D42
Sandhutton 57 A39
Sandiacre 41 B40
Sandilands 53 D51
Sandiway 49 E32
Sandleheath 10 C36
Sandleigh 21 A40
Sandling 14 B53
Sandness 107 B37
Sandon *Stf.* 40 C35
Sandon *Hfs.* 33 E49
Sandon *Esx* 24 A53
Sandown 11 F42
Sandown Airport 11 F41
Sandplace 4 E18
Sandquoy 104 B33
Sandridge *Wts.* 20 E35
Sandridge *Hfs.* 32 G47
Sandringham 44 C53
Sandrocks 13 D49
Sandsend 63 E44
Sand Side 55 A28
Sandside House 103 B25
Sandsound 107 C39
Sandtoft 51 B43
Sanduck 7 G23
Sandway 14 B54
Sandwich 15 B59
Sandwick *She.* 107 E40
Sandwick *Cum.* 60 E30
Sandwick *W.I.* 100 D10
Sandwith 60 E25
Sandy 32 D47
Sandycroft 48 F29
Sandygate *I.o.M.* 54 D25
Sandygate *Dev.* 5 C24
Sandy Haven 16 D14
Sandylands 55 C29
Sandy Lane *W.Y.* 57 F37
Sandy Lane *Wts.* 20 E35
Sandyway 28 F30
Sangobeg 102 B20
Sanna 79 A10
Sannaig 72 D11
Sanquhar 68 C23
Santon Bridge 60 F27
Santon Downham 44 G54
Sapcote 41 F40
Sapey Common 29 B32
Sapiston 34 A54
Sapperton *Glo.* 20 A35
Sapperton *Lcn.* 42 B46
Saracen's Head 43 C49
Sarclet 103 D29
Sardis 16 D15
Sarisbury 11 D40
Sarn *M.G.* 18 C25
Sarn *Pow.* 38 F27
Sarnau *Pow.* 38 D28
Sarnau *Gwy.* 37 B25
Sarnau *Dyf.* 26 C18
Sarnau *Dyf.* 17 C19
Sarn Bach 36 C18
Sarnesfield 28 C29
Sarn-Meyllteyrn 36 B18
Saron *Dyf.* 17 C22
Saron *Dyf.* 17 A19
Saron *Gwy.* 46 F21
Sarratt 22 B46
Sarre 25 E58
Sarsden 30 F38
Sarsgrum 101 B19
Sartfield 54 D25
Satley 62 B37
Satterleigh 6 C22
Satterthwaite 60 G29
Sauchen 91 B32
Saucher 82 D27
Sauchieburn 91 G32
Sauchrie 67 B18
Saughall 48 E29
Saughall Massie 48 D28
Saughtree 70 D31
Saul 20 A33
Saundaig 78 C5
Saundby 51 D43
Saundersfoot 16 D17
Saunderton 22 A43
Saunton 6 B20
Sausthorpe 53 F49
Savalbeg 96 A21
Savalmore 96 A21
Sawbridgeworth 33 G50
Sawdon 59 A45
Sawley *N.Y.* 57 C38
Sawley *Lan.* 56 E33
Sawley *Dby.* 41 B40
Sawston 33 D50
Sawtry 42 G47
Saxby *Lei.* 42 D44
Saxby *Lcn.* 52 D45
Saxby All Saints 52 A45
Saxelbye 41 C42
Saxilby 52 E44
Saxlingham 44 B55
Saxlingham Green 45 F58
Saxlingham Nethergate 45 F58
Saxlingham Thorpe 45 F58
Saxmundham 35 B59
Saxondale 41 A42
Saxon Street 33 C52
Saxtead Green 35 B58
Saxtead Little Green 35 B58
Saxthorpe 45 B57
Saxton 57 F40
Sayers Common 13 E48
Scackleton 58 B42
Scadabhagh 93 B7
Scaftworth 51 C42
Scagglethorpe 58 B44
Scalasaig 72 A9
Scalby *Hum.* 58 G44
Scalby *N.Y.* 59 A45
Scaldwell 31 A43
Scaleby 69 G30
Scalebyhill 69 G30
Scale Houses 61 B31
Scales *Cum.* 60 D29
Scales *Cum.* 55 B28
Scalford 42 C43
Scaling 63 E43
Scallasaig 86 C14
Scallastle 79 D12
Scalloway 107 D39
Scamadale 79 E14
Scamblesby 53 E48
Scamodale 86 G14
Scampston 58 B44
Scampton 52 E45
Scaniport 88 A22
Scapa 105 A30
Scar 104 B32
Scarborough 59 A46
Scarcewater 3 C15
Scarcliffe 51 F40
Scarcroft 57 E39
Scardroy 95 F17
Scarff 106 D38
Scarfskerry 103 A28
Scargill 62 E36
Scarinish 78 C6
Scarisbrick 48 A29
Scarning 44 D55
Scarrington 42 A43
Scarth Hill 48 B30
Scartho 53 B48
Scatraig 88 A22
Scaur 65 C24
Scawby 52 B45
Scawton 58 A41
Scayne's Hill 13 D49
Scealascro 100 E7
Scethrog 27 F26
Schaw 67 A20
Scholar Green 49 G34
Scholes *W.Y.* 50 B37
Scholes *W.Y.* 57 F39
Sciberscross 96 A23
Scilly Isles Airport 2 A11
Scleddau 16 A15
Scofton 51 D42
Scole 35 A57
Scolpaig 92 D3
Scolton 16 B15
Sconser 86 A11
Scoor 79 F10
Scopwick 52 G46
Scoraig 94 B15
Scorborough 59 E46
Scorrier 2 D13
Scorriton 5 D23
Scorton *N.Y.* 62 F38
Scorton *Lan.* 55 E30
Sco Ruston 45 C58
Scotby 60 A30
Scotch Corner 62 F38
Scotforth 55 D30
Scothern 52 E46
Scotland Gate 71 E38
Scotlandwell 82 G27
Scotnish 73 B13
Scotsburn 96 D22
Scots' Gap 71 E36
Scotston *Tay.* 81 C24
Scotston *Grm.* 91 F33
Scotstown 79 A14
Scotter 52 B44
Scotterthorpe 52 B44
Scottlethorpe 42 C46
Scotton *Lcn.* 52 C44
Scotton *N.Y.* 62 G37
Scotton *N.Y.* 57 D39
Scottow 45 C58
Scoulton 44 E55
Scourie 101 D17
Scourie More 101 D17
Scousburgh 107 D37
Scrabster 103 A26
Scrainwood 70 C35
Scrane End 43 A49
Scraptoft 41 E42
Scratby 45 D61
Scrayingham 58 C43
Scredington 42 A46
Scremby 53 F50
Scremerston 77 F35
Screveton 42 A43
Scriven 57 D39
Scrooby 51 C42
Scropton 40 B37
Scrub Hill 53 G48
Scruton 62 G38
Scunthorpe 52 A44
Seabank 79 C14
Seaborough 8 D30
Seacombe 48 C28
Seacroft *W.Y.* 57 F39
Seacroft *Lcn.* 53 F51
Seafield *Ltn* 75 D26
Seafield *Str.* 73 B13
Seafield *Str.* 67 A19
Seaford 13 G50
Seaforth 48 C29
Seagrave 41 D41
Seaham 62 A40
Seahouses 77 G37
Seal 23 F51
Sealand 48 F29
Seale 22 G44
Seamer *N.Y.* 62 E40
Seamer *N.Y.* 59 A46
Seamill 73 F17
Sea Palling 45 C60
Searby 52 B46
Seasalter 25 E56
Seascale 60 F26
Seathwaite 60 E28
Seatoller 60 E28
Seaton *Drm* 62 B39
Seaton *Cum.* 60 C25
Seaton *Hum.* 59 E47
Seaton *Nor.* 71 F39
Seaton *Cnw.* 4 E19
Seaton *Dev.* 8 E28
Seaton *Lei.* 42 F44
Seaton Burn 71 F38
Seaton Carew 63 C41
Seaton Delaval 71 F39
Seaton Junction 8 E28
Seaton Ross 58 E43
Seaton Sluice 71 F39
Seatown *Grm.* 99 D37
Seatown *Grm.* 98 C30
Seatown *Grm.* 98 C30
Seatown *Dor.* 8 E30
Seave Green 63 F41
Seaview 11 E42
Seaville 60 A27
Seavington St Mary 8 C29
Seavington St Michael 8 C30
Seawick 35 G57
Sebastopol 19 B28
Sebergham 60 B29
Seckington 40 E38
Second Coast 94 B14
Sedbergh 61 G32
Sedbury 19 B31
Sedbusk 61 G34
Sedgeberrow 29 E35
Sedgebrook 42 B44
Sedgefield 62 D39
Sedgehill 9 B34
Sedgley 40 F34
Sedgwick 55 A31
Sedlescombe 14 F53
Sedlescombe Street 14 F53
Seend 20 E35
Seend Cleeve 20 E35
Seer Green 22 B45
Seething 45 F59
Sefton 48 B29
Seghill 71 F38
Seighford 40 C34
Seilebost 92 B6
Seion 46 F21
Seisdon 40 F34
Seisiadar 101 D11
Selattyn 38 B28
Selborne 11 A43
Selby 58 F42
Selham 12 D45

Selkirk 69 A30
Sellack 28 F31
Sellafield 60 F26
Sellafirth 106 C41
Sellindge 15 D56
Selling 15 B56
Sells Green 20 E35
Selly Oak 40 G36
Selmeston 13 F51
Selsdon 23 E49
Selsey 12 G44
Selsfield Common 13 C49
Selside 56 B33
Selstead 15 C57
Selston 51 G40
Selworthy 7 A25
Semblister 107 B39
Semer 34 D55
Semington 20 E34
Semley 9 B34
Send 22 F46
Send Marsh 22 F46
Senghenydd 18 B26
Sennen 2 F9
Sennybridge 27 F24
Senwick 65 F22
Sequer's Bridge 5 E22
Sessay 57 B40
Setchey 44 D52
Setley 10 D38
Setter *She.* 107 C41
Setter *She.* 107 B39
Settiscarth 104 E29
Settle 56 C34
Settrington 58 B44
Seven Bridges 20 B37
Sevenhampton *Wts.* 20 B37
Sevenhampton *Glo.* 29 F36
Seven Kings 23 C50
Sevenoaks 23 F51
Sevenoaks Weald 23 F51
Seven Sisters 18 A23
Seven Springs 29 G35
Severn Beach 19 C31
Severn Stoke 29 D34
Sevington 15 C56
Sewards End 33 E51
Sewardstone 23 B49
Sewerby 59 C48
Seworgan 2 E13
Sewstern 42 C44
Sexhow 62 F40
Sgarasta Mhor 92 B6
Sgiogarstaigh 101 A11
Sgodachail 96 B20
Shabbington 21 A42
Shackerley 40 E34
Shackerstone 41 E39
Shackleford 22 G45
Shadfen 71 E38
Shadforth 62 B39
Shadingfield 45 G60
Shadoxhurst 14 D55
Shadwell 44 G55
Shaftesbury 9 B34
Shafton 51 A39
Shalbourne 21 E38
Shalcombe 11 F40
Shalden 21 G42
Shaldon 5 C25
Shalfleet 11 F40
Shalford *Sry* 22 G46
Shalford *Esx* 34 F53
Shalford Green 33 F52
Shallowford 7 A23
Shalmsford Street 15 B56
Shalmstry 103 B27
Shalstone 31 E42
Shalunt 73 C16
Shambellie 65 D25
Shamley Green 22 G46
Shandon 74 B18
Shandwick 97 D24
Shangton 41 F42
Shankend 70 C31
Shankhouse 71 F38
Shanklin 11 F41
Shannochie 66 A15
Shantron 74 B19
Shantullich 96 F22
Shanzie 82 B28
Shap 61 E31
Shapwick *Som.* 8 A29
Shapwick *Dor.* 9 D35
Shardlow 41 B40
Shareshill 40 E35
Sharlston 51 A39
Sharnbrook 32 C45
Sharnford 41 F40
Sharoe Green 55 F31
Sharow 57 B39
Sharpenhoe 32 E46
Sharperton 70 C35
Sharpham House 5 E24
Sharpness 19 A32
Sharpthorne 13 C49
Sharrington 44 B56
Shatterford 39 G33
Shaugh Prior 5 D21
Shavington 49 G33
Shaw *G.M.* 49 B35
Shaw *Wts.* 20 E34
Shaw *Wts.* 20 C37
Shaw *Brk.* 21 E40
Shawbury 38 C31
Shawclough 49 A34
Shawell 41 G41
Shawford 11 B40
Shawforth 56 G34
Shawhead 65 C24
Shaw Mills 57 C38
Shawtonhill 74 F22
Sheanachie 66 B13
Sheandow 98 F28
Shear Cross 20 G34
Shearington 69 G26
Shearsby 41 F42
Shebbear 6 E20
Shebdon 39 C33
Shebster 103 B25
Shedfield 11 C41
Sheen 50 F36
Sheepscombe 29 G34
Sheepstor 5 D21
Sheepwash *Nor.* 71 E38
Sheepwash *Dev.* 6 E20
Sheepway 19 D30
Sheepy Magna 41 E39
Sheepy Parva 41 E39
Sheering 33 G50
Sheerness 25 D55
Sheet 11 B43
Sheffield 51 D39
Sheffield Bottom 21 E42
Sheffield Green 13 D50
Shefford 32 E47
Shefford Woodlands 21 D39
Sheigra 101 B17
Sheinton 39 E32
Shelderton 28 A29
Sheldon *Dby.* 50 F37
Sheldon *Dev.* 7 E27
Sheldon *W.M.* 40 G37
Sheldwich 14 B55
Shelf 57 G37
Shelfanger 45 G57
Shelfield 40 E36
Shelford 41 A42
Shellachan *Str.* 80 E16
Shellachan *Str.* 79 F14
Shellbrook Hill 38 B29
Shelley *Sfk* 34 E56
Shelley *W.Y.* 50 A38
Shelley *Esx* 23 A51
Shellingford 21 B39
Shellow Bowells 23 A51
Shelsley Beauchamp 29 B33
Shelsley Walsh 29 B33
Shelton *Bfd.* 32 B46
Shelton *Shr.* 38 D30
Shelton *Nfk* 45 F58
Shelton *Not.* 42 A43
Shelton Green 45 F58
Shelve 38 F29
Shelwick 28 D31
Shenfield 24 B52
Shenington 30 D39
Shenley 22 A47
Shenley Brook End 32 E44
Shenleybury 22 A47
Shenley Church End 32 E44
Shenmore 28 E29
Shennanton 64 D19
Shenstone *Stf.* 40 E37
Shenstone *H.&W.* 29 A34
Shenstone Woodend 40 E36
Shenton 41 E39
Shenval 90 A27
Shepeau Stow 43 D48
Shephall 33 F48
Shepherd's Green 21 C42
Shepherdswell or Sibertswold 15 C58
Shepley 50 B37
Sheppardstown 103 E27
Shepperdine 19 B31
Shepperton 22 E46
Shepreth 33 D49
Shepshed 41 D40
Shepton Beauchamp 8 C30
Shepton Mallet 19 G32
Shepton Montague 9 A32
Shepway 14 B53
Sheraton 62 C40
Sherborne *Glo.* 30 G37
Sherborne *Dor.* 9 C32
Sherborne St John 21 F42
Sherbourne 30 B38
Sherburn *Drm* 62 B39
Sherburn *N.Y.* 59 B45
Sherburn in Elmet 57 F40
Shere 22 G46
Shereford 44 C54
Sherfield English 10 B38
Sherfield on Loddon 21 F42
Sherford 5 F23
Sheriffhales 39 D33
Sheriff Hutton 58 C42
Sheringham 45 A57
Sherington 32 D44
Sherramore 88 E21
Sherrington 9 A35
Sherston 20 C34
Sherwood Green 6 C21
Shettleston 74 D22
Shevington 48 B31
Shevington Moor 48 A31
Sheviock 4 E19
Shiel Bridge 86 C15
Shieldaig *Hgh.* 94 D14
Shieldaig *Hgh.* 94 F13
Shieldhill 75 C24
Shielfoot 79 A12
Shielhill 83 B30
Shiels 91 C32
Shifford 21 A39
Shifnal 39 E33
Shilbottle 71 C37
Shildon 62 D38
Shillingford *Dev.* 7 C25
Shillingford *Oxf.* 21 B41
Shillingford St George 7 G24
Shillingstone 9 C33
Shillington 32 E47
Shillmoor 70 C34
Shilstone 6 E22
Shilton *Oxf.* 21 A38
Shilton *War.* 41 G40
Shimpling *Nfk* 45 G57
Shimpling *Sfk* 34 C54
Shimpling Street 34 C54
Shincliffe 62 B38
Shiney Row 62 A39
Shinfield 22 E43
Shingay 33 D48
Shingle Street 35 D59
Shinner's Bridge 5 D23
Shinness Lodge 102 G21
Shipbourne 23 F51
Shipdham 44 E55
Shipham 19 F30
Shiphay 5 D24
Shiplake 22 D43
Shipley *W.S.* 12 D47
Shipley *W.Y.* 57 F37
Shipley *Nor.* 71 B37
Shipley *Shr.* 39 F33
Shipley Bridge *Dev.* 5 D22
Shipley Bridge *Sry* 23 G49
Shipmeadow 45 F59
Shippon 21 B40
Shipton *N.Y.* 58 D41
Shipton *Shr.* 38 F31
Shipton *Glo.* 30 G36
Shipton Bellinger 21 G38
Shipton Gorge 8 E30
Shipton Green 12 G44
Shipton Moyne 20 C34
Shipton-on-Cherwell 31 G40
Shipton on Stour 30 D38
Shiptonthorpe 58 E44
Shipton-under-Wychwood 30 G38
Shira 80 F17
Shirburn 22 B43
Shirdley Hill 48 A29
Shirebrook 51 F41
Shirehampton 19 D30
Shiremoor 71 F38
Shirenewton 19 B30
Shire Oak 40 E36
Shireoaks 51 D41
Shirland 51 G39
Shirley *G.L.* 23 E49
Shirley *Ham.* 11 C40
Shirley *Ham.* 10 E37
Shirley *Dby.* 40 A38
Shirley *W.M.* 30 A37
Shirl Heath 28 C30
Shirrell Heath 11 C41
Shirwell 6 B22
Shirwell Cross 6 B21
Shiskine 66 A14
Shobdon 28 B29
Shobrooke 7 E24
Shocklach 38 A30
Shoeburyness 25 C55
Sholden 15 B59
Sholing 11 C40
Shooter's Hill 23 D50
Shoot Hill 38 D30
Shop *Cnw.* 6 D18
Shop *Cnw.* 3 A14
Shop Corner 35 E58
Shoreditch 23 C49
Shoreham 23 E51
Shoreham Airport 12 F47
Shoreham-by-Sea 13 F48
Shoremill 96 E23
Shoresdean 77 F35
Shoreswood 77 F35
Shoretown 96 E21
Shorncote 20 B35
Shorne 24 D52
Shorne Ridgeway 24 D52
Shortacombe 6 G21
Short Cross 38 E28
Shortgate 13 E50
Short Green 44 G56
Shortgrove 33 E50
Short Heath *W.M.* 40 F36
Short Heath *Dby.* 40 D38
Shortlanesend 2 D13
Shorwell 11 F40
Shoscombe 20 F33
Shotesham 45 F58
Shotgate 24 B53
Shotley 35 E58
Shotley Bridge 62 A36
Shotleyfield 62 A36
Shotley Gate 35 E58
Shottenden 15 B56
Shottermill 12 C44
Shottery 30 C37
Shotteswell 30 D39
Shottisham 35 D59
Shottle 41 A39
Shottlegate 40 A38
Shotton *Clw.* 48 F28
Shotton *Nor.* 77 G34
Shotton *Drm* 62 C40
Shotton Colliery 62 B39
Shotts 75 D24
Shotwick 48 E29
Shoughlaige-e-Caine 54 E24
Shouldham 44 E52
Shouldham Thorpe 44 E52
Shoulton 29 C33
Shover's Green 13 C52
Shrawardine 38 D29
Shrawley 29 B33
Shrewley 30 B37
Shrewsbury 38 D30
Shrewton 20 G36
Shripney 12 F45
Shrivenham 21 C38
Shropham 44 F55
Shrub End 34 F55
Shucknall 28 D31
Shudy Camps 33 D51
Shurdington 29 G35
Shurlock Row 22 D44
Shurrery 103 C26
Shurrery Lodge 103 C26
Shurton 7 A27
Shustoke 40 F38
Shute 8 E28
Shutford 30 D39
Shut Heath 40 C34
Shuthonger 29 E34
Shutlanger 31 C43
Shuttington 40 E38
Shuttlewood 51 E40
Shuttleworth 49 A34
Siabost 100 C8
Siadar Iarach 100 B9
Siadar Uarach 100 B9
Sibbaldbie 69 E27
Sibbertoft 41 G42
Sibdon Carwood 38 G29
Sibford Ferris 30 E39
Sibford Gower 30 E39
Sible Hedingham 34 E53
Sibsey 53 G49
Sibson *Cbs.* 42 F46
Sibson *Lei.* 41 E39
Sibster 103 C29
Sibthorpe 42 A43
Sibton 35 B59
Sicklesmere 34 C54
Sicklinghall 57 E39
Sidbury *Shr.* 39 G32
Sidbury *Dev.* 7 F27
Sidcot 19 F30
Sidcup 23 D50
Siddington *Glo.* 20 B36
Siddington *Che.* 49 E34
Sidemoor 29 A35
Sidestrand 45 B58
Sidford 7 F27
Sidlesham 12 G44
Sidley 14 G53
Sidlowbridge 23 G48
Sidmouth 7 G27
Siefton 38 G30
Sigford 5 C23
Sigglesthorne 59 E47
Sigingstone 18 D25
Silchester 21 E42
Sileby 41 D41
Silecroft 54 A27
Silfield 45 F57
Silian 26 C21
Silkstone 50 B38
Silkstone Common 50 B38
Silksworth 62 A39
Silk Willoughby 42 A46
Silloth 60 A26
Sills 70 C34
Sillyearn 98 D30
Silpho 63 G45
Silsden 57 E36
Silsoe 32 E46
Silton 9 B33
Silverburn 75 D27
Silvercraigs 73 B14
Silverdale *Lan.* 55 B30
Silverdale *Stf.* 39 A33
Silver End 34 G53
Silver Hill *E.S.* 14 F54
Silver Hill *E.S.* 14 E53
Silverley's Green 35 A58
Silvermoss 99 F33
Silverstone 31 D42
Silverton 7 E25
Silvington 28 A31
Silwick 107 C38
Simonburn 70 F34
Simonsbath 7 B23
Simonstone 56 F33
Simprim 77 F34
Simpson 32 E44
Sinclair's Hill 77 E33
Sinclairston 67 B20
Sinderby 57 A39
Sinderhope 61 A34
Sindlesham 22 E43
Singdean 70 C31
Singleton *W.S.* 12 E44
Singleton *Lan.* 55 F29
Singlewell or Ifield 24 D52
Sinnahard 90 B30
Sinnington 58 A43
Sinton Green 29 B34
Sipson 22 D46
Sirhowy 28 G27
Sisland 45 F59
Sissinghurst 14 D53
Siston 19 D32
Sithney 2 F12
Sittingbourne 25 E55
Siulaisiadar 101 D11
Six Ashes 39 G33
Sixhills 52 D47
Six Mile Bottom 33 C51
Sixmile Cottages 15 C57
Sixpenny Handley 9 C35
Sizewell 35 B60
Skail 102 D23
Skaill *Ork.* 104 E28
Skaill *Ork.* 105 A31
Skares *Grm.* 98 F32
Skares *Str.* 67 B21
Skarpigarth 107 B37
Skateraw 77 C33
Skaw 107 A41
Skeabost 93 G9
Skeabrae 104 D28
Skeeby 62 F37
Skeffington 42 E43
Skeffling 53 A49
Skegby 51 F40
Skegness 53 F51
Skelberry 107 D37
Skelbo 96 B23
Skeldon 67 B19
Skeldyke 43 B49
Skellingthorpe 52 E44
Skellister 107 B40
Skellow 51 A41
Skelmanthorpe 50 A38
Skelmersdale 48 B30
Skelmonae 99 F34
Skelmorlie 73 D17
Skelmuir 99 E35
Skelton *Cum.* 60 C30
Skelton *Cle.* 63 E42
Skelton *N.Y.* 62 F36
Skelton *Hum.* 58 G43
Skelton *N.Y.* 58 D41
Skelton *N.Y.* 57 C39
Skelton Green 63 E42
Skelwick 104 B30
Skendleby 53 F50
Skenfrith 28 G30
Skerne 59 D46
Skeroblingarry 66 A12
Skerray 102 B22
Sketty 17 E22
Skewen 18 B23
Skewsby 58 B42
Skeyton 45 C58
Skidbrooke 53 C50
Skidby 59 F46
Skilgate 7 C25
Skillington 42 C44
Skinburness 60 A26
Skinidin 93 G8
Skinnet 103 B27
Skinningrove 63 D42

Skipness 73 E14
Skipsea 59 D47
Skipton 56 D35
Skipton-on-Swale 57 A39
Skipwith 58 F42
Skirbeck 43 A49
Skirling 75 G26
Skirmett 22 C43
Skirpenbeck 58 D43
Skirwith *Cum.* 61 C31
Skirwith *N.Y.* 56 B33
Skirza 103 B29
Skulamus 86 B12
Skullomie 102 B21
Skye of Curr 89 B25
Slack 98 F31
Slackhall 50 D36
Slackhead 98 C29
Slad 20 A34
Slade 6 A20
Slade Green 23 D51
Slaggyford 61 A32
Slaidburn 56 D33
Slains Park 91 F34
Slaithwaite 50 A36
Slaley 62 A35
Slamannan 75 C24
Slapton *Dev.* 5 F23
Slapton *Bkh.* 32 F45
Slapton *Nmp.* 31 D42
Slate Haugh 98 C30
Slatenber 56 B33
Slattadale 94 D14
Slattocks 49 B34
Slaugham 13 D48
Slaughden 35 C60
Slaughterford 20 D34
Slawston 42 F43
Sleaford *Ham.* 12 C44
Sleaford *Lcn.* 42 A46
Sleagill 61 E31
Sleapford 39 D32
Sledge Green 29 E34
Sledmere 59 C45
Sleights 63 F44
Slepe 9 E35
Slickly 103 B28
Sliddery 66 A15
Sliemore 89 B26
Sligachan 85 B10
Slimbridge 20 A33
Slindon *Stf.* 40 B34
Slindon *W.S.* 12 F45
Slinfold 12 C47
Slingsby 58 B42
Slioch 98 F31
Slip End *Bfd.* 33 E48
Slip End *Bfd.* 32 G46
Slipton 32 A45
Slochd 89 B24
Slockavullin 73 A13
Slogarie 65 D22
Sloley 45 C58
Slongaber 65 C23
Sloothby 53 E50
Slough 22 C45
Sluggan 89 B24
Slyne 55 C30
Smailholm 76 G32
Smallbridge 49 A35
Smallburgh 45 C59
Smallburn *Str.* 68 A22
Smallburn *Grm.* 99 E36
Small Dole 13 E48
Smalley 41 A39
Smallfield 23 G49
Small Hythe 14 D54
Smallridge 8 D28
Smallthorne 49 G34
Smallworth 44 G56
Smannell 21 G39
Smardale 61 F33
Smarden 14 C54
Smaull 72 D8
Smeale 54 C26
Smeatharpe 7 D27
Smeeth 15 D56
Smeeton Westerby 41 F42
Smelthouses 57 C37
Smerral 103 E27
Smethwick 40 G35
Smirisary 86 G12
Smisby 41 D39
Smith End Green 29 C33
Smithfield 69 G30
Smithincott 7 D26
Smith's Green 33 F51
Smithtown 96 G22
Smithy Green 49 E33
Smug Oak 22 A47
Smyrton 66 E16
Smythe's Green 34 G54
Snailbeach 38 E29
Snailwell 33 B52
Snainton 59 A45
Snaith 58 G42
Snape *N.Y.* 57 A38
Snape *Sfk* 35 C59
Snape Green 48 A29
Snarestone 41 E39
Snarford 52 D46
Snargate 14 E55
Snave 15 D56
Sneachill 29 C34
Snead 38 F28
Sneaton 63 F44
Sneatonthorpe 63 F44
Snelland 52 D46
Snellings 60 F25
Snelston 40 A37
Snetterton 44 F55
Snibston 41 D39
Snig's End 29 F33
Snishival 84 A3
Snitter 71 C36
Snitterby 52 C45
Snitterfield 30 C37
Snitton 28 A31
Snodhill 28 D29
Snodland 24 E52
Snowshill 30 E36
Soar *Dyf.* 17 B22
Soar *Dev.* 5 G22
Soberton 11 C42
Soberton Heath 11 C42
Sockburn 62 F39
Sodylt Bank 38 A29
Soham 33 A51
Solas 92 D4
Soldon Cross 6 D19
Soldridge 11 A42
Sole Street *Kent* 15 C56
Sole Street *Kent* 24 E52
Solihull 30 A37
Solihull Lodge 30 A36
Sollers Dilwyn 28 C30
Sollers Hope 29 E32
Sollom 48 A30
Solsgirth 75 A25
Solva 16 B13
Solwaybank 69 F28
Somerby 42 D43
Somercotes 51 G39
Somerford Keynes 20 B36
Somerley 11 E43
Somerleyton 45 F60
Somersal Herbert 40 B37
Somersby 53 E49
Somersham *Sfk* 34 D56
Somersham *Cbs.* 33 A49
Somerton *Oxf.* 31 F40
Somerton *Som.* 8 B30
Somerton *Sfk* 34 C53
Sompting 12 F47
Sonning 22 D43
Sonning Common 22 D43
Sonning Eye 22 D43
Sopley 10 E37
Sopworth 20 C33
Sorbie 64 F20
Sordale 103 B27
Sorisdale 78 A8
Sorn 67 A21
Sornhill 74 G21
Soroba 79 E14
Sortat 103 B28
Sotby 53 E48
Sots Hole 52 F47
Sotterly 45 G60
Soudley 39 C33
Soughton 48 F28
Soulbury 32 F44
Soulby 61 E33
Souldern 31 E41
Souldrop 32 B45
Sound *She.* 107 C40
Sound *Che.* 39 A32
Sound *She.* 107 B39
Soundwell 19 D32
Sourhope 70 A34
Sourin 104 C30
Sourton 6 G21
Soutergate 55 A28
South Acre 44 D53
Southall 22 C47
South Allington 5 G23
South Alloa 75 A24
Southam *War.* 31 B40
Southam *Glo.* 29 F35
South Ambersham 12 E45
Southampton 10 C39
Southampton Airport 11 C40
South Anston 51 D41
South Ascot 22 E45
South Ballachulish 80 B16
South Balloch 67 D18
South Bank 63 D41
Southbar 74 D20
South Barrow 8 B31
South Beddington 23 E48
South Benfleet 24 C53
South Bersted 12 G45
South Blackbog 99 F33
Southborough 23 G51
Southbourne *W.S.* 11 D43
Southbourne *Dor.* 10 E37
South Bowood 8 E30
South Brent 5 D22
South Brentor 6 G20
South Brewham 9 A33
South Broomhill 71 D38
Southburgh 44 E56
South Burlingham 45 E59
Southburn 59 D45
South Cadbury 9 B32
South Carlton 52 E45
South Cave 59 F45
South Cerney 20 B36
South Chard 8 D28
South Charlton 71 A37
South Cheriton 9 B32
Southchurch 24 C54
South Cliffe 58 F44
South Clifton 52 E44
South Cockerington 53 D49
South Common 13 E49
South Cornelly 18 D23
South Corrygills 73 G16
Southcott 6 F21
South Cove 45 G60
South Creagan 80 C15
South Croxton 41 D42
South Dalton 59 E45
South Darenth 23 E51
Southdean 70 C32
South Duffield 58 F42
Southease 13 F50
South Elkington 53 D48
South Elmsall 51 A40
South End *Cum.* 54 C27
South End *Hum.* 52 A47
South End *Bkh.* 32 F44
Southend *Str.* 66 C12
Southend *Grm.* 99 E33
Southend *Brk.* 21 D42
Southend Airport 24 C54
Southend-on-Sea 24 C54
Southerndown 18 D24
Southerness 65 E25
South Erradale 94 D13
Southery 43 F51
South Fambridge 24 B54
South Fawley 21 C39
South Ferriby 59 G45
Southfleet 24 D52
South Flobbets 99 F33
South Garth 106 C41
Southgate *Nfk* 45 C57
Southgate *G.L.* 23 B48
South Godstone 23 G49
South Gorley 10 C37
South Green *Esx* 24 B52
South Green *Nfk* 44 D56
South Hall 73 C16
South Hanningfield 24 B53
South Harting 11 C43
South Hayling 11 E43
South Hazelrigg 77 G36
South Heath 22 A45
South Heighton 13 F50
South Hetton 62 B39
South Hiendley 51 A39
South Hill 4 C19
South Hole 6 D18
South Holmwood 22 G47
South Hornchurch 23 C51
South Hourat 74 E18
South Huish 5 F22
South Hykeham 52 F45
South Hylton 62 A39
Southhill 32 D47
Southington 21 G40
South Kelsey 52 C46
South Kessock 96 G22
South Killingholme 52 A47
South Kilvington 57 A40
South Kilworth 41 G41
South Kirkby 51 B40
South Kirkton 91 C33
South Kyme 52 G47
South Lancing 12 F47
South Ledaig 80 D15
Southleigh 8 E28
South Leigh 21 A39
South Leverton 51 D43
South Littleton 30 D36
South Lopham 44 G56
South Luffenham 42 E45
South Malling 13 E50
South Marston 20 C37
South Milford 58 F41
South Milton 5 F23
South Mimms 23 A48
Southminster 25 B55
South Molton 7 C23
South Moor 62 A37
South Moreton 21 C41
Southmuir 82 B29
South Mundham 12 G44
South Muskham 51 G43
South Newbald 59 F45
South Newington 31 E40
South Newton 10 A36
South Normanton 51 G40
South Norwood 23 E49
South Nutfield 23 G48
South Ockendon 23 C51
Southoe 32 B47
Southolt 35 B57
South Ormsby 53 E49
Southorpe 42 E46
South Otterington 57 A39
Southowram 57 G36
South Oxhey 22 B46
South Park 23 G48
South Perrott 8 D30
South Petherton 8 C30
South Petherwin 6 G19
South Pickenham 44 E54
South Pool 5 F23
Southport 48 A28
South Queensferry 75 C27
South Radworthy 7 B23
South Rauceby 42 A46
South Raynham 44 C54
South Redbriggs 99 E33
Southrepps 45 B58
South Reston 53 D50
Southrey 52 F47
Southrop 20 A37
Southrope 21 G42
South Runcton 44 E52
South Scarle 52 F44
Southsea *Clw.* 48 G28
Southsea *Ham.* 11 E42
South Shian 80 C15
South Shields 71 G39
South Skirlaugh 59 F47
South Somercotes 53 C50
South Stainley 57 C39
Southstoke 20 E33
South Stoke *Oxf.* 21 C42
South Stoke *W.S.* 12 F46
South Street *E.S.* 13 E49
South Street *Kent* 24 E52
South Tawton 6 F22
South Thoresby 53 E50
South Tidworth 21 G38
South Town 11 A42
Southtown *Ork.* 105 B30
Southtown *Nfk* 45 E61
South Upper Barrack 99 E35
South View 107 C39
Southwaite *Cum.* 60 B30
Southwaite *Cum.* 61 F33
South Walsham 45 D59
Southwark 23 D49
South Warnborough 22 G43
Southwater 12 D47
Southway 19 G30
South Weald 23 B51
Southwell *Dor.* 9 G32
Southwell *Not.* 51 G42
South Weston 21 B42
South Wheatley *Not.* 51 D43
South Wheatley *Cnw.* 4 A18
Southwick *Ham.* 11 D42
Southwick *Wts.* 20 F34
Southwick *T.&W.* 62 A39
Southwick *W.S.* 13 F48
Southwick *Nmp.* 42 F46
South Widcombe 19 F31
South Wigston 41 F41
South Willesborough 14 C55
South Willingham 52 D47
South Wingate 62 C40
South Wingfield 51 G39
South Witham 42 D44
Southwold 35 A61
South Wonston 11 A40
Southwood *Som.* 8 A31
Southwood *Nfk* 45 E59
South Woodham Ferrers 24 B54
South Wootton 44 C52
South Wraxall 20 E34
South Yardley 40 G37
South Zeal 6 F22
Sowerby *W.Y.* 57 G36
Sowerby *N.Y.* 57 A40
Sowerby Bridge 57 G36
Sowerby Row 60 B29
Sowton 7 F25
Soyal 96 B21
Spa Common 45 B58
Spadeadam 70 F31
Spalding 43 C48
Spaldington 58 F43
Spaldwick 32 A46
Spalefield 83 G31
Spalford 52 F44
Spanby 42 B46
Sparham 44 C56
Spark Bridge 55 A29
Sparkford 8 B31
Sparkwell 5 E21
Sparrowpit 50 D36
Sparrow's Green 13 C52
Sparsholt *Ham.* 11 A40
Sparsholt *Oxf.* 21 C39
Spartylea 61 B34
Spaunton 63 G43
Spaxton 8 A28
Spean Bridge 87 F18
Speddoch 68 E24
Speen *Bkh.* 22 A44
Speen *Brk.* 21 E40
Speeton 59 B47
Speke 48 D30
Speldhurst 23 G51
Spellbrook 33 G50
Spelsbury 30 F39
Spencers Wood 22 E43
Spen Green 49 F34
Spennithorne 57 A37
Spennymoor 62 C38
Spetchley 29 C34
Spetisbury 9 D34
Spexhall 45 G59
Spey Bay 98 C29
Speybridge 89 B26
Speyview 98 E28
Spilsby 53 F50
Spindlestone 77 G37
Spinkhill 51 E40
Spinningdale 96 B22
Spirthill 20 D35
Spital *Hgh.* 103 C27
Spital *Brk.* 22 D45
Spitalbrook 23 A49
Spital in the Street 52 C45
Spithurst 13 E50
Spittal *D.&G.* 64 E19
Spittal *D.&G.* 64 D20
Spittal *Dyf.* 16 B15
Spittal *Nor.* 77 E36
Spittal *Ltn* 76 C30
Spittalfield 82 C26
Spittal of Glenmuick 90 E29
Spittal of Glenshee 89 G26
Spixworth 45 D58
Spofforth 57 D39
Spondon 41 B39
Spooner Row 44 F56
Spoonley 39 B32
Sporle 44 D54
Sportsman's Arms 47 F25
Spott 76 C32
Spratton 31 B43
Spreakley 22 G44
Spreyton 6 F22
Spridlington 52 D46
Springburn 74 D22
Springfield *Str.* 73 C16
Springfield *Tay.* 82 D27
Springfield *Fife* 82 F29
Springfield *Grm.* 97 E26
Springfield *D.&G.* 69 G28
Springfield *W.M.* 40 G36
Springholm 65 D23
Springkell 69 F28
Springleys 99 F33
Springside 74 G19
Springthorpe 52 D44
Springwell 62 A38
Sproatley 59 F48
Sproston Green 49 F33
Sprotbrough 51 B41
Sproughton 35 D57
Sprouston 77 G33
Sprowston 45 D58
Sproxton *N.Y.* 58 A42
Sproxton *Lei.* 42 C44
Spurstow 48 G31
Square Point 65 C23
Squires Gate 55 F28
Sron Doire 73 C14
Sronphadruig Lodge 88 G22
Stableford 39 B33
Stackhouse 56 C33
Stackpole 16 E15
Stacksteads 56 G34
Staddiscombe 5 E21
Staddlethorpe 58 G44
Stadhampton 21 B42
Stadhlaigearraidh 84 A3
Staffield 61 B31
Staffin 93 E10
Stafford 40 C35
Stagden Cross 33 G52
Stagsden 32 D45
Stagshaw Bank 70 G35
Stain 103 B29
Stainburn 57 E38
Stainby 42 C44
Staincross 51 B39
Staindrop 62 D37
Staines 22 D46
Stainfield *Lcn.* 42 C46
Stainfield *Lcn.* 52 E46
Stainforth *N.Y.* 56 C34

Stainforth *S.Y.* 51 A42
Staining 55 F29
Stainland 50 A36
Stainsacre 63 F44
Stainton *N.Y.* 62 G36
Stainton *Cle.* 62 E40
Stainton *Drm* 62 E36
Stainton *Cum.* 61 D30
Stainton *Cum.* 55 A31
Stainton *S.Y.* 51 C41
Stainton by Langworth 52 E46
Staintondale 63 G45
Stainton le Vale 52 C47
Stainton with Adgarley 55 B28
Stair *Str.* 67 A20
Stair *Cum.* 60 D28
Staithes 63 E43
Stakeford 71 E38
Stake Pool 55 E30
Stalbridge 9 C33
Stalbridge Weston 9 C33
Stalham 45 C59
Stalham Green 45 C59
Stalisfield Green 14 B55
Stallingborough 53 A48
Stalling Busk 56 A35
Stalmine 55 E29
Stalybridge 49 C35
Stambourne 33 E52
Stamford *Nor.* 71 B38
Stamford *Lcn.* 42 E45
Stamford Bridge 58 D43
Stamfordham 71 F36
Stanborough 32 G47
Stanbridge *Bfd.* 32 F45
Stanbridge *Dor.* 9 D35
Stanbridge Earls 10 B39
Stanbury 56 F35
Stand 75 D23
Standburn 75 C25
Standeford 40 E34
Standen 14 C54
Standford 12 C44
Standish 48 A31
Standlake 21 A39
Standon *Stf.* 39 B33
Standon *Hfs.* 33 F49
Standon *Ham.* 11 B40
Stane 75 E24
Stanfield 44 C55
Stanford *Kent* 15 D57
Stanford *Bfd.* 32 D47
Stanford Bishop 29 C32
Stanford Bridge 29 B33
Stanford Dingley 21 D41
Stanford in the Vale 21 B39
Stanford-le-Hope 24 C52
Stanford on Avon 31 A41
Stanford on Soar 41 C41
Stanford on Teme 29 B32
Stanford Rivers 23 A51
Stanghow 63 E42
Stanground 42 F47
Stanhope *Drm* 62 C35
Stanhope *Bor.* 69 A27
Stanion 42 G45
Stanley *Dby.* 41 A40
Stanley *Stf.* 49 G35
Stanley *Tay.* 82 D26
Stanley *Wts.* 20 D35
Stanley *Drm* 62 A37
Stanley *W.Y.* 57 G39
Stanley Common 41 A40
Stanmer 13 F49
Stanmore *G.L.* 22 B47
Stanmore *Brk.* 21 D40
Stannersburn 70 E32
Stanningfield 34 C54
Stannington *S.Y.* 50 D38
Stannington *Nor.* 71 F37
Stansbatch 28 B29
Stansfield 34 C53
Stanstead 34 D54
Stanstead Abbots 33 G49
Stansted 23 E51
Stansted Airport 33 F51
Stansted Mountfitchet 33 F50
Stanton *Stf.* 40 A37
Stanton *Nor.* 71 D37
Stanton *Sfk* 34 A55
Stanton *Glo.* 30 E36
Stanton *Dby.* 40 D38
Stanton by Bridge 41 C39
Stanton by Dale 41 B40
Stanton Drew 19 E31
Stanton Fitzwarren 20 B37
Stanton Harcourt 21 A39
Stanton Hill 51 F40
Stanton in Peak 50 F38
Stanton Lacy 28 A30
Stanton Long 38 F31
Stanton on the Wolds 41 C42
Stanton Prior 19 E32
Stanton St Bernard 20 E36
Stanton St John 21 A41
Stanton St Quintin 20 C34
Stanton Street 34 B55
Stanton under Bardon 41 D40
Stanton upon Hine Heath 38 C31
Stanton Wick 19 E31
Stanwardine in the Fields 38 C29
Stanway *Esx* 34 F55
Stanway *Glo.* 30 E36
Stanwell 22 D46
Stanwell Moor 22 D46
Stanwick 32 A45
Stanwix 60 A29
Stanydale 107 B38
Staoinebrig 84 A3
Stape 63 G43
Stapehill 10 D36
Stapeley 39 A32
Staple 15 B58
Staple Cross 14 E53
Staplefield 13 D48
Staple Fitzpaine 8 C28
Stapleford *Lcn.* 52 G44
Stapleford *Hfs.* 33 G48
Stapleford *Cbs.* 33 C50
Stapleford *Lei.* 42 D44
Stapleford *Not.* 41 B40
Stapleford *Wts.* 10 A36
Stapleford Abbotts 23 B50
Stapleford Tawney 23 B50
Staplegrove 7 C27
Staplehurst 14 C53
Staplers 11 F41
Stapleton *Lei.* 41 F40
Stapleton *H.&W.* 28 B29
Stapleton *Shr.* 38 E30
Stapleton *Cum.* 69 F31
Stapleton *Som.* 8 B30
Stapleton *N.Y.* 62 E38
Stapleton *Avon* 19 D31
Stapley 7 D27
Staploe 32 B47
Staplow 29 D32
Star *Avon* 19 F30
Star *Dyf.* 17 A18
Star *Fife* 82 G29
Starbotton 56 B35
Starcross 7 G25
Starkigarth 107 E40
Starling's Green 33 E50
Starr 67 D20
Starston 45 G58
Startforth 62 E36
Startley 20 C35
Statham 49 D32
Stathe 8 B29
Stathern 42 B43
Station Town 62 C40
Staughton Green 32 B47
Staughton Highway 32 B47
Staunton *Glo.* 29 F33
Staunton *Glo.* 28 G31
Staunton Harold Hall 41 C39
Staunton on Arrow 28 C29
Staunton on Wye 28 D29
Staveley *Cum.* 61 G30
Staveley *N.Y.* 57 C39
Staveley *Dby.* 51 E40
Staveley-in-Cartmel 55 A29
Staverton *Nmp.* 31 B41
Staverton *Dev.* 5 D23
Staverton *Glo.* 29 F34
Staverton *Wts.* 20 E34
Staverton Bridge 29 F34
Stawell 8 A29
Stawley 7 C26
Staxigoe 103 C29
Staylittle (Penffordd-Las) 37 F24
Staynall 55 E29
Staythorpe 51 G43
Stean 57 B36
Steane 31 E41
Stearsby 58 B41
Steart 19 G28
Stebbing 33 F52
Stebbing Green 33 F52
Stedham 12 D44
Steel Cross 13 C51
Steele Road 70 D31
Steel Works 19 C29
Steen's Bridge 28 C31
Steep 11 B43
Steeple *Dor.* 9 F35
Steeple *Esx* 25 A55
Steeple Ashton 20 F35
Steeple Aston 31 F40
Steeple Barton 31 F40
Steeple Bumpstead 33 D52
Steeple Claydon 31 F42
Steeple Gidding 42 G47
Steeple Langford 10 A36
Steeple Morden 33 D48
Steeton 57 E36
Stein 93 F8
Steinmanhill 99 E33
Stella 71 G37
Stelling Minnis 15 C57
Stemster *Hgh.* 103 B27
Stemster *Hgh.* 103 D27
Stemster House 103 B27
Stenalees 4 E16
Stenhousemuir 75 B24
Stenigot 53 D48
Stenness 106 E37
Stenscholl 93 E10
Stenton *Ltn* 76 C32
Stenton *Tay.* 82 C26
Stepaside 16 D17
Stepney 23 C49
Steppingley 32 E45
Stepps 74 D22
Sternfield 35 B59
Sterridge 6 A21
Stert 20 F36
Stetchworth 33 C52
Stevenage 33 F48
Stevenston 74 F18
Steventon *Oxf.* 21 B40
Steventon *Ham.* 21 G41
Stevington 32 C45
Stewartby 32 D46
Stewarton *D.&G.* 64 F20
Stewarton *Str.* 74 F20
Stewkley 32 F44
Stewton 53 D49
Steyning 12 E47
Steynton 16 D15
Stibb 6 D18
Stibbard 44 C55
Stibb Cross 6 D20
Stibb Green 21 E38
Stibbington 42 F46
Stichill 76 G32
Sticker 3 C15
Stickford 53 F49
Sticklepath 6 F21
Stickney 53 G49
Stiffkey 44 A55
Stifford's Bridge 29 D33
Stillingfleet 58 E41
Stillington *N.Y.* 58 C41
Stillington *Cle.* 62 D39
Stilton 42 G47
Stinchcombe 20 B33
Stinsford 9 E33
Stirchley *Shr.* 39 E32
Stirchley *W.M.* 40 G36
Stirkoke House 103 C28
Stirling *Grm.* 99 E37
Stirling *Cen.* 75 A23
Stisted 34 F53
Stithians 2 E12
Stittenham 96 D22
Stivichall 30 A39
Stix 81 C23
Stixwould 52 F47
Stoak 48 E30
Stobo 75 G27
Stoborough 9 F34
Stoborough Green 9 F35
Stobwood 75 E25
Stock 24 B52
Stockbridge *Cen.* 81 G23
Stockbridge *Ham.* 10 A39
Stockbury 24 E54
Stockcross 21 E40
Stockdalewath 60 B29
Stockerston 42 F44
Stock Green 29 B35
Stockingford 41 F39
Stocking Pelham 33 F50
Stockland 8 D28
Stockland Bristol 19 G28
Stock Lane 21 D38
Stockleigh English 7 E24
Stockleigh Pomeroy 7 E24
Stockley 20 E35
Stocklinch 8 C29
Stockport 49 D34
Stocksbridge 50 C38
Stocksfield 71 G36
Stockton *Wts.* 9 A35
Stockton *Nfk* 45 F59
Stockton *Shr.* 39 F33
Stockton *War.* 31 B40
Stockton *H.&W.* 28 B31
Stockton Heath 49 D32
Stockton-on-Tees 62 D39
Stockton on Teme 29 B33
Stockton on the Forest 58 D42
Stock Wood 29 C35
Stockwood 8 D31
Stodday 55 D30
Stodmarsh 25 E57
Stody 44 B56
Stoer 101 F16
Stoford *Som.* 8 C31
Stoford *Wts.* 10 A36
Stogumber 7 B26
Stogursey 7 A27
Stoke *W.M.* 30 A39
Stoke *Kent* 24 D54
Stoke *Dev.* 6 C18
Stoke *Ham.* 11 D43
Stoke *Ham.* 21 F39
Stoke Abbott 8 D30
Stoke Albany 42 G44
Stoke Ash 35 A57
Stoke Bardolph 41 A42
Stoke Bliss 29 B32
Stoke Bruerne 31 C43
Stoke by Clare 34 D53
Stoke-by-Nayland 34 E55
Stoke Canon 7 F25
Stoke Charity 11 A40
Stoke Climsland 4 C19
Stoke D'Abernon 22 F47
Stoke Doyle 42 G46
Stoke Dry 42 F44
Stoke Ferry 44 F52
Stoke Fleming 5 F24
Stokeford 9 F34
Stoke Gabriel 5 E24
Stoke Gifford 19 D32
Stoke Golding 41 F39
Stoke Goldington 32 D44
Stokeham 51 E43
Stoke Hammond 32 F44
Stoke Heath 39 C32
Stoke Holy Cross 45 E58
Stokeinteignhead 5 C25
Stoke Lacy 28 D31
Stoke Lyne 31 F41
Stoke Mandeville 22 A44
Stokenchurch 22 B43
Stoke Newington 23 C49
Stokenham 5 F23
Stoke on Tern 39 C32
Stoke-on-Trent 40 A34
Stoke Orchard 29 F35
Stoke Poges 22 C45
Stoke Prior *H.&W.* 28 C31
Stoke Prior *H.&W.* 29 B35
Stoke Rivers 6 B22
Stoke Rochford 42 C44
Stoke Row 21 C42
Stokesay 38 G29
Stokesby 45 D60
Stokesley 63 F41
Stoke St Gregory 8 B29
Stoke St Mary 8 B28
Stoke St Michael 19 G32
Stoke St Milborough 38 G31
Stoke sub Hamdon 8 C30
Stoke Talmage 21 B42
Stoke Trister 9 B33
Stoke Wake 9 D33
Stolford 19 G28
Stonar Cut 25 E59
Stondon Massey 23 A51
Stone *Kent* 23 D51
Stone *Kent* 14 E55
Stone *H.&W.* 29 A34
Stone *Bkh.* 31 G43
Stone *Stf.* 40 B35
Stone *Glo.* 19 B32
Stone Allerton 19 F29
Ston Easton 19 F32
Stonebridge *E.S.* 13 D51
Stonebridge *War.* 40 G38
Stonebroom 51 G39
Stone Cross *E.S.* 13 F52
Stone Cross *Kent* 13 C51
Stone Cross *Kent* 15 D56
Stoneferry 59 F46
Stonefield *Str.* 74 E22
Stonefield *Str.* 73 C14
Stonegate 13 D52
Stonegrave 58 B42
Stonehaugh 70 F33
Stonehaven 91 E34
Stonehouse *Nor.* 61 A32
Stone House 56 A33
Stonehouse *Str.* 75 F23
Stonehouse *Glo.* 20 A33
Stonehouse *Dev.* 4 E20
Stonehouse *D.&G.* 65 D24
Stoneleigh 30 A39
Stonely 32 B46
Stoner Hill 11 B43
Stonesby 42 C44
Stonesfield 30 G39
Stones Green 35 F57
Stone Street *Sfk* 45 G59
Stone Street *Kent* 23 F51
Stonestreet Green 15 D56
Stonethwaite 60 E28
Stoneyburn 75 D25
Stoney Cross 10 C38
Stoneygate 41 E41
Stoneyhills 25 B55
Stoney Houghton 51 F40
Stoneykirk 64 E16
Stoney Stanton 41 F40
Stoney Stoke 9 A33
Stoney Stratton 9 A32
Stoney Stretton 38 E29
Stoneywood 91 B34
Stonganess 106 B41
Stonham Aspal 35 C57
Stonnall 40 E36
Stonor 22 C43
Stonton Wyville 42 F43
Stonybreck 106 A37
Stonyhurst College 56 F32
Stony Stratford 31 D43
Stoodleigh 7 D24
Stopham 12 E46
Stopsley 32 F46
Stoptide 3 A15
Storeton 48 D28
Stornoway 100 D9
Stornoway Airport 100 D10
Storridge 29 D33
Storrington 12 E46
Storth 55 A30
Storwood 58 E42
Stotfield 98 B28
Stotfold 32 E47
Stottesdon 39 G32
Stoughton *Lei.* 41 E42
Stoughton *Sry* 22 F45
Stoughton *W.S.* 11 C43
Stoul 86 E13
Stoulton 29 C34
Stourbridge 40 G34
Stourpaine 9 D34
Stourport-on-Severn 29 A33
Stour Provost 9 B33
Stour Row 9 B34
Stourton *Wts.* 9 A33
Stourton *War.* 30 E38
Stourton *Stf.* 40 G34
Stourton Caundle 9 C33
Stove 104 C32
Stoven 45 G60
Stow *Bor.* 76 F30
Stow *Lcn.* 52 D44
Stow Bardolph 44 E52
Stow Bedon 44 F55
Stowbridge 43 E51
Stow cum Quy 33 B50
Stowe *Shr.* 28 A28
Stowe *Stf.* 40 C35
Stowe *Glo.* 19 A31
Stowell *Glo.* 30 G36
Stowell *Som.* 9 B32
Stowey 19 F31
Stowford 6 G20
Stowlangtoft 34 B54
Stow Longa 32 A47
Stow Maries 24 B54
Stowmarket 34 C56
Stow-on-the-Wold 30 F37
Stowting 15 C56
Stowupland 34 B56
Stracathro 91 G32
Strachan 91 D32
Strachur 80 G16
Stradbroke 35 A58
Stradishall 34 C53
Stradsett 44 E52
Stragglethorpe 52 G44
Straiton *Str.* 67 C19
Straiton *Ltn.* 76 D28
Straloch *Tay.* 82 A26
Straloch *Grm.* 91 A34
Stramshall 40 B36
Strang 54 F25
Strannda 92 C6
Stranraer 64 D16
Strata Florida 27 B23
Stratfield Mortimer 21 E42
Stratfield Saye 21 E42
Stratfield Turgis 21 F42
Stratford 29 E34
Stratford St Andrew 35 B59
Stratford St Mary 34 E56
Stratford sub Castle 10 A37
Stratford Tony 10 B36
Stratford-upon-Avon 30 C37
Strath 103 C28
Strathan *Hgh.* 86 E15
Strathan *Hgh.* 101 F16
Strathaven 74 F22
Strathblane 74 C21
Strathdon 90 B29
Strathgirnock 90 D29
Strathkanaird 95 A17
Strathkinness 83 F30
Strathmiglo 82 G27
Strathpeffer 96 F20
Strathrannoch 96 D19
Strathwhillan 73 G16
Strathy 102 B24
Strathyre 81 F21
Stratton *Glo.* 20 A35
Stratton *Dor.* 9 E32
Stratton *Cnw.* 6 E18
Stratton Audley 31 F42
Stratton-on-the-Fosse 19 F32
Stratton St Margaret 20 C37
Stratton St Michael 45 F58
Stratton Strawless 45 C58

Stravanan 73 E16
Stravithie 83 F31
Streat 13 E49
Streatham 23 D48
Streatley *Brk.* 21 C41
Streatley *Bfd.* 32 F46
Street *Som.* 8 A30
Street *N.Y.* 63 F43
Street *Lan.* 55 D31
Street Dinas 38 B29
Street End *Kent* 15 B57
Street End *W.S.* 12 G44
Streethay 40 D37
Streetlam 62 G39
Streetly 40 F36
Street on the Fosse 8 A31
Strefford 38 G30
Strensall 58 C42
Strensham 29 D34
Stretcholt 19 G28
Strete 5 F24
Stretford 49 C33
Stretford Court 28 C30
Strethall 33 E50
Stretham 33 A50
Strettington 12 F44
Stretton *Dby.* 51 F39
Stretton *Che.* 49 D32
Stretton *Che.* 48 G30
Stretton *Stf.* 40 C38
Stretton *Lei.* 42 D45
Stretton *Stf.* 40 D34
Stretton en le Field 41 D39
Stretton Grandison 29 D32
Stretton Heath 38 D29
Stretton-on-Dunsmore 31 A40
Stretton-on-Fosse 30 E37
Stretton Sugwas 28 D30
Stretton under Fosse 41 G40
Stretton Westwood 38 F31
Stribers 55 A29
Strichen 99 D35
Stringston 7 A27
Strixton 32 B44
Stroat 19 B31
Stromeferry 86 A14
Stromemore 86 A14
Stromness 105 A28
Stronachlachar 80 G19
Strone *Hgh.* 87 F17
Strone *Hgh.* 88 B21
Strone *Str.* 73 B17
Strone Cen. 81 F20
Stronechrubie 101 G18
Stronenaba 87 F17
Stronlonag 73 B16
Stronmilchan 80 E17
Stronsay Airport 104 D32
Strontian 79 A14
Strontoiller 79 E14
Stronvar 81 F21
Strood 24 E53
Strood Green 12 D46
Stroquhan 68 E24
Stroud *Glo.* 20 A34
Stroud *Ham.* 11 B43
Stroud Common 22 G46
Stroud Green 20 A34
Stroul 74 B18
Stroxton 42 B44
Struan *Hgh.* 85 A9
Struan *Tay.* 81 A23
Strubby 53 D50
Strumpshaw 45 E59
Struthers 82 G29
Struy 96 G19
Stryt-issa 38 A28
Stryt-yr-hwch 38 A29
Stuartfield 99 E35
Stubbington 11 D41
Stubbins 49 A33
Stubhampton 9 C34
Stubley 51 E39
Stub Place 60 G26
Stubton 42 A44
Stuck *Str.* 73 D16
Stuck *Str.* 73 A17
Stuckbeg 74 A18
Stuckgowan 80 G18
Stuckindroin 80 F18
Stuckreoch 73 A16
Stuckton 10 C37
Studdon 61 A34
Studfold 56 B34
Stud Green 22 D44
Studham 32 G46
Studholme 60 A28
Studland 10 F36
Studley *Wts.* 20 D35
Studley *War.* 30 B36
Studley Common 30 B36
Studley Roger 57 B38
Stuggadhoo 54 F24
Stump Cross 33 D50
Stuntney 33 A51
Stunts Green 13 E52
Sturbridge 40 B34
Sturmer 33 D52
Sturminster Common 9 C33
Sturminster Marshall 9 D35
Sturminster Newton 9 C33
Sturry 25 E57
Sturton by Stow 52 D44
Sturton le Steeple 51 D43
Stuston 35 A57
Stutton *Sfk* 35 E57
Stutton *N.Y.* 57 E40
Styal 49 D34
Styrrup 51 C41
Suainebost 101 A11
Suardail 100 D10
Succoth *Str.* 80 G18
Succoth *Grm.* 98 F30
Succothmore 80 G17
Suckley 29 C33
Sudborough 42 G45
Sudbourne 35 C60
Sudbrook *Gwe.* 19 C30
Sudbrook *Lcn.* 42 A45
Sudbrooke 52 E46
Sudbury *Dby.* 40 B37
Sudbury *Sfk* 34 D54
Sudbury *G.L.* 22 C47
Sudgrove 20 A35
Suffield *Nfk* 45 B58
Suffield *N.Y.* 63 G45
Sugarloaf 14 D55
Sugnall 39 B33
Suie Lodge Hotel 81 E20
Sulby 54 D25
Sulgrave 31 D41
Sulham 21 D42
Sulhamstead 21 E42
Sullington 12 E46
Sullom 106 E39
Sullom Voe Oil Terminal 106 E39
Sully 18 E27
Sumburgh 107 E37
Summer Bridge 57 C38
Summercourt 3 C14
Summerhill 48 G28
Summer-house 62 E37
Summerleaze 19 C29
Summerseat 49 A33
Summertown 21 A40
Summit 49 A35
Sunadale 73 F13
Sunbury 22 E46
Sundaywell 68 E23
Sunderland *T.&W.* 62 A39
Sunderland *Cum.* 60 C27
Sunderland Bridge 62 C38
Sundhope 69 A29
Sundon Park 32 F46
Sundridge 23 F50
Sundrum 67 A20
Sunhill 20 A36
Sunipol 78 B9
Sunk Island 53 A48
Sunningdale 22 E45
Sunninghill 22 E45
Sunningwell 21 B40
Sunniside *Drm.* 62 C38
Sunniside *T.&W.* 62 A38
Sunny Bank 60 G28
Sunnylaw 75 A23
Sunnymead 21 A40
Sunnyside *Nor.* 70 G35
Sunnyside *Grm.* 91 D34
Sunnyside *W.S.* 13 C49
Sunwick 77 E34
Surbiton 22 E47
Surfleet 43 C48
Surfleet Seas End 43 C48
Surlingham 45 E59
Sustead 45 B57
Susworth 52 B44
Sutcombe 6 D19
Suton 44 F56
Sutors of Cromarty 96 E23
Sutterton 43 B48
Sutton *Cbs.* 42 F46
Sutton *Not.* 42 B43
Sutton *W.S.* 12 E45
Sutton *G.L.* 23 E48
Sutton *Sry* 22 G47
Sutton *Lcn.* 52 G44
Sutton *Not.* 51 D42
Sutton *S.Y.* 51 A41
Sutton *Shr.* 39 G33
Sutton *Stf.* 39 C33
Sutton *Sfk* 35 D59
Sutton *Shr.* 38 E30
Sutton *Shr.* 39 B32
Sutton *Bfd.* 33 D48
Sutton *Cbs.* 33 A50
Sutton *Nfk* 45 C59
Sutton *Oxf.* 21 A40
Sutton *Kent* 15 C59
Sutton *Dyf.* 16 C15
Sutton at Hone 23 E51
Sutton Bassett 42 G43
Sutton Benger 20 D35
Sutton Bonington 41 C41
Sutton Bridge 43 C50
Sutton Cheney 41 E40
Sutton Coldfield 40 F37
Sutton Courtenay 21 B40
Sutton Crosses 43 C50
Sutton Grange 57 B38
Sutton Green 22 F46
Sutton Holms 10 C36
Sutton Howgrave 57 B38
Sutton in Ashfield 51 G41
Sutton-in-Craven 56 E35
Sutton in the Elms 41 F41
Sutton Lane Ends 49 E35
Sutton Leach 48 C31
Sutton le Marsh 53 D51
Sutton Maddock 39 E33
Sutton Mallet 8 A29
Sutton Mandeville 9 B35
Sutton Montis 9 B32
Sutton-on-Hull 59 F47
Sutton on Sea 53 D51
Sutton-on-the-Forest 58 C41
Sutton on the Hill 40 B38
Sutton on Trent 51 F43
Sutton Poyntz 9 F32
Sutton Scotney 11 A40
Sutton St Edmund 43 D49
Sutton St James 43 D50
Sutton St Nicholas 28 D31
Sutton-under-Brailes 30 E39
Sutton-under-Whitestonecliffe 57 A40
Sutton upon Derwent 58 E43
Sutton Valence 14 C54
Sutton Veny 20 G34
Sutton Waldron 9 C34
Sutton Weaver 48 E31
Sutton Wick 21 B40
Swaby 53 E49
Swadlincote 40 C38
Swaffham 44 E54
Swaffham Bulbeck 33 B51
Swaffham Prior 33 B51
Swafield 45 B58
Swainby 62 F40
Swainshill 28 D30
Swainsthorpe 45 E58
Swainswick 20 E33
Swalcliffe 30 E39
Swalecliffe 25 E57
Swallow 52 B47
Swallow Beck 52 F45
Swallowcliffe 9 B35
Swallowfield 22 E43
Swalwell 71 G37
Swampton 21 F40
Swanage 9 G35
Swanbach 39 A32
Swanbourne 31 F43
Swanbridge 18 E27
Swancote 39 F33
Swanlaws 70 B33
Swanley 23 E51
Swanmore 11 C41
Swannington *Lei.* 41 D39
Swannington *Nfk* 45 D57
Swanscombe 23 D51
Swansea 17 E22
Swansea Airport 17 E21
Swan Street 34 F54
Swanton Abbot 45 C58
Swanton Morley 44 D56
Swanton Novers 44 B56
Swanwick *Dby.* 51 G39
Swanwick *Ham.* 11 D41
Swarby 42 A46
Swardeston 45 E57
Swarkestone 41 C39
Swarland 71 C37
Swaton 42 B47
Swavesey 33 B49
Sway 10 E38
Swayfield 42 C45
Swaythling 11 C40
Swaythorpe 59 C46
Sweetshouse 4 D16
Sweffling 35 B59
Swell 8 B29
Swepstone 41 D39
Swerford 30 E39
Swettenham 49 F33
Swffryd 19 B28
Swiftsden 14 E53
Swilland 35 C57
Swillbrook 55 F30
Swillington 57 F39
Swimbridge 6 C21
Swimbridge Newland 6 B22
Swinbrook 30 G38
Swincliffe 57 D38
Swinderby 52 F44
Swindon *Glo.* 29 F35
Swindon *Wts.* 20 C37
Swindon *Stf.* 40 F34
Swine 59 F47
Swinefleet 58 G43
Swineshead *Bfd.* 32 B46
Swineshead *Lcn.* 43 A48
Swineshead Bridge 43 A48
Swiney 103 E28
Swinford *Oxf.* 21 A40
Swinford *Lei.* 31 A41
Swingfield Minnis 15 C58
Swinhoe 71 A37
Swinhope 52 C47
Swining 107 A40
Swinithwaite 57 A36
Swinscoe 40 A37
Swinside Hall 70 B33
Swinstead 42 C46
Swinton *S.Y.* 51 C40
Swinton *G.M.* 49 B33
Swinton *Bor.* 77 F34
Swinton *N.Y.* 58 B43
Swinton *N.Y.* 57 B38
Swintonmill 77 F33
Swithland 41 D41
Swordale 96 E21
Swordland 86 E13
Swordle 79 A11
Swordly 102 B23
Sworton Heath 49 D32
Swyddffynnon 27 B22
Swyncombe 21 B42
Swynnerton 40 B34
Swyre 8 F31
Syde 29 G35
Sydenham *Oxf.* 22 A43
Sydenham *G.L.* 23 D49
Sydenham Damerel 4 C20
Sydling St Nicholas 9 E32
Sydmonton 21 F40
Syerston 42 A43
Syke 49 A34
Sykehouse 51 A42
Sykes 56 D32
Sylen 17 D21
Symbister 107 A41
Symington *Str.* 75 G25
Symington *Str.* 74 G19
Symondsbury 8 E29
Symonds Yat 28 G31
Synod Inn 26 C19
Syre 102 D22
Syreford 30 F36
Syresham 31 D42
Syston *Lcn.* 42 A45
Syston *Lei.* 41 D42
Sytchampton 29 B34
Sywell 32 B44

T

Taagan 95 E16
Tabost *W.I.* 101 A11
Tabost *W.I.* 100 F9
Tacher 103 D27
Tackley 31 G40
Tacleit 100 D7
Tacolneston 45 F57
Tadcaster 57 E40
Tadden 9 D35
Taddington 50 E37
Taddiport 6 D20
Tadley 21 E42
Tadlow 33 D48
Tadmarton 30 E39
Tadworth 23 F48
Tafarnaubach 27 G26
Tafarn-y-bwlch 16 A16
Tafarn-y-Gelyn 47 F27
Taffs Well 18 C26
Tafolwern 37 E24
Tai-bach 38 C27
Taibach 18 C23
Tain *Hgh.* 103 B28
Tain *Hgh.* 96 C23
Tai'n Lon 46 G20
Tairbeart (Tarbert) 100 G7
Tai'r Bull 27 F25
Tairlaw 67 C20
Takeley 33 F51
Takeley Street 33 F51
Talachddu 27 E26
Talacre 47 D27
Talardd 37 C24
Talaton 7 F26
Talbenny 16 C14
Talbot Green 18 C26
Talerddig 37 E25
Talgarreg 26 C20
Talgarth 28 E27
Taliesin 37 F22
Talisker 85 B9
Talke 49 G34
Talkin 61 A31
Talla Bheith 81 B21
Talladale 94 D14
Talla Linnfoots 69 A27
Tallarn Green 38 A30
Tallentire 60 C26
Talley 17 A22
Tallington 42 E46
Talmine 102 B21
Talog 17 B19
Tal-sarn 26 C21
Talsarnau 36 B21
Talskiddy 3 B14
Talwrn *Clw.* 38 A28
Talwrn *Gwy.* 46 E20
Tal-y-bont *Gwy.* 47 F23
Tal-y-bont *Gwy.* 46 E21
Talybont 37 G22
Tal-y-bont *Gwy.* 36 C21
Talybont-on-Usk 27 F26
Tal-y-Cae 46 F21
Tal-y-cafn 47 E23
Talyllyn 27 F26
Tal-y-llyn 37 E22
Talysarn 46 G20
Tal-y-wern 37 E24
Tamavoid 74 A21
Tamerton Foliot 4 D20
Tamworth 40 E37
Tandridge 23 F49
Tanerdy 17 B20
Tanfield 62 A37
Tangiers 16 C15
Tanglandford 99 F34
Tangley 21 F39
Tangmere 12 F44
Tangwick 106 E38
Tangy 66 A12
Tankerness 105 A30
Tankersley 51 C39
Tan-lan 37 A22
Tannach 103 D29
Tannachie 91 E33
Tannachy 96 A23
Tannadice 83 B30
Tannington 35 B58
Tannochside 75 D23
Tansley 51 G39
Tansor 42 F46
Tantobie 62 A37
Tanton 63 E41
Tanworth in Arden 30 A37
Tan-y-fron 47 F25
Tan-y-graig 36 B18
Tanygrisiau 37 A22
Tan-y-groes 26 D18
Tan-y-pistyll 37 C26
Taobh A Deas Loch Baghasdail 84 C3
Taobh Tuath 92 C5
Taoth Siar 100 G7
Tapeley 6 C20
Taplow 22 C44
Taravocan 80 C15
Tarbat Ho. 96 D23
Tarbert (Tairbeart) 100 G7
Tarbert *Hgh.* 79 A12
Tarbert *Str.* 73 D14
Tarbert *Str.* 72 E12
Tarbert *Str.* 72 B12
Tarbet *Str.* 80 G19
Tarbet *Hgh.* 101 D17
Tarbet *Hgh.* 86 E13
Tarbolton 67 A19
Tarbrax 75 E26
Tardebigge 29 B35
Tardy Gate 55 G31
Tarfside 90 E30
Tarland 90 C30
Tarleton 55 G30
Tarlscough 48 A30
Tarlton 20 B35
Tarnbrook 55 D31
Tarnock 19 F29
Tarporley 48 F31
Tarr 7 B26
Tarrant Crawford 9 D35
Tarrant Gunville 9 C35
Tarrant Hinton 9 C35
Tarrant Keyneston 9 D35
Tarrant Launceston 9 D35
Tarrant Monkton 9 D35
Tarrant Rawston 9 D35
Tarrant Rushton 9 D35
Tarrel 97 C24
Tarring Neville 13 F50
Tarrington 28 D31
Tarrnacraig 73 G15
Tarsappie 82 E27
Tarskavaig 86 D11
Tarves 99 F34
Tarvie *Tay.* 82 A26
Tarvie *Hgh.* 96 F20
Tarvin 48 F30
Tarvin Sands 48 F30
Tasburgh 45 F58
Tasley 39 F32
Taston 30 F39
Tatenhill 40 C37
Tatham 55 C31

Tathwell 53 D49
Tatsfield 23 F50
Tattenhall 48 G30
Tatterford 44 C54
Tattershall 53 G48
Tattershall Bridge 52 G47
Tattershall Thorpe 53 G48
Tattingstone 35 E57
Tatworth 8 D29
Tauchers 98 E29
Taunton 8 B28
Tavelty 91 B33
Taverham 45 D57
Tavernspite 16 C17
Tavistock 4 C20
Taw Bridge 6 E22
Taw Green 6 F22
Tawstock 6 B21
Taxal 49 E35
Tayburn 74 F21
Tayinloan 72 F12
Taylors Cross 6 D18
Taynafead 80 F16
Taynish 73 B13
Taynton *Oxf.* 30 G38
Taynton *Glo.* 29 F33
Taynuilt 80 D15
Tayock 83 B32
Tayovullin 72 C8
Tayport 83 E30
Tayvallich 73 B13
Tealby 52 C47
Team Valley 71 G38
Teanamachar 92 E3
Teangue 86 D12
Teasses 82 G29
Tebay 61 F32
Tebworth 32 F45
Tedburn St Mary 7 F24
Teddington *Glo.* 29 E35
Teddington *G.L.* 22 D47
Tedstone Delamere 29 C32
Tedstone Wafre 29 C32
Tees-side Airport 62 E39
Teeton 31 A42
Teffont Evias 9 A35
Teffont Magna 9 A35
Tegryn 17 A18
Teigh 42 D44
Teigngrace 5 C24
Teignmouth 5 C25
Telford 39 E32
Telham 14 F53
Tellisford 20 F33
Telscombe 13 F50
Telscombe Cliffs 13 F49
Tempar 81 B22
Templand 69 E26
Temple *Cnw.* 4 C17
Temple *Ltn* 76 E29
Temple Bar 26 C21
Temple Cloud 19 F32
Templecombe 9 B32
Temple Ewell 15 C58
Temple Grafton 30 C36
Temple Guiting 30 F36
Temple Hirst 58 G42
Temple Normanton 51 F40
Temple Sowerby 61 D31
Templeton *Dyf.* 16 C16
Templeton *Dev.* 7 D24
Templeton Bridge 7 D24
Templewood 83 A31
Tempsford 32 C47
Tenbury Wells 28 B31
Tenby 16 D17
Tendring 35 F57
Tenga 79 C11
Ten Mile Bank 43 F51
Tenterden 14 D54
Tepersie Castle 90 A31
Terally 64 F17
Terling 34 G53
Ternhill 39 B32
Terregles 65 C25
Terrington 58 B42
Terrington St Clement 43 C51
Terrington St John 43 D51
Tervieside 98 F28
Teston 14 B53
Testwood 10 C39
Tetbury 20 B34
Tetbury Upton 20 B34
Tetchill 38 B29
Tetcott 6 F19
Tetford 53 E49
Tetney 53 B49
Tetney Lock 53 B49
Tetsworth 21 A42
Tettenhall 40 E34
Tettenhall Wood 40 F34
Tetworth 33 C48
Teuchan 99 F36
Teversal 51 F40
Teversham 33 C50
Teviothead 69 C29
Tewel 91 E34
Tewin 33 G48
Tewkesbury 29 E34
Teynham 25 E55
Thainston 91 F32
Thainstone 91 B33
Thakeham 12 E47
Thame 21 A42
Thames Ditton 22 E47
Thames Haven 24 C53
Thamesmead 23 C50
Thanington 15 B57
Thankerton 75 G25
Tharston 45 F57
Thatcham 21 E41
Thatto Heath 48 C30
Thaxted 33 E51
Theakston 57 A38
Thealby 52 A45
Theale *Som.* 19 G30
Theale *Brk.* 21 D42
Thearne 59 F46
The Bage 28 D28
The Banking 99 F33
The Bar 12 D47
Theberton 35 B60
The Birks 91 C33
The Bog 38 F29
The Bourne 22 G44
The Bratch 40 F34
The Bryn 19 A29
The Burf 29 B34
The Burn 90 F31
The Camp 20 A35
The Chequer 38 A30
The City 22 B43
The Common 10 A38
The Craigs 96 B20
The Cronk 54 D25
Thedden Grange 11 A42
Theddingworth 41 G42
Theddlethorpe All Saints 53 D50
Theddlethorpe St Helen 53 D50
The Den 74 E19
The Dicker 13 F51
The Drums 82 A29
The Eaves 19 A31
The Flatt 70 F31
The Folly 32 G47
The Grange *Shr.* 38 B29
The Grange *Sry* 23 G49
The Green *Str.* 78 C5
The Green *Wts.* 9 A34
The Haven 12 C46
The Hermitage 23 F48
The Howe 54 G24
The Isle 38 D30
The Knowle 23 G52
The Laurels 45 F59
Thelbridge Barton 7 D23
The Leacon 14 D55
The Lee 22 A44
The Lhen 54 C25
Thelnetham 34 A56
The Lodge 73 A17
Thelveton 45 G57
Thelwall 49 D32
The Marsh 38 F28
Themelthorpe 44 C56
The Moor 14 E53
The Mumbles 17 F22
The Mythe 29 E34
The Neuk 91 D33
Thenford 31 D41
The Node 32 G47
Therfield 33 E49
The Rhos 16 C15
The Rowe 40 B34
The Sands 22 G44
The Shoe 20 D34
The Smithies 39 F32
The Stocks 14 E55
Thetford 44 G54
The Vauld 28 D31
The Wrythe 23 E48
The Wyke 39 E33
Theydon Bois 23 B50
Thickwood 20 D34
Thimbleby *N.Y.* 62 G40
Thimbleby *Lcn.* 53 E48
Thirkleby 57 B40
Thirlby 57 A40
Thirlestane 76 F31
Thirn 57 A38
Thirsk 57 A40
Thistleton *Lei.* 42 D44
Thistleton *Lan.* 55 F30
Thistley Green 33 A52
Thixendale 58 C44
Thockrington 70 F35
Tholomas Drove 43 E50
Tholthorpe 57 C40
Thomas Chapel 16 D16
Thomastown 98 F31
Thompson 44 F54
Thomshill 97 F27
Thong 24 D52
Thoralby 56 A35
Thoresby 51 E42
Thoresway 52 C47
Thorganby *Lcn.* 52 C47
Thorganby *N.Y.* 58 E42
Thorgill 63 G42
Thorington 35 A60
Thorington Street 34 E56
Thorlby 56 D35
Thorley 33 G50
Thorley Street *Hfs.* 33 G50
Thorley Street *Ham.* 10 F39
Thormanby 57 B40
Thornaby-on-Tees 62 E40
Thornage 44 B56
Thornborough *N.Y.* 57 B38
Thornborough *Bkh.* 31 E43
Thornbury *H.&W.* 29 C32
Thornbury *Dev.* 6 E19
Thornbury *Avon* 19 B32
Thornby 31 A42
Thorncliff 49 G35
Thorncombe 8 D29
Thorncombe Street 22 G46
Thorncote Green 32 D47
Thorndon 35 B57
Thorne 51 A42
Thorner 57 E39
Thornes 40 E36
Thorne St Margaret 7 C26
Thorney *Not.* 52 E44
Thorney *Som.* 8 B30
Thorney *Cbs.* 43 E48
Thorney *Bkh.* 22 D46
Thorney Hill 10 D38
Thorn Falcon 8 B28
Thornford 8 C31
Thorngrove 8 A29
Thorngumbald 59 G48
Thornham 44 A53
Thornham Magna 34 A56
Thornham Parva 35 A57
Thornhaugh 42 E46
Thornhill *Ham.* 11 C40
Thornhill *Dby.* 50 D37
Thornhill *W.Y.* 50 A38
Thornhill *D.&G.* 68 D24
Thornhill *M.G.* 18 C27
Thornhill *Cen.* 81 G22
Thornholme 59 C47
Thornicombe 9 D34
Thornley *Drm* 62 B39
Thornley *Drm.* 62 C37
Thornliebank 74 E21
Thorns 34 C53
Thornsett 49 D35
Thornthwaite *Cum.* 60 D27
Thornthwaite *N.Y.* 57 D37
Thornton *Lan.* 55 E29
Thornton *Lei.* 41 E40
Thornton *Hum.* 58 E43
Thornton *W.Y.* 57 F36
Thornton *Mer.* 48 B29
Thornton *Nor.* 77 F35
Thornton *Fife* 76 A28
Thornton *Dyf.* 16 D15
Thornton *Tay.* 82 C26
Thornton *Tay.* 82 C29
Thornton *Cle.* 62 E40
Thornton *Lcn.* 53 F48
Thornton *Bkh.* 31 E43
Thornton Cross 6 F21
Thornton Curtis 52 A46
Thornton Dale 58 A44
Thorntonhall 74 E21
Thornton Hough 48 D29
Thornton-in-Craven 56 E35
Thornton-le-Beans 62 G40
Thornton-le-Clay 58 C42
Thornton-le-Moor 57 A39
Thornton le Moor 52 C46
Thornton-le-Moors 48 E30
Thornton-le -Street 57 A39
Thorntonloch 77 C33
Thornton Park 77 F35
Thornton Rust 56 A35
Thornton Steward 57 A37
Thornton Watlass 57 A38
Thornwood Common 23 A50
Thornyhill 91 F32
Thornylee 76 G29
Thoroton 42 A43
Thorp Arch 57 E40
Thorpe *Hum.* 59 E46
Thorpe *N.Y.* 57 C36
Thorpe *Nfk* 45 F60
Thorpe *Not.* 51 G43
Thorpe *Dby.* 50 G37
Thorpe *Lcn.* 53 D50
Thorpe *Sry* 22 E46
Thorpe Abbotts 45 G57
Thorpe Acre 41 D40
Thorpe Arnold 42 C43
Thorpe Audlin 51 A40
Thorpe Bassett 58 B44
Thorpe Bay 25 C55
Thorpe by Water 42 F44
Thorpe Constantine 40 E38
Thorpe Culvert 53 F50
Thorpe End Garden Village 45 D58
Thorpe Green 34 C55
Thorpe Hall 58 B41
Thorpe Hesley 51 C39
Thorpe in Balne 51 A41
Thorpe in the Fallows 52 D45
Thorpe Langton 42 F43
Thorpe Larches 62 D39
Thorpe-le-Soken 35 F57
Thorpe le Street 58 E44
Thorpe Malsor 32 A44
Thorpe Mandeville 31 D40
Thorpe Market 45 B58
Thorpe Morieux 34 C55
Thorpeness 35 C60
Thorpe on the Hill *Lcn.* 52 F44
Thorpe on the Hill *W.Y.* 57 G38
Thorpe Salvin 51 D41
Thorpe Satchville 42 D43
Thorpe St Andrew 45 E58
Thorpe St Peter 53 F50
Thorpe Thewles 62 D39
Thorpe Tilney Dales 52 G47
Thorpe Underwood 57 D40
Thorpe Waterville 42 G46
Thorpe Willoughby 58 F41
Thorpland 43 E51
Thorrington 34 G56
Thorverton 7 E24
Thrandeston 34 A56
Thrapston 32 A45
Threapland 56 C35
Threapwood 38 A30
Three Bridges 13 C48
Three Burrows 2 D13
Three Chimneys 14 D54
Three Cocks 28 E27
Three Crosses 17 E21
Three Cups Corner 13 D52
Three Holes 43 E51
Threekingham 42 B46
Three Leg Cross 13 C52
Three Legged Cross 10 D36
Three Mile Cross 22 E43
Threemilestone 2 D13
Threlkeld 60 D28
Threshers Bush 23 A50
Threshfield 56 C35
Threxton Hill 44 E54
Thriepley 82 D28
Thrigby 45 D60
Thringarth 61 D35
Thringstone 41 D40
Thrintoft 62 G39
Thriplow 33 D50
Throcking 33 E49
Throckley 71 G37
Throckmorton 29 C35
Throphill 71 E37
Thropton 71 C36
Throwleigh 6 F22
Throwley 14 B55
Throws 33 F52
Thrumpton 41 B40
Thrumster 103 D29
Thrunton 71 B36
Thrupp *Glo.* 20 A34
Thrupp *Oxf.* 31 G40
Thrushelton 6 G20
Thrussington 41 D42
Thruxton *H.&W.* 28 E30
Thruxton *Ham.* 21 G38
Thrybergh 51 C40
Thulston 41 B39
Thundergay 73 F14
Thundersley 24 C53
Thunderton 99 E36
Thundridge 33 G49
Thurcaston 41 D41
Thurcroft 51 D40
Thurdistoft 103 B27
Thurgarton *Nfk* 45 B57
Thurgarton *Not.* 41 A42
Thurgoland 50 B38
Thurlaston *War.* 31 A40
Thurlaston *Lei.* 41 F40
Thurlbear 8 B28
Thurlby *Lcn.* 52 F44
Thurlby *Lcn.* 42 D47
Thurleigh 32 C46
Thurlestone 5 F22
Thurloxton 8 A28
Thurlstone 50 B38
Thurlton 45 F60
Thurmaston 41 E41
Thurnby 41 E42
Thurne 45 D59
Thurnham 14 B54
Thurning *Nmp.* 42 G46
Thurning *Nfk* 44 C56
Thurnscoe 51 B40
Thursby 60 A29
Thursford 44 B55
Thursley 12 C44
Thurso 103 B26
Thurstaston 48 D28
Thurston 34 B55
Thurstonfield 60 A28
Thurstonland 50 B37
Thurton 45 E59
Thurvaston 40 B38
Thuster 103 C28
Thuxton 44 E56
Thwaite *N.Y.* 61 G34
Thwaite *Sfk* 34 B56
Thwaite Head 55 A29
Thwaite St Mary 45 F59
Thwing 59 C46
Tibbermore 82 E26
Tibberton *Shr.* 39 C32
Tibberton *Glo.* 29 F33
Tibberton *H.&W.* 29 C35
Tibbie Shiels Inn 69 A28
Tibenham 45 F57
Tibertich 79 G14
Tibshelf 51 F40
Tibthorpe 59 D45
Ticehurst 13 C52
Tichborne 11 A41
Tickencote 42 E45
Tickenham 19 D30
Tickhill 51 C41
Ticklerton 38 F30
Ticknall 41 C39
Tickton 59 E46
Tidcombe 21 F38
Tiddington *Oxf.* 21 A42
Tiddington *War.* 30 C37
Tidebrook 13 D52
Tideford 4 E19
Tidenham 19 B31
Tidenham Chase 19 B31
Tideswell 50 E37
Tidmarsh 21 D42
Tidmington 30 E38
Tidpit 10 C36
Tiers Cross 16 C15
Tiffield 31 C42
Tifty 99 E33
Tigerton 83 A31
Tighachnoic 79 C12
Tigh A Ghearraidh 92 D2
Tighnablair 81 F23
Tighnabruaich 73 C15
Tighnacomaire 80 A15
Tigley 5 D23
Tilbrook 32 B46
Tilbury 24 D52
Tile Cross 40 G37
Tile Hill 30 A38
Tilehurst 21 D42
Tilford 22 G44
Tillathrowie 98 F30
Tillers' Green 29 E32
Tillery 91 A35
Tilley 38 C30
Tillicoultry 75 A24
Tillingham 25 A55
Tillington *H.&W.* 28 D30
Tillington *W.S.* 12 D45
Tillington Common 28 D30
Tillyarblet 83 A30
Tillybirloch 91 C32
Tillycairn Castle 91 B32
Tillycorthie 91 A34
Tillydrine 90 D31
Tillyfar 99 E34
Tillyfour 90 B31
Tillyfourie 91 B32
Tillygreig 91 A34
Tillypronie 90 C30
Tilmanstone 15 B58
Tilney All Saints 43 D51
Tilney High End 43 D51
Tilney St Lawrence 43 D51
Tilshead 20 G36
Tilstock 38 B31
Tilston 48 G30
Tilstone Fearnall 48 F31
Tilsworth 32 F45
Tilton on the Hill 42 E43
Tiltups End 20 B34
Timberland 52 G47
Timberland Dales 52 F47
Timbersbrook 49 F34
Timberscombe 7 A25
Timble 57 D37
Timperley 49 D33
Timsbury *Avon* 19 F32
Timsbury *Ham.* 10 B39
Timsgearraidh 100 D6
Timworth Green 34 B54
Tincleton 9 E33
Tindale 61 A32
Tingewick 31 E42
Tingley 57 G38
Tingrith 32 E45

Tingwall 104 D29
Tinhay 6 G20
Tinney 4 A18
Tinshill 57 E38
Tinsley 51 C39
Tinsley Green 13 C48
Tintagel 4 B16
Tintern Parva 19 A31
Tintinhull 8 C30
Tintwistle 50 C36
Tinwald 68 E25
Tinwell 42 E45
Tipperty *Grm.* 91 E33
Tipperty *Grm.* 91 A35
Tiptoe 10 E38
Tipton 40 F35
Tipton St John 7 F26
Tiptree 34 G54
Tiptree Heath 34 G54
Tirabad 27 D24
Tirdeunaw 17 E22
Tiree Airport 78 C5
Tirindrish 87 F18
Tirley 29 F34
Tirphil 18 A27
Tirril 61 D30
Tir-y-dail 17 C22
Tisbury 9 B35
Tissington 50 G37
Tister 103 B27
Titchberry 6 C18
Titchfield 11 D41
Titchmarsh 32 A46
Titchwell 44 A53
Tithby 41 B42
Titley 28 B29
Titsey 23 F50
Titson 6 E18
Tittensor 40 B34
Tittleshall 44 C54
Tiverton *Dev.* 7 D25
Tiverton *Che.* 48 F31
Tivetshall St Margaret 45 G57
Tivetshall St Mary 45 G57
Tixall 40 C35
Tixover 42 E45
Toab *She.* 107 E37
Toab *Ork.* 105 A31
Tobermory 79 B10
Toberonochy 79 G13
Tobha Mor 84 A3
Tobson 100 D7
Tocher 98 F32
Tockenham 20 D36
Tockenham Wick 20 C36
Tockholes 56 G32
Tockington 19 C31
Tockwith 57 D40
Todber 9 C33
Toddington *Bfd.* 32 F45
Toddington *Glo.* 30 E36
Toddington *W.S.* 12 F46
Todenham 30 E38
Todhills *Cum.* 69 G29
Todhills *Tay.* 83 D30
Todlachie 91 B32
Todmorden 56 G35
Todwick 51 D40
Toft *She.* 106 E40
Toft *Cbs.* 33 C49
Toft *Lcn.* 42 D46
Toftcarl 103 D29
Toft Hill 62 D37
Toft Monks 45 F60
Toft next Newton 52 D46
Toftrees 44 C54
Tofts 103 B29
Toftwood 44 D55
Togston 71 C38
Tokavaig 86 C12
Tokers Green 22 D43
Tolastadh 101 C11
Tolastadh a Chaolais 100 D7
Tolastadh Ur 101 C11
Tolland 7 B26
Tollard Royal 9 C35
Tollcross 74 D22
Toller Down Gate 8 D31
Toller Fratrum 8 E31
Toller Porcorum 8 E31
Tollerton *Not.* 41 B41
Tollerton *N.Y.* 57 C40
Toller Whelme 8 D31
Tollesbury 25 A55
Tollesby 62 E40
Tolleshunt D'Arcy 34 G55
Tolleshunt Knights 34 G55
Tolleshunt Major 34 G54
Toll of Birness 99 F35
Tolpuddle 9 E33
Tolvah 89 E24
Tolworth 22 E47
Tom an Fhuadain 100 F9
Tomatin 88 B23
Tombreck 88 A22
Tomchrasky 87 C18
Tomdoun 87 D17
Tomdow 97 G25
Tomich *Hgh.* 87 B19
Tomich *Hgh.* 96 A22
Tomich *Hgh.* 96 D22
Tomintoul 90 B27
Tomnacross 96 G20
Tomnamoon 97 F26
Tomnaven 98 F29
Tomnavoulin 90 A27
Tomvaich 89 A26
Tonbridge 23 G51
Tondu 18 C24
Tonfanau 36 E21
Tong 39 E33
Tonge 41 C40
Tongham 22 G44
Tongland 65 E22
Tong Norton 39 E33
Tong Street 57 F37
Tongue 102 C21
Tongue Ho. 102 C21
Tongwynlais 18 C27
Tonna 18 B23
Ton-Pentre 18 B25
Ton-teg 18 C26
Tonwell 33 G49
Tonypandy 18 B25
Tonyrefail 18 C25
Toot Baldon 21 A41
Toot Hill 23 A50
Toothill 10 C39
Topcliffe 57 B39
Topcroft 45 F58
Topcroft Street 45 F58
Top End 32 B46
Toppesfield 34 E53
Toppings 49 A33
Topsham 7 G25
Topsham Bridge 5 E23
Torastan 78 A8
Torbain 90 B27
Torbeg *Grm.* 90 D29
Torbeg *Str.* 66 A14
Torbryan 5 D24
Torcastle 87 G17
Torcross 5 F24
Tordarroch 88 A22
Tore 96 F21
Toreduff 97 E26
Toremore 103 E27
Torgyle 87 C18
Torksey 52 E44
Torlum 92 F3
Torlundy 87 G17
Tormarton 20 D33
Tormisdale 72 E8
Tormore 73 G14
Tormsdale 103 C27
Tornagrain 96 G23
Tornahaish 90 C28
Tornaveen 90 C31
Torness 88 B21
Torpenhow 60 C27
Torphichen 75 C25
Torphins 90 C31
Torpoint 4 E20
Torquay 5 D25
Torquhan 76 F30
Torr 5 E21
Torran *Hgh.* 94 G11
Torran *Hgh.* 96 D22
Torran *Str.* 79 G14
Torrance *Str.* 74 E22
Torrance *Str.* 74 C22
Torrancroy 90 B29
Torrich 97 F24
Torridon 94 F15
Torrin 86 B11
Torrisdale *Hgh.* 102 B22
Torrisdale *Str.* 73 G13
Torrish 103 G25
Torrisholme 55 C30
Torroble 96 A21
Torry *Grm.* 91 C35
Torry *Grm.* 98 E30
Torryburn 75 B26
Torsonce 76 F30
Torterston 99 E36
Torthorwald 69 F26
Tortington 12 F45
Tortworth 19 B32
Torvaig 93 G10
Torver 60 G28
Torwood 75 B24
Torworth 51 D42
Tosberry 6 C18
Toscaig 86 A12
Toseland 33 B48
Tosside 56 D33
Tostarie 78 C9
Tostock 34 B55
Totaig 93 F8
Totamore 78 B7
Tote 93 G10
Totegan 102 B24
Totford 11 A41
Tothill 53 D50
Totland 10 F39
Totley 51 D39
Totnes 5 D23
Toton 41 B40
Totronald 78 B7
Tottenham 23 B49
Tottenhill 44 D52
Totteridge 23 B48
Totternhoe 32 F45
Tottington *G.M.* 49 A33
Tottington *Nfk* 44 F54
Totton 10 C39
Touchen-End 22 D44
Toulton 7 B27
Toux 99 D35
Tovil 14 B53
Toward 73 D17
Towcester 31 D42
Towednack 2 E10
Tower Hamlets 23 C49
Towersey 22 A43
Towie *Grm.* 99 C34
Towie *Grm.* 90 A31
Towie *Grm.* 90 B30
Towiemore 98 E29
Tow Law 62 C37
Town End *Cbs.* 43 F49
Townend 74 C20
Town End *Cum.* 55 A30
Town Green 48 B30
Townhead 65 F22
Townhead of Greenlaw 65 D23
Townhill 75 B26
Town Row 13 C51
Townshend 2 E11
Town Street 44 G53
Town Yetholm 70 A33
Towthorpe *N.Y.* 58 D42
Towthorpe *Hum.* 58 C44
Towton 57 F40
Towyn 47 E25
Toynton All Saints 53 F49
Toynton Fen Side 53 F49
Toynton St Peter 53 F50
Toy's Hill 23 F50
Trabboch 67 A20
Traboe 2 F13
Tradespark *Hgh.* 97 F24
Tradespark *Ork.* 105 A30
Trafford Park 49 C33
Trallong 27 F25
Tranch 19 A28
Tranent 76 C29
Trantlebeg 102 C24
Trantlemore 102 C24
Tranwell 71 E37
Trapp 17 C22
Traprain 76 C31
Traquair 76 G29
Trawden 56 F35
Trawsfynydd 37 B22
Trealaw 18 B25
Treales 55 F30
Trearddur 46 E18
Treaslane 93 F9
Trebanog 18 C26
Trebanos 17 D22
Trebarrow 4 A18
Trebartha 4 C18
Trebarwith 4 B16
Trebetherick 3 A15
Treborough 7 B25
Trebudannon 3 B15
Trebullett 4 C18
Treburley 4 C19
Trebyan 4 D16
Trecastle 27 F24
Trecwn 16 A15
Trecynon 18 A25
Tredavoe 2 F10
Tre-ddiog 16 B14
Tredegar 18 A27
Tredington *War.* 30 D38
Tredington *Glo.* 29 F34
Tredinnick *Cnw.* 4 E18
Tredinnick *Cnw.* 3 A15
Tredissi 16 A16
Tredomen 27 E26
Tredunnock 19 B29
Treen 2 F9
Treeton 51 D40
Trefaldwyn (Montgomery) 38 F28
Trefasser 16 A14
Trefdraeth 46 E19
Trefecca 28 E27
Trefeglwys 37 F25
Trefenter 26 B21
Treffgarne 16 B15
Treffynnon 16 B14
Trefgarn Owen 16 B14
Trefil 28 G27
Trefilan 26 C21
Treflach 38 C28
Trefnanney 38 D27
Trefnant 47 E26
Trefonen 38 C28
Trefor *Gwy.* 36 A19
Trefor *Gwy.* 46 D19
Treforest 18 C26
Treforest Ind. Est. 18 C26
Trefriw 47 F23
Trefynwy (Monmouth) 28 G30
Tregadillett 4 B18
Tregaian 46 E20
Tregare 28 G30
Tregaron 27 C22
Tregarth 46 F21
Tregavethan 2 D13
Tregear 3 C14
Tregeare 4 B18
Tregeiriog 38 B27
Tregele 46 C19
Tregidden 2 F13
Treglemais 16 B13
Tregolds 3 A14
Tregole 4 A17
Tregonetha 3 B15
Tregony 3 D15
Tregoyd 28 E27
Tre-groes *Dyf.* 26 D20
Tre-groes *M.G.* 18 C25
Treguff 18 D26
Tregurrian 3 B14
Tregynon 37 F26
Trehafod 18 B26
Treharris 18 B26
Treherbert 18 B25
Trekenner 4 C19
Trelash 4 A17
Trelassick 3 C14
Trelawnyd 47 E26
Trelech 17 A18
Trelech a'r Betws 17 B18
Trelewis 18 B26
Trelights 3 A15
Trelill 4 C16
Trelissick 3 E14
Trelleck 19 A30
Trelleck Grange 19 A30
Trelogan 47 D27
Trelystan 38 E28
Tremadog 36 A21
Tremail 4 B17
Tremain 26 D18
Tremaine 4 B18
Tremar 4 D18
Trematon 4 E19
Tremeirchion 47 E26
Tremethick Cross 2 E9
Trenance 3 B14
Trenarren 4 F16
Trench *Shr.* 39 D32
Trench *Clw.* 38 B29
Treneglos 4 B18
Trenewan 4 E17
Trent 8 C31
Trentham 40 A34
Trentishoe 6 A22
Treoes 18 D25
Treorchy 18 B25
Tre'r-ddol 37 F22
Tre-Rhys 26 D17
Trerule Foot 4 E19
Tresaith 26 C18
Trescott 40 F34
Trescowe 2 E11
Tresham 20 B33
Treshnish 78 C9
Tresillian 3 D14
Tresinney 4 B17
Tresinwen 16 A14
Treskinnick Cross 4 A18
Tresmeer 4 B18
Tresparrett 4 A17
Tresparrett Posts 4 A16
Tressait 81 A24
Tresta *She.* 107 B39
Tresta *She.* 106 C42
Treswell 51 E43
Trethurgy 4 E16
Tretio 16 B13
Tretire 28 F31
Tretower 28 F27
Treuddyn 48 G28
Trevalga 4 A16
Trevalyn 48 G29
Trevanson 3 A15
Trevarren 3 B15
Trevarrick 3 D15
Tre-vaughan 17 B19
Trevaughan 16 C17
Trevellas 2 C13
Trevelmond 4 D18
Treverva 2 E13
Trevescan 2 F9
Trevethin 19 A28
Trevigro 4 D19
Trevine *Dyf.* 16 A14
Trevine *Str.* 80 E16
Treviscoe 3 C15
Trevone 3 A14
Trevor 38 A28
Trewalder 4 B16
Trewarmett 4 B16
Trewarthenick 3 D14
Trewassa 4 B17
Trewellard 2 E9
Trewen 4 B18
Trewern 38 D28
Trewidland 4 E18
Trewilym 26 D17
Trewint 4 A17
Trewithian 3 E14
Trewoon 3 C15
Trewornan 3 A15
Treyarnon 3 A14
Treyford 12 E44
Triangle 57 G36
Trickett's Cross 10 D36
Trimdon 62 C39
Trimdon Colliery 62 C39
Trimdon Grange 62 C39
Trimingham 45 B58
Trimley St Martin 35 E58
Trimley St Mary 35 E58
Trimpley 29 A33
Trimsaran 17 D20
Trimstone 6 A21
Trinafour 81 A23
Trinant 18 B27
Tring 32 G45
Trinity 83 A31
Trislaig 87 G16
Trispen 3 C14
Tritlington 71 D37
Trochry 82 C25
Troedyraur 26 D19
Troedyrhiw 18 A26
Trondavoe 106 E39
Troon *Str.* 74 G19
Troon *Cnw.* 2 E12
Trosaraidh 84 C3
Troston 34 A54
Troswell 4 A18
Trottiscliffe 24 E52
Trotton 12 D44
Troughend 70 D34
Troustan 73 C16
Troutbeck 60 F29
Troutbeck Bridge 60 F29
Trowbridge 20 F34
Trow Green 19 A31
Trowle Common 20 F34
Trowley Bottom 32 G46
Trows 76 G32
Trowse Newton 45 E58
Trudernish 72 E10
Trudoxhill 20 G33
Trull 8 B28
Trumaisge Arraidh 92 D4
Trumpan 93 E8
Trumpet 29 E32
Trumpington 33 C50
Trunch 45 B58
Trunnah 55 E29
Truro 3 D14
Trusham 7 G24
Trusley 40 B38
Trusthorpe 53 D51
Truthan 3 C14
Trysull 40 F34
Tubney 21 B40
Tuckenhay 5 E23
Tuckingmill 2 D12
Tuddenham *Sfk* 34 A53
Tuddenham *Sfk* 35 D57
Tudeley 23 G52
Tudhoe 62 C38
Tudweiloig 36 B18
Tuffley 29 G34
Tufton *Dyf.* 16 B16
Tufton *Ham.* 21 G40
Tugby 42 E43
Tugford 38 G31
Tughall 71 A37
Tuirnaig 94 C14
Tulchan 82 E25
Tullibody 75 A24
Tullich *Str.* 80 F16
Tullich *Cen.* 81 D21
Tullich *Hgh.* 88 B22
Tullich *Grm.* 98 E29
Tullich *Str.* 79 F14
Tullich *Hgh.* 97 D24
Tullich Muir 96 D23
Tulliemet 82 B25
Tulloch *Hgh.* 96 B22
Tulloch *Grm.* 97 F26
Tulloch *Grm.* 99 F34
Tullochgorm 73 A15
Tullochgribban High 89 B25
Tullochvenus 90 C31
Tulloes 83 C30
Tullybannocher 81 E23
Tullybelton 82 D26

Tullyfergus 82 C27
Tullymurdoch 82 B27
Tullynessle 90 B31
Tumble 17 C21
Tumby 53 G48
Tumby Woodside 53 G48
Tummel Bridge 81 B23
Tundergarth Mains 69 E27
Tunga 100 D10
Tunstall *N.Y.* 62 G37
Tunstall *Nfk* 45 E60
Tunstall *Hum.* 59 F49
Tunstall *Lan.* 55 B31
Tunstall *Stf.* 49 G34
Tunstall *Sfk* 35 C59
Tunstall *Kent* 24 E54
Tunstead 45 C58
Tunworth 21 G42
Tupsley 28 E31
Turbiskill 73 B13
Turclossie 99 D34
Turgis Green 21 F42
Turin 83 B31
Turkdean 30 G36
Tur Langton 42 F43
Turnastone 28 E29
Turnberry 67 C17
Turnchapel 4 E20
Turnditch 40 A38
Turner's Green 30 A37
Turners Hill 13 C49
Turners Puddle 9 E34
Turnford 23 A49
Turnworth 9 D33
Turret Bridge 88 E19
Turriff 99 D33
Turton Bottoms 49 A33
Turvey 32 C45
Turville 22 B43
Turville Heath 22 B43
Turweston 31 E41
Tutbury 40 C37
Tutnall 29 A35
Tutshill 19 B31
Tuttington 45 C58
Tuxford 51 E43
Twatt *She.* 107 B39
Twatt *Ork.* 104 D28
Twechar 74 C22
Tweedmouth 77 E35
Tweedsmuir 69 A26
Twelveheads 2 D13
Twenty 42 C47
Twerton 19 E32
Twickenham 22 D47
Twigworth 29 F34
Twineham 13 D48
Twinhoe 20 F33
Twinstead 34 E54
Twiss Green 49 C32
Twitchen *Dev.* 7 B23
Twitchen *Shr.* 28 A29
Twizell House 71 A37
Two Bridges 5 C22
Two Dales 50 F38
Two Gates 40 E38
Twycross 41 E39
Twyford *Dby.* 41 C39
Twyford *Brk.* 22 D43
Twyford *Ham.* 11 B40
Twyford *Bkh.* 31 F42
Twyford *Nfk* 44 C56
Twyford *Dor.* 9 C34
Twyford *Lei.* 42 D43
Twyford Common 28 E31
Twynholm 65 E22
Twyning 29 E34
Twyning Green 29 E34
Twynllanan 27 F23
Twyn-yr-odyn 18 D26
Twyn-y-Sheriff 19 A29
Twywell 32 A45
Tyberton 28 D29
Tyburn 40 F37
Tycroes 17 C21
Tycrwyn 37 D26
Tydd Gote 43 D50
Tydd St Giles 43 D49
Tydd St Mary 43 D50
Tye Common 24 B52
Tye Green 34 F53
Ty-hen 36 B17
Tyldesley 49 B32
Tyle-garw 18 C26
Tyler Hill 25 E57
Tylers Green *Esx* 23 A51
Tylers Green *Bkh.* 22 B44
Tylorstown 18 B25
Tylwch 27 A25
Ty-mawr *Clw.* 38 A27
Ty-mawr *Clw.* 37 A25
Ty-nant *Gwy.* 37 C25
Ty-nant *Clw.* 37 A25
Tyndrum 80 D19
Tyneham 9 F34
Tynehead 76 E29
Tynemouth 71 F39
Tynewydd 18 B24
Tyninghame 76 C31
Tynribbie 80 C15
Tynron 68 D23
Tyn-y-cefn 37 A26
Tyn-y-Cwm 37 G24
Tyn-y-ffridd 37 B26
Tyn-y-graig 27 D25
Tynygraig 27 B22
Ty'n-y-groes 47 E23
Tyringham 32 D44
Tythegston 18 D24
Tytherington *Som.* 20 G33
Tytherington *Avon* 19 C32
Tytherington *Wts.* 20 G34
Tytherington *Che.* 49 E34
Tytherleigh 8 D28
Ty-uchaf 37 C25
Tywardreath 4 E16
Tywardreath Highway 4 E16
Tywyn *Gwy.* 36 E21
Tywyn *Gwy.* 47 E23

U

Uachdar 92 F3
Uags 86 A13
Ubbeston Green 35 A59
Ubley 19 F31
Uckerby 62 F38
Uckfield 13 D50
Uckinghall 29 E34
Uckington 29 F34
Uddingston 74 D22
Uddington 75 G24
Udimore 14 F54
Udny Green 91 A34
Udny Station 91 A34
Udstonhead 75 F23
Uffcott 20 D37
Uffculme 7 D26
Uffington *Shr.* 38 D31
Uffington *Lcn.* 42 E46
Uffington *Oxf.* 21 C39
Ufford *Cbs.* 42 E46
Ufford *Sfk* 35 C58
Ufton 30 B39
Ufton Nervet 21 E42
Ugborough 5 E22
Uggeshall 35 A60
Ugglebarnby 63 F44
Ugley 33 F51
Ugley Green 33 F50
Ugthorpe 63 E43
Uig *Hgh.* 93 E9
Uig *Hgh.* 93 F7
Uig *Str.* 78 B7
Uig *Str.* 73 B17
Uigen 100 D6
Uiginish 93 G8
Uigshader 93 G10
Uisgebhagh 92 G4
Uisken 78 F9
Ulbster 103 D29
Ulcat row 60 D29
Ulceby *Lcn.* 53 E50
Ulceby *Hum.* 52 A47
Ulceby Cross 53 E50
Ulcombe 14 C54
Uldale 60 C28
Uldale House 61 G33
Uley 20 B33
Ulgham 71 D38
Ullapool 95 B17
Ullenhall 30 B37
Ullenwood 29 G35
Ulleskelf 58 E41
Ullesthorpe 41 G40
Ulley 51 D40
Ullingswick 28 D31
Ullinish 85 A9
Ullock 60 D26
Ulpha 60 G27
Ulrome 59 D47
Ulsta 106 D40
Ulting 24 A53
Uluvalt 79 E11
Ulverston 55 B28
Ulwell 10 F36
Ulzieside 68 C23
Umberleigh 6 C22
Unapool 101 E18
Underbarrow 60 G30
Underhoull 106 B41
Underriver 23 F51
Underwood *Not.* 51 G40
Underwood *Gwe.* 19 C29
Undy 19 C30
Unifirth 107 B38
Union Croft 91 D34
Union Mills 54 F25
Unstone 51 E39
Unthank 60 C30
Upavon 20 F37
Up Cerne 9 D32
Upchurch 24 E54
Upcott *H.&W.* 28 C29
Upcott *Dev.* 6 F20
Upend 33 C52
Up Exe 7 E25
Uphall *Dor.* 8 D31
Uphall *Ltn* 75 C26
Uphall Station 75 C26
Upham *Dev.* 7 E24
Upham *Ham.* 11 B41
Uphampton 29 B34
Up Hatherley 29 F34
Uphill 19 F29
Up Holland 48 B31
Upleadon 29 F33
Upleatham 63 D42
Uplees 25 E55
Uploders 8 E31
Uplowman 7 D25
Uplyme 8 E29
Up Marden 11 C43
Upminster 23 C51
Up Nately 21 F42
Upottery 7 E27
Upper Affcot 38 G30
Upper Ardroscadale 73 D16
Upper Arley 39 G33
Upper Arncott 31 G42
Upper Aston 40 F34
Upper Astrop 31 E41
Upper Basildon 21 D41
Upper Beeding 12 E47
Upper Benefield 42 G45
Upper Bighouse 102 C24
Upper Boat 18 C26
Upper Boddington 31 C40
Upper Borth 36 G21
Upper Boyndlie 99 C35
Upper Brailes 30 D38
Upper Breakish 86 B12
Upper Breinton 28 D30
Upper Broughton 41 C42
Upper Bucklebury 21 E41
Upper Burgate 10 C37
Upper Burnhaugh 91 D34
Upper Caldecote 32 D47
Upper Camster 103 D28
Upper Catshill 29 A35
Upper Chapel 27 D26
Upper Chute 21 F38
Upper Clatford 21 G39
Upper Coberley 29 G35
Upper Cound 38 E31
Upper Cwmbran 19 B28
Upper Dallachy 98 C29
Upper Dean 32 B46
Upper Denby 50 B38
Upper Derraid 89 A26
Upper Diabaig 94 E14
Upper Dicker 13 E51
Upper Dovercourt 35 F58
Upper Dunsforth 57 C40
Upper Eastern Green 40 G38
Upper Eathie 96 E23
Upper Elkstone 50 G36
Upper End 50 E36
Upper Farringdon 11 A43
Upper Framilode 29 G33
Upper Froyle 22 G43
Upper Gills 103 A29
Upper Glendessarry 86 E15
Upper Godney 19 G30
Upper Gornal 40 F35
Upper Gravenhurst 32 E47
Upper Green *Esx* 33 E50
Upper Green *Gwe.* 28 G29
Upper Green *Brk.* 21 E39
Upper Gylen 79 E14
Upper Hackney 50 F38
Upper Halliford 22 E46
Upper Halling 24 E52
Upper Hambleton 42 E45
Upper Hardres Court 15 B57
Upper Hartfield 13 C50
Upper Hawkhillock 99 F36
Upper Hayton 38 G31
Upper Heath 38 G31
Upper Helmsley 58 D42
Upper Hergest 28 C28
Upper Heyford 31 F40
Upper Hill 28 C30
Upper Hopton 50 A37
Upper Horsebridge 13 E51
Upper Hulme 49 F35
Upper Inglesham 20 B37
Upper Kilchattan 72 A9
Upper Killay 17 E21
Upper Knockando 97 G27
Upper Lambourn 21 C38
Upper Langwith 51 E41
Upper Largo 83 G30
Upper Lochton 91 D33
Upper Longdon 40 D36
Upper Ludstone 40 F34
Upper Lybster 103 E28
Upper Lydbrook 29 G32
Upper Maes-coed 28 E29
Upper Midhope 50 C37
Uppermill 49 B35
Upper Minety 20 B36
Upper Mitton 29 A33
Upper North Dean 22 B44
Upper Norwood 23 D49
Upper Obney 82 D26
Upper Oddington 30 F37
Upper Ollach 85 A10
Upper Poppleton 58 D41
Upper Quinton 30 D37
Upper Ridinghill 99 D36
Upper Rochford 29 B32
Upper Sanday 105 A31
Upper Sapey 29 B32
Upper Seagry 20 C35
Upper Shelton 32 D45
Upper Sheringham 45 A57
Upper Skelmorlie 74 D18
Upper Slaughter 30 F37
Upper Sonachan 80 E16
Upper Soudley 29 G32
Upper Stoke 41 G39
Upper Stondon 32 E47
Upper Stowe 31 C42
Upper Street *Sfk* 35 E57
Upper Street *Nfk* 45 D59
Upper Street *Ham.* 10 C37
Upper Sundon 32 F46
Upper Swell 30 F37
Upper Tean 40 B35
Upperthong 50 B36
Upper Thurnham 55 D30
Upper Tillyrie 82 G26
Upperton 12 D45
Upper Tooting 23 D48
Uppertown 103 A29
Upper Town 19 E30
Upper Tysoe 30 D39
Upper Upham 21 D38
Upper Upnor 24 D53
Upper Victoria 83 D31
Upper Wardington 31 D40
Upper Weald 31 E43
Upper Weedon 31 C42
Upper Welson 28 C28
Upper Wield 11 A42
Upper Winchendon 31 G43
Upper Woodford 10 A37
Upper Wootton 21 F41
Upper Wraxall 20 D33
Upper Wyche 29 D33
Uppingham 42 F44
Uppington *Dor.* 10 D36
Uppington *Shr.* 38 E31
Upsall 57 A40
Upsettlington 77 F34
Upshire 23 A49
Up Somborne 11 A40
Upstreet 25 E57
Up Sydling 9 D32
Upton *Nfk* 45 D59
Upton *Som.* 7 C25
Upton *Dor.* 9 E35
Upton *Cnw.* 4 C18
Upton *Nmp.* 31 B43
Upton *Bkh.* 31 G43
Upton *Cbs.* 32 A47
Upton *Lcn.* 52 D44
Upton *Mer.* 48 D28
Upton *Dev.* 5 F23
Upton *Che.* 48 F30
Upton *W.Y.* 51 A40
Upton *Not.* 51 E43
Upton *Not.* 51 G43
Upton *Dev.* 7 E26
Upton *Ham.* 10 C39
Upton *Brk.* 22 D45
Upton *Ham.* 21 F39
Upton *Oxf.* 21 C40
Upton *Cbs.* 42 E47
Upton Bishop 29 F32
Upton Cheyney 19 D32
Upton Cressett 39 F32
Upton Cross 4 C18
Upton End 32 E47
Upton Green 45 D59
Upton Grey 22 G43
Upton Hellions 7 E24
Upton Lovell 20 G35
Upton Magna 38 D31
Upton Noble 9 A33
Upton Pyne 7 F25
Upton Scudamore 20 G34
Upton Snodsbury 29 C35
Upton St Leonards 29 G34
Upton upon Severn 29 D34
Upton Warren 29 B35
Upwaltham 12 E45
Upware 33 B51
Upwell 43 E51
Upwey 9 F32
Upwood 43 G48
Uradale 107 D39
Urafirth 106 E38
Urchany 97 G24
Urchfont 20 F36
Urdimarsh 28 D31
Ure 106 E38
Urgha 93 B7
Urlay Nook 62 E39
Urmston 49 C33
Urquhart *Grm.* 98 C28
Urquhart *Hgh.* 96 F21
Urra 63 F41
Urray 96 F20
Ushaw Moor 62 B38
Usk 19 A29
Usselby 52 C46
Utley 57 E36
Uton 7 F24
Utterby 53 C48
Uttoxeter 40 B36
Uwchmynydd 36 C17
Uxbridge 22 C46
Uyeasound 106 B41
Uzmaston 16 C15

V

Valley 46 E18
Valleyfield *Fife* 75 B25
Valleyfield *D.&G.* 65 E22
Valley Trudde 4 B17
Valsgarth 106 A42
Vange 24 C53
Vardre 17 D22
Varteg 19 A28
Vatten 93 G8
Vaul 78 C6
Vaynor 27 G26
Vaynor Park 38 E27
Veaullt 28 C27
Veensgarth 107 C39
Velindre *Dyf.* 16 A16
Velindre *Pow.* 28 E27
Vellow 7 B26
Veness 104 D31
Venn 5 F23
Vennington 38 E29
Venn Ottery 7 F26
Ventnor 11 G41
Vernham Dean 21 F39
Vernham Street 21 F39
Vernolds Common 38 G30
Verwig 26 D17
Verwood 10 D36
Veryan 3 E15
Vicarage 8 F28
Vickerstown 54 C27
Victoria 3 B15
Vidlin 107 A40
Viewfield 103 B26
Viewpark 75 D23
Vigo 40 E36
Vigo Village 24 E52
Villavin 6 D21
Vinehall Street 14 E53
Vine's Cross 13 E51
Viney Hill 19 A32
Virginia Water 22 E45
Virginstow 6 F19
Virley 34 G55
Vobster 19 G32
Voe *She.* 106 D39
Voe *She.* 107 A40
Vowchurch 28 E29
Voy 104 E28

W

Wackerfield 62 D37
Wacton 45 F57
Wadborough 29 D34
Waddesdon 31 G43
Waddingham 52 C45
Waddington *Lcn.* 52 F45
Waddington *Lan.* 56 E33
Waddingworth 52 E47
Wadebridge 3 A15
Wadeford 8 C28
Wadenhoe 42 G45
Wadesmill 33 G49
Wadhurst 13 C52
Wadshelf 50 E38
Wadsley Bridge 51 C39
Wadworth 51 C41
Wadworth Hill 59 G48
Waen 47 F26
Waen-fach 38 D28
Waen-wen 46 F21
Wag 103 F26
Wainfleet All Saints 53 G51
Wainfleet Bank 53 G50
Wainhouse Corner 4 A17
Wainscott 24 D53
Wainstalls 57 G36
Waitby 61 F33
Wakefield 57 G39
Wakerley 42 F45
Wakes Colne 34 F54

Walberswick **35 A60**
Walberton **12 F45**
Walcot *Lcn.* **42 B46**
Walcot *Shr.* **38 G29**
Walcot *Lcn.* **52 G47**
Walcot *Hum.* **58 G44**
Walcot *Shr.* **38 D31**
Walcot Dales **52 G47**
Walcote *War.* **30 C37**
Walcote *Lei.* **41 G41**
Walcot Green **45 G57**
Walcott **45 B59**
Walden **57 A36**
Walden Head **56 A35**
Walden Stubbs **51 A41**
Walderslade **24 E53**
Walderton **11 C43**
Walditch **8 E30**
Waldley **40 B37**
Waldridge **62 A38**
Waldringfield **35 D58**
Waldron **13 E51**
Wales **51 D40**
Walesby *Lcn.* **52 C47**
Walesby *Not.* **51 E42**
Walford *Shr.* **38 C30**
Walford *H.&W.* **28 F31**
Walford *H.&W.* **28 A29**
Walgherton **39 A32**
Walgrave **31 A43**
Walhampton **10 E39**
Walkden **49 B33**
Walker **71 G38**
Walkerburn **76 G29**
Walker Fold **56 E32**
Walkeringham **51 C43**
Walkerith **51 C43**
Walkern **33 F48**
Walker's Green **28 D30**
Walkerton **82 G28**
Walkhampton **5 D21**
Walk Mill **56 F34**
Walkwood **30 B36**
Wall *Nor.* **70 G35**
Wall *Stf.* **40 E36**
Wallacehall **69 F28**
Wallacetown **67 C18**
Wallasey **48 C28**
Wall Bank **38 F30**
Wallbottle **71 G37**
Wallend **24 D54**
Waller's Green **29 E32**
Wall Heath **40 G34**
Wallingford **21 C41**
Wallington *G.L.* **23 E48**
Wallington *Ham.* **11 D41**
Wallington *Hfs.* **33 E48**
Wallis **16 B16**
Wallisdown **10 E36**
Walliswood **12 C47**
Walls **107 C38**
Wallsend **71 G38**
Wall under Heywood **38 F31**
Wallyford **76 C29**
Walmer **15 B59**
Walmer Bridge **55 G30**
Walmersley **49 A33**
Walmley **40 F37**
Walpole **35 A59**
Walpole Cross Keys **43 C51**
Walpole Highway **43 D51**
Walpole St Andrew **43 D51**
Walpole St Peter **43 D51**
Walsall **40 F35**
Walsall Wood **40 E36**
Walsden **56 G35**
Walsgrave on Sowe **41 G39**
Walsham le Willows **34 A55**
Walsoken **43 D50**
Walston **75 F26**
Walsworth **32 E47**
Walterstone **28 F29**
Waltham *Kent* **15 C56**
Waltham *Hum.* **53 B48**
Waltham Abbey **23 A49**
Waltham Chase **11 C41**
Waltham Forest **23 B49**
Waltham on the Wolds **42 C44**
Waltham St Lawrence **22 D44**
Walthamstow **23 C49**
Walton *Cbs.* **42 E47**
Walton *Lei.* **41 G41**
Walton *Stf.* **40 B34**
Walton *Cum.* **70 G31**
Walton *N.Y.* **57 E40**
Walton *Pow.* **28 C28**
Walton *Bkh.* **32 G44**
Walton *War.* **30 C38**
Walton *Bkh.* **32 E44**
Walton *Shr.* **38 D31**
Walton *Sfk* **35 E58**
Walton *Dby.* **51 F39**
Walton *W.Y.* **51 A39**
Walton *Mer.* **48 C29**
Walton *Som.* **8 A30**
Walton Cardiff **29 E34**
Walton East **16 B15**
Walton-in-Gordano **19 D30**
Walton-le-Dale **55 G31**
Walton-on-Thames **22 E47**
Walton on the Hill **23 F48**
Walton-on-the-Hill **40 C35**
Walton on the Naze **35 F58**
Walton on the Wolds **41 D41**
Walton-on-Trent **40 D38**
Walton Park **65 C23**
Walton West **16 C14**
Walwen *Clw.* **47 E27**
Walwen *Clw.* **48 E28**
Walwick **70 F34**
Walworth **62 E38**
Walwyns Castle **16 C14**
Wambrook **8 D28**
Wanborough *Sry* **22 G45**
Wanborough *Wts.* **20 C37**
Wandel **68 A25**
Wandon **71 A36**
Wandsworth **23 D48**
Wandylaw **71 A37**
Wangford *Sfk* **44 G53**
Wangford *Sfk* **35 A60**
Wanlip **41 D41**
Wanlockhead **68 B24**
Wannock **13 F51**
Wansford *Nmp.* **42 F46**
Wansford *Hum.* **59 D46**
Wanstead **23 C49**
Wanstrow **19 G32**
Wanswell **19 A32**
Wantage **21 C39**
Wapley **19 D32**
Wappenbury **30 A39**
Wappenham **31 D41**
Warblebank **60 B28**
Warbleton **13 E52**
Warborough **21 B41**
Warboys **33 A48**
Warbstow **4 A18**
Warburton **49 D33**
Warcop **61 E33**
Warden *Kent* **25 D56**
Warden *Nor.* **70 G34**
Ward End **40 G37**
Wardgate **40 A38**
Ward Green **34 B56**
Wardhouse **98 F31**
Wardington **31 D40**
Wardle *G.M.* **49 A34**
Wardle *Che.* **48 G31**
Wardley **42 E44**
Wardlow **50 E37**
Wardy Hill **43 G50**
Ware *Hfs.* **33 G49**
Ware *Kent* **25 E58**
Wareham **9 F35**
Warehorne **14 D55**
Warenford **71 A37**
Waren Mill **77 G37**
Warenton **77 G36**
Wareside **33 G49**
Waresley **33 C48**
Warfield **22 D44**
Wargrave **22 D43**
Warham **44 A55**
Wark *Nor.* **77 G34**
Wark *Nor.* **70 F34**
Warkleigh **6 C22**
Warkton **32 A44**
Warkworth *Nmp.* **31 D40**
Warkworth *Nor.* **71 C38**
Warlaby **62 G39**
Warland **56 G35**
Warleggan **4 D17**
Warley **40 G35**
Warley Town **57 G36**
Warlingham **23 F49**
Warmfield **57 G39**
Warmingham **49 F32**
Warminghurst **12 E47**
Warmington *Nmp.* **42 F46**
Warmington *War.* **30 D39**
Warminster **20 G34**
Warmlake **14 C54**
Warmley **19 D32**
Warmsworth **51 B41**
Warmwell **9 F33**
Warndon **29 C34**
Warnford **11 B42**
Warnham **12 C47**
Warningcamp **12 F46**
Warninglid **13 D48**
Warren *Dyf.* **16 E15**
Warren *Che.* **49 E34**
Warrenby **63 D41**
Warren House **6 G22**
Warren Row **22 C44**
Warren Street **14 B55**
Warrington *Che.* **49 D32**
Warrington *Bkh.* **32 C44**
Warroch **82 G26**
Warsash **11 D40**
Warslow **50 G36**
Warsop **51 F41**
Warter **58 D44**
Warthill **58 D42**
Wartle **90 C31**
Wartling **13 F52**
Wartnaby **41 C42**
Warton *War.* **40 E38**
Warton *Lan.* **55 G30**
Warton *Lan.* **55 B30**
Warton *Nor.* **71 C36**
Warwick *War.* **30 B38**
Warwick *Cum.* **60 A30**
Warwick Bridge **61 A30**
Wasbister **104 C29**
Washaway **4 C16**
Washbourne **5 E24**
Wash Common **21 E40**
Washfield **7 D25**
Washfold **62 F36**
Washford **7 A26**
Washford Pyne **7 D24**
Washingborough **52 E46**
Washington *T.&W.* **62 A38**
Washington *W.S.* **12 E47**
Washmere Green **34 D55**
Wasing **21 E41**
Waskerley **62 B36**
Wasperton **30 C38**
Wass **58 B41**
Watchet **7 A26**
Watchfield *Som.* **19 G29**
Watchfield *Oxf.* **21 B38**
Watchgate **61 G31**
Watendlath **60 E28**
Water **56 G34**
Waterbeach **33 B50**
Waterbeck **69 F28**
Water Eaton **31 G41**
Water End *Hfs.* **32 G46**
Water End *Hfs.* **23 A48**
Waterfall **50 G36**
Waterfoot *Lan.* **56 G34**
Waterfoot *Str.* **74 E21**
Waterford **33 G48**
Waterhead *D.&G.* **68 E23**
Waterhead *Cum.* **60 F29**
Waterhill of Bruxie **99 E35**
Waterhouses *Drm* **62 B37**
Waterhouses *Stf.* **50 G36**
Wateringbury **23 F52**
Waterloo *Grm.* **99 F36**
Waterloo *Mer.* **48 C28**
Waterloo *Nfk* **45 D58**
Waterloo *Str.* **75 E24**
Waterloo *Dyf.* **16 D15**
Waterloo *Dor.* **9 E35**
Waterloo *Tay.* **82 D26**
Waterloo Cross **7 D26**
Waterloo Port **46 F20**
Waterlooville **11 C42**
Watermeetings **68 B25**
Watermillock **60 D30**
Water Newton **42 F47**
Water Orton **40 F37**
Waterperry **21 A42**
Waterrow **7 C26**
Watersfield **12 E46**
Waterside *Str.* **74 F20**
Waterside *Str.* **74 C22**
Waterside *Bkh.* **22 A45**
Waterside *Grm.* **90 B29**
Waterside *Grm.* **91 A36**
Waterside *Str.* **67 C20**
Waterstock **21 A42**
Waterston **16 D15**
Water Stratford **31 E42**
Waters Upton **39 D32**
Water Yeat **55 A28**
Watford *Nmp.* **31 B41**
Watford *Hfs.* **22 B47**
Wath *N.Y.* **57 C37**
Wath *N.Y.* **57 B39**
Wath Brow **60 E26**
Wath upon Dearne **51 B40**
Watlington *Nfk* **44 D52**
Watlington *Oxf.* **21 B42**
Watnall **41 A40**
Watten **103 C28**
Wattisfield **34 A56**
Wattisham **34 C55**
Watton *Nfk* **44 E54**
Watton *Hum.* **59 E46**
Watton at Stone **33 G49**
Watton Green **44 E55**
Wattston **75 D23**
Wattstown **18 B25**
Wattsville **18 B27**
Waunarlwydd **17 E21**
Waunclynda **17 A22**
Waunfawr **46 G21**
Waun Fawr **37 G22**
Waun y Clyn **17 D20**
Wavendon **32 E44**
Waverbridge **60 B27**
Waverton *Cum.* **60 B27**
Waverton *Che.* **48 F30**
Wawne **59 F46**
Waxham **45 C60**
Waxholme **59 G49**
Wayford **8 D29**
Way Gill **56 C35**
Waytown **8 E30**
Way Village **7 D24**
Weachyburn **98 D32**
Weald **21 A38**
Wealdstone **22 C47**
Weare **19 F29**
Weare Giffard **6 C20**
Wearhead **61 B34**
Wearne **8 B30**
Weasenham All Saints **44 C54**
Weasenham St Peter **44 C53**
Weathercote **56 B33**
Weatheroak Hill **30 A36**
Weaverham **49 E32**
Weaverthorpe **59 B45**
Webheath **29 B35**
Webton **28 E29**
Wedderlairs **99 F34**
Weddington **41 F39**
Wedhampton **20 F36**
Wedmore **19 G30**
Wednesbury **40 F35**
Wednesfield **40 E35**
Weedon **32 G44**
Weedon Bec **31 C42**
Weedon Lois **31 D42**
Weeford **40 E37**
Week **7 D23**
Weekley **42 G44**
Week Orchard **6 E18**
Week St Mary **4 A18**
Weeley **35 F57**
Weeley Heath **35 F57**
Weem **81 B24**
Weeping Cross **40 C35**
Weethley **30 C36**
Weeting **44 G53**
Weeton *Hum.* **59 G49**
Weeton *W.Y.* **57 E38**
Weeton *Lan.* **55 F29**
Weir *Lan.* **56 G34**
Weir *Esx* **24 C54**
Weirbrook **38 C29**
Welbeck Abbey **51 E41**
Welborne **44 E56**
Welbourn **52 G45**
Welburn **58 C43**
Welbury **62 F39**
Welby **42 B45**
Welches Dam **43 G50**
Welcombe **6 D18**
Weldon **42 G45**
Welford *Nmp.* **41 G42**
Welford *Brk.* **21 D40**
Welford-on-Avon **30 C37**
Welham *Not.* **51 D43**
Welham *Lei.* **42 F43**
Welham Green **23 A48**
Well *Ham.* **22 G43**
Well *Lcn.* **53 E50**
Well *N.Y.* **57 A38**
Welland **29 D33**
Wellbank **83 D30**
Well End **22 C44**
Wellesbourne **30 C38**
Well Hill **23 E50**
Welling **23 D50**
Wellingborough **32 B44**
Wellingham **44 C54**
Wellingore **52 G45**
Wellington *Shr.* **39 D32**
Wellington *H.&W.* **28 D30**
Wellington *Cum.* **60 F26**
Wellington *Som.* **7 C27**
Wellington Heath **29 D32**
Wellington Marsh **28 D30**
Wellow *Avon* **20 F33**
Wellow *Not.* **51 F42**
Wellow *I.o.W.* **10 F39**
Wells **19 G31**
Wellsborough **41 E39**
Wells-Next-The-Sea **44 A55**
Well Town **7 E25**
Wellwood **75 B26**
Welney **43 F51**
Welshampton **38 B30**
Welsh Bicknor **28 G31**
Welsh End **38 B30**
Welsh Frankton **38 B29**
Welsh Hook **16 B14**
Welsh Newton **28 G30**
Welshpool (Y Trallwng) **38 E27**
Welsh St Donats **18 D26**
Welton *Avon* **19 F32**
Welton *Cum.* **60 B29**
Welton *Nmp.* **31 B41**
Welton *Lcn.* **52 D45**
Welton *Hum.* **59 G45**
Welton le Marsh **53 F50**
Welton le Wold **53 D48**
Welwick **59 G49**
Welwyn **33 G48**
Welwyn Garden City **33 G48**
Wem **38 C31**
Wembdon **8 A28**
Wembley **22 C47**
Wembury **4 F20**
Wembworthy **6 E22**
Wemyss Bay **74 D18**
Wenallt *Gwy.* **37 C24**
Wenallt *Gwy.* **37 A25**
Wendens Ambo **33 E50**
Wendlebury **31 G41**
Wendling **44 D55**
Wendover **22 A44**
Wendron **2 E12**
Wendy **33 D49**
Wenhaston **35 A60**
Wenlli **47 F24**
Wennington *Lan.* **56 B32**
Wennington *Cbs.* **33 A48**
Wennington *Esx* **23 C51**
Wensley *Dby.* **50 F38**
Wensley *N.Y.* **62 G36**
Wentbridge **51 A40**
Went Hill **13 G51**
Wentnor **38 F29**
Wentworth *S.Y.* **51 C39**
Wentworth *Cbs.* **33 A50**
Wentworth Castle **51 B39**
Wenvoe **18 D27**
Weobley **28 C29**
Weobley Marsh **28 C30**
Wepham **12 F46**
Wepre **48 F28**
Wereham **44 E52**
Wergs **40 E34**
Wernyrheolydd **28 G29**
Werrington *Dev.* **6 G19**
Werrington *Nmp.* **42 E47**
Werrington *Stf.* **40 A35**
Wervil Brook **26 C19**
Wervin **48 E30**
Wesham **55 F30**
Wessington **51 G39**
West Aberthaw **18 E26**
West Acre **44 D53**
West Allerdean **77 F35**
West Alvington **5 F23**
West Amesbury **20 G37**
West Anstey **7 C24**
West Ashby **53 E48**
West Ashling **12 F44**
West Ashton **20 F34**
West Auckland **62 D37**
West Ayton **59 A45**
West Bagborough **7 B27**
West Barkwith **52 D47**
West Barnby **63 E44**
West Barns **76 C32**
West Bay **8 E30**
West Beckham **45 B57**
West Benhar **75 D24**
Westbere **25 E57**
West Bergholt **34 F55**
West Bexington **8 F30**
West Bilney **44 D53**
West Blatchington **13 F48**
West Boldon **71 G39**
Westborough **42 A44**
Westbourne *W.S.* **11 D43**
Westbourne *Dor.* **10 E36**
West Bradenham **44 E54**
West Bradford **56 E33**
West Bradley **8 A31**
West Bretton **50 A38**
West Bridgford **41 B41**
West Bromwich **40 F35**
Westbrook **21 D40**
West Buckland *Som.* **7 C27**
West Buckland *Dev.* **6 B22**
West Burrafirth **107 B38**
West Burton *N.Y.* **57 A36**
West Burton *W.S.* **12 E45**
Westbury *Wts.* **20 F34**
Westbury *Shr.* **38 E29**
Westbury *Bkh.* **31 E41**
Westbury Leigh **20 G34**
Westbury-on-Severn **29 G33**
Westbury on Trym **19 D31**
Westbury-sub-Mendip **19 G30**
West Butterwick **52 B44**
Westby **55 F29**
West Byfleet **22 F46**
West Cairncake **99 D34**
West Caister **45 D60**
West Calder **75 D25**
West Camel **8 B31**
West Cauldcoats **74 F22**
West Challow **21 C39**
West Charleton **5 F23**
West Chelborough **8 D31**
West Chevington **71 D38**
West Chiltington **12 E46**
West Chinnock **8 C30**
West Chisenbury **20 F37**
West Clandon **22 F46**

West Cliffe 15 C59
Westcliff-on-Sea 24 C54
West Clyne 97 A24
West Coker 8 C31
Westcombe 9 A32
West Compton *Dor.* 8 E31
West Compton *Som.* 19 G31
Westcote 30 F37
Westcott *Bkh.* 31 G42
Westcott *Dev.* 7 E26
Westcott *Sry* 22 G47
Westcott Barton 30 F39
West Cross 17 F22
West Curry 4 A18
West Curthwaite 60 B29
West Dean *Wts.* 10 B38
Westdean 13 G51
West Dean *W.S.* 12 E44
West Deeping 42 E47
West Derby 48 C30
West Dereham 44 E52
West Ditchburn 71 A37
West Down 6 A21
Westdowns 4 B16
West Drayton *G.L.* 22 D46
West Drayton *Not.* 51 E42
West Dullater 81 G21
West Dunnet 103 A27
West Edington 71 E37
West Ella 59 G46
West End *Hum.* 59 C46
West End *N.Y.* 57 D37
West End *Sfk* 45 G60
West End *Nfk* 45 D60
West End *Str.* 75 F25
West End *Oxf.* 21 A40
West End *Avon* 19 D30
West End *Lan.* 55 C30
West End *Lcn.* 53 C49
West End *Kent* 25 E57
West End *Bfd.* 32 C45
West End *Sry* 22 E45
West End *Sry* 22 E46
West End *Ham.* 11 C40
West End Green 21 E42
Wester Aberchalder 88 B21
Wester Badentyre 99 D33
Wester Culbeuchly 98 C32
Westerdale *N.Y.* 63 F42
Westerdale *Hgh.* 103 C26
Wester Dechmont 75 C26
Westerfield *She.* 107 B39
Westerfield *Sfk* 35 D57
Wester Fintray 91 B34
Westergate 12 F45
Wester Gruinards 96 B20
Westerham 23 F50
Wester Lealty 96 D21
Westerleigh 19 D32
Wester Lonvine 96 D22
Wester Newburn 83 G30
Wester Ord 91 C34
Wester Parkgate 69 E26
Wester Quarff 107 D40
Wester Skeld 107 C38
Westerton *Tay.* 83 B32
Westerton *Grm.* 91 D33
Westerton *Drm* 62 C38
Westerton *Tay.* 81 F24
Westerwick 107 C38
West Farleigh 14 B53
West Farndon 31 C41
West Felton 38 C29
Westfield *Nfk* 44 E55
Westfield *Cum.* 60 D25
Westfield *Ltn* 75 C25
Westfield *E.S.* 14 F53
Westfield *Hgh.* 103 B26
Westfield Moor 14 F54
West Firle 13 F50
West Fleetham 71 A37
West Garforth 57 F39
Westgate *Drm* 61 C34
Westgate *Nfk* 44 A55
Westgate *Nor.* 71 F37
Westgate *Hum.* 51 B43
Westgate Hill 57 G38
Westgate on Sea 25 D58
West Ginge 21 C40
West Glen 73 C16
West Grafton 21 E38
West Green 22 F43
West Grimstead 10 B38
West Grinstead 12 D47
West Haddlesey 58 G41
West Haddon 31 A42
West Hagbourne 21 C41
West Hagley 40 G34
West Hall 70 G31
Westhall *Sfk* 45 G59
Westhall *Grm.* 91 A32
West Hallam 41 A40
West Halton 59 G45
Westham *Som.* 19 G29
Westham *Dor.* 9 G32
Westham *E.S.* 13 F52
West Ham 23 C50
Westhampnett 12 F44
West Handley 51 E39
West Hanney 21 B39
West Hanningfield 24 B53
West Hardwick 51 A40
West Harptree 19 F31
West Harting 11 B43
West Hatch 8 B28
Westhay 19 G30
Westhead 48 B30
West Heath *W.M.* 30 A36
West Heath *Ham.* 22 F44
West Helmsdale 103 G25
West Hendred 21 C40
West Heslerton 59 B45
Westhide 28 D31
Westhill *Grm.* 91 C34
West Hill *Avon* 19 D30
West Hill *Dev.* 7 F26
Westhill *Hgh.* 96 G23
West Hoathly 13 C49
West Holme 9 F34
Westhope *H.&W.* 28 C30
Westhope *Shr.* 38 G30
West Horndon 24 C52
Westhorpe *Sfk* 34 B56
Westhorpe *Lcn.* 42 B47
West Horrington 19 G31
West Horsley 22 F46
West Horton 77 G36
West Hougham 15 C58
Westhoughton 49 B32
Westhouse 56 B32
Westhouses 51 G39
West Humble 22 F47
West Huntspill 19 G29
West Hyde 22 B46
West Hythe 15 D57
West Ilsley 21 C40
Westing 106 B41
West Itchenor 12 F44
West Keal 53 F49
West Kennett 20 E37
West Kilbride 74 F18
West Kingsdown 23 E51
West Kington 20 D34
West Kirby 47 D27
West Knapton 58 B44
West Knighton 9 F33
West Knoyle 9 A34
West Kyloe 77 F36
Westlake 5 E21
West Lambrook 8 C30
West Langdon 15 C59
West Langwell 96 A22
West Lavington *Wts.* 20 F36
West Lavington *Wts.* 12 D44
West Layton 62 E37
West Leake 41 C41
Westleigh *G.M.* 49 B32
Westleigh *Dev.* 6 C20
Westleigh *Dev.* 7 D26
Westleton 35 B60
West Lexham 44 D54
Westley *Shr.* 38 E29
Westley *Sfk* 34 B54
Westley Heights 24 C52
Westley Waterless 33 C51
West Lilling 58 C42
West Lingo 83 G30
Westlington 22 A43
West Linton 75 E27
Westlinton 69 G29
West Littleton 20 D33
Westloch 76 E28
West Lockinge 21 C40
West Looe 4 E18
West Lulworth 9 F33
West Lutton 59 C45
West Lydford 8 A31
West Lyng 8 B29
West Lynn 44 D52
West Mains 77 F36
West Malling 23 F52
West Malvern 29 D33
West Marden 11 C43
West Markham 51 E43
West Marsh 53 A48
Westmarsh 25 E58
West Marton 56 D34
West Melton 51 B40
West Meon 11 B42
West Meon Hut 11 B42
West Mersea 34 G56
Westmeston 13 E49
Westmill 33 F49
West Milton 8 E30
West Minster 25 D55
West Molesey 22 E47
West Monkton 8 B28
West Moors 10 D36
West Mostard 61 G32
Westmuir 82 B29
West Muir 83 A31
West Ness 58 B42
Westness 104 D29
Westnewton *Cum.* 60 B27
West Newton *Hum.* 59 F48
West Newton *Nfk* 44 C53
Westnewton *Nor.* 77 G34
West Norwood 23 D49
West Ogwell 5 D24
Weston *Dor.* 9 G32
Weston *Hfs.* 33 E48
Weston *Brk.* 21 D40
Weston *Avon* 20 E33
Weston *N.Y.* 57 E37
Weston *Dev.* 7 G27
Weston *Nmp.* 31 D41
Weston *Shr.* 38 F31
Weston *Shr.* 38 C31
Weston *Che.* 49 G33
Weston *Che.* 48 D30
Weston *Grm.* 98 C30
Weston *Not.* 51 F43
Weston *Ham.* 11 B43
Weston *Lcn.* 43 C48
Weston *Stf.* 40 C35
Weston Beggard 28 D31
Westonbirt 20 C34
Weston by Welland 42 F43
Weston Colville 33 C51
Weston Corbett 21 G42
Weston Coyney 40 A35
Weston Favell 31 B43
Weston Green *Cbs.* 33 C52
Weston Green *Nfk* 45 D57
Weston Green *Sry* 22 E47
Weston Heath 39 D33
Weston Hills 43 C48
Westoning 32 E46
Weston-in-Gordano 19 D30
Weston Jones 39 C33
Weston Longville 45 D57
Weston Lullingfields 38 C30
Weston-on-the-Green 31 G41
Weston-on-Trent 41 C39
Weston Patrick 21 G42
Weston Point 48 D30
Weston Rhyn 38 B28
Weston Subedge 30 D36
Weston-super-Mare 19 E28
Weston Turville 22 A44
Weston-under-Lizard 40 D34
Weston under Penyard 29 F32
Weston under Wetherley 30 A39
Weston Underwood *Bkh.* 32 C44
Weston Underwood *Dby.* 40 A38
Westonzoyland 8 A29
West Orchard 9 C34
West Overton 20 E37
Westow 58 C43
West Park *Grm.* 91 D33
West Park *Mer.* 48 C30
West Parley 10 E36
West Peckham 23 F52
West Pennard 8 A31
West Pentire 2 B13
West Perry 32 B47
West Porlock 7 A24
Westport *Som.* 8 C29
Westport *Str.* 66 A12
West Putford 6 D19
West Quantoxhead 7 A27
West Rainton 62 B39
West Rasen 52 C46
Westray Airport 104 A30
West Raynham 44 C54
Westrigg 75 D25
West Rounton 62 F39
West Row 33 A52
West Rudham 44 C54
West Runton 45 A57
Westruther 76 F32
Westry 43 F49
West Saltoun 76 D30
West Sandwick 106 D40
West Scrafton 57 A36
Westside 91 D34
West Somerton 45 D60
West Stafford 9 F33
West Stockwith 51 C43
West Stoke 12 F44
West Stonesdale 61 F34
West Stoughton 19 G29
West Stour 9 B33
West Stourmouth 25 E58
West Stow 34 A54
West Stowell 20 E37
West Stratton 21 G41
West Street 14 B55
West Tanfield 57 B38
West Taphouse 4 D17
West Tarbert 73 D14
West Tarring 12 F47
West Thorney 11 D43
West Thurrock 23 D51
West Tilbury 24 D52
West Tisted 11 B42
West Tofts *Nfk* 44 F54
West Tofts *Tay.* 82 D26
West Torrington 52 D47
West Town *Avon* 19 E30
West Town *Ham.* 11 E43
West Tytherley 10 A38
West Tytherton 20 D35
West Walton 43 D50
West Walton Highway 43 D50
Westward 60 B28
Westward Ho! 6 C19
Westwell *Oxf.* 30 G38
Westwell *Kent* 14 C55
Westwell Leacon 14 C55
West Wellow 10 B38
West Wemyss 76 A29
West Wick 19 E29
Westwick *Nfk* 45 C58
Westwick *Drm* 62 E36
Westwick *Cbs.* 33 B50
West Wickham *Cbs.* 33 D51
West Wickham *G.L.* 23 E49
West Williamston 16 D16
West Winch 44 D52
West Winterslow 10 A38
West Wittering 11 E43
West Witton 57 A36
Westwood *Wts.* 20 F34
Westwood *Dev.* 7 F26
West Woodburn 70 E34
West Woodhay 21 E39
Westwood Heath 30 A38
West Woodlands 20 G33
Westwoodside 51 C43
West Worldham 11 A43
West Worlington 7 D23
West Worthing 12 F47
West Wratting 33 C51
West Wycombe 22 B44
West Yell 106 D40
Wetheral 60 A30
Wetherby 57 E40
Wether Cote Fm 63 G42
Wetherden 34 B56
Wetheringsett 35 B57
Wethersfield 33 E52
Wethersta 107 A39
Wetherup Street 35 B57
Wetley Rocks 40 A35
Wettenhall 48 F31
Wettenhall Green 49 G32
Wetton 50 G36
Wetwang 59 D45
Wetwood 39 B33
Wexcombe 21 F38
Weybourne 45 A57
Weybread 45 G58
Weybridge 22 E46
Weycroft 8 D29
Weydale 103 B27
Weyhill 21 G39
Weymouth 9 G32
Whaddon *Cbs.* 33 D49
Whaddon *Bkh.* 31 E44
Whaddon *Glo.* 29 G34
Whaddon *Wts.* 10 B37
Whaddon Gap 33 D49
Whale 61 D31
Whaley 51 E40
Whaley Bridge 50 D36
Whaligoe 103 D29
Whalley 56 F33
Whalton 71 E37
Wham 56 C33
Whaplode 43 C49
Whaplode Drove 43 D49
Whaplode St Catherine 43 D49
Wharfe 56 C33
Wharles 55 F30
Wharncliffe Side 50 C38
Wharram le Street 58 C44
Wharram Percy 58 C44
Wharton *Che.* 49 F32
Wharton *H.&W.* 28 C30
Whashton 62 F37
Whatcote 30 D38
Whatfield 34 D56
Whatley 20 G33
Whatlington 14 F53
Whatstandwell 50 G38
Whatton 42 B43
Whauphill 64 F19
Whaw 62 F35
Wheatacre 45 F60
Wheatenhurst 20 A33
Wheathampstead 32 G47
Wheathill 39 G32
Wheatley *Ham.* 22 G43
Wheatley *Oxf.* 21 A41
Wheatley Hill 62 C39
Wheatley Lane 56 F34
Wheaton Aston 40 D34
Wheddon Cross 7 B25
Wheedlemont 90 A30
Wheelerstreet 22 G45
Wheelock 49 G33
Wheelton 56 G32
Wheen 90 F29
Wheldrake 58 E42
Whelford 20 B37
Whelpley Hill 22 A46
Whelpo 60 B28
Whenby 58 C42
Whepstead 34 C54
Wherstead 35 D57
Wherwell 21 G39
Wheston 50 E37
Whetley Cross 8 D30
Whetsted 23 G52
Whetstone 41 F41
Whicham 54 A27
Whichford 30 E38
Whickham 71 G37
Whiddon Down 6 F22
Whifflet 75 D23
Whigstreet 83 C30
Whilton 31 B42
Whim 76 E28
Whimple 7 F26
Whimpwell Green 45 C59
Whinburgh 44 E56
Whin Lane End 55 E29
Whinnyfold 99 F36
Whippingham 11 E40
Whipsnade 32 G45
Whipton 7 F25
Whisby 52 F44
Whissendine 42 D43
Whissonsett 44 C54
Whistley Green 22 D43
Whiston *S.Y.* 51 C40
Whiston *Mer.* 48 C30
Whiston *Nmp.* 32 B44
Whiston *Stf.* 40 D34
Whiston *Stf.* 40 A36
Whitbeck 54 A27
Whitbourne 29 C32
Whitburn *Ltn* 75 D25
Whitburn *T.&W.* 71 G39
Whitby *Che.* 48 E29
Whitby *N.Y.* 63 E44
Whitchurch *Oxf.* 21 D42
Whitchurch *Shr.* 38 A31
Whitchurch *Dev.* 4 C20
Whitchurch *Bkh.* 31 F43
Whitchurch *Avon* 19 E31
Whitchurch *Dyf.* 16 B14
Whitchurch *Ham.* 21 G40
Whitchurch *S.G.* 18 D27
Whitchurch Canonicorum 8 E29
Whitchurch Hill 21 D42
Whitcombe 9 F32
Whitcott Keysett 38 G28
Whiteacen 98 E28
Whiteash Green 34 E53
Whitebog 99 D35
Whitebridge *Hgh.* 103 A28
Whitebridge *Hgh.* 88 C20
Whitebrook 19 A31
Whiteburn 76 F31
Whitecairn 64 E17
Whitecairns 91 B34
Whitecastle 75 F25
White Chapel 55 E31
Whitechurch 16 A17
White Colne 34 F54
White Coppice 49 A32
Whitecraig 76 C29
Whitecroft 19 A32
Whitecrook 64 E17
White Cross *Dev.* 7 F26
White Cross *Cnw.* 3 B14
White Cross *H.&W.* 28 D30
Whitecross 2 E11
White End 29 F33
Whiteface 96 C22
Whitefield *Tay.* 82 D27
Whitefield *Grm.* 91 A33
Whitefield *Hgh.* 88 B21
Whitefield *Hgh.* 103 C28
Whitefield *G.M.* 49 B33
Whiteford 91 A32
Whitegate 49 F32
Whitehall 104 D32
Whitehaven 60 E25
Whitehill *Str.* 74 E18
Whitehill *Kent* 14 B55
Whitehill *Ham.* 11 A43
Whitehills 98 C32
Whitehouse *Str.* 73 D14
Whitehouse *Grm.* 91 B32
Whitekirk 76 B31
White Lackington 9 E33
Whitelackington 8 C29
White Ladies Aston 29 C35
Whitelaw 77 E34
Whiteleen 103 D29
Whitelees 74 G19
Whiteley 11 D41
Whiteley Bank 11 F41
Whiteleys 64 E16
Whiteley Village 22 E46
Whitemans Green 13 D49

White Mill 17 B20
Whitemire 97 F25
White Moor 41 A39
White Notley 34 G53
Whiteparish 10 B38
White Pit 53 E49
Whiterashes 91 A34
White Roding 33 G51
Whiterow 103 D29
Whiteshill 20 A34
Whiteside *Ltn* 75 D25
Whiteside *Nor.* 70 G33
Whitesmith 13 E50
Whitestaunton 8 C28
Whitestone *Str.* 73 G13
Whitestone *Dev.* 7 F24
Whitestone *Grm.* 91 D32
Whitestripe 99 D35
White Waltham 22 D44
Whiteway 29 G34
Whitewell *Lan.* 56 E32
Whitewell *Grm.* 99 C35
Whiteworks 5 C22
Whitewreath 98 D28
Whitfield *Kent* 15 C58
Whitfield *Nor.* 61 A33
Whitfield *Avon* 19 B32
Whitfield *Nmp.* 31 E41
Whitfield *H.&W.* 28 E30
Whitford *Dev.* 8 E28
Whitford *Clw.* 47 E27
Whitgift 58 G44
Whitgreave 40 C34
Whithorn 64 F20
Whiting Bay 66 A16
Whitkirk 57 F39
Whitlam 91 A34
Whitland 16 C17
Whitland Abbey 16 C17
Whitletts 67 A19
Whitley *N.Y.* 58 G41
Whitley *Brk.* 21 E42
Whitley Bay 71 F39
Whitley Chapel 61 A35
Whitley Lower 50 A38
Whitley Row 23 F50
Whitlock's End 30 A36
Whitminster 20 A33
Whitmore *Stf.* 39 A33
Whitmore *Dor.* 10 D36
Whitnage 7 D26
Whitnash 30 B39
Whitney 28 D28
Whitrigg *Cum.* 60 C28
Whitrigg *Cum.* 60 A28
Whitsbury 10 C37
Whitsome 77 E34
Whitson 19 C29
Whitstable 25 E56
Whitstone 4 A18
Whittingham 71 B36
Whittingslow 38 G29
Whittington *Shr.* 38 B29
Whittington *Dby.* 51 E39
Whittington *Glo.* 29 F36
Whittington *Nfk* 44 F52
Whittington *H.&W.* 29 C34
Whittington *Stf.* 40 G34
Whittington *Stf.* 40 E37
Whittington *Lan.* 55 B31
Whittlebury 31 D42
Whittle-le-Woods 55 G31
Whittlesey 43 F48
Whittlesford 33 D50
Whitton *Cle.* 62 D39
Whitton *Hum.* 59 G45
Whitton *Nor.* 71 C36
Whitton *Pow.* 28 B28
Whitton *Shr.* 28 A31
Whitton *Sfk* 35 D57
Whittonditch 21 D38
Whittonstall 62 A36
Whitway 21 F40
Whitwell *I.o.W.* 11 G41
Whitwell *Lei.* 42 E45
Whitwell *Nfk* 45 C57
Whitwell *N.Y.* 62 G38
Whitwell *Dby.* 51 E41
Whitwell *Hfs.* 32 F47
Whitwell-on-the-Hill 58 C42
Whitwick 41 D40
Whitwood 57 G39
Whitworth 49 A34
Whixall 38 B30
Whixley 57 D40
Whorlton *N.Y.* 62 F40
Whorlton *Drm* 62 E37
Whygate 70 F33
Whyle 28 B31
Whyteleafe 23 F49
Wibdon 19 B31
Wibsey 57 F37
Wibtoft 41 G40
Wichenford 29 B33
Wichling 14 B55
Wick *W.S.* 12 F46
Wick *Dor.* 10 E37
Wick *Wts.* 10 B37
Wick *H.&W.* 29 D35
Wick *Avon* 19 D32
Wick *M.G.* 18 D25
Wick *Hgh.* 103 C29
Wicken *Cbs.* 33 A51
Wicken *Nmp.* 31 E43
Wicken Bonhunt 33 E50
Wickenby 52 D46
Wickerslack 61 E31
Wickersley 51 C40
Wickford 24 B53
Wickham *Brk.* 21 D39
Wickham *Ham.* 11 C41
Wickham Bishops 34 G54
Wickhambreaux 15 B57
Wickhambrook 34 C53
Wickhamford 30 D36
Wickham Heath 21 E39
Wickham Market 35 C58
Wickhampton 45 E60
Wickham Skeith 34 B56
Wickham St Paul 34 E54
Wickham Street *Sfk* 34 C53
Wickham Street *Sfk* 34 A56
Wick Hill *Brk.* 22 E44
Wick Hill *Kent* 14 C54
Wicklewood 44 E56
Wickmere 45 B57
Wick St Lawrence 19 E29
Wickwar 20 C33
Widdington 33 E51
Widdop 56 F35
Widdrington 71 D38
Widecombe in the Moor 5 C22
Widegates 4 E18
Widemouth Bay 6 E18
Wide Open 71 F38
Widewall 105 B30
Widford *Hfs.* 33 G50
Widford *Esx* 24 A52
Widmerpool 41 C42
Widnes 48 D31
Widworthy 7 F27
Wigan 48 B31
Wiggaton 7 F27
Wiggenhall St Germans 44 D52
Wiggenhall St Mary Magdalen 43 D51
Wiggenhall St Mary the Virgin 43 D51
Wiggenhall St Peter 44 D52
Wiggington 58 D41
Wigginton *Hfs.* 32 G45
Wigginton *Oxf.* 30 E39
Wigginton *Stf.* 40 E37
Wigglesworth 56 D34
Wiggonby 60 A28
Wiggonholt 12 E46
Wighill 57 E40
Wighton 44 B55
Wightwizzle 50 C38
Wigmore *H.&W.* 28 B29
Wigmore *Kent* 24 E54
Wigsley 52 E44
Wigsthorpe 42 G46
Wigston 41 F41
Wigston Parva 41 F40
Wigthorpe 51 D41
Wigtoft 43 B48
Wigton 60 B28
Wigtown 64 E20
Wilbarston 42 G43
Wilberfoss 58 D43
Wilburton 33 A50
Wilby *Nmp.* 32 B44
Wilby *Nfk* 44 F56
Wilby *Sfk* 35 A58
Wilcot 20 E37
Wilcott 38 D29
Wilcrick 19 C29
Wildboarclough 49 F35
Wilden *H.&W.* 29 A34
Wilden *Bfd.* 32 C46
Wildhern 21 F39
Wildhill 23 A48
Wildsworth 51 C43
Wilford 41 B41
Wilkesley 38 A31
Wilkhaven 97 C25
Wilkieston 75 D26
Willand 7 D26
Willaston *Che.* 49 G32
Willaston *Che.* 48 E29
Willen 32 D44
Willenhall *W.M.* 30 A39
Willenhall *W.M.* 40 F35
Willerby 59 G46
Willersey 30 D36
Willersley
Willesborough 14 C55
Willesborough Lees 14 C55
Willesden 23 C48
Willesley 20 C34
Willett 7 B26
Willey *War.* 41 G40
Willey *Shr.* 39 F32
Williamscot 31 D40
Williamthorpe 51 F39
Willian 33 E48
Willimontswick 70 G33
Willingale 23 A51
Willingdon 13 F51
Willingham *Cbs.* 33 A49
Willingham *Lcn.* 52 D44
Willington *War.* 30 E38
Willington *T.&W.* 71 G38
Willington *Drm* 62 C37
Willington *Bfd.* 32 D46
Willington *Dby.* 40 C38
Willington Corner 48 F31
Willisham 34 C56
Willitoft 58 F43
Williton 7 A26
Willoughby *Lcn.* 53 E50
Willoughby *War.* 31 B40
Willoughby on the Wolds 41 C42
Willoughby Waterleys 41 F41
Willoughton 52 C45
Willows Green 34 G53
Willsworthy 6 G21
Wilmcote 30 C37
Wilmington *Dev.* 8 D28
Wilmington *W.S.* 13 F51
Wilmington *Kent* 23 D51
Wilmslow 49 D34
Wilnecote 40 E37
Wilpshire 56 F32
Wilsden 57 F36
Wilsford *Wts.* 20 G37
Wilsford *Wts.* 20 F36
Wilsford *Lcn.* 42 A45
Wilsill 57 C37
Wilsley Green 14 D53
Wilson 41 C39
Wilstead 32 D46
Wilsthorpe 42 D46
Wilstone 32 G44
Wilton *Bor.* 69 B30
Wilton *Som.* 8 B28
Wilton *Cum.* 60 E26
Wilton *N.Y.* 58 A44
Wilton *Cle.* 63 D41
Wilton *Wts.* 21 E38
Wilton *Wts.* 10 A36
Wimbish 33 E51
Wimbish Green 33 E52
Wimblebury 40 D35
Wimbledon 23 D48
Wimblington 43 F49
Wimborne Minster 9 E35
Wimborne St Giles 10 C36
Wimbotsham 44 E52
Wimpstone 30 D37
Wincanton 9 B32
Wincham 49 E32
Winchburgh 75 C26
Winchcombe 29 F35
Winchelsea 14 F55
Winchelsea Beach 14 F55
Winchester 10 B39
Winchet Hill 14 C53
Winchfield 22 F43
Winchmore Hill *G.L.* 23 B48
Winchmore Hill *Bkh.* 22 B45
Wincle 49 F35
Wincobank *Str.* 51 C39
Windermere 60 G30
Winderton 30 D39
Windhill 96 G21
Windlesham 22 E45
Windley 40 A38
Windley Meadows 41 A39
Windmill Hill *Som.* 8 C29
Windmill Hill *E.S.* 13 E52
Windrush 30 G37
Windsor 22 D45
Windygates 82 G29
Windy Yet 74 E20
Wineham 13 D48
Winestead 59 G49
Winewall 56 F35
Winfarthing 44 G56
Winford 19 E31
Winforton 28 D28
Winfrith Newburgh 9 F33
Wing *Bkh.* 32 F44
Wing *Lei.* 42 E44
Wingate 62 C39
Wingates *Nor.* 71 D36
Wingates *G.M.* 49 B32
Wingerworth 51 F39
Wingfield *Sfk* 35 A58
Wingfield *Bfd.* 32 F45
Wingfield *Wts.* 20 F34
Wingham 15 B58
Wingmore 15 C57
Wingrave 32 G44
Winkburn 51 G42
Winkfield 22 D44
Winkfield Row 22 D44
Winkhill 50 G36
Winkleigh 6 E21
Winksley 57 B38
Winksley Banks 57 B38
Winkton 10 E37
Winlaton 71 G37
Winlaton Mill 71 G37
Winless 103 C28
Winmarleigh 55 E30
Winnards Perch 3 B15
Winnersh 22 D43
Winscombe 19 F29
Winsford *Som.* 7 B24
Winsford *Che.* 49 F32
Winsham 8 D29
Winshill 40 C38
Winskill 61 C31
Winslade 21 G42
Winsley 20 E33
Winslow 31 F43
Winson 20 A36
Winsor 10 C39
Winster *Cum.* 60 G30
Winster *Dby.* 50 F38
Winston *Sfk* 35 B57
Winston *Drm* 62 E37
Winstone 20 A35
Winswell 6 D20
Winterborne Came 9 F32
Winterborne Clenston 9 D34
Winterborne Houghton 9 D34
Winterborne Kingston 9 E34
Winterborne Monkton 9 F32
Winterborne Stickland 9 D34
Winterborne Whitechurch 9 E34
Winterborne Zelston 9 E35
Winterbourne *Avon* 19 C32
Winterbourne *Brk.* 21 D40
Winterbourne Abbas 9 E32
Winterbourne Bassett 20 D36
Winterbourne Dauntsey 10 A37
Winterbourne Earls 10 A37
Winterbourne Gunner 10 A37
Winterbourne Monkton 20 D37
Winterbourne Steepleton 9 F32
Winterbourne Stoke 20 G36
Winterburn 56 D35
Wintercleugh 68 B25
Winteringham 59 G45
Winterley 49 G33
Wintersett 51 A39
Wintershill 11 C40
Winterslow 10 A38
Winterton 52 A45
Winterton-on-Sea 45 D60
Winthorpe *Lcn.* 53 F51
Winthorpe *Not.* 52 G44
Winton *Cum.* 61 E33
Winton *Dor.* 10 E36
Wintringham 58 B44
Winwick *Che.* 49 C32
Winwick *Nmp.* 31 A42
Winwick *Cbs.* 42 G46
Wirksworth 50 G38
Wirswall 38 A31
Wisbech 43 E50
Wisbech St Mary 43 E50
Wisborough Green 12 D46
Wiseton 51 D42
Wishaw *Str.* 75 E23
Wishaw *War.* 40 F37
Wisley 22 F46
Wispington 52 E47
Wissett 35 A59
Wissington 34 E55
Wistanstow 38 G30
Wistanswick 39 C32
Wistaston 49 G32
Wiston *Str.* 75 G25
Wiston *Dyf.* 16 C16
Wiston *W.S.* 12 E47
Wistow *N.Y.* 58 F41
Wistow *Cbs.* 43 G48
Wiswell 56 F33
Witcham 33 A50
Witchampton 9 D35
Witchburn 66 B12
Witchford 33 A50
Witcombe 8 B30
Witham 34 G53
Witham Friary 20 G33
Witham on the Hill 42 D46
Withcote 42 E43
Witherenden Hill 13 D52
Witherhurst 13 D52
Witheridge 7 D24
Witherley 41 F39
Withern 53 D50
Withernsea 59 G49
Withernwick 59 E48
Withersdale Street 45 G58
Withersfield 33 D52
Witherslack 55 A30
Witherslack Hall 55 A30
Withiel 3 B15
Withiel Florey 7 B25
Withington *G.M.* 49 C34
Withington *Shr.* 38 D31
Withington *H.&W.* 28 D31
Withington *Glo.* 30 G36
Withington *Stf.* 40 B36
Withington Green 49 E34
Withleigh 7 D24
Withnell 56 G32
Withybrook 41 G40
Withycombe 7 A25
Withycombe Raleigh 7 G26
Withyham 13 C50
Withypool 7 B24
Witley 12 C45
Witnesham 35 C57
Witney 30 G39
Wittering 42 E46
Wittersham 14 E54
Witton 90 F31
Witton Bridge 45 B59
Witton Gilbert 62 B38
Witton-le-Wear 62 C37
Witton Park 62 C37
Wiveliscombe 7 C26
Wivelsfield 13 D49
Wivelsfield Green 13 E49
Wivenhoe 34 F56
Wiveton 44 A56
Wix 35 F57
Wixford 30 C36
Wixoe 33 D52
Woburn 32 E45
Woburn Sands 32 E45
Wokefield Park 21 E42
Woking 22 F46
Wokingham 22 E44
Wolborough 5 D24
Woldingham 23 F49
Wold Newton 53 C48
Wolfelee 70 C31
Wolferlow 29 B32
Wolferton 44 C52
Wolfhampcote 31 B40
Wolfhill 82 D27
Wolfpits 28 C27
Wolf's Castle 16 B15
Wolfsdale 16 B15
Woll 69 A30
Wollaston *Nmp.* 32 B44
Wollaston *Shr.* 38 D29
Wollaston *Stf.* 40 G34
Wollerton 38 C31
Wolsingham 62 C36
Wolstenholme 49 A34
Wolston 30 A39
Wolvercote 21 A40
Wolverhampton 40 F34
Wolverley *Shr.* 38 B30
Wolverley *H.&W.* 29 A34
Wolverton *Bkh.* 31 D44
Wolverton *War.* 30 B38
Wolverton *Ham.* 21 F41
Wolvesnewton 19 B30
Wolvey 41 G40
Wolviston 62 D40
Wombleton 58 A42
Wombourne 40 F34
Wombwell 51 B40
Womenswold 15 B57
Womersley 51 A41
Wonastow 28 G30
Wonersh 22 G46
Wonson 6 G22
Wonston 11 A40
Wooburn 22 C44
Wooburn Green 22 C45
Woodale 57 B36
Woodbastwick 45 D59
Woodbeck 51 E43
Woodbine 16 C15
Woodborough *Wts.* 20 E36
Woodborough *Not.* 41 A42
Woodbridge 35 D58
Wood Burcote 31 D42
Woodbury 7 G26
Woodbury Salterton 7 G26
Woodchester 20 A34
Woodchurch *Mer.* 48 D28
Woodchurch *Kent* 14 D55
Woodcote *Oxf.* 21 C42
Woodcote *Shr.* 39 D33
Woodcott 21 F40
Woodcroft 19 B31
Woodcutts 9 C35
Wood Dalling 44 C56
Woodditton 33 C52
Woodeaton 31 G41
Wood End *Hfs.* 33 F49
Wood End *War.* 30 A36
Woodend *Nmp.* 31 D41
Wood End *Bfd.* 32 D45
Woodend *Hgh.* 88 B23
Woodend *Grm.* 91 B32

Woodend *Tay.* 81 C23
Woodend *W.S.* 12 F44
Woodend *Cum.* 60 G27
Wood End *War.* 40 F38
Woodend *Hgh.* 79 A13
Wood Enderby 53 F48
Woodfalls 10 B37
Woodford *G.L.* 23 B49
Woodford *Glo.* 19 B32
Woodford *Nmp.* 32 A45
Woodford *G.M.* 49 D34
Woodford *Cnw.* 6 D18
Woodford Bridge 23 B50
Woodford Green 23 B49
Woodford Halse 31 C41
Woodgate *H.&W.* 29 B35
Woodgate *Nfk* 44 D56
Woodgate *W.M.* 40 G35
Woodgate *W.S.* 12 F45
Wood Green 23 B48
Woodgreen 10 C37
Woodhall 62 G35
Woodhall Spa 52 F47
Woodham *Sry* 22 E46
Woodham *Drm* 62 D38
Woodham Ferrers 24 B53
Woodham Mortimer 24 A54
Woodham Walter 24 A53
Woodhaven 82 E29
Wood Hayes 40 E35
Woodhead 99 F33
Woodhill 39 G33
Woodhorn 71 E38
Woodhouse *Lei.* 41 D41
Woodhouse *Cum.* 55 A31
Woodhouse *S.Y.* 51 D39
Woodhouse Eaves 41 D41
Woodhouses 40 D37
Woodhuish 5 E25
Woodhurst 33 A48
Woodingdean 13 F49
Woodland *Dev.* 5 D23
Woodland *Drm* 62 D36
Woodlands *Shr.* 39 G32
Woodlands *Ham.* 10 C38
Woodlands *Dor.* 10 D36
Woodlands Park 22 D44
Woodleigh 5 F23
Woodlesford 57 G39
Woodley 22 D43
Woodmancote *W.S.* 13 E48
Woodmancote *W.S.* 11 D43
Wood-mancote 20 A35
Woodmancote *Glo.* 29 F35
Woodmancott 21 G41
Woodmansey 59 F46
Woodmansterne 23 F48
Woodminton 10 B36
Woodmoor 38 E28
Woodnesborough 15 B58
Woodnewton 42 F46
Wood Norton 44 C56
Woodplumpton 55 F30
Woodrising 44 E55
Woodseaves *Stf.* 39 C33
Woodseaves *Shr.* 39 B32
Woodsend 21 D38
Woodsetts 51 D41
Woodsford 9 E33
Woodside *Fife* 82 G28
Woodside *Grm.* 91 C35
Woodside *Tay.* 82 D27
Woodside *Str.* 74 E19
Woodside *Shr.* 38 G29
Woodside *D.&G.* 69 F26
Woodside *W.M.* 40 G34
Woodside *Hfs.* 23 A48
Woodside *Brk.* 22 D45
Woodstock 31 G40
Woodstock Slop 16 B16
Woodston 42 F47
Wood Street 22 F45
Woodthorpe *Lei.* 41 D41
Woodthorpe *Dby.* 51 E40
Woodton 45 F58
Woodtown *Grm.* 90 F31
Woodtown *Dev.* 6 C20
Woodville 40 D38
Woodwalton 42 G47
Woodyates 9 C35
Woofferton 28 B30
Wookey 19 G30
Wookey Hole 19 G31
Wool 9 F34
Woolacombe 6 A20
Woolaston 19 B31
Woolavington 19 G29
Woolbeding 12 D44
Wooler 70 A35
Woolfardisworthy *Dev.* 7 E23
Woolfardisworthy *Dev.* 6 C18
Woolfords Cottages 75 E25
Woolhampton 21 E41
Woolhope 28 E31
Woollage Green 15 C58
Woolland 9 D33
Woollard 19 E32
Woollaton 6 D20
Woolley *Cbs.* 32 A47
Woolley *Avon* 20 E33
Woolley *W.Y.* 51 A39
Woolmere Green 29 B35
Woolmer Green 33 G48
Woolmersdon 8 A28
Woolpit 34 B55
Woolscott 31 B40
Woolstaston 38 F30
Woolsthorpe *Lcn.* 42 C44
Woolsthorpe *Lcn.* 42 B44
Woolston *Ham.* 11 C40
Woolston *Shr.* 38 G30
Woolston *Shr.* 38 C29
Woolston *Che.* 49 D32
Woolstone 21 C38
Woolston Green 5 D23
Woolton 48 D30
Woolton Hill 21 E40
Woolverstone 35 E57
Woolverton 20 F33
Woolwich 23 D50
Woonton 28 C29
Wooperton 71 A36
Woore 39 A33
Wootton *Bfd.* 32 D45
Wootton *Nmp.* 31 C43
Wootton *Oxf.* 31 G40
Wootton *Oxf.* 21 A40
Wootton *Kent* 15 C57
Wootton *Stf.* 40 A37
Wootton *Shr.* 28 A30
Wootton *Ham.* 10 E38
Wootton *Stf.* 40 C34
Wootton *Hum.* 52 A46
Wootton Bassett 20 C36
Wootton Bridge 11 E41
Wootton Common 11 E41
Wootton Courtenay 7 A25
Wootton Fitzpaine 8 E29
Wootton Green 32 D45
Wootton Rivers 20 E37
Wootton St Lawrence 21 F41
Wootton Wawen 30 B37
Worcester 29 C34
Worcester Park 23 E48
Wordsley 40 G34
Wordwell 34 A54
Worfield 39 F33
Work 104 E30
Workington 60 D25
Worksop 51 E41
Worlaby 52 A46
Worlds End 11 C42
World's End 21 D40
Worle 19 E29
Worleston 49 G32
Worlingham 45 F60
Worlington 33 A52
Worlingworth 35 B58
Wormbridge 28 E29
Wormegay 44 D52
Wormelow Tump 28 E30
Wormhill 50 E37
Wormiehills 83 D31
Wormingford 34 E54
Worminghall 21 A42
Wormington 30 E36
Worminster 19 G31
Wormistone 83 G31
Wormit 82 E29
Wormleighton 31 C40
Wormley *Hfs.* 23 A49
Wormley *Sry* 12 C45
Wormshill 14 B54
Wormsley 28 D30
Worplesdon 22 F45
Worrall 50 C38
Worsbrough 51 B39
Worsley 49 B33
Worstead 45 C59
Worsted Lodge 33 C51
Worsthorne 56 F34
Worston 56 E33
Worswell 5 F21
Worth *Kent* 15 B59
Worth *W.S.* 13 C48
Wortham 34 A56
Worthen 38 E29
Worthenbury 38 A29
Worthing *Nfk* 44 D56
Worthing *W.S.* 12 F47
Worthington 41 C39
Worth Matravers 9 G35
Wortley *Glo.* 20 B33
Wortley *S.Y.* 50 C38
Worton 20 F35
Wortwell 45 G58
Wotherton 38 E28
Wotton 22 G47
Wotton-under-Edge 20 B33
Wotton Underwood 31 G42
Woughton on the Green 32 E44
Wouldham 24 E53
Wrabness 35 E57
Wrae 99 D33
Wrafton 6 B20
Wragby 52 E47
Wragholme 53 C49
Wramplingham 45 E57
Wrangham 98 F32
Wrangle 53 G50
Wrangle Lowgate 53 G50
Wrangway 7 D27
Wrantage 8 B28
Wrawby 52 B46
Wraxall *Avon* 19 D30
Wraxall *Som.* 8 A31
Wray 55 C31
Wray Castle 60 F29
Wraysbury 22 D46
Wrea Green 55 F29
Wreay *Cum.* 60 B30
Wreay *Cum.* 60 D30
Wrecclesham 22 G43
Wrekenton 62 A38
Wrelton 58 A43
Wrenbury 38 A31
Wreningham 45 F57
Wrentham 45 G60
Wrenthorpe 57 G39
Wrentnall 38 E29
Wressle 58 F43
Wrestlingworth 33 D48
Wretham 44 G54
Wretton 44 F52
Wrexham 38 A29
Wribbenhall 29 A33
Wrightington Bar 48 A31
Wrightpark 74 A22
Wrinehill 39 A33
Wrington 19 E30
Writhlington 19 F32
Writtle 24 A52
Wrockwardine 38 D31
Wroot 51 B43
Wrotham 23 F51
Wrotham Heath 23 F52
Wrotham Hill 24 E52
Wrotham Park 23 B48
Wroughton 20 C37
Wroxall 11 G41
Wroxeter 38 E31
Wroxhall 30 A38
Wroxham 45 D58
Wroxton 30 D39
Wstrws 26 D19
Wyaston 40 A37
Wyberton 43 A49
Wyboston 32 C47
Wybunbury 39 A32
Wychbold 29 B35
Wych Cross 13 C50
Wyck 11 A43
Wyck Rissington 30 F37
Wycliffe 62 E36
Wycoller 56 F35
Wycomb 42 C43
Wycombe Marsh 22 B44
Wyddial 33 E49
Wye 15 C56
Wyke *W.Y.* 57 G37
Wyke *Dor.* 9 B33
Wyke *Shr.* 39 E32
Wykeham *Hum.* 59 A45
Wykeham *N.Y.* 58 B44
Wyken 39 F33
Wyke Regis 9 G32
Wykey 38 C29
Wylam 71 G36
Wylde Green 40 F37
Wyllie 18 B27
Wylye 9 A35
Wymering 11 D42
Wymeswold 41 C41
Wymington 32 B45
Wymondham *Nfk* 45 E57
Wymondham *Lei.* 42 D44
Wyndham 18 B25
Wynford Eagle 8 E31
Wynnstay 38 A29
Wyre Piddle 29 D35
Wyresdale Tower 56 D32
Wysall 41 C41
Wyson 28 B30
Wythall 30 A36
Wytham 21 A40
Wythburn 60 E29
Wyton 33 A48
Wyverstone 34 B56
Wyverstone Street 34 B56
Wyville 42 C44
Wyvis Lodge 96 D20

Y

Yaddlethorpe 52 B44
Yafford 11 F40
Yafforth 62 G39
Yalding 14 C53
Yanworth 30 G36
Yapham 58 D43
Yapton 12 F45
Yarburgh 53 C49
Yarcombe 8 D28
Yardley 40 G37
Yardley Gobion 31 D43
Yardley Hastings 32 C44
Yardro 28 C28
Yarkhill 28 D31
Yarlet 40 C35
Yarley 19 G30
Yarlington 9 B32
Yarm 62 E40
Yarmouth 10 F39
Yarnacott 6 B22
Yarnbrook 20 F34
Yarnfield 40 B34
Yarnscombe 6 C21
Yarnton 31 G40
Yarpole 28 B30
Yarrow 69 A29
Yarrow Feus 69 A29
Yarrowford 69 A29
Yarsop 28 D29
Yarwell 42 F46
Yate 19 C32
Yateley 22 E43
Yatesbury 20 D36
Yattendon 21 D41
Yatton *Avon* 19 E30
Yatton *H.&W.* 28 B30
Yatton Keynell 20 D34
Yaverland 11 F42
Yaxham 44 D56
Yaxley *Sfk* 35 A57
Yaxley *Cbs.* 42 F47
Yazor 28 D29
Y Bryn 37 C24
Y Drenewydd (Newtown) 38 F27
Yeading 22 C46
Yeadon 57 E37
Yealand Conyers 55 B30
Yealand Redmayne 55 B30
Yealmpton 5 E21
Yearby 63 D41
Yearsley 58 B41
Yeaton 38 D30
Yeaveley 40 A37
Yedingham 58 B44
Yelford 21 A39
Yelland *Dev.* 6 B20
Yelland *Dev.* 6 F21
Yelling 33 B48
Yelvertoft 31 A41
Yelverton *Nfk* 45 E58
Yelverton *Dev.* 5 D21
Yenston 9 B32
Yeoford 7 F23
Yeolmbridge 4 B18
Yeomadon 6 E18
Yeo Vale 6 C20
Yeovil 8 C31
Yeovil Marsh 8 C31
Yeovilton 8 B31
Yerbeston 16 D16
Yesnaby 104 E28
Yetlington 70 C35
Yetminster 8 C31
Yettington 7 G26
Yetts o'Muckhart 82 G25
Y Fan 37 G25
Y Felinheli 46 F20
Y Ffor 36 B19
Yielden 32 B46
Yiewsley 22 D46
Ynysboeth 18 B26
Ynysddu 18 B27
Ynyshir 18 B26
Ynyslas 36 F21
Ynysmendwy 18 A23
Ynystawe 17 D22
Ynysybwl 18 B26
Yockenthwaite 56 B34
Yockleton 38 D29
Yokefleet 58 G43
Yoker 74 D20
Yonder Bognie 98 E31
York 58 D41
Yorkletts 25 E56
Yorkley 19 A32
Yorton 38 C30
Youldon 6 E18
Youldonmoor Cross 6 E19
Youlgreave 50 F37
Youlstone 6 D18
Youlthorpe 58 D43
Youlton 57 C40
Young's End 34 G53
Yoxall 40 D37
Yoxford 35 B59
Ysbyty Cynfyn 27 A23
Ysbyty Ifan 37 A24
Ysbyty Ystwyth 27 A23
Ysceifiog 47 E27
Ysgubor-y-coed 37 F22
Ystalyfera 18 A23
Ystrad 18 B25
Ystrad Aeron 26 C20
Ystradfellte 27 G25
Ystradffin 27 D23
Ystradgynlais 27 G23
Ystrad Meurig 27 B22
Ystrad Mynach 18 B27
Ystradowen *S.G.* 18 D26
Ystradowen *Dyf.* 27 G23
Ythanwells 98 F32
Ythsie 99 F34
Y Trallwng (Welshpool) 38 E27

Z

Zeal Monachorum 6 E22
Zeals 9 A33
Zelah 3 C14
Zennor 2 E10

Conversion Tables

DISTANCES AND SPEEDS

Miles to kilometres
Miles per hour to kilometres per hour

1	1.60	20	32.18	75	120.70
2	3.21	25	40.23	80	128.74
3	4.82	30	48.27	85	136.79
4	6.43	35	56.32	90	144.84
5	8.04	40	64.37	95	152.88
6	9.65	45	72.41	100	160.93
7	11.26	50	80.46	200	321.86
8	12.87	55	88.51	300	482.80
9	14.48	60	96.55	400	643.73
10	16.09	65	104.60	500	804.67
15	24.13	70	112.65	1000	1609.34

1 Mile = 1.6093 Km

1 Km = 0.6213 Miles

Kilometres to miles
Kilometres per hour to miles per hour

1	0.62	20	12.42	75	46.60
2	1.24	25	15.53	80	49.71
3	1.86	30	18.64	85	52.81
4	2.48	35	21.74	90	55.92
5	3.10	40	24.85	95	59.03
6	3.72	45	27.96	100	62.14
7	4.34	50	31.07	200	124.27
8	4.97	55	34.17	300	186.41
9	5.59	60	37.28	400	248.55
10	6.21	65	40.39	500	310.69
15	9.32	70	43.49	1000	621.37

1 Yard = 91.4 cm

1 Foot = 30.5 cm

1 Inch = 2.5 cm

Feet to metres		Metres to feet	
1	0.3	1	3.2
2	0.6	2	6.5
3	0.9	3	9.8
4	1.2	4	13.1
5	1.5	5	16.4
6	1.8	6	19.6
7	2.1	7	22.9
8	2.4	8	26.2
9	2.7	9	29.5
10	3.0	10	32.8
15	4.5	15	49.2
20	6.0	20	65.6
50	15.2	50	164.0
100	30.4	100	328.1

TYRE PRESSURES

Pounds per sq in to kg per sq cm

16	1.12	28	1.96
18	1.26	30	2.10
20	1.40	32	2.24
22	1.54	36	2.52
24	1.68	40	2.80
26	1.83	50	3.50

TEMPERATURE

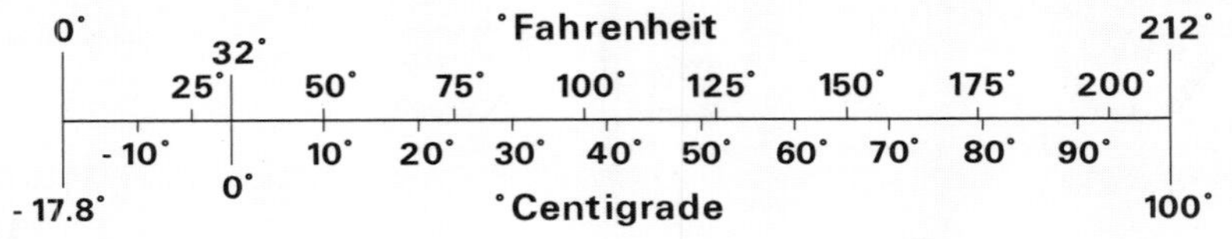

PETROL CONSUMPTION

Miles per gall to km per 10 litres

10	35	20	71
11	39	25	88
12	42	30	106
13	46	35	124
14	50	40	142
15	53	45	159

WEIGHTS

Pounds Avoirdupois	Kilogrammes
1	0.45
2	0.91
3	1.36
4	1.81
5	2.27
6	2.72
7	3.18
8	3.63
9	4.08
10	4.54
11	4.99
12	5.44
13	5.90
14	6.35
15	6.80
20	9.07
30	13.61
40	18.14
50	22.68
112	50.80

Kilogrammes	Pounds Avoirdupois
1	2.20
2	4.41
3	6.61
4	8.82
5	11.02
6	13.23
7	15.43
8	17.64
9	19.84
10	22.05
11	24.25
12	26.46
13	28.66
14	30.86
15	33.07
20	44.09
30	66.14
40	88.18
50	110.23
100	220.46

LIQUIDS

Pints	Litres
0.5	0.28
1	0.57
2	1.14
3	1.71
4	2.27
Gallons	**Litres**
1	4.5
2	9.1
3	13.6
4	18.2
5	22.7
6	27.3
7	31.8
8	36.4
9	40.9
10	45.5
25	113.6
50	227.3
100	454.6

Litres	Gallons
0.5	0.11
1	0.22
2	0.44
3	0.66
4	0.88
5	1.10
6	1.32
7	1.54
8	1.76
9	1.98
10	2.20
20	4.40
30	6.60
40	8.80
50	11.00
60	13.20
70	15.40
80	17.60
90	19.80
100	22.00

GRADIENTS

Grade	Percentage
1:3	33.3
1:4	25.0
1:5	20.0
1:6	16.7
1:7	14.3
1:8	12.5
1:9	11.1
1:10	10.0
1:11	9.1
1:12	8.3
1:13	7.7
1:14	7.1
1:15	6.7
1:16	6.3
1:17	5.9
1:18	5.6
1:19	5.3
1:20	5.0
1:25	4.0
1:30	3.3

Road Signs

THE SIGNING SYSTEM

The shapes give / **The colours give**

orders / warnings / information / a positive instruction / a negative instruction / general information / directions on primary routes

EXCEPTIONS ARE FOR EMPHASIS

SIGNS GIVING ORDERS — mostly circular

Stop and Give Way / Give way to traffic on major road / No vehicles / No entry for vehicles / No right turn / No left turn / No U turns / No overtaking / Give priority to vehicles from opposite direction

School Crossing Patrol / Maximum speed / National speed limit applies / No horse-drawn vehicles / No vehicles carrying explosives / Overall length of vehicle or combination of vehicles limit / Total weight limit / Axle weight limit / Width limit / Height limit

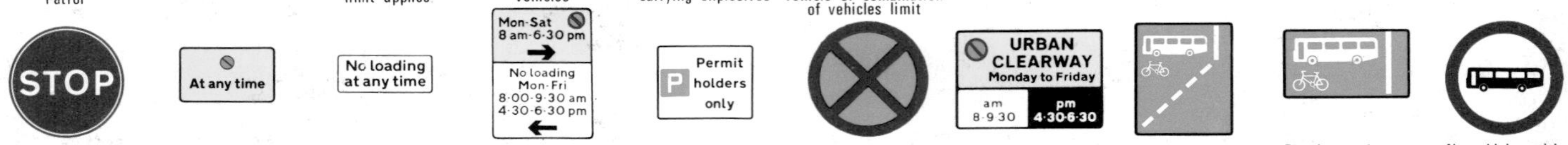

Manually operated temporary Stop sign / Continuous prohibition on waiting, except for loading/unloading / No loading/unloading / Times of (upper) no waiting, (lower) no loading/unloading / Parking reserved for permit holders / No stopping ('Clearway') / No stopping during times indicated except for up to 2 minutes to set down or pick up passengers / Lane ahead for buses and pedal cycles only / Bus lane – buses and pedal cycles only / No vehicles with over 12 seats except regular scheduled school and work buses

No pedestrians / No cycling / No goods vehicles over specified unladen weight / End of restriction on prohibition of goods vehicles / No motor vehicles / No motor vehicles except motor cycles without side-cars

Plates below some signs qualify their message

End of restriction / Exception for vehicles with over 12 seats / Exception for loading/unloading goods and access to off-street garaging

Ahead only / One-way traffic / Turn left (right if symbol reversed) / Turn left ahead (right if symbol reversed) / Keep left (right if symbol reversed) / Vehicles may pass either side to reach same destination / Mini-roundabout / Route to be used by pedal cyclists only / Minimum speed / End of minimum speed

WARNING SIGNS — mostly triangular

Cross roads / Side road / Staggered junction / T Junction / Traffic merging with equal priority from right / Traffic merging with equal priority from left / Bend to right (left if symbol reversed) / Double bend first to left / Double bend first to right / Sharp deviation of route to left / Sharp deviation of route to right

Priority through junction indicated by thickened line

Road narrows on both sides / Road narrows on right (left if symbol reversed) / Dual carriageway ends / Roundabout / Two-way traffic straight ahead / Two-way traffic crosses one-way road ahead / Right-hand lane of a three lane carriageway closed to traffic ahead / Change to opposite carriageway (may be reversed) / Steep hill upwards (gradient shown as ratio 1:6=16%) / Steep hill downwards (gradient shown as percentage 10%=1:10)

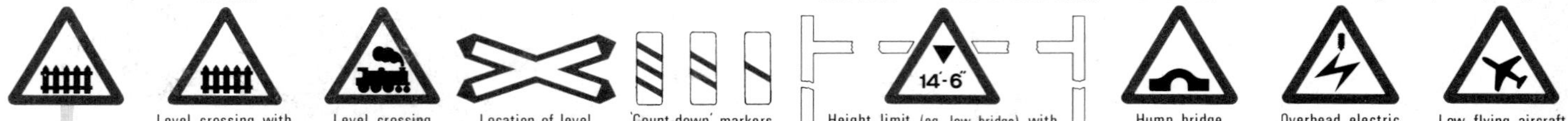

Level crossing with other barrier or gate ahead / Level crossing without barrier or gate ahead / Location of level crossing without barrier or gate / 'Count-down' markers approaching concealed level crossing / Height limit (eg. low bridge) with available width of headroom indicated / Hump bridge / Overhead electric cable / Low flying aircraft or sudden aircraft noise

Level crossing with automatic barrier and flashing lights / Traffic signals ahead / Pedestrian crossing ahead / Worded warning sign / Opening or swing bridge / Quayside or river bank / Slippery road / Uneven road / Risk of fallen or falling rocks / Loose chippings

Roadworks / Cattle / Wild animals / Accompanied horses or ponies crossing the road ahead / Children going to or from school / Other danger (plate indicates nature) / Distance to STOP sign ahead / Distance to GIVE WAY sign ahead / Hazard markers / Distance to hazard / Distance over which hazard extends